Days Out Guide 2011

AA Lifestyle Guides

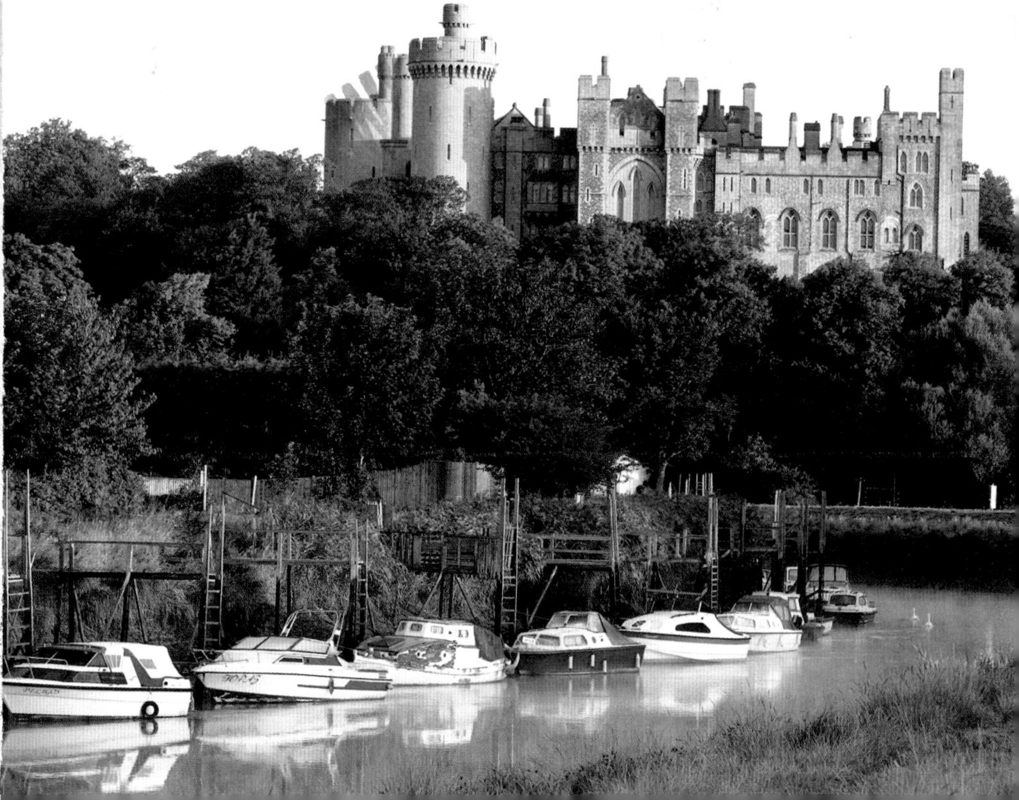

Produced by AA Publishing

Advertisement Sales: advertisingsales@theAA.com
Editorial: lifestyleguides@theAA.com

Front cover: (t) AA/N Jenkins; (bl) AA/J Tims; (br) AA/J Wood
Back cover: (l) AA/J Mottershaw; (c) AA/M Jourdan; (r) AA/M Birkitt

Typeset/Repro by Servis Filmsetting, Stockport, UK
Printed in Italy by Printer Trento SRL, Trento

Directory compiled by the AA Lifestyle Guides Department and managed in the Librios Information Management System and generated from the AA establishment database system.

theAA.com/shop

Published by AA Publishing, a trading name of AA Media Limited whose registered office is Fanum House, Basing View, Basingstoke, Hampshire, RG21 4EA
Registered number 06112600.

A CIP catalogue record for this book is available from the British Library

ISBN 978-0-7495-6742-2
A04465

Maps prepared by the Mapping Services Department of AA Publishing.

Contents

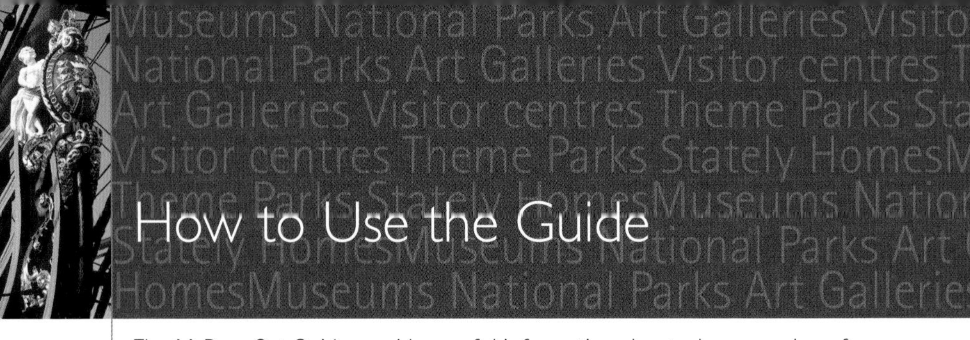

How to Use the Guide

The AA Days Out Guide provides useful information about a large number of museums, art galleries, theme parks, national parks, visitor centres, stately homes and other attractions across Britain and Ireland. Entries include contact details, along with a short description and details of opening times, prices and special facilities. We hope this guide will help you and your family get the most out of your visit.

The Directory

The directory is arranged in countries, counties, and in alphabetical location order within each county.

❶ **Map References and Atlas**
Map references for attractions are based on the National Grid, and can be used with the Atlas at the back of this book. First comes the map page number, followed by the National Grid reference. To find the location, read the first figure horizontally and the second figure vertically within the lettered square.

❷ **Directions** may be given after the address of each attraction and where shown have been provided by the attractions themselves.

❸ **Telephone Numbers** have the STD code shown before the telephone number. (If dialling Northern Ireland from England use the STD code, but for the Republic you need to prefix the number with 00353, and drop the first zero from the Irish area code).

❹ **Opening Times** quoted in the guide are inclusive - for instance, where you see Apr-Oct, that place will be open from the beginning of April to the end of October.

❺ **Fees** quoted for the majority of entries are current. If no price is quoted, you should check with the attraction concerned before you visit. Places which are open 'at all reasonable times' are usually free, and many places which do not charge admission at all may ask for a voluntary donation. Remember that prices can go up, and those provided to us by the attractions are provisional.

❶ **SOUTH MOLTON** Map 3 SS72

Quince Honey Farm **2 FOR 1**

EX36 3AZ

❸ ☎ 01769 572401 🖷 01769 574704

e-mail: info@quincehoney.co.uk

web: www.quincehoney.com

❷ **dir:** 3.5m W of A361, on N edge of South Molton

Follow the story of honey and beeswax from flower to table. The exhibition allows you to see the world of bees close up in complete safety; hives open at the press of a button revealing the honeybees' secret life. After viewing the bees at work, sample the fruits of their labour in the café or shop.

❹ **Times** Open daily, Apr-Sep 9-6; Oct 9-5; Shop only Nov-Etr 9-5, closed Sun. Closed 25 Dec-4 Jan.*

❺ **Fees** £4 (ch 5-16 £3, pen £3.50)* **Facilities** Ⓟ ☕ ⛩ (outdoor) ❻

❼ ♿ (partly accessible) (no lift to exhibition on first floor) toilets for disabled shop 🚭 ⊘ ❽

*__Admission prices__ followed by a star relate to 2010. It should be noted that in some entries the opening dates and times may also have been supplied as 2010. Please check with the establishment before making your journey.

Free Entry FREE
These attractions do not charge a fee for entry, although they may charge for use of audio equipment, for example. We have not included attractions that expect a donation in this category.

2-FOR-1 Voucher Scheme 2 FOR 1
This symbol indicates which attractions have chosen to participate in our 2-for-1 voucher scheme. Visitors using one of the vouchers from the back of this guide will be able to buy 2 tickets for the price of

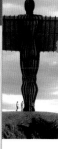

one, with certain restrictions that are detailed on the voucher itself. Some attractions also have individual restrictions, which are detailed in their entries.

6 **Facilities** This section includes parking, dogs allowed, refreshments etc. See this page for a key to Symbols and Abbreviations used in this guide.

7 **Visitors with Mobility Disabilities** should look for the wheelchair symbol showing where all or most of the establishment is accessible to the wheelchair-bound visitor. We strongly recommend that you telephone in advance of your visit to check the exact details, particularly regarding access to toilets and refreshment facilities. Assistance dogs are usually accepted where the attractions show the 'No Dogs' symbol. Please check with attraction before visit. For the hard of hearing induction loops are indicated by a symbol at the attraction itself.

8 **Credit & Charge cards** are taken by a large number of attractions for admission charges. To indicate which do not accept credit cards we have used this symbol at the end of the entry.

Photography is restricted in some places and there are many where it is only allowed in specific areas. Visitors are advised to check with places of interest on the rules for taking photographs and the use of video cameras.

Special events are held at many of these attractions, and although we have listed a few in individual entries, we cannot hope to give details of them all, so please ring the attractions for details of exhibitions, themed days, talks, guided walks and more.

Attractions with *italic* headings. These are entries that were unable to provide the relevant information in time for publication.

...and finally Opening times and admission prices can be subject to change. Please check with the attraction before making your journey.

Key to Symbols

- Telephone number
- Suitable for visitors in wheelchairs
- Parking at establishment
- Parking nearby
- Refreshment
- Picnic area
- Restaurant
- No dogs
- No coaches
- * Admission prices relate to 2010
- Cadw (Welsh Monuments)
- English Heritage
- National Trust
- The National Trust for Scotland
- Historic Scotland

Abbreviations

BHs Bank Hoildays
PH Public Holidays
Etr Easter
Xmas Christmas
hols holidays
ex except
ad adult
ch children
Pen senior citizens
Concessions (Students, unemployed etc)
mins minutes
wk week
wkday/s weekdays
wknd/s weekends

Public Holidays 2011

1 January	New Year's Day
4 January	New Year's Holiday (Scotland only)
17 March	St Patrick's Day (N.I & R.O.I)
22 April	Good Friday
25 April	Easter Monday
2 May	May Day Bank Holiday
30 May	Spring Bank Holiday (excluding R.O.I)
12 July	Battle of the Boyne (Orangemen's Day) (N.I)
1 August	Summer Bank Holiday (Scotland & R.O.I only)
29 August	Summer Bank Holiday (excluding R.O.I)
31 October	Bank Holiday (R.O.I)
26 December	Christmas Day (BH in lieu of 25th December)
27 December	Boxing Day (BH in lieu of 26th December) St Stephen's Day in R.O.I)

BEDFORDSHIRE

Shuttleworth Collection

ENGLAND

AMPTHILL — Map 4 TL03

Houghton House — FREE

web: www.english-heritage.org.uk
dir: 1m NE off A421

Now a ruin, the mansion was built for Mary Countess of Pembroke, the sister of Sir Philip Sidney. Inigo Jones is thought to have been involved in work on the house, which may have been the original 'House Beautiful' in Bunyan's *Pilgrim's Progress.*

Times Open at all reasonable times **Facilities** Ⓟ ⌗

BEDFORD — Map 4 TL04

Bedford Museum — FREE

Castle Ln MK40 3XD
☎ 01234 353323 📠 01234 273401
e-mail: bmuseum@bedford.gov.uk
web: www.bedfordmuseum.org
dir: close to town bridge and Embankment

Embark on a fascinating journey through the human and natural history of north Bedfordshire, pausing briefly to glimpse at wonders from more distant lands. Go back in time and visit the delightful rural room sets and the Old School Museum, where you will find Blackbeard's Sword; 'Old Billy' - the record breaking longest-living horse, and numerous other treasures and curiosities. Housed in the former Higgins and Sons Brewery, Bedford Museum is situated within the gardens of what was once Bedford Castle, beside the Great Ouse embankment. The courtyard and galleries provide an excellent setting for the varied collections.

Times Open all year, Tue-Sat 11-5, Sun 2-5. Closed Mon ex BH Mon, Good Fri, Xmas & New Year* **Facilities** Ⓟ ☕ ⛩ (outdoor) ♿ (fully accessible) toilets for disabled (lift available on request, subject to staff availability) shop 🚫

Cecil Higgins Art Gallery — FREE

Castle Ln MK40 3RP
☎ 01234 211222 📠 01234 327149
e-mail: chag@bedford.gov.uk
web: www.cecilhigginsartgallery.org
dir: in town centre close to Embankment

Bedford Gallery is the completed first phase of the re-development of Cecil Higgins Art Gallery and Bedford Museum. It is a new state-of-the-art exhibition venue which will house varied and exciting exhibitions including touring exhibitions from national museums and galleries.

Times The Cecil Higgins Art Gallery is undergoing re-development. The new Bedford Gallery in Castle Lane is now open Tue-Sat 11-5, Sun & BHs 2-5. Closed Xmas, New Year & Good Fri. During exhibition changeovers Bedford Gallery could also be closed so please check the website for further details* **Facilities** Ⓟ ⛩ (outdoor) ♿ (fully accessible) toilets for disabled (wheelchair available) 🚫

LEIGHTON BUZZARD — Map 4 SP92

Leighton Buzzard Railway — 2 FOR 1

Pages Park Station, Billington Rd LU7 4TN
☎ 01525 373888
e-mail: station@lbngrs.org.uk
web: www.buzzrail.co.uk
dir: 0.75m SE on A505/A4146 southern bypass, follow brown tourist signs at rdbt

The Leighton Buzzard Railway offers a 70-minute journey into the vanished world of the English light railway, with its sharp curves, steep gradients, level crossings and unique roadside running. Built in 1919 to serve the local sand industry, the railway has carried a steam passenger service, operated by volunteers, since 1968. Special events run throughout the year, including many locomotive anniversaries.

Times Open mid Mar-Oct, Sun & BHs, also Wed; Jun-Aug, Etr & Oct school hols **Fees** Return ticket £8 (ch 2-15 £4, ch under 2 free, pen £6). Family & day Rover tickets available. Different prices at Xmas **Facilities** Ⓟ ☕ ⛩ (outdoor) ♿ (partly accessible) (some museum exhibits not suitable, platform & train access for wheelchairs) toilets for disabled (designated parking) shop

LUTON — Map 4 TL02

Stockwood Discovery Centre

Stockwood Park, London Rd LU1 4LX
☎ 01582 548600 📠 01582 546763
e-mail: museum.gallery@lutonculture.com
web: www.stockwooddiscovery.com
dir: signed from M1 junct 10 & from Hitchin, Dunstable, Bedford, Luton town centre, entrance from London Rd

A museum and visitor attraction includes gardens featuring world, medicinal and sensory gardens, a visitor centre with a shop and café selling locally produced, free range products, and an outdoor discovery play area. There are also fascinating interactive displays about the history of Luton and the surrounding areas, as well as exciting events and special exhibitions.

Times Summer season; Apr-Oct, Mon-Fri 10-5, Sat-Sun 11-5. Winter season; Nov-Mar, Mon-Fri 10-4, Sat-Sun 11-4 **Fees** Free entry but charges apply to activity workshops, taught sessions & some events. Donations welcomed **Facilities** Ⓟ Ⓟ ☕ ⛩ (outdoor) ♿ (fully accessible) toilets for disabled (mobility scooter, w/chairs) shop 🚫

Wardown Park Museum

Wardown Park, Old Bedford Rd LU2 7HA
☎ 01582 546722 & 546739 📠 01582 546763
e-mail: museum.gallery@lutonculture.com
web: www.wardownparkmuseum.com
dir: Follow brown signs from town centre north. Turn off A6 towards Bedford

A Victorian mansion, with displays illustrating the natural and cultural history and industries of the area, including the development of Luton's hat industry, and the Bedfordshire and

Hertfordshire Regimental Collections. 'Luton Life' displays tell the story of the town and its residents over the past 200 years. Exhibitions and events throughout the year. Please telephone for details.

Times Open all year, Tue-Sat 10-5, Sun 1-5. Closed 25 Dec, 1 Jan & Mon (ex BH Mons)* **Fees** Free entry but charges will apply to activity workshops, taught sessions & some events. Donations welcomed **Facilities** (outdoor) (fully accessible) toilets for disabled (parking adjacent to entrance, lift to 1st floor) shop

OLD WARDEN Map 4 TL14

The Shuttleworth Collection

Old Warden Park SG18 9EP
01767 627927 01767 627949
e-mail: collection@shuttleworth.org
web: www.shuttleworth.org
dir: 2m W from rdbt on A1, Biggleswade by-pass

Housed in eight hangars on a classic grass aerodrome, 40 working historic aeroplanes span the progress of aviation with exhibits ranging from a 1909 Bleriot to a 1941 Spitfire. A garage of roadworthy motor vehicles explores the eras of the 1898 Panhard Levassor to the Railton sports car of 1937. The 19th-century coach house displays horse-drawn vehicles from 1880 to 1914. Flying displays of historic aeroplanes are held on the first Sunday and the third Saturday of the month between May and October.

Times Open Apr-Oct 10-5; Nov-Mar 10-4. (Last admission 1hr before closing) **Fees** Collection £10 (concessions £9). Swiss garden £5 (concessions £4). Birds of prey £10 (concessions £9). Combination ticket £20 (concessions £17). Air shows please check website. Accompanied ch under 16 free **Facilities** licensed (outdoor) (fully accessible) toilets for disabled (wheelchairs) shop

SANDY Map 4 TL14

RSPB The Lodge Nature Reserve

The Lodge SG19 2DL
01767 680541 01767 683508
e-mail: thelodgereserve@rspb.org.uk
web: www.rspb.org.uk
dir: 1m E of Sandy, on B1042 Potton road

The headquarters of the Royal Society for the Protection of Birds. Explore peaceful woodlands, colourful gardens and the Iron Age hill fort on Galley Hill. The house and buildings are not open to the public, but there are waymarked paths and formal gardens, and two species of woodpecker, nuthatches and woodland birds may be seen, as may rare breed sheep. Various events through the year include Shakespearean plays and Feed the Birds day.

Times Open all year, Nature Reserve: dawn to dusk. Shop: Mon-Fri 9-5, Sat, Sun & BHs 10-5. Closed 25-26 Dec* **Facilities** (outdoor) (partly accessible) (gardens some steps, nature trails vary some steep sections) toilets for disabled (wheelchair hire) shop

SILSOE Map 4 TL03

Wrest Park Gardens

MK45 4HS
01525 860152
web: www.english-heritage.org.uk
dir: 0.75m E off A6

A little-known but fascinating garden, Wrest Park's formality provides a history of gardening styles, laid out over 150 years and inspired by the great gardens of Versailles in France. The house was home to the De Grey family from the 13th century until 1917, and the gardens are centered on the early 18th-century pavilion designed by Thomas Archer. Subsequent additions include the Bath House and the Chinese Pavilion. There are also an Orangery, Italian Garden and Parterre with magnificent 19th-century lead statues.

Times Open, Apr-Jun & Sep, Sat-Sun & BH 10-6; Jul-Aug, Thu-Mon 10-6; Oct, Sat-Sun 10-5. The House and Gardens may close early if there is an event booked. Please call to check. **Fees** £5.50 (ch £2.80, concessions £4.70). Family £13.80. Prices and opening times are subject to change in March 2011. Please call 0870 333 1181 for the most up to date prices and opening times when planning your visit **Facilities**

ENGLAND

ENGLAND

STOTFOLD Map 5 TL23

Stotfold Watermill

Mill Ln SG5 4NU
☎ 01462 734541
e-mail: enquiries@stotfoldmill.com
web: www.stotfoldmill.com
dir: 1m from A1(M) junct 10

In an idyllic setting on the River Ivel, where a mill has stood since the 11th century, this working watermill still produces high-quality stone-ground flour. After a fire in 1992, the Mill was renovated by volunteers who started in 1998, and completed their work in 2006 when the Mill was opened to the public. There are twice-daily guided tours and a programme of special events.

Times Open Etr-Oct, alternate Sun (please check website) **Fees** Free entry, guided tours £1.50 **Facilities** (fully accessible) toilets for disabled shop

WHIPSNADE Map 4 TL01

Whipsnade Wild Animal Park

LU6 2LF
☎ 01582 872171 01582 872649
e-mail: marketing@zsl.org
web: www.whipsnade.co.uk
dir: signed from M1 junct 9 & 12

Located in beautiful Bedfordshire countryside, Whipsnade is home to more than 2,500 rare and exotic animals and is one of the largest conservation centres in Europe. Hop aboard the Jumbo Express, a fantastic steam train experience, and see elephants, rhino, yaks, camels and deer, along with wild horses, and learn about their lives in the wilds of Asia and Africa. Other highlights include the Lions of the Serengeti, the sealion pool, and Birds of the World. The Discover Centre is home to tamarins, turtles, big snakes and sea horses among others. Visitors can also enjoy the picnic areas, keeper talks and animal shows.

Times Open all year, daily. Closed 25 Dec. Closing times vary* **Facilities** (outdoor) toilets for disabled shop

WILDEN Map 4 TL05

Wild Britain

65A Renhold Rd MK44 2PX
☎ 01234 772770 01234 772773
e-mail: enquiries@wild-britain.co.uk
web: www.wild-britain.co.uk
dir: From A421 take Gt Barford slip road. Follow brown signs

Join the adventures of Urchin the hedgehog as he explores the countryside. Meet British animals in the presentation shows. Visit the steamy tropical butterfly house to experience what the future could hold for Britain. Children's arts and craft activities every day.

Times Open Etr-Oct, 10-5* **Facilities** (fully accessible) toilets for disabled shop

WOBURN Map 4 SP93

Woburn Abbey

MK17 9WA
☎ 01525 290333 01525 290271
e-mail: admissions@woburnabbey.co.uk
web: www.woburn.co.uk
dir: Just off M1 junct 12/13

Set in a beautiful 3,000 acre deer park, Woburn Abbey has been home to the Dukes of Bedford for over 300 years and is currently occupied by the 15th Duke and his family. The Abbey houses one of the most important private art collections in the world including paintings by Canaletto, Gainsborough, Reynolds, Van Dyck and Cuyp and collections of silver, gold and porcelain. Woburn was the setting for the origin of "Afternoon Tea", introduced by Anna Maria, wife of the 7th Duke. An audio tour is available (charged) and guided tours on request. There are extensive informal gardens, pottery and a fine antiques centre representing over 30 dealers. Various events throughout the year include Plays in the Park between June and August.

Times Open daily 27 Mar-3 Oct, 4-31 Oct, wknds only. Woburn Abbey closed Nov-Dec. Gardens & Deer Park all year (ex 24-26 Dec).* **Fees** £12.50 (ch 3-15 £6, pen £10.50). Passport ticket for Woburn Abbey and Woburn Safari Park allows one visit to each attraction on same or different days £22.50 (ch £15.50, pen £19). Please phone or check website for further details of opening times and prices* **Facilities** licensed (outdoor) (partly accessible) (limited access to house, only 3 rooms on ground floor. Other areas can only be accessed by stairs) toilets for disabled (mobility scooters available with pre-booking) shop

Woburn Safari Park

MK17 9QN
☎ 01525 290407 01525 290489
e-mail: info@woburnsafari.co.uk
web: www.woburn.co.uk
dir: Signed from M1 junct 13

Take a Safari Adventure at Woburn Safari Park and enjoy the beauty of wild animals in close-up. Tour the reserves from the safety of your car and experience the thrill of being alongside white rhino, buffalo, giraffes and Siberian tiger. The Leisure Park has indoor and outdoor adventure playgrounds, walkthrough areas with wallabies, squirrel monkeys and lemurs, and a full programme of keeper talks and demonstrations. All attractions are included in the entry price including the new Mammoth Play Ark, Great Woburn Railway and the Swanboats.

Times Open Mar-Oct, daily 10-5; Nov-28 Feb, wknds only 11-3. Check website for current information* **Fees** £13.50-£18.50 (ch 3-15 £13.50, pen £15.50)* **Facilities** licensed (indoor & outdoor) (partly accessible) (some steeper hills in leisure area) toilets for disabled (w/chairs pre-booking required) shop

BERKSHIRE

Skiffs and swans on the River Thames at Windsor

ENGLAND

BRACKNELL Map 4 SU86

The Look Out Discovery Centre 2 FOR 1

Nine Mile Ride RG12 7QW
☎ 01344 354400 🖷 01344 354422
e-mail: thelookout@bracknell-forest.gov.uk
web: www.bracknell-forest.gov.uk/be
dir: 3m S of town centre. From M3 junct 3, take A322 to Bracknell and from M4 junct 10, take A329M to Bracknell. Follow brown tourist signs

A hands-on, interactive science and nature exhibition where budding scientists can spend many hours exploring and discovering over 90 fun-filled exhibits within five themed zones, linked to the National Curriculum. Zones include Light and Colour, Forces and Movement and the Body and Perception. A new exciting zone, Woodland and Water; has a vortex, stream, ant colony and many more interactive exhibits. Climb the 88 steps to the Look Out tower and enjoy views towards Bracknell and beyond, or enjoy a nature walk in the surrounding 1,000 hectares of Crown Estate woodland. Interactive shows for the public and schools running throughout the year.

Times Open all year 10-5. Closed 24-26 Dec, 10-14 Jan* **Fees** £6.25 (ch & concessions £4.15). Family (2ad+2ch or 1ad+3ch) £16.60. Prices valid until 31 March 2011* **Facilities** Ⓟ ☕ ⛩ (outdoor) ♿ (partly accessible) (all ex 22mtrs tall tower) toilets for disabled (lift to 1st floor) shop ⊗

ETON Map 4 SU97

Dorney Court 2 FOR 1

Dorney SL4 6QP
☎ 01628 604638
e-mail: palmer@dorneycourt.co.uk
web: www.dorneycourt.co.uk
dir: signed from M4 junct 7

An enchanting brick and timber manor house (c1440) in a tranquil setting. With tall Tudor chimneys and a splendid great hall, it has been the home of the present family since 1510, and is often seen in films and TV programmes.

Times Open BH Sun & Mon in May 1.30-4. Apr-May, Mon-Fri 1.30-4 **Fees** £7.50 (ch £5, under 10's free) **Facilities** Ⓟ Ⓟ ☕ ♿ (partly accessible) (downstairs only accessible) toilets for disabled (DVD of upstairs, ramps) ⊗

HAMPSTEAD NORREYS Map 4 SU57

The Living Rainforest

RG18 0TN
☎ 01635 202444 🖷 01635 202440
e-mail: enquiries@livingrainforest.org
web: www.livingrainforest.org
dir: follow brown tourist signs from M4/A34

By providing education and supporting research into the relationship between humanity and the rainforests, this wonderful attraction hopes to promote a more sustainable future. Visitors to the Living Rainforest will see plants and wildlife that are under threat in their natural habitat, and be encouraged to take part in a large variety of activities, workshops and exhibitions.

Times Open all year daily 10-5. (Closed 24-26 Dec)* **Facilities** Ⓟ ☕ ⛩ (outdoor) ♿ (fully accessible) toilets for disabled shop ⊗

LOWER BASILDON Map 4 SU67

Basildon Park

RG8 9NR
☎ 0118 984 3040 🖷 0118 976 7370
e-mail: basildonpark@nationaltrust.org.uk
web: www.nationaltrust.org.uk/basildonpark
dir: 7m NW of Reading on W side of A329 between Pangbourne & Streatley

This 18th-century house, built of Bath stone, fell into decay in the 20th century, but was beautifully restored by Lord and Lady Iliffe in the 1950s. The classical front has a splendid central portico and pavilions, and inside there are delicate plasterwork decorations on the walls and ceilings. The Octagon drawing room has fine pictures and furniture, and there is a small formal garden. Please contact for details of special events.

Times House open mid Mar-Oct, Wed-Sun & BH Mon 12-5. Park & garden, shop & tea room mid Feb-mid Dec, Wed-Sun & BH Mon 11-3* **Fees** House & grounds £8.80 (ch £4.40)* **Facilities** Ⓟ 🍽 licensed ⛩ (outdoor) ♿ (partly accessible) (grd floor ramped access to exhibition rooms, tea rooms & shop - main showroom up 20 steps from gd floor) toilets for disabled (transfer buggy, virtual tour of upper showrooms) shop 🌿

Beale Park

Lower Basildon RG8 9NH
☎ 0870 777 7160 📠 0870 777 7120
web: www.bealepark.co.uk
dir: M4 junct 12, follow brown tourist signs to Pangbourne, A329 towards Oxford

Beale Park is home to an extraordinary collection of birds and animals including peacocks, swans, owls and parrots. It also offers a steam railway, rare breeds of farm animals, a great pet corner, meerkats, wallabies, ring-tailed lemurs, a deer park, three splash pools, a huge adventure playground, acres of gardens, and sculptures in a traditional, family park beside the Thames. There are summer riverboat trips and excellent lake and river fishing.

Times Open Mar-Oct* **Facilities** 🅟 ☕ 🍽 licensed ⛩ (outdoor) ♿ (partly accessible) toilets for disabled (wheelchair available, parking) shop 🚫🐕

NEWBURY Map 4 SU46

West Berkshire Museum FREE

The Wharf RG14 5AS
☎ 01635 519231 & 519562
e-mail: museum@westberks.gov.uk
web: www.westberkshiremuseum.org.uk
dir: from London take M4 junct 13, then southbound on A34, follow signs for town centre

Occupying two adjoining buildings in the centre of Newbury; the Cloth Hall built in 1627 and the Granary built in 1720, the West Berkshire Museum includes displays of fine and decorative art, costume, local history and archaeology.

Times Open Apr-Sep, Thu-Sat 10.30-5, Sun & BHs 11-4 **Facilities** 🅟 Ⓟ ♿ (partly accessible) (ground floor accessible) (induction loop at reception) shop 🚫🐕

OLD WINDSOR Map 4 SU97

Runnymede

North Lodge, Windsor Rd SL4 2JL
☎ 01784 432891 📠 01784 479007
e-mail: runnymede@nationaltrust.org.uk
web: www.nationaltrust.org.uk/runnymede
dir: From M25 junct 13. 2m W of Runnymede Bridge on S side of A308. 6m E of Windsor

Partly designated as a Site of Special Scientific Interest, Runnymede is an area of meadows, grassland, and woodland that sits alongside the Thames. Best known as the site where King John signed the Magna Carta in 1215, this momentous event was commemorated by the American Bar Association, who built a monument here in 1957. There is also a memorial to American President, John F Kennedy. Also there are the Fairhaven Lodges, designed by Edward Lutyens, one of which is now an art gallery.

Times Car parks: Oct-Mar 9-5; Apr-Sep 9-7 **Fees** Car parking £1.50-£6, Coaches £6 **Facilities** 🅟 Ⓟ ☕ 🍽 licensed ⛩ (outdoor) ♿ (partly accessible) (steps to front of tea rooms & art gallery) toilets for disabled (Braille guide) 🍃

READING Map 4 SU77

Museum of English Rural Life FREE

University of Reading, Redlands Rd RG1 5EX
☎ 0118 378 8660 📠 0118 378 5632
e-mail: merl@reading.ac.uk
web: www.merl.org.uk
dir: close to Royal Berkshire Hospital, museum 100mtrs on right

Recently moved to larger premises, this museum houses a national collection of agricultural, domestic and crafts exhibits, including wagons, tools and a wide range of other equipment used in the English countryside over the last 150 years. Special facilities are available for school parties. The museum also contains extensive documentary and photographic archives, which can be studied by appointment. There is a regular programme of events and activities, please see website for details.

Times Open all year, Tue-Fri, 9-5, Sat & Sun 2-4.30. Closed BHs & Xmas-New Year* **Facilities** 🅟 ⛩ (outdoor) ♿ (fully accessible) toilets for disabled (chair lifts, hearing loop) shop 🚫🐕

RISELEY Map 4 SU76

Wellington Country Park 2 FOR 1

RG7 1SP
☎ 0118 932 6444 📠 0118 932 6445
e-mail: info@wellington-country-park.co.uk
web: www.wellington-country-park.co.uk
dir: M4 junct 11 follow A33 S towards Basingstoke, M3 junct 6 follow A33 N towards Reading

Wellington Country Park consists of 350 acres of woodland walks and parkland, ideal for a family outing. Attractions appealing to younger children include; a miniature railway, a variety of play areas, crazy golf and nature trails. There is also an 80-acre family campsite, a nature trail maze and animal corner. The 2 for 1 voucher will admit one child free with each full paying adult and is not valid for camping.

Times Open Feb-Nov, daily 9.30-5 in low season, 9.30-5.30 in high season* **Fees** £6.50 (ch 2 and under free, 3-15 £5.50, pen £6) Family ticket (2ad+2ch) £21.50* **Facilities** 🅟 ☕ ⛩ (outdoor) ♿ (partly accessible) (most walks are forest floor but park area stone surface) toilets for disabled shop

ENGLAND

WINDSOR Map 4 SU97

Frogmore House

Home Park SL4 1NJ
☎ 020 7766 7305 020 7930 9625
e-mail: bookinginfo@royalcollection.org.uk
web: www.royalcollection.org.uk
dir: entrance via The Long Walk, from B3021 between Datchet & Old Windsor

Frogmore House has been a royal retreat since the 18th century, and is today used by the Royal Family for private entertaining. It is especially linked with Queen Charlotte, the wife of George III, and her daughters, whose love of botany and art is reflected throughout the house. Queen Victoria loved Frogmore so much that she broke with royal tradition and chose to build a mausoleum for herself and Prince Albert there. Please note the Royal Mausoleum is not open to visitors.

Times Open Aug BH wknd, 10-5.30 (last admission 4). Prebooked coach groups Aug-Sep, Tue-Thu* **Fees** Contact Ticket Sales and Information Office (020 7766 7305) for details of admission prices or see website **Facilities** (outdoor) (partly accessible) (gravel paths) (phone 020 7766 7324 for information) shop

LEGOLAND Windsor

Winkfield Rd SL4 4AY
01753 626119
e-mail: customer.services@legoland.co.uk
web: www.legoland.co.uk
dir: on B3022 (Windsor to Ascot road) signed from M3 junct 3 & M4 junct 6

With over 50 interactive rides, live shows, buil ding workshops, driving schools and attractions, LEGOLAND Windsor is set in 150 acres of beautiful parkland, and is a different sort of family theme park. This is an atmospheric and unique experience for the whole family.

Times Open daily 12 Mar-5 Nov* **Facilities** licensed (outdoor) (partly accessible) toilets for disabled (signing staff, wheelchair hire, parking) shop

The Royal Landscape

The Savill Garden, Wick Ln, Englefield Green TW20 0UU
☎ 01784 435544 & 01753 860222
e-mail: enquiries@theroyallandscape.co.uk
web: www.theroyallandscape.co.uk
dir: M25 junct 13, signed off A30 between Egham & Virginia Water

The work of master landscape gardener, Sir Eric Savill, this is one of the greatest woodland gardens in England. It was created in the 1930s and offers year-round interest with colourful displays of interesting and rare plants. The Savill Building is a visitor centre built to a unique and innovative gridshell design, made with timber harvested from Windsor Great Park. The Royal Landscape is an area of a thousand acres of gardens and parkland accessible to the public, at the southern end of Windsor Great Park. It includes The Savill Garden, The Valley Gardens and Virginia Water, and was shaped and planted over a period of 400 years.

Times Open all year, daily 10-6; Nov-Feb 10-4.30. Closed 25-26 Dec* **Fees** Mar-Oct: £8 (ch 6-16 £3.75, seniors £7.50). Family £20 (2ad+2ch). Groups (10+) £6.65. For prices from Nov 2010, please call, email or visit website* **Facilities** licensed (outdoor) (fully accessible) toilets for disabled (wheelchairs available) shop

St George's Chapel

SL4 1NJ
☎ 020 7766 7304 01753 620165
dir: M4 junct 6 & M3 junct 3

St George's Chapel, within the precincts of Windsor Castle, is one of the most beautiful ecclesiastical buildings in England. Founded by Edward IV in 1475, it is the burial place of ten monarchs, including Henry VIII and his favourite wife Jane Seymour. The Chapel is the spiritual home of the Order of the Garter, the most senior order of British Chivalry.

Times Open Mar-Oct 9.45-5.15; Nov-Feb 9.45-4.15 (last admission 1hr and 15mins before closing). Evening service daily 5.15, visitors welcome. May close at short notice - 24hr info line - 020 7766 7304 or see website. Closed Sun, worshippers welcome **Fees** Free entry to the Chapel is included in the price of entry to Windsor Castle* **Facilities** (fully accessible) shop

Windsor Castle

SL4 1NJ
☎ 020 7766 7304 020 7930 9625
e-mail: bookinginfo@royalcollection.org.uk
web: www.royalcollection.org.uk
dir: M4 junct 6 & M3 junct 3

Covering 13 acres, Windsor Castle is the official residence of HM The Queen, and the largest occupied castle in the world. Begun as a wooden fort by William the Conqueror, it has been added to by almost every monarch since. A visit takes in the magnificent State Apartments, St George's Chapel, Queen Mary's doll's house, the Drawings Gallery, and between October and March, the semi-state rooms created by George IV. A special exhibition of royal portraits by Marcus Adams is on display until February 2011.

Times Open daily except Good Fri & 25-26 Dec. Nov-Feb, 9.45-4.15; Mar-Oct, 9.45-5.15 (last admission 1hr and 15mins before closing). May be subject to change at short notice (24hr info line: 020 7766 7304 or see website) **Fees** £16 (ch under 17 £9.50, under 5's free, concessions £14.50) Family (2ad+3ch) £42. (see website for latest details of prices)* **Facilities** (fully accessible) toilets for disabled shop

BRISTOL

Brunel's *ss Great Britain*

ENGLAND

BRISTOL Map 3 ST57

Arnolfini 2 FOR 1

16 Narrow Quay BS1 4QA
☎ 0117 917 2300 & 917 2301 0117 917 2303
e-mail: boxoffice@arnolfini.org.uk
web: www.arnolfini.org.uk
dir: From M32 follow brown signs

In a fantastic location at the heart of Bristol's harbourside, Arnolfini is one of Europe's leading centres for the contemporary arts. Arnolfini stages art exhibitions, cinema, live art and dance performances, talks and events and has one of the country's best art bookshops. Entrance to the galleries is free, making Arnolfini a great place to spend a few minutes or a few hours. The 2 for 1 voucher only relates to cinema tickets. There will be a special programme of events during 2011 to celebrate the 50th anniversary of Arnolfini.

Times Open all year, Tue-Sun & BHs, 11-6 **Fees** Galleries free, Cinema £6 (concessions £4.50)* **Facilities** Ⓟ licensed (outdoor) (fully accessible) toilets for disabled shop

At-Bristol

Anchor Rd, Harbourside BS1 5DB
☎ 0845 345 1235 0117 915 7202
e-mail: information@at-bristol.org.uk
web: www.at-bristol.org.uk
dir: from city centre, A4 to Anchor Rd. Located on left opposite Cathedral

At-Bristol is one of the UK's largest and most exciting hands-on science centres with over 300 interactive exhibits, live shows and a planetarium. Join Morph and friends to make animations, have a game of virtual volley-ball or even climb inside a giant hamster wheel. Learn about the world by gazing at icy comets. Take a closer look at the beautiful patterns in ice and get in a spin in the turbulent orb. With so much interactive fun and a planetarium, there is something for everyone to enjoy. A new interactive exhibition using the latest technology opens in February 2011, looking at how intriguing the human body is.

Times Open all year, Bristol schools term-time wkdays 10-5, wknds & school hols 10-6. Closed 24-26 Dec* **Fees** With Gift Aid £11.90 (ch £7.70, concessions £9.90). Family ticket £34. Grand-parents family ticket £31.90 **Facilities** Ⓟ (indoor & outdoor) (fully accessible) toilets for disabled (induction loop & mini com 0117 914 3475) shop

Bristol's Blaise Castle House Museum FREE

Henbury Rd, Henbury BS10 7QS
☎ 0117 903 9818
e-mail: general.museum@bristol.gov.uk
web: www.bristol.gov.uk/museums
dir: M5 junct 19, 4m NW of city, off B4057

Built in the 18th century for a Quaker banker, this mansion is now Bristol's Museum of Social History. Set in 400 acres of parkland, nearby Blaise Hamlet is a picturesque estate village, and was designed by John Nash.

Times Open Etr-Oct, Wed-Sun; Jul-Aug, Tue-Sun; Nov-Etr, wknds only 10.30-4. Closed 25-26 Dec **Facilities** Ⓟ (outdoor) (partly accessible) (access ramp, no lift due to age of house) shop

Bristol's Blue Reef Aquarium

Anchor Rd, Harbourside BS1 5TT
☎ 0117 929 8929
e-mail: bristol@bluereefaquarium.co.uk
web: www.bluereefaquarium.co.uk
dir: M5 south, junct 18, take A4 to city centre or north M4/M5, take M32 to city centre. Follow harbourside signs to Anchor Road

Dive into a breathtaking 3D underwater world and be transported below the ocean surface in the Imax theatre. Visit 40 naturally themed habitats from the British Coast to exotic coral seas. Enjoy close encounters with sharks, stingrays, giant octopus and thousands of incredible aquatic creatures and see feeding displays in a free programme of daily events.

Times Open daily from 10. Closed 25 Dec **Fees** £13.50 (ch 3-15 £9.20, under 3 free, concessions £11.50)* **Facilities** Ⓟ (fully accessible) toilets for disabled shop

Bristol's City Museum & Art Gallery FREE

Queen's Rd, Clifton BS8 1RL
☎ 0117 922 3571 0117 922 2047
e-mail: general.museum@bristol.gov.uk
web: www.bristol.gov.uk/museums
dir: follow signs to city centre, then follow tourist board signs to City Museum & Art Gallery

Regional and international collections representing ancient history, natural sciences, and fine and applied arts. Displays include dinosaurs, Bristol ceramics, silver, and Chinese and Japanese ceramics. A full programme of special exhibitions take place throughout the year, including family activities and a mini museum.

Times Open all year, daily 10.30-5, late night opening every week until 8. Closed 25-26 Dec **Facilities** Ⓟ (partly accessible) (level access entrance, lift to some floors) toilets for disabled (lift) shop

ENGLAND

Bristol's Georgian House

FREE

7 Great George St, off Park St BS1 5RR
☎ 0117 921 1362 📠 0117 922 2047
e-mail: general.museum@bristol.gov.uk
web: www.bristol.gov.uk/museums
dir: 5 mins walk from city museum & art gallery

A carefully preserved example of a six-storey, late 18th-century merchant's town house, with many original features, furnished to illustrate life both above and below stairs. Displays allow visitors to examine the role that slavery played in 18th-century Bristol.

Times Open Etr-Oct, Wed-Thu & Sat-Sun 10.30-4; Jul-Aug, Tue-Sun **Facilities** Ⓟ ㊗

Bristol's Red Lodge

FREE

Park Row BS1 5LJ
☎ 0117 921 1360
e-mail: general.museum@bristol.gov.uk
web: www.bristol.gov.uk/museums
dir: 5 mins walk from city museum & art gallery

The house was built in 1590 and then altered in 1730. It has fine oak panelling and carved-stone chimney pieces, and is furnished in Elizabethan, Stuart and Georgian styles. The Great Oak Room is considered to be one of the finest Elizabethan rooms in the West Country, and has an original plasterwork ceiling. From here you can look down into the beautiful Knot Garden. The house has been home to many families over the centuries and was a reform school for girls in the 1800s.

Times Open Etr-Oct, Wed-Thu & Sat-Sun 10.30-4; Jul-Aug Tue-Sun **Facilities** Ⓟ ㊗

Bristol Zoo Gardens

Clifton BS8 3HA
☎ 0117 974 7399 📠 0117 973 6814
e-mail: information@bristolzoo.org.uk
web: www.bristolzoo.org.uk
dir: M5 junct 17, take A4018 then follow brown elephant signs. Also signed from city centre

Enjoy an amazing world of animals, all within these award-winning 12 acre gardens. With over 450 species, including nine animal houses undercover, you can enjoy your visit whatever the weather. Visit the primates in Monkey Jungle, stroll through the lemur garden, feed our colourful parrots at Feed the Lorikeets or come face to face with the inhabitants of the impressive Seal and Penguin Coast. The more adventurous can take the ZooRopia challenge and swing like a gibbon on this unique aerial ropes course. In July 2011, Bristol Zoo Gardens will celebrate its 175th birthday.

Times Open all year, daily (ex 25 Dec). 9-5.30 (British Summer Time), 9-5 (standard hrs)* **Fees** £12.50 (ch 3-14yrs £7.75, under 3 free, concessions £11). Family ticket (2ad+2ch) £36.50* **Facilities** 🅟 ☕ 🍽 licensed ⛩ (outdoor) ♿ (fully accessible) toilets for disabled (wheelchairs/electric scooters for use in zoo grounds) shop ㊗

Brunel's ss Great Britain

Great Western Dock, Gas Ferry Rd BS1 6TY
☎ 0117 926 0680 📠 0117 925 5788
e-mail: admin@ssgreatbritain.org
web: www.ssgreatbritain.org
dir: off Cumberland Rd

Built and launched in Bristol in 1843, Isambard Kingdom Brunel's maritime masterpiece was the first ocean-going, propeller-driven, iron ship. Launched in 1843 to provide luxury travel to New York, the world's first great ocean liner set new standards in engineering, reliability and speed. Find out about passengers and crew - from the rich and famous to those leaving 1850s England to begin a new life. Steer the ship on a westerly course, prepare her for sail and climb to the crow's nest. Descend beneath the glass 'sea' for a close up view of the ship's giant hull and propeller and the state-of-the-art equipment which will save her for the next hundred years. Another feature is the Dockyard Museum charting the history of Brunel's masterpiece. A replica of the square rigger *Matthew* is moored at the same site when in Bristol. Special events are held all year - please see the website for details.

Times Open all year daily 10-6, 4.30 in winter. Closed 17, 24-25 Dec* **Fees** £11.95 (ch 4 & under free, 16 & under £5.95, concessions £9.50)* **Facilities** 🅟 Ⓟ ☕ ♿ (fully accessible) toilets for disabled (audio guides, free entry for dedicated carers) shop ㊗

ENGLAND

BRISTOL *continued*

HorseWorld

2 FOR 1

Staunton Manor Farm, Staunton Ln, Whitchurch BS14 0QJ
☎ 01275 540173 🖷 01275 540119
e-mail: visitor.centre@horseworld.org.uk
web: www.horseworld.org.uk
dir: A37 Bristol to Wells road, follow brown signs from Maes Knoll traffic lights

Set in beautiful stone farm buildings on the southern edge of Bristol, HorseWorld's Visitor Centre is an award winning attraction that offers a great day for everyone. Meet the friendly horses, ponies and donkeys.

Times Open all year, Apr-Oct, daily 10-5; Nov-Mar, Wed-Sun 10-4 **Fees** £6.95 (ch 3-15yrs £4.95, concessions £5.95). Family (2ad+2ch) £20.95* **Facilities** Ⓟ ☕ 🍽 licensed ⛩ (indoor & outdoor) ♿ (fully accessible) toilets for disabled shop

M Shed (formerly Bristol's Industrial Museum)

FREE

Prince's Wharf, Prince St, City Docks BS1 4RN
☎ 0117 925 1470
e-mail: general.museum@bristol.gov.uk
web: www.mshed.org
dir: within walking distance of the city centre

M Shed is due to re-open in spring 2011 following a major refurbishment, and explores the history of Bristol over the last 2,000 years. Working exhibits, including steamboats, trains and cranes on the harbour side, personal accounts and rare film footage, will challenge your perception of the City. Thought provoking and fun, learn about Bristol's trading past, the city's war-time experiences and industrial heritage. A large collection of artefacts, display's and exhibitions help to bring this 'living museum' alive.

Times Due to re-open in Spring 2011. See website or contact for details **Facilities** Ⓟ ☕ 🍽 licensed ⛩ ♿ (fully accessible) toilets for disabled shop 🚫

BUCKINGHAMSHIRE

Waddesdon Manor

ENGLAND

AYLESBURY Map 4 SP81

Boarstall Duck Decoy

Boarstall HP18 9UX
☎ 01280 822850
e-mail: stowegarden@nationaltrust.org.uk
web: www.nationaltrust.org.uk
dir: A41/B4011, towards Long Crendon. Turn right to Boarstall & follow brown sign. 200yds on right, through Manor Farm

A rare survival of a 17th-century decoy in working order. Working decoy demonstration on Saturday and Sunday, please phone for more details.

Times Open 3 Apr-29 Aug, Sat-Sun 10-4; 7 Apr-25 Aug, also Wed 3.30-6* **Facilities** (outdoor) (fully accessible)

King's Head

King's Head Passage, Market Square HP20 2RW
☎ 01296 381501 01296 381502
e-mail: kingshead@nationaltrust.org.uk
web: www.nationaltrust.org.uk
dir: A41 follow signs for town centre, located at top of Market Sq

This historic coaching inn was established in 1455 and is still trading today. It has many notable architectural features, including a medieval stained glass window, extensive timber framing and an ancient cobbled courtyard. Once a base for Oliver Cromwell, it now houses a history centre among other features.

Times Open all year, NT bookshop/coffee shop Tue-Sat, 10.30-4. (Inn Mon-Sat 11-11 & Sun 12-10.30)* **Facilities** licensed (partly accessible) (cobbled courtyard, narrow corridors, steep stairs) toilets for disabled (hearing loop)

Tiggywinkles Visitor Centre & Hedgehog World Museum

Aston Rd HP17 8AF
☎ 01844 292511
e-mail: mail@sttiggywinkles.org.uk
web: www.tiggywinkles.com
dir: Turn off A418 towards Haddenham then follow signs to 'Wildlife Hospital'

Look through the glass into bird and mammal nursery wards in the hospital. Find out all about the hospital, the patients and their treatment on education boards dotted around the gardens. See some of the other hospital wards on CCTV monitor. Wander round the world's first Hedgehog Memorabilia Museum, or watch the foxes in their permanent enclosure. Try to catch a glimpse of one of the resident badgers or see the deer in the recovery paddocks. The animals live as natural a life as possible, so don't be surprised if they do not come out to visit.

Times Open Etr-Sep, daily 10-4* **Facilities** shop

BEACONSFIELD Map 4 SU99

Bekonscot Model Village and Railway

2 FOR 1

Warwick Rd HP9 2PL
☎ 01494 672919 01494 675284
e-mail: info@bekonscot.co.uk
web: www.bekonscot.co.uk
dir: M40 junct 2, 4m M25 junct 16, take A355 and follow signs to Model Village

A miniature world, depicting rural England in the 1930s. A Gauge 1 model railway meanders through six little villages, each with their own tiny population. Rides on the sit-on miniature railway take place at weekends and local school holidays. Remote control boats are available. The 2-for-1 voucher will admit a child free with a full-paying adult.

Times Open 19 Feb-Oct, 10-5 **Fees** £8.50 (ch £5, concessions £6)* **Facilities** (indoor & outdoor) (fully accessible) toilets for disabled (wheelchair loan by prior booking) shop

BLETCHLEY Map 4 SP93

Bletchley Park

The Mansion, Bletchley Park MK3 6EB
☎ 01908 640404 01908 274381
e-mail: info@bletchleypark.org.uk
web: www.bletchleypark.org.uk
dir: Approach Bletchley from V7 Saxon St. At rdbt, southern end of Saxon St under railway bridge towards Buckingham & follow signs to Bletchley Park

Known as 'Station X' during World War II, this was the home of the secret scientific team that worked to decipher German military messages sent using the Enigma code machine. Visitors can find out more about the Enigma machine; the 'bombes', computers used to crack the code; Alan Turing, one of the leading mathematicians of his day, who worked on the project; as well as see a number of other displays including the use of pigeons during the war, wartime vehicles, and a Churchill collection.

Times Open daily 9.30-5.30 (Tours at 11 & 2). Wknds open 10.30-5. Closed 25 & 26 Dec* **Facilities** licensed toilets for disabled shop

CHALFONT ST GILES **Map 4 SU99**

Chiltern Open Air Museum

Newland Park, Gorelands Ln HP8 4AB
01494 871117 01494 872774
e-mail: coamuseum@netscape.net
web: www.coam.org.uk
dir: M25 junct 17, M40 junct 2. Follow brown signs

Chiltern Open Air Museum is an independent charity, established over 30 years ago, with the aim of preserving some of the historic buildings that are unique examples of the heritage of the Chilterns. The museum is now home to more than 30 historic buildings all rescued from demolition and re-erected on this 45-acre woodland and parkland site. Events take place weekends and school holidays throughout the season, please check website for details.

Times Open 27 Mar-29 Oct, daily 10-5 (last admission 3.30)* **Facilities** (indoor & outdoor) (partly accessible) (Some paths/areas and buildings not accessible for all on this 45 acre site - full details on website or phone) toilets for disabled (Braille & audio guides, w/chairs pre-booking advised) shop

Milton's Cottage

Dean Way HP8 4JH
01494 872313
e-mail: info@miltonscottage.org
web: www.miltonscottage.org
dir: 0.5m W of A413. 3m N of M40 junct 2

A timber-framed, 16th-century cottage with a charming garden, the only surviving home in which John Milton lived and worked. He completed *Paradise Lost* and started *Paradise Regained* here. First editions of these works are among the many rare books and artefacts on display.

Times Open Mar-Oct, Tue-Sun 10-1 & 2-6. Also open Spring & Summer BH **Fees** £5 (ch 15 £3). Group rate 20+ £4 each **Facilities** licensed (partly accessible) (ground floor only accessible) (special parking area closer to cottage) shop

CLIVEDEN **Map 4 SU98**

Cliveden

SL6 0JA
01628 605069 01628 669461
e-mail: cliveden@nationaltrust.org.uk
web: www.nationaltrust.org.uk
dir: 2m N of Taplow, follow brown signs on A4

Cliveden's 375 acres of garden and woodland overlook the River Thames, and include a magnificent parterre, topiary, lawns with box hedges, and water gardens. The palatial house, former home of the Astors, is now a hotel - The Great Hall and French Dining Room can be visited on certain afternoons.

Times Open Grounds Mar-Oct daily 11-6, Nov-23 Dec daily 11-4 House Apr-Oct, Thu & Sun 3-5.30 by timed ticket* **Facilities** licensed (outdoor) (partly accessible) (most garden paths accessible) toilets for disabled (wheelchairs available, parking) shop

GREAT MISSENDEN **Map 6 SP80**

The Roald Dahl Museum & Story Centre

81-83 High St HP16 0AL
01494 892192 01494 892191
e-mail: admin@roalddahlmuseum.org
web: www.roalddahlmuseum.org
dir: From London/Amersham turn left off A413 into Great Missenden link road

This award-winning museum is aimed at 6 to 12 year olds and their families. Two interactive and biographical galleries tell the fascinating story of Roald Dahl's life, while the Story Centre puts imagination centre-stage, and encourages everyone (young and old) to dress up, make up stories, words and poems, or get arty in the craft room. Situated in Great Missenden where Dahl lived for over 36 years, it was created as a home for the author's archive (which visitors can see on regular tours) and as a place to inspire creativity and a love of reading in children, about which Dahl was passionate. 13th September every year - Roald Dahl Day national celebrations.

Times Open all year, Tue-Sun & BH Mon 10-5* **Facilities** (indoor & outdoor) (partly accessible) toilets for disabled (audio loops, tactile maps, wheelchair) shop

ENGLAND

HIGH WYCOMBE Map 4 SU89

Hughenden Manor

HP14 4LA
☎ 01494 755573 📠 01494 474284
e-mail: hughenden@nationaltrust.org.uk
web: www.nationaltrust.org.uk
dir: 1.5m N of High Wycombe, on W side of A4128

This fascinating Victorian manor was home to Prime Minister Benjamin Disraeli from 1848 to 1881. Many of his possessions are still on display, along with beautiful gardens designed by his wife Mary-Anne. Other facilities include circular woodland walks, family tracker packs, I-spy sheets in the Manor and an exhibition revealing Hughenden's role in WWII. See website for special event details.

Times House open 19 Feb-Dec (closed 25 Dec), Wed-Sun & BH Mon 12-5 (Feb, Nov & Dec 11-3). Gardens 19 Feb-Dec (closed 25 Dec), 11-5 (Feb, Nov & Dec 11-4). Park open all year* **Fees** £8 (ch £4.10). Family ticket £20. Garden only £3.20 (ch £2.20). Park free **Facilities** licensed (outdoor) (partly accessible) (Ground floor only fully accessible) toilets for disabled (Braille leaflet, wheelchairs, ramp to house) shop

West Wycombe Park

West Wycombe HP14 3AJ
☎ 01494 513569 📠 01494 474284
e-mail: westwycombe@nationaltrust.org.uk
web: www.nationaltrust.org.uk
dir: S of A40, at W end of West Wycombe

Set in 300 acres of beautiful parkland, the house was rebuilt in the Palladian style, between 1745 and 1771, for Sir Francis Dashwood. Of particular note are the painted ceilings by Borgnis. The park was laid out in the 18th century and given an artificial lake and classical temples.

Times Open, House & grounds 29 May-Aug, Sun-Thu 2-6. Grounds only 3 Apr-26 May, Sun-Thu 2-6 & BH Sun & Mon 2-6 (last admission 5.15). Entry by timed tickets. Parties must book in advance. **Fees** House & grounds £8 (ch £4). Family £20. Groups £6.60. Grounds only £4 (ch £2.35) **Facilities** (partly accessible) (partial access to ground floor & gardens)

Wycombe Museum

Castle Hill House, Priory Av HP13 6PX
☎ 01494 421895
e-mail: museum@wycombe.gov.uk
web: www.wycombe.gov.uk/museum
dir: A404 (Amersham Hill) N of High Wycombe just past railway station or from Marlow Hill A404, follow brown signs

High Wycombe is famous for chair making and the Museum has an extensive collection of chairs and artefacts from the furniture industry. There is also a gallery featuring local scenes and artists. Other aspects of Wycombe's history are also explored in a local history gallery. New for 2010/2011 is a changing exhibition gallery, including displays on the Women's Institute and the Wildlife of the Chilterns. The beautiful Museum Gardens provide an ideal spot for a picnic

Times Open all year, Mon-Sat 10-5, Sun 2-5. Closed on BHs except special events - ring for details* **Fees** Free admission (charges made for special events) **Facilities** (outdoor) (partly accessible) (ground floor and museum gardens only accessible) toilets for disabled (portable induction loop, special parking & drop off point) shop

LONG CRENDON Map 4 SP60

Courthouse

HP18 9AN
☎ 01280 822850
e-mail: stowegardens@nationaltrust.org.uk
web: www.nationaltrust.org.uk
dir: 2m N of Thame, via B4011, on entering village turn right into High St. Courthouse on left at end of High St next to parish church

One of the finest examples of early timber-framed building in the area, the Courthouse was probably built as a wool store in the early 1400s. It was also used as a manorial courthouse until the late 19th century, and still stands out, even in this picturesque village. Although the windows and doors have been altered and the chimney stack is Tudor, the magnificent timber roof is original.

Times Open, Upper storey 3 Apr-26 Sep, Sat-Sun 11-6; 7 Apr-29 Sep, also Wed 2-6* **Facilities**

MIDDLE CLAYDON Map 4 SP72

Claydon House

MK18 2EY
☎ 01296 730349 01296 738511
e-mail: claydon@nationaltrust.org.uk
web: www.nationaltrust.org.uk
dir: M40 junct 9 off A413 in Padbury, follow National Trust signs. Entrance by north drive only

The rather sober exterior of this 18th-century house gives no clue to the extravagances that lie inside, in the form of fantastic rococo carvings. Ceilings, cornices, walls and overmantels are adorned with delicately carved fruits, birds, beasts and flowers by Luke Lightfoot. The Chinese room is particularly splendid. There is also a spectacular parquetry staircase. Florence Nightingale was a regular visitor to the house from 1859-1890. The Costume Collection Displays are a recent addition.

Times House open 7 Mar-1 Nov, Sat-Wed 1-5 (last admission 4.30)* **Facilities** licensed (outdoor) (partly accessible) (ground floor accessible) toilets for disabled (Braille guide, photograph albums)

QUAINTON Map 4 SP72

Buckinghamshire Railway Centre 2 FOR 1

Quainton Road Station HP22 4BY
☎ 01296 655720 & 655450 01296 658569
e-mail: office@bucksrailcentre.org
web: www.bucksrailcentre.org
dir: Signed off A41 (Aylesbury-Bicester road) at Waddesdon, 7m NW of Aylesbury

Housed in a former Grade II listed building, the Centre features an interesting and varied collection of about 20 locomotives with 40 carriages and wagons from places as far afield as South Africa, Egypt and America. Items date from the 1800s up to the 1960s. Visitors can take a ride on full-size and miniature steam trains, and stroll around the 20-acre site to see locomotives and rolling stock. The Centre runs locomotive driving courses for visitors. Regular 'Days out with Thomas' events take place throughout the year. The 2 for 1 voucher is not valid for 'Days out with Thomas'.

Times Open with engines in steam Apr-Oct, Sun & BH; also Wed in school hols 10.30-4.30. (Open most days for restricted viewing)* **Fees** Gift aid incl prices. Steaming Days: £9 (ch £5.50, under 5's free, concessions £7.70). Family ticket (2ad+up to 4 ch) £23.50. Special events £10 (ch £7, under 5's free, concessions £9). Family ticket £27. Special prices apply for Day Out with Thomas* **Facilities** licensed (indoor & outdoor) (partly accessible) (some trains not accessible) toilets for disabled (ramped bridge with lift for wheelchairs) shop

STOWE Map 4 SP63

Stowe House

MK18 5EH
☎ 01280 818229 01280 818186
e-mail: amcevoy@stowe.co.uk
web: www.shpt.org
dir: 3m NW Buckingham

Set in the famous landscaped gardens, now owned by the National Trust, Stowe House is a splendid 18th-century neo-classical palace. The leading architects of the day - Vanbrugh, Gibbs, Kent and Leoni - all had a hand in the design of both the house and the gardens. A public school since 1923, Stowe House Preservation Trust now owns the building and is raising money for a six-phase restoration plan. The newly restored State Library is now open.

Times Open various dates & times. Call information line 01280 818166 **Fees** £4.40 (ch 2.70). Family ticket (2ad+3ch) £13.20. NT members £3.80 (ch £2.20). Family ticket £11* **Facilities** (fully accessible) toilets for disabled (lift to 1st floor) shop

Stowe Landscape Gardens

MK18 5DQ
☎ 01280 822850 01280 822437
e-mail: stowegarden@nationaltrust.org.uk
web: www.nationaltrust.org.uk
dir: 3m NW of Buckingham via Stowe Ave, off A422

Stowe is a breathtaking 18th-century creation, an idealised version of nature and is one of the first and foremost of the great English landscape gardens. Hidden amongst spectacular views and vast open spaces there are over 40 monuments, temples and secret corners to be discovered.

Times Open all year Jan-Mar, Sat-Sun, 10.30-4; Mar-Nov, Wed-Sun 10.30-5.30 (last entry 4); Nov-Feb, Sat-Sun 10.30-4. Open BHs* **Facilities** licensed (outdoor) (partly accessible) (some hills) toilets for disabled (batricars) shop

WADDESDON Map 4 SP71

Waddesdon Manor

HP18 0JH
☎ 01296 653226 & 653203 📠 01296 653212
e-mail: waddesdonmanor@nationaltrust.org.uk
web: www.waddesdon.org.uk
dir: entrance off A41, 6m NW of Aylesbury

Built in the 19th century by Baron Ferdinand de Rothschild, this French-style chateau was created as a showcase for his fine collection of French decorative arts. The Victorian gardens are known for seasonal displays, a parterre, walks, views, fountains and statues. The aviary is stocked with species that were once part of Baron Ferdinand's collection and the wine cellar contains Rothschild wines dating back to 1868. Special events throughout the year.

Times Gardens: 2 Jan-28 Mar, wknds only; 31 Mar-Dec, Wed-Sun & BHs also Mon-Tue 20-21 & 27-28 Dec; House: 31 Mar-Oct, Wed-Sun & BHs. Bachelors Wing 31 Mar-Oct Wed-Fri 12-2. Xmas season 17 Nov-Dec Wed-Sun & BHs also Mon-Tue 20-21 & 27-28 Dec* **Fees** Gardens, 2 Jan-28 Mar (wknds only) £7 (ch £3.50) Family £17.50; 31 Mar-Dec, (Wed-Fri) £5.50 (ch £2.75) Family £13.75. Wknds & BHs £7 (ch £3.50) Family £17.50. House & gardens, 31 Mar-Dec (Wed-Fri) £13.20 (ch £9.35), wknds & BHs £15 (ch £11). Batchelors Wing £3.30* **Facilities** Ⓟ 🍽 licensed ♿ (fully accessible) toilets for disabled (wheelchairs, Braille guide, scented plants, audio guide) shop ㊙ ✣

WEST WYCOMBE Map 4 SU89

The Hell-Fire Caves

HP14 3AJ
☎ 01494 524411 (office) & 533739 (caves)
📠 01494 471617
e-mail: mary@west-wycombe-estate.co.uk
web: www.hellfirecaves.co.uk
dir: just off A40 in West Wycombe

Go underground into the Hell-Fire Caves for a unique day out. Sir Francis Dashwood had these extraordinary caves excavated in the 1750s. The caves were reputed to have hosted the notorious Hell-Fire Club whose members included some of Britain's most senior aristocrats and statesmen. A tour of the caves takes you past various small chambers to the Banqueting Hall, down over the River Styx to the Inner Temple, which is about 300 feet beneath the church on the top of the hill. The caves are scattered with statues in costume and a commentary with sound effects are included throughout the tour.

Times Open all year, Apr-Oct, daily, 11-5.30; Nov-Mar, wknds & school hols 11-5.30* **Facilities** Ⓟ ℗ ☕ ⛩ (outdoor) ♿ (partly accessible) (cafe and toilets accessible) toilets for disabled shop ㊙

WING Map 4 SP82

Ascott

LU7 0PS
☎ 01296 688242 📠 01296 681904
e-mail: info@ascottestate.co.uk
web: www.ascottestate.com
dir: 0.5m E of Wing, 3m SW of Leighton Buzzard on S side of A418

A National Trust property since 1949, Ascott holds an exceptional collection of paintings, Chinese porcelain, and English and French furniture. The 30-acre garden is a fine example of Victorian gardening, and the grounds are stunning at any time of year.

Times House & Gardens: 23 Mar-25 Apr, daily (ex Mon); 27 Apr-22 Jul, Tue-Thu; 27 Jul-10 Sep, daily (ex Mon) & open BH Mon, 2-6 (last admission 5)* **Facilities** Ⓟ ♿ (fully accessible) toilets for disabled (w/chairs avail, assistance required, large print guide) ㊙ ✣

CAMBRIDGESHIRE

Ely Cathedral

ENGLAND

CAMBRIDGE Map 5 TL45

Cambridge & County Folk Museum 2 FOR 1

2/3 Castle St CB3 0AQ
☎ 01223 355159
e-mail: info@folkmuseum.org.uk
web: www.folkmuseum.org.uk
dir: off A14 onto A3019, museum NW of town

This timber-framed inn houses items covering the everyday life of the people of Cambridgeshire from early times to the present day. There are also temporary exhibitions and children's activity days taking place throughout the year. Please telephone for details.

Times Open all year, Apr-Sep, Tue-Sat 10.30-5, Sun 2-5; Oct-Mar, Tue-Sat 10.30-5, Sun 2-5. Also open BH Mon 2-5 (last admission 30 mins before closing). Closed 24-31 Dec & 1 Jan* **Fees** £3.50 (ch 5-12 £1, one free ch with every full paying adult, concessions £2)* **Facilities** Ⓟ (outdoor) (fully accessible) toilets for disabled (lift) shop

Cambridge University Botanic Garden

1 Brookside CB2 1JE
☎ 01223 336265 01223 336278
e-mail: enquiries@botanic.cam.ac.uk
web: www.botanic.cam.ac.uk
dir: 1m S of city centre, 5min from train station. Brookside Gate entrance at corner of Trumpington Road (A1309) & Bateman St. Station Rd entrance at junct of Hills Rd (A1307) & Station Rd

The Cambridge University Botanic Garden is a 40-acre oasis of beautifully landscaped gardens and glasshouses close to the heart of the historic city. Opened on its present site in 1846, the garden showcases a collection of some 8,000 plant species. This Grade II heritage landscape features the Rock Garden, displaying alpine plants; the Winter and Autumn Gardens; tropical rainforest and seasonal displays in the Glasshouses; the historic Systematic Beds; the Scented Garden; Herbaceous Beds and the finest collection of trees in the east of England.

Times Open all year daily, Apr-Sep 10-6; Feb-Mar, Oct 10-5, Nov-Jan 10-4. (Glasshouses & cafe close 30 mins before garden). Please call to check Xmas closure. Both Brookside Gate & Station Rd Gate now open daily* **Facilities** Ⓟ (outdoor) (partly accessible) (Some historic areas of the garden inaccessible for wheelchairs, such as the rock garden) toilets for disabled (manual & motorised wheelchairs-prebooked) shop

Fitzwilliam Museum FREE

Trumpington St CB2 1RB
☎ 01223 332900 01223 332923
e-mail: fitzmuseum-enquiries@lists.cam.ac.uk
web: www.fitzmuseum.cam.ac.uk
dir: M11 junct 11, 12 or 13. Near city centre

The Fitzwilliam is the art museum of the University of Cambridge and one of the oldest public museums in Britain. It contains magnificent collections spanning centuries and civilisations, including antiquities from Ancient Egypt, Greece and Rome; sculpture, furniture, armour, ceramics, manuscripts, coins and medals, paintings, drawings and prints.

Times Open all year Tue-Sat 10-5, Sun 12-5. Closed Mon ex BHs, 24-26 & 31 Dec, 1 Jan & Good Fri* **Facilities** Ⓟ (outdoor) (fully accessible) toilets for disabled (induction loop) shop

The Polar Museum, Scott Polar Research Institute

Lensfield Rd CB2 1ER
☎ 01223 336540 01223 336549
e-mail: enquiries@spri.cam.ac.uk
web: www.spri.cam.ac.uk
dir: 1km S of city centre

An international centre for polar studies, including a museum featuring displays of Arctic and Antarctic expeditions, with special emphasis on those of Captain Scott and the exploration of the Northwest Passage. Other exhibits include Inuit work and other arts of the polar region, as well as displays on current scientific exploration. Public lectures run from October to December and February to April. The Polar Museum reopened after a major renovation in June 2010. Please check website for exhibitions.

Times Open Tue-Sat, 10-4. Closed BH wknds. Please call 01223 336540 or check the website for further details **Fees** Free admission, donations welcome **Facilities** Ⓟ (fully accessible) toilets for disabled (induction loop at kiosk) shop

University Museum of Archaeology & Anthropology FREE

Downing St CB2 3DZ
☎ 01223 333516 01223 333517
e-mail: cumaa@hermes.cam.ac.uk
web: www.maa.cam.ac.uk
dir: opposite Crowne Plaza Hotel in city centre

The museum is part of the Faculty of Archaeology and Anthropology of the University of Cambridge. It was established in 1884 and is still housed in its 1916 building on the Downing Site in the city centre. Some of the highlights are Pacific material collected on Captain Cook's voyages of exploration and a 46-foot high totem pole from Canada. Find out about local, national and world archaeology in the Archaeology Galleries, including painted pottery from Peru, giled Anglo-Saxon brooches, and Roman altar stones.

Times Open Tue-Sat, 10.30-4.30* **Facilities** Ⓟ (partly accessible) toilets for disabled (lift available) shop

DUXFORD Map 5 TL44

Imperial War Museum Duxford

CB22 4QR
☎ 01223 835000 01223 837267
e-mail: duxford@iwm.org.uk
web: www.iwm.org.uk/duxford
dir: off M11 junct 10, on A505

Set within the best preserved Battle of Britain's airfield, Duxford is a vibrant museum that marries its historic past with modern displays, interactive exhibitions, events and attractions. Come and wander amongst two hundred aircraft to discover the science, engineering and fascinating human stories behind the machines that changed our world forever. The Museum holds four air shows throughout the year plus many other exciting events such as American Air Day, Military Vehicle Show, car shows, family activities during school holidays, talks, tours and much more.

Times Open all year, 15 Mar-14 Oct, daily 10-6; 15 Oct-14 Mar, daily 10-4. Closed 24-26 Dec **Fees** £16 (ch under 16 free, concessions £12.80). Events & airshow prices vary* **Facilities** licensed (indoor & outdoor) (fully accessible) toilets for disabled (w/chair available - phone in advance, ramps, lifts) shop

ELY — Map 5 TL58

Ely Cathedral

CB7 4DL

☎ 01353 667735 Fax 01353 665658

e-mail: receptionist@cathedral.ely.anglican.org

web: www.cathedral.ely.anglican.org

dir: A10 or A142, 15m from Cambridge

The Octagon Tower of Ely Cathedral can be seen for miles as it rises above the surrounding flat fenland. A monastery was founded on the site by St Etheldreda in 673, but the present cathedral church dates from 1083 and is a magnificent example of Romanesque architecture. Choral music is a big attraction at the Cathedral, and visitors can hear Evensong at 5.30pm on weekdays and Saturdays, and 4pm on a Sunday.

Times Open daily, Summer 7-7, Winter 7.30-6 (5pm Sun) **Fees** £6 (services & students £5)* **Facilities** licensed (outdoor) (fully accessible) toilets for disabled (touch tour for blind/partially sighted) shop

Ely Museum — 2 FOR 1

The Old Gaol, Market St CB7 4LS

☎ 01353 666655 Fax 01353 659259

e-mail: admin@elymuseum.org.uk

web: www.elymuseum.org.uk

dir: On corner of Market St and Lynn Rd. In centre of Ely, 250mtrs from west door of Ely Cathedral

Centre of history for the Isle of Ely and the Fens, telling the story of the area from prehistoric times to the 20th century. The museum is within a building dating from the 13th century that has been a private house, a tavern, a registry office and most famously the Bishop's Gaol. Sensitively renovated in 1997 much of the building's history can still be seen, including prisoner's graffiti, hidden doorways and original planking on the walls.

Times Open during summer, Mon-Sat 10.30-5 & Sun 1-5. Winter Mon-Sat 10.30-4 (closed Tue), Sun 1-4 **Fees** £3.50 (up to 4 accompanied children free with each paying adult, concessions £2.50)* **Facilities** (fully accessible) toilets for disabled (Stair lift, auto doors) shop

Oliver Cromwell's House — 2 FOR 1

29 St Mary's St CB7 4HF

☎ 01353 662062 Fax 01353 668518

e-mail: tic@eastcambs.gov.uk

web: www.visitely.org.uk

dir: follow brown tourist signs from main roads. Adjacent to Saint Mary's Church

Cromwell inherited the house and local estates from a maternal uncle and moved here in 1636, along with his mother, sisters, wife and eight children. There are displays and period rooms dealing with Cromwell's life, the Civil War and domestic life in the 17th century, as well as the history of The Fens and the house itself, from its medieval origins to its role as an inn in the 19th century. Various special events are held during the year including Living History days.

Times Open all year: Apr-Oct, daily 10-5; Nov-Mar, Mon-Fri 11-4, Sat 10-5. Sun 11.15-4* **Fees** £4.50 (ch £3.10, concessions £4). Family ticket £13* **Facilities** (partly accessible) (wheelchair access to two rooms & interactive booth) (written script of audio features) shop

The Stained Glass Museum

The South Triforium, Ely Cathedral CB7 4DL

☎ 01353 660347 Fax 01353 665025

e-mail: curator@stainedglassmuseum.com

web: www.stainedglassmuseum.com

dir: Museum inside Ely Cathedral on corner of Market St & Lynn Rd

800 years of stained-glass history are illustrated in this unique museum inside Ely Cathedral. Over 100 panels of original stained-glass windows rescued from the UK and abroad are on display. The medieval section includes important loans from the Victoria and Albert Museum in London. There are also exhibits from Buckingham Palace and Windsor Castle, work by William Morris and John Piper, and changing exhibitions of contemporary work.

Times Open all year (ex Good Fri & 25-26 Dec) Etr-Oct, Mon-Fri 10.30-5, Sat 10.30-5, Sun 12-6; Nov-Etr, Mon-Sat 10.30-5, Sun 12-4.30 **Fees** £3.50 (ch under 16 & concessions £2.50). Family ticket (up to 4 with 1 under 16) £7 **Facilities** licensed (outdoor) (partly accessible) (wheelchair access to interactive station at lower level) toilets for disabled shop

HOUGHTON — Map 4 TL27

Houghton Mill

PE28 2AZ

☎ 01480 301494

e-mail: houghtonmill@nationaltrust.org.uk

web: www.nationaltrust.org.uk

dir: in Houghton signed off A1123 Huntingdon to St Ives

The last working watermill on the Great Ouse, Houghton Mill has hands-on exhibits for all the family and has most of its machinery intact.

Times Open Mill/Bookshop: 2 May-26 Sep, Sat 11-5; 27 Apr-27 Sep, Mon-Wed & Sun 11-5; Mar-Apr & Oct, Sat 11-5. Also open BHs & Good Fri* **Facilities** (partly accessible)

ENGLAND

LINTON Map 5 TL54

Chilford Hall Vineyard

Chilford Hall, Balsham Rd CB21 4LE
☎ 01223 895600 📠 01223 895605
e-mail: info@chilfordhall.co.uk
web: www.chilfordhall.co.uk
dir: Brown Tourist Info signs from A1307 & A11

Taste and buy award-winning wines from the largest vineyard in Cambridgeshire. See the grapes growing in the 18 acre vineyard and take a winery tour to learn how English wine is made and appreciate the subtle difference between each of the Chilford quality wines. Please telephone for details of special events.

Times Open Mar-Oct, Fri-Sun & BHs 10.30-5. Please telephone outside of these times* **Fees** Guided tours & tasting £9.95 (ch free). Party 15+ (please call for group rate)* **Facilities** licensed (outdoor) (fully accessible) toilets for disabled (ramps, lift, all areas are ground floor) shop

Linton Zoological Gardens

Hadstock Rd CB21 4NT
☎ 01223 891308 📠 01223 891308
web: www.lintonzoo.co.uk
dir: M11 junct 9/10, on B1052 off A1307 between Cambridge & Haverhill, signed

Linton Zoo places emphasis on conservation and education where visitors can see a combination of beautiful gardens and a wealth of wildlife from all over the world. There are many rare and exotic creatures to see including tapirs, snow leopards, tigers, lions, zebra, tamarin monkeys, lemurs, owls, parrots, giant tortoises, snakes, tarantulas and many others. The zoo is set in 16 acres of gardens with plenty of picnic areas, children's play area and bouncy castle.

Times Open all year, daily 10.30-4 (last admission 3). Hours extended during summer. Closed 25-26 Dec.* **Facilities** (outdoor) (fully accessible) toilets for disabled shop

LODE Map 5 TL56

Anglesey Abbey, Gardens & Lode Mill

CB25 9EJ
☎ 01223 810080 📠 01223 810088
e-mail: angleseyabbey@nationaltrust.org.uk
web: www.nationaltrust.org.uk/angleseyabbey
dir: 6m NE of Cambridge on B1102, signed from A14

A medieval undercroft has survived from the priory founded here in 1135, but the house dates mainly from 1600. Thomas Hobson of 'Hobson's Choice' was one of the owners. A later owner was Lord Fairhaven, who amassed the huge collection of pictures, and laid out the beautiful 114 acre gardens with its beautifully restored watermill, wildlife discovery centre and classical sculptures. A programme of exhibitions and events can be enjoyed all year round, including an outdoor theatre in August, garden study days and children's events.

Times Open House: 7 Mar-30 Oct, Wed-Sun 11-5. Gardens open daily Jan-6 Mar & 31 Oct-Dec, 10.30-4.30 & 7 Mar-30 Oct, 10.30-5.30. Closed 24-26 Dec. Lode Mill open Jan-Dec, Wed-Sun 11-1 & 2-4 **Fees** House, garden & mill £9.75 (ch £4.90). Family ticket £24.40. Garden & mill £5.80 (ch £2.90). Family ticket £14.50* **Facilities** licensed (outdoor) (partly accessible) (2 rooms accessible in house, lower floor only in Mill, good paths through most of garden) toilets for disabled (electric buggy, wheelchairs, large print & Braille guides) shop

PETERBOROUGH Map 4 TL19

Flag Fen Archaeology Park

The Droveway, Northey Rd PE6 7QJ
☎ 01733 313414 📠 01733 349957
e-mail: info@flagfen.org
web: www.flagfen.org
dir: From A1139 exit at Boongate junct. At rdbt 3rd exit, through lights, turn right. At T-junct turn right, Flag Fen signed

Although visitors enter this site through a 21st-century roundhouse, the rest of their day will be spent in the Bronze Age, some 3,000 years ago. Flag Fen's Museum contains artefacts found over the last 20 years of excavating on site, and includes among them the oldest wheel in Britain. In the Park there is a reconstructed Bronze Age settlement and Iron Age roundhouse, while in the Preservation Hall visitors can see the excavated Bronze Age processional way that spanned over one mile. The Hall also contains a 60-ft mural depicting the fens in ancient times.

Times Open daily Mar-Oct 10-5 (last admission 4)* **Facilities** (outdoor) (fully accessible) toilets for disabled (electric mobility scooter and wheelchairs available) shop

Peterborough Cathedral

PE1 1XS
☎ 01733 355300 & 343342 📠 01733 355316
e-mail: richard.cattle@peterborough-cathedral.org.uk
web: www.peterborough-cathedral.org.uk
dir: access from A1 junct with A605 or A47, follow signs for city centre

With one of the most dramatic West fronts in the country, its three arches an extraordinary creation of medieval architecture, it would be easy for the interior to be an anticlimax, but it is not. The dramatic Romanesque interior is little altered since its completion 800 years ago. Particular highlights of a visit include the unique painted nave ceiling, the elaborate fan vaulting of the 'new' building, Saxon carvings from an earlier church and the burial place of two Queens. An exhibition in the North aisle tells the story of the cathedral. A range of tours can be booked in advance: please contact the Chapter office for details.

Times Open all year, Mon-Fri 9-6.30 (limited access from 5.30), Sat 9-5, Sun services from 7.30 visitors from 12. Closed 25-26 Dec **Fees** Donations appreciated. Group tours: £5 (concessions £3.50)* **Facilities** licensed (fully accessible) toilets for disabled (touch & hearing centre, Braille guide, ramps) shop

Railworld

Oundle Rd PE2 9NR
☎ 01733 344240 & 319362 📠 01733 319362
e-mail: info@railworld.net
web: www.railworld.net
dir: from A1(M) Peterborough onto A1139 then exit at junct 5 to city centre. At 1st rdbt, follow "Little Puffer" tourist signs. Entrance for Railworld off Oundle Rd at city end through car park

Railworld is a sustainable transport centre and 21st-century rail showcase. Its main focus is on the future of rail transport and how it can meet the challenges of climate change and other environmental issues. It features a large model railway, displays on rail history, showcases of rail technology and innovation, an environmental maze, hovertrains, and much more.

Times Open Etr-Oct, Tue-Thu & Sat-Sun 11-4. Closed Mon (ex school hols & BH) & Fri (ex school hols). Closed Nov-Etr unless by appointment & special events **Fees** £3 (ch free, concessions £2) **Facilities** Ⓟ Ⓟ ☕ ⛩ (outdoor) ♿ (fully accessible) toilets for disabled shop ⊗

RAMSEY — Map 4 TL28

Ramsey Abbey Gatehouse

Abbey School PE17 1DH
☎ 01480 301494 📠 01263 734924
e-mail: ramseyabbey@nationaltrust.org.uk
web: www.nationaltrust.org.uk
dir: SE edge of Ramsey, at Chatteris Road & B1096 junct

The ruins of this 15th-century gatehouse, together with the 13th-century Lady Chapel, are all that remain of the abbey. Half of the gatehouse was taken away after the Dissolution. Built in ornate late-Gothic style, it has panelled buttresses and friezes.

Times Open Apr-Sep, first Sun of the month 1-5 (Group visits by appt only other wknds)* **Facilities** ⊗ ✤

THORNHAUGH — Map 4 TL00

Sacrewell Farm & Country Centre — 2 FOR 1

PE8 6HJ
☎ 01780 782254 📠 01780 781370
e-mail: info@sacrewell.org.uk
web: www.sacrewell.org.uk
dir: E of A1/A47 junct. Follow brown tourist signs from both directions

Treasures of farming and the country await discovery at this farm and 18th-century watermill. All aspects of agriculture and country life through the ages are here, listed buildings, working 18th-century watermill, mill house and farm bygones. Friendly farm animals are here to be fed, and tractor rides, straw bale maze, soft play area and pedal tractors are just a few of the activities to be experienced. Events throughout the year include lambing at Easter, Halloween rides and a Christmas Victorian spectacular. The 2 for 1 voucher admits one child free with each full paying adult.

Times Open all year daily Mar-Sep, 9.30-5; Oct-Feb, 10-4. Closed 24 Dec-2 Jan **Fees** £6.50 (ch £4.85, ch under 3 free, pen £5.50). Please check dates & prices before visiting* **Facilities** Ⓟ ☕ 🍽 licensed ⛩ (indoor & outdoor) ♿ (partly accessible) (upstairs in watermill not accessible) toilets for disabled shop

WANSFORD — Map 4 TL09

Nene Valley Railway — 2 FOR 1

Wansford Station, Stibbington PE8 6LR
☎ 01780 784444 📠 01780 784440
e-mail: nvrorg@nvr.org.co.uk
web: www.nvr.org.uk
dir: A1 at Stibbington, W of Peterborough, 1m S of A47 junct

Originally opened as a working railway in 1845, closed in 1966, then re-opened in 1977 as a tourist railway, Nene Valley Railway has steam and diesel engines, carriages and wagons from the UK and Europe. Travelling between Yarwell Junction, Wansford and Peterborough, the 7.5 miles of track pass through the heart of the 500-acre Ferry Meadows Country Park. Nene Valley Railway is also the home of Thomas the Tank Engine. Thomas and other themed events from February to December.

Times Train services operate on Sun from Jan; wknds from Apr-Oct; Wed from May, plus other mid-week services in summer* **Fees** £12 (ch 3-15 £6, concessions £9). Family ticket £30* **Facilities** Ⓟ Ⓟ ☕ ⛩ (outdoor) ♿ (fully accessible) toilets for disabled (disabled access to trains) shop

WATERBEACH — Map 5 TL46

The Farmland Museum and Denny Abbey

Ely Rd CB25 9PQ
☎ 01223 860988 📠 01223 860988
e-mail: info@farmlandmuseum.org.uk
web: www.dennyfarmlandmuseum.org.uk
dir: on A10 between Cambridge & Ely

Explore two areas of rural life at this fascinating museum. The Abbey tells the story of those who have lived there, including Benedictine monks, Franciscan nuns, and the mysterious Knights Templar. The farm museum features the craft workshops of a wheelwright, a basketmaker, and a blacksmith. There is also a 1940s farmworker's cottage and a village shop. Special events on Easter, May and August Bank Holidays.

Times Open daily, Apr-Oct, 12-5* **Facilities** Ⓟ ☕ ⛩ (outdoor) ♿ (partly accessible) toilets for disabled (wheelchairs, guides upstairs) shop

WICKEN Map 5 TL57

Wicken Fen National Nature Reserve

Lode Ln CB7 5XP
☎ 01353 720274
e-mail: wickenfen@nationaltrust.org.uk
web: www.nationaltrust.org.uk/main
dir: S of Wicken A1123

An ancient fenland landscape and internationally renowned wetland site, Wicken Fen is home to the Wicken Vision Project, the Trust's most ambitious landscape-scale habitat restoration project.

Times Reserve & Visitor Centre open all year daily 10-5 **Fees** £5.99 (ch 5-17yrs £2.99). Family £14.99 **Facilities** (outdoor) (partly accessible) (boardwalk 0.75m circular walk suitable for wheelchairs) shop

WIMPOLE Map 5 TL35

Wimpole Hall

SG8 0BW
☎ 01223 206000 01223 207838
e-mail: wimpolehall@nationaltrust.org.uk
web: www.nationaltrust.org.uk/wimpole
dir: M11 junct 12, 8m SW of Cambridge off A603

Wimpole Hall is one of the grandest mansions in East Anglia, and has 360 acres of parkland devised and planted by no less than four celebrated landscape designers, Charles Bridgeman, Lancelot 'Capability' Brown, Sanderson Miller and Humphry Repton. The house dates back to 1640, but was altered into a large 18th-century mansion with a Georgian façade. The chapel has a trompe l'oeil ceiling.

Times Hall 28 Feb-15 Jul, 29 Aug-1 Nov, Mon-Wed, Sat & Sun 10.30-5; 18 Jul-27 Aug, Mon-Thu, Sat & Sun 10.30-5. Garden 1-25 Feb, 2 Nov-23 Dec, 2-31 Jan, Mon-Wed, Sat & Sun 11-4; 28 Feb-15 Jul, Mon-Wed, Sat & Sun; 18 Jul-27 Aug, 10.30-5. BH Mon & Good Fri 10.30-5 (Hall 11-5 & Good Fri 1-5). Park: all year dawn-dusk daily* **Facilities** licensed (outdoor) (partly accessible) toilets for disabled (Braille & large print guide, buggies, stairlift, w/chair) shop

Wimpole Home Farm

SG8 0BW
☎ 01223 206000 01223 207838
e-mail: wimpolefarm@nationaltrust.org.uk
web: www.nationaltrust.org.uk/wimpole
dir: M11 junct 12, 8m SW of Cambridge off A603

When built in 1794, the Home Farm was one of the most advanced agricultural enterprises in the country. The Great Barn, now restored, holds a display of farm machinery and implements of the kind used at Wimpole over the past two centuries. On the farm there are rare breeds of domestic animals, and visitors can see the new lambs in spring, and sheep shearing in June. Please ring for details of special events.

Times Open 1-25 Feb, Sat & Sun 11-4; 28 Feb-15 Jul, Mon-Wed, Sat & Sun 10.30-5; Jul-27 Aug, Mon-Thu, Sat & Sun 10.30-5; 29 Aug-1 Nov, Mon-Wed, Sat & Sun 10.30-5; 7 Nov-20 Dec, Sat-Sun 11-4; 27-31 Dec, Tue-Thu, Sat & Sun 11-4; 2-31 Jan, Sat-Sun 11-4. BH Mon & Good Fri 10.30-5* **Facilities** licensed (outdoor) (partly accessible) toilets for disabled (large print guide, wheelchairs, electric buggies) shop

WISBECH Map 9 TF40

Peckover House & Garden

North Brink PE13 1JR
☎ 01945 583463 01945 583463
e-mail: peckover@nationaltrust.org.uk
web: www.nationaltrust.org.uk/peckover
dir: Exit A47, follow town centre signs, then brown tourist signs

Dating from 1722, Peckover House is an elegant Georgian brick townhouse with an outstanding two-acre walled town garden. Over 70 types of rose grow here, along with a number of notable specimen trees such as Maidenhead Tree and Tulip Tree. The Victorian glasshouses include a propagation house, and an orangery with 300-year-old trees that still bear fruit. Visitors can borrow a croquet set and play on the lawn. There is a children's handling collection in the basement. Lots of special events each year, ring for details. 2011 marks the centenary of the death of Octavia Hill who started the National Trust and who was born in Wisbech, opposite Peckover House.

Times House open 12 Mar-30 Oct, Mon-Wed & wknds 1-5, garden 12-5 (last admission 4.30) **Fees** £6.60 (ch £3.30). Garden only £4.30 (ch £2.15) **Facilities** (outdoor) (partly accessible) (garden fully accessible) toilets for disabled (Batricar, induction loops) shop

WOODHURST Map 5 TL37

The Raptor Foundation

The Heath, St Ives Rd PE28 3BT
☎ 01487 741140 01487 841140
e-mail: heleowl@aol.com
web: www.raptorfoundation.org.uk
dir: B1040 to Somersham, follow brown signs

Permanent home to over 250 birds of which there are 40 different varieties. This is a unique opportunity to meet and learn about birds of prey. Depending on weather and time of year flying demonstrations are held, usually three times a day and audiences have the chance to participate in displays. There are nearly 60 birds in the flying team, so each display has a different set of birds. Educational trail linking to new education room. New indoor flying area. Ask about activity days, membership and adoption.

Times Open all year, daily 10-5. Closed 25-26 Dec & 1 Jan* **Facilities** licensed (outdoor) (fully accessible) toilets for disabled (ramped areas, blocked paved paths) shop

CHESHIRE

Little Moreton Hall, Congleton

ENGLAND

BEESTON Map 7 SJ55

Beeston Castle

Chapel Ln CW6 9TX
☎ 01829 260464
web: www.english-heritage.org.uk
dir: on minor road off A49 or A41

Known as the 'Castle of the Rock', Beeston Castle is at the top of an impressive crag which enjoys breathtaking views over eight counties, from the Pennines to the Welsh mountains. An exhibition details 4,000 years of Beeston Castle's history, from Bronze Age settlement to Iron Age hill fort. Legend tells of a vast treasure hidden here by King Richard II, but a treasure more easily found is the 40 acres of unspoiled woodland full of wildlife and trails to explore.

Times Open all year, Apr-Sep, daily 10-6; Oct-Mar, Thu-Mon 10-4. Closed 24-26 Dec & 1 Jan **Fees** £5.30 (ch £2.70, concessions £4.50). Prices and opening times are subject to change in March 2011. Please call 0870 333 1181 for the most up to date prices and opening times when planning your visit **Facilities** Ⓟ ⛩ shop ⊗ ⌗

CAPESTHORNE Map 7 SJ87

Capesthorne Hall

SK11 9JY
☎ 01625 861221 🖷 01625 861619
e-mail: info@capesthorne.com
web: www.capesthorne.com
dir: On A34 between Congleton and Wilmslow

Capesthorne has been the home of the Bromley-Davenport family and their ancestors since Domesday times. The present house dates from 1719 and was designed by the Smiths of Warwick. It was subsequently altered by Edward Blore in 1837, and after a disastrous fire in 1861 the whole of the centre portion was rebuilt by Anthony Salvin. Capesthorne contains a great variety of sculptures, paintings and other items including a collection of boxes, from a Victorian oak letterbox to hat and cigar boxes. There are also lakeside gardens including swallow hole and ice house.

Times Open Apr-Oct, Sun & Mon (incl BH). Park & Garden 12-5, Hall 1.30-3.30. Closed Xmas & New Year.* **Fees** Park, Garden & Chapel £4.50 (ch £2.50). Park, Gardens, Chapel & Hall £7 (ch £3.50 & concessions £6). Family ticket £16. Special deal on Mon's £10 per car (up to 4 persons). Coach £70, Mini-bus £35* **Facilities** Ⓟ ☕ ♿ (partly accessible) (ground floor of hall accessible) toilets for disabled (ramp access to ground floor of hall & gardens) ⊗

CHESTER Map 7 SJ46

The Cheshire Military Museum — 2 FOR 1

The Castle CH1 2DN
☎ 01244 327617 🖷 01244 401700
e-mail: museum@chester.ac.uk
web: www.chester.ac.uk/militarymuseum
dir: follow signs to Military Museum from town centre

This military museum boasts exhibits from the history of the Cheshire Regiment, Cheshire Yeomanry, 5th Royal Inniskilling Dragoon Guards, and 3rd Carabiniers. There is a display of the work of George Jones, Victorian battle artist, and an exhibition of life in barracks in the 1950s. Research resources are available by written appointment and donation. There are special events throughout the year, please phone for details. The War Horse exhibition shows the equine species at war - from the Persian Wars through to the present day.

Times Open all year, daily 10-5 (last entry 4). Closed 22 Dec-3 Jan* **Fees** £3 (ch & concessions £2)* **Facilities** Ⓟ ♿ (fully accessible) toilets for disabled (wheelchair accessible) shop ⊗

Chester Cathedral — 2 FOR 1

Saint Werburgh St CH1 2HU
☎ 01244 324756 🖷 01244 699040
e-mail: visits@chestercathedral.com
web: www.chestercathedral.com
dir: St Werburgh Str, opposite Town Hall

With 1000 years of history, a visit to Chester Cathedral opens a window onto a rich and varied story of monks, kings and craftsmen. The Cathedral is an extraordinary mixture of old and new, with something for everyone to enjoy. From Norman arches to gothic columns, spectacular 14th-century woodcarvings to afternoon teas in the Refectory Café. There is so much here to discover from modern works of art to the tranquil Cloister Garden, a haven of peace and calm on a busy day. The cathedral hosts a wide range of special events and concerts throughout the year.

Times Open Mon-Sat, 9-5, Sun 1-4.30, please telephone to check* **Fees** £5 (ch £2.50 free up to age 3 with paying adult, concessions £4). Groups £4 (ch £2)* **Facilities** Ⓟ ☕ 🍽 licensed ♿ (partly accessible) (steps to some areas, uneven floors) toilets for disabled (induction loop, wide doors) shop ⊗

Chester Visitor Centre

FREE

Vicars Ln CH1 1QX

☎ 01244 401796 & 329580 📠 01244 403188

e-mail: rowscafe@hotmail.co.uk

web: www.chestervisitorcentre.co.uk

dir: opposite St Johns Church Roman Amphitheatre

Among the attractions at this large visitor information centre are guided walks of Chester, displays on the history of Chester, a café and a gift shop. Chester is the most complete walled city in Britain, and was originally settled by the Romans in the first century AD. The city also played its part in battles with the Vikings, the Norman invasion, and the Civil War. The newly refurbished amphitheatre is directly opposite the building.

Times Open all year Apr-Oct, Mon-Sat 9-5, Sun 10-4; Nov-Mar, Mon-Fri 9-4, Sat 9-5, Sun 10-4 **Facilities** Ⓟ ☕ 🛒 (outdoor) ♿ (fully accessible) toilets for disabled (ramped access from Vicars Lane) shop 🚭

Chester Zoo

Upton-by-Chester CH2 1LH

☎ 01244 380280 📠 01244 371273

e-mail: marketing@chesterzoo.org

web: www.chesterzoo.org

dir: 2m N of city centre off A41 & M53 junct 10 southbound, junct 12 all other directions

Chester Zoo is the UK's number one charity zoo, with over 7,000 animals and 400 different species, some of them amongst the most endangered species on the planet. There's plenty to see and do, like the Realm of the Red Ape enclosure, home to the Bornean and Sumatran orang-utans. Experience the sights and sounds of Assam, with the herd of Asian elephants, hornbills, tree shrews and rare fish inside Elephants of the Asian Forest. View the world's fastest land mammal, the cheetah, from the new Bat's Bridge. See a wide variety of beautifully coloured African birds housed in African Aviaries and Philippine crocodiles in their new enclosure in the Tropical Realm.

Times Open all year, daily from 10 (last admission varies with season). Closed 25-26 Dec* **Facilities** 🅟 Ⓟ ☕ 🍽 licensed 🛒 (indoor & outdoor) ♿ (fully accessible) toilets for disabled (electric scooters, wheelchairs for hire) shop 🚭

Dewa Roman Experience

2 FOR 1

Pierpoint Ln, (off Bridge St) CH1 1NL

☎ 01244 343407 📠 01244 347737

e-mail: info@dewaromanexperience.co.uk

web: www.dewaromanexperience.co.uk

dir: city centre

Stroll along reconstructed streets experiencing the sights, sounds and smells of Roman Chester. From the streets of Dewa (the Roman name for Chester) you return to the present day on an extensive archaeological 'dig', where you can discover the substantial Roman, Saxon and medieval remains beneath modern Chester. Try on Roman armour, solve puzzles and make brass rubbings and mosaics in the hands-on/activity room. Roman soldier patrols available.

Times Open all year daily, Feb-Nov 9-5 (Sun 10-5), Dec-Jan 10-4 . Closed 25-26 & 31 Dec & 1 Jan **Fees** £4.95 (ch 5-16 £3.25, under 5 free, senior/student £4.50). Group 10+ £4.25. Family (2ad & up to 3 ch £15)* **Facilities** Ⓟ ♿ (partly accessible) (2 flights of stairs but can be avoided) shop 🚭

CHOLMONDELEY — **Map 7 SJ55**

Cholmondeley Castle Gardens

SY14 8AH

☎ 01829 720383 📠 01829 720877

e-mail: office@cholmondeleycastle.co.uk

web: www.cholmondeleycastle.com

dir: off A49 Tarporley to Whitchurch road

Dominated by a romantic Gothic Castle built in 1801 of local sandstone, the gardens are laid out with fine trees and water gardens, and have been replanted with rhododendrons, azaleas, cornus, and acer. There is also a rose and lavender garden, lakeside and woodland walks, and unusual breeds of farm animals. The Duckery, a derelict 19th-century lakeside pleasure ground has recently been developed and restored. The castle is not open to the public. Plenty of events throughout the year, including classic car rallies, open-air theatre and fireworks. Please contact for details.

Times Open 2 Apr-26 Sep, Wed-Thu, Sun & BHs 11-5* **Fees** £5 (ch £2)* **Facilities** 🅟 ☕ 🛒 (outdoor) ♿ (partly accessible) (designated wheelchair route) toilets for disabled (disabled car park) shop

CONGLETON Map 7 SJ86

Little Moreton Hall

CW12 4SD
☎ 01260 272018
e-mail: littlemoretonhall@nationaltrust.org.uk
web: www.nationaltrust.org.uk
dir: 4m SW of Congleton, on E side of A34

One of the best-known examples of moated, half-timbered architecture in England. By 1580 the house was much as it is today, and the long gallery, chapel and the great hall are very impressive. The garden has a knot garden, orchard and herbaceous borders. Wall paintings are also of some significant interest, and the house has featured in a TV documentary series, *How We Built Britain*. Please ring for details of special events.

Times Open 27 Feb-14 Mar & 6 Nov-19 Dec, Sat-Sun 11-4; 17 Mar-Oct, Wed-Sun 11-5* **Fees** £7 (ch £3.50). Family ticket £17.50* **Facilities** licensed (outdoor) (partly accessible) (access restricted, no lift to other floors, some steps & cobbles in ground) toilets for disabled (w/chairs, Braille/large print guides, induction loop) shop

DISLEY Map 7 SJ98

Lyme Park

SK12 2NX
☎ 01663 762023 & 766492 01663 765035
e-mail: lymepark@nationaltrust.org.uk
web: www.nationaltrust.org.uk
dir: off A6, 6.5m SE of Stockport. 12m NW of Buxton. House & car park 1m from entrance

Originally Tudor, Lyme Park now resembles a huge, Italianate palace following its transformation in the 18th century. Inside, a colourful family history is brought to life in beautifully furnished rooms. Outside, enjoy the opulent Victorian and Edwardian gardens with their sunken parterre, lake, and Wyatt-designed orangery. The surrounding deer park stretches up to the moors and is stocked with native species of deer.

Times Open 27 Feb-Oct, House Fri-Tue, Garden daily, 11-5. Park: open all year daily 8-6* **Fees** House & Garden £9 (ch £4). Family ticket £22. House £5.95 (ch £3). Garden £5.60 (ch £2.80)* **Facilities** licensed (outdoor) (partly accessible) (access restricted, no lift to other floors, grounds have some slopes and uneven gravel paths) toilets for disabled (large print guide, induction loop, w/chairs, shuttle bus) shop

ELLESMERE PORT Map 7 SJ47

Blue Planet Aquarium

Cheshire Oaks CH65 9LF
☎ 0151 357 8800 0151 356 7288
e-mail: info@blueplanetaquarium.co.uk
web: www.blueplanetaquarium.com
dir: M53 junct 10 at Cheshire Oaks, M56 junct 15 follow Aquarium signs

A voyage of discovery on one of the longest moving walkways in the world. Beneath the waters of the Caribbean Reef, see giant rays and awesome sharks pass inches from your face, stroke some favourite fish in the special rock pools, or pay a visit to the incredible world of poisonous frogs. Divers hand feed the fish throughout the day and can answer questions via state of the art communication systems. Home to Europe's largest collection of sharks, including the large sand tiger sharks. Check website for details of special events.

Times Open all year, daily from 10. Closed 25 Dec. Seasonal variations in closing times, please call to confirm* **Facilities** licensed (outdoor) (fully accessible) toilets for disabled (wheelchair hire, lifts, hearing loop) shop

The National Waterways Museum 2 FOR 1

South Pier Rd CH65 4FW
☎ 0151 373 4373 0151 355 4079
e-mail: ellesmereport@thewaterwaystrust.org.uk
web: www.nwm.org.uk
dir: M53 junct 9

The National Waterways Museum aims to bring Britain's canal history to life. The fascinating museum is set within a 200-year-old seven acre dock complex and includes the world's largest floating collection of canal craft. With the dock workers cottages, blacksmiths forge, boat trips and events throughout the year there is something for everyone to enjoy. Check website or telephone for details of future events.

Times Open Summer daily 10-5. Winter Thu-Sun 10-4. Closed 1 Jan* **Fees** £6 (ch 5-16 £4, under 5 free)* **Facilities** (indoor & outdoor) (partly accessible) (85% of the site is accessible to wheelchairs) toilets for disabled (tactile map for blind, induction loop, free wheelchair use) shop

GAWSWORTH Map 7 SJ86

Gawsworth Hall 2 FOR 1

SK11 9RN
☎ 01260 223456 01260 223469
e-mail: gawsworthhall@btinternet.com
web: www.gawsworthhall.com
dir: 2.5m S of Macclesfield on A536

This fine Tudor black-and-white manor house was the birthplace of Mary Fitton, thought by some to be the 'Dark Lady' of Shakespeare's sonnets. Pictures and armour can be seen in the house, which also has a tilting ground - now thought to be a rare example of an Elizabethan pleasure garden. Watch out for open-air theatre in July and August, and craft fairs in spring and autumn.

Times Open 4 May-22 Jun & 31 Aug-21 Sep, Sun-Wed 2-5 (& special events); 22 Jun-27 Aug daily 2-5* **Fees** £6 (ch £3). Party 20+ £5 each* **Facilities** (outdoor) (partly accessible) (house not suitable for wheelchairs or prams, tea room accessible) toilets for disabled (disabled parking in front of house) shop

JODRELL BANK VISITOR CENTRE & ARBORETUM Map 7 SJ77

Jodrell Bank Visitor Centre & Arboretum

SK11 9DL
☎ 01477 571339 Fax 01477 571695
web: www.manchester.ac.uk/jodrellbank
dir: M6 junct 18, A535 Holmes Chapel to Chelford road

At Jodrell Bank, a scientific and engineering wonder awaits you - the magnificent Lovell telescope, one of the largest radio telescopes in the world. A pathway leads you 180 degrees around the telescope as it towers above you surveying and exploring the universe. Then, the visitor can wander along pathways amongst the trees of the extensive arboretum. The Centre is currently under a redevelopment, which will take 2-3 years to complete.

Times Open daily Nov-mid Mar 10.30-3, wknds 11-4; mid Mar-end Oct 10.30-5.30* **Facilities** (outdoor) (fully accessible) toilets for disabled (wheelchair loan) shop

KNUTSFORD Map 7 SJ77

Tabley House

WA16 0HB
☎ 01565 750151 Fax 01565 653230
e-mail: enquiries@tableyhouse.co.uk
web: www.tableyhouse.co.uk
dir: M6 junct 19 onto A556 S towards Chester. Entrance for cars off A5033, 2m W of Knutsford

The finest Palladian house in the North West, Tabley holds the first great collection of English pictures ever made, including works by Turner, Lawrence, Fuseli and Reynolds. There is also furniture by Chippendale, Gillow and Bullock, and fascinating Leicester family memorabilia. Friendly stewards are available to talk about the Leicesters' 700 years at Tabley.

Times House: Open Apr-end Oct, Thu-Sun & BHs, 2-5 (last entry 4.30)* **Facilities** licensed toilets for disabled (phone administrator in advance for help) shop

Tatton Park

WA16 6QN
☎ 01625 374400 & 374435 Fax 01625 374403
e-mail: tatton@cheshireeast.gov.uk
web: www.tattonpark.org.uk
dir: Signed on A556, 4m S of Altrincham. Entrance to Tatton Park on Ashley Rd, 1.5m NE of junct A5034 with A50

Tatton Park is one of England's most complete historic estates, with gardens and a 1,000-acre country park. The centrepiece is the Georgian mansion, with gardens laid out by Humphry Repton and Sir Joseph Paxton. More recently, a Japanese garden with a Shinto temple was created. The Tudor Old Hall is the original manor house, where a guided tour is available on special open days. There is also a working 1930s farm and a children's adventure playground. Special events most weekends include the RHS flower show and open air concerts.

Times 27 Mar-3 Oct, 10-7; 4 Oct-25 Mar 11-5. Closed Mon low season* **Fees** Car entry £5. Each attraction £4.50 (ch £2.50). Family ticket £11.50. Totally Tatton Ticket (up to 3 attractions) £7 (ch £3.50). Family £17* **Facilities** licensed (outdoor) (partly accessible) (old hall, areas of farm & mansion 2nd floor not accessible) toilets for disabled (Braille guides) shop

MACCLESFIELD Map 7 SJ97

Hare Hill

Over Alderley SK10 4QB
☎ 01625 584412 Fax 01625 587555
e-mail: harehill@nationaltrust.org.uk
web: www.nationaltrust.org.uk
dir: Off B5087. Turn N into Prestbury Road, left at T-junct after 200yds, continue 0.75m. Entrance on left

The beautiful parkland at Hare Hill also features a pretty walled garden and pergola. There are woodland paths and ponds, and, in late spring, a brilliant display of rhododendrons and azaleas. The grounds were originally developed as the setting for a Georgian mansion.

Times Open 2 Apr-2 May & 2 Jun-28 Oct, Wed-Thu & Sat-Sun; 3-30 May, daily, 10-5. Also open BH Mon & Good Fri* **Fees** £3.40 (ch £1.70). Car park fee applies but refundable on entry to garden* **Facilities** (outdoor) (partly accessible) (access difficult in some areas, slopes, steps, grass & uneven paths) toilets for disabled (Braille guides)

Macclesfield Silk Museum — 2 FOR 1

Heritage Centre, Roe St SK11 6UT
☎ 01625 613210 Fax 01625 617880
e-mail: info@macclesfield.silk.museum
web: www.macclesfield.silk.museum
dir: Turn off A523 & follow brown signs. Museum in town centre

The story of silk in Macclesfield, told through a colourful audio-visual programme, exhibitions, textiles, garments, models and room settings. The Silk Museum is part of the Heritage centre, a restored Georgian Sunday school, which runs a full programme of musical and artistic events throughout the year.

Times Open all year, Mon-Sat 11-5, BH Mon 1-5. Closed 25-26 Dec, 1 Jan & Good Fri. Please ring for winter opening times* **Fees** £4.25 (concessions £3.90). Joint ticket with 3 museums £9 (concessions £8). Accompanied ch free* **Facilities** licensed (partly accessible) toilets for disabled (ramps, chairlift, audio guides, induction loop) shop

ENGLAND

MACCLESFIELD *continued*

Paradise Mill & Silk Industry Museum

2 FOR 1

Park Ln SK11 6TJ
☎ 01625 612045 01625 612048
e-mail: info@macclesfield.silk.museum
web: www.macclesfield.silk.museum
dir: turn off A523 'The Silk Rd' & follow brown signs

A working silk mill until 1981, with restored jacquard hand looms in their original location. Knowledgeable guides, many of them former silk mill workers, illustrate the silk production process with the help of demonstrations from weavers. Exhibitions and room settings give an impression of working conditions at the mill during the 1930s. The adjacent Silk Industry Museum opened in 2002 and focuses on design and manufacturing processes.

Times Open all year, Mill: BH Mon & Mon-Sat 11-5. Closed Sun, 25-26 Dec & 1 Jan, Good Fri. Silk museum open until 31 Oct. Please ring for winter opening times* **Fees** £5.20 (concessions £4.65) includes Park Lane Galleries & Paradise Mill, all inclusive ticket £9 (concessions £8)* **Facilities** Ⓟ ♿ (partly accessible) (care needed on uneven floors in Paradise Mill) toilets for disabled shop

NANTWICH Map 7 SJ65

Hack Green Secret Nuclear Bunker

French Ln, Hack Green CW5 8AP
☎ 01270 629219 01270 629218
e-mail: coldwar@hackgreen.co.uk
web: www.hackgreen.co.uk
dir: from Nantwich take A530 towards Whitchurch, follow brown signs

One of the nation's most secret defence sites. Declassified in 1993, this underground bunker would have been the centre of regional government had nuclear war broken out. Observe the preparations the government made for nuclear war and step into the lives of people who worked here. View the Minister of State's office, life support, communication centre, decontamination facilities, telephone exchange and much more.

Times Open 20 Apr-30 Oct, daily 10.30-5.30; Nov, Jan, Feb wknds, 11-4. Closed Dec* **Fees** £6.80 (ch £4.90, concessions £6.50). Family £21* **Facilities** Ⓟ Ⓟ licensed (outdoor) ♿ (partly accessible) (1st floor & bistro partly accessible) toilets for disabled (facilities for blind & hard of hearing) shop

Stapeley Water Gardens

London Rd, Stapeley CW5 7LH
☎ 01270 623868 & 628628 01270 624919
e-mail: info@stapeleywg.com
web: www.stapeleywg.com
dir: off M6 junct 16, 1m S of Nantwich on A51

There is plenty to do at Stapeley Water Gardens. The Palms Tropical Oasis is home to piranhas, parrots, skunks and exotic flowers, as well as tamarin monkeys, poisonous frogs and a crocodile. The two-acre Water Garden Centre houses a fantastic collection of water-lilies, as well as Koi carp and other water features. There is also a large garden centre, and various children's activities, including 'Meet the Keeper', which take place during school holidays.

Times Open Summer: Mon-Sat 9-6, BHs 10-6, Sun 10-4, Wed 9-8; Winter: Mon-Sat 9-5, BHs 10-5, Sun 10-4. The Palms Tropical Oasis open from 10* **Facilities** Ⓟ licensed (outdoor) ♿ (fully accessible) toilets for disabled (free wheelchair loan service) shop

NESTON Map 7 SJ27

Ness Botanic Gardens

2 FOR 1

Liverpool University CH64 4AY
☎ 0151 353 0123 0151 353 1004
e-mail: nessgdns@liv.ac.uk
web: www.nessgardens.org.uk
dir: off A540 near Ness, follow signs

This 64 acre garden overlooks the Dee Estuary. Founded in 1898 by Arthur Kilpin Bulley, a Liverpool cotton merchant, original specimens such as 'Pieris forrestii' and the eponymously named 'Primula bulleyana', still flourish today. A long association with plant collectors ensures a wide range of plants, providing interest for academics, horticulturists and amateurs alike. Visit 'Ness Botanische', a display garden created by Chris Beardshaw. A regular programme of lectures, courses and special events take place throughout the year. A visitor centre, including meeting and conference facilities, offers a warm welcome. The 2-for-1 voucher can only be used against the purchase of an adult ticket.

Times Open all year, Feb-Oct, daily 10-5; Nov-Jan, daily 10-4.30. Closed 25-26 Dec **Fees** Feb-Oct £6.50 (ch 5-16 £3, under 5's free, concessions £5.50). Family (2ad+3ch) £18. Groups 20+ £5.25, guide up to 30 people £30. Nov-Jan, £4.50 (ch 5-16 £1, concessions £4.50). Family ticket (2ad+3ch) £10, Groups 20+ £4.25, Guide up to 30 people £30* **Facilities** Ⓟ Ⓟ (outdoor) ♿ (partly accessible) (visitor centre & 65% of gardens accessible) toilets for disabled (w/chair route, induction loop, scooters & w/chairs) shop

NORTHWICH **Map 7 SJ67**

Arley Hall & Gardens

CW9 6NA

☎ 01565 777353 & 777284 01565 777465

e-mail: enquiries@arleyhallandgardens.com

web: www.arleyhallandgardens.com

dir: 5m N of Northwich on B5075. 5m NW of Knutsford A556, signed from M56 juncts 9/10 and M6 juncts 19/20

Owned by the same family since medieval times, the present Arley Hall is a good example of the early Victorian Jacobean style and contains fine furniture, plasterwork, panelling and family portraits. The gardens include a walled garden, unique clipped ilex avenue, herb garden, scented garden and a woodland garden with rhododendrons, azaleas and exotic trees, as well as the double herbaceous borders, some of the earliest to be established in England (1846).

Times Gardens, grounds & chapel: Open Apr-Sep, Tue-Sun & BH 11-5. For Hall dates please call 01565 777353* **Facilities** licensed (outdoor) (partly accessible) (lower levels of hall & garden accessible) toilets for disabled (ramps, parking by entrance) shop

Weaver Hall Museum & Workhouse **2 FOR 1**

162 London Rd CW9 8AB

☎ 01606 271640 01606 350420

e-mail: cheshiremuseums@cheshire.gov.uk

dir: on A533, 0.5m S of town centre & 0.5m N of A556. Well signed from A556

Weaver Hall Museum and Workhouse is the new name for the Salt Museum in Northwich. Discover the fascinating history of West Cheshire as well as exploring the workhouse history of the imposing Victorian building.

Times Open Tue-Fri 10-5, Sat-Sun 2-5. Open BH & Mons (in school hols except Dec). Early winter closure Tue-Fri 10-4, Sat-Sun 1-4* **Fees** £2.50 (ch £2, concessions £1.30). Family £6* **Facilities** (outdoor) (fully accessible) toilets for disabled (introductory video with induction loop facilities) shop

RUNCORN **Map 7 SJ58**

Norton Priory Museum & Gardens

Tudor Rd, Manor Park WA7 1SX

☎ 01928 569895 01928 589266

e-mail: info@nortonpriory.org

web: www.nortonpriory.org

dir: from M56 junct 11 towards Warrington, follow brown signs

Thirty-eight acres of peaceful woodland gardens are the setting for the medieval priory remains, museum and Walled Garden. Displays tell the story of the transformation of the priory into a Tudor manor house and then into an elegant Georgian mansion.

Times Open all year, Apr-Oct, Mon-Fri 12-5; Sat, Sun & BHs 12-6; Nov-Mar daily 12-4. Closed 24-26 Dec & 1 Jan. Walled Garden open Apr-Oct, daily 1.30-4.30* **Facilities** (outdoor) (fully accessible) toilets for disabled (wheelchairs, large print & audio guides, induction loop) shop

STYAL **Map 7 SJ88**

Quarry Bank Mill & Styal Estate

SK9 4LA

☎ 01625 527468 & 445896 01625 539267

e-mail: quarrybankmill@nationaltrust.org.uk

web: www.quarrybankmill.org.uk

dir: 1.5m N of Wilmslow off B5166, 2.5m from M56 junct 5. Follow heritage signs from A34 & M56

Founded in 1784, Quarry Bank Mill is one of the finest surviving cotton mills of the period. Inside the water and steam-powered mill there are hands-on exhibits and demonstrations that show how traditional spinning and weaving was transformed through the ingenuity of early textile engineers. Using the most powerful working waterwheel in Europe, two mill engines bring the past to life. At the Apprentice House you can discover what home life was like for the pauper children who worked in the mill in the 1830s. Visit the Mill Owner's secret garden, a picturesque valley retreat. After all this history take a walk through surrounding woods and farmland along the River Bollin.

Times Open Mar-Oct, daily 11-5; Nov-12 Dec, Wed-Sun 11-4; 18-19 Dec, Sat-Sun 11-4; 26-31 Dec, daily 11-4 (last admission 1hr before closing). Apprentice House timed tours. Garden open Mar-Oct* **Fees** Mill & Apprentice House or Garden £10.50 (ch £5.25). Family ticket £25.20. Mill only £7.35 (ch £3.90). Family ticket £18.60* **Facilities** licensed (partly accessible) (Apprentice House level access to ground floor only) toilets for disabled (wheelchairs, chairlift, ramps, Braille & induction loops) shop

WIDNES **Map 7 SJ58**

Catalyst Science Discovery Centre

Mersey Rd WA8 0DF

☎ 0151 420 1121 0151 495 2030

e-mail: info@catalyst.org.uk

web: www.catalyst.org.uk

dir: signed from M62 junct 7 & M56 junct 12

Enter a colourful world of science and technology in interactive galleries, and experience an amazing journey of discovery in the interactive theatre. Take a trip in an all-glass external lift to the Observatory, 100 feet above the River Mersey. A range of special events is planned throughout the year. Please ring for details.

Times Open all year, Tue-Fri daily & BH Mon 10-5, wknds 11-5. Closed Mon ex BHs, 24-26 & 31 Dec & 1 Jan* **Facilities** toilets for disabled shop

CORNWALL & THE ISLES OF SCILLY

Eden Project, St Austell

BODMIN Map 2 SX06

Cornwall's Regimental Museum

The Keep PL31 1EG
☎ 01208 72810 ▤ 01208 269516
e-mail: dclimus@talk21.com
dir: on B3268, Lostwithiel Rd, beside steam railway station

The history of a famous County Regiment with fascinating displays of uniforms, weapons, medals, badges and much more. Please telephone for details of events planned throughout the year. There is also an extensive archive/reference library available and volunteer archivists to assist with research. The Volunteer Militia History as well as The Light Infantry collection, have been incorporated into the display. The Museum is home to the largest single section of The Berlin wall in the country.

Times Open all year Mon-Fri 9-5 and BH. Closed Xmas **Fees** £2.50 (ch 50p). Parties 10+ £2 each. Half price with valid Bodmin & Wenford railway ticket (ch Free) **Facilities** Ⓟ Ⓟ ⛩ (indoor & outdoor) ♿ (partly accessible) (ground floor, archive library & virtual tour of museum accessible) toilets for disabled (presentation of inaccessible areas, virtual tour to come) shop

Pencarrow **2 FOR 1**

Washaway PL30 3AG
☎ 01208 841369 ▤ 01208 841722
e-mail: info@pencarrow.co.uk
web: www.pencarrow.co.uk
dir: 4m NW of Bodmin, signed off A389 & B3266

Still a family home, this Georgian house has a superb collection of pictures, furniture and porcelain. The 50 acres of formal and woodland gardens include a Victorian rockery, a lake, 700 different rhododendrons and an acclaimed conifer collection. There is also a children's play area. Special events throughout the year. Please ring for details. The 2 for 1 voucher applies to the gardens only.

Times House: 3 Apr-29 Sep, Sun-Thu 11-3; Gardens: Mar-Oct, daily 10-5.30.Cafe, craft shop & plants, 3 Apr-29 Sep, Sun-Thu 11-5 **Fees** House & Gardens £8.50 (ch 5-16yrs £4, ch under 5 free). Gardens only £4 (ch 5-16yrs £1, ch under 5 free). Groups from £6 **Facilities** Ⓟ ☕ ⛩ (outdoor) ♿ (partly accessible) (ground floor rooms of house accessible) (1 w/chair, disabled parking, DVD tour) shop

CALSTOCK Map 2 SX46

Cotehele

St Dominick PL12 6TA
☎ 01579 351346 & 352739 (info) ▤ 01579 351222
e-mail: cotehele@nationaltrust.org.uk
web: www.nationaltrust.org.uk
dir: between Tavistock & Callington. Turn off A390 at St. Ann's Chapel, signed 2.5m S of junct

A 15th-century house that contains tapestries, embroideries, furniture and armour; and outside, a beautiful garden on different levels, including a formal Italian-style garden, medieval stewpond, dovecote, and an 18th-century tower with lovely views. There is a restored water mill in the valley below, and at the Victorian riverside quay is a Maritime Museum.

Times Open 13 Mar-Oct. Garden open all year daily 10-dusk. Limited opening Nov-24 Dec* **Facilities** Ⓟ ☕ 🍴 licensed ⛩ (outdoor) ♿ (partly accessible) (garden & house limited access) toilets for disabled (Braille guide, audio loop, wheelchairs) shop ⊗ ✤

CHYSAUSTER ANCIENT VILLAGE Map 2 SW43

Chysauster Ancient Village

TR20 8XA
☎ 07831 757934
web: www.english-heritage.org.uk
dir: 2.5m NW of Gulval, off B3311

Chysauster Ancient Village is what remains of an Iron Age settlement, occupied almost 2,000 years ago. The village consisted of stone-walled homes known as 'courtyard houses', found only on the Land's End peninsula and the Isles of Scilly. The houses line a 'village street', and each had an open central courtyard surrounded by a number of thatched rooms. The site also has the remains of an enigmatic 'fogou' underground passage.

Times Open Apr-Jun & Sep, daily 10-5; Jul-Aug, daily 10-6; Oct, daily 10-4. Closed Nov-Mar **Fees** £3.20 (ch £1.60, concessions £2.70). Prices and opening times are subject to change in March 2011. Please call 0870 333 1181 for the most up to date prices and opening times when planning your visit **Facilities** Ⓟ ⊗ ⌗

FALMOUTH Map 2 SW83

National Maritime Museum Cornwall

Discovery Quay TR11 3QY
☎ 01326 313388 01326 317878
e-mail: enquiries@nmmc.co.uk
web: www.nmmc.co.uk
dir: follow signs from A39 for park/float ride and museum

Recently voted the south west's Visitor Attraction of the Year, this award-winning museum offers something for everyone from ever changing exhibitions, hands-on family activities, talks, lectures, displays, events, crabbing and the opportunity to sail and see marine and bird life. Admire the views from the 29 metre tower, descend the depths in one of only three natural underwater viewing galleries in the world. The purchase of a full price individual ticket gives you free entry to the Museum for a year.

Times Open daily 10-5. Closed 25-26 Dec* **Facilities** licensed (fully accessible) toilets for disabled (wheelchairs provided on arrival) shop

Pendennis Castle

Pendennis Headland TR11 4LP
☎ 01326 316594 01326 212044
web: www.english-heritage.org.uk
dir: 1m SE

Together with St Mawes Castle, Pendennis forms the end of a chain of castles built by Henry VIII along the south coast as protection from attack from France. Journey through 450 years of history and discover the castle's wartime secrets.

Times Open all year, Apr-Jun & Sep, daily 10-5 (Sat 10-4); Jul-Aug, daily 10-6 (Sat 10-4); Oct-Mar, daily 10-4. Closed 24-26 Dec & 1 Jan **Fees** £6 (ch £3, concessions £5.10). Family £15. Prices and opening times are subject to change in March 2011. Please call 0870 333 1181 for the most up to date prices and opening times when planning your visit **Facilities** (partly accessible) (two steep steps ticket point, spiral staircase, difficult steps to upper floor) toilets for disabled (Braille, large print handouts, tactile exhibits) shop

FOWEY Map 2 SX15

St Catherine's Castle **FREE**

web: www.english-heritage.org.uk
dir: 0.75m SW of Fowey along footpath off A3082

A small sixteenth-century fort built by Henry VIII to defend Fowey Harbour. It has two storeys with gun ports at ground level.

Times Open at any reasonable time **Facilities**

GODOLPHIN CROSS Map 2 SW53

Godolphin House

TR13 9RE
☎ 01736 763194
web: www.nationaltrust.org.uk/godolphin
dir: on minor road from Godolphin Cross to Townsend

The garden is one of the oldest in Europe, with many surviving Tudor raised walkways and walls. Side Garden has three original compartments from a 9-square compartment garden dating back to 1300. Limited access to the house during major building work project.

Times Estate open all year. Garden 29 Mar-Oct, Sat-Wed, 10-5. House closed as major conservation is underway. Small pre-booked tours may be available. Please phone property for details* **Facilities** (outdoor) (partly accessible) (some rough surfaces on path to garden, cobbles in areas, steep slopes in garden) toilets for disabled

GORRAN Map 2 SW94

Caerhays Castle Gardens **2 FOR 1**

PL26 6LY
☎ 01872 501144 & 500025 01872 501870
e-mail: estateoffice@caerhays.co.uk
web: www.caerhays.co.uk
dir: off A390 onto B3287. Right at T-junct, left at next T-junct, next left to Porthluney Beach car park

For centuries this magnolia-filled garden was a deer park, and it was not until the late 19th century that John Charles Williams ("JCW") inherited Caerhays, and not until the early 20th that new and exotic plants were introduced here. Now the gardens are a blaze of plants from Chile, China, New Zealand, the Himalayas, and many other distant lands. Magnolias, Rhododendrons, Camellia, and Japonicas can all be seen on marked walks, and the house can be visited in small groups during the spring.

Times Gardens open 15 Feb-May 10-5. House open 15 Mar-May* **Fees** £5.50 house or garden; £9.50 combined ticket* **Facilities** (partly accessible) (House & lower area of garden accessible) toilets for disabled shop

ENGLAND

GWEEK Map 2 SW72

National Seal Sanctuary **2 FOR 1**

TR12 6UG
☎ 0871 423 2110 Fax 01326 221210
e-mail: seals@sealsanctuary.com
web: www.sealsanctuary.co.uk
dir: pass RNAS Culdrose, take A3293, then B3291 to Gweek. Sanctuary signed from village

Come face to face with an array of creatures from vast oceans to the local shoreline. Enjoy streamlined seals, playful otters, exciting sea lions, comical penguins and happy ponies, goats and sheep. Delve beneath the waves at the rock pool experience and hold a crab or starfish!

Times Open all year, daily 10-5 (winter 10-4). (Last entry 1hr before closing). Closed 25 Dec **Fees** £13.95 (ch under 3 free, 3-14 £11.95, concessions £12.95). Family ticket (2ad+2ch) £42 **Facilities** (outdoor) (fully accessible) toilets for disabled shop

HELSTON Map 2 SW62

The Flambards Experience

Culdrose Manor TR13 0QA
☎ 01326 573404 Fax 01326 573344
e-mail: info@flambards.co.uk
web: www.flambards.co.uk
dir: 0.5m SE of Helston on A3083, Lizard road

Three award-winning, all-weather attractions can be visited on one site here. Flambards Victorian Village is a recreation of streets, shops and houses from 1830-1910. Britain in the Blitz is a life-size wartime street featuring shops, a pub and a living room complete with Morrison shelter. The Science Centre is a science playground that brings physics alive for the whole family. Along with the Thunderbolt and Extreme Force, Flambards also offers the Hornet Rollercoaster, the Family Log Flume, Go-Kart circuit, and rides and play areas for the very young. The Wildlife Experience show features lizards, snakes, large spiders and birds of prey. See the website for special events.

Times Open Etr-Nov, summer opening. Nov-Mar, winter opening* **Facilities** (indoor & outdoor) (partly accessible) (some rivers not accessible) toilets for disabled (free loan of wheelchairs, route guides) shop

Goonhilly Satellite Earth Station Experience

Goonhilly Downs TR12 6LQ
☎ 0800 679593 Fax 01326 221438
e-mail: goonhilly.visitorscentre@bt.com
web: www.goonhilly.bt.com
dir: From Helston follow the brown direction signs

Future World is on the site of what was the largest satellite earth station in the world, with over 60 dishes, which makes a dramatic impression on the Lizard Peninsula landscape. Enter a world of historic predictions, past inventions and ideas and see artefacts from jet packs and space helmets to the Sinclair C5 and the first mobile phones, complete with 'brick' size batteries. Journey into a zone of interactive displays where you can record your own visions of the future. Discover the history and heritage of Goonhilly itself in the main visitors' centre, and learn how international communications have developed over the past 200 years. You an also book a tour into the heart of 'Arthur', the Grade II listed iconic satellite dish.

Times Open 15 Mar-27 Jun & 6 Sep-Oct 10-5; 28 Jun-5 Sep 10-6; Nov-27 Mar 11-4.Closed 24-26 Dec & 1 Jan* **Facilities** licensed (outdoor) (fully accessible) toilets for disabled (induction loop, wheelchair height terminals, lifts, ramps) shop

Trevarno Estate Garden & Museum of Gardening **2 FOR 1**

Trevarno Manor, Crowntown TR13 0RU
☎ 01326 574274 Fax 01326 574282
e-mail: enquiry@trevarno.co.uk
web: www.trevarno.co.uk
dir: E of Crowntown. Leave Helston on Penzance road signed B3302

Victorian gardens with the splendid fountain garden conservatory, tea room and the National Museum of Gardening. In the tranquil gardens and grounds, follow the progress of restoration projects, visit craft areas including handmade soap and toy workshops, explore Britain's largest and most comprehensive collection of antique tools, implements, memorabilia and ephemera, creatively displayed to illustrate how gardens and gardening influences most people's lives. Adventure play area for the youngsters, extended estate walk and viewing platform. Home of the national daffodil collection showgarden (flowering Jan-mid May). Special family events run every Wednesday during school holidays, and there is a Winter Wonderland Christmas fair, first weekend in December.

Times Open daily 10.30-5. Closed 25-26 Dec **Fees** £6.85 (ch 5-14 £2.40, concessions £5.95, disabled £3.45). Group 12+* **Facilities** (outdoor) (fully accessible) toilets for disabled (parking, extended disabled route) shop

LANHYDROCK Map 2 SX06

Lanhydrock

PL30 5AD
☎ 01208 265950 📠 01208 265959
e-mail: lanhydrock@nationaltrust.org.uk
web: www.nationaltrust.org.uk
dir: 2.5m SE of Bodmin, signed from A30, A38 & B3268

Part-Jacobean, part-Victorian building that gives a vivid picture of life in Victorian times. The 'below stairs' sections have a huge kitchen, larders, dairy, bakehouse, cellars, and servants' quarters. The long gallery has a moulded ceiling showing Old Testament scenes, and overlooks the formal gardens with their clipped yews and bronze urns. The higher garden, famed for its magnolias and rhododendrons, climbs the hillside behind the house.

Times House open 13 Mar-Oct daily (ex Mon) 11-5 (Apr-Sep 5.30), open BH Mon & Mon during school hols. Gardens open all year, daily 10-6* **Facilities** Ⓟ Ⓟ ☕ 🍽 licensed ⛩ (outdoor) ♿ (fully accessible) toilets for disabled (lift, self drive buggy (pre-book), wheelchairs) shop ⓧ ✿

LAUNCESTON Map 2 SX38

Launceston Castle

Castle Lodge PL15 7DR
☎ 01566 772365 📠 01566 772396
web: www.english-heritage.org.uk

Launceston Castle is set on a large natural mound, and dominates the surrounding landscape. Begun soon after the Norman Conquest, it has an unusual keep consisting of a 13th-century round tower built by Richard, Earl of Cornwall, inside an earlier circular keep. The tower top is reached via an internal staircase. The castle was used as a prison and George Fox, founder of the Quakers, was confined here in 1656. A display traces 1,000 years of history, with finds from site excavations.

Times Open Apr-Jun & Sep, daily 10-5; Jul-Aug, daily 10-6; Oct, daily 10-4. Closed Nov-Mar **Fees** £3.20 (ch £1.60, concessions £2.70). Prices and opening times are subject to change in March 2011. Please call 0870 333 1181 for the most up to date prices and opening times when planning your visit **Facilities** ⛩ ♿ (partly accessible) (outer bailey only) shop ⓧ #

Launceston Steam Railway

St Thomas Rd PL15 8DA
☎ 01566 775665
web: www.launcestonsr.co.uk
dir: turn off A30 Launceston, well signed

The Launceston Steam Railway links the historic town of Launceston with the hamlet of New Mills. Tickets are valid for unlimited travel on the day of issue and you can break your journey. Launceston Station houses railway workshops, a transport museum, gift shop and book shop.

Times Open Good Fri, 22-29 Apr. Whitsun 29 May-3 Jun. Summer, daily (ex Sat), 2 Jul-23 Sep. Please check website for opening dates in Jun **Fees** £8.25 (ch £5.50, concessions £6.50). Family ticket £25 (2 ad & up to 4 ch). Dogs 50p* **Facilities** Ⓟ Ⓟ ☕ ⛩ (outdoor) ♿ (partly accessible) (no access to upstairs of museum or bookshop) shop

Tamar Otter & Wildlife Centre

North Petherwin PL15 8GW
☎ 01566 785646
e-mail: info@tamarotters.co.uk
web: www.tamarotters.co.uk
dir: 5m NW off B3254 Bude road

Visitors to this wildlife centre will see British and Asian short-clawed otters in large natural enclosures. They will also be able to see fallow and Muntjac deer, and wallabies roaming around the grounds. There are also owls, a pair of Scottish wild cats, peacocks, and a large selection of waterfowl on two lakes. Otters are fed at noon and 3pm and this is accompanied by an informative talk.

Times Open Apr-Oct, daily 10.30-6. Opens Good Fri if earlier than 1 Apr **Fees** £7 (ch 3-15yrs £3.50, concessions £6) Family (2 ad+3 ch) £18* **Facilities** Ⓟ ☕ ⛩ (outdoor) ♿ (partly accessible) (steep slope to otter pens/woodland walk) toilets for disabled shop ⓧ

LOOE Map 2 SX25

The Monkey Sanctuary

St Martins PL13 1NZ
☎ 01503 262532 📠 01503 262532
e-mail: info@wildfutures.org
web: www.monkeysanctuary.org
dir: signed on B3253 at No Man's Land between East Looe & Hessenford

The Wild Futures' Monkey Sanctuary has been caring for unwanted and ex-pet monkeys for over 45 years. Initially rescuing South American woolly monkeys from the pet trade in the 1950s and 60s, it now cares for four different species of monkeys, all rescued from the UK and international primate pet trades. Visitors can meet some of these characters, dependent on the stage of their rehabilitation, and keepers are on hand all day to talk about the Sanctuary's work in rescue and rehabilitation, as well as informative talks on the charity's wider work.

Times Open Sun-Thu from the Sun before Etr-Sep. Also open Autumn Half Term. 11-4.30 **Fees** £7.50 (ch £3.50, under 5's free & concessions £5). Family (2ad+3ch) £20* **Facilities** (outdoor) (partly accessible) toilets for disabled shop

MARAZION Map 2 SW53

St Michael's Mount

TR17 0HT

01736 710507 & 710265 01736 719930

e-mail: mail@stmichaelsmount.co.uk

web: www.stmichaelsmount.co.uk

dir: access is by Causeway on foot at low tide. 0.5m S of A394 at Marazion or by motorboat in summer

After the Norman Conquest, the abbey on St Michael's Mount was granted to the Benedictine order and the church on the island's summit was built by the French abbot in charge of the abbey. Miracles, said to have occurred here in the 1260s, increased the island's religious attraction to pilgrims. The Mount was besieged in 1473 during the War of the Roses, in 1588 it was the place where the first beacon was lit to warn of the arrival of the Spanish Armada, and in the Civil War it was a Royalist stronghold attacked by Cromwell's forces. Today it is the home of the St Aubyn family who have lived here since the 17th century. The island is separated from the mainland by a causeway which is covered by the sea at high tide.

Times Open: Castle 27 Mar-30 Oct 10.30-5 (last entry 45mins before closing). Winter Tue & Fri by guided tour only (ring in advance). Garden May-Jun Mon-Fri, Jul-Oct Thu & Fri 10.30-5. All visits subject to favourable weather **Fees** £7 (ch £3.50) Family ticket £17.50 (1ad family £10.50). Groups 15+ £6. Garden £3.50 (ch £1.50). Castle & gardens free to NT members* **Facilities** licensed (outdoor) (partly accessible) (cobbled & uneven surfaces, steep climb) (sandchair available) shop

MAWNAN SMITH Map 2 SW72

Glendurgan

TR11 5JZ

01872 862090 01872 865808

e-mail: glendurgan@nationaltrust.org.uk

web: www.nationaltrust.org.uk

dir: 4m SW of Falmouth. 0.5m SW of Mawnan Smith on road to Helford Passage

This delightful garden, set in a valley above the River Helford, was started by Alfred Fox in 1820. The informal landscape contains trees and shrubs from all over the world, including the Japanese loquat and tree ferns from New Zealand. There is a laurel maze, and a Giant's Stride which is popular with children. The house is not open to the public.

Times Open 13 Feb-Jul & Sep-Oct, Tue-Sat, 10.30-5.30; Aug, Mon-Sat, 10.30-5.30. Open BH Mons. Closed Good Fri* **Facilities** (partly accessible) (limited access to gardens/ground floor) toilets for disabled (Braille guide) shop

Trebah Garden

TR11 5JZ

01326 252200 01326 250781

e-mail: mail@trebah-garden.co.uk

web: www.trebah-garden.co.uk

dir: signed at Treliever Cross rdbt at junct of A39/A394 & follow brown tourist signs

A 26-acre wooded valley garden, descending 200 feet from the 18th-century house down to a private cove on the Helford River. The cascading Water Garden has pools of giant koi and exotic water plants, winding through two acres of blue and white hydrangeas to the beach. There are glades of sub-tropical tree ferns and palms, as well as rhododendrons and many other trees and shrubs from all over the world. The beach is open to visitors and there are children's trails and activities all year.

Times Open daily 10-5. In winter 10 til dusk* **Facilities** licensed (outdoor) (partly accessible) (disabled easy access route) toilets for disabled (3 powered wheelchairs, 1 carer-controlled buggy) shop

NEWQUAY Map 2 SW86

Blue Reef Aquarium — 2 FOR 1

Towan Promenade TR7 1DU

01637 878134 01637 872578

e-mail: newquay@bluereefaquarium.co.uk

web: www.bluereefaquarium.co.uk

dir: from A30 follow signs to Newquay, follow Blue Reef Aquarium signs to car park in town centre. Disabled access please ring

Take the ultimate undersea safari at the Blue Reef Aquarium. Discover Cornish marine life from native sharks and rays to the incredibly intelligent and playful octopus. From here journey through warmer waters to watch the magical seahorses, unusual shape shifting, jet-propelled cuttlefish and the vibrant, swaying tentacles of living sponges and anemones. Continue your safari through the underwater tunnel below a tropical sea. Here you will encounter the activities of a coral reef alive with shoals of brightly coloured fish and the graceful, black tip reef sharks which glide silently overhead. Daily talks and regular feeding demonstrations bring the experience to life. Events all year, please see website for details.

Times Open all year, daily 10-5. Closed 25 Dec. Open until 6 during summer holidays **Fees** £9.20 (ch £7.20, concessions £8.20)* **Facilities** (outdoor) (partly accessible) (small area, only accessible via steps) toilets for disabled (lifts, wheelchairs & beach wheelchair, ramps) shop

NEWQUAY *continued*

Dairy Land Farm World

Summercourt TR8 5AA
☎ 01872 510246 📠 01872 510349
e-mail: info@dairylandfarmworld.co.uk
web: www.dairylandfarmworld.com
dir: Signed from A30 at exit for Mitchell/Summercourt

Visitors can watch while the cows are milked to music on a spectacular merry-go-round milking machine. The life of a Victorian farmer and his neighbours is explored in the Heritage Centre, and a Farm Nature Trail features informative displays along pleasant walks. Children will have fun getting to know the farm animals in the Farm Park. They will also enjoy the playground, assault course and indoor play areas.

Times Open daily, late Mar-Oct 10-5. (Bull pen additional winter openings Thu-Sun & school hols, please telephone for more information)* **Facilities** Ⓟ ☕ ⛩ (indoor & outdoor) ♿ (partly accessible) toilets for disabled (wheelchairs for loan; disabled viewing gallery - milking) shop 🚫

Newquay Zoo

Trenance Gardens TR7 2LZ
☎ 0844 474 2244 📠 01637 851318
e-mail: info@newquayzoo.org.uk
web: www.newquayzoo.org.uk
dir: off A3075 and follow signs to Zoo

Experience the world's wildlife at award-winning Newquay Zoo. Set within exotic lakeside gardens and with over 130 species, Newquay Zoo is one of Cornwall's most popular attractions. The Madagascar Walkthrough features crowned lemurs, vasa parrots, striped mongoose and more. Gaze across the African savanna from the viewing platform and see animals of the African plains graze and wander as they would in the wild. Animal feeds and informative talks run throughout the day. Kids can also enjoy the Tarzan Trail and Dragon Maze. Other highlights include the Tropical house, Oriental Garden, Penguin pool, Village Farm and lots more animals.

Times Open all year Apr-Sep, daily 9.30-6; Oct-Mar, 10-5 (last entry 1hr before closing) **Fees** With voluntary 10% Gift Aid donation: £10.95 (ch 3-15 £8.20, 2 & under free, pen & students £8.25, disabled rates £10.45 (ch £7.70, pen & students £7.75). Family Saver ticket (2ad+2ch) £30.50. Please see website for current prices* **Facilities** Ⓟ Ⓟ ☕ 🍽 licensed ⛩ (outdoor) ♿ (partly accessible) (80% access, stairs in Tropical House & upto the Owls & Tarzan Trail) toilets for disabled (wheelchairs, guided tours) shop 🚫

PADSTOW Map 2 SW97

Prideaux Place

PL28 8RP
☎ 01841 532411 📠 01841 532945
e-mail: office@prideauxplace.co.uk
web: www.prideauxplace.co.uk
dir: off B3276 Padstow to Newquay road. Follow brown heritage signs

Situated above the picturesque port of Padstow is the Elizabethan Prideaux Place. Completed in 1592 by Nicholas Prideaux and still lived in by the family who can trace back their ancestry to William the Conqueror. Surrounded by 40 acres of landscaped gardens and overlooking a deer park, this splendid house contains a wealth of family and royal portraits, a fine porcelain collection, a growing teddy bear collection and a magnificent 16th-century plaster ceiling in the Great Chamber, which has some marvellous views across countryside to Bodmin Moor. There's plenty of opportunity for walking in both formal gardens and woodland, and there is also a peaceful tearoom. The house has been featured in many film and TV productions.

Times Open House: Etr Sun, 8 Apr & 9 May-7 Oct, Sun-Thu 1.30-4. Grounds & tearoom: 12.30-5. Open all year to pre-booked groups (15+)* **Facilities** Ⓟ Ⓟ ☕ ♿ (partly accessible) (2 upstairs rooms not accessible to wheelchair users) toilets for disabled (ramps to main entrance and tea room) shop

PENDEEN Map 2 SW33

Geevor Tin Mine

TR19 7EW

☎ 01736 788662 📠 01736 786059

e-mail: bookings@geevor.com

web: www.geevor.com

dir: From Penzance take A3071 towards St Just, then B3318 towards Pendeen. From St Ives follow B3306 to Pendeen

A preserved tin mine and museum provide an insight into the methods and equipment used in the industry that was once so important in the area. The Geevor Tin Mine only actually stopped operation in 1990. Guided tours let visitors see the tin treatment plant, and a video illustrates the techniques employed. A museum of hard rock mining has recently opened, and the underground tour is well worth the trip.

Times Open daily (ex Sat) 9-5 (9-4 Nov-Mar). Closed 21-26 Dec & 1 Jan* **Facilities** Ⓟ Ⓟ ☕ 🍽 licensed ⛩ (outdoor) ♿ (partly accessible) (access to new museum, shop & cafe) toilets for disabled (lift, ramps) shop ⊗

PENTEWAN Map 2 SX04

The Lost Gardens of Heligan

PL26 6EN

☎ 01726 845100 📠 01726 845101

e-mail: info@heligan.com

web: www.heligan.com

dir: signed from A390 & B3273

Heligan, seat of the Tremayne family for more than 400 years, is one of the most mysterious estates in England. At the end of the 19th-century its thousand acres were at their zenith, but only a few years after the Great War, bramble and ivy were already drawing a green veil over this sleeping beauty. Today the garden offers 200 acres for exploration, which include productive gardens, pleasure grounds, a sub-tropical jungle, sustainably-managed farmland, wetlands, ancient woodlands and a pioneering wildlife project. Please telephone for details of spring-time and harvest-time events and for summer evening theatre. In February 2011 The Lost Gardens of Heligan celebrates its 21st birthday.

Times Open Apr-Sep, daily 10-6; Oct-Mar, daily 10-5 (last tickets 1hr before closing) **Fees** £10 (ch £6, pen £9). Family (2ad+3ch) £27* **Facilities** Ⓟ Ⓟ ☕ ⛩ (indoor & outdoor) ♿ (partly accessible) (northern gardens, wildlife project, shop, plant sales & tearooms all accessible) toilets for disabled (free loan of wheelchairs & trained access advisors) shop ⊗

PENZANCE Map 2 SW43

Trengwainton Garden

TR20 8RZ

☎ 01736 363148 📠 01736 367762

e-mail: trengwainton@nationaltrust.org.uk

web: www.nationaltrust.org.uk

dir: 2m NW Penzance, 0.5m W of Heamoor off Penzance - Morvah road

With plants from around the globe scattered throughout this 25 acre garden, there is something to inspire around every corner. Champion magnolias and vibrant rhododendrons make way for lush banana plants and soaring echiums. Unusually, the restored walled kitchen garden was built to the dimensions of Noah's Ark and showcases contemporary varieties of fruit and vegetables. A colourfully bordered stream leads up to a shady pond and sunny terrace, with stunning views across Mount's Bay.

Times Open 13 Feb-30 Oct, daily (ex Fri & Sat) 10.30-5. Open Good Fri 10.30-5 **Fees** £6.50 (ch £3.20). Family & group tickets available. Reduced rate when arriving by cycle or public transport **Facilities** Ⓟ ☕ ⛩ (outdoor) ♿ (partly accessible) (hard gravel paths, map of accessible route. Approx. 75% of garden accessible to wheelchair users) toilets for disabled (2 wheelchairs for bkg) shop ✿

POOL Map 2 SW64

East Pool Mine

TR15 3NP

☎ 01209 315027 & 210900

e-mail: jane.affleck@nationaltrust.org.uk

web: www.nationaltrust.org.uk

dir: 2m W of Redruth on A3047, signed from A30, Pool exit

Impressive relics of the tin mining industry, these great beam engines were used for pumping water from 2000ft down, and for lifting men and ore from the workings below ground. The mine at East Pool has been converted into the Cornwall Industrial Heritage Centre which includes audio-visual theatre giving background to all aspects of Cornwall's industrial heritage.

Times Open Apr-Jun & Sep-Oct, Sun-Mon & Wed-Fri 11-5; Jul-Aug daily (ex Tue) 11-5 **Fees** Voluntary Gift Aid donation £6.80 (ch £3.30). Family Gift Aid £16.80. Standard admission available. Please check website **Facilities** Ⓟ Ⓟ ⛩ (outdoor) ♿ (partly accessible) (1 engine house only downstairs accessible) toilets for disabled (lift to all levels) shop ⊗ ✿

ENGLAND

PROBUS Map 2 SW84

Trewithen Gardens

Grampound Rd TR2 4DD
☎ 01726 883647 📠 01726 882301
e-mail: gardens@trewithen-estate.demon.co.uk
web: www.trewithengardens.co.uk
dir. on A390 between Truro & St Austell

The Hawkins family has lived in this charming, intimate country house since it was built in 1720. The internationally renowned landscaped garden covers some 30 acres and grows camellias, magnolias and rhododendrons as well as many rare trees and shrubs seldom seen elsewhere. The nurseries are open all year.

Times Open Mar-Sep, Mon-Sat 10-4.30; Mar-May daily **Fees** £5 (group 20+ £4.50)* **Facilities** Ⓟ ☕ ⛩ (outdoor) ♿ (partly accessible) (some steeper areas of garden not accessible) toilets for disabled shop

RESTORMEL Map 2 SX16

Restormel Castle

PL22 0BD
☎ 01208 872687
web: www.english-heritage.org.uk
dir: 1.5m N of Lostwithiel off A390

The great 13th-century circular shell-keep of Restormel encloses the principal rooms of the castle. It stands on an earlier Norman mound surrounded by a deep dry ditch, on top of a spur beside the River Fowey. Twice visited by Edward, Prince of Wales (The Black Prince) in the 14th century, it has only seen military action once, during the Civil War in 1644. It commands fantastic views and is a favourite picnic spot.

Times Open Apr-Jun & Sep, daily 10-5; Jul-Aug, daily 10-6; Oct, daily 10-4. Closed Nov-Mar **Fees** £3.20 (ch £1.60, concessions £2.70). Prices and opening times are subject to change in March 2011. Please call 0870 333 1181 for the most up to date prices and opening times when planning your visit **Facilities** Ⓟ ⛩ shop #

ST AUSTELL Map 2 SX05

Charlestown Shipwreck & Heritage Centre

Quay Rd, Charlestown PL25 3NJ
☎ 01726 69897 📠 01726 69897
e-mail: admin@shipwreckcharlestown.com
web: www.shipwreckcharlestown.com
dir: signed off A390 from St. Austell close to Eden Project

Charlestown is a small and unspoilt village with a unique sea-lock, china-clay port, purpose built in the 18th century. The Shipwreck and Heritage Centre was originally a dry house for china clay built on underground tunnels. Now it houses the largest display of shipwreck artefacts in the UK, along with local heritage, diving exhibits, and an *RMS Titanic* display. A recent addition is a Nelson display which commemorates the 200th anniversary of the Battle of Trafalgar.

Times Open Mar-Oct, daily 10-5 (last admission 1 hour before closing)* **Facilities** Ⓟ ⓟ ☕ 🍽 licensed ♿ (fully accessible) toilets for disabled shop

The China Clay Country Park 2 FOR 1

Carthew PL26 8XG
☎ 01726 850362 📠 01726 850362
e-mail: info@chinaclaycountry.co.uk
web: www.wheal-martyn.com
dir: turn off A30 at Innis Downs onto A391 to Bugle, follow brown signs 'China Clay Museum' located on B3274, 2m N of St Austell

Set within 26 acres of woodland, Wheal Martyn provides a fascinating day out for everyone. The site includes the UK's only China Clay Museum, set within a complete 19th-century clay works. It tells the story of Cornwall's most important present day industry. Key features are Cornwall's largest working water wheel, spectacular views of a wooden working clay pit with monstrous machines at work, nature trails, children's challenge trail, play area, indoor interactive displays, café and gift shop. Fun, discovery and adventure for all the family.

Times Open all year, Apr-Oct 10-6; Nov-Mar 10-5 (last admission 1hr and 30mins before closing) **Fees** £7.50 (ch 6-16 £4.50, 5 & under free, concessions £6) Family ticket (2ad+2ch) £20, (2ad+up to 4ch) £22.50. Group discount available* **Facilities** Ⓟ ⓟ ☕ 🍽 licensed ⛩ (outdoor) ♿ (partly accessible) (all buildings accessible, some outdoor walks not suitable due to nature of landscape) toilets for disabled (interactive museum gallery) shop

Eden Project 2 FOR 1

Bodelva PL24 2SG
☎ 01726 811911 📠 01726 811912
e-mail: information@edenproject.com
web: www.edenproject.com
dir: overlooking St Austell Bay signed from A390/A30/A391

An unforgettable experience in a breathtaking location, the Eden Project is a gateway into the fascinating world of plants and human society. Space-age technology meets "The Lost World" in the biggest greenhouse ever built. Located in a 50 metre-deep crater the size of 30 football pitches, are two gigantic geodesic conservatories: the Humid Tropics Biome and the Warm Temperate Biome. This is a startling and unique day out. There's an ice-rink in the winter (Nov-Feb) and concerts in the summer - see the website for details. 2011 is the 10th anniversary of the Eden Project.

Times Open Mar-Oct, daily 9-6; Nov-Mar 10-4.30; 20 Jul-4 Sep open until 8 on Tue, Wed & Thu (last admission 1hr 30 mins before close). Closed 24-25 Dec & 25-26 Jan **Fees** £16 (ch £5, under 5's free, students £8, concessions £11). Family ticket (2ad+ up to 3ch) £38. Annual membership available* **Facilities** licensed (indoor & outdoor) (partly accessible) toilets for disabled (wheelchairs, car shuttle to visitor centre/biomes) shop

ST IVES — Map 2 SW54

Park your car at Lelant Station and take advantage of the park and ride service. The fee includes parking and journeys on the train between Lelant and St Ives during the day.

Barbara Hepworth Museum & Sculpture Garden

Barnoon Hill TR26 1AD
01736 796226 01736 794480
e-mail: tatestivesinfo@tate.org.uk
web: www.tate.org.uk/stives
dir: M5 to Exeter, A30 onto Penzance & St Ives, in town centre

Visiting the museum and garden is a unique experience, which offers a remarkable insight into the work and outlook of one of Britain's most important 20th-century artists, Dame Barbara Hepworth.

Times Open Mar-Oct, daily 10-5.30; Nov-Feb, Tue-Sun 10-4.30 (last admission 30mins before closing). Closed 25 Dec* **Facilities** toilets for disabled

Tate St Ives

Porthmeor Beach TR26 1TG
01736 796226 01736 794480
e-mail: tatestivesinfo@tate.org.uk
web: www.tate.org.uk/stives
dir: M5 to Exeter, then A30 onto Penzance & St Ives. Located on Porthmeor Beach

Home of post-war British Modernism, St Ives provides the artistic foundations for Tate St Ives. Built in 1993, the gallery celebrates the surroundings and atmosphere that inspired the Modernists, and its unique architecture recalls the 'White Relief' work of Ben Nicholson as well as the unexpected twists and turns of the town itself. The gallery presents a varied programme of both Cornish and international artists, from the past and present, including displays on loan from Tate Modern.

Times Open Mar-Oct, daily 10-5.30; Nov-Feb, Tue-Sun 10-4.30. Closed 24-26 Dec* **Facilities** licensed (partly accessible) toilets for disabled (access ramp, lift, wheelchairs) shop

ST MARY'S — Map 2

Isles of Scilly Museum

Church St, Hugh Town TR21 0JT
01720 422337
e-mail: info@iosmuseum.org
web: www.iosmuseum.org
dir: In centre of Hugh Town

A small, independent museum, which seeks to safeguard and promote the islands' history and traditions, and reflect every aspect of island life.

Times Open Etr-Sep, Mon-Fri 10-4.30, Sat 10-12; Oct-Etr, Mon-Sat 10-12 **Fees** £4 (ch £1, concessions £3) **Facilities** (fully accessible) (stair lift to upper and lower floors)

ST MAWES — Map 2 SW83

St Mawes Castle

TR2 3AA
01326 270526
web: www.english-heritage.org.uk
dir: on A3078

In a wonderful location alongside the pretty fishing village of St Mawes, this castle was Henry VIII's most picturesque fort, one of a defensive chain built between 1539 and 1545 to counter an invasion threat from Catholic France and Spain. Although it was designed to mount heavy guns, great care was taken with its design, including carved Latin inscriptions in praise of Henry VIII and his son, Edward VI. It fell to Parliamentarian forces in 1646 with only a single shot being fired, which is one reason why it remains in such good condition.

Times Open all year Apr-Jun & Sep, Sun-Fri 10-5; Jul-Aug, Sun-Fri 10-6; Oct, daily 10-4; Nov-Mar, Fri-Mon 10-4. Closed Sat. (May close at 4 on Sun & Fri for private events). Closed 24-26 Dec & 1 Jan **Fees** £4.20 (ch £2.10, concessions £3.60). Prices and opening times are subject to change in March 2011. Please call 0870 333 1181 for the most up to date prices and opening times when planning your visit **Facilities** shop

SANCREED — Map 2 SW42

Carn Euny Ancient Village — FREE

web: www.english-heritage.org.uk
dir: 1.25m SW of Sancreed, off A30

The remains of an Iron Age settlement. Surviving features include the foundations of stone huts and an intriguing curved underground passage or 'fogou'.

Times Open at any reasonable time **Facilities**

ENGLAND

TINTAGEL Map 2 SX08

Tintagel Castle

PL34 0HE
☎ 01840 770328 📠 01841 772105
web: www.english-heritage.org.uk
dir: on Tintagel Head, 0.5m along uneven track from Tintagel, no vehicles

Overlooking the wild Cornish coast, Tintagel is one of the most spectacular spots in the country and is associated with King Arthur and Merlin. Recent excavations revealed Dark Age connections between Spain and Cornwall, alongside the discovery of the 'Arthnou' stone suggesting that this was a royal place for the Dark Age rulers of Cornwall.

Times Open all year, Apr-Sep, daily 10-6; Oct, daily 10-5; Nov-Mar, daily 10-4. Closed 24-26 Dec & 1 Jan. Beach cafe open daily, Apr-Oct (closes 1/2hr before castle) Nov-Mar 11-3.30 **Fees** £5.20 (ch £2.60, concessions £4.40). Family ticket £13. Prices and opening times are subject to change in March 2011. Please call 0870 333 1181 for the most up to date prices and opening times when planning your visit **Facilities** Ⓟ shop #

Tintagel Old Post Office

PL34 0DB
☎ 01840 770024
e-mail: tintageloldpo@nationaltrust.org.uk
web: www.nationaltrust.org.uk/main/w-tintageloldpostoffice
dir: In centre of Tintagel village

A rare survival of Cornish domestic medieval architecture, this 14th-century yeoman's farmhouse is well furnished with local oak pieces. One room was used during the Victorian era as the letter receiving office for the district.

Times Open daily, 19-27 Feb & 12 Mar-1 Apr 11-4; 2 Apr-Sep 10.30-5.30; 1 Oct-6 Nov 11-4 **Fees** £3.80 (ch £1.90, under 5's & NT members free). Family tickets available. Group 10+ £2.80, (reduced entry prices apply Mar-Jun & Oct, please contact for details) **Facilities** Ⓟ ♿ (partly accessible) (Braille guide, induction loop, virtual tour) shop ⊗ ✤

TORPOINT Map 2 SX45

Antony House

PL11 2QA
☎ 01752 812191 📠 01752 815724
e-mail: philip.brunsdon@nationaltrust.org.uk
web: www.nationaltrust.org.uk/antony
dir: 2m NW, off A374 from Trerulefoot rdbt, 2m from Torpoint Ferry

A fine, largely unaltered mansion, built in brick and Pentewan stone for Sir William Carew between 1711 and 1721. The stable block and outhouses remain from an earlier 17th-century building. The house contains contemporary furniture and family portraits. The grounds include a dovecote and the Bath Pond House.

Times Open Apr-28 May & Sep-29 Oct, Tue-Thu; 2 Jun-Aug, also Sun. Open BH Mon* **Facilities** Ⓟ Ⓟ 🍴 licensed ♿ (partly accessible) toilets for disabled (Braille guide, recommended route in garden) shop ⊗ ✤

Mount Edgcumbe House & Country Park

Cremyll PL10 1HZ
☎ 01752 822236 📠 01752 822199
e-mail: mt.edgcumbe@plymouth.gov.uk
web: www.mountedgcumbe.gov.uk
dir: from Plymouth via Cremyll Foot Ferry, Torpoint ferry or Saltash Bridge. Via Liskeard to A374, B3247 follow brown heritage signs

Covering some 800 acres, the country park surrounding Mount Edgcumbe contains a deer park, an amphitheatre, formal gardens, sculpture, the 18th-century Earl's Garden, and woodlands containing California redwoods. The coastal footpath runs along the shores of the Park from Cremyll to Whitsand Bay. Sir Richard Edgcumbe of Cotehele built Mount Edgcumbe between 1547 and 1553. It survived a direct hit by bombs in 1941, and was restored in the 1950s. It now contains antique paintings and furniture, 16th-century tapestries, and 18th-century porcelain. Events and exhibitions held each year.

Times Open: House & Earl's Garden Apr-Sep, Sun-Thu & BH Mon, 11-4.30. Country Park open all year* **Facilities** Ⓟ Ⓟ ☕ 🍴 licensed ⛩ (outdoor) toilets for disabled shop ⊗

TRELISSICK GARDEN Map 2 SW83

Trelissick Garden

TR3 6QL
☎ 01872 862090 📠 01872 865808
e-mail: trelissick@nationaltrust.org.uk
web: www.nationaltrust.org.uk
dir: 4m S of Truro on both sides of B3289, King Harry Ferry Road

Set amidst more than 500 acres of park and farmland, with panoramic views down the Carrick Roads to Falmouth and the sea, Trelissick Garden is well known for its large collection of hydrangeas, camellias, rhododendrons and exotic and tender plants. The Cornish Apple Orchard contains the definitive collection of Cornish apple varieties and is particularly lovely in the spring. Two galleries on the property display Cornish Arts and Crafts.

Times Open 2 Jan-12 Feb & Nov-23 Dec, daily 11-4; 13 Feb-Oct, daily, 10.30-5.30; 27-31 Dec, Mon-Fri, 11-4. Closed 24-26 Dec & 1 Jan* **Facilities** licensed (outdoor) (partly accessible) (certain areas some steps) toilets for disabled (audio guide, wheelchairs, batricar, induction loops) shop

TRERICE Map 2 SW85

Trerice

TR8 4PG
☎ 01637 875404 📠 01637 879300
e-mail: trerice@nationaltrust.org.uk
web: www.nationaltrust.org.uk
dir: 3m SE of Newquay off A3058 at Kestle Mill

Trerice was built in 1571 by Sir John Arundell IV and, having suffered no major changes since then due to a succession of absentee landlords, it appears very much the same as when it was built. The plaster ceilings in the Great Hall and Great Chamber are of particular merit and the façade of the building is thought to be the oldest of its kind in the country. The house contains many fine pieces of furniture and a large collection of clocks. The garden is planted to provide colour and interest throughout the year, and features an orchard with many varieties of Cornish apple trees.

Times Open Mar-Oct, daily (ex Fri) 11-4.30* **Facilities** licensed (outdoor) (fully accessible) toilets for disabled (Braille/large print guide, tape tour, 2 wheelchairs) shop

TRURO Map 2 SW84

Royal Cornwall Museum

River St TR1 2SJ
☎ 01872 272205 📠 01872 240514
e-mail: enquiries@royalcornwallmuseum.org.uk
web: www.royalcornwallmuseum.org.uk
dir: follow A390 towards town centre

Cornwall's oldest and most prestigious museum is famed for its internationally important collections. Visitors can see large collections of minerals, a real Egyptian mummy and the Cornish Giant. The art gallery has a fine collection of painting from the Newlyn and St Ives Schools, and regular temporary exhibitions of local, national and international artists. The museum runs a range of family activities throughout the year along with a regular programme of lectures. Contact the museum for details of events and activities.

Times Open all year, Mon-Sat 10-4.45. Library closes 1-2, all day Thu & Sat pm. Closed BHs & Sun* **Fees** Charges may apply **Facilities** licensed (fully accessible) toilets for disabled (lift, ramps to main entrances, Braille floor plan) shop

WENDRON Map 2 SW63

Poldark Mine and Heritage Complex

TR13 0ER
☎ 01326 573173 📠 01326 563166
e-mail: info@poldark-mine.com
web: www.poldark-mine.com
dir: 3m from Helston on B3297 Redruth road, follow brown signs

The centre of this attraction is the 18th-century tin mine where visitors can join a guided tour of workings which retain much of their original character. The site's Museum explains the history of tin production in Cornwall from 1800BC through to the 19th century and the fascinating story of the Cornish overseas. In addition to the Museum, the audio-visual presentation gives more insight into Cornwall's mining heritage. Ghost tours through July and August, please phone for details.

Times Open Etr-end Oct, 10-5.30 (last tour 4)* **Facilities** licensed (indoor & outdoor) (partly accessible) (surface area only) toilets for disabled (w/chair hire) shop

ZENNOR Map 2 SW43

Wayside Folk Museum & Trewey Watermill

TR26 3DA
☎ 01736 796945
dir: 4m W of St Ives, on B3306

Founded in 1937, this museum and watermill covers every aspect of life in Zennor and the surrounding area from 3000BC to the 1930s. Over 5000 items are displayed in 12 workshops and rooms covering wheelwrights, blacksmiths, agriculture, fishing, wrecks, mining, schools, dairy, domestic and archaeological artefacts. A photographic exhibition entitled 'People of the Past' tells the story of the village. The museum also contains a fully working watermill with original 19th-century machinery restored to working order grinding grain to flour. Flour for sale in shop.

Times Open Etr-end Oct, daily 10.30-5.30* **Fees** £3.75 (ch £2.75). Family ticket (2ad+2ch) £12. Party rates 10+* **Facilities** (outdoor) (not suitable for wheelchair users) shop

CUMBRIA

View over Grasmere, Lake District National Park

ALSTON Map 12 NY74

Nenthead Mines

Nenthead CA9 3PD
☎ 01434 382294 Fax 01434 382043
e-mail: mines@npht.com
web: www.npht.com/ntheadmines
dir: 5m E of Alston, on A689

Set in 200 acres in the North Pennines, this hands-on heritage centre contains exhibitions and displays on geology, local wildlife, and social history. Visitors can operate three enormous water wheels, gaze down a 328ft deep brewery shaft, and take an underground trip through the Nenthead mines, last worked for lead in 1915. Special events take place throughout the year.

Times Open Etr-Oct, daily 11-5 (last entry to mine 3.30)* **Fees** £4-£7 (ch free-£3). Family ticket from £15* **Facilities** (indoor & outdoor) (partly accessible) (ltd disabled access underground) toilets for disabled (ramps & motorised scooter) shop

South Tynedale Railway — 2 FOR 1

The Railway Station, Hexham Rd CA9 3JB
☎ 01434 381696 & 01434 382828
e-mail: strps@hotmail.com
web: www.strps.org.uk
dir: 0.25m N, on A686

Running along the beautiful South Tyne valley, this narrow-gauge railway follows the route of the former Alston to Haltwhistle branch. At present the line runs between Alston and Kirkhaugh.

Times Open Etr-Oct, wknds & BHs; mid Jul-Aug daily. Santa Specials all wknds in Dec. Please enquire for exact details **Fees** Return £6 (ch 3-15 £3). Single £4 (ch 3-15 £2). All day £10 (ch 3-15 £5, dog £1, bicycle 50p) **Facilities** (outdoor) (fully accessible) toilets for disabled (railway carriage for wheelchairs, pre-booking required) shop

AMBLESIDE Map 7 NY30

The Armitt Collection

Rydal Rd LA22 9BL
☎ 015394 31212 Fax 015394 31313
e-mail: info@armitt.com
web: www.armitt.com
dir: On A591 opposite Rydal Rd car park in Ambleside. Next to St Martins College

A fascinating and entertaining place that celebrates over 2000 years of Lake District history, from the time of Ambleside's Roman occupation to the 20th century. Facts, artefacts, historic photographs and renowned works of art by not only the area's better known former inhabitants such as Beatrix Potter, Kurt Schwitters and John Ruskin, but also displays about the daily lives of its hard-working townspeople in past times. Over 11,000 books are contained within a reference library and there is a changing programme of exhibitions. The Collection is pre-eminently a research source, using the gallery to demonstrate the range of material within the collection.

Times Open all year, daily 10-5 (last entrance 4.30). Closed 24-26 Dec* **Facilities** (fully accessible) toilets for disabled (chairlift to upstairs library, parking at establishment) shop

BARROW-IN-FURNESS Map 7 SD26

The Dock Museum — FREE

North Rd LA14 2PW
☎ 01229 876400 Fax 01229 811361
e-mail: dockmuseum@barrowbc.gov.uk
web: www.dockmuseum.org.uk
dir: A590 to Barrow-in-Furness. Follow brown tourist signs

Explore this museum and relive the fascinating history of Barrow-in-Furness. Discover how the industrial revolution prompted the growth of the town from a small hamlet into a major industrial power through models, graphics and film shows.

Times Open Apr-Nov, Tue-Fri 10-5, Sat-Sun 11-5; Nov-Mar, Wed-Fri 10.30-4, Sat-Sun 11-4.30. **Facilities** (outdoor) (fully accessible) toilets for disabled (hearing & induction loops, 2 w/chairs, lift) shop

BARROW-IN-FURNESS *continued*

Furness Abbey

LH13 0TJ

☎ 01229 823420

web: www.english-heritage.org.uk

dir: 1.5m NE on unclass road

Located in a peaceful valley, the majestic red sandstone remains of this beautiful abbey that dates from the 12th century, housed a wealthy Cistercian monastic order. Set in the 'vale of nightshade', the romantic ruins were celebrated by Wordsworth in his poem *The Prelude* of 1805. View the fine stone carvings and visit the exhibition to find out more about the powerful religious community that was once based here.

Times Open all year, Apr-Sep, Thu-Mon 10-5; Oct-Mar, Sat-Sun 10-4. Closed 24-26 Dec & 1 Jan **Fees** £3.70 (ch £1.90, concessions £3.10). Prices and opening times are subject to change in March 2011. Please call 0870 333 1181 for the most up to date prices and opening times when planning your visit **Facilities** P ♿ (partly accessible) (some low walls, steps, slopes) toilets for disabled (audio tour, hearing loop) shop #

BASSENTHWAITE — Map 11 NY23

Trotters World of Animals — 2 FOR 1

Coalbeck Farm CA12 4RD

☎ 017687 76239 017687 76598

e-mail: info@trottersworld.com

web: www.trottersworld.com

dir: follow brown signs on A591/A66 from Bassenthwaite Lake, 8m from Keswick

Set in breathtaking scenery enjoy a fun and educational day out at this award-winning wildlife park. From antelopes to zebras, see over 100 species from every corner of the world, ranging from cheeky mandrills and meerkats to endangered species like gibbons and Asian fishing cats. Fun for all ages.

Times Open all year 10-5.30 or dusk if earlier. Closed 25 Dec & 1 Jan* **Fees** £7.50 (ch £5.50, pen £6.50) **Facilities** P licensed (indoor & outdoor) ♿ (fully accessible) toilets for disabled shop

BIRDOSWALD — Map 12 NY66

Birdoswald Roman Fort

CA8 7DD

☎ 016977 47602 016977 47605

e-mail: birdoswald.romanfort@english-heritage.org.uk

web: www.english-heritage.org.uk

dir: signed off A69 between Brampton & Hexham

A visitor centre introduces you to Hadrian's Wall and the Roman Fort. This unique section of Hadrian's Wall overlooks the Irthing Gorge, and is the only point along the Wall where all the components of the Roman frontier system can be found together. Birdoswald isn't just about the Romans, though, it's also about border raids in the Middle Ages, and recent archaeological discoveries. Please telephone for details of re-enactments and family activities.

Times Open Apr-Sep, daily 10-5.30 (last admission 5). Oct-1 Nov, daily 10-4 **Fees** £4.80 (ch £2.40, concessions £4.10) **Facilities** P (P) (outdoor) ♿ (partly accessible) toilets for disabled (ramp outside, disabled parking, lift) shop #

BORROWDALE — Map 11 NY21

Honister Slate Mine

Honister Pass CA12 5XN

☎ 01768 777230 01768 777958

e-mail: info@honister.com

web: www.honister.com

dir: from Keswick take B5289 through Borrowdale & Rosthwaite, follow road to top of pass. From Cockermouth take B5292 towards Keswick for 4m, turn right onto B5289 to Low Larton & Buttermere. Follow road to top of pass

The last working slate mine in England. Fully guided tours allow you to explore the caverns hacked out by Victorian miners. Learn the history of the famous Honister green slate, how to rive slates, and see local skills in action.

Times Open Mon-Fri 9-5, wknds 10-5. Closed 19 Dec-12 Jan* **Facilities** P (P) licensed ♿ (partly accessible) toilets for disabled shop

BOWNESS-ON-WINDERMERE — Map 7 SD49

Blackwell The Arts & Crafts House

LA23 3JT

☎ 015394 46139 015394 88486

e-mail: info@blackwell.org.uk

web: www.blackwell.org.uk

dir: M6 junct 36. 1.5m S of Bowness on B5360, off A5074

Blackwell is one of Britain's finest houses from the turn of the last century and survives in a truly remarkable state of preservation retaining almost all of its original decorative features. Blackwell offers more than most historic houses, with several of its first floor rooms adapted for use as exhibition galleries. These are perfect spaces for showing contemporary work by established and emerging craft-makers, and for displaying historical exhibitions that explore different aspects of the Arts & Crafts Movement.

Times Open 16 Jan-3 Jan daily, 10.30-5. Closes 4pm Jan-Mar & Nov-Dec* **Fees** £6.50 (ch £3.80). Family ticket £17.25* **Facilities** P ♿ (partly accessible) (some rooms have no disabled access but visual guides available) toilets for disabled (lift to upper floor, photos for inaccessible rooms) shop

BRAMPTON Map 12 NY56

Lanercost Priory

CA8 2HQ
☎ 01697 73030
web: www.english-heritage.org.uk
dir: 2.5m NE

The atmospheric ruins of this Augustinian priory, founded in the 12th century, are close to Hadrian's Wall.

Times Open Apr-Sep, daily 10-5; Oct-1 Nov, Thu-Mon, 10-4 **Fees** £3.20 (ch £1.60, concessions £2.70). Prices and opening times are subject to change in March 2011. Please call 0870 333 1181 for the most up to date prices and opening times when planning your visit **Facilities** Ⓟ shop #

BROUGH Map 12 NY71

Brough Castle FREE

CA17 4EJ
☎ 0191 261 1585
web: www.english-heritage.org.uk
dir: 8m SE of Appleby, S of A66

Dating from Roman times the 12th-century keep at this site replaced an earlier stronghold destroyed by the Scots in 1174. It was restored by Lady Anne Clifford in the 17th century. You can still see the outline of her kitchen gardens.

Times Apr-Sep, daily 10-5; Oct-Mar 10-4. Closed 24-26 Dec & 1 Jan. Please call 0870 333 1181 for details of opening times **Facilities** Ⓟ #

BROUGHAM Map 12 NY52

Brougham Castle

CA10 2AA
☎ 01768 862488
web: www.english-heritage.org.uk
dir: 1.5m SE of Penrith on minor road off A66

Explore the maze of stairs and passages in the ruins of this once glorious 11th-century castle on the banks of the River Eamont. Enjoy the lively exhibition where you'll see relics from the nearby Roman Fort.

Times Open Apr-Sep, daily 10-5 **Fees** £3.70 (ch £1.90, concessions £3.10). Family £9.30. Prices and opening times are subject to change in March 2011. Please call 0870 333 1181 for the most up to date prices and opening times when planning your visit **Facilities** Ⓟ ⛩ ♿ (partly accessible) (no w/chair access to keep) (wheelchair route, interpretation panels) shop #

CARLISLE Map 11 NY35

Carlisle Castle

CA3 8UR
☎ 01228 591992 📠 01228 514880
web: www.english-heritage.org.uk
dir: north side of city centre, close to station

Discover a thrilling and bloody past and enjoy panoramic views over the city and hills of the Lake District and Southern Scotland. Uncover an exciting history through lively exhibitions, which tell of William Rufus, Mary Queen of Scots and Bonnie Prince Charlie.

Times Open all year, Apr-Sep, daily 9.30-5; Oct-Mar, daily 10-4. Closed 24-26 Dec & 1 Jan **Fees** £4.80 (ch £2.40, concessions £4.10). Prices and opening times are subject to change in March 2011. Please call 0870 333 1181 for the most up to date prices and opening times when planning your visit **Facilities** Ⓟ shop ㊗ #

Carlisle Cathedral

Castle St CA3 8TZ
☎ 01228 535169 & 548151 📠 01228 547049
e-mail: office@carlislecathedral.org.uk
web: www.carlislecathedral.org.uk
dir: M6 junct 42,43 or 44, located in City Centre

The Cathedral, founded in 1122 as a Norman Priory for Augustinian canons, has conducted services for nearly 900 years. Items of special interest include the East Window, with its tracery containing some very fine 14th-century stained glass, and the Brougham Triptych, a magnificent 16th-century carved Flemish altarpiece in St. Wilfrid's Chapel. There is an interesting 14th-century barrel-vaulted painted ceiling in the Choir, and in the north and south aisles medieval paintings depict the Life of St. Cuthbert and St. Anthony and the figures of the 12 Apostles.

Times Open all year daily, Mon-Sat 7.30-6.15, Sun 7.30-5, summer BHs 9.45-6.15, winter BHs, Xmas & New Year 9.45-4 (may vary during special events) **Fees** Suggested donation of £4 per adult. Treasury £1 charge. **Facilities** Ⓟ 🍴 licensed ⛩ (outdoor) ♿ (partly accessible) (cathedral mostly accessible) toilets for disabled (parking, ramps, loop system, large print books, chairlifts) shop ㊗

The Guildhall Museum FREE

Green Market CA3 8JE
☎ 01228 625400 📠 01228 810249
e-mail: enquiries@tulliehouse.co.uk
web: www.tulliehouse.co.uk
dir: town centre, behind Tourist Information Centre

Experience the unique atmosphere of the oldest town centre building in the city. The Guildhall was originally a row of shops and workshops attached to a wealthy merchant's town house. It has been owned by the City of Carlisle since the 14th century and is now home to a museum of civic history, such as Carlisle Bells, the oldest horseracing prizes in the country and the impressive medieval monument chest, Victorian civic regalia, and Guild Silver collections.

Times Open Good Fri-Oct, 12-4.30* **Facilities** Ⓟ shop ㊗

ENGLAND

CARLISLE *continued*

Tullie House Museum & Art Gallery

Castle St CA3 8TP
☎ 01228 618718 📠 01228 810249
e-mail: enquiries@tulliehouse.co.uk
web: www.tulliehouse.co.uk
dir: M6 junct 42, 43 or 44 follow signs to city centre. Car park in Devonshire Walk

Set in newly re-designed Roman and Jacobean gardens, Old Tullie House is home to an impressive collection of Pre-Raphaelite art, with many of the classical features of the 17th-century building still remaining, including the stunning staircase. Along with painting and sculpture, there are plenty of interactive exhibits that explore Roman life as well as 'Freshwater Life'. Lots of events throughout the year, contact for details.

Times Open Nov-Mar, Mon-Sat 10-4, Sun 12-4; Apr-Jun & Sep-Oct, Mon-Sat 10-5, Sun 12-5; Jul-Aug, Mon-Sat 10-5, Sun 11-5. Closed 25-26 Dec & 1 Jan* **Facilities** Ⓟ licensed (partly accessible) (Old Tullie House restricted access) toilets for disabled (chair lift, ramped access, lifts to all floors) shop

COCKERMOUTH — Map 11 NY13

Jennings Brewery Tour and Shop

The Castle Brewery CA13 9NE
☎ 0845 129 7190 📠 0845 129 7186
e-mail: jenningsbreweryshop@marstons.co.uk
web: www.jenningsbrewery.co.uk
dir: A66 to Cockermouth, follow tourist signs to brewery

Jennings Brewery was originally established as a family business in 1828 and moved to its current location in 1874. It is a traditional brewer, using Lakeland water drawn from the Brewery's own well. English Pale Ale Malt is used in all beers.

Times Tours: Jan-Feb & Nov-Dec, Mon-Sat at 2; Mar-Jun & Sep-Oct, Mon-Sat at 11 & 2; Jul-Aug, daily at 11 & 2* **Fees** £6 (ch over 12 £3) **Facilities** Ⓟ (partly accessible) (ground floor shop & amenities accessible) toilets for disabled shop

Wordsworth House

Main St CA13 9RX
☎ 01900 820882 📠 01900 820883
e-mail: wordsworthhouse@nationaltrust.org.uk
web: www.wordsworthhouse.org.uk
dir: W end of Main Street

William Wordsworth was born here on 7th April 1770, and happy memories of the house had a great effect on his work. The house is imaginatively presented for the first time as the home of the Wordsworth family in the 1770s. It offers a lively and interactive visit with hands-on activities and costumed living history.

Times Open 13 Mar-Oct, Sat-Tue 11-5; Jul, Aug & BHs Mon-Sat, other times Tue-Sat. School hols Sat-Thu 11-5* **Fees** £6.20 (ch £3.10). Family ticket £15.50* **Facilities** Ⓟ (partly accessible) toilets for disabled (Braille guide, touch list, computer) shop

CONISTON — Map 7 SD39

Brantwood

LA21 8AD
☎ 015394 41396 📠 015394 41263
e-mail: enquiries@brantwood.org.uk
web: www.brantwood.org.uk
dir: 2.5m SE off B5285, unclass road. Regular ferry services from Coniston Pier

Brantwood, home of John Ruskin, is a beautifully situated house with fine views across Coniston Water. Inside, there is a large collection of Ruskin paintings and memorabilia, and visitors can enjoy delightful nature walks through the Brantwood Estate.

Times Open mid Mar-mid Nov, daily 11-5.30. Winter, Wed-Sun 11-4.30. Closed 25-26 Dec **Fees** House & Garden: £6.30 (ch 5-15 £1.35, students £5). Familty ticket (2ad+3ch) £13.15. Garden only: £4.50 (ch 5-15 £1.35, students £3.60). Family ticket (2ad+3ch) £8.60 **Facilities** Ⓟ licensed (partly accessible) (access restricted to ground floor of house, stairs to upper floor) toilets for disabled (wheelchairs, photos of inaccessible areas, Braille guides) shop

The Ruskin Museum

Yewdale Rd LA21 8DU
☎ 015394 41164 📠 015394 41132
web: www.ruskinmuseum.com
dir: A593 from A591 at Ambleside; A593 from A590 at Greenodd; B5285 from Hawkshead. In village centre opposite fire station, accessed from Mines Rd between Black Bull and Co-op

John Ruskin (1819-1900) was one of Britain's most versatile and important political thinkers and artists. The museum contains many of his watercolours, drawings, letters, sketchbooks and other relics. The geology, mines and quarries of the area and Arthur Ransome's *Swallows and Amazons* country are also explored in the Museum. The conservation rebuild of Donald Campbell's iconic hydroplane is underway, and should be completed by autumn 2010. Permission has been granted for future low-speed engineering proving trials on Coniston Water. The housing of *Bluebird A7* in a new museum wing is also planned.

Times Open 2-4 Jan, 6 Jan-5 Mar, Wed-Sun 10.30-3.30; from 6 Mar, daily 10-5.30. Contact or see website for details of winter opening hours.* **Facilities** (fully accessible) toilets for disabled (handling specimens, guided walks) shop

Steam Yacht Gondola

Coniston Pier LA21 8AJ

015394 41288 015394 41962

e-mail: gondola@nationaltrust.org.uk

web: www.nationaltrust.org.uk/gondola

dir: A593 to Coniston, follow signs near garage 'to boats' & S Y Gondola. Coniston Pier at end of Lake Road

Originally launched in 1859, the graceful Gondola plied the waters of Coniston Water until 1936. Beautifully rebuilt, she came back into service in 1980, and visitors can once again enjoy her silent progress and old-fashioned comfort.

Times Open Apr-Oct to scheduled daily timetable* **Fees** Round trip £8.50 (ch £4.50). Family ticket (2ad+3ch) £21.50, including NT members* **Facilities** (partly accessible) (Gondola not accessible to wheelchair bound visitors) shop

DALEMAIN Map 12 NY42

Dalemain Mansion & Historic Gardens

2 FOR 1

CA11 0HB

017684 86450 017684 86223

e-mail: admin@dalemain.com

web: www.dalemain.com

dir: M6 junct 40, between Penrith & Ullswater on A592

Originally a mediaeval pele tower, Dalemain was added to in Tudor times, and the imposing Georgian facade was completed in 1745. It has oak panelling, Chinese wallpaper, Tudor plasterwork and fine period furniture. The tower contains the Westmorland and Cumberland Yeomanry Museum, and there is a countryside collection in the 16th-century Great Barn. The gardens include a collection of old fashioned roses, wild flower spiral, earth sculpture and in early summer a magnificent display of blue Himalayan poppies.

Times Open House: 3 Apr-27 Oct, Sun-Thu 11.15-4 (3 in Oct). Gardens, tea room & giftshop: Sun-Thu 10.30-5 (4 in Oct) **Fees** House & Garden £9.50, garden only £6.50 **Facilities** licensed (outdoor) (partly accessible) (downstairs of house accessible, pictures of upstairs available) toilets for disabled (ramp access at entrance, electric scooter) shop

DALTON-IN-FURNESS Map 7 SD27

South Lakes Wild Animal Park

2 FOR 1

Crossgates LA15 8JR

01229 466086 01229 461310

e-mail: office@wildanimalpark.co.uk

web: www.wildanimalpark.co.uk

dir: M6 junct 36, A590 to Dalton-in-Furness, follow tourist signs

A day you'll never forget at one of Cumbria's top attractions. Hand feed giraffes, penguins and kangaroos every day. Get up close to rhinos, tigers, bears, hippos, monkeys, vultures, and lemurs. There are new aerial walkways and viewpoints, the Wild Things gift shop and Maki restaurant, all overlooking a recreated African Savannah where rhinos, giraffes and baboons wander.

Times Open all year, daily 10-5; Nov-Feb 10-4.30 (last admission 45mins before close). Closed 25 Dec **Fees** £11.50 (ch & concessions £8). Free entry during Dec 2010 & Jan 2011 **Facilities** licensed (indoor & outdoor) (fully accessible) toilets for disabled (wheelchair users may need help) shop

GRASMERE Map 11 NY30

Dove Cottage and The Wordsworth Museum

LA22 9SH

015394 35544 015394 35748

e-mail: enquiries@wordsworth.org.uk

web: www.wordsworth.org.uk

dir: A591S of rdbt for Grasmere village

Dove Cottage was the inspirational home of William Wordsworth between 1799-1808, and it was here that he wrote some of his best-known poetry. The cottage has been open to the public since 1891, and is kept in its original condition. The museum displays manuscripts, works of art and items that belonged to the poet. There is a changing programme of special events, both historical and modern. Please visit website for details.

Times Open daily 9.30-5.30; Oct-Feb, 9.30-4.30 (last admission 30mins before close). Closed 25 Dec & most of Jan (yearly maintenance) **Fees** £7.50 (ch £4.50). Family ticket £17.20. Discounts for pre-booked groups **Facilities** licensed (partly accessible) (Museum, galleries & ground floor of cottage accessible) toilets for disabled (ramps, induction loop, virtual tour) shop

ENGLAND

HAWKSHEAD Map 7 SD39

Beatrix Potter Gallery

Main St LA22 0NS
☎ 015394 36269 📠 015394 36811
e-mail: beatrixpottergallery@nationaltrust.org.uk
web: www.nationaltrust.org.uk
dir: on main street in village centre

An annually changing exhibition of Beatrix Potter's original illustrations from her children's storybooks, housed in the former office of her husband, solicitor William Heelis.

Times Open 13 Feb-25 Mar, Sat-Thu 11-3.30; 27 Mar-Oct, Sat-Thu 11-5. Admission by timed ticket including NT members* **Fees** £4.40 (ch £2.10). Family ticket (2ad+3ch) £10.50.* **Facilities** Ⓟ ♿ (partly accessible) (Braille guide) shop

HOLKER Map 7 SD37

Holker Hall & Gardens 2 FOR 1

Cark in Cartmel, Grange over Sands LA11 7PL
☎ 015395 58328 📠 015395 58378
e-mail: info@holker.co.uk
web: www.holker.co.uk
dir: from M6 junct 36, follow A590, signed lake District Peninsulas and then Holker Hall. Located on B5278, 0.5m from Cark-in-Cartmel

Dating from the 17th century, the new wing of the Hall was rebuilt in 1871, after a fire. It has notable woodcarving and many fine pieces of furniture which mix happily with family photographs from the present day. There are magnificent gardens, both formal and woodland, and further attractions include the beautiful deer park, children's play and picnic areas. The Holker Garden Festival will take place between 3-5 June 2011.

Times Hall & Gardens: Open 14 Mar-Oct, Sun-Fri. Hall open 11-4 & Garden 10.30-5.30. Café & Gift shop open daily 31 Jan-24 Dec, 10.30-5.30. Closes 4 in winter* **Fees** Hall & Gardens £10 (ch £5.50, concessions £9). Family ticket £27.50. Gardens & Park £6.50 (ch £3.50, concessions £5.50)* **Facilities** Ⓟ licensed (outdoor) ♿ (partly accessible) (first floor of Hall not accessible) toilets for disabled (ramps, wheelchairs & scooters available for hire) shop

KENDAL Map 7 SD59

Abbot Hall Art Gallery

LA9 5AL
☎ 01539 722464 📠 01539 722494
e-mail: info@abbothall.org.uk
web: www.abbothall.org.uk
dir: M6 junct 36, follow signs to Kendal. Located at south end of town centre beside parish church

The Gallery is housed in one of Kendal's most important buildings; a Grade I listed Georgian Villa on the banks of the River Kent. The Gallery offers two floors of light-filled spaces, a temporary exhibition programme that has achieved a national profile, and the permanent collection of works by George Romney spanning his entire career. The upstairs galleries feature commanding views of the River Kent and Kendal Castle and show works by major British artists including Sean Scully, Frank Auerbach, and Ben and Winifred Nicholson.

Times Open 6 Jan-18 Dec, Mon-Sat 10.30-5. Closes 4 Jan-Mar & Nov-Dec* **Fees** £5.75 (ch up to 18 & students up to 25 free)* **Facilities** Ⓟ Ⓟ ♿ (fully accessible) toilets for disabled (chair lifts in split level galleries, large print labels) shop

Kendal Museum 2 FOR 1

Station Rd LA9 6BT
☎ 01539 815597 📠 01539 737976
e-mail: info@kendalmuseum.org.uk
web: www.kendalmuseum.org.uk
dir: opposite railway station

The archaeology and natural history of the Lakes is explored in this popular museum which also features a world wildlife exhibition and a display devoted to author Alfred Wainwright, who was honorary clerk to the museum.

Times Open Thu-Sat noon-5* **Fees** £2.80 (ch & full time students free, pen £2.20)* **Facilities** Ⓟ Ⓟ ♿ (partly accessible) (2 of 4 galleries accessible - access via disabled doors from ramp) toilets for disabled shop

Museum of Lakeland Life

Abbot Hall LA9 5AL
☎ 01539 722464 📠 01539 722494
e-mail: info@lakelandmuseum.org.uk
web: www.lakelandmuseum.org.uk
dir: M6 junct 36, follow signs to Kendal. Located at south end of Kendal beside Abbot Hall Art Gallery

Recreated period rooms and workshops reveal how people lived and worked, the toys that children played with, and how different Georgian and Victorian life was from today. Explore a farmhouse kitchen with traditional recipes and utensils, a bedroom full of vernacular furniture, including a magnificent 16th-century four-poster bed, and a parlour with rare 17th-century oak panelling. Other displays include a traditional chemist's shop, farming, Lakeland industries, and the local Arts & Crafts Movement.
A visit to the Arthur Ransome Room allows you to immerse yourself in the world of *Swallows and Amazons* with the author's typewriter, desk, personal mementos and original illustrations.

Times Open 13 Jan-18 Dec, Mon-Sat 10.30-5 (Jan-Mar & Nov-Dec closing at 4)* **Fees** £4.75 (ch £3.40). Family ticket £13.60* **Facilities** Ⓟ Ⓟ ♿ (partly accessible) (partial wheelchair access on the ground floor) toilets for disabled shop

KESWICK Map 11 NY22

The Bond Museum

Southey Hill Trading Estate CA12 5NR
☎ 017687 75007 & 72090 📠 017687 72090
e-mail: thebondmuseum@aol.com
web: www.thebondmuseum.com
dir: M6 junct 40, follow signs to Keswick on A66. Museum in town centre behind Cumberland Pencil Museum

A must for all James Bond fans, see Aston Martins, Lotus, planes and a T55 Russian tank from the film *Goldeneye*. Enjoy film clips showing car chases in the cinema and visit the Bond souvenir shop.

Times Open daily Feb half term & 1 wk prior to Etr until end Oct 10-5 **Fees** £6 (ch 4-15 £4). Family ticket (2ad+2ch) £20, incl brochure, photo, pass & quiz* **Facilities** 🅟 Ⓟ ♿ (fully accessible) toilets for disabled shop

Cars of the Stars Motor Museum

Standish St CA12 5LS
☎ 017687 73757 📠 017687 72090
e-mail: cotsmm@aol.com
web: www.carsofthestars.com
dir: M6 junct 40, A66 to Keswick, continue to town centre, close to Bell Close car park

This unusual museum features celebrity TV and film vehicles. Some notable exhibits to look out for are *Chitty Chitty Bang Bang*, James Bond's DB5 Aston Martin, Harry Potter's Ford Anglia, Del Boy's Robin Reliant, thw A-Team van and the Batmobile. Each vehicle is displayed in its individual film set.

Times Open Feb half term, daily Etr-Nov (wknds Dec) 10-5 **Fees** £5 (ch £3)* **Facilities** Ⓟ ♿ (fully accessible) shop

Cumberland Pencil Museum

Southey Works, Greta Bridge CA12 5NG
☎ 017687 73626 📠 01900 602489
e-mail: kes_museum@acco.com
web: www.pencilmuseum.co.uk
dir: M6 N onto A66 at Penrith. Left at 2nd Keswick exit, left at T-junct, left over Greta Bridge

Investigating the history and technology of an object most of us take utterly for granted, this interesting museum includes a replica of the Borrowdale mine where graphite was first discovered, the world's longest pencil, children's activity area, and various artistic techniques that use pencils. Artist demonstrations and workshops will take place throughout the year.

Times Open daily 9.30-4 (hours may be extended during peak season). Closed 25-26 Dec & 1 Jan* **Facilities** 🅟 Ⓟ ☕ ⛩ (outdoor) ♿ (fully accessible) toilets for disabled shop

Mirehouse

CA12 4QE
☎ 017687 72287
e-mail: info@mirehouse.com
web: www.mirehouse.com
dir: 3m N of Keswick on A591

Visitors return to Mirehouse for many reasons: close links to Tennyson and Wordsworth, the spectacular setting of mountain and lake, the varied gardens, changing displays on the Poetry Walk, free family trail, four woodland playgrounds, live piano music in the house, generous Cumbrian cooking in the tearoom, and a relaxed, friendly welcome. Please contact for details of special events.

Times Open Apr-Oct. Grounds: daily 10.30-5. House: Wed, Sun, (also Fri in Aug) 2-last entry 4.30 **Fees** House & grounds £6.50 (ch £3). Grounds only £3 (ch £1.50). Family ticket £18 (2ad & up to 4ch)* **Facilities** 🅟 ☕ ⛩ (outdoor) ♿ (fully accessible) toilets for disabled

LAKESIDE Map 7 SD38

Lakes Aquarium

LA12 8AS
☎ 015395 30153 📠 015395 30152
e-mail: info@lakesaquarium.co.uk
web: www.lakesaquarium.co.uk
dir: M6, junct 36, take A590 to Newby Bridge. Turn right over bridge, follow Hawkshead Rd to Lakeside

Lakes Aquarium is now home to creatures that live in and around freshwater lakes across the globe. See things that swim, fly and bite in beautifully-themed displays. Discover mischievous otters in the Asia area, piranhas in the Americas and cheeky marmosets in the rainforest displays, not forgetting all your favourite creatures that live a bit closer to home. This includes diving ducks in the spectacular underwater tunnel and fresh water rays and seahorses in the Seashore Discover Zone. Don't miss the worlds first virtual dive bell. Experience a spectacular interactive adventure and come face to face with awesome virtual creatures, including a terrifying shark, charging hippo and fierce crocodile - without getting wet. Special themed events take place throughout the year, please see website for details.

Times Open all year, daily 9-5 (winter) 9-6 (summer) last admission 1hr prior to closing. Closed 25 Dec* **Fees** £8.95 (ch 3-15 £5.95, concessions £7.50). Family ticket (2ad+2ch) £26.95* **Facilities** 🅟 ☕ 🍽 licensed ⛩ (outdoor) ♿ (fully accessible) toilets for disabled (lift to first floor, wheelchair) shop 🚭

LEVENS **Map 7 SD48**

Levens Hall

LA8 0PD
☎ 015395 60321 015395 60669
e-mail: houseopening@levenshall.co.uk
web: www.levenshall.co.uk
dir: M6 junct 36. 5m S of Kendal, on A6

An Elizabethan mansion, built onto a 13th-century pele tower, with fine plasterwork, panelling and leatherwork. The topiary garden, laid out in 1694, survives virtually unchanged.

Times Open: House & gardens mid Apr-mid Oct, Sun-Thu. Gardens 10-5. House 12-4.30 (last admission 4) **Facilities** (outdoor) (partly accessible) (house-no access for wheelchairs/buggies) toilets for disabled shop

NEAR SAWREY **Map 7 SD39**

Hill Top

LA22 0LF
☎ 015394 36269 015394 36811
e-mail: hilltop@nationaltrust.org.uk
web: www.nationaltrust.org.uk
dir: 2m S of Hawkshead or 2m from Bowness Car Ferry

This small 17th-century house is where Beatrix Potter wrote many of her famous children's stories. It remains as she left it, and in each room can be found something that appears in one of her books.

Times House open 13 Feb-25 Mar, Sat-Thu 11-3.30; 27 Mar-Oct, Sat-Thu 10.30-4.30. Garden open 13 Feb-26 Mar, daily 11-4; 27 Mar-Oct, daily 10-5; Nov-24 Dec, daily 10-4* **Fees** £6.50 (ch £3.10). Family ticket £16 (2ad+3ch). Entry to garden free on Fri when house is closed* **Facilities** (partly accessible) (access by arrangement) (Braille guide, handling items) shop

PENRITH **Map 12 NY53**

The Rheged Centre

Redhills CA11 0DQ
☎ 01768 868000 01768 868002
e-mail: enquiries@rheged.com
web: www.rheged.com
dir: M6 junct 40, on A66 near Penrith

Rheged's ten shops reflect the unique nature of the region, while the indoor and outdoor activities provide challenges for children of all ages. The centre has introduced large format 3D films, three films show twice a day. From a relaxed family lunch to a quick coffee and cake, Rheged's three cafes offer fresh food, made on the premises using the finest local ingredients.

Times Open daily 10-5.30. Closed 25-26 Dec & 1 Jan* **Facilities** licensed (outdoor) (fully accessible) toilets for disabled (Wheelchairs and motorised scooters) shop

Wetheriggs Animal Rescue & Conservation Centre

Clifton Dykes CA10 2DH
☎ 01768 866657 01768 866657
web: www.wetheriggsanimalrescue.co.uk
dir: approx 2m off A6, S from Penrith, signed

Wetheriggs is an animal rescue centre with a mixture of farm and exotic animals. Operated as a registered charity, all proceeds go towards rescuing and looking after the animals. You can also learn about the heritage of the steam-powered pottery and engine room, and paint your own pot. There is a newt pond, play area and a petting farm and reptile house, café and gift shop, all set in 7.5 acres of the beautiful Eden Valley.

Times Open daily, Apr-Oct 10-4; Nov-Mar 10-3. Closed 25-26 Dec & 1 Jan* **Fees** £3.95 (ch £2.95). Family ticket (2ad+4ch) £12.50* **Facilities** (outdoor) toilets for disabled shop

RAVENGLASS **Map 6 SD09**

Ravenglass & Eskdale Railway

CA18 1SW
☎ 01229 717171 01229 717011
e-mail: steam@ravenglass-railway.co.uk
web: www.ravenglass-railway.co.uk
dir: close to A595, Barrow to Carlisle road

The Lake District's oldest, longest and most scenic steam railway, stretching from the coast at Ravenglass, through two of Lakeland's loveliest valleys for seven miles to Dalegarth Visitor Centre and the foot of England's highest mountains. At least seven trains daily from March to November, plus winter weekends and holiday periods. Packages for walkers and cyclists, children's activities with Ratty the Water-vole Stationmaster and special event days.

Times Open: trains operate daily mid Mar-early Nov, most winter wknds, daily between Xmas & New Year & Feb half term **Fees** Return fare £11.20 (ch £5.60, under 5's free). Family discounts available* **Facilities** licensed (outdoor) (fully accessible) toilets for disabled (special coaches - prior notice advisable) shop

RYDAL Map 11 NY30

Rydal Mount and Gardens

LA22 9LU

☎ 015394 33002 015394 31738

e-mail: info@rydalmount.co.uk

web: www.rydalmount.co.uk

dir: 1.5m from Ambleside on A591 to Grasmere

The family home of William Wordsworth from 1813 until his death in 1850. The house contains important family portraits, furniture, and many of the poet's personal possessions, together with first editions of his work. In a lovely setting overlooking Windermere and Rydal Water, the gardens were designed by Wordsworth himself. Evening visits for groups can be organised.

Times Open Mar-Oct, daily 9.30-5; Nov, Dec & Feb, Wed-Sun 11-4. Closed 24-25 Dec & Jan **Fees** £6 (ch 5-15 £2.50, concessions & students £5). Garden only £4* **Facilities** (outdoor) (partly accessible) (assistance to front door & ramp) shop

SHAP Map 12 NY51

Shap Abbey

FREE

CA10 3NB

web: www.english-heritage.org.uk

dir: 1.5m W of Shap on bank of River Lowther

Dedicated to St Mary Magdalene, the abbey was founded by the Premonstratensian order in 1199, but most of the ruins are of 13th-century date. The most impressive feature is the 16th-century west tower of the church.

Times Open at any reasonable time **Facilities**

SIZERGH Map 7 SD48

Sizergh Castle & Garden

LA8 8AE

☎ 015395 60951

e-mail: sizergh@nationaltrust.org.uk

web: www.nationaltrust.org.uk

dir: 3.5m S of Kendal, signed from A590

The castle has a 60-foot high tower, built in the 14th century, but most of the castle dates from the 15th to the 18th centuries. There are panelled rooms with fine carved overmantles and adze-hewn floors, and the gardens, laid out in the 18th century, contain the National Trust's largest limestone rock garden.

Times Open Apr-Oct, Sun-Thu 1-5; Garden open Apr-Oct, from 11 (last admission 4)* **Fees** House & Garden £7.90 (ch £4). Family ticket £19.80. Garden only £5.15 (ch £2.65)* **Facilities** (partly accessible) (ramps) toilets for disabled (Braille guide, wheelchair, powered buggy) shop

SKELTON Map 12 NY43

Hutton-in-the-Forest

CA11 9TH

☎ 017684 84449 017684 84571

e-mail: info@hutton-in-the-forest.co.uk

web: www.hutton-in-the-forest.co.uk

dir: 6m NW of Penrith on B5305 to Wigton, 2.5m from M6 junct 41

A beautiful house, set in woods which were once part of the medieval forest of Inglewood, belonging to the Inglewood family since 1605. The house consists of a 14th-century pele tower with later additions, and contains a fine collection of furniture, portraits, tapestries and china, a 17th-century gallery and cupid staircase. The walled garden has a large collection of herbaceous plants, and there are 19th-century topiary terraces, a 17th-century dovecote and a woodland walk with impressive specimen trees. Special events include a plant and food fair in May, open-air Shakespeare in June and vintage cars in July. See website for details.

Times Open: Gardens Apr-Oct, daily (ex Sat) 11-5. House 17 Apr-20 Oct, Wed-Thu, Sun & BH Mon 12.30-4 **Fees** £8 (ch £3). Family ticket £19. Gardens £5 (ch free) **Facilities** (outdoor) (partly accessible) (garden gravel paths) toilets for disabled shop

TEMPLE SOWERBY Map 12 NY62

Acorn Bank Garden and Watermill

CA10 1SP

☎ 017683 61893 017683 66824

e-mail: acornbank@nationaltrust.org.uk

web: www.nationaltrust.org.uk

dir: 6m E of Penrith on A66

A delightful garden of some two and a half acres, where an extensive collection of over 250 varieties of medicinal and culinary herbs is grown. Scented plants are grown in the small greenhouse, and a circular walk runs beside the Crowdundle Beck to the partially restored watermill. Please ring for details of special events.

Times Open late Mar-Oct, Wed-Sun 10-5 (last admission 4.30)* **Fees** £4.20 (ch £2.10). Family ticket £10.50* **Facilities** (outdoor) (partly accessible) toilets for disabled (Braille/large print guide, wheelchairs available) shop

ENGLAND

TROUTBECK Map 7 NY40

Townend

LA23 1LB
☎ 015394 32628 🖹 015394 32628
e-mail: townend@nationaltrust.org.uk
web: www.nationaltrust.org.uk
dir: 3m SE of Ambleside at S end of village

The house is one of the finest examples of a 'statesman' (wealthy yeoman) farmer's house in Cumbria, built in 1626 for George Browne, whose descendents lived here until 1943. Inside is the original home-made carved furniture, with domestic utensils, letters and papers of the farm.

Times Open Apr-Oct, Wed-Sun & BH Mon 1-5 or dusk if earlier (last admission 4.30)* **Fees** £4.70 (ch £2.35). Family ticket £10.50* **Facilities** Ⓟ ♿ (partly accessible) (Braille and sensory guide) 🚫🐕

WHITEHAVEN Map 11 NX91

The Beacon 2 FOR 1

West Strand CA28 7LY
☎ 01946 592302 🖹 01946 598150
e-mail: thebeacon@copelandbc.gov.uk
web: www.thebeacon-whitehaven.co.uk
dir: A595, after Parton right onto New Rd. Follow one way system & town museum tourist signs

Home to Copeland's museum collection, The Beacon tells the story of this fascinating corner of the Western Lake District using interactive displays and activities. Enjoy panoramic views of the town and coast from the fourth floor gallery. Regular art exhibitions are held in the Harbour Gallery.

Times Open all year, Tue-Sun 10-4.30. Closed Mon except school hols & BHs. Closed 25-26 Dec. **Fees** Art gallery free. Museum £5 (under 16's free, concessions £4)* **Facilities** Ⓟ Ⓟ 🍽 licensed ♿ (fully accessible) toilets for disabled (chair/stair lift, Braille signs) shop 🚫🐕

The Rum Story 2 FOR 1

27 Lowther St CA28 7DN
☎ 01946 592933 🖹 01946 590595
e-mail: dutymanagers@rumstory.co.uk
web: www.rumstory.co.uk
dir: A595, follow town centre signs

Set in the original shop, courtyards, cellars and bonded warehouses of the Jefferson family - the oldest rum trading family in the UK - this fascinating story takes the visitor back in time to the early days of the rum trade, its links with the slave trade, sugar plantations, the Royal Navy, barrel-making and more. Set pieces include a tropical rainforest, an African village, a slave ship, and a cooper's workshop.

Times Open daily, 10-4.30. Closed 25-26 Dec & 1 Jan. Also closed 3rd wk in Jan for maintenance **Fees** £5.45 (ch £3.45, concessions £4.45) Family ticket (2ad+2ch) £16.45. Group rate 15+ £3.50, child group 15+ £2.50 **Facilities** Ⓟ ☕ ♿ (partly accessible) (exhibition courtyard facilities only accessible) toilets for disabled (wheelchairs, wide doors, lifts) shop 🚫🐕

WINDERMERE Map 7 SD49

Holehird Gardens

Lakeland Horticultural Society, Patterdale Rd LA23 1NP
☎ 015394 46008
web: www.holehirdgardens.org.uk
dir: A591 Windermere, turn right at rdbt onto A592 gardens 1m on right just past school

The garden is maintained by its members who are all volunteers. It lies on a splendid hillside site with stream gardens and rocky outcrops looking to Windermere and the Langdale Pikes. The garden includes specimen trees and flowering shrubs for all seasons. Among the highlights are autumn heather and shrubs, spring bulbs and alpines. There are also national collections of astilbe, hydrangea and polystichum, as well as fine herbaceous borders, herbs and climbers. The Lakeland Horticultural Society was founded in 1969, and there are a number of LHS events throughout the year.

Times Open all year, daily dawn to dusk. (Wardens available for advice Etr-Oct)* **Facilities** Ⓟ ♿ (partly accessible) (steep slopes to upper gardens) toilets for disabled (parking) 🚫🐕

Lake District Visitor Centre at Brockhole

LA23 1LJ
☎ 015394 46601 🖹 015394 43523
e-mail: infodesk@lake-district.gov.uk
web: www.lake-district.gov.uk
dir: on A591, between Windermere and Ambleside, follow brown tourist signs

Set in 32 acres of landscaped gardens and grounds, on the shore of Lake Windermere, this house became England's first National Park Visitor Centre in 1969. It offers permanent and temporary exhibitions, lake cruises, an adventure playground and an extensive events programme. Contact the Centre for a copy of their free events guide. Canoe and sailing tuition available in school holidays and boats available for hire in summer, weekends and school holidays.

Times Open all year, daily 10-5; Nov-Mar 10-4. Closed 25 Dec. Grounds & Garden open all year **Fees** Free admission but pay & display parking **Facilities** Ⓟ ☕ 🍽 licensed ⛩ (indoor & outdoor) ♿ (fully accessible) toilets for disabled (manual & electric wheelchairs, lifts, induction loops) shop

DERBYSHIRE

Tramway Village, Crich

ENGLAND

BOLSOVER Map 8 SK47

Bolsover Castle

Castle St S44 6PR
☎ 01246 822844 fax 01246 241569
web: www.english-heritage.org.uk
dir: on A632

This award-winning property has the air of a romantic storybook castle, with its turrets and battlements rising from a wooded hilltop. See the stunning Venus garden with its beautiful statuary and fountain. State of the art audio tours are available.

Times Open all year, Apr-Oct, daily 10-5, (Fri-Sat 10-4); Nov-Mar, Thu-Mon 10-4. Closed 24-26 Dec & 1 Jan. Part of castle may close for one hour if an event is booked, please call to check **Fees** £7.40 (ch £3.70, concessions £6.30). Family £18.50. Prices and opening times are subject to change in March 2011. Please call 0870 333 1181 for the most up to date prices and opening times when planning your visit **Facilities** (partly accessible) (little castle not accessible to wheelchair users, some steps) (audio tour with hearing loop, tactile exhibits) shop

BUXTON Map 7 SK07

Poole's Cavern (Buxton Country Park)

2 FOR 1

Green Ln SK17 9DH
☎ 01298 26978 fax 01298 73563
e-mail: info@poolescavern.co.uk
web: www.poolescavern.co.uk
dir: 1m from Buxton town centre, off A6 and A515

Limestone rock, water, and millions of years created this natural cavern containing thousands of crystal formations. A 45-minute guided tour leads the visitor through chambers used as a shelter by Bronze Age cave dwellers, Roman metal workers and as a hideout by the infamous robber Poole. Attractions include the underground source of the River Wye, the 'Poached Egg Chamber', Mary, Queen of Scots' Pillar, the Grand Cascade and underground sculpture formations. Set in 100 acres of woodland, Buxton Country Park has leafy trails to Grinlow viewpoint and panoramic peakland scenery.

Times Open all year, 5 Mar-Oct, daily 9.30-5; Nov-Feb, timed tours 10-4. Closed 25 Dec & 1 Jan **Fees** £8 (ch £4.75, concessions £7). Family ticket £23. Please check website or telephone for current prices **Facilities** licensed (outdoor) (partly accessible) (access to visitor centre & 1st 100mtrs of cave tour to main chamber, no access to woods) toilets for disabled shop

CALKE Map 8 SK32

Calke Abbey

DE73 7LE
☎ 01332 863822 fax 01332 865272
e-mail: calkeabbey@nationaltrust.org.uk
web: www.nationaltrust.org.uk
dir: on A514 between Swadlincote and Melbourne

A country house and estate preserved in 20th-century decline. A place poised somewhere between gentle neglect and downright dereliction, telling the tale of an eccentric family who amassed a huge collection of hidden treasures. The house has had little restoration portraying a period when great country houses struggled to survive. In the walled gardens explore the Orangery, the flower and kitchen gardens or walk around the fragile habitats of Calke Park National Nature Reserve. All visitors (including NT members) require a ticket for the house and garden or garden only from the Visitor Reception.

Times Open 1-9 Mar, Sat-Sun; 15 Mar-2 Nov, Mon-Wed & Sat-Sun & Good Fri. House 12.30-5; Gardens & Church 11-5; Restaurant & Shop 10.30-5. Note: Timed house tickets apply and delays on entry will occur at busy times and BHs* **Facilities** licensed (outdoor) (partly accessible) (access to 3 rooms on ground floor only. Stairs to other floors) toilets for disabled (Braille guide, hearing system, wheelchair, map) shop

CASTLETON Map 7 SK18

Blue-John Cavern & Mine

Buxton Rd S33 8WP
☎ 01433 620638 & 620642 fax 01433 621586
e-mail: lesley@bluejohn.gemsoft.co.uk
web: www.bluejohn.gemsoft.co.uk
dir: follow brown 'Blue-John Cavern' signs from Castleton

A remarkable example of a water-worn cave, over a third of a mile long, with chambers 200ft high. It contains 8 of the world's 14 veins of Blue John stone, and has been the major source of this unique form of fluorspar for nearly 300 years.

Times Open all year, daily, 9.30-5 (or dusk). Guided tours of approx 1hr every 10 mins tour. Closed 25-26 Dec & 1 Jan **Fees** £9 (ch £4.50, pen & students £7) Family ticket £25. Party rates on request **Facilities** (not suitable for disabled visitors) shop

Peak Cavern

S33 8WS
☎ 01433 620285
e-mail: info@peakcavern.co.uk
web: www.devilsarse.com
dir: on A6187, in centre of Castleton

One of the most spectacular natural limestone caves in the Peak District, with an electrically-lit underground walk of about half a mile. Ropes have been made for over 500 years in the 'Grand Entrance Hall', and traces of a row of cottages can be seen. Rope-making demonstrations are included on every tour.

Times Open all year, daily 10-5. Nov-Mar limited tours, please call in advance for times. Closed 25 Dec **Fees** £7.75 (ch £5.75, other concessions £6.75). Family ticket (2ad+2ch) £24* **Facilities** (indoor & outdoor) (partly accessible) (number of stairs throughout the cave) shop

Peveril Castle

Market Place S33 8WQ
☎ 01433 620613
web: www.english-heritage.org.uk
dir: on S side of Castleton

The romantic ruins of this Norman fortress are situated high on a rocky crag and the views from the great square tower of the surrounding Peak District are breathtaking. Sir Walter Scott glamourised the castle in his novel, *Peveril of the Peak*.

Times Open Apr-Oct, Thu-Mon 10-5; Jul-Aug, daily 10-6; Nov-Mar, Thu-Mon 10-4. Closed 24-26 Dec & 1 Jan **Fees** £4.20 (ch £2.10, concessions £3.60). Family £10.50. Prices and opening times are subject to change in March 2011. Please call 0870 333 1181 for the most up to date prices and opening times when planning your visit **Facilities** shop

Speedwell Cavern

Winnats Pass S33 8WA
☎ 01433 620512 01433 621888
e-mail: info@speedwellcavern.co.uk
web: www.speedwellcavern.co.uk
dir: A625 becomes A6187 at Hathersage. 0.5m W of Castleton

Descend 105 steps to a boat that takes you on a one-mile underground exploration of floodlit caverns part of which was once a lead mine. The hand-carved tunnels open out into a network of natural caverns and underground rivers. See the Bottomless Pit, a huge subterranean lake in a huge, cathedral-like cavern.

Times Open all year, daily 10-5. Closed 25 Dec. Phone to check winter opening times due to weather. Last boat 4 **Fees** £8.25 (ch £6.25)* **Facilities** (partly accessible) (105 steps in one flight down to boat & back up again to surface) shop

Treak Cliff Cavern

S33 8WP
☎ 01433 620571 01433 620519
e-mail: treakcliff@bluejohnstone.com
web: www.bluejohnstone.com
dir: 0.75m W of Castleton on A6187

An underground world of stalactites, stalagmites, flowstone, rock and cave formations, minerals and fossils. There are rich deposits of the rare and beautiful Blue John stone, including 'The Pillar', the largest piece ever found. Show caves include the Witch's Cave, Aladdin's Cave, Dream Cave and Fairyland Grotto. These caves contain some of the most impressive stalactites in the Peak District. Visitors can also polish their own Blue John stone in school holidays, and purchase Blue John stone jewellery and ornaments in the Castleton Gift Shop.

Times Open all year, Mar-Oct, daily 10-last tour 4.20; Nov-Feb daily - call for special tour times. All tours are guided & last about 40 mins. Enquire for last tour of day & possible closures. Closed 24-26 & 31 Dec & 1 Jan. All dates & times are subject to change without notice* **Fees** £7.95 (ch 5-15 £4). Family ticket (2ad+2ch) £22* **Facilities** (indoor & outdoor) (partly accessible) (no wheelchair access, walking disabled only) (hearing loop & picture word guides, details on website) shop

ENGLAND

CHATSWORTH Map 8 SK27

Chatsworth

DE45 1PP
☎ 01246 565300 🖷 01246 583536
e-mail: visit@chatsworth.org
web: www.chatsworth.org
dir: 8m N of Matlock off B6012. 16m from M1 junct 29, signed via Chesterfield, follow brown signs

Home of the Duke and Duchess of Devonshire, Chatsworth contains a massive private collection of fine and decorative arts. There is a splendid painted hall, and a great staircase leads to the chapel, decorated with statues and paintings. There are pictures, furniture and porcelain, and a trompe l'oeil painting of a violin on the music room door. The park was laid out by 'Capability' Brown, but is most famous as the work of Joseph Paxton, head gardener in the 19th century. The park is also home to the Duke and Duchess' personal collection of contemporary sculpture.

Times Open mid Mar-23 Dec, House & Garden 11-5.30, Farmyard 10.30-5.30* **Facilities** licensed (partly accessible) toilets for disabled (3 electric wheelchairs available for garden) shop

CHESTERFIELD

Chesterfield Museum and Art Gallery FREE

St Mary's Gate S41 7TD
☎ 01246 345727
e-mail: museum@chesterfield.gov.uk
web: www.visitchesterfield.info
dir: In town centre

The Museum tells the story of Chesterfield from its beginning as a Roman fort on Rykneild Street to the building of the 'Crooked Spire' Church and its growth as a market town. Chesterfield's most famous Victorian resident, George Stephenson, the 'Father of the Railways' is also featured. The displays continue the story of the town to the present day.

Times Open all year, Mon-Tue & Thu-Sat, 10-4 **Facilities** (fully accessible) shop

CRESWELL Map 8 SK57

Creswell Crags Museum and Education Centre

Crags Rd, Welbeck S80 3LH
☎ 01909 720378 🖷 01909 724726
e-mail: info@creswell-crags.org.uk
web: www.creswell-crags.org.uk
dir: off B6042, Crags Road, between A616 & A60, 1m E of Creswell village

Creswell Crags, a picturesque limestone gorge with lakes and caves, is one of Britain's most important archaeological sites. The many caves on the site have yielded Ice Age remains, including bones of woolly mammoth, reindeer, hyena and bison, stone tools of Ice Age hunters from over 10,000 years ago and new research has revealed the only Ice Age rock art in Britain (about 13,000 years old). Visit the Museum and Education Centre to learn more about your Ice Age ancestors through an exhibition, touch-screen computers and video. Join a 'Virtually the Ice Age' cave tour, picnic in Crags Meadow, or try the new activity trail. Plenty of special events year round, contact for details.

Times Feb-Oct, daily 10-5.30; Nov-Jan, wknds only 10-4.30. Cave tours only wknds* **Fees** Exhibition £3 (ch £1.50, concessions £2); Ice Age Tour £6.50 (ch £4.50, concessions £5); Rock Art Tour £8 (ch £6, concessions £7)* **Facilities** (outdoor) (partly accessible) (accessible round Gorge. Tour may be unsuitable for mobility scooters, due to steps) toilets for disabled shop

CRICH Map 8 SK35

Crich Tramway Village

DE4 5DP
☎ 01773 854321 🖷 01773 854320
e-mail: enquiry@tramway.co.uk
web: www.tramway.co.uk
dir: off B5035, 8m from M1 junct 28

A mile-long scenic journey through a period street to open countryside with panoramic views. You can enjoy unlimited vintage tram rides, and the exhibition hall houses the largest collection of vintage electric trams in Britain. The village street contains a bar and restaurant, tearooms, a sweet shop, ice cream shop, and police sentry box, among others. There is also a Workshop Viewing Gallery where you can see the trams being restored. Ring for details of special events.

Times Open Apr-Oct, daily 10-5.30 (6.30 wknds Jun-Aug & BH wknds). 10.30-4 until Nov* **Fees** £10.50 (ch 4-15 £5.50, pen £9.50). Family ticket (2ad+3ch)* **Facilities** licensed (outdoor) (fully accessible) toilets for disabled (Braille guidebooks, talktype facility) shop

DENBY Map 8 SK34

Denby Pottery Visitor Centre

Derby Rd DE5 8NX
☎ 01773 740799 📠 01773 740749
e-mail: tours.reception@denby.co.uk
web: www.denbyvisitorcentre.co.uk
dir: 8m N of Derby off A38, on B6179, 2m S of Ripley

Situated around a cobbled courtyard with shops and a restaurant. Pottery tours are available daily February to October including hands-on activities such as paint-a-plate and make-a-clay-souvenir. Extensive cookshop with free half hour demonstrations daily. There are lots of bargains on Denby seconds in the factory shop; Dartington Crystal Shop, gift shop, garden shop and hand painted Denby.

Times Centre open all year. Factory tours, Mon-Thu 10.30 & 1. Craftroom tour, daily 11-3. Visitor Centre Mon-Sat 9.30-5, Sun 10-5. No tours Nov-Jan. Closed 25-26 Dec* **Fees** Free. Factory tour £5.95 (ch £4.95). Craftroom tour £4.95 (ch £3.95)* **Facilities** licensed (outdoor) (partly accessible) (factory tour not accessible) toilets for disabled (lift) shop

DERBY Map 8 SK33

Derby Museum & Art Gallery — FREE

The Strand DE1 1BS
☎ 01332 641901 📠 01332 716670
e-mail: museums@derby.gov.uk
web: www.derby.gov.uk/museums
dir: follow directions to city centre

The museum has a wide range of displays, notably of Derby porcelain, and paintings by the artist Joseph Wright (1734-97). Also antiquities, natural history and a new military gallery 'Soldiers Story', as well as many temporary exhibitions.

Times Open all year, Mon 11-5, Tue-Sat 10-5, Sun & BHs 1-4. Closed Xmas & New Year, telephone for details* **Facilities** (partly accessible) (parts of building are not accessible to powered wheelchair users) toilets for disabled (lift to all floors, portable mini-loop, large print labels) shop

Pickford's House Museum — FREE

41 Friar Gate DE1 1DA
☎ 01332 255363 📠 01332 255277
e-mail: museums@derby.gov.uk
web: www.derby.gov.uk/museums
dir: from A38 into Derby, follow signs to city centre

The house was built in 1770 by the architect Joseph Pickford as a combined workplace and family home. It now shows domestic life at different periods, with Georgian reception rooms and service areas and a 1930s bathroom. Other galleries display part of the museum's collections of historic costume and toy theatres. There is a lively programme of changing temporary exhibitions and events throughout the year.

Times Open all year, Mon 11-5, Tue-Sat 10-5, Sun & BHs 1-4. Closed Xmas & New Year, telephone for details* **Facilities** (partly accessible) (wheelchair access to ground & lower ground floors) (video with sign language subtitles) shop

Royal Crown Derby Visitor Centre — 2 FOR 1

194 Osmaston Rd DE23 8JZ
☎ 01332 712800 📠 01332 712899
e-mail: enquiries@royalcrownderby.co.uk
web: www.royalcrownderby.co.uk
dir: on A514, opposite Derby Royal Infirmary

This museum traces the history of the company from 1750 to the present day, while the factory tour demonstrates the making of Royal Crown Derby in detail from clay through to the finished product. A demonstration studio gives you the opportunity to watch craftspeople at close quarters and try out a variety of different skills.

Times Tours, Tue-Fri 11 & 1.30 (booking essential), (shop, Mon-Sat 10-5, cafe Mon-Fri 10-4)* **Fees** £4.95* **Facilities** licensed (partly accessible) (museum set on upper level) toilets for disabled (ramps) shop

The Silk Mill - Derby's Museum of Industry and History — FREE

Silk Mill Ln, off Full St DE1 3AR
☎ 01332 255308 📠 01332 255108
e-mail: museums@derby.gov.uk
web: www.derby.gov.uk/museums
dir: From Derby inner ring road, head for Cathedral & Assembly Rooms car park. 5 mins walk

The museum is set in a re-built 18th-century silk mill and adjacent flour mill on the site of the world's first modern factory. Displays cover local industries, and include a major collection of Rolls Royce aero-engines from 1915 to the present. There is also a section covering the history of railway engineering in Derby. The building is now part of the Derwent Valley Mills World Heritage Site.

Times Open all year, Mon 11-5, Tue-Sat 10-5, Sun & BHs 1-4. Closed Xmas & New Year, telephone for details **Facilities** (outdoor) (fully accessible) toilets for disabled (lift to all floors) shop

EYAM Map 8 SK27

Eyam Hall

S32 5QW
☎ 01433 631976 📠 01433 631603
e-mail: nicola@eyamhall.com
web: www.eyamhall.com
dir: Turn off A623 just after Calver Crossroads & village of Stoney Middleton. Turn left at top of hill. Eyam Hall in village centre opposite stocks

An intimate 17th-century manor house in the heart of the famous "plague village". Home to the Wright family since 1671, the Hall offers a glimpse of domestic history through the eyes of one family, in portraits, furniture, tapestries, costumes and memorabilia. Converted farm buildings house the Eyam Hall Craft Centre. Please telephone for details of musical and theatrical events throughout the season.

Times Open House & Garden: Etr week Sun, Mon, Wed & Thu. May & Spring BH Sun & Mon. Jul & Aug: Wed, Thu, Sun, BH Mon. Xmas wknds in Dec. All 12-4. Craft Centre year round Tue-Sun 11-5* **Facilities** licensed (outdoor) (partly accessible) toilets for disabled (disabled entrance via special gate, ramps) shop

HADDON HALL Map 8 SK26

Haddon Hall

DE45 1LA
☎ 01629 812855 📠 01629 814379
e-mail: info@haddonhall.co.uk
web: www.haddonhall.co.uk
dir: 1.5m S of Bakewell off A6

Originally held by the illegitimate son of William the Conqueror, Haddon has been owned by the Manners family since the 16th century. Little has been added since the reign of Henry VIII, and, despite its time-worn steps, few medieval houses have so successfully withstood the ravages of time.

Times Open Apr-Oct, Sat-Mon; Etr Good Fri-Tue; May-Sep, daily 12-5; 5-13 Dec 10.30-4 Closed 27-28 Jul* **Facilities** licensed (partly accessible) (steps & uneven floors, not accessible for w/chairs due to distance from carpark) toilets for disabled shop

HARDWICK HALL Map 8 SK46

Hardwick Hall

Doe Lea S44 5QJ
☎ 01246 850430 & 858400 📠 01246 858424
e-mail: hardwickhall@nationaltrust.org.uk
web: www.nationaltrust.org.uk/main/w-hardwickhall
dir: 2m S M1 junct 29 via A6175. Access by Stainsby Mill entrance only

One of the most splendid houses in England. Built by Bess of Hardwick in the 1590s and unaltered since, its huge windows and high ceilings make it feel strikingly modern. Its six towers make a dramatic skyline. Climbing up through the house, from one floor to the next, is a thrilling architectural experience. Rich tapestries, plaster friezes and alabaster fireplaces colour the rooms, culminating in the hauntingly atmospheric Long Gallery. Note: The Old Hall is owned by the NT and administered by English Heritage.

Times Open Hall & Garden: 17 Feb Oct, Wed-Sun 11-4.30 (Garden 11-5); 4-19 Dec, 11-3 Sat-Sun. Hardwick Old Hall: Apr-Oct, Wed-Sun 10-5. Parkland Gates: Open daily all year, 8.30-6. Open BH Mon & Good Fri* **Fees** With Gift Aid donation: House & Garden £10.50 (ch £5.25). Family ticket £26.25. Garden only: £5.30 (ch £2.65). Family ticket £13.25. Combined ticket old & new halls: £12.80 (ch £6.40). Family ticket £32. Please see website for current opening times, closing details & prices* **Facilities** licensed (outdoor) (partly accessible) (ramped entrance. Ground floor accessible, stairs with handrail to other floors, grounds partly accessible with slopes, grass paths & some cobbles) toilets for disabled (large print & Braille guide, wheelchair, touch screens) shop

KEDLESTON HALL Map 8 SK34

Kedleston Hall

DE22 5JH
☎ 01332 842191 📠 01332 841972
e-mail: kedlestonhall@nationaltrust.org.uk
web: www.nationaltrust.org.uk
dir: 5m NW of Derby, entrance off Kedleston Rd, signed from rdbt where A38 crosses A52, close to Markeaton Park

Take a trip back in time to the 1760s at this spectacular neo-classical mansion framed by historic parkland. Designed for lavish entertaining and displaying an extensive collection of paintings, sculpture and original furnishings, Kedleston is a stunning example of the work of architect Robert Adam. The Curzon family have lived here since the 12th century and continue to live at the Hall. Lord Curzon's Eastern Museum is a treasure trove of fascinating objects acquired on his travels in Asia and while Viceroy of India (1899-1905). Used as a key location for *The Duchess*, a 2008 Paramount film. Note: Medieval All Saints Church, containing many family monuments is run by the Churches Conservation Trust.

Times Open all year: House; Mar-2 Nov, Sat-Wed 12-5 (last admission 4.15). Garden; same as house but open daily 10-6. Park open daily, Mar-2 Nov 10-6 & 3 Nov-27 Feb 10-4. Closed 25-26 Dec & some restrictions may apply in Dec & Jan* **Facilities** licensed (partly accessible) (steps to main entrance, access via shop. Ground floor fully accessible but stairs to state floor. Grounds have steps, grass paths & cobbles) toilets for disabled (Braille guide, w/chair, self-drive vehicle) shop

MATLOCK BATH Map 8 SK25

The Heights of Abraham Cable Cars, Caverns & Hilltop Park

DE4 3PD

☎ 01629 582365 📠 01629 581128

e-mail: office@heightsofabraham.com

web: www.heightsofabraham.com

dir: on A6, signed from M1 junct 28 & A6. Base station next to Matlock Bath railway station

The Heights of Abraham, a unique Hilltop Park, reached using the country's most up-to-date cable cars. Once you are at the summit you can join exciting underground tours of two spectacular show caverns. Above ground there are play areas, picnic spots, exhibitions, shops, café and summit bar all with stunning views across the surrounding Peak District. New attractions are the Heath and Heaven and Fossil Factory exhibitions, plus brand new, state-of-the-art lighting in the Great Masson Cavern which reveals its magnitude as it has never been seen before.

Times Open 14-22 Feb, daily 10-4.30; 28 Feb-14 Mar, wknds 10-4.30; 21 Mar-Sep, daily 10-4.30 (later at wknds & in high season). Oct-1 Nov, daily 10-4.30* **Fees** £11.50 (ch 5-16yrs £8.50, under 5's free (one per full paying adult). Senior ticket £8.50. Family (2ad+2ch) £35 (2ad+3 ch) £42. Please telephone or check website for details* **Facilities** Ⓟ ☕ 🍴 licensed ⛩ (outdoor) ♿ (partly accessible) toilets for disabled shop 🚫

Peak District Mining Museum

The Pavilion DE4 3NR

☎ 01629 583834

e-mail: mail@peakmines.co.uk

web: www.peakmines.co.uk

dir: On A6 alongside River Derwent

A large display explains the history of the Derbyshire lead industry from Roman times to the present day. The geology of the area, mining and smelting processes, the quarrying and the people who worked in the industry, are illustrated by a series of static and moving exhibits. The museum also features an early 19th-century water pressure pumping engine. There is a recycling display in the Pump Room.

Times Open all year, daily Apr-end Sep 10-5, Oct-end Mar 11-3. Closed 25 Dec **Fees** £3.50 (ch £2.50, concessions £3). Family ticket (2ad+4ch) £10 **Facilities** 🅟 Ⓟ ☕ ♿ (fully accessible) (chair lift to mezzanine, larger print) shop 🚫

Temple Mine

Temple Rd DE4 3NR

☎ 01629 583834

e-mail: mail@peakmines.co.uk

web: www.peakmines.co.uk

dir: off A6. Please telephone for directions

A typical Derbyshire mine which was worked from the early 1920s until the mid 1950s for fluorspar and associated minerals. See examples of mining methods which give an insight into working conditions underground.

Times Open Apr-end Sep timed visits noon & 2pm daily, Oct-Mar timed visits noon & 2pm wknds only **Fees** £3.50 (ch £2.50, concessions & students £3). Family ticket (2ad+4ch) £10 **Facilities** Ⓟ 🚫

MELBOURNE Map 8 SK32

Melbourne Hall & Gardens

DE73 8EN

☎ 01332 862502 📠 01332 862263

e-mail: melbhall@globalnet.co.uk

web: www.melbournehall.com

dir: 9m S of Derby on A514, in Melbourne take turn by bus shelter in Market Place, follow road to Church Square

Sir John Coke (Charles I's Secretary of State) leased Melbourne Hall in 1628 and the house has been home to two Prime Ministers: Lord Melbourne and Lord Palmerston. The glorious formal gardens are among the finest in Britain.

Times Open, house daily throughout Aug only (ex first three Mons) 2-5 (last admission 4.15). Prebooked parties by appointment in Aug. Gardens Apr-Sep, Wed, Sat, Sun & BH Mon 1.30-5.30 & when hall open in Aug. Upstairs rooms available by appointment **Fees** House Tue-Sat (guided tour) £3.50 (ch £2, pen £3), Sun & BH Mon (no guided tour) £3 (ch £1.50, pen £2.50). House & Garden (Aug only) £5.50 (ch £3.50, pen £4.50). Garden only £3.50 (pen £2.50). Family £9.50* **Facilities** Ⓟ ☕ ♿ (partly accessible) (Hall guided tours on ground floor, only one wheelchair per tour) (ramps at house & garden entrance) shop 🚫

MIDDLETON BY WIRKSWORTH Map 8 SK25

Middleton Top Engine House

Middleton Top Visitor Centre DE4 4LS

☎ 01629 823204 📠 01629 825336

e-mail: middletontop@derbyshire.gov.uk

web: www.derbyshire.gov.uk/countryside

dir: Signed off A6 in Cromford then, 0.5m S from B5036 Cromford/Wirksworth road

A beam engine built in 1829 for the Cromford and High Peak Railway, and its octagonal engine house. The engine's job was to haul wagons up the Middleton Incline, and its last trip was in 1963 after 134 years' work. The visitor centre tells the story of this historic railway.

Times Open: Information Centre, daily, wknds only winter. Engine House Etr-Oct 1st wknd in month (engine in motion)* **Fees** Working Engine £2 (ch & concessions £1)* **Facilities** 🅟 ⛩ (outdoor) ♿ (partly accessible) (trail & visitor centre accessible, engine house has a number of steep steps) toilets for disabled shop

ENGLAND

OLD WHITTINGTON Map 8 SK37

Revolution House FREE

High St S41 9JZ
☎ 01246 345727 01246 345720
e-mail: museum@chesterfield.gov.uk
web: www.visitchesterfield.info
dir: 3m N of Chesterfield town centre, on B6052 off A61, signed

Revolution House takes its name from the Revolution of 1688, when this cottage was an ale house - the "Cock and Pynot". It was here that three local noblemen met and began planning their parts in events which led to the overthrow of King James II, in favour of William and Mary of Orange.

Times Open 2 Apr-26 Sep, Fri-Sun & BHs, 11-4* **Facilities** Ⓟ (partly accessible) (Ground floor access only for wheelchairs) shop

RIPLEY Map 8 SK35

Midland Railway Butterley 2 FOR 1

Butterley Station DE5 3QZ
☎ 01773 747674 & 749788 01773 570721
e-mail: midland.railway@btconnect.com
web: www.midlandrailwaycentre.co.uk
dir: M1 junct 28, A38 towards Derby, then signed

A regular steam-train passenger service runs here, to the centre where the aim is to depict every aspect of the golden days of the Midland Railway and its successors. Exhibits range from the steam locomotives of 1866 to an electric locomotive, with a large section of rolling stock spanning the last 100 years. Also a country park, along with narrow gauge, miniature and model railways. Regular rail-related special events throughout the year. Contact for details.

Times Open all year, trains run wknds Feb-Dec & most school holidays* **Fees** £12 (ch 5-16 £6, ch under 5 free, pen £11). Party 15+* **Facilities** Ⓟ (outdoor) (partly accessible) (most trains with wheelchair access, museum & country park partly accessible) toilets for disabled (special accommodation on trains) shop

SUDBURY Map 7 SK13

Sudbury Hall and Museum of Childhood

DE6 5HT
☎ 01283 585305 01283 585139
e-mail: sudburyhall@nationaltrust.org.uk
web: www.nationaltrust.org.uk
dir: 6m E of Uttoxeter at junct of A50 & A515

Two totally different experiences sitting side by side. The country home of the Lords Vernon features exquisite plasterwork, wood carvings, murals based on classical stories and fine 17th-century craftsmanship. The Great Staircase and Long Gallery are extremely impressive. The Museum of Childhood is a delight for all ages with something for everyone. Explore the childhoods of times gone by, make stories, play with toys and share your childhood with others. You can be a chimney weep, a scullion or a Victorian pupil, and be captivated by the archive film, interactives and displays.

Times Opening details not confirmed. Please telephone or see website for details* **Facilities** Ⓟ licensed (partly accessible) (Access via steps & 4 flights of steps to first floor. Lift to all Museum floors. Grounds partly accessible, grass & loose gravel paths, some steps) toilets for disabled (w/chair available, large print/Braille guide & touch list) shop

WIRKSWORTH Map 8 SK25

Wirksworth Heritage Centre

Crown Yard DE4 4ET
☎ 01629 825225
e-mail: enquiries@storyofwirksworth.co.uk
web: www.storyofwirksworth.co.uk
dir: on B5023 off A6 in centre of Wirksworth

The Centre has been created in an old silk and velvet mill. The three floors of the mill have interpretative displays of the town's past history as a prosperous lead-mining centre. Each floor offers many features of interest including a computer game called 'Rescue the injured lead-miner', a mock-up of a natural cavern, and a Quarryman's House. During the Spring Bank Holiday you can also see the famous Well Dressings. Exhibits on the top floor include one on quarrying, information about local round-the-world yachtswoman, Ellen MacArthur, and local memories from World War II. There's also a small art gallery carrying local works.

Times Open Etr-Sep, Wed-Sun & BHs 10.30-4.30 & Oct half term* **Facilities** Ⓟ licensed (partly accessible) (4 steps to ground floor) (portable ramp) shop

DEVON

Harbour Bridge, Torquay

ENGLAND

ARLINGTON Map 2 SS64

Arlington Court

EX31 4LP
☎ 01271 850296 📠 01271 851108
e-mail: arlingtoncourt@nationaltrust.org.uk
web: www.nationaltrust.org.uk/main/w-arlingtoncourt
dir: 7m NE of Barnstaple, on A39

Arlington Court was built in 1823 and is situated in the thickly wooded Yeo Valley. The centrepiece is the Victorian mansion, surrounded by formal and informal gardens. Also open to visitors is the working stable yard, housing a collection of carriages and horse-drawn vehicles. The extensive parkland around the house is grazed by Jacob sheep and Red Devon cattle. Please telephone for details of events running throughout the year.

Times Open 12 Mar-Oct, daily 10.30-5 (last admission 4.30). Grounds open during daylight hours **Fees** House, carriage museum & grounds £9 (ch £4.50). Family ticket £22.60 **Facilities** (outdoor) (partly accessible) (access ground floor only of house) toilets for disabled (wheelchairs, ramps at house, batricar, Braille guide) shop

BARNSTAPLE Map 2 SS53

Marwood Hill Gardens

Marwood EX31 4EB
☎ 01271 342528
web: www.marwoodhillgarden.co.uk
dir: off A361, follow brown tourist signs

The 18-acre gardens with their three small lakes contain many rare trees and shrubs. There is a large bog garden and a walled garden, collections of clematis, camellias and eucalyptus. Alpine plants are also a feature, and there are plants for sale.

Times Open Mar-Oct, daily 9.30-5.30* **Facilities**

BEER Map 3 SY28

Pecorama Pleasure Gardens

Underleys EX12 3NA
☎ 01297 21542 📠 01297 20229
e-mail: pecorama@btconnect.com
web: www.peco-uk.com
dir: from A3052 take B3174, Beer road, signed

The gardens are high on a hillside, overlooking Beer. A miniature steam and diesel passenger line offers visitors a stunning view of Lyme Bay as it runs through the Pleasure Gardens. Attractions include an aviary, crazy golf, children's activity area and the Peco Millennium Garden. The main building houses an exhibition of railway modelling in various small gauges. There are souvenir and railway model shops, plus full catering facilities. Please telephone for details of events running throughout the year.

Times Open Etr-Oct , Mon-Fri 10-5.30, Sat 10-1. Open Sun at Etr, then 1 & 29 May-11 Sep **Fees** £7.50 (ch 4-16 £5.50, concessions £7) **Facilities** licensed (outdoor) (partly accessible) (no wheelchairs on miniature railway, garden steep in places) toilets for disabled (access with helper, wheelchair) shop

BICTON Map 3 SY08

Bicton Park Botanical Gardens

East Budleigh EX9 7BJ
☎ 01395 568465 📠 01395 568374
e-mail: info@bictongardens.co.uk
web: www.bictongardens.co.uk
dir: 2m N of Budleigh Salterton on B3178, leave M5 at junct 30 & follow brown tourist signs

Unique Grade I-listed, 18th-century historic gardens with palm house, orangery, plant collections, extensive countryside museum, indoor and outdoor activity play areas, pinetum, arboretum, nature trail, woodland railway garden centre and restaurant. All this set in 63 acres of beautiful parkland that has been cherished for 300 years. Open air concerts take place in July and August.

Times Open Winter 10-5, Summer 10-6. Closed 25 & 26 Dec* **Facilities** licensed (outdoor) (partly accessible) toilets for disabled (adapted carriage on woodland railway, wheelchairs) shop

BLACKMOOR GATE Map 3 SS64

Exmoor Zoological Park **2 FOR 1**

South Stowford, Bratton Fleming EX31 4SG
☎ 01598 763352 📠 01598 763352
e-mail: exmoorzoo@btconnect.com
web: www.exmoorzoo.co.uk
dir: off A361 link road onto A399, follow tourist signs

Exmoor Zoo is both personal and friendly. Open since 1982 it is an ideal family venue, catering particularly for the younger generation. The zoo specialises in smaller animals, many endangered, such as the golden-headed lion tamarins. There are new exhibits for animals such as cheetahs, maned wolves, tapirs, sitatungas and of course the "Exmoor Beast".

Times Open daily, Mar-4 May & 16 Sep-2 Nov 10-5; 3 Nov-30 Mar 10-4; 5 May-15 Sep 10-6* **Fees** £9.25 (ch £6.75, concessions £8.25). Family ticket (2ad+2ch) £29.50* **Facilities** (indoor) (partly accessible) (tarmac paths on hill, no steps) toilets for disabled shop

BRANSCOMBE Map 3 SY29

Branscombe - The Old Bakery, Manor Mill and Forge

EX12 3DB
☎ 01752 346585 📠 01752 346585
e-mail: branscombe@nationaltrust.org.uk
web: www.nationaltrust.org.uk
dir: In Branscombe village, off A3052

Charming vernacular buildings with mill and forge restored to working order. The forge is open daily and the blacksmith sells the ironwork he produces.

Times Open Old Bakery: Apr-30 Oct, Wed-Sun 10.30-5; Jul-Aug, Mon-Sun 10.30-5; Manor Mill 17 Apr-30 Oct, Sun 2-5; Jul-Aug, Wed & Sun 2-5; Forge - phone for opening times. **Fees** Entry free but donations welcome* **Facilities** (partly accessible) (Manor Mill has narrow doorways, corridors & steep stairs) toilets for disabled (small interpretation area)

BUCKFASTLEIGH Map 3 SX76

Buckfast Abbey

FREE

TQ11 0EE
01364 645500 01364 643891
e-mail: enquiries@buckfast.org.uk
web: www.buckfast.org.uk
dir: 0.5m from A38, midway between Exeter and Plymouth. Turn off at 'Dart Bridge' junct and follow brown tourist signs

The Abbey, founded in 1018, was dissolved by Henry VIII in the 16th century. Restoration began in 1907, when four monks with little building experience began the work. The church was built on the old foundations, using local blue limestone and Ham Hill stone. The precinct contains several medieval monastic buildings, including the 14th-century guest hall which contains an exhibition of the history of the Abbey.

Times Open all year daily. Closed Good Fri & 24-26 Dec* **Facilities** licensed (outdoor) (fully accessible) toilets for disabled (Braille & audio information) shop

Buckfast Butterfly Farm & Dartmoor Otter Sanctuary

TQ11 0DZ
01364 642916
e-mail: contact@ottersandbutterflies.co.uk
web: www.ottersandbutterflies.co.uk
dir: off A38, at Dart Bridge junct, follow tourist signs, adjacent to steam railway

Visitors can wander around a specially designed, undercover tropical garden, where free-flying butterflies and moths from around the world can be seen. The otter sanctuary has large enclosures with underwater viewing areas. Three types of otters can be seen - the native British otter along with Asian and North American otters.

Times Open Apr-Oct, daily 10-5 or dusk (if earlier). For rest of year please see website* **Fees** £6.95 (ch £4.95, concessions £5.95). Family ticket £19.95* **Facilities** (outdoor) (partly accessible) (fence height around some otter enclosures can make it difficult for w/chair users to see) (wheelchair ramps) shop

BUCKLAND ABBEY Map 2 SX46

Buckland Abbey

PL20 6EY
01822 853607 01822 855448
e-mail: bucklandabbey@nationaltrust.org.uk
web: www.nationaltrust.org.uk/main
dir: off A386 0.25m S of Yelverton, signed

Originally a prosperous 13th-century Cistercian Abbey, and then home of the Grenville family, Buckland Abbey was sold to Sir Francis Drake in 1581, who lived there until his death in 1596. Several restored buildings house a fascinating exhibition about the Abbey's history. Among the exhibits is Drake's Drum, which is said to give warning of danger to England. There is an Elizabethan garden, estate walks and a letterbox trail. 2011 marks the 60th Anniversary of the Abbey being open to the public.

Times Open 18-27 Feb daily 11-4; 4-6 Mar, Fri-Sun; 12 Mar-30 Oct, daily 10.30-5.30 **Fees** Abbey & grounds £9. Grounds only £4.50 **Facilities** licensed (outdoor) (partly accessible) (upper floors in house not accessible. Some steep slopes in grounds) toilets for disabled (wheelchairs & motorised buggy available) shop

CHITTLEHAMPTON Map 3 SS62

Cobbaton Combat Collection

Cobbaton EX37 9RZ
01769 540740
e-mail: info@cobbatoncombat.co.uk
web: www.cobbatoncombat.co.uk
dir: signed from A361 & A377

World War II British and Canadian military vehicles, war documents and military equipment can be seen in this private collection. There are over 60 vehicles including tanks, one a Gulf War Centurian, and a recently added Warsaw Pact section. There is also a section on 'Mum's War' and the Home Front. The Home Front section is now in a new purpose-built building.

Times Open Apr-Oct, daily (ex Sat) 10-5; Jul-Aug, daily. Winter most wkdays, phone for details.* **Fees** £6.50 (ch £4, concessions £5.50)* **Facilities** (outdoor) (fully accessible) toilets for disabled shop

CHUDLEIGH Map 3 SX87

Canonteign Falls

EX6 7NT
01647 252434 01647 52617
e-mail: info@canonteignfalls.com
web: www.canonteignfalls.com
dir: off A38 at Chudleigh/Teign Valley junct onto B3193 and follow tourist signs for 3m

A magical combination of waterfalls, woodlands and lakes. 3 graded walks marked with colour ferns.

Times Open Mar-Oct 10-4 **Fees** £5.90 (ch £4.50, concessions £5). Family £19.50 **Facilities** licensed (indoor & outdoor) (partly accessible) (grounds partly accessible but not up to falls) toilets for disabled shop

CHURSTON FERRERS — Map 3 SX95

Greenway

TQ5 0ES
☎ 01803 842382 📠 01803 661900
e-mail: greenway@nationaltrust.org.uk
web: www.nationaltrust.org.uk/devoncornwall
dir: off A3022 into Galmpton. Follow Manor Vale Rd into village then follow brown signs for gardens

Greenway House re-opened in 2009 after a major restoration project. Pre-booking for car parking is essential; those arriving by 'green' means will have slots made available to see this unique and magical property with its many collections, including archaeology, Tunbridgeware, silver, botanical china and books, the atmospheric house set in the 1950s, and the glorious woodland garden with its wild edges and rare plantings, all allow a glimpse into the private holiday home of the famous and well-loved author, Agatha Christie, and her family. Enjoy the adventure of arriving here by ferry alighting at Greenway Quay, with the dramatic views of the house from the river. Greenway is not easily accessible having some steep and slippery paths. All visitors are asked to wear walking shoes and to follow routes and directions according to their suitability on the day.

Times Open 28 Feb-19 Jul & 2 Sep-25 Oct, Wed-Sun; 21 Jul-30 Aug, Tue-Sun 10.30-5* **Facilities** Ⓟ ☕ ⛩ (outdoor) ♿ (partly accessible) (Ground floor of house and part of garden only accessible) toilets for disabled (Braille guide, large print, T Loop) shop

CLOVELLY — Map 2 SS32

The Milky Way Adventure Park

EX39 5RY
☎ 01237 431255 📠 01237 431735
e-mail: info@themilkyway.co.uk
web: www.themilkyway.co.uk
dir: on A39, 2m from Clovelly

An all-inclusive, all-weather adventure park in the country, with five major rides and live shows, including Merlin the Escapologist. There certainly is something fun and educational for everyone. Get close and personal with a bird of prey, lose yourself in a maze or take a trip out of this world whatever the weather. Ride Devon's tallest, fastest and longest rollercoaster, The Cosmic Typhoon or pilot the Droid Destroyer dodgems. Smaller adventurers can ride on The Big Apple, or enjoy ball pools, sand pits or play tractors. Challenge the family to archery, golf or laser shooting or just sit back and relax. There is plenty to do even on rainy days in the North Coast's largest indoor play area.

Times Open Etr-Oct, daily 10.30-6. Also open wknds & school hols in winter **Fees** £11 (under 3's free, concessions £8.50) **Facilities** Ⓟ ☕ ⛩ (indoor & outdoor) ♿ (fully accessible) toilets for disabled (ramps) shop

CLYST ST MARY — Map 3 SX99

Crealy Adventure Park

Sidmouth Rd EX5 1DR
☎ 01395 233200 📠 01395 233211
e-mail: fun@crealy.co.uk
web: www.crealy.co.uk
dir: M5 junct 30 onto A3052 Exeter to Sidmouth road

Crealy Adventure Park offers an unforgettable day for all the family with Tidal Wave log flume, El Pastil Loco Coaster, Queen Bess Pirate Ship, Techno Race Karts, Bumper Boats, Victorian Carousel, Funosaurus show and all-weather play area. Visit the Animal Realm to ride, feed, milk, groom or cuddle the animals, and relax on the Prairie Train tour around the Sunflower Maze.

Times Open all year, Jan-mid Jul & 6 Sep-Dec, daily 10-5. Closed winter term time Mon-Tue; mid Jul-5 Sep, daily 10-6* **Fees** £13.50 (ch £13.50, ch under 92cms free). £14.50 during Festival* **Facilities** Ⓟ Ⓟ ☕ 🍽 licensed ⛩ (indoor & outdoor) ♿ (fully accessible) toilets for disabled (carers admitted free, rollercoaster has disabled facility) shop

COMBE MARTIN — Map 2 SS54

Combe Martin Wildlife Park & Dinosaur Park — 2 FOR 1

EX34 0NG
☎ 01271 882486 📠 01271 889077
e-mail: info@dinosaur-park.com
web: www.dinosaur-park.com
dir: M5 junct 27 then A361 towards Barnstaple, turn right onto A399

Come and see the UK's only full-size animatronic Tyrannosaurus Rex, along with a pair of vicious, interacting Meglosaurs, a Velociraptor and Dilophosaurus, the 'Spitting Dinosaur'. Explore 26 acres of stunning gardens with cascading waterfalls and hundreds of exotic birds and animals. There are daily sea lion shows, falconry displays, lemur encounters and handling sessions. Other attractions include the Earthquake Canyon Train Ride, Tomb of the Pharoahs, Tropical House, T Rex photographic studio, and much more.

Times Open Feb half term-6 Nov, daily 10-5 (last admission 3) **Fees** £14 (ch 3-15 £8.50, ch under 3 free, pen £10). Family (2ad+2ch) £40 **Facilities** Ⓟ Ⓟ ☕ ⛩ (outdoor) ♿ (partly accessible) (bottom part of park has sharp decline, not suitable for wheelchairs or severe disabilities) toilets for disabled shop

COMPTON Map 3 SX86

Compton Castle

TQ3 1TA

☎ 01803 842382 📠 01803 661900

e-mail: compton@nationaltrust.org.uk

web: www.nationaltrust.org.uk/devoncornwall

dir: Off A381 at Ipplepen. Or, off A380 Torquay, Paignton ring road at Marldon - no coaches on this road

Home to the Gilbert family for an almost unbroken 600 years, this imposing castle set against a backdrop of rolling hills and orchards evokes a bewitching mixture of romance and history. This is the last truly fortified dwelling to be built in Devon, and its extremely high curtain walls, symmetrical towers and portcullis create an unforgettable approach. Inside there are machiolations, spiral staircases and squints, making Compton a place of discovery and adventure for imaginative children and adults alike.

Times Open 30 Mar-29 Oct Mon, Wed & Thu 11-5* **Facilities** Ⓟ Ⓟ (outdoor) (partly accessible) (Please phone for guidance, accessiblity limited) (large print, Braille notes, portable ramp)

CULLOMPTON Map 3 ST00

Diggerland

Verbeer Manor EX15 2PE

☎ 0871 227 7007 📠 0901 2010 300

e-mail: mail@diggerland.com

web: www.diggerland.com

dir: M5 junct 27. E on A38 & at rdbt turn right onto A3181. Diggerland is 3m on left

An adventure park with a difference, where kids of all ages can experience the thrills of driving real earth-moving equipment. Choose from various types of diggers and dumpers ranging from 1 ton to 8 and a half tons. Supervised by an instructor, complete the Dumper Truck Challenge or dig for buried treasure. New rides include JCB Robots, Diggerland Dodgems, Go-karts, Landrover Safari and Spin Dizzy. Even under 5's can join in, with mum or dad's help. Please telephone for details of events during school and Bank Holidays.

Times Open 12 Feb-Oct, 10-5, wknds, BHs & school hols (including half terms)* **Facilities** Ⓟ (outdoor) (fully accessible) toilets for disabled shop

DARTMOUTH Map 3 SX85

Bayard's Cove Fort

FREE

TQ6 9AT

web: www.english-heritage.org.uk

dir: in Dartmouth on riverfront

Built by the townspeople to protect the harbour, the remains of the circular stronghold still stand at the southern end of the harbour.

Times Open at any reasonable time **Facilities**

INDOOR OUTDOOR
ALL DAY VALUE
Woodlands
FAMILY THEME PARK
DARTMOUTH
FAMILY RIDES
ZOO-FARM
ALL AGES
Discover our Caravan Park
Woodlands Family Theme Park, Dartmouth, South Devon TQ9 7DQ
Tel: 01803 712598 • www.woodlandspark.com
Woodlands Leisure reserve the right to close the park or any attractions without prior notice.

Dartmouth Castle

Castle Rd TQ6 0JN

☎ 01803 833588 📠 01803 834445

web: www.english-heritage.org.uk

dir: 1m SE off B3205, narrow approach road

Built at the water's edge in a superb scenic setting, the castle's military history spans well over 500 years.

Times Open all year, Apr-Jun & Sep, daily 10-5; Jul-Aug, daily 10-6; Oct, daily 10-4; Nov-Mar, Sat-Sun, 10-4. Closed 24-26 Dec & 1 Jan **Fees** £4.50 (ch £2.30, concessions £3.80). Prices and opening times are subject to change in March 2011. Please call 0870 333 1181 for the most up to date prices and opening times when planning your visit **Facilities** Ⓟ shop

ENGLAND

DARTMOUTH *continued*

Woodlands Family Theme Park

Blackawton TQ9 7DQ

☎ 01803 712598 📠 01803 712680

e-mail: fun@woodlandspark.com

web: www.woodlandspark.com

dir: 5m from Dartmouth on A3122. From A38 follow brown tourist signs

An all-weather attraction packed with variety for all ages at one inclusive cost. The Ninja Towers has tree top aerial runways, sky high rope bridges and incredible slides. The baffling illusion of the Seascape Mirror Maze has bewildering pathways and weird sea monsters that disappear. There are 16 family rides, including exhilarating water coasters, Swing Ship, 500m Toboggan Run and Avalanche, and ten massive play zones to entertain the kids for hours. Great for rainy days with 100,000sq ft of undercover action. Explore the Empire, 5 floors of challenging climbs, rides and slides, hang on to the Trauma Tower and zap your buddies in the Master Blaster. Incredible Zoo-in-a-Farm, amazing night and day creatures, insects and birds. Get close to the animals and ride big U-Drive tractors. There is also a falconry centre with fascinating flying displays; and live entertainers in the summer holidays.

Times Open daily 2 Apr-6 Nov at 9.30. Winter open wknds & Devon school hols **Fees** £12.60 (ch £12.60, under 92cms free)* **Facilities** P ☕ 🪑 (indoor & outdoor) ♿ (partly accessible) (some rides not suitable) toilets for disabled (ramps) shop 🚫🐕

See advert on page 75

DREWSTEIGNTON Map 3 SX79

Castle Drogo

EX6 6PB

☎ 01647 433306 📠 01647 433186

e-mail: castledrogo@nationaltrust.org.uk

web: www.nationaltrust.org.uk/main

dir: 5m S of A30 Exeter-Okehampton. Coaches turn off A382 at Sandy Park

India tea baron Julius Drewe's dream house, this granite castle, built between 1910 and 1930, is one of the most remarkable works of Sir Edward Lutyens, and combines the grandeur of a medieval castle with the comfort of the 20th century. A great country house with terraced formal garden, woodland spring garden, huge circular croquet lawn and colourful herbaceous borders. Standing at more than 900 feet overlooking the wooded gorge of the River Teign with stunning views of Dartmoor, and delightful walks. Lots of events in school holidays, ring for details. 100th Anniversary of the foundation stone for Castle Drogo was laid. Special events throughout the year.

Times Castle open 14 Mar-1 Nov, daily 11-5; Garden, tearooms & shop open 14 Mar-1 Nov 10.30-5.30 **Fees** House & garden £9.10 (ch £4.60). Family £22.70. Garden only £5.75 (ch £3.15) **Facilities** P ☕ 🪑 (outdoor) ♿ (partly accessible) (Gardens, Hall & Library fully accessible, other areas only accessible via stairs) toilets for disabled (Braille & large print guide, touch list) shop 🚫🐕 🌿

EXETER Map 3 SX99

Exeter Cathedral

1 The Cloisters EX1 1HS

☎ 01392 285983 📠 01392 285986

e-mail: visitors@exeter-cathedral.org.uk

web: www.exeter-cathedral.org.uk

dir: Follow signs for city centre

A fine example of a medieval cathedral, famous for its two Norman towers, impressive West Front carvings and the longest unbroken stretch of Gothic vaulting in the world. It has been the seat of the bishops of Exeter for over one thousand years and remains a vibrant worshipping community. The Cathedral has an on-going programme of concerts and recitals throughout the year.

Times Open all year, Mon-Sat 9.30-5, for general visiting. (Restrictions may apply when the cathedral is being used for special services & events. Check website before travelling)* **Facilities** Ⓟ ☕ 🍽 licensed 🪑 (outdoor) ♿ (partly accessible) (wheelchair access avoiding steps can be made available) toilets for disabled shop 🚫🐕

Exeter's Underground Passages

2 Paris St EX1 1GA
☎ 01392 665887 & 665832 📠 01392 265625
e-mail: underground.passages@exeter.gov.uk
web: www.exeter.gov.uk/passages
dir: Follow signs for city centre

Dating from the 14th century, these medieval passages under Exeter High Street are a unique ancient monument. No similar system of passages can be explored by the public anywhere else in Britain. The passages were built to house the pipes that brought fresh water to the city. Visitors to the Underground Interpretation Centre pass through an exhibition and video presentation before their guided tour. The centre is packed with interactive exhibits but the passages remain the same: narrow, dark and exciting.

Times Open Jun-Sep (incl school hols outside this period), Mon-Sat 9.30-5.30. Sun 10.30-4. Oct-May, Tue-Fri 11.30-5.30. Sat 9.30-5.30, Sun 11.30-4 (ast tour 1 hour before closing) **Fees** £5 (ch 5-18 £3.50, under 5 free access to exhibition only, concessions £4). Family ticket (2ad+3ch) £15 **Facilities** Ⓟ ♿ (partly accessible) (exhibition accessible to wheelchairs, tours of passages not suitable) toilets for disabled shop 🚭

Quay House Visitor Centre FREE

46 The Quay EX2 4AN
☎ 01392 271611 📠 01392 265625
e-mail: quayhouse@exeter.gov.uk
web: www.exeter.gov.uk/quayhouse
dir: Turn off A30 onto A366. Follow signs to historic quayside

Two thousand years of Exeter's history in an audio-visual presentation of the city from Roman times to the present day. The newly refurbished centre provides the opportunity to learn about the history of the Quayside through lively displays, illustrations and artefacts.

Times Open all year, Apr-Oct, daily 10-5; Nov-Mar, Sat-Sun 11-4 **Facilities** Ⓟ ♿ (partly accessible) (access to downstairs only) (induction loop, audio visual presentation) shop 🚭

St Nicholas Priory

The Mint, off Fore St EX4 3BL
☎ 01392 665858 📠 01392 421252
e-mail: priory@exeter.gov.uk
web: www.exeter.gov.uk/priory
dir: follow signs for city centre

Originally part of a Medieval Priory, this splendid building was later lived in by the wealthy Hurst family. It is now presented as their furnished Elizabethan town house with replica furniture, sumptious fabrics and rich colours. Come and feel at home in this historical family house.

Times Open Sat & Mon-Sat Devon school hols, 10-5; Term time Mon-Fri prebooked groups & school parties. Closed BHs* **Fees** £2.50 (ch £1). Prebooked groups £3 (ch £2.25)* **Facilities** Ⓟ ♿ (partly accessible) (Ground floor) toilets for disabled (audio visuals of inaccessible rooms) shop 🚭

EXMOUTH **Map 3 SY08**

A la Ronde

Summer Ln EX8 5BD
☎ 01395 265514
e-mail: alaronde@nationaltrust.org.uk
web: www.nationaltrust.org.uk
dir: 2m N of Exmouth on A376

A unique 16-sided house built on the instructions of two spinster cousins on their return from a grand tour of Europe. It has fascinating interior decorations and collections.

Times Open 27 Feb-7 Mar, Sat-Sun 11-5; 13 Mar-Jun & 4 Sep-Oct, Sat-Wed 11-5; 2 Jul-3 Sep, Fri-Wed 11-5, also open Good Fri* **Fees** £6.70 (ch £3.40, under 5's free). Family tickets available. Groups 15+ £5.70 each. Reduced rate when arriving by public transport £5.70* **Facilities** 🅟 ☕ 🛆 (outdoor) ♿ (partly accessible) (grounds partly accessible, steep stairs to 1st floor) toilets for disabled (Braille guide, large print, photo album) shop 🚭 🌿

The World of Country Life

Sandy Bay EX8 5BU
☎ 01395 274533
e-mail: info@worldofcountrylife.co.uk
web: www.worldofcountrylife.co.uk
dir: M5 junct 30, take A376 to Exmouth. Follow signs to Sandy Bay

All-weather family attraction including falconry displays, and a safari train that travels through a forty acre deer park. Kids will enjoy the friendly farm animals, pets centre and animal nursery. There is also a Victorian street, working models and thousands of exhibits from a bygone age, including steam and vintage vehicles.

Times Open Apr-Oct, daily 10-5* **Fees** £9.85 (ch 3-17 & pen £7.85). Family ticket (2ad+2ch) £32.50, (2ad+3ch) £37.50* **Facilities** 🅟 Ⓟ ☕ 🍽 licensed 🛆 (indoor & outdoor) ♿ (partly accessible) (no wheelchair access in pet centre, deer train & play areas) toilets for disabled shop 🚭

ENGLAND

GREAT TORRINGTON Map 2 SS41

Dartington Crystal 2 FOR 1

EX38 7AN

☎ 01805 626242 📠 01805 626263
e-mail: tours@dartington.co.uk
web: www.dartington.co.uk
dir: Turn off A386 in centre of Great Torrington, down School Lane (opposite church). Dartington Crystal 200mtrs on left. Follow brown signs for directions

Dartington Crystal has won many international design awards in recognition of its excellence. The all new factory experience allows visitors to watch skilled craftsmen at work from ground level or from an elevated viewing gallery. Excellent shopping outlets and café. There is something for all age groups in the Visitor Centre.

Times Open all year. Visitor centre, Factory experience, Cafe and Shops Mon-Fri 9-5 (last tour 3.15), Sat 10-5, Sun 10-4 (tours closed wknds). For Xmas, New Year and BH opening please telephone for opening time details* **Fees** £6 (ch under 16 free, pen £5). Max 5 ch with every full paying adult* **Facilities** Ⓟ Ⓟ ☕ 🍴 licensed ⛩ (outdoor) ♿ (fully accessible) toilets for disabled (wheelchairs available) shop 🚫

RHS Garden Rosemoor

EX38 8PH

☎ 01805 624067 📠 01805 624717
e-mail: rosemooradmin@rhs.org.uk
web: www.rhs.org.uk/rosemoor
dir: 1m SE of Great Torrington on A3124

RHS Garden Rosemoor is 65 acres of enchanting garden and woodland set in Torridge Valley. Rich in variety with year-round interest, Rosemoor includes inspiring displays of formal and informal planting. The garden has two beautiful rose gardens, a winter garden, cottage garden, fruit and vegetable garden, lake, arboretum and much more. Over 80 events are held each year, phone 01805 626800 for details.

Times Open: Gardens all year; Apr-Sep 10-6; Oct-Mar 10-5. Closed 25 Dec. Visitor Centre as for gardens but closed 24-26 Dec* **Facilities** Ⓟ Ⓟ ☕ 🍴 licensed ⛩ (outdoor) ♿ (fully accessible) toilets for disabled (herb garden for disabled, wheelchair available) shop 🚫

HONITON Map 3 ST10

Allhallows Museum

High St EX14 1PG

☎ 01404 44966 & 42996
e-mail: info@honitonmuseum.co.uk
web: www.honitonmuseum.co.uk
dir: next to parish church of St Paul in High Street

The museum, housed in a chapel dating back to around 1200, has a wonderful display of Honiton lace, and there are lace demonstrations from June to August. The town's history is also illustrated.

Times Open Mon before Etr-Sep; Mon-Fri 9.30-4.30 & Sat 9.30-1; Oct, Mon-Fri 9.30-3.30, Sat 9.30-12.30* **Facilities** Ⓟ ♿ (partly accessible) (stair lift, wheelchair, hearing loop) shop 🚫

ILFRACOMBE Map 2 SS54

Watermouth Castle & Family Theme Park

EX34 9SL

☎ 01271 863879 📠 01271 865864
web: www.watermouthcastle.com
dir: 3m NE off A399, midway between Ilfracombe & Combe Martin

A popular family attraction including mechanical music demonstrations, musical water show, dungeon labyrinths, Victorian displays, bygone pier machines, animated fairy tale scenes, tube slide, mini golf, children's carousel, swingboats, aeroplane ride, water fountains, river ride, gardens and a maze.

Times Open Apr-end Oct, closed Sat. (Also closed some Mon & Fri off season). Ring for further details* **Fees** £12 (ch £10, under 92cm free & pen £8)* **Facilities** Ⓟ ☕ ⛩ (outdoor) ♿ (partly accessible) toilets for disabled (special wheelchair route) shop 🚫

KILLERTON HOUSE & GARDEN Map 3 SS90

Killerton House & Garden

EX5 3LE

☎ 01392 881345 📠 01392 883112
e-mail: killerton@nationaltrust.org.uk
web: www.nationaltrust.org.uk
dir: off B3181 Exeter to Cullompton road

Elegant 18th-century house set in an 18-acre garden with sloping lawns and herbaceous borders. A majestic avenue of beech trees runs up the hillside, past an arboretum of rhododendrons and conifers. The garden has an ice house and rustic summer house where the family's pet bear was once kept, as well as a Victorian chapel. Inside the house are displays from the Killerton Dress Collection, and a Victorian laundry. Please telephone for details of annual events.

Times Open: House, 12 Feb-13 Mar 2-5, 14 Mar-Oct 11-5. Last entry 4.30. Gardens open all year daily 10.30-dusk or 7 **Fees** Gift aid admission House & garden: £8.80 (ch £4.40) Family £21.70. Garden & park only: £6.50 (ch £3.25). Standard admission £8 (ch £4). Family ticket £19.70. Garden & Park only £5.80 (ch £2.40) **Facilities** Ⓟ ☕ ⛩ (outdoor) ♿ (partly accessible) (Costume collection on 1st floor not accessible. Some steep paths in garden) toilets for disabled (wheelchairs & motorised buggy, photo album) shop ⊛ ✿

KINGSBRIDGE Map 3 SX74

Cookworthy Museum of Rural Life

The Old Grammar School, 108 Fore St TQ7 1AW
☎ 01548 853235
e-mail: wcookworthy@talk21.com
web: www.kingsbridgemuseum.net
dir: A38 onto A384, then A381 to Kingsbridge, museum at top of town

The 17th-century schoolrooms of this former grammar school are now the setting for another kind of education. A Victorian kitchen, a costume room and extensive collection of local historical items are gathered to illustrate South Devon life. A walled garden and farm gallery are also features of this museum, founded to commemorate William Cookworthy, 'father' of the English china clay industry. The Local Heritage Resource Centre with public access databases, microfilm of local newspapers since 1855 and Devon record service point are available to visitors. Extensive photographic collection available to view in kiosks. Please ring for details of special events.

Times Open 4 Apr-Sep, Mon-Sat 10.30-5; Oct 10.30-4. Nov-Mar groups by arrangement. Local Heritage Resource Centre open all year, Mon-Thu 10-12 & Wed also 2-4, other times by appointment **Fees** £2.50 (ch £1, concessions £2). Family (2ad+ up to 4ch) £6 **Facilities** ⓟ ⛩ (outdoor) ♿ (partly accessible) (Wheelchair access ground floor, walled garden & Resource Centre) toilets for disabled (Braille labels on selected exhibits, viewing gallery) shop ⊛

KINGSWEAR Map 3 SX85

Coleton Fishacre House & Garden

Brownstone Rd TQ6 0EQ
☎ 01803 752466 📠 01803 753017
e-mail: coletonfishacre@nationaltrust.org.uk
web: www.nationaltrust.org.uk
dir: 3m from Kingswear. Take Ferry Rd and turn off at Toll House, follow brown tourist signs

In this enchanting corner of South Devon, house, garden and sea meet in perfect harmony. Lose yourself in the magical garden, where tender plants from the Mediterranean, South Africa and New Zealand thrive. Explore the secluded cove below and enjoy the far-reaching views out over the sea. In this most evocative of holiday homes, built for Rupert D'Oyly Carte, there is true 1920s elegance. A light, joyful atmosphere fills the rooms and music is usually playing, echoing the family's Gilbert and Sullivan connections.

Times Garden open 1-30 Mar, Sat & Sun only 11-5; 31 Mar-29 Oct, Wed-Sun & BH Mon 10.30-5. House open 29 Mar-29 Oct, Wed-Sun & BH Mon 11-4.30* **Facilities** Ⓟ ⓟ ☕ ⛩ (outdoor) ♿ (partly accessible) toilets for disabled (wheelchairs available, Braille guides, mobile T loop) shop ⊛ ✿

KNIGHTSHAYES COURT Map 3 SS91

Knightshayes Court — 2 FOR 1

EX16 7RQ
☎ 01884 254665 & 257381
e-mail: knightshayes@nationaltrust.org.uk
web: www.nationaltrust.org.uk/knightshayes
dir: M5 junct 27, 2m N of Tiverton off A396

This fine Victorian mansion, a rare example of William Burges' work, offers much of interest to all ages. The garden is one of the most beautiful in Devon, with formal terraces, amusing topiary, a pool garden and woodland walks.

Times Open 19-27 Feb, 11-4, 12 Mar-30 Oct, 11-5. **Fees** House, gardens & parkland £9 (ch £4.50). Family (2ad+3ch) £22.50, (1ad+3ch) £14. Groups 15+ £7.50. Gardens & parkland only £7.15 (ch £3.65) Groups 15+ £6.05 **Facilities** Ⓟ ☕ 🍽 licensed ⛩ (outdoor) ♿ (partly accessible) (woodland paths not accessible. Ground floor only in mansion accessible) toilets for disabled (wheelchairs available, lift & Braille) shop ⊛ ✿

LYDFORD Map 2 SX58

Lydford Castle and Saxon Town — FREE

EX20 4BH
web: www.english-heritage.org.uk
dir: in Lydford off A386

Standing above the gorge of the River Lyd, this tower, dating back to the 12th-century, was notorious as a prison. The earthworks of the original Norman fort lie to the south.

Times Open at any reasonable time **Facilities** Ⓟ #

Lydford Gorge

EX20 4BH
☎ 01822 820320 & 820441 📠 01822 822000
e-mail: lydfordgorge@nationaltrust.org.uk
web: www.nationaltrust.org.uk/lydfordgorge
dir: off A386, between Okehampton & Tavistock, 7m S of A30

This lush oak-wooded steep-sided river gorge, with its fascinating history and many legends, can be explored through a variety of short and long walks. See the spectacular White Lady Waterfall, pass over the tumbling water at Tunnel Falls and watch the river bubble in the Devil's Cauldron. There's an abundance of wildlife to spot.

Times Open 12 Mar-30 Oct, daily 10-5 (Oct 10-4). Winter opening - please ring for details **Fees** £6.40 (ch £3.20). Family ticket (2ad+3ch) £16 **Facilities** Ⓟ ⓟ ☕ ⛩ (outdoor) ♿ (partly accessible) (initial steep section to bird hide) toilets for disabled (audio tapes, Braille guide, railway line) shop ✿

ENGLAND

MORWELLHAM Map 2 SX47

Morwellham Quay

PL19 8JL
☎ 01822 832766 & 833808 📠 01822 833808
e-mail: enquiries@morwellham-quay.co.uk
web: www.morwellham-quay.co.uk
dir: 4m W of Tavistock, off A390. Midway between Gunnislake & Tavistock. Signed

A unique, open-air museum based around the ancient port and copper mine workings in the heart of the Tamar Valley. Journey back into another time as costumed interpreters help you re-live the daily life of a 19th-century mining village and shipping quay. A tramway takes you deep into the workings of the George and Charlotte mine. Special events include music festivals, classic car shows, and a Victorian food festival.

Times Open Jul-Aug 10-5.30; Sep-Oct 10-5; Nov-Dec please phone or check website* **Fees** £5.95 (grounds) £3.50 (mine trip), (ch £3.95 grounds, £2.50 mine trip, concessions £4.95 grounds £3 mine trip) **Facilities** Ⓟ ☕ ⛩ (indoor & outdoor) ♿ (partly accessible) (Blue trail not accessible, smooth paths, but difficult areas in Victorian village) toilets for disabled shop

NEWTON ABBOT Map 3 SX87

Bradley Manor

TQ12 6BN
☎ 01803 843235 📠 01803 661900
e-mail: bradley@nationaltrust.org
web: www.nationaltrust.org.uk/devoncornwall
dir: SW of Newton Abbot on A381 Totnes road. 1m from town centre

Set in an area of 'wild space' on the outskirts of the market town of Newton Abbot, Bradley Manor is a charming, unspoilt historic house still lived in by the donor family. Predominantly 15th century, parts of the building date back to the 13th century, and some original decoration survives from that time. This little-changed, relaxed family home contains a superb collection of furniture and paintings. The meadows and woodland surrounding it are ideal for family walks.

Times Open 31 Mar-1 Oct, Tue-Thu 2-5; Oct wkdays by appointment only* **Facilities** Ⓟ ⓟ ⛩ (outdoor) ♿ (partly accessible) (T loop, large print guide, portable ramps)

Prickly Ball Farm and Hedgehog Hospital — 2 FOR 1

Denbury Rd, East Ogwell TQ12 6BZ
☎ 01626 362319
e-mail: enquiries@pricklyballfarm.co.uk
web: www.pricklyballfarm.com
dir: 1.5m from Newton Abbot on A381 towards Totnes, follow brown heritage signs

See, touch and learn about this wild animal and spend time in a wildlife garden. In mid-season see baby hogs bottle feeding. Find out how to encourage hedgehogs into your garden and how they are put back into the wild. Talks on hedgehogs are held throughout the day. There is goat walking, pony grooming, lamb feeding (in season), a barnyard grand prix, petting zoo, pig and sheep feeding and a mini pitch and putt course.

Times Open Apr-Sep, Oct wknds & half term week 10-5. (Recommended last admission 3.30)* **Fees** £6.95 (ch 3-16 £6.25, concessions £6.50). Family ticket (2ad+2ch) £25* **Facilities** Ⓟ ☕ ⛩ (indoor & outdoor) ♿ (fully accessible) toilets for disabled (parking) shop

Tuckers Maltings

Teign Rd TQ12 4AA
☎ 01626 334734 📠 01626 330153
e-mail: info@tuckersmaltings.com
web: www.tuckersmaltings.com
dir: follow brown tourist signs from Newton Abbot railway station

The only working Malthouse in England open to the public, producing malt from barley for over 30 West Country breweries. Learn all about the process of malting - and taste the end product at the in-house brewery. Guided tours last an hour.

Times Open Good Fri-end Oct, Mon-Sat. Speciality bottled beer shop open throughout the year. Phone to check winter opening* **Facilities** ⓟ ⛩ ♿ (partly accessible) (only shop accessible) toilets for disabled shop

OKEHAMPTON Map 2 SX59

Museum of Dartmoor Life — 2 FOR 1

3 West St EX20 1HQ
☎ 01837 52295
e-mail: dartmoormuseum@eclipse.co.uk
web: www.museumofdartmoorlife.eclipse.co.uk
dir: follow brown signs off all major roads into Okehampton. Museum on main road next to White Hart Hotel

Housed on three floors in an early 19th-century mill, the museum tells the story of how people have lived, worked and played on and around Dartmoor through the centuries. It shows how the moorland has shaped their lives just as their work has shaped the moorland. In the Cranmere Gallery, temporary exhibitions feature local history, art and crafts.

Times Open Etr-Oct, Mon-Sat 10.15-4. Phone for Winter opening times* **Fees** £3.50 (students £1). Family (2ad+2ch) £7.50* **Facilities** Ⓟ ⓟ ☕ ♿ (fully accessible) toilets for disabled (Braille, desk loop, lift) shop

Okehampton Castle

Castle Lodge EX20 1JB
☎ 01837 52844
web: www.english-heritage.org.uk
dir: 1m SW of town centre

Once the largest castle in Devon set amongst the stunning Dartmoor foothills. A free audio tour brings this romantic ruin to life.

Times Open Apr-Jun & Sep, daily 10-5; Jul-Aug, daily 10-6; Closed Oct-Mar **Fees** £3.50 (ch £1.80, concessions £3). Prices and opening times are subject to change in March 2011. Please call 0870 333 1181 for the most up to date prices and opening times when planning your visit **Facilities** toilets for disabled shop

OTTERTON Map 3 SY08

Otterton Mill

FREE

EX9 7HG
☎ 01392 568521
e-mail: escape@ottertonmill.com
web: www.ottertonmill.com
dir: on B3178 between Budleigh Salterton & Newton Poppleford

Set beside the River Otter in one of Devon's loveliest valleys, Otterton Mill is a centuries-old working watermill, a famous bakery and shop full of local produce, a restaurant, and a gallery of arts and crafts from local artists. Please see website for details of music nights and art events

Times Open daily, 10-5* **Facilities** licensed (partly accessible) toilets for disabled (free entry to ground floor) shop

PAIGNTON Map 3 SX86

Dartmouth Steam Railway & River Boat Company

Queens Park Station, Torbay Rd TQ4 6AF
☎ 01803 555872 01803 664313
e-mail: bookings@dsrrb.co.uk
web: www.dartmouthrailriver.co.uk
dir: from Paignton follow brown tourist signs

Steam trains run for seven miles from Paignton to Kingswear on the former Great Western line, stopping at Goodrington Sands, Churston, and Kingswear, connecting with the ferry crossing to Dartmouth. Combined river excursions available. Please ring for details of special events. In 2011 there will be celebrations to mark the 150th Anniversary of the railway line reaching Churston Station.

Times Open on Fri 1 Apr. Open daily from May-Sep. Santa specials in Dec **Fees** Paignton to Kingswear £9 (ch £5.50, pen £8). Family £25. Paignton to Dartmouth (including ferry) £11 (ch £6.50, pen £10). Family £30* **Facilities** (fully accessible) toilets for disabled (wheelchair ramp for boarding train) shop

Paignton Zoo Environmental Park

Totnes Rd TQ4 7EU
☎ 0844 474 2222 01803 523457
e-mail: info@paigntonzoo.org.uk
web: www.paigntonzoo.org.uk
dir: 1m from Paignton town centre on A3022 Totnes road. Follow brown signs

Paignton is one of Britain's biggest zoos, set in a beautiful and secluded woodland valley, where new enclosures are spacious and naturalistic. Your visit will take you through some of the world's threatened habitats - Forest, Savannah, Wetland and Desert, with hundreds of species, many of them endangered and part of conservation breeding programmes. There is a new crocodile swamp. There are regular keeper talks, a children's play area, and special events throughout the year. Visitors can obtain special joint tickets which allow them to visit nearby Living Coasts.

Times Open all year, daily 10-6 (5 in winter) (last admission 5 (4 in winter). Closed 25 Dec **Fees** £11.35 (ch 3-15 £7.60, concessions £9.35). Family ticket (2ad & 2ch) £34.10. Joint family saver ticket with Living Coasts £49.15* **Facilities** licensed (indoor & outdoor) (partly accessible) (footpaths have slight gradient, some steep hills) toilets for disabled (wheelchair loan-booking essential) shop

ENGLAND

PLYMOUTH Map 2 SX45

The Elizabethan House

32 New St, The Barbican PL1 2NA
☎ 01752 304774 📠 01752 304775
e-mail: museum@plymouth.gov.uk
web: www.plymouth.gov.uk/museums
dir: A38/A374 follow signs to city centre then The Barbican, house just behind Southside Street

On Plymouth's historic Barbican, find an ancient doorway and go back in time to Drake's Plymouth. Home of an Elizabethan merchant or sea captain, the house is an opportunity to see how an Elizabethan mariner might have lived. A rare Tudor time-capsule with furniture and fabrics dating back to the 1600s. A recently restored kitchen and gardens add to the authentic feel.

Times Open Apr-Sep, Tue-Sat & BH Mon, 10-5 (last entry 4.30)* **Fees** £2 (ch £1). Family & other concessions available* **Facilities** Ⓟ ♿ (partly accessible) (ground floor & kitchen garden partly accessible) shop 🚭

National Marine Aquarium

Rope Walk, Coxside PL4 0LF
☎ 01752 600301 📠 01752 600593
e-mail: enquiries@national-aquarium.co.uk
web: www.national-aquarium.co.uk
dir: A38 to Marsh Mills (Sainsbury's) then towards city centre & follow brown signs for Barbican & Coxside car park

Europe's biggest tank has now got Europe's biggest collection of sharks and rays - Atlantic Ocean is a must see exhibit. Next to this is Ocean Drifters the UK's largest collection of jellyfish. The National Marine Aquarium is noted for being the safest attraction in the South West so come and enjoy the under water world.

Times Open all year daily, mid Mar-Oct 10-6; Nov-mid Mar 10-5* **Facilities** Ⓟ ☕ ⛩ (outdoor) ♿ (fully accessible) toilets for disabled shop 🚭

Plymouth City Museum & Art Gallery

FREE

Drake Circus PL4 8AJ
☎ 01752 304774 📠 01752 304775
e-mail: museum@plymouth.gov.uk
web: www.plymouthmuseum.gov.uk
dir: off A38 onto A374, museum on NW of city centre, opposite university

The City Museum and Art Gallery runs an exciting programme of exhibitions, talks, concerts, family workshops and other events alongside its gallery collections. There is an interactive natural history gallery and an impressive porcelain and silver collection, as well as the internationally important Cottonian collection. For further details please visit the website.

Times Open all year Tue-Fri 10-5.30, Sat & BH Mons 10-5. Closed Good Fri & Xmas* **Facilities** Ⓟ ☕ ⛩ (outdoor) ♿ (fully accessible) toilets for disabled (wheelchair available) shop 🚭

PLYMPTON Map 2 SX55

Saltram

PL7 1UH
☎ 01752 333500 & 333503 📠 01752 336474
e-mail: saltram@nationaltrust.org.uk
web: www.nationaltrust.org.uk
dir: 3.5m E of Plymouth, between A38 & A379. Take Plympton turn at Marsh Mill rdbt, right at 4th lights to Cot Hill. At T-junct right into Merafield Rd. Saltram 0.25m on right

This magnificent George II house still has its original contents. The collection of paintings was begun at the suggestion of Sir Joshua Reynolds and includes many of his portraits. The saloon and dining room were designed by Robert Adam and have superb decorative plasterwork and period furniture. The extensive gardens include a working Orangery and several follies, and part of their 500 acres is alongside the River Plym.

Times Open House: Apr-Oct, 12-4.30 (ex Fri). Garden open all year, 11-4.30. Park open all year, dawn to dusk* **Facilities** 🅟 🍽 licensed ⛩ (outdoor) ♿ (partly accessible) toilets for disabled (wheelchairs available, Braille & audio guides) shop 🚭 🌿

POWDERHAM Map 3 SX98

Powderham Castle

EX6 8JQ
☎ 01626 890243 📠 01626 890729
e-mail: castle@powderham.co.uk
web: www.powderham.co.uk
dir: signed off A379 Exeter/Dawlish road

Set in a tranquil deer park along the Exe estuary. Built in 1391 by Sir Philip Courtenay, it has long been the family home of the Earl of Devon. There is a beautiful rose garden and spring walks through the woodland garden. Guided tours showcase the castle's intriguing history, majestic interiors and fine collection of treasures. Special events throughout the year.

Times Open Etr-Oct, 10-5.30 (last admission 4.30). Closed Sat.* **Facilities** 🅟 Ⓟ ☕ 🍽 licensed ⛩ (outdoor) ♿ (partly accessible) toilets for disabled (ramps) shop 🚭

SALCOMBE Map 3 SX73

Overbeck's

Sharpitor TQ8 8LW
☎ 01548 842893 📠 01548 845020
e-mail: overbecks@nationaltrust.org.uk
web: www.nationaltrust.org.uk
dir: 1.5m SW of Salcombe, signed from Malborough & Salcombe, narrow approach road

This famous garden is home to an unusual collection of rare and tropical plants creating a dramatic display of hot colours and exotic scents. Perching on high cliffs overlooking Salcombe, the views are breathtaking. Once home to the eccentric Dr Overbeck, the house contains some quirky collections from around the world.

Times Open Garden, museum & facilities 13 Mar-Oct, daily 11-5. Gardens only Nov-Jan, Mon-Thu 11-4 **Fees** Gardens & House £6.70 (ch £3.40). Family ticket £16.80 (1ad family £10.10). Groups £5.70 each **Facilities** (outdoor) (partly accessible) (steep paths to access garden & house) (ramp from garden, Braille guide, hearing loop, audio tour) shop

SOUTH MOLTON Map 3 SS72

Quince Honey Farm 2 FOR 1

EX36 3AZ

☎ 01769 572401 01769 574704

e-mail: info@quincehoney.co.uk

web: www.quincehoney.com

dir: 3.5m W of A361, on N edge of South Molton

Follow the story of honey and beeswax from flower to table. The exhibition allows you to see the world of bees close up in complete safety; hives open at the press of a button revealing the honeybees' secret life. After viewing the bees at work, sample the fruits of their labour in the café or shop.

Times Open daily, Apr-Sep 9-6; Oct 9-5; Shop only Nov-Etr 9-5, closed Sun. Closed 25 Dec-4 Jan **Fees** £5.25 (ch 5-16 £4.25, pen £4.60)* **Facilities** (outdoor) (partly accessible) (no lift to exhibition on first floor) toilets for disabled shop

STICKLEPATH Map 3 SX69

Finch Foundry

EX20 2NW

☎ 01837 840046 01837 840809

e-mail: finchfoundry@nationaltrust,org.uk

web: www.nationaltrust.org.uk

dir: off A30 at Okehampton junct, follow brown signs to Finch Foundry. Located in main street of village

Finch Foundry was, in the 19th century, a water-powered factory for making sickles, scythes, shovels and other hand tools. Although no longer in production, three waterwheels can still be seen driving huge hammers, shears, grindstone and other machinery, with daily working demonstrations. These demonstrations explain the key role the foundry played in the local community. Special Event: St Clement's Day (St Clement is the patron saint of blacksmiths) third Saturday in November.

Times Open 20 Mar-Oct, daily (ex Tue), 11-5 (Last entry 4.30)* **Fees** £4.40 (ch £2.20)* **Facilities** (outdoor) (partly accessible) (steps to workshop & interpretation gallery) (access to shop/tea room, view main foundry via shop) shop

TIVERTON Map 3 SS91

Tiverton Castle 2 FOR 1

EX16 6RP

☎ 01884 253200 & 255200 01884 254200

e-mail: tiverton.castle@ukf.net

web: www.tivertoncastle.com

dir: M5 junct 27, then 7m on A361 towards Tiverton to rdbt. Castle signed

The original castle, built in 1106 by order of Henry I, was rebuilt in the late 13th-14th centuries. It resisted General Fairfax during the Civil War but fell to him when a lucky shot hit the drawbridge chain. Now a private house, the gardens are lovely and there's a fine Civil War armoury, some pieces of which can be tried on.

Times Open Etr Sun-end Oct, Sun, Thu & BH Mon only 2.30-5.30 (last admission 5) **Fees** £6 (ch 7-16 £2.50, under 7 free). Disabled half price if accessing ground floor only **Facilities** (partly accessible) (garden & ground floor accessible) toilets for disabled shop

Tiverton Museum of Mid Devon Life 2 FOR 1

Beck's Square EX16 6PJ

☎ 01884 256295

e-mail: curator04@tivertonmuseum.org.uk

web: www.tivertonmuseum.org.uk

dir: in centre of town next to Beck's Square car park

This large and comprehensive museum now with 15 galleries, re-opened after extensive rebuilding throughout. It is housed in a 19th-century school and the exhibits include a Heathcoat Lace Gallery featuring items from the local lace-making industry. There is also an agricultural section with a collection of farm wagons and implements. Other large exhibits include two waterwheels and a railway locomotive with many GWR items.

Times Open Feb-mid Dec, Mon-Fri 10.30-4.30, Sat 10-1. Open BHs **Fees** £4.50 (ch £1, pen £3.50). Family ticket (2ad+4ch) £10 **Facilities** (fully accessible) toilets for disabled (lift, induction loop) shop

TORQUAY Map 3 SX96

Babbacombe Model Village

Hampton Av, Babbacombe TQ1 3LA

☎ 01803 315315 01803 315173

e-mail: sw@model-village.co.uk

web: www.model-village.co.uk

dir: follow brown tourist signs from outskirts of town

See the world recreated in miniature. Thousands of miniature buildings, people and vehicles capture the essence of England's past, present and future, set in four acres of award-winning gardens. Various events are planned, please contact for details.

Times Open all year, times vary* **Facilities** licensed (partly accessible) (very steep slopes but access is possible) toilets for disabled (push button audio information) shop

ENGLAND

TORQUAY *continued*

'Bygones'

Fore St, St Marychurch TQ1 4PR
☎ 01803 326108 📠 01803 326108
web: www.bygones.co.uk
dir: follow tourist signs into Torquay and St Marychurch

Step back in time in this life-size Victorian exhibition street of over 20 shops including a forge, pub and period display rooms, housed in a former cinema. Exhibits include a large model railway layout, illuminated fantasyland, railwayana and military exhibits including a walk-through World War I trench. At Christmas the street is turned into a winter wonderland. A new set piece features Babbacombe's John Lee ('the man they couldn't hang') in his cell. There is something here for all the family including a 1940s/50s shopping arcade.

Times Open all year, Spring- Autumn 10-6; Winter 10-4, wknds & school hols 10-5 (last entry 1hr before closing)* **Facilities** Ⓟ ☕ ♿ (partly accessible) (ground floor only accessible) (ramp) shop

Kents Cavern

Cavern House, 91 Ilsham Rd, Wellswood TQ1 2JF
☎ 01803 215136
e-mail: caves@kents-cavern.co.uk
web: www.kents-cavern.co.uk
dir: 1.25m NE off B3199, follow brown tourist signs. 1m from Torquay harbour

Probably the most important Palaeolithic site in Britain and recognised as one of the country's most significant archaeological areas. This is not only a world of spectacular natural beauty, but also a priceless record of past times, where a multitude of secrets of mankind, animals and nature have become trapped and preserved over the last 500,000 years. 170 years after the first excavations and with over 80,000 remains already unearthed, modern research is still discovering new clues to our past. Please visit website for details of special events.

Times Open all year daily from 10, last tour 3.30 Nov-Feb, 4 Mar-Jun & Sep-Oct, 4.30 Jul-Aug* **Facilities** Ⓟ Ⓟ ☕ 🍽 licensed ⛩ (outdoor) ♿ (partly accessible) toilets for disabled shop

Living Coasts

Beacon Quay TQ1 2BG
☎ 01803 202470 📠 01803 202471
e-mail: info@livingcoasts.org.uk
web: www.livingcoasts.org.uk
dir: once in Torquay follow A379 and brown tourist signs to harbour

Living Coasts is a coastal zoo that allows visitors to take a trip around the coastlines of the world without leaving Torquay. Specially designed environments are home to fur seals, puffins, penguins, ducks, rats, and waders among others. All the animals can be seen above and below the water, while the huge meshed aviary allows the birds to fly free over your head. Visitors can obtain special joint tickets which will allow them to visit nearby Paignton Zoo. Contact or see website for details of special events.

Times Open daily from 10. Closed 25 Dec* **Fees** £9.65 (ch over 3 £7.25, concessions £7.50). Family ticket (2ad+2ch) £30.40* **Facilities** Ⓟ Ⓟ ☕ 🍽 licensed ♿ (fully accessible) toilets for disabled (pre-booked wheelchair hire) shop

Torre Abbey

The Kings Dr TQ2 5JE
☎ 01803 293593 📠 01803 215948
e-mail: torre.abbey@torbay.gov.uk
web: www.torre-abbey.org.uk
dir: A389 turn right at Torre railway station, follow brown signs for 1.5m. On seafront, next to Riviera Centre

Torre Abbey is the oldest building in Torquay, founded in 1196 as a monastery and later adapted as a country house. It has a story spanning 800 years and was once the most important Abbey of its kind in England, the brothers who lived here then were known as the White Canons. Following a massive three-year restoration project, visitors can now explore the most ancient and hallowed parts of the building and gardens where some stunning finds have been unearthed.

Times Open Feb-Mar 10-5; Apr-Dec 10-6 **Fees** £5.75 (ch £2.45, concessions £4.80). Group rates available. Family ticket £14.50* **Facilities** Ⓟ Ⓟ ☕ 🍽 licensed ⛩ (outdoor) ♿ (fully accessible) toilets for disabled shop

ENGLAND

TOTNES Map 3 SX86

Berry Pomeroy Castle

Berry Pomeroy TQ9 6NJ
☎ 01803 866618
web: www.english-heritage.org.uk
dir: 2.5m E off A385

Building of this now ruined shell, inside the 15th-century defences of the Pomeroy family castle, began around the mid-16th century and ambitiously enlarged at the beginning of the 17th century. It was intended to become the most spectacular house in Devon, but the project was abandoned by 1700 and has become the focus of spooky ghost stories.

Times Open Apr-Jun & Sep, daily 10-5; Jul-Aug, daily 10-6; Oct, daily 10-4. Closed Nov-Mar **Fees** £4.50 (ch £2.30, concessions £3.80). Prices and opening times are subject to change in March 2011. Please call 0870 333 1181 for the most up to date prices and opening times when planning your visit **Facilities** (partly accessible) (narrow spiral staircases, stone pathways) toilets for disabled shop

The Guildhall 2 FOR 1

Ramparts Walk, off High St TQ9 5QH
☎ 01803 862147 01803 864275
e-mail: office@totnestowncouncil.gov.uk
web: www.totnestowncouncil.gov.uk
dir: behind St Mary's Church on the main street

Originally the refectory, kitchens, brewery and bakery for the Benedictine Priory of Totnes (1088-1536), the building was established as the Guildhall in 1553 during the reign of Edward VI. A magistrates' court and a prison opened in 1624, and the council chamber is still used today.

Times Open Apr-Oct, Mon-Fri 10.30-4.30, other times by appointment* **Fees** £1.25 (ch 30p) **Facilities** (partly accessible) (some steps to view lower chamber and other areas)

Totnes Castle

Castle St TQ9 5NU
☎ 01803 864406
web: www.english-heritage.org.uk
dir: on hill overlooking town

One of the best surviving examples of a Norman motte and bailey castle with spectacular views. The once great ditch that surrounded the keep is today filled with the cottages and gardens of the town.

Times Open Apr-Jun & Sep, daily 10-5; Jul-Aug, daily 10-6; Oct, daily 10-4. Closed Nov-Mar **Fees** £3.20 (ch £1.60, concessions £2.70). Prices and opening times are subject to change in March 2011. Please call 0870 333 1181 for the most up to date prices and opening times when planning your visit **Facilities** shop

Totnes Museum 2 FOR 1

70 Fore St TQ9 5RU
☎ 01803 863821
e-mail: totnesmuseum@btconnect.com
web: www.devonmuseums.net/totnes
dir: from bottom of Totnes Town, turn into Fore St, museum on left of main street, just before East Gate Arch Clock Tower

An Elizabethan house, dating from 1575, said to have been built for Walter Kelland, a wealthy merchant. The building houses archaeological and social history collections and a room dedicated to Charles Babbage, inventor of the first computer. Study centre archives located at the rear of the museum.

Times Open 14 Mar-28 Oct, Mon-Fri 10.30-5. Last entry 4.30 **Fees** £2.50 (ch £1, concessions £1.75) **Facilities** (partly accessible) (spiral staircase) (personal guided tours, virtual/audio tours available) shop

UFFCULME Map 3 ST01

Coldharbour Mill Working Wool Museum

Coldharbour Mill EX15 3EE
☎ 01884 840960
e-mail: info@coldharbourmill.org.uk
web: www.coldharbourmill.org.uk
dir: 2m from M5 junct 27, off B3181. Follow signs to Willand, then brown signs to museum

The picturesque Coldharbour Mill is set in idyllic Devon countryside. It has been producing textiles since 1799 and is now a working museum, still making knitting wools and fabrics on period machinery. With machine demonstrations, a water wheel and steam engines, Coldharbour Mill is a wonderful and very different family day out. There are engines in steam regularly throughout the year plus special events, please see the website for details. The new self-guided tour of the Woollen Mill is available every day.

Times Open all year, daily 10-4. Closed at wknds during winter **Fees** General visit £5 (ch £2.50 concessions £4): Steam Up Event £7.50 (ch £4, concessions £7) **Facilities** licensed (outdoor) (partly accessible) (indoor restaurant not accessible but assistance given) toilets for disabled (helpful disabled guides & lift) shop

YELVERTON Map 2 SX56

Yelverton Paperweight Centre FREE

4 Buckland Ter, Leg O'Mutton Corner PL20 6AD
☎ 01822 854250 01822 854250
e-mail: paperweightcentre@btinternet.com
web: www.paperweightcentre.co.uk
dir: at Yelverton off A386, Plymouth to Tavistock road

This unusual centre is home to a glittering permanent collection of glass paperweights of all sizes and designs. The centre also has an extensive range of modern glass paperweights for sale, starting from only a few pounds. More expensive collectable paperweights can also be purchased. There is also a series of limited edition prints of Dartmoor scenes by David W Young.

Times Open Apr-Oct, daily 10.30-5 **Facilities** (fully accessible) (ramp on request) shop

DORSET

Corfe Castle

ABBOTSBURY Map 3 SY58

Abbotsbury Swannery 2 FOR 1

New Barn Rd DT3 4JG
☎ 01305 871858 & 871130 📠 01305 871092
e-mail: info@abbotsbury-tourism.co.uk
web: www.abbotsbury-tourism.co.uk
dir: turn off A35 at Winterborne Abbas near Dorchester. Abbotsbury on B3157 (coastal road), between Weymouth & Bridport

Abbotsbury is the breeding ground of the only managed colony of mute swans. The swans can be seen safely at close quarters, and the site is also home or stopping point for many wild birds. The highlight of the year is the cygnet season, end of May to the end of June, when there may be over 100 nests on site. Visitors can often take pictures of cygnets emerging from eggs at close quarters. There is an audio-visual show, as well as mass feeding at noon and 4pm daily, and an ugly duckling trail. Children's play area available and a new giant maze planted with willow in the shape of a swan. Find your way to the giant egg at the centre!

Times Open 19 Mar-30 Oct, daily 10-6 (last admission 5) **Fees** £10 (ch £6.50 & concessions £9.50) **Facilities** licensed (outdoor) (fully accessible) toilets for disabled (free wheelchair loan, herb garden for blind) shop

ATHELHAMPTON Map 3 SY79

Athelhampton House & Gardens 2 FOR 1

DT2 7LG
☎ 01305 848363
e-mail: enquiry@athelhampton.co.uk
web: www.athelhampton.co.uk
dir: off A35 Northbrook junct, follow brown tourist signs towards Puddletown. Left at lights. House & Gardens approx 1m on left

Athelhampton, one of the finest 15th-century houses in England, contains magnificently furnished rooms including The Great Hall of 1485 and the library, which contains 3,000 books and an original 1915 Riley Imperial billiard table. The glorious Grade I gardens contain the world-famous topiary pyramids, fountains, and collections of tulips, magnolias, roses, clematis and lilies in season. The West Wing Gallery features paintings by Marevna (1892-1984), a Russian painter who lived and painted at Athelhampton.

Times Open Mar-Oct, Sun-Thu & Nov-Feb, Sun 10.30-5 (ex Xmas). Closed Fri & Sat, open Good Fri **Fees** House & Garden £9.25 (ch free, pen £8.75, student & disabled £6.25). After 2.30 £6.25 (with lunch receipt). Groups 12+ £7.50* **Facilities** licensed (outdoor) (partly accessible) (access only to ground floor in house) toilets for disabled (wheelchairs available) shop

BEAMINSTER Map 3 ST40

Mapperton 2 FOR 1

DT8 3NR
☎ 01308 862645 📠 01308 861082
e-mail: office@mapperton.com
web: www.mapperton.com
dir: 2m SE off A356 & B3163

Several acres of terraced valley gardens with specimen trees and shrubs and formal borders surround a manor house that dates back to the 16th century. There are also fountains, grottoes, stone sculpture, fishponds and an orangery, and the garden offers good views and walks. A plant fair is held twice annually, usually in April and September.

Times Gardens open: Apr-Oct, daily (ex Sat) 11-5. House open 30 May, 11 Jul-12 Aug, 29 Aug wkdays only, 2-4.30 (last admission 4) **Fees** Gardens £5 (ch 5-18 £2.50, under 5 free). House £4.50, Groups 20+ £9 (house & garden), £4.50 (house or garden) **Facilities** (partly accessible) (ramp from parking area to garden) toilets for disabled shop

BLANDFORD FORUM Map 3 ST80

Royal Signals Museum

Blandford Camp DT11 8RH
☎ 01258 482248 📠 01258 482084
e-mail: info@royalsignalsmuseum.com
web: www.royalsignalsmuseum.com
dir: signed off B3082 (Blandford/Wimborne road) & A354 (Salisbury road). Follow brown signs for Royal Signals Museum

The Royal Signals Museum depicts the history of military communications, science and technology from the Crimea to current day. As well as displays on all major conflicts involving British forces, there are the stories of the ATS, the Long Range Desert Group, Air Support, Airborne, Para and SAS Signals. D-Day and Dorset explores the Royal Signals involvement in Operation Overlord. For children there are trails and interactive exhibits.

Times Open Mar-Oct, Mon-Fri 10-5, Sat-Sun 10-4* **Facilities** (fully accessible) toilets for disabled (ramps & lifts) shop

ENGLAND

BOURNEMOUTH Map 4 SZ09

Oceanarium

Pier Approach, West Beach BH2 5AA
☎ 01202 311993 📠 01202 311990
e-mail: info@oceanarium.co.uk
web: www.oceanarium.co.uk
dir: from A338 Wessex Way, follow Oceanarium tourist signs

Take an underwater adventure around the waters of the world and come face to face with hundreds of awesome creatures. Home to all your favourites from flamboyant clownfish and tiny terrapins, to stunning sharks and the infamous piranha, immerse yourself in a sea of colour, with 10 spectacular recreated environments including the Great Barrier Reef underwater tunnel. Experience the world's first Interactive Dive Cage - take a virtual adventure to discover more about magnificent sea creatures, without getting wet. And don't miss the Global Meltdown experience and find out what would happen if the ice caps melted and the world was flooded with water. Spectacular theming, state-of-the-art technology and amazing interactive displays, make Global Meltdown an experience not to be missed.

Times Open all year, daily from 10. Late night opening during school summer hols. Closed 25 Dec* **Facilities** Ⓟ 🍴 licensed ♿ (fully accessible) toilets for disabled (lift) shop 🚫🐕

BOVINGTON CAMP Map 3 SY88

Clouds Hill

BH20 7NQ
☎ 01929 405616
e-mail: cloudshill@nationaltrust.org.uk
web: www.nationaltrust.org.uk
dir: 1m N of Bovington Camp & Tank Museum, 1.5m E of Waddock x-rds B3390, 4m S of A35

T E Lawrence 'Lawrence of Arabia' bought this cottage in 1925 when he was a private in the Tank Corps at Bovington. He would escape here to play records and entertain friends to feasts of baked beans and China tea. The furniture and contents were Lawrence's own and a new display tells the story of Lawrence's life.

Times Open 20 Mar-26 Oct, Thu-Sun. 12-5* **Facilities** 🅿 ♿ (partly accessible) (Braille guide, ramped access available) shop 🚫🐕 🚫🚌 ✤

The Tank Museum

BH20 6JG
☎ 01929 405096 📠 01929 405360
e-mail: info@tankmuseum.org
web: www.tankmuseum.org
dir: off A352 or A35, follow brown tank signs from Bere Regis & Wool

The Tank Museum houses the world's best collection of tanks. From the first tank ever built to the modern Challenger II, the Museum houses examples from all over the world. This definitive collection comprises of over 250 vehicles dating back to 1909. The Tank Museum is the only place where many of these rare and historic vehicles can be seen. You will come face to face with tanks that have seen action in all the major wars of the 20th century. There are plenty of live action displays all year, please see website for details.

Times Open all year, daily 10-5; (Aug until 8 wkdays). Closed 24-26 Dec & 1 Jan **Fees** £11 (ch 5-16 £7.50, concessions £9). Family saver ticket (2ad+2ch) £30 or (1ad+3ch) £27. Group rates available* **Facilities** 🅿 Ⓟ ☕ 🍴 licensed ⛩ (indoor & outdoor) ♿ (fully accessible) toilets for disabled (wheelchairs available) shop 🚫🐕

BROWNSEA ISLAND Map 3 SZ08

Brownsea Island

BH13 7EE
☎ 01202 707744 📠 01202 701635
e-mail: brownseaisland@nationaltrust.org.uk
web: www.nationaltrust.org.uk
dir: located in Poole Harbour

Peaceful island of woodland, wetland and heath with a rich diversity of wildlife. The island is most famous for its rare red squirrels and as the site of the first experimental Scout camp held by Lord Baden-Powell in 1907.

Times Open 13 Mar-Oct, daily, 10-5 (13-26 Mar boats from Sandbanks only, 27-31 Mar full boat service from Poole Quay & Sandbanks)* **Facilities** licensed (outdoor) (partly accessible) (countryside property with rough terrain in places. Contact ferry operators to discuss carrying of wheelchairs on boats) toilets for disabled (Braille guide, DVD, tractor trailor service) shop

CANFORD CLIFFS Map 4 SZ08

Compton Acres Gardens

164 Canford Cliffs Rd BH13 7ES
☎ 01202 700778 📠 01202 707537
e-mail: events@comptonacres.co.uk
web: www.comptonacres.co.uk
dir: on B3065, follow brown tourist signs

The ten acres of Compton Acres incorporate Japanese and Italian gardens, rock and water gardens, and heather gardens. There are fine views over Poole Harbour and the Purbeck Hills. The beautiful wooded valley is an amazing place to explore the wide range of plants. The Italian garden was used as a location in Stanley Kubrick's 1975 movie, *Barry Lyndon*. There is also a model railway, restaurants, a tea room, and a craft shop.

Times Open Apr-Oct 9-dusk, Nov-Mar 10-4 (last entry 1hr before close). Closed 25-26 Dec* **Facilities** Ⓟ licensed (fully accessible) toilets for disabled shop

CHRISTCHURCH Map 4 SZ19

Christchurch Castle & Norman House FREE

web: www.english-heritage.org.uk
dir: near Christchurch Priory

Set on the river bank, the ruins of this Norman keep and constable's house date back to the 12th-century.

Times Open at any reasonable time **Facilities**

Red House Museum & Gardens FREE

Quay Rd BH23 1BU
☎ 01202 482860 📠 01202 481924
e-mail: paul.willis@hants.gov.uk
web: www.hants.gov.uk/museum/redhouse
dir: follow brown tourist signs from Christchurch, Red House is on corner of Quay Rd

A museum with plenty of variety, featuring local history and archaeology, displayed in a beautiful Georgian house. There's an excellent costume collection, some Arthur Romney-Green furniture and gardens with a woodland walk and herb garden. Regularly changing temporary exhibitions include contemporary art and crafts, plus historical displays. The museum celebrates its 60th anniversary in 2011.

Times Open Tue-Sat 10-5, Sun 2-5 (last admission 4.30). Open BHs (spring & summer) Closed 25 Dec-1 Jan & Good Fri. **Facilities** Ⓟ (partly accessible) (ground floor and gardens accessible) toilets for disabled (hearing loop in reception only) shop

CORFE CASTLE Map 3 SY98

Corfe Castle

BH20 5EZ
☎ 01929 481294 📠 01929 477067
e-mail: corfecastle@nationaltrust.org.uk
web: www.nationaltrust.org.uk
dir: follow A351 from Wareham to Swanage. Corfe Castle approx 5m

Built in Norman times, the castle was added to by King John. It was defended during the Civil War by Lady Bankes, who surrendered after a stout resistance. Parliament ordered the demolition of the castle, and today it is one of the most impressive ruins in England. Please ring for details of special events.

Times Open all year, daily Mar & Oct 10-5; Apr-Sep 10-6; Nov-Feb 10-4 (last admission 30 mins before closing). Closed 25-26 Dec* **Facilities** Ⓟ licensed (partly accessible) (steep, uneven cobbled paths & steps, wheelchair access restricted to Outer Bailey only) toilets for disabled (Braille/large print guide, menu) shop

Corfe Castle Museum

West St BH20 5HA
☎ 01929 480666
e-mail: steven.hitchins@gmail.com
dir: to side of church on left of West St upon leaving village square

The tiny, rectangular building was partly rebuilt in brick after a fire in 1780, and is the smallest town hall building in England. It has old village relics, and dinosaur footprints 130 million years old. The Ancient Order of Marblers meets here each Shrove Tuesday.

Times Open all year, Apr-Oct, daily 9.30-6; Nov-Mar, wknds & Xmas hols 10-5 **Fees** Donations welcome **Facilities** Ⓟ (fully accessible)

ENGLAND

DORCHESTER Map 3 SY69

Dinosaur Museum

Icen Way DT1 1EW
☎ 01305 269880 📠 01305 268885
e-mail: info@thedinosaurmuseum.com
web: www.thedinosaurmuseum.com
dir: off A35 into Dorchester, museum in town centre just off High East St

Britain's award-winning museum devoted to dinosaurs has a fascinating mixture of fossils, skeletons, life-size reconstructions and interactive displays such as the 'feelies', colour box and parasaurlophus sound. There are multi-media presentations providing an all-round family attraction with something new each year. There is a Great Dinosaur Easter Egg Hunt every Easter weekend.

Times Open all year, daily 9.30-5.30; Nov-Mar 10-4.30. Closed 24-26 Dec **Fees** £6.95 (ch £5.50, under 4's free, concessions £5.95). Family ticket £22.50* **Facilities** Ⓟ ♿ (partly accessible) (ground floor only accessible) (many low level displays) shop

Dorset County Museum — 2 FOR 1

High West St DT1 1XA
☎ 01305 262735 📠 01305 257180
e-mail: enquiries@dorsetcountymuseum.org
web: www.dorsetcountymuseum.org
dir: off A354 signed Dorchester, attraction on right half way up main street

Displays cover prehistoric and Roman times, including sites such as Maiden Castle, and there's a gallery on Dorset writers with sections on the poet William Barnes, Thomas Hardy (with a reconstruction of his study), and 20th-century writers. Also geology, local wildlife and social history are explored in the museum. The Jurassic Coast geology gallery was opened by Sir David Attenborough in summer 2006.

Times Open Apr-Oct, Mon-Sat 10-5; Nov-Mar 10-4* **Fees** £6.50 (up to 2 accompanied ch free, additional ch £2, concessions £5)* **Facilities** Ⓟ ♿ (partly accessible) (access via lift to Geology Gallery on 1st floor) toilets for disabled (free entry for disabled visitors, ramp, audio commentary) shop ⊗

Hardy's Cottage

Higher Bockhampton DT2 8QJ
☎ 01305 262366
e-mail: hardyscottage@nationaltrust.org.uk
web: www.nationaltrust.org.uk
dir: 3m NE of Dorchester, 0.5m S of A35. Turn off A35 at Kingston Maurward rdbt towards Stinsford and Bockhampton. Left onto Bockhampton Ln, signed to Hardy's Cottage

The small cob and thatch cottage where novelist and poet Thomas Hardy was born in 1840 and from where he would walk six miles to school in Dorchester every day. It was built by his great-grandfather and is little altered since. The interior has been furnished by the Trust. It was here that he wrote his early novels *Under the Greenwood Tree* and *Far from the Madding Crowd*. It has a charming cottage garden.

Times Open Apr-Oct, Sun-Thu 11-5* **Facilities** Ⓟ (parking by arrangement, large print/Braille guide) shop ⊗ ✤

The Keep Military Museum — 2 FOR 1

The Keep, Bridport Rd DT1 1RN
☎ 01305 264066 📠 01305 250373
e-mail: info@keepmilitarymuseum.org
web: www.keepmilitarymuseum.org
dir: near top of High West St leading out of town towards Bridport

Three hundred years of military history, with displays on the Devon Regiment, Dorset Regiment, Dorset Militia and Volunteers, the Queen's Own Dorset Yeomanry, and Devonshire and Dorset Regiment (from 1958). The Museum uses modern technology, interactive and creative displays to tell the stories of the Infantry, Cavalry and Artillerymen.

Times Open Apr-Sep, Mon-Sat 9.30-5; Oct-Mar, Tue-Fri 10-4.30 (last admission 1 hour before close). Closed 2 wks at Xmas & New Year **Fees** £6 (ch £2, under 8 free, pen £4). Family £13* **Facilities** 🅟 Ⓟ ♿ (partly accessible) (wheelchairs cannot access roof) toilets for disabled (lift availble to 3 floors) shop ⊗

Maiden Castle — FREE

DT1 9PR
web: www.english-heritage.org.uk
dir: 2m S of Dorchester, access off A354, N of bypass

The Iron Age fort ranks among the finest in Britain. It covers 47 acres, and has daunting earthworks, with a complicated defensive system around the entrances. One of its main purposes may well have been to protect grain from marauding bands. The first single-rampart fort dates from around 700BC, and by 100BC the earthworks covered the whole plateau. It was finally overrun by Roman troops in AD43.

Times Open at any reasonable time **Facilities** 🅟 ⌗

Teddy Bear Museum

High East St & Salisbury St DT1 1JU
☎ 01305 266040 📠 01305 268885
e-mail: info@teddybearmuseum.co.uk
web: www.teddybearmuseum.co.uk
dir: off A35, museum in town centre near Dinosaur Museum

Meet Edward Bear and his extended family of people-sized bears. See them relaxing and busying themselves in their Edwardian-style house. From the earliest teddies of 100 years ago to today's TV favourites, they are all on display in this family museum.

Times Open daily, 10-5 (4.30 in winter). Closed 24-26 Dec **Fees** £5.75 (ch £4, under 4's free, concessions £5). Family £18* **Facilities** Ⓟ shop ⊗

Tutankhamun Exhibition

High West St DT1 1UW
☎ 01305 269571 🖷 01305 268885
e-mail: info@tutankhamun-exhibition.co.uk
web: www.tutankhamun-exhibition.co.uk
dir: off A35 into Dorchester town centre

The exhibition recreates the excitement of one of the world's greatest discoveries of ancient treasure. A reconstruction of the tomb and recreations of its treasures are displayed. The superbly preserved mummified body of the boy king can be seen, wonderfully recreated in every detail. Facsimiles of some of the most famous treasures, including the golden funerary mask and the harpooner can be seen in the final gallery.

Times Open all year daily, Apr-Oct, 9.30-5.30; Nov-Mar, wkdays 9.30-5, wknds 10-4.30. Closed 24-26 Dec* **Fees** £6.95 (ch £5.50, under 5 free, concessions £5.95). Family ticket £22.50* **Facilities** Ⓟ ♿ (fully accessible) shop ⊗

MINTERNE MAGNA — **Map 3 ST60**

Minterne Gardens — 2 FOR 1

DT2 7AU
☎ 01300 341370 🖷 01300 341747
e-mail: enquiries@minterne.co.uk
web: www.minterne.co.uk
dir: 2m N of Cerne Abbas on A352

Landscaped in the manner of 'Capability' Brown in the 18th century, Minterne's unique garden has been described by Simon Jenkins as "a corner of paradise". 20 wild woodland acres abound with magnolias, rhododendrons and eucryphias, providing a new vista at each turn, with small lakes, streams and cascades. Over 200 maples and acers provide stunning autumn colouring. Home to the Churchill and Digby families for 350 years, the house is open for organised groups only.

Times Open Mar-9 Nov, daily 10-6 **Fees** £5 (accompanied ch free up to 12) **Facilities** 🅟 ⛩ (outdoor)

ORGANFORD — **Map 3 SY99**

Farmer Palmer's Farm Park

BH16 6EU
☎ 01202 622022 🖷 01202 622182
e-mail: info@farmerpalmers.co.uk
web: www.farmerpalmers.co.uk
dir: From Poole, just off A35 straight over rdbt past Bakers Arms, signed on left, take 2nd turn, 0.5m after rdbt

Family owned and run Farmer Palmers has been specially designed for families with children 8 years and under. Many activities include meeting and learning about the animals, climbing the straw mountain, going for a tractor trailer ride and exercising in the soft play area. A fun and busy day for the family.

Times Open 5 Feb-26 Mar, daily 10-4; 27 Mar-22 Oct, daily 10-5.30; 23 Oct-18 Dec, daily 10-4. Closed 19 Dec-4 Jan **Fees** 5 Feb-26 Mar £4.15 (ch £4.15, 2 yr olds £1.50, pen £3.45). 27 Mar-22 Oct £4.50 (ch £4.50, 2 yr olds £1.80, pen £3.95). 40% discount for groups. Please check prices before visit **Facilities** 🅟 Ⓟ ☕ 🍴 licensed ⛩ (indoor & outdoor) ♿ (partly accessible) (woodland walk & outside animal pen not level) toilets for disabled (ramps & woodland walk) shop ⊗

POOLE — **Map 3 SZ09**

Poole Museum — FREE

4 High St BH15 1BW
☎ 01202 262600 🖷 01202 262622
e-mail: museums@poole.gov.uk
web: www.boroughofpoole.com/museums
dir: off Poole Quay

After major redevelopment the museum opens its doors again. The museum tells the story of Poole's history, including the Studland Bay wreck and trade with Newfoundland with displays and hands-on activities.

Times Open 6 Apr-1 Nov, Mon-Sat 10-5, Sun 12-5. Closed 25-26 Dec* **Facilities** Ⓟ ☕ ♿ (partly accessible) (Scaplen's Court not accessible) toilets for disabled shop ⊗

PORTLAND — **Map 3 SY67**

Portland Castle

Castleton DT5 1AZ
☎ 01305 820539 🖷 01305 860853
web: www.english-heritage.org.uk
dir: overlooking Portland harbour

Visit one of Henry VIII's finest coastal forts, in use right up to World War II. Home to the Wrens and scene of the US troops' embarkation for the D-Day invasion in 1944. Explore the Captain's House and Gardens.

Times Open Apr-Jun & Sep, daily 10-5; Jul-Aug, daily 10-6; Oct, daily 10-4. Closed Nov-Mar **Fees** £4.20 (ch £2.10, concessions £3.60). Family ticket £10.50. Prices and opening times are subject to change in March 2011. Please call 0870 333 1181 for the most up to date prices and opening times when planning your visit **Facilities** 🅟 ☕ toilets for disabled shop ⊗ #

PORTLAND *continued*

Portland Museum

2 FOR 1

217 Wakeham DT5 1HS
☎ 01305 821804
e-mail: portlandmuseum@gmail.com
web: www.portlandmuseum.co.uk
dir: A354, through Fortuneswell to Portland Heights Hotel, then English Heritage signs

Avice's cottage in Thomas Hardy's book *The Well-Beloved*, this building is now a museum of local and historical interest, with varied displays. Regular temporary exhibitions are held. The adjoining Marie Stopes cottage houses shows a display of the maritime and local history while the Avice's cottage tells the history of Portland Stone and the Jurassic coast. Exhibitions and events throughout the year. Shop and refreshments available on site. Contact for details.

Times Open daily Jul-Aug, 11-4.30; Sep-Oct, Fri-Tue 11-4.30.; Nov-19 Dec, open wknds only 11-4.30* **Fees** £2.50 (ch under 16 free, concessions £1.50)* **Facilities** Ⓟ ⛩ (outdoor) ♿ (partly accessible) (access to ground floor areas) shop ⊗

SHAFTESBURY — Map 3 ST82

Shaftesbury Abbey Museum & Garden

2 FOR 1

Park Walk SP7 8JR
☎ 01747 852910 📠 01747 852910
e-mail: user@shaftesburyabbey.fsnet.co.uk
web: www.shaftesburyheritage.org.uk
dir: Follow signs to town centre parking. Take passage way to the Abbey, located alongside King Alfred's Restaurant in town centre, Park Walk

The Abbey at Shaftesbury was part of a nunnery founded by King Alfred in 888. Patronage and pilgrims to the shrine of St Edward helped to make the abbey both rich and famous. It became one of the wealthiest in the country but was destroyed during the Dissolution in 1539. The excavated ruins show the foundations of the abbey church. The story is told through an audio guide and the use of carved stone and medieval floor tiles and illustrations from ancient manuscripts. Please visit the website for event listings.

Times Open Apr-Oct, daily, 10-5* **Fees** £2.50 (ch £1, concessions £2). Please ask for more information on the new joint ticket which also allows entry into 'Gold Hill Museum & Garden'* **Facilities** Ⓟ ♿ (partly accessible) (parts of garden not accessible) toilets for disabled (large print guides, audio tour, interactive display) shop

SHERBORNE — Map 3 ST61

Sherborne Castle

New Rd DT9 5NR
☎ 01935 813182 (office) & 812072 (castle)
📠 01935 816727
e-mail: enquiries@sherbornecastle.com
web: www.sherbornecastle.com
dir: off A30/A352, 0.5m SE of Sherborne, follow brown signs

Built by Sir Walter Raleigh in 1594, Sherborne Castle has been the home of the Digby family since 1617. Prince William of Orange was entertained here in 1688, and George III visited in 1789. Splendid collections of art, furniture and porcelain are on show in the Castle. Lancelot 'Capability' Brown created the lake in 1753 and 30 acres of beautiful gardens and grounds surround it. Special events include a country fair, classic car shows, outdoor theatre, music and sports events and fireworks. Contact for details.

Times Open Apr-Oct, Tue-Thu, Sat-Sun & BH Mon 11-4.30 (last admission 4.30) Castle interior open from 2 on Sat* **Fees** £9.50 (concessions £9). Gardens only £5 (ch under 15 free, max 4 ch per adult). Party 15+ £8. Helpers of wheelchair users & blind visitors admitted free* **Facilities** Ⓟ Ⓟ ☕ ⛩ (outdoor) ♿ (partly accessible) (access to ground floor only of castle) toilets for disabled (Braille guide book) shop

Sherborne Museum

Abbey Gate House, Church Ln DT9 3BP
☎ 01935 812252
e-mail: info@sherbornemuseum.co.uk
web: www.sherbornemuseum.co.uk
dir: From bottom of Cheap St, walk through Church Ln towards Abbey, museum on left

The museum features a model of Sherborne's original Norman castle, as well as a fine Victorian doll's house and other domestic and agricultural bygones. There are also items of local geological, natural history and archaeological interest, including Roman material. The Sherborne Missal, one of the greatest medieval manuscripts, can be seen using the latest digital technology which enables the visitor to 'turn the pages' of the manuscript with the sweep of a hand - with touch, zoom and audio facilities.

Times Open Apr-7 Nov, Tue-Sat 10.30-4.30* **Fees** £1 (ch, concessions & members free)* **Facilities** Ⓟ ♿ (partly accessible) (Ground floor only accessible, one to one visits can be arranged) toilets for disabled (video of upper floor displays) shop ⊗

Sherborne Old Castle

Castleton D19 3SA
☎ 01935 812730
web: www.english-heritage.org.uk
dir: 0.5m E off B3145

The ruins of this early 12th-century castle are a testament to the 16 days Oliver Cromwell's army took to capture it during the Civil War.

Times Open Apr-Jun & Sep, daily 10-5; Jul-Aug, daily 10-6; Oct, daily 10-4. Closed Nov-Mar **Fees** £3.20 (ch £1.60, concessions £2.70). Joint ticket with Sherborne Castle grounds £7. Prices and opening times are subject to change in March 2011. Please call 0870 333 1181 for the most up to date prices and opening times when planning your visit **Facilities** (partly accessible) (access to castle and grounds by sloping timber bridge, some steps) toilets for disabled shop

SWANAGE — Map 3 SZ07

Swanage Railway

Station House BH19 1HB
☎ 01929 425800 01929 426680
e-mail: info@swanage-railway.co.uk
web: www.swanagerailway.co.uk
dir: signed from A351

The railway from Swanage to Wareham was closed in 1972, and in 1976 the Swanage Railway took possession and have gradually restored the line, which now runs for 6 miles, passing the ruins of Corfe Castle. Steam trains run daily April to October, as well as week-ends most of the year. Special events throughout the year including Santa Specials.

Times Open every wknd ex Jan, daily Apr-Oct* **Fees** Swanage-Corfe/Norden £9 return (ch £7 return). Family ticket £26. Day Rover £14.50 (ch £11)* **Facilities** licensed (outdoor) (fully accessible) toilets for disabled (disabled persons coach) shop

TOLPUDDLE — Map 3 SY79

Tolpuddle Martyrs Museum FREE

DT2 7EH
☎ 01305 848237 01305 848237
e-mail: jpickering@tuc.org.uk
web: www.tolpuddlemartyrs.org.uk
dir: off A35 from Dorchester Tolpuddle signed at Troytown turn off. Continue on old A35. If coming from the East, the museum has Brown Heritage sign

One dawn, in the bitter February of 1834, six Tolpuddle farm labourers were arrested after forming a trade union. A frightened squire's trumped up charge triggered one of the most celebrated stories in the history of human rights. That dawn arrest created the Tolpuddle Martyrs, who were punished with transportation as convicts to Australia. Packed with illustrative displays, this interactive exhibition tells the Tolpuddle Martyrs' story. Every summer on the weekend of the third Sunday in July, the museum holds the Tolpuddle Martyrs Festival. The weekend combines celebration with tradition offering traditional and contemporary music as well as many other attractions.

Times Open all year, Apr-Oct, Tue-Sat 10-5, Sun 11-5; Nov-Mar, Thu-Sat 10-4, Sun 11-4. Also open BHs. Closed 19 Dec-4 Jan **Facilities** (outdoor) (fully accessible) toilets for disabled (parking, interactive computers at wheelchair height) shop

WEST LULWORTH — Map 3 SY88

Lulworth Castle & Park

BH20 5QS
☎ 0845 450 1054 01929 400563
e-mail: estate.office@lulworth.com
web: www.lulworth.com
dir: from Wareham, W on A352 for 1m, left onto B3070 to E Lulworth, follow tourist signs

Glimpse life below stairs in the restored kitchen, and enjoy glorious views from the top of the tower of this historic castle set in beautiful parkland. The 18th-century chapel is the first Catholic chapel built in England after the Reformation. Children will enjoy the animal farm, play area, indoor activity room and pitch and putt. Visit website for details of future events.

Times Open Castle & Park: all year, Sun-Fri, Sat before Etr, 3 Apr & 18 Sep. Summer 10.30-6, winter 10.30-4. Entrance to Lulworth Castle House, the Weld family home, on Heritage Open Days 9 & 10 Sep or by appointment. Closed 3-16 Jan, 29 Jul-2 Aug & 24-25 Dec* **Facilities** (outdoor) (partly accessible) (access limited in castle due to grade one listing) toilets for disabled (electric scooters & wheelchairs for hire) shop

ENGLAND

WEYMOUTH Map 3 SY67

RSPB Nature Reserve Radipole Lake

The Swannery Car Park DT4 7TZ
☎ 01305 778313 📠 01305 778313
web: www.rspb.org.uk
dir: close to seafront & railway station

Covering 222 acres, the Reserve offers firm paths, a hide and a visitor centre. Several types of warblers, mute swans, gadwalls, teals and great crested grebes may be seen, and the visitor centre has viewing windows overlooking the lake. Phone for details of special events.

Times Open daily 9-5* **Facilities** toilets for disabled shop

Weymouth Sea Life Adventure Park & Marine Sanctuary

Lodmoor Country Park DT4 7SX
☎ 0871 423 2110 & 01305 761070 📠 01305 760165
e-mail: slcweymouth@merlinentertainments.biz
web: www.sealifeeurope.com
dir: on A353

A unique mix of indoor and outdoor attractions set in 7 acres. The park offers a day of fun, bringing you face to face with penguins, otters, seals and much more.

Times Open all year, daily from 10. Closed 25 Dec* **Facilities** licensed (indoor & outdoor) (fully accessible) toilets for disabled shop

WIMBORNE Map 3 SZ09

Kingston Lacy

BH21 4EA
☎ 01202 883402 (Mon-Fri) 📠 01202 882402
e-mail: kingstonlacy@nationaltrust.org.uk
web: www.nationaltrust.org.uk
dir: 1.5m W of Wimborne, B3082

Kingston Lacy House was the home of the Bankes family for over 300 years. The original house is 17th century, but in the 1830s was given a stone façade. The Italian marble staircase, Venetian ceiling, treasures from Spain and an Egyptian obelisk were also added. There are outstanding pictures by Titian, Rubens, Velasquez, Reynolds and Van Dyck. No photography is allowed in the house.

Times Open: House 13 Mar-Oct, Wed-Sun, 11-4. Garden & Park 13 Mar-Oct, daily, 10.30-6* **Fees** House, Garden & Park £12 (ch £6) Family £30. Park & Gardens £6 (ch £3) Family £15* **Facilities** licensed (outdoor) (partly accessible) (ground floor accessible, with touch screen virtual tour available) toilets for disabled (wheelchairs, large print & Braille guides, parking) shop

The Priest's House Museum and Garden

23-27 High St BH21 1HR
☎ 01202 882533
e-mail: priestshouse@eastdorset.gov.uk
web: www.priest-house.co.uk
dir: opposite The Minster

An award-winning local history museum, set in an historic house. The 17th-century hall, Georgian parlour and working Victorian kitchen reveal the history of the building and its inhabitants. The museum houses exhibitions on East Dorset from prehistoric to modern times. There are regular special exhibitions and a walled garden to explore.

Times Open Apr-Oct, Mon-Sat 10-4.30 **Fees** £3.50 (ch £1, concesssions £2.50). Family £8.50. Season ticket £10 **Facilities** (outdoor) (partly accessible) (ground floor & garden) (hands on archaeology & childhood galleries) shop

WOOL Map 3 SY88

Monkey World-Ape Rescue Centre

Longthorns BH20 6HH
☎ 01929 462537 & 0800 456600 📠 01929 405414
e-mail: apes@monkeyworld.org
web: www.monkeyworld.org
dir: 1m N of Wool on Bere Regis road, follow brown tourist signs

Set up in order to rescue monkeys and apes from abuse and illegal smuggling, Monkey World houses over 230 primates in 65 acres of Dorset woodland. There is the largest group of chimpanzees outside Africa, as well as orang-utans, gibbons, woolly monkeys, lemurs, macaques and marmosets. Those wishing to help the centre continue in its quest to rescue primates from lives of misery may like to take part in the adoption scheme, which includes free admission to the park for one year. There are keeper talks every half hour, and the south's largest Great Ape Play Area for kids.

Times Open daily 10-5; Jul-Aug 10-6 (last admission 1hr before closing). Closed 25 Dec* **Fees** £10.75 (ch 3-15, senior, disabled & carer £7.50, students £9). Family ticket (1ad+2ch) £23, (2ad+2ch) £33. Group rates available* **Facilities** (indoor & outdoor) (partly accessible) (woodland walk uneaven surface) toilets for disabled (sensory statues, motorised scooters, wheelchairs, swings) shop

CO DURHAM

Durham Cathedral

BARNARD CASTLE Map 12 NZ01

Barnard Castle

DL12 9AT

☎ 01833 638212

web: www.english-heritage.org.uk

Imposing remains of one of England's largest medieval castles perched high on a rugged escarpment above the banks of the River Tees.

Times Open all year, Apr-Sep, daily 10-6; Oct-Mar, Sat & Sun 10-4. Closed 24-26 Dec & 1 Jan **Fees** £4.20 (ch £2.10, concessions £3.60). Prices and opening times are subject to change in March 2011. Please call 0870 333 1181 for the most up to date prices and opening times when planning your visit **Facilities** shop ⌗

The Bowes Museum **2 FOR 1**

DL12 8NP

☎ 01833 690606 📠 01833 637163

e-mail: info@thebowesmuseum.org.uk

web: www.thebowesmuseum.org.uk

dir: in Barnard Castle, just off A66

John and Joséphine Bowes founded The Bowes Museum over 100 years ago. The magnificent building houses a collection of treasures from fine and decorative art to major temporary exhibitions of international quality and interest. The icon of the collection is the Silver Swan, a unique life-size, musical automaton which plays every day. There are also works by El Greco, Goya and Canaletto. The Café Bowes, shop and beautiful grounds add to a wonderful day out for all.

Times Open daily 10-5. Closed 25-26 Dec & 1 Jan* **Fees** £8 (ch under 16 free, concessions £7)* **Facilities** Ⓟ ⓟ ☕ ⛩ (outdoor) ♿ (fully accessible) toilets for disabled (lift, ramped entrance, reserved parking, audio guide/loop) shop ⊗

Egglestone Abbey **FREE**

DL12 8QN

web: www.english-heritage.org.uk

dir: 1m S of Barnard Castle on minor road off B6277

The scant, but charming remains of a small medieval monastery. The picturesque ruins of Egglestone are located above a bend in the River Tees. A large part of the church can be seen, as can remnants of monastic buildings.

Times Open daily, 10-6 **Facilities** Ⓟ ⌗

BEAMISH Map 12 NZ25

Beamish Museum

DH9 0RG

☎ 0191 370 4000 📠 0191 370 4001

e-mail: museum@beamish.org.uk

web: www.beamish.org.uk

dir: off A693 & A6076. Signed from A1M junct 63

Set in 300 acres of countryside, award-winning Beamish recreates life in the early 1800s and 1900s. Costumed staff welcome visitors to a 1913 town street, colliery village, farm and railway station; a re-creation of how people lived and worked. Ride on early electric tramcars, take a ride on a replica of an 1825 steam railway and visit Pockerley Manor where a yeoman farmer and his family would have lived.

Times Open Apr-Oct, daily 10-5; Oct-Mar 10-4 (last admission 3). Closed Mon, Fri & 25 Dec. Christmas at Beamish 20 Nov-2 Jan 10-4* **Fees** Summer £16 (ch £10, concessions £13). Winter £6 (ch & concessions £6). Winter visit is centered on town, colliery village & tramway only, other areas are closed. Christmas at Beamish £10 (ch £8)* **Facilities** Ⓟ ☕ ⛩ (outdoor) ♿ (partly accessible) (some 1st floor areas inaccessible, some ground floor areas have steeped access & narrow doorways) toilets for disabled (not ideal for wheelchairs, assistance recommended) shop ⊗

ENGLAND

BISHOP AUCKLAND Map 8 NZ22

Auckland Castle

DL14 7NR
☎ 01388 602576 📠 01388 605264
e-mail: secretary@bishopdunelm.co.uk
web: www.auckland-castle.co.uk
dir: follow signs to Market Place then brown tourist sign for Castle

Serving as the principal county residence of the Prince Bishops since the 12th century, Auckland Castle is the home of the Bishop of Durham. Built on a promontory overlooking the River Wear and the Roman Fort of Binchester, the Castle has been added to and adapted over the centuries. St Peter's Chapel houses many of the treasures of past Bishops. Special events take place throughout the year, please contact for details.

Times Open Etr Mon-Jun, Sun & Mon 2-5; Jul-Aug, Sun-Mon & Wed 11-5. Sep, Sun-Mon 2-5 **Fees** £4 (ch under 12 free, concessions £3)* **Facilities** Ⓟ Ⓟ ♿ (fully accessible) toilets for disabled (chair walker available by prior arrangement) shop

BOWES Map 12 NY91

Bowes Castle FREE

DL12 9LD
web: www.english-heritage.org.uk
dir: in Bowes village, just off A66

Massive ruins of Henry II's tower keep, three storeys high, set within the earthworks of a Roman fort and overlooking the valley of the River Greta.

Times Open at any reasonable time **Facilities**

COWSHILL Map 12 NY84

Killhope The North of England Lead Mining Museum 2 FOR 1

DL13 1AR
☎ 01388 537505 📠 01388 537617
e-mail: info@killhope.org.uk
web: www.killhope.org.uk
dir: beside A689 midway between Stanhope & Alston

Equipped with hard hats and lamps, you can explore the working conditions of Victorian lead miners. The lead mine and 19th-century crushing mill have been restored to look as they would have done in the 1870s, and the 34ft water wheel has been restored to working order. There is also a visitor centre and mineral exhibition, a woodland walk, children's play area and red squirrel and bird hides. Please ring for information on workshops and events.

Times Open Apr-Oct, daily 10.30-5 **Fees** Mine & Site: £7 (ch £4, concessions £6.50). Family £21. Site: £5 (ch £2, concessions £4.50). Family £13* **Facilities** Ⓟ (indoor & outdoor) ♿ (partly accessible) (accessible hide for wildlife viewing, Visitor Centre fully accessible, parts of Victorian site rough grounds) toilets for disabled (electric scooter, sympathetic hearing scheme) shop

DARLINGTON Map 8 NZ21

Head of Steam-Darlington Railway Museum 2 FOR 1

North Road Station DL3 6ST
☎ 01325 460532 📠 01325 287746
e-mail: headofsteam@darlington.gov.uk
web: www.head-of-steam.co.uk
dir: 0.75m N, off A167

Housed in the carefully restored North Road Station, this museum's prize exhibit is *Locomotion No 1*, which pulled the first passenger train on the Stockton to Darlington railway and was built by Robert Stephenson & Co in 1825. Several other steam locomotives are also shown, together with models and other exhibits relating to the Stockton and Darlington and the North Eastern Railway companies.

Times Open Oct-Mar, Tue-Sun 11-3.30; Apr-Sep, Tue-Sun 10-4* **Fees** £4.95 (ch 6-16 £3, concessions £3.75). Family ticket (2ad+4ch) £10* **Facilities** Ⓟ Ⓟ (outdoor) ♿ (fully accessible) toilets for disabled (hearing loop at reception) shop

DURHAM Map 12 NZ24

Crook Hall & Gardens 2 FOR 1

Sidegate DH1 5SZ
☎ 0191 384 8028 📠 0191 386 4521
e-mail: info@kbacrookhall.co.uk
web: www.crookhallgardens.co.uk
dir: In city centre

Grade I listed medieval manor house with attractive gardens. A few minutes' walk from the city centre and close to the River Wear. Special events include Fairytale Week in May/June, Hallowe'en, Teddy Bear Day and Easter and Christmas events.

Times Open 17 Apr-Sep, Sun-Thu 11-5 **Fees** £6.50 (concessions £5.50, ch £5). Family ticket (2ad & 2ch) £19* **Facilities** Ⓟ Ⓟ (outdoor) ♿ (partly accessible) shop

Durham Cathedral

DH1 3EH
☎ 0191 386 4266 📠 0191 386 4267
e-mail: enquiries@durhamcathedral.co.uk
web: www.durhamcathedral.co.uk
dir: A690 into city, follow signs to car parks

Founded in 1093 as a shrine to St Cuthbert, the cathedral is a remarkable example of Norman architecture, set in an impressive position high above the River Wear. A full programme of concerts takes place throughout the year, and there is a St Cuthbert's Day Procession in March (phone for details).

Times Open all year, Mon-Sat, 9.30-5; Sun, 12.30-5. During school summer holidays open until 8. Access restricted during services and events.* **Facilities** Ⓟ licensed ♿ (partly accessible) (some areas are not accessible to wheelchairs) toilets for disabled (large print guides, stair climbers) shop

ENGLAND

DURHAM *continued*

Durham Light Infantry Museum & Durham Art Gallery

Aykley Heads DH1 5TU
☎ 0191 384 2214 0191 386 1770
e-mail: dli@durham.gov.uk
web: www.durham.gov.uk/dli
dir: 0.5m N of City Centre on A691

The history of the Regiment is told in displays of artefacts, medals, uniforms and vehicles. The Art Gallery has a continuous programme of temporary exhibitions, and holds regular lectures and concerts.

Times Open all year, Apr-Oct, daily 10-5; Nov-Mar, daily 10-4. Closed 24-25 Dec **Fees** Annual Pass: £4.50 (ch £2.50, under 5's free, concessions £3.50) **Facilities** (outdoor) (fully accessible) toilets for disabled (wheelchair available, lift, ramps) shop

Finchale Priory — FREE

Brasside, Newton Hall DH1 5SH
☎ 0191 386 6528
web: www.english-heritage.org.uk
dir: 3m NE

Dating from the 13th-century, these beautiful priory ruins are in a wooded setting beside the River Wear.

Times Any reasonable time **Facilities** shop

Old Fulling Mill Museum of Archaeology — 2 FOR 1

The Banks DH1 3EB
☎ 0191 334 1823 0191 334 5694
e-mail: archaeology.museum@durham.ac.uk
web: www.dur.ac.uk/fulling.mill
dir: On river bank directly below Cathedral

Once a key part of Durham's cloth making industry, the Old Fulling Mill is now home to Durham University's Museum of Archaeology. The collections on display provide a fascinating insight into the rich heritage of the north east of England, as well as showcasing items from across Europe. Highlights include outstanding Roman collections together with Anglo-Saxon, Medieval and Tudor finds from Durham City and the local area. Up to date details of exhibitions and the lively programme of family activities at weekends and during school holidays can be found on the museum's website

Times Open Apr-Oct, daily 10-4; Nov-Mar, Fri-Mon 11.30-3.30 **Fees** £1 (ch & concessions 50p, students free). Family ticket £2.50 **Facilities** (partly accessible) (ground floor only accessible) (parking can be arranged in advance) shop

Oriental Museum — 2 FOR 1

University of Durham, Elvet Hill DH1 3TH
☎ 0191 334 5694 0191 334 5694
e-mail: oriental.museum@durham.ac.uk
web: www.dur.ac.uk/oriental.museum
dir: signed from A167 & A177

The Oriental Museum is the only museum in northern Britain dedicated solely to the art and archaeology of the Orient. The remarkable collections reveal to the visitor the history and prehistory of the great cultures of Asia, the Near and Middle East and North Africa. Highlights include one of the largest and finest Chinese collections in Europe and an ancient Egyptian collection of international importance.

Times Open Mon-Fri 10-5, wknds & BHs 12-5. Closed Xmas & New Year **Fees** £1.50 (concessions 75p, students in HE free). Family ticket £3.50 **Facilities** (outdoor) (fully accessible) toilets for disabled (lifts to all floors) shop

HARTLEPOOL Map 8 NZ53

Hartlepool's Maritime Experience

Maritime Av TS24 0XZ

☎ 01429 860077 & 523445 📠 01429 867332

e-mail: info@hartlepoolsmaritimeexperience.com

web: www.hartlepoolsmaritimeexperience.com

dir: from N A19 take A179 and follow signs for marina then historic quay. From S A19 take A689 and follow signs for marina then historic quay

Britain's maritime heritage is brought to life, with the sights and sounds of a 1800s quayside. Learn about the birth of the Royal Navy, and visit the Quayside shops, the admiral's house, Europe's oldest warship afloat - *HMS Trincomalee*, and the children's Maritime Adventure Centre. Other features include regular demonstrations of sword fighting, and cannon firing.

Times Open all year daily summer 10-5, winter 10.30-4. Closed 25-26 Dec & 1 Jan **Fees** £7.95 (ch £4.95, concessions £4.95-£5.95). Family ticket (2ad+3ch) £21. Prices valid until 31 Mar 2011, please check website for updates. Museum is free* **Facilities** licensed (outdoor) (partly accessible) (no lift to top deck of paddle steam ship. Lift on board HMS Trincomalee) toilets for disabled (all areas ramped or lift access, auto doors, parking) shop

LANGLEY PARK Map 12 NZ24

Diggerland

DH7 9TT

☎ 0871 227 7007 📠 09012 010300

e-mail: mail@diggerland.com

web: www.diggerland.com

dir: A1(M) junct 62. W & follow Consett signs. After 6m left at rdbt, signed Langley Park, then right into Riverside Industrial Estate

An adventure park with a difference, where kids of all ages can experience the thrills of driving real earth-moving equipment. Choose from various types of diggers and dumpers ranging from 1 ton to 8.5 tons. Supervised by an instructor, complete the Dumper Truck Challenge or dig for buried treasure. New rides include JCB Robots, Diggerland Dodgems, Go-karts, Landrover Safari and Spin Dizzy. Even under 5's can join in, with mum or dad's help.

Times Open 12 Feb-end Oct, 10-5, wknds BHs & school hols only (including half terms).* **Facilities** (fully accessible) toilets for disabled shop

SHILDON Map 8 NZ22

Locomotion: The National Railway Museum at Shildon

DL4 1PQ

☎ 01388 777999 📠 01388 771448

e-mail: locomotion@nrm.org.uk

web: www.nrm.org.uk/locomotion

dir: A1(M) junct 68, take A68 & A6072 to Shildon, attraction is 0.25m SE of town centre

Timothy Hackwood (1786-1850) was an important figure in the development of steam travel. He constructed *Puffing Billy* for William Hedley, ran Stephenson's Newcastle Works, and also became the first superintendent of the Stockton & Darlington Railway. Locomotion is one of the greatest changing railway collections of the North East; offering interactive displays, free school holiday activities and an exciting events programme. Star attractions include many vehicles from the National collection such as the Timothy Hackworth's pioneering locomotive *Sans Pareil*.

Times Open 29 Mar-31 Oct, daily 10-5 (except 3-31 Oct 10-4); Nov-3 Apr, Wed-Sun 10-4 (limited opening Mon-Tue). Closed 22 Dec-3 Jan* **Fees** Free admission but small charge for train rides* **Facilities** (indoor & outdoor) (fully accessible) toilets for disabled (bus available to transport guests, please contact) shop

STAINDROP Map 12 NZ12

Raby Castle

DL2 3AH

☎ 01833 660202 01833 660169

e-mail: admin@rabycastle.com

web: www.rabycastle.com

dir: on A688, Barnard Castle to Bishop Auckland road, 1m N of Staindrop

This dramatic 14th-century castle, built by the Nevills has been home to Lord Barnard's family since 1626. It has an impressive gateway, nine towers, a vast hall and an octagonal Victorian drawing room displaying one of the most striking interiors from the 19th century. Rooms contain fine furniture, impressive artworks and elaborate architecture. In the grounds are a deer park, large walled gardens, coach and carriage collections, a woodland adventure playground, a picnic area and gift shop.

Times Open May, Jun & Sep, Sun-Wed. Jul-Aug, open daily (ex Sat) 11-5, open BH wknds & Etr.* **Facilities** Ⓟ Ⓟ (outdoor) ♿ (partly accessible) (most of ground floor accessible, 40 steps in castle, walkways in garden) toilets for disabled (DVD interpretation) shop

TANFIELD Map 12 NZ15

Tanfield Railway

Old Marley Hill NE16 5ET

☎ 0191 388 7545 0191 387 4784

e-mail: tanfield@ingsoc.demon.co.uk

web: www.tanfield_railway.co.uk

dir: on A6076 1m S of Sunniside

A 3-mile working steam railway which is the oldest existing railway in the world. The Causey Arch, the first large railway bridge of its era, is the centrepiece of a deep wooded valley, with picturesque walks. You can ride in carriages that first saw use in Victorian times, and visit Marley Hill shed, the home of 35 engines; inside the shed you can see the stationary steam engine at work driving some of the vintage machine tools. The blacksmith is also often at work forging new parts for the restoration work. Special events are held throughout the year, please telephone for details.

Times Open all year, Summer daily 10-5; Winter daily 10-4. Trains: Sun & Summer BHs wknds; also Thu & Sat mid Jul-Aug. Santa's Specials Sat & Sun in Dec (booking essential). Mince pie specials Boxing Day* **Facilities** Ⓟ Ⓟ ♿ (partly accessible) toilets for disabled (all trains carry ramps for wheelchair access) shop

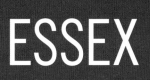

ESSEX

Lee Valley Park, Waltham Abbey

AUDLEY END Map 5 TL53

Audley End House & Gardens

CB11 4JF
☎ 01799 522842 📠 01799 521276
web: www.english-heritage.org.uk
dir: 1m W of Saffron Walden on B1383

Onc of thc most significant Jacobean houses in England with 31 opulent rooms on view. Set in a 'Capability' Brown landscaped park, with walled Victorian kitchen garden.

Times Open Apr-Sep, Wed-Sun & BH 11-5; Oct, Wed-Sun 11-4. House closed Nov-Mar (last entry 1hr before closing) **Fees** House & Gardens: £11.90 (ch £6, concessions £10.10). Family £29.80. Full estate £8.30 (ch £4.20, concessions £7.10). Family £20.70. Stables, Service Wing & Gardens not available on event days. Prices & opening times are subject to change in March 2011. Please call 0870 333 1181 for the most up to date prices and opening times **Facilities** Ⓟ ☕ ⛩ ♿ (partly accessible) (bridges either have a step or steep slope) toilets for disabled (4 wheelchairs, 4 motorised scooters book on 01799 522842) shop ⌗

BRENTWOOD Map 5 TQ69

Kelvedon Hatch Secret Nuclear Bunker

2 FOR 1

CM14 5TL
☎ 01277 364883 📠 01277 365260
e-mail: bunker@japar.demon.co.uk
web: www.secretnuclearbunker.co.uk
dir: on A128 at Kelvedon Hatch

Witness the three phases of the bunker's life. From its role with the RAF where the overall tactical controller could react to a nuclear attack from Britain's enemies, through to its role as Regional Government HQ, when there could have been up to 600 personnel, possibly including the Prime Minister, organising the survival of the civilian population in the aftermath of nuclear war. See for yourself the equipment and rooms needed to support the plotting of nuclear fall-out patterns. This is an all-weather, all-age group educational venue.

Times Open Mar-Oct, wkdays 10-4 wknds 10-5; Nov-Feb, Thu-Sun 10-4 **Fees** £6.50 (ch £4.50). Family ticket (2ad+2ch) £16 **Facilities** Ⓟ ☕ 🍽 licensed ⛩ (outdoor) ♿ (partly accessible) (top two floors accessible) toilets for disabled (stairlift, ramps) shop ⊗

CASTLE HEDINGHAM Map 5 TL73

Colne Valley Railway & Museum

Castle Hedingham Station CO9 3DZ
☎ 01787 461174
e-mail: info@colnevalleyrailway.co.uk
web: www.colnevalleyrailway.co.uk
dir: 4m NW of Halstead on A1017

Many former Colne Valley and Halstead railway buildings have been rebuilt here. Stock includes seven steam locomotives plus 80 other engines, carriages and wagons. Visitors can dine in style in restored Pullman carriages while travelling along the line. Please telephone for a free timetable and details of the many special events.

Times Open all year, daily 10-dusk. Steam days, rides from 12-4. Closed 23 Dec-1 Feb. Steam days every Sun and BH from Mothering Sun to end Oct, Wed of school summer hols & special events. Railway Farm Park open May-Sep. Phone 01787 461174 for timetable information or visit website for details.* **Facilities** Ⓟ ☕ 🍽 licensed ⛩ (outdoor) ♿ (partly accessible) (some steps) toilets for disabled (ramps for wheelchairs to get onto carriages) shop ⊗

Hedingham Castle

CO9 3DJ
☎ 01787 460261 📠 01787 461473
e-mail: mail@hedinghamcastle
web: www.hedinghamcastle.co.uk
dir: on B1508, 1m off A1017 Colchester/Cambridge. Follow brown heritage signs to Hedingham Castle

This impressive Norman castle was built in 1140. It was besieged by King John, visited by Henry VII, Henry VIII and Elizabeth I, and was home to the de Veres, Earls of Oxford, for over 500 years. During the summer months Hedingham's colourful heritage comes to life with a full programme of special events. There are medieval jousts and sieges with authentic living history displays and encampments. Please telephone for details.

Times Open Apr-28 Oct, Sun-Thu 10-5* **Facilities** Ⓟ ☕ ⛩ (outdoor) ♿ (partly accessible) (paved access) toilets for disabled shop ⊗

CHELMSFORD Map 5 TL70

RHS Garden Hyde Hall

Westerns Approach, Rettendon CM3 8AT
☎ 01245 402006 & 400256 📠 01245 402100
e-mail: suecarter@rhs.org.uk
web: www.rhs.org.uk
dir: from M25 junct 29 (signed A127 Southend) or A12 junct 17 (signed A130 signed Southend/Basildon). From A130 Rettendon Turnpike rdbt, follow tourist signs towards South Woodham Ferrers on A132. At Shaw Farm rdbt turn into Willow Grove/ Creephedge Lane

RHS Garden Hyde Hall is an oasis of calm and serenity and a visit to the 360-acre estate is unforgettable in any season. The developed area of the garden, in excess of 24 acres, demonstrates an eclectic range of inspirational horticultural styles, from the formality of clipped hedges to large swathes of naturalistic planting. Highlights include the Rose Garden, colour themed herbaceous borders, ponds, dry garden and developing woodland. A range of workshops and family fun events are run throughout the year, please see the website for details.

Times Open all year (ex 25 Dec) from 10, closing times vary with season - contact garden for details* **Fees** £7 (ch 6-16 £2.50, ch under 6 free)* **Facilities** Ⓟ ☕ 🍽 licensed ⛩ (outdoor) ♿ (partly accessible) (ramps and easy access to visitor centre and restaurant) toilets for disabled (manual wheelchairs for loan) shop ⊗

COGGESHALL Map 5 TL82

Paycocke's

West St CO6 1NS
☎ 01376 561305
web: www.nationaltrust.org.uk
dir: Signed from A120, on S side of West Street

This timber-framed house is a fine example of a medieval merchant's home. It was completed in about 1505 and has interesting carvings on the outside timbers, including the Paycocke trade sign. Inside there are further elaborate carvings and linenfold panelling. Behind the house is a pretty garden.

Times Open 5 Apr-11 Oct, Tue, Thu, Sun & BH Mon* **Facilities** Ⓟ ♿ (partly accessible) (Large print & Braille guide, photo album) ⊗ ✿

COLCHESTER Map 5 TL92

The Beth Chatto Gardens

Elmstead Market CO7 7DB
☎ 01206 822007 📠 01206 825933
e-mail: info@bethchatto.fsnet.co.uk
web: www.bethchatto.co.uk
dir: 5m E of Colchester on A133

For over 50 years Beth Chatto has worked on transforming acres of wasteland into beautifully landscaped gardens, where magnificent water, gravel and shaded oak gardens await you. See unusual plants grown in a variety of conditions or visit the extensive plant nursery.

Times Open all year, Mar-Oct, Mon-Sat 9-5, Sun 10-5; Nov-Feb, Mon-Sat 9-4, Sun 10-4* **Fees** £5 (accompanied ch under 14 free) **Facilities** Ⓟ ☕ ⛩ (outdoor) ♿ (partly accessible) (steep slope in garden) toilets for disabled ⊗

Colchester Castle Museum

Castle Park, High St CO1 1TJ
☎ 01206 282939 📠 01206 282925
e-mail: museums@colchester.gov.uk
web: www.colchestermuseums.org.uk
dir: at E end of High St

The largest Norman castle keep in Europe - built over the remains of the magnificent Roman Temple of Claudius which was destroyed by Boudicca in AD60. Colchester was the first capital of Roman Britain, and the archaeological collections are among the finest in the country. Please telephone or visit website for details of a range of events held throughout the year.

Times Open all year, Mon-Sat 10-5, Sun 11-5. Closed Xmas/New Year* **Facilities** Ⓟ ⛩ (indoor & outdoor) ♿ (partly accessible) (Roman vaults not accessible) toilets for disabled (touch stations, alternative tours) shop ⊗

Colchester Zoo

Stanway, Maldon Rd CO3 0SL
☎ 01206 331292 📠 01206 331392
e-mail: enquiries@colchester-zoo.co.uk
web: www.colchester-zoo.com
dir: turn off A12 onto A1124, follow elephant signs

One of England's finest zoos, Colchester Zoo has over 250 species of animal. Visitors can feed the elephants and giraffes themselves, and enjoy up to 50 daily displays. Enclosures include Spirit of Africa with the breeding group of African elephants, Playa Patagonia where sea lions swim above your head in a 24 metre underwater tunnel, Penguin Shores, Chimp World, and the Kingdom of the Wild, with giraffes, zebras, rhinos and Orangutan Forest. There is also an undercover soft play complex, two road trains, four adventure play areas, eating places and gift shops, all set in 60 acres of gardens.

Times Open all year, daily from 9.30. Last admission 5.30 (1hr before dusk out of season). Closed 25 Dec* **Fees** £13.99-£16.99 (ch £7.99-£9.99, seniors £9.99-£12.99). Prices vary according to season* **Facilities** Ⓟ ☕ 🍽 licensed ⛩ ♿ (partly accessible) (easy routes developed but zoo has hills) toilets for disabled (wheelchairs for hire) shop ⊗

ENGLAND

HADLEIGH Map 5 TQ88

Hadleigh Castle FREE

☎ 01760 755161
web: www.english-heritage.org.uk
dir: 0.75m S of A13

The subject of several of Constable's paintings, the castle has fine views of the Thames estuary. It is defended by ditches on three sides, and the north-east and south-east towers are still impressive.

Times Open at any reasonable time **Facilities** ⌗

HARWICH Map 5 TM23

Harwich Redoubt Fort 2 FOR 1

CO12 3TE
☎ 01255 503429 📠 01255 503429
e-mail: theharwichsociety@quista.net
web: www.harwich-society.com
dir: behind 29 Main Rd

The 180ft-diameter circular fort was built in 1808 in case of invasion by Napoleon. It has a dry moat and 8ft-thick walls, with 18 rooms for stores, ammunition and quarters for 300 men. The Redoubt is being restored by the Harwich Society, and contains three small museums. Ten guns can be seen on the battlements.

Times Open May-Aug, daily 10-4; Sep-Apr, Sun only 10-4 **Fees** £3 (accompanied ch free) **Facilities** Ⓟ ♿ (partly accessible) (ground floor only accessible) shop

LAYER MARNEY Map 5 TL91

Layer Marney Tower 2 FOR 1

CO5 9US
☎ 01206 330784 📠 01206 330884
e-mail: info@layermarneytower.co.uk
web: www.layermarneytower.co.uk
dir: off B1022 Colchester to Maldon road, signposted

The tallest Tudor gatehouse in the country, intended to be the entrance to a courtyard which would have rivalled Hampton Court Palace. The death of Henry, 1st Lord Marney in 1523, and of his son in 1525, meant that the building work ceased before completion. The beautiful parish church lies within the grounds. Visit the medieval barn and playground. Special events throughout the year, please see website.

Times Open 3 Apr-25 Sep, Apr-Jun & Sep, Sun & Wed; Jul-Aug, Sun-Thu 12-5; also open BH Sun-Mon, 11-5 **Fees** £5 (ch £3). Family ticket (2ad+2ch) £14* **Facilities** 🅟 ☕ ⛩ (outdoor) ♿ (partly accessible) (ramps in garden) toilets for disabled shop

SAFFRON WALDEN Map 5 TL53

Saffron Walden Museum 2 FOR 1

Museum St CB10 1JL
☎ 01799 510333 📠 01799 510334
e-mail: museum@uttlesford.gov.uk
web: www.saffronwaldenmuseum.org
dir: Close to M11, take B184/B1052 & follow signs to Saffron Walden

Opened in 1835, this friendly, family-size museum lies near the castle ruins in the centre of town. Its collections include local history and archaeology, natural history, ceramics, glass, costume, furniture, toys, an ancient Egyptian room, a natural history gallery, Discovery Centre and important ethnography collections. This museum has won the Museum of the Year award for being the best museum of social history, and awards for disabled access. There is a regular programme of special exhibitions, events and family holiday activities.

Times Open all year, Mar-Oct, Mon-Sat 10-5, Sun & BHs 2-5; Nov-Feb, Mon-Sat 10-4.30, Sun & BHs 2-4.30. Closed 24 & 25 Dec **Fees** £1.50 (ch 18 & under free, concessions 75p) **Facilities** 🅟 Ⓟ ⛩ (outdoor) ♿ (partly accessible) (2 small raised platforms unaccessible to wheelchairs, steps with stairlift to two mezzanine floors) toilets for disabled (ramps, wheelchairs, stairlifts, hearing loop) shop 🚫

SOUTHEND-ON-SEA Map 5 TQ88

Southend Museum and Planetarium 2 FOR 1

Victoria Av SS2 6EW
☎ 01702 434449 📠 01702 349806
e-mail: southendmuseum@hotmail.com
web: www.southendmuseums.co.uk
dir: take A127 or A13 towards town centre. Museum is adjacent to Southend Victoria Railway Station

A fine Edwardian building housing displays of archaeology, natural history and local history, telling the story of man in the south-east Essex area. Ring for details of special events, or see website.

Times Open Central Museum: Tue-Sat 10-5; Planetarium: Wed-Sat, shows at 11, 2 & 4 **Fees** Planetarium £3.95 (ch & pen £2.95). Museum free admission* **Facilities** Ⓟ ♿ (partly accessible) (planetarium & toilets not accessible) shop 🚫

Southend Pier Museum

Western Esplanade, Sounthend Pier SS1 2EL
☎ 01702 611214 & 614553
web: www.southendpiermuseum.co.uk
dir: A127 follow signs to seafront and pier, attraction is at shore end of pier, access from shore train station

Southend Pier is one and a third miles long and was built in 1830. This living museum portrays the history of the pier, its railway, its disasters, and the people who have lived and worked there. Exhibits include ex-pier rolling stock, a reconstructed signal box with working levers, and antique slot machines. Children can have fun learning about their heritage.

Times Open Apr-Sep Sun-Wed & BH 11-5 (during school hols 5.30). Due to open Etr 2011 after 6mths refurbishment **Fees** £1 (accompanied ch up to 12yrs free). Families only **Facilities** Ⓟ ♿ (fully accessible) shop ㊙

STANSTED — Map 5 TL52

Mountfitchet Castle Experience

CM24 8SP
☎ 01279 813237 📠 01279 816391
e-mail: office@mountfitchetcastle.com
web: www.mountfitchetcastle.com
dir: off B1383, in village. 2m from M11 junct 8

Come and see a Norman motte and bailey castle and village reconstructed as it was in Norman England of 1066, on its original historic site. A vivid illustration of village life in Domesday England, complete with houses, church, seige tower, seige weapons, and many types of animals roaming freely. Animated wax figures in all the buildings give historical information to visitors. Adjacent to the castle is the House on the Hill Toy Museum, a nostalgic trip through memories of childhood days. The whole experience is a unique all-weather, all-in-one heritage entertainment complex.

Times Open daily, mid Mar-mid Nov, 10-5 **Fees** £9.50 (ch £7.50, concessions £9) **Facilities** 🅟 Ⓟ ☕ ⛩ (outdoor) ♿ (partly accessible) (grassy slopes, cobbled areas & steps) toilets for disabled (laser commentaries) shop ㊙

TILBURY — Map 5 TQ67

Tilbury Fort

No 2 Office Block, The Fort RM18 7NR
☎ 01375 858489
web: www.english-heritage.org.uk
dir: 0.5m E off A126

View the finest example of 17th-century military engineering, a spectacular sight on the River Thames. View the World War I and II gun emplacements and even fire a real anti-aircraft gun.

Times Open all year, Apr-Oct, daily 10-5; Nov-Mar, Thu-Mon 10-4. Closed 24-26 Dec & 1 Jan **Fees** £4.20 (ch £2.10, concessions £3.60). Family £10.50. Prices and opening times are subject to change in March 2011. Please call 0870 333 1181 for the most up to date prices and opening times when planning your visit **Facilities** shop ㊙ #

WALTHAM ABBEY — Map 5 TL30

Lee Valley Park Farms — 2 FOR 1

Stubbins Hall Ln, Crooked Mile EN9 2EF
☎ 01992 892781 & 702200 📠 01992 899561
e-mail: farms@leevalleypark.org.uk
web: www.leevalleypark.org.uk/farms
dir: M25 junct 26, follow to Waltham Abbey. 2m from Waltham Abbey on B914

Lee Valley Park has over 200 animals, including pigs, goats and rare breeds. Meet Tallulah and Barbara the pigs, and Ella and Eve the goats. Ride on a mini tractor, dig in the pit or bounce on a new giant pillow. Play in the Bundle Barn indoor soft play area or visit the working dairy farm. There is a series of special events, including falconry displays, and tractor rides every second Saturday. The 2-for-1 voucher will admit a child free with a full paying adult.

Times Open Feb half term-Oct, daily 10-5 **Fees** £7 (ch 2-16 & concessions £5.60). Family tickets from £23. (Prices due for review)* **Facilities** 🅟 Ⓟ ☕ ⛩ (indoor & outdoor) ♿ (fully accessible) toilets for disabled (graded concrete paths, signed routes) shop

Royal Gunpowder Mills

Beaulieu Dr EN9 1JY
☎ 01992 707370 📠 01992 707372
e-mail: info@royalgunpowdermills.com
web: www.royalgunpowdermills.com
dir: M25 junct 26. Follow signs for A121 to Waltham Abbey at rdbt, entrance in Beaulieu Drive

Set in 170 acres of natural parkland with 20 buildings of major historic importance, the site mixes fascinating history, exciting science and beautiful surroundings to produce a magical day out for all ages. Over 20 special weekend events with many living history re-enactments, VE Day celebrations, Steam & Country Show, Rocket & Space event and a Classic Vehicle Show. Easy access, children's activities, exhibitions, guided land train tours, a woodland walk and much more.

Times Open end Apr-end Sep, 11-5, last entry 3.30. (Wknds, BHs & Wed in summer school hols)* **Fees** £7.20 (ch 5-15 £4.40, concessions £6.20, under 5's free) Family ticket (2ad & 3ch) £23.20* **Facilities** 🅟 Ⓟ ☕ ⛩ (outdoor) ♿ (partly accessible) (stairs provide access to top of Wildlife Tower. Some paths on nature walk are uneven. Lift available in main exhibition, number of ramps on site) toilets for disabled (wheelchairs & mobility scooters for loan) shop ㊙

Waltham Abbey Gatehouse, Bridge & Entrance to Cloisters — FREE

☎ 01992 702200
web: www.english-heritage.org.uk
dir: in Waltham Abbey off A112

Beside the great Norman church at Waltham are the slight remains of the abbey buildings - bridge, gatehouse and part of the north cloister. The bridge is named after King Harold, founder of the abbey.

Times Open at any reasonable time **Facilities** ♿ (partly accessible) (sensory trail guide) #

GLOUCESTERSHIRE

Snowshill

ALDSWORTH **Map 4 SP11**

Lodge Park & Sherborne Estate

GL54 3PP
☎ 01451 844130 & 844257 📠 01451 844131
e-mail: lodgepark@nationaltrust.org.uk
web: www.nationaltrust.org.uk/lodgepark
dir: approach from A40 only, between Northleach & Burford rdbts

Situated on the picturesque Sherborne Estate in the Cotswolds, Lodge Park was created in 1634 by John 'Crump' Dutton. Inspired by his passion for gambling and banqueting it is a unique survival of what would have been called a grandstand, with its deer course and park. Many special events are held including outdoor theatre shows.

Times Open mid Mar-Oct, Fri-Sun 11-4 **Fees** Grandstand: £5.25 (ch £3). Family £13.50. Estate: free. (£1 donation per car to support work on the estate). NT members free* **Facilities** Ⓟ Ⓟ (outdoor) ♿ (partly accessible) (ground floor only accessible) toilets for disabled (Braille guide, manual wheelchair, drop off point) shop ⊗

BERKELEY **Map 3 ST69**

Berkeley Castle **2 FOR 1**

GL13 9BQ
☎ 01453 810332 📠 01453 512995
e-mail: info@berkeley-castle.com
web: www.berkeley-castle.com
dir: M5 junct 13 or 14, just off A38 midway between Bristol & Gloucester

Berkeley Castle is the amazing fortress home of the Berkeley family, who have lived in the building since the Keep was completed in 1153. The castle is still intact, from dungeon to elegant drawing rooms, and reflects nearly a thousand years of English history: a king's murder, the American Colonies, London's Berkeley Square. Rose-clad terraces surround this most romantic castle.

Times Open 3 Apr-30 Oct, Thu, Sun & BH 11-5.30; Sun-Thu during school hols **Fees** Castle & Gardens & Butterfly House: £9.50 (ch 5-15 £5, pen £7.50). Family ticket (2ad+2ch) £24. Groups 25+ £9 (ch £4, concessions £7) **Facilities** Ⓟ (outdoor) ♿ (partly accessible) (some ground floor rooms accessible for wheelchair users) (audio personal tours) shop ⊗

Edward Jenner Museum **2 FOR 1**

Church Ln, High St GL13 9BN
☎ 01453 810631 📠 01453 811690
e-mail: info@edwardjenner.co.uk
web: www.jennermuseum.com
dir: follow tourist signs from A38 to town centre, left into High St & left again into Church Lane

This beautiful Queen Anne house was the home of Edward Jenner, the pioneer of vaccination against smallpox in 1796. The house and the garden, with its thatched Temple of Vaccinia, are much as they were in Jenner's day. The displays record Jenner's life as an 18th-century country doctor, his work on vaccination and his interest in natural history. 2011 marks the 45th anniversary of the decision by the World Health Assembly to embark on a global eradication of smallpox programme.

Times Open Apr-Sep, Tue-Sat 12.30-5.30, Sun 12-5.30; Oct, Sun 1-5.30, (25-31 Oct 12.30-5.30); daily in Jul & Aug. Open BH Mon 12-5.30. Last entry 5. Groups by appointment year round* **Fees** £5 **Facilities** Ⓟ Ⓟ (indoor & outdoor) ♿ (partly accessible) (ground floor accessible) toilets for disabled (some information in large print) shop ⊗

BOURTON-ON-THE-WATER **Map 4 SP12**

Birdland **2 FOR 1**

Rissington Rd GL54 2BN
☎ 01451 820480 📠 01451 822398
e-mail: simonb@birdland.co.uk
web: www.birdland.co.uk
dir: on A429

Birdland is a natural setting of woodland, river and gardens, which is inhabited by over 500 birds; flamingos, pelicans, penguins, cranes, storks, cassowary and waterfowl can be seen on various aspects of the water habitat. Over 50 aviaries of parrots, falcons, pheasants, hornbills, touracos, pigeons, ibis and many more. Toucan and Desert Houses are home to the more delicate species, and Birdland has the only group of king penguins in England. There's a new nature trail, 'Marshmouth Reserve' and 'Discovery Zone' indoor educational area, plus Trigg Hall with its conference and meeting rooms.

Times Open all year, Apr-Oct, daily 10-6; Nov-Mar, daily 10-4 (last admission 1hr before closing). Closed 25 Dec **Fees** £6.50 (concessions £5.50). Family ticket (2ad+2ch) £19.80 **Facilities** Ⓟ (indoor & outdoor) ♿ (fully accessible) toilets for disabled shop

ENGLAND

CHEDWORTH Map 4 SP01

Chedworth Roman Villa

Yanworth GL54 3LJ
☎ 01242 890256 📠 01242 890909
e-mail: chedworth@nationaltrust.org.uk
web: www.nationaltrust.org.uk/chedworth
dir: 3m NW of Fossebridge on A429

The remains of a Romano-British villa, excavated 1864-65 and known as 'Britains oldest county house'. Set in a beautiful wooded combe, there are fine 4th-century mosaics, two bath houses, and a temple with spring. The museum houses the smaller finds and there is an 18-minute AV programme. Telephone for further details of special events. Major redevelopment of the site will take place between 2010-2011 with a chance to see work in progress.

Times Open 13-27 Mar & 2-14 Nov, Tue-Sun 10-4; 28 Mar-Oct, Tue-Sun 10-5. (Open BH Mon)* **Fees** £7 (ch £4). Family ticket £18. NT members free* **Facilities** (outdoor) (partly accessible) (steps to mosaics and museum) toilets for disabled (audio tour, induction loop, Braille guide) shop

CHELTENHAM Map 3 SO92

Holst Birthplace Museum

4 Clarence Rd GL52 2AY
☎ 01242 524846 📠 01242 580182
e-mail: holstmuseum@btconnect.com
web: www.holstmuseum.org.uk
dir: opposite gateway of Pittville Park. 10 min walk from town centre

Gustav Holst, composer of *The Planets*, was born at this Regency house in 1874. The museum contains unique displays on Holst's life, including his original piano. The rooms of the house have been carefully restored, each area evoking a different period in the history of the house from Regency to Edwardian times.

Times Open Tue-Sat 10-4. Open BH Mon & mid Dec-mid Jan, ex pre-booked groups **Fees** £4.50 (ch & concessions £4). Family ticket (2ad+3ch) £10 **Facilities** (partly accessible) (ground floor accessible but steps to front door) (large print & Braille guide, special hands-on tours) shop

CIRENCESTER Map 4 SP00

Corinium Museum 2 FOR 1

Park St GL7 2BX
☎ 01285 655611
e-mail: museums@cotswold.gov.uk
web: www.cotswold.gov.uk/go/museum
dir: in town centre

Discover the treasures of the Cotswolds at the Corinium Museum. Two years and over £5 million in the making, it has been transformed into a must-see attraction. Featuring archaeological and historical material from Cirencester and the Cotswolds, from prehistoric times to the 19th century. The museum is known for its Roman mosaic sculpture and other material from one of Britain's largest Roman towns. On display are Anglo-Saxon treasures from Lechlade bringing to life this little-known period. The museum also houses Medieval, Tudor, Civil War and 18th-19th century displays.

Times Open Mon-Sat 10-5, Sun 2-5; Nov-Mar 10-4. Closed Xmas & New Year **Fees** £4.50 (ch £2.25, concessions £3.75, students £3). Family ticket (2ad+5ch) 10% discount off standard admission prices* **Facilities** licensed (indoor) (fully accessible) toilets for disabled (large print & Braille guides) shop

CLEARWELL Map 3 SO50

Clearwell Caves Ancient Iron Mines 2 FOR 1

GL16 8JR
☎ 01594 832535 📠 01594 833362
e-mail: jw@clearwellcaves.com
web: www.clearwellcaves.com
dir: 1.5m S of Coleford town centre, off B4228 follow brown tourist signs

These impressive natural caves have been mined since the earliest times for paint pigment and iron ore. Today visitors explore nine large caverns with displays of local mining and geology. There is a colour room where ochre pigments are still produced, and a blacksmith shop. Deep level excursions are available for more adventurous visitors, but must be pre-booked. There is a Christmas fantasy event when the caverns are transformed into a magical world of light and sound. The 2 for 1 voucher cannot be used for the Christmas Fantasy event in Nov and Dec.

Times Open Mar-Oct, daily 10-5; Jan-Feb, Sat-Sun 10-5; Xmas Fantasy 1-24 Dec, daily 10-5 **Fees** £5.80 (ch £3.80, concessions £5.30) Family ticket £17.30 **Facilities** (outdoor) (partly accessible) (w/chair need 2 helpers on steep pathway) toilets for disabled (hands-on exhibits, Braille guide book, contact in advance) shop

CRANHAM Map 3 SO81

Prinknash Abbey

GL4 8EX
☎ 01452 812066 📠 01452 812066
web: www.prinknashabbey.org.uk
dir: on A46 between Cheltenham & Stroud

Set in a large park, the old priory building is a 12th to 16th-century house, used by Benedictine monks and guests of Gloucester Abbey until 1539. It became an abbey for Benedictine monks from Caldey in 1928. Home to the reconstruction of the Great Orpheus Pavement, the largest mosaic in Britain, as mentioned in the Guinness Book of Records. Also visit the bird and deer park.

Times Open all year Wed-Sun 10-4. Closed Good Fri, 25-26 Dec & 1 Jan.* **Facilities** (outdoor) (fully accessible) toilets for disabled (Radar approved)

Prinknash Bird & Deer Park — 2 FOR 1

GL4 8EX
☎ 01452 812727 📠 01452 812727
e-mail: office@thebirdpark.com
web: www.thebirdpark.com
dir: M5 junct 11a, A417 towards Cirencester, take 1st exit signed A46 Stroud. Follow brown tourist signs

Nine acres of parkland and lakes make a beautiful home for black swans, geese and other water birds. There are also exotic birds such as white and Indian blue peacocks, reindeer, miniature Mediterranean donkeys, tame fallow deer and pygmy goats. The Golden Wood is stocked with ornamental pheasants, and leads to the reputedly haunted monks' fishpond, which contains trout. An 80-year old, free-standing, 16-foot tall Wendy House in Tudor style is located near the picnic area. A pair of reindeer, the only ones to be found in the Cotswolds, can also be seen. 2-for-1 voucher will admit a child free with a full paying adult (not accepted on event days or Bank Holidays).

Times Open all year, summer 10-5, winter 10-4. Closed 25 Dec & Good Fri **Fees** £6.50 (ch £4.50, concessions £5.50)* **Facilities** (outdoor) (partly accessible) (steep entrance & some hills as park is set in a valley) toilets for disabled (no charge for wheelchairs or helpers) shop

DEERHURST Map 3 SO82

Odda's Chapel

web: www.english-heritage.org.uk
dir: off B4213 near River Severn at Abbots Court SW of parish church

This rare Saxon chapel was built by Earl Odda and dedicated in 1056. When it was discovered, it had been incorporated into a farmhouse. It has now been carefully restored.

Times Open Apr-Oct, daily 10-6; Nov-Mar, daily 10-4. Closed 24-26 Dec & 1 Jan **Facilities**

DYRHAM Map 3 ST77

Dyrham Park

SN14 8ER
☎ 0117 937 2501 📠 0117 937 1353
e-mail: dyrhampark@nationaltrust.org.uk
web: www.nationaltrust.org.uk
dir: 8m N of Bath, 2m S from M4 junct 18 on A46

Dyrham Park is an elegant 17th-century mansion, set in a dramatic deer park. Inside, the lavish collections reflect the fashion for all things Dutch, whilst the Victorian servants' quarters give an idea of life below stairs. Weekly guided park and garden walks. 2011 is the 50th anniversary of the opening of Dyrham Park to the public by the National Trust.

Times Open: House 19 Feb-Oct, Fri-Tue, 11-5, Jul-Aug, daily (limited offer Wed-Thu); 5 Nov-18 Dec, wknds only (limited offer). Garden, shop & tearoom, 19 Feb-Oct, Fri-Tue, 10-5; Jul-Aug daily; 5 Nov-18 Dec wknds only. Park open daily all year 10-5 **Fees** Gift Aid admission prices. House, Park & Garden £11.55 (ch £6). Family £28.90. Garden & Park £4.65 (ch £2.35). Family £10.30. Park only £2.90 (ch £1.70). Family £6.60 **Facilities** licensed (outdoor) (partly accessible) (steps to house entrance but access via domestic rooms, no electric wheelchairs allowed in house, tea room/shop & garden accessible) toilets for disabled (Braille, 4 wheelchairs to borrow, free bus from car park) shop

GLOUCESTER Map 3 SO81

Gloucester City Museum & Art Gallery — FREE

Brunswick Rd GL1 1HP
☎ 01452 396131 📠 01452 410898
e-mail: city.museum@gloucester.gov.uk
web: www.gloucester.gov.uk/citymuseum
dir: A38 Bristol Rd to Southgate St, situated between Spa Rd & Brunswick Rd

An impressive range of Roman artefacts including the Rufus Sita tombstone; the amazing Iron Age Birdlip mirror; one of the earliest backgammon sets in the world; dinosaur fossils; and paintings by famous artists such as Turner and Gainsborough. There is something for everyone, full-sized dinosaurs; wildlife from the city and the Gloucestershire countryside; beautiful antique furniture, glass, ceramics and silver; hands-on displays, computer quizzes and activity workstations throughout the galleries. There is an exciting range of temporary exhibitions from contemporary art and textiles to dinosaurs and local history; children's holiday activities and regular special events.

Times Open all year, Tue-Sat 10-5* **Facilities** (fully accessible) toilets for disabled (lift to 1st floor galleries, induction loops) shop

ENGLAND

GLOUCESTER *continued*

Gloucester Folk Museum FREE

99-103 Westgate St GL1 2PG
☎ 01452 396868 & 396869 📠 01452 330495
e-mail: folk.museum@gloucester.gov.uk
web: www.gloucester.gov.uk/folkmuseum
dir: from W - A40 & A48; from N - A38 & M5, from E - A40 & B4073; from S - A4173 & A38

Three floors of splendid Tudor and Jacobean timber-framed buildings dating from the 16th and 17th centuries along with new buildings housing the dairy, ironmonger's shop and wheelwright and carpenter workshops. Local history, domestic life, crafts, trades and industries from 1500 to the present, including Toys and Childhood gallery with hands-on toys and a puppet theatre, the Siege of Gloucester, a Victorian class room, Victorian kitchen and laundry equipment. A wide range of exhibitions, hands-on activities, events, demonstrations and role play sessions are held throughout the year. There is an attractive cottage garden and courtyard for events, often with live animals, and outside games.

Times Open all year, Tue-Sat, 10-5* **Facilities** Ⓟ (outdoor) ♿ (partly accessible) (virtual tour in Postal gallery, induction loops) shop

The National Waterways Museum

Llanthony Warehouse, The Docks GL1 2EH
☎ 01452 318200 📠 01452 318202
e-mail: gloucester@thewaterwaystrust.org.uk
web: www.nwm.org.uk
dir: From M5, A40. In city follow brown signs for historic docks

Based in Gloucester Docks, this museum takes up three floors of a seven-storey Victorian warehouse, and documents the 200-year history of Britain's water-based transport. The emphasis is on hands-on experience, including working models and engines, interactive displays, actual craft, computer interactions and the national collection of inland waterways. Boat trips are also available between Easter and October.

Times Open all year, daily 10-5 (last admission 4). Closed 25 Dec* **Facilities** Ⓟ Ⓟ licensed (outdoor) ♿ (fully accessible) toilets for disabled (wheelchair, lifts, limited access to floating exhibits) shop

Nature in Art 2 FOR 1

Wallsworth Hall, Tewkesbury Rd, Twigworth GL2 9PA
☎ 01452 731422 & 0845 450 0233 📠 01452 730937
e-mail: enquiries@nature-in-art.org.uk
web: www.nature-in-art.org.uk
dir: 0.5m off main A38 between Gloucester and Tewkesbury, 2m N of Gloucester. Follow brown tourist signs

Nature in Art is unique - it is the world's only museum dedicated exclusively to art inspired by nature. Within the fine Georgian mansion can be found a truly diverse range of world-class art: displays embrace two and three-dimensional work in all mediums and styles ranging from Picasso to Shepherd. Spanning 1500 years, the collection contains work by 600 artists from over 50 countries. So typically, as well as a temporary exhibition, you'll find watercolour landscapes, contemporary glass, the Flemish masters, modern abstract interpretations, bronze sculpture and even some exotic oriental treasures. Visitors can also meet an artist in residence as they work on their next creation, which can range from painting to woodcarving (Feb-Nov).

Times Open all year, Tue-Sun & BHs 10-5. Closed 24-26 Dec **Fees** £4.75 (ch under 8 free, ch & concessions £4.25). Family ticket £13.50. Party 15+ 50p discount per person* **Facilities** Ⓟ licensed (outdoor) ♿ (fully accessible) toilets for disabled (lift & ramps at entrance) shop

Soldiers of Gloucestershire Museum 2 FOR 1

Custom House, Gloucester Docks GL1 2HE
☎ 01452 522682 📠 01452 311116
e-mail: curator@sogm.co.uk
web: www.glosters.org.uk
dir: follow brown tourist signs to historic dockyard, A38 Southgate Street/Bristol Road

'Soldiers of Gloucestershire' tells the remarkable story of those who have served in the regiments of Gloucestershire since 1694. Their courage, humour and sacrifice are brought together in exciting and colourful exhibitions. Walk through a First World War trench, feel and hear the deafening sound of guns or enjoy interactive and hands on displays. See memorabilia from the

18th, 19th and 20th centuries, including uniforms, medals and moving accounts of individual acts of bravery.

Times Open all year, daily 10-5 incl BHs. Closed Mon in winter **Fees** £4.25 (ch £2.25, under 5 free, concessions £3.25). Family ticket (2ad+2ch) £13 **Facilities** Ⓟ (outdoor) ♿ (partly accessible) toilets for disabled (lift, w/chairs) shop

GUITING POWER Map 4 SP02

Cotswold Farm Park 2 FOR 1

GL54 5UG

☎ 01451 850307 01451 850423

e-mail: info@cotswoldfarmpark.co.uk

web: www.cotswoldfarmpark.co.uk

dir: signed off B4077 from M5 junct 9

Meet over 50 breeding flocks and herds of rare farm animals. There are lots of activities for the youngsters, with rabbits and guinea pigs to cuddle, lambs and goat kids to bottle feed, tractor and trailer-rides, battery powered tractors, Touch Barn, Maze Quest, Jumping Pillows and safe rustic-themed play areas both indoors and outside. Lambing occurs in early May, followed by shearing and then milking demonstrations later in the season. The Cotswold Farm Park also has its own 40-pitch camping and caravanning site. In 2011 the park celebrates its 40th anniversary.

Times Open mid Mar-mid Sep, daily (then open wknds only until end Oct & Autumn half term 10.30-5)* **Fees** £6.95 (ch £5.65, concessions £6.45). Family ticket £22.75* **Facilities** Ⓟ (outdoor) ♿ (partly accessible) toilets for disabled (ramps) shop

HAILES Map 4 SP02

Hailes Abbey

GL54 5PB

☎ 01242 602398

web: www.english-heritage.org.uk

dir: 2m NE of Winchcombe off B4632

Explore the atmospheric ruins of this great medieval pilgrimage abbey, in the midst of the Cotswolds. Built in the 13th century Hailes became famous when presented with a phial that was said to contain the blood of Christ.

Times Open Apr-Jun & Sep, daily 10-5; Jul-Aug, daily 10-6; Oct, daily 10-4. Closed Nov-Mar **Fees** £4 (ch £2, concessions £3.40). Nat Trust members free, but charge of £1 for audio tour & special events. Prices and opening times are subject to change in March 2011. Please call 0870 333 1181 for the most up to date prices and opening times when planning your visit **Facilities** Ⓟ shop

LYDNEY Map 3 SO60

Dean Forest Railway

Forest Rd GL15 4ET

☎ 01594 843423 (info) & 845840 (enquiries)

e-mail: info@deanforestrailway.co.uk

web: www.deanforestrailway.co.uk

dir: At Lydney, turn off A48. Follow brown tourist signs to Norchard Station, on B4234

Travel on a heritage railway operated by steam trains (and the occasional diesel) through the beautiful and historic Forest of Dean. A relaxing round trip of over 8 miles to the recently opened Parkend Station. There's free car parking at Norchard Station (near Lydney) with a well-stocked gift shop, interesting museum and cafe. Regular family events include days out with Thomas and Santa Specials.

Times Open Apr-Oct, Sun; Jun-Sep, Wed, Sat, Sun; also Thu in Aug & BHs; Dec wknds (Santa Specials) & New Year.* **Facilities** Ⓟ licensed (outdoor) ♿ (fully accessible) toilets for disabled (specially adapted coach for wheelchairs, phone for details) shop

ENGLAND

MICKLETON Map 4 SP14

Hidcote Manor Garden

Chipping Campden GL55 6LR
☎ 01386 438333 01386 438817
e-mail: hidcote@nationaltrust.org.uk
web: www.nationaltrust.org.uk/hidcote
dir: 1m E of B4632, near village of Mickleton

One of the most delightful arts and crafts gardens in England, created by the horticulturist Major Lawrence Johnston and comprising a series of small gardens within the whole, separated by walls and hedges of different species. It is famous for its rare shrubs and trees, outstanding herbaceous borders and unusual worldwide plant species.

Times Garden mid Mar-Jun & Sep, Sat-Wed & Jul-Aug daily 10-6; 2-end Oct, Sat-Wed 10-5 (last admission 1hr before closing)* **Fees** £9.50 (ch £4.75). Family £23.75. Groups £8.20 (ch £4.10)* **Facilities** licensed (outdoor) (partly accessible) (uneven pathways, steps, gravelled surfaces) toilets for disabled (wheelchair, Braille) shop

Kiftsgate Court Garden

GL55 6LN
☎ 01386 438777 01386 438777
e-mail: info@kiftsgate.co.uk
web: www.kiftsgate.co.uk
dir: 0.5m S off A46, adjacent Hidcote NT garden

Kiftsgate Garden is spectacularly set on the edge of the Cotswold Escarpment, with views over the Vale of Evesham. It contains many rare plants collected by three generations of women gardeners, including the largest rose in England, the R. Filipes Kiftsgate.

Times Open Apr, Aug & Sep; Sun, Mon & Wed 2-6; May-Jul, daily (ex Thu & Fri) 12-6 **Fees** £7 (ch £2.50) **Facilities** (partly accessible) (top garden only accessible, very steep banks) shop

MORETON-IN-MARSH Map 4 SP23

Cotswold Falconry Centre

Batsford Park GL56 9AB
☎ 01386 701043
e-mail: mail@cotswold-falconry.co.uk
web: www.cotswold-falconry.co.uk
dir: 1m W of Moreton-in-Marsh on A44

Conveniently located by the Batsford Park Arboretum, the Cotswold Falconry gives daily demonstrations in the art of falconry. The emphasis here is on breeding and conservation, and over 100 eagles, hawks, owls and falcons can be seen.

Times Open mid Feb-mid Nov, 10.30-5.30 (last admission 5)* **Facilities** (outdoor) (partly accessible) toilets for disabled (no steps, wide doorways) shop

Sezincote

GL56 9AW
☎ 01386 700444
e-mail: edwardpeake64@hotmail.com
web: www.sezincote.co.uk
dir: 1.5m out of Moreton-in-Marsh on A44, Evesham road

The Indian-style house at Sezincote was the inspiration for Brighton Pavilion; its charming water garden adds to its exotic aura and features trees of unusual size.

Times Open: House, May-Sep, Thu, Fri & BH Mon 2.30-6. Garden only, all year (ex Dec) Thu, Fri & BH Mon 2-6 or dusk if earlier* **Fees** House & garden £10, Garden only £5 (ch £1.50). Children not allowed in the House. Groups by appointment only **Facilities** (partly accessible) (some hills & gravel paths) toilets for disabled

NEWENT Map 3 SO72

The National Birds of Prey Centre

GL18 1JJ
☎ 0870 9901992 01531 821389
e-mail: kb@nbpc.co.uk
web: www.nbpc.co.uk
dir: follow A40, right onto B4219 towards Newent. Follow brown tourist signs from Newent town

Trained birds can be seen at close quarters in the Hawk Walk and the Owl Courtyard and there are also breeding aviaries, a gift shop, bookshop, picnic areas, coffee shop and children's play area. Birds are flown three times daily in summer and winter, giving an exciting and educational display. There are over 80 aviaries on view with 40 species.

Times Open all year daily 10.30-5.30 (closed 25-26 Dec).* **Facilities** (partly accessible) toilets for disabled (special tours available, pre-booking required) shop

NORTHLEACH Map 4 SP11

Keith Harding's World of Mechanical Music

The Oak House, High St GL54 3ET
☎ 01451 860181 📠 01451 861133
e-mail: keith@mechanicalmusic.co.uk
web: www.mechanicalmusic.co.uk
dir: at crossroads of A40 & A429

A fascinating collection of antique clocks, musical boxes, automata and mechanical musical instruments, restored and maintained in the world-famous workshops, displayed in a period setting, presented as a live entertainment, and played during regular tours. There is an exhibition of coin operated instruments which visitors can play.

Times Open all year, daily 10-5. Last tour 4. Closed 25-26 Dec.* **Facilities** Ⓟ Ⓟ ♿ (fully accessible) toilets for disabled (Safety rails, non-slip floor) shop

OWLPEN Map 3 ST89

Owlpen Manor **2 FOR 1**

GL11 5BZ
☎ 01453 860261 📠 01453 860819
e-mail: sales@owlpen.com
web: www.owlpen.com
dir: 3m E of Dursley, signed at village green in Uley off B4066

A romantic Tudor manor house set in small formal terraced gardens, on a 215 acre estate. The house is being refurbished and is closed until further notice. The 2 for 1 voucher can only be used against garden tickets.

Times House closed for conservation. Open Garden: May-Sep, Mon, Wed-Thu from 12* **Fees** House closed. Garden only: £4 (ch £2.40). Family ticket (2ad+4ch) £12.50* **Facilities** Ⓟ licensed ♿ (partly accessible) (access restricted to top terrace of garden)

PAINSWICK Map 3 SO80

Painswick Rococo Garden

GL6 6TH
☎ 01452 813204 📠 01452 814888
e-mail: info@rococogarden.org.uk
web: www.rococogarden.org.uk
dir: on B4073 0.5m NW of Painswick

This beautiful Rococo garden (a compromise between formality and informality) is the only one of its period to survive complete. There are ponds, woodland walks, a maze, kitchen garden and herbacious borders, all set in a Cotswold valley famous for snowdrops in the early spring. Please ring for details of special events.

Times Open 10 Jan-Oct, daily 11-5* **Fees** £6 (ch £3, concessions £5) **Facilities** Ⓟ Ⓟ licensed (outdoor) ♿ (partly accessible) (steep slopes) toilets for disabled shop

SLIMBRIDGE Map 3 SO70

WWT Slimbridge

GL2 7BT
☎ 01453 891900 📠 01453 890827
e-mail: info.slimbridge@wwt.org.uk
web: www.wwt.org.uk
dir: off A38, signed from M5 junct 13 & 14

Slimbridge is home to the world's largest collection of swans, geese, ducks and flamingos. An internationally renowned reserve with an astounding array of wildlife from water voles to waders, hares to dragonflies and wetland mammal exhibit. Facilities include a tropical house, discovery centre, children's outdoor play area, canoe safari, shop and restaurant.

Times Open all year, daily from 9.30-5.30 (winter 5). Closed 25 Dec **Fees** £8.86 (ch £4.82, under 4's free, concessions £6.82). Family £24.82* **Facilities** Ⓟ licensed (outdoor) ♿ (fully accessible) toilets for disabled (wheelchair & scooter loan, hearing loops) shop

ENGLAND

SNOWSHILL Map 4 SP03

Snowshill Manor and Garden

WR12 7JU
☎ 01386 852410 01386 842822
e-mail: snowshillmanor@nationaltrust.org.uk
web: www.nationaltrust.org.uk
dir: 2m SW of Broadway, off A44

Charles Wade embodied his family motto 'Let nothing perish', spending his life and inherited wealth amassing a spectacular collection of everyday and extraordinary objects from across the globe. He bought objects because of their colour, craftsmanship and design, restoring the ancient, golden-yellow Cotswold manor house to display them. Laid out theatrically according to Mr Wade's wishes, the Manor is literally packed to the rafters with 22,000 or so unusual objects - from tiny toys to splendid suits of Samurai armour. The Manor is surrounded by an intriguing terraced hillside garden designed in the Arts & Crafts style.

Times Open 12 Mar-30 Oct, Wed-Sun & BHs; House 12-5, Garden: 11-5.30* **Fees** House & Garden: £9.50, (ch £4.80). Family £24. Garden, Restaurant & Shop: £5.20, (ch £2.60). Family £12.70* **Facilities** licensed (outdoor) (partly accessible) (limited wheelchair access, 3 steps to front of manor, terraced garden) toilets for disabled (Braille guides, audio tapes, 2 w/chairs, virtual tour) shop

SOUDLEY Map 3 SO61

Dean Heritage Centre

Camp Mill GL14 2UB
☎ 01594 822170 01594 823711
e-mail: info@deanheritagemuseum.com
web: www.deanheritagemuseum.com
dir: A40, A48 in Forest of Dean

The Dean Heritage Centre is the ideal starting point for a visit to the Forest. With five modern museum galleries, and a range of features designed to create a living history experience, there is plenty for all ages to enjoy, including Forester's Cottage, Freemine Entrance, Charcoal Burner's Camp and an adventure playground. There is a regular events programme and there are plenty of activities involving history, crafts and the Forest's wildlife. The lovely mill pond and surrounding five acres of woodland are home to lots of wildlife.

Times Open summer 10-5, winter 10-4, open BHs (ex 24-26 Dec), 1 Jan 11-4.* **Fees** £5.40 (ch £2.75, under 5's free, concessions £4.65). Family £15.40, Party 10+* **Facilities** (outdoor) (partly accessible) (access to woodland area restricted due to uneven ground) toilets for disabled (lift, ramps, staff assistance) shop

TETBURY Map 3 ST89

Chavenage House 2 FOR 1

Chavenage GL8 8XP
☎ 01666 502329 01666 504696
e-mail: info@chavenage.com
web: www.chavenage.com
dir: 2m NW of Tetbury signed off B4014, 7m SE of Stroud, signed off A46

Built in 1576, this unspoilt Elizabethan house contains stained glass from the 16th century and earlier with some good furniture and tapestries. The owner during the Civil War was a Parliamentarian, and the house contains Cromwellian relics. In more recent years, the house has been the location or Candleford Manor in the BBC's *Lark Rise to Candleford*, and in 2008 scenes for the adaptation of *Tess of the D'Ubervilles* were shot at Chavenage. Tours of the house are enlivened by ghost stories.

Times Open May-Sep, Thu, Sun & BHs 2-5 (last tour 4). Also Etr Sun & Mon. Other days by appointment only* **Fees** £7 (ch £3.50)* **Facilities** (partly accessible) (no lift to 2 rooms upstairs)

TODDINGTON Map 4 SP03

Gloucestershire Warwickshire Steam Railway

The Railway Station GL54 5DT
☎ 01242 621405
e-mail: enquiries@gwsr.com
web: www.gwsr.com
dir: 10m E of M5 junct 9 near junct of B4077 & B4632 between Winchcombe & Broadway

The railway runs along a part of the former Great Western Railway's mainline from Birmingham to Cheltenham, via Stratford-upon-Avon. The line commands wonderful views of the sleepy hamlets and villages, as it runs though the beautiful Cotswold countryside. The line was primarily built (1900-1906) to improve through services from Birmingham to Bristol and the West Country.

Times Open Mar-Dec, selected days & times. Call 01242 621405 for details* **Fees** £11 (ch 5-15 £6.50, under 5 free, concessions

£9.50). Family (2 ad+3 ch) £30* **Facilities** (outdoor) (partly accessible) (steep slope to platform at Cheltenham, some uneven surfaces at Winchcombe) toilets for disabled (specially converted carriage) shop

ULEY Map 3 ST79

Uley Long Barrow (Hetty Pegler's Tump)

FREE

web: www.english-heritage.org.uk
dir: 3.5m NE of Dursley on B4066

This 180-foot long Neolithic long barrow is popularly known as Hetty Pegler's Tump. The mound, surrounded by a wall, is about 85 feet wide. It contains a stone central passage, and three burial chambers.

Times Open at any reasonable time **Facilities**

WESTBURY ON SEVERN Map 3 SO71

Westbury Court Garden

GL14 1PD
01452 760461 01452 760461
e-mail: westburycourt@nationaltrust.org.uk
web: www.nationaltrust.org.uk
dir: 9m SW of Gloucester on A48

This formal water garden with canals and yew hedges was laid out between 1696 and 1705 and is the earliest of its kind remaining in England. It was restored in 1971, and planted with species dated pre-1700, including apple, pear and plum trees.

Times Open 10 Mar-Jun & Sep-Oct, Wed-Sun, 10-5; Jul-Aug, daily 10-5; Nov-Feb by appointment. Open BHs.* **Facilities** (partly accessible) (several steps up to Pavilion and Summerhouse) toilets for disabled (Braille guide, w/chair available)

WESTONBIRT Map 3 ST88

Westonbirt, The National Arboretum

GL8 8QS
01666 880220 01666 880559
e-mail: westonbirt@forestry.gov.uk
web: www.forestry.gov.uk/westonbirt
dir: 3m S Tetbury on A433

Begun in 1829, this arboretum contains one of the finest and most important collections of trees and shrubs in the world. There are 18,000 specimens, planted from 1829 to the present day, covering 600 acres of landscaped Cotswold countryside. Magnificent displays of Rhododendrons, Azaleas, Magnolias and wild flowers, and a blaze of colour in the autumn from the national collection of Japanese Maples. Special events include the Festival of the Tree (Aug BH) and the Enchanted Christmas Trail (every Fri, Sat, Sun in December until Xmas).

Times Open all year. Opening times subject to seasonal variation* **Fees** £6-£9 (ch £2-£4, concessions available) Prices are subject to seasonal variation* **Facilities** licensed (outdoor) (fully accessible) toilets for disabled (electric & manual wheelchair for loan - phone to book) shop

WINCHCOMBE Map 4 SP02

Sudeley Castle, Gardens & Exhibitions

GL54 5JD
01242 602308 01242 602959
e-mail: enquiries@sudeley.org.uk
web: www.sudeleycastle.co.uk
dir: B4632 to Winchcombe. Castle signed from town

Sudeley Castle was home to Katherine Parr, who is buried in the Chapel. Henry VIII, Anne Boleyn, Lady Jane Grey and Elizabeth I all stayed or visited here; and it was the headquarters of Prince Rupert during the Civil War. The Queen's Garden is famous for its rose collection. There are exhibitions, a gift shop and plant centre. New exhibitions include '1535: Romance and Intrigue at Sudeley' commemorating Henry VIII's visit with Anne Boleyn, and 'Textile Treasures'.

Times Open 29 Mar-Oct, daily 10.30-5. Closed 9 Oct*
Fees £7.20 (ch 5-15 £4.20, concessions £6.20). Family ticket £20.80* **Facilities** (outdoor) (partly accessible) (part of exhibition up stairs) toilets for disabled shop

GREATER MANCHESTER

Timber-framed facade, Bramall Hall

ENGLAND

ALTRINCHAM Map 7 SJ78

Dunham Massey

WA14 4SJ
☎ 0161 941 1025 0161 929 7508
e-mail: dunhammassey@nationaltrust.org.uk
web: www.nationaltrust.org.uk
dir: 3m SW of Altrincham (off A56), M6 junct 19 or M56 junct 7, then follow brown signs

A fine 18th-century house, garden and park, home of the Earls of Stamford until 1976. The house contains fine furniture and silverware, and some thirty rooms, including the library, billiard room, fully-equipped kitchen, butler's pantry and laundry. The garden is on an ancient site with waterside plantings, mixed borders and fine lawns. The ancient deer park has beautiful avenues and several ponds as well as a working sawmill where the waterwheel is demonstrated on afternoons in high season.

Times Open House: 26 Feb-Oct, Sat-Wed 11-5; Garden: all year daily, 11-4* **Fees** House & Garden £9.40 (ch £4.70). Family £23.50. Garden only £6.60 (ch £3.30). Family £16.50* **Facilities** licensed (outdoor) (partly accessible) (access restricted, steps with handrail to Great Hall & other floors) toilets for disabled (w/chairs, lift, Braille & large print guide, pmv, parking) shop

ASHTON-UNDER-LYNE Map 7 SJ99

Central Art Gallery FREE

Central Library Building, Old St OL6 7SG
☎ 0161 342 2650 0161 342 2650
e-mail: central.artgallery@tameside.gov.uk
web: www.tameside.gov.uk
dir: Near centre of town, off A635 (large Victorian building)

Set in a fine Victorian Gothic building, Central Art Gallery has three gallery spaces, each of which offers a varied programme of contemporary exhibitions. A range of tastes and styles are covered, with group and solo shows of work by artists from the region including paintings, sculpture, installation and textiles. Extensive education programmes for schools, children, families, adults and teenagers.

Times Open all year, Tue, Wed & Fri 10-5, Thu 1-7.30 & Sat 9-4.* **Facilities** (fully accessible) toilets for disabled (induction loop) shop

Museum of The Manchester Regiment FREE

The Town Hall, Market Place OL6 6DL
☎ 0161 342 2812 & 3710 0161 343 2869
e-mail: portland.basin@tameside.gov.uk
web: www.tameside.gov.uk
dir: in town centre, on market square, follow signs for museum

The social and regimental history of the Manchesters is explored at this museum, tracing the story back to its origins in the 18th century. Children can try on military headwear, experience a First World War trench, and try out the interactive 'A Soldier's Life'.

Times Open all year, Mon-Sat, 10-4 **Facilities** (fully accessible) toilets for disabled (lift)

Portland Basin Museum FREE

Portland Place OL7 0QA
☎ 0161 343 2878 0161 343 2869
e-mail: portland.basin@tameside.gov.uk
web: www.tameside.gov.uk
dir: M60 junct 23 into town centre. Museum near Cross Hill Street & car park. Follow brown signs with canal boat image

Exploring the social and industrial history of Tameside, this museum is part of the recently rebuilt Ashton Canal Warehouse, constructed in 1834. Visitors can walk around a 1920s street, dress up in old hats and gloves, steer a virtual canal boat, and see the original canal powered waterwheel that once drove the warehouse machinery. Portland Basin Museum also features changing exhibitions and event programme- so there's always something new to see!

Times Open all year, Tue-Sun 10-5. Open BH Mon **Facilities** licensed (outdoor) (fully accessible) toilets for disabled (wheelchair, lift, loop system) shop

BRAMHALL Map 7 SJ88

Bramall Hall & Park 2 FOR 1

SK7 3NX
☎ 0161 485 3708 0161 486 6959
e-mail: bramall.hall@stockport.gov.uk
web: www.bramallhall.org.uk
dir: from A6 right at Blossoms public house through Davenport village then right - signed

This large timber-framed hall dates from the 14th century, and is one of the finest black-and-white houses in the North West. It has rare 16th-century wall paintings and period furniture, and was the home of the Davenport family for 500 years. Much of the house is open to the public and available for hire. Open air concerts and plays are a feature in summer.

Times Open all year, Apr-Oct, Fri-Sat 1-4, Sun & Tue-Thu 1-5; Nov-Mar, Sat-Sun only 1-4. Closed 25-26 Dec* **Fees** £4.05 (ch & pen £3.05)* **Facilities** (outdoor) (partly accessible) (ground floor on different levels but accessible to wheelchairs) toilets for disabled (access for wheelchair users, guide book) shop

MANCHESTER Map 7 SJ89

Gallery of Costume FREE

Platt Hall, Rusholme M14 5LL
☎ 0161 245 7245
e-mail: m.lambert@manchester.gov.uk
web: www.manchestergalleries.org.uk
dir: in Platt Fields Park, Rusholme, access from Wilmslow Rd. 2m S of city centre

With one of the most comprehensive costume collections in Great Britain, this gallery makes captivating viewing. Housed in a fine Georgian mansion, the displays focus on the changing styles of everyday fashion and accessories over the last 400 years. Contemporary fashion is also illustrated. Because of the vast amount of material in the collection, no one period is permanently illustrated.

Times Open from Apr, Wed-Sat 1.30-4.30* **Facilities** Ⓟ (outdoor) (partly accessible) (ground floor full access, stairs with handrails to first floor) toilets for disabled (ramp, video presentation, handling material) shop

Imperial War Museum North FREE

The Quays, Trafford Wharf Rd, Trafford Park M17 1TZ
☎ 0161 836 4090 0161 836 4012
e-mail: iwmnorth@iwm.org.uk
web: www.iwm.org.uk
dir: M60 junct 9, join Parkway (A5081) towards Trafford Park. At 1st island take 3rd exit onto Village Way. At next island take 2nd exit onto Warren Bruce Rd. Right at T-junct onto Trafford Wharf Rd. Alternatively, leave M602 junct 3 and follow signs

Imperial War Museum North features a wide range of permanent and temporary exhibitions exploring the ways in which human life is affected by war and conflict. The award-winning building (designed by architect Daniel Libeskind) symbolises the world torn apart by conflict.

Times Open all year, Mar-Oct, daily 10-6; Nov-Feb 10-5. Closed 24-26 Dec **Facilities** Ⓟ Ⓟ (indoor) (fully accessible) toilets for disabled (lifts, parking, wheelchairs, induction loop, BSL & audio tour) shop

The John Rylands Library FREE

150 Deansgate M3 3EH
☎ 0161 275 8742 & 306 0555
e-mail: jrl.visitors@manchester.ac.uk
web: www.manchester.ac.uk/library
dir: off A56, at southern end of Deansgate

Founded as a memorial to Manchester cotton-magnate and millionaire John Rylands, this is a public library, and also the Special Collections Division. It is widely regarded as one of the most beautiful libraries in the world. It extends to four million books, manuscripts and archival items representing some fifty cultures and ranging in date from the third millennium BC to the present day. Changing exhibitions throughout the year, and a full public events programme.

Times Open all year Sun-Mon 12-5, Tue-Sat 10-5. Closed 23 Dec-3 Jan **Facilities** Ⓟ licensed (fully accessible) toilets for disabled shop

Manchester Art Gallery

Mosley St M2 3JL
☎ 0161 235 8888 0161 235 8805
web: www.manchestergalleries.org
dir: from M60 follow signs to city centre. Gallery close to Town Hall & Central Library

Manchester Art Gallery houses the city's magnificent art collection in stunning Victorian and contemporary surroundings. Highlights of the collection include outstanding Pre-Raphaelite works, crafts and design, and early 20th-century British art. The Clore Interactive Gallery has lively exhibits and multimedia facilities. There are also a wide range of events, from talks and tours to hands-on activities for children and adults. Contact for details of events and changing exhibitions.

Times Open all year, Tue-Sun, 10-5. Open BH Mon. Closed Good Fri, 24-26 & 31 Dec & 1 Jan* **Fees** £6 (concessions £4, under 18 & Manchester Art Gallery Friends free). For up to date prices please refer to website* **Facilities** Ⓟ licensed (fully accessible) toilets for disabled (w/chairs, induction loops, audio/Braille guides) shop

Manchester Museum

FREE

The University of Manchester, Oxford Rd M13 9PL
☎ 0161 275 2634 & 2643 ▤ 0161 275 2676
e-mail: museum@manchester.ac.uk
web: www.manchester.ac.uk/museum
dir: S of city centre on B5117

Discover the natural wonders of the world and the many cultures it is home to. The objects in the Museum's 15 galleries tell the story of the past, present and future of our planet. Come face to face with live poison dart frogs, fossils of prehistoric creatures and much more besides. Handle objects from the collection, take part in hands-on activities or enjoy a glass of wine or cup of coffee whilst exploring the latest ideas in science, culture and the arts. See website for details of family and adult events. Animal life 1 gallery is undergoing a major redevelopment and will reopen in April 2011.

Times Open all year, Tue-Sat 10-5, Sun-Mon, BHs & 27-31 Dec 11-4. Closed 24-26 Dec & 1 Jan **Facilities** licensed (indoor) (fully accessible) toilets for disabled (hearing loops, Braille & large print, audio guides) shop

Manchester United Museum & Tour Centre

2 FOR 1

Sir Matt Busby Way, Old Trafford M16 0RA
☎ 0161 868 8000 ▤ 0161 868 8861
e-mail: toursenquiry@manutd.co.uk
web: www.manutd.com/museum
dir: 2m from city centre, off A56

This museum was opened in 1986 and was the first purpose-built British football museum. It covers the history of Manchester United, bringing this remarkable story to life through historical exhibits and interactive experiences, from its inception in 1878 to the present day.

Times Open daily 9.30-5. Closed 25 Dec & Match days
Fees Stadium tour & Museum: £13 (ch under 16 & concessions £9.50). Family ticket (4) £42, (5) £50. Museum only £10 (ch & concessions £8). Family ticket (4) £32, (5) £40 **Facilities** licensed (indoor) (fully accessible) toilets for disabled (w/chair, audio visual scripts) shop

See advert on this page

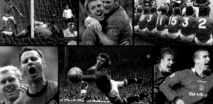

MOSI (Museum of Science and Industry)

Liverpool Rd, Castlefield M3 4FP
☎ 0161 832 2244 ▤ 0161 833 1471
e-mail: marketing@mosi.org.uk
web: www.mosi.org.uk
dir: follow brown tourist signs from city centre

Uncover Manchester's industrial past and learn the fascinating stories of the people who contributed to the history and science of a city which helped shape the modern world. Located on the site of the world's oldest surviving passenger railway station, MoSI's action-packed galleries, working exhibits and costumed

continued

ENGLAND

MANCHESTER *continued*

characters tell the amazing story of revolutionary discoveries and remarkable inventions both past and present. There is a programme of changing exhibitions, please see the website for details.

Times Open all year, daily 10-5 (last admission 4.30). Closed 24-26 Dec & 1 Jan **Fees** All permanent galleries - Free. Charges apply for special exhibitions* **Facilities** Ⓟ Ⓟ ☕ 🍽 licensed ⛩ (indoor) ♿ (fully accessible) toilets for disabled (lifts, wheelchair loan service) shop 🚫

Museum of Transport

Boyle St, Cheetham M8 8UW
☎ 0161 205 2122 📠 0161 205 1110
e-mail: e-mail@gmts.co.uk
web: www.gmts.co.uk
dir: museum adjacent to Queens Rd bus depot. 1.25m N of city centre on Boyle St

This museum is a must-see for fans of public transport. Among the many interesting exhibits are more than 80 beautifully restored buses and coaches from the region - the biggest collection in the UK. Displays of old photographs, tickets and other memorabilia complement the vehicles, some of which date back to 1890. Please telephone for details of special events, most of which, unsurprisingly, relate to transport in some way.

Times Open all year Mar-Oct, 10-5; Nov-Feb, 10-4; Wed, Sat, Sun & BH ex Xmas* **Facilities** Ⓟ Ⓟ ☕ ♿ (fully accessible) toilets for disabled shop 🚫

People's History Museum — FREE

Left Bank, Spinningfields M3 3ER
☎ 0161 838 9190 📠 0161 838 9190
e-mail: info@phm.org.uk
web: www.phm.org.uk
dir: City centre, corner of Left Bank and Bridge St

Following a £12.5m redevelopment, the new and improved people's history museum re-opened in early 2010. Come and see this iconic new building and magnificently restored historic Edwardian Pump House. The museum contains materials that relate to the history of the working people of Britain and the struggle for democracy over two centuries. The galleries are now bigger and better, with even more interactive activities for visitors of all ages.

Times Open all year, daily 10-5. Closed 24-26 Dec, 1 Jan & Good Fri **Facilities** Ⓟ ☕ 🍽 licensed ⛩ (indoor) ♿ (fully accessible) toilets for disabled shop 🚫

The Whitworth Art Gallery — FREE

The University of Manchester, Oxford Rd M15 6ER
☎ 0161 275 7450 📠 0161 275 7451
e-mail: whitworth@manchester.ac.uk
web: www.manchester.ac.uk/whitworth
dir: follow brown tourist signs, on Oxford Rd (B5117) to S of city centre. Gallery in Whitworth Park, opp Manchester Royal Infirmary

The gallery houses an impressive range of modern and historic drawings, prints, paintings and sculpture, as well as the largest collection of textiles and wallpapers outside London, and an internationally famous collection of British watercolours. The gallery hosts an innovative programme of touring exhibitions. A selection of tour lectures, workshops and concerts complement the exhibition programme.

Times Open all year, Mon-Sat 10-5, Sun 12-4. Closed Good Fri & Xmas-New Year* **Facilities** Ⓟ Ⓟ ☕ ⛩ (outdoor) ♿ (fully accessible) toilets for disabled (wheelchair available, induction loop, Braille lift buttons) shop 🚫

PRESTWICH — Map 7 SD80

Heaton Park — FREE

Heaton Park M25 2SW
☎ 0161 773 1085 📠 0161 798 0107
e-mail: heatonpark@manchester.gov.uk
web: www.heatonpark.org.uk
dir: 4m N of Manchester city centre. M60 junct 19, S on A576, then onto A6044 & A665, into St Margaret's Road. Park 100yds on right

600 acres of rolling parkland on the edge of Manchester; a traditional park for the whole family. Facilities include a Tram Museum, sports pitches, stables, farm and animals centres, and a horticultural centre. The hall was designed by James Wyatt for Sir Thomas Egerton in 1772, the house has magnificent period interiors decorated with fine plasterwork, paintings and furniture. Other attractions include a unique circular room with Pompeian-style paintings, and the original Samuel Green organ still in working order.

Times Park: Open all year, daily 8-dusk; Hall: Open Etr-early Sep, Thu-Sun & BH 11-5.30* **Facilities** Ⓟ Ⓟ ☕ ⛩ (outdoor) ♿ (partly accessible) (top floor not accessible) toilets for disabled (disabled parking, land train from car park to facilities) shop 🚫

SALFORD — Map 7 SJ89

The Lowry — FREE

Pier Eight, Salford Quays M50 3AZ
☎ 0843 208 6000 📠 0161 876 2001
e-mail: info@thelowry.com
web: www.thelowry.com
dir: M60 junct 12 for M602. Salford Quays is 0.25m from junct 3 of M602, follow brown Lowry signs

The Lowry is an award-winning building housing galleries, shops, cafés and a restaurant, plus three theatres showing everything from West End plays and musicals, comedians, ballet and live bands. With regular family activity too, you can make a whole day of your visit.

Times Open all year, daily from 10. Galleries, Sun-Fri from 11, Sat from 10. Closed 25 Dec* **Facilities** licensed (fully accessible) toilets for disabled (Sennheiser System, signed, audio & stage text) shop

Salford Museum & Art Gallery

Peel Park, Crescent M5 4WU

0161 778 0800 0161 745 9490

e-mail: salford.museum@salford.gov.uk

web: www.salford.gov.uk/museums.htm

dir: from N leave M60 at junct 16 (A666). From S follow signs from end of M602

The museum features a reconstruction of a 19th-20th century Northern street with original shop fronts. Upstairs in the galleries there are temporary exhibitions and a gallery displaying paintings, sculptures and ceramics. Additions include the lifetimes gallery, featuring audio, IT zones, temporary exhibitions, a spectacular Pilkington's display and lots of hands-on activities and dressing up areas. There are family friendly events running all year at the museum. Please see website for more details.

Times Open all year, Mon-Fri 10-4.45, Sat & Sun 1-5. Closed Good Fri, Etr Sat, 25 & 26 Dec, 1 Jan. **Fees** Free admission, some events & family fun days are chargeable **Facilities** (fully accessible) toilets for disabled (Braille & large print labels & visitor packs, hearing loop) shop

STALYBRIDGE Map 7 SJ99

Astley Cheetham Art Gallery

FREE

Trinity St GK15 2BN

0161 338 6767

e-mail: astley.cheetham@tameside.gov.uk

web: www.tameside.gov.uk

dir: N of town centre

Built as a gift to the town in 1901 by mill owner John Frederick Cheetham, this one-time lecture hall has been an art gallery since 1932 when Cheetham left his collection to the town. Among the works are Italian paintings from the Renaissance, British masters such as Cox and Burne-Jones, and more recent gifts such as works by Turner and local artist Harry Rutherford. The gallery hosts a programme of temporary exhibitions of the collection and regional artists, and a variety of workshops are run for families throughout the year.

Times Open all year, Mon-Wed & Fri 10-12.30, 1-5; Sat 9-12.30, 1-4. **Facilities** (partly accessible) (induction loop)

STOCKPORT Map 7 SJ89

Hat Works Museum

Wellington Mill, Wellington Road South SK3 0EU

0161 355 7770 0161 480 8735

e-mail: bookings.hatworks@stockport.gov.uk

web: www.hatworks.org.uk

dir: M60 junct 1, on A6, Stockport town centre, follow signs for town centre. Museum opp bus station

Hat Works is the UK's only museum of the hatting industry, hats and headwear, offering an insight into a once flourishing industry. See how hats are made with a unique working collection of Victorian millinery machinery and take a tour with expert guides who will give visitors an insight into the Hatter's World. Browse an extensive collection of hats before relaxing in the Level 2 café. Exhibitions and events throughout the year, contact for details.

Times Open all year, Tue-Fri 10-5, Sat, Sun & BHs 11-5. Please telephone for Xmas opening times* **Fees** Free. (Guided tours £2.60 per person) **Facilities** (fully accessible) toilets for disabled (hearing loops) shop

UPPERMILL Map 7 SD90

Saddleworth Museum & Art Gallery

High St OL3 6HS

01457 874093 01457 870336

e-mail: curator@saddleworthmuseum.co.uk

web: www.saddleworthmuseum.co.uk

dir: M62 E junct 22 or M62 W junct 21. On A670

Based in an old mill building next to the Huddersfield canal, the museum explores the history of the Saddleworth area. Wool weaving is the traditional industry, displayed in the 18th-century Weaver's Cottage and the Victoria Mill Gallery. The textile machinery is run regularly by arrangement. The Art Gallery has regular exhibitions.

Times Open all year: Apr-Oct, Mon-Sat 10-4.30; Sun 12-4; Nov-Mar, Mon-Sun 1-4. Closed 24-25 & 31 Dec & 1 Jan* **Fees** Museum £2 (concessions £1) Family ticket £4. Art gallery free* **Facilities** (partly accessible) (chairlift to art gallery, ramp to ground floor galleries) toilets for disabled (Braille & large print guides, wheelchair) shop

HAMPSHIRE

Historic Dockyard, Portsmouth

ALDERSHOT Map 4 SU85

Aldershot Military Museum 2 FOR 1

Evelyn Woods Rd, Queens Av GU11 2LG
☎ 0845 6035635 🖷 01252 342942
e-mail: sally.1.day@hants.gov.uk
web: www.hants.gov.uk/museum/aldershot-museum
dir: A331 exit for 'Aldershot Military Town (North)', attraction near to North Camp

Follow the development of the 'Home of the British army' and the 'Birthplace of British aviation' through brand new displays. Also discover the fascinating local history of Aldershot and Farnborough including the first British powered flight, which took place in October 1908.

Times Open all year, daily 10-5 (last admission 4.30)* **Fees** £2.50 (ch under 5 free, ch & concessions £1, pen £2)* **Facilities** Ⓟ Ⓟ ⛩ (outdoor) ♿ (fully accessible) toilets for disabled shop ⊗

AMPFIELD Map 4 SU42

The Sir Harold Hillier Gardens 2 FOR 1

Jermyns Ln SO51 0QA
☎ 01794 369318 🖷 01794 368027
e-mail: info@hilliergardens.org.uk
web: www.hilliergardens.org.uk
dir: 2m NE of Romsey, signed off A3090 & A3057

Sir Harold Hillier Gardens offers 180 acres of beauty, inspiration and discovery. Over 42,000 plants from temperate regions around the world grow in a variety of landscapes. Visit the Children's Education Garden and Europe's largest Winter Garden. Events, exhibitions and workshops all year round. During May to October visit the spectacular Art in the Garden annual outdoor exhibition, which features 150 sculptures set around the gardens. New play features include the stunning tree house. The 2 for 1 voucher will admit a free concession with each full paying adult.

Times Open all year, daily, 10-6 (or dusk if earlier). Closed 25-26 Dec **Fees** £8.25 (ch under 16 free, concessions £7.15). Group bookings £6.60 (subject to change, please check website) **Facilities** Ⓟ ☕ 🍽 licensed ⛩ (outdoor) ♿ (partly accessible) (most pathways are fully accessible) toilets for disabled (wheelchairs & mobility scooters for hire pre-bookable) shop ⊗

ANDOVER Map 4 SU34

Finkley Down Farm Park

SP11 6NF
☎ 01264 352195 🖷 01264 363172
e-mail: admin@finkleydownfarm.co.uk
web: www.finkleydownfarm.co.uk
dir: signed from A303 & A343, 1.5m N of A303 & 2m E of Andover

This fun family farm park is jam packed with things to do. You can join in with feeding time, groom a pony, or cuddle a rabbit. Lots of activities are scheduled throughout the day, or kids can just let off steam in the playground or on the trampolines. From chipmunks to chinchillas, pygmy goats to peacocks, and lambs to llamas, Finkley Down Farm has something for everyone.

Times Open mid Mar-Oct, daily 10-6 (last admission 5) **Fees** £7 (ch £6). Family ticket (2ad+2ch) £25* **Facilities** Ⓟ ☕ ⛩ (outdoor) ♿ (fully accessible) toilets for disabled shop ⊗

ASHURST Map 4 SU31

Longdown Activity Farm 2 FOR 1

Longdown SO40 7EH
☎ 023 8029 2837 🖷 023 8029 3376
e-mail: enquiries@longdownfarm.co.uk
web: www.longdownfarm.co.uk
dir: off A35 between Lyndhurst & Southampton

Fun for all the family with a variety of hands-on activities every day, including small animal handling and bottle feeding calves and goat kids. Indoor and outdoor play areas, with trampolines and ball pools and bumpy tractor rides. Tearoom, picnic area and excellent gift shop. Farm shop selling locally sourced produce.

Times Open Feb-Oct, daily 10-5; Nov wknds only; Xmas period daily **Fees** £7 (ch 3-14 & concessions £6. Saver ticket £24 (2ad+2ch). (Refer to website for current prices)* **Facilities** Ⓟ ☕ ⛩ (indoor & outdoor) ♿ (partly accessible) (concrete path for wheelchairs) toilets for disabled shop ⊗

AVINGTON Map 4 SU53

Avington Park

SO21 1DB
☎ 01962 779260
e-mail: enquiries@avingtonpark.co.uk
web: www.avingtonpark.co.uk
dir: off B3047 at Itchen Abbas between Winchester & Alresford. 4m from both on River Itchen

Avington Park is a privately-owned house, which was once described by William Cobbett as "one of the prettiest places in the county", and has played host to Charles II and George IV. The state rooms consist of the beautifully painted main hall, the library overlooking the south lawns, adjoining and leading onto a unique pair of conservatories, the old dining room and the ballroom upstairs with a magnificent gold plasterwork ceiling and painted panels.

Times Open May-Sep, Sun & BHs 2.30-5.30 (10-11 Sep 2.30-5). Also open Mon in Aug.* **Facilities** Ⓟ ☕ ♿ (partly accessible) (2 staterooms only accessible by stairs) toilets for disabled

ENGLAND

BASINGSTOKE Map 4 SU65

Milestones - Hampshire's Living History Museum

Basingstoke Leisure Park, Churchill Way West RG22 6PG
☎ 01256 477766 📠 01256 477784
e-mail: louise.mackay@hants.gov.uk
web: www.milestones-museum.com
dir: M3 junct 6, take ringway road (West). Follow brown Leisure Park signs

Milestones brings Hampshire's recent past to life through stunning period street scenes and exciting interactive areas, all under one very large roof. Nationally important collections of transport, technology and everyday life are presented in an entertaining way. Staff in period costumes, mannequins and sounds all bring the streets to life. Various events through the year.

Times Open all year, Tue-Fri & BHs 10-5, Sat-Sun 11-5. Closed 25-26 Dec & 1 Jan* **Facilities** Ⓟ Ⓟ ☕ ⛩ (indoor & outdoor) ♿ (partly accessible) toilets for disabled (induction loops, subtitles screens, scooters, wheelchairs) shop ⊛

BEAULIEU Map 4 SU30

Beaulieu : National Motor Museum

SO42 7ZN
☎ 01590 612345 📠 01590 612624
e-mail: info@beaulieu.co.uk
web: www.beaulieu.co.uk
dir: M27 junct 2, A326, B3054, then follow tourist signs

Set in the heart of William the Conqueror's New Forest, on the banks of the Beaulieu River, stands this 16th-century house. It has become most famous as the home of the National Motor Museum. The site also contains the picturesque abbey ruins, which have an exhibition on life in the middle ages, and various family treasures and memorabilia. Visit the "World of Top Gear" and see actual cars from some of the show's most ambitious challenges. The Secret Army Exhibition tells the story of the secret agents trained at the Beaulieu 'Finishing School' during WWII. There are rides and drives for all the family.

Times Open all year - Palace House & Gardens, National Motor Museum, Beaulieu Abbey & Exhibition of Monastic Life, May-Sep 10-6; Oct-Apr 10-5. Closed 25 Dec **Fees** £16 (ch 5-12 £8.60, 13-17 £9.60, senior £15). Family ticket (1ad+4ch or 2 ad+3ch) £43.50. Please see website for current prices* **Facilities** Ⓟ Ⓟ ☕ 🍽 licensed ⛩ (outdoor) ♿ (partly accessible) (upper level of Palace house & Beaulieu Abbey not accessible by w/chair, visual guides available as alternative) toilets for disabled (ramp access, lift to upper level, induction loop) shop

BISHOP'S WALTHAM Map 4 SU51

Bishop's Waltham Palace

FREE

SO32 1DH
☎ 01489 892460
web: www.english-heritage.org.uk
dir: on B3045

Discover the medieval seat of the Bishops of Winchester. Enjoy the wonderful moated grounds and an exhibition about the powerful Winchester Bishops.

Times Grounds only: May-Sep, Sun-Fri 10-5. Farmhouse May-Sep, Sat-Sun 2-4. Grounds may open Sat please ring before visiting **Facilities** Ⓟ ⛩ shop ⊛ #

BOLDRE Map 4 SZ39

Spinners Garden and Nursery

School Ln SO41 5QE
☎ 01590 675488 & 07545 432090
e-mail: info@spinnersgarden.co.uk
web: www.spinnersgarden.co.uk
dir: off A337, between Brockenhurst & Lymington, follow brown signs

The garden has been entirely created by the owners since 1960. It has azaleas, rhododendrons, camellias, magnolias and Japanese maples interspersed with a huge range of woodland and bog plants. The nursery is well known for its rare trees, shrubs and plants.

Times Open Apr-Sep, Mon-Sat 10-5.* **Fees** £4 **Facilities** Ⓟ Ⓟ ⛩ (outdoor) ♿ (partly accessible) (part of garden unaccessible) (help provided where possible) ⊛

BREAMORE Map 4 SU11

Breamore House & Countryside Museum

SP6 2DF
☎ 01725 512468 📠 01725 512858
e-mail: breamore@btinternet.com
web: www.breamorehouse.com
dir: exit A338 between Salisbury & Fordingbridge. Follow signs for 1m

The handsome manor house was completed in around 1583 and has a fine collection of paintings, china and tapestries. The museum has good examples of steam engines, and uses reconstructed workshops and other displays to show how people lived and worked a century or so ago. There is also a children's playground.

Times Open Apr, Tue, Sun & Etr, May-Sep, Tue-Thu & Sat, Sun & all BH; 2-5.30 (Countryside Museum 1pm).* **Facilities** Ⓟ Ⓟ ☕ ♿ (partly accessible) toilets for disabled (ramps, parking, recorded message & book about 1st floor) shop ⊗

BUCKLERS HARD **Map 4 SU40**

Buckler's Hard Village & Maritime Museum

SO42 7XB

☎ 01590 616203 📠 01590 612624

e-mail: info@bucklershard.co.uk

web: www.bucklershard.co.uk

dir: M27 junct 2, A326, B3054 then follow tourist signs to Beaulieu & Buckler's Hard

An enticing port of call, the historic and picturesque shipbuilding village of Buckler's Hard is where ships from Nelson's fleet were built. Enjoy the Buckler's Hard Story, *SS Persia* Exhibition and the authentically reconstructed 18th-century historic cottages. Savour the sights and sounds of the countryside on a ramble through the woodland walk or along the Riverside Walk. Enjoy a cruise on the Beaulieu River between Easter and October.

Times Open all year daily from 10. Closed 25 Dec **Fees** £5.95 (ch 5-17 £4.30, senior £5.60). Family ticket (1ad+4ch or 2ad+3ch) £17.50. Annual pass also available £10. Please see website for current prices* **Facilities** Ⓟ ☕ 🍴 licensed ⛩ (outdoor) ♿ (partly accessible) toilets for disabled shop

BURGHCLERE **Map 4 SU46**

Sandham Memorial Chapel

Harts Ln RG20 9JT

☎ 01635 278394 📠 01635 278394

e-mail: sandham@nationaltrust.org.uk

web: www.nationaltrust.org.uk/sandham

dir: 4m S Newbury, 0.5m E of A34. Follow signs to Highclere/ Burghclere, then brown signs or white NT signs to Sandham Memorial Chapel

This red brick chapel was built in the 1920s for the artist Stanley Spencer to fill with paintings inspired by his experiences in WWI. Influenced by Giotto's Arena Chapel in Padua, Spencer took 5 years to complete what is arguably his finest achievement. The chapel is set amongst lawns and orchards with views over Watership Down. The chapel has no internal lighting, so it's best to visit on a bright day. 2011 marks the 85th anniversary of the completion of the Sandham Memorial Chapel. The architect Lionel Pearson of Adams, Holden and Pearson was also involved in the design of the Royal Artillery Memorial in London.

Times Open wknds 5-27 Mar & 5-18 Dec, 11-3; 30 Mar-2 Oct, Wed-Sun 11-5; 5-30 Oct, Wed-Sun 11-3 **Fees** £4 (ch £2) **Facilities** Ⓟ ⛩ (outdoor) ♿ (partly accessible) (portable ramps available for manual wheelchairs to chapel) (Braille guide, large print guide, hearing loop, ramps) ⊗ ✿

CHAWTON **Map 4 SU73**

Jane Austen's House Museum

GU34 1SD

☎ 01420 83262

e-mail: enquiries@jane-austens-house-museum.org.uk

web: www.jane-austens-house-museum.org.uk

dir: 1m SW of Alton, in centre of village

Jane Austen lived and wrote here from 1809 to 1817. Restored to look as it would have done in the early 1800s, with items such as the author's donkey cart and writing table to be seen. Celebrations and events to commemorate 200th anniversary of the publication of Jane's first book *Sense and Sensibility.* Details available on the website.

Times Open daily Feb half-term, 1-2 Jan-mid Feb wknds only. Closed 25-26 Dec **Fees** £7.50 (ch 2-16 £2 under 2 free, concessions £6) **Facilities** Ⓟ ⛩ (outdoor) ♿ (partly accessible) (ground floor & garden fully accessible, no access to first floor) toilets for disabled (wheelchair ramp) shop ⊗

EXBURY **Map 4 SU40**

Exbury Gardens & Railway

Exbury Estate Office SO45 1AZ

☎ 023 8089 1203 📠 023 8089 9940

e-mail: nigel.philpott@exbury.co.uk

web: www.exbury.co.uk

dir: from M27 W junct 2, 3m from Beaulieu, off B3054

A 200-acre landscaped woodland garden on the east bank of the Beaulieu River, with one of the finest collections of rhododendrons, azaleas, camellias and magnolias in the world - as well as many rare and beautiful shrubs and trees. A labyrinth of tracks and paths enable you to explore the beautiful gardens and walks. Year round interest is ensured in various parts of the gardens and a steam railway has several features. Exbury is National Collection holder for Nyssa and Oxydendrum, spectacular trees for autumn colour. The Five Arrows Gallery hosts a number of art exhibitions and plant displays during the year.

Times Open 19 Mar-6 Nov, daily 10-5 (last admission); Santa Steam Specials on selected dates in Dec **Fees** £8.50 (ch under 3 free, ch 3-15 £1.50, concessions £8). Family ticket (2ad+3ch) £19. Railway £3.50. The railway has 4 carriages accessible to wheelchairs* **Facilities** Ⓟ Ⓟ 🍴 licensed ⛩ (outdoor) ♿ (partly accessible) (most pathways accessible) toilets for disabled (free wheelchair loans, access maps, buggy tours £3.50-£4) shop

ENGLAND

FAREHAM Map 4 SU50

Royal Armouries Fort Nelson

Portsdown Hill Rd PO17 6AN
☎ 01329 233734 01329 822092
e-mail: fnenquiries@armouries.org.uk
web: www.royalarmouries.org
dir: from M27 junct 11, follow brown tourist signs for Royal Armouries

Home to the Royal Armouries' collection of over 350 big guns and cannon, this superbly restored Victorian fort overlooks Portsmouth Harbour. Built in the 1860s to deter a threatened French invasion, there are secret tunnels, underground chambers and grass ramparts to explore with daily guided tours and explosive gun firings. There are free children's activity days on Tuesday and Thursday during school holidays.

Times Open all year, Apr-Oct, daily 10-5 (Wed 11-5); Nov-Mar, daily 10.30-4 (Wed 11.30-4). Closed 24-26 Dec.* **Facilities** (outdoor) (fully accessible) toilets for disabled (access & audio guide, ramps, induction loop, wheelchair) shop

GOSPORT Map 4 SZ69

Explosion Museum of Naval Firepower

2 FOR 1

Priddy's Hard PO12 4LE
☎ 023 9250 5600 023 9250 5605
e-mail: info@explosion.org.uk
web: www.explosion.org.uk
dir: M27 junct 11, A32 and follow signs

Explosion The Museum of Naval Firepower is set in the green Heritage Area of Priddy's Hard in Gosport on the shores of Portsmouth Harbour, telling the story of naval firepower from the days of gunpowder to modern missiles. Come face to face with the atom bomb, the Exocet missile and the Gatling Gun and take a trip into the fascinating story of the men and women who supplied the Royal Navy. Walk around the buildings that were a state secret for 200 years and discover the Grand Magazine, an amazing vault once packed full with gunpowder, now a stunning multimedia film show.

Times Open Apr-Oct daily 10-5; Nov-Mar wknds only 10-4 **Fees** £10 (ch £5, pen £7)* **Facilities** licensed (outdoor) (partly accessible) (ideal for w/chair users) toilets for disabled (induction loop) shop

Royal Navy Submarine Museum

Haslar Rd PO12 2AS
☎ 023 9251 0354 023 9251 1349
e-mail: enquiries@submarine-museum.co.uk
web: www.submarine-museum.co.uk
dir: M27 junct 11, follow brown tourist signs

Dive into history and go onboard a WWII submarine - *HMS Alliance*, with a veteran submariner to hear his stories about living beneath the waves. Peer into the only surviving WWII midget submarine, climb inside the Royal Navy's first submarine, *Holland I* and relax in the harbour-side coffee shop.

Times Open all year, Apr-Oct 10-5.30; Nov-Mar 10-4.30 (last tour 1 hour before closing). Closed 24-26 Dec & 1 Jan **Fees** £10 (ch £7, pen £8). Family (2ad+3ch) £28* **Facilities** (indoor & outdoor) (partly accessible) (no wheelchair access to the Alliance WWII submarine) toilets for disabled (Braille info, hearing loop, lift to upper gallery) shop

HARTLEY WINTNEY Map 4 SU75

West Green House Gardens

West Green RG27 8JB
☎ 01252 844611 01252 844611
e-mail: enquiries@westgreenhouse.co.uk
web: www.westgreenhouse.co.uk
dir: off A30, at Phoenix Green take sign to West Green, along Thackhams Lane. House last left

The gardens are considered to be one of the top 50 gardens in England and were the subject of a whole edition of the BBC's *Gardener's World*. Today the Queen Anne house is surrounded by four walled gardens, lakes, follies, the green theatre, nymphaeum, mixed border and potager. The owner is a noted garden writer and lecturer. Music and opera performances are a regular feature.

Times Open Etr Sat & Sun then Wed, Thu, Sat, Sun until 19 Sep, 11-4.30.* **Facilities** licensed (outdoor) (partly accessible) shop

HAVANT Map 4 SU70

Staunton Country Park

2 FOR 1

Middle Park Way PO9 5HB
☎ 023 9245 3405 023 9249 8156
e-mail: staunton.park@hants.gov.uk
web: www.hants.gov.uk/staunton
dir: off B2149, between Havant & Horndean

Set in the Regency pleasure grounds of Sir George Staunton, 19th-century traveller, Orientalist and patron of horticulture, Staunton boasts an ornamental farm, the largest ornamental glasshouses on the South Coast, 1,000 acres of parkland, with ancient woodland and intriguing follies and much, much more. Children can feed farm animals, or visit the play area while the grown-ups stroll through the walled gardens or get lost in the Golden Jubilee Maze.

Times Open all year, daily 10-5 (4 winter) **Fees** £6.20 (ch & pen £4.60). Prices subject to change* **Facilities** licensed (outdoor) (partly accessible) (most areas accessible) toilets for disabled (wheelchair for visitors, lift) shop

HIGHCLERE Map 4 SU45

Highclere Castle & Gardens

RG20 9RN
☎ 01635 253210 Fax 01635 255315
e-mail: theoffice@highclerecastle.co.uk
web: www.highclerecastle.co.uk
dir: 4.5m S of Newbury, off A34

This splendid early Victorian mansion stands in beautiful parkland on the site of a previous house, which in turn was built on the site of an even earlier house owned by the Bishops of Winchester. The Castle cellars have been redeveloped firstly to display the family's collection of Egyptian artefacts and secondly to recreate the discovery of the tomb of Tutankhamun in 1922, by the 5th Earl and Howard Carter.

Times Open Jul-Aug, Sun-Thu, last entry 3.30. Telephone 01635 253210 before travelling as Highclere Castle reserves the right to close at other times **Facilities** (outdoor) (partly accessible) (first floor landing/bedrooms not accessible) toilets for disabled (wheelchair available) shop

HINTON AMPNER Map 4 SU62

Hinton Ampner

SO24 0LA
☎ 01962 771305 Fax 01962 793101
e-mail: hintonampner@nationaltrust.org.uk
web: www.nationaltrust.org.uk
dir: off A272, 1m W of Bramdean

A masterpiece of design by Ralph Dutton, 8th and last Lord Sherborne, the 12 acre garden unites a formal layout with varied and informal plantings in pastel shades. There are magnificent vistas over 80 acres of parkland and rolling Hampshire countryside. The house, which is tenanted, contains Ralph Dutton's fine collection of Regency furniture, Italian paintings and hardstone items.

Times Garden, Shop & Tea room open: 19 Feb-30 Oct, Sat-Thu 10-5; 31 Oct-Nov, Sat-Wed, 10-5. House: 19 Feb-30 Oct, Sat-Thu 11-5; 31 Oct-30 Nov, Sat-Wed 11-5. All open 3-11 Dec daily 11-4. 9 Dec all open 11-7. Open on Good Fri usual times* **Fees** With voluntary Gift Aid donation: House and Garden £8.25 (ch £4). Group £7 each. Garden only £7 (ch £3.50) **Facilities** (outdoor) (partly accessible) (ground floor of house only accessible) toilets for disabled (Braille guides, special parking, wheelchair loan) shop

HURST CASTLE Map 4 SZ38

Hurst Castle

SO4 0FF
☎ 01590 642344
web: www.english-heritage.org.uk
dir: on Pebble Spit S of Keyhaven

Built by Henry VIII, Hurst Castle was the pride of Tudor England's coastal defences. Crouched menacingly on a shingle spit, the castle has a fascinating history, including involvement in the smuggling trade in the 17th and 18th centuries.

Times Open Apr-Sep, daily 10.30-5.30; Oct closes 4pm **Fees** £3.60 (ch £2.30, concessions £3.30). Prices and opening times are subject to change in March 2011. Please call 0870 333 1181 for the most up to date prices and opening times when planning your visit **Facilities**

LIPHOOK Map 4 SU83

Hollycombe Steam In The Country

Iron Hill, Midhurst Rd GU30 7LP
☎ 01428 724900 Fax 01428 723682
e-mail: info@hollycombe.co.uk
web: www.hollycombe.co.uk
dir: 1m SE Liphook on Midhurst road, follow brown tourist signs

A comprehensive collection of working steam-power, including a large Edwardian fairground, railways, one with spectacular views of the South Downs, traction engine hauled rides, steam agricultural machinery, sawmill and even a paddle steamer engine. The museum celebrates its 40th Anniversary in July 2011.

Times Open Apr-Oct, Sun & BHs, 4 wks to Aug BH, daily ex Mon & Sat (apart from BH wknd), 11-5* **Fees** £12 (ch 3-15 £10 & pen £10)* **Facilities** (outdoor) (partly accessible) (some rough paths, some rides inacessible) toilets for disabled shop

LYNDHURST Map 4 SU30

The New Forest Centre

Main Car Park, High St SO43 7NY
☎ 023 8028 3444 fax 023 8028 4236
e-mail: office@newforestmuseum.org.uk
web: www.newforestmuseum.org.uk
dir: leave M27 at Cadnam & follow A337 to Lyndhurst. Visitor Centre signed

The story of the New Forest - history, traditions, character and wildlife, told through an audio-visual show and exhibition displays. With life-size models of Forest characters, and the famous New Forest embroidery. Events and exhibitions throughout the year, and children's activities on Tuesdays and Thursdays during every school holiday. Contact for details.

Times Open all year daily, from 10. Closed 25-26 Dec & 1 Feb* **Facilities** P (fully accessible) toilets for disabled shop

MARWELL Map 4 SU52

Marwell Zoological Park

Colden Common SO21 1JH
☎ 01962 777407 fax 01962 777511
e-mail: marwell@marwell.org.uk
web: www.marwell.org.uk
dir: M3 junct 11 or M27 junct 5. On B2177, follow brown tourist signs

Marwell has over 200 species of rare and wonderful animals including tigers, snow leopards, rhino, meerkats, hippo and zebra. Highlights include The World of Lemurs, Encounter Village, Tropical World with its rainforest environment, Into Africa for giraffes and monkeys, Penguin World and Desert Carnivores. Recent additions include an exciting new snow leopard enclosure and a walkway that enables visitors to come face to face with the giraffes. Marwell is dedicated to saving endangered species and every visit helps conservation work. With road and rail trains, holiday activities, gift shop and adventure playgrounds Marwell provides fun and interest for all ages.

Times Open all year, daily 10-6 (summer), 10-4 (winter) (last admission 90 mins before closing). Closed 25 Dec* **Facilities** P licensed (outdoor) (partly accessible) toilets for disabled shop

MIDDLE WALLOP Map 4 SU23

Museum of Army Flying

SO20 8DY
☎ 01264 784421 fax 01264 781694
e-mail: administration@flying-museum.org.uk
web: www.flying-museum.org.uk
dir: on A343, between Andover & Salisbury

One of the country's finest historical collections of military kites, gliders, aeroplanes and helicopters. Imaginative dioramas and displays trace the development of Army flying from before the First World War to more recent conflicts in Ireland, the Falklands and the Gulf. Sit at the controls of a real Scout or Apache attack helicopters and test your skills on the flight simulator, plus children's education centre and 1940s house.

Times Open all year, daily 10-4.30. Closed week prior to Xmas. Evening visits by special arrangement. Private functions welcome.* **Facilities** P licensed (outdoor) (fully accessible) toilets for disabled (lifts to upper levels) shop

MINSTEAD Map 4 SU21

Furzey Gardens

SO43 7GL
☎ 023 8081 2464 & 8081 2297 fax 023 8081 2297
e-mail: info@furzey-gardens.org
web: www.furzey-gardens.org
dir: 1m S of junct A31/M3 Cadnam off A31 or A337 near Lyndhurst

A large thatched gallery is the venue for refreshments and displays of local arts and crafts, and the eight acres of peaceful glades which surround it include winter and summer heathers, rare flowering trees and shrubs and a mass of spring bulbs. There is a 16th-century cottage, lake, and the nursery, run by the Minstead Training Project for Young People with Learning Disabilities, sells a wide range of produce.

Times Gardens open daily, 10-5 (or dusk if earlier). Gallery open Mar-Oct, 10-5* **Facilities** P P (outdoor) (partly accessible) (garden access for wheelchair visitors with assistance) toilets for disabled shop

MOTTISFONT Map 4 SU32

Mottisfont Abbey & Garden

SO51 0LP
☎ 01794 340757 fax 01794 341492
e-mail: mottisfontabbey@nationaltrust.org.uk
web: www.nationaltrust.org.uk/mottisfontabbey
dir: 4.5m NW of Romsey, 1m W of A3057

In a picturesque setting by the River Test, Mottisfont Abbey is an 18th-century house adapted from a 12th-century priory. The north front shows its medieval church origins quite clearly, and the garden has splendid old trees and a walled garden planted

with the national collection of old-fashioned roses. The estate includes Mottisfont village and surrounding farmland and woods.

Times House: Open daily Mar-29 Oct 11-5. Garden: Open all year daily Mar-29 Oct 11-5; Nov-Feb Sat & Sun only. Closed Fri 21 Apr-25 May & 30 Jun-29 Oct* **Facilities** Ⓟ licensed (outdoor) (partly accessible) toilets for disabled (Braille guide, wheelchair available, driven buggy) shop

NETLEY Map 4 SU40

Netley Abbey

FREE

SO31 5FB
☎ 023 9258 1059
web: www.english-heritage.org.uk
dir: 4m SE of Southampton, facing Southampton Water

A romantic ruin, set among green lawns and trees, this 13th-century Cistercian abbey was founded by Peter des Roches, tutor to Henry III. Nearby is the 19th-century Gothic Netley Castle.

Times Open all year, Apr-Sep, daily 10-6; Oct-Mar, Sat-Sun 10-3. Closed 24-26 Dec & 1 Jan **Facilities** Ⓟ

NEW ALRESFORD Map 4 SU53

Watercress Line

2 FOR 1

The Railway Station SO24 9JG
☎ 01962 733810 fax 01962 735448
e-mail: info@watercressline.co.uk
web: www.watercressline.co.uk
dir: stations at Alton & Alresford signed off A31, follow brown tourist signs

The Watercress Line runs through ten miles of rolling scenic countryside between Alton and Alresford. All four stations are 'dressed' in period style, and there's a locomotive yard and picnic area at Ropley. Special events throughout the year including Thomas the Tank Engine, War on the Line and Santa Specials. The 2 for 1 voucher is not valid for special event days.

Times Open Jan-Oct wknds, May-Sep midwk, Aug daily.*
Fees Unlimited travel for the day, £14 (ch £7). Family ticket £35 (2ad+2ch). Charge for dogs. Pre-booked groups 15+ discount available **Facilities** Ⓟ Ⓟ licensed (outdoor) (partly accessible) (ramp access to trains) toilets for disabled shop

NEW MILTON Map 4 SZ29

Sammy Miller Motorcycle Museum

Bashley Cross Rd BH25 5SZ
☎ 01425 620777 & 616644 fax 01425 639407
e-mail: info@sammymiller.co.uk
web: www.sammymiller.co.uk
dir: signed off A35, 15m W of Southampton, 10m E of Bournemouth, N of New Milton town centre

Run by motorcycling legend Sammy Miller MBE, the museum houses over 300 rare and classic bikes and, with machines dating back to 1900, some are the only surviving examples of their type. The Racing collection features world record-breaking bikes and their history, including the first bike to lap a Grand Prix course at over 100 miles per hour. The collection constantly evolves as new bikes are acquired; almost every bike is in full running order.

Times Open all year, daily 10-4.30. Closed wkdys Dec-Feb.*
Facilities Ⓟ Ⓟ licensed (outdoor) (partly accessible) (upstairs inaccessible) toilets for disabled (special rates for disabled people) shop

OLD BASING Map 4 SU65

Basing House

Redbridge Ln RG24 7HB
☎ 01256 467294 fax 01256 326283
dir: signed from Basingstoke ring road

The largest private house of Tudor England, almost entirely destroyed by Parliamentary forces during a two-year siege ending in 1645. Built on the site of a Norman castle in 1530, the ruins include a 300ft long tunnel. There is a re-creation of a garden of 1600 and exhibitions showing the history of the house. A fine 16th-century barn stands nearby.

Times Open Apr-Sep, Wed-Sun & BH 2-6.* **Facilities** Ⓟ (outdoor) (partly accessible) toilets for disabled (disabled parking by prior arangement) shop

ENGLAND

OWER Map 4 SU31

Paultons Park

SO51 6AL
☎ 023 8081 4442 023 8081 3025
e-mail: guestservices@paultons.co.uk
web: www.paultonspark.co.uk
dir: exit M27 junct 2, near junct A31 & A36

Paultons Park offers a great day out for all the family with over 50 different attractions. Many fun activities and rides include EDGE, The Cobra, The Stinger, Raging River Ride log flume, Sky Swinger, and many more. Attractions for younger children include Water Kingdom, Tiny Tots Town, Rabbit Ride, the Magic Forest, Wonderful World of Wind in the Willows and the Ladybird ride. New for 2011 is Peppa Pig World. In beautiful parkland setting with extensive 'Capability' Brown gardens landscaped with ponds and aviaries for exotic birds, including a colony of penguins; lake and hedge maze. There is also the Village Life Museum. Something for everyone.

Times Open mid Mar-Oct, daily 10-6; Nov & Dec, wknds only until Xmas.* **Fees** £18.50 (adults & ch over 1mtr tall). (Free entry only for children under 1mtr tall). Range of Family Supersavers. Refer to website for up to date details* **Facilities** licensed (outdoor) (partly accessible) (some rides accessible for disabled guests) toilets for disabled (pre-booked wheelchair hire, some rides unsuitable) shop

PORTCHESTER Map 4 SU60

Portchester Castle

Castle St PO16 9QW
☎ 023 9237 8291
web: www.english-heritage.org.uk
dir: off A27

Discover 2,000 years of history from its Roman beginnings to the years of medieval splendour. Stand where Henry V rallied his troops before setting out to the battle of Agincourt in 1415.

Times Open all year, Apr-Sep, daily 10-6; Oct-Mar, daily 10-4. Closed 24-26 Dec & 1 Jan **Fees** £4.50 (ch £2.30, concessions £3.80). Family £11.30. Prices and opening times are subject to change in March 2011. Please call 0870 333 1181 for the most up to date prices and opening times when planning your visit **Facilities** shop

PORTSMOUTH Map 4 SU60

Blue Reef Aquarium

Clarence Esplanade PO5 3PB
☎ 023 9287 5222 023 9229 4443
e-mail: portsmouth@bluereefaquarium.co.uk
web: www.bluereefaquarium.co.uk
dir: on approach to city follow brown tourist signs to seafront or Aquarium. Located on Southsea seafront between D-Day Museum and The Hoverport

Spectacular underwater walkthrough tunnels offer amazing sights of exotic coral reefs - home to sharks and shimmering shoals of brightly-coloured fish. Mediterranean and tropical waters are recreated in giant ocean tanks, home to a stunning array of undersea life including seahorses, puffer fish, coral, piranhas, and incredible crustaceans. Visit the website for current special events.

Times Open all year, daily from 10. Closing times vary with season, please telephone for details.* **Facilities** (outdoor) (fully accessible) toilets for disabled (all on 1 level) shop

Charles Dickens' Birthplace Museum

393 Old Commercial Rd PO1 4QL
☎ 023 9282 7261 023 9287 5276
e-mail: mvs@portsmouthcc.gov.uk
web: www.charlesdickensbirthplace.co.uk
dir: M27/M275 into Portsmouth, from M275 turn left at 'The News' rdbt. Signed

A small terraced house built in 1805 which became the birthplace and early home of the famous novelist, born in 1812. On display are items pertaining to Dickens' work, portraits of the Dickens' family, and the couch on which he died. Dickens readings are given in the exhibition room on the first Sunday of each month at 3pm.

Times Open Apr-Sep, daily 10-5.30 (last admission 5)* **Facilities** shop

City Museum & Records Office FREE

Museum Rd PO1 2LJ
☎ 023 9282 7261 023 9287 5276
e-mail: mvs@portsmouthcc.gov.uk
web: www.portsmouthcitymuseums.co.uk/
dir: M27/M275 into Portsmouth, follow museum symbol, City Museum on Brown signposts

Dedicated to local history, fine and decorative art, 'The Story of Portsmouth' displays room settings showing life here from the 17th century to the 1950s. The 'Portsmouth at Play' exhibition features leisure pursuits from the Victorian period to the 1970s. The museum has a fine and decorative art gallery, plus a temporary exhibition gallery with regular changing exhibitions. The Record Office contains the official records of the City of Portsmouth from the 14th century.

Times Open all year, Apr-Sep, daily 10-5.30; Oct-Mar, 10-5. Closed 24-26 Dec & Record Office closed on PH* **Facilities** (outdoor) (fully accessible) toilets for disabled (induction loops, lift & wheelchairs, parking) shop

D-Day Museum & Overlord Embroidery

Clarence Esplanade PO5 3NT
☎ 023 9282 7261 📠 023 9287 5276
e-mail: mvs@portsmouthcc.gov.uk
web: www.ddaymuseum.co.uk
dir: M27/M275 or M27/A2030 into Portsmouth, follow signs for seafront then D-Day museum name signs

Portsmouth's D-Day Museum tells the dramatic story of the Allied landings in Normandy in 1944. The centrepiece is the magnificent 'Overlord Embroidery', 34 individual panels and 83 metres in length. Experience the world's largest ever seaborne invasion, and step back in time to scenes of wartime Britain. Military equipment, vehicles, landing craft and personal memories complete this special story.

Times Open all year, Apr-Sep, daily 10-5.30; Oct-Mar, 10-5. Closed 24-26 Dec* **Facilities** 🅟 Ⓟ ☕ 🛒 (outdoor) ♿ (fully accessible) toilets for disabled (induction loops, sound aids, w/chairs available) shop ⊗

Eastney Beam Engine House FREE

Henderson Rd, Eastney PO4 9JF
☎ 023 9282 7261 📠 023 9287 5276
e-mail: mvs@portsmouthcc.gov.uk
web: www.portsmouthmuseums.co.uk
dir: accessible from A3(M), A27 & A2030 into Southsea, turn left at Bransbury Park lights towards seafront or follow signs

The main attraction here is a magnificent pair of James Watt Beam Engines still housed in their original High Victorian engine house opened in 1887. One of these engines is in steam when the museum is open. A variety of other pumping engines, many in running order, are also on display.

Times Open last wknd of month 1-5 (last admission 30 minutes before closing). Closed Dec* **Facilities** Ⓟ shop ⊗

Natural History Museum & Butterfly House FREE

Cumberland House, Eastern Pde PO4 9RF
☎ 023 9282 7261 📠 023 9282 5276
e-mail: mvs@portsmouthcc.gov.uk
web: www.portsmouthnaturalhistory.co.uk
dir: accessed via A3(M), A27 or A2030, follow signs to seafront

Focusing on the natural history and geology of the area, with wildlife dioramas including a riverbank scene with fresh water aquarium. During the summer British and European butterflies fly free in the Butterfly House.

Times Open all year daily, Apr-Oct 10-5.30; Nov-Mar 10-5.* **Facilities** Ⓟ shop ⊗

Portsmouth Historic Dockyard

HM Naval Base PO1 3LJ
☎ 023 9283 9766 📠 023 9283 8228
e-mail: enquiries@historicdockyard.co.uk
web: www.historicdockyard.co.uk
dir: M27/M275 & follow brown historic waterfront and dockyard signs

Portsmouth Historic Dockyard is home to the world's greatest historic ships: *HMS Victory* - Lord Nelson's flagship at the Battle of Trafalgar and *HMS Warrior* - the first iron-hulled warship. In addition, the National Museum of the Royal Navy has the most significant, permanent collections relating to Nelson and the Battle of Trafalgar, and Action Stations gives an interactive insight into the modern day Royal Navy. View the exceptional collection of thousands of personal, domestic and military objects in the Mary Rose Museum (Henry VIII's favourite ship). 2011 is the 150th anniversary of *HMS Warrior*'s first year of service.

Times Open Apr-Oct, daily 10-6; Nov-Mar, daily 10-5.30 (last entry 1hr 30mins before closing) **Fees** £19.50 (ch & student £14, under 5 free, pen £16.50) Family £55* **Facilities** 🅟 Ⓟ ☕ 🍽 licensed 🛒 (outdoor) ♿ (partly accessible) (varying degrees of accessibility, please check website) toilets for disabled (wheelchairs, facilities for visually & hearing impaired) shop ⊗

The Royal Marines Museum

Southsea PO4 9PX
☎ 023 9281 9385 📠 023 9283 8420
e-mail: info@royalmarinesmuseum.co.uk
web: www.royalmarinesmuseum.co.uk
dir: signed from seafront

The Royal Marines Museum celebrates the famous fighting spirit and long history of the Royal Marines. Based in the lavishly decorated former Officers' Mess of Eastney Barracks, built in the 1860s for the Royal Marine Artillery, the Museum is situated in the very heart of the Corps history. With displays and exhibits highlighting the history of the Royal Marines from their beginnings in 1664 through to the present day, 'The Making of the Royal Marines Commando' exhibition and the Special Exhibition Gallery, the Museum brings to life the history, character and humour of the Royal Marines.

Times Open all year, daily 10-5. Closed 24-26 Dec* **Fees** £6.95 (ch 5-16 & student £4.75, pen £5.50). Family ticket (2ad+4ch) £16.50. Registered disabled £3 (free admission for one assistant)* **Facilities** 🅟 Ⓟ ☕ 🛒 (outdoor) ♿ (fully accessible) toilets for disabled (wheelchairs, hearing loops, special tours-prior notice) shop ⊗

ENGLAND

PORTSMOUTH *continued*

Southsea Castle

Clarence Esplanade PO5 3PA

☎ 023 9282 7261 🖷 023 9287 5276

e-mail: mvs@portsmouthcc.gov.uk

web: www.southseacastle.co.uk

dir: Follow seafront symbol then Southsea Castle brown signs.

Part of Henry VIII's national coastal defences, this fort was built in 1544. In the 'Time Tunnel' experience, the ghost of the castle's first master gunner guides you through the dramatic scenes from the castle's eventful history. Audio-visual presentation, underground passages, Tudor military history displays, artillery, and panoramic views of the Solent and Isle of Wight.

Times Open Apr-Sep, daily 10-5.30.* **Facilities** (outdoor) (partly accessible) (wheelchair available) shop

Spinnaker Tower

Gunwharf Quays PO1 3TT

☎ 023 9285 7521 🖷 023 9285 7539

e-mail: info@spinnakertower.co.uk

web: www.spinnakertower.co.uk

dir: From M275 follow tourist signs for Tower

Elegant, sculptural and inspired by Portsmouth's maritime heritage, the Spinnaker Tower is a new national icon - a 'must-see' landmark for visitors worldwide. Soaring 170 metres above Portsmouth Harbour, with three viewing decks, the Spinnaker Tower is now open to view. Take the high speed internal lift and step right out into the best view in the country. Dare you 'walk on air' on the glass floor, the largest in Europe? Watch history unfold through unique 'Time Telescopes'. Back down to earth and shop for souvenirs or talk about your travels over a snack in the waterfront Tower Café bar.

Times Open Sep-Jul daily 10-6; Aug Sun-Thu 10-7, Fri-Sat 10-6* **Fees** Standard £7.25 (ch 3-15 £5.75, ch under 3 free, concessions £6.50); Resident £5.25 (ch 3-15 £4.15, ch under 3 free, concessions £4.75)* **Facilities** licensed (partly accessible) (view deck 3 has no wheelchair access) toilets for disabled (hearing loop) shop

RINGWOOD — Map 4 SU10

Moors Valley Country Park

Horton Rd, Ashley Heath BH24 2ET

☎ 01425 470721 🖷 01425 471656

e-mail: moorsvalley@eastdorset.gov.uk

web: www.moors-valley.co.uk

dir: 1.5m from Ashley Heath rdbt on A31 near Three Legged Cross

One thousand acres of forest, woodland, heathland, lakes, river and meadows provide a home for a wide variety of plants and animals, and there's a Visitor Centre, Adventure Playgrounds, picnic area, Moors Valley Railway, Tree Top Trail and 'Go Ape'-high ropes course (book on 0845 643 9215). Cycle hire is also available.

Times Open all year, 8-dusk (8pm at latest). Visitor centre open 9-4.30 (later in summer). Closed 25 Dec **Fees** No admission charge but parking up to £8 per day* **Facilities** licensed (outdoor) (partly accessible) (some footpaths in forest unacessible) toilets for disabled (scooters & wheelchair to hire - book in advance) shop

ROCKBOURNE — Map 4 SU11

Rockbourne Roman Villa — 2 FOR 1

SP6 3PG

☎ 0845 603 5635

web: www.hants.gov.uk/rockbourne-roman-villa

dir: from Salisbury exit A338 at Fordingbridge, take B3078 west through Sandleheath & follow signs. Or turn off A354 (Salisbury to Blandford road), W of Coombe Bissett

Discovered in 1942, the site features the remains of a 40-room Roman villa and is the largest in the area. Displays include mosaics and a very rare hypocaust system. The museum displays the many artefacts found on the site during excavations. Summer Sunday activities - please ring for details.

Times Open Apr-Sep, daily 10.30-6 (last admission 5.30) **Fees** £2.50 (concessions £1.50). Family (2ad+2ch) £7* **Facilities** (outdoor) (fully accessible) toilets for disabled (ramps in & out of museum) shop

ROWLAND'S CASTLE — Map 4 SU71

Stansted Park — 2 FOR 1

PO9 6DX

☎ 023 9241 2265 🖷 023 9241 3773

e-mail: enquiry@stanstedpark.co.uk

web: www.stanstedpark.co.uk

dir: follow brown heritage 'Stansted House' signs from A3 Horndean exit, or A27 Havant exit

Stansted Park is set in 1750 acres of park and woodland. The mansion rooms house the Bessborough family collection of furniture and paintings, and below stairs the restored servants quarters can be found, with an extensive collection of household artefacts giving an insight into the running of the house. The ancient Chapel of St Paul was an inspiration to the poet John Keats and is open in conjunction with the house. Various events through the summer and Christmas.

Times Open Etr-Sep, Sun & BH 1-4; Jun-Aug, Sun-Wed 1-4 & by appt for schools & groups on other days* **Fees** £7 (ch £3.50, concessions £6). Family ticket (2ad+2ch) £18 **Facilities** licensed (outdoor) (partly accessible) (wheelchair lift not suitable for motorised chairs) toilets for disabled (wheelchair lift to house)

ENGLAND

SELBORNE Map 4 SU73

Gilbert White's House, Garden and the Oates Collection

High St GU34 3JH
☎ 01420 511275 Fax 01420 511040
e-mail: info@gilbertwhiteshouse.org.uk
web: www.gilbertwhiteshouse.org.uk
dir: on village High St

Charming 18th-century house, home of famous naturalist, the Rev Gilbert White, author of *The Natural History and Antiquities of Selborne.* Over 20 acres of garden and parkland, shop and tea parlour serving some 18th-century fare. There is also an exhibition on Captain Lawrence Oates and his ill-fated expedition to the South Pole in 1911. Events, courses, exhibitions and lectures throughout the year.

Times Open Jan-28 Mar & 2 Oct-23 Dec, Tue-Sun 11-4; 30 Mar-1 Oct, Tue-Sun (plus BH Mon) 10.30-5.30* **Fees** £7.50 (ch 5-16 £2 under 5 free, concessions £6.50)* **Facilities** Ⓟ ☕ picnic ♿ (partly accessible) (garden fully accessible, upstairs of house not accessible) toilets for disabled (wheelchair users pay 1/2 price) shop 🚫dogs

SHERBORNE ST JOHN Map 4 SU65

The Vyne

RG24 9HL
☎ 01256 883858 Fax 01256 881720
e-mail: thevyne@nationaltrust.org.uk
web: www.nationaltrust.org.uk
dir: 4m N of Basingstoke, off A340, signed from A33, A339 & A340

Built in the early 16th-century for Lord Sandys, the Vyne was visited by Henry VIII at least three times. The house later became home to the Chute family for 350 years. The building is a fascinating microcosm of architectural and design fads and fashions through the centuries. Visitors can view the family's original collection of art and sculpture, and the garden and grounds are very popular for walking. A wetlands area with bird hide attracts a wide diversity of wildlife. The recently restored Victorian glass house is within the walled kitchen garden.

Times House, 14 Mar-1 Nov, Sat & Sun 11-5; 16 Mar-28 Oct, Mon, Tue & Wed. 1-5. Gardens, shop & restaurant Feb-8 Mar; Sat & Sun 11-5; 14 Mar-1 Nov, Sat-Wed, 11-5.* **Facilities** Ⓟ ☕ restaurant licensed picnic (outdoor) ♿ (partly accessible) (Deep gravel in some parts of gardens, along with slopes make access difficult. Access to shop, restaurant & ground floor of house) toilets for disabled (Braille guides, hearing loop & touch tours) shop 🚫dogs National Trust

SOUTHAMPTON Map 4 SU41

Museum of Archaeology FREE

God's House Tower, Winkle St SO14 2NY
☎ 023 8063 5904 & 8083 2768 Fax 023 8033 9601
e-mail: museums@southampton.gov.uk
web: www.southampton.gov.uk/leisure
dir: near waterfront, close to Queen's Park & Town Quay

The museum is housed in an early fortified building, dating from the 1400s and takes its name from the nearby medieval hospital. Exhibits on the Roman, Saxon and medieval towns of Southampton are displayed.

Times Open Tue-Fri 10-4, Sat 10-12, 1-4, Sun 1-4* **Facilities** Ⓟ shop 🚫dogs

Southampton City Art Gallery FREE

Civic Centre, Commercial Rd SO14 7LP
☎ 023 8083 2277 Fax 023 8083 2153
e-mail: art.gallery@southampton.gov.uk
web: www.southampton.gov.uk/art
dir: situated on the Watts Park side of the Civic Centre, a short walk from the station, on Commercial Rd

The largest gallery in the south of England, with the finest collection of British contemporary art in the country outside London. Varied displays of landscapes, portrait paintings or recent British art are always available, as well as a special display, selected by students.

Times Open all year, Tue-Sat 10-5, Sun 1-4. Closed 25-26 & 31 Dec. **Facilities** Ⓟ ☕ restaurant licensed ♿ (fully accessible) toilets for disabled (free BSL signed tours by arrangement, 'touch tour') shop 🚫dogs

SOUTHAMPTON *continued*

Southampton Maritime Museum FREE

The Wool House, Town Quay SO14 2AR
☎ 023 8022 3941 & 8063 5904 📠 023 8033 9601
e-mail: museums@southampton.gov.uk
web: www.southampton.gov.uk/leisure
dir: on the waterfront, near to the Town Quay

The Wool House was built in the 14th century as a warehouse for wool, and now houses a maritime museum, with models and displays telling the history of the Victorian and modern port of Southampton. There are exhibitions on the Titanic, The Queen Mary and an interactive area for children.

Times Open all year, Tue-Fri 10-4; Sat 10-1 & 2-4; Sun 1-4* **Facilities** Ⓟ ♿ (partly accessible) (hearing loop on Titanic presentation) shop ㊗

TITCHFIELD Map 4 SU50

Titchfield Abbey FREE

Place House Studio, Mill Ln PO15 5RA
☎ 01329 842133
dir: 0.5m N off Titchfield, off A27

Also known as 'Place House', in Tudor times this was the seat of the Earl of Southampton, built on the site of the abbey founded in 1232. He incorporated the gatehouse and the nave of the church into his house.

Times Open all year, Apr-Sep, daily 10-5; Oct-Mar, daily 10-4. Closed 25 Dec **Facilities** 🅟 ⛩

WEYHILL Map 4 SU34

Hawk Conservancy Trust 2 FOR 1

SP11 8DY
☎ 01264 773850 📠 01264 773772
e-mail: info@hawkconservancy.org
web: www.hawkconservancy.org
dir: 3m W of Andover, signed from A303

The Hawk Conservancy Trust is a registered charity and award-winning visitor attraction that has for many years been working in the fields of conservation, education, rehabilitation and research of birds of prey. The Trust is set in 22 acres of woodland and wild flower meadow, where there are over 150 birds of prey on view, from the tiny Pygmy Owl to the impressive European Black Vulture. A day at the Trust has a packed itinerary including three flying demonstrations that include owls, kites, hawks, falcons and eagles showing off their skills. There is even an opportunity for visitors to hold a British bird of prey.

Times Open all year. Closed 25-26 Dec **Fees** £11.50 (ch £7.50, pen & student £10). Family ticket (2ad+2ch) £35 **Facilities** 🅟 ☕ ⛩ (indoor & outdoor) ♿ (fully accessible) toilets for disabled (wheelchairs, viewing areas in hides, ramps) shop ㊗

WHITCHURCH Map 4 SU44

Whitchurch Silk Mill 2 FOR 1

28 Winchester St RG28 7AL
☎ 01256 892065 📠 01256 893882
e-mail: silkmill@btinternet.com
web: www.whitchurchsilkmill.org.uk
dir: halfway between Winchester & Newbury, take exit off A34 to Whitchurch. Located in town centre, signed

Whitchurch Silk Mill is idyllically located on the River Test, and is the oldest working silk mill in Britain, still weaving in its original building. Fine silks and ribbons are still woven for interiors, churches and costume dramas. See the 19th-century waterwheel pounding and learn about winding, warping and have a go at hand weaving. There is a programme of exhibitions, workshops and children's activities.

Times Open all year, Tue-Sun & BH Mon 10.30-5 (last admission 4.15). Closed 24 Dec-1 Jan* **Fees** £4 (ch £2.25, pen & student £3.50). Family ticket £9.25 **Facilities** 🅟 Ⓟ ☕ ⛩ (indoor & outdoor) ♿ (partly accessible) (1st floor only accessible via stair lift) toilets for disabled (parking adjacent, AV presentations, induction loops, ramps) shop ㊗

WINCHESTER Map 4 SU42

The Great Hall FREE

Castle Av SO23 8PJ
☎ 01962 846476 📠 01962 841326
e-mail: the.great.hall@hants.gov.uk
web: www.hants.gov.uk/greathall
dir: at top of High St. Park & Ride recommended

The only surviving part of Winchester Castle, once home to the Domesday Book, this 13th-century hall was the centre of court and government life. Built between 1222-1235, during the reign of Henry III, it is one of the largest and finest five bay halls in England to have survived to the present day. The Round Table based on the Arthurian Legend and built between 1230-1280 hangs in the hall. Queen Eleanor's Garden is a re-creation of a late 13th-century ornamental garden.

Times Open all year daily, Mar-Oct, 10-5; Nov-Feb, 10-4. Closed 25-26 Dec.* **Facilities** Ⓟ ♿ (fully accessible) toilets for disabled shop ㊗

Gurkha Museum

Peninsula Barracks, Romsey Rd SO23 8TS
☎ 01962 842832 📠 01962 877597
e-mail: curator@thegurkhamuseum.co.uk
web: www.thegurkhamuseum.co.uk
dir: M3 junct 9 to Winchester, follow one-way system into High St, 1st left after Westgate

This museum tells the fascinating story of the Gurkhas' involvement with the British Army. Travel from Nepal to the North-West Frontier and beyond, with the help of life-sized dioramas, interactive exhibits and sound displays.

Times Open all year, Mon-Sat 10-5, Sun 12-4. Closed 25-26 Dec & 1 Jan* **Fees** £2 (ch under 16 free, pen £1)* **Facilities** (fully accessible) toilets for disabled (lift & chair lift) shop

Horse Power, The King's Royal Hussars Regimental Museum — FREE

Peninsula Barracks, Romsey Rd SO23 8TS
☎ 01962 828539 & 828541 📠 01962 828538
e-mail: curator@horsepowermuseum.co.uk
web: www.krh.org.uk
dir: M3 junct 9/10 follow city centre signs, then hospital A&E red signs to Romsey Rd. Vehicle access from Romsey Rd

Horse Power, the museum of the King's Royal Hussars, tells the exciting story of an English cavalry regiment, mounted on horses and in tanks or armoured cars.

Times Open 6 Jan-18 Dec, Tue-Fri 10-4, wknds & BHs, 12-4. Closed daily between 12.45-1.15* **Facilities** (fully accessible) toilets for disabled (lift to first floor) shop

Hospital of St Cross — 2 FOR 1

St Cross SO23 9SD
☎ 01962 851375 📠 01962 878221
e-mail: visitors@stcrosshospital.co.uk
web: www.stcrosshospital.co.uk
dir: on B3335, 0.5m from M3 junct 11

A beautiful group of Grade I listed medieval and Tudor buildings, in a tranquil setting by the water meadows, St Cross is home to 25 elderly Brothers. In keeping with tradition, they wear gowns and trencher hats and act as visitor guides. The hospital is world-famous for its ancient and unique tradition of the Wayfarers Dole - a beaker of beer and a morsel of bread is given by the porter to all visitors who request it. Visitors can admire the medieval and Tudor architecture, explore the medieval hall, the Georgian kitchen and the Tudor cloister as well as the walled garden with many plants of American origin.

Times Open all year, Apr-Oct, 9.30-5; Nov-Mar 10.30-3.30. Closed Good Fri, 25 Dec, Sun mornings (summer) & Sun (winter) **Fees** £3.50 (ch £1.50, pen £3)* **Facilities** (outdoor) (partly accessible) (ramp access to church & some buildings, gravel paths to gardens) toilets for disabled shop

INTECH - Science Centre & Planetarium — 2 FOR 1

Telegraph Way, Morn Hill SO21 1HZ
☎ 01962 863791 📠 01962 868524
e-mail: htct@intech-uk.com
web: www.intech-uk.com
dir: M3 junct 10 (S) or junct 9 (N) onto A31 then B3404 (Alresford road)

This purpose-built, all-weather, family attraction houses 100 interactive exhibits, which demonstrate the science and technology of the world around us in an engaging and exciting way. The philosophy is most definitely 'hands-on', and the motto of the centre is 'Doing is Believing'. Activities take place during school holidays. INTECH also has the UK's largest capacity planetarium. This digital cinema has a 17-metre high dome that makes the audience feel like it's floating through the universe. Dramatic, awesome and entertaining.

Times Open all year, daily 10-4, Aug 10-5. Closed 3 days at Xmas **Fees** £8 (ch £5.50, pen £6.50) Family ticket (2ad+2ch) £24.30. Planetarium £2.20 with admission **Facilities** (outdoor) (fully accessible) toilets for disabled shop

Royal Hampshire Regiment Museum & Memorial Garden — FREE

Serle's House, Southgate St SO23 9EG
☎ 01962 863658
e-mail: museum@serleshouse.co.uk
web: www.royalhampshireregimentmuseum.co.uk
dir: near city centre. 150mtrs from lights in High St

Regimental Museum of the Royal Hampshire Regiment 1702-1992, housed in 18th-century Serles house, surrounded by the regiment's Memorial Garden. The museum tells the history of the regiment, its regulars, militia, volunteers and Territorials.

Times Normally open all year (ex 2 wks Xmas & New Year), Mon-Fri 10-4; Apr-Oct wknds & BH 12-4* **Facilities** (fully accessible) shop

ENGLAND

WINCHESTER *continued*

Winchester Cathedral

1 The Close SO23 9LS
☎ 01962 857200 & 866854 📠 01962 857201
e-mail: cathedral.office@winchester-cathedral.org.uk
web: www.winchester-cathedral.org.uk
dir: in city centre - follow city heritage signs

The longest medieval church in Europe, founded in 1079 on a site where Christian worship had already been offered for over 400 years. Among its treasures are the 12th-century illuminated Winchester Bible, the font, medieval wall paintings and Triforium Gallery Museum. Items of interest include Jane Austen's tomb and the statue of the Winchester diver, William Walker, who in 1905 saved the cathedral from collapse by underpinning its foundations, working up to six hours a day over a period of six years, often in 20 feet of water. Visitors can also descend into the crypt to see a sculpture by Anthony Gormley, best known as creator of *The Angel of The North*, or ascend to the tower and bell chamber. Christmas Market from Nov to Dec, and Ice Rink from Nov to Jan. Contact for details.

Times Open all year, Mon-Sat 8.30-6, Sun 8.30-5.30 (Subject to services and special events).* **Facilities** Ⓟ ☕ 🍽 licensed ♿ (partly accessible) toilets for disabled (chair lift to east end of Cathedral, touch & hearing model) shop ⊗

Winchester City Mill

Bridge St SO23 8EJ
☎ 01962 870057 📠 01962 870057
e-mail: winchestercitymill@nationaltrust.org.uk
web: www.nationaltrust.org.uk
dir: by city bridge between King Alfred's statue & Chesil St

Built over the fastflowing River Itchen in 1744, the mill has a delightful small island garden and an impressive millrace. There are regular milling demonstrations and guided wildlife walks, as well as other special events and hands-on activities throughout the year.

Times Open: Mill & Shop, 13-21 Feb daily 10.30-4, 12 Mar-12 Jul & 15 Sep-24 Oct Wed-Sun 10.30-5, 13 Jul-12 Sep & 25 Oct-24 Dec daily 10.30-5* **Facilities** Ⓟ ♿ (partly accessible) (hearing loop, large print guide, Braille of video text) shop ⊗ 🌿

Winchester College

73 College St SO23 9NA
☎ 01962 621209 📠 01962 621166
e-mail: enterprises@wincoll.ac.uk
web: www.winchestercollege.org
dir: S of Cathedral Close, beyond Kingsgate arch. Limited vehicle access along College St

Founded in 1382, Winchester College is believed to be the oldest continuously running school in England. The College has greatly expanded over the years but the original buildings remain intact. Visitors can follow in the footsteps of John Keats, and see the College's many historic buildings, including the 14th-century gothic chapel with one of the earliest examples of a fan-vaulted roof constructed from wood rather than stone, the original scholars' dining room and the cloister containing memorials to former members of the college including one to Mallory the Mountaineer.

Times Open all year. Guided tours available Mon, Wed, Fri & Sat; 10.45, 12, 2.15 & 3.30. Tue & Thu 10.45 & 12. Sun 2.15 & 3.30. Groups of 10+ at times to suit by arrangement only. Closed 24 Dec-1 Jan (Tours may be subject to change/cancellation by the college) **Fees** £6 (concessions £5) **Facilities** Ⓟ ♿ (partly accessible) (one building in the tour has access via staircase) toilets for disabled (access ramps) shop ⊗

HEREFORDSHIRE

Hereford Cathedral

ASHTON Map 3 SO56

Berrington Hall

Berrington HR6 0DW

☎ 01568 615721 📠 01568 613263

e-mail: berrington@nationaltrust.org.uk

web: www.nationaltrust.org.uk/main/w-berringtonhall

dir: 3m N of Leominster, on A49

An elegant neo-classical house of the late 18th century, designed by Henry Holland and set in a park landscape by 'Capability' Brown. Visitors can explore life as a servant at Berrington. The butler's pantry and bedroom tell the story of William Kemp, the butler. Join one of the "maids" on a daily below stairs tour. The corner bedroom and back stairs are brought to life with sounds and smells. Events throughout the year please contact for details.

Times Open 1-16 Mar, Sat-Sun; 17 Mar-2 Nov, Mon-Wed, wknds & Good Fri 11-5 (last admission 30mins before closing). Garden open 11-5 (4.30 6-21 Dec). Park walk open 16 Jun-2 Nov; wknds 12-4.30 1-16 Dec. Open Good Fri* **Fees** £7.50 (ch £3.75) Family ticket £18.75. Garden only £6 (ch £3) Family ticket £15. Joint ticket with Croft Castle £10.50 **Facilities** Ⓟ licensed (outdoor) (partly accessible) (lift to tea room) toilets for disabled (wheelchairs/batricar, steps to entrance) shop

BROCKHAMPTON Map 3 SO65

Brockhampton Estate

WR6 5TB

☎ 01885 482077 & 488099 📠 01885 482151

e-mail: brockhampton@nationaltrust.org.uk

web: www.nationaltrust.org.uk

dir: 2m E of Bromyard on A44

This traditionally formed 1700 acre estate has extensive areas of wood and parkland, with a rich variety of wildlife and over five miles of walks. At the heart of the estate lies Lower Brockhampton House, a late 14th-century moated manor house with a beautiful timber-framed gatehouse and ruined chapel.

Times Open House and Tearoom: 6 Mar-4 Apr, Wed-Sun 11-4; 5 Apr-18 Apr & Jul-Aug daily 11-5; 21 Apr-Jun & Sep-Oct, Wed-Sun 11-5; 6 Nov-19 Dec Sat-Sun 11-4.Open BH Mon* **Fees** Lower Brockhampton £5.25 (ch £2.60) Family £13. Parkland only £2.50* **Facilities** Ⓟ (outdoor) (partly accessible) (grounds, shop and ground floor of Lower Brockhampton all accessible) toilets for disabled (special parking, ramps, Braille guide) shop

CROFT Map 3 SO46

Croft Castle & Parkland

Yarpole HR6 9PW

☎ 01568 780246 📠 01568 780462

e-mail: croftcastle@nationaltrust.org.uk

web: www.nationaltrust.org.uk/main/w-croftcastle

dir: off B4362 N of Leominster

Home to the Croft family since Domesday, the walls and towers date from the 14th and 15th centuries, while the interior is mainly 18th century. Set in 1500 acres of Herefordshire countryside, there is a splendid avenue of 350-year-old Spanish chestnuts, and an Iron Age Fort (Croft Ambrey), which may be reached by footpath. Explore the walled garden, church and parkland or enjoy a family walk. There are also many annual events, including outdoor theatre; please telephone for details.

Times Park open all year, daily dawn-dusk. Castle (on open days 11-1 by tour), Garden, shop, tea room & play area open 6 Mar-Oct, Wed-Sun 11-5; 29 Mar-11 Apr & 22-31 May & Jul-Aug & 23-31 Oct, daily 11-5; 6 Nov-19 Dec, Sat-Sun 11-4. Open BH Mons. Tea room & play area also open daily 2-31 Jan & 13-21 & 27-28 Feb 11-4; 27-31 Dec 11-3* **Fees** Gift Aid admission House & gardens £7.50 (ch £3.60) Family ticket £17.90; groups £6.05. Garden & grounds: £4.20 (ch £3.15). Family ticket £10.50. Ground & garden Jan-Feb £2.10 (ch £1.05). Joint ticket with Berrington Hall £10.50. Standard prices also available, see website or display at property* **Facilities** Ⓟ licensed (outdoor) (fully accessible) toilets for disabled (parking, Braille guide, w/chair buggy, Tramper vehicle) shop

GOODRICH Map 3 SO51

Goodrich Castle

HR9 6HY

☎ 01600 890538

web: www.english-heritage.org.uk

dir: 5m S of Ross-on-Wye, off A40

A magnificent red sandstone fortress rising out of a rocky outcrop above the Wye Valley. Climb the huge towers for exhilarating views and explore a maze of small rooms and passageways. Hear about the doomed Civil War lovers on our audio tour.

Times Open all year, Mar, Wed-Sun 10-5; Apr-Jun & Sep-Oct, daily 10-5; Jul-Aug, daily 10-6; Nov-Feb, Wed-Sun 10-4. Closed 24-26 Dec & 1 Jan **Fees** £5.50 (ch £2.80, concessions £4.70). Family £13.80. Prices and opening times are subject to change in March 2011. Please call 0870 333 1181 for the most up to date prices and opening times when planning your visit **Facilities** Ⓟ shop

HEREFORD Map 3 SO53

Cider Museum & King Offa Distillery 2 FOR 1

21 Ryelands St HR4 0LW
☎ 01432 354207
e-mail: enquiries@cidermuseum.co.uk
web: www.cidermuseum.co.uk
dir: off A438 (Hereford to Brecon road)

Explore the fascinating history of cider making - view cidermaking equipment, the cooper's workshop and the vat house. Walk through original champagne cider cellars, see 18th-century English lead crystal cider glasses and 19th-century watercolours of apples and pears.

Times Open all year, Apr-Oct 10-5; Nov-Mar 11-3, closed Sun-Mon. Open BHs **Fees** £4 (ch & students £2.50, concessions £3.50). Party 15+, 50p reduction per person **Facilities** Ⓟ Ⓟ ☕ ⛩ (outdoor) ♿ (partly accessible) (limited access to ground floor) toilets for disabled (audiotapes, large print guide sheets) shop ⓧ

Hereford Cathedral

HR1 2NG
☎ 01432 374200 📠 01432 374220
e-mail: office@herefordcathedral.org
web: www.herefordcathedral.org
dir: A49 signed from city inner ring roads

Built on the site of a place of worship that dates back to Saxon times, Hereford Cathedral contains some of the finest examples of architecture from the Norman era to the present day, including the 13th-century Shrine of St Thomas of Hereford, the recently restored 14th-century Lady Chapel, and the award-winning new library building. The Mappa Mundi and Chained Library exhibition tells the stories of these famous national treasures through models, artefacts and changing exhibitions.

Times Cathedral open daily 7.30-Evensong; Mappa Mundi & Chained Library Exhibition Summer: Mon-Sat 10-4.30, Sun 11-3.30. Winter: Mon-Sat 11-3.30* **Facilities** Ⓟ ☕ ⛩ ♿ (partly accessible) toilets for disabled (touch facility for blind, Braille & large print info) shop ⓧ

Old House FREE

High Town HR1 2AA
☎ 01432 260694 📠 01432 342492
e-mail: herefordmuseums@herefordshire.gov.uk
web: www.herefordshire.gov.uk
dir: in centre of High Town

The Old House is a fine Jacobean building dating from around 1621, and was once in a row of similar houses. Its rooms are furnished in 17th-century style and give visitors the chance to learn what life was like in Cromwell's time.

Times Open all year, Tue-Sat 10-5; Apr-Sep Sun & BH Mon 10-4.* **Facilities** Ⓟ ♿ (partly accessible) (ground floor accessible) (virtual tour, Braille guide, tactile images) shop ⓧ

KINGTON Map 3 SO25

Hergest Croft Gardens

The Hergest Estate Office, Ridgebourne HR5 3EG
☎ 01544 230160 📠 01544 232031
e-mail: gardens@hergest.co.uk
web: www.hergest.co.uk
dir: off A44 W of Kington and follow signs

From spring bulbs to autumn colour, this is a garden for all seasons. A fine collection of trees and shrubs surrounds the Edwardian house. There's an old fashioned kitchen garden with spring and summer borders, and Park Wood, a hidden valley with magnificent rhododendrons. Please contact for details of special events.

Times Open Mar wknds, 28 Mar-1 Nov daily 12.30-5.30.* **Facilities** Ⓟ ☕ ⛩ (outdoor) ♿ (partly accessible) (most of the garden accessible except park wood as it has steep gravel paths) toilets for disabled (portable ramp & wheelchair available) shop

LEDBURY Map 3 SO73

Eastnor Castle

Eastnor HR8 1RL
☎ 01531 633160 📠 01531 631776
e-mail: enquiries@eastnorcastle.com
web: www.eastnorcastle.com
dir: 2.5m E of Ledbury on A438 (Tewkesbury road)

A magnificent Georgian castle in a lovely setting, with a deer park, arboretum and lake. Inside are tapestries, fine art and armour, and the Italianate and Gothic interiors have been beautifully restored. There are an adventure playground, nature trails and lakeside walks. Events take place throughout the year.

Times Open 22-25 Apr; 1-2 & 29-30 May; 5 Jun-25 Sep, Sun; 17 Jul-Aug, Sun-Thu 11-4.30 (last admission 4) **Fees** Castle & grounds £8.50 (ch £5.50, pen £7.50). Family £22.50. Grounds only £5.50 (ch £3.50, pen £4.50). Family £14.50 **Facilities** Ⓟ ☕ ⛩ (outdoor) ♿ (partly accessible) (wheelchair climber, lift) shop

MUCH MARCLE

Westons Cider 2 FOR 1

The Bounds HR8 2NQ
☎ 01531 660108 📠 01531 660619
e-mail: enquiries@westons-cider.co.uk
web: www.westons-cider.co.uk
dir: Turn opp A449 at Much Marcle x-rds (with old garage & Walwyn Arms). Westons about 0.5m up road clearly signed

It's not just about a drop of cider (adults only) on this fun day out. Visitors can take in the Henry Weston courtyard garden; the Bottle Museum tea room; shire horse dray rides (ring first for availability); traditional and rare breeds farm park and orchard walk; a children's playground; visitor centre and Scrumpy House restaurant and bar. The 2-for-1 voucher will admit a child free with a full paying adult.

Times Open wkdays 9-4.30, Sat, Sun & BHs 10-4* **Fees** Mill tours £6 (ch £3.25), Traditional & Rare Breeds Farm Park £3.25 (ch £2.25), Shire Horse Dray Rides £3 (ch £2). Picnic area, childrens play area & Henry Weston Courtyard Garden free* **Facilities** licensed (outdoor) (partly accessible) (restaurant, courtyard, garden and shop all accessible) toilets for disabled shop

SWAINSHILL Map 3 SO44

The Weir Gardens

HR4 7QF
☎ 01981 590509 📠 01981 590000
e-mail: theweir@nationaltrust.org.uk
web: www.nationaltrust.org.uk
dir: 5m W of Hereford, on A438

A unique riverside garden created in the 1920s. This peaceful 10 acre garden offers dramatic views of the Wye Valley and Herefordshire countryside beyond. In spring, drifts of early flowering bulbs are followed by a succession of summer wildflowers, managed to create a varied habitat for a wide range of wildlife. Autumn gives a final flourish of colour and the River Wye provides a moving backdrop to this tranquil garden. Bring a picnic and spend a day by the river in this special place. Discover the secret garden created in 2009.

Times Open Feb Wed-Sun 11-4; Mar-3 May daily 11-5; 6 May-1 Nov Wed-Sun 11-5; 23-31 Jan Sat-Sun 11-4* **Facilities** (outdoor) (partly accessible) (garden has steep banks with narrow paths and steps in some places) toilets for disabled (disabled parking near toilets)

HERTFORDSHIRE

Knebworth House

ENGLAND

AYOT ST LAWRENCE Map 4 TL11

Shaw's Corner

AL6 9BX
☎ 01438 820307 Fax 01438 820307
e-mail: shawscorner@nationaltrust.org.uk
web: www.nationaltrust.org.uk/shawscorner
dir: A1(M) junct 4 or M1 junct 10. Follow B653 signed Wheathampstead & follow National Trust signs to Shaw's Corner

An Edwardian 'Arts and Crafts'influenced house, this was the home of George Bernard Shaw from 1906 until his death in 1950. The rooms remain much as he left them, with many literary and personal effects evoking the individuality and genius of this great dramatist. The kitchen and outbuildings are evocative of early 20th-century domestic life. Shaw's writing hut is hidden at the bottom of the garden, which has richly planted borders and views over the Hertfordshire countryside. A selection of plants in addition to a small collection of George Bernard Shaw plays are available to buy.

Times House: 14 Mar-1 Nov, Wed-Sun 1-5. Garden: 14 Mar-1 Nov, Wed-Sun 12-5.30 & all BHs* **Facilities** Ⓟ ⛩ ♿ (partly accessible) (Ground floor limited access, stairs to other floors, grounds partly accessible for wheelchairs) (Braille/large print guides, scented plants, items to touch) ⊗ ✿

BERKHAMSTED Map 4 SP90

Ashridge Estate Visitor Centre

Moneybury Hill, Ringshall HP4 1LT
☎ 01442 851227 & 755557 Fax 01442 850000
e-mail: ashridge@nationaltrust.org.uk
web: www.nationaltrust.org.uk
dir: between Northchurch & Ringshall, just off B4506

Miles of paths through woodland and open country with spring bluebells, ancient trees, fungi and breath-taking views. Discover more about the wildlife in the visitor centre next to the Bridgewater monument, with an interactive exhibition room. A wide range of activities and events for all the family take place through out the year.

Times Open: Estate all year. Visitor Centre: 13 Feb-19 Dec 10-5, Monument: 3 Apr-Oct 12-4.30.* **Facilities** Ⓟ Ⓟ ☕ ♿ (partly accessible) (visitor centre & cafe accessible) toilets for disabled (disabled parking, mobility vehicles available) shop ✿

Berkhamsted Castle FREE

HP4 1HF
web: www.english-heritage.org.uk
dir: by Berkhamsted station

Roads and a railway have cut into the castle site, but its huge banks and ditches remain impressive. The original motte-and-bailey was built after the Norman Conquest, and there is a later stone keep, once owned by the Black Prince, eldest son of King Edward III, where King John of France was imprisoned.

Times Open all year, daily, summer 10-6; winter 10-4. Closed 25 Dec & 1 Jan **Facilities** ⌗

HATFIELD Map 4 TL20

Hatfield House, Park and Gardens

AL9 5NQ
☎ 01707 287010 Fax 01707 287033
e-mail: visitors@hatfield-house.co.uk
web: www.hatfield-house.co.uk
dir: 2m from junct 4 A1(M) on A1000, 7m from M25 junct 23. House opposite Hatfield railway station

The house, built by Robert Cecil in 1611, is the home of the 7th Marquess of Salisbury and is full of exquisite tapestries, furniture and famous paintings. The 42 acres of gardens include formal, knot, scented and wilderness areas, and reflect their Jacobean history. Includes the national collection of model soldiers and children's play area. The Tudor Palace of Hatfield, close by the house, was the childhood home of Elizabeth I and where she held her first Council of State when she became Queen in 1558. 400th anniversary of the completion of Hatfield House in 2011. Events take place throughout the year - see website for details.

Times Open Etr Sat-Sep, Wed-Sun & BH Mon, House 12-4; Park & West Garden 11-5.30. **Fees** Henry Moore exhibition £12 (inc West Garden & Park). House £6. West Garden (Wed) £4 **Facilities** Ⓟ ☕ 🍽 licensed ⛩ (outdoor) ♿ (partly accessible) (lift to 1st floor) toilets for disabled (wheelchairs) shop ⊗

KNEBWORTH Map 4 TL22

Knebworth House, Gardens & Country Park

SG3 6PY
☎ 01438 812661 Fax 01438 811908
e-mail: info@knebworthhouse.com
web: www.knebworthhouse.com
dir: direct access from A1(M) junct 7 Stevenage South

Home of the Lytton family since 1490, the original Tudor Manor was transformed in 1843 by the spectacular high Gothic decoration of Victorian novelist Sir Edward Bulwer-Lytton. The formal gardens, laid out by Edwin Lutyens in 1908, include a Gertrude Jekyll herb garden, a maze, an organically-run, walled kitchen garden and a dinosaur trail, comprising 72 life-size models set grazing and hunting amongst the rhododendrons and the redwoods. The 250-acres of rolling parkland include a giant adventure playground and miniature railway. There are many special events.

Times Open daily 9-25 Apr, 28 May-5 Jun, 2 Jul-Aug; 26 Mar-3 Apr, 30 Apr-22 May, 11-26 Jun, 3-25 Sep, wknds & BHs. Park, gardens & playground 11-5 (last admission 4.15). House 12-5. (last admission 4) **Fees** House, gardens & park £10.50 (ch & pen £10). Family ticket £37. Gardens & park £8. Family ticket £28 **Facilities** (outdoor) (partly accessible) (house has no lift, history of building can be conveyed to visitors on ground floor) toilets for disabled (transport to door by prior arrangement, w/chair available) shop

LETCHWORTH — Map 4 TL23

Letchworth Museum & Art Gallery — FREE

Broadway SG6 3PF
☎ 01462 685647 01462 481879
e-mail: letchworth.museum@north-herts.gov.uk
web: www.north-herts.gov.uk
dir: next door to Public Library in town centre, near Broadway Cinema

Opened in 1914 to house the collections of the Letchworth Naturalists' Society, this friendly town-centre museum has exhibits on local wildlife, geology, arts and crafts, and archaeology. There is also a museum shop and a regular programme of art exhibitions and workshops.

Times Open all year Mon-Tue & Thu-Sat 10-5. Closed BHs* **Facilities** (partly accessible) (ground floor only accessible) (ramp, touch screen computer) shop

LONDON COLNEY — Map 4 TL10

de Havilland Aircraft Heritage Centre — 2 FOR 1

Salisbury Hall AL2 1BU
☎ 01727 826400 & 822051(info) 01727 826400
e-mail: w4050.dhamt@fsmail.net
web: www.dehavillandmuseum.co.uk
dir: M25 junct 22. Follow signs for 'Mosquito Aircraft Museum' onto B556

The site of the hall and museum is a very old one. The aircraft museum opened in 1959 to preserve and display the de Havilland Mosquito prototype on the site of its conception. A working museum with displays of 20 de Havilland aircraft and sections together with a comprehensive collection of de Havilland engines and memorabilia. Selective cockpits are open to enter. Education storyboard 'maze style' gives an outline history of de Havilland Enterprise.

Times Open first Sun Mar-last Sun Oct, Sun & BHs 10.30-5.30, Tue, Thu & Sat 2-5.30* **Fees** £5 (ch under 5 free, ch 5-16 £3, pen £4) Family ticket (2ad+2ch) £13* **Facilities** (indoor & outdoor) (fully accessible) toilets for disabled shop

ST ALBANS — Map 4 TL10

Clock Tower

Market Place AL3 3DR
☎ 01727 819340 01727 837472
e-mail: museum@stalbans.gov.uk
web: www.stalbansmuseums.org.uk
dir: city centre, junct of High St (A1081) & Market Place

Built between 1403 and 1412, this is the only medieval town belfry in England. Inside you can hear the great bell Gabriel (also 600 years old), find out about the original clock, the Napoleonic War telegraph station (1808-14), and see fine Victorian turret clock in action.

Times Open Etr-Sep, Sat, Sun & BH 10.30-5 **Fees** £1 (ch under 12 free) **Facilities** (wheelchair access not possible) shop

The Gardens of The Rose (Royal National Rose Society)

Chiswell Green Ln AL2 3NR
☎ 01727 850461 & 0845 833 4344 01727 850360
e-mail: mail@rnrs.org.uk
web: www.rnrs.org
dir: 2m S off B4630 Watford Rd in Chiswell Green Ln. Turn into lane by Three Hammers pub

The Royal National Rose Society's Gardens of the Rose boasts a comprehensive collection of roses of all types, as well as a good selection of complementary trees, shrubs, summer bulbs and herbaceous perennials in a garden setting together with a grass maze. A stunning new 72 arch pergola supports a wide selection of climbing roses with clematis and other flowering species. There are three new pools containing a variety of marginal plants and water lilies.

Times Open 4 Jun-28 Sep, Wed-Sun, 11-5* **Facilities** (fully accessible) toilets for disabled (ramps where necessary)

Gorhambury

AL3 6AH
☎ 01727 855000 01727 843675
dir: Gorhambury Drive off Bluehouse Hill A4147

This house was built by Sir Robert Taylor between 1774 and 1784 to house an extensive picture collection of 17th-century portraits of the Grimston and Bacon families and their contemporaries. Also of note is the 16th-century enamelled glass collection and an early English pile carpet.

Times Open May-Sep, Thu 2-5 (last admission 4) **Fees** £7.50 (ch £4, concessions £6.50) **Facilities** (partly accessible) (steps to first floor, smaller tour available on ground floor) toilets for disabled shop

ENGLAND

ST ALBANS *continued*

Museum of St Albans

FREE

9A Hatfield Rd AL1 3RR
☎ 01727 819340 📠 01727 837472
e-mail: history@stalbans.gov.uk
web: www.stalbansmuseums.org.uk
dir: city centre on A1057 Hatfield road

The story of St Albans is traced from the departure of the Romans up to the present day. A variety of exhibitions are held throughout the year. The Museum is also the home of the Salaman Collection of trade and craft tools. Outside is a wildlife garden suitable for picnics.

Times Open all year, daily 10-5, Sun 2-5. Closed 25-26 Dec & 1 Jan* **Facilities** (outdoor) (partly accessible) toilets for disabled (ramp at entrance) shop

Roman Theatre of Verulamium

St Michaels AL3 6AE
☎ 01727 835035 📠 01727 843675
e-mail: romantheatre@grimstontrust.co.uk
web: www.romantheatre.co.uk
dir: Gorhambury Drive off Bluehouse Hill A4147

The theatre was first found in 1847, and was fully excavated by 1935. It is semicircular in shape with a stage area. The seating would have accommodated over 2000 spectators.

Times Open all year, daily 10-5 (4 in winter). Closed 25-26 Dec. 1 Jan by appointment only **Fees** £2.50 (ch £1.50, concessions £2, school parties £1) **Facilities** (partly accessible) (theatre fully accessible - steps down to the house, limited access to viewing path) shop

St Albans Cathedral

Sumpter Yard AL1 1BY
☎ 01727 890204 📠 01727 850944
e-mail: mail@stalbanscathedral.org.uk
web: www.stalbanscathedral.org
dir: M25 junct 22a, in the centre of St Albans

An imposing Norman abbey church built on the site of the execution of St Alban, Britain's first martyr (c250AD). The cathedral is constructed from recycled Roman brick taken from nearby Verulamium. It is the oldest site of continuous Christian worship in the country.

Times Open all year, daily 8.30-5.45 **Fees** Admission free. Suggested donation £4 per adult **Facilities** licensed (outdoor) (partly accessible) (vast majority of cathedral accessible but some restrictions) toilets for disabled (touch & hearing centre, Braille guides) shop

Verulamium Museum

St Michaels AL3 4SW
☎ 01727 751810 📠 01727 859919
e-mail: museum@stalbans.gov.uk
web: www.stalbansmuseums.org.uk
dir: follow signs for St Albans, museum signed

Verulamium was one of the largest and most important Roman towns in Britain - by the Ist century AD it was declared a 'municipium', giving its inhabitants the rights of Roman citizenship, the only British city granted this honour. A mosaic and underfloor heating system can be seen in a separate building, and the museum has wall paintings, jewellery, pottery and other domestic items. On the second weekend of every month legionaries occupy the galleries and describe the tactics and equipment of the Roman Imperial Army and the life of a legionary.

Times Open all year Mon-Fri 10-5.30, Sun 2-5.30. Closed 25-26 Dec.* **Facilities** (outdoor) (fully accessible) toilets for disabled (ramp access to main entrance) shop

TRING — Map 4 SP91

The Natural History Museum at Tring

FREE

The Walter Rothschild Building, Akeman St HP23 6AP
☎ 020 7942 6171 📠 020 7942 6150
e-mail: tring-enquiries@nhm.ac.uk
web: www.nhm.ac.uk/tring
dir: signed from A41

An unusual museum exhibiting a range of animals, collected by its founder Lionel Walter, 2nd Baron Rothschild, scientist, eccentric and natural history enthusiast. Home to the world-class research and collections of the Natural History Museum's Bird Group. A programme of temporary exhibitions, activities and events make any visit a unique day out.

Times Open all year, Mon-Sat 10-5, Sun 2-5. Closed 24-26 Dec.* **Facilities** (outdoor) (partly accessible) toilets for disabled (ramps, virtual tour, disabled parking space) shop

WARE — Map 5 TL31

Scott's Grotto

24 Scott's Rd SG12 9JQ
☎ 01920 464131
e-mail: tourism@ware-herts.org.uk
web: www.scotts-grotto.org
dir: off A119

Scott's Grotto, built in the 1760s by the Quaker poet John Scott, has been described by English Heritage as 'one of the finest in England'. Restored by the Ware Society, it consists of underground passages and chambers decorated with flints, shells, minerals and stones, and extends 67ft into the side of the hill. Please wear flat shoes and bring a torch, as the grotto is not lit, this is essential.

Times Open Apr-Sep, Sat & BH Mon 2-4.30. Other times by appointment only **Fees** Donations welcome* **Facilities** (partly accessible) (many steps, not suitable for wheelchair users) (web link virtual tour)

KENT

Apple orchards

AYLESFORD Map 5 TQ75

Aylesford Priory

The Friars ME20 7BX
☎ 01622 717272 📠 01622 715575
e-mail: gm@thefriars.org.uk
web: www.thefriars.org.uk
dir: M20 junct 6 or M2 junct 3 onto A229, signed

Built in the 13th and 14th centuries, the Priory has been restored and is now a house of prayer, guest house, conference centre and a place of pilgrimage and retreat. It has fine cloisters, and displays sculpture and ceramics by modern artists.

Times Open all year, daily 9-dusk. Gift, book shop & tea rooms May-Sep, 10-5; Oct-Apr, 10-4 (Sun 11am). Guided tours of the priory by arrangement.* **Facilities** (outdoor) (partly accessible) toilets for disabled (wheelchairs available, ramps) shop

BEKESBOURNE Map 5 TR15

Howletts Wild Animal Park

Beekesbourne Rd CT4 5EL
☎ 0844 8424 647 📠 01303 264944
e-mail: info@howletts.net
web: www.totallywild.net
dir: Signed off A2, 3m S of Canterbury, follow brown tourist signs

Set in 90 acres, Howletts includes the largest group of western lowland gorillas in captivity in the world, and the largest herd of African elephants in the UK. A number of glass-fronted tiger enclosures allow for amazing views of the Sumatran and Indian tigers. In addition, Howletts is home to assorted primates, clouded leopards, tapirs, Javan langurs, black rhinos and Iberian wolves. There are plenty of other rare and endangered species from around the world. Visitors can walk in an open air enclosure where a family of amazingly agile and lively lemurs roam freely. Picnic areas are spread around the park and a variety of hot and cold dishes are available in the Pavilion Restaurant.

Times Open all year, daily 10-6 summer; winter 10-5 (last admission 1hr 30mins before closing). Closed 25 Dec* **Facilities** licensed (outdoor) (fully accessible) toilets for disabled (wheelchairs for hire, book in advance) shop

BELTRING Map 5 TQ64

The Hop Farm **2 FOR 1**

TN12 6PY
☎ 01622 872068 📠 01622 872630
e-mail: info@thehopfarm.co.uk
web: www.thehopfarm.co.uk
dir: on A228 at Paddock Wood

The Hop Farm is set among the largest collection of Victorian oast houses, and its attractions include museums and exhibitions, indoor and outdoor play areas, animal farm and shire horses, and restaurant and gift shop. The recently opened Driving School and Jumping Pillows offer non-stop fun for children; and for the adults there is Legends in Wax and the story of the Hop Farm. The new Great Goblin Hunt transports children into a fantasy world with 3D attractions. Events and shows all year such as the renowned War and Peace Show, Kent County Fair, The Hop Festival and Paws in the Park. For further details see website. The 2-for-1 voucher cannot be used for special events.

Times Open Apr-Nov daily from 10* **Fees** £13. Supersaver for 4 £45, for 5 £55* **Facilities** licensed (outdoor) (fully accessible) toilets for disabled (lifts, ramps) shop

BIDDENDEN Map 5 TQ83

Biddenden Vineyards & Cider Works

Gribble Bridge Ln TN27 8DF
☎ 01580 291726 📠 01580 291933
e-mail: info@biddendenvineyards.co.uk
web: www.biddendenvineyards.com
dir: 0.5m S off A262, 0.5m from Biddenden Village. Bear right at Woolpack Corner

The present vineyard was established in 1969 and now covers 22 acres. Visitors are welcome to stroll around the vineyard and to taste wines, ciders and apple juice available at the shop. English wine week is held here at the end of May.

Times Open all year, Shop: Mon-Sat 10-5, Sun & BH 11-5. Closed noon 24 Dec-2 Jan & Sun in Jan & Feb* **Fees** Non-guided groups and individuals free. Pre-booked guided tours (min 15) £5.10 (ch 10-17 £2.50, ch under 10 £1). Evening guided tour max 35 people £7.25* **Facilities** (outdoor) (partly accessible) shop

BIRCHINGTON Map 5 TR36

Powell - Cotton Museum, Quex House & Gardens **2 FOR 1**

Quex Park CT7 0BH
☎ 01843 842168 📠 01843 846661
e-mail: enquiries@quexmuseum.org
web: www.quexmuseum.org
dir: A28 to Birchington right into Park Lane before rdbt in town centre. Entrance 600yds on left

Major Powell-Cotton (1866-1940) devoted his life to the study of the animals and many different cultures of Africa. This museum, founded in 1895, is his legacy, consisting of animal dioramas, ethnography, weaponry, archaeology, ceramics and artefacts from around the world. Also on display in Quex House, the family home, are collections of paintings, Eastern and Asian furniture, and English period furniture. All set within 15 acres of mature gardens, including a Victorian walled garden, fountains, children's maze and resident doves, ducks and peacocks. A full programme of family events throughout the summer can be found on the website.

Times Open Apr-Oct, Tue-Sun & BH Mons 11-5, Quex House 2-5. Nov-Mar museum & gardens, Sun 1-4 house closed **Fees** £7 (under 5s free, ch & concessions £5). Family ticket (2ad+3ch) £20. Garden only £2 (ch & concessions £1.50) **Facilities**

☕ 🍴 licensed ⛩ (outdoor) ♿ (partly accessible) toilets for disabled (two wheelchairs available) shop 🚫

BOROUGH GREEN **Map 5 TQ65**

Great Comp Garden

TN15 8QS
☎ 01732 886154
e-mail: greatcompgarden@aol.com
web: www.greatcomp.co.uk
dir: 2m E off B2016, follow brown signs

A beautiful seven-acre garden surrounds an early 17th-century Manor (not open). There is a plantsmans' collection of trees, shrubs, heathers and herbaceous plants in a setting of fine lawns and grass paths. Each area of the garden reveals a different character. From the large collection of magnolias, rhododendrons and azaleas in the spring to the rare and exotic shrubs and perennial plants through the remainder of the year. Great Comp is home to the Dyson Salvia Collection.

Times Open Apr-Oct, daily 11-5.* **Facilities** Ⓟ ☕ 🍴 licensed ♿ (fully accessible) toilets for disabled (free wheelchair for hire) shop 🚫

BRASTED **Map 5 TQ45**

Emmetts Garden

Ide Hill TN14 6AY
☎ 01732 868381 📠 01732 750490
e-mail: emmetts@nationaltrust.org.uk
web: www.nationaltrust.org.uk/emmettsgarden
dir: 1m S of A25, Sundridge-Ide Hill road

Emmetts is a charming hillside shrub garden, with bluebells, azaleas and rhododendrons in spring and fine autumn colours. It has magnificent views over Bough Beech Reservoir and the Weald. Events include family picnic days and guided walks.

Times Open 12 Mar-30 Oct, Sat-Wed, 11-5 **Fees** £6.50 (ch £1.70, under 5, carers & NT members free). Family ticket (2ad+3ch) £14.70. Please telephone for details or see website for current prices* **Facilities** Ⓟ ☕ ⛩ (outdoor) ♿ (partly accessible) (access steps & steep slopes) toilets for disabled (wheelchairs, buggy service, Braille/large print guide) shop

BROADSTAIRS **Map 5 TR36**

Dickens House Museum — 2 FOR 1

2 Victoria Pde CT10 1QS
☎ 01843 863453 📠 01843 863453
e-mail: l.ault@btinternet.com
web: www.dickenshouse.co.uk
dir: on seafront

The house was immortalised by Charles Dickens in *David Copperfield* as the home of the hero's aunt, Betsy Trotwood, whom Dickens based on owner Miss Mary Pearson Strong. Dickens' letters and possessions are shown, with local and Dickensian prints, costumes and general Victoriana.

Times Open Etr-Oct, daily 2-5, Jul-Sep 10-5 **Fees** £3.25 (ch £1.80). Family ticket (2ad+2ch) £7.90 **Facilities** Ⓟ ♿ (partly accessible) shop 🚫

CANTERBURY **Map 5 TR15**

Canterbury Roman Museum — 2 FOR 1

Butchery Ln, Longmarket CT1 2JR
☎ 01227 785575 📠 01227 455047
e-mail: museums@canterbury.gov.uk
web: www.canterbury-museums.co.uk
dir: in centre close to cathedral & city centre car parks

Step below today's Canterbury to discover an exciting part of the Roman town including the real remains of a house with fine mosaics. Experience everyday life in the reconstructed market place and see exquisite silver and glass. Try your skills on the touch screen computer, and in the hands-on area with actual finds. Use the computer animation of Roman Canterbury to join the search for the lost temple.

Times Open all year, Mon-Sat 10-4 & Sun, Jun-Oct 1.30-4 (last admission 4). Closed Good Fri & Xmas period* **Fees** £3.10 (ch 5-18, concessions £2.10). Family ticket £8 (2ad+up to 3 ch) **Facilities** Ⓟ ♿ (fully accessible) toilets for disabled (lift) shop 🚫

The Canterbury Tales — 2 FOR 1

St. Margaret's St CT1 2TG
☎ 01227 479227 📠 01227 765584
e-mail: info@canterburytales.org.uk
web: www.canterburytales.org.uk
dir: In heart of city centre, located in St Margaret's St

Step back in time to experience the sights, sounds and smells of the Middle Ages in this reconstruction of 14th-century England. Travel from the Tabard Inn in London, to St. Thomas Becket's Shrine in Canterbury with Chaucer's colourful pilgrims. Their tales of chivalry, romance and intrigue are brought vividly to life along the way.

Times Open all year, Mar-Jun 10-5; Jul-Aug 9.30-5; Sep-Oct 10-5 & Nov-Feb 10-4.30. Closed 25 & 26 Dec, 1 Jan* **Fees** £7.75 (ch £5.75, concessions £6.75)* **Facilities** Ⓟ ♿ (fully accessible) toilets for disabled (notice required for wheelchairs, hearing loop facilities) shop 🚫

ENGLAND

CANTERBURY *continued*

Canterbury West Gate Towers **2 FOR 1**

St. Peter's St CT1 2BQ
☎ 01227 789576 & 452747 📠 01227 455047
e-mail: museums@canterbury.gov.uk
web: www.canterbury-museum.co.uk
dir: at end of main street beside river. Entrance under main arch

The last of the city's fortified gatehouses sits astride the London road with the river as a moat. Rebuilt in around 1380 by Archbishop Sudbury, it was used as a prison for many years. The battlements give a splendid panoramic view of the city and are a good vantage point for photographs. Arms and armour can be seen in the guardroom, and there are cells in the towers. Brass rubbings can be made and children can try on replica armour.

Times Open all year Sat only; 11-12.30 & 1.30-3.30 (last admission 15 mins before closure). Also by special arrangement for groups* **Fees** £1.30 (concessions 80p). Family ticket (2ad+up to 3ch) £3 **Facilities** Ⓟ shop ⊛

Druidstone Park **2 FOR 1**

Honey Hill, Blean CT2 9JR
☎ 01227 765168 📠 01227 768860
web: www.druidstone.net
dir: 3m NW on A290 from Canterbury

Idyllic garden setting with enchanted woodland walks "where dwells the sleeping dragon". See the mystical Oak Circle with the Old Man of the Oaks. Children's farmyard, play areas, gift shop and cafeteria.

Times Open Etr-Nov, Fri-Mon, 10-5.30; daily during school hols* **Fees** £4.50 (ch under 3 free) **Facilities** Ⓟ ☕ ⛩ (outdoor) ♿ (fully accessible) toilets for disabled shop ⊛

Museum of Canterbury **2 FOR 1**

Stour St CT1 2NR
☎ 01227 475202 📠 01227 455047
e-mail: museums@canterbury.gov.uk
web: www.canterbury-museums.co.uk
dir: in the Medieval Poor Priests' Hospital, just off St Margaret's St or High St

Discover the story of Canterbury in new interactive displays for all the family. See the city's treasures including the famous Canterbury Cross. Try the fun activities in the Medieval Discovery Gallery, find out about the mysteries surrounding Christopher Marlowe's life and death, and spot friend or foe planes in the WW2 Blitz gallery. Meet favourite children's TV character Bagpuss and friends, and enjoy the Rupert Bear Museum.

Times Open all year, Mon-Sat 11-4 & Jun-Sep, Sun 1.30-4 (last admission 4). Closed Good Fri & Xmas period* **Fees** £3.60 (concessions £2.30). Family ticket £9.20 (2ad+3 ch) **Facilities** Ⓟ ♿ (fully accessible) toilets for disabled shop ⊛

St Augustine's Abbey

CT1 1TF
☎ 01227 767345
web: www.english-heritage.org.uk
dir: off A28

Part of the Canterbury World Heritage site, this is considered by many as the birthplace of Christianity in England. Visit the fascinating museum and take the free interactive audio tour.

Times Open all year, Apr-Sep, Wed-Sun 10-5; Jul-Aug, daily 10-6; Sep-Mar, Sat-Sun 10-5; Nov-Mar, Sat-Sun 10-4. Closed 24-26 Dec & 1 Jan **Fees** £4.50 (ch £2.30, concessions £3.80). Family ticket £11.30. Prices and opening times are subject to change in March 2011. Please call 0870 333 1181 for the most up to date prices and opening times when planning your visit **Facilities** Ⓟ shop ⌗

CHARTWELL **Map 5 TQ45**

Chartwell

TN16 1PS
☎ 01732 868381 📠 01732 868193
e-mail: chartwell@nationaltrust.org.uk
web: www.nationaltrust.org.uk/chartwell
dir: off A25 onto B2026 at Westerham, Chartwell 2m S of village

The former home of Sir Winston Churchill is filled with reminders of the great statesman, from his hats and uniforms to gifts presented by Stalin, Roosevelt, de Gaulle and many other State leaders. There are portraits of Churchill and other works by notable artists, and also many paintings by Churchill himself. The gardens command breathtaking views over the Weald of Kent.

Times Open House, 12 Mar-30 Oct, Wed-Sun 11-5; BH Mon & Tue in Jul & Aug (last admission 4.15). Garden, exhibition, shop & restaurant open all year, Wed-Sun; Jul-Aug, Tue-Sun **Fees** With 10% or more voluntary Gift Aid donation: House, Garden & Studio £11.80 (ch £5.90). Garden & Studio £5.90 (ch £2.95). Family ticket £29.50. Visitors can choose to pay standard admission prices which are displayed at the property & on NT website* **Facilities** Ⓟ 🍽 licensed ⛩ (outdoor) ♿ (partly accessible) (house stairs to 1st, lower floors & steps, steep slopes in garden) toilets for disabled (parking, guides, sensory facilities) shop ⊛ 🌿

CHATHAM Map 5 TQ76

Dickens World

2 FOR 1

Leviathan Way ME4 4LL

☎ 01634 890421 📠 01634 891972

e-mail: enquiries@dickensworld.co.uk

web: www.dickensworld.co.uk

dir: Signed from junct 1, 3, & 4 of the M2, follow brown anchor signs

Dickens World is an exciting indoor complex themed around the life, books and times of Charles Dickens. It takes visitors on a fascinating journey through the author's lifetime as you step back into Dickensian England and are immersed in the streets, sounds and smells of the 19th century. Dickens World includes The Great Expectations boat ride; The Haunted Man; Victorian School Room; a 4D Hi-def show in Peggotty's Boathouse; Fagin's Den, a soft play area for younger children; and The Britannia Theatre, an animatronic stage show.

Times Open all year, daily from 10, closing time varies seasonally. Closed 25 Dec **Fees** £12.50 (ch 5-15 £7.50, concessions £10.50)* **Facilities** Ⓟ Ⓟ ☕ 🍽 licensed ♿ (partly accessible) (to board boat ride, wheelchair users must be able to get in/out of chair unaided) toilets for disabled (lifts, hearing loops, essential carers, disabled parking) shop 🚫

The Historic Dockyard Chatham

ME4 4TZ

☎ 01634 823807 & 823800 📠 01634 823801

e-mail: info@chdt.org.uk

web: www.thedockyard.co.uk

dir: Follow brown tourist signs from M2 junct 1 or 4 via A289 or M20 junct 6 via town centre

Costumed guides bring this spectacular maritime heritage site alive. Discover over 400 years of maritime history as you explore the most complete dockyard of the Age of Sail, set in a stunning 80-acre estate. Various special events take place throughout the year, please see the website for details.

Times Open daily at 10 from 12 Feb-mid Dec* **Fees** £14 (ch £9.50, concessions £11.50). Family (2ad+2ch) £42.50, additional ch £6.50* **Facilities** Ⓟ Ⓟ ☕ 🍽 licensed ⛩ (indoor & outdoor) ♿ (partly accessible) (Historic warships not fully accessible. Cobbles & uneven surfaces on site) toilets for disabled (wheelchair available, virtual tours) shop

DEAL Map 5 TR35

Deal Castle

Victoria Rd CT14 7BA

☎ 01304 372762

web: www.english-heritage.org.uk

dir: SW of Deal town centre

Discover the history of this formidable fortress as you explore the long, dark passages that once linked a garrison of 119 guns.

Times Open Apr-Sep, daily 10-6. Closed Oct-Mar **Fees** £4.50 (ch £2.30, concessions £3.80). Family Ticket £11.30. Prices and opening times are subject to change in March 2011. Please call 0870 333 1181 for the most up to date prices and opening times when planning your visit **Facilities** ♿ (partly accessible) (spiral staircase, some steps, narrow doorways) (hearning loop, parking available) shop 🚫 #

Walmer Castle & Gardens

Kingsdown Rd CT14 7LJ

☎ 01304 364288 📠 01304 364829

web: www.english-heritage.org.uk

dir: 1m S on coast, off A258

Originally built by Henry VIII as a formidable and austere fortress, the castle has since been transformed into an elegant stately home, formerly used by HM The Queen Mother. Many of her rooms are open to view, but the special highlight is the magnificent gardens.

Times Open Apr-Sep, daily 10-6; Mar & Oct, Wed-Sun 10-4. Closed Nov-Feb & when Lord Warden in residence 9-11 Jul **Fees** £7 (ch £3.50, concessions £6). Family ticket £17.50. Prices and opening times are subject to change in March 2011. Please call 0870 333 1181 for the most up to date prices and opening times when planning your visit **Facilities** Ⓟ ☕ ♿ (partly accessible) (cobbled & flagstone walkway, wooden drawbridge) (audio tour, hearing loop) shop 🚫 #

DOVER Map 5 TR34

Dover Castle & Secret Wartime Tunnels

CT16 1HU

☎ 01304 211067 📠 01304 214739

web: www.english-heritage.org.uk

Various exhibitions demonstrate how Dover Castle has served as a vital strategic centre for the Iron Age onwards. In May 1940 the tunnels under the castle became the nerve centre for 'Operation Dynamo' - the evacuation of Dunkirk. These wartime secrets are now revealed for all to see. From early autumn 2010 to early summer 2011 English Heritage will be starting work within the Secret Wartime Tunnels to improve the visitor facilities and interpretation. This is likely to result in closure of some or all areas of the tunnel complex at various times during this period. We advise that from early autumn 2010 check the Dover Castle website www.english-heritage.org.uk/dovercastle or telephone the site direct on 01304 211067 for full details of available access to the Secret Wartime Tunnels. The Great Tower and other attractions within the castle remain fully open throughout the year.

Times Open Apr-Jul & Sep, daily 10-6; Aug, daily 9.30-6; Oct, daily 10-5; Nov-Jan, Thu-Mon 10-4; Feb-Mar, daily 10-4. Closed 24-26 Dec & 1 Jan (last admission 1 hr before closing). Secret Wartime Tunnel tour - time ticket system in operation (last tour 1 hour before closing) **Fees** £13.90 (ch £7, concessions £11.80). Family £34.80. Includes Secret Wartime Tunnels tour. Additional charges for members and non-members may apply on event days. All prices and opening times are subject to change in March 2011. Please call 0870 333 1181 for the most up to date prices and opening times when planning your visit **Facilities** Ⓟ Ⓟ 🍽 licensed ♿ (partly accessible) (steep slopes) toilets for disabled (mobility scooters for hire, Braille, hearing loop) shop 🚫 #

ENGLAND

DOVER *continued*

Roman Painted House — 2 FOR 1

New St CT17 9AJ
☎ 01304 203279
dir: follow A20 to York St bypass, located in town centre

Visit five rooms of a Roman hotel built 1800 years ago, famous for its unique, well-preserved Bacchic frescos. The Roman underfloor heating system and part of a late-Roman defensive wall are also on view. There are extensive displays on Roman Dover.

Times Open 1-15 Apr daily, 16 Apr-May, Tue & Sat only. Jun-15 Sep daily except Mon **Fees** £3 (ch & concessions £2) **Facilities** (outdoor) (partly accessible) (basement area reachable via stairs) toilets for disabled (touch table, glass panels on gallery for wheelchairs) shop

The White Cliffs of Dover

Visitor Centre, Langdon Cliffs, Upper Rd CT16 1HJ
☎ 01304 202756 01304 215484
e-mail: whitecliffs@nationaltrust.org.uk
web: www.nationaltrust.org.uk
dir: A2/A258 towards Dover town centre, in 1m turn left into Upper Rd, 0.75m turn right into entrance

The White Cliffs of Dover are one of England's most spectacular natural features, as well as being an important national icon. Visitors enjoy their special appeal through the seasons by taking the cliff top paths offering views of the French coast, and savouring the rare flora and fauna that can be found across this chalk grassland. On offer are a range of guided walks and special events are held throughout the year.

Times Open all year. Visitor Centre: Nov-Feb, 11-4, Mar-Oct, 10-5. Car park Nov-Feb, 8-5, Mar-Oct, 8-6 **Fees** Free admission. Parking charges car £3, mobile home £4, coach £7 **Facilities** (outdoor) (partly accessible) (some uneven and steep paths) toilets for disabled (designated parking) shop

DYMCHURCH — Map 5 TR12

Dymchurch Martello Tower — FREE

High St CT16 1HU
☎ 01304 211067
web: www.english-heritage.org.uk
dir: access from High St not seafront

This artillery tower formed part of a chain of strongholds intended to resist invasion by Napoleon.

Times Open Aug BH and Heritage Open Days. As we go to print the tower is temporarily closed **Facilities**

EDENBRIDGE

See Hever

EYNSFORD — Map 5 TQ56

Eagle Heights

Lullingstone Ln DA4 0JB
☎ 01322 866466 01322 861024
e-mail: office@eagleheights.co.uk
web: www.eagleheights.co.uk
dir: M25 junct 3/A20 towards West Kingsdown. Right after 2 rdbts onto A225. Follow brown signs

Eagle Heights is an impressive display of birds of prey from all over the world. Many are flown out across the Darenth valley twice daily. There are also owls, pygmy goat and rabbits in the paddock. New Africa show including cheetah.

Times Open Mar-Oct daily 10.30-5; Nov, Jan-Feb wknd only 11-4* **Fees** £8.50 (ch £5, concessions £7)* **Facilities** (outdoor) (fully accessible) toilets for disabled (loop system) shop

Eynsford Castle — FREE

web: www.english-heritage.org.uk
dir: in Eynsford, off A225

One of the first stone castles to be built by the Normans. The moat and remains of the curtain wall and hall can still be seen.

Times Open all year, Apr-Sep, daily 10-6; Oct-Nov & Feb-Mar, daily 10-4; Dec-Jan, Wed-Sun, 10-4. Closed 24-26 Dec & 1 Jan **Facilities**

Lullingstone Castle

DA4 0JA
☎ 01322 862114 01322 862115
web: www.lullingstonecastle.co.uk
dir: 1m SW of Eynsford via A225 & Lullingstone Roman Villa

The house was altered extensively in Queen Anne's time, and has fine state rooms and beautiful grounds. The 15th-century gate tower was one of the first gatehouses in England to be made entirely of bricks, and there is a church with family monuments. The two-acre walled garden is currently being turned into a 'World Garden of Plants', which will contain 10,000 different plant species. Please telephone for details of special events.

Times Open Apr-Sep, Fri & Sat, garden 12-5, Sun & BHs (ex Good Fri) garden 2-6. Guided groups by arrangement Wed & Thu. House open BH wknds & special events (times same as garden)* **Fees** House & Gardens £6 (ch £3 & concessions £5.50). Family £15* **Facilities** (partly accessible) (ground floor only accessible) toilets for disabled shop

FAVERSHAM Map 5 TR06

Fleur de Lis Heritage Centre 2 FOR 1

10-13 Preston St ME13 8NS
☎ 01795 534542
e-mail: ticfaversham@btconnect.com
web: www.faversham.org/society
dir: 3 minutes drive from M2 junct 6

Expanded and updated, and housed in 16th-century premises, the Centre features colourful displays and room settings that vividly evoke the 2000 year history of Faversham. Special features include the 'Gunpowder Experience' and a working old-style village telephone exchange, one of only two remaining in Britain. In July, during the Faversham Open House Scheme, over 20 historic properties in the town are opened to the public.

Times Open all year, Mon-Sat, 10-4; Sun 10-1 **Fees** £3 (ch & pen £1.50) **Facilities** Ⓟ ♿ (partly accessible) (access to 75% of premises) toilets for disabled (DVD show of parts that are inaccessible) shop

GILLINGHAM Map 5 TQ76

Royal Engineers Museum, Library & Archive 2 FOR 1

Prince Arthur Rd ME4 4UG
☎ 01634 822839 🖹 01634 822371
e-mail: mail@re-museum.co.uk
web: www.remuseum.org.uk
dir: follow brown signs from Gillingham & Chatham town centres

The museum covers the diverse and sometimes surprising work of the Royal Engineers. Learn about the first military divers, photographers, aviators and surveyors; see memorabilia relating to General Gordon and Field Marshal Lord Kitchener, Wellington's battle map from Waterloo and a Harrier jump-jet. The superb medal displays include 25 Victoria Crosses, among 6,000 medals. Among the exhibits are locomotives, tanks, the first wire guided torpedo, bridges, and models. Special events sometimes take place in conjunction with Chatham Historic Dockyard.

Times Open all year, Tue-Fri 9-5, Sat-Sun & BH Mon 11.30-5. Closed Good Fri, Xmas week & 1 Jan. Library open by appointment (ex wknds)* **Fees** £7.13 (concessions £4.75) Family £19. Gift aid ticket for 1 year entry* **Facilities** Ⓟ Ⓟ ⛩ (indoor & outdoor) ♿ (partly accessible) (one gallery not easily accessible) toilets for disabled (help available if required, chair lift to upper level) shop ⊗

ENGLAND

GOUDHURST Map 5 TQ73

Finchcocks Musical Museum

TN17 1HH

☎ 01580 211702 📠 01580 211007
e-mail: katrina@finchcocks.co.uk
web: www.finchcocks.co.uk
dir: off A21 on the A262, 2m W of Goudhurst village, entrance by Green Cross Inn

This magnificent manor set in a beautiful garden surrounded by parkland provides the backdrop for a large and varied programme of open days, private visits, concerts, courses and much more. Now in its 28th year of operation, Finchcocks is a Georgian manor house with a very special collection of historical musical instruments: The Richard Burnett keyboard collection. Finchcocks is truly a living museum with entertaining demonstrations of the instruments for all visitors, which are as appealing to the non-musician as they are to the specialist. Various musical events through the year.

Times Open Apr-Sep, Sun & BH Mon 2-6; Aug, Wed, Thu 2-6. Private groups on other days by appointment Apr-Dec **Fees** £10 daytime £12 evening (ch £5, students £7). Family ticket (with school age children) £22. Garden only £3 **Facilities** Ⓟ ☕ 🍽 licensed 🛒 (outdoor) ♿ (partly accessible) (accessible use of ramps & rails) toilets for disabled (wheelchair available, Braille signs) shop 🚫

GROOMBRIDGE PLACE Map 5 TQ53

Groombridge Place Gardens & Enchanted Forest

TN3 9QG

☎ 01892 861444 📠 01892 863996
e-mail: office@groombridge.co.uk
web: www.groombridge.co.uk
dir: M25 junct 5, follow A21 S, exit at A26 (signed Tunbridge Wells), then take A264 - follow signs to village and Groombridge Place Gardens

This award-winning attraction, set in 200 acres, features a series of magnificent walled gardens set against the backdrop of a romantic 17th-century moated manor. Explore the herbaceous border, the white rose garden, the 'Drunken Topiary', the 'Secret Garden' and the peacock walk. By way of contrast, in the ancient woodland of the 'Enchanted Forest', the imagination is stimulated by mysterious features such as the 'Dark Walk', 'Dinosaur and Dragon Valley' and 'Groms' Village'. Groombridge was used as a major location in the recent movie adaptation of Jane Austen's *Pride and Prejudice*. There are also bird of prey flying displays, canal boat cruises, and a full programme of special events.

Times Open Apr-Nov, daily 10-5.30* **Facilities** Ⓟ 🍽 licensed 🛒 (outdoor) ♿ (partly accessible) toilets for disabled shop 🚫

HAWKINGE Map 5 TR23

Kent Battle of Britain Museum

Aerodrome Rd CT18 7AG

☎ 01303 893140
e-mail: kentbattleofbritainmuseum@btinternet.com
web: www.kbobm.org
dir: off A260, 1m along Aerodrome road

Once a Battle of Britain Station, today it houses the largest collection of relics and related memorabilia of British and German aircraft involved in the fighting. Also on display are full-size replicas of the Hurricane, Spitfire and Me109 used in Battle of Britain films. The year 2000 was the 60th anniversary of the Battle of Britain and a new memorial was dedicated. Artefacts on show, recovered from over 650 Battle of Britain aircraft, all form a lasting memorial to all those involved in the conflict.

Times Open Good Fri-May & Oct, 10-4; Jun-Sep, 10-5 (last admission 1 hour before closing). Closed Mon ex BHs.* **Facilities** Ⓟ ⓟ ☕ 🛒 (outdoor) ♿ (fully accessible) shop 🚫

HEVER Map 5 TQ44

Hever Castle & Gardens

TN8 7NG

☎ 01732 865224 📠 01732 866796
e-mail: mail@hevercastle.co.uk
web: www.hevercastle.co.uk
dir: M25 junct 5 or 6, 3m SE of Edenbridge, off B2026

This enchanting, double-moated, 13th-century castle was the childhood home of Anne Boleyn. Restored by the American millionaire William Waldorf Astor at the beginning of the 20th century, it shows superb Edwardian craftsmanship. Astor also transformed the grounds, creating topiary, a yew maze, 35 acre lake and Italian gardens filled with antique sculptures. There is also a 100 metre herbaceous border, a 'splashing' water maze' on the Sixteen Acre Island, and a woodland walk known as Sunday Walk. Adventure play area with the Henry VIII Tower Maze.

Times Open Mar-Nov, daily. Castle 12-6, Gardens 11-6 (last admission 5). Closes 4pm Mar & Nov* **Facilities** Ⓟ ☕ 🍽 licensed 🛒 (outdoor) ♿ (partly accessible) toilets for disabled (wheelchairs available, book in advance) shop

HYTHE Map 5 TR13

Romney, Hythe & Dymchurch Railway

TN28 8PL

☎ 01797 362353 & 363256 01797 363591
e-mail: info@rhdr.org.uk
web: www.rhdr.org.uk
dir: M20 junct 11, follow signs to Hythe Station

The world's smallest public railway has its headquarters here. The concept of two enthusiasts coincided with Southern Railway's plans for expansion, and so the 13.5 mile stretch of 15-inch gauge railway came into being, running from Hythe through New Romney and Dymchurch to Dungeness Lighthouse.

Times Open Etr-Oct; daily; Jan-Mar, wknds **Fees** Romney Rover all day ticket £15 (ch over 3 £7.50) **Facilities** licensed (indoor & outdoor) (fully accessible) toilets for disabled (stairlift to Model Museum) shop

IGHTHAM Map 5 TQ55

Ightham Mote

TN15 0NT

☎ 01732 811731 & 811145 (info line) 01732 811029
e-mail: igthammote@nationaltrust.org.uk
web: www.nationaltrust.org.uk
dir: 2.5m S off A227, 6m E of Sevenoaks

This moated manor house, nestling in a sunken valley, dates from 1320. The main features of the house span many centuries and include the Great Hall, an old chapel and crypt, a Tudor chapel with painted ceiling, and a drawing room with Jacobean fireplace, frieze and 18th-century hand-painted Chinese wallpaper. There is an extensive garden as well as interesting walks in the surrounding woodland. Following completion of all conservation work, visitors can enjoy the most extensive visitor route to date, including the bedroom of Charles Henry Robinson who bequeathed Ightham Mote to the National Trust.

Times Open daily 12 Mar-Oct, (ex Tue & Wed), 11-5. Open BH & Good Fri (last admission 4.30) **Fees** £11.50 (ch £5.75). Family ticket £27.30. Includes a voluntary Gift Aid donation of 10% or more. Visitors can choose to pay the standard admission price **Facilities** licensed (outdoor) (partly accessible) (only gardens & ground floor rooms in house accessible) toilets for disabled (wheelchairs, special parking ask at office, virtual tour) shop

LAMBERHURST Map 5 TQ63

Bayham Old Abbey

TN3 8DE

☎ 01892 890381
web: www.english-heritage.org.uk
dir: off B2169, 2m W in East Sussex

Explore the romantic ruins of this 13th-century abbey built by French monks in an 18th-century landscaped setting.

Times Open Apr-Sep, daily 11-5. Closed Oct-Mar **Fees** £4 (ch £2, concessions £3.40). Prices and opening times are subject to change in March 2011. Please call 0870 333 1181 for the most up to date prices and opening times when planning your visit **Facilities** (partly accessible) (mostly accessible except Dower House, some steps, loose gravel paths) toilets for disabled (alternative side gate into grounds)

Scotney Castle

TN3 8JN

☎ 01892 893868 01892 890110
e-mail: scotneycastle@nationaltrust.org.uk
web: www.nationaltrust.org.uk/scotneycastle
dir: 1m, S of Lamberhurst on A21

Scotney Castle is a hidden gem, set in one of the most romantic gardens in England. Home of the Hussey family since the late 18th century, Scotney Castle was remodelled in the 1830s by Edward Hussey III. The beautiful gardens were planned around the remains of the old, moated castle. There is something to see all year round, with spring flowers followed by rhododendrons, azaleas and kalmia in May and June, wisteria and roses in summer, and then superb autumn colours. There are fine estate walks all year, through 770 acres of woodlands, hop farm and meadows. The house has limited rooms open, reflecting the lives and times of family members.

Times Open House 28 Feb-1 Nov, Wed-Sun 11-5; (Garden 11-5.30). 7 Nov-20 Dec, Sat-Sun 11-4.* **Facilities** licensed (outdoor) (partly accessible) (access to all floors via stairs, garden steep slopes) toilets for disabled (w/chair hire, virtual tour, Braille/large print guidebook) shop

LYDD Map 5 TR02

RSPB Nature Reserve

Boulderwall Farm, Dungeness Rd TN29 9PN

☎ 01797 320588 01797 321962
e-mail: dungeness@rspb.org.uk
web: www.rspb.org.uk
dir: off Lydd to Dungeness road, 1m SE of Lydd, follow tourist signs

Occupying over 2,000 acres of the Dungeness peninsula, this is the largest shingle beach of its kind in Europe. About 60 species of birds breed on the reserve each year, including large numbers of waterfowl and waders. Marsh harriers and bearded tits nest in the reed beds along with more common reed and sage warblers and reed buntings. In spring and autumn migrating birds such as warblers and waders pass through Dungeness, while in winter the reserve plays host to hundreds of wildfowl, including pintail, smew and goldeneye. Many plants, butterflies and dragonflies can also be seen around the nature trail. The Dungeness Wildlife and Countryside fair takes place in August each year, with free entry to all.

Times Open: Visitor Centre all year, daily 10-5 (10-4 Nov-Feb). Reserve open all year, daily 9am-9pm (or sunset if earlier). Closed 25-26 Dec.* **Facilities** (outdoor) (partly accessible) (visitor centre & most trails accessible for wheelchair users & access by car to all but one hide) toilets for disabled shop

ENGLAND

LYMPNE Map 5 TR13

Port Lympne Wild Animal Park

CT21 4LR
☎ 0844 8424 647 🖹 01303 264944
e-mail: info@howletts.net
web: www.totallywild.net
dir: M20 junct 11, follow brown tourist signs

An historic mansion and landscaped gardens set in 600 acres, Port Lympne Park also houses the largest breeding herd of black rhino outside Africa as well as African elephants, Siberian and Indian tigers, small cats, monkeys, Malayan tapirs, Barbary lions and many more rare and endangered species. Other exciting features include the 'African Experience', Livingstone Safari Lodge, Day and Sunset safaris, Enrichment Centre Workshops and the chance to be a keeper for a day (subject to availability and at an additional charge) Pre-booking essential for some activities, please see website.

Times Open all year, daily summer 10-6; winter 10-5 (last admission 1hr & 30mins before close). Closed 25 Dec* **Facilities** Ⓟ licensed (outdoor) ♿ (partly accessible) (very limited access for disabled, special route available) toilets for disabled shop

MAIDSTONE Map 5 TQ75

Kent Life

Lock Ln, Sandling ME14 3AU
☎ 01622 763936 🖹 01622 662024
e-mail: enquiries@kentlife.org.uk
web: www.kentlife.org.uk
dir: from M20 junct 6 onto A229 Maidstone road, follow signs for Aylesford

Kent Life is Kent's premier farm attraction featuring 28 acres of fun including a new indoor play barn and outdoor play area. Lots of hands on activities and an animal cuddle corner. See website for a full list of seasonal events.

Times Open Summer 2 Apr-6 Nov, wkdays 10-5; wknds & hols 10-6; winter 7 Nov-Mar, daily 10-4 (last admission 1 hour before close)* **Fees** Summer £8.50 (ch 4-15 £6.50, ch under 4 free, concessions £7.50); Winter £5 (ch 4-15 £3, ch under 4 free, concessions £4)* **Facilities** Ⓟ licensed (outdoor) ♿ (partly accessible) (access to upper floors restricted, no lifts) toilets for disabled (wheelchairs & transport available, ramps) shop

Leeds Castle

ME17 1PL
☎ 01622 765400 🖹 01622 735616
e-mail: enquiries@leeds-castle.co.uk
web: www.leeds-castle.com
dir: 7m E of Maidstone at junct 8 of M20/A20, clearly signed

Set in 500 acres of beautiful parkland, a visit to Leeds Castle is full of discovery. With over 900 years of fascinating history, the castle has been a Norman stronghold, a royal residence for six medieval queens of England, a favourite palace of Henry VIII and a grand country house. Its blend of history and heritage, glorious gardens, aviary and birds of prey, maze and grotto, dog collar museum, craft centre and children's playground, make it the perfect choice for a day out. Special events all year, contact for details or visit the website.

Times Open all year, Grounds: Apr-Sep, daily 10-6 (Castle 10.30-5.30 last admission 4.30). Grounds: Oct-Mar 10-4 (Castle 10.30-4 last admission 3). Last entry to the castle is 30min after the last admission time* **Fees** £17.50 (ch £10, under 4 free, concessions £15). Every ticket purchased for entry to Leeds Castle is valid for unlimited use for an entire year (excluding special ticketed events). Prices are valid until 31 March 2011 **Facilities** Ⓟ licensed (outdoor) ♿ (partly accessible) (only ground floor of castle accessible) toilets for disabled (Braille information, induction loops, wheelchair & lift) shop

Maidstone Museum & Bentlif Art Gallery FREE

St Faith's St ME14 1LH
☎ 01622 602838
e-mail: museum@maidstone.gov.uk
web: www.museum.maidstone.gov.uk
dir: close to County Hall & Maidstone E train station, opposite Fremlin's Walk

Set in an Elizabethan manor house which has been much extended over the years, this museum contains an outstanding collection of fine and applied arts, including watercolours, furniture, ceramics, and a collection of Japanese art and artefacts. The museum of the Queen's Own Royal West Kent Regiment is also housed here. Please apply for details of temporary exhibitions, workshops etc. Opening of the New Art Gallery in Summer 2011.

Times Open all year, Mon-Sat 10-5.15, Sun & BH Mon 11-4. Closed 25-26 Dec & 1 Jan **Facilities** Ⓟ ♿ (partly accessible) (Lifts) shop

Tyrwhitt Drake Museum of Carriages FREE

The Archbishop's Stables, Mill St ME15 6YE
☎ 01622 602838
e-mail: museuminfo@maidstone.gov.uk
web: www.museum.maidstone.gov.uk
dir: close to River Medway & Archbishops Palace, just off A229 in town centre

The museum is home to a unique collection of horse-drawn vehicles and transport curiosities. More than 60 vehicles are on display, from grand carriages and ornate sleighs to antique sedan chairs and Victorian cabs, there is even an original ice-cream cart.

Times Open May-Aug, Wed-Sun & BH, 10.30-4.30. **Facilities** Ⓟ ♿ (partly accessible) shop

PENSHURST Map 5 TQ54

Penshurst Place & Gardens 2 FOR 1

TN11 8DG
☎ 01892 870307 📠 01892 870866
e-mail: enquiries@penshurstplace.com
web: www.penshurstplace.com
dir: M25 junct 5 take A21 Hastings road then exit at Hildenborough & follow brown signs

Built between 1340 and 1345, the original house is perfectly preserved. Enlarged by successive owners during the 15th, 16th and 17th centuries, the great variety of architectural styles creates a dramatic backdrop for the extensive collections of English, French and Italian furniture, tapestries and paintings. The chestnut-beamed Baron's Hall is one of the oldest and finest in the country, and the house is set in magnificent formal gardens. There is a toy museum, venture playground, woodland trail, 10 acres of walled formal gardens and events throughout the season. Two major restoration projects will be completed in 2011, tapestries and fabric conservation and the re-design of the double herbaceous border. Penshurst is a popular choice as a movie and television location.

Times Open: wknds Mar; daily from Good Fri-Oct. Gardens open 10.30-6. House open noon-4. See website for more information **Fees** House, garden, grounds £9.50 (ch 5-16 £6). Family ticket (2ad+2ch) £25. Grounds including garden £7.50 (ch 5-16 £5.50). Family ticket (2ad+2ch) £22* **Facilities** Ⓟ Ⓟ ☕ 🍽 licensed ⛩ (outdoor) ♿ (partly accessible) (garden accessible from visitor entrance, Baron's Hall and Nether Gallery all on ground floor, DVD show of other state rooms) toilets for disabled (ramp into Baron's Hall, Braille & large print guides) shop 🚫

RAMSGATE Map 5 TR36

Ramsgate Maritime Museum

Clock House, Pier Yard, Royal Harbour CT11 8LS
☎ 01843 570622
e-mail: curatorramsgate@btconnect.com
web: www.ramsgatemaritimemuseum.org.uk
dir: Follow A299 to Ramsgate, then Harbour signs

Ramsgate Maritime Museum is housed in the early 19th-century Clock House, focal point of the town's historic Royal Harbour. Four galleries explore the maritime heritage of east Kent. Themes include the fishing industry, transport, shipwreck and salvage, the area during two World Wars and the archaeology of the Goodwin Sands. A fifth display and conservation room features a 17th-century naval gun.

Times Open Jul-Sep, Wed-Sun 10-5.* **Facilities** Ⓟ Ⓟ ♿ (partly accessible) (access restricted to ground floor, no easy access to upper galleries) shop 🚫

RECULVER Map 5 TR26

Reculver Towers & Roman Fort FREE

CT6 6SU
☎ 01227 740676
web: www.english-heritage.org.uk
dir: 3m E of Herne Bay

An imposing 12th-century landmark: twin towers and the walls of a Roman fort.

Times Open any reasonable time, external viewing only
Facilities Ⓟ #

RICHBOROUGH Map 5 TR36

Richborough Roman Fort & Amphitheatre

CT13 9JW
☎ 01304 612013
web: www.english-heritage.org.uk
dir: 1.5m N of Sandwich off A257

Explore the site of the first Roman landing in Britain and visit the museum with its collection of artefacts uncovered on site. See the remains of the huge triumphal arch, once 25 metres high.

Times Amphitheatre: Any reasonable time, access across grazed land from footpath. Please call 01304 612013 for details. Fort: Apr-Sep, daily 10-6 **Fees** £4.50 (ch £2.30, concessions £3.80). Family ticket £11.30. Prices and opening times are subject to change in March 2011. Please call 0870 333 1181 for the most up to date prices and opening times when planning your visit
Facilities Ⓟ shop #

ROCHESTER Map 5 TQ76

Guildhall Museum FREE

High St ME1 1PY
☎ 01634 848717 📠 01634 832919
e-mail: guildhall.museum@medway.gov.uk
web: www.medway.gov.uk
dir: follow signs from A2 to Rochester city centre, museum is at N end of High St

Housed in two adjacent buildings, one dating from 1687 and the other from 1909, the collections are arranged chronologically from Prehistory to the Victorian and Edwardian periods. They cover local history and archaeology, fine and decorative art. There is a gallery devoted to the prison hulks of the River Medway, and a new room detailing the links between Charles Dickens and the Medway Towns. The museum stages a regular programme of temporary exhibitions.

Times Open all year, daily (ex Mon) 10-4.30 (last admission 4). Closed Xmas, New Year & some BHs* **Facilities** Ⓟ ♿ (partly accessible) (limited wheelchair access to Guildhall ground floor, by prior arrangement) shop 🚫

ENGLAND

ROCHESTER *continued*

Rochester Castle

ME1 1SX
☎ 01634 402276
web: www.english-heritage.org.uk
dir: M2 junct 1 & M25 junct 2, A2, by Rochester Bridge

Built on the Roman City Wall, this Norman bishop's castle was a vital royal stronghold.

Times Open all year, Apr-Sep, daily 10-6; Oct-Mar, daily 10-4 (last admission 45mins before closing). Closed 24-26 Dec & 1 Jan **Fees** £5 (ch & concessions £3.50). Family ticket £13.50. Prices and opening times are subject to change in March 2011. Please call 0870 333 1181 for the most up to date prices and opening times when planning your visit **Facilities** shop

ROLVENDEN — Map 5 TQ83

C M Booth Collection of Historic Vehicles

Falstaff Antiques, 63 High St TN17 4LP
☎ 01580 241234
e-mail: info@morganmuseum.org.uk
web: www.morganmuseum.org.uk
dir: on A28, 3m from Tenterden

Not just vehicles, but various other items of interest connected with transport. There is a unique collection of three-wheel Morgan cars, dating from 1913, and the only known Humber tri-car of 1904, as well as a 1929 Morris van, a 1936 Bampton caravan, motorcycles and bicycles. There is also a toy and model car display.

Times Open all year, Mon-Sat 10-5.30. Closed 25-26 Dec* **Fees** £3 (ch £1) **Facilities** (partly accessible) (very narrow access path and in museum) shop

SEVENOAKS — Map 5 TQ55

Knole

TN15 0RP
☎ 01732 462100 & 450608 (info line) 01732 465528
e-mail: knole@nationaltrust.org.uk
web: www.nationaltrust.org.uk/main/w-knole
dir: From town centre, off A225 Tonbridge road, opposite St. Nicholas' Church

Knole's fascinating links with Kings, Queens and nobility, as well as its literary connections with Vita Sackville-West and Virginia Woolf, make this one of the most intriguing houses in England. Thirteen superb state-rooms are laid out much as they were in the 18th century, to impress visitors with the status of the Sackville family, who continue to live at Knole today. The house includes rare furniture and important paintings, as well as many 17th-century tapestries.

Times House open 13 Mar-Oct, Wed-Sun 12-4; open BH Mon. 27 Jul-5 Sep, Tue-Sun 11-4.30* **Fees** Voluntary Gift Aid donation: £10.45 (ch £5.20). Family ticket £26.10. Garden (standard admission) £2 (ch £1). Including a voluntary donation of 10% or more. Visitors can choose to pay the standard admission prices which are displayed* **Facilities** (partly accessible) (access to the Great Hall, shop, tea room, orangery & visitor centre) toilets for disabled (audio loop, Braille guide, large print guide, virtual tour) shop

SISSINGHURST — Map 5 TQ73

Sissinghurst Castle

TN17 2AB
☎ 01580 710700 01580 710702
e-mail: sissinghurst@nationaltrust.org.uk
web: www.nationaltrust.org.uk/sissinghurst
dir: 1m E of Sissinghurst village on A262

Created in the ruins of a large Elizabethan house and set in unspoilt countryside, Sissinghurst Castle Garden is one of the most celebrated gardens made by Vita Sackville-West and her husband Sir Harold Nicolson. Fruit and vegetables grown on the estate are used in the Granary restaurant and the estate is open all year for walks.

Times Open: Gardens 13 Mar-Oct, Fri-Tue 11-5.30. (Peace & Tranquillity after 3.30). Check website for current opening times* **Fees** £10.50 (ch £5.20). Family ticket £26. Prices include a voluntary donation of 10% or more. (Visitors can choose to pay standard admission price)* **Facilities** licensed (outdoor) (partly accessible) (steps to tower, some steps in garden, buggy service to vegetable garden when open) toilets for disabled (buggy service from car park to visitor reception) shop

SMALLHYTHE — Map 5 TQ83

Smallhythe Place

TN30 7NG
☎ 01580 762334 01580 762334
e-mail: smallhytheplace@nationaltrust.org.uk
web: www.nationaltrust.org.uk
dir: 2m S of Tenterden, on E side of the Rye Road on B2082

This half-timbered, 16th-century building was the home of Dame Ellen Terry, a Victorian actress, until her death in 1928. Built when Smallhythe was a thriving shipbuilding yard, the cottage is now a museum of Ellen Terry memorabilia. The cottage grounds include her rose garden, orchard, nuttery and the working Barn Theatre. The anniversary of her death is celebrated every July.

Times Open 26 Feb-30 Oct, Sat-Wed 11-5 (last admission 4.30) **Fees** With 10% Gift Aid donation: £7 (ch £3.80). Family ticket £17. Without Gift Aid donation £6.20 (ch £3.40, group £5.50). Family ticket £15.50 **Facilities** (outdoor) (partly accessible) (access restricted to ground floor of House. Garden partly accessible, slopes, uneven paths, undulating terrain) (album of descriptions & photos of upstairs, Braille guide)

STROOD Map 5 TQ76

Diggerland

Medway Valley Leisure Park, Roman Way ME2 2NU
☎ 0871 227 7007 🖹 09012 010300
e-mail: mail@diggerland.com
web: www.diggerland.com
dir: M2 junct 2, follow A228 towards Rochester. At rdbt turn right. Diggerland on right

An adventure park with a difference. Experience the thrills of driving real earth-moving equipment. Choose from various types of diggers and dumpers ranging from 1 ton to 8.5 tons. Complete the Dumper Truck Challenge or dig for buried treasure supervised by an instructor. New rides include JCB Robots, Diggerland Dodgems, Go-karts, Landrover Safari, Spin Dizzy and the Diggerland Tractors.

Times Open 12 Feb-end Oct, 10-5, wknds, BHs & school hols only (including half term).* **Facilities** 🅟 Ⓟ ☕ ⛩ (outdoor) ♿ (fully accessible) toilets for disabled shop 🚫

SWINGFIELD MINNIS Map 5 TR24

MacFarlane's World of Butterflies

2 FOR 1

MacFarlanes Garden Centre CT15 7HX
☎ 01303 844244 🖹 01303 844244
e-mail: macfarlanes.nursery@hotmail.co.uk
web: www.macfarlanesgardens.co.uk
dir: on A260 by junction with Elham-Lydden road

A tropical greenhouse garden with scores of colourful free-flying butterflies from all over the world among exotic plants such as bougainvillea, oleander and banana. The garden centre celebrates its 90th anniversary in 2011.

Times Open Apr-end Sep, daily 10-5. Closed Etr Sun **Fees** £3 (ch £2 & concessions £2.50). Family ticket (2ad+2ch) £8.50 **Facilities** 🅟 ☕ 🍽 licensed ⛩ (outdoor) ♿ (fully accessible) toilets for disabled shop 🚫

TENTERDEN Map 5 TQ83

Kent & East Sussex Railway

Tenterden Town Station, Station Rd TN30 6HE
☎ 01580 765155 🖹 01580 765654
e-mail: enquiries@kesr.org.uk
web: www.kesr.org.uk
dir: A28 turn into Station Rd beside The Vine Public House, station 200yds on right

Ten and a half miles of pure nostalgia, this is England's finest rural light railway. Beautifully restored coaches and locomotives dating from Victorian times enable visitors to experience travel and service from a bygone age. The picturesque line weaves between Tenterden and Bodiam, terminating in the shadow of the castle.

Times Open Etr-Sep wkdays & wknds. Other times of the year wknds & school hols. Five trains per day* **Facilities** 🅟 Ⓟ ☕ 🍽 licensed ⛩ (outdoor) ♿ (fully accessible) toilets for disabled (converted coach for w/chairs, induction loop) shop

TUNBRIDGE WELLS (ROYAL) Map 5 TQ53

Tunbridge Wells Museum and Art Gallery

FREE

Civic Centre, Mount Pleasant TN1 1JN
☎ 01892 554171 & 526121 🖹 01892 554131
e-mail: museum@tunbridgewells.gov.uk
web: www.tunbridgewellsmuseum.org
dir: adjacent to Town Hall, off A264

This combined museum and art gallery tells the story of the borough of Tunbridge Wells. There are collections of costume, art, dolls and toys along with natural and local history from dinosaur bones to the original Pantiles. There is also a large collection of Tunbridge ware, the intricate wooden souvenirs made for visitors to the Wells. The art gallery features a changing programme of contemporary and historic art, touring exhibitions, and local art and craft.

Times Open all year, daily 9.30-5. Sun 10-4. Closed BHs & Etr Sat* **Facilities** Ⓟ shop 🚫

UPNOR Map 5 TQ77

Upnor Castle

ME2 4XG
☎ 01634 718742 & 338110
web: www.english-heritage.org.uk
dir: on unclass road off A228

16th-century gun fort built to protect Elizabeth I's warships. It saw action in 1667, when the Dutch navy sailed up the Medway to attack the dockyard at Chatham.

Times Open Apr-Oct, daily 10-6 (last admission 45mins before closing). Closed in winter. May close early on Fri & Sat for weddings, please call in advance to check **Fees** £5 (ch & concessions £3.50). Family ticket £13.50. Prices and opening times are subject to change in March 2011. Please call 0870 333 1181 for the most up to date prices and opening times when planning your visit **Facilities** Ⓟ #

WEST MALLING Map 5 TQ65

St Leonard's Tower

FREE

ME19 6PE
☎ 01732 870872
web: www.english-heritage.org.uk
dir: on unclass road W of A228

Early example of a Norman tower keep, built c.1080 by Gundulf, Bishop of Rochester. The tower stands almost to its original height and takes its name from a chapel dedicated to St Leonard that once stood nearby.

Times Open any reasonable time for exterior viewing. Internal viewing by appointment only, please call 01732 870872 **Facilities** #

WESTERHAM Map 5 TQ45

Quebec House

TN16 1TD

☎ 01732 868381 ▤ 01732 868193
e-mail: chartwell@nationaltrust.org.uk
web: www.nationaltrust.org.uk
dir: at E end of village on N side of A25 facing junct with B2026 Edenbridge Road

A house of architectural and historical interest situated near the village green in Westerham. For some years the childhood home of General James Wolfe, it contains family and military memorabilia and an exhibition on the Battle of Quebec.

Times Open: House 12 Mar-30 Oct, Wed-Sun & BH Mon 1-5. Garden & Exhibition 12-5 (last admission 4.30) **Fees** 10% or more voluntary Gift Aid donation: £4.50 (ch £1.70). Family ticket £10.70. Booked groups £3.50. Adult joint ticket with Emmetts Garden £9. Visitors can choose to pay the standard admission prices which are displayed at the property & on NT website* **Facilities** Ⓟ ♿ (partly accessible) (ground floor accessible, stairs to other floors, grounds partly accessible, loose gravel paths) toilets for disabled (wheelchair, tactile items, Braille & large print guide) shop

Squerryes Court 2 FOR 1

TN16 1SJ

☎ 01959 562345 ▤ 01959 565949
e-mail: enquiries@squerryes.co.uk
web: www.squerryes.co.uk
dir: 0.5m W of town centre, signed off A25

This beautiful manor house, built in 1681 by Sir Nicholas Crisp, has been the home of the Wardes since 1731. It contains a fine collection of pictures, furniture, porcelain and tapestries. The lovely garden was landscaped in the 18th century and has a lake, restored formal garden, and woodland walks.

Times Open Apr-Sep, Wed, Sun & BH Mon. Garden open 11.30-5, House 12.30-5 (last entry 4.30)* **Fees** House & grounds £7 (ch under 16 £4, concessions £6.50). Family ticket (2ad+2ch) £14. Grounds £4.50 (ch under 16 £2.50, concessions £4). Family ticket (2ad+2ch) £9* **Facilities** Ⓟ Ⓟ ☕ (outdoor) ♿ (partly accessible) (ground floor of house accessible and level area around formal garden, phone for more detail) toilets for disabled shop

YALDING Map 5 TQ75

Yalding Organic Centre

Benover Rd ME18 6EX

☎ 01622 814650 ▤ 01622 814650
e-mail: enquiry@gardenorganic.org.uk
web: www.yaldingorganics.com
dir: on B2162, 0.5m S of Yalding

Eighteen gardens tell the history of gardening in an imaginatively landscaped setting. Travel through representations of ancient woodlands, medieval physic, knot and paradise gardens, a 19th-century artisan's plot, and borders inspired by Gertrude Jekyll's ideas before reaching a 1950s 'Dig for Victory' allotment. The remainder of the garden is devoted to the vision of the 'organic' future of horticulture, growing flowers, fruit and vegetables without added chemicals. The garden was founded, and is still owned by, Garden Organic, the national charity for organic growing, almost fifty years ago.

Times Open all year, daily 9-6* **Facilities** Ⓟ ☕ ♿ (fully accessible) toilets for disabled shop

LANCASHIRE

Whitewell, Forest of Bowland

ENGLAND

BLACKPOOL Map 7 SD33

Blackpool Zoo

East Park Dr FY3 8PP
☎ 01253 830830 📠 01253 830800
e-mail: info@blackpoolzoo.org.uk
web: www.blackpoolzoo.org.uk
dir: M55 junct 4, follow brown tourist signs

This multi-award-winning zoo, built in 1972, houses over 1500 animals within its 32 acres of landscaped gardens. There is a miniature railway, lots of close encounters and animals in action, a children's play area, animal feeding times and keeper talks throughout the day. New animal attractions include Giraffe Heights and Penguin Pool. Many special events throughout the year.

Times Open all year daily, summer 10-6; winter 10-dusk. Jul-Aug, Wed 10-9. Closed 25 Dec.* **Facilities** Ⓟ Ⓟ ☕ 🍽 licensed ⛩ (outdoor) ♿ (fully accessible) toilets for disabled (wheelchair loan, talking & signing tours - booked) shop 🚫

BURNLEY Map 7 SD83

Towneley Hall Art Gallery & Museums 2 FOR 1

Towneley Park BB11 3RQ
☎ 01282 424213 📠 01282 436138
e-mail: towneleyhall@burnley.gov.uk
web: www.burnley.gov.uk/towneley
dir: M65 junct 9 signed Halifax (A646) and follow signs for Towneley Hall

This 14th-century house contains the art gallery and museum. Today a variety of displays encompass natural history, Egyptology, textiles and art. Special exhibitions and events are held throughout the year, telephone for details. There are nature trails and Natural History Collections. Look out for the Wildabout Burnley. Educational facilities are available for schools.

Times Open all year, Sat-Thu 12-5 **Fees** £3.70 (ch & students free)* **Facilities** Ⓟ Ⓟ ☕ 🍽 licensed ⛩ (outdoor) ♿ (partly accessible) (no access due to stairs in Historic Long Gallery) toilets for disabled (virtual tour on computer) shop 🚫

CHARNOCK RICHARD Map 7 SD51

Camelot Theme Park

PR7 5LP
☎ 01257 452100 📠 01257 452395
e-mail: kingarthur@camelotthemepark.co.uk
web: www.camelotthemepark.co.uk
dir: from M6 junct 27/28, or M61 junct 8 follow brown tourist signs

Join Merlin, King Arthur and the Knights of the Round Table at the magical kingdom of Camelot. Explore five magic lands filled with thrilling rides, spectacular shows, and many more attractions. From white-knuckle thrills on Knightmare, The Whirlwind spinning rollercoaster, to wet-knuckle thrills on Pendragon's Plunge, there's something for everyone.

Times Open 31 Mar-28 Oct.* **Facilities** Ⓟ ☕ ⛩ (indoor & outdoor) ♿ (partly accessible) toilets for disabled (disabled car parking) shop 🚫

CHORLEY Map 7 SD51

Astley Hall Museum & Art Gallery FREE

Astley Park PR7 1NP
☎ 01257 515555 📠 01257 515923
e-mail: astley.hall@chorley.gov.uk
web: www.astleyhall.co.uk
dir: M61 junct 8, signed Botany Bay. Follow brown signs

A charming Tudor/Stuart building set in beautiful parkland, this lovely Hall retains a comfortable 'lived-in' atmosphere. There are pictures and pottery to see, as well as fine furniture and rare plasterwork ceilings. Special events throughout the year.

Times Open Apr (or Etr)-Oct, Sat-Sun & BH Mon 12-5; By appointment only during the week* **Facilities** Ⓟ Ⓟ ⛩ (outdoor) ♿ (partly accessible) (video of upper floors, print/Braille guide, CD audio guide) shop 🚫

CLITHEROE Map 7 SD74

Clitheroe Castle Museum

Castle Hill BB7 1BA
☎ 01200 424568 📠 01200 421008
e-mail: clitheroecastlemuseum@lancashire.gov.uk
web: www.lancashire.gov.uk
dir: follow Clitheroe signs from A59 Preston-Skipton by-pass. Museum located in castle grounds near town centre

Clitheroe Castle Museum covers 350 million years of history of the local area. The galleries include displays and hands-on interactives on geology, wildlife, the history of Clitheroe's castle keep and buildings; the history of the town, its people, industry and transport.

Times Open all year, Apr-Oct, daily 11-5; Nov-Mar, daily noon-4. Closed 25-26 Dec & 1 Jan **Fees** £3.50 (ch under 16 free but must be accompanied by an adult, concessions £2.50). LCMS Xplorer tickets welcome. **Facilities** Ⓟ ☕ ♿ (fully accessible) toilets for disabled (lift) shop 🚫

LANCASTER Map 7 SD46

Lancaster Castle 2 FOR 1

The Shire Hall, Castle Pde LA1 1YJ
☎ 01524 64998 📠 01524 847914
e-mail: christine.goodier@lancashire.gov.uk
web: www.lancastercastle.com
dir: follow brown tourist signs from M6 junct 33/34

Founded on the site of three Roman forts, Lancaster Castle dominates Castle Hill, above the River Lune. The Norman keep was built in about 1170 and King John added a curtain wall and Hadrian's Tower. The Shire Hall, noted for its Gothic revival design, contains a splendid display of heraldry. The Crown Court was notorious as having handed out the greatest number of death sentences of any court in the land. Various events through the year.

Times Open all year, daily 10.30 (1st tour)-4 (last tour). Court sittings permitting - it is advisable to telephone before visiting. Closed Xmas & New Year* **Fees** £5 (concessions £4). Family ticket £14* **Facilities** Ⓟ Ⓟ ♿ (partly accessible) (Shire Hall courtroom accessible to wheelchair users) shop 🚫

Lancaster City Museum FREE

Market Sq LA1 1HT
☎ 01524 64637 📠 01524 841692
e-mail: lancastercitymuseum@lancashire.gov.uk
web: www.lancashire.gov.uk/museums
dir: in city centre just off A6

The fine Georgian town hall is the setting for the museum, which explores the history and archaeology of the city from prehistoric and Roman times onwards. Also housed here is the museum of the King's Own Royal Lancaster Regiment. The Cottage Museum, furnished in the style of an artisan's house of around 1820, faces Lancaster Castle.

Times Open all year, Mon-Sat, 10-5. Closed 25 Dec-1 Jan* **Facilities** Ⓟ ♿ (partly accessible) (ramp to entrance/ground floor, 2 stairlifts) shop 🚫

Lancaster Maritime Museum 2 FOR 1

St George's Quay LA1 1RB
☎ 01524 382264 📠 01524 841692
e-mail: lancastermaritimemuseum@lancashire.gov.uk
web: www.lancashire.gov.uk/museums
dir: close to M6, junct 33 & 34. From A6 follow signs to town centre & then brown tourist signs to the Quay

Graceful Ionic columns adorn the front of the Custom House, built in 1764. Inside, the histories of the 18th-century transatlantic maritime trade of Lancaster, the Lancaster Canal and the fishing industry of Morecambe Bay are well illustrated. Changing programme of special exhibitions and holiday events, please ring or see website for details.

Times Open all year, daily, Etr-Oct 11-5; Nov-Etr 12.30-4 **Fees** £3 (concessions £2). Free to accompanied children and residents of Lancaster district* **Facilities** Ⓟ Ⓟ ☕ 🪑 (indoor) ♿ (partly accessible) (mezzanine floor inaccessible) toilets for disabled shop 🚫

LEIGHTON HALL Map 7 SD47

Leighton Hall 2 FOR 1

LA5 9ST
☎ 01524 734474 📠 01524 720357
e-mail: info@leightonhall.co.uk
web: www.leightonhall.co.uk
dir: M6 junct 35 onto A6 & follow signs

This is the historic family home of the Gillow furniture makers, and early Gillow furniture is displayed among other treasures in the fine interior of the neo-Gothic mansion. There are also fine gardens, a maze and a woodland walk. A varied programme of special events throughout the year, for full details please see website.

Times Open May-Sep, Tue-Fri & BH Sun & Mon; Aug, Tue-Fri, Sun & BH Mon 2-5. Groups all year by arrangement **Fees** £6.95 (ch 5-12 £4.75, pen £6). Family ticket £22 **Facilities** Ⓟ ☕ 🪑 (outdoor) ♿ (partly accessible) (upstairs not accessible) toilets for disabled (ramps, parking close to entrance) shop 🚫

LEYLAND Map 7 SD52

British Commercial Vehicle Museum 2 FOR 1

King St PR25 2LE
☎ 01772 451011 📠 01772 451015
e-mail: enquiries@bcvm.co.uk
web: www.bcvm.co.uk
dir: 0.75m from M6 junct 28 in town centre

A unique line-up of historic commercial vehicles and buses spanning a century of truck and bus building. There are more than 60 exhibits on permanent display, the 'Engine Room' which tells the story of engine development and how drivers can care for their vehicle engines, a cinema showing classic transport films, and a photographic archive containing over 250,000 images of past times.

Times Open Mar-Oct, Sat-Sun & BHs plus during school hols Thu-Fri, 10-5 **Fees** £5.50 (ch £3, pen £5). Family ticket (2ad+3ch) £14 **Facilities** Ⓟ Ⓟ ☕ 🪑 (outdoor) ♿ (fully accessible) toilets for disabled (ramps to decked viewing area) shop 🚫

MARTIN MERE Map 7 SD41

WWT Martin Mere

L40 0TA

☎ 01704 895181 📠 01704 892343

e-mail: info@martinmere.co.uk

web: www.wwt.org.uk/martinmere

dir: signed from M61, M58 & M6, 6m from Ormskirk, off A59

One of Britain's most important wetland sites, where you can get really close to a variety of ducks, geese and swans from all over the world as well as two flocks of flamingos and beavers. Thousands of wildfowl, including pink-footed geese, Bewick's and Whooper swans, winter here. Other features include a children's adventure playground, craft area, shop and an educational centre.

Times Open all year, daily 9.30-5.30 (5 in winter). Closed 25 Dec.* **Facilities** Ⓟ ☕ ⛩ (indoor & outdoor) ♿ (fully accessible) toilets for disabled (wheelchair loan, heated hide) shop

PADIHAM Map 7 SD73

Gawthorpe Hall

BB12 8UA

☎ 01282 771004 📠 01282 770178

e-mail: gawthorpehall@nationaltrust.org.uk

web: www.nationaltrust.org.uk/main/w-gawthorpehall

dir: on E outskirts of Padiham, 0.75m on A671

An early 17th-century manor house, built around Britain's most southerly pele tower, restored in 1850. A collection of portraits from the National Portrait Gallery and the Kay Shuttleworth Collections of costume, embroidery and lace are on show in the exhibition areas. The wooded park and riverside location offer wonderful walks.

Times Open Garden: daily 10-6. House: Apr-Oct, Tue-Thu & Sat-Sun. Also open BH Mon & Good Fri* **Fees** House: £4 (ch & concessions £3). Children free if accompanied by adult. Garden: free. Please telephone or check website for further details* **Facilities** Ⓟ ☕ ⛩ (outdoor) ♿ (partly accessible) (House accessed via 4 steps and stairs to all floors. Grounds route to lawn and entrance to tea room are level) toilets for disabled (Braille & large print guide, photo album & car drop off) 🚫 ✽

PRESTON Map 7 SD52

Harris Museum & Art Gallery FREE

Market Square PR1 2PP

☎ 01772 258248 📠 01772 886764

e-mail: harris.museum@preston.gov.uk

web: www.harrismuseum.org.uk

dir: M6 junct 31, follow signs for city centre, park at bus stn car park

An impressive Grade I listed Greek Revival building containing extensive collections of fine and decorative art including a gallery of clothes and fashion. The Story of Preston covers the city's history and the lively exhibition programmes of contemporary art and social history are accompanied by events and activities throughout the year.

Times Open all year, Mon & Wed-Sat 10-5, Tue 11-5. Closed Sun & BHs* **Facilities** Ⓟ ☕ ♿ (partly accessible) (lift to all floors with exception of Egyptian Balcony. Wheelchair available, chair lift to mezzanine galleries, ramp to entrance) toilets for disabled (audio visual guide to Egyptian Balcony is on 2nd floor) shop 🚫

See advert on opposite page

ROSSENDALE Map 7 SD72

Rossendale Museum FREE

Whitaker Park, Haslingden Rd, Rawtenstall BB4 6RE

☎ 01706 260785 📠 01706 250037

e-mail: rossendale.museum@lancashire.gov.uk

web: www.lancashire.gov.uk/museums

dir: off A681, 0.25m W of Rawtenstall centre

Former mill owner's house, built in 1840 and set in the delightful Whitaker Park. Displays include fine and decorative arts, a Victorian drawing room, natural history, costume, local and social history and regular temporary exhibitions.

Times Open all year, Apr-Oct, Tue-Thu, Sat-Sun & BHs, 1-4.30; Nov-Mar, 1-4* **Facilities** Ⓟ Ⓟ ♿ (fully accessible) toilets for disabled (large print, audio guides, induction loop, lift) shop 🚫

RUFFORD Map 7 SD41

Rufford Old Hall

L40 1SG

☎ 01704 821254 📠 01704 823823

e-mail: ruffordoldhall@nationaltrust.org.uk

web: www.nationaltrust.org.ukmain/w-ruffordoldhall

dir: M6 junct 27 & follow signs to Rufford. Hall on E side of A59

Rufford is one of Lancashire's finest Tudor buildings, and is where a young William Shakespeare is believed to have performed for its owner, Sir Thomas Hesketh. Visitors can wander around the house and view the fine collections of furniture, arms, armour and tapestries. Outside there are the gardens, topiary and sculptures. Enjoy a walk in the woodlands alongside the canal, and then have some freshly-prepared local food in the tea room.

Times Open 27 Feb-7 Mar, wknds only 11-5; 13 Mar-Oct, Sun-Wed 11-5 & Sat 1-5. Garden, shop & tea room, 5 Nov-19 Dec, Fri-Sun 12-4* **Fees** House & Garden: £6.20 (ch £3.10). Family ticket £15.50. Garden only: £4.30 (ch £2.20)* **Facilities** Ⓟ licensed (outdoor) ♿ (partly accessible) (ground floor accessible, but steps from Great Hall & some loose cobbles & gravel in grounds) toilets for disabled (Braille & large print guide, wheelchairs, induction loop) shop

SAMLESBURY Map 7 SD53

Samlesbury Hall

Preston New Rd PR5 0UP

☎ 01254 812010 & 812229 📠 01254 812174

e-mail: enquiries@samlesburyhall.co.uk

web: www.samlesburyhall.co.uk

dir: M6 junct 31/A677 for 3m, as indicated by brown tourist signs

A well restored half-timbered manor house, built during the 14th and 15th centuries, and set in five acres of beautiful grounds. Sales of antiques and collector's items, craft shows and temporary exhibitions are held all year round. Live theatre productions and seasonal events throughout the year.

Times Open all year, Sun-Fri 11-4.30. Closed 25-26 Dec & 1 Jan and Sat* **Fees** £3 (ch 4-16 £1)* **Facilities** Ⓟ Ⓟ licensed ♿ (partly accessible) (ground floor fully accessible, upper floor accessible via chair lift) toilets for disabled (stair lift) shop

ENGLAND

SILVERDALE Map 7 SD47

RSPB Leighton Moss Nature Reserve

2 FOR 1

Myers Farm LA5 0SW
☎ 01524 701601 01524 702092
e-mail: leighton.moss@rspb.org.uk
web: www.rspb.org.uk
dir: M6 junct 35, west on A501(M) for 0.5m. Turn right and head N on A6. Follow brown tourist signs

Leighton Moss is the largest remaining reedbed in north-west England, with special birds, breeding bitterns, bearded tits, marsh harriers, avocets and other spectacular wildlife. Enjoy nature trails and visit the RSPB shop and visitor centre.

Times Reserve: open daily 9-dusk. Visitor Centre daily Feb-Oct 9.30-5; Nov-Jan 9.30-4.30. Closed 25 Dec* **Fees** £4.50 (ch £1, concessions £3) Family £9. RSPB members Free* **Facilities** licensed (outdoor) (partly accessible) (some nature trails accessible) toilets for disabled (stairlift available to cafe) shop

TURTON BOTTOMS Map 7 SD71

Turton Tower

BL7 0HG
☎ 01204 852203 01204 853759
e-mail: turton.tower@mus.lanscc.gov.uk
dir: on B6391, off A666 or A676

A historic house incorporating a 15th-century tower house and Elizabethan half-timbered buildings, and displaying a major collection of carved wood furniture. During the 19th century, the house became associated with the Gothic revival and later typified the idealism of the Arts and Crafts movement. The gardens are being restored in late-Victorian style.

Times Open May-Sep, Mon-Thu 11-5, wknds 1-5; Mar-Oct, Mon-Wed 1-5, wknds 1-4; Apr Sat-Wed 1-5; Nov & Feb, Sun 1-4. Other times by prior arrangement.* **Facilities** toilets for disabled shop

WHALLEY Map 7 SD73

Whalley Abbey

2 FOR 1

BB7 9SS
☎ 01254 828400 01254 825519
e-mail: office@whalleyabbey.org
web: www.whalleyabbey.co.uk
dir: off A59 4m S of Clitheroe

Whalley Abbey was established in the 13th century and the ruins of this former Cistercian Monastery are now open to the public. It is set in beautiful grounds in the glorious countryside of the Ribble Valley.

Times Open daily, 10-5. Closed 25-26 Dec & New Year **Fees** Grounds and ruins £2 (ch 50p). Please check for current prices* **Facilities** Ⓟ (outdoor) (partly accessible) toilets for disabled (chair lifts, ramps, wheelchairs available) shop

LEICESTERSHIRE

Bosworth battlefield, Market Bosworth

ASHBY-DE-LA-ZOUCH Map 8 SK31

Ashby-de-la-Zouch Castle

South St LE65 1BR

☎ 01530 413343 📠 01530 411677

web: www.english-heritage.org.uk

Impressive ruins of a late medieval castle. The magnificent 24 metre Hastings Tower offers panoramic views of the surrounding countryside. Ashby was the setting for the famous jousting scene in Sir Walter Scott's classic romance *Ivanhoe*.

Times Open all year, Apr-Jun & Sep-Oct, Thu-Mon 10-5; Jul-Aug, daily 10-5; Nov-Mar, Thu-Mon 12-4. Closed 24-26 Dec & 1 Jan **Fees** £4.30 (ch £2.10, concessions £3.60). Family ticket £10.50. Prices and opening times are subject to change in March 2011. Please call 0870 333 1181 for the most up to date prices and opening times when planning your visit **Facilities** Ⓟ shop ⌗

BELVOIR Map 8 SK83

Belvoir Castle 2 FOR 1

NG32 1PE

☎ 01476 871002 📠 01476 870443

e-mail: sales@belvoircastle.com

web: www.belvoircastle.com

dir: between A52 & A607, follow the brown heritage signs from A1, A52, A607 & A46

Although Belvoir Castle has been the home of the Dukes of Rutland for many centuries, the turrets, battlements, towers and pinnacles of the house are a 19th-century fantasy. Amongst the many treasures to be seen inside are paintings by Murillo, Holbein and other famous artists, military treasures of the guardroom and stunning state rooms. Lovingly restored gardens are also open to visitors. Special events planned throughout the season, phone for details or visit the website.

Times Open: Jul-Sep, Mon-Tue (Coach parties only by prior arrangement); Aug, Sun-Thu; 1-3 Dec (eve only); 12-17 Dec (daytime only)* **Fees** £10 (ch £6). Family ticket £28* **Facilities** Ⓟ Ⓟ ☕ 🍽 licensed ⛩ (outdoor) ♿ (partly accessible) (castle limited to ground floor, gardens limited access) toilets for disabled (permitted to be driven/drive right up to castle entrance) shop ⊗

COALVILLE Map 8 SK41

Snibston Discovery Museum

Ashby Rd LE67 3LN

☎ 01530 278444 📠 01530 813301

e-mail: snibston@leics.gov.uk

web: www.snibston.com

dir: 4.5m from M1 junct 22 or from A42/M42 junct 13 on A511 on W side of Coalville

Snibston is the largest science and technology museum in the East Midlands, displaying a wealth of nationally important collections that explore ways in which technology, design and industry impact upon our everyday lives. Visitors to the museum can lift a mini, join one of our former miners on a colliery tour and hear what it was like to work underground (subject to availability), journey back to the industrial revolution with the beam engines or experience the largest fashion gallery outside London. With something for everyone, regardless of age or interest, you will be amazed at what is on offer to discover.

Times Open all year, Apr-Oct, daily 10-5; Nov-Mar 10-3. School hols & wknds 10-5. Closed 2 wks in Jan for maintenance **Fees** £6.75 (ch £4.50, concessions £4.75). Family ticket £20. Please call or see website for up to date admission prices* **Facilities** Ⓟ Ⓟ ☕ ⛩ (indoor & outdoor) ♿ (fully accessible) toilets for disabled (Braille labels, touch tables, hearing loop, parking) shop ⊗

DONINGTON-LE-HEATH Map 5 SK41

Donington-le-Heath Manor House FREE

Manor Rd LE67 2FW

☎ 01530 831259 📠 01530 831259

e-mail: dlhmanorhouse@leics.gov.uk

web: www.leics.gov.uk/donington

dir: S of Coalville

This is a rare example of a medieval manor house, tracing its history back to about 1280. It has now been restored as a period house, with fine oak furnishings. The surrounding grounds include period gardens, and the adjoining stone barn houses a restaurant.

Times Open Mar-Nov, daily 11-4; Dec-Feb, Sat-Sun 11-4* **Facilities** Ⓟ ☕ 🍽 licensed ⛩ ♿ (partly accessible) toilets for disabled shop ⊗

LEICESTER Map 4 SK50

Abbey Pumping Station

Corporation Rd, Abbey Ln LE4 5PX

☎ 0116 299 5111 📠 0116 299 5125

e-mail: museums@leicester.gov.uk

web: www.leicester.gov.uk/museums

dir: off A6, 1m N from city centre

Explore Leicester's industrial, technological and scientific heritage at Abbey Pumping Station. Built in 1891, this fascinating museum features some of the largest steam beam engines in the country and a working model railway. Exhibitions include historic transport, light and optics, and public health. There are plenty of interactive exhibits, popular with children.

Times Open Feb-Oct, daily 11-4.30. Open Nov-Jan for special events **Fees** Admission free, a small charge made for some events. Donations welcome **Facilities** (outdoor) (partly accessible) (limited wheelchair access) toilets for disabled (loan of wheelchairs, wheelchair lift) shop

Belgrave Hall Museum & Gardens

Church Rd, off Thurcaston Rd, Belgrave LE4 5PE
0116 266 6590 0116 261 3063
e-mail: museums@leicester.gov.uk
web: www.leicester.gov.uk/museums
dir: off Belgrave/Loughborough road, 1m from city centre

A delightful three-storey Queen Anne house which dates from 1709 with beautiful period and botanic gardens. Authentic room settings contrast Georgian elegance with Victorian cosiness and include the kitchen, drawing room, music room and nursery. Believed to be haunted, ghost hunters regularly investigate the site.

Times Open Feb-Oct, Sat-Wed 11-4.30, Sun 1-4.30. Open every day during school hols, ex Xmas **Fees** Free admission, donations welcome. Small charge for some events **Facilities** (outdoor) (partly accessible) (no access upstairs in Hall) toilets for disabled (loan of wheelchair) shop

The Guildhall

Guildhall Ln LE1 5FQ
0116 253 2569 0116 253 9626
e-mail: museums@leicester.gov.uk
web: www.leicester.gov.uk/museums
dir: next to Leicester Cathedral

A preserved medieval building dating back to the 14th century, the Guildhall is one of Leicester's oldest buildings still in use. Over the centuries it has served as the Hall of the Guild of Corpus Christi, the Civic Centre and Town Hall, a judicial centre for court sessions and home to Leicester's first police force. The Guildhall now houses one of the oldest libraries in the country, as well as hosting events, activities and performances.

Times Open all year. Feb-Nov, Sat-Wed 11-4.30, Sun 1-4.30. Open Dec-Jan for special events **Fees** Admission free. Donations welcome **Facilities** (partly accessible) (No disabled access upstairs) toilets for disabled (wheelchair loan, induction loop, voice minicom) shop

Jewry Wall Museum

St Nicholas Circle LE1 4LB
0116 225 4971 0116 225 4966
e-mail: museums@leicester.gov.uk
web: www.leicester.gov.uk/museums
dir: opposite the Holiday Inn

Behind the massive fragment of the Roman Jewry Wall and a Roman Baths site from the 2nd century AD, is the Museum of Leicestershire Archaeology, which includes finds from the earliest times to the Middle Ages.

Times Open Feb-Oct, daily 11-4.30. Open Nov-Jan for special events **Fees** Admission free, however a charge is made for some events. Donations welcome **Facilities** (partly accessible) (access for wheelchair users via the staff entrance on Holy Bones) toilets for disabled shop

National Space Centre

Exploration Dr LE4 5NS
0845 605 2001 0116 258 2100
e-mail: info@spacecentre.co.uk
web: www.spacecentre.co.uk
dir: off A6, 2m N of city centre midway between Leicester's central & outer ring roads. Follow brown rocket signs from M1 (junct 21, 21a or 22) & all arterial routes around Leicester

The award-winning National Space Centre offers a great family day out, with six interactive galleries, a full-domed Space Theatre, a 42-metre high Rocket Tower, and the new Human Spaceflight Experience with 3D SIM ride. Explore the universe, orbit Earth, join the crew on the lunar base, and take the astronaut fitness tests, all without leaving Leicester! Project Apollo is the latest interactive experience celebrating the 40th anniversary of the Apollo moon landing. In 2011 the centre celebrates its 10th anniversary. Throughout the year there are numerous events relating to space reality and science fiction, so contact the Centre for more details.

Times Open during school term: Tue-Fri, 10-4, Sat-Sun 10-5. During school hols: daily, 10-5* **Fees** £13 (ch 5-16 & concessions £11). Family ticket (2ad+2ch) £41, (2ad+3ch) £51. All tickets valid for a full year **Facilities** licensed (outdoor) (fully accessible) toilets for disabled (induction loop, large text, wheelchairs, lifts) shop

Newarke Houses Museum & Gardens

The Newarke LE2 7BY
0116 225 4980 0116 225 4982
e-mail: museums@leicester.gov.uk
web: www.leicester.gov.uk/museums
dir: opposite De Montfort University

Recently renovated, this museum tells the story of the Royal Leicestershire Regiment and the city's social history in the 20th century. Displays include a reconstruction of a First World War trench, typical room settings from the 1950s and 1970s, a 1950s street and two community galleries, telling the stories of 'Moving Here' and settling in Leicester.

continued

ENGLAND

LEICESTER *continued*

Times Open all year, daily 10-5, Sun 11-5. Closed 24-26 & 31 Dec & 1 Jan **Fees** Admission free but small charge for some events. Donations welcome **Facilities** Ⓟ (outdoor) (partly accessible) (some parts of the garden are not accessible) (car parking can be arranged) shop

New Walk Museum & Art Gallery

53 New Walk LE1 7EA
☎ 0116 225 4900 0116 225 4927
e-mail: museums@leicester.gov.uk
web: www.leicester.gov.uk/museums
dir: situated on New Walk. Access by car from A6 onto Waterloo Way at Railway Stn. Right into Regent Rd, right onto West St, right onto Princess Rd which leads to car park

This major regional venue houses local and national collections. There's an internationally famous collection of German Expressionism and other displays include the Rutland Dinosaur and the Egyptian Gallery. An extensive Natural History collection augmented by art from the renaissance to contemporary.

Times Open all year, Mon-Sat 10-5, Sun 11-5. Closed 24-26 & 31 Dec, 1 Jan (some downstairs art galleries may close at 12 on Sat for weddings) **Fees** Admission free. Donations welcome. Small charge for some events **Facilities** Ⓟ (fully accessible) toilets for disabled (wheelchairs for loan, minicom, induction loop) shop

The Record Office for Leicestershire & Rutland

FREE

Long St, Wigston Magna LE18 2AH
☎ 0116 257 1080 0116 257 1120
e-mail: recordoffice@leics.gov.uk
web: www.leics.gov.uk/recordoffice
dir: old A50, S of Leicester City

Housed in a converted 19th-century school in Wigston, the Record Office holds photographs, electoral registers and archive film, files of local newspapers, history tapes and sound recordings, all of which can be studied.

Times Open all year, Mon, Tue & Thu 9.15-5, Wed 9.15-7.30, Fri 9.15-4.45, Sat 9.15-12.15. Closed Sun & BH wknds Sat-Tue* **Facilities** Ⓟ (fully accessible) toilets for disabled

University of Leicester Harold Martin Botanic Garden

Beaumont Hall, Stoughton Drive South, Oadby LE2 2NA
☎ 0116 271 7725 & 2933 (tours)
e-mail: bldal@le.ac.uk
web: www.le.ac.uk/biology/botanicgarden/
dir: 3m SE A6, entrance at 'The Knoll', Glebe Rd, Oadby

The grounds of four houses, now used as student residences and not open to the public, make up this 16-acre garden. A great variety of plants in different settings provide a delightful place to walk, including rock, water and sunken gardens, trees, borders, glasshouses and national collections of hardy fuchsias, aubrieta, skimmia and Lawson cypress.

Times Open all year, Mon-Fri 10-4, Sat-Sun 10-4 (from 3rd wknd in Mar to 2nd wknd in Nov inclusive). Closed 25-26 Dec & 1 Jan.* **Facilities** Ⓟ (partly accessible) (some steps) toilets for disabled

LOUGHBOROUGH — Map 8 SK51

Great Central Railway

Great Central Rd LE11 1RW
☎ 01509 230726 01509 239791
e-mail: sales@gcrailway.co.uk
web: www.gcrailway.co.uk
dir: signed from A6, follow brown tourist signs

This private steam railway runs over eight miles from Loughborough Central to Leicester North, with all trains calling at Quorn & Woodhouse and Rothley. The locomotive depot and museum are at Loughborough Central. A buffet car runs on most trains.

Times Open all year daily, trains run every wknd & BHs throughout the year, May-Sep, Wed; Jun, Jul & Aug daily ex Fri.* **Facilities** Ⓟ licensed (outdoor) (fully accessible) toilets for disabled shop

MARKET BOSWORTH — Map 4 SK40

Bosworth Battlefield Visitor Centre & Country Park

Ambion Hill, Sutton Cheney CV13 0AD
☎ 01455 290429 01455 292841
e-mail: bosworth@leics.gov.uk
web: www.leics.gov.uk
dir: follow brown tourist signs from A447, A444 & A5

The Battle of Bosworth Field was fought in 1485 between the armies of Richard III and the future Henry VII. The visitor centre offers a comprehensive interpretation of the battle, with exhibitions, models and a film theatre. Special medieval attractions are held in the summer months.

Times Open: Country Park daily Apr-Sep, 8.30-5.30; Oct-Mar 8.30-4.40. Heritage Centre open daily Apr-Oct, 10-5; Nov-Mar, 10-4 (last admission 1hr before closing). Closed Jan & 24-27 Dec* **Facilities** Ⓟ licensed (outdoor) (partly accessible) toilets for disabled (wheelchair & electric scooter hire, tactile exhibits) shop

MOIRA — Map 8 SK31

Conkers

2 FOR 1

Millennium Av, Rawdon Rd DE12 6GA
☎ 01283 216633 01283 210321
e-mail: info@visitconkers.com
web: www.visitconkers.com
dir: on B5003 in Moira, signed from A444 and M42

Explore over one hundred indoor interactive exhibits, together with 120 acres that contain lakeside walks and trails, habitats, an assault course, adventure play areas and a miniature train. There are also events in the covered amphitheatre, and many other opportunities for you and your family to be entertained and educated.

Times Open all year, daily, summer 10-6, autumn 10-5, winter 10-4.30. Closed 25 Dec* **Fees** £7.95 (ch 3-15yrs £5.95, ch under 3 free, concessions £6.95). Family ticket (2ad+2ch) £24.95. Prices include a 10% donation to The Heart of the National Forest* **Facilities** Ⓟ ☕ 🍴 licensed ⛩ (indoor & outdoor) ♿ (fully accessible) toilets for disabled (multi access walks & trails accessible to wheelchairs) shop ⊗

SHACKERSTONE — Map 4 SK30

Battlefield Line Railway

Shackerstone Station CV13 6NW
☎ 01827 880754 📠 01827 881050
web: www.battlefield-line-railway.co.uk
dir: located between Ashby-de-la-Zouch & Hinckley. Follow brown signs from A444 & A447

The Battlefield Line is the last remaining part of the former Ashby and Nuneaton Joint Railway which was opened in 1873. It runs from Shackerstone via Market Bosworth to Shenton in Leicestershire and is operated by the Shackerstone Railway Society. There are regular train trips to Bosworth battlefield with a variety of locomotives, steam and diesel-hauled trains and heritage railcars. Special events take place all year - please contact for details.

Times Open Etr-Oct wknds & BH 10.30-5.30. Closed Xmas. Trains runs Etr-Oct, Santa trains Dec* **Facilities** Ⓟ ☕ ⛩ (outdoor) ♿ (partly accessible) (not all carriages & parts of museum suitable for wheelchairs) toilets for disabled (parking & toilets at Shackerstone & Shenton Stations) shop

SWINFORD — Map 4 SP57

Stanford Hall

LE17 6DH
☎ 01788 860250 📠 01788 860870
e-mail: enquiries@stanfordhall.co.uk
web: www.stanfordhall.co.uk
dir: 7.5m NE of Rugby, 1.5m from Swinford. 2m from the M1, M6, A14 junct

A beautiful William and Mary house, built in 1697 by Sir Roger Cave, ancestor of the present owner. The house contains antique furniture, paintings (including the Stuart Collection) and family costumes. Special events include car and motorcycle owners' club rallies.

Times Open 12-26 Apr, daily, 1.30-5.30; also open selected days in conjunction with Park events & BH Mons.* **Facilities** Ⓟ ☕ ♿ (partly accessible) toilets for disabled shop ⊗

TWYCROSS — Map 4 SK30

Twycross Zoo

CV9 3PX
☎ 01827 880250 📠 01827 880700
web: www.twycrosszoo.org
dir: on A444 Burton to Nuneaton road, directly off M42 junct 11

Twycross Zoo appeals to all ages and spans some 50 acres that are home to around 1000 animals, including the most comprehensive collection of primate species in the world. Twycross is the only zoo in Great Britain to house bonobos - humanity's 'closest living relative'. While at the zoo, visitors can visit a genuine Borneo Longhouse, brought to life in the Leicestershire countryside, where many exotic birds, animal species and traditional artefacts can be seen. See the new Asian elephant walkway "Uda Walewe" and the new visitor centre and restaurant "Himalaya", a unique dining experience. Also enjoy a children's area with adventure playground, rides for little explorers and pets from around the world.

Times Open all year, daily 10-5.30 (4 in winter). Closed 25 Dec **Fees** £9.50 (ch £6, pen £7). Family Ticket £29. See website for current prices* **Facilities** Ⓟ ☕ 🍴 licensed ⛩ (outdoor) ♿ (fully accessible) toilets for disabled shop ⊗

LINCOLNSHIRE

Tattershall Castle

BELTON **Map 8 SK93**

Belton House Park & Gardens

NG32 2LS
☎ 01476 566116 📠 01476 579071
e-mail: belton@nationaltrust.org.uk
web: www.nationaltrust.org.uk
dir: 3m NE Grantham on A607

17th-century country house, set in its own extensive deer park, Belton was designed to impress with opulent décor, stunning silverware and fine furnishings. Delightful gardens, luxuriantly planted Orangery and lakeside walks are a pleasure to explore.

Times Open: House: 1-14 Mar, Sat & Sun 12.30-4.30; 15 Mar-Oct, Wed-Sun. Open BH Mon, 12.30-4.30. Garden: 6-28 Feb, Sat & Sun 12-4; Mar-Oct, Wed-Sun 10.30-5.30 (daily during Lincolnshire school hols Mar-Oct)* **Facilities** Ⓟ ☕ 🍽 licensed ♿ (partly accessible) (House: steps to entrance. Stairclimber available. Ground floor accessible Grounds: partly accessible, loose gravel paths) toilets for disabled (Braille guide, hearing scheme, audio guide, wheelchairs available) shop 🚫 ✤

CLEETHORPES **Map 8 TA30**

Pleasure Island Family Theme Park

Kings Rd DN35 0PL
☎ 01472 211511 📠 01472 211087
e-mail: reception@pleasure-island.co.uk
web: www.pleasure-island.co.uk
dir: M180 then A180, follow signs to park

Pleasure Island is packed with over seventy rides and attractions. Hold on tight as the colossal wheel of steel rockets you into the sky at a G-force of 2.5, then hurtles you around 360 degrees, sending riders into orbit and giving the sensation of complete weightlessness. It's not just grown ups and thrill seekers who are catered for at Pleasure Island. For youngsters there's hours of fun in Tinkaboo Town, an indoor themed area full of rides and attractions. There's also five family shows.

Times Open daily Apr-1 Sep ex Mon & Tue in Jun & wknds in Sep & Oct. Call for further info* **Fees** £17.50 (ch under 4 free, concessions £10.50)* **Facilities** Ⓟ ☕ 🍽 licensed ⛩ (outdoor) ♿ (partly accessible) (shops & restaurants are wheelchair accessible) toilets for disabled shop

CONINGSBY **Map 8 TF25**

Battle of Britain Memorial Flight Visitor Centre

LN4 4SY
☎ 01522 782040 📠 01526 342330
e-mail: bbmf@lincolnshire.gov.uk
web: www.lincolnshire.gov.uk/bbmf
dir: on A153 in Coningsby village - follow heritage signs

View the aircraft of the Battle of Britain Memorial Flight, including the only flying Lancaster in Europe, five Spitfires, two Hurricanes, a Dakota and two Chipmunks. Because of operational commitments, specific aircraft may not be available. Please ring for information before planning a visit.

Times Open Mon-Fri, conducted tours 10.30-3.30; (winter 10.30-3). Closed 2 wks Xmas. Times may be reviewed, please check before visiting.* **Facilities** Ⓟ Ⓟ ⛩ (outdoor) ♿ (fully accessible) toilets for disabled (electric wheelchairs not allowed in hangar) shop 🚫

ENGLAND

EAST KIRKBY Map 8 TF36

Lincolnshire Aviation Heritage Centre

East Kirkby Airfield PE23 4DE
☎ 01790 763207 📠 01790 763207
e-mail: enquiries@lincsaviation.co.uk
web: www.lincsaviation.co.uk
dir: off A16 onto A155, museum on east side of village

Relive a World War Two bomber airfield here at East Kirkby. Experience the sights and sounds, smells and atmosphere. The only place in the country to see and ride in a Lancaster bomber on its original airfield.

Times Open 2 Jan-Etr, 10-4; Etr-Nov, 10-5. Closed Sun.* **Facilities** licensed (outdoor) toilets for disabled shop

EPWORTH Map 8 SE70

Old Rectory

1 Rectory St DN9 1HX
☎ 01427 872268
e-mail: curator@epwortholdrectory.org.uk
web: www.epwortholdrectory.org.uk
dir: on A161, 3m S of M180 junct 2. Follow brown signs through Epworth

John and Charles Wesley and their sisters were brought up in this Queen Anne style rectory, built in 1709. Maintained by the Methodist Church as 'The Home of the Wesleys', the house displays items which belonged to John and Charles Wesley and their parents Samuel and Susanna. The house is an accredited museum. Samuel Wesley was Rector of the Parish of St Andrews from 1695-1735. The Anglican Church sold the rectory to the Methodist Church in 1954. From 1957, it has been open to the public as a museum and heritage house.

Times Open daily Mar-Apr & Oct, Mon-Sat 10.30-3.30; Mar-Oct, Sun 2-4.30; May-Sep, Mon-Sat 10-4.30; Good Fri 2-4.30* **Fees** £5 (ch under 16 £2, concessions £4, student £3). Family £11. Groups £4 each. School £1.50 per child with up to 3 adults free.* **Facilities** (outdoor) (partly accessible) (access limited to ground floor) toilets for disabled (ramp, written scripts, rails) shop

GAINSBOROUGH Map 8 SK88

Gainsborough Old Hall

Parnell St DN21 2NB
☎ 01427 612669 📠 01427 612779
e-mail: gainsborougholdhall@lincolnshire.gov.uk
web: www.english-heritage.org.uk
dir: turn off A1 onto A57 to Gainsborough. Follow brown heritage signs in city centre. Old Hall is adjacent to town centre.

A complete medieval manor house dating back to 1460-80 and containing a remarkable Great Hall and original kitchen with a variety of room settings. Richard III, Henry VIII, the Mayflower Pilgrims and John Wesley all visited the Old Hall.

Times Open all year, early Mar-Oct, Mon-Fri 10-5, Sat & Sun 11-5; Nov-Feb, Mon-Fri 10-4, Sat 11-4. Closed for 2 wks over Xmas, please call for details **Fees** Admission charged, please contact site for details **Facilities** (partly accessible) toilets for disabled (audio tour, induction loop, wheelchair for visitors use) shop

GRIMSBY Map 0 TA20

Fishing Heritage Centre

Alexandra Dock DN31 1UZ
☎ 01472 323345 📠 01472 323555
web: www.nelincs.gov.uk/leisure/museums
dir: follow signs off M180

Sign on as a crew member for a journey of discovery, and experience the harsh reality of life on board a deep sea trawler built inside the Centre. Through interactive games and displays, your challenge is to navigate the icy waters of the Arctic in search of the catch.

Times Open Nov-Apr, Mon-Fri 10-4, wknds & BHs 11-9* **Facilities** (partly accessible) (Ross Tiger Trawler not recommended to those with mobility problems) toilets for disabled shop

GRIMSTHORPE Map 8 TF02

Grimsthorpe Castle

PE10 0LY
☎ 01778 591205 📠 01778 591259
e-mail: ray@grimsthorpe.co.uk
web: www.grimsthorpe.co.uk
dir: on A151, 8m E of Colsterworth on A1

Seat of the Willoughby de Eresby family since 1516, the castle has a medieval tower and a Tudor quadrangular house with a Baroque north front by Vanbrugh. There are eight state rooms, two picture galleries, and an important collection of furniture, pictures and tapestries. There is also a family cycle trail, woodland adventure playground and ranger-guided tours of the park by minibus. A cycle hire service is in operation allowing visitors to explore trails in the park.

Times Open Apr-May, Sun, Thu & BH Mon; Jun-Sep, Sun-Thu. Park & Gardens 11-6. Castle 1-4.30 **Fees** Park & Gardens £5 (ch £2, concessions £4). Combined ticket with castle £10 (ch £4, concessions £9) **Facilities** licensed (outdoor) (partly accessible) (no wheelchair access to 1st floor) toilets for disabled (Virtual castle tour, Braille guide, w/chair loan) shop

LINCOLN Map 8 SK97

The Collection: Art & Archaeology in Lincolnshire

Danes Ter LN2 1LP
☎ 01522 550990 📠 01522 550991
e-mail: thecollection@lincolnshire.gov.uk
web: www.thecollection.lincoln.museum/
dir: follow signs for Lincoln City Centre, then parking for cultural quarter then pedestrian signs to The Collection

Housed in an impressive new building, the Collection consists of the combined collections of the City and County Museum and the Usher Gallery. The art collection includes contemporary art and craft, paintings, sculpture, porcelain, clocks and watches. There are paintings by Turner, Stubbs and Lowry, major porcelain collections and clocks by Robert Sutton. The archaeological collection covers 300,000 years of history up to the 18th-century.

Times Open all year daily, 10-4 (last entry 3.30). Closed 25-26 Dec & 1 Jan* **Fees** Free entry, but may be a charge for some temporary exhibitions. See website for group & school admission prices **Facilities** Ⓟ ☕ 🍽 licensed ⛩ (outdoor) ♿ (fully accessible) toilets for disabled (parking for disabled, induction loop, w/chairs) shop 🚭

Lincoln Castle

Castle Hill LN1 3AA
☎ 01522 511068 📠 01522 512150
e-mail: lincoln_castle@lincolnshire.gov.uk
web: www.lincolnshire.gov.uk/lincolncastle
dir: off A46 Lincoln Ring Road in heart of historic city

Situated in the centre of Lincoln, the Castle, built in 1068 by William the Conqueror, dominates the Bailgate area alongside the great Cathedral. In addition to its many medieval features, Lincoln Castle has strong 19th-century connections and the unique Victorian prison chapel is awe-inspiring. The beautiful surroundings are ideal for historical adventures, picnics and special events that include jousting, Roman re-enactments, and vintage vehicle rallies. The Castle is the home of the Magna Carta and there is an exhibition interpreting and displaying this important document.

Times Open all year daily, May-Aug 10-6; Apr & Sep 10-5; Oct-Mar 10-4* **Facilities** Ⓟ ☕ ⛩ (outdoor) ♿ (partly accessible) (wheelchair lift into prison, ramps in grounds) toilets for disabled (hearing loop, audio visual tour, wheelchair, lift) shop 🚭

Museum of Lincolnshire Life FREE

Burton Rd LN1 3LY
☎ 01522 528448 📠 01522 521264
e-mail: lincolnshirelife.museum@lincolnshire.gov.uk
web: www.lincolnshire.gov.uk/museumoflincolnshirelife
dir: 5 min walk from Lincoln Castle

A large and varied social history museum, where two centuries of Lincolnshire life are illustrated by enthralling displays of domestic implements, industrial machinery, agricultural tools and a collection of horse-drawn vehicles. The exciting and interactive Royal Lincolnshire Regiment Museum contains videos, an audio tour, and touch screen computers. Various events throughout the year.

Times Open all year, Apr-Sep, daily 10-4; Oct-Mar, Mon-Sat 10-4 (last admission 3.30). Closed 24-26 & 31 Dec, 1 Jan* **Facilities** 🅟 Ⓟ ☕ ♿ (fully accessible) toilets for disabled (wheelchair available, parking space) shop 🚭

Usher Gallery FREE

Lindum Rd LN2 1NN
☎ 01522 550990 📠 01522 550991
e-mail: thecollection@lincolnshire.gov.uk
web: www.thecollection.lincoln.museum/
dir: follow signs for Lincoln City Centre, then parking for cultural quarter, then pedestrian signs to The Collection

Built as the result of a bequest by Lincoln jeweller James Ward Usher, the Gallery houses his magnificent collection of watches, porcelain and miniatures, as well as topographical works, watercolours by Peter de Wint, Tennyson memorabilia and coins. The gallery has a popular and changing display of contemporary visual arts and crafts. There is a lively lecture programme and children's activity diary.

Times Open all year, daily 10-4 ex 24-26 Dec & 1 Jan (last entry 3.30)* **Facilities** Ⓟ ☕ ⛩ (outdoor) ♿ (fully accessible) toilets for disabled (large print guides, induction loop, parking) shop 🚭

SCUNTHORPE Map 8 SE81

Normanby Hall Country Park

Normanby DN15 9HU
☎ 01724 720588 📠 01724 721248
e-mail: normanby.hall@northlincs.gov.uk
web: www.northlincs.gov.uk/normanby
dir: 4m N of Scunthorpe off B1430

A whole host of activities and attractions are offered in the 300 acres of grounds that surround Normanby Hall, including riding, nature trails and a farming museum. Inside the Regency mansion the fine rooms are decorated and furnished in period style. There is a fully restored and working Victorian kitchen garden, and a walled garden selling a wide range of plants, from barrows located at the gift shop and Farming Museum.

Times Open: Park all year, daily, 9-dusk. Walled garden, daily 10.30-5 (4 in winter). Hall & Farming Museum, Apr-Sep, daily 1-5.* **Facilities** 🅟 ☕ 🍽 licensed ⛩ (outdoor) ♿ (partly accessible) (ground floor of Great Hall, walled garden, farming museum, cafe, giftshops & toilets accessible) toilets for disabled (audio tour, wheelchair/scooter (must be pre-booked) shop

ENGLAND

SKEGNESS Map 9 TF56

Church Farm Museum

Church Road South PE25 2HF

☎ 01754 766658 📠 01754 898243

e-mail: churchfarmmuseum@lincolnshire.gov.uk

web: www.lincolnshire.gov.uk/churchfarmmuseum

dir: follow brown museum signs on entering Skegness

A farmhouse and outbuildings, restored to show the way of life on a Lincolnshire farm at the end of the 19th century, with farm implements and machinery plus household equipment on display. Temporary exhibitions are held in the barn and there is a restored timber-framed mud and stud cottage on site. Telephone for details of special events held throughout the season.

Times Open Apr-Oct, daily 10-4 (last entry 3.30).* **Facilities** Ⓟ ☕ ⛩ (outdoor) ♿ (partly accessible) (grounds accessible with care) toilets for disabled (wheelchair available) shop ⊗

Skegness Natureland Seal Sanctuary

North Pde PE25 1DB

☎ 01754 764345 📠 01754 764345

web: www.skegnessnatureland.co.uk

dir: N end of seafront

Natureland houses seals, penguins, tropical birds, aquarium and reptiles, as well as a pets' corner. Also free-flight tropical butterflies (Apr-Oct). Natureland is well known for its rescue of abandoned seal pups, and has successfully reared and returned to the wild a large number of them. The hospital unit incorporates a public viewing area, and a large seascape seal pool (with underwater viewing).

Times Open all year, daily at 10. Closing times vary according to season. Closed 25-26 Dec & 1 Jan* **Fees** £6.80 (ch £4.40, concessions £5.60). Family ticket £20.20 (2ad+2ch)* **Facilities** Ⓟ ☕ 🍽 licensed ⛩ (outdoor) ♿ (fully accessible) toilets for disabled (low windows on seal pools) shop

SPALDING Map 8 TF22

Butterfly & Wildlife Park

Long Sutton PE12 9LE

☎ 01406 363833 & 363209 📠 01406 363182

e-mail: info@butterflyandwildlifepark@.co.uk

web: www.butterflyandwildlifepark.co.uk

dir: off A17 at Long Sutton

The Park contains one of Britain's largest walk-through tropical gardens, in which hundreds of butterflies from all over the world fly freely. The tropical gardens are also home to crocodiles, snakes and lizards. Outside are 15 acres of butterfly and bee gardens, wildflower meadows, nature trail, farm animals, a pets' corner and a large adventure playground. At The Lincolnshire Birds of Prey Centre, there are daily birds of prey displays. In the ant room visitors can observe leaf-cutting ants in their natural working habitat.

Times Open 15 Mar-2 Nov, daily 10-5 (Sep & Oct 10-4)* **Facilities** Ⓟ ☕ ⛩ (outdoor) ♿ (fully accessible) toilets for disabled (wheelchairs available) shop ⊗

STAMFORD Map 4 TF00

Burghley House

PE9 3JY

☎ 01780 752451 📠 01780 480125

e-mail: burghley@burghley.co.uk

web: www.burghley.co.uk

dir: 1.5m off A1 at Stamford

This great Elizabethan house, built by William Cecil, has all the hallmarks of that ostentatious period. The vast house is three storeys high and the roof is a riot of pinnacles, cupolas and paired chimneys in classic Tudor style. However, the interior was restyled in the 17th century, and the state rooms are now Baroque, with silver fireplaces, elaborate plasterwork and painted ceilings. These were painted by Antonio Verrio, whose Heaven Room is quite awe-inspiring. The Sculpture Garden is dedicated to exhibiting the best in contemporary sculpture, in pleasant surroundings.

Times Open 20 Mar-Oct, daily (ex Fri). Please telephone for details.* **Fees** £11.80 (ch £5.80, concessions £10.40). Family (2ad+2ch) £30* **Facilities** Ⓟ ☕ 🍽 licensed ⛩ (outdoor) ♿ (partly accessible) toilets for disabled (chairlift access, some mobility required) shop ⊗

Stamford Museum FREE

Broad St PE9 1PJ

☎ 01780 766317 📠 01780 480363

e-mail: stamford_museum@lincolnshire.gov.uk

web: www.lincolnshire.gov.uk/stamfordmuseum

dir: from A1 follow town centre signs from any Stamford exit

Displays illustrate the history of this fine stone town and include Stamford Ware pottery, the visit of Daniel Lambert and the Town's more recent industrial past. The Stamford Tapestry depicts the history of the town in wool.

Times Open all year, Mon-Sat 10-4. Closed 24-26 & 31 Dec & 1 Jan **Facilities** Ⓟ ♿ (fully accessible) (audio loop, lift, semi auto doors, Braille leaflets) shop ⊗

TATTERSHALL Map 8 TF25

Tattershall Castle

LN4 4LR

☎ 01526 342543

e-mail: tattershallcastle@nationaltrust.org.uk

web: www.nationaltrust.org.uk

dir: S of A153, 15m NE of Sleaford

Explore the six floors of this 130ft tall, rare red-brick medieval castle built by Ralph Cromwell, Lord Treasurer of England and one of the most powerful men in the country. Let the audio guide create a picture of what life was like at Tattershall Castle in the 15th century. Climb the 150 steps from the basement to the battlements and enjoy the magnificent views of the Lincolnshire countryside, then explore the grounds, moats, bridges and neighbouring church, also built by Ralph Cromwell.

Times Open 1-14 Mar & 3 Nov-16 Dec, Sat & Sun, 12-4; 15 Mar-1 Oct, Mon-Wed & Sat-Sun, 11-5.30; Open Good Fri

11-5.30.* **Facilities** Ⓟ ♿ (partly accessible) (ramped entrance, ground floor has ramp available. Many stairs to other floors. Some visitors may require assistance) toilets for disabled (Braille guide, one wheelchair available, must prebook) shop

THORNTON **Map 8 TA11**

Thornton Abbey and Gatehouse

Thornton Abbey Rd, Ulceby DN39 6TU
web: www.english-heritage.org.uk
dir: 7m SE of Humber Bridge, on road E of A1077

This abbey, founded in 1139 for a community of Augustinian canons, was reconstructed from the 1260s onwards, as its prestige and riches grew. The remains of a beautiful octagonal chapter-house are notably fine. Most impressive is the 14th-century gatehouse, recognised as one of the grandest in England.

Times Open Abbey Grounds: Apr-Jun, Wed-Sun & BHs 10-5; Jul-Aug, daily 10-5; Sep-Mar, Fri-Sun 10-4. Closed 24-26 Dec & 1 Jan **Fees** £4.20 (ch £2.10, concessions £3.60). Prices and opening times are subject to change in March 2011. Please call 0870 333 1181 for the most up to date prices and opening times when planning your visit **Facilities** Ⓟ ♿ (partly accessible) (mostly accessible apart from gatehouse)

WOOLSTHORPE **Map 8 SK92**

Woolsthorpe Manor

23 Newton Way NG33 5PD
☎ 01476 860338 01476 862826
e-mail: woolsthorpemanor@nationaltrust.org.uk
web: www.nationaltrust.org.uk/main/w-woolsthorpemanor
dir: 7m S of Grantham, 1m W of A1

Isaac Newton was born in this modest manor house in the mid 1600s and he made many of his most important discoveries about light and gravity here. A complex figure, Newton notched up careers as diverse as Cambridge Professor and Master of the Royal Mint; spent years studying alchemy and the Bible as well as science, and was President of the Royal Society. You can still see the famous apple tree from Isaac's bedroom window and enjoy the new Discovery Centre.

Times Open 5-13 Mar, Sat-Sun 11-5; 16 Mar-30 Oct, Wed-Sun & BHs 11-5 **Fees** With Gift Aid donation: £6.40 (ch 3.20). Family ticket £16 **Facilities** Ⓟ (outdoor) ♿ (partly accessible) (narrow doorways & small rooms, ramps available. Stairs to other floors. Grounds partly accessible, uneven & loose gravel paths, some steps) toilets for disabled (Braille & large print guide, wheelchair available) shop

ENGLAND

LONDON

Changing of the Guard, Buckingham Palace

E2

Geffrye Museum

136 Kingsland Rd, Shoreditch E2 8EA
☎ 020 7739 9893 020 7729 5647
e-mail: info@geffrye-museum.org.uk
web: www.geffrye-museum.org.uk
dir: S end of Kingsland Rd A10 in Shoreditch between Cremer St & Pearson St

The only museum in the UK to specialise in the domestic interiors and furniture of the urban middle classes. Displays span the 400 years from 1600 to the present day, forming a sequence of period rooms which capture the nature of English interior style. The museum is set in elegant, 18th-century buildings, surrounded by delightful gardens including an award-winning walled herb garden and a series of historical gardens which highlight changes in town gardens from the 17th to 20th centuries. One of the museum's historic almshouses has been fully restored to its original condition and is open on selected days (ring for details). Each December, the museum's period rooms are decorated in authentic, festive style to reflect 400 years of Christmas traditions in English homes.

Times Open all year, Tue-Sat 10-5, Sun & BH Mon 12-5. Closed Mon, Good Fri, 24-26 Dec & New Year **Fees** Free admission to museum & exhibitions. Prices for special lectures on request **Facilities** Ⓟ licensed (outdoor) (fully accessible) toilets for disabled (ramps, lift, wheelchair available, induction loop) shop

V & A Museum of Childhood

FREE

Cambridge Heath Rd E2 9PA
☎ 020 8983 5200 020 8983 5225
e-mail: moc@vam.ac.uk
web: www.museumofchildhood.org.uk
dir: Underground - Bethnal Green

The V&A Museum of Childhood re-opened following an extensive transformation a few years ago. There is a stunning new entrance, fully updated galleries and displays, a brand new gallery and expanded public spaces. Galleries include Creativity, Moving Toys and Childhood Galleries. There is also a full programme of activities. Exhibitions include Sit Down, Seating for kids.

Times Open all year, daily 10-5.45. Closed 24-26 Dec & 1 Jan **Facilities** Ⓟ (outdoor) (fully accessible) toilets for disabled (disabled parking by arrangement) shop

E9

Sutton House

2 & 4 Homerton High St E9 6JQ
☎ 020 8986 2264 020 8525 9051
e-mail: suttonhouse@nationaltrust.org.uk
web: www.nationaltrust.org.uk
dir: 10 min walk from Hackney Central train station

In London's East End, the building is a rare example of a Tudor red-brick house. Built in 1535 by Sir Ralph Sadleir, Principal Secretary of State for Henry VIII, the house has 18th-century alterations and later additions. There are regular exhibitions of contemporary art by local artists.

Times Open Feb-19 Dec, Thu-Sun & BH Mon, 12.30-4.30, closed Good Fri.* **Facilities** Ⓟ licensed (partly accessible) (wheelchair accessible on ground floor) toilets for disabled (induction loop, Braille/large print/audio guide) shop

E14

Museum of London Docklands

FREE

No 1 Warehouse, West India Quay E14 4AL
☎ 020 7001 9844
e-mail: info@museumoflondon.org.uk
web: www.museumoflondon.org.uk/docklands
dir: Signed from West India Quay DLR

From Roman settlement to Docklands' regeneration, unlock the history of London's river, port and people, in this historic warehouse. Discover a wealth of objects from whale bones to WWII gas masks in state-of-the-art galleries, including Mudlarks, an interactive area for kids; Sailortown, an atmospheric recreation of 19th century riverside Wapping; and London, Sugar & Slavery, which reveals the city's involvement in the transatlantic slave trade.

Times Open all year, daily 10-6. Closed 24-26 Dec* **Facilities** Ⓟ licensed (indoor) (fully accessible) toilets for disabled (w/chairs, power scooters & various aids) shop

ENGLAND

E17

William Morris Gallery

FREE

Lloyd Park, Forest Rd, Walthamstow E17 4PP
☎ 020 8496 4390 📠 020 8527 7070
e-mail: wmg.enquiries@walthamforest.gov.uk
web: www.walthamforest.gov.uk/william-morris
dir: Underground - Blackhorse Rd, take bus no. 123 along Forest Rd, get off at the Lloyd Park stop or Walthamstow Central, N 15m along Hoe St, left into Gaywood Rd to Lloyd Park

Victorian artist, craftsman, poet and free thinker William Morris lived here from 1848 to 1856, and the gallery houses displays illustrating his life and work. Exhibits include fabrics, stained glass, wallpaper and furniture, as well as Pre-Raphaelite paintings, ceramics and a collection of pictures by Frank Brangwyn, who worked briefly for Morris.

Times Open all year, Wed-Sun 10-5* **Facilities** Ⓟ ♿ (partly accessible) (ground floor only) shop ⊛

EC1

Museum of The Order of St John

St John's Gate, St John's Ln, Clerkenwell EC1M 4DA
☎ 020 7324 4005 📠 020 7336 0587
e-mail: museum@nhq.sja.org.uk
web: www.sja.org.uk/museum
dir: Underground - Farringdon, Barbican

The Priory of Clerkenwell was built in the 1140s by the Hospitallers and it is their remarkable story which lies behind the modern work of St John Ambulance. The Knights' surprising tale is revealed in the ground floor galleries housed in the Tudor gatehouse and includes furniture, paintings, silver, armour, stained glass and interactive, multimedia galleries. Re-opening in November 2010, the museum will have many new galleries and attractions (see website). Supported by the National Lottery through the Heritage Lottery Fund.

Times Open Mon-Sat 10-5. Closed Xmas wk & BH wknds. Guided tours Tue, Fri & Sat 11 & 2.30 **Fees** Museum free. For tours of St John's Gate & Grand Priory Church a donation of £5 (concessions £4) is requested **Facilities** Ⓟ ♿ (partly accessible) (part of first floor accessible by lift) toilets for disabled (lift) shop ⊛

Wesley's Chapel, House & Museum of Methodism

49 City Rd EC1Y 1AU
☎ 020 7253 2262 📠 020 7608 3825
e-mail: museum@wesleyschapel.org.uk
web: www.wesleyschapel.org.uk
dir: Underground - Old Street - exit number 4

Wesley's Chapel has been the Mother Church of World Methodism since its construction in 1778. The crypt houses a museum which traces the development of Methodism from the 18th century to the present day. Wesley's house - built by him in 1779 - was his home when not touring and preaching. Special events are held on May 24th (the anniversary of Wesley's conversion), and November 1st (the anniversary of the Chapel's opening).

Times Open all year, Mon-Sat, 10-4, Sun 12-2. Closed Thu 12.45-1.30, Xmas-New Year, BHs (last entry 30mins before closing)* **Fees** Donations welcome **Facilities** Ⓟ ⛩ ♿ (partly accessible) (chapel & museum fully accessible. Many stairs and no lift make the house inaccessible) toilets for disabled (lift to the crypt of the chapel) shop ⊛

EC2

Bank of England Museum

FREE

Bartholomew Ln EC2R 8AH
☎ 020 7601 5545 📠 020 7601 5808
e-mail: museum@bankofengland.co.uk
web: www.bankofengland.co.uk/museum
dir: museum housed in Bank of London, entrance in Bartholomew Lane. Bank underground, exit 2

The museum tells the story of the Bank of England from its foundation in 1694 to its role in today's economy. Interactive programmes with graphics and video help explain its many and varied roles. Popular exhibits include a unique collection of banknotes and a genuine gold bar, which may be handled.

Times Open all year, Mon-Fri 10-5. Closed wknds & BHs. Open on day of Lord Mayor's Show & Open House London* **Facilities** Ⓟ ♿ (fully accessible) toilets for disabled (audio guides, induction loop. Advance notice helpful) shop ⊛

The Guildhall

FREE

Gresham St EC2V 5AE
☎ 020 7606 3030
e-mail: pro@cityoflondon.gov.uk
web: www.cityoflondon.gov.uk/guildhall
dir: Underground - Bank, St Paul's

The Court of Common Council (presided over by the Lord Mayor) administers the City of London and meets in the Guildhall. Dating from 1411, the building was badly damaged in the Great Fire and again in the Blitz. The great hall, traditionally used for the Lord Mayor's Banquet and other important civic functions, is impressively decorated with the banners and shields of the livery companies, of which there are more than 90. The Clock Museum, which has a collection of 700 exhibits, charts the history of 500 years of time-keeping.

Times Open all year, May-Sep, daily 10-5; Oct-Apr, Mon-Sat 10-5 (last entry 4.30). Closed Xmas, New Year, Good Fri & Civic occasions. Please contact 020 7606 3030 before visit to be certain of access **Facilities** Ⓟ ♿ (partly accessible) toilets for disabled (lift for east and west crypts) shop ⊛

Museum of London

FREE

150 London Wall EC2Y 5HN
☎ 0870 444 3851 📠 0870 444 3853
e-mail: info@museumoflondon.org.uk
web: www.museumoflondon.org.uk
dir: Underground - St Paul's, Barbican. N of St Paul's Cathedral at the end of St Martins le Grand and S of the Barbican. S of Aldersgate St

Dedicated to the story of London and its people, the Museum of London exists to inspire a passion for London in all who visit it.

As well as the permanent collection, the Museum has a varied exhibition programme with major temporary exhibitions and topical displays each year. There are also smaller exhibitions in the foyer gallery. A wide programme of lectures and events explore London's history and its evolution into the city of today.

Times Open all year, daily 10-6 (last admission 5.30). Closed 24-26 Dec* **Facilities** licensed (indoor) (partly accessible) toilets for disabled (w/chairs & power scooters, lifts & induction loops) shop

EC3

The Monument

Monument St EC3R 8AH
020 7626 2717 020 7403 4477
e-mail: enquiries@towerbridge.org.uk
web: www.towerbridge.org.uk
dir: Underground - Monument

Designed by Wren and Hooke and erected in 1671-7, the Monument commemorates the Great Fire of 1666 which is reputed to have started in nearby Pudding Lane. The fire destroyed nearly 90 churches and about 13,000 houses. This fluted Doric column stands 202ft high (Pudding Lane is exactly 202ft from its base) and you can climb the 311 steps to a platform at the summit, and receive a certificate as proof of your athletic abilities.

Times Open all year, daily, 9.30-5.30, (last admission 5) **Fees** £3 (ch £1, concessions £2). Combined ticket with Tower Bridge Exhibition £8 (ch £3.50, concessions £5.50)* **Facilities**

Tower of London

Tower Hill EC3N 4AB
0870 756 6060
web: www.hrp.org.uk
dir: Underground - Tower Hill

Perhaps the most famous castle in the world, the Tower of London has played a central part in British history. Discover the stories of this awesome fortress; from gruesome tales of torture and escape to fascinating traditions that can still be seen today. Learn the legend of the ravens and be dazzled by the Crown Jewels. Join a Yeoman Warder tour and listen to their captivating tales of pain and passion, treachery and torture, all delivered with a smile and a swagger!

Times Open all year, Mar-Oct, Sun-Mon 10-5.30, Tue-Sat 9-5.30; Nov-Feb, Tue-Sat 9-4.30, Sun-Mon 10-4.30 (last admission 30mins before close). Closed 24-26 Dec & 1 Jan* **Facilities** licensed (partly accessible) toilets for disabled (access guide can be obtained in advance call 020 7488 5694) shop

EC4

Dr Johnson's House — 2 FOR 1

17 Gough Square EC4A 3DE
020 7353 3745 020 7353 3745
e-mail: curator@drjohnsonshouse.org
web: www.drjohnsonshouse.org
dir: Underground - Temple, Chancery Lane

The celebrated literary figure, Dr Samuel Johnson, lived here between 1748 and 1759. He wrote his English Dictionary here, and a facsimile edition is on display at the house. The dictionary took nine and a half years to complete and contained over 40,000 words. The house is a handsome example of early 18th-century architecture, with many original features, and includes a collection of prints, letters and other Johnson memorabilia. The 100th anniversary of the house being saved from demolition and opened to the public will be celebrated in 2011.

Times Open all year, May-Sep, Mon-Sat 11-5.30; Oct-Apr 11-5. Closed Sun, BHs, Good Fri. Please check website for Xmas opening times **Fees** £4.50 (ch £1.50, concessions £3.50). Family £10 **Facilities** (partly accessible) (wheelchair access difficult, many steps) (large print info sheets, handrails, seating) shop

Middle Temple Hall — FREE

The Temple EC4Y 9AT
020 7427 4800 & 4820 020 7427 4801
e-mail: banqueting@middletemple.org.uk
web: www.middletemple.org.uk
dir: Underground - Temple, Blackfriars. Turn left at the embankment & left into Middle Temple Lane. Hall half way up on left

Between Fleet Street and the Thames are the Middle and Inner Temples, separate Inns of Court, so named after the Knights Templar who occupied the site from about 1160. Middle Temple Hall is a fine example of Tudor architecture, completed in about 1570, and has a double hammerbeam roof and beautiful stained glass. The 29ft-long high table was made from a single oak tree from Windsor Forest. Sir Francis Drake was a visitor to and friend of the Middle Temple, and a table made from timbers from his ship, the *Golden Hind*, survives to this day.

Times Open all year, Mon-Fri 10-12 & 3-4. Closed BH & legal vacations* **Facilities** licensed (fully accessible) toilets for disabled shop

ENGLAND

EC4 *continued*

St Paul's Cathedral

St Pauls Churchyard EC4M 8AD
☎ 020 7246 8348 📠 020 7248 3104
e-mail: chapterhouse@stpaulscathedral.org.uk
web: www.stpauls.co.uk
dir: St Paul's Tube

Completed in 1710, Sir Christopher Wren's architectural masterpiece is the cathedral church of the Bishop of London, and arose, like so much of this area of London, from the ashes of the Great Fire of London in 1666. Among the worthies buried here are Nelson and the Duke of Wellington, while Holman Hunt's masterpiece, *Light of the World* hangs in the Middlesex Chapel. St Paul's also hosted the weddings of Charles and Diana, and the funeral of Sir Winston Churchill. Impressive views of London can be seen from the Golden Gallery. The 300th anniversary of the completion of the cathedral will continue to be celebrated into early 2011.

Times Open Cathedral, Crypt, Ambulatory, Mon-Sat 8.30. Galleries 9.30 (last admission 4). Cathedral may close for special services **Fees** £12.50 (ch £4.50, concessions £11.50, students £9.50). Family (2ad+2ch) £29.50* **Facilities** Ⓟ ☕ 🍽 licensed ♿ (partly accessible) (cathedral floor and crypt are accessible, but not the galleries) toilets for disabled (lift for wheelchairs between the crypt and cathedral floor) shop ⊗

N1

The London Canal Museum

12/13 New Wharf Rd N1 9RT
☎ 020 7713 0836 📠 020 7689 6679
e-mail: info@canalmuseum.org.uk
web: www.canalmuseum.org.uk
dir: Underground - Kings Cross. Follow York Way along East side of King's Cross Stn, turn right at Wharfdale Rd, then left into New Wharf Rd

The museum covers the development of London's canals (particularly Regent's Canal), canal vessels and trade, and the way of life of the canal people. Housed in a former ice warehouse and stables, it also illustrates horse transport and the unusual trade of importing ice from Norway; there are two large ice wells under the floor. Facilities include temporary moorings, so you can arrive by boat if you want. There are regular special exhibitions, and special events include evening illustrated talks, towpath walks, and tunnel boat trips.

Times Open all year, Tue-Sun & BH Mon 10-4.30 (last admission 3.45). 1st Thu each mth 10-7.30. Closed 24-26 & 31 Dec **Fees** £3 (ch £1.50, under 5s free, concessions £2). Groups 10+* **Facilities** Ⓟ ⛩ (indoor & outdoor) ♿ (fully accessible) toilets for disabled (large print guides, induction loop, Braille signs, audio tour) shop ⊗

N6

Highgate Cemetery

Swains Ln N6 6PJ
☎ 020 8340 1834
web: www.highgate-cemetery.org.uk
dir: Underground - Archway, see directions posted at exit

Highgate Cemetery is the most impressive of a series of large, formally arranged and landscaped cemeteries which were established around the perimeter of London in the mid-19th century. There's a wealth of fine sculpture and architecture amongst the tombstones, monuments and mausoleums as well as the graves of such notables as the Rossetti family, George Eliot, Michael Faraday and Karl Marx. It is also a Grade I listed park.

Times Open all year. Eastern Cemetery: daily 10 (11 wknds)-5 (4 in winter). Western Cemetery by guided tour only: Sat & Sun 11-4 (3 in winter); midweek tours at 2, advisable to book. Closed 25-26 Dec & during funerals. **Fees** East cemetery £3. Tour of West cemetery £7 (ch 8-16 £3, no ch under 8 on tours). Donations encouraged to assist restoration. No video or flash allowed **Facilities** ⊗

NW1

The Jewish Museum

Raymond Burton House, 129-131 Albert St, Camden Town NW1 7NB
☎ 020 7284 7384 📠 020 7284 7385
e-mail: admin@jewishmuseum.org.uk
web: www.jewishmuseum.org.uk
dir: Underground - Camden Town, 3 mins walk from station

Following a major redevelopment project, the new Jewish Museum is open. Housing internationally acclaimed collections, the Museum provides an inspirational environment in which the Jewish culture, heritage and identity can be explored. Engaging with people of all ages, backgrounds and faiths the new galleries bring a series of collections to life, including a look at religious life and Jewish settlement in Britain. A photographic archive helps tell the Jewish story, providing snapshots of the changing face of Jewish and British life.

Times Open all year Sun-Wed 10-5, Thu 10-9, Fri 10-2. Closed Jewish Festivals, 25-26 Dec & 1 Jan **Fees** £7 (ch 5-16 £3, under 5 free, concessions £6). Family ticket (2ad+4ch) £17. Price includes voluntary Gift Aid donation **Facilities** Ⓟ ☕ ♿ (fully accessible) toilets for disabled (induction loop in lecture room linked to audio-visual unit) shop ⊗

Madame Tussauds

Marylebone Rd NW1 5LR
☎ 0870 400 3000
e-mail: csc@madame-tussauds.com
web: www.madame-tussauds.com
dir: Underground - Baker Street

Madame Tussaud's world-famous waxwork collection was founded in Paris in 1770. It moved to England in 1802 and found a permanent home in London's Marylebone Road in 1884. The 21st century has brought new innovations and new levels of interactivity. Listen to Kylie Minogue whisper in your ear, become an A-list celeb in the 'Blush' nightclub, and take your chances in a high security prison populated by dangerous serial killers.

Times Open all year 9.30-5.30 (9-6 wknds/summer). Closed 25 Dec.* **Facilities** Ⓟ licensed ♿ (fully accessible) toilets for disabled shop

ZSL London Zoo

Regents Park NW1 4RY
☎ 020 7449 6231 020 7586 6177
e-mail: marketing@zsl.org
web: www.zsl.org
dir: Underground - Camden Town or Regents Park

ZSL London Zoo is home to over 12,000 animals, insects, reptiles and fish. First opened in 1828, the Zoo can claim the world's first aquarium, insect and reptile house. Get closer to your favourite animals, learn about them at the keeper talks and watch them show off their skills at special events. Enjoy Gorilla Kingdom, a walk through the rainforest where you can get close to a group of Western Lowland gorillas. The newest exhibit is Giants of the Galapagos, featuring three Galapagos tortoises.

Times Open all year, daily from 10, (closing time dependant on time of year). Closed 25 Dec.* **Facilities** Ⓟ Ⓟ licensed ♿ (partly accessible) toilets for disabled (wheelchairs & booster scooter available) shop

NW3

Fenton House

Windmill Hill, Hampstead Grove NW3 6RT
☎ 020 7435 3471 020 7435 3471
e-mail: fentonhouse@nationaltrust.org.uk
web: www.nationaltrust.org.uk
dir: Underground - Hampstead, right out of station. Cross Heath St, up Holly Hill. Take right fork at top of hill into Hampstead Grove. Entrance on left

A William and Mary merchant's house built about 1686 and set in a walled garden, Fenton House is now owned by the National Trust. It contains outstanding displays of Oriental and European porcelain, 17th-century needlework pictures and Georgian furniture as well as the Benton Fletcher collection of early keyboard instruments. In 2007 a collection of British pictures of the 19th and early 20th centuries was bequeathed to Fenton House by the actor Peter Barkworth.

Times Open 5 Mar-Oct, Wed-Sun & BHs 11-5, Jun-Jul, Thu 2 (due to lunchtime concerts, TBC) **Fees** £6 (ch £3). Family ticket £15. Group 15+ £5.10. Garden only £1 (ch free)* **Facilities** Ⓟ ♿ (partly accessible) (temporary ramps to ground floor, wheelchair access) (photographs of areas which are not accessible)

Freud Museum

20 Maresfield Gardens, Hampstead NW3 5SX
☎ 020 7435 2002 & 7435 5167 020 7431 5452
e-mail: info@freud.org.uk
web: www.freud.org.uk
dir: Underground - Finchley Road, follow brown signs to museum

In 1938, Sigmund Freud left Vienna as a refugee from the Nazi occupation and chose exile in England, transferring his entire domestic and working environment to this house. He worked here until his death a year later. His extraordinary collection of Egyptian, Greek, Roman and Oriental antiquities, his working library and papers, and his fine furniture including the famous desk and couch are all here.

Times Open all year, Wed-Sun 12-5. Closed BHs, telephone for Xmas holiday times* **Fees** £6 (pen £4.50, students £3)* **Facilities** Ⓟ ♿ (partly accessible) (access to ground floor only) (personal tours can be arranged if booked in advance) shop

Keats House

Keats Grove, Hampstead NW3 2RR
☎ 020 7332 3868
e-mail: keatshouse@corpoflondon.gov.uk
web: www.cityoflondon.gov.uk/keatshousehampstead
dir: Underground - Hampstead, about 15 mins walk from station

The poet John Keats lived in this house from 1818-1820 and wrote some of his most famous poems, including *Ode to a Nightingale*. Here he met and fell in love with Fanny Browne and it was from this house that, weakened by tuberculosis, he left England to spend the winter of 1820-1821 in the warmer climate of southern Italy. Keats never returned but died in Rome in February of the following year at the age of 25.

Times Open all year, Etr-Oct, Tue-Sun, 1-5; Oct-Etr, Fri-Sun 1-5 **Fees** £5 (ch under 16 free, concessions £3) **Facilities** Ⓟ (outdoor) ♿ (partly accessible) (ground floor accessible) toilets for disabled shop

Kenwood House FREE

Hampstead Ln NW3 7JR
☎ 020 8348 1286 020 7973 3891
web: www.english-heritage.org.uk
dir: Underground - Hampstead

In splendid grounds beside Hampstead Heath, this outstanding neo-classical house contains one of the most important collections of paintings ever given to the nation. Works by Rembrandt, Vermeer, Turner, Gainsborough and Reynolds are all set against a backdrop of sumptuous rooms. Scenes from *Notting Hill* and *Mansfield Park* were filmed here.

Times Open all year, Apr-Mar, daily 11.30-4. Closed 24-26 Dec & 1 Jan. The park stays open later, please see site notices **Facilities** Ⓟ licensed toilets for disabled shop

ENGLAND

NW3 *continued*

2 Willow Road

2 Willow Rd, Hampstead NW3 1TH
☎ 020 7435 6166 020 7435 6166
e-mail: 2willowroad@nationaltrust.org.uk
web: www.nationaltrust.org.uk
dir: Hampstead tube (Northern Line), along High Street, left Flask Walk, right at end into Willow Rd or Hampstead Heath train station (London overground line)

Discover the 1939 home built by the architect Ernö Goldfinger for himself and his family. On display is his modern art collection including works by Henry Moore, Bridget Riley, Max Ernst and Marcel Duchamp as well as an extensive collection of original furniture designed by the architect.

Times Open 5 Mar-Oct, Thu-Sun 11-5. Entry by timed tour only at 11, 12, 1 & 2. Non-guided viewing 3-5 (last admission 4.30) **Fees** £5.80 (ch £2.90). Joint admission with Fenton House £9. Family ticket £14.50 **Facilities** Ⓟ ♿ (partly accessible) (wheelchair accessible on ground floor only) (video tour of house in cinema)

NW8

Ben Uri Gallery, The London Jewish Museum of Art

108A Boundary Rd, St John's Wood NW8 0RH
☎ 020 7604 3991 020 7604 3992
e-mail: info@benuri.org.uk
web: www.benuri.org.uk
dir: straight on West End Lane (B510), left onto Abbey Rd (B507), pass Beatle landmark, left onto Boundary Rd

Ben Uri Gallery, The London Jewish Museum of Art, is Britain's oldest Jewish cultural organisation. The Ben Uri Art Society was established in 1915 in London's East End to provide support for the many Jewish artists and craftspeople who were flourishing there in the face of poverty, anti-Semitism and isolation from mainstream culture. It was founded by Lazar Berson, a Lithuanian-born decorative artist.

Times Open all year, summer, Mon-Fri 10-5.30, Sun 12-4; winter, Mon-Thu 10-5.30, Fri 10-3, Sun 12-4.* **Facilities** Ⓟ ♿ (fully accessible)

Lord's Tour & M.C.C. Museum

Lord's Ground NW8 8QN
☎ 020 7616 8595 & 7616 8596 020 7266 3825
e-mail: tours@mcc.org.uk
web: www.lords.org
dir: Underground - St John's Wood

Established in 1787, Lord's is the home of the MCC and cricket. Guided tours take you behind the scenes, and highlights include the Long Room and the MCC Museum, where the Ashes and a large collection of paintings and memorabilia are displayed. The Museum is open on match days for spectators.

Times Open all year, Nov-Mar tours at 12 & 2; Apr-Oct 10, 12 & 2 (restrictions on some match days). Telephone for details & bookings.* **Facilities** Ⓟ licensed ♿ (partly accessible) (everything is accessible apart from 1st floor of museum) toilets for disabled shop

NW9

Royal Air Force Museum London FREE

Grahame Park Way, Colindale NW9 5LL
☎ 020 8205 2266 020 8358 4981
e-mail: groups@rafmuseum.org
web: www.rafmuseum.org
dir: within easy reach of the A5, A41, M1 and North Circular A406 roads. Tube on Northern Line to Colindale. Rail to Mill Hill Broadway station. Bus route 303 passes the door

Take off to the Royal Air Force Museum London and soar through the history of aviation from the earliest balloon flights to the latest jetfighter, the Eurofighter. This is a world-class collection of over 100 aircraft, aviation/wartime memorabilia and artefacts together with an impressive sound and light show 'Our Finest Hour' that takes you back to the Battle of Britain. The 3D cinema, located in Milestones of Flight, will thrill children of all ages. Also visit the Aeronauts Interactive Centre, specially designed for younger visitors, offering hands-on entertainment, including cockpit controls, co-ordination tests, engine lifting, pilot testing and more. See website for a full calendar of special events.

Times Open all year, daily 10-6 (last admission 5.30). Closed 24-26 Dec, 1 & 10-14 Jan **Facilities** Ⓟ licensed (indoor & outdoor) ♿ (fully accessible) toilets for disabled (lifts, ramps & wheelchairs available) shop

SE1

Bankside Gallery FREE

48 Hopton St SE1 9JH
☎ 020 7928 7521 📠 020 7928 2820
e-mail: info@banksidegallery.com
web: www.banksidegallery.com
dir: E of Blackfriars Bridge, South Bank of the Thames, adjacent to Tate Modern and the Millennium Bridge

Bankside Gallery is the home of the Royal Watercolour Society (RWS) and the Royal Society of Painter-Printmakers (RE). A series of regularly changing exhibitions throughout the year displays the work of both societies, and other prestigious contemporary artists.

Times Open all year, daily during exhibitions 11-6 **Facilities** Ⓟ ♿ (fully accessible) shop

Dali Universe

County Hall Gallery, Riverside Building, South Bank SE1 7PB
☎ 0870 744 7485 📠 020 7620 3120
e-mail: marketing@thedaliuniverse.com
web: www.thedaliuniverse.co.uk
dir: Waterloo Station - follow signs to South Bank and County Hall, attraction next to London Eye. Westminster Underground - cross Westminster Bridge, County Hall on left

An amazing collection of over 500 artworks by the master of surrealism, Salvador Dali, including the world's largest collection of his sculptures plus original artworks by Picasso and Chagall. Fine art gallery, bookshop and café.

Times Open all year, daily 9.30-6 (7 on Fri & BHs). Closed 25 Dec.* **Facilities** Ⓟ licensed ♿ (partly accessible)

Design Museum

Shad Thames SE1 2YD
☎ 0870 909 9009 📠 0870 909 1909
e-mail: info@designmuseum.org
web: www.designmuseum.org
dir: Turn off Tooley St onto Shad Thames. Underground - London Bridge or Tower Hill

The Design Museum is the first museum in the world to be dedicated to 20th and 21st century design. Since opening in 1989, it has won international acclaim for its ground-breaking exhibition and education programmes. As one of the leading museums of design, fashion and architecture, the Design Museum has a changing programme of exhibitions, combining insights into design history with innovative contemporary design.

Times Open all year, daily 10-5.45 (last entry 5.15). Closed 25-26 Dec* **Facilities** Ⓟ licensed ♿ (fully accessible) toilets for disabled (ramped entrance, wheelchair & lift) shop

Florence Nightingale Museum

St Thomas' Hospital, Gassiot House, 2 Lambeth Palace Rd SE1 7EW
☎ 020 7620 0374 📠 020 7928 1760
e-mail: info@florence-nightingale.co.uk
web: www.florence-nightingale.co.uk
dir: Underground - Westminster, Waterloo, Lambeth North

Dedicated to the life and nursing innovations of 'the Lady with the Lamp' (1820-1910), this beautifully designed museum has three pavilions reliving Florence's childhood, her experiences in the Crimean War and her pioneering nursing practices.

Times Open all year, daily 10-5. Closed Good Fri, 25-26 Dec **Fees** £5.80 (ch & concessions £4.80). Family ticket (2ad+ up to 5ch) £16. Discounted rates for pre-booked groups of 15+ **Facilities** Ⓟ ♿ (fully accessible) toilets for disabled shop

The Garden Museum 2 FOR 1

Lambeth Palace Rd SE1 7LB
☎ 020 7401 8865 📠 020 7401 8869
e-mail: info@gardenmuseum.org.uk
web: www.gardenmuseum.org.uk
dir: Underground - Waterloo, Westminster, Vauxhall. Next to Lambeth Palace, near Lambeth Bridge

Situated in the restored church of St. Mary-At-Lambeth, adjacent to Lambeth Palace, the Garden Museum provides an insight into the history and development of gardens and gardening in the UK. It houses a fine public display of tools and artefacts. In addition, there is a replica 17th-century knot garden filled with flowers and shrubs of the period, created around the tombs of the famous plant hunters, the John Tradescants, father and son, and Captain William Bligh of *HMS Bounty*. Visit the new exhibition gallery to see temporary exhibitions of garden design, history and botanical art.

Times Open daily Sun-Fri 10.30-5, Sat 10.30-4. Closed 1st Mon of each month except BHs **Fees** £6 (concessions £5, Art Fund members £3) Free for children, students & carers of disabled visitors **Facilities** Ⓟ ♿ (fully accessible) toilets for disabled shop

Golden Hinde Educational Trust

182 Pickfords Wharf, Clink St SE1 9DG
☎ 020 7403 0123 📠 020 7407 5908
e-mail: info@goldenhinde.org
web: www.goldenhinde.org
dir: On the Thames path between Southwark Cathedral and the new Globe Theatre

An authentic replica of the galleon in which Sir Francis Drake sailed around the world in 1577-1580. This ship has travelled over 140,000 miles, many more than the original. She is now permanently berthed on London's South Bank.

Times Open all year, daily 10-5.30. Visitors are advised to check opening times as they may vary due to closures for functions.* **Facilities** Ⓟ ♿ (partly accessible) (stairs on main deck so no access to wheelchairs) shop

ENGLAND

SE1 ***continued***

HMS Belfast

Morgans Ln, Tooley St SE1 2JH
☎ 020 7940 6300 📠 020 7403 0719
e-mail: hmsbelfast@iwm.org.uk
web: www.iwm.org.uk/hmsbelfast
dir: Underground - London Bridge/Tower Hill/Monument. Rail - London Bridge

Europe's last surviving big gun armoured warship from the Second World War, *HMS Belfast* was launched in 1938 and served in the North Atlantic and Arctic with the Home Fleet. She led the Allied naval bombardment of German positions on D-Day, and was saved for the nation in 1971. A tour of the ship will take you from the Captain's Bridge through nine decks to the massive Boiler and Engine Rooms. You can visit the cramped Mess Decks, Officers' Cabins, Galley, Sick Bay, Dentist and Laundry.

Times Open all year, daily. Mar-Oct 10-6; Nov-Feb 10-5 (last admission 1 hour before close). Closed 24-26 Dec* **Facilities** ☕ 🛆 (indoor) ♿ (partly accessible) (wheelchair access to main decks, but not all decks) toilets for disabled (wheelchair lift for access on board) shop 🚫

Imperial War Museum

Lambeth Rd SE1 6HZ
☎ 020 7416 5320 & 7416 5321 📠 020 7416 5374
e-mail: mail@iwm.org.uk
web: www.iwm.org.uk
dir: Underground - Lambeth North, Elephant & Castle or Waterloo

Founded in 1917, this museum illustrates and records all aspects of the two World Wars and other military operations involving Britain and the Commonwealth since 1914. There are always special exhibitions and the programme of special and family events includes film shows and lectures. The museum also has an extensive film, photography, sound, document and art archive as well as a library, although some reference departments are open to the public by appointment only.

Times Open all year, daily 10-6. Closed 24-26 Dec* **Facilities** Ⓟ ☕ 🍴 licensed 🛆 (indoor & outdoor) ♿ (fully accessible) toilets for disabled (parking & w/chair hire book in advance, study room, T-Loop) shop 🚫

London Aquarium

County Hall, Riverside Building, Westminster Bridge Rd SE1 7PB
☎ 020 7967 8000 📠 020 7967 8029
e-mail: info@londonaquarium.co.uk
web: www.londonaquarium.co.uk
dir: Underground-Waterloo & Westminster. On south bank next to Westminster Bridge, nr Big Ben & London Eye

The London Aquarium is one of Europe's largest displays of global aquatic life with over 350 species in over 50 displays, ranging from the mystical seahorse to the deadly stonefish. The huge Pacific display is home to a variety of jacks, stingrays and seven sharks. Come and witness the spectacular Atlantic feed where a team of divers hand-feed rays and native British sharks. The rainforest feed incorporates a frenzied piranha attack with the amazing marksmanship of the archerfish. There is also a range of education tours and literature to enhance any visit.

Times Open all year, daily 10-6. Late opening over summer months (last admission 1hr before closing). Closed 25 Dec* **Facilities** Ⓟ ☕ ♿ (partly accessible) toilets for disabled (wheelchairs available) shop 🚫

The London Dungeon

28-34 Tooley St SE1 2SZ
☎ 020 7403 7221 📠 020 7378 1529
e-mail: london.dungeon@merlinentertainments.biz
web: www.thedungeons.com
dir: Next to London Bridge Station

Transport yourself back to the darkest moments in the capital's history within the depths of the London Dungeon. Live actors, shows, rides and interactive special effects ensure that you face your fears head-on in this unique experience. Everything you see is based on real events, from Jack the Ripper to the Great Fire, torture and the Plague. Now with two scary rides including Extremis: Drop Ride to Doom, the Dungeon provides a thrilling experience.

Times Open all year, daily, Apr-Sep 10-5.30; Oct-Mar 10.30-5. Late night opening in the Summer. Telephone for exact times.* **Facilities** Ⓟ ♿ (fully accessible) toilets for disabled (cards for deaf visitors) shop 🚫

London Eye

Riverside Building, County Hall, Westminster Bridge Rd SE1 7PB
☎ 0870 500 0600 📠 0870 990 8882
e-mail: customer.services@londoneye.com
web: www.londoneye.com
dir: Underground - Waterloo/Westminster

The London Eye is one of the most inspiring and visually dramatic additions to the London skyline. At 135m/443ft high, it is the world's tallest observation wheel, allowing you to see one of the world's most exciting cities from a completely new perspective. The London Eye takes you on a gradual, 30 minute, 360 degree rotation, revealing parts of the city, which are simply not visible from the ground. For Londoners and visitors alike, it is the best way to see London and its many celebrated landmarks. The London Eye provides the perfect location for private parties and entertaining, and offers a wide variety of 'in-flight' hospitality packages, like champagne and canapés, which are available to enjoy in the privacy of your own capsule.

Times Open all year, daily, Oct-May 10-8; Jun-Sep, 10-9. Closed 25 Dec & annual maintenance.* **Facilities** Ⓟ ☕ ♿ (partly accessible) toilets for disabled (Braille guidebooks, w/chair hire, T-loop, carer ticket) shop 🚫

Shakespeare's Globe Exhibition & Theatre Tour

21 New Globe Walk, Bankside SE1 9DT
☎ 020 7902 1500 020 7902 1515
e-mail: info@shakespearesglobe.com
web: www.shakespeares-globe.org
dir: Underground - London Bridge, walk along Bankside. Mansion House, walk across Southwark Bridge. St Pauls, walk across Millennium Bridge

Guides help to bring England's theatrical heritage to life at the 'unparalleled and astonishing' recreation of this famous theatre. Discover what an Elizabethan audience would have been like, find out about the rivalry between the Bankside theatres, the bear baiting and the stews, hear about the penny stinkards and find out what a bodger is. Shakespeare's Globe Exhibition is the world's largest exhibition devoted to Shakespeare and the London in which he lived and worked. Housed beneath the reconstructed theatre, the exhibition explores the remarkable story of the Globe, and brings Shakespeare's world to life using a range of interactive display and live demonstrations.

Times Open all year, 23 Apr-early Oct, daily 9-12 (1-5 Rose Theatre tour); Oct-22 Apr 10-5 **Fees** £10.50 (ch 5-15 £6.50, pen & students £8.50). Family ticket (2ad+3ch) £28.* **Facilities** Ⓟ licensed (fully accessible) toilets for disabled (parking spaces, 'touch tours' available by appointment) shop

Southwark Cathedral

London Bridge SE1 9DA
☎ 020 7367 6700 & 7367 6734 020 7367 6730
e-mail: cathedral@southwark.anglican.org
web: www.southwarkcathedral.org.uk
dir: adjacent to London Bridge, off Borough High St

Originally an Augustinian priory, this is London's oldest gothic church, and has been a place of worship for more than 1,400 years. It became a cathedral for the Diocese of Southwark in 1905, and has links with Chaucer, Dickens and Shakespeare. John Gower and Shakespeare's brother Edmund are buried here. John Harvard of US university fame was baptised here in 1607, and there is a chapel to his memory. Visitors can view part of a Roman road, 14th-century cloister work, and kilns used for Southwark delftware in the 17th/18th centuries.

Times Open all year, daily 9-6. No tourism permitted on Good Fri & 25 Dec **Fees** Free, suggested donation £4 per person. Mandatory charge for groups, which should pre-book on 020 7367 6734 **Facilities** Ⓟ licensed (outdoor) (fully accessible) toilets for disabled (induction loop, wheelchair available, large print) shop

Tate Modern

Bankside SE1 9TG
☎ 020 7887 8008 (info) & 7887 8888 020 7401 5052
e-mail: visiting.modern@tate.org.uk
web: www.tate.org.uk
dir: Underground - Southwark

This is the UK's largest museum of modern art and is housed in the impressive Bankside power station. Entrance to the permanent collection, which includes works from artists like Picasso, Warhol and Dalí, is free. Tate Modern also holds world-acclaimed temporary exhibitions as well as education programmes, events and activities.

Times Open all year, Sun-Thu 10-6, Fri & Sat 10am-10pm (last admission 45 mins before close). Closed 24-26 Dec* **Fees** Free. A charge is made for special exhibitions **Facilities** Ⓟ licensed (fully accessible) toilets for disabled (parking & wheelchairs available call 020 7887 8888) shop

The Tower Bridge Exhibition

Tower Bridge Rd SE1 2UP
☎ 020 7940 3985 020 7357 7935
e-mail: enquiries@towerbridge.org.uk
web: www.towerbridge.org.uk
dir: Underground - Tower Hill or London Bridge

Enter the most famous bridge in the world and experience stunning panoramic views across London from glass-covered walkways, 142ft above the Thames. One of the capital's most famous landmarks, learn about the history of the bridge before visiting the magnificent Victorian engine rooms, where much of the original machinery can be seen. The Tower Bridge Exhibition uses state-of-the-art effects to present the story of the bridge in a dramatic and exciting fashion. Experience a virtual bridge lift shown on a giant projector screen and watch footage of the amazing bridge jump by Red Bull stunt rider Robbie Maddison.

Times Open all year, Apr-Sep 10-6.30. Last ticket 5.30. Oct-Mar 9.30-5.30. Last ticket 5. Closed 25-26 Dec **Fees** £7 (ch £3, under 5 free, concessions £5). Family tickets available, Groups 10+. See website* **Facilities** Ⓟ (fully accessible) toilets for disabled (loop systems) shop

Vinopolis, City of Wine

1 Bank End SE1 9BU
☎ 0870 241 4040 020 7940 8302
e-mail: sales@vinopolis.co.uk
web: www.vinopolis.co.uk
dir: Underground-London Bridge. Borough High St West exit, right into Stoney St, then left into Park St & follow road round to Vinopolis main entrance

Vinopolis is London's premiere wine attraction, situated on a 2.5 acre site on the vibrant Bankside. It offers an imaginative, interactive tour around the world of wine as well as great tastings. The setting is delightful, with Victorian vaulted ceilings and intricate, almost rustic red brickwork.

Times Open all year, Mon, Fri & Sat 12-9, Tue-Thu & Sun 12-6 (last admission 2 hrs before closing). Please call for opening hours in Dec & BHs* **Facilities** Ⓟ licensed toilets for disabled (lifts & ramps) shop

ENGLAND

SE1 *continued*

Winston Churchill's Britain at War Experience

2 FOR 1

64/66 Tooley St SE1 2TF

☎ 020 7403 3171 📠 020 7403 5104

e-mail: info@britainatwar.org.uk

web: www.britainatwar.co.uk

dir: mid way down Tooley St, between London Bridge & Tower Bridge. 2min walk from London Bridge Stn

Step back in time to the 1940s and experience a realistic adventure of life in war-torn London. Take the lift to the underground where many spent sleepless nights. Explore evacuation, food and clothes rationing, the blackout and much more. Uniforms, gas masks and tin helmets are available to try on and photography is allowed.

Times Open all year, Apr-Oct 10-5; Nov-Mar 10-4.30 **Fees** £11.45 (ch under 5 free, ch 5-16 £5.50, concessions £6.50). Family (2ad+2ch) £29* **Facilities** Ⓟ ♿ (fully accessible) toilets for disabled shop ⊗

SE5

South London Gallery

FREE

65 Peckham Rd SE5 8UH

☎ 020 7703 6120 & 7703 9799 (info) 📠 020 7252 4730

e-mail: mail@southlondongallery.org

web: www.southlondongallery.org

dir: from Vauxhall take A202 to Camberwell Green. Gallery halfway between Camberwell Green and Peckham

The gallery presents a programme of up to six exhibitions a year of cutting-edge contemporary art, and has established itself as South East London's premier venue for contemporary visual arts. The Gallery also programmes regular talks, screenings, live art projects and a range of activities for families and young people.

Times Open all year, Tue-Sun 11-6, Wed 11-9. Closed Mon **Facilities** Ⓟ ☕ ♿ (fully accessible) toilets for disabled (disabled access, induction loop) shop ⊗

SE9

Eltham Palace

Court Yard SE9 5QE

☎ 020 8294 2548 ex209 📠 020 8294 2621

web: www.english-heritage.org.uk

Stephen and Virginia Courtauld's stunning country house shows the glamour and allure of 1930s Art Deco style and is a feast of luxurious design ideas. The house incorporates the medieval Great Hall and stunning moated gardens.

Times Open Apr-Oct, Sun-Wed 10-5; Nov-Dec & Feb-Mar, Sun-Wed 11-4. Closed Jan **Fees** House & Garden: £8.70 (ch £4.40, concessions £7.40). Family ticket £21.80. Garden only: £5.60 (ch £2.80, concessions £4.80). Prices and opening times are subject to change in March 2011. Please call 0870 333 1181 for the most up to date prices and opening times when planning your visit **Facilities** Ⓟ shop ⊗ 🚌 #

SE10

The Fan Museum

2 FOR 1

12 Crooms Hill SE10 8ER

☎ 020 8305 1441 📠 020 8293 1889

e-mail: admin@fan-museum.org

web: www.fan-museum.org

dir: approached via DLR

Two elegant Georgian houses have been beautifully restored as the setting for the first museum in the world devoted entirely to all aspects of the ancient art and craft of fan making. More than 4,000 fans and fan leaves dating back as far as the 11th century are displayed in changing exhibitions.

Times Open all year, Tue-Sat, 11-5 & Sun noon-5. Closed 25-26 Dec, 31 Dec-1 Jan* **Fees** £4 (ch under 7 free, concessions £3). Free for OAPs & disabled on Tue after 2 (ex groups)* **Facilities** Ⓟ ♿ (fully accessible) toilets for disabled (lift, ramp) shop ⊗

National Maritime Museum

Romney Rd SE10 9NF

☎ 020 8312 6589 📠 020 8312 6632

e-mail: marketing@nmm.ac.uk

web: www.nmm.ac.uk

dir: central Greenwich A206

Britain's seafaring history is displayed in this impressive modern museum. Themes include exploration and discovery, Nelson, trade and empire, passenger shipping and luxury liners, maritime London, costume, art and the sea, and the future of the sea. There are interactive displays for children.

Times Open all year, daily 10-5. Closed 24-26 Dec. (Partial closures 31 Dec, 1 Jan & Marathon day) **Fees** Free, except some special events & exhibtions **Facilities** Ⓟ ☕ ⛩ (outdoor) ♿ (fully accessible) toilets for disabled (wheelchair, advisory service for hearing/sight impaired) shop ⊗

See advert on opposite page

Old Royal Naval College

Greenwich SE10 9LW
☎ 020 8269 4747 📠 020 8269 4757
e-mail: info@greenwichfoundation.org.uk
web: www.oldroyalnavalcollege.org
dir: In centre of Greenwich, off one way system, (College Approach), on the Thames next to Greenwich Pier

The Old Royal Naval College is one of London's most famous riverside landmarks and a masterpiece of Baroque architecture. The Grade I listed group of buildings, designed by Sir Christopher Wren as the Greenwich Hospital, occupy the site of the Tudor palace where Henry VIII and Elizabeth I were born. The buildings incorporate the magnificent Painted Hall by James Thornhill and the Chapel by James Stuart. The public can visit the beautiful grounds of the estate and also Discover Greenwich, a major new education and interpretation centre, opened winter 2009, telling the continuing history of the Old Royal Naval College and Maritime Greenwich.

Times Open all year ex 24-26 Dec. (Painted Hall & Chapel), daily 10-5 . Chapel open to visitors from 12.30 on Sun, public worship from 11.* **Facilities** Ⓟ 🍴 licensed ⛩ (outdoor) ♿ (partly accessible) (several stairs make access difficult, stairmate carries wheelchair users up and into Painted Hall & Chapel) toilets for disabled (parking, wheelchair, stairmate - notice required) 🚫

The Queens House

Romney Rd, Greenwich SE10 9NF
☎ 020 8312 6589 📠 020 8312 6632
e-mail: marketing@nmm.ac.uk
web: www.nmm.ac.uk
dir: central Greenwich A206

The first Palladian-style villa in England, designed by Inigo Jones for Anne of Denmark and completed for Queen Henrietta Maria, wife of Charles I. The Great Hall, the State Rooms and a Loggia overlooking Greenwich Park are notable features. Also displays the extensive art collection of the National Maritime Museum including Tudor and Stuart royalty.

Times Open all year, daily 10-5. Closed 24-26 Dec. (Partial closures 31 Dec, 1 Jan & Marathon day) **Fees** Free, except some special events & exhibitions **Facilities** Ⓟ ☕ ⛩ (outdoor) ♿ (fully accessible) toilets for disabled (lift, wheelchairs) shop 🚫

Royal Observatory Greenwich **2 FOR 1**

Greenwich Park, Greenwich SE10 8XJ
☎ 020 8312 6589 📠 020 8312 6632
e-mail: bookings@nmm.ac.uk
web: www.nmm.ac.uk
dir: off A2, Greenwich Park, enter from Blackheath Gate only

Charles II founded the Royal Observatory in 1675 'for perfecting navigation and astronomy'. It stands at zero meridian longitude and is the original home of Greenwich Mean Time. Astronomy galleries and the Peter Harrison Planetarium house an extensive collection of historic timekeeping, astronomical and navigational instruments. The 2-for-1 voucher can be used for the Peter Harrison Planetarium.

Times Open all year, daily 10-5. Closed 24-26 Dec (Partial closures 31 Dec, 1 Jan and Marathon day) **Fees** Free, except for Planetarium shows £6.50 (ch £4.50). Family ticket £17.50* **Facilities** Ⓟ ☕ ⛩ (outdoor) ♿ (partly accessible) (narrow staircase to Octagon room) toilets for disabled (assistance on request) shop 🚫

The Wernher Collection at Ranger's House

Chesterfield Walk, Blackheath SE10 8QY
☎ 020 8853 0035 📠 020 8853 0090
web: www.english-heritage.org.uk

Handsome 18th-century house with lovely views over London, Greenwich Park, Blackheath and the Thames. View the 'Wernher Collection' of self-made millionaire Julius Wernher, who made his fortune in the diamond mines of South Africa.

Times Open Apr-Sep, Mon-Wed 11.30-2.30 entry by guided tours only, booking advisable on 020 8853 0035; Apr-Sep, Sun 11-5; Oct-Mar available for group tours, please call for details. The property may close at short notice, please ring in advance for details **Fees** £6 (ch £3, concessions £5.10). Prices and opening times are subject to change in March 2011. Please call 0870 333 1181 for the most up to date prices and opening times when planning your visit **Facilities** Ⓟ toilets for disabled shop ⌗

SE18

Firepower Royal Artillery Museum

Royal Arsenal, Woolwich SE18 6ST
☎ 020 8855 7755 📠 020 8855 7100
e-mail: info@firepower.org.uk
web: www.firepower.org.uk
dir: A205, right at Woolwich ferry onto A206, attraction signed

Firepower is the Royal Artillery Museum in the historic Royal Arsenal. It spans 2,000 years of artillery, and shows the development from Roman catapult to guided missile, to self-propelled gun. Put science into action with touchscreen displays, and be awed by the big guns.

Times Open all year, Wed-Sun & BHs 11-5.30. Phone for winter opening times* **Facilities** Ⓟ Ⓟ ⛩ ♿ (partly accessible) toilets for disabled (wheelchairs available) shop ⊗

Thames Barrier Information & Learning Centre **2 FOR 1**

1 Unity Way SE18 5NJ
☎ 020 8305 4188 📠 020 8855 2146
e-mail: learningcentre@environment-agency.gov.uk
web: www.environment-agency.gov.uk/thamesbarrier
dir: Turn off A102(M) onto A206, turn onto Eastmoor St and follow signs

The Thames Barrier is one of the largest movable flood barriers in the world. It protects 125 square kilometres of Central London. That's 1.25 million people, historic buildings including the Houses of Parliament, offices, power supplies, tube lines and hospitals to name a few. Visit the Thames Barrier Information Centre to find out how the Thames Barrier was designed and built and how it works. Also learn more about the history and environment of the River Thames.

Times Open Apr-Sep, 10.30-4.30; Oct-Mar, 11-3.30. Closed for Xmas, please call for details **Fees** £3.50 (ch £2, concessions £3) **Facilities** Ⓟ ☕ ⛩ (outdoor) ♿ (fully accessible) toilets for disabled (lift from river pier approach) shop ⊗

SE21

Dulwich Picture Gallery **2 FOR 1**

Gallery Rd, Dulwich SE21 7AD
☎ 020 8693 5254 📠 020 8299 8700
e-mail: info@dulwichpicturegallery.org.uk
web: www.dulwichpicturegallery.org.uk
dir: off South Circular A205, follow signs to Dulwich village

This is the oldest public art gallery in England, housing a magnificent collection of Old Masters, including works by Poussin, Claude, Rubens, Murillo, Van Dyck, Rembrandt, Watteau and Gainsborough. The gallery was designed by Sir John Soane in 1811. The collection, the building and the critically acclaimed loan exhibitions make the gallery a must see for art lovers. Various exhibitions throughout the year. 2011 is the gallery's bicentenary and in celebration a loan masterpiece from some of the world's greatest artists will be displayed each month.

Times Open all year Tue-Fri 10-5, wknds & BH Mon 11-5. Closed 24-26 Dec & 1 Jan **Fees** £5 (concessions £4, ch, students, unemployed & disabled free), + £4 for special exhibitions **Facilities** Ⓟ Ⓟ ☕ 🍽 licensed ⛩ (outdoor) ♿ (fully accessible) toilets for disabled (wheelchairs available, hearing loop) shop ⊗

SE23

The Horniman Museum & Gardens FREE

London Rd, Forest Hill SE23 3PQ
☎ 020 8699 1872 📠 020 8291 5506
e-mail: enquiry@horniman.ac.uk
web: www.horniman.ac.uk
dir: situated on A205

Founder Frederick Horniman, a tea merchant, gave the museum to the people of London in 1901. The collection covers the natural and cultural world including Natural History with displays on Vanishing Birds and African Worlds, The Music Gallery, which displays Britain's largest collection of musical instruments and the Centenary Gallery which showcases world cultures. There are 16 acres of gardens, and the museum hosts a variety of workshops and activities for all ages.

Times Open all year, daily 10.30-5.30. Closed 24-26 Dec. Gardens close at sunset.* **Facilities** Ⓟ ☕ ⛩ (outdoor) ♿ (partly accessible) toilets for disabled (large print leaflets, induction loop) shop 🚫

SW1

The Banqueting House, Whitehall

Whitehall SW1A 2ER
☎ 0870 751 5178 📠 020 7930 8268
e-mail: banquetinghouse@hrp.org.uk
web: www.hrp.org.uk
dir: Underground - Westminster, Charing Cross or Embankment

Designed by Inigo Jones, this is the only surviving building of the vast Whitehall Palace, destroyed by fire 300 years ago. The Palace has seen many significant royal events, including the execution of Charles I in 1649. The Banqueting House's Rubens ceiling paintings are stunning examples of the larger works of the Flemish Master and its classical Palladian style set the fashion for much of London's later architecture.

Times Open all year, Mon-Sat 10-5. Closed Sun, BHs, 24 Dec-1 Jan. Subject to closure at short notice.* **Facilities** Ⓟ ♿ (fully accessible) toilets for disabled (Braille guide, Induction loops) shop 🚫

Buckingham Palace

Buckingham Palace Rd SW1A 1AA
☎ 020 7766 7300 📠 020 7930 9625
e-mail: bookinginfo@royalcollection.org.uk
web: www.royalcollection.org.uk
dir: Underground - Victoria, Green Park, St James' Park, entrance in Buckingham Palace Road

Buckingham Palace has been the official London residence of Britain's sovereigns since 1837. Today it serves as both the home and office of Her Majesty The Queen. Its nineteen State Rooms, which open for eight weeks a year, form the heart of the working palace and more than 50,000 people visit each year as guests at State, ceremonial and official occasions and garden parties. After visiting the State Rooms, visitors can enjoy a walk along the south side of the garden, which offers superb views of the west front of the Palace and the 19th-century lake.

Times Open Aug-Sep 9.45-6 (last admission 3.45). Entry by timed-ticket* **Fees** £17 (ch under 17 £10, ch under 5 free, students & pen £15.50). Family ticket (2ad+3ch) £45. See website www.royalcollection.org.uk for current prices* **Facilities** Ⓟ ☕ ♿ (fully accessible) toilets for disabled (ex gardens, pre-booking essential - 020 7766 7324) shop 🚫

Churchill War Rooms

Clive Steps, King Charles St SW1A 2AQ
☎ 020 7930 6961 📠 020 7839 5897
e-mail: cwr@iwm.org.uk
web: www.iwm.org.uk/cabinet
dir: Underground - Westminster (exit 6) or St James Park

Learn more about the man who inspired Britain's finest hour at the interactive and innovative Churchill Museum, the world's first major museum dedicated to the life of the 'Greatest Briton'. Step back in time and discover the secret underground headquarters that were the nerve centre of Britain's war effort. Located in the heart of Westminster, visitors can view this complex of historic rooms left as they were in 1945, while at the same time taking in the Churchill Museum.

Times Open all year, daily 9.30-6 (last admission 5). Closed 24-26 Dec **Fees** £14.95 (concessions £12). Group rates available* **Facilities** Ⓟ ☕ ♿ (partly accessible) (2 wheelchairs available) toilets for disabled (education service, object handling session, induction loop) shop 🚫

ENGLAND

SW1 *continued*

The Household Cavalry Museum 2 FOR 1

Horse Guards, Whitehall SW1A 2AX
☎ 020 7930 3070
e-mail: museum@householdcavalry.co.uk
web: www.householdcavalrymuseum.co.uk
dir: Underground - Charing Cross, Embankment & Westminster

The Household Cavalry Museum is unlike any other military attraction because it offers a unique 'behind-the-scenes' look at the work that goes into the ceremonial duties and operational role of the Household Cavalry. Watch troopers working with their horses in the original 18th-century stables (via a glazed screen) and hear accounts of their demanding training. Plus children's trails, activity packs and dressing up areas.

Times Open all year daily, Mar-Sep 10-6, Oct-Feb 10-5. Closed 24-26 Dec* **Fees** £6 (ch 5-16 & concessions £4). Family ticket (2ad+3ch) £15. Group rate 10% discount* **Facilities** Ⓟ ♿ (fully accessible) toilets for disabled shop ⊗

Houses of Parliament

Westminster SW1A 0AA
☎ 020 7219 4272 📠 020 7219 5839
web: www.parliament.uk
dir: Underground - Westminster

The Houses of Parliament occupy the Palace of Westminster, a royal palace for nearly 1000 years. Visitors will see the Queen's Robing Room, the Royal Gallery, the Chambers of both the House of Lords and House of Commons, the voting lobbies, historic Westminster Hall (c.1097) where Charles I and Guy Fawkes were put on trial, plus other areas normally hidden from public view.

Times Open all year, Sat 9.15-4.30 **Fees** £14 (ch £6, concessions £9). Family ticket £35* **Facilities** Ⓟ ☕ ♿ (partly accessible) (visitor route 95% accessible, one short detour required for wheelchair users) toilets for disabled shop ⊗

Mall Galleries

The Mall SW1Y 5BD
☎ 020 7930 6844 📠 020 7839 7830
e-mail: info@mallgalleries.com
web: www.mallgalleries.org.uk
dir: Underground - Charing Cross, situated on the Mall, near Trafalgar Square and Admiralty Arch

The venue for the annual open exhibitions of nine national art societies. There is also a wide range of individual and group shows. The galleries display work which is both traditional and contemporary by a large number of prominent international artists. A variety of subjects are displayed in a number of mediums, including oil, watercolour, drawings and sculpture. Phone for details of special events.

Times Open all year, daily 10-5. Closed between exhibitions and at Xmas. Some late night opening, please phone for details.* **Facilities** Ⓟ ☕ ♿ (fully accessible) toilets for disabled (platform lift to galleries) shop ⊗

The Queen's Gallery

Buckingham Palace, Buckingham Palace Rd SW1A 1AA
☎ 020 7766 7301 📠 020 7930 9625
e-mail: bookinginfo@royalcollection.org.uk
web: www.royalcollection.org.uk
dir: Underground - Victoria, Green Park & St. James' Park. Entrance in Buckingham Palace Road

The Queen's Gallery is a permanent space dedicated to changing exhibitions of items from the Royal Collection, a wide-ranging collection of art, furniture, jewellery and other pieces held in trust by The Queen for the Nation.

Times Open daily, 10-5.30 (last admission 4.30). Closed Nov-14 Apr **Fees** £9 (ch under 5 free, ch under 17 £4.50, concessions £8). Family ticket (2ad+3ch) £23. See website for current prices* **Facilities** Ⓟ ♿ (fully accessible) toilets for disabled shop ⊗

The Royal Mews

Buckingham Palace, Buckingham Palace Rd SW1W 0QH
☎ 020 7766 7302 📠 020 7930 9625
e-mail: bookinginfo@royalcollection.org.uk
web: www.royalcollection.org.uk
dir: Underground - Victoria, Green Park, St. James Park. Entrance in Buckingham Palace Road

Designed by John Nash and completed in 1825, the Royal Mews houses the State Coaches, horse-drawn carriages and motor cars used for Coronations, State Visits, Royal Weddings and the State Opening of Parliament. These include the Gold State Coach made in 1762, with panels painted by the Florentine artist Cipriani. As one of the finest working stables in existence, the Royal Mews provides a unique opportunity for you to see a working department of the Royal Household.

Times Open Jan-Mar, Mon-Fri 11-4; Mar-Nov, Sat-Thu 11-4; Aug-Sep, daily 10-5 (last admission 45 mins before close). Closed during state visits, see website for details **Fees** £8 (ch under 17 £5, ch under 5 free, concessions £7) Family (2ad+3ch) £21.50* **Facilities** Ⓟ ♿ (fully accessible) toilets for disabled (phone 020 7766 7324 for access information) shop ⊗

Tate Britain

Millbank SW1P 4RG
☎ 020 7887 8888 & 8008
e-mail: information@tate.org.uk
web: www.tate.org.uk
dir: Underground - Pimlico

Tate Britain is the national gallery of British art from 1500 to the present day, from Tudors to the Turner Prize. Tate holds the greatest collection of British art in the world, including works by Blake, Constable, Epstein, Gainsborough, Gilbert and George, Hatoum, Hirst, Hockney, Hodgkin, Hogarth, Moore, Rossetti, Sickert, Spencer, Stubbs and Turner. The gallery is the world centre for the understanding and enjoyment of British art.

Times Open all year, daily 10-6. Closed 24-26 Dec* **Fees** Admission free but charge for special exhibitions **Facilities** Ⓟ ☕ 🍽 licensed ⛩ (indoor & outdoor) ♿ (fully accessible) toilets for disabled (wheelchairs on request, parking by prior arrangement) shop ⊗

Westminster Abbey

Broad Sanctuary SW1P 3PA
☎ 020 7222 5152 020 7233 2072
e-mail: info@westminster-abbey.org
web: www.westminster-abbey.org
dir: Underground - Westminster, St James's Park. Next to Parliament Square and opposite the Houses of Parliament

Westminster Abbey was originally a Benedictine monastery. In the 11th century, it was re-founded by St Edward the Confessor. The great Romanesque abbey Edward built next to his royal palace became his burial place shortly after it was completed. Over the centuries that followed, many more kings and queens have been buried, and many great figures commemorated, in the abbey. The abbey has been the setting for nearly every coronation since that of William the Conqueror in 1066, and for numerous other royal occasions. The present building, begun by Henry III in 1245, is one of the most visited churches in the world.

Times Open all year, Mon-Fri 9.30-3.30, Sat 9.30-1.30 (summer 9.30-3.30). Wed late night til 6.30 (last admission 1hr before closing). No tourist visiting on Sun, however visitors are welcome at services. The Abbey may at short notice be closed for special services & other events* **Fees** £15 (school ch £6, under 11 free, concessions £12). Family tickets available* **Facilities** Ⓟ (partly accessible) (some areas dimly lit, floor and steps uneven, low doorways) toilets for disabled (induction loop, wheelchairs, large print / Braille guides) shop

Westminster Cathedral FREE

Victoria St SW1P 1QW
☎ 020 7798 9055 020 7798 9090
e-mail: barrypalmer@rcdow.org.uk
web: www.westminstercathedral.org.uk
dir: 300 yds from Victoria Station

Westminster Cathedral is a fascinating example of Victorian architecture. Designed in the Early Christian Byzantine style by John Francis Bentley, its strongly oriental appearance makes it very distinctive. The foundation stone was laid in 1895 but the interior decorations are not fully completed. The Campanile Bell Tower is 273ft high and has a four-sided viewing gallery with magnificent views over London. The lift is open daily 9am-5pm Mar-Nov but shut Mon-Wed from Dec-Feb.

Times Open all year, daily 7am-7pm. **Facilities** Ⓟ (partly accessible) (all parts accessible except side chapels) (loop system) shop

SW3

Carlyle's House

24 Cheyne Row SW3 5HL
☎ 020 7352 7087 020 7352 5108
e-mail: carlyleshouse@nationaltrust.org.uk
web: www.nationaltrust.org.uk/carlyleshouse
dir: Underground - Sloane Square. Off Cheyne Walk between Battersea & Albert Bridges

'The Sage of Chelsea' - distinguished essayist and writer of historical works, Thomas Carlyle - lived here, with his wife Jane, from 1834 until his death in 1881. Such literary notables as Tennyson, Thackeray, Browning, Ruskin and Dickens were frequent visitors.

Times Open 5 Mar-30 Oct, Wed-Sun & BH Mon 11-5 (last admission 4.30) **Fees** £5.10 (ch £2.60) Family £12.80 **Facilities** Ⓟ (partly accessible) (not suitable for wheelchair users)

Chelsea Physic Garden

66 Royal Hospital Rd, (entrance in Swan Walk) SW3 4HS
☎ 020 7352 5646 020 7376 3910
e-mail: enquiries@chelseaphysicgarden.co.uk
web: www.chelseaphysicgarden.co.uk
dir: Underground - Sloane Square

Begun in 1673 for the study of plants used by the Society of Apothecaries, this garden is one of Europe's oldest botanic gardens and is the only one to retain the title 'Physic' after the old name for the healing arts. The garden is still used for botanical and medicinal research, and offers displays of many fascinating plants in lovely surroundings.

Times Open Apr-Oct, Wed 12-5, Sun 12-6. (Additional opening during Chelsea Flower Show week, late May & Chelsea Festival week late Jun. Groups at other times by appointment).* **Facilities** Ⓟ (fully accessible) toilets for disabled (disabled parking in road, wheelchair loan) shop

National Army Museum FREE

Royal Hospital Rd, Chelsea SW3 4HT
☎ 020 7730 0717 020 7823 6573
e-mail: info@national-army-museum.ac.uk
web: www.national-army-museum.ac.uk
dir: Underground - Sloane Square

The museum will guide you through Britain's Military History and its effect on Britain and the world today. Permanent gallery displays, exhibitions, celebrity speakers, lectures and special events will both engage and entertain you.

Times Open all year, daily 10-5.30. Closed 24-26 Dec & 1 Jan* **Facilities** Ⓟ Ⓟ (fully accessible) toilets for disabled (wheelchair lift to access lower ground floor) shop

ENGLAND

SW3 *continued*

Royal Hospital Chelsea

FREE

Royal Hospital Rd SW3 4SR
☎ 020 7881 5200 020 7881 5463
e-mail: friends@chelsea-pensioners.org.uk
web: www.chelsea-pensioners.org.uk
dir: near Sloane Square, off A3216 & A3031

Founded in 1682 by Charles II as a retreat for army veterans who had become unfit for duty, through injury or long service, the Royal Hospital Chelsea was built on the site of a theological college founded by James I in 1610. The buildings were designed and built by Sir Christopher Wren, and then added to by Robert Adam and Sir John Soane. The hospital houses some 300 'In-Pensioners', some of whom do voluntary work as tour guides, clerical assistants and ground staff. Visitors can stroll around the grounds, gain admission to the Chapel, Great Hall and visit the Museum.

Times Open all year, daily Mon-Sat, 10-12 & 2-4, Sun 2-4. (Museum closed on Sun Oct-Mar). Closed 25-26 Dec & Good Fri* **Facilities** Ⓟ (outdoor) (partly accessible) toilets for disabled (induction loop in post office) shop

SW7

The Natural History Museum

Cromwell Rd SW7 5BD
☎ 020 7942 5000 020 7942 5075
e-mail: feedback@nhm.ac.uk
web: www.nhm.ac.uk
dir: Underground - South Kensington

This vast and elaborate Romanesque-style building, with its terracotta tiles showing relief mouldings of animals, birds and fishes, covers an area of four acres. Holding over 70 million specimens from all over the globe, from dinosaurs to diamonds and earthquakes to ants, the museum provides a journey into Earth's past, present and future. Discover more about the work of the museum through a daily programme of talks from museum scientists or go behind the scenes of the Darwin Centre, the museum's scientific research centre.

Times Open all year, daily 10-5.50 (last admission 5.30). Closed 24-26 Dec* **Facilities** Ⓟ licensed (indoor) (partly accessible) (top floor/one gallery not accessible) toilets for disabled (wheelchair hire) shop

Science Museum

Exhibition Rd, South Kensington SW7 2DD
☎ 0870 870 4868 020 7942 4421
e-mail: sciencemuseum@sciencemuseum.org.uk
web: www.sciencemuseum.org.uk
dir: Underground - South Kensington, signed from tube stn

See iconic objects from the history of science, from Stephenson's Rocket to the Apollo 10 command module; be amazed by a 3D IMAX movie; take a ride in a simulator; visit an exhibition; and encounter the past, present and future of technology in seven floors of free galleries, including the famous hands-on section where children can have fun investigating science with the Museum's dedicated Explainers. Opening in March 2011 "Watt's Workshop".

Times Open all year, daily 10-6. Closed 24-26 Dec
Fees Admission free. Charges apply for IMAX 3D cinema, simulators & some special exhibitions **Facilities** Ⓟ licensed (indoor) (fully accessible) toilets for disabled (personal 2hr tour of museum, hearing loop) shop

Victoria and Albert Museum

Cromwell Rd, South Kensington SW7 2RL
☎ 020 7942 2000
e-mail: vanda@vam.ac.uk
web: www.vam.ac.uk
dir: Underground - South Kensington, Museum situated on A4, Buses C1, 14, 74, 414 stop outside the Cromwell Road entrance

The V&A is the world's greatest museum of art and design. It was established in 1852 to make important works of art available to all, and also to inspire British designers and manufacturers. The Museum's rich and diverse collections span over three thousand years of human creativity from many parts of the world, and include ceramics, furniture, fashion, glass, jewellery, metalwork, sculpture, textiles and paintings. Highlights include the British Galleries 1500-1900, the Jameel Gallery of Islamic Art, the enormous Cast Courts, and the magnificent John Madejski Garden.

Times Open all year, daily 10-5.45. Fri 10am-10pm*
Facilities Ⓟ licensed (outdoor) (partly accessible) toilets for disabled (call 020 7942 2211 for details of disabled facilities) shop

SW13

WWT London Wetland Centre

Queen Elizabeth Walk SW13 9WT
☎ 020 8409 4400 020 8409 4401
e-mail: info.london@wwt.org.uk
web: www.wwt.org.uk
dir: Situated just off A306 in Barnes, or a 5 min bus ride from Hammersmith tube

An inspiring wetland landscape that stretches over 105 acres, in the heart of London. Thirty wild wetland habitats have been created from reservoir lagoon to ponds, lakes and reedbeds and all are home to a wealth of wildlife, including birds, bats, water voles, frogs and butterflies. Each week there is a wide range of activities on offer, from guided walks and talks to children's events. There are two children's adventure zones.

Times Open all year: winter 9.30-5; summer 9.30-6 (last admission 1 hour before close) **Fees** £9.50 (ch £5.25, concessions £7.10). Family ticket £26.55 **Facilities** Ⓟ licensed (outdoor) (fully accessible) toilets for disabled (ramps, lifts) shop

ENGLAND

SW19

Wimbledon Lawn Tennis Museum

Museum Building, The All England Club, Church Rd SW19 5AE

☎ 020 8946 6131 📠 020 8947 8752

e-mail: museum@aeltc.com

web: www.wimbledon.org/museum

dir: Underground - Southfields, 15mins walk. By road - from central London take A3 Portsmouth road, just before Tibbet's Corner left onto A219 towards Wimbledon, down Parkside, left onto Church Rd

Visitors to the Wimbledon Lawn Tennis Museum are invited to explore the game's evolution from a garden party pastime to a multi-million dollar professional sport played worldwide. Highlights include the Championship Trophies, a cinema that captures the Science of Tennis using CGI special effects, film and video footage of some of the most memorable matches, an extensive collection of memorabilia dating back to 1555, and a holographic John McEnroe who walks through a recreated 1980s changing room.

Times Open all year, daily 10-5. Closed middle Sun of Championships, Mon immediately following Championships, 24-26 Dec & 1 Jan* **Facilities** Ⓟ Ⓟ ☕ ♿ (fully accessible) toilets for disabled (audio guides in 8 languages) shop ⊗

W1

Apsley House, The Wellington Museum

148 Piccadilly, Hyde Park Corner WIJ 7NT

☎ 020 7499 5676 📠 020 7493 6576

web: www.english-heritage.org.uk

dir: Underground - Hyde Park Corner, exit 1 overlooking rdbt

Number One, London, is the popular name for one of the Capital's finest private residences, 19th-century home of the first Duke of Wellington. Built in the 1770s, its rich interiors have been returned to their former glory, and house the Duke's magnificent collection of paintings, silver, porcelain, sculpture and furniture.

Times Open all year Apr-Oct, Wed-Sun & BHs 11-5; Nov-Mar, Wed-Sun 11-4. Closed 24-26 Dec & 1 Jan **Fees** £6 (ch £3, concessions £5.10). Prices & opening times are subject to change in March 2011. Please call 0870 333 1181 for the most up to date prices and opening times **Facilities** Ⓟ (lift) shop ⊗ #

Handel House Museum

25 Brook St W1K 4HB

☎ 020 7495 1685 📠 020 7495 1759

e-mail: mail@handelhouse.org

web: www.handelhouse.org

dir: off Park Lane into Brook Gate, then Upper Brook Street. Pass Claridge's Hotel on right. The entrance is in Lancashire Court

Home to George Frideric Handel from 1723 until his death in 1759, the Handel House Museum celebrates Handel's music and life. It was here that Handel composed *Messiah, Zadok the Priest* and *Music for the Royal Fireworks.* Over 200 years later, live music, educational projects and public events continue to bring Handel's former home to life.

Times Open all year Tue, Wed, Fri & Sat 10-6, Thu 10-8, Sun 12-6. Closed Mon & BHs, 25-26 Dec & 1-2 Jan.* **Facilities** Ⓟ toilets for disabled (lift) shop ⊗

Pollock's Toy Museum

1 Scala St W1T 2HL

☎ 020 7636 3452

e-mail: pollocks@btconnect.com

web: www.pollockstoytheatre.com

dir: Underground - Goodge St

Teddy bears, wax and china dolls, dolls' houses, board games, toy theatres, tin toys, mechanical and optical toys, folk toys and nursery furniture, are among the attractions to be seen in this appealing museum. Items from all over the world and from all periods are displayed in two small, interconnecting houses with winding staircases and charming little rooms.

Times Open all year, Mon-Sat 10-5. Closed BH, Sun & Xmas.* **Facilities** Ⓟ ♿ (partly accessible) (wheelchair access to shop only) shop

Royal Academy Of Arts

Burlington House, Piccadilly W1J 0BD

☎ 020 7300 5729 📠 020 7300 8032

e-mail: maria.salvatierra@royalacademy.org.uk

web: www.royalacademy.org.uk

dir: Underground - Piccadilly Circus, head towards Green Park

Known principally for international loan exhibitions, the Royal Academy of Arts was founded in 1768 and is Britain's oldest Fine Arts institution. Two of its founding principles were to provide a free school and to mount an annual exhibition open to all artists of distinguished merit, now known as the Summer Exhibition. The Royal Academy's most prized possession, Michelangelo's *Tondo, 'The Virgin and Child with the Infant St John'*, one of only four marble sculptures by the artist outside Italy, is on permanent display in the Sackler Wing.

Times Open all year, daily 10-6. Late night opening Fri 10am-10pm. Closed 24-26 Dec **Fees** £8-£12 (ch, concessions & group visitors reduced price). Prices vary for each exhibition. Free entry to permanent collection. Please contact for details of exhibitions and prices* **Facilities** Ⓟ ☕ 🍴 licensed ♿ (fully accessible) toilets for disabled (large-print guides/labels, sign language) shop ⊗

W1 *continued*

The Wallace Collection FREE

Hertford House, Manchester Square W1U 3BN
☎ 020 7563 9500 📠 020 7224 2155
e-mail: visiting@wallacecollection.org
web: www.wallacecollection.org
dir: Underground - Bond St, Baker St, Oxford Circus, located minutes from Oxford St, in garden square behind Selfridges

Founded by the 1st Marquis of Hertford, the Wallace Collection was bequeathed to the nation in 1897 and came on public display three years later. This is one of the world's finest collections of art ever assembled by one family. The collection is shown in the family home, a tranquil oasis just a few minutes from Oxford Street. There are paintings by Titian, Canaletto, Rembrandt, Rubens, Hals, Fragonard, Velazquez, Gainsborough and many more. There is a very important collection of French porcelain and furniture, much of it of Royal providence, as well as amazing arms and armour, sculpture and Renaissance treasures. Many rooms have been recently restored creating wonderful intimate and opulent settings for the works of art.

Times Open all year, daily 10-5, closed 24-26 Dec & 1 Jan **Facilities** Ⓟ ☕ 🍽 licensed ♿ (fully accessible) toilets for disabled (lift, ramp, wheelchair available, induction loop) shop 🚫

W2

Serpentine Gallery FREE

Kensington Gardens W2 3XA
☎ 020 7402 6075 📠 020 7402 4103
e-mail: press@serpentinegallery.org
web: www.serpentinegallery.org
dir: Underground - Knightsbridge, Lancaster Gate, South Kensington. Bus 9, 10, 12, 52, 94

The Serpentine Gallery, named after the lake in Hyde Park, is situated in the heart of Kensington Gardens in a 1934 tea pavilion, and was founded in 1970 by the Arts Council of Great Britain. Today the Gallery attracts over 400,000 visitors a year and is one the best places in London for modern and contemporary art and architecture.

Times Open all year, daily 10-6 **Facilities** 🧺 ♿ (fully accessible) toilets for disabled shop 🚫

W4

Chiswick House

Burlington Ln, Chiswick W4 2RP
☎ 020 8995 0508 📠 020 8742 3104
web: www.english-heritage.org.uk
dir: Underground - Gunnersbury

Discover the story of this celebrated Palladian villa, a fine example of 18th-century English architecture with lavish interiors and classical landscaping.

Times Open Apr, daily 10-5; May-Oct, Sun-Wed & BHs 10-5; Nov-Mar available for group access please call for details **Fees** £5 (ch £2.50, concessions £4.30). Family ticket £12.50. Prices and opening times are subject to change in March 2011. Please call 0870 333 1181 for the most up to date prices and opening times when planning your visit **Facilities** Ⓟ ☕ 🧺 ♿ (partly accessible) (telephone in advance for wheelchair facilities) shop #

Hogarth's House FREE

Hogarth Ln, Great West Rd W4 2QN
☎ 020 8994 6757 📠 0845 456 2880
e-mail: info@cip.org.uk
web: www.hounslow.info
dir: 50yds W of Hogarth rdbt on Great West Road A4

This 18th-century house was the country home of artist William Hogarth (1697-1764) during the last 15 years of his life. The house contains displays on the artist's life, and many of his satirical engravings. The gardens contain Hogarth's famous mulberry tree.

Times Open all year, Apr-Oct, Tue-Fri 1-5, Sat-Sun 1-6; Nov-Mar, Tue-Fri 1-4, Sat-Sun 1-5. Closed Mon (ex BHs), Jan, Good Fri & 25-26 Dec.* **Facilities** Ⓟ ♿ (partly accessible) toilets for disabled (telephone in advance to confirm) shop 🚫

W8

Kensington Palace State Apartments & Royal Ceremonial Dress Collection

Kensington Gardens W8 4PX
☎ 0844 482 7777 📠 020 3166 6110
e-mail: kensingtonpalace@hrp.org.uk
web: www.hrp.org.uk
dir: Underground - High Street Kensington or Notting Hill Gate

Highlights of a visit to Kensington include the King's and Queen's Apartments with a fine collection of paintings from the Royal Collection. The rooms used by Princess Victoria are also shown, including her bedroom, where she was woken to be told she was Queen. The Royal Ceremonial Dress Collection includes representations of tailor's and dressmaker's workshops, and a display of dresses that belonged to Diana, Princess of Wales. Kensington Palace is undergoing major re-presentation with completion due in 2012.

Times Open all year, Mar-Oct 10-6, Nov-Feb 10-5 (last admission 1hr before closing). Closed 24-26 Dec* **Facilities** Ⓟ ☕ ♿ (partly accessible) (ground floor & lower ground floor accessible) toilets for disabled (audio guide, cafe has wheelchair access ramp) shop 🚫

Linley Sambourne House

18 Stafford Ter W8 7BH
☎ 020 7602 3316 📠 020 7371 2467
e-mail: museums@rbkc.gov.uk
web: www.rbkc.gov.uk/linleysambournehouse
dir: Underground - High Street Kensington

The home of Linley Sambourne (1844-1910), chief political cartoonist at Punch magazine, has had its magnificent artistic interior preserved, almost unchanged, since the late 19th century. Also displayed are many of Sambourne's own drawings and photographs. Tours are lead by costumed actors with scripts developed from the Sambourne family archive.

Times All access by guided tour, mid Mar-mid Dec. Sat & Sun tours 11.15, 1, 2.15, 3.30.* **Facilities** Ⓟ shop ⊗

W11

Museum of Brands, Packaging & Advertising

2 Colville Mews, Lonsdale Rd W11 2AR
☎ 020 7908 0880 & 020 7908 0881 📠 020 7908 0950
e-mail: info@museumofbrands.com
web: www.museumofbrands.com
dir: A4026 signed Notting Hill. From Westbourne Grove turn onto Ledbury Rd then left onto Lonsdale Rd

Featuring over 12,000 original items from the Robert Opie Collection, MOBPA details the history of consumer culture, revealed decade by decade in the "time tunnel", from Victorian times to the present day. Exhibits include all aspects of daily cultural consumer life, from washing powder packaging to newspapers, from radio and television to the rise of trains and planes. Regular changing exhibitions.

Times Open all year, Tue-Sat 10-6, Sun & BH Mon 11-5. Closed 25 Dec & Notting Hill carnival 28-29 Aug (dates to be confirmed) **Fees** £6.50 (ch 7-16 £2.25, ch under 7 free, concessions £4). Group discount 10% (ad price includes gift aid donation) **Facilities** Ⓟ ☕ ♿ (fully accessible) toilets for disabled shop ⊗

W12

BBC Television Centre Tours

BBC Television Centre, Wood Ln W12 7RJ
☎ 0370 901 1227 📠 020 8576 7466
e-mail: bbctours@bbc.co.uk
web: www.bbc.co.uk/tours
dir: Underground - Central Line/White City. Wood Lane - Hammersmith & City Line

On a tour of BBC Television Centre you will see behind the scenes of the most famous TV Centre in the world. You may see studios, the News Centre, Weather Centre, the interactive studio, and dressing rooms, but due to the operational nature of the building guarantees cannot be made. The CBBC Interactive Tour is aimed at 7-12 year olds - visit the Blue Peter Garden, have fun making a programme in the interactive studio, take part in the Raven challenge, and become 'Diddy Dick & Dom'. Both tours last up to two hours. Tours of Broadcasting House run weekly on Sundays. The UK's first purpose-built broadcast centre has been undergoing a major restoration and modernisation as part of a ten year development project. Tours are fitted round the working building's activities and you will see a range of areas such as the newly restored radio theatre, the council chamber and an interactive radio drama experience. Please telephone for details.

Times Open all year, Mon-Sat 10-6. Tours at 10, 10.15, 10.30, 10.45, 1.15, 1.30, 1.45, 2, 3.30, 3.45, 4 & 4.15. Closed Xmas & BHs. All tours must be pre-booked* **Fees** £9.95 (ch & students £7.50, concessions £8.95). Family £30* **Facilities** Ⓟ ♿ (fully accessible) toilets for disabled (wheelchair & sign language available) shop ⊗

W14

Leighton House Museum

12 Holland Park Rd W14 8LZ
☎ 020 7602 3316
e-mail: museums@rbkc.gov.uk
web: www.leightonhouse.co.uk
dir: Underground - High St Kensington. Museum is N of Kensington High St, off Melbury Rd

An opulent and exotic example of high Victorian taste, Leighton House was built for the President of the Royal Academy, Frederic Lord Leighton. The main body of the house was built in 1866 but the fabulous Arab Hall, an arresting 'Arabian Nights' creation, was not completed until 13 years later.

Times Open all year, daily (ex Tue) 11-5.30. Closed 25-26 Dec & 1 Jan* **Facilities** Ⓟ shop ⊗

WC1

British Museum

Great Russell St WC1B 3DG
☎ 020 7323 8000 📠 020 7323 8616
e-mail: information@britishmuseum.org
web: www.thebritishmuseum.ac.uk
dir: Underground - Russell Sq, Tottenham Court Rd, Holborn

"Of the world and for the world", the British Museum brings together astounding examples of universal heritage, for free. Enter through the largest covered square in Europe. Pick up your audio guide, children's pack or What's On programme, then discover the world through objects like the Aztec mosaics, the Rosetta Stone, El Anatsui's African textiles or the colossal Ramesses II. And if you want a more intimate look, a fantastic evening meal or some world cinema, come late - every Thursday and Friday.

Times Open all year, Gallery: 10-5.30 selected galleries open late Thu-Fri until 8.30. Great Court: Sun-Wed 9-6, Thu-Sat 9am-11pm. Closed Good Fri, 24-26 Dec & 1 Jan.* **Facilities** Ⓟ ☕ 🍽 licensed ⛩ (indoor) toilets for disabled ♿ (parking by arrangement) shop ⊗

The Cartoon Museum — 2 FOR 1

35 Little Russell St WC1A 2HH
☎ 020 7580 8155 📠 020 7631 0793
e-mail: info@cartoonmuseum.org
web: www.cartoonmuseum.org
dir: left off New Oxford St into Museum St, then left into Little Russell St

The main galleries display over 200 original cartoons, comics, cartoon strips and caricatures by many of the greatest and funniest of British cartoonists past and present. There is also a programme of temporary exhibitions which change regularly.

Times Open all year Tue-Sat 10.30-5.30, Sun 12-5.30. Closed 25 Dec-3 Jan **Fees** £5.50 (ch under 18 free, concessions £4, students with ID £3), Art fund members free* **Facilities** Ⓟ ♿ (partly accessible) (only ground floor acessible to wheelchairs) toilets for disabled (hearing loop, large print labels) shop ⊗

ENGLAND

WC1 *continued*

The Charles Dickens Museum London

48 Doughty St WC1N 2LX
☎ 020 7405 2127 ▤ 020 7831 5175
e-mail: info@dickensmuseum.com
web: www.dickensmuseum.com
dir: Underground - Russell Square or Chancery Lane

Charles Dickens lived in Doughty Street in his twenties and it was here he worked on his first full-length novel, *The Pickwick Papers*, and later *Oliver Twist* and *Nicholas Nickleby*. Pages of the original manuscripts are on display, together with valuable first editions, his marriage licence and many other personal mementoes.

Times Open all year, Mon-Sat 10-5, Sun 11-5.* **Facilities** Ⓟ shop ⊛

Petrie Museum of Egyptian Archaeology FREE

Malet Place, Univerity College London WC1E 6BT
☎ 020 7679 2884 ▤ 020 7679 2886
e-mail: petrie.museum@ucl.ac.uk
web: www.petrie.ucl.ac.uk
dir: on 1st floor of the D M S Watson building, in Malet Place, off Torrington Place, UCL Main Campus

One of the largest and most inspiring collections of Egyptian archaeology anywhere in the world. The displays illustrate life in the Nile Valley from prehistory, through the era of the Pharoahs to Roman and Islamic times. Especially noted for its collection of the personal items that illustrate life and death in Ancient Egypt, including the world's earliest surviving dress (c 2800BC).

Times Open all year, Tue-Sat 1-5. Closed for 1 wk at Xmas & Etr. **Facilities** ♿ (partly accessible) (objects on rear staircase which make it inaccessible to wheelchairs) toilets for disabled (wheelchair lift) shop ⊛

WC2

Benjamin Franklin House

36 Craven St WC2N 5NF
☎ 020 7839 2006
e-mail: info@benjaminfranklinhouse.org
web: www.benjaminfranklinhouse.org
dir: Between Charing Cross & Embankment

The house is not only a museum, but an educational facility as well. Between 1757 and 1775 Dr Benjamin Franklin - scientist, diplomat, philosopher and inventor lived here. The Historical Experience Show presents the excitement and uncertainty of Franklin's London years.

Times Open all year, Wed-Sun, shows at 12, 1, 2 & 3.15 & 6.15. Closed Xmas & BHs.* **Facilities** shop ⊛

The Courtauld Gallery 2 FOR 1

Somerset House, Strand WC2R 0RN
☎ 020 7848 2526 ▤ 020 7848 2589
e-mail: galleryinfo@courtauld.ac.uk
web: www.courtauld.ac.uk
dir: Underground - Temple, Embankment, Covent Garden & Charing Cross

Famous for its Impressionist and Post-impressionist masterpieces as well as outstanding earlier paintings and drawings, The Courtauld Gallery is one of the finest small museums in the world. Ranging from Botticelli, Cranach and Rubens to Monet, Gauguin and Van Gogh, this magnificent collection is displayed in the elegant 18th-century setting of Somerset House. World-famous paintings include Monet's *Bar at the Folies-Bergere*, Van Gogh's *Self Portrait with Bandaged Ear* and Renoir's *La Loge*. In addition, The Courtauld Gallery offers a highly acclaimed programme of temporary exhibitions.

Times Open all year, daily 10-6 (last admission 5.30). 24 Dec 10-4. Closed 25-26 Dec. See website for late night openings **Fees** £6 (concessions £4.50). Free Mon 10-2 (ex BHs). Under 18's, full time UK students, registered unwaged, staff of UK universities, Friends of The Courtauld & Helper for disabled visitors free **Facilities** Ⓟ ☕ 🍽 licensed ♿ (fully accessible) toilets for disabled (lift, disabled parking by arrangement call 020 7845 4600) shop ⊛

Hunterian Museum at The Royal College of Surgeons 2 FOR 1 FREE

35-43 Lincoln's Inn Fields WC2A 3PE
☎ 020 7869 6560 ▤ 020 7869 6564
e-mail: museums@rcseng.ac.uk
web: www.rcseng.ac.uk
dir: Underground - Holborn

The Hunterian Museum at the Royal College of Surgeons houses over 3000 anatomical and pathological preparations collected by the surgeon John Hunter (1728-1793). New interpretive displays explore Hunter's life and work, the history of the Hunterian Museum and the College, and the development of surgery from the 18th century to the present. The MacRae Gallery provides a dedicated space for learning based on the museum's reserve collections. The museum also stages a changing programme of temporary exhibitions, lectures and other public events on themes related to the history and current practice of surgery. The 2 for 1 offer can be used for the audio commentaries available.

Times Open all year, Tue-Sat 10-5. Closed Good Fri, Etr Sat, Xmas & New Year. Refer to website for precise dates **Facilities** Ⓟ ☕ ♿ (fully accessible) toilets for disabled (descriptive tours by arrangement) shop ⊛

London Transport Museum 2 FOR 1

The Piazza, Covent Garden WC2E 7BB
☎ 020 7379 6344 & 7565 7299 📠 020 7565 7250
e-mail: enquiry@ltmuseum.co.uk
web: www.ltmuseum.co.uk
dir: Underground - Covent Garden, Leicester Sq, Holborn or Charing Cross

Situated in the old Victorian flower market, London Transport Museum tells the story of the development of London, its transport system and how it shaped the lives of people living and working in the Capital. One of the world's best collections of graphic art and design is showcased in the 'Design for Travel' gallery including Harry Beck's famous Underground map, iconic transport posters, architecture and the story of a pioneering corporate identity. The museum also features past and present public transport including the Routemaster bus and the world's first Underground steam train.

Times Open all year Sat-Thu 10-6, Fri 11-6 (last admission 5.15). See website for Xmas & New Year opening times* **Fees** With voluntary Gift Aid donation: £10 (under 16 free, pen £8, concessions £6)* **Facilities** Ⓟ ☕ 🛋 (indoor) ♿ (fully accessible) toilets for disabled (lift & ramps) shop ⊛

National Gallery

Trafalgar Square WC2N 5DN
☎ 020 7747 2885 📠 020 7747 2423
e-mail: information@ng-london.org.uk
web: www.nationalgallery.org.uk
dir: Underground - Charing Cross, Leicester Square, Embankment & Piccadilly Circus. Rail - Charing Cross. Located on N side of Trafalgar Sq

All the great periods of Western European painting from the Middle Ages to the early 20th century are represented here. Artists on display include Leonardo da Vinci, Rembrandt, Titian, Caravaggio, Turner, Monet and Van Gogh. Major exhibitions and events throughout the year.

Times Open all year, daily 10-6, (Fri until 9). Special exhibitions open normal gallery times. Closed 24-26 Dec & 1 Jan **Fees** Free. Admission charged for some major exhibitions **Facilities** Ⓟ ☕ 🍴 licensed ♿ (fully accessible) toilets for disabled (w/chairs, induction loop, lift, deaf/blind tours/events) shop ⊛

National Portrait Gallery

St Martin's Place WC2H 0HE
☎ 020 7306 0055 📠 020 7306 0056
web: www.npg.org.uk
dir: Underground - Charing Cross, Leicester Square. Buses to Trafalgar Square

The National Portrait Gallery is home to the largest collection of portraiture in the world featuring famous British men and woman who have created history from the Middle Ages until the present day. Over 1000 portraits are on display across three floors from Henry VIII and Florence Nightingale to The Beatles and HM The Queen. If you want to rest your weary feet, visit the fabulous Portrait Restaurant on the top floor with roof-top views across London. Special events take place throughout the year, see website for details.

Times Open all year, Mon-Wed & Sat-Sun 10-6, Thu-Fri 10-9. Closed Good Fri, 24-26 Dec & 1 Jan. Gallery closure commences 10 mins prior to stated time* **Fees** Free ex special exhibitions **Facilities** Ⓟ ☕ 🍴 licensed ♿ (fully accessible) toilets for disabled (stairclimber, touch tours, audio guide, print captions) shop ⊛

Sir John Soane's Museum

13 Lincoln's Inn Fields WC2A 3BP
☎ 020 7440 4279 📠 020 7831 3957
e-mail: sbhatti@soane.org.uk
web: www.soane.org
dir: Underground - Holborn

Sir John Soane was responsible for some of the most splendid architecture in London, and his house, built in 1812, contains his collections of antiquities, sculpture, paintings, drawings and books. Amongst his treasures are the Rake's Progess, the Election series of paintings by Hogarth and the Sarcophagus of Seti I.

Times Open all year, Tue-Sat 10-5. Also first Tue of month 6-9pm. Closed BH, Good Fri & 24 Dec. Lecture tour Sat 11am (limited no of tickets sold from 10.30)* **Fees** Free entry, donations welcome **Facilities** Ⓟ ♿ (partly accessible) (phone 020 7440 4263 for details) (wheelchair available) shop ⊛

ENGLAND

LONDON, GREATER

BARNET Map 4 TQ29

Museum of Domestic Design & Architecture

Middlesex University, Cat Hill EN4 8HT
☎ 020 8411 5244 020 8411 6639
e-mail: moda@mdx.ac.uk
web: www.moda.mdx.ac.uk
dir: from M25, junct 24 signed A111 Cockfosters to Cat Hill rdbt, straight over onto Chase side. Entrance 1st right opposite Chicken Shed Theatre on Cat Hill Campus

MoDA is a museum of the history of the home. It holds one of the world's most comprehensive collections of decorative design for the period 1870 to 1960, and is a rich source of information on how people decorated and lived in their homes. MoDA has two galleries, a lecture theatre for study days, a seminar room with practical workshops for both adults and children, and a study room which gives visitors access to the collections.

Times Open all year, Tue-Sat 10-5, Sun 2-5. Closed Mon, Etr, Xmas & New Year (the museum will be relocating in summer 2011, see website for details)* **Fees** Free entrance. Charges for study days, workshop & group tours* **Facilities** (fully accessible) toilets for disabled (induction loop fitted in lecture theatre & at reception) shop

BEXLEY Map 5 TQ47

Hall Place and Gardens

Bourne Rd DA5 1PQ
☎ 01322 526574 & 621236 01322 522921
e-mail: info@hallplace.org.uk
web: www.hallplace.org.uk
dir: A2 Black Prince interchange 5m from M25 junct 2 towards London

Hall Place is an attractive Grade I listed mansion of chequered flint and brick, with wonderful gardens. It was built during the reign of Henry VIII and extended during the 17th century. It sits in 65 hectares of gardens which boast a stunning topiary lawn including the Queen's Beasts, planted to mark the Coronation of Queen Elizabeth II. An extensive restoration has made it possible for the public to see the first floor rooms for the first time. New displays, galleries and visitor centre with riverside tea room have added to the visitor enjoyment.

Times Open all year: House, Mon-Sat 10-5, Sun 11-5. Garden, daily 9am-dusk. Please contact for current opening times*
Fees Entry free, but a charge may be made for special events
Facilities licensed (outdoor) (fully accessible) toilets for disabled (lift, ramps) shop

BEXLEYHEATH Map 5 TQ47

Danson House **2 FOR 1**

Danson Park, Danson Rd DA6 8HL
☎ 020 8303 6699 020 8304 6641
e-mail: info@dansonhouse.org.uk
web: www.dansonhouse.org.uk
dir: From Danson interchange of the A2 via Danson Rd (A221) located in Danson Park

Danson House is a Palladian villa that was completed in 1766 to designs by Sir Robert Taylor for his client, Sir John Boyd, whose family fortune was founded on the West Indian sugar trade. The house was built for Boyd's young bride, Catherine Chapone, and so the interiors and layout reflect themes of love and enjoyment. The principal floor has a cycle of 17 original wall paintings, and there is a restored George England organ in the library.

Times Open Apr-Oct, Wed-Thu, Sun & BH Mon (Tue-Thu & Sun Jun-Aug) 11-5 (last admission 4.15) **Fees** £6 (concessions £5). English Heritage Members £4.50 **Facilities** licensed (outdoor) (fully accessible) toilets for disabled (lifts) shop

Red House

Red House Ln DA6 8JF
☎ 020 8304 9878 020 8303 6359
e-mail: red.house@nationaltrust.org.uk
web: www.nationaltrust.org.uk/redhouse
dir: Exit A2 at Danson Interchange & follow A221 to Bexleyheath. Right at Bean Rd, left onto Red House Lane

Commissioned by William Morris in 1859 and designed by Philip Webb, Red House is of enormous international significance in the history of domestic architecture and garden design. The building is constructed of warm red brick, under a steep red-tiled roof, with an emphasis on natural materials and a strong gothic influence. The garden was designed to 'clothe' the house with a series of subdivided areas which still exist. Inside, the house retains many of the original features and fixed items of furniture designed by Morris and Webb.

Times Open Mar-Oct, Wed-Sun 11-4.45: Nov-Dec Fri-Sun 11-4.45. Last entry 4.15 **Fees** £7.20 (ch 5-15 £3.60). Family ticket (2ad & 3ch) £18. Group price £6.20 **Facilities** Ⓟ ☕ ⛩ (outdoor) ♿ (partly accessible) (upper floor not accessible, ramp to allow access over small step on ground floor) shop ⊗ ✿

BRENTFORD Map 4 TQ17

Kew Bridge Steam Museum

Green Dragon Ln TW8 0EN
☎ 020 8568 4757 📠 020 8569 9978
e-mail: info@kbsm.org
web: www.kbsm.org
dir: Underground - Kew Gardens, District line then 391 bus. Museum 100yds from N side of Kew Bridge, on A315

This Victorian pumping station has steam engines and six beam engines, five of which are working and one of which is the largest in the world. The Grand Junction 90 inch engine is over 40 feet high, and weighs around 250 tons. A diesel house and waterwheel can also be seen along with London's only steam narrow-gauge railway, which operates every Sunday (Mar-Nov). The Water for Life Gallery tells the story of London's water supply from Pre-Roman times.

Times Open Tue-Sun, Jan-18 Dec & BH (excl Good Fri), 11-4. Closed 6-7 Oct **Fees** Multi-entry for one year £9.50 (ch free, concessions £8.50)* **Facilities** Ⓟ Ⓟ ☕ ⛩ (indoor & outdoor) ♿ (partly accessible) (access restricted to ground floor) toilets for disabled (wheelchairs, large print guide, lifts) shop ⊗

The Musical Museum **2 FOR 1**

399 High St TW8 0DU
☎ 020 8560 8108 📠 020 8847 9383
e-mail: fred.stone@musicalmuseum.co.uk
web: www.musicalmuseum.co.uk
dir: Underground - Gunnersbury, near Kew Bridge. Railway - Kew Bridge

This museum takes the visitor back to a bygone age to hear and see a marvellous working collection of automatic musical instruments from small musical boxes to a Mighty Wurlitzer theatre organ. Working demonstrations at weekends and for pre-booked groups.

Times Open all year, Tue-Sun (& most BH Mons), 11-5.30 (last admission 4.30)* **Fees** £8 (accompanied ch under 16 free, concessions £6.50)* **Facilities** Ⓟ Ⓟ ☕ ♿ (fully accessible) toilets for disabled shop ⊗

CHESSINGTON Map 4 TQ16

Chessington World of Adventures

Leatherhead Rd KT9 2NE
☎ 0871 663 4477
web: www.chessington.com
dir: M25 junct 9/10, on A243

One of Britain's premiere theme parks. Explore the ancient ruins of Wild Asia, a new and mythical land where a ride on the spinning disc ride Kobra is a must. Visit Lorikeet Lagoon to see exotic birds and journey on to Wanyama Village and African Reserve where Grevy's zebras and the rare Scimitar horned oryx roam free. Soar on the Vampire roller coaster through the depths of Transylvania, take a fiery spin round Dragon's Fury or discover the mystery of Tomb Blaster in Forbidden Kingdom. Take a walk on the wild side with tigers, lions and gorillas in the Trail of the Kings and come face to face with sharks and curious stingrays in the park's very own Sea Life Centre and safari themed hotel.

Times Open 27 Mar-1 Nov, times vary (main season). Zoo only days 14-16, 21-23, 28-30 Sep; 5-7, 12-14 Oct; wknds from 6 Nov & daily from 11-26. Closed 25 Dec* **Fees** £36 (ch under 12 £26, under 1 metre free). Family ticket (2ad+1ch or 1ad+2ch) £75; (2ad+2ch or 1ad+3ch) £98; (2ad+3ch or 1ad+4ch) £120 (Discounts apply when booking online)* **Facilities** Ⓟ ☕ 🍽 licensed ⛩ (outdoor) ♿ (partly accessible) toilets for disabled (some rides not accessible, guide available) shop ⊗

CHISLEHURST Map 5 TQ47

Chislehurst Caves **2 FOR 1**

Old Hill BR7 5NL
☎ 020 8467 3264 📠 020 8295 0407
e-mail: enquiries@chislehurstcaves.co.uk
web: www.chislehurstcaves.co.uk
dir: off A222 near Chislehurst railway stn. Turn into station approach, then right & right again into Caveside Close

Miles of mystery and history beneath your feet. Grab a lantern and get ready for an amazing adventure. Visit the caves and your whole family can travel back in time as you explore the maze of passageways dug through the chalk deep beneath Chislehurst. Accompanied by an experienced guide on a 45-minute tour you'll see the tunnels made famous as a shelter during the Second World War, visit the cave's church, druid altar, the haunted pool and much more.

Times Open all year, Wed-Sun, 10-4. Daily during local school hols (incl half terms). Closed Xmas **Fees** £5 (ch & pen £3) **Facilities** Ⓟ ☕ 🍽 licensed ⛩ (outdoor) ♿ (partly accessible) (uneven floors in the caves may cause some difficulties) toilets for disabled shop ⊗

ENGLAND

ESHER Map 4 TQ16

Claremont Landscape Garden

Portsmouth Rd KT10 9JG
☎ 01372 467806 📠 01372 476420
e-mail: claremont@nationaltrust.org.uk
web: www.nationaltrust.org.uk/main/w-claremontlandscapegarden
dir: 1m S of Esher on A307

Laid out by Vanbrugh and Bridgeman before 1720, extended and naturalised by Kent, this is one of the earliest surviving examples of an English landscaped garden. Its 50 acres include a lake with an island pavilion, a grotto, a turf amphitheatre and a new children's play area. Full programme of events throughout the year.

Times Open all year, daily, Apr-Oct, 10-6 including BH Mons; Nov-30 Jan, Tue-Sun 10-4; Feb-Mar, Tue-Sun 10-5 **Fees** With voluntary Gift Aid donation 10% or more: £6.40 (ch £3.20). Family ticket £16. Visitors can choose to pay the standard admission price displayed* **Facilities** Ⓟ Ⓟ ☕ ♿ (partly accessible) (some steep paths) toilets for disabled (wheelchairs available, Braille guide) shop ⊗ ✿

HAM Map 4 TQ17

Ham House & Garden

Ham St TW10 7RS
☎ 020 8940 1951 📠 020 8940 1950
e-mail: hamhouse@nationaltrust.org.uk
web: www.nationaltrust.org.uk/hamhouse
dir: W of A307, between Kingston & Richmond

Ham House is a fine example of 17th-century fashion and power. Built in 1610 and decorated by William Murray before the English Civil War, the house was enlarged in the 1670s by his daughter, the Duchess of Lauderdale, when it was at the heart of Restoration court life and intrigue. It was then occupied by the same family until 1948. The formal garden is significant for its survival in an area known as the cradle of the English Landscape Movement. The intriguing outbuildings include an orangery, an ice house, a still house (a 17th-century equivalent of an in-house pharmacy), and a dairy with unusual cast-iron "cow's legs". Rich in history and atmosphere Ham was built to impress in its day and continues to do so today.

Times House 12 Feb-Mar, Sat-Thu 11.30-3.30; 2 Apr-30 Oct, Sat-Thu 12-4 (open Good Fri); 31 Oct-29 Nov, Sat-Tue 11.30-3. Garden, shop, cafe open daily, Jan-11 Feb, 11-4; 12 Feb-30 Oct, 11-5; 31 Oct-18 Dec, 11-4. Special Christmas opening times see website for details (last admission 30mins before closing time) **Fees** Gift aid prices. House & Garden 12 Feb-30 Oct, £10.90 (ch £6.05). Family £27.90. Garden £3.65 (ch £2.45). Family £9.75; 31 Oct-29 Nov, £9.10 (ch £4.85). Family £23.05. Garden only, Jan-11 Feb & 31 Oct-16 Dec (ex 3,4,10,11 Dec), £1.85 (ch £1.25). Family £4.45. Groups £8.40 (£14.70 outside normal hours) **Facilities** Ⓟ Ⓟ ☕ ⛩ (outdoor) ♿ (partly accessible) (onsite lift suitable for most manual wheelchairs) toilets for disabled (Braille guide, induction loop, lift, mobility vehicle) shop ⊗ ✿

HAMPTON COURT Map 4 TQ16

Hampton Court Palace

KT8 9AU
☎ 0870 752 7777 📠 020 8781 9669
e-mail: hamptoncourt@hrp.org.uk
web: www.hrp.org.uk
dir: A3 to Hook underpass then A309. Train from Waterloo - Hampton Court, 2mins walk from station

Step into a living Tudor world at Henry VIII's favourite palace, celebrating the 500th anniversary of his accession to the throne. Join Henry as his Tudor Kitchens fire up to prepare a king's feast and be a guest at his royal wedding, to his 6th wife! Creep along the eerie Haunted Gallery, relax in the acres of beautiful gardens running alongside the River Thames, and lose yourself in the world famous Maze.

Times Open all year, palace & maze 29 Mar-24 Oct, daily 10-6 (last ticket sold at 5, last entry into maze 5.15) 25 Oct-27 Mar, daily 10-4.30 (last ticket sold at 3.30, last entry into maze 3.45). Closed 24-26 Dec.* **Facilities** Ⓟ Ⓟ ☕ 🍽 licensed ⛩ ♿ (fully accessible) toilets for disabled (lifts, buggies for gardens, wheelchairs, wardens, Braille) shop ⊗

ISLEWORTH Map 4 TQ17

Syon House

TW8 8JF
☎ 020 8560 0882 & 0883 📠 020 8568 0936
e-mail: info@syonpark.co.uk
web: www.syonpark.co.uk
dir: A310 Twickenham road into Park Rd

Set in 200 acres of parkland, Syon House is the London home of the Duke of Northumberland, whose family have lived here since the late 16th century. During the second half of the 18th century the first Duke of Northumberland engaged Robert Adam to remodel the interior and 'Capability' Brown to landscape the grounds. Adam was also responsible for the furniture and decorations, and the result is particularly spectacular in the superbly coloured Ante-Room and Long Gallery.

Times Open 19 Apr-Oct, Wed-Thu, Sun & BH 11-5 (last ticket 4.15)* **Facilities** 🅟 ☕ ♿ (partly accessible) toilets for disabled (stairclimber available) shop 🚫🐕

Syon Park

TW9 8JF
☎ 020 8560 0882 📠 020 8568 0936
e-mail: info@syonpark.co.uk
web: www.syonpark.co.uk
dir: A310 Twickenham road into Park Rd

Contained within the 40 acres that make up Syon Park Gardens is one of the inspirations for the Crystal Palace at the Great Exhibition of 1851: a vast crescent of metal and glass, the first construction of its kind in the world and known as the Great Conservatory. Although the horticultural reputation of Syon Park goes back to the 16th century, its beauty today is thanks to the master of landscape design, 'Capability' Brown.

Times Open all year, Mar-Oct daily, 10.30-5.30; (4pm Nov-Feb, wknds & 1 Jan)* **Facilities** 🅟 ☕ toilets for disabled shop 🚫🐕

KEW Map 4 TQ17

Kew Gardens (Royal Botanic Gardens)

TW9 3AB
☎ 020 8332 5655 📠 020 8332 5197
e-mail: info@kew.org
web: www.kew.org
dir: 1m from M4 on South Circular (A205)

Kew Gardens is a paradise throughout the seasons. Lose yourself in the magnificent glasshouses and discover plants from the world's deserts, mountains and oceans. Wide-open spaces, stunning vistas, listed buildings and wildlife contribute to the Gardens' unique atmosphere. As well as being famous for its beautiful gardens, Kew is world renowned for its contribution to botanical and horticultural science.

Times Open all year, Gardens daily 9.30. Closing times vary (seasonal, phone to verify). Closed 24-25 Dec* **Facilities** 🅟 Ⓟ ☕ 🍴 licensed ♿ (partly accessible) (access restricted in Palm House basement & galleries, Temperate House & steps to upper level in the Princess of Wales Conservatory) toilets for disabled (large print map, w/chair, 16 seat bus tour ring 020 8332 5643) shop 🚫🐕

Kew Palace

Royal Botanic Gardens TW9 3AB
☎ 0870 751 5179
e-mail: kewpalace@hrp.org.uk
web: www.hrp.org.uk
dir: Underground - Kew Bridge

A fairly modest red-brick building, built in the Dutch style with gables, Kew Palace was built in 1631 and used until 1818 when Queen Charlotte died. Visitors can see artefacts that belonged to George III and his family, and gain access to the second floor, which has never before been open to the public. There are also rooms on the second floor, faithfully recreated with décor and furnishings as George III and his family would have known them in the early 1800s.

Times Open 10 Apr-27 Sep, Mon 11-5, Tue-Sun 10-5 (last admission 4.15)* **Facilities** 🅟 Ⓟ ♿ (fully accessible) toilets for disabled shop 🚫🐕

The National Archives FREE

Bessant Dr TW9 4DU
☎ 020 8876 3444
web: www.nationalarchives.gov.uk
dir: Underground - Kew Gardens or South circular A205, parking must be pre-purchased via website

The National Archives houses one of the finest, most complete archives in Europe, comprising the records of the central government and law courts from the Norman Conquest to the present century. It is a mine of information and includes the Domesday Book.

Times Open all year, Tue & Thu, 9-7; Wed, Fri & Sat, 9-5. Closed PH wknds **Facilities** 🅟 Ⓟ ☕ 🧺 (outdoor) ♿ (fully accessible) toilets for disabled (hearing loops & large print text in museum) shop 🚫🐕

Queen Charlotte's Cottage

Royal Botanic Gardens TW9 3AB
☎ 0870 751 5175
web: www.hrp.org.uk
dir: Underground - Kew Gardens

Typical of the fashionable rustic style popular with the gentry in the 18th century, the cottage was built for George III and Queen Charlotte as a home for their menagerie of exotic pets, as well as a picnic spot and summer house.

Times Open wknds Jul & Aug.* **Facilities** Ⓟ 🚫🐕

MORDEN Map 5 TQ26

Morden Hall Park FREE

Morden Hall Rd SM4 5JD
☎ 020 8545 6850
e-mail: mordenhallpark@nationaltrust.org.uk
web: www.nationaltrust.org.uk/main/w-mordenhallpark-2
dir: A298 (Bushey Rd), right at 2nd lights into Martin Way. Morden Hall signed

A green oasis in the heart of South West London. A former deer park, with a network of waterways including meadow, wetland and woodland habitats. Also discover the picturesque rose garden with over 2000 roses, fragrant from May to September.

Times Open all year, daily 8-6* **Facilities** 🅟 ☕ 🍴 licensed 🧺 (outdoor) ♿ (partly accessible) (access to natural areas of the park may be difficult in some conditions) toilets for disabled (wheelchair, Braille guides, large handled cutlery) shop 🌿

ENGLAND

OSTERLEY Map 4 TQ17

Osterley Park and House

Jersey Rd TW7 4RB
☎ 020 8232 5050 020 8232 5080
e-mail: osterley@nationaltrust.org.uk
web: www.nationaltrust.org.uk/main/w-osterleypark
dir: signed from A4. Underground - Osterley

This spectacular mansion and its surrounding gardens, park and farmland is one of the last surviving country estates in London. Transformed in the late 18th century for the wealthy Child family by the architect Robert Adam, the house and garden were designed for entertaining and impressing this banking family's friends and clients. With a series of stunning show rooms affording views over extensive parkland, Osterley continues to impress visitors today. The gardens are currently being restored to their former 18th-century splendour and there are pleasant walks around the park as well as wide open green spaces for families to enjoy. Look out for Osterley fun day, an annual event held each summer, entry free.

Times House 3 Mar-Oct, Wed-Sun & BHs 12-4.30; 4-19 Dec 12-2.30. Garden 3 Mar-Oct, Wed-Sun & BHs 11-5. Park & car park, daily until 27 Mar 8-6; 28 Mar-30 Oct 8-7.30; 31 Oct onwards 8-6 (car park closed 25-26 Dec & 1 Jan)* **Fees** House & Garden £8.80 (ch £4.40). Family ticket £22. Group 15+(booked in advance) £7.50. Garden only £3.85 (ch £1.95, under 5 free). Car park £3.50, park free* **Facilities** (outdoor) (partly accessible) (house-steps to principle floor, please call for full details) toilets for disabled (Braille guide, wheelchairs, electric carts, stair climber) shop

TWICKENHAM Map 4 TQ17

Marble Hill House

Richmond Rd TW1 2NL
☎ 020 8892 5115 020 8607 9976
web: www.english-heritage.org.uk

A magnificent Thames-side Palladian villa built for Henrietta Howard, mistress of King George II, set in 66 acres of riverside parklands.

Times Open Apr-Oct, Sat 10-2; Sun & BHs 10-5. Guided tours at noon on Sat, 11 & 2.30 on Sun; Nov-Mar available for group tours - please call for details **Fees** £5 (ch £2.50, concessions £4.30). Family £12.50. Prices and opening times are subject to change in March 2011. Please call 0870 333 1181 for the most up to date prices and opening times when planning your visit **Facilities** licensed toilets for disabled shop

Orleans House Gallery FREE

Riverside TW1 3DJ
☎ 020 8831 6000 020 8744 0501
e-mail: m.denovellis@richmond.gov.uk
web: www.richmond.gov.uk
dir: Richmond road (A305), Orleans Rd is on right just past Orleans Park School

Stroll beside the Thames and through the woodland gardens of Orleans House, where you will find stunning 18th-century interior design and an excellent public art gallery. Visitors of all ages can try out their own artistic talents in pre-booked workshops, and wide-ranging temporary exhibitions are held throughout the year - please telephone for details.

Times Open all year, Apr-Sep Tue-Sat 1-5.30, Sun & BH 2-5.30; Oct-Mar, Tue-Sat 1-4.30, Sun & BH 2-4.30* **Facilities** (partly accessible) toilets for disabled (handling objects & large print labels for some exhibitions) shop

World Rugby Museum & Twickenham Stadium Tours

Twickenham Stadium, Rugby Rd TW1 1DZ
☎ 020 8891 8877 & 8831 6685 020 8892 2817
e-mail: museum@rfu.com
web: www.rfu.com/museum/
dir: A316, follow signs to Twickenham Stadium

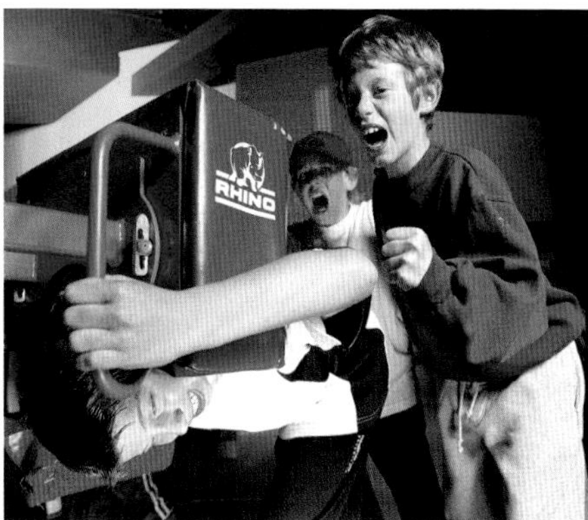

Combine a behind-the-scenes guided tour of the world's most famous rugby stadium with a visit to the World Rugby Museum. The tour includes breathtaking views from the top of the Stand, a visit to the England dressing room and ends by walking through the players tunnel to pitch side. The multi-media museum appeals to enthusiasts of all ages and charts the history and world-wide growth of rugby. You can also test your skills on the scrum machine.

Times Open all year, Tue-Sat 10-5, Sun 11-5 (last admission 30 mins before close). Closed post Twickenham match days, Etr Sun, 24-26 Dec & 1 Jan. On match days museum only available to match ticket holders. Please pre book all tours* **Fees** Museum & Tour £14 (concessions £8). Family (2ad+up to 3ch) £40* **Facilities** licensed (fully accessible) toilets for disabled shop

MERSEYSIDE

The Liver Building, Liverpool

ENGLAND

BIRKENHEAD Map 7 SJ38

U-Boat Story 2 FOR 1

Woodside Ferry Terminal, Woodside CH41 6DU
☎ 0151 330 1000 & 330 1444
web: www.u-boatstory.co.uk
dir: M53 junct 1, take A5139 signed docks, right at A554 rdbt, or A41 Birkenhead. Follow signs for Woodside

Visit the real life story of the U-534 U-boat, raised from the seabed in 1993 and lovingly restored. With its amazing interior exhibited in four sections through glass viewing panels, discover the story of the U-boat who refused to surrender and was sunk in 1945. Experience a unique insight into life aboard a submarine during wartime and enjoy well preserved artefacts including a rare Enigma machine. Audiovisual tours, interactive exhibits and an interpretation centre complete this unique experience.

Times Open all year, daily 10.30-5.30 (last admission 5). Closed 25-26 Dec & 1 Jan* **Fees** £5 (ch 5+ £3, under 5 free, concessions £4). Family ticket (2ad+3ch) £15* **Facilities** (fully accessible) toilets for disabled shop

LIVERPOOL Map 7 SJ39

The Beatles' Childhood Homes - 20 Forthlin Road

L24 1YP
☎ 0844 8004791
e-mail: 20forthlinroad@nationaltrust.org.uk
web: www.nationaltrust.org.uk/main/w-the_beatles.htm
dir: No direct access by car or on foot. Visits are by combined minibus tour only with Mendips, childhood home of John Lennon

The Beatles' Childhood Homes at 20 Forthlin Road and Mendips are part of a combined minibus tour. 20 Forthlin Road is the former home of the McCartney family, a 1950s terraced house where the Beatles met, rehearsed and wrote many of their earliest songs. Displays include contemporary photographs by Michael McCartney and early Beatles memorabilia.

Times Open 27 Feb-28 Nov, Wed-Sun. Times vary* **Fees** Joint ticket 20 Forthlin Road & Mendips £16.80 (ch £3.15, NT members £7.90)* **Facilities** (partly accessible) toilets for disabled

The Beatles' Childhood Homes - Mendips

251 Menlove Av, Woolton L25 7SA
☎ 0151 427 7231 & 0844 800 4791
e-mail: mendips@nationaltrust.org.uk
web: www.nationaltrust.org.uk/beatles
dir: No direct access by car or on foot. Visits are by combined minibus tour only with 20 Forthlin Road, childhood home of Sir Paul McCartney

Visit Mendips and 20 Forthlin Road as part of a combined minibus tour. The childhood home of John Lennon, Mendips is a 1930s semi where his passion for music began and where some of his early songs were written. The house evokes the time he spent here during his formative years.

Times Open 28 Feb-15 Mar & 7-29 Nov, Wed-Sun. Times vary **Fees** Joint ticket Mendips & 20 Forthlin Road £16.80 (ch £3.15, NT members £7.90)* **Facilities** (partly accessible) toilets for disabled

The Beatles Story

Britannia Pavilion, Albert Dock L3 4AD
☎ 0151 709 1963 Fax 0151 203 3089
e-mail: info@beatlesstory.com
web: www.beatlesstory.com
dir: follow signs to Albert Dock. Located outside Britannia Pavilion, next to Premier Inn

Located within Liverpool's historic Albert Dock, the Beatles Story is a unique visitor attraction that transports you on an enlightening and atmospheric journey into the life, times, culture and music of The Beatles.

Times Open all year, daily Oct-Mar 10-6; Apr-Sep 9-7
Fees £12.95 (ch 5-16 yrs £6.50 & concessions £8.50)
Facilities (fully accessible) toilets for disabled (hearing loop, large print guide) shop

The Grand National Experience & Visitor Centre

Aintree Racecourse, Ormskirk Rd L9 5AS
☎ 0151 522 2927
e-mail: aintree@jockeyclubracecourses.com
web: www.aintree.co.uk
dir: Aintree Racecourse on A59 (Liverpool to Preston road) clearly signed

A fascinating look at Britain's most famous horserace, the Grand National. Visitors can sit in the jockeys' weighing-in chair, walk around the dressing rooms, visit the stables, watch video presentations, and view a gallery of paintings, photography and artefacts depicting the race.

Times Open late May-mid Oct, Tue-Fri 9-5 **Fees** £10*
Facilities licensed (outdoor) (fully accessible) toilets for disabled

International Slavery Museum FREE

Albert Dock L3 4AQ
☎ 0151 478 4499 Fax 0151 478 4590
web: www.liverpoolmuseums.org.uk
dir: enter Albert Dock from the Strand

2007 saw the bicentenary of the abolition of the slave trade in Britain, and this museum was opened at Albert Dock. It looks at the impact of the transatlantic slave trade and includes thought-provoking displays on issues such as freedom, identity, human rights, racial discrimination and cultural change.

Times Open all year, daily 10-5 & 24 Dec 10-2. Closed 25-26 Dec & 1 Jan. **Facilities** licensed (outdoor) (partly accessible) (restricted wheelchair access, no access to basement) toilets for disabled shop

Liverpool Cathedral

St James' Mount L1 7AZ
☎ 0151 709 6271 📠 0151 702 7292
e-mail: eryl.parry@liverpoolcathedral.org.uk
web: www.liverpoolcathedral.org.uk
dir: follow city centre signs 'Cathedrals'. St James' Mount is off Upper Duke St in S side of city centre, adjacent to 'Chinatown'

Although it appears at first sight to be as old as any other monumental cathedral in Britain, Liverpool Cathedral is in fact a 20th-century structure that was only completed in 1978. Its foundation stone was laid in 1904, and through two World Wars the building continued. It is the largest Anglican Cathedral in Europe, and has the largest pipe organ and the heaviest ringing peal of bells in the world. In addition to great views from the tower, the Cathedral now has an award-winning new visitor centre, the Great Space, with a film, audio tours and interactive stations. The Cathedral hosts a full calendar of family activities and cultural events.

Times Open all year, daily 8-6 (25 Dec 8-3)* **Facilities** Ⓟ Ⓟ ☕ 🍽 licensed ♿ (partly accessible) (Tower & Nave Bridge have steps) toilets for disabled (Braille leaflets, handrails, lift, induction loop) shop ㊗

Liverpool Football Club Museum and Stadium Tour

Anfield Rd L4 0TH
☎ 0151 260 6677 📠 0151 264 0149
e-mail: Stephen.done@liverpoolfc.tv
web: www.liverpoolfc.tv

Touch the famous "This is Anfield" sign as you walk down the tunnel to the sound of the crowd at the LFC museum and tour centre. Celebrate all things Liverpool, past and present. Bright displays and videos chart the history of one of England's most successful football clubs.

Times Open all year: Museum daily 10-5 (last admission 4). Closed 25-26 Dec. Match days 9 until last admission - 1hr before kick off. Museum & Tour - tours are run subject to daily demand. Advance booking is essential to avoid disappointment* **Facilities** Ⓟ Ⓟ 🍽 licensed toilets for disabled ♿ (lifts, ramps to all areas for wheelchairs) shop ㊗

Merseyside Maritime Museum FREE

Albert Dock L3 4AQ
☎ 0151 478 4499 📠 0151 478 4590
web: www.liverpoolmuseums.org.uk
dir: enter Albert Dock from the Strand

Discover the story behind one of the world's greatest ports and the people who used it. For many, Liverpool was a gateway to a new life in other countries. For others its importance to the slave trade had less happy consequences. From slavers to luxury liners, submarine hunters to passenger ferries, explore Liverpool's central role.

Times Open all year, daily 10-5 & 24 Dec 10-2. Closed 25-26 Dec & 1 Jan.* **Facilities** Ⓟ ☕ 🍽 licensed ⛩ (outdoor) toilets for disabled ♿ (lifts, wheelchairs, ramps, ex pilot boat & basement) shop ㊗

Metropolitan Cathedral of Christ the King

Mount Pleasant L3 5TQ
☎ 0151 709 9222 📠 0151 708 7274
e-mail: info@metcathedral.org.uk
web: www.liverpoolmetrocathedral.org.uk
dir: 10 mins walk from either Liverpool Lime St or Liverpool Central Railway Station. Cathedral well signed from city centre

A modern Roman Catholic cathedral which provides a focal point on the Liverpool skyline. The imposing structure of concrete ribs and coloured glass was designed by Sir Frederick Gibberd and consecrated in 1967. Monumental crypt of brick and granite by Sir Edwin Lutyens 1933. Numerous modern works of art.

Times Open all year, daily 8-6 (Sun 5 in winter). Crypt, Mon-Sat 10-4. **Fees** Free admission to cathedral, although donation of £3 requested. Crypt admission £3.* **Facilities** Ⓟ Ⓟ ☕ 🍽 licensed ♿ (fully accessible) toilets for disabled (lift, loop system) shop ㊗

Museum of Liverpool Life FREE

Pier Head L3 4AA
☎ 0151 478 4080 📠 0151 478 4090
dir: follow signs for Albert Dock, museum is on Pier Head side

The Museum of Liverpool Life celebrates the contribution of the people of Liverpool to national life. Recently expanded to include three new galleries, City Lives exploring the richness of Liverpool's cultural diversity, The River Room featuring life around the river Mersey and City Soldiers about the King's Regiment. Other galleries include Mersey Culture from *Brookside* to the Grand National, Making a Living and Demanding a Voice.

Times Open all year, daily 10-5. Closed from 2 on 24 Dec and all day 25-26 Dec & 1 Jan* **Facilities** Ⓟ Ⓟ ⛩ (indoor & outdoor) ♿ (partly accessible) toilets for disabled (wheelchairs, audio handsets, subtitles on video terminals) shop ㊗

National Conservation Centre FREE

Whitechapel L1 6HZ
☎ 0151 478 4999 📠 0151 478 4990
web: www.liverpoolmuseums.org.uk
dir: follow brown tourist signs to Whitechapel

Award-winning centre, the only one of its kind, gives the public an insight into the world of museum and gallery conservation. There is a regular changing exhibition programme.

Times Open all year, daily 10-5 & 24 Dec 10-2. Closed 25-26 Dec & 1 Jan **Facilities** Ⓟ Ⓟ ☕ ♿ (fully accessible) toilets for disabled (induction loop, support for visual impairments) shop ㊗

ENGLAND

LIVERPOOL *continued*

National Wildflower Centre **2 FOR 1**

Court Hey Park, Roby Rd L16 3NA
☎ 0151 738 1913 📠 0151 737 1820
e-mail: info@nwc.org.uk
web: www.nwc.org.uk
dir: M62 junct 5, take A5080 to rdbt. Exit into Roby Rd, entrance 0.5m on left

Set in a public park on the outskirts of Liverpool, the award-winning National Wildflower Centre promotes the creation of wildflower habitats around the country and provides educational materials, wildflower seeds and interactive facilities. The Centre has demonstration areas, children's activities, a working nursery, compost display and rooftop walk. There is a comprehensive programme of events through the summer. Special Events: Green Fayre in June, Knowsley Flower Show in August, Winter Celebration in December. 2011 marks the centre's 10th anniversary.

Times Open Mar-Aug, daily 10-5 (last admission 4) **Fees** £3.50 (ch & concessions £1.75). Family ticket (2ad+2ch) £9. Group discount tickets available & supporter packages **Facilities** P ☕ ⛩ (outdoor) ♿ (partly accessible) (90% of the centre accessible, lift to roof top walkway currently out of order) toilets for disabled (electric buggy & wheelchair available on pre-booking) shop ⊗

Sudley House **FREE**

Mossley Hill Rd L18 8BX
☎ 0151 724 3245
web: www.liverpoolmuseums.org.uk
dir: near Aigburth Station and Mossley Hill Station

Sudley, Liverpool's hidden gem, is unique, a Victorian merchant's house with an art collection displayed in its original setting. Works on show include paintings by Landseer and Turner, major pre-Raphaelite pictures and a group of 18th-century portraits by Gainsborough, Reynolds, Romney and Lawrence. Sudley houses an introductory display telling the history of the house, a Toy Zone (a display of dolls, toys and doll's house with a children's activities area), a display of items from the historic costume and fashion collection, and a new temporary exhibition gallery.

Times Open all year, daily 10-5 & 24 Dec 10-2. Closed 25-26 Dec & 1 Jan.* **Facilities** P ☕ ♿ (fully accessible) shop ⊗

Tate Liverpool

Albert Dock L3 4BB
☎ 0151 702 7400 & 7402 📠 0151 702 7401
e-mail: visiting.liverpool@tate.org.uk
web: www.tate.org.uk/liverpool/
dir: within walking distance of Liverpool Lime Street train station, on the Albert Dock. Follow the brown tourist signs from motorway

Tate Liverpool is one of the largest galleries of modern and contemporary art outside London and is housed in a converted warehouse in the historic Albert Dock. The gallery is home to the National Collection of Modern Art in the North, and has four floors displaying work selected from the Tate Collection, as well as special exhibitions which bring together artwork loaned from around the world.

Times Open all year Sep-May, Tue-Sun 10-5.50 (open BH Mon); Jun-Aug, daily 10-5.50. Closed Good Fri & 24-26 Dec **Fees** Admission free. Charge for special exhibitions, phone for details **Facilities** Ⓟ ☕ ♿ (fully accessible) toilets for disabled (wheelchairs, Braille leaflets, hearing loop, large print) shop ⊗

Walker Art Gallery **FREE**

William Brown St L3 8EL
☎ 0151 478 4199 📠 0151 478 4190
e-mail: thewalker@liverpoolmuseums.org.uk
web: www.liverpoolmuseums.org.uk
dir: city centre adjacent to St George's Hall & Lime St

The National Gallery of the North, this is one of the finest art galleries in Europe, housing an outstanding collection of British and European art from the 14th to the 20th century. Many visitors will already be familiar with some of the much-loved paintings in the gallery's permanent collection, including the tense Civil War scene *And When Did You Last See Your Father?* and the famous Tudor portraits of Henry VII and Elizabeth I. There are also temporary exhibitions and a programme of special events, please see the website for details.

Times Open all year, daily 10-5 & 24 Dec 10-2. Closed 25-26 Dec & 1 Jan **Facilities** P Ⓟ ☕ 🍴 licensed ♿ (fully accessible) toilets for disabled (prior notice appreciated, w/chair on request, parking) shop ⊗

World Museum Liverpool **FREE**

William Brown St L3 8EN
☎ 0151 478 4393 📠 0151 478 4350
web: www.liverpoolmuseums.org.uk
dir: in city centre next to St George's Hall and Lime St, follow brown signs

The World Museum Liverpool offers a journey of discovery from the oceans to the stars. Collections cover natural and physical sciences, ancient history and archaeology, and there are also frequently changing exhibitions, special events and other permanent attractions, such as the Bug House.

Times Open all year, daily 10-5 & 24 Dec 10-2. Closed 25-26 Dec & 1 Jan. **Facilities** P Ⓟ ☕ 🍴 licensed ⛩ (indoor) ♿ (fully accessible) toilets for disabled shop ⊗

ENGLAND

PORT SUNLIGHT Map 7 SJ38

Lady Lever Art Gallery

FREE

CH62 5EQ

☎ 0151 478 4136 📠 0151 478 4140

web: www.liverpoolmuseums.org.uk

dir: M53 junct 4 or from Liverpool/Birkenhead tunnel follow A41 towards Port Sunlight & follow brown heritage signs

The Lady Lever Art Gallery is one of the most beautiful galleries in the country and the perfect place to introduce younger members of the family to art. Home to the extensive personal collection of founder William Hesketh Lever, first Lord Leverhulme, this wonderful gallery is best known for its outstanding Victorian and pre-Raphaelite paintings by artists such as Leighton and Rossetti as well as other treasures just waiting to be discovered around every corner.

Times Open all year, daily 10-5 & 24 Dec 10-2. Closed 25-26 Dec & 1 Jan **Facilities** Ⓟ Ⓟ ☕ ⛩ (indoor & outdoor) ♿ (fully accessible) toilets for disabled (prior notice appreciated, wheelchair on request) shop ㊗

PRESCOT Map 7 SJ49

Knowsley Safari Park

L34 4AN

☎ 0151 430 9009 📠 0151 426 3677

e-mail: safari.park@knowsley.com

web: www.knowsley.com

dir: M57 junct 2. Follow 'safari park' signs

A five-mile drive through the reserves enables visitors to see lions, tigers, elephants, rhinos, monkeys and many other animals in spacious, natural surroundings. Also a children's amusement park, reptile house, pets' corner plus sealion shows. Other attractions include an amusement park and a miniature railway.

Times Open all year, Mar-Oct, daily 10-4; Nov-Feb, 11-3. Closed 25 Dec **Fees** £14 (ch & concessions £10)* **Facilities** Ⓟ ☕ ⛩ (outdoor) ♿ (fully accessible) toilets for disabled shop ㊗

Prescot Museum

FREE

34 Church St L34 3LA

☎ 0151 430 7787 📠 0151 430 7219

e-mail: prescot.museum.dlcs@knowsley.gov.uk

web: www.knowsley.gov.uk/leisure

dir: situated on corner of High St (A57) & Church St. Follow brown heritage signs

Permanent exhibitions reflecting the local history of the area, including its important clock and watch making heritage. There is a programme of special exhibitions, events and holiday activities, telephone for details.

Times Open all year, Tue-Sat 10-5 (closed 1-2), Sun 2-5, Mon by appointment. Closed BHs* **Facilities** Ⓟ ♿ (partly accessible) (wheelchair access to ground floor) (ramp) shop ㊗

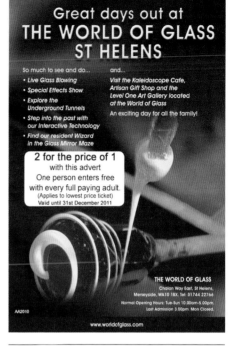

ST HELENS Map 7 SJ59

World of Glass

2 FOR 1

Chalon Way East WA10 1BX

☎ 01744 22766 📠 01744 616966

e-mail: info@worldofglass.com

web: www.worldofglass.com

dir: 5mins from M62 junct 7

Ideal for all the family, this fascinating attraction is in the heart of St Helens, a town shaped by glass-making. Features include the world's first continuous glass-making furnace, and two museum galleries that show glass from antiquity and Victorian

continued

ENGLAND

ST HELENS *continued*

life in St Helens. Live glass-blowing demonstrations and a special effects film show are the highlight of any visit.

Times Open all year, Etr-Oct, Tue-Sun & BH, 10-5; Nov-Etr, Tue-Sun, 10-4. Closed 25-26 Dec & 1 Jan **Fees** £6 (ch & pen £4) Family & group discounts **Facilities** (fully accessible) toilets for disabled (induction loop) shop

See advert on page 207

SEACOMBE **Map 7 SJ38**

Spaceport **2 FOR 1**

Victoria Place CH44 6QY
0151 330 1566
e-mail: info@spaceport.org.uk
web: www.spaceport.org.uk
dir: From M56 westbound, take M53 junct 11, exit junct 1 A5139. Over rdbt to A554, Spaceport on right

Visit Spaceport and enjoy an inspirational journey through space, walk through several themed galleries featuring a large variety of interactive hands-on exhibits and audio visual experiences. See the new Wallace & Gromit Space exhibition and planetarium dome show or take a ride on a motion simulator.

Times Open all year, Tue-Sun 10.30-6 (last admission 4.30). Closed Mon ex BHs and school breaks* **Fees** £8 (ch 3-15 £4.50, concessions £5.50). Family ticket (2ad+3ch) £20* **Facilities** (fully accessible) toilets for disabled shop

SOUTHPORT **Map 7 SD31**

The British Lawnmower Museum **2 FOR 1**

106-114 Shakespeare St PR8 5AJ
01704 501336 01704 500564
e-mail: info@lawnmowerworld.com
web: www.lawnmowerworld.com
dir: From M6, M58 or M57 follow signs towards town centre, then brown heritage signs to museum

This award-winning museum houses a private collection of over 250 rare exhibits of garden machinery of special interest dating from 1799. There is also the largest collection of vintage toy lawnmowers and games in the world. See the fastest and most expensive mowers, a genuine 2-inch lawnmower, the first electric and robot lawnmowers, and the Lawnmowers of the Rich and Famous, including machines that belonged to Princess Diana, Nicholas Parsons, Prince Charles, Brian May, Hilda Ogden and many more.

Times Open all year, daily, 9-5.30, ex Sun & BH Mon* **Fees** £2 (ch £1) includes Audio tour. Guided tours by appointment* **Facilities** (partly accessible) (ramps to front entrance only) shop

SPEKE **Map 7 SJ48**

Speke Hall

The Walk L24 1XD
0151 427 7231 & 0844 800 4799 0151 427 9860
e-mail: spekehall@nationaltrust.org.uk
web: www.nationaltrust.org.uk/main/w-spekehall
dir: on N bank of Mersey, 1m off A561 on W side of Liverpool Airport, follow brown signs

A remarkable timber-framed manor house set in tranquil gardens and grounds. The house has a Tudor Great Hall, Stuart plasterwork, and William Morris wallpapers. Outside are varied grounds, including a rose garden, bluebell woods and woodland walks. Also, live interpretation by costumed guides, children's quiz-trail and adventure playground. Lots of events throughout the year, contact for details.

Times House open: 27 Feb-14 Mar, 6 Nov-12 Dec, Sat & Sun 11-4.30; 17 Mar-Oct, Wed-Sun 11-5 Garden open daily 2 Jan-30 Dec, 11-4.30* **Fees** Hall & Garden: £8.40 (ch £4.20). Family ticket £21. Gardens only: £5 (ch £2.60). Family ticket £12.60* **Facilities** licensed (outdoor) (partly accessible) (ground floor accessible. Level entrance to shop & restaurant. Accessible route in grounds) toilets for disabled (wheelchairs, electric car, Braille guide, induction loop) shop

NORFOLK

Cutting the lavender

ENGLAND

BACONSTHORPE Map 9 TG13

Baconsthorpe Castle FREE

NR25 6LN
☎ 01799 322399
web: www.english-heritage.org.uk
dir: 0.75m N of Baconsthorpe off unclass road, 3m E of Holt

The remains of a 15th-century castle, built by Sir John Heydon during the Wars of the Roses. The exact date when the building was started is not known, since Sir John did not apply for the statutory royal licence necessary to construct a fortified house. In the 1560s, Sir John's grandson added the outer gatehouse, which was inhabited until the 1920s, when one of the turrets fell down. The remains of red brick and knapped flint are reflected in the lake, which partly embraces the castle as a moat.

Times Open at any reasonable time **Facilities** Ⓟ ⌗

BANHAM Map 5 TM08

Banham Zoo

The Grove NR16 2HE
☎ 01953 887771 & 887773 📠 01953 887445
e-mail: info@banhamzoo.co.uk
web: www.banhamzoo.co.uk
dir: on B1113, signed off A11 and A140. Follow brown tourist signs

Set in 35 acres of magnificent parkland, see hundreds of animals ranging from big cats to birds of prey and siamangs to shire horses. Tiger Territory is a purpose-built enclosure for Siberian tigers, including a rock pool and woodland setting. See also Lemur Island and Tamarin and Marmoset Islands. The Heritage Farm Stables and Falconry displays Norfolk's rural heritage with majestic shire horses and birds of prey. Other attractions include Children's Farmyard Barn and Adventure Play Area.

Times Open all year, daily from 10 (last admission 1 hour before closing). Closed 25 & 26 Dec* **Facilities** Ⓟ Ⓟ ☕ 🍴 licensed ⛩ ♿ (partly accessible) toilets for disabled (3 wheelchairs for hire, parking) shop ⊗

BLICKLING Map 9 TG12

Blickling Hall

NR11 6NF
☎ 01263 738030 📠 01263 738035
e-mail: blickling@nationaltrust.org.uk
web: www.nationaltrust.org.uk/blickling
dir: on B1354, 1.5m NW of Aylsham, signed off A140 Norwich to Cromer road

Flanked by dark yew hedges and topped by pinnacles, the warm red brick front of Blickling is a memorable sight. Fifty five acres of grounds include woodland and a lake, a formal parterre, topiary yew hedges, a Secret Garden, an orangery, and a dry moat filled with roses, camellias and other plants. Inside there are fine collections of furniture, paintings and tapestries, along with a spectacular Jacobean plaster ceiling, and a library of some 12,000 books.

Times Hall: 28 Feb-12 Jul, 15 Jul-6 Sep, 9 Sep-1 Nov, Wed-Sun 11-5, Garden: 2 Jan-27 Feb, 2 Nov-Jan, Thu-Sun 11-4; 28 Feb-1 Nov Wed-Sun10.15-5.15. Park: all year dawn to dusk. Open all BHs* **Facilities** Ⓟ ☕ 🍴 licensed ⛩ (outdoor) ♿ (partly accessible) (stairs to basement rooms) toilets for disabled (wheelchairs & batricars, Braille guide, lift, parking) shop ⊗ ✾

BRESSINGHAM Map 5 TM08

Bressingham Steam Museum & Gardens

IP22 2AB
☎ 01379 686900 & 687386 📠 01379 686907
e-mail: info@bressingham.co.uk
web: www.bressingham.co.uk
dir: on A1066 2.5m W of Diss, between Thetford & Diss

Alan Bloom is an internationally recognised nurseryman and a steam enthusiast, and has combined his interests to great effect at Bressingham. There are three miniature steam-hauled trains, including a 15-inch gauge running through two and a half miles of the wooded Waveney Valley. The Dell Garden has 5000 species of perennials and alpines; Foggy Bottom has wide vistas, pathways, trees, shrubs, conifers and winter colour (restricted opening). A steam roundabout is another attraction, and the Norfolk Fire Museum is housed here. Various events are held, including Dad's Army Day, Friends of Thomas the Tank Engine, and the home of the Royal Scot locomotive, please telephone for details.

Times Open: Steam Museum, Dad's Army collection, Foggy Bottom & Dell Garden Mar, Apr, May, Sep & Oct, daily 10.30-4.30. Jun, Jul & Aug, 10.30-5.30. Check before travelling* **Facilities** Ⓟ ☕ 🍴 licensed ⛩ (outdoor) ♿ (partly accessible) (Nursery and Waveney lines accessible to wheelchairs) toilets for disabled shop ⊗

BURGH CASTLE Map 5 TG40

Burgh Castle

FREE

NR31 9PZ
web: www.english-heritage.org.uk
dir: at far W end of Breydon Water on unclass road, 3m W of Great Yarmouth

Burgh Castle was built in the third century AD by the Romans, as one of a chain of forts along the Saxon Shore - the coast where Saxon invaders landed. Sections of the massive walls still stand.

Times Open at any reasonable time **Facilities** ⊗ ⌗

CAISTER-ON-SEA Map 9 TG51

Caister Roman Site

FREE

web: www.english-heritage.org.uk
dir: 3m N of Great Yarmouth

The name Caister has Roman origins, and this was in fact a Roman naval base. The remains include the south gateway, a town wall built of flint with brick courses and part of what may have been a seamen's hostel.

Times Open at any reasonable time **Facilities** ⊗ ⌗

CASTLE ACRE Map 9 TF81

Castle Acre Priory and Castle

Stocks Green PE32 2XD
☎ 01760 755394 📠 01760 755594
web: www.english-heritage.org.uk

Britain's best-preserved Cluniac priory with walled herb garden where visitors can find out about the medieval uses of herbs. Nearby Castle Acre Castle is also well worth a visit.

Times Open all year, Apr-Jun & Sep, daily 10-5; Jul-Aug, daily 10-6; Oct-Mar, Thu-Mon 10-4. Closed 24-26 Dec & 1 Jan.* **Facilities** Ⓟ ⛩ ♿ (partly accessible) (slopes, steps, narrow spiral staircase) (audio tour, hearing loop) shop ⌗

CASTLE RISING Map 9 TF62

Castle Rising Castle

PE31 6AH
☎ 01553 631330
web: www.english-heritage.org.uk
dir: off A149

A fine 12th-century domestic keep, set amid huge defensive earthworks, once the palace and home to Isabella, the 'She Wolf' of France, dowager Queen of England. The keep walls stand to their original height.

Times Open all year, Apr-Nov, daily 10-6 (closes at dusk if earlier in Oct); 2 Nov-Mar, Wed-Sun 10-4. Closed 24-26 Dec.* **Facilities** Ⓟ toilets for disabled shop ⌗

CROMER Map 9 TG24

Cromer Museum

East Cottages, Tucker St NR27 9HB
☎ 01263 513543 📠 01263 511651
e-mail: cromer.museum@norfolk.gov.uk
web: www.norfolk.gov.uk/tourism/museums
dir: On Church St next to Cromer Church

The museum is housed in five 19th-century fishermen's cottages, one of which has period furnishings. There are pictures and exhibits from Victorian Cromer, with collections illustrating local natural history, archaeology, social history and geology. Items to discover include the scandal of mixed bathing, the daring rescues of Henry Blogg and the Cromer Lifeboatmen, and the incredible story of the West Runton elephant, Britain's oldest and most complete elephant fossil. Contact for details of special events.

Times Open all year, Mar-Oct, Mon-Sat 10-5, Sun 1-4; Nov-26 Feb, Mon-Sat 10-4. Closed Sun* **Fees** £3.20 (ch £1.80, concessions £2.70)* **Facilities** Ⓟ ♿ (partly accessible) toilets for disabled (lift and ramps) shop ⊗

RNLI Henry Blogg Museum

FREE

The Rocket House, The Gangway NR27 9ET
☎ 01263 511294 📠 01263 513047
e-mail: blogg_museum@rnli.org.uk
web: www.rnli.org.uk/henryblogg
dir: located at the bottom of East Gangway

A lifeboat has been stationed at Cromer since 1804, and the museum at the bottom of The Gangway covers local lifeboat history and the RNLI in general. The main exhibit is the WWII Watson Class lifeboat *H F Bailey*, the boat Henry Blogg coxed. In ten years he helped to save over 500 lives, and is still the RNLI's most decorated crew member. The museum has much to offer for people of all ages and welcomes families.

Times Open all year Apr-Sep, Tue-Sun 10-5; Oct-Nov & Feb-Mar 10-4. Closed Dec-Jan **Facilities** Ⓟ ♿ (fully accessible) toilets for disabled (lift from cliff top to Museum and internal lift) shop ⊗

ERPINGHAM Map 9 TG13

Wolterton Park

2 FOR 1

NR11 7LY
☎ 01263 584175 & 768444 📠 01263 761214
e-mail: admin@walpoleestate.co.uk
web: www.manningtongardens.co.uk
dir: signed from A140 Norwich to Cromer

Covering some 800 hectares this estate contains managed conservation areas, 18th-century landscaped gardens, and Wolterton Hall, built in the 1720s for Horatio Walpole, younger brother of Britain's first Prime Minister, Sir Robert Walpole. Special events include music, drama, history, costume and textile, plus art and craft exhibitions.

Times Open: Park daily; Hall, late Apr-end Oct, Fri 2-5 (last entry 4) **Fees** Hall £5. Car park £2 (free for hall visitors)* **Facilities** Ⓟ ⛩ (outdoor) ♿ (partly accessible) toilets for disabled (chair lift to first floor) shop ⊗

ENGLAND

FAKENHAM — Map 9 TF93

See also Thursford Green

Pensthorpe Nature Reserve & Gardens — 2 FOR 1

Pensthorpe NR21 0LN
☎ 01328 851465 📠 01328 855905
e-mail: info@pensthorpe.com
web: www.pensthorpe.co.uk
dir: 1m from Fakenham on the A1067 to Norwich

Explore the beautiful lakes, nature trails and gardens designed by Chelsea Flower Show gold medallists, and look out for the large collection of cranes in the recently opened Conservation Centre. Pensthorpe is currently host to the BBC *Springwatch* programme.

Times Open Jan-Mar, daily 10-4. Apr-Dec, 10-5. Closed 25-26 Dec* **Fees** £8.50 (ch 4-16 £5, concessions £7). Family ticket (2ad+2ch) £23. Please telephone or see website for current prices* **Facilities** (outdoor) (partly accessible) (network of hard surfaced pathways ensures access around some of the reserve) toilets for disabled (parking for the disabled) shop

FELBRIGG — Map 9 TG23

Felbrigg Hall

NR11 8PR
☎ 01263 837444 📠 01263 837032
e-mail: felbrigg@nationaltrust.org.uk
web: www.nationaltrust.org.uk/main/w-felbrigghallgardenandpark
dir: off B1436 betweeen A148 Cromer to Kings Lynn & A140 Cromer to Norwich

Felbrigg is a 17th-century house built on the site of an existing medieval hall. It contains a superb collection of 18th-century furniture and pictures and an outstanding library. A 550-acre wood shelters the house from the North Sea and contains waymarked walks and a working dovecot. Please telephone for details of special events.

Times House & Garden: Open Mar-Oct, Mon-Sun 11-5* **Fees** £8.70 (ch £4.10). Family ticket £21.50 (incl. voluntary donation, but visitors can choose standard prices displayed at the property and on website). Garden only £4.10 (ch £1.80)* **Facilities** licensed (outdoor) (partly accessible) (access to ground floor of hall only) toilets for disabled (electric wheelchair for garden, Braille guide) shop

FILBY — Map 9 TG41

Thrigby Hall Wildlife Gardens

NR29 3DR
☎ 01493 369477 📠 01493 368256
web: www.thrigbyhall.co.uk
dir: on unclass road off A1064, between Acle & Caister-on-Sea

The 250-year-old park of Thrigby Hall is now the home of animals and birds from Asia, and the lake has ornamental wildfowl. There are tropical bird houses, a unique blue willow pattern garden and tree walk and a summer house as old as the park. The enormous jungled swamp hall has special features such as underwater viewing of large crocodiles.

Times Open all year, daily from 10 **Fees** £9.90 (ch 4-14 £7.90, concessions £8.90) **Facilities** (indoor & outdoor) (fully accessible) toilets for disabled (wheelchairs available, ramps, parking) shop

GREAT BIRCHAM — Map 9 TF73

Bircham Windmill — 2 FOR 1

PE31 6SJ
☎ 01485 578393
e-mail: info@birchamwindmill.co.uk
web: www.birchamwindmill.co.uk
dir: 0.5m W off unclassified Snettisham road

This windmill is one of the last remaining in Norfolk. Sails turn on windy days, and the adjacent tea room serves home-made cakes, light lunches and cream teas. There is also a bakery shop and cycle hire. In addition, crafts people feature on a number of weekends throughout the year.

Times Open Etr-Sep, 10-5 **Fees** £3.75 (ch £2, pen £3)* **Facilities** (partly accessible) (accessible in windmill, no access to upper floors) toilets for disabled shop

GREAT YARMOUTH — Map 5 TG50

Elizabethan House Museum

4 South Quay NR30 2QH
☎ 01493 855746 📠 01493 745459
e-mail: yarmouth.museums@norfolk.gov.uk
web: www.museums.norfolk.gov.uk
dir: from A12 & A47 follow town centre signs, then Historic South Quay signs, leading onto South Quay

Experience the lives of families who lived in this splendid quayside house from Tudor to Victorian times. Decide for yourself if the death of Charles I was plotted in the Conspiracy Room. Dress the family in Tudor costumes. Discover Victorian life, upstairs and downstairs, and find out what it was like to work in the kitchen and scullery. Children can play in the toy room, while parents relax in the small but delightful walled garden.

Times Open Apr-Oct, Mon-Fri 10-5, Sat & Sun 12-4* **Fees** £3.50 (ch £1.90, concessions £2.90)* **Facilities** (partly accessible) (Braille guide) shop

Great Yarmouth Row 111 Houses & Greyfriars' Cloister

South Quay NR30 2RQ
☎ 01493 857900
web: www.english-heritage.org.uk
dir: follow signs to dock and south quay

Visit these 17th-century houses unique to Great Yarmouth, and the remains of a Franciscan friary with rare early wall paintings. Guided tours explain how the rich and poor lived in these properties through history.

Times Open Apr-Sep, daily 12-5 **Fees** £4.20 (ch £2.10, concessions £3.60). Family ticket £10.50. Prices and opening times are subject to change in March 2011. Please call 0870 333 1181 for the most up to date prices and opening times when planning your visit **Facilities** shop ⊛ ⌗

Merrivale Model Village

Marine Pde NR30 3JG

☎ 01493 842097

web: www.merrivalemodelvillage.co.uk

dir: Marine parade seafront, next to Wellington Pier

Set in more than an acre of attractive landscaped gardens, this comprehensive miniature village is built on a scale of 1:12, and features streams, a lake and waterfalls. Among the models are a working fairground, a stone quarry, houses, shops, and a garden railway. At some times of the year there are illuminations at dusk. The Penny Arcade gives you the chance to play old amusements.

Times Open Etr-Oct, daily from 10* **Facilities** Ⓟ ☕ ⛩ (outdoor) ♿ (fully accessible) toilets for disabled shop

Time and Tide Museum of Great Yarmouth Life

Tower Curing Works, Blackfriar's Rd NR30 3BX

☎ 01493 743930 📠 01493 743940

e-mail: yarmouth.museums@norfolk.gov.uk

web: www.museums.norfolk.gov.uk

dir: from A12 & A47 follow brown signs

An award-winning museum set in a Grade II listed Victorian herring-curing factory. Time and Tide tells Great Yarmouth's fascinating story, from prehistoric times to the present day; displays include fishing, wreck and rescue, seaside holidays, port and trade, and the World Wars. It also brings to life the herring curing industry and the lives of the people who worked here. The Museum's unique collections are interpreted using both traditional and interactive technology.

Times Open all year, Apr-Oct daily 10-5; Nov-Mar, Mon-Fri 10-4, Sat & Sun 12-4 **Fees** £4.50 (ch £3.30, concessions £3.80)* **Facilities** Ⓟ ☕ ♿ (fully accessible) toilets for disabled (lift) shop ⊛

Tolhouse Museum

Tolhouse St NR30 2SH

☎ 01493 858900 📠 01493 745459

e-mail: yarmouth.museums@norfolk.gov.uk

web: www.museums.norfolk.gov.uk

dir: from A12 & A47 follow AA signs to town centre, then signs to South Quay. Museum attached to Central Library.

Visit one of the oldest prisons in the country and explore Great Yarmouth's story of crime and punishment. With the free audio guide you can hear the gaoler and his prisoners describe their experiences. Discover the fate of the thieves, smugglers, witches, pirates and murderers at a time when punishments included transportation or execution. Other exhibits detail the history of this 12th-century former merchant's house that went on to become one of the town's most important civic buildings.

Times Open Apr-Oct, Mon-Fri 10-5, Sat & Sun 12-4* **Fees** £3.50 (ch £1.90, concessions £2.90)* **Facilities** Ⓟ ♿ (partly accessible) (lift to ground & 2nd floor, notice preferable) shop ⊛

Yesterday's World Great Yarmouth

2 FOR 1

34 Marine Pde NR30 2EN

☎ 01493 331148 📠 01493 330700

e-mail: enquiries@yesterdaysworld.co.uk

web: www.yesterdaysworld.co.uk

dir: From A12/A47 follow signs Great Yarmouth seafront. Located opposite Marine Centre

Step back into the past and enjoy an amazing journey through one hundred and twenty five years of British social history. This award winning museum brings to life history in exciting street scenes, with evocative sounds and smells. Take a ride on a Victorian carousel or enjoy over 150,000 artefacts, virtual and interactive exhibits.

Times Open Mar & Oct-Dec 10-4; Apr-Sep 10-5 **Fees** £7 (ch & concessions £6). Family ticket (2ad+2ch) £20* **Facilities** Ⓟ ☕ ♿ (fully accessible) toilets for disabled shop ⊛

GRESSENHALL **Map 9 TF91**

Gressenhall Farm and Workhouse

NR20 4DR

☎ 01362 860563 📠 01362 860385

e-mail: gressenhall.museum@norfolk.gov.uk

web: www.museums.norfolk.gov.uk

dir: on B1146 3m NW of Dereham, follow brown signs

Enjoy a fascinating journey through the story of rural Norfolk with a thrilling woodland adventure playground, an historic workhouse, traditional farm and many indoor displays, Gressenhall is the perfect setting for a day out.

Times Open Mar-Nov, 10-5* **Facilities** Ⓟ ☕ ⛩ (indoor & outdoor) ♿ (fully accessible) toilets for disabled (sound guide, wheelchair loan) shop ⊛

GRIMES GRAVES **Map 5 TL88**

Grimes Graves

IP26 5DE

☎ 01842 810656

web: www.english-heritage.org.uk

dir: 7m NW of Thetford off A134

These unique and remarkable Neolithic flint mines are the earliest major industrial site in Europe.

Times Open Mar & Oct, Thu-Mon 10-5; Apr-Jun & Sep, daily 10-5; Jul-Aug, daily 10-6. Closed Nov-Feb **Fees** £3.20 (ch £1.60, concessions £2.70). Family ticket £8. No entry to mines for children under 5. Prices and opening times are subject to change in March 2011. Please call 0870 333 1181 for the most up to date prices and opening times when planning your visit **Facilities** Ⓟ ♿ (partly accessible) (exhibition area only; access track rough) shop ⌗

ENGLAND

HEACHAM Map 9 TF63

Norfolk Lavender

2 FOR 1

Caley Mill PE31 7JE
☎ 01485 570384 & 07787 550286 📠 01485 571176
e-mail: admin@norfolk-lavender.co.uk
web: www.norfolk-lavender.co.uk
dir: follow signs on A149 & A148. Car park entrance on B1454, 100yds E of junct with A149

Norfolk lavender is England's premier lavender farm, and home to the National Collection of Lavender. There are plants for sale and tours are available (including the distillery) between May-August. There is a Lavender Festival in July. Facilities include an animal rare breeds centre, a play barn and farm shop and the new ceramics café within the children's play area, where children and parents can choose ceramic pottery to paint and have fired in kilns to take home.

Times Open all year, daily, Apr-Oct 9-5; Nov-Mar 9-4. Closed 25-26 Dec & 1 Jan **Fees** Admission to grounds free. Extended gardens and animal rare breeds area £3.50 (concessions £2.50). Family ticket (2ad+3ch) £10. Season tickets available **Facilities** licensed (fully accessible) toilets for disabled (wheelchair for loan) shop

HOLKHAM Map 9 TF84

Holkham Hall & Bygones Museum

NR23 1AB
☎ 01328 710227 📠 01328 711707
e-mail: enquiries@holkham.co.uk
web: www.holkham.co.uk
dir: off A149, 2m W of Wells-next-the-Sea, coaches should use B1105 at New Holkham, signed "Holkham Coaches"

The 18th-century Palladian mansion Holkham Hall is privately owned and lived in by descendants of the builder of the house, the 1st Earl of Leicester. The Coke family takes great pride in sharing the house and its treasures with visitors, offering the opportunity to see the superb collections of ancient statuary, original furniture, tapestries and paintings by Rubens, Van Dyck, Gaspar Poussin and Gainsborough. Set in a 3,000 acre deer park and close to the award-winning Holkham Beach, visitors can also enjoy lake cruises, a nature trail, or take a walk to the extensive 18th-century walled gardens to see work in progress as it undergoes a 5-year restoration project.

Times Open Apr-Oct : Hall Sun, Mon & Thu 12-4; Museum daily, 10-5. See website for up to date information* **Fees** Hall £9 (ch £4.50). Bygones £4 (ch £2). Combined ticket Hall & Bygones: £11 (ch £5.50). Family ticket £27. See website for up to date information* **Facilities** (outdoor) (fully accessible) toilets for disabled (wheelchair ramps, stairclimbing equipment) shop

HORSEY Map 9 TG42

Horsey Windpump

NR29 4EF
☎ 01263 740241
e-mail: horseywindpump@nationaltrust.org.uk
web: www.nationaltrust.co.uk
dir: 15m N of Great Yarmouth, on the B1159 4m NE of Martham

Set in a remote part of the Norfolk Broads, the windpump mill was built 200 years ago to drain the area, and then rebuilt in 1912 by Dan England, a noted Norfolk millwright. It has been restored since being struck by lightning in 1943, and overlooks Horsey Mere and marshes, noted for their wild birds and insects, as a site of International Importance for Nature Conservation.

Times Open 28 Feb-29 Mar, Sat & Sun, 10-5; 1-5 Apr, 9 Sep-18 Oct, 28 Oct-1 Nov, Wed-Sun, 10-5; 6 Apr-6 Sep, 19 Oct-25 Oct, daily, 10-5, Open Good Fri & BH Mons* **Facilities** (partly accessible) (nature garden is wheelchair accessible) toilets for disabled (parking, ramps to ground floor) shop

HORSHAM ST FAITH Map 9 TG21

City of Norwich Aviation Museum

Old Norwich Rd NR10 3JF
☎ 01603 893080 📠 01603 893080
e-mail: admin@cnam.co.uk
web: www.cnam.co.uk
dir: follow brown tourist signs from A140 Norwich to Cromer road

A massive Avro Vulcan bomber, veteran of the Falklands War, dominates the collection of military and civilian aircraft at this museum. There are several displays relating to the aeronautical history of Norfolk, including some on the role played by Norfolk-based RAF and USAAF planes during World War II, and a section dedicated to the operations of RAF Bomber Command's 100 group.

Times Open all year, Apr-Oct, Tue-Sat 10-5, Sun & BH Mons 12-5; Nov-Mar, Wed & Sat 10-4, Sun 12-4* **Fees** £4.25 (ch £2.10, concessions £4). Family ticket £12* **Facilities** (outdoor) (partly accessible) (assistance available) shop

HOUGHTON Map 9 TF72

Houghton Hall

2 FOR 1

PE31 6UE
☎ 01485 528569 📠 01485 528167
e-mail: info@houghtonhall.com
web: www.houghtonhall.com
dir: 1.25m off A148. 13m E of King's Lynn & 10m W of Fakenham on A148

Houghton Hall built in the 1720s by Sir Robert Walpole, Britain's first Prime Minister, is one of the grandest surviving Palladian Houses in England. Now owned by the 7th Marquess of Cholmondeley. The spectacular 5-acre walled garden, restored by Lord Cholmondeley, has been divided into areas for fruit and vegetables, spacious herbaceous borders, and formal rose gardens with over 150 varieties. A collection of Model

Soldiers contains over 20,000 models laid out in various battle formations. Look out for the herd of white fallow deer that live in the grounds, and contemporary sculptures in the garden. There are musical events in the summer, and the Houghton International Horse Trials in May.

Times Open Park, Walled Garden, Soldier Museum 24 Apr-29 Sep, Wed, Thu, Sun & BHs 11.30-5.30. House open 1.30-5 (last entry 4.30) **Fees** £8.80 (ch £3.50). Family ticket £22. Grounds only: £6 (ch £2.50) Family ticket £15 **Facilities** licensed (outdoor) (fully accessible) toilets for disabled (lift in house, motorised buggies in garden) shop

HUNSTANTON **Map 9 TF64**

Hunstanton Sea Life Sanctuary

Southern Promenade PE36 5BH
01485 533576 01485 533531
web: www.sealsanctuary.co.uk
dir: A149 King's Lynn to Hunstanton, then follow brown sealife signs

With over 30 displays of marine life, this fascinating aquarium offers close encounters with starfish, sharks, octopus, eels and many other underwater wonders. Feeding demonstrations, talks and special presentations. Also see: Claws. Six displays featuring strange clawed creatures from around the world.

Times Open all year, daily from 10. Closed 25 Dec* **Facilities** toilets for disabled shop

KING'S LYNN **Map 9 TF62**

African Violet Centre

FREE

Terrington St Clement PE34 4PL
01553 828374 01553 828376
e-mail: manager@africanvioletandgardencentre.com
web: www.africanvioletandgardencentre.com
dir: situated beside A17 5m from Kings Lynn and 3m from A47/A17 junct

A warm and friendly welcome awaits you at the African Violet Centre. As a major plant specialist the centre offers a wide variety of plants for any enthusiast. The African Violet Centre is a winner of many Chelsea Gold Medals.

Times Open all year Mon-Sat 9-5, Sun 10-5. Closed Xmas & New Year. **Facilities** toilets for disabled (ramps & wide doors) shop

Lynn Museum

Market St PE30 1NL
01553 775001 01553 775001
e-mail: lynn.museum@norfolk.gov.uk
web: www.museums.norfolk.gov.uk
dir: Entrance opposite King's Lynn bus station

Following a £1.2 million redevelopment, this charming museum tells the story of West Norfolk, and is home to Seahenge, the astonishing Bronze Age timber circle. A whole gallery is devoted to these unique 4000 year old timbers, and includes a life size replica of the circle. Original timbers are also displayed. The main gallery narrates the history of the area from the Iron Age to the 20th century. The museum also features the Iron Age gold coin hoard from Sedgeford, a display of pilgrims' badges and the beautiful 19th-century fairground gallopers made by Savages of Lynn.

Times Open all year, Tue-Sat, 10-5* **Fees** £3.10 (ch 4-16 £1.70, concessions £2.60). Free admission from Oct-Mar* **Facilities** (fully accessible) toilets for disabled shop

Town House Museum

46 Queen St PE30 5DQ
01553 773450
e-mail: lynn.museum@norfolk.gov.uk
web: www.museums.norfolk.gov.uk
dir: In Queen St in heart of historic 'Old Lynn' close to Saturday Market Place & St Margarets Church

A charming museum set in a 19th-century town house. Explore everyday life in King's Lynn through the ages in a series of carefully re-constructed rooms, from medieval times to the 1950s. Enjoy collections of historic toys and costumes, and take the air in the delightful garden. Dotted around the displays are colourful games and activities that will keep the children amused.

Times Open Feb-Apr, Mon-Sat 10-4; May-Oct, Mon-Sat 10-5* **Facilities** (partly accessible) (only ground floor accessible) shop

LENWADE **Map 9 TG01**

Dinosaur Adventure Park

Weston Park NR9 5JW
01603 876310 01603 876315
e-mail: info@dinosaurpark.co.uk
web: www.dinosaurpark.co.uk
dir: From A47 or A1067 follow brown signs to Park

Visitors can help the Ranger 'Track: T-Rex' on the Dinosaur Trail and meet giants from the past including the new spinosaurus. They can also make friends with animals from hedgehogs to wallabies, or bugs and snakes in the secret animal garden. There is also an adventure play area including a Climb-o-saurus, Raptor Racers, Jurassic Putt Crazy Golf, and the Lost World Amazing Adventure.

Times Open daily from 10 Sep & Oct half term; 11 Sep-22 Oct, Fri-Sun* **Facilities** (indoor & outdoor) toilets for disabled shop

LITTLE WALSINGHAM Map 9 TF93

Walsingham Abbey Grounds & Shirehall Museum

NR22 6BP
☎ 01328 820510 & 820259 📠 01328 820098
e-mail: jackie@walsingham-estate.co.uk
dir: follow B1105 from Fakenham. Entrance to museum through tourist info centre in village

In the grounds of the Abbey are the ruins of the original Augustinian priory built in the 1100s. The priory was built over the shrine of Our Lady of Walsingham which had been established in 1061. Shirehall Museum consists of an original Georgian Courthouse, displays on the history of Walsingham and local artefacts. The museum is situated in 20 acres of tranquil and picturesque gardens with access to woodland and river walks across the historic parkland.

Times Open Feb daily 10-4. 2 Apr-30 Oct, daily 10-4.30; Nov-Dec, Mon-Fri 10-4 **Fees** £3.50 (concessions £2.50) **Facilities** Ⓟ (outdoor) ♿ (partly accessible) (gravel/hard paths accessible but not woodland & river) toilets for disabled shop

NORTH CREAKE Map 9 TF83

Creake Abbey FREE

NR21 9LF
web: www.english-heritage.org.uk
dir: off B1355

The ruins of the church of an Augustinian abbey, later converted to an almshouse.

Times Open at any reasonable time **Facilities**

NORWICH Map 5 TG20

Air Defence Radar Museum 2 FOR 1

RAF Neatishead NR12 8YB
☎ 01692 631485
e-mail: curator@radarmuseum.co.uk
web: www.radarmuseum.co.uk
dir: follow brown signs from A1062 at Horning

This multi-award winning Museum, housed in the original 1942 Radar Operations building, features the Battle of Britain Room, 1942 Ground Controlled Interception Room, Radar Engineering, Military Communications Systems, Cold War Operations Room, Royal Observer Corps, Space Defence, Bloodhound Missiles and Original Mobile Radar Vehicles. The newest addition is the RAF Coltishall Memorial Room.

Times Open year round 2nd Sat each month; Apr-Oct, Tue & Thu & BH Mons 10-5 **Fees** £4.50 (ch £3.50, under 13 free, concessions £4) **Facilities** Ⓟ (outdoor) ♿ (partly accessible) (two rooms not accessible to wheelchairs) toilets for disabled (video tour for inaccessible areas) shop

Norwich Castle Museum & Art Gallery

Castle Meadow NR1 3JU
☎ 01603 493625 📠 01603 493623
e-mail: museums@norfolk.gov.uk
web: www.museums.norfolk.gov.uk
dir: in city centre

The Castle keep was built in the 12th century, and the museum houses displays of art, archaeology, natural history, Lowestoft porcelain, Norwich silver, a large collection of paintings (with special emphasis on the Norwich School of Painters) and British ceramic teapots. There are also guided tours of the dungeons and battlements. A programme of exhibitions, children's events, gallery and evening talks takes place throughout the year. Please ring for details.

Times Open all year, Mon-Sat from 10 (Sun from 1) Apr-27 Jun & 4 Oct-3 Jul, Mon-Sat 10-4.30, Sun 1-4.30. 28 Jun-3 Oct, Mon-Sat 10-5, Sun 1-5* **Fees** Castle Ticket £6.20 (ch £4.40, concessions £5.30), Special exhibitions £3.30 (ch £2.80, concessions £2.40)* **Facilities** Ⓟ (indoor) ♿ (fully accessible) toilets for disabled (lift, disabled parking, virtual tour, audio loops) shop

Norwich Cathedral

12 The Close NR1 4DH
☎ 01603 218300 📠 01603 766032
e-mail: reception@cathedral.org.uk
web: www.cathedral.org.uk
dir: A47, A11 to city centre, inner ring road to Barrack St rdbt, take road towards city centre to Tombland

The splendour and tranquility of Norwich Cathedral have attracted visitors and pilgrims for nearly 1,000 years. Norwich has the second highest spire, and the largest monastic cloister in England, and the 1,000 carved medieval roof bosses are amazing. The building remains a place of quiet reflection and prayer as well as for participation in daily worship or the rich pageantry of the Church's festivals. An education and visitors centre is now open.

Times Open all year, daily, 7.30am-6pm* **Facilities** Ⓟ licensed (outdoor) ♿ (fully accessible) toilets for disabled (lift, touch & hearing centre, audio-induction loop) shop

Royal Norfolk Regimental Museum

Shirehall, Market Av NR1 3JQ
☎ 01603 493649 📠 01603 493623
e-mail: regimental.museum@norfolk.gov.uk
web: www.norfolk.gov.uk
dir: adjacent to Norwich Castle Museum

Museum displays deal with the social as well as military history of the county regiment from 1685, including the daily life of a soldier. Audio-visual displays and graphics complement the collection.

Times Open School term-time & Xmas hols: Tue-Fri 10-4.30, Sat 10-5; School half-terms, Easter & Summer hols: Tue-Sat 10-5* **Facilities** Ⓟ ♿ (partly accessible) (stair lift available, ring for details) shop

ENGLAND

Sainsbury Centre for Visual Arts

University of East Anglia NR4 7TJ
☎ 01603 593199 📠 01603 591053
e-mail: scva@uea.ac.uk
web: www.scva.ac.uk
dir: A47 bypass W towards Swaffham. 1st exit onto B1108, follow brown signs

The Sainsbury Centre for Visual Arts is an inspirational public art museum exhibiting outstanding public art for free. The centre which opened in 1978 to house the Robert and Lisa Sainsbury's collection, is a world class building designed by Norman Foster, at the University of East Anglia. Visitors can see modern and world art in permanent collections in addition to special exhibitions which change every few months.

Times Open all year, Tue-Sun 10-5 **Fees** Permanent collection free, special exhibitions £4 (concessions £2)* **Facilities** licensed (indoor & outdoor) (fully accessible) toilets for disabled (parking at main entrance, wheelchair available on loan) shop

OXBOROUGH Map 5 TF70

Oxburgh Hall

PE33 9PS
☎ 01366 328258 📠 01366 328066
e-mail: oxburghhall@nationaltrust.org.uk
web: www.nationaltrust.org.uk/main/w-oxburghhall
dir: Signed from A134 at Stoke ferry & Swaffham

The outstanding feature of this 15th-century moated building is the 80ft high Tudor gatehouse which has remained unaltered throughout the centuries. Henry VII lodged in the King's Room in 1487. A parterre garden of French design stands outside the moat. Rare needlework by Mary Queen of Scots and Bess of Hardwick is on display. A particular attraction is a genuine 16th-century priests hole, which is accessible to members of the public.

Times Open House: 28 Feb-8 Mar, Sat & Sun, 11-5; 14 Mar-1 Nov, daily 11-5* **Fees** £7.45, (ch £3.90). Family Ticket £19.95* Garden only £3.90 (ch £2.25). Includes a voluntary donation but visitors can choose to pay the standard prices displayed at the property and on the website* **Facilities** licensed (outdoor) (partly accessible) (no access for w/chair users to upper floor, woodland walks partially accessible for w/chairs & pushchairs) toilets for disabled (DVD tour of first floor, wheelchairs available, touch tour) shop

REEDHAM Map 5 TG40

Pettitts Animal Adventure Park

NR13 3UA
☎ 01493 700094 & 701403 📠 01493 700933
e-mail: pettittsreedham@aol.com
web: www.pettittsadventurepark.co.uk
dir: off A47 at Acle then follow brown signs

Three parks in one, aimed at the younger child. Rides include a railway and roller coaster; the adventure play area has a golf course, ball pond and tearoom; and entertainment is provided by clowns, puppets and live musicians. Among the animals that can be seen are small horses, wallabies, birds of prey, goats, alpacas and reindeer.

Times Open daily 15 Mar-2 Nov, 10-5/5.30; wknds in Nov & Dec. Daily during Xmas hols. Closed 25 Dec* **Facilities** (outdoor) toilets for disabled (ramps to all areas) shop

ST OLAVES Map 5 TM49

St Olave's Priory

FREE

web: www.english-heritage.org.uk
dir: 5.5m SW of Great Yarmouth on A143

Remains of an Augustinian priory founded nearly 2000 years after the death in 1030 of the patron saint of Norway, after whom it was named.

Times Open at any reasonable time **Facilities**

SANDRINGHAM Map 9 TF62

Sandringham House, Gardens & Museum

PE35 6EN
☎ 01553 612908 📠 01485 541571
e-mail: visits@sandringhamestate.co.uk
web: www.sandringhamestate.co.uk
dir: off A148

The private country retreat of Her Majesty The Queen, this neo-Jacobean house was built in 1870 for King Edward VII. The main rooms used by the Royal Family when in residence are all open to the public. Sixty acres of glorious grounds surround the House and offer beauty and colour throughout the season. Sandringham Museum contains fascinating displays of Royal memorabilia. The ballroom exhibition changes each year.

Times Open Etr Sat-mid Jul & early Aug-Oct. House open 11-4.45, Museum 11-5 & Grounds 10.30-5 **Fees** House, Museum & Grounds: £10 (ch £5, pen £8). Family ticket £25* **Facilities** licensed (outdoor) (fully accessible) toilets for disabled (wheelchair loan, free transport in grounds, Braille guide) shop

ENGLAND

SAXTHORPE Map 9 TG13

Mannington Gardens & Countryside 2 FOR 1

Mannington Hall NR11 7BB
☎ 01263 584175 & 768444 01263 761214
e-mail: admin@walpoleestate.co.uk
web: www.manningtongardens.co.uk
dir: signed from Corpusty/Saxthorpe on B1149 Norwich-Holt road. Follow signs

The moated manor house, built in 1460 and still a family home, forms a centre-piece for the pretty gardens which surround it. Visitors can take in the Heritage rose garden, lakes, a scented garden, a ruined church, and horse graves. Music and theatre events are a regular feature. Contact for more details.

Times Open: Gardens Jun-Aug, Wed-Fri 11-5; also Sun noon-5; 30 Apr-1 Oct. Walks open every day from 9. Hall open by prior appointment only **Fees** Garden £5 (accompanied ch under 16 free, concessions £4). Walkers & car park £2 (free garden visitors)* **Facilities** (outdoor) (partly accessible) (grass & gravel paths, some steep) toilets for disabled (boardwalk across meadow, wheelchair entrance) shop

SHERINGHAM Map 9 TG14

North Norfolk Railway (The Poppy Line)

Sheringham Station NR26 8RA
☎ 01263 820800 01263 820801
e-mail: enquiries@nnrailway.co.uk
web: www.nnrailway.co.uk
dir: from A148 take A1082. Next to large car park by rdbt in town centre. Just off A149 coast road

A full size heritage steam railway running between Sheringham and Holt, with an intermediate station at Weybourne. The route runs for 5.5m along the coast, and up through the heathland, and features three genuine Victorian stations. The William Marriott Railway Museum is housed in a replica goods shed at Holt Station. There are special events throughout the year, please contact for details. "North Norfolkman" dining train offers timetabled lunch and dinner services - contact for dates.

Times Open Feb-Mar, wknds. Apr-Oct, daily. Santa Specials in Dec **Fees** £10.50 (ch 5-15 yrs £7, under 5 free, concessions £9.50). Family ticket £35 incl £5 voucher to spend on refreshments. Cycles & dogs £1* **Facilities** (outdoor) (fully accessible) toilets for disabled (ramps to trains, carriage converted for wheelchair access) shop

SOUTH WALSHAM Map 9 TG31

Fairhaven Woodland & Water Garden 2 FOR 1

School Rd NR13 6DZ
☎ 01603 270449 & 270683 01603 270449
e-mail: fairhavengarden@btconnect.com
web: www.fairhavengarden.co.uk
dir: follow brown heritage signs from A47 onto B1140 to South Walsham. Through village towards Gt Yarmouth. Left into School Rd, 100yds on left, opposite South Walsham Village Hall

131 acres of ancient woodland and water garden with private broad. Excellent bird-watching from the boat. In spring there are masses of primroses and bluebells, with azaleas and rhododendrons in several areas. Candelabra primulas and some unusual plants grow near the waterways, and in summer the wild flowers provide food for butterflies, bees and dragonflies. Summer flowers include Day Lilies, Ligularia, Hostas, Hydrangeas and flowering shrubs, including Viburnum Mariesii (Wedding Cake Viburnum), Cornus Kousa Chinensis and Cornus Florida Rubra. See website for details of special events.

Times Open all year, daily 10-5, (10-4 winter). May-Aug, Wed-Thu 10-9pm. Closed 25 Dec **Fees** £5 (ch £2.50, concessions £4.50). Single membership tickets £18.50. Family membership ticket £45* **Facilities** (outdoor) (fully accessible) toilets for disabled (ramp, grab rail, sensory gardens, hearing loop) shop

THETFORD Map 5 TL88

Ancient House Museum

21-23 White Hart St IP24 1AA
☎ 01842 752599
e-mail: ancient.house.museum@norfolk.gov.uk
web: www.norfolk.gov.uk/tourism/museums
dir: in town centre

An early Tudor timber-framed house with beautifully carved beamed ceilings, it now houses an exhibition on Thetford and Breckland life. This has been traced back to very early times, and there are examples from local Neolithic settlements. Brass-rubbing facilities are available and there is a small period garden recreated in the rear courtyard.

Times Open all year Apr-Sep, Tue-Sat 10-5; Oct-Mar 10-4* **Fees** £3.50 (ch £1.90, concessions £2.90). Free admission Nov-Mar* **Facilities** (partly accessible) toilets for disabled shop

Thetford Priory FREE

web: www.english-heritage.org.uk
dir: on W side of Thetford near station

A glimpse of medieval religious life before the dissolution of the monasteries. The Priory of Our Lady of Thetford belonged to the Order of Cluny, and was founded in 1103 by Roger Bigod, an old soldier and friend of William the Conqueror.

Times Open all year at any reasonable time **Facilities** #

Thetford Warren Lodge

FREE

web: www.english-heritage.org.uk
dir: 2m W of Thetford, off B1107

The remains of a two-storey hunting lodge, built in the 15th-century of flint with stone dressings.

Times Open at any reasonable time **Facilities** ⌗

THURSFORD GREEN — Map 9 TF93

Thursford Collection

2 FOR 1

NR21 0AS
☎ 01328 878477 📠 01328 878415
e-mail: admin@thursfordcollection.co.uk
web: www.thursford.com
dir: 1m off A148. Halfway between Fakenham and Holt

Only open during the summer, Thursford Collection is a working museum of mechanical organs, Wurlitzer shows, silent movies, old-fashioned fairground carousels and static displays of both fairground and road engines, along with all kinds of related memorabilia. There are two behind-the-scenes tours: the first goes back stage, taking in dressing rooms, costume stores, wardrobe and Fantasy Land, while the second visits the old forge and engine yard, with videos explaining how the engines would have been used. During November and December, Christmas Spectacular Shows and also Santa's Magical Journey are staged.

Times Open Good Fri-last Sun in Sep, daily, 12-5. Closed Sat **Fees** £8 (ch under 4 free, ch 4-14 £4, students & pen £7). Party 20+ £7 each **Facilities** Ⓟ ☕ 🍽 licensed ⛩ (outdoor) ♿ (fully accessible) toilets for disabled shop ⊛

TITCHWELL — Map 9 TF74

RSPB Nature Reserve

PE31 8BB
☎ 01485 210779 📠 01485 210779
e-mail: titchwell@rspb.org.uk
web: www.rspb@org.uk
dir: 6m E of Hunstanton on A149, signed entrance

On the Norfolk coast, Titchwell Marsh is the RSPB's most popular reserve. Hundreds and thousands of migrating birds pass through in spring and autumn and many stay during winter, providing an opportunity to see many species of ducks, waders, seabirds and geese and also the RSPB emblem bird, the Avocet. A great day out for the entire family.

Times Open at all times. Visitor Centre 4 Nov-Mar daily 9.30-5* **Fees** Facilities charge for non RSPB members* **Facilities** Ⓟ ☕ ⛩ (outdoor) ♿ (fully accessible) toilets for disabled (ramps to hides, wheelchair bays in hides) shop

UPPER SHERINGHAM — Map 9 TG14

Sheringham Park

Visitor Centre, Wood Farm NR26 8TL
☎ 01263 820550
e-mail: sheringhampark@nationaltrust.org.uk
web: www.nationaltrust.org.uk/main/w-sheringhampark
dir: 2m SW of Sheringham, main entrance at junct of A148 Cromer-Holt road & B1157

Fabulous displays of rhododendrons and azaleas from mid May to June, as well as a gazebo and viewing towers with stunning coastal vistas, make Sheringham one of the finest examples of landscape design in the country.

Times Open Park: all year, dawn-dusk; Visitor Centre: Feb-14 Mar & Nov-Jan Sat-Sun 11-4; 15 Mar-Sep daily 10-5; Oct Wed-Sun 10-5* **Fees** £4.50* **Facilities** Ⓟ ☕ ♿ (partly accessible) (grass & hard gravel paths, undulating terrain in garden) toilets for disabled (designated parking, free mobility scooter/wheelchair hire) shop ✿

WEETING — Map 5 TL78

Weeting Castle

FREE

IP27 0RQ
web: www.english-heritage.org.uk
dir: 2m N of Brandon off B1106

This ruined 11th-century fortified manor house stands in a moated enclosure. There are interesting but slight remains of a three-storey cross-wing.

Times Open at any reasonable time **Facilities** ⌗

WELLS-NEXT-THE-SEA — Map 9 TF94

Wells & Walsingham Light Railway

NR23 1QB
☎ 01328 711630
dir: A149 Cromer road

The railway covers the four miles between Wells and Walsingham, and is the longest ten and a quarter inch gauge track in the world. The line passes through some very attractive countryside, particularly noted for its wild flowers and butterflies. This is the home of the unique Garratt Steam Locomotive specially built for this line.

Times Open Good Fri-end Oct daily **Fees** £8 return (ch £6.50 return)* **Facilities** Ⓟ ♿ (fully accessible) shop

ENGLAND

WELNEY Map 5 TL59

WWT Welney Wetland Centre

Hundred Foot Bank PE14 9TN
☎ 01353 860711 📠 01353 863524
e-mail: info.welney@wwt.org.uk
web: www.wwt.org.uk
dir: off A1101, N of Ely

This important wetland site on the beautiful Ouse Washes is famed for the breathtaking winter spectacle of wild ducks, geese and swans. Impressive observation facilities, including hides and a heated main observatory, offer outstanding views of the huge numbers of wildfowl which include Bewick's and Whooper swans, wigeon, teal and shoveler. Floodlit evening swan feeds take place between November and February. In summer the reserve is alive with over 40% of all British wetland plant flowers. Butterflies, dragonflies and damselflies are in abundance, and the summer walk gives a unique access to the wetland habitat.

Times Open all year, Mar-Oct, daily 9.30-5; Nov-Feb, Mon-Wed 10-5, Thu-Sun 10-8. Closed 25 Dec **Fees** £7.10 (ch £3.50, concessions £5.35). Family ticket £18.95 **Facilities** Ⓟ ☕ ⛩ (outdoor) ♿ (partly accessible) (Visitor Centre & half reserve access for all. Further reaches of reserve limited access) toilets for disabled (w/chair loan (book in advance), hearing loops) shop ⊗

WEST RUNTON Map 9 TG14

Hillside Shire Horse Sanctuary

Sandy Ln NR27 9QH
☎ 01603 736200
e-mail: contact@hillside.org.uk
web: www.hillside.org.uk
dir: off A149 in village of West Runton half-way between Cromer & Sheringham, follow brown signs for Shire Horse Sanctuary

Come and see the heavy horses, ponies and donkeys as well as sheep, pigs, rabbits, ducks, hens, goats and many more rescued animals in their home in the beautiful north Norfolk countryside. Visit the museum and relive the farming days of yesteryear surrounded by an extensive collection of carts, wagons and farm machinery. There's lots of space for children to play in the activity areas. Try 'animal friendly' refreshments in the cafe and take home a souvenir from the gift shop. You may even 'adopt' a rescued animal.

Times Open 28 Mar-28 Oct daily; Apr-May after Etr; Jun-Aug; Sep-Oct. Closed Fri & Sat Apr-May & Sep-Oct, Sat only in Jun* **Facilities** Ⓟ ☕ ⛩ (outdoor) ♿ (partly accessible) toilets for disabled (video room, concrete yards all ramped) shop

WEYBOURNE Map 9 TG14

The Muckleburgh Collection

Weybourne Military Camp NR25 7EG
☎ 01263 588210 & 588608 📠 01263 588425
e-mail: info@muckleburgh.co.uk
web: www.muckleburgh.co.uk
dir: on A149, coast road, 3m W of Sheringham

The largest privately-owned military collection of its kind in Norfolk, which incorporates the Museum of the Suffolk and Norfolk Yeomanry. Exhibits include restored and working tanks, armoured cars, trucks and artillery of WWII, and equipment and weapons from the Falklands and the Gulf War. Live tank demonstrations are run daily (except Sat) during school holidays.

Times Open 20 Mar-Oct daily* **Fees** £7 (ch £5, pen £6). Family ticket £20 **Facilities** Ⓟ ☕ 🍽 licensed ⛩ (outdoor) ♿ (fully accessible) toilets for disabled (ramped access, wheelchairs available) shop ⊗

NORTHAMPTONSHIRE

Althorp House

ENGLAND

ALTHORP Map 4 SP66

Althorp

NN7 4HQ
☎ 01604 770107 📠 01604 770042
e-mail: mail@althorp.com
web: www.althorp.com
dir: from S, exit M1 junct 16, & N junct 18, follow signs towards Northampton until directed by brown Althorp signs

Althorp House has been the home of the Spencer family since 1508. The house was built in the 16th century, but has been changed since, most notably by Henry Holland in the 18th century. Restored by the present Earl, the house is carefully maintained and in immaculate condition. The award-winning exhibition 'Diana, A Celebration' is located in six rooms and depicts the life and work of Diana, Princess of Wales. There is in addition, a room which depicts the work of the Diana, Princess of Wales Memorial Fund.

Times Open Jul-30 Aug, daily 11-5* **Fees** £12.50 (ch £6, concessions £10.50). Family ticket (2ad+2ch) £29.50. Upstairs rooms £2.50* **Facilities** Ⓟ ☕ ⛩ (outdoor) ♿ (partly accessible) (no assisted access to upstairs rooms, but alternative arrangements can be made) toilets for disabled (disabled parking, wheelchairs, audio tour, shuttle bus) shop ®

CANONS ASHBY Map 4 SP55

Canons Ashby House

NN11 3SD
☎ 01327 861900 📠 01327 861909
e-mail: canonsashby@nationaltrust.org.uk
web: www.nationaltrust.org.uk
dir: easy access from either M40 junct 11 or M1 junct 16

Canon Ashby was first built by the Dryden family during the Elizabethan period, using stone from the Augustinian priory which previously occupied the site. The private church is all that remains of the priory. The interior is welcoming and atmospheric, with Jacobean wall paintings, plasterwork and tapestries. The house was updated in the 18th century, with the south facing rooms remodelled again in the 19th century, when Sir Henry Dryden 'The Antiquarian' recorded much of the history of the estate and the surrounding area. The gardens are currently being restored to their colourful 19th-century designs from Sir Henry's records.

Times Open: House & Gardens 28 Feb-8 Mar, Sat-Sun 11-5; 14 Mar-1 Nov, daily (ex Thu & Fri) 11-5; 7 Nov-20 Dec , daily (ex Thu & Fri) 12-4. House 6-21 Dec, Sat-Sun 12-4. Gardens, Park & Church 28 Feb-8 Mar,11-5.30; 14 Mar-1 Nov, daily (ex Thu & Fri) 11-5; 7 Nov-20 Dec, Sat-Sun 12-4. Open Good Fri 11-5. House tour timed tickets only before 1pm* **Facilities** Ⓟ ☕ ♿ (partly accessible) (access limited, ground floor has steps, uneven floors, little turning space. Stairs to other floors. Grounds have gravel paths & some steps) toilets for disabled (Braille/large print guide, taped guide, w/chair available) shop 🌿

DEENE Map 4 SP99

Deene Park

NN17 3EW
☎ 01780 450278 & 450223 📠 01780 450282
e-mail: admin@deenepark.com
web: www.deenepark.com
dir: 0.5m off A43, between Kettering & Stamford

A mainly 16th-century house of great architectural importance, and home of the Brudenell family since 1514 (including the 7th Earl of Cardigan who led the Charge of the Light Brigade). There's a large lake and park, and extensive gardens with old-fashioned roses, rare trees and shrubs. Phone for details of garden openings and any other special events.

Times Open Sun & Mon Etr; Sun & BH Mon May-Aug; Wed in May-Jun, plus 8, 15, 22 Sep 2-5. Party 20+ by prior arrangement with the Administrator* **Fees** House & Gardens: £8 (ch 10-14 £4, under 10 with adult free, concessions £7). Gardens only: £5.50 (ch £2.50)* **Facilities** Ⓟ ☕ ♿ (partly accessible) (majority of ground floor & gardens) (ramps to cafeteria and gardens) shop ®

Kirby Hall

NN17 5EN
☎ 01536 203230 📠 01536 403088
web: www.english-heritage.org.uk
dir: on unclass road off A43, 4m NE of Corby

An outstanding Elizabethan mansion with unusually strict symmetry and amazing Renaissance detail. The beautiful formal gardens gained a reputation in the 17th century as being the finest in England.

Times Open Apr-Jun & Sep-Oct, Thu-Mon 10-5; Jul-Aug, daily 10-5; Nov-Mar, Thu-Mon noon-4. Closed 24-26 Dec & 1 Jan. May close early for private events, please call to check **Fees** £5.30 (ch £2.70, concessions £4.50) Family £13.30. Prices and opening times are subject to change in March 2011. Please call 0870 333 1181 for the most up to date prices and opening times when planning your visit **Facilities** Ⓟ ♿ (fully accessible) toilets for disabled shop #

KETTERING Map 4 SP87

Alfred East Art Gallery FREE

Sheep St NN16 0AN
☎ 01536 534274
e-mail: museumandgallery@kettering.gov.uk
web: www.kettering.gov.uk/art
dir: A43/A14, located in town centre, next to library, 5 min walk from railway station

The Gallery has a permanent exhibition space showing work by Sir Alfred East, Thomas Cooper Gotch and other local artists, as well as selections from the Gallery's contemporary collection. Two further display spaces are dedicated to temporary changing exhibitions of art, craft and photography by regional and national artists. There is also a monthly lunchtime talks programme and regular family events.

Times Open all year, Tue-Sat 9.30-5* **Facilities** Ⓟ ⛩ (outdoor) ♿ (partly accessible) (wheelchair access via Kettering Library, during gallery opening hrs) shop ®

LYVEDEN NEW BIELD Map 4 SP98

Lyveden New Bield

2 FOR 1

PE8 5AT
☎ 01832 205358
e-mail: lyvedennewbield@nationaltrust.org.uk
web: www.nationaltrust.org.uk
dir: 4m SW Oundle via A427

In the heart of rural Northamptonshire, Lyveden is a remarkable survival of the Elizabethan age. Begun by Sir Thomas Tresham to symbolise his Catholic faith, Lyveden remains incomplete and virtually unaltered since work stopped on his death in 1605. Discover the mysterious garden lodge and explore the Elizabethan garden with spiral mounts, terracing and canals. Wander through the new orchard, containing many old varieties of apples and pears, or explore the Lyveden Way, a circular path through beautiful meadows, woodland and villages.

Times Open 18 Mar-Oct, Wed-Sun 10.30-5; Jul-Aug, daily 10.30-5; Feb-29 Nov, Sat & Sun 11-4. Open BH Mon's & Good Fri 10.30-5* **Fees** With Gift Aid donation: £5 (ch & NT members free) **Facilities** Ⓟ ♿ (partly accessible) (9 steps to low entrance, grounds partly accessible, grass and uneven paths)

NORTHAMPTON Map 4 SP76

Northampton Museum & Art Gallery

FREE

Guildhall Rd NN1 1DP
☎ 01604 838111 01604 838720
e-mail: museums@northampton.gov.uk
web: www.northampton.gov.uk/museums
dir: situated in town centre, in Guildhall Rd

Home to the world's largest collection of shoes, Northampton Museum and Art Gallery displays shoes that have been in fashion through the ages, from Ferragamo to Vivienne Westwood. 'Life and Sole' tells the history of footwear, and other displays detail the history of Northampton, and British and Oriental ceramics and glass. There is also a gallery of Italian paintings depicting scenes from the Bible and ancient mythology. There is a changing programme of exhibitions.

Times Open all year, Tue-Sun. Closed 25-26 Dec & 1 Jan. Contact museum for current opening hours* **Facilities** Ⓟ ♿ (fully accessible) toilets for disabled shop

ROCKINGHAM Map 4 SP89

Rockingham Castle

2 FOR 1

LE16 8TH
☎ 01536 770240 01536 771692
e-mail: a.norman@rockinghamcastle.com
web: www.rockinghamcastle.com
dir: 2m N of Corby, off A6003

Set on a hill overlooking five counties, the castle was built by William the Conqueror. The site of the original keep is now a rose garden, but the outline of the curtain wall remains, as do the foundations of the Norman hall, and the twin towers of the gatehouse. A royal residence for 450 years, the castle was granted to Edward Watson in the 16th century, and the Watson family have lived there ever since.

Times Open 17 Apr-May, Sun & BH Mon; Jun-Sep, Tue, Sun & BH Mon 12-5. Grounds open from 12. Castle open from 1 (last entry 4.30) **Fees** House & Gardens £8.50 (ch 5-16 £5, pen £7.50). Family ticket (2ad+2ch) £22. Gardens & Salvin's Tower only all tickets £5 (not available during special events). Group tours 20+ by appt only. See website for current prices* **Facilities** Ⓟ (outdoor) ♿ (partly accessible) (ramps are available, ground floor accessible, 1st floor & tower not accessible due to spiral staircase) toilets for disabled (audio tour, large print guide, parking next to castle) shop

RUSHTON Map 4 SP88

Rushton Triangular Lodge

NN14 1RP
☎ 01536 710761
web: www.english-heritage.org.uk

A delightful Elizabethan folly designed to symbolise the Holy Trinity, with its three sides, three floors, trefoil windows and three triangular gables on each side. Designed and built by Sir Thomas Gresham.

Times Open Apr-Oct, Thu-Mon 11-4 **Fees** £3.20 (ch £1.60, concessions £2.70). Prices and opening times are subject to change in March 2011. Please call 0870 333 1181 for the most up to date prices and opening times when planning your visit **Facilities** Ⓟ shop #

SULGRAVE Map 4 SP54

Sulgrave Manor

2 FOR 1

Manor Rd OX17 2SD
☎ 01295 760205 01295 768056
e-mail: enquiries@sulgravemanor.org.uk
web: www.sulgravemanor.org.uk
dir: off B4525 Banbury to Northampton road

A splendid example of a Tudor manor house with a Georgian wing, housing excellent collections of authentic period furniture and fabrics. Set in pleasant gardens in the English formal style.

Times Open Apr-Oct (wknds only in Apr). From May Tue-Thu from 2 (last entry 4). Open for pre-booked groups all year **Fees** Standard admission without Gift aid: £6.55 (ch 5-16 £3.15). Family ticket £18.50. Special event days £7.50 (ch £3.50). Family ticket £20 **Facilities** Ⓟ Ⓟ (outdoor) ♿ (partly accessible) (fully accessible visitor centre and grounds, House partially accessible on ground floor) toilets for disabled (wheelchair, large print menu) shop

NORTHUMBERLAND

Dunstanburgh Castle

ALNWICK **Map 12 NU11**

Alnwick Castle

NE66 1NQ
☎ 01665 510777 📠 01665 510876
e-mail: enquiries@alnwickcastle.com
web: www.alnwickcastle.com
dir: off A1 on outskirts of town, signed

Set in a stunning landscape, Alnwick Castle overlooks the historic market town of Alnwick. Although it was originally built for the Percy family, who have lived here since 1309, - the current Duke and Duchess of Northumberland being the current tenants - the castle is best known as one of the locations that served as Hogwarts School in the Harry Potter movies. The castle is full of art and treasures and there are plenty of activities for all the family.

Times Open Etr-Oct, daily 10-6 (last admission 4.30)* **Facilities** Ⓟ ☕ 🍽 licensed ⛩ (outdoor) ♿ (partly accessible) (some areas not suitable for wheelchair users) toilets for disabled (castle lift if able to walk a little, 8 parking bays) shop ⊗

The Alnwick Garden

Denwick Ln NE66 1YU
☎ 01665 511350 📠 01665 511351
e-mail: info@alnwickgarden.com
web: www.alnwickgarden.com
dir: 1m from A1. Follow signs & access garden from Denwick Lane

The Alnwick Garden is a vision of the Duchess of Northumberland and a leading garden visitor attraction in North East England. The 40-acre landscape is the creation of Belgian designers Wirtz International, and British architect Sir Michael Hopkins designed The Pavilion and Visitor Centre. This unique project in a deprived rural area has transformed a derelict and forgotten plot into a stimulating landscape. Having completed its second phase of development, the garden includes one of the largest wooden tree houses in the world, a Poison Garden, Bamboo Labyrinth and Serpent Garden. An all-weather attraction for all ages and accessible to all. A varied programme of events and activities is available throughout the year.

Times Open all year, Apr-Sep, 10-6; Oct-Mar, 10-4. Closed 25 Dec* **Facilities** 🅟 Ⓟ ☕ 🍽 licensed ⛩ (outdoor) ♿ (fully accessible) toilets for disabled (ramps, w/chairs & scooters for hire) shop ⊗

ASHINGTON **Map 12 NZ29**

Woodhorn

Northumberland Museum, Archives & Country Park, QEII Country Park NE63 9YF
☎ 01670 528080 📠 01670 528083
e-mail: dtate@woodhorn.org.uk
web: www.experiencewoodhorn.com
dir: Just off A189 E of Ashington

Inspired by monster coal-cutting machines, the Cutter building houses emotive displays about life in the mining community, colourful banners and exhibition galleries. It is also home to the archives for Northumberland with records dating back 800 years. Unique listed colliery buildings have also been brought back to life for the Colliery Experience.

Times Open all year, Apr-Oct, Wed-Sun& BH Mon 10-5; Nov-Mar, Wed-Sun, & BHs 10-4. Open Tue in school hols **Fees** Entrance free (£2.50 parking)* **Facilities** 🅟 Ⓟ ☕ ⛩ (outdoor) ♿ (partly accessible) (accessibility limited to 95%, due to Grade II building status) toilets for disabled (tactile map, large print text, hearing loop) shop ⊗

BAMBURGH **Map 12 NU13**

Bamburgh Castle

NE69 7DF
☎ 01668 214515 & 214208
web: www.bamburghcastle.com
dir: A1 Belford by-pass, E on B1342 to Bamburgh

Rising dramatically from a rocky outcrop, Bamburgh Castle is a huge, square Norman castle. Last restored in the 19th century, it has an impressive hall and an armoury with a large collection of armour from the Tower of London. These formidable stone walls have witnessed dark tales of royal rebellion, bloody battles, spellbinding legends and millionaire benefactors. Experience the sights, stories and atmosphere of over two thousand years of exhilarating history.

Times Open Mar-Oct, daily 10-5 (last admission 4)* **Facilities** 🅟 Ⓟ ☕ ⛩ (outdoor) ♿ (partly accessible) (5 castle rooms accessible to wheelchairs) toilets for disabled (DVD showing remainder of castle) shop ⊗

Grace Darling Museum

Radcliffe Rd NE69 7AE
☎ 01668 214910 📠 01668 214912
dir: follow A1, turn off at Bamburgh & follow signs to Northumbria Coastal route, museum on left

Pictures, documents and other reminders of the heroine are on display, including the boat in which Grace Darling and her father, keeper of Longstone Lighthouse, Farne Islands, rescued nine survivors from the wrecked *SS Forfarshire* in 1838. New exhibitions include audio visual displays and a replica of the Longstone Lighthouse.

Times Open all year, Etr-Sep, daily (ex Mon) 10-5; Oct-Etr 10-4* **Facilities** Ⓟ ♿ (fully accessible) toilets for disabled (ramps) shop ⊗

ENGLAND

BARDON MILL Map 12 NY76

Vindolanda (Chesterholm)

Vindolanda Trust NE47 7JN
☎ 01434 344277 📠 01434 344060
e-mail: info@vindolanda.com
web: www.vindolanda.com
dir: signed from A69 or B6318

Vindolanda was a Roman fort and frontier town. It was started well before Hadrian's Wall, and became a base for 500 soldiers. The civilian settlement lay just west of the fort and has been excavated. The excellent museum in the country house of Chesterholm nearby has displays and reconstructions. There are also formal gardens and an open-air museum with Roman Temple, shop, house and Northumbrian croft.

Times Open Feb-Mar & Oct, daily 10-5; Apr-Sep, 10-6. Limited winter opening, please contact site for further details **Fees** £5.90 (ch £3.50, concessions £4.90). Family ticket (2ad+2ch) £16. Saver ticket for joint admission to the Roman Army Museum £9 (ch £5, concessions £7.50). Family ticket £25* **Facilities** (outdoor) (partly accessible) (please contact for further info) toilets for disabled shop

BELSAY Map 12 NZ07

Belsay Hall, Castle and Gardens

NE20 0DX
☎ 01661 881636 📠 01661 881043
web: www.english-heritage.org.uk
dir: on A696

Beautiful neo-classical hall, built from its own quarries with a spectacular garden, listed Grade I in the Register of Gardens. It is slightly unclear who built the 'Grecian-style hall', however it was designed by Sir Charles in 1807, in Greek Revival style. The magnificent 30 acres of grounds contain the ruins of a 14th-century castle.

Times Open all year, Apr-Sep, daily 10-6; Oct, daily 10-4; Nov-Mar, Thu-Mon 10-4. Closed 24-26 Dec & 1 Jan. Open Feb half-term for snowdrop displays. **Fees** £6.80 (ch £3.40, concessions £5.80). Family ticket £17. During Expo £8 (ch£4, concessions £6.80. Family ticket £20. Prices and opening times are subject to change in March 2011. Please call 0870 333 1181 for the most up to date prices and opening times when planning your visit **Facilities** toilets for disabled shop #

BERWICK-UPON-TWEED Map 12 NT95

Berwick-Upon-Tweed Barracks

The Parade TD15 1DF
☎ 01289 304493
web: www.english-heritage.org.uk
dir: on the Parade, off Church St, in town centre

Designed by Nicholas Hawksmoor, and begun in 1717, Berwick Barracks were among the first in England to be purpose-built. The Barracks hosts an exhibition on the life of the British infantryman, the King's Own Scottish Borderers Museum, the Berwick Gymnasium Art Gallery and the Berwick Borough Museum. There is also a Georgian Guard House near the quay. It displays 'The Story of a Border Garrison Town' exhibition.

Times Open Barracks: Apr-Sep, Wed-Sun & BHs 10-5. Please call site for details of Main Guard **Fees** £3.70 (ch £1.90, concessions £3.10). Prices and opening times are subject to change in March 2011. Please call 0870 333 1181 for the most up to date prices and opening times when planning your visit **Facilities** Ⓟ shop #

Paxton House, Gallery & Country Park

TD15 1SZ
☎ 01289 386291 📠 01289 386660
e-mail: info@paxtonhouse.com
web: www.paxtonhouse.com
dir: 3m from A1 Berwick-upon-Tweed bypass on B6461 Kelso road

Built in 1758 for the Laird of Wedderburn, the house is a fine example of neo-Palladian architecture. Much of the house is furnished by Chippendale and there is a large picture gallery. The house is set in 80 acres beside the River Tweed, and the grounds include an adventure playground. Visit website for details of special events.

Times Open daily from Apr-Oct, house & gallery 11-5 (last tour of house 4). Grounds 10-sunset **Fees** £7.50 (ch £3.50) Family £20 **Facilities** licensed (outdoor) (partly accessible) toilets for disabled (lifts to main areas of house, parking close to reception) shop

CAMBO Map 12 NZ08

Wallington House Walled Garden & Grounds

NE61 4AR
☎ 01670 773600 📠 01670 774420
e-mail: wallington@nationaltrust.org.uk
web: www.nationaltrust.org.uk/main
dir: 6m NW of Belsay off the A696

Wallington is the largest country estate protected by the National Trust. With 13,500 acres that include the entire village of Cambo, the main attraction is the country house set among woods and gardens. There is a Pre-Raphaelite central hall, a small museum of curiosities and a display of dolls' houses. There are plenty of walks exploring the historic landscape, and a walled garden created by the Trevelyan family in the 1920s. 2011 marks the bicentenary of artist William Bell Scott who painted the famous scenes of Northumbrian history around the central hall in the house. Series of special events to celebrate this event. Contact the estate for details of Wallington's varied events programme.

Times Open: House daily (ex Tue) 5 Mar-30 Oct, Sat-Sun 11-5, Mon-Fri 1-5. Grounds open all year dawn-dusk. Walled garden open daily, Apr-Sep 10-7; Mar & Oct 10-4; Jan, Feb & Nov-Dec 10-4 **Fees** House, walled garden & grounds: £10.80 (ch £5.40). Family £27; Garden & grounds only £7.50 (ch £3.75). Family £18.75 **Facilities** (outdoor) (partly accessible) (top floor of house not accessible but lift to other floors, some paths not suitable for wheelchairs, access to shop, cafe and farm shop) toilets for disabled (wheelchairs available, lift) shop

CARRAWBROUGH Map 12 NY87

Temple of Mithras (Hadrian's Wall) FREE

web: www.english-heritage.org.uk
dir: 3.75m W of Chollerford on B6318

This fascinating Mithraic temple was uncovered by a farmer in 1949. Its three altars to the war god Mithras, date from the third century AD, and are now in the Museum of Antiquities in Newcastle, but there are copies on site.

Times Open all reasonable times **Facilities** Ⓟ ⌗

CHILLINGHAM Map 12 NU02

Chillingham Castle

NE66 5NJ
☎ 01668 215359 📠 01668 215463
e-mail: enquiries@chillingham-castle.com
web: www.chillingham-castle.com
dir: signed from A1 & A697

Chillingham is a magnificent medieval fortress with Tudor additions. Romantic grounds laid out by Sir Jeffry Wyatville command views over the Cheviots and include topiary gardens and woodland walks. Weddings, private functions and meals can be arranged, and fishing is available. Please ring for details of special events.

Times Open Etr-end Oct, Sun-Fri (last admission 4.30). Other times by prior arrangement. Castle 1-5, grounds & tearoom 12-5 **Fees** £6.75 (ch £3, pen £5.50)* **Facilities** Ⓟ ☕ ♿ (partly accessible) (limited access to gardens) shop 🚫

Chillingham Wild Cattle Park

NE66 5NP
☎ 01668 215250
web: www.chillinghamwildcattle.com
dir: off B6348, follow brown tourist signs off A1 and A697

The Park at Chillingham has been home to a unique herd of wild white cattle for around 700 years. Visitors are welcome to experience the Park and approach the cattle in the company of the Warden, who can provide information on the cattle and their history.

Times Open Apr-Oct, daily tours at 10, 11, 12 & 2, 3, 4. Closed Sat & Sun am* **Fees** £5 (ch 4-16 £2, concessions £3). Family ticket (2ad+2ch) £12, forest walk-free* **Facilities** Ⓟ ⛩ (outdoor) ♿ (partly accessible) (guided tour with warden by prior arrangement) 🚫

CORBRIDGE Map 12 NY96

Corbridge Roman Site and Museum

NE45 5NT
☎ 01434 632349
web: www.english-heritage.org.uk
dir: 0.5m NW of Corbridge on minor road - signed

Originally a fort, which evolved into a prosperous town during the Roman era. An excellent starting point to explore Hadrian's Wall. The museum houses a fascinating collection of finds.

Times Open all year, Apr-Sep, daily 10-5.30 (last admission 5); Oct, daily 10-4; Nov-Mar, Sat-Sun 10-4. Closed 24-26 Dec & 1 Jan **Fees** £4.80 (ch £2.40, concessions £4.10). Prices and opening times are subject to change in March 2011. Please call 0870 333 1181 for the most up to date prices and opening times when planning your visit **Facilities** Ⓟ toilets for disabled ⌗

EMBLETON Map 12 NU22

Dunstanburgh Castle

Craster NE66 2RD
☎ 01665 576231
web: www.english-heritage.org.uk
dir: 1.5m E on footpaths from Craster or Embleton

An easy two mile coastal walk leads to the eerie skeleton of this wonderful 14th-century castle situated on a basalt crag more than 30 metres high with breathtaking views. The castle was built by Thomas Earl of Lancaster, nephew to King Edward II.

Times Open all year, Apr-Sep, daily 10-5; Oct-Nov, daily 10-4; Nov-Mar, Thu-Mon 10-4. Closed 24-26 Dec & 1 Jan **Fees** £3.80 (ch £1.90, concessions £3.20). Prices and opening times are subject to change in March 2011. Please call 0870 333 1181 for the most up to date prices and opening times when planning your visit **Facilities** Ⓟ ⛩ ⌗

GREENHEAD Map 12 NY66

Roman Army Museum

Carvoran CA8 7JB
☎ 016977 47485
e-mail: info@vindolanda.com
web: www.vindolanda.com
dir: follow brown tourist signs from A69 or B6318

Situated alongside the Walltown Grags Section of Hadrian's Wall, the museum is a great introduction to the Roman Army. Find out about Roman weapons, training, pay, off-duty activities and much more. See if you can be persuaded to join up by watching the recruitment film, or view the Eagle's Eye film and soar with the eagle over Hadrian's Wall.

Times Open Mar & Oct, 10-5; Apr-Sep 10-6* **Fees** £4.50 (ch £2.50, concessions £4). Family ticket (2ad+2ch) £12.50. Joint site saver ticket with Vindolanda £9 (ch £5, concessions £7.50). Family ticket £25* **Facilities** Ⓟ Ⓟ ☕ ⛩ (outdoor) ♿ (fully accessible) toilets for disabled (ramps, subtitles on main film) shop 🚫

HOLY ISLAND (LINDISFARNE) Map 12 NU14

Lindisfarne Castle

TD15 2SH
☎ 01289 389244 Fax 01289 389909
e-mail: lindisfarne@nationaltrust.org.uk
web: www.nationaltrust.org.uk
dir: 8m S Berwick from A1 on Holy Island via 3m tidal causeway

This 16th-century fort was restored by Sir Edwin Lutyens in 1903. The austere outside walls belie the Edwardian comfort within, which includes antique Flemish and English furniture, porcelain and polished brass. A small walled garden designed by Gertrude Jekyll is set on the southward facing slope, some 500 metres to the north of the castle. Spectacular views from the ramparts to the Farne Islands, Bamburgh Castle and beyond. 100th Anniversary of creation of Gertrude Jekyll Garden.

Times Open daily 19-27 Feb, 12 Mar-Oct (closed Mon ex BHs & open daily in Aug, alternate wkds in winter). As Lindisfarne is a tidal island, the Castle opening times will vary, 10-3 or 12-5 **Fees** Castle & garden £7.20 (ch £3.60) Family ticket £18. Garden only £1.50 donation **Facilities** Ⓟ ♿ (partly accessible) (castle is at top of 180 mtrs cobbled ramp, with steep steps inside) (Braille guide) shop

Lindisfarne Priory

TD15 2RX
☎ 01289 389200
web: www.english-heritage.org.uk
dir: can only be reached at low tide across a causeway. Tide tables posted at each end of the causeway

One of the holiest Anglo-Saxon sites in England, renowned for the original burial place of St Cuthbert whose corpse was discovered 11 years after his burial and found to be mysteriously undecayed. An award-winning museum.

Times Open all year, Apr-Sep, daily 9.30-5; Oct, daily 9.30-4; Nov-Jan, Sat-Mon 10-2; Feb-Mar, daily 10-4. Closed 24-26 Dec & 1 Jan **Fees** £4.50 (ch £2.30, concessions £3.80). Prices and opening times are subject to change in March 2011. Please call 0870 333 1181 for the most up to date prices and opening times when planning your visit **Facilities** toilets for disabled shop

HOUSESTEADS Map 12 NY76

Housesteads Roman Fort

Haydon Bridge NE47 6NN
☎ 01434 344363
web: www.english-heritage.org.uk
dir: 2.5m NE of Bardon Mill on B6318

The jewel in the crown of Hadrian's Wall and the most complete Roman fort in Britain, these superb remains offer a fascinating glimpse into the past glories of one of the world's greatest empires.

Times Open all year, Apr-Sep, daily 10-6; Oct-Mar, daily 10-4. Closed 24-26 Dec & 1 Jan **Fees** £4.80 (ch £2.40, concessions £4.10). Free entry to NT members. Prices and opening times are subject to change in March 2011. Please check web site or call 0870 333 1181 for the most up to date prices and opening times when planning your visit **Facilities** Ⓟ shop

LONGFRAMLINGTON Map 12 NU10

Brinkburn Priory

NE65 8AF
☎ 01665 570628
web: www.english-heritage.org.uk
dir: off B6344

This late 12th-century church is a fine example of early gothic architecture set in beautiful riverside surroundings. Look out for some unusual modern sculptures.

Times Open Apr-Sep, Thu-Mon 11-4 **Fees** £3.20 (ch £1.60, concessions £2.70). Prices and opening times are subject to change in March 2011. Please check web site or call 0870 333 1181 for the most up to date prices and opening times when planning your visit **Facilities** Ⓟ shop

MORPETH Map 12 NZ28

Morpeth Chantry Bagpipe Museum FREE

Bridge St NE61 1PD
☎ 01670 500717 Fax 01670 500710
web: www.northumberland.gov.uk
dir: off A1, in Morpeth town centre

This unusual museum specialises in the history and development of Northumbrian small pipes and their music. They are set in the context of bagpipes from around the world, from India to Inverness. It is also host to the Morpeth Northumbrian Gathering, with music and crafts the weekend after Easter and a traditional music festival through the month of October.

Times Open all year, Mon-Sat 9.30-5, open Sun in Aug & Dec. Closed 25-26 Dec, 1 Jan & Etr Mon. **Facilities** Ⓟ ♿ (partly accessible) (lift to 1st floor) toilets for disabled (induction loop, large print text, DVD guide to museum) shop

NORHAM Map 12 NT94

Norham Castle FREE

TD15 2JY
☎ 01289 382329
web: www.english-heritage.org.uk

A mighty border fortress built in 1160, was one of the strongest of the border castles. Take an audio tour conjuring up four centuries of sieges and war with the Scots.

Times Open all year Sat-Sun & BHs 10-5. Please call 01289 304493 for details **Facilities** Ⓟ

PRUDHOE Map 12 NZ06

Prudhoe Castle

NE42 6NA
☎ 01661 833459
web: www.english-heritage.org.uk
dir: on minor road off A695

Explore the romantic remains of this 13th-century fortress perched on a steep wooded spur rising above the Tyne and set in lovely grounds.

Times Open Apr-Sep, Thu-Mon 10-5 **Fees** £4.20 (ch £2.10, concessions £3.60). Prices and opening times are subject to change in March 2011. Please check web site or call 0870 333 1181 for the most up to date prices and opening times when planning your visit **Facilities** Ⓟ shop ⌗

ROTHBURY Map 12 NU00

Cragside **2 FOR 1**

NE65 7PX

☎ 01669 620333 & 620150 📠 01669 620066

e-mail: cragside@nationaltrust.org.uk

web: www.nationaltrust.org.uk/main/w-cragsidehousegardenandestate

dir: 15m NW of Morpeth on A697, left onto B6341, entrance 1m N of Rothbury

The aptly named Cragside was the home of Victorian inventor and landscape genius, Lord Armstrong, and sits on a rocky crag high above the Debden Burn. Crammed with ingenious gadgets it was the first house in the world to be lit by water-powered electricity. In the 1880s it also had hot and cold running water, central heating, fire alarms, telephones, and a passenger lift. In the estate there are forty miles of footpaths to explore, including a stroll through some of the best Victorian gardens in the country.

Times Open, Estate & Gardens: Mar-Dec, Tue-Sun & BH Mons 10.30-7 (last admission 1hr before closing). House: Mar-Oct, Tue-Sun 11-5. Opening dates & times vary, please contact or see web for information **Fees** House, Gardens & Estate £14.60 (ch £7.35). Family ticket £36.50. Admission free for NT members **Facilities** Ⓟ ☕ 🍽 licensed ⛩ (outdoor) ♿ (partly accessible) (very steep paths, slopes, steps & uneven surfaces) toilets for disabled (virtual tour, Braille guide, wheelchair path, lift) shop ✿

WALWICK Map 12 NY97

Chesters Roman Fort

Chollerford NE46 4EP

☎ 01434 681379

web: www.english-heritage.org.uk

dir: 0.5m W of Chollerford on B6318

The best-preserved Roman cavalry fort in Britain. The museum holds displays of carved stones, altars and sculptures from all along Hadrian's Wall.

Times Open all year, Apr-Sep, daily 10-6; Oct-Mar, daily 10-4. Closed 24-26 Dec & 1 Jan. **Fees** £4.80 (ch £2.40, concessions £4.10). Prices and opening times are subject to change in March 2011. Please check web site or call 0870 333 1181 for the most up to date prices and opening times when planning your visit **Facilities** Ⓟ ☕ ♿ (wheelchair access limited) shop ⌗

WARKWORTH Map 12 NU20

Warkworth Castle & Hermitage

NE66 0UJ

☎ 01665 711423

web: www.english-heritage.org.uk

The magnificent eight-towered keep of Warkworth Castle stands on a hill high above the River Coquet, dominating all around it. A complex stronghold, it was home to the Percy family, which at times wielded more power in the North than the King himself.

Times Open all year. Castle: Apr-Sep, daily 10-5; Oct, daily 10-4; Nov-Mar, Sat-Mon 10-4. Hermitage: Apr-Sep, Wed, Sun & BH 11-5. Closed 24-26 Dec & 1 Jan **Fees** Castle: £4.50 (ch £2.30, concessions £3.80). Family ticket £11.30. Hermitage: £3.20 (ch £1.60, concessions £2.70). Prices and opening times are subject to change in March 2011. Please check web site or call 0870 333 1181 for the most up to date prices and opening times when planning your visit **Facilities** Ⓟ ♿ (partly accessible) (limited access, steps) toilets for disabled (ramp, audio tour, hearing loop) shop ⌗

WYLAM Map 12 NZ16

George Stephenson's Birthplace **2 FOR 1**

NE41 8BP

☎ 01661 853457

e-mail: georgestephensons@nationaltrust.org.uk

web: www.nationaltrust.org.uk/ main/w-georgestephensonsbirthplace

dir: 1.5m S of A69 at Wylam

Birthplace of the world famous railway engineer, this small stone tenement was built around 1760 to accommodate mining families. The furnishings reflect the year of Stephenson's birth here in 1781, his whole family living in one room.

Times Open 26 Mar-Oct, Thu-Sun 12-5 & BH Mon **Fees** With Gift Aid donation: £2 (ch £1) **Facilities** Ⓟ ☕ ♿ (partly accessible) (one indoor step at cottage entrance, no parking, access via bridleway) toilets for disabled (induction loop, Braille guide, wheelchair) ⊗ ✿

NOTTINGHAMSHIRE

Upper Lake, Newstead Abbey Park

EASTWOOD Map 8 SK44

D. H. Lawrence Heritage — 2 FOR 1

Durban House Heritage Centre, Mansfield Rd NG16 3DZ
☎ 01773 717353 📠 01773 713509
e-mail: culture@broxtowe.gov.uk
web: www.dhlawrenceheritage.org
dir: A610or A608, follow brown tourist signs

D H Lawrence Heritage, in the writer's home town of Eastwood, brings together the D H Lawrence Birthplace Museum and the Durban House Heritage Centre, along with two quality gift shops, a contemporary art gallery and a bistro. Discover more about the son of a miner who went on to become one of the 20th century's most influential writers. The annual D H Lawrence Festival is held throughout September.

Times Open all year Apr-Oct, Tue-Fri & Sun 10-5; Nov-Mar, Tue-Fri & Sun 10-4. Closed over Xmas & New Year **Fees** £2.50 (concessions £1.75) Family ticket £5.60* **Facilities** licensed (outdoor) (partly accessible) (Durban house is fully accessible, but the Birthplace Museum has steep stairs and no lift) toilets for disabled (lift to exhibition, wheelchair available Braille signage) shop

EDWINSTOWE Map 8 SK66

Sherwood Forest Country Park & Visitor Centre — FREE

NG21 9HN
☎ 01623 823202 & 824490 📠 01623 823202
e-mail: sherwood.forest@nottscc.gov.uk
web: www.nottinghamshire.gov.uk/sherwoodforestcp
dir: on B6034 N of Edwinstowe between A6075 and A616

At the heart of the Robin Hood legend is Sherwood Forest. Today it is a country park and visitor centre with 450 acres of ancient oaks and shimmering silver birches. Waymarked pathways guide you through the forest. A year round programme of events includes the spectacular annual Robin Hood Festival.

Times Open all year. Country Park: open daily dawn to dusk. Visitor Centre: open daily 10-5, 4.30 Nov-Mar. Closed 25 Dec **Facilities** (outdoor) (partly accessible) toilets for disabled (wheelchair and electric buggy loan) shop

FARNSFIELD Map 8 SK65

White Post Farm

NG22 8HL
☎ 01623 882977 & 882026 📠 01623 883499
e-mail: admin@whitepostfarm.co.uk
web: www.whitepostfarm.co.uk
dir: 12m N of Nottingham on A614

With over 25 acres there's lots to see and do at the White Post Farm. There are more than 3000 animals including pigs, goats and sheep, along with more exotic animals like deer, reptiles and wallabies. The new indoor play area is ideal for small children, and there's also a sledge run, trampolines and pedal go-karts.

Times Open daily from 10* **Facilities** licensed (indoor & outdoor) (fully accessible) toilets for disabled (free hire wheelchairs, book if more than 6) shop

NEWARK-ON-TRENT Map 8 SK75

Newark Air Museum

The Airfield, Winthorpe NG24 2NY
☎ 01636 707170 📠 01636 707170
e-mail: newarkair@onetel.com
web: www.newarkairmuseum.org
dir: easy access from A1, A46, A17 & Newark relief road, follow tourist signs, next to county showground

A diverse collection of transport, training and reconnaissance aircraft, jet fighters, bombers and helicopters, now numbering more than seventy. Two Undercover Aircraft Display Halls and an Engine Hall make the museum an all-weather attraction. Everything is displayed around a WWII airfield. Special events through the year includes the Annual Cockpit Fest and Aeroboot in mid-June.

Times Open all year, Mar-Sep, daily 10-5; Oct-Feb, daily 10-4. Closed 24-26 Dec & 1 Jan. Other times by appointment* **Fees** £6.25 (ch £4, concessions £5.75). Family ticket (2ad+3ch) £18.50. Party 15+* **Facilities** (outdoor) (fully accessible) toilets for disabled shop

Newark Millgate Museum — FREE

48 Millgate NG24 4TS
☎ 01636 655730 📠 01636 655735
e-mail: museums@nsdc.info
web: www.newark-sherwooddc.gov.uk/museums
dir: easy access from A1 & A46

The museum is home to diverse social history collections and features fascinating exhibitions - recreated streets, shops and houses in period settings. There are also children's activities. The mezzanine gallery, home to a number of temporary exhibitions shows the work of local artists, designers and photographers.

Times Open all year, daily 10.30-4.30 **Facilities** (partly accessible) (access to ground floor only for wheelchair users) toilets for disabled shop

Vina Cooke Museum of Dolls & Bygone Childhood — 2 FOR 1

The Old Rectory, Cromwell NG23 6JE
☎ 01636 821364
e-mail: info@vinasdolls.co.uk
web: www.vinasdolls.co.uk
dir: 5m N of Newark off A1

All kinds of childhood memorabilia are displayed in this 17th-century house: prams, toys, dolls' houses, costumes and a large collection of Victorian and Edwardian dolls including Vina Cooke hand-made character dolls.

Times Open all year, appointment advisable; please ring to verify times* **Fees** Please ring to verify admission charges* **Facilities** (outdoor) (partly accessible) (5 steps to front door with handrail on both sides)

NEWSTEAD Map 9 SK55

Newstead Abbey, Historic House & Gardens

Newstead Abbey Park NG15 8NA
☎ 01623 455900 📠 01623 455904
e-mail: sally.winfield@nottinghamcity.gov.uk
web: www.newsteadabbey.org.uk
dir: off A60, between Nottingham & Mansfield, at Ravenshead

This beautiful house is best known as the home of poet Lord Byron. Visitors can see Byron's own rooms, mementoes of the poet and other splendidly decorated rooms. The grounds of over 300 acres include waterfalls, ponds, water gardens and Japanese gardens. Special events include outdoor theatre and opera, Christmas events and Ghost Tours. Please telephone for details of events running throughout the year.

Times Open: Grounds all year, daily 9-dusk or 6 whichever is earliest (ex last Fri in Nov & 25 Dec); House Apr-Sep, Fri-Mon 12-5 (last admission 4)* **Fees** House & Grounds £8 (ch £3.50, concessions £6) Family ticket £20. Grounds only £4 (concessions £3.50) Family ticket £10.50. Subject to change* **Facilities** (outdoor) (partly accessible) (grounds & ground floor of house accessible) toilets for disabled (audio tour & wheelchair for loan Apr-Sep) shop

NOTTINGHAM Map 8 SK53

Galleries of Justice

The Shire Hall, High Pavement, Lace Market NG1 1HN
☎ 0115 952 0555 📠 0115 993 9828
e-mail: info@galleriesofjustice.uk
web: www.galleriesofjustice.org.uk
dir: follow signs to city centre, brown heritage signs to Lace Market & Galleries of Justice

The Galleries of Justice are located on the site of an original Court and County Gaol. Recent developments include the arrival of the HM Prison Service Collection, which will now be permanently housed in the 1833 wing. Never before seen artefacts from prisons across the country offer visitors the chance to experience some of Britain's most gruesome, yet often touching, reminders of what prison life would have been for inmates and prison staff over the last three centuries.

Times Open all year, Tue-Sun & BH Mon 10-5. Also open Mon in school hols (last admission one hour before closing). Contact for Xmas opening times* **Facilities** (indoor) (partly accessible) toilets for disabled (Braille control lifts, induction loop, large print lables) shop

Green's Windmill

Windmill Ln, Sneinton NG2 4QB
☎ 0115 915 6878 📠 0115 915 6875
e-mail: greensmill@nottinghamcity.gov.uk
web: www.nottingham.gov.uk/windmill
dir: off B686, 500yds from Ice Centre

Restored to working order, take a look around the mill and see how grain is turned into flour by harnessing the power of the wind. Find out about the "mathematician miller", George Green and his theories, and test your mind with hands-on puzzles and experiments. There is also a Science Centre, an Under 5's Discovery Zone and a brand new outdoor play park.

Times Open all year, Wed-Sun (also BHs), 10-4. Phone for Xmas & New Year closing* **Fees** Admission free, but small charge for some events and activities. Kids Club Members access events for free* **Facilities** (outdoor) (partly accessible) (Centre & ground floor of Mill are accessible to wheelchair users, but there is short flight of steps from car park) toilets for disabled (parking in Millyard, induction loops) shop

The Museum of Nottingham Life **2 FOR 1**

Brewhouse Yard, Castle Boulevard NG7 1FB
☎ 0115 915 3640 📠 0115 915 3601
e-mail: anni@ncmg.org.uk
web: www.nottingham.gov.uk/nottinghamlife
dir: follow signs to city centre, the museum is a 5 min walk from city centre with easy access from train, tram and bus

Nestled in the rock below Nottingham Castle and housed in a row of 17th-century cottages, the museum presents a realistic glimpse of life in Nottingham over the last 300 years. Discover the caves behind the museum and peer through 1920s shop windows.

Times Open all year, Tue-Sun, 10-4.30 (last admission 4). Closed 24-26 Dec, 1-2 Jan **Fees** £5.50 (concessions £4). Family ticket (2ad+3ch) £15* **Facilities** (outdoor) (partly accessible) (ground floor fully accessible to all, but no lifts in main museum or Rock Cottage) toilets for disabled (video of upper floors and room displays) shop

Nottingham Castle Museum & Art Gallery **2 FOR 1**

Off Friar Ln NG1 6EL
☎ 0115 915 3700 📠 0115 915 3653
e-mail: castle@ncmg.org.uk
web: www.nottingham.gov.uk/nottinghamcastle
dir: Follow signs to city centre, then signs to castle.

This 17th-century building is both museum and art gallery, with major temporary exhibitions, by historical and contemporary artists, as well as the permanent collections. There is a 'Story of Nottingham' exhibition and a gallery designed especially to entertain young children. Guided tours of the underground passages take place on most days.

Times Open all year, Tue-Sun, Mar-Sep 10-5; Oct-Feb 10-4 (last entry 30 mins before closing) **Fees** £5.50 (concessions £4). Family ticket (2ad+3ch) £15* **Facilities** (outdoor) (fully accessible) toilets for disabled shop

Wollaton Hall, Gardens & Park

Wollaton NG8 2AE
☎ 0115 915 3900 📠 0115 915 3942
e-mail: info@wollatonhall.org.uk
web: www.nottingham.gov.uk/wollatonhall
dir: M1 junct 25 signed from A52, A609, A6514, A60 and city centre

A stunning Elizabethan mansion, housing a Natural History Museum with special exhibitions in the Yard Gallery, located in the courtyard. The Hall itself is set in 500 acres of historic deer park, with herds of red and fallow deer roaming wild. There are also formal gardens, a lake, nature trails and adventure playgrounds.

Times Open all year, daily, Apr-Oct 11-5; Nov-Mar 11-4. Please phone for Xmas & New Year closing times* **Fees** Free entry. Charge for guided tours and car parking **Facilities** (outdoor) (fully accessible) toilets for disabled shop

OLLERTON **Map 8 SK66**

Rufford Abbey Country Park

NG22 9DF
01623 821338 & 821328 01623 824840
e-mail: info.rufford@nottscc.gov.uk
web: www.nottinghamshire.gov.uk/ruffordcp
dir: 3m S of Ollerton, directly off A614

At the heart of the wooded country park stand the remains of a 12th-century Cistercian Abbey, housing an exhibition on the life of a Cistercian Monk at Rufford. Many species of wildlife can be seen on the lake, and there are lovely formal gardens with sculptures, plus exhibitions of contemporary crafts in the gallery.

Times Open all year, daily 10-5 (4.30 in winter). Closed 25 Dec **Fees** Free admission. Small seasonal charge for car parking, £3 **Facilities** licensed (outdoor) (partly accessible) (visitor facilities accessible, advanced booking for w/chair hire) toilets for disabled (lift to craft centre, w/chair & electric buggy loan) shop

SOUTHWELL **Map 8 SK65**

The Workhouse **2 FOR 1**

Upton Rd NG25 0PT
01636 817250 01636 817251
e-mail: theworkhouse@nationaltrust.org.uk
web: www.nationaltrust.org.uk/main/w-theworkhouse
dir: 13m from Nottingham on A612

Discover the most complete workhouse in existence. Meet the Reverend Becher, the founder of the Workhouse, by watching the introductory film and immerse yourself in the unique atmosphere evoked by the audio guide. Based on real archive records, the guide helps bring the 19th-century inhabitants back to life. Discover how society dealt with poverty through the centuries. Explore the segregated work yards, day rooms, dormitories, master's quarters and cellars, then see the recreated working 19th century garden and find out what food the paupers would have eaten.

Times Open 2 Mar-30 Oct, Wed-Sun 12-5. Open BH Mons & Good Fri. Guided external tours daily 11-12 (last admission 1hr before closing) **Fees** With voluntary Gift Aid donation: £6.10 (ch £3.15). Family ticket (2ad+3ch) £15.35. Family ticket (1ad) £9.25* **Facilities** (partly accessible) (ground floor accessible, stairs to other floors, not suitable for motorised wheelchairs, grounds partly accessible, loose gravel paths) toilets for disabled (virtual tour, photo album, wheelchairs available)

SUTTON-CUM-LOUND **Map 8 SK68**

Wetlands Waterfowl Reserve & Exotic Bird Park

Off Loundlow Rd DN22 8SB
01777 818099
dir: signed on A638

The Reserve is a 32-acre site for both wild and exotic waterfowl. Visitors can see a collection of birds of prey, parrots, geese, ducks, and wigeon among others. There are also many small mammals and farm and wild animals, including llamas, wallabies, emus, monkeys, red squirrels, deer and goats.

Times Open all year, daily 10-5.30 or dusk - whichever is earlier. Closed 25 Dec* **Facilities** (partly accessible) (wheelchair available) shop

WORKSOP **Map 8 SK57**

Clumber Park

The Estate Office, Clumber Park S80 3AZ
01909 476592 01909 500721
e-mail: clumberpark@nationaltrust.org.uk
web: www.nationaltrust.org.uk
dir: 4.5m SE of Worksop, 6.5m SW of Retford, 1m from A1/A57

Clumber was once the country estate of the Dukes of Newcastle. Although the house no longer exists, the Walled Kitchen Garden, magnificent Gothic Revival Chapel, Pleasure Ground and lake remain as clues to its past. Covering 3,800 acres, Clumber's mosaic of important and varied habitats are home to a world of hidden nature and a haven for visitors. Bikes are available for hire.

Times Open: Park daily.* **Facilities** licensed (partly accessible) (ramped access to chapel & walled kitchen garden & from conservatory to garden) toilets for disabled (powered self-drive vehicle available if booked) shop

OXFORDSHIRE

Temple Island, Henley on Thames

BANBURY Map 4 SP44

Banbury Museum

FREE

Spiceball Park Rd OX16 2PQ
☎ 01295 753752
e-mail: banburymuseum@cherwell-dc.gov.uk
web: www.cherwell.gov.uk/banburymuseum
dir: M40 junct 11 straight across at first rdbt into Hennef Way, left at next rdbt into Concord Ave, right at next rdbt & left at next rdbt, Castle Quay Shopping Centre & Museum on right

The Banbury Museum is situated in an attractive canal-side location in the centre of Banbury. Exciting modern displays tell of Banbury's origins and historic past. The Civil War; the plush manufacturing industry; the Victorian market town; costume from the 17th century to the present day; Tooley's Boatyard and the Oxford Canal, are just some of the subjects illustrated in the new museum.

Times Open all year, Mon-Sat 10-5* **Facilities** Ⓟ 🍽 licensed ♿ (fully accessible) toilets for disabled shop ㊗

BROUGHTON Map 4 SP43

Broughton Castle

2 FOR 1

OX15 5EB
☎ 01295 276070
e-mail: info@broughtoncastle.com
web: www.broughtoncastle.com
dir: 2m W of Banbury Cross on B4035 Shipston-on-Stour in Broughton village, turn off B4035 by Saye & Sele Arms

Built by Sir John de Broughton, then owned by William of Wykeham, and later by the first Lord Saye and Sele, the castle is an early 14th-and mid 16th-century house with a moat and gatehouse. Period furniture, paintings and Civil War relics are displayed. There are fine borders in the walled garden, and against the castle walls.

Times Open Etr Sun & Mon; May-15 Sep, Wed, Sun & BH Mon 2-5 (also open Thu in Jul & Aug) (last admission 4.30) **Fees** £7 (ch £3, concessions £6)* **Facilities** Ⓟ ☕ 🛋 (outdoor) ♿ (partly accessible) (ground floor & garden only for wheelchair users) toilets for disabled shop

BURFORD Map 4 SP21

Cotswold Wildlife Park

OX18 4JP
☎ 01993 823006 📠 01993 823807
web: www.cotswoldwildlifepark.co.uk
dir: on A361 2m S of A40 at Burford

This 160-acre landscaped zoological park surrounds a listed Gothic-style manor house. There is a varied collection of animals from all over the world, many of which are endangered species such as Asiatic lions, leopards, white rhinos and red pandas. See the new giraffe enclosure, built to mark the 40th anniversary of the park opening. There's an adventure playground, a children's farmyard, and train rides during the summer. The park has also become one of the Cotswolds' leading attractions for garden enthusiasts, with its exotic summer displays and varied plantings offering interest all year.

Times Open all year, daily from 10 (last admission 4.30 Mar-Sep, 3.30 Oct-Feb). Closed 25 Dec* **Fees** £11.50 (ch 3-16 & over 65's £8)* **Facilities** Ⓟ ☕ 🍽 licensed 🛋 (indoor & outdoor) ♿ (fully accessible) toilets for disabled (parking, free hire of wheelchairs, access to train) shop

BUSCOT Map 4 SU29

Buscot Park

SN7 8BU
☎ 01367 240786 📠 01367 241794
e-mail: estbuscot@aol.com
web: www.buscotpark.com
dir: on south side of A417 between Faringdon & Lechlade

A late 18th-century house set in enchanting landscaped grounds and home to the Faringdon collection of art, including Burne-Jones's *Legend of the Briar Rose.* The extensive park contains the famous water garden designed in 1904 by Harold Peto and the four seasons walled garden.

Times Open: House and Grounds Apr-Sep, Wed-Fri 2-6 (last entry 5). Also open Sat-Sun & BHs: 9-10, 23-25, 30 Apr; 1-2, 14-15, 28-30 May; 11-12, 25-26 Jun; 9-10, 23-24 Jul; 13-14, 27-29, Aug; 10-11, 24-25 Sep. Grounds only 6 Apr-29 Sep, Mon-Tue 2-6 **Fees** House & Grounds £8 (ch £4). Grounds only £5 (ch £2.50) **Facilities** Ⓟ ☕ 🛋 (outdoor) ♿ (partly accessible) (14 steps to house, no wheelchair access) toilets for disabled (3 powered mobility vehicles-must pre-book) ㊗ ✽

CHASTLETON Map 4 SP22

Chastleton House

GL56 0SU
☎ 01608 674981 📠 01608 674355
e-mail: chastleton@nationaltrust.org.uk
web: www.nationaltrust.org.uk
dir: 6m from Stow-on-the-Wold. Approach from A436 towards Chipping Norton

One of England's finest and most complete Jacobean houses, Chastleton House is filled with a mixture of rare and everyday

continued

ENGLAND

CHASTLETON *continued*

objects, furniture and textiles maintaining the atmosphere of this 400-year-old home. The gardens have a typical Elizabethan and Jacobean layout with a ring of topiary. The National Trust has focussed on conserving rather than restoring the house. Events include Summer Garden Party in July and Christmas concerts in early December.

Times Open 28 Mar-29 Sep 1-5, 3-27 Oct, 1-4. Custodians tour every Wed at 10 throughout season* **Facilities** Ⓟ ♿ (partly accessible) (access restricted to lower floor & gardens) toilets for disabled (visual material on ground floor) ⊗ ✿

DEDDINGTON **Map 4 SP43**

Deddington Castle

FREE

OX5 4TE
web: www.english-heritage.org.uk
dir: S of B4031 on E side of Deddington

The large earthworks of the outer and inner baileys can be seen, and the remains of 12th-century castle buildings have been excavated, but they are not now visible.

Times Open any reasonable time **Facilities** ⌗

DIDCOT **Map 4 SU58**

Didcot Railway Centre

2 FOR 1

OX11 7NJ
☎ 01235 817200 📠 01235 510621
e-mail: info@didcotrailwaycentre.org.uk
web: www.didcotrailwaycentre.org.uk
dir: M4 junct 13, A34, located on A4130 at Didcot Parkway Station

Based around the original GWR engine shed, the Centre is home to the biggest collection anywhere of Great Western Railway steam locomotives, carriages and wagons. A typical GWR station has been re-created and a section of Brunel's original broad gauge track relaid, with a replica of the *Fire Fly* locomotive of 1840. There is a full programme of steamdays, including the now-traditional Thomas the Tank and Santa specials. Contact for a timetable.

Times Open all year, Sat-Sun; daily 13-21 Feb; 2-18 Apr; 22 May-12 Sep; 23-31 Oct, 27 Dec-2 Jan. Day out with Thomas 6-7 Mar, 2-3 Oct & 4-23 Dec, Sat-Sun* **Fees** £5-£10 depending on event (ch £4-£9, concessions £4.50-£9.50) **Facilities** Ⓟ ☕ 🍴 licensed ⛩ (outdoor) ♿ (partly accessible) (18 awkward steps at entrance) toilets for disabled (advance notice recommended) shop

See advert on opposite page

FILKINS **Map 4 SP20**

Cotswold Woollen Weavers

FREE

GL7 3JJ
☎ 01367 860491 & 07713 636415 📠 01367 860661
e-mail: richard@naturalbest.co.uk
web: www.naturalbest.co.uk
dir: A361 between Burford & Lechlade

This traditional 18th-century woollen mill is home to the Cotswold Woollen Weavers. Located in the idyllic village of Filkins, the mill houses a textile museum, design studio, shop and gallery. See traditionally-woven cloth, interior textiles and traditionally-made upholstered furniture, all hand-worked on site. Enjoy constantly changing collections, inspired by the limestone landscape of the Cotswolds.

Times Open all year daily, Mon-Sat 10-6, Sun 2-6 **Facilities** Ⓟ Ⓟ ☕ 🍴 licensed ⛩ (outdoor) ♿ (partly accessible) (stairs to upper floor) toilets for disabled shop ⊗

GREAT COXWELL **Map 4 SU29**

Great Coxwell Barn

SN7 7LZ
☎ 01793 762209
e-mail: greatcoxwellbarn@nationaltrust.org.uk
web: www.nationaltrust.org.uk/main/w-greatcoxwellbarn
dir: 2m SW of Faringdon between A420 & B4019

William Morris said that the barn was 'as noble as a cathedral', and this is a good example of what he meant. Great Coxwell is a 13th-century stone-built tithe barn, 152ft long and 44ft wide, with a beautifully crafted framework of timbers supporting the lofty stone roof. The barn was built for the Cistercians.

Times Open all reasonable times. For details please contact Estate Office* **Fees** £1* **Facilities** Ⓟ ♿ (fully accessible) ✿

HENLEY-ON-THAMES **Map 4 SU78**

Greys Court

Rotherfield Greys RG9 4PG
☎ 01491 628529 📠 01491 628935
e-mail: greyscourt@nationaltrust.org.uk
web: www.nationaltrust.org.uk
dir: A4130 take B481. Property signed 3m on left. From town centre follow signs to Peppard/Greys for 3m

A picturesque house originating from the 14th century but with later additions. There is a beautiful courtyard and the surviving tower which dates from 1347. The outbuildings include a Tudor wheelhouse - one supplying water to the house, walled gardens and an ornamental vegetable garden. Check online for details of special events.

Times House open: Apr-Oct, BH Mon, Wed-Sun 1-5 (last entry 4.30). Garden & Tearoom 11-5 **Fees** With Gift Aid donation: House & Garden £8.20 (ch £5.40). Family ticket £21.90. Garden only £6 (ch £3.20). Family ticket £15.30 Without Gift Aid donation: House & garden £7.45 (ch £4.90). Family ticket £19.90* **Facilities** (outdoor) (partly accessible) (ground floor access limited & no access to top floor of house. Full access to gardens) toilets for disabled shop

River & Rowing Museum **2 FOR 1**

Mill Meadows RG9 1BF
01491 415600 01491 415601
e-mail: museum@rrm.co.uk
web: www.rrm.co.uk
dir: off A4130, signed to Mill Meadows

Discover the River Thames, the sport of rowing and the town of Henley-on-Thames at this award-winning museum, a contemporary building overlooking the river and bordered by meadows. You can also meet Mr Toad, Ratty, Badger and Mole at the *Wind in the Willows* exhibition. E.H. Shepard's famous illustrations are brought to life by 3-D models of their adventures. See Ratty and Mole's picnic on the riverbank, get lost in the Wild Wood or watch the weasels at Toad Hall.

Times Open: May-Aug 10-5.30; Sep-Apr 10-5. Closed 24-25 & 31 Dec & 1 Jan **Fees** £7.50 (ch 4 & over & concessions £5.50), tickets give unlimited entry for 12 months* **Facilities** licensed (fully accessible) toilets for disabled (lift access to upstairs galleries, ramps at entrance) shop

LONG WITTENHAM Map 4 SU59

Pendon Museum **2 FOR 1**

OX14 4QD
01865 407365 0870 236 8125
e-mail: sandra@pendon.plus.com
web: www.pendonmuseum.com
dir: follow brown signs from A4130 Didcot-Wallingford or A415 Abingdon-Wallingford road

This charming exhibition shows highly detailed and historically accurate model railway and village scenes transporting the visitor back into 1930s country landscapes. Enjoy a working

continued

LONG WITTENHAM *continued*

scenic model railway, the 'Madder Valley' exhibit, run four times a year and watch skilled modellers, who can often be seen at work on the exhibits.

Times Open Sat & Sun 2-5, BH wknds from 11, also Wed in school hols (last admission 4.45). Closed Dec **Fees** £5.50 (ch 7-16 £3.50, under 7 free, over 60 £4.50). Family ticket (2ad+3ch) £18 **Facilities** Ⓟ Ⓟ ☕ ♿ (fully accessible) toilets for disabled (phone in advance, special seating with handrails, lift) shop ⊗

MAPLEDURHAM — Map 4 SU67

Mapledurham House

RG4 7TR
☎ 0118 972 3350 📠 0118 972 4016
e-mail: enquiries@mapledurham.co.uk
web: www.mapledurham.co.uk
dir: off A4074, follow brown heritage signs from Reading

The small community at Mapledurham includes the house, a watermill and a church. The fine Elizabethan mansion, surrounded by quiet parkland that runs down to the River Thames, was built by the Blount family in the 16th century. The estate has literary connections with the poet Alexander Pope, with Galsworthy's *Forsyte Saga* and Kenneth Graham's *Wind in the Willows*, and was a location for the film *The Eagle has Landed*. Open-air theatre is a summer feature.

Times Open Etr-Sep, Sat, Sun & BHs 2-5.30. Picnic area 2-5.30 (last admission 5). Group visits midweek by arrangement* **Fees** Combined house, watermill & grounds £7 (ch 5-16 £3, under 5 free). House & grounds £4.50 (ch 5-16 £2, under 5 free). Watermill & grounds £3.50 (ch 5-16, £1.50, under 5 free)* **Facilities** Ⓟ ☕ ⛩ (outdoor) ♿ (partly accessible) shop ⊗

Mapledurham Watermill

RG4 7TR
☎ 0118 972 3350 📠 0118 972 4016
e-mail: enquiries@mapledurham.co.uk
web: www.mapledurham.co.uk
dir: off A4074, follow brown heritage signs from Reading

Close to Mapledurham House stands the last working corn and grist mill on the Thames, still using traditional wooden machinery and producing flour for local bakers and shops. The watermill's products can be purchased in the shop. When Mapledurham House is open the mill can be reached by boat from nearby Caversham.

Times Open Etr-Sep, Sat, Sun & BHs 2-5.30. Picnic area 2-5.30 (last admission 5). Groups midweek by arrangement* **Fees** Watermill & grounds £3.50 (ch £1.50)* **Facilities** Ⓟ ☕ ⛩ (outdoor) shop ⊗

MINSTER LOVELL — Map 4 SP31

Minster Lovell Hall & Dovecote — FREE

OX8 5RN
web: www.english-heritage.org.uk
dir: adjacent to Minster Lovell Church, 3m W of Witney off A40

Home of the ill-fated Lovell family, the ruins of the 15th-century house are steeped in history and legend. One of the main features of the estate is the medieval dovecote.

Times Open any reasonable time. Dovecote-exterior only **Facilities** ⌗

NORTH LEIGH — Map 4 SP31

North Leigh Roman Villa — FREE

OX8 6QB
web: www.english-heritage.org.uk
dir: 2m N of North Leigh

This is the remains of a large and well-build Roman courtyard villa. The most important feature is an almost complete mosaic tile floor, which is intricately patterned in reds and browns.

Times Grounds open any reasonable time. Viewing window for mosaic tile floor. Pedestrian access only from main road 600yds **Facilities** Ⓟ ⌗

OXFORD — Map 4 SP50

Ashmolean Museum of Art & Archaeology — FREE

Beaumont St OX1 2PH
☎ 01865 278000 📠 01865 278018
web: www.ashmolean.org
dir: city centre, opposite The Randolph Hotel

The oldest museum in the country, opened in 1683, the Ashmolean contains Oxford University's priceless collections. Many important historical art pieces and artefacts are on display, including work from Ancient Greece through to the 20th century. The museum has undergone a massive redevelopment, including the building of 39 new galleries, an education centre, conservation studios and a walkway.

Times Open all year, Tue-Sun 10-5, BH Mons 10-5. Closed during St Giles Fair (7-9 Sep) Xmas & 1 Jan* **Facilities** Ⓟ ☕ 🍽 licensed ♿ (fully accessible) toilets for disabled (entry ramp from Beaumont St - phone before visit) shop ⊗

Harcourt Arboretum

Nuneham Courtenay OX44 9PX
☎ 01865 343501
e-mail: piers.newth@obg.ox.ac.uk
web: www.botanic-garden.ox.ac.uk
dir: 400yds S of Nuneham Courtenay on A4074

The gardens consist of 75 acres of mixed woodland, meadow, pond, rhododendron walks and fine specimen trees.

Times Open all year, Apr-Nov, daily 10-5; Dec-Mar, Mon-Fri 10-4.30. Closed 22 Dec-4 Jan.* **Facilities** (partly accessible) (access for wheelchairs via path around Arboretum) toilets for disabled

Museum of Oxford FREE

St Aldate's OX1 1DZ
☎ 01865 252761 01865 252555
e-mail: museum@oxford.gov.uk
web: www.museumofoxford.org.uk

Permanent displays depict the archaeology and history of the city through the ages. There are temporary exhibitions, facilities for school parties and groups, and an audio tour. A programme of family, community events and activities also operates throughout the year.

Times Open all year, Tue-Fri 10-5, Sat & Sun 12-5. Closed 25-26 Dec.* **Facilities** (partly accessible) (main entrance steps, alternative access to ground floor via Town Hall next door) toilets for disabled (virtual tour online, audio tour for adults) shop

Museum of the History of Science FREE

Broad St OX1 3AZ
☎ 01865 277280 01865 277288
e-mail: museum@mhs.ox.ac.uk
web: www.mhs.ox.ac.uk
dir: next to Sheldonian Theatre in city centre, on Broad St

The first purpose-built museum in Britain, containing the world's finest collection of early scientific instruments used in astronomy, navigation, surveying, physics and chemistry. Various events through the year.

Times Open all year, Tue-Fri 12-5, Sat 10-5, Sun 2-5. Closed Xmas and Etr Sun **Facilities** (partly accessible) (lift to basement) toilets for disabled shop

Oxford Castle - Unlocked 2 FOR 1

44-46 Oxford Castle OX1 1AY
☎ 01865 260666 01865 260667
e-mail: info@oxfordcastleunlocked.co.uk
web: www.oxfordcastleunlocked.co.uk
dir: in city centre off New Rd

For the first time in 1000 years, the secrets of Oxford Castle will be "Unlocked" revealing episodes of violence, executions, great escapes, betrayal and even romance. Walk through these ancient buildings and experience the stories that connect the real people of the past to these extraordinary events. At weekends enjoy a Sights and Secrets walking tour.

Times Open all year, daily 10-5.30 (last tour 4.20). Closed 24-26 Dec **Fees** £7.75 (ch £5.50, concessions £6.50)* **Facilities** (outdoor) (partly accessible) (St Georges Tower & Castle Mound not accessible) toilets for disabled (lift & ramp) shop

Oxford University Museum of Natural History FREE

Parks Rd OX1 3PW
☎ 01865 272950 01865 272970
e-mail: info@oum.ox.ac.uk
web: www.oum.ox.ac.uk
dir: opposite Keble College

Built between 1855 and 1860, this museum of "the natural sciences" was intended to satisfy a growing interest in biology, botany, archaeology, zoology, entomology and so on. The museum reflects Oxford University's position as a 19th-century centre of learning, with displays of early dinosaur discoveries, Darwinian evolution and Elias Ashmole's collection of preserved animals. Although visitors to the Pitt-Rivers Museum must pass through the University Museum, the two should not be confused.

Times Open daily 10-5. Times vary at Xmas & Etr **Facilities** (outdoor) (fully accessible) toilets for disabled (lift access to gallery) shop

Pitt Rivers Museum FREE

South Parks Rd OX1 3PP
☎ 01865 270927 01865 270943
e-mail: prm@prm.ox.ac.uk
web: www.prm.ox.ac.uk
dir: 10 min walk from city centre, visitors entrance on Parks Rd through the Oxford University Museum of Natural History

The museum is one of the city's most popular attractions. It is part of the University of Oxford and was founded in 1884. The collections held at the museum are internationally acclaimed, and contain many objects from different cultures of the world and from various periods, all grouped by type, or purpose. Highlights include a 2500 year old Egyptian mummy, a striking 11 metre high totem pole and a firearms display in the newly re-opened upper gallery.

Times Open all year, Tue-Sun & BH Mon 10-4.30, Mon 12-4.30. Contact museum for Xmas & Etr opening times **Facilities** (fully accessible) toilets for disabled (audio loop, accessible trail-print audio tour) shop

St Edmund Hall FREE

College of Oxford University OX1 4AR
☎ 01865 279000 01865 279090
e-mail: bursary@seh.ox.ac.uk
web: www.seh.ox.ac.uk
dir: Queen's Lane Oxford at end of High St

This is the only surviving medieval academic hall and has a Norman crypt, 17th-century dining hall, chapel and quadrangle. Other buildings are of the 18th and 20th centuries.

Times Open all year. Closed 20-30 Mar, 23-26 Aug, 21 Dec-5 Jan* **Facilities** (partly accessible) toilets for disabled

ENGLAND

OXFORD *continued*

University of Oxford Botanic Garden

Rose Ln OX1 4AZ
☎ 01865 286690 01865 286693
e-mail: postmaster@obg.ox.ac.uk
web: www.botanic-garden.ox.ac.uk
dir: E end of High St on banks of River Cherwell

Founded in 1621, this botanic garden is the oldest in the United Kingdom. There is a collection of over 6000 species of plants from all over the world. Consisting of three sections, the Glasshouses contain plants that need protection from the British weather. The area outside the Walled Garden contains a water garden and rock garden as well as the spring border and autumn border. Within the Walled Garden plants are grouped by country of origin, botanic family or economic use.

Times Open all year daily: 9-4.30 Jan-Feb & Nov-Dec; Mar-Apr, Sep-Oct 9-5; May-Aug 9-6 (last admission 45 mins before close). Closed Good Fri & 25 Dec* **Fees** £3.50 (ch & disabled with 1 carer free, concessions £3). Annual pass £12* **Facilities** Ⓟ ♿ (fully accessible) toilets for disabled shop

ROUSHAM Map 4 SP42

Rousham House — 2 FOR 1

OX25 4QX
☎ 01869 347110 01869 347110
e-mail: ccd@rousham.org
web: www.rousham.org
dir: 1m E of A4260. 0.5m S of B4030

This attractive mansion was built by Sir Robert Dormer in 1635. During the Civil War it was a Royalist garrison. The house contains over 150 portraits and other pictures, and also much fine contemporary furniture. The gardens are a masterpiece by William Kent, and are his only work to survive unspoiled.

Times Open all year, garden only, daily 10-4.30 (last entry). House, May-Sep. Groups by arrangement* **Fees** Garden £5, House & Garden groups 12+ £10 (min charge £120)* **Facilities** Ⓟ ♿ (partly accessible) (restricted access as some areas of garden quite steep)

RYCOTE Map 4 SP60

Rycote Chapel

OX9 2PE
web: www.english-heritage.org.uk
dir: off B4013

This small private chapel was founded in 1449 by Richard Quatremayne. It has its original font, and a particularly fine 17th-century interior. The chapel was visited by both Elizabeth I and Charles I.

Times Open Apr-Sep, Fri-Sun, 2-6. May close at short notice for services or functions, please phone for details.* **Facilities** Ⓟ shop

STONOR Map 4 SU78

Stonor House & Park

RG9 6HF
☎ 01491 638587 01491 639348
e-mail: administrator@stonor.com
web: www.stonor.com
dir: On B480, approx 5m N of Henley-on-Thames

The house dates back to 1190 but features a Tudor façade. It has a medieval Catholic chapel which is still in use today, and shows some of the earliest domestic architecture in Oxfordshire. Its treasures include rare furniture, paintings, sculptures and tapestries from Britain, Europe and America. The house is set in beautiful gardens with commanding views of the surrounding deer park. Special events June and August.

Times Open 5 Apr-13 Sep, Sun 2-5.30; Jul-Aug, also Wed 2-5.30; BH Mon. Parties by appointment Tue-Thu, Apr-Sep **Fees** House £8 (ch 5-16 £4; under 5 free). Gardens only £4 (ch 5-16 £2, under 5 free). Private guided tours £9 each by appointment Tue-Thu **Facilities** Ⓟ (outdoor) ♿ (partly accessible) shop

UFFINGTON Map 4 SU38

Uffington Castle, White Horse & Dragon Hill — FREE

☎ 01793 762209
web: www.nationaltrust.org.uk/main
dir: S of B4507

The 'castle' is an Iron Age fort on the ancient Ridgeway Path. It covers about eight acres and has only one gateway. On the hill below the fort is the White Horse, a 375ft prehistoric figure carved in the chalk hillside and thought to be about 3000 years old.

Times Open at any reasonable time* **Facilities** Ⓟ (outdoor) ♿ (partly accessible) (disabled car parking and access to view points)

WATERPERRY Map 4 SP60

Waterperry Gardens

OX33 1JZ
☎ 01844 339226 & 339254 01844 339883
e-mail: office@waterperrygardens.co.uk
web: www.waterperrygardens.co.uk
dir: 7.5m from city centre. From E M40 junct 8, from N M40 junct 8a. Waterperry 2.5m from A40, exit a Wheatley and follow brown tourist signs

Waterperry has eight acres of ornamental gardens, including formal and rose gardens, a river walk, lily canal and classical herbaceous border. The Gallery and Long Barn feature works of art, and the shop carries a large range of locally grown apples and juices. Look out for outdoor theatre in the gardens in the summer. Ring for details of this and a full programme of events or visit website.

Times Open daily all year, Jan-Feb & Nov-Dec 10-5; Mar-Oct 10-5.30. Closed Xmas, New Year & during "Art in Action" 16-19

Jul* **Fees** £3.50 (ch 16 & under free, concessions £3.50). Party 20+ £3.50, Jan-Feb. £5.45 (ch under 10 free, ch 10-16 £3.65, concessions £4.35). Party 20+ £4.25, Mar-Oct. £3.85 (ch 16 & under free, concessions £3.85). Party 20+ £3.85, Nov-Dec. (Party rates available for coaches)* **Facilities** Ⓟ ☕ 🍽 licensed ⛩ (outdoor) ♿ (fully accessible) toilets for disabled shop 🚭

WITNEY Map 4 SP31

Cogges Manor Farm Museum

Church Ln, Cogges OX28 3LA
☎ 01993 772602 📠 01993 703056
web: www.cogges.org
dir: 0.5m SE off A4022

The museum includes the Manor, dairy and walled garden, and has breeds of animals typical of the Victorian period. The first floor of the manor contains period rooms. Special events take place through the season.

Times Open Apr-Oct, Tue-Fri 10.30-5.30, Sat, Sun & BH Mon, 12-5.30. Early closing Oct. Closed Good Fri.* **Facilities** Ⓟ Ⓟ ☕ ⛩ (outdoor) ♿ (partly accessible) toilets for disabled (wheelchair available, audio tour) shop

WOODSTOCK Map 4 SP41

Blenheim Palace

OX20 1PP
☎ 0800 849 6500 & 01993 811091 📠 01993 810570
e-mail: operations@blenheimpalace.com
web: www.blenheimpalace.com
dir: M40 junct 9, follow signs to Blenheim Palace, on A44 8m N of Oxford

Home of the Duke and Duchess of Marlborough and birthplace of Sir Winston Churchill, Blenheim Palace is an English Baroque masterpiece. Fine furniture, sculpture, paintings and tapestries are set in magnificent gilded staterooms that overlook sweeping lawns and formal gardens. 'Capability' Brown landscaped the 2100-acre park, which is open to visitors for pleasant walks and beautiful views. A permanent exhibit 'Blenheim Palace: The Untold Story' explores the lives of those who have lived here, through the eyes of the servants. Please telephone for details of the full event programme throughout the year including a Jousting Tournament and the Battle Proms.

Times Open daily Palace, Park & Gardens 12 Feb-11 Dec (ex Mon-Tue in Nov & Dec) 10.30-6. Park daily all year 9-6 (last admission 4.45). Closed 25 Dec **Fees** Palace, Park & Gardens £18 (ch £10, concessions £14.50). Familly £48. Park & Gardens £10.30 (ch £5, concessions £7.70). Family £26* **Facilities** Ⓟ Ⓟ ☕ 🍽 licensed ⛩ (outdoor) ♿ (partly accessible) (wheelchair access via lift in Palace) toilets for disabled (ramps, disabled parking, buggies, wheelchairs) shop 🚭

Oxfordshire Museum FREE

Fletcher's House, Park St OX20 1SN
☎ 01993 811456 📠 01993 813239
e-mail: oxon.museum@oxfordshire.go.uk
web: www.tomocc.org.uk
dir: A44 Evesham-Oxford, follow signs for Blenheim Palace. Museum opposite church

Situated in the heart of the historic town of Woodstock, the award-winning redevelopment of Fletcher's House provides a home for the county museum. Set in attractive gardens, the new museum celebrates Oxfordshire in all its diversity and features collections of local history, art, archaeology, landscape and wildlife as well as a gallery exploring the County's innovative industries from nuclear power to nanotechnology. Interactive exhibits offer new learning experiences for visitors of all ages. The museum's purpose-built Garden Gallery houses a variety of touring exhibitions of regional and national interest. A new display of dinosaur footprints from Ardley Quarry and a replica megalosaurus, are located in the walled garden.

Times Open all year, Tue-Sat 10-5, Sun 2-5. Closed Good Fri, 25-26 Dec & 1 Jan. Open BH Mons. Please check for opening hours **Facilities** Ⓟ ☕ 🍽 licensed ⛩ (outdoor) ♿ (fully accessible) toilets for disabled (chair lifts to all galleries) shop 🚭

RUTLAND

The Great Hall, Oakham Castle

LYDDINGTON Map 4 SP89

Lyddington Bede House

Blue Coat Ln LE15 9LZ
☎ 01572 822438 📠 01572 822780
web: www.english-heritage.org.uk

Once a prominent medieval palace, later converted into an almshouse for the poor. Its history is bought to life in an evocative audio tour.

Times Open Apr-Nov, Thu-Mon 10-5 **Fees** £4.20 (ch £2.10, concessions £3.60). Family ticket £10.50. Prices and opening times are subject to change in March 2011. Please check web site or call 0870 333 1181 for the most up to date prices and opening times when planning your visit **Facilities** ♿ (partly accessible) (ground floor only) ⊗ #

OAKHAM Map 4 SK80

Oakham Castle FREE

Catmos St LE15 6HW
☎ 01572 758440 📠 01572 758445
e-mail: museum@rutland.gov.uk
web: www.rutland.gov.uk/castle
dir: off Market Place

An exceptionally fine Norman Great Hall built in the 12th century. Earthworks, walls and remains of an earlier motte can be seen along with medieval sculptures and unique presentation horseshoes forfeited by peers of the realm and royalty to the Lord of the Manor. The castle is now a popular venue for civil marriages, meetings and special events.

Times Open all year, Tue-Fri 10-5, Sat 10-4. Closed Sun-Mon & Xmas, New Year & Good Fri **Facilities** Ⓟ ♿ (partly accessible) shop ⊗

Rutland County Museum & Visitor Centre FREE

Catmos St LE15 6HW
☎ 01572 758440 📠 01572 758445
e-mail: museum@rutland.gov.uk
web: www.rutland.gov.uk/museum
dir: on A6003, S of town centre

Rutland County Museum is the perfect introduction to England's smallest county. Displays include local archaeology, discoveries, vintage tractors and carts, the Oakham Drop Gallows and a Dinosaur Discovery area for children. The museum holds regular cinema screenings and has a popular gift shop.

Times Open all year, Tue-Fri 10-5, Sat 10-4. Closed Sun-Mon & Xmas, New Year & Good Fri **Facilities** 🅟 Ⓟ ♿ (partly accessible) toilets for disabled (induction loop in meeting room) shop ⊗

SHROPSHIRE

Ludlow Castle

ACTON BURNELL Map 7 SJ50

Acton Burnell Castle

FREE

SY5 7PE
web: www.english-heritage.org.uk
dir: in Acton Burnell on unclass road 8m S of Shrewsbury

Not so much a castle, more a fortified 13th-century manor house, Acton Burnell Castle is now just a shell, but it is believed that the first parliament at which the commons were fully represented was held here in 1283.

Times Open at all reasonable times **Facilities** ⌗

ATCHAM Map 7 SJ50

Attingham Park

SY4 4TP
☎ 01743 708123 📠 01743 708175
e-mail: attingham@nationaltrust.org.uk
web: www.nationaltrust.org.uk/attinghampark
dir: 4m SE of Shrewsbury on B4380

Attingham Park is centred on one of Britain's finest regency mansions, set in a landscaped deer park designed by Humphry Repton. The house is undergoing a major project to revive and re-discover the original lavish decorative schemes, with new upstairs rooms open for the first time. The park is an ideal place for a country walk, and there is a programme of events throughout the year.

Times Park & grounds open daily, 9-6. House: daily. 11-5.30, tours 13-28 Nov, 11-3.* **Facilities** Ⓟ ☕ ⛩ (outdoor) ♿ (partly accessible) (level access, lift to first floor, top floor only accessible via stairs) toilets for disabled (2 electric self drive buggies, 1 staff driven 8-seater) shop ✿

BENTHALL Map 7 SJ60

Benthall Hall

TF12 5RX
☎ 01952 882159
e-mail: benthall@nationaltrust.org.uk
web: www.nationaltrust.org.uk/main/w-benthallhall
dir: on B4375

The main part of the house was built around 1585. A wing at the back, which has been altered at various times, dates originally from about 1520. It is an attractive sandstone building with mullioned windows, fine oak panelling and a splendid carved staircase.

Times Open Apr-Jun, Tue-Wed 2-5.30; also Sun Jul-Sep. Open BH Mon. Garden opens 1.30* **Fees** House & garden £5.50 (ch £2.80). Garden only £3.50 (ch £1.75)* **Facilities** Ⓟ ♿ (partly accessible) toilets for disabled (Braille, large print guides) ⊗ ✿

BOSCOBEL Map 7 SJ80

Boscobel House and The Royal Oak

Brewood ST19 9AR
☎ 01902 850244 📠 01902 850244
web: www.english-heritage.org.uk
dir: on unclass road between A41 and A5

Built around 1632, Boscobel House has been fully restored and refurbished and is essentially a farmhouse that was converted into a hunting lodge. After his defeat at the Battle of Worcester in 1651, the future King Charles II hid from Cromwell's troops in an oak tree in the grounds, and then in a priest-hole in the attic of the house. The Royal Oak that visitors can see now was grown from an acorn taken from the original tree.

Times Open Apr-Oct, Wed-Sun & BH 10-5 (last entry 1hr before closing) **Fees** £5.50 (ch £2.80, concessions £4.70). Family ticket £13.80. Prices and opening times are subject to change in March 2011. Please check web site or call 0870 333 1181 for the most up to date prices and opening times when planning your visit **Facilities** Ⓟ ☕ ⛩ shop ⊗ ⌗

Whiteladies Priory

FREE

web: www.english-heritage.org.uk
dir: 1m SW of Boscobel House, off an unclass road between A41 and A5

Only the ruins are left of this Augustinian nunnery, which dates from 1158 and was destroyed in the Civil War. After the Battle of Worcester Charles II hid here and in the nearby woods before going on to Boscobel House.

Times Open daylight hours **Facilities** ⌗

BUILDWAS Map 7 SJ60

Buildwas Abbey

Iron Bridge TF8 7BW
☎ 01952 433274
web: www.english-heritage.org.uk
dir: on S bank of River Severn on B4378

Set against a backdrop of wooded grounds beside the River Severn, are the extensive remains of this Cistercian abbey founded in 1135.

Times Open Apr-Sep, Wed-Sun & BH Mon 10-5 **Fees** £3.20 (ch £1.60, concessions £2.70). Prices and opening times are subject to change in March 2011. Please check web site or call 0870 333 1181 for the most up to date prices and opening times when planning your visit **Facilities** Ⓟ shop ⊗ ⌗

BURFORD Map 3 SO56

Burford House Gardens

WR15 8HQ
☎ 01584 810777 01584 810673
e-mail: info@burford.co.uk
web: www.burford.co.uk
dir: off A456, 1m W of Tenbury Wells, 8m from Ludlow

Burford House and Garden Centre set within 15 acres, incorporates a Georgian mansion, which houses a shop and riverside gardens where you will find the National Clematis Collection.

Times Open all year 9-6 or dusk if earlier. Closed 25-26 Dec.* **Facilities** licensed (outdoor) (partly accessible) toilets for disabled (ramp into gardens, sloping paths, wheelchairs available) shop

COSFORD Map 7 SJ70

The Royal Air Force Museum

TF11 8UP
☎ 01902 376200 01902 376211
e-mail: cosford@rafmuseum.org
web: www.rafmuseum.org
dir: on A41, 1m S of M54 junct 3

The Royal Air Force Museum Cosford has one of the largest aviation collections in the UK, with 70 historic aircraft on display. Visitors will be able to see Britain's V bombers - Vulcan, Victor and Valiant and other aircraft suspended in flying attitudes in the national Cold War exhibition, housed in a landmark building covering 8000sqm.

Times Open all year daily, 10-6 (last admission 4). Closed 24-26 Dec, 1 & 7-11 Jan.* **Facilities** licensed (outdoor) (fully accessible) toilets for disabled (free loan of 3 manual w/chairs and 3 motor scooters) shop

CRAVEN ARMS Map 7 SO48

The Shropshire Hills Discovery Centre

School Rd SY7 9RS
☎ 01588 676000 01588 676030
e-mail: zoe.griffin@shropshire-cc.gov.uk
web: www.shropshirehillsdiscoverycentre.co.uk
dir: on A49, on S edge of Craven Arms

This attraction explores the history, nature and geography of the Shropshire Hills, through a series of interactive displays and simulations. The award-winning Centre has been revamped over the winter and now has a brand new Secret Hills exhibition. Become a landscape detective as you follow the new family Timeline Trail, which takes you from the Ice Age to the present day. On the way meet the Shropshire Mammoth, look inside an Iron Age Round House, dress up in Celtic clothing, make a mediaeval seal and float over Shropshire by watching the panoramic hot air balloon film. Other features include the Ice Age Orienteering trail around Onny Meadows, a Craft Room and a Riverside Ramble. Also try Geocaching, a kind of treasure-hunt that uses hand-held GPS.

Times Open all year, daily from 10 (last admission Nov-Mar 3.30, Apr-Oct 4.30)* **Facilities** licensed (outdoor) (partly accessible) toilets for disabled (wheelchair available) shop

HAUGHMOND ABBEY Map 7 SJ51

Haughmond Abbey

Upton Magna SY4 4RW
☎ 01743 709661
web: www.english-heritage.org.uk
dir: off B5062

Absorb these extensive 12th-century Augustinian abbey ruins, and visit the small museum.

Times Open Apr-Sep, Wed-Sun & BH Mon 10-5 **Fees** £3.20 (ch £1.60, concessions £2.70). Prices and opening times are subject to change in March 2011. Please check web site or call 0870 333 1181 for the most up to date prices and opening times when planning your visit **Facilities** shop

ENGLAND

IRONBRIDGE Map 7 SJ60

Ironbridge Gorge Museums

Coach Rd TF8 7DQ
☎ 01952 884391 & 0800 590258 📠 01952 884391
e-mail: tic@ironbridge.org.uk
web: www.ironbridge.org.uk
dir: M54 junct 4, signed

Ironbridge is the site of the world's first iron bridge. It was cast and built here in 1779, to span a narrow gorge over the River Severn. Now Ironbridge is the site of a remarkable series of museums relating the story of the bridge, recreating life in Victorian times and featuring ceramics and social history displays.

Times Open all year, 10-5. Some small sites closed Nov-Mar. Telephone for exact winter details.* **Facilities** licensed (outdoor) (fully accessible) toilets for disabled (wheelchairs, potters wheel, Braille guide, hearing loop) shop

LILLESHALL Map 7 SJ71

Lilleshall Abbey FREE

TF10 9HW
☎ 0121 625 6820
web: www.english-heritage.org.uk
dir: off A518 on unclass road

In the beautiful grounds of Lilleshall Hall, ruined Lilleshall Abbey was founded shortly before the middle of the 12th century and from the high west front visitors can look down the entire 228ft length of the abbey church.

Times Open Apr-Sep, daily 10-5. Closed Oct-Mar **Facilities**

LUDLOW Map 7 SO57

Ludlow Castle

Castle Square SY8 1AY
☎ 01584 873355 & 874465 📠 01584 874465
e-mail: info@ludlowcastle.com
web: www.ludlowcastle.com
dir: A49 to town centre

Ludlow Castle dates from 1086. In 1473, Edward IV sent the Prince of Wales and his brother - later to become the Princes in the Tower - to live here, and Ludlow Castle became a seat of government. John Milton's *Comus* was first performed at Ludlow Castle in 1634; now contemporary performances of Shakespeare's plays, together with concerts, are put on in the castle grounds during the Ludlow Festival (end June-early July). Please telephone for details of events running throughout the year.

Times Open all year, Dec-Jan, Sat-Sun 10-4; Feb-Mar & Oct-Nov, daily 10-4; Apr-Jul & Sep, daily 10-5; Aug, daily 10-7; (last admission 30 minutes before closing). Closed 25 Dec **Fees** £4.50 (ch under 6 free, ch £2.50, pen £4). Family ticket £12.50* **Facilities** (outdoor) (partly accessible) toilets for disabled shop

MORETON CORBET Map 7 SJ52

Moreton Corbet Castle FREE

web: www.english-heritage.org.uk
dir: In Moreton Corbet off B5063 (a turning off A49), 7 miles NE of Shrewsbury

Inherited by the Corbets in 1235, who are thought to have remodelled the great keep, this castle may already have been standing for over 100 years. It was remodelled in the 16th century and then partially demolished to make way for a great Elizabethan mansion. Although damaged in the Civil War, the castle and mansion stand today as one of the most picturesque ruins of the Shropshire Marches.

Times Open at any reasonable time **Facilities**

MUCH WENLOCK Map 7 SO69

Wenlock Priory

TA3 6HS
☎ 01952 727466
web: www.english-heritage.org.uk

Experience the ruins of this large Cluniac priory and the atmospheric remains of the 13th-century church and Norman chapter house. The audio tour offers a fascinating insight into its history. Impressive topiary figures guard the priory ruins.

Times Open all year, Mar-Apr, Wed-Sun & BH 10-5; May-Aug, daily 10-5; Sep-Oct, Wed-Sun 10-5; Nov-Feb, Thu-Sun 10-4. Closed 24-26 Dec & 1 Jan **Fees** £3.80 (ch £1.90, concessions £3.20). Prices and opening times are subject to change in March 2011. Please check web site or call 0870 333 1181 for the most up to date prices and opening times when planning your visit **Facilities** (fully accessible) toilets for disabled (audio tour, hearing loop)

OSWESTRY Map 7 SJ22

Old Oswestry Hill Fort FREE

web: www.english-heritage.org.uk
dir: 1m N of Oswestry, off an unclass road off A483

An impressive Iron Age hill-fort of 68 acres, defended by a series of five ramparts, with an elaborate western entrance and unusual earthwork cisterns.

Times Open at any reasonable time **Facilities**

QUATT **Map 7 SO78**

Dudmaston Estate

WV15 6QN
☎ 01746 780866 📠 01746 780744
e-mail: dudmaston@nationaltrust.org.uk
web: www.nationaltrust.org.uk/main/w-dudmaston
dir: 4m SE of Bridgnorth on A442

The 17th-century flower paintings which belonged to Francis Darby of Coalbrookdale are exhibited in this house of the same period, with modern works, botanical art and fine furniture. The house stands in an extensive park and garden and there are woodland and lakeside walks.

Times Open House Apr-Sep, Tue-Wed, Sun & BH Mon, 2-5. Garden, tea room & shop Sun-Wed, noon-5.30. Closed Good Fri* **Fees** House, Garden & Grounds £7 (ch £3.50). Family ticket £17.50. Garden & Grounds £5.50 (ch £2.75). Family ticket £13.75* **Facilities** Ⓟ Ⓟ ☕ ⛩ (outdoor) ♿ (partly accessible) (all ground floors are accessible, first floor galleries are currently unaccessible) toilets for disabled (Braille & large print guides, taped tours, hearing loops) shop 🚫 ✤

SHREWSBURY **Map 7 SJ41**

Shrewsbury Castle and Shropshire Regimental Museum

The Castle, Castle St SY1 2AT
☎ 01743 358516
e-mail: shropsrm@zoom.co.uk
web: www.shrewsburymuseums.com
dir: located in town centre, adjacent to railway station

Shrewsbury Castle commands fantastic views over the town and surrounding area. Dating originally from the 1070s it was 'restored' in the 18th century by Thomas Telford, who built the romantic Laura's Tower. In the main building is the Shropshire Regimental Museum, where, as well as fascinating displays, you will find staff ready to help with enquiries about your family's role in Shropshire's military life. The Circular Room at Shrewsbury Castle is licensed for civil ceremonies. The grounds are a magnificent setting for photographs and a varied programme of summer events.

Times Open all year, 27 May-10 Sep, Mon-Sat, 10-5; Sun 10-4; 11 Sep-22 Dec, Tue-Sat, 10-4* **Facilities** Ⓟ ⛩ (outdoor) ♿ (partly accessible) (ramped access to main museum, steps and steep slopes around monument) toilets for disabled shop 🚫

STOKESAY **Map 7 SO48**

Stokesay Castle

SY7 9AH
☎ 01588 672544
web: www.english-heritage.org.uk
dir: 1m S of Craven Arms off A49

Most perfectly preserved 13th-century fortified manor house. See its superb timber-framed Jacobean gatehouse and stroll through the impressive great hall. Delightful cottage gardens.

Times Open all year, Apr-Sep, daily 10-5; Oct & Mar, Wed-Sun 10-5; Nov-Feb, Thu-Sun 10-4. Closed 24-26 Dec & 1 Jan. Castle may close early for functions, please call to check **Fees** £5.50 (ch £2.80, concessions £4.70) Family £13.80. Prices and opening times are subject to change in March 2011. Please check web site or call 0870 333 1181 for the most up to date prices and opening times when planning your visit **Facilities** Ⓟ ⛩ ♿ (partly accessible) (some steps, narrow gate) toilets for disabled (tape tour for visually impaired, ramp for wheelchairs) 🚫 #

TELFORD **Map 7 SJ60**

Hoo Farm Animal Kingdom

Preston-on-the-Weald Moors TF6 6DJ
☎ 01952 677917 📠 01952 677944
e-mail: info@hoofarm.com
web: www.hoofarm.com
dir: M54 junct 6, follow brown tourist signs

Hoo Farm is a real children's paradise where there is always something happening. A clean, friendly farm that appeals to all ages and offers close contact with a wide variety of animals from fluffy chicks and lambs to foxes, llamas, deer and ostriches. A daily programme of events encourages audience participation in the form of bottle feeding lambs, pig feeding, ferret racing and collecting freshly-laid eggs. The Craft Area offers the chance to try your hand at candle dipping, glass or pottery painting or even throwing a pot on the potters wheel. There are junior quad bikes and a rifle range, pony rides, powered mini-tractors as well as indoor and outdoor play areas and a games room. Please telephone for details of special events throughout the year.

Times Open 25 Mar-9 Sep, Tue-Sun 10-6; 10 Sep-24 Nov, Tue-Sun, 10-5. 25; Nov-24 Dec, daily 10-5. Closes at 1 on 24 Dec* **Facilities** Ⓟ ☕ ⛩ (indoor & outdoor) ♿ (partly accessible) toilets for disabled shop 🚫

WELLINGTON Map 7 SJ61

Sunnycroft

200 Holyhead Rd TF1 2DR
☎ 01952 242884
e-mail: sunnycroft@nationaltrust.org.uk
web: www.nationaltrust.org.uk/sunnycroft
dir: M54 junct 7, 2m E of Wellington off B5061

A late Victorian gentleman's villa, typical of houses built for prosperous business and professional people on the fringe of towns and cities. The house is a time capsule of early 20th-century life both above and below stairs, when it was home to the Lander family. Displays of embroidery by Joan Lander can be seen within the house. The gardens and grounds are very attractive, and taking tea in the old smoking room overlooking the croquet lawn is a quintessential English experience.

Times House & Gardens open 12 Mar-Oct & 17-20 Dec, Fri-Sun 1-5.* **Facilities** Ⓟ Ⓟ ☕ ⛩ (outdoor)

WESTON-UNDER-REDCASTLE Map 7 SJ52

Hawkstone Historic Park & Follies

SY4 5UY
☎ 01948 841700 01939 200335
e-mail: enquiries@hawkstone.co.uk
web: www.principal-hayley.co.uk
dir: 3m from Hodnet off A53, follow brown heritage signs

Created in the 18th century by the Hill family, Hawkstone is one of the greatest historic parklands in Britain. After almost 100 years of neglect it has now been restored and designated a Grade I historic landscape. Visitors can once again experience the magical world of intricate pathways, arches and bridges, towering cliffs and follies, and an awesome grotto. The Grand Valley and woodlands have centuries-old oaks, wild rhododendrons and lofty monkey puzzles. The park covers nearly 100 acres of hilly terrain and visitors are advised to wear sensible shoes and clothing and to bring a torch. Allow 3-4 hours for the tour, which is well signposted - a route map is included in the admission price. Attractions include 'Hear King Arthur' and meeting the Duke of Wellington in the White Tower to discuss the Battle of Waterloo.

Times Open from 10 Mar, Sat & Sun; Apr-May, & Sep-Oct, Wed-Sun; Jun-Aug, daily* **Fees** Wkdays £6.95 (ch £4 pen & students £5.95). Family ticket £20* **Facilities** Ⓟ ☕ licensed (outdoor) ♿ (partly accessible) (access to tearooms, gift shop and grand valley) toilets for disabled shop

WROXETER Map 7 SJ50

Wroxeter Roman City

SY5 6PH
☎ 01743 761330 01743 761990
web: www.english-heritage.org.uk
dir: 5m E of Shrewsbury, 1m S of A5

Discover what urban life was like 2,000 years ago in the fourth largest city in Roman Britain. See the remains of the impressive 2nd-century municipal baths and view the excavated treasures in the museum.

Times Open all year, Mar-Oct, daily 10-5; Nov-Feb, Wed-Sun 10-4. Closed 24-26 Dec & 1 Jan **Fees** £4.40 (ch £2.20, concessions £3.70). Family ticket £11. Prices and opening times are subject to change in March 2011. Please check web site or call 0870 333 1181 for the most up to date prices and opening times when planning your visit **Facilities** Ⓟ toilets for disabled shop #

SOMERSET

Moated entrance to the Bishop's Palace, Wells

AXBRIDGE **Map 3 ST45**

King John's Hunting Lodge

The Square BS26 2AP

☎ 01934 732012

e-mail: kingjohns@nationaltrust.org.uk

web: www.nationaltrust.org.uk

dir: on corner of Axbridge High St, in the Square

Nothing to do with King John or with hunting, this jettied and timber-framed house was built around 1500. It gives a good indication of the wealth of the merchants of that time and is now a museum of local history, with old photographs, paintings and items such as the town stocks and constables' staves.

Times Open 21 Mar-Sep, daily 1-4* **Facilities** Ⓟ shop

BARRINGTON **Map 3 ST31**

Barrington Court

TA19 0NQ

☎ 01460 241938 & 242614 01460 243133

e-mail: barringtoncourt@nationaltrust.org.uk

web: www.nationaltrust.org.uk

dir: 5m NE of Ilminster on B3168

The house is a Tudor manor, the interior of which is currently displayed empty, though with changing exhibitions. The gardens were created in the 1920s, with the help (through the post) of Gertrude Jekyll. They are laid out in 'rooms' and there is a large walled kitchen garden supplying fresh fruit and vegetables to the restaurant.

Times Open Mar, Thu-Tue 11-4.30; Apr-Sep daily (ex Wed) 11-5; 2 Oct-2 Nov, Thu-Tue 11-4.30. 6-14 Dec, Sat & Sun 11-4.* **Facilities** Ⓟ licensed (outdoor) (partly accessible) (Court House not easily accessible due to many stairs) toilets for disabled (Batricars, Braille and large print guides, w/chairs) shop

BATH **Map 3 ST76**

American Museum in Britain **2 FOR 1**

Claverton Manor BA2 7BD

☎ 01225 460503 01225 469160

e-mail: info@americanmuseum.org

web: www.americanmuseum.org

dir: Signed from city centre & A36 Warminster road

Claverton Manor is just two miles south east of Bath, in a beautiful setting above the River Avon. The house was built in 1820 by Sir Jeffrey Wyatville, and is now a museum of American decorative arts. The gardens are well worth seeing, and include an American arboretum and a replica of George Washington's garden at Mount Vernon. Each year the museum holds special exhibitions and runs a full programme of special events with kids' activities, live music, living history events and Quilting Bees. 2011 is the 50th anniversary year of the museum, there will be many events including a special exhibition featuring costume and memorabilia of Marilyn Monroe.

Times Open 13 Mar-Oct, Tue-Sun 12-5. Open Mon in Aug & BHs. Also open 26 Nov-19 Dec Tue-Sun 12-4.30* **Fees** £8 (ch £4.50, concessions £7). Family ticket £21.50* **Facilities** Ⓟ (outdoor) (partly accessible) (grounds not fully accessible) toilets for disabled (lift to all floors) shop

Bath Abbey

Abbey Churchyard BA1 1LY

☎ 01225 422462 & 303310 01225 429990

e-mail: office@bathabbey.org

web: www.bathabbey.org

dir: M4 junct 18, centre of Bath, next to Pump Rooms & The Roman Baths. Orange Grove drop off and collection point for coaches-east end

The 15th-century abbey church was built on the site of the Saxon abbey where King Edgar was crowned in 973. The church is Perpendicular style with Norman arches and superb fan-vaulting. The famous West Front carvings represent the founder-bishop's dream of angels ascending and descending from heaven.

Times Abbey: Apr-Oct, Mon-Sat 9-6; Nov-Mar, Mon-Sat 9-4.30, Sun all year 1-2.30 & 4.30-5.30. Museum: Apr-Oct, Mon-Sat 10-5; Nov-Mar, Mon-Sat 10-4. Closed 25 Dec & Good Fri **Fees** Visitors invited to donate £2.50 per adult & £1 per student. Tower Tours £5 (ch 5-14 must be accompanied £2.50). Tickets available from shop **Facilities** Ⓟ (fully accessible) toilets for disabled (level access, induction loop, large print leaflet, lift) shop

Bath Aqua Theatre of Glass **2 FOR 1**

105-107 Walcot St BA1 5BW

☎ 01225 428146

e-mail: sales@bathaquaglass.com

web: www.bathaquaglass.com

View old stained-glass windows renovated from Bath Abbey Chambers. In the heart of the city's artisan quarter, this is an ideal centre to learn about the history of glass and watch the ancient craft of free glass-blowing.

Times Open all year, daily (ex Sun) 9.30-5. Gift shop open Mon-Sat 9.30-5. Glass Blowing demonstration, Mon-Sat 11.15 & 2.15* **Fees** £4 (ch under 16 & concessions £2.50). Family ticket (2ad+2ch) £10* **Facilities** Ⓟ (partly accessible) (shop and visitor area all on one level) shop

BATH *continued*

Bath Postal Museum

2 FOR 1

27 Northgate St BA1 1AJ
☎ 01225 460333 Fax 01225 460333
e-mail: info@bathpostalmuseum.org
web: www.bathpostalmuseum.org
dir: On entering city fork left at mini rdbt. After all lights into Walcot St. Podium car park facing

The first letter sent with a stamp was sent from Bath, and this museum helps you to discover how 18th-century Bath influenced and developed the Postal System, including the story of the Penny Post. Visitors can explore the history of written communication from ancient Egyptian clay tablets, to the first Airmail flight from Bath to London in 1912. See the Victorian Post Office and watch continuous video films including the in-house production entitled 'History of Writing'. The museum is full of hands-on and interactive features to engage the whole family.

Times Open all year, Mon-Sat 11-5 (last admission 4.30 winter)* **Fees** £3.50 (ch under 5 free, ch £1.50, concessions £3, students £1.50). Family and Party 10+ tickets available* **Facilities** Ⓟ ♿ (fully accessible) (films and computer games for hearing impaired) shop ®

Fashion Museum

Bennett St BA1 2QH
☎ 01225 477789 Fax 01225 477173
e-mail: fashion_bookings@bathnes.gov.uk
web: www.fashionmuseum.co.uk
dir: Museum near city centre. Parking in Charlotte Street Car park

The Fashion Museum showcases a world-class collection of historical and contemporary dress and includes opportunities to try on replica corsets and crinolines. It is housed in Bath's famous 18th-century Assembly Rooms designed by John Wood the Younger in 1771. Special exhibitions are held every summer, see website for details.

Times Open all year, daily Jan-Feb 10.30-4; Mar-Oct 10.30-5; Nov-Dec 10.30-4. Closed 25-26 Dec **Fees** £7 (ch £5). Family ticket £20. Combined ticket with Roman Baths, £14.50 (ch £8.70)* **Facilities** Ⓟ ☕ ♿ (fully accessible) toilets for disabled (audio guides available) shop ®

The Herschel Museum of Astronomy

2 FOR 1

19 New King St BA1 2BL
☎ 01225 446865 Fax 01225 446865
e-mail: herschelbpt@btconnect.com
web: www.bath-preservation-trust.org.uk
dir: in Bath city centre

This 18th-century town house celebrates the achievements of William Herschel and his sister Caroline, who were both distinguished astronomers. William discovered Uranus in 1781. The house is decorated and furnished in the style of the period of Georgian Bath, while the gardens are semi-formal in design and include different plants and herbs popular at the time. There is also a star vault astronomy auditorium.

Times Open daily (ex Wed) 31 Jan-11 Dec, Mon-Tue & Thu-Fri 1-5, Sat, Sun & BHs 11-5 **Fees** £4.50 (ch £2.50, students £3, concessions £4). Family ticket £11 **Facilities** Ⓟ ♿ (partly accessible) (audio & virtual tours, handling collections, sub titles) shop ®

The Holburne Museum

Great Pulteney St BA2 4DB
☎ 01225 466669 Fax 01225 333121
e-mail: holburne@bath.ac.uk
web: www.bath.ac.uk/holburne
dir: M4 junct 18 to A4 and follow brown signs

This jewel in Bath's crown re-opens its doors in spring 2011, following a major development project. Once the Georgian Sydney Hotel, this Grade I listed building has been lovingly restored with a striking new extension in the garden, designed by Eric Parry. It displays the treasures collected by Sir William Holbourne: superb English and continental silver, porcelain, majolica, glass, Renaissance bronzes and embroidery. Since Sir William's time the collection has been greatly expanded and now includes portraits by Stubbs, Ramsay, Raeburn and Bath's own artist Gainsborough. The Museum will provide access to all, offer creative learning opportunities and an exciting events and exhibition programme.

Times Scheduled to re-open Spring 2011, following a major redevelopment project. See website for current opening times **Fees** Free entry, but charge made for some temporary exhibitions **Facilities** (outdoor) (fully accessible) (lift to 1st floor) shop

The Jane Austen Centre 2 FOR 1

40 Gay St, Queen Square BA1 2NT
01225 443000 01225 443018
e-mail: jackie@janeausten.co.uk
web: www.janeausten.co.uk
dir: in heart of Bath by Queen Square

Celebrating Bath's most famous resident, the centre offers a snapshot of life during Regency times and explores how living in this city affected Jane Austen's life and writing. Every September, Bath holds a Jane Austen festival.

Times Open all year, daily 9.45-5.30; Jul-Aug, Thu-Sat 9.45-7; Nov-Mar, Sun-Fri 11-4.30, Sat 9.45-5.30. Closed 24-26 Dec & 1 Jan **Fees** £6.95 (ch £3.95, concessions £5.50). Family ticket (2 ad+up to 4 ch) £18* **Facilities** licensed (partly accessible) (access to exhibition on ground floor only) shop

Museum of Bath at Work 2 FOR 1

Julian Rd BA1 2RH
01225 318348 01225 318348
e-mail: mobaw@hotmail.com
web: www.bath-at-work.org.uk
dir: from city centre, off Lansdown Rd into Julian Rd. Museum next to church on right

Two thousand years of Bath's commercial and industrial development are explored with exhibits on 'The Story of Bath Stone', a Bath cabinet makers' workshop, a 1914 Horstmann car and a reconstruction of J B Bowlers' engineering and mineral water business. A local history gallery, education room and a display about local inventions add further interest.

Times Open all year, Apr-1 Nov, daily 10.30-5; Nov-Apr, wknds 10.30-5. Closed Dec **Fees** £5 (concessions £3.50). Family ticket £12* **Facilities** (indoor) (partly accessible) (audio guides, ramps, wheelchair access to exhibition floor) shop

No 1 Royal Crescent

No 1 Royal Cresent BA1 2LR
01225 428126 01225 481850
e-mail: no1musuem@bptrust.org.uk
web: www.bath-preservation-trust.org.uk
dir: 1st house in Royal Crescent situated above Victoria Ave & Victoria Park, Charlotte St car park

Bath is renowned as a Georgian city, but most of its houses have been altered over the years to suit changing tastes and lifestyles. Built in 1768 by John Wood the Elder, No 1 Royal Crescent has been restored to look as it would have done some 200 years ago. Visitors can see a grand townhouse of the late 18th century with authentic furniture, paintings and carpets. On the ground floor are the study and dining room, and on the first floor a lady's bedroom and drawing room. In the basement there is a period kitchen and the museum shop.

Times Open 19 Feb-30 Oct, 10.30-5; 31 Oct-10 Dec, 10.30-4. Open BH Mon & Good Fri (last admission 30 mins before closing) **Fees** £6 (concessions £5). Family ticket £12. Group rate 10+ £4 each. Schools £2.50 each **Facilities** (partly accessible) (DVD virtual tour, induction loop, Braille guide) shop

Prior Park Landscape Garden

Ralph Allen Dr BA2 5AH
01225 833422 & 0900 133 5242
e-mail: priorpark@nationaltrust.org.uk
web: www.nationaltrust.org.uk/main/w-priorpark
dir: close to city centre, 30 mins walk from Bath Spa railway station

Created by local entrepreneur Ralph Allen with advice from Alexander Pope and 'Capability' Brown, this garden in set in a sweeping valley with magnificent views of the city of Bath. Many interesting features include an 18th-century Palladian Bridge, three lakes, a wooded glade and a recently restored wilderness.

Times Open all year, Jan-6 Feb & 5 Nov-Dec, Sat-Sun 11-dusk; 12 Feb-30 Oct, daily 11-5.30. Closed 25 Dec **Fees** £5.80 (ch £3.25). Family (2ad+2ch) £14.80 **Facilities** (outdoor) (partly accessible) (the wilderness and view point are fully accessible) toilets for disabled (Braille, large print guides, designated parking)

ENGLAND

BATH *continued*

Roman Baths & Pump Room

Abbey Church Yard BA1 1LZ
☎ 01225 477785 & 477867 📠 01225 477743
e-mail: romanbaths_bookings@bathnes.gov.uk
web: www.romanbaths.co.uk
dir: M4 junct 18, A46 into city centre

The remains of the Roman baths and temple give a vivid impression of life nearly 2,000 years ago. New displays and costumed characters re-tell the story. Built next to Britain's only hot spring, the baths served the sick, and the pilgrims visiting the adjacent Temple of Sulis Minerva. Above the Temple Courtyard, the Pump Room became a popular meeting place in the 18th century. The site still flows with natural hot water and no visit is complete without a taste of the famous hot spa water.

Times Open all year, Mar-Jun & Sep-Oct, daily 9-5; Jul & Aug, daily 9am-9pm; Jan-Feb & Nov-Dec, daily 9.30-4-30 (last exit 1hr after these times). Closed 25-26 Dec. Summer evening opening by torch light until 10, in Jul-Aug, (last entry 9) **Fees** £11 (£11.50 Jul-Aug) (ch £7.20). Family ticket £32. Combined ticket with Fashion Museum £14.50 (ch £8.70)* **Facilities** Ⓟ licensed (partly accessible) (lift to lower museum, some steps) toilets for disabled (sign language, audioguide) shop

Sally Lunn's Refreshment House & Museum

4 North Parade Passage BA1 1NX
☎ 01225 461634 📠 01225 447090
e-mail: enquiries@sallylunns.co.uk
web: www.sallylunns.co.uk
dir: centre of Bath, follow signs, next to Bath Abbey

This Tudor building is Bath's oldest house and was a popular 17th-century meeting place. The traditional 'Sally Lunn' is similar to a brioche, and it is popularly believed to carry the name of its inventor who came to Bath in 1680. The bun is still served in the restaurant, and the original oven, Georgian cooking range and a collection of baking utensils are displayed in the museum.

Times Open all year, Museum, Mon-Fri 10-6, Sat 10-5, Sun 11-5. Closed 25-26 Dec. House open Mon-Fri 10-9, Sat 10-10, Sun 11-9 **Fees** 30p (concessions free) **Facilities** Ⓟ licensed (partly accessible) (toilets and museum only accessible via stairs) (Braille menu available) shop

CHARD Map 3 ST30

Forde Abbey

TA20 4LU
☎ 01460 221290 📠 01460 220296
e-mail: info@fordeabbey.co.uk
web: www.fordeabbey.co.uk
dir: 4m SE of Chard, signed from A30 and A358

As one of the top gardens in England, Forde Abbey has much to offer keen gardeners. The 30 acres include a colourful bog garden, a walled kitchen garden, cascades, ponds, Ionic temple, rockery, herbaceous borders and the Centenary Fountain, the highest powered fountain in England. The privately owned magnificent 12th-century house contains outstanding Mortlake tapestries, spectacularly decorated plaster ceilings and fine furniture and paintings.

Times Gardens, open all year, daily 10-4.30. House open Apr-Oct, Tue-Fri, Sun & BH 12-4* **Facilities** Ⓟ licensed (outdoor) (partly accessible) (parts of bog garden not wheelchair accessible. Only great hall accessible in house) toilets for disabled (large print guide, computer presentation, w/chair) shop

CLEVEDON Map 3 ST47

Clevedon Court

Tickenham Rd BS21 6QU
☎ 01275 872257
e-mail: clevedoncourt@nationaltrust.org.uk
web: www.nationaltrust.org.uk
dir: M5 junct 20, off B3130 1.5m E of Clevedon

Clevedon Court is a remarkably complete manor house of around 1320. Additions have been made in each century, so it has a pleasing variety of styles, with an 18th-century terraced garden.

Times Open Apr-Sep, Wed-Thu, Sun & BH Mon 2-5. Car park & Gardens will open at 1.15* **Fees** £6.60 (ch £3.10). Party 20+ by arrangement* **Facilities** Ⓟ (partly accessible) (access via steps) (Braille/large print guide)

CRANMORE Map 3 ST64

East Somerset Railway

Cranmore Railway Station BA4 4QP
☎ 01749 880417 📠 01749 880764
e-mail: info@eastsomersetrailway.com
web: www.eastsomersetrailway.com
dir: on A361 between Frome & Shepton Mallet

Steam through the rolling Mendip countryside on a day out at The East Somerset Railway. Take a ride on one of the steam trains and travel back in time. There are plenty of events throughout the year, from Thomas the Tank Engine and Santa Specials to Enthusiast Gala Weekends. Telephone for details.

Times Open Apr-Oct, wknds; Jun-Aug, Wed & BHs (& Thu in Aug). December for Santa Specials. Please call for details **Fees** £7.50 (ch £5.50 & pen £6.50)* **Facilities** (P) licensed (fully accessible) toilets for disabled (ramp from road to platform & to train) shop

CRICKET ST THOMAS Map 3 ST30

The Wildlife Park at Cricket St Thomas

TA20 4DB
01460 30111 & 30892 01460 30817
e-mail: wildlifepark.cst@bourne-leisure.co.uk
web: www.wild.org.uk
dir: 3m E of Chard on A30, follow brown heritage signs

The Wildlife Park offers you the chance to see more than 500 animals at close quarters. Visitors can learn about what is being done to save endangered species, take a walk through the Lemur Wood, or ride on the Safari Train. During peak season, park mascot Larry the Lemur stars in his own show.

Times Open all year, daily 10-6 (last admission 4); winter 10-4.30 (last admission 3). Closed 25 Dec.* **Facilities** (P) licensed (outdoor) (partly accessible) toilets for disabled (some steep slopes) shop

DUNSTER Map 3 SS94

Dunster Castle

TA24 6SL
01643 821314 & 823004 (info only) 01643 823000
e-mail: dunstercastle@nationaltrust.org.uk
web: www.nationaltrust.org.uk
dir: 3m SE of Minehead, approach from A39. Approx 2m from Dunster Stn

The castle's picturesque appearance is largely due to 19th-century work, but older features can also be seen, the superb 17th-century oak staircase for example. Sub-tropical plants flourish in the 28-acre park and the terraced gardens are noted for exotica such as a giant lemon tree, yuccas, mimosa and palms.

Times Castle: 12 Mar-30 Oct, daily (ex Thu) 11-5 (last entry 4), 9-24 Apr & 16 Jul-28 Aug open on Thu. Garden & Park: Jan-11 Mar & Oct-Dec, daily 11-4, 12 Mar-30 Oct daily 10-5 **Fees** Castle, Garden & Park £9.40 (ch under 16 £4.60). Family ticket £22.50 (1 ad £14). Garden & Park only £5.20 (ch under 16 £2.40). Family ticket £12.80 (1 ad £7.60) **Facilities** (P) (P) (outdoor) (partly accessible) (ground floor wheelchair accessible, wheelchair routes through gardens) toilets for disabled (Braille, large print guides, Batricar & 2 w/chairs) shop

EAST LAMBROOK Map 3 ST41

East Lambrook Manor Gardens **2 FOR 1**

TA13 5HH
01460 240328
e-mail: enquiries@eastlambrook.com
web: www.eastlambrook.com
dir: signed off A303, at South Petherton rdbt. Follow brown signs to East Lambrook

It was the celebrated plantswoman and gardening writer, the late Margery Fish, who popularised the 'cottage garden' style of gardening in the 1950s and 1960s. Her wonderful Grade I listed cottage garden is known to garden lovers throughout the world. The garden now houses specialist collections of snowdrops and hardy geraniums, a specialist plant nursery and art gallery. Please contact or see website for more details.

Times Open Feb and May-17 Jul, daily 10-5; Mar-Apr and 20 Jul-Oct, Tue-Sat & BH Mon 10-5. Opening times 2011 not yet confirmed, please check before visit* **Fees** £4.50 (ch under 16 free). Group 10+ £4. Opening times & prices not yet confirmed for 2011, please check before visit* **Facilities** (P) (partly accessible) (narrow paths & steps restrict access to some parts of garden) toilets for disabled

FARLEIGH HUNGERFORD Map 3 ST85

Farleigh Hungerford Castle

BA2 7RS
01225 754026
web: www.english-heritage.org.uk
dir: 3.5m W of Trowbridge on A366

Set in a picturesque valley, this castle hides many secrets and a sinister past. An audio tour reveals all.

Times Open all year, Apr-Jun & Sep, daily 10-5; Jul-Aug, daily 10-6; Oct-1 Nov, daily 10-4; 2 Nov-Mar, Sat-Sun 10-4. Closed 24-26 Dec & 1 Jan.* **Facilities** (P) shop #

ENGLAND

GLASTONBURY Map 3 ST43

Glastonbury Abbey 2 FOR 1

Abbey Gatehouse, Magdalene St BA6 9EL
☎ 01458 832267 📠 01458 836117
e-mail: info@glastonburyabbey.com
web: www.glastonburyabbey.com
dir: M5 junct 23 to A39, on A361 between Frome & Taunton

Few places in Britain are as rich in myth and legend as Glastonbury. Tradition maintains that the impressive ruins mark the birthplace of Christianity in Britain. Joseph of Arimathea is said to have founded a chapel here in AD61, planting his staff in the ground where it flowered both at Christmas and Easter. Later, it is said, King Arthur and Guinevere were buried here, and the abbey has been a place of pilgrimage since the Middle Ages. The present abbey ruins date mostly from the 12th and 13th centuries. The display area contains artefacts and a model of the Abbey as it might have been in 1539. During the summer months meet a character from the past, who will tell you something of this wonderful place. Thirty-six acres of grounds including two ponds, an orchard and wildlife areas. Special events throughout the year, see website for details.

Times Open all year, daily, Jun-Aug 9-6; Sep-May 9.30-6 or dusk, whichever is the earliest. Dec-Feb open at 10. Closed 25 Dec* **Fees** £5.50 (ch 5-15 £3.50, pen £5). Family ticket £16.50* **Facilities** Ⓟ Ⓟ ☕ ⛩ (outdoor) ♿ (partly accessible) toilets for disabled (audio tape, hearing loop, wheelchairs, large print leaflet) shop

KINGSDON Map 3 ST52

Lytes Cary Manor

TA11 7HU
☎ 01458 224471 📠 01458 224471
e-mail: lytescarymanor@nationaltrust.org.uk
web: www.nationaltrust.org.uk/main/w-lytescarymanor
dir: off A303, signed from Padimore rdbt at junct of A303 & A37, take A372

Fine medieval manor house and delightful 14th-century chapel, surrounded by gardens with an enchanting mixture of formality and simplicity. Much of the present house was built in the 16th century although the oldest part, the chapel, dates from 1343. The Great Hall was a 15th-century addition. Unfortunately the gardens did not survive, but the present formal gardens are being restocked with plants that were commonly grown at the time of building, according to the 'Lytes Cary Herbal'-a manuscript still on display within the property. High yew topiary hedges enclose large borders and hidden paths.

Times Open 12 Mar-30 Oct, daily (ex Thu) 11-5 (last entry into house 4.30) **Fees** £8.10 (ch £4.10). Family £20.30. Garden only £5.75 (ch £2.95) **Facilities** Ⓟ ☕ ⛩ (outdoor) ♿ (partly accessible) (Downstairs of house only, some parts of garden are uneven) toilets for disabled (Braille guide, scented plants) shop ㊗ ✿

MINEHEAD Map 3 SS94

West Somerset Railway

The Railway Station TA24 5BG
☎ 01643 704996 📠 01643 706349
e-mail: info@west-somerset-railway.co.uk
web: www.west-somerset-railway.co.uk
dir: Follow brown WSR sign through Taunton & onto A358. Left after 3m for Bishops Lydeard Station car park

Take a journey of discovery, relive your childhood, or simply sit back and relax as you travel along one of Britain's best and longest Heritage Railways.

Times Open May-Sep, daily; Mar, Apr & Oct, Tue-Thu & Sat-Sun; Nov wknds only 10.15-5.15* **Fees** £14.80 (ch £7.40, pen £13.60). Cheaper for shorter journeys* **Facilities** Ⓟ Ⓟ ☕ ⛩ (outdoor) ♿ (fully accessible) toilets for disabled shop

MONTACUTE Map 3 ST41

Montacute House

TA15 6XP
☎ 01935 823289 📠 01935 826921
e-mail: montacute@nationaltrust.org.uk
web: www.nationaltrust.org.uk
dir: 4m W of Yeovil, on S side of A3088, 3m E of A303

Set amidst formal gardens, Montacute House was built by Sir Edward Phelips. He was a successful lawyer, and became Speaker of the House of Commons in 1604. Inside there are decorated ceilings, ornate fireplaces, heraldic glass and fine wood panelling. The Long Gallery displays a permanent collection of Tudor and Jacobean portraits from the National Portrait Gallery in London. Montacute has been used as the setting for successful films such as the 1995 version of *Sense and Sensibility*.

Times Open House & Gardens 13 Mar-Oct.* **Facilities** Ⓟ ☕ 🍴 licensed ⛩ (outdoor) ♿ (partly accessible) (wheelchair access restricted to ground floor) toilets for disabled (Braille guide, 3 manual wheelchairs) shop ㊗ ✿

MUCHELNEY Map 3 ST42

Muchelney Abbey

TA10 0DQ
☎ 01458 250664 01458 253842
web: www.english-heritage.org.uk

The monastery was first established at Muchelney by Ine, a 7th-century king of Wessex. It did not survive the Viking invasions, but the abbey was re-founded about AD950 and lasted for nearly six centuries. The present remains date largely from the 12th century. The best preserved feature of the site today is the Abbot's lodging, which had only just been completed in 1539 when the abbey was surrendered to Henry VIII.

Times Open Apr-Jun & Sep, daily 10-5; Jul-Aug, daily 10-6; Oct, daily 10-4. Closed Nov-Mar **Fees** £4 (ch £2, concessions £3.40). Prices and opening times are subject to change in March 2011. Please check web site or call 0870 333 1181 for the most up to date prices and opening times when planning your visit **Facilities** (partly accessible) (stairs to upper floor are uneven and steep) shop

NETHER STOWEY Map 3 ST13

Coleridge Cottage

35 Lime St TA5 1NQ
☎ 01278 732662
e-mail: coleridgecottage@nationaltrust.org.uk
web: www.nationaltrust.org.uk
dir: at W end of Nether Stowey, on S side of A39, 8m W of Bridgwater

Discover the former home of Coleridge, who lived in the cottage for three years from 1797. It was here that he wrote *The Rime of the Ancient Mariner*, part of *Christabel*, *Frost at Midnight* and *Kubla Khan*. The Coleridge family moved to Nether Stowey in 1797 and became friendly with the Wordsworths who lived nearby.

Times Open Apr-26 Sep, Thu-Sun & BHs 2-5.* **Facilities** (partly accessible) (steps to entrance, Braille & large print guides)

NUNNEY Map 3 ST74

Nunney Castle FREE

web: www.english-heritage.org.uk
dir: 3.5m SW of Frome, off A361

Built in 1373, and supposedly modelled on France's Bastille, this crenellated manor house has one of the deepest moats in England. It was ruined by Parliamentarian forces in the Civil War.

Times Open at any reasonable time **Facilities**

SPARKFORD Map 3 ST62

Haynes International Motor Museum

BA22 7LH
☎ 01963 440804 & 442783 01963 441004
e-mail: info@haynesmotormuseum.co.uk
web: www.haynesmotormuseum.co.uk
dir: from A303 follow A359 towards Castle Cary, museum clearly signed

An excellent day out for everyone - with more than 400 cars and bikes stunningly displayed, dating from 1885 to the present day, this is the largest international motor museum in Britain. If you want a nostalgic trip down memory lane the museum offers a host of familiar names such as Austin, MG and Morris, while for those seeking something more exotic there is a vast array of performance cars, from modern classics such as the Dodge Viper, Jaguar XJ220 and the Ferrari 360, plus the classic Jaguar E Type and AC Cobra. Also on show is a large collection of American cars, including the jewels in the Haynes crown, the V16 Cadillac, and the million-dollar Duesenberg. There's a Kids' Race Track, themed play area, soft play-bus, Super Diggers and plenty of other activities.

Times Open all year, Apr-Sep, daily 9.30-5.30; Oct-Mar, 10-4.30. Closed 24-26 Dec & 1 Jan **Fees** £8.95 (ch £4.25, concessions £7.50). Family (1ad+1ch) £11.50, (2ad+3ch) £25 **Facilities** (outdoor) (fully accessible) toilets for disabled (ramps & loan wheelchairs available) shop

STOKE ST GREGORY Map 3 ST32

Willow & Wetlands Visitor Centre FREE

Meare Green Court TA3 6HY
☎ 01823 490249 01823 490814
e-mail: info@englishwillowbaskets.co.uk
web: www.englishwillowbaskets.co.uk
dir: between North Curry & Stoke St Gregory, signed from A361 & A378

The centre is owned and run by Somerset Basketmakers and willow growers P H Coate & Son. The environmental exhibition gives a fascinating insight into the Somerset Levels and Moors. Optional guided tours are available during the week.

Times Open all year incl BHs, daily (ex Sun) 9.30-5. Optional guided tours are available wkdays at 11 & 2.30 (charged) **Facilities** (outdoor) (partly accessible) (some areas of the garden, up stairs museum & exhibition inaccessible) toilets for disabled shop

ENGLAND

STOKE-SUB-HAMDON Map 3 ST41

Stoke-Sub-Hamdon Priory FREE

North St TA4 6QP
☎ 01935 823289
web: www.nationaltrust.org.uk
dir: between A303 & A3088

A complex of buildings, begun in the 14th century for the priests of the Chantry Chapel of St Nicholas (now destroyed).

Times Open 13 Mar-Oct, daily 10-6 or dusk if earlier.* **Facilities** Ⓟ ♿ (partly accessible) (steps & rough ground)

STREET Map 3 ST43

The Shoe Museum FREE

C & J Clark Ltd, High St BA16 0EQ
☎ 01458 842169 01458 442226
e-mail: linda.stevens@clarks.com
dir: A39 to Street, follow signs for Clarks Village

The museum is in the oldest part of the shoe factory set up by Cyrus and James Clark in 1825. It contains shoes from Roman times to the present, buckles, engravings, fashion plates, machinery, hand tools and advertising material.

Times Open all year, Mon-Fri 10-4.45. Closed over Xmas, BH & wknds **Facilities** Ⓟ ♿ (fully accessible) (check in advance if wheelchair access available) shop

See advert on opposite page

TAUNTON Map 3 ST22

Hestercombe Gardens 2 FOR 1

Cheddon Fitzpaine TA2 8LG
☎ 01823 413923 01823 413747
e-mail: info@hestercombe.com
web: www.hestercombe.com
dir: 3m N of Taunton near Cheddon Fitzpaine. Signed from all main roads

There are three period gardens to enjoy at Hestercombe: the 50-acre Georgian pleasure grounds with woodland walks, temples, Witch House and Great Cascade; the Victorian terrace and recently established Victorian shrubbery; and the Edwardian gardens, where the work of Gertrude Jekyll and architect Edwin Lutyens are shown off to full effect. Restoration of a 17th-century watermill creating a centre for education is now open.

Times Open all year, daily, 10-6 (last admission 5). Closed 25 Dec **Fees** £8.90 (ch 5-15 £3.30, pen £8.30). W/chair users £4.40 helper free* **Facilities** Ⓟ licensed (outdoor) ♿ (partly accessible) (those with limited mobility may find some paths difficult, easy access marked on guide map) toilets for disabled shop

TINTINHULL Map 3 ST41

Tintinhull Garden

Farm St BA22 8PZ
☎ 01935 823289 01935 826357
e-mail: tintinhull@nationaltrust.org.uk
web: www.nationaltrust.org.uk
dir: 0.5m S off A303. Follow signs to Tintinhull village, garden is well signed

An attractive, mainly 17th-century manor house with a Queen Anne facade, it stands in two acres of beautiful formal gardens. The gardens were largely created by Mrs Reiss, who gave the property to the National Trust in 1953.

Times Open 13 Mar-Oct, Wed-Sun & BH Mons 11-5.* **Facilities** Ⓟ (outdoor) ♿ (partly accessible) (some areas of garden not accessible to wheelchairs) (1 wheelchair, Braille & large print guide)

WASHFORD Map 3 ST04

Cleeve Abbey

TA23 0PS
☎ 01984 640377 01984 641348
web: www.english-heritage.org.uk
dir: 0.25m S of A39

This 13th-century monastic site features some of the finest cloister buildings in England; medieval wall paintings, a mosaic tiled floor and an interesting exhibition.

Times Open Apr-Jun & Sep, daily 10-5; Jul-Aug, daily 10-6; Oct, daily 10-4. Closed Nov-Mar **Fees** £4 (ch £2, concessions £3.40). Prices and opening times are subject to change in March 2011. Please check web site or call 0870 333 1181 for the most up to date prices and opening times when planning your visit **Facilities** Ⓟ shop

Tropiquaria Animal and Adventure Park

2 FOR 1

TA23 0QB
☎ 01984 640688
e-mail: info@tropiquaria.co.uk
web: www.tropiquaria.co.uk
dir: on A39, between Williton and Minehead

Housed in a 1930s BBC transmitting station, the main hall has been converted into an indoor jungle with a 15-foot waterfall, tropical plants and free-flying birds. (Snakes, lizards, iguanas, spiders, toads and terrapins are caged!) Downstairs is the submarine crypt with local and tropical marine life. Other features include landscaped gardens, the Shadowstring Puppet Theatre, and 'Wireless in the West' museum. Also two new full size pirate adventure ships are moored on the front lawn accessible to pirates of all ages! The park has an indoor playcastle for adventure and fun whatever the weather.

Times Open all year, Apr-Sep, daily 10.30-5 (last entry 4.30); Oct daily 11-5 (last entry 4); Nov-Mar Mon & wknds 11-4 (last entry 3) **Fees** £8 (ch & concessions £7)* **Facilities** Ⓟ ☕ ⛩ (indoor & outdoor) ♿ (partly accessible) (aquarium not accessible) toilets for disabled (ramp to pirate galleon & indoor castle) shop 🚫

WELLS — Map 3 ST54

The Bishop's Palace

2 FOR 1

Henderson Rooms BA5 2PD
☎ 01749 988111
e-mail: info@bishopspalace.org.uk
web: www.bishopspalace.org.uk
dir: Follow city centre signs, turn left into Market Place and enter archway between National Trust shop and post office

Close to the cathedral is the moated bishop's palace. The early part of the palace, the bishop's chapel and the ruins of the banqueting hall date from the 13th century and the undercroft remains virtually unchanged from this time. There are several state rooms and a long gallery which houses portraits of former Bishops. The spectacular gardens contain the wells which give the city its name.

Times Open Apr-Oct, daily 10.30-5* **Fees** £5 (ch £2, concessions £4). Family ticket £12* **Facilities** Ⓟ ☕ 🍽 licensed ⛩ (outdoor) ♿ (partly accessible) (85% accessible) (stair lift to first floor) shop

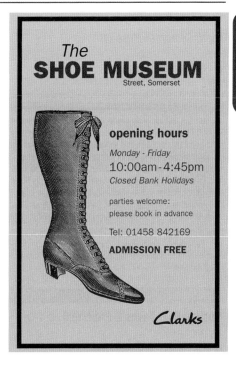

WESTON-SUPER-MARE — Map 3 ST36

The Helicopter Museum

The Heliport, Locking Moor Rd BS24 8PP
☎ 01934 635227 📠 01934 645230
e-mail: helimuseum@btconnect.com
web: www.helicoptermuseum.co.uk
dir: outskirts of town on A371, nr M5 junct 21, follow propellor signs

The world's largest rotary-wing collection and the only helicopter museum in Britain, home of the Queen's Royal flight helicopters. More than 70 helicopters and autogyros are on display - including examples from France, Germany, Poland, Russia and the United States, from 1935 to the present day - with displays of models, engines and other components explaining the history and development of the rotorcraft. Special events include 'Open Cockpit Days', when visitors can learn more about how the helicopter works. Helicopter flights available on set dates throughout the year.

Times Open all year, Nov-Mar, Wed-Sun 10-4.30; Apr-Oct 10-5.30. Open daily during Etr & summer school hols 10-5.30. Closed 24-26 Dec & 1 Jan* **Fees** £5.50 (ch under 5 free, ch 5-16 £3.50, concessions £4.50). Family ticket (2ad+2ch) £15.50, (2ad+3ch) £17.50* **Facilities** Ⓟ ☕ ⛩ (outdoor) ♿ (fully accessible) toilets for disabled (large print and Braille information sheet) shop

ENGLAND

WESTON-SUPER-MARE *continued*

North Somerset Museum

Burlington St BS23 1PR
☎ 01934 621028 01934 612526
e-mail: museum.service@n-somerset.gov.uk
web: www.n-somerset.gov.uk/museum
dir: in centre of Weston-super-Mare

This museum, housed in the former workshops of the Edwardian Gaslight Company, has displays on the seaside holiday, an old chemist's shop, a dairy and Victorian pavement mosaics. Adjoining the museum is Clara's Cottage, a Westonian home of the 1900s with period kitchen, parlour, bedroom and back yard. One of the rooms has an additional display of Peggy Nisbet dolls. Other displays include wildlife gallery, mining and local archaeology, costume and ceramics. There is even a display on secret weapons developed on Birnbeck Island during WWII.

Times Open all year Mon-Sat 10-4.30. Closed 24-26 Dec & 1 Jan.* **Facilities** Ⓟ (partly accessible) (ground floor of main museum accessible) toilets for disabled (hearing loop at reception) shop

WOOKEY HOLE — Map 3 ST54

Wookey Hole Caves & Papermill **2 FOR 1**

BA5 1BB
☎ 01749 672243 01749 677749
e-mail: witch@wookey.co.uk
web: www.wookey.co.uk
dir: M5 junct 22 follow signs via A38 & A371, from Bristol & Bath A39 to Wells then 2m to Wookey Hole

Britain's most spectacular caves and legendary home of the infamous Witch of Wookey. The 19th-century paper mill houses a variety of fascinating attractions including a Cave Museum, Victorian Penny Arcade, Magical Mirror Maze, Haunted Corridor of Crazy Mirrors, and the Wizard's Castle play area. Visitors can also see paper being made in Britain's only surviving handmade paper mill. Theatre shows, an enchanted fairy garden and Dinosaur Valley round off this family day out in Wookey Hole.

Times Open all year daily Apr-Oct 10-5; Nov-Mar 10-4; Dec-Jan, open wknds & school hols. Closed 25-26 Dec **Fees** £16 (under 3s free, ch & concessions £11)* **Facilities** Ⓟ licensed (outdoor) (partly accessible) (papermill only accessible) toilets for disabled shop

YEOVILTON — Map 3 ST52

Fleet Air Arm Museum **2 FOR 1**

Royal Naval Air Station BA22 8HT
☎ 01935 840565 & 842638 01935 842630
e-mail: info@fleetairarm.com
web: www.fleetairarm.com
dir: on B3151, just off junct of A303 and A37

The Fleet Air Arm Museum is where museum meets theatre. 'Fly' by helicopter to the replica flight deck of aircraft carrier *HMS Ark Royal*. See fighter aircraft and two enormous projection screens showing jet fighters taking off and landing, and even see a nuclear bomb. The Museum has Europe's largest collection of naval aircraft and the first British-built Concorde. Go on board and visit the cockpit. There's an adventure playground, and the museum is located alongside Europe's busiest military air station at RNAS Yeovilton. 2 for 1 voucher not valid on special event days and will only admit 1 free child with a full paying adult.

Times Open all year: Apr-Oct, daily 10-5.30; Nov-Mar, Wed-Sun 10-4.30. Closed 24-26 Dec* **Fees** £12 (ch under 17 £8.50, under 5 free, concessions £10). Family (2ad+3ch) £36* **Facilities** Ⓟ Ⓟ licensed (outdoor) (fully accessible) toilets for disabled (wheelchairs available) shop

STAFFORDSHIRE

Manifold Valley, Peak District National Park

ENGLAND

ALTON Map 7 SK04

Alton Towers

ST10 4DB

☎ 08705 204060 🖷 01538 704097

e-mail: info@alton-towers.com

web: www.altontowers.com

dir: from S - M1 junct 23a or M6 junct 15. From N - M1 junct 24a or M6 junct 16

Alton Towers Resort is a fantastic day out for all the family. With world-class rides and attractions as well as some beautiful gardens, this is more than just a theme park. The Resort is a popular UK short break destination for familiesand consists of the Alton Towers Theme Park, waterpark, spa, two fully themed hotels and two nine-hole golf courses. See website for details of special events.

Times Open daily 19-27 Feb & 26 Mar-6 Nov. Hotels, waterpark, spa and golf open all year **Fees** £30.40 (ch £23.20, concessions £15.40). Family ticket (3 £64.80, 4 £86.40, 5 £108, 6 £129.60). Prices apply when booked online* **Facilities** licensed (outdoor) (fully accessible) toilets for disabled (disabled guest guide books) shop

BIDDULPH Map 7 SJ85

Biddulph Grange Garden

Grange Rd ST8 7SD

☎ 01782 517999 🖷 01782 510624

e-mail: biddulphgrange@nationaltrust.org.uk

web: www.nationaltrust.org.uk/main/w-biddulphgrangegarden

dir: access from A527, Tunstall-Congleton road. Entrance on Grange Rd 0.5m N of Biddulph

Amazing Victorian garden and Geological Gallery created by Darwin contemporary James Bateman as an extension of his beliefs and scientific interests. His plant collection comes from all over the world - visitors take a global journey from an Italian terrace to an Egyptian pyramid. Discover the fabulous collection of rhododendrons, dahlia walk and oldest surviving golden larch in Britain, brought from China by the great plant hunter Robert Fortune. A garden for all seasons. The 200th anniversary of James Bateman's birth will be celebrated in July 2011.

Times Open 3-31 Mar, Wed-Sun 11-5; 9 Apr-Oct, daily 11-5; 6 Nov-19 Dec, Sat-Sun 11-3.30* **Fees** Mar-Oct £6.40 (ch £3.20). Family ticket £14.90; Nov-Dec £2.40 (ch £1.20). Family ticket £5.60* **Facilities** (outdoor) (partly accessible) (steps to entrance & on ground floor, steep slopes, many steps. Narrow gravel paths, tunnels and stepping stones throughout garden) toilets for disabled shop

CHEDDLETON Map 7 SJ95

Cheddleton Flint Mill

Beside Caldon Canal, Cheadle Rd ST13 7HL

☎ 01782 818654

web: www.tinyurl.com/chedmill

dir: 3m S of Leek on A520

Twin water-wheels on the River Churnet drive flint-grinding pans in the two mills, and the museum houses a collection of machinery used in the preparation of materials for the ceramic industry. This includes a 100 HP Robey horizontal steam engine, a model Newcomen beam engine, and an edge-runner mill. Display panels explain the processes of winning and treating clays, stone and flint for the pottery industry. Other attractions include Caldon Canal, Miller's cottage and garden.

Times Open Mar-Oct (groups by arrangement). Phone to check recorded message current opening times **Fees** Free entry, but donations welcome **Facilities** (partly accessible) (access restricted to ground floor and outside exhibits, parts of site uneven) toilets for disabled

Churnet Valley Railway — 2 FOR 1

The Station ST13 7EE

☎ 01538 360522

e-mail: enquiries@churnetvalleyrailway.co.uk

web: www.churnetvalleyrailway.co.uk

dir: 3m S from Leek, 3m N from Cellarhead along A520. Kingsley & Froghall Station is situated on the Stoke to Ashbourne road, A52

The Churnet Valley Railway runs through the hidden countryside between Cheddleton, with its Grade II Victorian station, and Kingsley and Froghall, with the newly built station and Canal Wharf. The journey incorporates Consall, a sleepy rural station and nature reserve, and Leekbrook with one of the longest tunnels on a preserved railway. Special Events include 1940s weekend in April, Ghost Train in October, and Santa & Steam in December.

Times Open Etr-Sep Sun, May-Sep Sat, Jul-Aug Wed & all BH Mons **Fees** All day travel £10 (ch £5, concessions £8) **Facilities** (outdoor) (fully accessible) toilets for disabled (ramps) shop

HALFPENNY GREEN Map 7 SO89

Halfpenny Green Vineyards FREE

DY7 5EP

☎ 01384 221122 📠 01384 221101

e-mail: enquiries@halfpenny-green-vineyards.co.uk

web: www.halfpenny-green-vineyards.co.uk

dir: 0.5m off B4176 Dudley to Telford road

Using German, French and hybrid varieties that can prosper even in the poorest British summer, this vineyard offers "The complete English wine experience." This includes a self-guided vineyard trail as well as guided tours, wine-tasting, a craft centre and a visitor centre. Visitors can purchase wines with personalised labels for special occasions. Coarse fishing is also available.

Times Open all year, daily 9.30-5* **Facilities** licensed (fully accessible) toilets for disabled shop

HIMLEY Map 7 SO89

Himley Hall & Park

DY3 4DF

☎ 01384 817817 📠 01384 817818

e-mail: himley.hall@dudley.gov.uk

web: www.dudley.gov.uk/himleyhall

dir: off A449, on B4176

The extensive parkland offers a range of attractions, including a nine-hole golf course and coarse fishing. The hall is open to the public when exhibitions are taking place. There is a permanent orienteering course, and a charge is made for the maps. Group guided tours at the hall available by prior arrangement. The Hall is available for private hire. There are also a large variety of outdoor events and concerts, please contact for details.

Times Open Hall: 5 Apr-6 Sep, Tue-Sun 2-5, BH Mon 2-5* **Facilities** (fully accessible) toilets for disabled

LEEK Map 7 SJ95

Blackbrook Zoological Park

Winkhill ST13 7QR

☎ 01538 308293 📠 01538 308293

e-mail: enquiries@blackbrookzoologicalpark.co.uk

web: www.blackbrookzoologicalpark.co.uk

dir: off A523 Leek to Ashbourne road

Blackbrook Zoological Park is a fun and educational day for all. A continually growing attraction, always with something new to see. The zoo features: mammals, rare birds, reptiles, insects and aquatics; owl flights, pelican, penguin and lemur feeds. Blackbrook Zoological Park is fully accessible for pushchairs and wheelchairs.

Times Open daily 10-5.30; winter 10.30-dusk (last admission 4)* **Facilities** (outdoor) (fully accessible) toilets for disabled shop

LICHFIELD Map 7 SK10

Erasmus Darwin House

Beacon St WS13 7AD

☎ 01543 306260 📠 01543 306261

e-mail: enquiries@erasmusdarwin.org

web: www.erasmusdarwin.org

dir: signed to Lichfield Cathedral. Access by foot through cathedral close at West End

The House is dedicated to Erasmus Darwin, the grandfather of Charles Darwin, and a talented doctor, inventor, philosopher, poet and founder member of the Lunar Society. A resident of Lichfield for more than 20 years, the displays are contained within his beautiful 18th-century home, and recreate the story of Erasmus' life, ideas and inventions, through period rooms, audio visual and interactive displays.

Times Open all year, Apr-Oct, Tue-Sun 11-5; Nov-Mar, 12-4.30 (last admission 4.15)* **Fees** £3 (ch £1, concessions £2). Family ticket (2ad+2ch) £6* **Facilities** (fully accessible) toilets for disabled (audio tour) shop

Lichfield Cathedral

WS13 7LD

☎ 01543 306100 📠 01543 306109

e-mail: enquiries@lichfield-cathedral.org

web: www.lichfield-cathedral.org

dir: Signed from all major roads and within city

The Cathedral's three spires, known as the Ladies of the Vale, dominate the landscape. The first cathedral here was founded in AD700 to house the shrine of St Chad. The present building, with its elaborate carvings, has been much restored since it was attacked during the Civil War. Among its treasures are the St Chad Gospels, an 8th-century illuminated manuscript; a collection of modern silver, and the 16th-century Flemish glass in the Lady Chapel. Please check website for details of latest events.

Times Open all year, daily 7.30am-6.15pm* **Fees** Entry free, suggested donation of £5 for each adult visitor **Facilities** licensed (partly accessible) (most areas accessible) toilets for disabled (touch & hearing centre for blind) shop

LICHFIELD *continued*

Samuel Johnson Birthplace Museum

FREE

Breadmarket St WS13 6LG

☎ 01543 264972 📠 01543 258441

e-mail: sjmuseum@lichfield.gov.uk

web: www.samueljohnsonbirthplace.org.uk

dir: located in city centre market place

Dr Samuel Johnson, author of the famous English dictionary of 1755, lexicographer, poet, literary critic, biographer and moralist was born in this house in 1709. The birthplace now houses a museum dedicated to his extraordinary life, work and personality. Five floors of exhibits featuring period room settings, introductory video and personal items owned by Johnson, his family and his famous friends. Johnson's birthday is celebrated annually in September. Please see the website for special events.

Times Open all year, daily Apr-Sep 10.30-4.30; Oct-Mar 11-3.30.* **Facilities** Ⓟ ♿ (partly accessible) (Grade 1 listed & many unavoidable stairs) (large print text literature, induction loop system) shop ⊗

SHUGBOROUGH — Map 7 SJ92

Shugborough Estate

2 FOR 1

ST17 0XB

☎ 01889 881388 📠 01889 881323

e-mail: enquiries@shugborough.org.uk

web: www.shugborough.org.uk

dir: 6m E of Stafford off A513, signed from M6 junct 13

Journey through the historic estate of Shugborough and discover a bygone era as the costumed living history characters bring the past to life. The story begins in the walled garden - meet the gardeners of 1805 and find out how fruit and vegetables are grown on the estate. At the farm the servants are busy making butter and cheese and the farm hands tend to the animals. Then take a short ride on Lucy the Train or walk across the stunning parkland. The story continues in the Servants' Quarters where cooks and kitchen maids scurry about, preparing food on the range, starching the whites in the laundry and brewing ale in the wood-fired brewery. The Mansion House completes the story, where the 1805 Viscount and Lady Anson are often present. Please contact or see website for details of special events. The 2-for-1 voucher excludes special events, season pass, group purchases and garden tickets.

Times Open 18 Mar-28 Oct, daily 11-5. Site open all year to pre-booked parties* **Fees** £12 (ch £7, under 5 free, concessions £9.50). Family ticket (2ad+3ch) £30, (1ad+1ch) £15* **Facilities** 🅟 ☕ 🍽 licensed ⛩ (outdoor) ♿ (partly accessible) (steps to house, stairclimber available) toilets for disabled (6 wheelchairs, 2 batricars, hearing loop, ramps) shop ⊗ 🌿

STAFFORD — Map 7 SJ92

Shire Hall Gallery

FREE

Market Square ST16 2LD

☎ 01785 278345 📠 02785 278327

e-mail: shirehallgallery@staffordshire.gov.uk

web: www.staffordshire.gov.uk/shirehallgallery

dir: In pedestrianised area of the town centre, 5 min walk from railway station

With free entry and an exciting activities programme, there's something for everyone at the Shire Hall Gallery - Staffordshire's largest venue for contemporary arts and crafts. Visit the historic courtroom, or book a play session in the multi-sensory room. Contact the gallery for info on the latest exhibitions and activities.

Times Open all year, Mon & Wed-Sat 9.30-5; Tue 10-5; Sun 1-4. Gallery closes for exhibition changes and at BHs, please call for further details **Facilities** Ⓟ ☕ ♿ (partly accessible) (some areas only accessible by lift, limited wheelchair access to the Court room) toilets for disabled (lifts to some areas, hearing loop, Braille & large print) shop ⊗

STOKE-ON-TRENT — Map 7 SJ84

Ceramica

Market Place, Burslem ST6 3DS

☎ 01782 832001 📠 01782 823300

e-mail: info@ceramicauk.com

web: www.ceramicauk.com

dir: A4527 (signed Tunstall). After 0.5m right onto B5051 for Burslem. Ceramica is in Old Town Hall in centre of town.

A unique experience for all the family, Ceramica is housed in the Old Town Hall in the centre of Burslem, Mother Town of the Potteries. Explore the hands-on activities in Bizarreland, and learn how clay is transformed into china. Dig into history with the time team and take a magic carpet ride over the town. Discover the past, present and future of ceramics with the interactive displays in the Pavillions. Explore the Memory Bank and read the local news on Ceramica TV.

Times Open all year, Mon-Sat 9.30-5, Sun 10.30-4.30. For Xmas opening please telephone.* **Facilities** 🅟 Ⓟ ⛩ (indoor) ♿ (partly accessible) toilets for disabled (ramps, lift to all floors, tactile displays) shop ⊗

Etruria Industrial Museum — 2 FOR 1

Lower Bedford St, Etruria ST4 7AF
☎ 01782 233144
e-mail: etruria@stoke.gov.uk
web: www.stoke.gov.uk/museums
dir: M6 junct 16, A500 onto Stoke Rd (A5006)

The Etruria Industrial Museum is Britain's sole surviving, steam-powered potters' mill in Britain and includes Jesse Shirley's Bone and Flint Mill, listed an ancient monument in 1975. The Mill is "in steam" several times a year when the 1903 boiler is fired and the 1820s *Princess* beam engine powers the historic machinery.

Times Open 6 Apr-4 Dec, Wed-Sun 12-4.30 **Fees** £3 (ch under 5 free & concessions £2, wheelchair users free). Family ticket £6.50* **Facilities** (outdoor) (partly accessible) (The Mill inaccessible to wheelchairs. Access to Visitor centre and canal wharf) toilets for disabled (virtual tour) shop

Ford Green Hall — 2 FOR 1

Ford Green Rd, Smallthorne ST6 1NG
☎ 01782 233195
e-mail: ford.green.hall@stoke.gov.uk
web: www.stoke.gov.uk/museums
dir: on the B5051

Home to the Ford family for nearly 200 years, the Ford Green Hall is 17th century timber-framed farmhouse, complete with period garden. An award-winning museum, the Hall offers visitors a fascinating insight into life in the 17th century. The rooms are furnished with an outstanding collection of textiles, ceramics and furniture.

Times Open all year, Sun-Thu 1-5. Closed 25 Dec-2 Jan **Fees** £3 (ch under 5 free & concessions £2, wheelchair users free). Family ticket £6.50* **Facilities** (outdoor) (partly accessible) (1st floor inaccessible to wheelchair users) toilets for disabled (interactive virtual tour) shop

Gladstone Pottery Museum — 2 FOR 1

Uttoxeter Rd, Longton ST3 1PQ
☎ 01782 237777
e-mail: gladstone@stoke.gov.uk
web: www.stoke.gov.uk/museums
dir: A50 then follow brown heritage signs

Gladstone is the only complete Victorian pottery factory from the days when coal burning ovens made the World's finest bone china. The original workshops, the cobbled yard and huge bottle kilns create an atmosphere time-warp that has no equal.

Times Open all year, daily 10-5. Closed 25 Dec-2 Jan **Fees** £6.95 (ch £4.75, concessions £5.50). Family (2ad+2ch) £20* **Facilities** licensed (outdoor) (partly accessible) (cobbled courtyard and 2 museum's rooms inacessible to wheelchair users) toilets for disabled (lift, ramp, electric buggy available on loan) shop

The Potteries Museum & Art Gallery — FREE

Bethesda St, Hanley ST1 3DW
☎ 01782 232323 01782 232500
e-mail: museums@stoke.gov.uk
web: www.stoke.gov.uk/museums
dir: M6 junct 15/16 take A500 to Stoke-on-Trent. Follow signs for city centre (Hanley), Cultural Quarter & The Potteries Museum

The history of the Potteries under one roof, including a dazzling display of the world's finest collection of Staffordshire ceramics. Other displays introduce natural, local and archaeological history from in and around The Potteries, and a Mark 16 Spitfire commemorating its locally born designer - Reginald Mitchell. The museum has a continual display of the Staffordshire Hoard - the largest Hoard of Anglo-Saxon gold ever found.

Times Open all year, Mon-Sat 10-5, Sun 2-5. Closed 25 Dec-1 Jan* **Facilities** (fully accessible) toilets for disabled (lift, induction loop, 2 wheelchairs available) shop

Wedgwood Visitor Centre

Barlaston ST12 9ES
☎ 01782 282986 01782 223063
e-mail: bookings@wedgwood.com
web: www.wedgwoodvisitorcentre.com
dir: From M1, via A50 follow tourist signs to Stoke. From M6 junct 15 follow brown tourist signs

Set in 250 acres of lush parkland in the heart of Staffordshire, visitors can take a fascinating trip behind the scenes at one of the world's famous pottery companies. The award-winning tour allows visitors to enjoy the entire experience at their own pace. Hands-on activities such as throwing your own pot or painting your own plate, are available in the demonstration area, where individuals craft artisans demonstrate their skills. These may include Coalport painter, jewellery maker, hand painter and flower maker. Add to this, exhibition areas, film theatre and an exclusive Wedgwood shop, the centre offers an all-inclusive day for everyone.

Times Open all year, Mon-Fri 9-5, Sat & Sun 10-5. Shop open Sun 10-4 (ex Etr Sun). Closed Xmas week.* **Facilities** licensed (fully accessible) toilets for disabled shop

ENGLAND

TAMWORTH Map 7 SK20

Drayton Manor Theme Park

B78 3TW

☎ 0844 4721950 & 4721960 📠 01827 288916

e-mail: info@draytonmanor.co.uk

web: www.draytonmanor.co.uk

dir: M42 junct 9, on A4091. Exit at T2 of M6 toll

A popular family theme park with over 100 rides and attractions suitable for all the family, set in 280 acres of parkland and lakes. Drayton Manor has been run by the same family for 60 years, and features world-class rides like rollercoaster sensation G-Force, Apocalypse- the world's first stand-up tower drop, Stormforce 10 and Shockwave - Europe's only stand-up rollercoaster. ThomasLand features Thomas and Percy trains and themed rides for adults and children. There's an award-winning zoo and a penny slot machine museum plus plenty of special events throughout the year.

Times Park & Rides open mid Mar-Oct. Rides from 10.30-5, 6 or 7. Zoo open all year. 'ThomasLand' also open end Nov-3 Jan (except 24-26 Dec) **Fees** £25 (ch under 4 free, 4-11 £21, pen 60+ £12, disabled & helper £19 each). Please telephone 0844 4721950 to check prices or 0844 4721960 for ticket offers, or visit website for details* **Facilities** Ⓟ ☕ 🍽 licensed ⛩ (indoor & outdoor) ♿ (partly accessible) (some rides limited access due to steps, with ramps or lifts to most rides) toilets for disabled shop 🚫

Tamworth Castle 2 FOR 1

Holbway Lodge B79 7NA

☎ 01827 709629 & 709626 📠 01827 709630

e-mail: heritage@tamworth.gov.uk

web: www.tamworthcastle.co.uk

dir: M42 junct 10 & M6 junct 12, access via A5

Tamworth Castle is located in the centre of the town. Owned by six wealthy and influential families over the centuries, the medieval motte and bailey castle has welcomed a number of royal visitors including King Henry II, King James I and his son Prince Charles. The ancient sand stone tower and shell wall still dominate views of the Castle today. While visiting this scheduled ancient monument witness the magnificent late medieval Great Hall, grand Tudor chambers and Victorian suite of reception rooms. The castle hosts a varied and exciting events programme, education service and is also the ideal wedding location.

Times Open all year, Apr-Sep, Tue-Sun 12-5.15; Oct-Mar, Sat & Sun 12-5.15 (last admission 4.30)* **Fees** £5 (ch under 2 free, 2-4 £1, 5+ £3, concessions £4). Family ticket (2ad+2ch) £14.50* **Facilities** Ⓟ ☕ ⛩ (outdoor) ♿ (partly accessible) (ground floor access only) (one wheelchair for use inside the castle) shop 🚫

TRENTHAM Map 7 SJ94

Trentham Gardens

Trentham Estate, Stone Rd ST4 8AX

☎ 01782 646646 📠 01782 644536

e-mail: enquiry@trentham.co.uk

web: www.trentham.co.uk

dir: M6 junct 15 onto A500 towards Stoke, after 1m take A34 to Trentham & Stone. Estate on right in 1m

This Italianate award-winning landscape garden has a variety of innovative horticultural displays. A mile long lake, fountains and model show gardens displays different techniques, crafts and ideas. For the younger visitor there is an adventure play area and Barfuss Britain's first bare foot walking park.

Times Open all year Northern entrance daily 9-8. Southern entrance 9-6. Both entrances 9-4, 2 Nov-Mar. (Last entry 1hr before closing at northern entrance).* **Facilities** Ⓟ ☕ ⛩ (outdoor) toilets for disabled shop

Trentham Monkey Forest

Trentham Estate, Southern Entrance, Stone Rd ST4 8AY

☎ 01782 659845 📠 01782 644699

e-mail: info@monkey-forest.com

web: www.monkey-forest.com

dir: M6 junct 15, 5 mins drive to A34 in direction of Stone

A unique experience for everyone - come to the only place in Britain where you can walk amongst 140 Barbary macaques roaming free in 60 acres of forest. Walking in the park, you are transported into a different world through close contact with the monkeys. Guides are situated all along the path to give information and there are feeding talks every hour.

Times Open Feb-Mar & Nov, wknds & school hols, 10-4; daily Apr-Oct 10-5 (school summer hols 10-6) **Fees** £6.50 (ch under 3 free, ch 3-14 £4.50), groups 20+ £5.50 (ch £3.50). Check website for current prices **Facilities** (outdoor) (partly accessible) (hills in forest) toilets for disabled shop

WALL Map 7 SK10

Wall Roman Site

FREE

Watling St WS14 0AW
☎ 01543 480768
web: www.english-heritage.org.uk
dir: off A5

Explore the haunting remains of a 2,000 year old wayside staging post situated along Watling Street, the famous Kent to North Wales Roman road.

Times Site open: Mar-Oct, daily 10-5; Nov-Feb, daily 10-4. Museum 4-5 & 24-25 Apr, 2-3 & 29-31 May, 26-27 Jun, 24-25 Jul, 28-30 Aug, 25-26 Sep & 30-31 Oct. Closed Nov-Feb **Facilities** shop

WESTON PARK Map 7 SJ81

Weston Park

2 FOR 1

TF11 8LE
☎ 01952 852100 01952 850430
e-mail: enquiries@weston-park.com
web: www.weston-park.com
dir: on A5 at Weston-under-Lizard, 30 min from central Birmingham 3m off M54 junct 3 and 8m off M6 junct 12

Built in 1671, this fine mansion stands in elegant gardens and a vast park designed by 'Capability' Brown. Three lakes, a miniature railway, and a woodland adventure playground are to be found in the grounds, and in the house itself there is a magnificent collection of pictures, furniture and tapestries. There is also a farm shop, art gallery and restaurant.

Times House open: daily 28 May-4 Sep 1-5 (guided tours to house only every 45 mins). Park & Garden open: daily 10.30-6 (last admission 4.30) **Fees** House: £8 (ch 4-17 £5.50, pen £7). Park & Gardens: £5 (ch 4-14 £3, pen £4.50). Family ticket House, Park & Gardens (2ad+3ch or 1ad+4ch) £20* **Facilities** licensed (outdoor) (partly accessible) (some steps in garden, w/chair users can access via stair climber) toilets for disabled (disabled route, access to restaurant & shop) shop

WHITTINGTON Map 7 SK10

Staffordshire Regiment Museum

Whittington Barracks WS14 9PY
☎ 01543 434394 & 434395 01543 434391
e-mail: curator@staffordshireregimentmuseum.com
dir: on A51 between Lichfield/Tamworth

Located next to Whittington Barracks, the museum tells the story of the soldiers of the Staffordshire Regiment and its predecessors. Exhibits include vehicles, uniforms, weapons, medals and memorabilia relating to three hundred years of regimental history, including distinguished service in the First and Second World Wars and the Gulf War. Visitors can experience a World War I trench system with sound effects and a World War II Anderson shelter.

Times Open all year, Mon-Fri 10-4.30 (last admission 4). Also Apr-Oct wknds & BH 12.30-4.30. Closed Xmas-New Year. Parties at other times by arrangement* **Fees** £3 (ch £2, concessions £2). Family ticket £6. Regimental Association Members & serving Mercian soldiers free* **Facilities** (outdoor) (fully accessible) toilets for disabled (ramps, lowered kerbs, graded access to attraction) shop

WILLOUGHBRIDGE Map 7 SJ74

The Dorothy Clive Garden

TF9 4EU
☎ 01630 647237
e-mail: info@dorothyclivegarden.co.uk
web: www.dorothyclivegarden.co.uk
dir: on A51 between Nantwich & Stone

This 12-acre, 200-year-old gravel quarry was converted by Colonel Harry Clive, who began landscaping in 1939 to create a garden for his wife, Dorothy. Today the garden boasts superb woodland with cascading waterfall, an alpine scree and spectacular summer borders which drift along the hillside down to a tranquil lily pond. A host of spring bulbs, magnificent displays of Rhododendrons and Azaleas, and stunning autumn colours are among the seasonal highlights.

Times Open daily 19 Mar-25 Sep, 10-5.30 (last admission 4.30). Tea room 11-5 **Fees** £5.50 (ch up to 19 free, pen £4.75). Groups 20+ £4.50* **Facilities** (outdoor) (partly accessible) (garden 90% accessible) toilets for disabled (ramps, w/chairs, special route, garden guides, parking)

SUFFOLK

The Tide Mill, Woodbridge

BURY ST EDMUNDS Map 5 TL86

Moyse's Hall Museum

Cornhill IP33 1DX
☎ 01284 706183 📠 01284 765373
e-mail: moyses.hall@stedsbc/gov.uk
web: www.moyseshall.org
dir: take Bury central exit from A14, follow signs for town centre, museum situated in town centre

Moyse's Hall is a 12th-century Norman house built of flint and stone which now serves as a local history museum, and among the fascinating exhibits are memorabilia of the notorious William Corder "Murder in the Red Barn". Other collections include the history of the town, Suffolk Regiment, fine art, toys, clocks and timepieces.

Times Open all year, Mon-Fri 10-5 (last entry at 4), Sat & Sun 11-4. Closed 25-27 Dec & all BH **Fees** £4 (under 5 free, ch & concessions £2). Family Heritage ticket £9 (allows 5 additional visits free) **Facilities** Ⓟ ♿ (fully accessible) toilets for disabled (stairlift, lift, hearing loop, w/chair) shop 🚫

EAST BERGHOLT Map 5 TM03

Flatford: Bridge Cottage FREE

Flatford CO7 6UL
☎ 01206 298260 & 297201
e-mail: flatfordbridgecottage@nationaltrust.org.uk
web: www.nationaltrust.org.uk/flatford
dir: On N bank of Stour, 1m S of East Bergholt B1070

Bridge Cottage, Flatford Mill and Willy Lott's House were the subject of several of John Constable's paintings. You can take a tour of the sites of his paintings and enjoy some of the best walks you could wish for in the beautiful unspoilt countryside of the Dedham Vale.

Times Open all year, Jan-Feb Sat-Sun 11-3.30; Mar Wed-Sun 11-4; Apr daily 11-5; May-Sep daily 10.30-5.30; Oct daily 11-4.30; Nov-23 Dec Wed-Sun 11-3.30 **Facilities** 🅟 ☕ ♿ (fully accessible) toilets for disabled (wheelchair/electric runaround available) shop 🚫

EASTON Map 5 TM25

Easton Farm Park

IP13 0EQ
☎ 01728 746475
e-mail: info@eastonfarmpark.co.uk
web: www.eastonfarmpark.co.uk
dir: signed from A12 at Wickham Market, and from A1120

Award-winning farm park on the banks of the River Deben. There are lots of breeds of farm animals, including Suffolk Punch horses, ponies, pigs, lambs, calves, goats, rabbits, guinea pigs and poultry. Chicks hatching and egg collecting daily. Free hug-a-bunny and pony rides every day.

Times Open Mar-end Sep, daily 10.30-6. Also open Feb & Oct half term hols & wknds in Dec* **Facilities** 🅟 ☕ ⛩ (indoor & outdoor) ♿ (partly accessible) (mainly hard standing surfaces) toilets for disabled (special parking and wheelchairs) shop

EUSTON Map 5 TL87

Euston Hall

IP24 2QP
☎ 01842 766366 📠 01842 766764
e-mail: lcampbell@euston-estate.co.uk
web: www.eustonhall.co.uk
dir: on A1088, 3m S of Thetford

Home of the Duke and Duchess of Grafton, this 18th-century house is notable for its fine collection of pictures, by Stubbs, Lely, Van Dyck and other Masters. The grounds were laid out by John Evelyn, William Kent and 'Capability' Brown, and include a 17th-century church in the style of Wren and a river walk to the restored watermill.

Times Open 18 Jun-17 Sep, Thu only. Also open Sun 28 Jun, 12 Jul & 6 Sep.* **Facilities** 🅟 ☕ ⛩ (outdoor) ♿ (partly accessible) (first floor of hall not accessible) toilets for disabled shop 🚫

FLIXTON Map 5 TM38

Norfolk & Suffolk Aviation Museum

Buckeroo Way, The Street NR35 1NZ
☎ 01986 896644 & 01508 532646
e-mail: nsam.flixton@tesco.net
web: www.aviationmuseum.net
dir: off A143, take B1062, 2m W of Bungay

Situated in the Waveney Valley, the museum has over 60 historic aircraft. There is also a Bloodhound surface-to-air missile, the 446th Bomb Group Museum, RAF Bomber Command Museum, the Royal Observer Corps Museum, RAF Air-Sea Rescue and Coastal Command and a souvenir shop. Among the displays are Decoy Sites and Wartime Deception, Fallen Eagles - Wartime Luftwaffe Crashes and an ex-Ipswich airport hangar made by Norwich company Boulton and Paul Ltd.

Times Open all year, Apr-Oct, Sun-Thu 10-5; Nov-Mar, Tue, Wed & Sun 10-4 (last admission 1hr before close). Closed late Dec-early Jan **Fees** Free entry. Donations are welcomed **Facilities** 🅟 Ⓟ ☕ ⛩ (outdoor) ♿ (fully accessible) toilets for disabled (helper advised, ramps/paths to all buildings) shop

FRAMLINGHAM Map 5 TM26

Framlingham Castle

IP8 9BT
☎ 01728 724189
web: www.english-heritage.org.uk
dir: on B1116

Walk the 12th-century battlements that encircle the castle site with their impressive thirteen towers. Exceptional views over the countryside and a very popular audio tour.

Times Open Apr-Jun & Sep-Oct, daily 10-5; Jul-Aug, daily 10-6; Nov-Mar, Thu-Mon 10-4. (May close early for events, please call to check) Closed 24-26 Dec & 1 Jan **Fees** £6 (ch £3, concessions £5.10). Family ticket £15. Prices and opening times are subject to change in March 2011. Please check web site or call 0870

continued

ENGLAND

FRAMLINGHAM *continued*

333 1181 for the most up to date prices and opening times when planning your visit **Facilities** (partly accessible) (steep spiral stairs to upper floors & wall walk) toilets for disabled (interactive audio tour, hearing loop) shop

HORRINGER **Map 5 TL86**

Ickworth House, Park & Gardens

The Rotunda IP29 5QE
☎ 01284 735270 01284 735175
e-mail: ickworth@nationaltrust.org.uk
web: www.nationaltrust.org.uk/ickworth
dir: 2.5m SW of Bury St Edmunds in village of Horringer on A143

The eccentric Earl of Bristol created this equally eccentric house, begun in 1795, to display his collection of European art. The Georgian Silver Collection is considered the finest in private hands. 'Capability' Brown designed the parkland, and also featured are a vineyard, waymarked walks and an adventure playground.

Times Open all year: House 14 Mar-1 Nov, Mon-Tue, Fri-Sun & BHs, 11-5, Oct-2 Nov, Mon-Tue, Fri-Sun & BHs. Garden Feb-13 Mar & 2 Nov-Jan daily, 11-4; 14 Mar-1 Nov daily 10-5. Park: daily 8-8.* **Facilities** licensed (outdoor) (partly accessible) (loose gravel paths, steep slopes, terraces, steps) toilets for disabled (Braille guide, batricars, hearing loop, large print guides) shop

IPSWICH **Map 5 TM14**

Christchurch Mansion **FREE**

Soane St IP4 2BE
☎ 01473 433554 & 213761 01473 433564
e-mail: museums.service@ipswich.gov.uk
web: www.ipswich.gov.uk
dir: S side of Christchurch Park, close to town centre

The house was built in 1548 on the site of an Augustinian priory. Set in a beautiful park, it displays period rooms and an art gallery which has changing exhibitions. The Suffolk Artists' Gallery has a collection of paintings by Constable and Gainsborough.

Times Open all year, Mon-Sun 10-5. Closed Good Fri, 24-26 Dec & 1 Jan.* **Facilities** (partly accessible) toilets for disabled shop

Ipswich Museum **FREE**

High St IP1 3QH
☎ 01473 433550 01473 433558
e-mail: museum.service@ipswich.gov.uk
web: www.ipswich.gov.uk
dir: follow tourist signs to Crown St car park. Museum 3 mins walk

The Museum has sections on Victorian Natural History, Suffolk wildlife, Suffolk geology, Roman Suffolk, Anglo-Saxon Ipswich and Peoples of the World. There is also one of the best bird collections in the country.

Times Open all year, Tue-Sat 10-5. Closed Good Fri, 24-26 Dec & 1 Jan* **Facilities** (fully accessible) toilets for disabled (lift) shop

LAVENHAM **Map 5 TL94**

Lavenham The Guildhall of Corpus Christi

Market Place CO10 9QZ
☎ 01787 247646 01787 246345
e-mail: lavenhamguildhall@nationaltrust.org.uk
web: www.nationaltrust.org.uk/main/w-lavenham
dir: Lavenham Market Place. A1141 & B1071

The Guildhall of Corpus Christi is one of the finest timber framed buildings in Britain. It was built around 1530 by the prosperous Corpus Christi Guild, for religious rather than commercial reasons. The hall now houses a local history museum telling the story of Lavenham's 15th- and 16th-century cloth-trade riches. Visitors can also see the walled garden with its 19th-century lock-up and mortuary. 2011 marks the 60th anniversary of the National Trust acquiring this site.

Times Open 5-27 Mar, Wed-Sun; 28 Mar-30 Oct daily 11-5; 5-27 Nov, Sat-Sun 11-4 **Fees** With voluntary Gift Aid donation: £4.50 (ch £1.90). Family ticket £10.90. Visitors can choose to pay the standard admission prices displayed **Facilities** (partly accessible) (stairs to first floor, large beams across thresholds) toilets for disabled (photo album of museum, Braille guide) shop

LEISTON **Map 5 TM46**

Leiston Abbey **FREE**

IP16 4TD
☎ 01728 831354 & 832500 01728 635378
e-mail: admin@leistonabbey.co.uk
web: www.leistonabbey.co.uk
dir: N of Leiston, off B1069

For hundreds of years this 14th-century abbey was used as a farm and its church became a barn. A Georgian house, now used as a school for young musicians, was built into its fabric and remains of the choir, the church transepts and parts of the cloisters still stand.

Times Open at any reasonable time **Facilities** (partly accessible) (wheelchair access restricted in some areas) (disabled parking bay close to ruins)

Long Shop Museum **2 FOR 1**

Main St IP16 4ES
☎ 01728 832189 01728 832189
e-mail: longshop@care4free.net
web: www.longshopmuseum.co.uk
dir: Turn off A12, follow B1119 from Saxmundham to Leiston. Museum is in the middle of town

Discover the Magic of Steam through a visit to the world famous traction engine manufacturers. Trace the history of the factory and Richard Garrett engineering. See the traction engines and road rollers in the very place that they were built. Soak up the atmosphere of the Long Shop, built in 1852 as one of the first production line engineering halls in the world. An award-winning museum with five exhibition halls full of items from the glorious age of steam and covering 200 years of local, social and industrial history.

Times Open Apr-Oct, Mon-Sat 10-5, Sun 11-5* **Fees** £5 (ch £2, ch under 5 free, concessions £4.50) Family ticket £12* **Facilities** Ⓟ Ⓟ (outdoor) (partly accessible) (90% access, one upper gallery not wheelchair accessible) toilets for disabled (wheelchair available) shop

LINDSEY — Map 5 TL94

St James' Chapel (Lindsey) — FREE

Rose Green
web: www.english-heritage.org.uk
dir: on unclass road 0.5m E of Rose Green

Built mainly in the 13th century, this small thatched, flint-and-stone chapel incorporates some earlier work.

Times Open all year, daily 10-4 **Facilities**

LONG MELFORD — Map 5 TL84

Kentwell Hall

CO10 9BA
☎ 01787 310207 Fax 01787 379318
e-mail: enquiries@kentwell.co.uk
web: www.kentwell.co.uk
dir: signed off A134, between Bury St Edmunds & Sudbury

Kentwell Hall is a moated red brick Tudor manor with gardens, woodland walks and a rare breeds farm. Restoration started in 1971 and still continues today. The house and grounds are open to the public at certain times of the year, and recreations of Tudor and 1940s life take place at weekends. Ring for details.

Times Open Mar-Oct. Please contact estate office for opening times or refer to website* **Fees** Please refer to website for up to date details* **Facilities** Ⓟ (outdoor) (partly accessible) (first floor of hall not accessible) toilets for disabled (wheelchair ramps & 3 wheelchairs for loan) shop

Melford Hall

CO10 9AA
☎ 01787 379228 & 376395 Fax 01787 379228
e-mail: melford@nationaltrust.org.uk
web: www.nationaltrust.org.uk/melford
dir: off A134, 3m N of Sudbury, next to village green

Set in the unspoilt village of Long Melford, the house has changed little externally since 1578 when Queen Elizabeth I was entertained here, and retains its original panelled banqueting hall. It has been the home of the Hyde Parker Family since 1786. There is a Regency library, Victorian bedrooms, good collections of furniture and porcelain and a small display of items connected with Beatrix Potter, who was related to the family. The garden contains some spectacular specimen trees and a banqueting house and there is an attractive walk through the park.

Times Open all year, Apr-Oct, Sat-Sun 1.30-5; May-Sep, Wed-Sun 1.30-5 & BH Mon (last entry to the house 4.30) **Fees** House & Garden: £6.30 (ch £3.15). Family ticket £15.50. Garden only: £3.15 (ch £1.60). Family ticket £8. Please phone or see website for current prices* **Facilities** Ⓟ Ⓟ (outdoor) (partly accessible) (slopes & some steps in grounds) toilets for disabled (stairlift, ramp, Braille & large print guides) shop

LOWESTOFT — Map 5 TM59

Africa Alive!

Kessingland NR33 7TF
☎ 01502 740291 Fax 01502 741104
e-mail: info@africa-alive.co.uk
web: www.africa-alive.co.uk
dir: 25min S of Gt. Yarmouth just S of Lowestoft off A12

Set in 80 acres of dramatic coastal parkland, visitors can explore the sights and sounds of Africa at Africa Alive! There are giraffes, rhinos, cheetah, hyenas and many more, including a bird's eye view of the new lion enclosure. There are lots of daily feeding talks and animal encounter sessions, a magnificent bird of prey display, and free journey round the park with live commentary.

Times Open all year, daily from 10. Closed 25-26 Dec.* **Facilities** Ⓟ licensed (partly accessible) toilets for disabled (wheelchairs available for hire) shop

East Anglia Transport Museum

Chapel Rd, Carlton Colville NR33 8BL
☎ 01502 518459 Fax 01502 584658
e-mail: enquiries@eatm.org.uk
web: www.eatm.org.uk
dir: 3m SW of Lowestoft, follow brown signs from A12, A146 & A1117

A particular attraction of this museum is the reconstructed 1930s street scene which is used as a setting for working vehicles: visitors can ride by tram, trolley bus and narrow gauge railway. Other motor, steam and electrical vehicles are exhibited. There is also a woodland picnic area served by trams.

Times Open: Apr-Sep, Sun & BH 11-5. From Jun, Thu & Sat, 2-5* **Facilities** Ⓟ (outdoor) (partly accessible) toilets for disabled shop

Maritime Museum — 2 FOR 1

Sparrow Nest Gardens, Whapload Rd NR32 1XG
☎ 01502 561963
web: www.lowestoftmaritimemuseum.org.uk
dir: on A12, 100mtrs N of Lowestoft Lighthouse, turn right down Ravine

Themed exhibits tracing the history of Lowestoft and its connections with the sea, displaying ancient and modern fishing, commercial boats, fishing gear, shipwrights tools, life boats, wheelhouse, steam drifter cabin and fish market, including models and paintings. New audio visual room.

Times Open 22 Apr-30 Oct, daily 10-5 (last admission 4) **Fees** £2 (ch & students 50p, pen £1) **Facilities** Ⓟ Ⓟ (outdoor) (fully accessible) toilets for disabled (hear for all) shop

LOWESTOFT *continued*

Pleasurewood Hills

Leisure Way, Corton NR32 5DZ
☎ 01502 586000 (admin) 01502 567393
e-mail: info@pleasurewoodhills.com
web: www.pleasurewoodhills.com
dir: off A12 at Lowestoft

Set in 50 acres of coastal parkland, Pleasurewood Hills has all the ingredients for a great day out for all the family. Adrenalin-fuelled thrills and spills for the bravest adventurers, such as the newest attraction, Wipeout, which claims to be the most extreme rollercoaster in the East of England. Fun rides for all the family including some for younger children. Wonderful shows with sealions, parrots, acrobats and the breathtaking Magic Circus spectacular. When the action gets too much, take a leisurely ride on the alpine chairlift or jump aboard one of two railways that weave their way through the park.

Times Open Apr-Oct from 10. Please telephone for details or visit website **Fees** £16.50 (ch 3-11 £14.50, under 3 free, pen/special needs/carers £10.50)* **Facilities** licensed (outdoor) (fully accessible) toilets for disabled (all shows accessible, most ride operators able to assist) shop

NEWMARKET — Map 5 TL66

National Horseracing Museum and Tours — 2 FOR 1

99 High St CB8 8JH
☎ 01638 667333 01638 665600
e-mail: admin@nhrm.co.uk
web: www.nhrm.co.uk
dir: located in centre of High St

This friendly award-winning museum tells the story of the people and horses involved in racing in Britain. Have a go on the horse simulator in the hands-on gallery and chat to retired jockeys and trainers about their experiences. Special mini bus tours visit the gallops, a stable and horses' swimming pool.

Times Open Etr-Oct, daily 11-5, 10am on race days. Open BH Mon* **Fees** £6 (ch £3, concessions £5). Family (2ad+2ch) £13* **Facilities** licensed (outdoor) (fully accessible) toilets for disabled (ramps & lift) shop

ORFORD — Map 5 TM45

Orford Castle

IP12 2ND
☎ 01394 450472
web: www.english-heritage.org.uk
dir: on B1084

A great keep of Henry II with three huge towers and commanding views over Orford Ness. Climb the spiral staircase leading to a maze of rooms and passageways.

Times Open all year, Apr-Jun & Sep, daily 10-5; Jul-Aug, daily 10-6; Oct-Mar, Thu-Mon 10-4. Closed 24-26 Dec & 1 Jan.* **Facilities** shop

SAXTEAD GREEN — Map 5 TM26

Saxtead Green Post Mill

The Mill House IP13 9QQ
☎ 01728 685789
web: www.english-heritage.org.uk
dir: 2.5m NW of Framlingham on A1120

A post mill since 1287, Saxtead Green Post Mill is still in working order. Climb the wooden stairs to the various floors full of fascinating mill machinery. An audio tour explains the workings of the mill.

Times Open Apr-Sep, Fri-Sat & BHs 12-5 **Fees** £3.50 (ch £1.80, concessions £3). Prices and opening times are subject to change in March 2011. Please check web site or call 0870 333 1181 for the most up to date prices and opening times when planning your visit **Facilities** shop

STOWMARKET — Map 5 TM05

Museum of East Anglian Life

IP14 1DL
☎ 01449 612229 01449 672307
e-mail: enquiries@eastanglianlife.org.uk
web: www.eastanglianlife.org.uk
dir: in centre of Stowmarket, signed from A14 & B1115

This 70-acre, all-weather museum is set in an attractive river-valley site with 3km of woodland and riverside nature trails. There are reconstructed buildings, including a working water mill, a smithy and also a wind pump, and the Boby Building houses craft workshops. There are displays on Victorian domestic life, gypsies, farming and industry. These include working steam traction engines, the only surviving pair of Burrell ploughing engines of 1879, and a Suffolk Punch horse. The William Bone Building illustrates the history of Ransomes of Ipswich.

Times Open late March-end Oct.* **Facilities** (outdoor) (partly accessible) toilets for disabled (w/chairs & 2 buggies available, special vehicle facilities) shop

SUDBURY — Map 5 TL84

Gainsborough's House — 2 FOR 1

46 Gainsborough St CO10 2EU
☎ 01787 372958 01787 376991
e-mail: mail@gainsborough.org
web: www.gainsborough.org
dir: in centre of Sudbury. Follow pedestrian signs from town centre car parks or from train stn

The birthplace of Thomas Gainsborough RA (1727-88). The Georgian-fronted town house, with an attractive walled garden, displays more of the artist's work at any one time than any other gallery, together with 18th-century furniture and memorabilia. A varied programme of temporary exhibitions on British art is shown throughout the year.

Times Open all year, Mon-Sat 10-5. Closed Sun, Good Fri & Xmas-New Year **Fees** £4.50 (ch and students £2, concessions

£3.60). Family ticket £10 **Facilities** Ⓟ ☕ ♿ (partly accessible) (3rd floor not accessible) toilets for disabled (lift to 1st/2nd floor) shop

WEST STOW **Map 5 TL87**

West Stow Anglo Saxon Village

West Stow Country Park, Icklingham Rd IP28 6HG
☎ 01284 728718 📠 01284 728277
e-mail: weststow@stedsbc.gov.uk
web: www.weststow.org
dir: off A1101, 7m NW of Bury St Edmunds. Follow brown heritage signs

The village is a reconstruction of a pagan Anglo-Saxon settlement dated 420-650 AD. Seven buildings have been reconstructed on the site of the excavated settlement. There is a Visitors' Centre which includes a new archaeology exhibition, DVD area and a children's play area. A new Anglo-Saxon Centre houses the original objects found on the site. Located in the 125 acre West Stow Country Park with river, lake, woodland and heath, plus many trails and paths.

Times Open all year, daily 10-5 (last entry 4, winter 3.30) except Xmas period* **Facilities** Ⓟ Ⓟ ☕ (outdoor) ♿ (partly accessible) toilets for disabled (ramps) shop

WESTLETON **Map 5 TM46**

RSPB Nature Reserve Minsmere

IP17 3BY
☎ 01728 648281 & 648780 📠 01728 648770
e-mail: minsmere@rspb.org.uk
web: www.rspb.org.uk/reserves/minsmere
dir: signed from A12 at Yoxford & Blythburgh and from Westleton Village

Set on the beautiful Suffolk coast, Minsmere offers an enjoyable day out for all. Nature trails take you through a variety of habitats to the excellent birdwatching hides. Spring is a time for birdsong, including nightingales and booming bitterns. In summer, you can watch breeding avocets and marsh harriers. Autumn is excellent for migrants, and in winter, hundreds of ducks visit the reserve. Look out for otters and red deer. The visitor centre has a well-stocked shop and licensed tearoom, and you can find out more about the reserve. There is a programme of events throughout the year, including several for children and families. Self-guided activity booklets for families.

Times Open all year, daily 9-9 or dusk if earlier, visitor centre 9-5, Nov-Jan 9-4. Closed 25-26 Dec **Fees** £5 (ch £1.50, concessions £3). Family ticket £10. RSPB members free **Facilities** Ⓟ Ⓟ ☕ (outdoor) ♿ (partly accessible) (visitor centre, parts of nature trail and some hides are accessible) toilets for disabled (batricar available for loan, booking advised) shop

WOODBRIDGE **Map 5 TM24**

Sutton Hoo

IP12 3DJ
☎ 01394 389700 📠 01394 389702
e-mail: suttonhoo@nationaltrust.org.uk
web: www.nationaltrust.org.uk/suttonhoo
dir: off B1083 Woodbridge to Bawdsey road. Follow signs from A12 avoiding Woodbridge itself

Discovered in 1939 and described as 'page one of English history', this is the site of one of the most important archaeological finds in Britain's history: the complete 7th-century ship burial of an Anglo-Saxon king, which had been missed by grave-robbers, and lay undisturbed for 1300 years. Sutton Hoo displays reveal how Anglo-Saxon nobles lived, went to war and founded a new kingdom in East Anglia. The centre-piece is a full sized replica of an Anglo-Saxon warrior king's burial chamber. The discoveries at Sutton Hoo changed forever our perceptions of the 'Dark Ages', by revealing a culture rich in craftsmanship, trade and legend.

Times Open all year Jun & Sep-Oct, Wed-Sun, 10.30-5; Jul-Aug, daily 10.30-5; Nov-Feb, Sat-Sun, 11-4. Open BHs **Fees** Gift Aid Admission prices £6.50, (ch £3.40). Family tickets £16.45. Gift aid admission includes a voluntary donation but visitors can choose to pay the standard prices displayed at the property and on the website **Facilities** Ⓟ licensed ♿ (partly accessible) (slopes, burial mound tours not accessible to w/chairs or PMV) toilets for disabled (ramps, electric buggy hire) shop

Woodbridge Tide Mill

Tide Mill Way IP12
☎ 01728 746959 📠 01728 748226
e-mail: wtm.terina.booker@btinternet.com
web: www.tidemill.org.uk
dir: follow signs for Woodbridge off A12, 7m E of Ipswich-Tide Mill is on riverside

The machinery of this 18th-century mill has been completely restored. There are photographs and working models on display. Situated on a busy quayside, the unique building looks over towards the historic site of the Sutton Hoo Ship Burial. Every effort is made to run the machinery for a while whenever the mill is open and the tides are favourable.

Times Open Etr, then daily May-Sep; Apr, Oct wknds only, 11-5* **Facilities** Ⓟ ♿ (partly accessible) (ground floor & viewing area only accessible) shop

SURREY

Day-rental narrowboat, River Wey, Guildford

ENGLAND

ASH VALE — Map 4 SU85

Army Medical Services Museum — FREE

Keogh Barracks GU12 5RQ

☎ 01252 868612 📠 01252 868832

e-mail: armymedicalmuseum@btinternet.com

web: www.ams-museum.org.uk

dir: M3 junct 4 on A331 to Mytchett then follow tourist signs

The museum traces the history of Army medicine, nursing, dentistry and veterinary science from 1660 until the present day. Medical equipment and ambulances complement displays including uniforms and medals.

Times Open all year, Mon-Fri 10-3.30. Closed Xmas, New Year & BH. Wknds by appointment only.* **Facilities** Ⓟ (partly accessible) toilets for disabled (audio guide, Braille guides) shop

CHERTSEY — Map 4 TQ06

Thorpe Park

Staines Rd KT16 8PN

☎ 0870 444 4466 📠 01932 566367

web: www.thorpepark.com

dir: M25 junct 11 or 13 and follow signs via A320 to Thorpe Park

For hardcore adrenaline junkies, Thorpe Park is the must-do destination for insanely thrilling rollercoaster fun. Unleash the daredevil within and take on the loops, spins, vertical drops and incredible speeds of the nation's thrill capital.

Times Open 15 Mar-9 Nov. Opening times vary throughout, check in advance.* **Facilities** licensed (fully accessible) toilets for disabled (wheelchair hire available) shop

EAST CLANDON — Map 4 TQ05

Hatchlands Park

GU4 7RT

☎ 01483 222482 📠 01483 223176

e-mail: hatchlands@nationaltrust.org.uk

web: www.nationaltrust.org.uk/main/hatchlands

dir: E of Guildford, off A246

Built in the 1750s for Admiral Boscawen, hero of the battle of Louisburg, and set in a beautiful 430-acre park designed by Humphry Repton, offering a variety of park and woodlands walks, Hatchlands boasts the earliest known decorative works by Robert Adam. Hatchlands is home to the Cobbe collection, the world's largest group of keyboard instruments associated with famous composers. There is also a small garden by Gertrude Jekyll and a beautiful bluebell wood in May. Please telephone for details of family activities and other events.

Times House & Gardens: Apr-30 Oct, Tue-Thu & Sun, 2-5.30. Park walks daily, Apr-30 Oct, 11-6 **Fees** Gift Aid donation: £7 (ch £3.60) Family ticket £18.90. Park walks £4 (ch £2). Joint ticket with Clandon Park £12.20 (ch £6.10). Family £35.10. Includes a voluntary donation of 10% or more. Visitors can choose to pay the standard admission which is displayed at the property and on NT website **Facilities** licensed (outdoor) (partly accessible) (park walks unsuitable and not accessible) toilets for disabled (wheelchair available, parking and assistance to house) shop

FARNHAM — Map 4 SU84

Birdworld & Underwaterworld — 2 FOR 1

Holt Pound GU10 4LD

☎ 01420 22140 📠 01420 23715

e-mail: bookings@birdworld.co.uk

web: www.birdworld.co.uk

dir: 3m S of Farnham on A325

Birdworld is the largest bird collection in the country and includes toucans, pelicans, flamingoes, ostriches and many others. Underwater World is a tropical aquarium with brilliant lighting that shows off collections of marine and freshwater fish, as well as the swampy depths of the alligator exhibit. Visitors can also visit some beautiful gardens, the Jenny Wren farm and the Heron Theatre.

Times Open all year, daily, summer 10-6; winter 10-4.30. Closed 25-26 Dec **Fees** £13.95 (ch 3-6 £10.95 & 7-15 £11.95, concessions £11.95). Family ticket (2ad+2ch) £45* **Facilities** Ⓟ licensed (outdoor) (fully accessible) toilets for disabled (wheelchairs available) shop

Farnham Castle Keep — FREE

Castle St GU6 0AG

☎ 01252 713393

web: www.english-heritage.org.uk

dir: 0.5m N on A287

A motte and bailey castle, once one of the seats of the bishop of Winchester, has been in continuous occupation since the 12th century.

Times Open Feb-23 Dec, Mon-Fri 9-5 or dusk if earlier, Sat-Sun 9-4. 1 May opening subject to change as building works may take place. Please call the site to avoid disappointment. Closed 24 Dec-1 Jan **Facilities** shop

GODSTONE — Map 5 TQ35

Godstone Farm

RH9 8LX

☎ 01883 742546 📠 01883 740380

e-mail: havefun@godstonefarm.co.uk

web: www.godstonefarm.co.uk

dir: M25 junct 6, S of village, signed

An ideal day out for children, Godstone Farm has lots of friendly animals, big sand pits and play areas, including an indoor play barn for rainy days.

Times Open all year, Mar-Oct, 10-6; Nov-Feb 10-5 (last admission 1hr before close). Closed 25 & 26 Dec **Fees** Contact for admission prices **Facilities** (indoor & outdoor) (fully accessible) toilets for disabled shop

ENGLAND

GREAT BOOKHAM Map 4 TQ15

Polesden Lacey

RH5 6BD

☎ 01372 452048 01372 452023

e-mail: polesdenlacey@nationaltrust.org.uk

web: www.nationaltrust.org.uk/polesdenlacey

dir: 2m S off A246 from village of Bookham

King George VI and Queen Elizabeth the Queen Mother spent part of their honeymoon here, and photographs of other notable guests can be seen. The house is handsomely furnished and full of charm, and it is set in spacious grounds. There is also a summer festival, where concerts and plays are performed. Please phone for details of special events.

Times Open all year; Grounds & Garden: daily 10-5. House: 15 Mar-25 Oct,11-5 (last admission 30 mins before closing).* **Facilities** licensed (outdoor) (partly accessible) (no access for w/chairs to house upper floors. Some steps & uneven paths in garden. Courtesy shuttle from car park to front of house) toilets for disabled (Braille guide, parking & mobility vehicles/wheelchairs) shop

GUILDFORD Map 4 SU94

Dapdune Wharf

Wharf Rd GU1 4RR

☎ 01483 561389 01483 531667

e-mail: riverwey@nationaltrust.org.uk

web: www.nationaltrust.org.uk/riverwey

dir: off Woodbridge Rd to rear of Surrey County Cricket Ground

The visitor centre at Dapdune Wharf is the centrepiece of one of the National Trust's most unusual properties, the River Way Navigations. A series of interactive exhibits and displays allow you to discover the fascinating story of Surrey's secret waterway, one of the first British rivers to be made navigable. See where huge Wey barges were built and climb aboard *Reliance*, one of the last surviving barges. Children's trails and special events run throughout the season.

Times Open 12 Mar-30 Oct, Thu-Mon 11-5. River trips Thu-Mon, 11-5 (conditions permitting) **Fees** £4 (ch £2). Family ticket £10.50. NT Members free **Facilities** (outdoor) (partly accessible) (Unable to take visitors with disabilities on the boat trip) toilets for disabled (Braille guide) shop

Guildford House Gallery FREE

155 High St GU1 3AJ

☎ 01483 444751 01483 458563

e-mail: guildfordhouse@guildford.gov.uk

web: www.guildfordhouse.co.uk

dir: N side of High St, opposite Sainsbury's

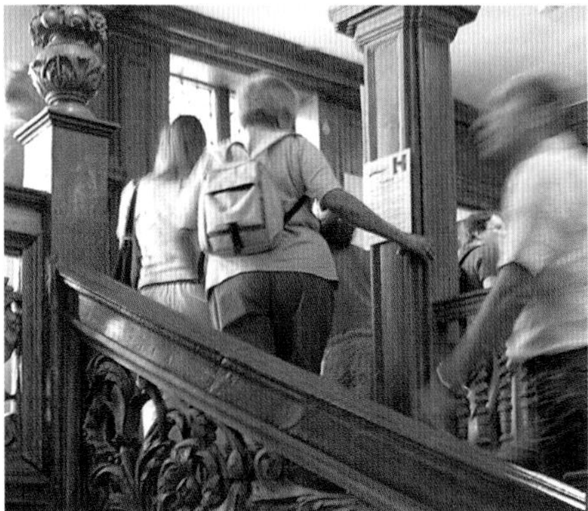

An impressive building in its own right, Guildford House dates from 1660 and has been Guildford's art gallery since 1959. A changing selection from the Borough's Art Collection is on display, including pastel portraits by John Russell, topographical paintings and contemporary craftwork, as well as temporary exhibitions.

Times Open all year Tue-Sat 10-4.45. Closed Good Fri & 25-26 Dec **Facilities** licensed (partly accessible) (ramps available for w/chair access to ground floor) shop

Loseley Park

GU3 1HS

☎ 01483 304440 01483 302036

e-mail: enquiries@loseleypark.co.uk

web: www.loseleypark.com

dir: 2m SW of Guildford, off A3 onto B3000

Magnificent Elizabethan mansion, home of the More-Molyneux family for over 500 years. Set in magnificent parkland scenery. Based on a Gertrude Jekyll design, the walled garden contains five gardens each with its own theme and character. These include the award-winning Rose Garden, Vine Walk, fruit, vegetable and flower gardens and the Serene White Fountain Garden. For information on events throughout the year please refer to website.

Times Open Grounds and Walled Garden: May-Sep, Tue-Sun & BH 11-5. House May-Aug, Tue-Thu, Sun & BH 1-5 **Fees** House & Gardens £8 (ch £4, ch under 5 free, concessions £7.50). Family £20. Gardens only £4.50 (ch £2.25, concessions £4). Discount for pre-booked groups **Facilities** (outdoor) (partly accessible) (Only ground floor of house accessible) toilets for disabled (wheelchair available, parking) shop

HASCOMBE Map 4 SU94

Winkworth Arboretum

Hascombe Rd GU8 4AD
01483 208477 01483 208252
e-mail: winkwortharboretum@nationaltrust.org.uk
web: www.nationaltrust.org.uk/main/w-winkwortharboretum
dir: 2m SE of Godalming, E side of B2130, follow brown tourist signs from Godalming

This lovely woodland covers a hillside of nearly 100 acres, with fine views over the North Downs. The best times to visit are April and May, for the azaleas, bluebells and other flowers, and October for the autumn colours. A delightful Victorian boathouse is open Apr-Oct with fine views over Rowes Flashe lake. Many rare trees and shrubs in group plantings for spring and autumn colour effect.

Times Open all year, daily 10-5 or sunset if earlier (could close in bad weather conditions such as high winds) **Fees** With a voluntary Gift Aid donation of 10% or more: £5.90 (ch £2.95). Family ticket £14.70. Visitors can choose to pay the standard admission price displayed. Reduction if arriving by public transport/cycle* **Facilities** (partly accessible) toilets for disabled (suggested route, free entry for helpers)

OCKLEY Map 5 TQ14

The Hannah Peschar Sculpture Garden

Black and White Cottage, Standon Ln RH5 5QR
01306 627269
e-mail: info@hannahpescharsculpture.com
web: www.hannahpescharsculpture.com
dir: M25 junct 9, take A24 signed Dorking. Leave A24 onto A29 signed Bognor Regis/Ockley, right into Cathill Lane at village end, left at T-junct Standon Lane, garden on right past Okewood Church

Broadleaved plants and mature trees frame a changing collection of contemporary sculptures in this stunning garden, created by landscape designer Anthony Paul. The ranges of work on display, selected by Hannah Peschar, include figurative and abstract styles using both contemporary and traditional materials. Each sculpture is placed in harmony with other works already featured in the garden to create an inspired and peaceful setting.

Times Open May-Oct, Fri-Sat 11-6, Sun & BHs 2-5. (Tue-Thu open to groups 4+ by appt only). Nov-Apr by appt only* **Fees** £10 (ch £7, concessions £8). Group visits, lecture tours and school visits by appointment only* **Facilities** (outdoor) (fully accessible)

PAINSHILL PARK Map 4 TQ06

Painshill Park

2 FOR 1

Portsmouth Rd KT11 1JE
01932 868113 01932 868001
e-mail: info@painshill.co.uk
web: www.painshill.co.uk
dir: W of Cobham on A245

Covering 158 acres, this magnificent 18th-century landscape garden was created by Charles Hamilton as a series of subtle and surprising vistas. Its landscape includes authentic 18th-century plantings, a working vineyard, unusual follies, and a unique grotto. The garden is also home to the John Bartram Heritage Collection of North American Trees and Shrubs. There are events for the whole family throughout the year and Father Christmas visits the grotto in December.

Times Open all year, Apr-Oct, 10.30-6 (last entry 4.30). Nov-Mar, 10.30-4 (last entry 3). Closed 25-26 Dec. Limited opening times to grotto **Fees** £6.60 (ch 5-16 £3.85, under 5 free, concessions £5.80). Family ticket (2ad+4ch) £22. Free admission for carer of disabled person. Pre-booked adult groups 10+ £5.80* **Facilities** (outdoor) (partly accessible) (accessible route covering 2/3rds of the landscape) toilets for disabled (pre-booked w/chairs & guided buggy tour available) shop

REIGATE Map 4 TQ24

Reigate Priory Museum

Bell St RH2 7RL
01737 222550
e-mail: museum@reigate-priory.surrey.sch.uk
web: www.reigatepriorymuseum.org.uk
dir: in Priory Park close to town centre, use Bell St car park on A217

The Priory Museum is housed in Reigate Priory. Originally founded in the early 13th century, this Grade I listed building was converted to a mansion in Tudor times. Notable features include the magnificent Holbein fireplace, 18th-century oak staircase and murals. The small museum has changing exhibitions on a wide range of subjects, designed to appeal to both adults and children. The collection includes domestic bygones, local history and costume.

Times Open Etr-early Dec, Wed & Sat, 2-4.30 in term time **Fees** Free admission. Donations welcome **Facilities** (fully accessible) (hands on facilities) shop

ENGLAND

TILFORD Map 4 SU84

Rural Life Centre

2 FOR 1

Reeds Rd GU10 2DL
☎ 01252 795571 📠 01252 795571
e-mail: info@rural-life.org.uk
web: www.rural-life.org.uk
dir: off A287, 3m S of Farnham, signed

The museum covers village life from 1750 to 1960. It is set in over ten acres of garden and woodland and incorporates purpose-built and reconstructed buildings, including a chapel, pavilion, village hall, schoolroom and 'prefab'. Displays show village crafts and trades, such as wheelwrighting, thatching, ploughing and gardening. The historic village playground provides entertainment for children and a narrow gauge railway operates on Sundays during the summer months. There is an arboretum featuring over 100 trees from around the world. An extensive programme of events takes place throughout the year, please contact for details.

Times Open mid Mar-end Oct, Wed-Sun & BH 10-5; Winter Wed & Sun only 11-4 **Fees** £8 (ch £6, concessions £7). Family ticket (2ad+2ch) £25 **Facilities** licensed (indoor & outdoor) (partly accessible) (2 buildings not wheelchair accessible but can be viewed from outside) toilets for disabled (3 wheelchairs for use) shop

WEST CLANDON Map 4 TQ05

Clandon Park

GU4 7RQ
☎ 01483 222482 📠 01483 223479
e-mail: clandonpark@nationaltrust.org.uk
web: www.nationaltrust.org.uk/clandonpark
dir: E of Guildford on A247

A grand Palladian mansion built c.1730 by the Venetian architect Giacomo Leoni, and notable for its magnificent marble hall. The house is filled with the superb Gubbay collection of 18th-century furniture, porcelain, textiles and carpets. The attractive gardens contain a parterre, grotto, sunken Dutch garden and a Maori meeting house. Please telephone or see website for details of special events and family activities.

Times House & Garden: open 14 Mar-Oct, Tue-Thu & Sun 11-5; museum 12-5 **Fees** Gift Aid donation: House & Garden £8.10 (ch £4). Family ticket £22. Joint ticket with Hatchlands Park £11.60 (ch £5.80). Family £33.40. Includes a voluntary donation of 10% or more. Visitors can however, choose to pay the standard admission which is displayed at the property and on NT website **Facilities** licensed (outdoor) (partly accessible) (7 steps to house entrance with handrail. Grounds partly accessible, grass & loose gravel paths, slopes, some steps & ramped access) toilets for disabled (wheelchairs, Braille guide, lifts, disabled parking) shop

WEYBRIDGE Map 4 TQ06

Brooklands Museum

Brooklands Rd KT13 0QN
☎ 01932 857381 📠 01932 855465
e-mail: info@brooklandsmuseum.com
web: www.brooklandsmuseum.com
dir: M25 junct 10/11, museum off B374, follow brown signs

Brooklands racing circuit was the birthplace of British motorsport and aviation. From 1907 to 1987 it was a world-renowned centre of engineering excellence. The Museum features old banked track and the 1-in-4 Test Hill. Many of the original buildings have been restored including the Clubhouse, the Shell and BP Petrol Pagodas, and the Malcolm Campbell Sheds in the Motoring Village. Many motorcycles, cars and aircraft are on display. Ring or see website for details of special events.

Times Open all year, daily 10-5 (4 in winter). Closed for a few days after Xmas **Fees** £9 (ch 5-16 £5.50, concessions £8). Family ticket (2ad+3ch) £25* **Facilities** (outdoor) (partly accessible) (no wheelchair access to aircraft) toilets for disabled shop

WISLEY Map 4 TQ05

RHS Garden Wisley

GU23 6QB
☎ 01483 226523 📠 01483 211750
web: www.rhs.org.uk/wisley
dir: on A3, close to M25 junct 10

With over 100 years of gardening, RHS Garden Wisley is the flagship garden of the Royal Horticultural Society. The garden stretches over 170 acres and there are countless opportunities for visitors to draw inspiration and gather new ideas. A 'must see' is the famous Glasshouse, with exotics from around the world in two climate zones. The mixed borders and vegetable garden are glories of summer, while the country garden, Battleston Hill and wild garden are magnificent in spring. Whatever the season the garden is full of interest.

Times Open all year, Mon-Fri 10-6, Sat-Sun 9-6; Nov-Feb 4.30. Closed 25 Dec* **Fees** £9.50 (ch 6-16 £3 under 6 free). RHS members plus one family guest free* **Facilities** licensed (outdoor) (partly accessible) (garden partly accessible, some difficult paths) toilets for disabled (free wheelchairs, mobility buggy/scooter, wheelchair route) shop

EAST SUSSEX

Bluebell Railway, Sheffield Park Station

ENGLAND

ALFRISTON Map 5 TQ50

Alfriston Clergy House

The Tye BN26 5TL
☎ 01323 870001 01323 871318
e-mail: alfriston@nationaltrust.org.uk
web: www.nationaltrust.org.uk/main/w-alfristonclergyhouse
dir: 4m NE of Seaford, E of B2108, next to church

This 14th-century thatched Wealden 'hall house' was the first building to be acquired by the National Trust in 1896. It has an unusual chalk and sour milk floor, and its pretty cottage garden is in an idyllic setting beside Alfriston's parish church, with views across the meandering Cuckmere River. Special Events: Please telephone or check website for details of events running throughout the year.

Times Open 26 Feb-13 Mar, daily ex Thu & Fri 11-4; 14 Mar-Jul & 29 Aug-30 Oct, daily ex Thu & Fri 10.30-5; 1-28 Aug, daily ex Fri 10.30-5; 31 Oct-18 Dec, daily, ex Thu & Fri 11-4 **Fees** With a voluntary Gift Aid donation of 10% or more: £4.30 (ch £2.15). Family ticket £10.75. Visitors can choose to pay the standard admission price displayed* **Facilities** ℗ ♿ (partly accessible) (slopes in garden to some limited areas, steps in house and garden make it inaccessible in wheelchair) (Braille/large print guides, sensory guide) shop

Drusillas Park

Alfriston Rd BN26 5QS
☎ 01323 874100 01323 874101
e-mail: info@drusillas.co.uk
web: www.drusillas.co.uk
dir: off A27 near Alfriston 12m from Brighton & 7m from Eastbourne

Widely regarded as the best small zoo in the country, Drusillas Park offers an opportunity to get nose to nose with nature, with hundreds of exotic animals, from monkeys and crocodiles to penguins and meerkats. But animals are only half the fun - Go Wild! Go Bananas! and Amazon Adventure are paradise for anyone who needs to let off steam and Thomas the Tank Engine offers a train service 362 days a year. Don't miss close encounters in Lemurland, or the brand new adventure maze quest - Eden's Eye.

Times Open all year, daily 10-5, winter 10-4. Closed 24-26 Dec* **Fees** Family of 4: peak £53.20, standard £49.20, off peak £41.20* **Facilities** ℗ licensed (indoor & outdoor) ♿ (fully accessible) toilets for disabled shop

BATTLE Map 5 TQ71

1066 Battle of Hastings Abbey & Battlefield

TN33 0AD
☎ 01424 773792 01424 775059
web: www.english-heritage.org.uk
dir: A21 onto A2100

Explore the site of the Battle of Hastings, where on 14th October 1066, one of the most famous events in English history took place. Free interactive wand tour of the battlefield and atmospheric abbey ruins.

Times Open all year, Apr-Sep, daily 10-6; Oct-Mar, daily 10-4. Closed 24-26 Dec & 1 Jan **Fees** £7 (ch £3.50, concessions £6). Family £17.50. Opening times and prices are subject to change from March 2011, for further details please phone 0870 333 118 **Facilities** ℗ ♿ (partly accessible) (steps to enter all abbey buildings) toilets for disabled (wheelchair access via gatehouse, hearing loop) shop #

Yesterday's World - Battle 2 FOR 1

89-90 High St TN33 0AQ
☎ 01424 777226 & 894314 01424 893316
e-mail: info@yesterdaysworld.co.uk
web: www.yesterdaysworld.co.uk
dir: M25 junct 5, A21 onto A2100 towards Battle, opposite Battle Abbey Gatehouse

This award-winning attraction brings 125 years of British social history to life. Discover 150,000 nostalgic artefacts, virtual and interactive exhibits superbly recaptured with evocative sounds and smells in life-size street scenes and shop displays. Secure gardens with children's play village.

Times Open all year daily; winter 10-4; summer 10-5. Closed 25-26 Dec & 1 Jan* **Fees** £7 (ch £5, concessions £6). Family ticket (2ad+2ch) £20* **Facilities** ℗ (outdoor) ♿ (partly accessible) (medieval building accessible) toilets for disabled shop

BODIAM Map 5 TQ72

Bodiam Castle

TN32 5UA
☎ 01580 830196 01580 830398
e-mail: bodiamcastle@nationaltrust.org.uk
web: www.nationaltrust.org.uk/main/w-bodiamcastle
dir: 2m E of A21 Hurst Green

With its tall round drum towers at each corner, Bodiam is something of a fairytale castle. It was built in 1385 by Sir Edward Dalyngrigge, for comfort and defence. The ramparts rise dramatically above a broad moat and the great gatehouse contains the original portcullis - a very rare example of its kind.

Times Open all year, Jan-Oct, daily 10.30-4.30; 3 Nov-23 Dec, Wed-Sun 11-3.30 **Fees** With voluntary Gift Aid donation of 10% or more: £6.40 (ch £3.20). Family ticket £17. Group 15+ £5 (ch £2.50). Visitors can choose to pay the standard admission price displayed* **Facilities** ℗ ♿ (partly accessible) (ground floor level is fully accessible, spiral staircase to upper levels) toilets for disabled (Braille/large print guides, sensory objects, audio loops) shop

BRIGHTON Map 4 TQ30

Booth Museum of Natural History FREE

194 Dyke Rd BN1 5AA
☎ 01273 292777 📠 01273 292778
e-mail: boothmuseum@brighton-hove.gov.uk
web: www.virtualmuseum.info
dir: from A27 Brighton by pass, 1.5m NW of town centre, opposite Dyke Rd Park

The museum was built in 1874 to house the bird collection of Edward Thomas Booth (1840-1890). His collection is still on display, but the museum has expanded considerably since Booth's day and now includes thousands of butterfly and insect specimens, geology galleries with fossils, rocks and local dinosaur bones, a magnificent collection of animal skeletons, largely collected by the Brighton solicitor F W Lucas (1842-1932), and an interactive discovery gallery.

Times Open all year, Mon-Sat (ex Thu) 10-5, Sun 2-5. Closed Good Fri, Xmas & 1 Jan **Facilities** Ⓟ ♿ (partly accessible) (rear access, otherwise accessible) toilets for disabled shop ⊗

Brighton Museum & Art Gallery

Royal Pavilion Gardens BN1 1EE
☎ 03000 290900 📠 03000 290908
e-mail: museums@brighton-hove.gov.uk
web: www.brighton.virtualmuseum.info
dir: M23/A23 from London. In city centre near seafront. New entrance in Royal Pavilion Gardens

A £10 million redevelopment transformed Brighton Museum into a state-of-the-art visitor attraction. Dynamic and innovative galleries, including two new Egyptian galleries, fashion, 20th-century design and world art, feature exciting interactive displays appealing to all ages. The museum also benefits from a spacious entrance located in the Royal Pavilion gardens and full disabled access. See website for details of special events and exhibitions.

Times Open all year, Tue 10-7, Wed-Sat 10-5, Sun 2-5. Open BHs 10-5 **Fees** Free admission (charge made for touring exhibitions) **Facilities** Ⓟ ☕ ⛩ (outdoor) ♿ (fully accessible) toilets for disabled (lift, tactile exhibits, induction loops, ramps) shop ⊗

Brighton Toy and Model Museum 2 FOR 1

52-55 Trafalgar St BN1 4EB
☎ 01273 749494
e-mail: info@brightontoymuseum.co.uk
web: www.brightontoymuseum.co.uk
dir: underneath Brighton Railway Station

A fascinating collection of over 10,000 exhibits, includes collections of toys from the last one hundred years. Toys from the top toy makers and a priceless model train collection are some examples to be viewed.

Times Open all year, Tue-Fri 10-5, Sat 11-5 **Fees** £4 (ch & concessions £3) Family (2ad & 2ch) £12* **Facilities** Ⓟ ♿ (fully accessible) toilets for disabled (ramp, wide door, rails & bars) shop ⊗

Preston Manor

Preston Drove BN1 6SD
☎ 01273 292770 & 03000 290900 📠 01273 292771
e-mail: museums@brighton-hove.gov.uk
web: www.prestonmanor.virtualmuseum.info
dir: off A23, 2m N of Brighton

This charming Edwardian manor house is beautifully furnished with notable collections of silver, furniture and paintings and presents a unique opportunity to see an Edwardian home both 'upstairs' and 'downstairs'. The servants' quarters can also be seen, featuring kitchen, butler's pantry and boot hall. The house is set in beautiful gardens, which include a pet cemetery and the 13th-century parish church of St Peter.

Times Open Apr-Sep, Tue-Sat 10-5, Sun 2-5* **Facilities** 🅟 Ⓟ ♿ (partly accessible) (lower floor only, call prior to visit to discuss access requirements) shop ⊗

Royal Pavilion

BN1 1EE
☎ 03000 290900 📠 03000 292871
e-mail: visitor.services@brighton-hove.gov.uk
web: www.royalpavilion.org.uk
dir: M23/A23 from London. In city centre near seafront. 15 min walk from rail station

Acclaimed as one of the most exotically beautiful buildings in the British Isles, the Royal Pavilion was the magnificent seaside residence of George IV. This breathtaking Regency palace is decorated in Chinese style, with a romanticised Indian exterior, and surrounded by restored Regency gardens.

Times Open all year daily, Apr-Sep, 9.30-5.45; Oct-Mar, 10-5.15 (last admission 45 mins before close 4.30). Closed 25-26 Dec **Fees** £9.50 (ch £5.40). Family ticket (1ad+2ch) £14.90, (2ad+2ch) £24.40. Group rates available **Facilities** Ⓟ ☕ 🍽 licensed ⛩ (outdoor) ♿ (partly accessible) (ground floor only accessible) toilets for disabled (wheelchairs, audio guides) shop ⊗

Sea Life Centre

Marine Pde BN2 1TB
☎ 01273 604234 📠 01273 681840
e-mail: slcbrighton@merlinentertainments.biz
web: www.sealife.co.uk
dir: next to Brighton Pier between Marine Parade & Madeira Drive

The Brighton Sea Life Centre offers a fun and educational day out what ever the weather, with over 150 species and 50 displays. Watch giant turtles and sharks glide above you in the underwater tunnel. Visit the Tropical Reef complete with a shark encircled wreck and tropical coral. A new feature is the UK's first glass bottom boat which floats atop the centre's huge open tank. It's the ultimate way to experience the wonder and beauty of the deep without getting your feet wet.

Times Open all year, daily 6 Sep-25 Jul 10-6; 26 Jul-5 Sep 10-7 (last admission 1 hour before close)* **Fees** £15.50 (ch £10.50, concessions £13). Family £45* **Facilities** Ⓟ ☕ ♿ (partly accessible) (no access to auditorium) toilets for disabled shop ⊗

ENGLAND

BURWASH Map 5 TQ62

Bateman's

TN19 7DS
☎ 01435 882302 📠 01435 882811
e-mail: batemans@nationaltrust.org.uk
web: www.nationaltrust.org.uk
dir: 0.5m SW off A265

Rudyard Kipling lived for over 34 years in this 17th-century manor house and it remains much the same as it was during his lifetime. His 1928 Rolls Royce Phantom is on display, and the watermill at the bottom of the garden grinds wheat into flour on Saturday afternoons and Wednesdays.

Times Open 12 Mar-30 Oct, Sat-Wed 11-5, also open Good Fri (last admission 4.30), House closes at 5 **Fees** Gift Aid donation: £8.20 (ch £4.10). Family ticket £20.50. Party £6.45 (ch £3.15). Includes a voluntary donation of 10% or more. Visitors can choose to pay the standard admission price* **Facilities** licensed (outdoor) (partly accessible) (access to first floor & water mill restricted) toilets for disabled (Braille guide, touch test, virtual tour) shop

EAST DEAN Map 5 TV59

Seven Sisters Sheep Centre

Gilberts Dr BN20 0AA
☎ 01323 423302 📠 01323 423302
e-mail: sevensisters.sheepcentre@talk21.com
web: www.sheepcentre.co.uk
dir: 3m W of Eastbourne on A259. Turn left in village of East Dean to Birling Gap and sea, 0.5m on left

Possibly the largest collection of sheep in the world, where over 40 different breeds can be visited at this family run farm. See lambs being born, sheep sheared and milked, cheese making and spinning. Take in the agricultural heritage and history of sheep on the South Downs.

Times Open 3 Mar-7 May & 30 Jun-2 Sep, 2-5 (11-5 wknds/E Sussex school hols)* **Facilities** (indoor & outdoor) shop

EASTBOURNE Map 5 TV69

"How We Lived Then" Museum of Shops & Social History

20 Cornfield Ter BN21 4NS
☎ 01323 737143
e-mail: howwelivedthen@btconnect.com
web: www.how-we-lived-then.co.uk
dir: just off seafront, between town centre & theatres, signed

Over the last 50 years, Jan and Graham Upton have collected over 100,000 items which are now displayed on four floors of authentic old shops. Room settings and displays transport visitors back to their parents' and grandparents' eras.

Times Open all year, daily from 10. Closing times vary according to season, please check **Fees** £5 (ch 5-15 £4, under 5's free, concessions £4.50). Family ticket available. Party rates for 10+ **Facilities** (partly accessible) (ground floor access only) (no charge for disabled) shop

FIRLE Map 5 TQ40

Firle Place

BN8 6LP
☎ 01273 858307 📠 01273 858145
e-mail: gage@firleplace.co.uk
web: www.firleplace.co.uk
dir: off A27, Eastbourne to Brighton road near Lewes

Home of the Gage family for over 500 years, the house has a Tudor core but was remodelled in the 18th century. Its treasures include important European and English Old Master paintings, fine English and French furniture, and porcelain, including notable examples from Sèvres and English factories. There are family monuments and brasses in the church at West Firle.

Times Open Jun-Sep, Sun, Wed, Thu & BHs 2-4.30 (last admission 4.15)* **Facilities** licensed (partly accessible) (access to ground floor only) toilets for disabled shop

FOREST ROW Map 5 TQ43

Ashdown Forest Llama Park

Wych Cross RH18 5JN
☎ 01825 712040 📠 01825 713698
e-mail: info@llamapark.co.uk
web: www.llamapark.co.uk
dir: on A22 between Uckfield & East Grinstead, 250mtrs S of junct with A275

Ashdown Forest Llama Park is home to more than 100 llamas and alpacas and these beautiful and gentle woolly animals, native to the high Andes of South America, are very much at home in Sussex. There are also now three reindeer who, in December, are an important part of the Christmas celebrations and Santa's Grotto. The park has wonderful views over Ashdown Forest and there is a marked trail around the Park, a picnic area and adventure play area. In the information Centre, learn about the fascinating world of llamas and alpacas and other fibre producing animals and plants. The coffee shop is open daily and local produce is used as much as possible. You can visit the coffee shop at any time without paying to visit the park. The park is holder of a Green Tourist Award.

Times Open all year, daily 10-5. Closed 25-26 Dec & 1 Jan* **Facilities** licensed (outdoor) (partly accessible) (shop and coffee shop accessible, some gravel areas in park but limited access to wheelchair users) toilets for disabled (ramps, wheelchairs provided) shop

HAILSHAM Map 5 TQ50

Michelham Priory

Upper Dicker BN27 3QS
01323 844224 01323 844030
e-mail: adminmich@sussexpast.co.uk
web: www.sussexpast.co.uk
dir: off A22 & A27 signed, 2m W of Hailsham, 8m NW of Eastbourne

Set on a moated island surrounded by glorious gardens, Michelham Priory is one of the most beautiful historic houses in Sussex. Founded in 1229 for Augustinian canons, the Priory is approached through a 14th-century gatehouse spanning the longest water-filled medieval moat in the country. Most of the original priory was demolished during the Dissolution, but the remains were incorporated into a Tudor farm that became a country house. Outside, the gardens are enhanced by a fully restored medieval watermill, physic garden, smithy, rope museum and the dramatic Elizabethan Great Barn. A variety of special events take place throughout the year.

Times Open Mar-Oct, Tue-Sun (daily in Aug & BH Mons). Mar & Oct 10.30-4.30, Apr-Jul & Sep 10.30-5, Aug 10.30-5.30.* **Facilities** licensed (outdoor) (partly accessible) toilets for disabled (wheelchairs, Braille guide & tactile tours) shop

HALLAND Map 5 TQ51

Bentley Wildfowl & Motor Museum

BN8 5AF
01825 840573 01825 841322
e-mail: barrysutherland@pavilion.co.uk
web: www.bentley.org.uk
dir: 7m NE of Lewes, signed off A22, A26 & B2192

Hundreds of swans, geese and ducks from all over the world can be seen on lakes and ponds along with flamingoes and peacocks. There is a fine array of Veteran, Edwardian and Vintage vehicles, and the house has splendid antiques and wildfowl paintings. The gardens specialise in old fashioned roses. Other attractions include woodland walks, a nature trail, education centre, adventure playground and a miniature train.

Times Open 17 Mar-Oct, daily 10.30-4.30. House open from noon, Apr-Nov, Feb & part of Mar, wknds only. Estate closed Dec & Jan. House closed all winter* **Facilities** (partly accessible) toilets for disabled (wheelchairs available) shop

HASTINGS Map 5 TQ80

Blue Reef Aquarium — 2 FOR 1

Rock-a-nore Rd TN34 3DW
01424 718776 01424 721483
e-mail: hastings@bluereefaquarium.co.uk
web: www.bluereefaquarium.co.uk
dir: Follow signs to end of Rock-a-nore Rd on seafront

Undersea safari in Hastings. Come face to face with seahorses, sharks, giant crabs, stingrays and many other aquatic creatures. At the aquarium's heart is a giant ocean tank where an underwater walkthrough tunnel offers close encounters with giant wrasse, tropical sharks and hundreds of colourful fish. Talks and feeding displays take place throughout the day.

Times Open all year daily 10-5, winter 10-4. Closed 25 Dec **Fees** £7.75 (ch £5.75, concessions £6.75, disabled & carers £4.99). Family ticket (2ad+2ch) £24, (2ad+3ch) £27.50. Please refer to website for current details* **Facilities** (partly accessible) (steps to tunnel) toilets for disabled shop

Old Town Hall Museum of Local History — FREE

Old Town Hall, High St TN34 1EW
01424 451052
e-mail: oldtownmuseum@hastings.gov.uk
web: www.hmag.org.uk
dir: off A259 coast road into High St in Hastings old town. Signed

Situated in the heart of Hastings Old Town, the museum was originally a Georgian Town Hall built in 1823. Displays tell the story of Hastings Old Town as a walk back in time, with features including a Cinque Ports ship, and interactive displays.

Times Open all year, Apr-Sep, Mon-Sat 10-5, Sun 11-5.; Oct-Mar, Mon-Fri 10-4, Sat-Sun 11-4 **Facilities** (fully accessible) toilets for disabled (lift, evac chair, low-level displays) shop

1066 Story in Hastings Castle

Castle Hill Rd, West Hill TN34 3RG
01424 781111 & 781112 (info line) 01424 781186
e-mail: bookings@discoverhastings.co.uk
web: www.discoverhastings.co.uk/hastings-castle-1066/
dir: close to A259 seafront, 2m from B2093

The ruins of the Norman castle stand on the cliffs, close to the site of William the Conqueror's first motte-and-bailey castle in England. It was excavated in 1825 and 1968, and old dungeons were discovered in 1894. An unusual approach to the castle can be made via the West Hill Cliff Railway.

Times Open daily, 27 Mar-Sep 10-5; Oct-26 Mar 11-3.30. Closed 24-26 Dec.* **Facilities** shop

ENGLAND

HASTINGS *continued*

Shipwreck & Coastal Heritage Centre

Rock-a-Nore TN34 3DW
☎ 01424 437452
e-mail: info@shipwreck-heritage.org.uk
web: www.shipwreck-heritage.org.uk
dir: old town E end of A259, turn into Rock-A-Nore rd. On right between Fishermans Museum & Blue Reef Aquarium

Sited in the historic town of Hastings, in the middle of the 'Maritime Park' shoreline, the Centre opened in 1986 and tells the story of shipwrecks around the area. It also explores the geological and environmental circumstances that have preserved these wrecks, two of which can be visited, where they sank, at certain very low tides. The audio-visual presentation is narrated by Christopher Lee. There are also fossils of dinosaurs and plants on display. In 2011 the centre celebrates its 25th anniversary.

Times Open Apr-Oct, daily 10-5; Nov-Mar, wknds only 11-4. Groups by arrangement **Fees** £1 donation for ad, ch free* **Facilities** Ⓟ ♿ (fully accessible) shop

Smugglers Adventure **2 FOR 1**

St Clements Caves, West Hill TN34 3HY
☎ 01424 422964
e-mail: smugglers@discoverhastings.co.uk
web: www.discoverhastings.co.uk
dir: follow brown signs on A259, coast road, through Hastings. Use seafront car park, then take West Cliff railway or follow signed footpath

Journey deep into the heart of Hastings historic West Hill to discover the fascinating world of the Smugglers Adventure in St Cements Caves. Join notorious smuggler 'Hairy Jack' as he leads you through acres of underground caverns, passages and tunnels on a voyage back through time to the heyday of smuggling. Several events throughout the year.

Times Open all year daily, Apr-Sep 10-5; Oct-Mar 11-4* **Fees** £7 (ch £5, concessions £6). Family ticket (2ad+2ch) £21, (2ad+3ch) £25. Please refer to website for current details* **Facilities** Ⓟ ♿ (partly accessible) (40 steps to entrance & exit the attraction) shop

HERSTMONCEUX **Map 5 TQ61**

The Observatory Science Centre

BN27 1RN
☎ 01323 832731 📠 01323 832741
e-mail: info@the-observatory.org
web: www.the-observatory.org
dir: 0.75m N of Wartling village

From the 1950s to the 1980s this was part of the Royal Greenwich Observatory, and was used by astronomers to observe and chart movements in the night sky. Visitors can learn about not only astronomy, but also other areas of science in a series of interactive and engaging displays. There are also exhibitions, a discovery park, and a collection of unusual giant exhibits.

Times Open daily 26 Jan-Nov & 6-7 Dec* **Facilities** Ⓟ (indoor & outdoor) ♿ (partly accessible) toilets for disabled (ramps & disabled entrance, lift to 1st floor) shop

The Truggery **FREE**

Coopers Croft BN27 1QL
☎ 01323 832314
e-mail: info@truggery.co.uk
web: www.truggery.co.uk
dir: from A22 at Hailsham, Boship rdbt, take A271 towards Bexhill for 4m

The art of Sussex trug making can be seen through all the work processes including preparing timber, use of the draw knife and assembly of trug. There is a wide selection of Sussex Trugs and locally made garden related items.

Times Open all year Thu-Sat 10-1, or by appointment **Facilities** Ⓟ Ⓟ ♿ (partly accessible) (path to workshop is over rough ground) shop

LEWES Map 5 TQ41

Anne of Cleves House 2 FOR 1

52 Southover High St BN7 1JA
☎ 01273 474610 📠 01273 486990
e-mail: anne@sussexpast.co.uk
web: www.sussexpast.co.uk
dir: S of town centre off A27/A26/A275

Henry VIII gave this beautiful timber-framed house to Anne of Cleves, his fourth wife, as part of her divorce settlement. Today there are collections of early English furniture, Sussex pottery and stone from Lewes Priory, plus a local social history exhibition. The Wealden Iron Gallery tells the story of the industrial past of Sussex and contains a large collection of iron artefacts.

Times Open Mar-Oct, Tue-Thu 10-5; Sun, Mon & BHs 11-5; Mon-Fri during Feb & Oct half term hols **Fees** £4.20 (ch 5-15 £2.10, concessions £3.70). Family ticket (2ad+2ch) £11.30* **Facilities** Ⓟ ♿ (partly accessible) (wheelchair access to house & garden limited, changes of level) (ramp available to enter east room) shop 🚫

Charleston

Firle BN8 6LL
☎ 01323 811265 & 811626 📠 01323 811628
e-mail: info@charleston.org.uk
web: www.charleston.org.uk
dir: Signed off A27, 7m E of Lewes between the villages of Firle and Selmeston

From 1916 Charleston was the home of the artists Vanessa Bell and Duncan Grant, and a rural retreat for the Bloomsbury Group. Over the years the house was transformed and filled with furniture, textiles and art by them and their contemporaries including Picasso, Renoir, Sickert, Derain and Lamb. The Downland setting captures their pioneering, creative and Bohemian way of life. The walled garden was redesigned in a style reminiscent of southern Europe, with mosaics, box hedges, gravel pathways and ponds, but with a touch of Bloomsbury humour in the placing of the statuary. Special events: The Charleston Literary Festival every May, plus other events throughout the year.

Times Open Apr-Oct Wed-Sat & BH 1-6 (Jul-Aug 12-6)* **Facilities** Ⓟ ☕ 🅰 (outdoor) ♿ (partly accessible) (only ground floor of house accessible) toilets for disabled shop 🚫

Lewes Castle & Barbican House Museum 2 FOR 1

169 High St BN7 1YE
☎ 01273 486290 📠 01273 486990
e-mail: castle@sussexpast.co.uk
web: www.sussexpast.co.uk
dir: N of High St off A27/A26/A275

One of the oldest castles in England, built soon after the Norman Conquest, and one of only two in England to be built on two mounds. The views over Lewes, the River Ouse and surrounding Downs are worth the climb up the Keep. Barbican House Museum, opposite the Castle tells the story of Sussex from the Stone Age to the end of the medieval period, and displays include flint tools, pottery, weapons, jewellery and other archaeological discoveries, as well as a model of Lewes in about 1870. Special family sessions on archaeological and historical themes are run throughout the year. Other events include a Medieval Day in May and open-air theatre.

Times Open all year, daily, Tue-Sat 10-5.30, Sun, Mon & BHs 11-5.30 (last admission 30 mins before closing). Closed Xmas & Mon in Jan **Fees** £6 (ch 5-15 £3, concessions £5.40, carer £3). Family ticket (2ad+2ch) £16.20* **Facilities** Ⓟ ♿ (partly accessible) (wheelchair access is limited to the lower Gun Garden of the Castle) toilets for disabled (some interpretation panels are provided in Braille) shop 🚫

NEWHAVEN Map 5 TQ40

Paradise Park, Heritage Trail & Gardens

Avis Rd BN9 0DH
☎ 01273 512123 📠 01273 616005
e-mail: promotions@paradisepark.co.uk
web: www.paradisepark.co.uk
dir: signed off A26 & A259

A perfect day out for plant lovers whatever the season. Discover the unusual garden designs with waterfalls, fountains and lakes, including the Caribbean garden and the tranquil Oriental garden. The Conservatory Gardens complex contains a large variety of the world's flora divided into several zones. There's also a Sussex history trail and Planet Earth with moving dinosaurs and interactive displays, plus rides and amusements for children.

Times Open all year, daily 9-6. Closed 25-26 Dec.* **Facilities** Ⓟ ☕ 🍴 licensed 🅰 (outdoor) ♿ (fully accessible) toilets for disabled (all areas level or ramped) shop 🚫

NORTHIAM Map 5 TQ82

Great Dixter House & Gardens

TN31 6PH
☎ 01797 252878 📠 01797 252879
e-mail: office@greatdixter.co.uk
web: www.greatdixter.co.uk
dir: off A28, signed

Birthplace and home of Christopher Lloyd, gardening writer, Great Dixter was built in 1460 and boasts one of the largest timber-framed buildings in the country. Lutyens was employed to restore both the house and gardens in 1910. The gardens are now a combination of meadows, ponds, topiary and notably the Long Border and Exotic Garden.

Times Open Apr-Oct Tue-Sun & BH Mon, Garden 11-5.30; House 2-5* **Fees** House & Gardens £8.50 (ch £4). Gardens only £7 (ch £3.50)* **Facilities** Ⓟ 🛆 (outdoor) ♿ (partly accessible) (wheelchair users need assistance in garden) toilets for disabled (2 wheelchairs available free of charge) shop ⊗

PEVENSEY Map 5 TQ60

Pevensey Castle

BN24 5LE
☎ 01323 762604
web: www.english-heritage.org.uk
dir: off A259

William the Conqueror landed here in 1066 and established his first stronghold. Discover the history of the Norman castle and the remains of an unusual keep through the free audio tour.

Times Open all year, Apr-Sep, daily 10-6; Oct, daily 10-4; Nov-Mar, Sat-Sun 10-4. Closed 24-26 Dec & 1 Jan **Fees** £4.50 (ch £2.30, concessions £3.80). Family £11.30. Prices and opening times are subject to change in March 2011. Please check web site or call 0870 333 1181 for the most up to date prices and opening times when planning your visit **Facilities** Ⓟ ☕ shop #

RYE Map 5 TQ92

Lamb House

West St TN31 7ES
☎ 01580 762334 📠 01580 762334
e-mail: lambhouse@nationaltrust.org.uk
web: www.nationaltrust.org.uk/main/w-lambhouse
dir: facing W end of Church

This 18th-century house was the home of novelist Henry James from 1898 until his death in 1916, and was later occupied by the writer E F Benson, who used Lamb House as the model for 'Mallards' in his Mapp and Lucia novels. Some of James' personal possessions can be seen. There is also a charming walled garden.

Times Open 15 Mar-29 Oct, Thu & Sat 2-6 (last admission 5.30) **Fees** £4.30 (ch £2.20). Family ticket £10.75. Groups £4 per person **Facilities** Ⓟ ♿ (partly accessible) (steps into house, no wheelchair access) (scented plants & herbs) ⊗ 🌿

Rye Castle Museum **2 FOR 1**

3 East St TN31 7JY
☎ 01797 226728
e-mail: info@ryemuseum.co.uk
web: www.ryemuseum.co.uk
dir: in town centre, on A259. Museum is on 2 sites, East St & Ypres Tower

Part of the museum is housed in a stone tower built as a fortification in 1249. The museum's collection of ironwork, medieval pots and smuggling items are on display here, while the East Street site contains the rest of the collection, including pottery made in Rye, fashions, an 18th-century fire engine, toys, cinque port regalia, a special exhibition on Rye between the wars, descriptions of the changes to the harbour and shipbuilding in Rye and businesses and leisure in Rye during the 19th and 20th centuries. The museum tells the story of Rye's long and illustrious history.

Times Ypres Tower: Open daily from 1 Apr, 10.30-5. East St: Open wknds only, 10.30-5; Nov-Mar: Ypres Tower only, wknds 10.30-3.30 (last entry 30 mins before close) **Fees** Ypres Tower: £3 (concessions £2.50). East St: £2.50 (concessions £2). Joint ticket £5 (ch free, concessions £4) **Facilities** Ⓟ ♿ (partly accessible) (ramp to ground floor of Ypres Tower, East St fully accessible) toilets for disabled shop ⊗

SHEFFIELD PARK Map 5 TQ42

Sheffield Park Garden

TN22 3QX
☎ 01825 790231 📠 01825 791264
e-mail: sheffieldpark@nationaltrust.org.uk
web: www.nationaltrust.org.uk/main/w-sheffieldparkgarden
dir: midway between East Grinstead & Lewes, 5m NW of Uckfield, on E side of A275, between A272 & A22

Sheffield Park was originally landscaped by 'Capability' Brown, in about 1775 to create a beautiful park with four lakes and cascades. Further extensive planting was done at the beginning of the 20th century, to give emphasis to autumn colour among the trees. In May and June masses of azaleas and rhododendrons bloom and later there are magnificent waterlillies on the lakes. Autumn brings stunning colours from the many rare trees and shrubs. Also visit South Park, a 265-acre historic parkland with stunning views. Special events run throughout the year, check the website for details.

Times Open all year. Closed 25 Dec. Please phone for details or check website **Fees** Gift Aid donation: £7.70 (ch £3.85). Family ticket £19.25. Groups 15+ £6.50. Joint ticket with Bluebell Railway available. RHS members free. Includes a voluntary donation of 10% or more. Visitors can pay standard admission, see website for current details* **Facilities** Ⓟ ☕ 🛆 (outdoor) ♿ (partly accessible) (most of the garden is accessible, please phone for further details) toilets for disabled (powered self drive cars pre-book, w/chairs, Braille guide) shop 🌿

SHEFFIELD PARK STATION Map 5 TQ42

Bluebell Railway

Sheffield Park Station TN22 3QL
☎ 01825 720800 & 722370 📠 01825 720804
e-mail: info@bluebell-railway.co.uk
web: www.bluebell-railway.co.uk
dir: 4.5m E of Haywards Heath, off A275, 10m S of East Grinstead A22-A275

A volunteer-run heritage steam railway with nine miles of track running through pretty Sussex countryside. Please note that there is no parking at Kingscote Station. If you wish to board the train here, catch the bus (service 473) which connects Kingscote and East Grinstead.

Times Open all year, Sat & Sun, daily Apr-Oct & during school hols. Santa Specials run Dec. Please contact for timetable and information regarding trains* **Facilities** Ⓟ Ⓟ ☕ ⛩ (indoor) ♿ (partly accessible) toilets for disabled (special carriage for wheelchairs & carers with lift) shop

TICEHURST Map 5 TQ63

Pashley Manor Gardens

TN5 7HE
☎ 01580 200888 📠 01580 200102
e-mail: info@pashleymanorgardens.com
web: www.pashleymanorgardens.com
dir: on B2099 between A21 and Ticehurst village, follow brown tourist signs

Once belonging to the family of Anne Boleyn, Pashley Manor has a beautiful traditional English garden. Visitors can wander among fine old trees, fountains, springs and large ponds, all surrounded by romantic landscaping and imaginative plantings, and interspersed with statues and sculptures by leading European sculptors. Special events take place throughout the year. Please telephone for details.

Times Open Apr-Sep, Tue-Thu, Sat, BH Mons & special event days 11-5; Garden only Oct, Mon-Fri 10-4 **Fees** £8 (ch £5) Group rate 15+ £7.50. Tulip festival £8.50. See website for up to date prices* **Facilities** Ⓟ 🍽 licensed ⛩ (outdoor) ♿ (partly accessible) (formal gardens, gift shop & cafe accessible. No access to woodland, and some areas of garden have sloping and gravel paths) toilets for disabled (ramps, 2 w/chairs for loan) shop ⊗

WEST SUSSEX

Straw bales below the South Downs

AMBERLEY Map 4 TQ01

Amberley Working Museum

BN18 9LT

☎ 01798 831370 📠 01798 831831

e-mail: office@amberleymuseum.co.uk

web: www.amberleymuseum.co.uk

dir: on B2139, between Arundel and Storrington, adjacent to Amberley railway station

36 acre open-air museum dedicated to the industrial heritage of the south east of England. Traditional craftspeople on site (including a blacksmith and potter), working narrow-gauge railway and vintage bus collection, Connected Earth telecommunications display, Seeboard Electricity Hall, stationary engines, print workshop, woodturners, wheelwrights, nature trails, restaurant, shop and much more.

Times Open 12 Mar-2 Nov, Wed-Sun & BH Mon 10-5.30 (last admission 4.30). Also open daily during school hols.* **Facilities** 🅟 ☕ 🛒 ♿ (partly accessible) toilets for disabled (wheelchairs available for loan & large print guides) shop

ARDINGLY Map 5 TQ32

Wakehurst Place & Millennium Seed Bank

Royal Botanic Gardens RH17 6TN

☎ 01444 894066 📠 01444 894069

e-mail: wakehurst@kew.org

web: www.kew.org

dir: M23 junct 10, 1.5m NW of Ardingly, on B2028, follow brown tourist signs

Woodland and lakes linked by a pretty watercourse make this large garden a beautiful place to walk, with an amazing variety of interesting trees and shrubs, a winter garden, and a rock walk. Also on site is the Millennium Seed Bank, dedicated to the conservation of seeds from wild plants. The garden is administered and maintained by the Royal Botanic Gardens, Kew.

Times Open all year, Mar-Oct 10-6, Nov-Feb 10-4.30. Closed 24-25 Dec **Fees** £9 (under 17's free)* **Facilities** 🅟 ☕ 🍴 licensed 🛒 (indoor & outdoor) ♿ (partly accessible) (some areas of the estate accessible only by very steep paths) toilets for disabled (manual & electric wheelchairs available) shop 🚫

ARUNDEL Map 4 TQ00

Arundel Castle

BN18 9AB

☎ 01903 882173 📠 01903 884581

e-mail: info@arundelcastle.org

web: www.arundelcastle.org

dir: on A27 between Chichester & Worthing

Set high on a hill in West Sussex, this magnificent castle and stately home, seat of the Dukes of Norfolk for nearly 1000 years, commands stunning views across the river Arun and out to sea. Climb to the keep and battlements; marvel at a fine collection of 16th-century furniture; portraits by Van Dyke, Gainsborough, Canaletto and others; tapestries and the personal possessions of Mary, Queen of Scots; wander in the grounds and renovated Victorian flower and vegetable gardens. The garden is divided into formal courts with a centre canal pond, tufa-lined cascade and a wild flyover labyrinth. Enjoy regular 'living history' events.

Arundel Castle

Times Open Apr-Oct, Tue-Sun 10-5, Castle open 12-5 (last admission 4). Open BH Mon **Fees** Silver tickets £9 (ch £7.50, concessions £9). See website for other ticket options incl family rate* **Facilities** 🅟 Ⓟ ☕ 🍴 licensed ♿ (partly accessible) (some steep & narrow staircases) toilets for disabled (chair lift) shop 🚫

See advert on this page

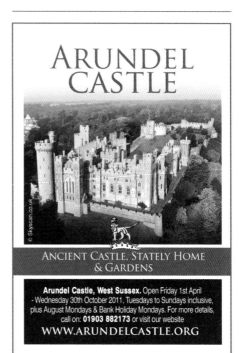

ENGLAND

ARUNDEL *continued*

WWT Arundel Wetland Centre

Mill Rd BN18 9PB
☎ 01903 881525 📠 01903 884834
e-mail: arundel@wwt.org.uk
web: www.wwt.org.uk
dir: signed from A27 & A29

Come nose to beak with exotic ducks, geese and swans from all over the world. Visitors can walk through the reed beds to hear warblers or spot water voles on the daily boat safaris. The children's areas combine learning and play; climb on the giant bird feeders at tree creepers play area; jump from lily pads at 'Pond Skaters' and get lost with the giant ants in the 'Meadow Maze'.

Times Open all year, daily; summer 9.30-5.30; winter 9.30-4.30 (last admission 30 mins before closing). Closed 25 Dec **Fees** £9.70 (ch £4.85 concessions £8.10). Family ticket £25.90. Group rates available* **Facilities** licensed (outdoor) (fully accessible) toilets for disabled (level paths, free wheelchair loan) shop

BIGNOR — **Map 4 SU91**

Bignor Roman Villa & Museum

RH20 1PH
☎ 01798 869259 📠 01798 869259
e-mail: enquiries@bignorromanvilla.co.uk
web: www.bignorromanvilla.co.uk
dir: 6m S of Pulborough & 6m N of Arundel on A29, signed. 8m S of Petworth on A285, signed

Rediscovered in 1811, this Roman house was built on a grand scale. It is one of the largest known, and has spectacular mosaics. The heating system can also be seen, and various finds from excavations are on show. The longest mosaic in Britain (82ft) is on display here in its original position. 18th July 2011 will be the 200th Anniversary of the rediscovering of Bignor Roman Villa.

Times Open Mar-Oct daily, Mar-May & Sep-Oct 10-5, Jun-Aug 10-6 **Fees** £5.50 (ch under 16 £2.50, pen & students £4). Family £14. Party 10+ 20% discount. Guided tours by arrangement **Facilities** (outdoor) (partly accessible) (most areas accessible) shop

BRAMBER — **Map 4 TQ11**

Bramber Castle

FREE

BN4 3FB
web: www.english-heritage.org.uk
dir: on W side of village off A283

The remains of a Norman motte and bailey castle. The gatehouse (still standing almost to its original height) and walls are still visible.

Times Open any reasonable time **Facilities**

CHICHESTER — **Map 4 SU80**

Chichester Cathedral

West St PO19 1PX
☎ 01243 782595 📠 01243 812499
e-mail: visitors@chichestercathedral.org.uk
web: www.chichestercathedral.org.uk
dir: in city centre, approach from M27 (A27) and turn northwards at one of the bypass rdbts following signs for the city centre

This magnificent 900-year-old Cathedral is both ancient and modern, where unique medieval features can be found alongside world famous 20th-century artworks. There are various exhibitions and a pleasant cloisters café. Talks and free guided tours take place throughout the year

Times Open end Mar-end Sep, daily 7.15-7; end Sep-end Mar 7.15-6 **Fees** Free, donations appreciated **Facilities** licensed (outdoor) (fully accessible) toilets for disabled (touch & hearing centre, loop system) shop

Pallant House Gallery

9 North Pallant PO19 1TJ
☎ 01243 774557 📠 01243 536038
e-mail: info@pallant.org.uk
web: www.pallant.org.uk
dir: from city centre (the Cross) take East St turning right at Superdrug. Gallery at end of North Pallant on left

A Queen Anne townhouse and a modern building have been combined to house a fine collection of 20th-century British art. The permanent collection includes pieces by: Auerbach, Blake, Bomberg, Caulfield, Freud, Hamilton, Hitchens, Leger, Moore, Nicholson, Piper, Richards, Severini, Sickert and Sutherland. Telephone or visit website for details of temporary exhibitions.

Times Open Tue-Sat, 10-5 (Thu 10-8), Sun & BHs, 12.30-5.* **Facilities** licensed (fully accessible) toilets for disabled shop

EAST GRINSTEAD — **Map 5 TQ33**

Standen

West Hoathly Rd RH19 4NE
☎ 01342 323029 📠 01342 316424
e-mail: standen@nationaltrust.org.uk
web: www.nationaltrust.org.uk/main/w-standen
dir: 2m S of East Grinstead, signed from B2110

Life in a Victorian family home is brought vividly to life in this gem of the Arts & Crafts movement. Standen is hidden at the end of a quiet Sussex lane with fine views over the High Weald and Weir Wood Reservoir. The design of the house, which incorporates the original medieval farmhouse, is a monument to the combined genius of architect Philip Webb and his friend William Morris. All the big names of the Arts & Crafts period are represented including ceramics by William de Morgan, furniture by George Jack and metal work by W. A. S. Benson. The beautiful hillside gardens provide year-round interest and the woodlands now offer a number of easily accessible, and picturesque, walks. 2011 is the 150th Anniversary of the Founding of Morris & Co, whose furnishings decorate the interiors of Standen.

Times House open: 19 Feb-6 Mar, Sat & Sun & 12 Mar-30 Oct, Wed-Sun, Mon in school hols & BH 11-4.30; 5 Nov-18 Dec, Sat-Sun & 19-21 Dec, Mon-Wed 11-3 (last entry 30 mins before closing) **Fees** Gift Aid donation: House & garden £9 (ch £4.50). Family ticket £22.50, Groups £7.80. Visitors can pay standard admission displayed **Facilities** Ⓟ 🍽 licensed ⛩ (outdoor) ♿ (partly accessible) (ground floor of house accessible, some parts of garden steep with steps) toilets for disabled (Braille guide, large print, garden level route map) shop ✿

FISHBOURNE Map 4 SU80

Fishbourne Roman Palace 2 FOR 1

Salthill Rd PO19 3QR
☎ 01243 789829 & 785859 📠 01243 539266
e-mail: adminfish@sussexpast.co.uk
web: www.sussexpast.co.uk
dir: off A27 onto A259 into Fishbourne. Turn right into Salthill Rd & right into Roman Way

The remains of the Roman Palace at Fishbourne were discovered in 1960. Here you can see Britain's largest collection of in-situ Roman floor mosaics. More everyday Roman objects found during the excavations are displayed in the museum gallery. A short film uses computer-generated images to interpret the site. Outside the garden has been replanted to its original plan, using plants that may have grown there when the palace was inhabited. The Collections Discovery Centre displays more artefacts from both Fishbourne and Chichester district. See website for daily activities.

Times Open all year, daily Feb-15 Dec. Feb, Nov-mid Dec 10-4; Mar-Jul & Sep-Oct 10-5; Aug 10-6. Winter wknds 10-4* **Fees** £7.60 (ch £4, concessions £6.80). Family ticket £21, Registered disabled £7.60. Group (over 20) £6.30* **Facilities** Ⓟ ☕ ⛩ (outdoor) ♿ (fully accessible) toilets for disabled (self guiding tapes & tactile objects, audio/visual room) shop ⊗

FONTWELL Map 4 SU90

Denmans Garden 2 FOR 1

Denmans Ln BN18 0SU
☎ 01243 542808 📠 01243 544064
e-mail: denmans@denmans-garden.co.uk
web: www.denmans-garden.co.uk
dir: 5m E of Chichester off A27 W between Chichester and Arundel, adjacent to Fontwell racecourse

The garden, jointly owned by John Brookes MBE and Michael Neve, is planted for all-year interest with emphasis on shape, colour and texture, and although four acres in size, is full of planting and design ideas that can be adapted to suit any size of garden. Gravel is used extensively in the garden, both to walk on and as a growing medium, so that you can walk through plantings rather than past them. Individual plants are allowed to self-seed and ramble.

Times Open all year, daily 9-5. Closed 25-26 Dec & 1 Jan. Please check website for winter opening times **Fees** £4.95 (ch £3.95, ch 4 & under free, pen £4.75, carers £2.95). Party 15+ £4.50 each* **Facilities** Ⓟ ℗ ☕ 🍽 licensed ♿ (fully accessible) toilets for disabled shop ⊗

GOODWOOD Map 4 SU81

Goodwood House

PO18 0PX
☎ 01243 755048 📠 01243 755005
e-mail: curator@goodwood.com
web: www.goodwood.com
dir: 3m NE of Chichester

The Sussex Downs and 12,000 acre working country estate provide a glorious backdrop to the magnificent Regency house, which has been the home of the Dukes of Richmond for over 300 years. The gilded, richly-decorated State Apartments include the luxurious Yellow Drawing Room and the unique Egyptian Dining Room. The art collection includes paintings by George Stubbs and Canaletto.

Times Open end Mar-early Oct, Sun-Mon, 1-5 (open Tue also after Etr & BHs); Aug, Sun-Thu. Closed for occasional events **Fees** £9 (ch under 12 free, ch & student £4, pen £7.50). Family ticket £20* **Facilities** Ⓟ ☕ ♿ (fully accessible) toilets for disabled (ramp at front of house, disabled parking area) ⊗

HANDCROSS Map 4 TQ22

Nymans 2 FOR 1

RH17 6EB
☎ 01444 405250
e-mail: nymans@nationaltrust.org.uk
web: www.nationaltrust.org.uk/main/w-nymansgarden2
dir: A23 London to Brighton road, on B2114 at Handcross, 4m S of Crawley, 10m S of Gatwick

One of the great 20th-century gardens, with an important collection of rare plants, set around a romantic house and ruins in a beautiful woodland estate. Theatrically designed with plants from around the world, Nymans is internationally renowned for its garden design, rare plant collection and intimacy. Visit the Messel family rooms in the house, and see the dramatic ruins, which form a backdrop to the main lawn. Enjoy fine views across the Sussex countryside and explore the wide estate with walks through ancient woodland, lakes and wild flowers. Nymans is one of the leading 'green' gardens in the National Trust, actively engaging visitors with its methods of sustainable gardening. Buggy tours are available, along with learning opportunities for the kids, and an all-round programme of events and workshops.

Times Garden: Open all year, Jan-Feb & Nov-Dec, daily 10-4; Mar-Oct, daily 10-5. House: 2 Mar-Oct, Mon, Wed-Sun 11-3 (last admission 30 mins before closing). Closed 25-31 Dec **Fees** With voluntary Gift Aid donation of 10% or more: £9.50 (ch £5), Family ticket (2ad+3ch) £24 (1ad+3ch) £14.50. Group 15+ £8 (ch £4). Visitors can choose to pay the standard admission displayed. N.T. members free **Facilities** Ⓟ ☕ 🍽 licensed ⛩ (outdoor) ♿ (fully accessible) toilets for disabled (wheelchairs, mobility buggy tours) shop ⊗ ✿

ENGLAND

HAYWARDS HEATH Map 5 TQ32

Borde Hill Garden

Balcombe Rd RH16 1XP
☎ 01444 450326 🖹 01444 440427
e-mail: info@bordehill.co.uk
web: www.bordehill.co.uk
dir: 0.5m N of Haywards Heath on Balcombe Rd, 3m from A23

This glorious garden flows into linked garden rooms, boasting their own distinctive character and style. Year-round colour and interest with spring flowering rhododendrons, azaleas, camellias, magnolias and the many champion trees. The Rose and Italian Gardens with the herbaceous borders provide colour for summer and into autumn. Set in 200 acres of parkland with panoramic views, woodland and lakeside walks.

Times Open Apr-Oct, 10-6.* **Facilities** 🅿 Ⓟ ☕ 🍽 licensed ⛩ (outdoor) ♿ (fully accessible) toilets for disabled (wheelchairs available, audio/Braille guides) shop

HIGHDOWN Map 4 SU91

Highdown FREE

Highdown Gardens BN12 6PE
☎ 01903 501054 🖹 01903 218757
e-mail: chris.beardsley@worthing.gov.uk
web: www.worthing.gov.uk/wbc
dir: N off A259 between Worthing & Littlehampton. Access off dual carriageway, when coming from E proceed to rdbt

Set on downland countryside this unique garden overlooks the sea, and has been deemed a National Collection due to the unique assortment of rare plants and trees. The garden was the achievement of Sir Frederick and Lady Stern, who worked for fifty years to prove that plants could grow on chalk. Many of the original plants were collected in China and the Himalayas.

Times Open all year: Apr-Sep, Mon-Fri 10-6. Winter: Oct-Nov & Feb-Mar, Mon-Fri, 10-4.30; Dec-Jan, 10-4.* **Facilities** 🅿 ⛩ (outdoor) ♿ (partly accessible) (gardens on a sloping site, may prove difficult for wheelchair users) toilets for disabled 🚫🐕

LITTLEHAMPTON Map 4 TQ00

Harbour Park 2 FOR 1

Seafront BN17 5LL
☎ 01903 721200 🖹 01903 716663
e-mail: fun@harbourpark.com
web: www.harbourpark.com
dir: A259 & A284 connect Littlehampton. Take B2140 follow signs to seafront, attraction is next to Windmill Theatre and River Arun.

Located next to the sandy beaches and marina at Littlehampton, Harbour Park includes traditional rides and attractions like the Dodgems, Adventure Golf, Water Chute and Indoor Play Area. With its 'New England' fishing village setting, wide grass picnic area and stunning views of the River Arun, this attraction offers a great day out for the whole family. Entry is free and the 2-for-1 voucher can be used for the ride ticket books.

Times Open all year. Closed 25 Dec. Outdoor attractions closed Nov-Feb, open wknds until Etr and every day during hols* **Fees** Admission free. Book of 10 ride tickets £15 or tokens can be purchased individually. Play area £3* **Facilities** 🅿 Ⓟ ☕ 🍽 licensed ⛩ (outdoor) ♿ (fully accessible) toilets for disabled shop

Look & Sea! Visitor Centre

63-65 Surrey St BN17 5AW
☎ 01903 718984 🖹 01903 718036
e-mail: info@lookandsea.co.uk
web: www.lookandsea.co.uk
dir: on harbour front 10 mins walk from Littlehampton Station

An interactive museum exploring the history and geography of Littlehampton and the surrounding area. Inside the modern waterfront building you can meet the 500,000 year old Boxgrove Man, become a ship's captain in an interactive computer game, and enjoy spectacular panoramic views of the Sussex coast from the circular glass tower.

Times Open all year, daily 9-5* **Fees** £1.50 (ch & concessions £1)* **Facilities** 🅿 Ⓟ ☕ 🍽 licensed ♿ (fully accessible) toilets for disabled shop 🚫🐕

PETWORTH Map 4 SU92

Petworth Cottage Museum 2 FOR 1

346 High St GU28 0AU
☎ 01798 342100
e-mail: petworthcottagemuseum@yahoo.co.uk
web: www.petworthcottagemuseum.co.uk
dir: Take High St from main Petworth car park, past Middle St, museum 2nd building on left.

A Leaconfield Estate worker's cottage restored to recreate the 1910 nostalgic look at the life of Mrs Mary Cummings, a seamstress and former tenant.

Times Open Apr-Oct, Tue-Sat, BHs & Etr Sun 2-4.30 **Fees** £3 (ch under 14 50p) **Facilities** Ⓟ ♿ (partly accessible) (access restricted to ground floor, incline to main approach) 🚫🐕

Petworth House & Park

GU28 0AE
☎ 01798 342207 & 343929 📠 01798 342963
e-mail: petworth@nationaltrust.org.uk
web: www.nationaltrust.org.uk/main/w-petworthhouse
dir: in town centre, A272/283

Petworth House is an impressive 17th-century mansion set in a 700 acre Deer Park, landscaped by 'Capability' Brown, and immortalised in Turner's paintings. At Petworth you will find the National Trust's finest art collection including work by Van Dyck, Titian, Blake and Turner, as well as sculpture, ceramics and fine furniture. Fascinating Servants' Quarters show the domestic side of life of this great estate.

Times Open Mar-Oct, Sat-Wed 11-5 (last entry 4.30) **Fees** With voluntary Gift Aid donation: £10.90 (ch £5.50). Family ticket £27.30. NT members free. Pleasure Ground £4.20 (ch £2.10)* **Facilities** licensed (partly accessible) (staircase to first floor bedrooms and steps down into chapel) toilets for disabled (wheelchairs, Braille guide, induction loop, virtual tour) shop

PULBOROUGH — Map 4 TQ01

Parham House & Gardens

Parham Park, Storrington RH20 4HS
☎ 01903 744888 & 742021 📠 01903 746557
e-mail: enquiries@parhaminsussex.co.uk
web: www.parhaminsussex.co.uk
dir: midway between A29 & A24, off A283 between Pulborough & Storrington

Surrounded by a deer park, fine gardens and 18th-century pleasure grounds in a beautiful downland setting, this Elizabethan family home contains an important collection of paintings, furniture and rare needlework. There are four acres of walled garden with huge herbaceous borders, greenhouse, orchard and herb garden.

Times Open House: Etr Sun-Sep, Wed, Thu, Sun & BH Mons (also open Tue & Fri in Aug), 2-5. Garden: Etr Sun-Sep, Tue-Fri 12-5. (Both House & Garden open Sun in Oct). See website for up to date opening times* **Fees** House & Gardens £8 (ch 5-15 £3.50, concessions £7). Family ticket £22. Gardens only £6 (ch free, concessions £5). Party rates available. See website for up to date prices **Facilities** (outdoor) (partly accessible) (access to house restricted to ground floor) toilets for disabled (wheelchairs, ramps, parking) shop

RSPB Pulborough Brooks Nature Reserve — 2 FOR 1

Uppertons Barn Visitor Centre, Wiggonholt RH20 2EL
☎ 01798 875851
e-mail: pulborough.brooks@rspb.org.uk
web: www.rspb.org.uk/pulboroughbrooks
dir: signed on A283, 2m SE of Pulborough & 2m NW of Storrington

Set in the scenic Arun Valley this is an excellent reserve for year-round family visits. A nature trail winds through hedgerow-lined lanes to viewing hides overlooking water-meadows. Breeding summer birds include nightingales and warblers, ducks and wading birds, and nightjars and hobbies on nearby heathland. Unusual wading birds and hedgerow birds regularly pass through on spring and autumn migration. Contact for details of special events or see website.

Times Open daily, Reserve: sunrise-sunset, closed 25 Dec. Visitor centre: 9.30-5. Closed 25-26 Dec **Fees** £3.50 (ch £1, concessions £2.50). Family ticket £7* **Facilities** (outdoor) (partly accessible) (visitor centre one level, circular trails suitable for most wheelchairs) toilets for disabled (free hire electric buggy and wheelchair) shop

SINGLETON — Map 4 SU81

Weald & Downland Open Air Museum

PO18 0EU
☎ 01243 811348 📠 01243 811475
e-mail: office@wealddown.co.uk
web: www.wealddown.co.uk
dir: 6m N of Chichester on A286

A showcase of English architectural heritage, where historic buildings have been rescued from destruction and rebuilt in a parkland setting. Vividly demonstrating the evolution of building techniques and use of local materials, these fascinating buildings bring to life the homes, farms and rural industries of the south east of the past 500 years. See also working Shire horses, cattle and traditional breeds of farm animals.

Times Open all year, during BST, 10.30-6 & 10.30-4 the rest of the year. Winter opening days vary, see website for details

continued

SINGLETON *continued*

Fees £9 (ch £4.80, pen £8.15). Family ticket (2ad+3ch) £24.75* **Facilities** Ⓟ ☕ ⛩ (indoor & outdoor) ♿ (partly accessible) (some areas of museum not suitable for disabled visitiors, but most key areas and exhibits are accessible) toilets for disabled (separate entrance and ramps available for some buildings) shop

SOUTH HARTING — Map 4 SU71

Uppark

GU31 5QR

☎ 01730 825415 & 825857 📠 01730 825873

e-mail: uppark@nationaltrust.org.uk

web: www.nationaltrust.org.uk/main/w-uppark

dir: A3 take A272, B2146 to South Harting, follow signs to Uppark

A late 17th-century house set high on the South Downs with magnificent sweeping views to the sea. The elegant Georgian interior houses a famous Grand Tour collection that includes paintings, furniture and ceramics. An 18th-century dolls' house with original features is one of the more impressive items. The servants' quarters appear as they did in Victorian days, when H G Wells' mother was housekeeper, while the garden is restored in the early 19th-century 'Picturesque' style.

Times Open 20 Mar-30 Oct, Sun-Thu. Garden 11.30-5. House: 12.30-4.30. Shop & restaurant 11.30-5 **Fees** With voluntary Gift Aid donation of 10% or more: £8.80 (ch £4.40). Family £22. Garden only £4.40 (ch £2.20). Visitors can choose to pay the standard admission price displayed **Facilities** Ⓟ ☕ 🍽 licensed ⛩ (outdoor) ♿ (fully accessible) toilets for disabled (ramps, lift to basement) shop ⊗ ✿

TANGMERE — Map 4 SU90

Tangmere Military Aviation Museum

PO20 2ES

☎ 01243 790090 📠 01243 789490

e-mail: info@tangmere-museum.org.uk

web: www.tangmere-museum.org.uk

dir: off A27, 3m E of Chichester towards Arundel

Based at an airfield that played an important role during the World Wars, this museum spans 80 years of military aviation. There are photographs, documents, aircraft and aircraft parts on display along with a Hurricane replica, prototype Spitfire replica and cockpit simulator. Hangars house a Supermarine Swift, English Electric Lightning and the record-breaking aircraft Meteor and Hunter. Aircraft outside include; Lockheed T33, De Havilland Sea Vixen, McDonnell Douglas Phantom F4, Gloster Meteor and a Westland Wessex helicopter.

Times Open Mar-Oct, daily 10-5.30; Feb & Nov, daily 10-4.30* **Fees** £7.50 (ch £2 & over 60s £6) Family £17 (2ad+2ch). **Facilities** Ⓟ ☕ ⛩ (outdoor) ♿ (fully accessible) toilets for disabled (wheelchairs available) shop ⊗

WEST DEAN — Map 4 SU81

West Dean Gardens

PO18 0QZ

☎ 01243 818210 & 811301 📠 01243 811342

e-mail: gardens@westdean.org.uk

web: www.westdean.org.uk

dir: 6m N of Chichester and 7m S of Midhurst on A286

Award winning historic garden of 35 acres in a tranquil downland setting. Noted for its 300ft long Harold Peto pergola, mixed and herbaceous borders, rustic summerhouses and specimen trees. Walled kitchen garden with magnificent collection of 16 Victorian glasshouses and frames. St Roche Arboretum offers a wonderful walk, including a new treehouse installation. The visitors' centre provides a high level of facilities with a beautiful prospect of the River Lavant and West Dean Park.

Times Open all year, Mar-Oct, daily 10.30-5; Nov-Feb, 10.30-4. Closed 24 Dec-end Jan **Fees** Summer: £7.50 (ch £3.50, pen £7). Family ticket £18.50. Groups £6. Winter: £4.75 (ch £2.25, pen £4.25). Family ticket £11.75. Groups £4* **Facilities** Ⓟ ☕ 🍽 licensed ⛩ (outdoor) ♿ (partly accessible) (shop, restaurant & majority of gardens accessible. Parkland walk not accessible) toilets for disabled (reserved parking, 2 wheelchairs available) shop ⊗

WISBOROUGH GREEN — Map 4 TQ02

Fishers Farm Park

Newpound Ln RH14 0EG

☎ 01403 700063 📠 01403 700823

e-mail: info@fishersfarmpark.co.uk

web: www.fishersfarmpark.co.uk

dir: follow brown & white tourist boards on all roads approaching Wisborough Green

All weather, all year farm and adventure park, providing a mixture of farmyard and dynamic adventure play. Please contact for details of special events.

Times Open all year, daily, 10-5. Closed 25-26 Dec **Fees** Please phone for details* **Facilities** Ⓟ ⓟ ☕ 🍽 licensed ⛩ (outdoor) ♿ (partly accessible) (woodland walkway inaccessible to wheelchairs) toilets for disabled (wheelchairs, mobility scooters) shop ⊗

TYNE & WEAR

Illuminated Milennium Bridge, Newcastle-upon-Tyne

ENGLAND

GATESHEAD Map 12 NZ26

BALTIC Centre for Contemporary Art FREE

South Shore Rd, Gateshead Quays NE8 3BA
☎ 0191 478 1810 & 440 4915 📠 0191 478 1922
e-mail: info@balticmill.com
web: www.balticmill.com
dir: follow signs for Quayside, Millennium Bridge. 15 mins' walk from Gateshead Metro & Newcastle Central Station

Once a 1950s grain warehouse, part of the old BALTIC Flour Mills, BALTIC Centre for Contemporary Art is an international centre presenting a dynamic and ambitious programme of complementary exhibitions and events. It consists of five art spaces, cinema, auditorium, library and archive, eating and drinking areas and a shop. Check website for current events information.

Times Open all year daily 10-6 (Tue 10.30-6). Closed 25-26 Dec & 1 Jan **Facilities** licensed (fully accessible) toilets for disabled (wheelchairs/scooters, Braille/large-print guides) shop

JARROW Map 12 NZ36

Bede's World 2 FOR 1

Church Bank NE32 3DY
☎ 0191 489 2106 📠 0191 428 2361
e-mail: visitor.info@bedesworld.co.uk
web: www.bedesworld.co.uk
dir: off A185 near S end of Tyne tunnel

Bede's World is an ambitious museum based around the extraordinary life and work of the Venerable Bede (AD673-735) early Medieval Europe's greatest scholar and England's first historian. Attractions include an 'Age of Bede' exhibition in the museum, which displays finds excavated from the site of St Paul's monastery. Alongside the museum, Bede's World has developed Gyrwe, an Anglo-Saxon demonstration farm, which brings together the animals, timber buildings, crops and vegetables that would have featured in the Northumbrian Landscape of Bede's Day. Special events throughout the year. See website for details.

Times Open all year, Feb-Dec, Mon-Sat 10-5, Sun noon-5; Closed Good Fri. Please contact for Xmas/New Year opening times. **Fees** £5.50 (ch & concessions £3.50). Family ticket £12.50 **Facilities** licensed (outdoor) (partly accessible) toilets for disabled (manual & electric w/chairs on request, disabled parking) shop

NEWCASTLE UPON TYNE Map 12 NZ26

Discovery Museum FREE

Blandford Square NE1 4JA
☎ 0191 232 6789 📠 0191 230 2614
e-mail: discovery@twmuseums.org.uk
web: www.twmuseums.org.uk/discovery
dir: off A6115/A6125. 5 mins walk from Newcastle Central Station

Newcastle Discovery Museum offers something for everyone. There are displays covering fashion, military history, maritime splendours and scientific curiosities. Local history is covered in the fascinating Great City story. There is a gallery housing *Turbinia*, once the world's fastest ship.

Times Open all year, Mon-Sat 10-5; Sun 2-5. Closed 25-26 Dec & 1 Jan* **Facilities** (fully accessible) toilets for disabled (textured floor in some galleries) shop

Hancock Museum

Barras Bridge NE2 4PT
☎ 0191 222 7418 📠 0191 261 7537
e-mail: hancock@twmuseums.org.uk
web: www.twmuseums.org.uk/hancock
dir: follow exit signs for city centre A167, off A1

Newcastle's premier Natural History museum unravels the natural world, through sensational galleries and close encounters with resident reptiles and insects. For more than 100 years the Hancock Museum has provided visitors with a glimpse of the animal kingdom and the powerful and often destructive forces of nature. From the dinosaurs to live animals, the Hancock is home to creatures past and present and the odd Egyptian mummy or two.

Times Open all year, Mon-Sat, 10-5, Sun 2-5. Closed 25-26 Dec & 1 Jan.* **Facilities** (partly accessible) toilets for disabled (stair lift, audio & Braille guide, sign language) shop

Life Science Centre

Times Square NE1 4EP
☎ 0191 243 8210 📠 0191 243 8201
e-mail: info@life.org.uk
web: www.life.org.uk
dir: A1M, A69, A184, A1058 & A167, follow signs to Centre for Life or Central Station

Life is an exciting place where science comes alive in a fun and funky environment. Aiming to inspire curiosity and encourage visitors to uncover new things about life, whatever age. If you are curious about the world around you, there is something for all the family at Life. Enjoy exhibitions, live science theatre shows and the north's biggest planetarium.

Times Open all year, Mon-Sat 10-6, Sun 11-6 . Closed 25-26 Dec & 1 Jan. Last entry subject to seasonal demand **Fees** £8 (ch 5-16 £5.85, concessions £6.95). Family ticket (1ad&3ch) £24.20 (2ad&2ch) £24.20* **Facilities** licensed (indoor) (fully accessible) toilets for disabled (ramps, wheelchairs, induction loops) shop

ROWLANDS GILL Map 12 NZ15

Gibside

NE16 6BG
☎ 01207 541820 📠 01207 541830
e-mail: gibside@nationaltrust.org.uk
web: www.nationaltrust.org.uk/main/gibside
dir: 3m W of Metro Centre & 6m SW of Newcastle-upon-Tyne near Rowlands Gill, clearly signed from the A1. Regular buses from Newcastle-Consett

This 18th-century landscaped garden, forest and nature reserve is the former home of the Bowes-Lyon family, with miles of walks through the wooded slopes and riverside of the Derwent valley. Discover hidden vistas, wildlife or wild flowers, or just enjoy a fresh seasonal Georgian style lunch in the Potting Shed Café. A perfect place for family adventures with a nature playscape and ropes challenge. Anglican weddings can be held in the unique Palladian Chapel. Various events throughout the year.

Times Landscape Garden: all year Mar-Oct 10-6; Nov-Feb 10-4 (last entry 1hr before closing). Chapel, shop, café: Mar-Oct 11-5; Nov-Feb 11-3.30. Closed 24-25 Dec **Fees** £6.50 (ch £4). Family £18.50, single parent family £13 **Facilities** Ⓟ ☕ ⛩ (indoor & outdoor) ♿ (partly accessible) (grass and loose gravel paths, some steep slopes and steps, map of accessible route available) toilets for disabled (Braille guide, w/chairs, induction loop) shop ✿

SOUTH SHIELDS Map 12 NZ36

Arbeia Roman Fort & Museum FREE

Baring St NE33 2BB
☎ 0191 456 1369 📠 0191 427 6862
web: www.twmuseums.org.uk/arbeia
dir: 5 mins walk from town centre, vehicle approach via Lowe Road & Fort St

These are the extensive remains of Arbeia, a Roman fort in use from the 2nd to 4th century. It was the supply base for the Roman army's campaign against Scotland. On site there are full size reconstructions of The West Gate, a barrack block and part of the commanding officer's house. Archaeological evacuations are in progress throughout the summer.

Times Open Apr-Oct, Mon-Sat 10-5, Sun 1-5. Closed Nov-Mar except for pre-booked guided tours **Facilities** Ⓟ ⛩ (outdoor) ♿ (partly accessible) (rough terrain of site, restricted access to upper floors of West Gate reconstruction) toilets for disabled (pre-visit info pack and portable induction loop) shop 🚫

SUNDERLAND Map 12 NZ35

Monkwearmouth Station Museum FREE

North Bridge St SR5 1AP
☎ 0191 567 7075
e-mail: monkwearmouth@twmuseums.org.uk
web: www.twmuseums.org.uk/monkwearmouth
dir: off A1018, at the end of Wearmouth bridge next to St Peter's Metro Station

Time stands still in this beautifully restored Victorian station. Travel and transport in the early 1900s are recorded with a look behind the scenes of the booking offices and guard's van. The brand new 'Play Station' activities area has been specifically designed for young visitors with regular organised events for children.

Times Open all year, Mon-Sat 10-5, Sun 2-5. Closed 25-26 Dec & 1 Jan **Facilities** Ⓟ Ⓟ ⛩ (indoor) ♿ (fully accessible) toilets for disabled (lift, ramp & induction loop) shop 🚫

National Glass Centre FREE

Liberty Way SR6 0GL
☎ 0191 515 5555 📠 0191 515 5556
e-mail: info@nationalglasscentre.com
web: www.nationalglasscentre.com
dir: A19 onto A1231, signed from all major roads

The National Glass Centre offers galleries showing an international programme of exhibitions. Home to the largest art glass making facility for kiln forming, a unique venue and a hub for activity inspired by glass. Artists' studios, glass production facilities and much more are located in an innovative glass and steel building on the banks of the River Wear. Explore with behind-the-scenes tours.

Times Open all year, daily 10-5 (last admission to glass tour 4.30). Closed 25 Dec & 1 Jan.* **Facilities** Ⓟ ☕ 🍴 licensed ♿ (fully accessible) toilets for disabled (lifts, ramps, w/chairs, Braille info, induction loops) shop 🚫

ENGLAND

SUNDERLAND *continued*

Sunderland Museum & Winter Gardens

FREE

Burdon Rd SR1 1PP
☎ 0191 553 2323 📠 0191 553 7828
e-mail: sunderland@twmuseums.org.uk
web: www.twmuseums.org.uk/sunderland
dir: in city centre on Burdon Rd, short walk from Sunderland metro and mainline stations

An award-winning attraction with wide-ranging displays and many hands-on exhibits that cover the archaeology and geology of Sunderland, the coal mines and shipyards of the area and the spectacular glass and pottery made on Wearside. Other galleries show the changes in the lifestyles of Sunderland women over the past century, works by LS Lowry and wildlife from all corners of the globe. The Winter Gardens are a horticultural wonderland where the exotic plants from around the world can be seen growing to their full natural height in a spectacular glass and steel rotunda.

Times Open all year, Mon-Sat 10-5, Sun 2-5 **Facilities** Ⓟ ☕ 🍽 licensed ♿ (fully accessible) toilets for disabled (lifts to all floors, induction loops) shop 🚭

TYNEMOUTH — Map 12 NZ36

Blue Reef Aquarium

2 FOR 1

Grand Pde NE30 4JF
☎ 0191 258 1031 📠 0191 257 2116
e-mail: tynemouth@bluereefaquarium.co.uk
web: www.bluereefaquarium.co.uk
dir: follow A19, taking A1058 (coast road), signed Tynemouth. Situated on seafront

From its position overlooking one of the North East's prettiest beaches, Blue Reef is home to a dazzling variety of creatures. Enjoy close encounters with seals, seahorses, sharks, stingrays, giant octopus, frogs, otters and hundreds of other aquatic lifeforms. Explore a dazzling coral reef and journey through the spectacular tropical ocean display in a transparent underwater tunnel. Informative, entertaining talks and feeding displays throughout the day. A recent addition is Amazing Amazon, a tropical rainforest that includes fish, plants and monkeys! For details of a packed events calendar, check the website.

Times Open all year, daily from 10. Closed 25 Dec **Fees** £7.95 (ch 3-14 £5.95, concessions £7). Family (2ad+2ch) £25.80 (2ad+3ch) £30.75* **Facilities** 🅟 Ⓟ ☕ 🛒 (outdoor) ♿ (fully accessible) toilets for disabled shop 🚭

Tynemouth Priory and Castle

NE30 4BZ
☎ 0191 257 1090
web: www.english-heritage.org.uk
dir: near North Pier

Discover a rich and varied history as you explore the priory, castle and underground chambers beneath a World War I gun battery.

Times Open all year, Apr-Sep, daily 10-5; Oct-Mar, Thu-Mon, daily during Feb & Oct half-terms 10-4. Closed 24-26 Dec & 1 Jan. Gun Battery access limited, please ask site staff for details **Fees** £4.20 (ch £2.10, concessions £3.60). Family ticket £10.50. Prices and opening times are subject to change in March 2011. Please check web site or call 0870 333 1181 for the most up to date prices and opening times when planning your visit **Facilities** 🛒 ♿ (partly accessible) (some steps) shop #

WALLSEND — Map 12 NZ26

Segedunum Roman Fort, Baths & Museum

Buddle St NE28 6HR
☎ 0191 236 9347 📠 0191 295 5858
e-mail: segedunum@twmuseums.org.uk
web: www.twmuseums.org.uk/sege
dir: A187 from Tyne Tunnel, signed

Hadrian's Wall was built by the Roman Emperor Hadrian in 122AD, Segedunum was built as part of the Wall, serving as a garrison for 600 soldiers until the collapse of Roman rule around 410AD. This major historical venture shows what life would have been like then, using artefacts, audio-visuals, reconstructed buildings and a 34m high viewing tower. Plenty of special events including craft activities and re-enactments from Roman cavalry and soldiers. Contact for details.

Times Open all year, Apr-Oct 10-5; Nov-Mar 10-3* **Facilities** 🅟 Ⓟ ☕ 🛒 (outdoor) ♿ (fully accessible) toilets for disabled (lifts) shop 🚭

WASHINGTON Map 12 NZ35

Washington Old Hall

2 FOR 1

The Avenue, Washington Village NE38 7LE
☎ 0191 416 6879 📠 0191 4192065
e-mail: washingtonoldhall@nationaltrust.org.uk
web: www.nationaltrust.org.uk
dir: 7m S of Newcastle-upon-Tyne. From A1 and A19 follow signs to A1231 to Washington, then District 4. The Avenue, next to Holy Trinity Church

Washington Old Hall, a delightful 17th-century manor incorporating parts of an earlier medieval home, was the home of George Washington's ancestors from 1183 to 1613. It was from here the family took their name. The house has been restored and filled with period furniture, and contains displays on George Washington and the history of American Independence. Enjoy a peaceful walk in the formal Jacobean garden or wildflower nuttery.

Times Open 13 Mar-Oct, Sun-Wed & Good Fri 11-5. Tea-room: 11-4 **Fees** £5.50 (ch £3.50). Family ticket £14.50. Group 10+ £4.50 **Facilities** (outdoor) (partly accessible) (access hall restricted to ground floor w/chair users, lift to lower garden) toilets for disabled (Braille guide, sensory scented gardens, induction loop, w/chair) shop

WWT Washington Wetland Centre

Pattinson NE38 8LE
☎ 0191 416 5454 📠 0191 416 5801
e-mail: info.washington@wwt.org.uk
web: www.wwt.org.uk/visit/washington
dir: signed off A195, A1231 & A182

Explore 45 hectares of wetland, woodland and wildlife reserve at Washington Wetland Centre - one of the North East's biggest conservation success stories. Home to exotic birds, amazing insects and beautiful wild scenery. Get nose to beak with rare waterbirds at Close Encounters and meet the pink Chilean Flamingos. See Grey Herons at Wade Lake, Great-spotted Woodpeckers in Hawthorn Wood and tiny ducklings at Waterfowl Nursery (May-July). Plus wildflower meadows, dragonflies, frogs, bats, goats and ancient woodland. Excellent year-round events calendar, award-winning educational programmes, excellent disabled access and free wheelchair hire.

Times Open all year: summer 9.30-5.30; winter 9.30-4.30 (last admission 30mins before close). Closed 25 Dec* **Facilities** licensed (outdoor) (partly accessible) (majority of pathways are tarmac and most hides are accessible) (free manual & electric wheelchairs to hire) shop

WHITBURN Map 12 NZ46

Souter Lighthouse & The Leas

Coast Rd SR6 7NH
☎ 0191 529 3161 📠 0191 529 0902
e-mail: souter@nationaltrust.org.uk
web: www.nationaltrust.org.uk/main
dir: on A183 coast road, 2m S of South Shields, 3m N of Sunderland

When it opened in 1871, Souter was the most advanced lighthouse in the world, and warned shipping off the notorious rocks in the river approaches of the Tyne and the Wear. Painted red and white and standing at 150ft high, it is a dramatic building, and hands-on displays and volunteers help bring it to life. Visitors can explore the whole building, with its engine room and lighthouse keeper's cottage. You can also take part in activities concerning shipwrecks and the workings of the lighthouse. Climb to the top of the lighthouse, or walk along the Leas, a 2.5 mile stretch of spectacular coastline.

Times Open 12 Mar-30 Oct, daily (ex Fri but open Good Fri) 11-5. Gallery, café & facilities open Fri in Jul-Aug* **Fees** £5 (ch £3.50). Family ticket £13.50. Group 10+ £4.50 **Facilities** licensed (outdoor) (partly accessible) (76 steps to top of Lighthouse Tower, CCTV available for those unable to climb) toilets for disabled (Braille guide, induction loops, tactile exhibits) shop

WARWICKSHIRE

Shakespeare's birthplace, Stratford-upon-Avon

ALCESTER Map 4 SP05

Ragley Hall

B49 5NJ

☎ 01789 762090 01789 764791

e-mail: ragley@ragleyhall.com

web: www.ragleyhall.com

dir: 8m SW of Stratford-upon-Avon, off A46/A435, follow brown tourist signs

Built in 1680, Ragley is the family home of the Marquess and Marchioness of Hertford, and has been for nine generations. Set in 400 acres of parkland, woodland and landscaped gardens, Ragley has something for all the family. Younger visitors will enjoy Adventure Wood with its swings, trampoline, 3-D maze, rope bridges and wooden fortress, while the Lakeside Café is ideal for parents to rest and enjoy a cuppa while the kids play safely. There are also 27 acres of formal gardens, the Woodland Walk featuring the Jerwood Sculpture Park, and the 18th-century stable block that houses a collection of historic carriages and equestrian memorabilia.

Times Open Feb-Oct wknds & during Warwickshire school hols. Please refer to website for details **Fees** £8.50 (ch £5, concessions £7). Family £27 **Facilities** (outdoor) (partly accessible) (some areas of garden accessible) toilets for disabled (lift) shop

BADDESLEY CLINTON Map 4 SP27

Baddesley Clinton

B93 0DQ

☎ 01564 783294 01564 782706

e-mail: baddesleyclinton@nationaltrust.org.uk

web: www.nationaltrust.org.uk/main/w-baddesleyclinton

dir: 0.75m W off A4141, 7.5m NW of Warwick

A romantically-sited medieval moated house, dating from the 15th century, that has changed very little since 1634. With family portraits, priest's holes, chapel, garden, ponds, nature trail and lake walk.

Times Open: 10 Feb-Oct, Wed-Sun 11-5; 29 Mar-18 Apr; 31 May-6 Jun; 26 Jul-5 Sep; 25-31 Oct, daily 11-5. Grounds, shops, restaurant: 3 Nov-19 Dec, Wed-Sun 11-4. House: 1-19 Dec, Wed-Sun 11-4* **Fees** With Gift Aid donation: Garden only £4.65 (ch £2.35). House & Garden £9.25 (ch £4.65). Family ticket £23.10. Joint ticket with Packwood House £13 (ch £6.55). Family ticket £32.50. Joint ticket for gardens only £6.95 (ch £3.50)* **Facilities** licensed (outdoor) (partly accessible) (grounds partly accessible, some steps and gravel paths) toilets for disabled (Braille guides, tactile route and 4 wheelchairs) shop

CHARLECOTE Map 4 SP25

Charlecote Park

CV35 9ER

☎ 01789 470277 01789 470544

e-mail: charlecote.park@nationaltrust.org.uk

web: www.nationaltrust.org.uk/main/w-charlecotepark

dir: 5m E of Stratford Upon Avon, 1m W of Wellesbourne, off B4086

Queen Elizabeth I and William Shakespeare knew Charlecote Park well. Follow in their footsteps at this impressive Warwickshire house and ancient deer park. Special events held every month, from outdoor picnic concerts to family events, outdoor theatre and specialist tours. Call for event details.

Times Open Mar-28 Oct, Fri-Tue grounds 10.30-5.30 park until 6. House noon-5. Open wknds Nov & Dec* **Fees** House & Grounds; £9 (ch £4.50). Family £22.50. Garden & Grounds £4.50 (ch £2.25). Family £11.25* **Facilities** licensed (outdoor) (partly accessible) (access restricted to ground floor of mansion & outbuildings, parts of garden & park accessible) toilets for disabled (virtual tour available, ramp to kitchens, shop & restaurant) shop

COMPTON VERNEY Map 4 SP35

Compton Verney

2 FOR 1

CV35 9HZ

☎ 01926 645500 01926 645501

e-mail: info@comptonverney.org.uk

web: www.comptonverney.org.uk

dir: 9m from Stratford-upon-Avon/Warwick/Leamington Spa on B4086 between Wellesbourne & Kineton

Visitors of all ages are warmly welcomed to this award-winning art gallery, housed in a restored 18th-century mansion. Explore works of art from around the world in the permanent collections, be enthralled by the diverse programme of changing exhibitions and events before relaxing in the 120 acres of landscaped parkland.

Times Open 26 Mar-11 Dec, Tue-Sun, 11-5. Open BH **Fees** £8 (ch under 5's free, 5-16 £2, concessions £6) Family £18 (2ad+up to 4 ch).* **Facilities** licensed (outdoor) (fully accessible) toilets for disabled (w/chairs, large print guides, hearing loop, BSL tours) shop

ENGLAND

COUGHTON Map 4 SP06

Coughton Court

B49 5JA
☎ 01789 400777 01789 765544
e-mail: coughtoncourt@nationaltrust.ork.uk
web: www.nationaltrust.org.uk/main/w-coughtoncourt
dir: 2m N of Alcester on E side of A435

This imposing Tudor house is set in beautiful gardens, and has been home to the Throckmortons for 600 years. The house contains many family portraits, and much in the way of fascinating furniture, fabrics and ornaments. The estate has two churches, a 19th-century Catholic church, and the parish church of St Peter's. The Throckmorton family created and maintain the grounds, including the walled garden and the award-winning displays of roses.

Times Open House, Garden & Restaurant: 13-28 Mar, Sat-Sun; Apr-Jun & Sep, Wed-Sun; Jul-Aug Tue-Sun; Oct-7 Nov, Thu-Sun 11-5; 4-12 Dec daily 12-6. Walled garden open 11.30-4.45 (parts of garden may be closed Mar, Oct-Dec)* **Fees** House and Garden: £9.40 (ch £4.70). Family £23.50. Garden only: £6.50 (ch £3.25). Family £16.30. Walled garden: £2.50 for NT members. (inc. in admission price for non-members)* **Facilities** licensed (outdoor) (partly accessible) (access only to to ground floor of mansion house, loose gravel and hoggin paths in garden) toilets for disabled (Braille guide, DDA Album, parking, 3 w/chairs available) shop

FARNBOROUGH Map 4 SP44

Farnborough Hall

OX17 1DU
☎ 01295 690002
web: www.nationaltrust.org.uk
dir: 6m N of Banbury, 0.5m W of A423

A classical mid 18th-century stone house with notable plasterwork; the entrance hall, staircase and two principal rooms are shown. The grounds contain charming 18th-century temples, terrace walk and an obelisk.

Times House, Grounds & Terrace walk open 3 Apr-29 Sep, Wed & Sat 2-5.30; 2-3 May, Sun & Mon only 2-5.30 (last admission 5)* **Fees** House, Garden & Terrace walk £5.25 (ch £2.60), Family £13.20* **Facilities** (partly accessible) (access only to ground floor, 2 steps to entrance and grounds partly accessible)

GAYDON Map 4 SP35

Heritage Motor Centre **2 FOR 1**

Banbury Rd CV35 0BJ
☎ 01926 641188 01926 641555
e-mail: enquiries@heritage-motor-centre.co.uk
web: www.heritage-motor-centre.co.uk
dir: M40 junct 12 and take B4100. Attraction signed

The Heritage Motor Centre is home to the world's largest collection of historic British cars. The museum boasts exciting and interactive exhibitions which uncover the story of the British motor industry from the 1890s to the present day. Fun for all the family with children's activity packs, special school holiday and lecture programs, plus free guided tours twice a day, onsite café and gift shop and a selection of outdoor activities including children's play area, picnic site, 4x4 Experience and Go-Karts. 2-for-1 voucher not valid on special event days.

Times Open all year, daily 10-5. Closed 24 Dec-1 Jan **Fees** £9 (ch 5-16 £7, under 5 free, concessions £8). Group rates available **Facilities** (outdoor) (fully accessible) toilets for disabled (lift to all floors, manual w/chair loan, hearing loop) shop

KENILWORTH Map 4 SP27

Kenilworth Castle

CV8 1NE
☎ 01926 852078 01926 851514
web: www.english-heritage.org.uk

Explore the largest and most extensive castle ruin in England, with a past rich in famous names and events. Its massive red sandstone towers, keep and wall glow brightly in the sunlight. Discover the history of Kenilworth through the interactive model in Leicester's Barn.

Times Open all year, Mar-Oct, daily 10-5; Nov-Feb, daily 10-4. Closed 24-26 Dec & 1 Jan. Gatehouse may close early for private events, please check before visit **Fees** £7.60 (ch £3.80, concessions £6.50). Family ticket £19. Prices and opening times are subject to change in March 2011. Please check web site or call 0870 333 1181 for the most up to date prices and opening times when planning your visit **Facilities** (partly accessible) (uneven surfaces, steep slopes, steps) toilets for disabled (audio tour, hearing loop, Braille) shop

Stoneleigh Abbey

2 FOR 1

CV8 2LF

☎ 01926 858535 & 858585 📠 01926 850724

e-mail: enquire@stoneleighabbey.org

web: www.stoneleighabbey.org

dir: entrance off B4115 close to junct of A46 and A452

Stoneleigh Abbey is one of the finest country house estates in the Midlands and has been the subject of considerable restoration work. The abbey, founded in the reign of Henry II, is now managed by a charitable trust. Visitors will experience a wealth of architectural styles spanning more than 800 years. The magnificent state rooms and chapel, the medieval Gatehouse and the Regency stables are some of the major areas to be admired. Set in 690 acres of parkland, 'Through the Keyhole' tours enable visitors to see parts of the Abbey that are not generally open to the public and on Sundays and Wednesdays to explore the Abbey's close links with Jane Austen. 2-for-1 voucher cannot be used for any special events such as Jane Austen Evenings or Halloween Special.

Times Open Good Fri-Oct, Tue-Thu, Sun & BHs for guided tours at 11, 1 & 3. Grounds open 10-5 **Fees** Grounds only, £3. Guided tour of house, £7 (1ch 5-12 free, additional ch £3, pen £6.50)* **Facilities** Ⓟ ☕ ♿ (partly accessible) (access over exterior gravel paths will require assistance & lift access to state rooms) toilets for disabled shop 🚫

MIDDLETON — Map 7 SP19

Ash End House Children's Farm

Middleton Ln B78 2BL

☎ 0121 329 3240 📠 0121 329 3240

e-mail: contact@thechildrensfarm.co.uk

web: www.childrensfarm.co.uk

dir: signed from A4091

Ideal for young children, this is a small family-owned farm with many friendly animals to feed and stroke, including some rare breeds. Café, gift shop, play areas, jumping pillow, picnic barns and lots of undercover activities. New for 2011 indoor play barn.

Times Open all year, daily 10-5 or dusk in winter. Closed 25 Dec until 2nd wknd in Jan **Fees** £5.50 (ch £6.50 includes animal feed, farm badge, fresh egg & all activities)* **Facilities** Ⓟ ☕ 🍴 (indoor & outdoor) ♿ (fully accessible) toilets for disabled shop 🚫

NUNEATON — Map 4 SP39

Arbury Hall

CV10 7PT

☎ 024 7638 2804 📠 024 7664 1147

e-mail: brenda.newell@arburyhall.net

dir: 2m SW of Nuneaton, off B4102 Meriden road

The 16th-century Elizabethan house, Gothicised in the 18th century, has been the home of the Newdegate family for over 450 years. It is the finest complete example of Gothic revival architecture in existence, and contains pictures, furniture, and beautiful plasterwork ceilings. The 17th-century stable block, with a central doorway by Wren, houses the tearooms and there are lovely gardens with lakes and wooded walks.

Times Open Apr-Sep. Hall & Gardens: Sun & Mon of BH wknds only. For other opening days & times, contact Administrator **Fees** £7 (ch £4.50) Gardens only £5 (ch £3.50)* **Facilities** Ⓟ Ⓟ ☕ ♿ (partly accessible) (access restricted to ground floor rooms) toilets for disabled shop 🚫

PACKWOOD HOUSE — Map 7 SP17

Packwood House

B94 6AT

☎ 01564 782024 📠 01564 787920

e-mail: packwood@nationaltrust.org.uk

web: www.nationaltrust.org.uk/main/w-packwoodhouse

dir: on unclass road off A3400

Dating from the 16th century, Packwood House has been extended and much changed over the years. An important collection of tapestries and textiles is displayed. Equally important are the stunning gardens with renowned herbaceous borders, attracting many visitors, and the almost surreal topiary garden based on the Sermon on the Mount. During summer months there is open air theatre in the garden.

Times Park : open all year, Mon-Sun dawn-dusk. House, garden & shop : 10 Feb-Oct, Wed-Sun 11-5; 29 Mar-18 Apr, 31 May-6 Jun, 26 Jul-5 Sep & 25-31 Oct, daily 11-5* **Fees** House & Garden £8.10 (ch £4.10, ch under 5 free). Family ticket £20.25. Garden only £4.65 (ch £2.35). Joint ticket with Baddesley Clinton £13 (ch £6.55). Family ticket £32.50, joint ticket for gardens only £6.95 (ch £3.50)* **Facilities** Ⓟ 🍴 (outdoor) ♿ (partly accessible) (ground floor of house, apart from great hall, accessible and loose gravel and some steps in garden) toilets for disabled (2 w/chairs available, tactile tour, Braille guide) shop 🚫 ✤

RUGBY — Map 4 SP57

The Webb Ellis Rugby Football Museum

FREE

5 Saint Matthew's St CV21 3BY

☎ 01788 567777 📠 01788 537400

e-mail: sales@webb-ellis.co.uk

web: www.webb-ellis.co.uk

dir: on A428 opposite Rugby School

An intriguing collection of Rugby football memorabilia is housed in the shop in which rugby balls have been made since 1842. Visitors can watch a craftsman at work, hand-stitching the footballs. Situated near to Rugby School and its famous playing field.

Times Open all year, Mon-Sat 9-5. Phone for hol opening times **Facilities** Ⓟ ♿ (partly accessible) (Wheelchairs can be accommodated. Narrow doorways in museum restrict full access) shop 🚫

RYTON-ON-DUNSMORE Map 4 SP37

Ryton Gardens 2 FOR 1

Wolston Ln CV8 3LG
☎ 024 7630 3517 📠 024 7663 9229
e-mail: enquiry@gardenorganic.org.uk
web: www.gardenorganic.org.uk
dir: 5m SE of Coventry signed off A45, on road to village of Wolston

Ryton Gardens is home to garden organic, the UK's leading authority on organic growing. The site has over 30 glorious organic gardens in ten acres of grounds to explore and discover. Designed around getting more people to grow organically, the gardens demonstrate the effectiveness of gardening in harmony with nature and how easy it is to grow your own fruit and vegetables. Also on site is the charity's world renowned Heritage Seed Library, which protects hundreds of endangered vegetable varieties, the Vegetable Kingdom interactive experience, and an award winning organic café, restaurant and shop. The site also hosts special event days and garden tours. Winner of BBC Gardeners' World Magazine favourite garden in Central England. The 2 for 1 voucher is not valid on special event days.

Times Open all year, daily 9-5. Restricted opening hours over Xmas period **Fees** £6 (ch £3 (one ch incl in adult ticket), concessions £5.45)* **Facilities** Ⓟ ☕ 🍽 licensed 🪑 (outdoor) ♿ (fully accessible) toilets for disabled (wheelchairs & scooter available) shop 🚫

SHOTTERY Map 4 SP15

Anne Hathaway's Cottage

Cottage Ln CV37 9HH
☎ 01789 292100 📠 01789 263138
e-mail: info@shakespeare.org.uk
web: www.shakespeare.org.uk
dir: House in Shottery Village, 1m from Stratford

This world-famous thatched cottage was the childhood home of Anne Hathaway, William Shakespeare's wife. The cottage still contains many family items including the beautiful 'Hathaway Bed'. In the stunning grounds there is a quintessential English cottage garden, orchard, sculpture garden, a romantic willow cabin and a maze.

Times Open all year, Apr-May & Oct-Nov, Mon-Sat 9.30-5, Sun 10-5; Jun-Aug, Mon-Sat 9-5, Sun 9.30-5; Nov-Mar, daily 10-4* **Facilities** Ⓟ ☕ ♿ (partly accessible) toilets for disabled (access room with virtual reality tours of cottage) shop 🚫

STRATFORD-UPON-AVON Map 4 SP25

Hall's Croft

Old Town CV37 6EP
☎ 01789 292107 📠 01789 263138
e-mail: info@shakespeare.org.uk
web: www.shakespeare.org.uk
dir: located in the centre of Stratford-upon-Avon

This elegant 17th-century house belonged to Shakespeare's eldest daughter, Susanna and her husband, the physician John Hall. It is an impressive building with many exquisite furnishing and paintings of the period, and an exhibition on early medicine.

Times Open all year, Apr-May and Sep-Oct, daily 11-5; Jun-Aug, Mon-Sat 9.30-5, Sun 10-5; Nov-Mar, daily 11-4.* **Facilities** Ⓟ ☕ ♿ (partly accessible) toilets for disabled shop 🚫

Nash's House & New Place

Chapel St CV37 6EP
☎ 01789 292325 📠 01789 263138
e-mail: info@shakespeare.org.uk
web: www.shakespeare.org.uk
dir: located in centre of Stratford upon Avon

The elegant home of Shakespeare's granddaughter Elizabeth Hall's first husband, Thomas Nash. The adjacent site of New Place, where Shakespeare retired and subsequently died in 1616, is now preserved as a picturesque garden space with an attractive Elizabethan knot garden.

Times Open all year, Apr-May & Sep-Oct, daily 11-5; Jun-Aug, Mon-Sat 9.30-5, Sun 10-5.30; Nov-Mar, daily 11-4;.* **Facilities** Ⓟ ♿ (partly accessible) toilets for disabled shop 🚫

Royal Shakespeare Company Collection

Royal Shakespeare Theatre, Waterside CV37 6BB
☎ 01789 262870 📠 01789 262870
e-mail: info@rsc.org.uk
web: www.rsc.org.uk
dir: M40 junct 14 take A46 S. At 1st rdbt take 2nd exit (A439). At next rdbt follow signs to park & ride. In town centre follow RSC signs

The RSC gallery opened in 1881, and was part of the first Shakespeare Memorial Theatre. In 1926 fire destroyed the theatre leaving only a semi circular wall and the gallery. The rebuilt theatre was opened in 1932. In 2007 the theatre, known as the Royal Shakespeare Theatre since 1961, was closed for redevelopment work. It is due to re-open in November 2010. 2011 celebrates the 50th Anniversary of RSC.

Times Royal Shakespeare Theatre closed for redevelopment in 2010. Due to open in Nov 2010 with activities and exhibitions including displays from the RSC Collections* **Fees** Fees will be charged for specific activities within the theatre building **Facilities** Ⓟ ☕ 🍽 licensed ♿ (fully accessible) toilets for disabled (Theatre induction loop & signed performances) shop 🚫

Shakespeare's Birthplace 2 FOR 1

Henley St CV37 6QW
☎ 01789 201 845 📠 01789 263138
e-mail: info@shakespeare.org.uk
web: www.shakespeare.org.uk
dir: in town centre

Visit the house where the world's most famous playwright was born and grew up. Discover the fascinating story of William Shakespeare's life and see it brought to life by the costumed guides. Enjoy the state of the art Life, Love and Legacy exhibition and see live performances in the garden with Shakespeare Aloud!

Times Open all year, daily Apr-Oct 9-5; Nov-Mar 10-4
Fees Birthplace including Nash's/Halls Croft £12.50 (ch £8, concessions £11.50) Family ticket £33.50. All five Shakespeare Houses £19 (ch £12, concessions £17). Family ticket £49. Mary Arden's Farm £8.50 (ch £5.50, concessions £7.50). Family ticket £22.50. Please call or see website for up to date prices*
Facilities Ⓟ ♿ (partly accessible) toilets for disabled (computer based virtual reality tour of upper floor) shop 🚫

Stratford Butterfly Farm 2 FOR 1

Tramway Walk, Swan's Nest Ln CV37 7LS
☎ 01789 299288 📠 01789 415878
e-mail: sales@butterflyfarm.co.uk
web: www.butterflyfarm.co.uk
dir: south bank of River Avon opposite RSC

The UK's largest live butterfly and insect exhibit. Hundreds of the world's most spectacular and colourful butterflies, in the unique setting of a lush tropical landscape, with splashing waterfalls and fish-filled pools. See also the strange and fascinating Insect City, a bustling metropolis of ants, stick insects, beetles and other remarkable insects. See the dangerous and deadly in Arachnoland!

Times Open all year, daily 10-6 (winter 10-dusk). Closed 25 Dec **Fees** £5.95 (ch £4.95, concessions £5.45). Family £17.50*
Facilities Ⓟ (outdoor) ♿ (fully accessible) shop 🚫

UPTON HOUSE — Map 4 SP34

Upton House & Gardens

OX15 6HT
☎ 01295 670266 📠 01295 671144
e-mail: uptonhouse@nationaltrust.org.uk
web: www.nationaltrust.org.uk/main/w-uptonhouse
dir: M40 junct 12, on A422, 7m NW of Banbury, 12m SE of Stratford

Join the guests of Lord and Lady Bearsted and experience the weekend house party of a 1930s millionaire. Surrounded by the internationally important art and porcelain collections, hear and discover more about family life and join in the atmosphere of the party. See the red and silver art deco bathroom and get close to art works by Hogarth, Stubbs and Bosch. The stunning garden is being returned to its 1930s heyday, the sweeping lawn which gives way to a series of terraces and herbaceous borders leading to a kitchen garden, tranquil water garden and the National Collection of Asters.

Times House & Garden open: 13 Feb-10 Mar, Sat-Wed & 13 Mar-Oct, Fri-Wed 11-5; Nov-3 Jan, Sat-Wed 12-4* **Fees** £9 (ch £4.50). Family ticket £22.50. Garden only £5.50 (ch £2.70) Family ticket £13.70* **Facilities** Ⓟ licensed (outdoor) ♿ (partly accessible) (access restricted to ground floor of house & main garden) toilets for disabled (close parking, buggy, w/chair, virtual tour) shop 🚫

WARWICK — Map 4 SP26

Warwick Castle 2 FOR 1

CV34 4QU
☎ 0871 265 2000
e-mail: customer.information@warwick-castle.com
web: www.warwick-castle.com
dir: 2m from M40 junct 15

From the days of William the Conqueror to the reign of Queen Victoria, Warwick Castle has provided a backdrop for many turbulent times. Attractions include the world's largest siege engine, thrilling jousting tournaments, birds of prey, daredevil knights, and an entire castle full of colourful characters. The newest addition is the immersive and interactive "Dream of Battle". Immerse yourself in a thousand years of history, come rain or shine.

Times Open all year, daily 10-6; Oct-Mar 5pm. Closed 25 Dec*
Fees £19.95 (ch 4-16 £11.95, seniors £13.95, students £12.95, disabled & carer £8.95). Family ticket (2ad+2ch) £55, prices exclude Castle Dungeon. Please check website for current admission prices & discounts if booking online **Facilities** Ⓟ Ⓟ licensed ♿ (partly accessible) toilets for disabled (hearing loop, large print guides, DVD, audio guides) shop 🚫

WARWICK *continued*

Warwickshire Yeomanry Museum

The Court House Vaults, Jury St CV34 4EW
☎ 01926 492212 & 428434 📠 01926 494837
e-mail: wtc.admin@bt.click.com
web: www.warwickhireyeomanrymuseum.co.uk
dir: situated on corner of Jury St & Castle St, 2m E of M40 junct 15

The vaults of the courthouse display militaria from the county Yeomanry, dating from 1794 to 1945. It includes regimental silver, paintings, uniforms and weapons. A small room in the cellars now houses the HUJ Gun project, a field gun captured by the Yeomanry in 1917.

Times Open Good Fri-Rememberance Sun, Sat, Sun & BH only. Private individuals or parties (max 15) can be admitted by arrangement at any time **Fees** Free admission and research. Donation welcome **Facilities** Ⓟ (outdoor) shop

WILMCOTE **Map 4 SP15**

Mary Arden's

Station Rd CV37 9UN
☎ 01789 293455 📠 01789 292083
e-mail: info@shakespeare.org.uk
web: www.shakespeare.org.uk
dir: 3m NW of Stratford-upon-Avon off A3400

The site includes two Tudor buildings, including the childhood home of Shakespeare's mother, Mary Arden. Experience the sights and sounds of a Tudor farm as the farmer, maids and labourers bring the farm to life. Take a walk on the nature trail and track down the Longhorn cattle, Cotswold sheep and other rare breeds.

Times Open all year daily, Apr-May & Sep-Oct, 10-5; Jun-Aug, 9.30-5; Nov-Mar, 10-4* **Facilities** Ⓟ (outdoor) (partly accessible) toilets for disabled shop

WEST MIDLANDS

Old cathedral ruins, Coventry

BIRMINGHAM Map 7 SP08

Aston Hall FREE

Trinity Rd, Aston B6 6JD
☎ 0121 464 2193 0121 675 4740
e-mail: bmag-enquiries@birmingham.gov.uk
web: www.bmag.org.uk/aston-hall
dir: E of Birmingham, just off the A4040 in Yardley

Built by Sir Thomas Holte, Aston Hall is a fine Jacobean mansion complete with a panelled Long Gallery, balustraded staircase and magnificent plaster friezes and ceilings. King Charles I spent a night here during the Civil War and the house was damaged by Parliamentary troops. It was also leased to James Watt Junior, the son of the great industrial pioneer.

Times Open Etr-Oct, Tue-Sun 11.30-4. Closed Mon ex BHs & wknds on Aston Villa home match days.* **Facilities** (partly accessible) shop

Birmingham Botanical Gardens & Glasshouses 2 FOR 1

Westbourne Rd, Edgbaston B15 3TR
☎ 0121 454 1860 0121 454 7835
e-mail: admin@birminghambotanicalgardens.org.uk
web: www.birminghambotanicalgardens.org.uk
dir: 2m W of city centre, follow signs for Edgbaston, then brown heritage signs

Originally opened in 1832, the gardens include the Tropical House, which has a 24ft-wide lily pool and lush vegetation. The Mediterranean house features a wide variety of citrus fruits and the Arid House has a desert scene with its giant agaves and opuntias. Outside, a tour of the gardens includes rhododendrons and azalea borders, 7000 plants and shrubs and a collection of over 200 trees. Young children's discovery garden and a sculpture trail. There are a large number of events to choose from, contact the gardens for a brochure.

Times Open all year, wkdays 9-7, Sun 10-7. Closed 25 Dec* **Fees** £7.50 (concessions £4.75). Family £22. Groups 10+ £6.50 (concessions £4.50) **Facilities** licensed (outdoor) (fully accessible) toilets for disabled (3 wheelchairs, 2 electric scooters & Braille guides) shop

Birmingham Museum & Art Gallery

Chamberlain Sq B3 3DH
☎ 0121 303 2834 0121 303 1379
e-mail: bmag-enquiries@birmingham.gov.uk
web: www.bmag.org.uk
dir: 5 mins walk from Birmingham New St Station, by Town Hall, Council House & Central Library

One of the world's best collections of Pre-Raphaelite paintings can be seen here, including important works by Burne-Jones, a native of Birmingham. Also on display are fine silver, ceramics and glass. The archaeology section has prehistoric Egyptian, Greek and Roman antiquities, and also objects from the Near East, Mexico and Peru. Galleries also explore the creation of art, while the In Touch gallery includes talking sculptures, and Samurai armour. The Bull Ring explores the 800 year history of this well-known area. A selection of artefacts from the Staffordshire Hoard, the largest find of Anglo-Saxon gold are also on display. There is a regular programme of temporary art and history exhibitions every year. Building of the new Birmingham history galleries has started, check in advance for details of any closures.

Times Open all year, Mon-Thu & Sat 10-5, Fri 10.30-5 & Sun 12.30-5. Please check for seasonal closures **Fees** Admission free but charge may be made for some temporary exhibitions & family art & craft activities **Facilities** licensed (fully accessible) toilets for disabled (lift) shop

Blakesley Hall FREE

Blakesley Rd, Yardley B25 8RN
☎ 0121 464 2193 0121 464 0400
e-mail: laura_r_cox@birmingham.gov.uk
web: www.bmag.org.uk
dir: A4040 onto Blakesley Rd, Hall 100yds on right

Blakesley Hall is a fine Yeoman farmer's residence, built by Richard Smalbroke in 1590. It has a half-timbered exterior and a Stuart interior, with a wonderful herb garden. The visitor centre has a varied exhibition programme, tea room and gift shop. Regular weekend events take place throughout the open season.

Times Open Apr-Oct, Tue-Sun & BHs, 12-4* **Facilities** (outdoor) (partly accessible) toilets for disabled shop

Museum of the Jewellery Quarter FREE

75-80 Vyse St, Hockley B18 6HA
☎ 0121 554 3598 0121 554 9700
e-mail: bmag-enquiries@birmingham.gov.uk
web: www.bmag.org.uk
dir: off A41 into Vyse St, museum on left after 1st side street

The Museum tells the story of jewellery making in Birmingham from its origins in the Middle Ages right through to the present day. Discover the skill of the jeweller's craft and enjoy a unique tour of an original jewellery factory frozen in time. For over eighty years the family firm of Smith and Pepper produced jewellery from the factory. This perfectly preserved 'time capsule' workshop has changed little since the beginning of the 20th century. The Jewellery Quarter is still very much at the forefront of jewellery manufacture in Britain and the Museum showcases the work of the city's most exciting new designers.

Times Open all year **Facilities** Ⓟ ♿ (fully accessible) toilets for disabled (tours for hearing/visually impaired booked in advance) shop 🚫

RSPB Sandwell Valley Nature Reserve

FREE

20 Tanhouse Av, Great Barr B43 5AG
☎ 0121 357 7395 📠 0121 358 3013
e-mail: sandwellvalley@rspb.org.uk
web: www.rspb.org.uk
dir: off B4167 Hamstead Rd into Tanhouse Ave

Opened in 1983 on the site of an old colliery, Sandwell Valley is home to hundreds of bird, animal and insect species in five different habitats. Summer is the best time to see the yellow wagtail or reed warblers, while wintertime attracts goosanders, snipe, and redshanks. There are guided walks and events for the kids in summer, and a visitor centre. The visitor centre is being re-built please contact for details of any closures.

Times Open Tue-Fri 9-5, Sat & Sun 10-5, dusk in winter. Closed 24 Dec-2 Jan **Facilities** 🅟 Ⓟ ⛩ (outdoor) ♿ (partly accessible) (some steep gradients, wheelchair users may need assistance) toilets for disabled

Sarehole Mill

FREE

Cole Bank Rd, Hall Green B13 0BD
☎ 0121 777 6612 📠 0121 303 2891
e-mail: bmag-enquiries@birmingham.gov.uk
web: www.bmag.org.uk
dir: A34 towards Birmingham. After 5m turn left on B4146, attraction on left

Sarehole Mill was built in the 1760s. Used for both flour production and metal-rolling up to the last century, the Mill can still be seen in action first Sunday each month during the summer months. Restored with financial backing from JRR Tolkien, who grew up in the area and cites Sarehole as an influence for writing *The Hobbit* and *Lord of the Rings*. Tolkien Weekend takes place during May each year.

Times Open Etr-Oct, Tue-Sun noon-4. Open BH Mon **Facilities** 🅟 ☕ ♿ (partly accessible) (ground floor of mill accessible to wheelchairs)

Soho House

FREE

Soho Av, Handsworth B18 5LB
☎ 0121 554 9122 📠 0121 554 5929
e-mail: bmag-enquiries@birmingham.gov.uk
web: www.bmag.org.uk
dir: from city centre follow A41 to Soho Rd, follow brown heritage signs to Soho Ave

Soho House was the elegant home of industrial pioneer Matthew Boulton between 1766 and 1809. Here, he met with some of the most important thinkers and scientists of his day. The house has been carefully restored and contains many of Boulton's possessions including furniture, clocks, silverware and the original dining table where the Lunar Society met.

Times Open Etr-Oct, Tue-Sun 12-4. Open BH Mon **Facilities** 🅟 ☕ ⛩ ♿ (fully accessible) toilets for disabled (induction loop) shop 🚫

Thinktank at Millennium Point

Millennium Point, Curzon St B4 7XG
☎ 0121 202 2222 📠 0121 202 2280
e-mail: findout@thinktank.ac
web: www.thinktank.ac
dir: Situated within Millennium Point & located on Curzon St, Digbeth. The nearest motorways are M6, M5 & M42

Thinktank offers a fun-packed day out for all the family. From steam engines to intestines this exciting museum has over 200 amazing artefacts and interactive exhibits on science and discovery. A state-of-the-art planetarium means you can tour the night sky and fly through the galaxy without stepping outside. There is an ever-changing programme of demonstrations, workshops and events. Contact for details. September 2011 is the 10th Anniversary for the museum.

Times Open daily 10-5 (last entry 4). Closed 24-26 Dec* **Fees** £11.75 (ch & concessions £7.95). Family ticket (2ad+2ch) £36.80* **Facilities** 🅟 Ⓟ ☕ ⛩ (indoor) ♿ (fully accessible) toilets for disabled (induction loop, w/chair loan, Braille, parking) shop 🚫

BOURNVILLE — Map 7 SP08

Cadbury World

Linden Rd B30 2LU
☎ 0845 450 3599 📠 0121 451 1366
e-mail: cadbury.world@csplc.com
web: www.cadburyworld.co.uk
dir: 1m S of A38 Bristol Rd, on A4040 Ring Rd. Follow brown signs from M5 junct 2 and junct 4

Get involved in the chocolate making process, and find out how the chocolate is used to make famous confectionery. Visitors can learn about the early struggles and triumphs of the Cadbury business, and follow the history of Cadbury television advertising. Two recently added attractions are: Essence, where visitors can create their own unique product by combining liquid chocolate with different tastes, and Purple Planet, where you can chase a creme egg, grow cocoa beans, and see yourself moulded in chocolate. A new visitor centre explores the innovative values of the Cadbury Brothers that make Bournville the place it is.

Times Opening times vary throughout the year please contact the information line 0845 450 3599* **Facilities** 🅟 ☕ 🍽 licensed ⛩ (outdoor) ♿ (partly accessible) (limited access to landing area) toilets for disabled (adapted ride & lift to 2nd floor, subtitles) shop 🚫

Selly Manor

Maple Rd, Bournville B30 2AE
☎ 0121 472 0199
e-mail: sellymanor@bvt.org.uk
web: www.bvt.org.uk/sellymanor
dir: off A4040 at Bournville Village Green

These two timber-framed manor houses date from the 13th and early 14th centuries, and have been re-erected in the 'garden suburb' of Bournville. There is a herb garden and events are held all year.

continued

ENGLAND

BOURNEVILLE *continued*

Times Open all year, Tue-Fri 10-5; Etr-Sep, Sat-Sun & BH Mon 2-5 **Fees** £3.50 (ch £1.50, concessions £2.50). Family ticket (2ad+3ch) £9.50* **Facilities** Ⓟ
(outdoor) ♿ (partly accessible) (ground floors, gardens & toilets) toilets for disabled (audio guides) shop

CASTLE BROMWICH Map 7 SP18

Castle Bromwich Hall Gardens

Chester Rd B36 9BT

☎ 0121 749 4100 📠 0121 749 4100

e-mail: admin@cbhgt.org.uk

web: www.cbhgt.org.uk

dir: M6 junct 5, follow brown tourist signs

This recently-restored 17th-century formal garden illustrates a period of history in an unusual and fascinating way. Although the garden is an accurate reconstruction of the garden as it was around 1680-1740, there is an addition: the holly maze, which was created in the 19th century, based on 17th-century plans.

Times Open: Apr-Sep, Sat-Sun & BH Mon 1.30-5.30, Tue-Thu 11-4, Fri 11-3.30* **Facilities** 🅟 Ⓟ ☕ (outdoor) ♿ (fully accessible) toilets for disabled (free wheelchairs available) shop

COVENTRY Map 4 SP37

Coventry Cathedral — 2 FOR 1

Priory St CV1 5ES

☎ 024 7652 1200 📠 024 7652 1200

e-mail: information@coventrycathedral.org.uk

web: www.coventrycathedral.org.uk

dir: signed on all approaches to the city

Coventry's old cathedral was bombed during an air raid on 14th November 1940 which devastated the city. The remains have been carefully preserved. The new cathedral was designed by Sir Basil Spence and consecrated in May 1962. It contains outstanding modern works of art, including a huge tapestry designed by Graham Sutherland, the west screen (a wall of glass engraved by John Hutton with saints and angels), bronzes by Epstein, and the great baptistry window by John Piper.

Times Open all year, daily 9-5. See website for occasional closures* **Fees** £4.50 (concessions £3.50) Tours: £7 (concessions £4.50)* **Facilities** Ⓟ ☕ 🍴 licensed (indoor & outdoor) ♿ (partly accessible) (two of the smaller chapels are inaccessible) toilets for disabled (large print service sheets) shop 🚫

Coventry Transport Museum — FREE

Millennium Place, Hales St CV1 1JD

☎ 024 7623 4270 📠 024 7623 4284

e-mail: enquiries@transport-museum.com

web: www.transport-museum.com

dir: just off junct 1, Coventry ring road, Tower St in city centre

Coventry is the traditional home of the British motor industry, and the museum's world-renowned collection displays over 150 years of its history. You can design your own car, feel what its like to break the sound barrier at 763mph and even travel into the future. The Festival of Motoring takes place over the first weekend in September and features vintage, veteran and classic vehicles with family activities and stunt show riders culminating in a car and motorcycle rally around the region.

Times Open all year, daily 10-5. Closed 24-26 Dec & 1 Jan **Facilities** Ⓟ ☕ ♿ (fully accessible) toilets for disabled (lifts & ramps available) shop 🚫

Herbert Art Gallery & Museum — FREE

Jordan Well CV1 5QP

☎ 024 7629 4734

e-mail: info@theherbert.org

web: www.theherbert.org

dir: in city centre near Cathedral

The Herbert Art and Gallery Museum, located next to Coventry Cathedral, has undergone a £20 million redevelopment. The site has eight permanent galleries, history centre and media suites. There is also an active programme of temporary exhibitions including plenty of events and activities for children. Please contact for details of forthcoming events.

Times Open all year, Mon-Sat 10-4, Sun 12-4. Closed 25-26 Dec & 1 Jan **Facilities** Ⓟ ☕ ♿ (fully accessible) toilets for disabled (disabled parking, automatic doors) shop 🚫

Jaguar Daimler Heritage Centre — FREE

Browns Ln, Allesley CV5 9DR

☎ 024 7620 3322 📠 024 7620 2835

e-mail: jagtrust@jaguar.com

web: www.jdht.com

dir: on A45, follow signs for Browns Lane Plant

Established in 1983, the Jaguar-Daimler Heritage Trust maintains a unique collection of motor vehicles and artefacts manufactured by Jaguar Cars Ltd, and the many other renowned marques associated with the company.

Times Open wkdays by appointment, no appointment required on last Sun of mth. **Facilities** 🅟 ☕ toilets for disabled shop 🚫

Lunt Roman Fort

Coventry Rd, Baginton CV8 3AJ

☎ 024 7629 4734 📠 024 7622 0171

e-mail: info@theherbert.org

web: www.theherbert.org

dir: S side of city, off Stonebridge highway, A45

The turf and timber Roman fort from around the end of the 1st century has been faithfully reconstructed. An Interpretation Centre is housed in the granary.

Times Open Apr-Oct, Sat-Sun & BH Mon 10.30-4.30 & Wed-Fri during school hols; 28 Jul-6 Sep, Wed-Sun 10.30-4.30 **Fees** £2.50 (concessions £1.25). Family ticket £7 **Facilities** 🅟 (outdoor) ♿ (fully accessible) toilets for disabled (ramp to Granary Interpretation Centre) shop 🚫

Priory Visitor Centre FREE

Priory Row CV1 5EX
☎ 024 7655 2242 📠 024 7622 0171
e-mail: prioryvisitorcentre@btconnect.com
web: www.theherbert.org
dir: in city centre near Cathedral

Earl Leofric and his wife Lady Godiva founded a monastery in Coventry in the 11th century. This priory disappeared somewhere beneath the cathedral that was built on the site, until this cathedral was in turn demolished by Henry VIII in the 16th century. Soon after that most of the buildings on the site had been reduced to ground level, leaving modern archaeologists to discover the outlines of history. This visitor centre displays finds from the site as well as telling the story of Coventry's first cathedral.

Times Open Mon-Sat 10-5, Sun noon-4 **Facilities** Ⓟ ♿ (fully accessible) toilets for disabled shop ⊗

St Mary's Guildhall FREE

Bayley Ln CV1 5RN
☎ 024 7683 3328 📠 024 7683 3329
e-mail: mark.twissell@coventry.gov.uk
web: www.coventry.gov.uk/stmarys
dir: in city centre near Herbert Art Gallery & south side of old Cathedral ruins

This impressive medieval Guildhall has stood in the heart of Coventry for over 650 years, and has played its part in the history of the area. It served as Henry VI's court during the War of the Roses, was a prison to Mary Queen of Scots, and was used as a setting by George Eliot in her novel *Adam Bede*. The Great Hall contains a Tournai tapestry commissioned for the visit of Henry VII and Queen Elizabeth in 1500.

Times Open Mar-Oct, Sun-Thu 10-4 **Facilities** Ⓟ 🍽 licensed ♿ (partly accessible) (ground floor, restaurant & WCs accessible) toilets for disabled (wheelchair stairlift) shop ⊗

DUDLEY Map 7 SO99

Black Country Living Museum 2 FOR 1

Tipton Rd DY1 4SQ
☎ 0121 557 9643 & 520 8054 📠 0121 557 4242
e-mail: info@bclm.co.uk
web: www.bclm.co.uk
dir: on A4037, near Showcase cinema

On the 26-acre site is a recreated canal-side village, with shops, houses and workshops. Meet the costumed characters and find out what life was like around 1900. Ride on a tramcar, explore the underground mine, venture into the limestone caverns or visit the olde tyme fairground (additional charge). There are also demonstrations of chainmaking, glass engraving and sweet-making. Watch a silent movie in the Limelight cinema, taste fish and chips cooked on a 1930s range, and finish your visit with a glass of real ale or dandelion and burdock in the Bottle and Glass Inn. Lots of varied events throughout the year, contact for details. 2-for-1 voucher not valid on Bank Holidays or pre-bookable events. Also not valid with on line bookings

Times Open all year, Mar-Oct, daily 10-5; Nov-Dec, daily 10-4; Jan-Feb, Wed-Sun 10-4. Closed 25-26 Dec & 3-4 Jan **Fees** £13.20 (ch 5-16 £6.60, under 5s free, student with NUS card £6.60, pen £10.70). Family ticket (1ad+1ch) £18 & (2ad+3ch) £34.95* **Facilities** Ⓟ ☕ 🍽 licensed ⛩ (indoor & outdoor) ♿ (partly accessible) (access to most buildings requires use of temporary ramp. Staff will assist visitors with restricted mobility) toilets for disabled (wheelchairs & ramps available, carers free entry) shop ⊗

Dudley Zoological Gardens

2 The Broadway DY1 4QB
☎ 01384 215313 📠 01384 456048
e-mail: marketing@dudleyzoo.org.uk
web: www.dudleyzoo.org.uk
dir: M5 junct 2 towards Wolverhampton/Dudley, signed

From lions and tigers to snakes and spiders, go wild at Dudley Zoo. Come face to face with lemurs as they roam in the trees. Watch amazing birds of prey, meet friends on the farm and look out for Ghosts in the Castle. Gift shop, restaurant, face painting and land train.

continued

DUDLEY *continued*

Times Open all year daily, Etr-mid Sep, 10-4; mid Sep-Etr, 10-3. Closed 25 Dec **Fees** £11.90 (ch 3 £7.70 under 3's free, concessions £8.70)* **Facilities** Ⓟ Ⓟ ☕ 🍽 licensed ⛩ (outdoor) ♿ (partly accessible) (not all accessible for wheelchairs due to hilly site) toilets for disabled (land train from gates-castle, w/chair pre book) shop 🚫

Museum & Art Gallery FREE

St James's Rd DY1 1HU
☎ 01384 815575 📠 01384 815576
e-mail: dudley.museum@dudley.gov.uk
web: www.dudley.gov.uk
dir: M5 N junct 2. Take A4123 signed to Dudley

The museum houses the Brooke Robinson collection of 17th-, 18th- and 19th-century European painting, furniture, ceramics and enamels. A fine geological gallery, 'The Time Trail' has spectacular displays of fossils from the local Wenlock limestone and coal measures. A changing programme of exhibitions including the new Saxons and Vikings exhibition, permanent Duncan Edwards and Local Heroes exhibition.

Times Open all year, Mon-Sat 10-4. Closed BHs & Good Fri **Facilities** Ⓟ ♿ (fully accessible) toilets for disabled (Braille & large print text, tactile objects) shop 🚫

KINGSWINFORD Map 7 SO88

Broadfield House Glass Museum FREE

Compton Dr DY6 9NS
☎ 01384 812745
e-mail: glass.museum@dudley.gov.uk
web: www.glassmuseum.org.uk
dir: Off A491 Stourbridge to Wolverhampton road, just S of Kingswinford Village Centre, follow brown tourist signs

Situated in the historic Stourbridge Glass Quarter, Broadfield House Glass Museum is one of the best glass museums in the world. Home to a magnificent collection of British glass from the 17th century to the present day, the museum hosts an exciting programme of exhibitions and events. The museum also has a gift shop and a hot glass studio, where visitors can watch the glassblowers at work.

Times Open all year, Tue-Sun 12-4. Please phone for Xmas & Etr openings **Facilities** Ⓟ ♿ (partly accessible) (access restricted to ground floor galleries, studio, shop & temporary exhibitions) toilets for disabled (photo album & dvd tour) shop 🚫

SOLIHULL Map 7 SP17

National Motorcycle Museum 2 FOR 1

Coventry Rd, Bickenhill B92 0EJ
☎ 01675 443311 📠 0121 711 3153
web: www.nationalmotorcyclemuseum.co.uk
dir: M42 junct 6, off A45 near NEC

The National Motorcycle Museum is recognised as the finest and largest motorcycle museum in the world, with machines always being added to the collection. It is a place where legends live on and it is a tribute to and a living record of this once great British industry that dominated world markets for some sixty years. The museum records for posterity the engineering achievements of the last century.

Times Open all year, daily 9.30-5.30. Closed 24-25 Dec **Fees** £6.95 (ch 12 & pen £4.95). Party 20+ £5.95 **Facilities** Ⓟ 🍽 licensed ♿ (fully accessible) toilets for disabled shop 🚫

STOURBRIDGE Map 7 SO88

The Falconry Centre

Hurrans Garden Centre, Kidderminster Road South, Hagley DY9 0JB
☎ 01562 700014 📠 01562 700014
e-mail: info@thefalconrycentre.co.uk
web: www.thefalconrycentre.co.uk
dir: off A456

The centre houses some 70 birds of prey including owls, hawks and falcons and is also a rehabilitation centre for sick and injured birds of prey. Spectacular flying displays are put on daily from midday. There are picnic areas, special fun days and training courses available.

Times Open all year, daily 10-5 & Sun 11-5. Closed 25, 26 Dec & Etr Sun.* **Facilities** Ⓟ ☕ ⛩ toilets for disabled ♿ (ramps in most places) shop 🚫

WALSALL Map 7 SP09

The New Art Gallery Walsall FREE

Gallery Square WS2 8LG
☎ 01922 654400 📠 01922 654401
e-mail: info@artatwalsall.org.uk
web: www.thenewartgallerywalsall.org.uk
dir: signed from all major routes into town centre

The New Art Gallery Walsall is home to the distinguished Garman Ryan Collection. This unique collection is displayed on two floors and consists of 365 works of art by artists including Sir Jacob Epstein, Van Gogh, Monet, Turner, Renoir, Constable and Freud. The temporary exhibition galleries offer the very best in contemporary art. DiSCO The Family Gallery is a safe place for families to explore art together.

Times Open all year, Mon-Sat 10-5, Sun 11-4 & BHs. Closed 25-28 Dec & 1 Jan. Please phone to confirm* **Facilities** Ⓟ ☕ ♿ (fully accessible) toilets for disabled (lift, access guide facilities, induction loop, large print) shop 🚫

Walsall Leather Museum FREE

Littleton Street West WS2 8EQ
☎ 01922 721153 📠 01922 725827
e-mail: leathermuseum@walsall.gov.uk
web: www.walsall.gov.uk/leathermuseum
dir: On Walsall ring-road A4148 on N side of town

Award winning working museum in the saddlery and leathergoods 'capital' of Britain. Watch skilled craftsmen and women at work in this restored Victorian leather factory. Displays tell the story of Walsall's leatherworkers past and present. Large shop stocks range of Walsall-made leathergoods, many at bargain prices. Groups very welcome, guided tours available.

Times Open all year, Tue-Sat 10-5, 4pm Nov-Mar. Open BH Mon. Closed 24-26 Dec, 1 Jan, Good Fri, Etr Sun & May Day* **Facilities** Ⓟ ☕ ⛩ (outdoor) ♿ (fully accessible) toilets for disabled (staff with sign language skills, tactile activities) shop 🚫

WOLVERHAMPTON — Map 7 SO99

Bantock House and Park — FREE

Finchfield Rd WV3 9LQ
☎ 01902 552195 📠 01902 552196
e-mail: bantockhouse@wolverhampton.gov.uk
web: www.wolverhamptonart.org.uk
dir: follow signs for Wolverhampton. Bantock House 1m out of city & well signed from ring road

A restored Georgian farmhouse set within 43 acres and surrounded by beautiful formal gardens. Visitors can explore the period settings of the Bantock's former home and discover stories about the family and other Victorians that helped to shape Wolverhampton. The house has permanent displays of exquisite locally made japanned-ware, enamels and steel jewellery, as well as a programme of changing exhibitions. Picnic areas, children's playground and pitch and putt. Please telephone or email for a quarterly events leaflet.

Times Open all year, Apr-Oct, 11-5; Nov-Mar, 12-4, open BH Mon **Facilities** Ⓟ ☕ ⛩ (outdoor) ♿ (fully accessible) toilets for disabled (wheelchair, induction loop, Braille guide) shop 🚫

Moseley Old Hall

Moseley Old Hall Ln, Fordhouses WV10 7HY
☎ 01902 782808 & 625451 📠 01902 625454
e-mail: moseleyoldhall@nationaltrust.org.uk
web: www.nationaltrust.org.uk/main/w-moseleyoldhall
dir: 4m N of Wolverhampton, off A460 and A449, M54 between junct 1 & 2

Originally built at the start of the 17th century, Moseley Old Hall is steeped in history. In 1651, the Prince of Wales, (later King Charles II) hid at Moseley Old Hall following his defeat at the Battle of Worcester. This romantic and daring story of the uncrowned king's escape is brought to life for visitors who enjoy stories from one of England's most turbulent times. Visitors can see the bed Charles slept on and the priest hole that concealed him. The impressive knot garden is based on a design of 1640. Details of special events can be found on the website.

Times Open 6 Mar-Oct, Sat-Sun & Wed, BH Mon & following Tue (except 4 May); 5 Jul-14 Sep, Mon-Tue 12-5; 7 Nov-19 Dec, Sun 12-4; BH Mon 11-5 & BH Tue 12-5* **Fees** Gift Aid donation: £6.60 (ch £3.30, under 5 free). Family ticket £16.50. Group tickets £5.60 & on Wed £5.30, out of hours £7.70* **Facilities** Ⓟ ☕ ⛩ (outdoor) ♿ (partly accessible) (access restricted to the ground floor of the house & garden) toilets for disabled (Braille & large print, 1 wheelchair, thick handled cutlery) shop 🌿

Wightwick Manor & Gardens

WV6 8EE
☎ 01902 761400
e-mail: wightwickmanor@nationaltrust.org.uk
web: www.nationaltrust.org.uk/main/w-wightwickmanor
dir: 3m W, Wolverhampton off A454 Bridgnorth

This house was begun in 1887 and is one of the finest examples of 19th-century Arts & Crafts decorative style. All aspects of William Morris's talents are shown in the house - wallpapers, textiles, carpets, tiles, embroidery and even books. The garden reflects late Victorian and Edwardian design. Please telephone for details of special events. In 2011 there is a year-long calendar of events to mark the 150th anniversary of the founding of the Morris' company.

Times Open 20 Feb-Oct, Wed-Sun & BH Mons 12.30-5; 6 Nov-19 Dec, Sat-Sun 11-5 (last admission 4.30). Gardens open daily & through school hols* **Fees** Gift Aid donation: House & gardens £8.70 (ch & concessions £4.30). Family ticket £21. Group rate £6.50. Garden only £4.30 (ch £2.10). Family ticket £12.60* **Facilities** Ⓟ Ⓟ ☕ ⛩ (outdoor) ♿ (partly accessible) (access to lower hall via 2 steps, to kitchen up 2 steps from ground floor) toilets for disabled (car parking call 01902 760100 for details) shop 🚫 🌿

WORDSLEY — Map 7 SO88

The Red House Glass Cone — FREE

High St DY8 4AZ
☎ 01384 812750 📠 01384 812751
e-mail: redhouse.cone@dudley.gov.uk
web: www.redhousecone.co.uk
dir: A491 just N of Stourbridge

One of only four cones left in the UK and one of the most complete glass cone sites in Europe, over one hundred feet tall, Red House was built in the 18th century. The cone was in use until 1936, and housed a furnace around which men blew glass. This is a busy heritage site hosting exhibitions, events, children's activities, tours, a schools' programme, live glass-making and craft studios.

Times Open all year, daily, 10-4. Please check for Xmas opening times. **Facilities** Ⓟ ☕ ⛩ (outdoor) ♿ (partly accessible) toilets for disabled (lift from first floor to gallery) shop 🚫

ISLE OF WIGHT

Low tide at dusk, Bembridge

ALUM BAY Map 4 SZ38

The Needles Old Battery & New Battery

West High Down PO30 0JH
☎ 01983 754772 📠 01983 756978
e-mail: isleofwight@nationaltrust.org.uk
web: www.nationaltrust.org.uk/isleofwight
dir: at Needles Headland, W of Freshwater Bay and Alum Bay, B3322

The threat of a French invasion prompted the construction in 1862 of this spectacularly sited fort, which now contains exhibitions on the Battery's involvement in both World Wars. Two of the original gun barrels are displayed in the parade ground and a 60-yard tunnel leads to a searchlight emplacement perched above the Needles Rocks giving magnificent views of the Dorset coastline beyond. An exhibition about the secret rocket testing programme is housed further up the headland at the Needles New Battery.

Times Old battery open: 12 Mar-30 Oct, daily 10.30-5 (last admission 4.30). New battery 12 Mar-30 Oct, Tue, Sat-Sun 11-4 (both properties close in high winds) **Fees** Old battery with Gift Aid: £5 (ch £2.50). Family ticket £12.10. New battery free **Facilities** Ⓟ ☕ ♿ (partly accessible) (access to the tunnel at Old Battery via spiral staircase, uneven surfaces & steep paths, access to New battery via steps to exhibition room) toilets for disabled (ramp, audio tours, hearing loops, photo album, w/chair) shop ❦

The Needles Park

PO39 0JD
☎ 0871 720 0022 📠 01983 755260
e-mail: info@theneedles.co.uk
web: www.theneedles.co.uk
dir: signed on B3322

Overlooking the Needles on the western edge of the island, the park has attractions for all the family: included in the wide range of facilities is the spectacular chair lift to the beach to view the famous coloured sand cliffs, Needles Rocks and lighthouse. Other popular attractions are Alum Bay Glass and the Isle of Wight Sweet Manufactory. Kids will enjoy the Junior Driver roadway, the Jurassic golf course and the Spins and Needles tea cup ride. The Park was also the site of Gugielmo Marconi's earliest experimental radio transmissions, and there is a monument to this. Please contact for special events.

Times Open Etr-Oct, daily from 10 (some attractions available in winter)* **Facilities** Ⓟ ☕ 🍽 licensed ⛩ (outdoor) ♿ (partly accessible) (some slopes) toilets for disabled (10 designated parking bays) shop

ARRETON Map 4 SZ58

Robin Hill Country Park

Downend PO30 2NU
☎ 01983 527352 📠 01983 527347
e-mail: dj@robin-hill.com
web: www.robin-hill.com
dir: 0.5m from Arreton next to Hare & Hounds pub

Set in 88 acres of beautiful woodland gardens and countryside, Robin Hill provides fun for all the family, with a wide variety of activities and attractions. There are twice-daily falconry displays at 11.30 and 2.45, and plenty of rides, like the Toboggan Run, Colossus Galleon and Time Machine. New attractions include a Roman villa interpretation barn and The Cows Express children's train ride. Robin Hill is also well-known as a great place to spot red squirrels.

Times Open Mar-Oct, daily 10-5 (last admission 4).* **Facilities** Ⓟ ☕ 🍽 licensed ⛩ (outdoor) ♿ (partly accessible) (most areas accessible, but some steep paths & rides may be unsuitable) toilets for disabled (ramps access, guide on request) shop

BEMBRIDGE Map 4 SZ68

Bembridge Windmill

PO35 5SQ
☎ 01983 873945 📠 01983 873 945
e-mail: isleofwight@nationaltrust.org.uk
web: www.nationaltrust.org.uk/isleofwight
dir: 0.5m S of Bembridge on B3395

Built around 1700, this is the only surviving windmill on the island and has much of its original machinery intact. It was last used in 1913, and the stone-built tower with its wooden cap and machinery has been restored so that visitors can explore its four floors. The mill also provides breathtaking views across glorious, unspoilt countryside and has a new working model so visitors can see how all the parts would have worked together. 2011 marks the 50th anniversary of National Trust ownership of the windmill.

Times Open 12 Mar-30 Oct, daily 11-5 (last admission 4.30 or dusk if earlier) **Fees** With voluntary gift Gift aid donation: £3.10 (ch £1.55) Family ticket £7.75 **Facilities** Ⓟ ♿ (partly accessible) (restricted access to ground floor, steps & narrow doorways, stairs to other floors) (hearing loop, pictorial guide, audio guide, Braille guide) shop ❦

ENGLAND

BLACKGANG — Map 4 SZ47

Blackgang Chine Fantasy Park

PO38 2HN
☎ 01983 730330 📠 01983 731267
e-mail: info@blackgangchine.com
web: www.blackgangchine.com
dir: follow signs from Ventnor for Whitnell & Niton. From Niton follow signs for Blackgang

Opened as scenic gardens in 1843 covering some 40 acres, the park has imaginative play areas, water gardens, maze and coastal gardens. Set on the steep wooded slopes of the chine are the themed areas Smugglerland, Nurseryland, Dinosaurland, Fantasyland and Frontierland. New is the Disappearing Village. This area of Blackgang includes a BBC *Coast* exhibition, The World of Timber and aerial film cinema, Wight Experience, which adults can visit separately.

Times Open late Mar-end Oct daily, 10-5; school summer hols open until 6* **Fees** All in ticket to Blackgang £9.95. Saver ticket (4 people) £37.50. Village only £4.95 **Facilities** licensed (outdoor) (partly accessible) (park on cliff edge, sloping paths) toilets for disabled shop

BRADING — Map 4 SZ68

Brading The Experience

46 High St PO36 0DQ
☎ 01983 407286 📠 01983 402112
e-mail: info@bradingtheexperience.co.uk
web: www.bradingtheexperience.co.uk
dir: on A3055, in Brading High St

Brading The Experience is more than just a waxworks. Comprising Great British Legends Gallery, this 16th-century rectory mansion is filled with famous and infamous characters from the past. There's also a Chamber of Horrors, award-winning courtyards, Animal World, World of Wheels and The Pier.

Times Open all year, Etr-Oct 10-5; Nov-Etr please contact establishment for details. (last admission 1.5 hrs before closing)* **Facilities** (partly accessible) toilets for disabled (disabled route planner, virtual tour) shop

Lilliput Antique Doll & Toy Museum

High St PO36 0DJ
☎ 01983 407231
e-mail: lilliput.museum@btconnect.com
web: www.lilliputmuseum.org.uk
dir: A3055 Ryde/Sandown road, in Brading High St

This private museum contains one of the finest collections of antique dolls and toys in Britain. There are over 2000 exhibits, ranging in age from 2000BC to 1950 with examples of almost every seriously collectable doll, many with royal connections. Also dolls' houses, teddy bears and rare and unusual toys.

Times Open all year, daily, 10-5 **Fees** £2.50 (ch £1.25, ch under 5 free, concessions £1.95). Party on request* **Facilities** (fully accessible) (ramps provided on request) shop

Nunwell House & Gardens — 2 FOR 1

Coach Ln PO36 0JQ
☎ 01983 407240
dir: Off Ryde-Sandown Rd, A3055, follow brown tourist signs

Set in beautiful gardens, Nunwell is an impressive, lived-in and much loved house where King Charles I spent his last night of freedom. It has fine furniture and interesting collections of family militaria. In summer, concerts are occasionally held in the music room. There are also five acres of gardens with some lovely views.

Times Open 30-31 May, 5 Jul-8 Sep, Mon-Wed 1-5. Tours of House 2 & 3.30* **Fees** £5 (ch under 10 £1, concessions £4.50). Garden £3* **Facilities** (outdoor) toilets for disabled

BRIGHSTONE — Map 4 SZ48

Brighstone Shop and Museum — FREE

North St PO30 4AX
☎ 01983 740689 📠 01983 740689
e-mail: isleofwight@nationaltrust.org.uk
web: www.nationaltrust.org.uk/isleofwight
dir: off B3399 in Brighstone into North Street, next to Post Office

Situated within a row of attractive, thatched cottages you will find this museum which contains an evocative tableau, an interesting exhibition on village life in the 19th century, and the Island's National Trust shop.

Times Open all year, Mon-Sat; 3 Jan-21 Apr 10-1; 22 Apr-27 May & 26 Sep-23 Dec 10-4; 28 May-24 Sep 10-5; 29 May-25 Sep, Sun 12-5 **Facilities** (fully accessible) (hearing loop) shop

CARISBROOKE — Map 4 SZ48

Carisbrooke Castle

Castle Hill PO30 1XY
☎ 01983 522107 📠 01983 528632
web: www.english-heritage.org.uk
dir: 1.25m SW of Newport, off B3401

A royal fortress and prison to King Charles I, Carisbrooke is set on a sweeping ridge at the heart of the Isle of Wight. Don't miss the donkeys that can be seen working a 16th-century wheel to draw water from the well.

Times Open all year, Apr-Sep, daily 10-5; Oct-Mar, daily 10-4. Closed 24-26 Dec & 1 Jan **Fees** £7 (ch £3.50, concessions £6). Family £17.50. Prices and opening times are subject to change in March 2011. Please check web site or call 0870 333 1181 for the most up to date prices and opening times when planning your visit **Facilities** toilets for disabled shop #

FRESHWATER Map 4 SZ38

Dimbola Lodge Museum

Terrace Ln, Freshwater Bay PO40 9QE
☎ 01983 756814 🖷 01983 755578
e-mail: administrator@dimbola.co.uk
web: www.dimbola.co.uk
dir: off A3054, visible from Freshwater Bay

Home of Julia Margaret Cameron, the pioneer Victorian portrait photographer. The house has the largest permanent collection of Cameron prints on display in the UK, as well as galleries exhibiting work by young, up and coming, and acclaimed modern photographers; and a large display of cameras and accessories.

Times Open all year Tue-Sun. Closed 5 days at Xmas. Open BH Mons & daily during school summer hols* **Facilities** licensed (fully accessible) toilets for disabled (chairlifts) shop

MOTTISTONE Map 4 SZ48

Mottistone Manor Garden

PO30 4ED
☎ 01983 741302 🖷 01983 741302
e-mail: isleofwight@nationaltrust.org.uk
web: www.nationaltrust.org.uk/isleofwight
dir: Situated between Brighstone & Brook on B3399

This magical garden is set in a sheltered valley with views to the sea, and surrounds an Elizabethan manor house, which is tenanted. With its colourful borders, shrub-filled banks and grassy terraces, it provides a tranquil and interesting place to visit. There is also a small organic kitchen garden, children's activity packs, a flowerpot trail, and some delightful walks onto the downs across the adjoining Mottistone Estate.

Times Open 13 Mar-27 Oct, Sun-Thu 11-5 (last admission 4.30 or dusk if earlier) **Fees** With voluntary Gift Aid donation: £4.20 (ch £2.10). Family ticket £10.50 **Facilities** (partly accessible) (access to entrance has steps, with loose gravel paths & some slopes & steps in garden) toilets for disabled (hearing loop, large print menu, photo album, 1 w/chair) shop

NEWTOWN Map 4 SZ49

Newtown Old Town Hall

Town Ln PO30 4PA
☎ 01983 531785 🖷 01983 741154
e-mail: isleofwight@nationaltrust.org.uk
web: www.nationaltrust.org.uk/isleofwight
dir: 1m N of A3054 between Yarmouth & Newport

The small, now tranquil, village of Newtown once sent two members to parliament and the Town Hall was the setting for often turbulent elections. This historic building contains exhibits on local history including the exploits of 'Ferguson's Gang', a mysterious group of anonymous benefactors. There are splendid views across unspoilt countryside to the town and footpaths leading to the nearby estuary. Regular art and photographic exhibitions.

Times Open 13 Mar-27 Oct, Sun & Tue-Thu 2-5, Jul & Aug, Sun-Thu 2-5 (last admission 4.45) **Fees** £2.30 (ch £1.15). Family ticket £5.75 **Facilities** (partly accessible) (access restricted to ground floor, 10 steps with handrail to entrance, stairs to upper floors) toilets for disabled (photo album, hearing loops)

OSBORNE HOUSE Map 4 SZ59

Osborne House

PO32 6JY
☎ 01983 200022 🖷 01983 281380
web: www.english-heritage.org.uk
dir: 1m SE of East Cowes

The beloved seaside retreat of Queen Victoria offers a glimpse into the private life of Britain's longest reigning monarch. The royal apartments are full of treasured mementos; and Queen Victoria's role as Empress of India is celebrated in the decoration of the Durbar Room. Visit the gardens and the charming Swiss Cottage.

Times Open all year, Apr-Sep, daily 10-6, house closes at 5; Oct, daily 10-4; 3 Nov-Mar, Wed-Sun 10-4 (pre-booked guided tours, last tour 2.30. Xmas themed tour season Dec-2 Jan). Closed 24-26 Dec & 1 Jan. May close early for special events on occasional days in Jul & Aug **Fees** House & Grounds: £10.90 (ch £5.50, concessions £9.30). Family £27.30. Prices and opening times are subject to change in March 2011. Please check web or call 0870 333 1181 for the most up to date prices and opening times **Facilities** shop #

PORCHFIELD Map 4 SZ49

Colemans Farm Park

Colemans Ln PO30 4LX
☎ 01983 522831
e-mail: chris@colemansfarmpark.co.uk
web: www.colemansfarmpark.co.uk
dir: A3054 Newport to Yarmouth road, follow brown tourist signs

Ideal for young children, this extensive petting farm has hands-on daily activities, tractor-trailer adventure rides and juniors play tower. There is also a straw fun barn with slides and swings, railway garden, a Tractor driving experience for children aged 12 and over and an Old Barn Café for adults who need to relax. Visitors can cuddle, stroke and feed the animals at special times throughout the day. Other special events run all day.

Times Open daily: Barns open all year; petting farm & tractor driving experience Mar-Oct 10-5* **Fees** Play barns & petting farm combined £6.95 (ch £5.95). Single entry to only one activity £4.95. Tractor driving experience £6* **Facilities** (indoor & outdoor) (partly accessible) (90% accessible) toilets for disabled shop

ENGLAND

SANDOWN Map 4 SZ58

Dinosaur Isle

2 FOR 1

Culver Pde PO36 8QA

☎ 01983 404344 📠 01983 407502

e-mail: dinosaur@iow.gov.uk

web: www.dinosaurisle.com

dir: In Sandown follow brown tourist signs to Dinosaur Isle, situated on B3395 on seafront

Britain's first purpose-built dinosaur attraction where, in a building reminiscent of a Pterosaur flying across the Cretaceous skies, you can walk back through fossilised time. In recreated landscape meet life-sized models of the island's five famous dinosaurs - Neovenator, Eotyrannus, Iguandon, Hypsilophodon and Polacanthus. Look out for the flying Pterodactyls and skeletons as they are found, watch volunteers preparing the latest finds or try the many hands-on activities. A guided fossil hunt (which must be pre-booked) has proven a popular addition.

Times Open all year daily, Apr-Sep 10-6; Oct 10-5; Nov-Mar 10-4. Closed 24-26 Dec & 1 Jan. Please phone to confirm opening 5 Jan-6 Feb (last admission 1hr before closing) **Fees** £5 (ch 3-15 £3.25, concessions £4). Family ticket (2ad+2ch) £15* **Facilities** Ⓟ Ⓟ ⛩ (outdoor) ♿ (fully accessible) toilets for disabled (lift for access to 2nd floor) shop ⊗

SHANKLIN Map 4 SZ58

Shanklin Chine

12 Pomona Rd PO37 6PF

☎ 01983 866432 📠 01983 866145

e-mail: jillshanklinchine1@msn.com

web: www.shanklinchine.co.uk

dir: turn off A3055 at lights, left into Hope Rd & continue onto Esplanade for entrance

Part of Britain's national heritage, this scenic gorge at Shanklin is a magical world of unique beauty and a haven for rare plants and wildlife. A path winds through the ravine with overhanging trees, ferns and other flora covering the steep sides. 'The Island - Then and Now' is an exhibition detailing the history of the Isle of Wight, including its military importance in WWII.

Times Open 31 Mar-25 May & 11 Sep-29 Oct, 10-5; 26 May-10 Sep, 10-10* **Facilities** Ⓟ ☕ ♿ (partly accessible) toilets for disabled (access via lower entry only) shop

VENTNOR Map 4 SZ57

Ventnor Botanic Garden

Undercliff Dr PO38 1UL

☎ 01983 855397 📠 01983 856756

e-mail: alison.ellsbury@iow.gov.uk

web: www.botanic.co.uk

dir: on A3055 coastal road, 1.5m W of Ventnor

Due to the unique microclimate of the 'Undercliff', plants that can only survive in a Mediterranean climate thrive on the Isle of Wight. Built on the site of a Victorian hospital for TB sufferers, the garden was founded in 1970 by Sir Harold Hillier, and opened in 1972 by Earl Mountbatten. The garden has plants from Australasia, Africa, America, the Mediterranean, and the Far East, and is a great day out for anyone remotely interested in exotic flora.

Times Gardens: open all year; Visitor Centre & Green House: Mar-Oct, daily 10-5 & Nov-Feb, wknds only 10-4* **Facilities** Ⓟ ☕ ⛩ (outdoor) ♿ (partly accessible) toilets for disabled (lifts in visitor centre, wheelchairs, 2 lifts) shop ⊗

WROXALL Map 4 SZ57

Appuldurcombe House

PO38 3EW

☎ 01983 852484

web: www.english-heritage.org.uk

dir: off B3327, 0.5m W

The shell of Appuldurcombe, once the grandest house on the Isle of Wight, stands in its own grounds, designed by 'Capability' Brown. An exhibition of prints and photographs depicts the house and its history.

Times Open Apr-Sep, daily 10-4, noon Sat (last entry 1hr before closing) **Fees** £3.50 (ch £2.50, concessions £3.25). Family ticket £12. Prices and opening times are subject to change in March 2011. Please check web site or call 0870 333 1181 for the most up to date prices and opening times when planning your visit **Facilities** Ⓟ shop #

YARMOUTH Map 4 SZ38

Yarmouth Castle

Quay St PO4 1OP

☎ 01983 760678

web: www.english-heritage.org.uk

dir: adjacent to car ferry terminal

The last addition to Henry VIII's coastal defences completed in 1547, the Tudor castle is set in a beautiful old seaside town. See the Isle of Wight paintings and memorable photographs of Old Yarmouth.

Times Open Apr-Sep, Sun-Thu 11-4 **Fees** £3.80 (ch £1.90, concessions £3.20). Prices and opening times are subject to change in March 2011. Please check web site or call 0870 333 1181 for the most up to date prices and opening times when planning your visit **Facilities** Ⓟ ♿ (partly accessible) (ground floor only) shop #

WILTSHIRE

The folly at Stourhead gardens

ENGLAND

AVEBURY Map 4 SU06

Alexander Keiller Museum

High St SN8 1RF
☎ 01672 539250 🖹 01672 538038
e-mail: avebury@nationaltrust.org.uk
web: www.nationaltrust.org.uk
dir: 6m W of Marlborough. 1m N of Bath Rd (A4) on A4361 and B4003

Avebury is one of the most important megalithic monuments in Europe, and was built before Stonehenge. The museum, including an exhibition in the 17th-century threshing barn, presents the full archaeological story of the stones using finds from the site, along with interactive and audio-visual displays.

Times Open all year, Apr-Oct, daily 10-6; Nov-Mar, 10-4. Closed 25-26 Dec **Fees** £4.90 (ch £2.45) Family £13.45 (with Gift Aid); £4.20 (ch £2.20) Family £12.20 (without Gift Aid) **Facilities** Ⓟ Ⓟ licensed (fully accessible) toilets for disabled (Braille guide, large print guide, drop off point) shop

Avebury Manor & Garden

SN8 1RF
☎ 01672 539250 🖹 01672 538038
e-mail: avebury@nationaltrust.org.uk
web: www.nationaltrust.org.uk
dir: from A4 take A4361/B4003

Avebury Manor has a monastic origin, and has been much altered since then. The present buildings date from the early 16th century, with notable Queen Anne alterations and Edwardian renovation. The flower gardens contain medieval walls, and there are examples of topiary.

Times House & Garden: Apr-Oct daily 11-5 **Fees** House & Garden £4.90 (ch £2.45) **Facilities** Ⓟ Ⓟ licensed (outdoor) (partly accessible) (ground floor accessible, stairs to rest of house) toilets for disabled (audio visual, Braille/large print guide, induction loop) shop

BRADFORD-ON-AVON Map 3 ST86

Bradford-on-Avon Tithe Barn FREE

web: www.english-heritage.org.uk
dir: 0.25m S of town centre, off B3109

This impressive tithe barn, over 160ft long by 30ft wide, once belonged to Shaftesbury Abbey. The roof is of stone slates, supported outside by buttresses and inside by massive beams and a network of rafters.

Times Open all year, daily 10.30-4. Closed 25 Dec **Facilities** Ⓟ

Great Chalfield Manor and Garden

SN12 8NH
☎ 01225 782239
e-mail: greatchalfieldmanor@nationaltrust.org.uk
web: www.nationaltrust.org.uk
dir: 3m SW of Melksham off B3107 via Broughton Gifford Common

Built during the Wars of the Roses, the manor is a beautiful, mellow, moated house restored from 1905-1912. There is a small 13th-century parish church next to the house.

Times House open Apr-Oct, Tue-Thu, guided tours only at 11, noon, 2, 3, 4. Sun 2-5 tours at 2, 3, 4. Garden open Tue-Thu 11-5, Sun 2-5.* **Facilities** Ⓟ (partly accessible) toilets for disabled (drop off point, wheelchair, Braille guide)

The Peto Garden at Iford Manor 2 FOR 1

Iford Manor BA15 2BA
☎ 01225 863146 🖹 01225 862364
e-mail: ifordmanor@countryside.uk.net
web: www.ifordmanor.co.uk
dir: Brown tourist signs 0.5m S of Bradford-on-Avon on B3109

An award-winning garden in the romantic setting of the Frome Valley. Designed by Harold Peto between 1899 and 1933, this Italian style garden features terraces, statues and ponds. Recitals and operas take place in the garden throughout the summer season as part of the Iford Arts programme. Homemade Housekeeper's teas at weekends (non-garden visitors welcome).

Times Open May-Sep, Tue-Thu, Sat & Sun. Apr & Oct open Sun only 2-5. Closed Mon & Fri except BH Mons. Groups by appointments at other times.* **Fees** £5 (ch under 10 free, concessions £4.50). Groups out of hours £5.50 per person **Facilities** Ⓟ (partly accessible) (please phone in advance for assistance and guidance) toilets for disabled

CALNE Map 3 ST97

Bowood House & Gardens 2 FOR 1

SN11 0LZ
☎ 01249 812102 🖹 01249 821757
e-mail: houseandgardens@bowood.org
web: www.bowood.org
dir: off A4 Chippenham to Calne road, in Derry Hill village

Built in 1624, the house was finished by the first Earl of Shelburne, who employed celebrated architects, notably Robert Adam, to complete the work. Adam's library is particularly admired, and also in the house is the laboratory where Dr Joseph Priestley discovered the existence of oxygen in 1774. The house overlooks terraced gardens towards the 40-acre lake and some beautiful parkland. The gardens were laid out by 'Capability' Brown in the 1760s, and are carpeted with daffodils, narcissi and bluebells in spring. For children between 2 and 12 years there is the superb adventure playground, which boasts a life size pirate galleon and the famous space dive. There is also an indoor soft play palace for younger children.

Times Open daily Apr-Oct 11-6, incl BH. Rhododendron Gardens (separate entrance off A342) open 6 wks during mid Apr-early Jun, 11-6 **Fees** House & Gardens £8.60 (ch 2-4 £4.85; 5-15 £7;

pen £7.60). Family ticket (2ad+2ch) £26.50. Rhododendrons only £5.90 (pen £5.40). £1 discount if house visited on same day* **Facilities** Ⓟ ☕ 🍽 licensed ⛩ (outdoor) ♿ (partly accessible) (restricted access to upper exhibition rooms) toilets for disabled (parking by arrangement, DVD tour of upstairs) shop ⊗

CORSHAM Map 3 ST87

Corsham Court

SN13 0BZ
☎ 01249 701610 📠 01249 701610
e-mail: staterooms@corsham-court.co.uk
web: www.corsham-court.co.uk
dir: 4m W of Chippenham off the A4

The Elizabethan manor was built in 1582, and later bought by the Methuen family in the 18th century to house their collections of paintings and statues. 'Capability' Brown made additions to the house and laid out the park, and later John Nash made further changes. There is furniture by Chippendale, Adam, Cobb and Johnson inside, as well as the Methuen collection of Old Master paintings. The garden has flowering shrubs, herbaceous borders, a Georgian bath house and peacocks.

Times Open: 20 Mar-Sep, daily (ex Mon & Fri), but incl BHs 2-5.30. Oct-19 Mar open wknds only 2-4.30. (last admission 30 minutes before closing). Closed Dec. Open throughout year by appointment for groups 15+* **Facilities** Ⓟ ⛩ (outdoor) ♿ (fully accessible) toilets for disabled (platform lift) shop ⊗

HOLT Map 3 ST86

The Courts Garden

BA14 6RR
☎ 01225 782875 📠 01225 782340
e-mail: courtsgarden@nationaltrust.org.uk
web: www.nationaltrust.org.uk
dir: 3m SW of Melksham, 2.5m E of Bradford on Avon, on south side of B3107 follow signs to Holt

The house is not open, but it makes an attractive backdrop to the gardens - a network of stone paths, yew hedges, pools and borders with a strange, almost magical atmosphere. The peaceful water gardens are planted with irises and lilies.

Times Open 13 Feb-Oct, daily (ex Wed) 11-5.30; out of season by appointment only.* **Facilities** Ⓟ ☕ ♿ (partly accessible) (garden largely flat & accessible) toilets for disabled (wheelchair, ramp access, Braille & large print guide) ⊗ 🌿

LACOCK Map 3 ST96

Lacock Abbey, Fox Talbot Museum & Village

SN15 2LG
☎ 01249 730459 📠 01249 730501
e-mail: lacockabbey@nationaltrust.org.uk
web: www.nationaltrust.org.uk/lacock
dir: 3m S of Chippenham, E of A350, car park signed

Lacock Abbey is the former home of William Henry Fox Talbot, who invented the photographic negative process. The oldest negative in existence is of a photograph of Lacock Abbey. As well as the museum there are newly-restored botanic gardens and greenhouse and a well-preserved country village. The Abbey has also been used as a film location, and can be seen in *Harry Potter, Pride and Prejudice, Cranford, The Other Boleyn Girl* and *Wolfman.*

Times Abbey, Grounds & Museum: 2 Jan-12 Feb & Nov-19 Dec wknds 11-4, 13 Feb-Oct daily 11-5. Access to Abbey on Tue & winter wknds limited to Cloisters only. Closed Good Fri.* **Facilities** Ⓟ ☕ 🍽 licensed ⛩ (outdoor) ♿ (partly accessible) (Cloisters, museum & garden accessible) toilets for disabled (manual wheelchairs, Braille/large print & audio guides) shop ⊗ 🌿

LONGLEAT Map 3 ST84

Longleat

The Estate Office BA12 7NW
☎ 01985 844400 📠 01985 844885
e-mail: enquiries@longleat.co.uk
web: www.longleat.co.uk
dir: turn off A36 Bath-Salisbury road onto A362 Warminster-Frome road

Nestling within magnificent 'Capability' Brown landscaped grounds in the heart of Wiltshire, Longleat House is widely regarded as one of the most beautiful stately homes open to the public. Built by Sir John Thynne and completed in 1580, it has remained the home of the same family ever since. Many treasures are contained within the house: paintings by Tintoretto

continued

ENGLAND

LONGLEAT *continued*

and Wootton, exquisite Flemish tapestries, fine French furniture and elaborate ceilings by John Dibblee Crace. The murals in the family apartments in the West Wing were painted by Alexander Thynne, the present Marquess, and are fascinating and remarkable additions to the collection. Apart from the ancestral home, Longleat is also renowned for its safari park, which was the first of its kind in the UK. Here, visitors have the rare opportunity to see hundreds of animals in natural woodland and parkland settings. Among the most magnificent sights are the famous pride of lions, wolves, tigers and zebra. Other attractions which ensure a fun family day out include the Longleat Hedge Maze, the Adventure Castle, Longleat Railway, Animal Adventure and the Safari Boats.

Times Open 13-21 Feb & 27 Mar-Oct daily, 27 Feb-21 Mar wknds only. Longleat House open daily. Closed 25 Dec. See website for current opening times* **Fees** Longleat passport: £24 (ch 3-14 £17, concessions £19). See website for current prices* **Facilities** licensed (outdoor) (partly accessible) (restricted wheelchair access on train & in house, some park attractions not accessible, steps, narrow cobbled paths) toilets for disabled (lift in house, w/chair hire, info leaflet, ramps) shop

LUDGERSHALL Map 4 SU25

Ludgershall Castle and Cross FREE

SP11 9QR
web: www.english-heritage.org.uk
dir: 7m NW of Andover on A342

Ruins of an early 12th-century royal hunting palace and medieval cross. The visitor can see large earthworks of the Norman motte-and-bailey castle and the flint walls of the later hunting palace. The stump of a medieval cross stands in the village street.

Times Open at any reasonable time **Facilities**

LYDIARD PARK Map 4 SU18

Lydiard Park

Lydiard Tregoze SN5 3PA
☎ 01793 770401 01793 770968
e-mail: lydiardpark@swindon.gov.uk
web: www.lydiardpark.org.uk
dir: M4 junct 16, follow brown tourist signs

Set in country parkland, Lydiard Park belonged to the St John family (the Bolingbrokes) for 500 years up until 1943 when the Swindon Corporation purchased it. Since then the house has been restored and many of the original furnishings returned, together with a family portrait collection dating from Elizabethan to Victorian times. Exceptional plaster work, early wallpaper, a rare painted glass window, and a room devoted to the talented 18th-century artist, Lady Diana Spencer (Beauclerk), can also be seen. The restored 18th-century ornamental fruit and flower walled garden opened in 2007.

Times Open all year, House & walled garden, Tue-Sun & BH Mons 11-5. Nov-Feb closing 4. Park: all year, daily closing at dusk. Times may be subject to change, please call 01793 770401 or check website* **Fees** House £3.50 (ch £1.75 , concessions £3). House & Walled Garden £4.50 (ch £2.25, pen £4). Walled Garden only £1.85 (ch £1, pen £1.50) Entry to grounds is free* **Facilities** (outdoor) (fully accessible) toilets for disabled (audio box in state room) shop

MARLBOROUGH Map 4 SU16

Crofton Beam Engines

Crofton Pumping Station, Crofton SN8 3DW
☎ 01672 870300
e-mail: enquiries@croftonbeamengines.org
web: www.croftonbeamengines.org
dir: signed from A4/A338/A346 & B3087 at Burbage

The oldest working beam engine in the world still in its original building and still doing its original job, the Boulton and Watt 1812, can be found in this rural spot. Its companion is a Harvey's of Hayle of 1845. Both are steam driven, from a hand-stoked, coal-fired boiler, and pump water into the summit level of the Kennet and Avon Canal with a lift of 40ft.

Times Open Etr-Sep daily (ex Wed) 10.30-5 (last entry 4.30). 'In Steam' Etr, BH wknds & last wknd of Jun, Jul & 1st week Oct **Fees** In Steam wknd: £8 (ch £3, pen £7). Family ticket £18. Non-In Steam days £5 (ch £3, pen £4.50). Family ticket £12.50 **Facilities** (outdoor) (partly accessible) (access restricted to ground floor pumphouse) (phone warden in advance, sighted guides provided) shop

MIDDLE WOODFORD Map 4 SU13

Heale Gardens

SP4 6NT
☎ 01722 782504 01722 782504
dir: 4m N of Salisbury, between A360 & A345

Heale House and its eight acres of beautiful garden lie beside the River Avon at Middle Woodford. Much of the house is unchanged since King Charles II sheltered here after the Battle of Worcester in 1651. The garden provides a wonderfully varied collection of plants, shrubs, and musk and other roses, growing in the formal setting of clipped hedges and mellow stonework. Special Event: Snowdrop Sundays in Feb.

Times Open: Gardens daily, plant centre daily 10-5, open BH Mon* **Facilities** (outdoor) (partly accessible) shop

SALISBURY **Map 4 SU12**

The Medieval Hall

Cathedral Close SP1 2EY

☎ 01722 412472 & 324731 📠 01722 339983

e-mail: medieval.hall@ntworld.com

web: www.medieval-hall.co.uk

dir: look for signs within Salisbury Cathedral Close

Visit the historic 13th-century Medieval Hall and watch the fascinating 40 minute sound and picture guide to the city and region. A witty and informative soundtrack, (available in six different languages) specially composed music and some startling effects accompany hundreds of images to provide an insight into Salisbury's extraordinary past, the colourful city of today, and many of the attractions in the area. Enjoy refreshments 'while you watch'. Contact the Hall for full details of special events.

Times Open Apr-Sep, 11-5. Also open throughout year for pre-booked groups. Occasionally closed for special events.* **Facilities** 🅟 Ⓟ ☕ ♿ (ramp access) shop

Mompesson House

The Close SP1 2EL

☎ 01722 335659 & 420980 (info only) 📠 01722 321559

e-mail: mompessonhouse@nationaltrust.org.uk

web: www.nationaltrust.org.uk

dir: on N side of Choristers Green in Cathedral Close, near High St Gate

With its high wrought-iron railings and perfect proportions, this Queen Anne house makes an impressive addition to the elegant Cathedral Close in Salisbury. Inside are stucco ceilings, a carved oak staircase and period furniture plus an important collection of 18th-century glasses, china and some fine paintings.

Times Open 12 Mar-30 Oct, daily (ex Thu & Fri) 11-5. Open Good Fri **Fees** £5.75 (ch £2.90). Group rate £4.70. Garden only £1. Family £14.40 **Facilities** Ⓟ ☕ ♿ (partly accessible) (ground floor & garden accessible) toilets for disabled (ramps, Braille & large print guide) shop 🚭 ✤

Old Sarum

Castle Rd SP1 3SD

☎ 01722 335398 📠 01722 416037

web: www.english-heritage.org.uk

dir: 2m N on A345

The site of the original city of Salisbury. The 56-acre ruins of this once bustling town are rich in history and woodland. Founded in the Iron Age and occupied until the 16th century. Romans, Saxons and Normans have all left their mark.

Times Open Apr-Jun & Sep, daily 10-5; Jul-Aug, daily 9-6; Oct-1 Nov & Mar, daily 10-4; 2 Nov-Jan, daily 11-3; Feb, daily 11-4. Closed 24-26 Dec & 1 Jan.* **Facilities** 🅟 ⛩ ♿ (partly accessible) (Monument has grass slopes, narrow paths, loose gravel surfaces) (assess to outer bailey and grounds only) shop ⌗

Salisbury & South Wiltshire Museum **2 FOR 1**

The King's House, 65 The Close SP1 2EN

☎ 01722 332151 📠 01722 325611

e-mail: museum@salisburymuseum.org.uk

web: www.salisburymuseum.org.com

dir: in Cathedral Close

One of the most outstanding of the beautiful buildings in Cathedral Close houses this local museum. Galleries feature Stonehenge, History of Salisbury, the Pitt Rivers collection, ceramics and pictures and the Wedgwood room, a reconstruction of a pre-NHS surgery, and a costume, lace and embroidery gallery.

Times Open all year Mon-Sat 10-5; also Sun Jul & Aug, 12-5. Closed Xmas* **Fees** Gift Aid charges £6 (ch 5+ £2, concessions & groups £4). Family ticket £12* **Facilities** Ⓟ ☕ ♿ (partly accessible) toilets for disabled (parking, induction loop, wheelchair, interactive computers) shop 🚭

Salisbury Cathedral

33 The Close SP1 2EJ

☎ 01722 555120 📠 01722 555116

e-mail: visitors@salcath.co.uk

web: www.salisburycathedral.org.uk

dir: S of city centre & Market Sq

Discover nearly 800 years of history on a visit to this magnificent 13th-century Gothic Cathedral. Situated in the largest and best preserved Close in Britain, amid historic buildings and ancient stone walls, Salisbury Cathedral is surrounded by eight acres of lawns. Explore the Cathedral with a volunteer guide and discover Britain's tallest spire (123m), finest preserved original Magna Carta (AD 1215) and Europe's oldest working clock (AD 1386). A recent addition is the new font and water sculpture by William Pye that now stands proudly in the centre of the Nave. Experience and enjoy the choral traditions which have existed here for almost eight centuries or relax in the glass-roofed Refectory Restaurant with its stunning views of the spire above.

Times Open all year, Mon-Sat 7.15am-6.15pm, Sun 12.30-2.30 & 4-6.15 **Fees** £5.50 (ch 5-17 & pen £4.50). Family £13 (2ad+3ch) **Facilities** Ⓟ ☕ 🍽 licensed ⛩ (indoor & outdoor) ♿ (partly accessible) toilets for disabled (loop system, interpretative model for blind, wheelchairs) shop

STONEHENGE Map 4 SU14

Stonehenge

SP4 7DE
☎ 0870 333 1181 & 01722 343834 📠 01722 343831
web: www.english-heritage.org.uk
dir: 2m W of Amesbury on junct A303 and A344/A360

Britain's greatest prehistoric monument and a World Heritage Site. What visitors see today are the substantial remains of the last in a series of monuments erected between around 3000 and 1600BC.

Times Open all year, Apr-May & Sep-15 Oct, daily 9.30-6; Jun-Aug, daily 9-7; 16 Oct-15 Mar, daily 9.30-4; 26 Dec & 1 Jan, 10-4. Closed 24-25 Dec. Opening times may vary around Summer Solstice 20-22 Jun & bad weather may restrict access **Fees** £6.90 (ch £3.50, concessions £5.90). Family ticket £17.30. NT members free. Prices and opening times are subject to change in March 2011. Please check web site or call 0870 333 1181 for the most up to date prices and opening times when planning your visit **Facilities** shop

STOURHEAD Map 3 ST73

Stourhead

Stourhead Estate Office BA12 6QD
☎ 01747 841152 📠 01747 842005
e-mail: stourhead@nationaltrust.org.uk
web: www.nationaltrust.org.uk/main/w-stourhead
dir: At Stourton off B3092, 3m NW Mere A303, follow brown tourist signs

An outstanding example of the English landscape style, this splendid garden was designed by Henry Hoare II and laid out between 1741 and 1780. Classical temples, including the Pantheon and Temple of Apollo, are set around the central lake at the end of a series of vistas, which change as the visitor moves around the paths and through the mature woodland with its extensive collection of exotic trees.

Times Garden open all year 9-7 or dusk if earlier. House open 12 Mar-30 Oct, Fri-Tue 11-5. King Alfred's Tower open 12 Mar-30 Oct, Fri-Tue 11-5 **Fees** With voluntary Gift aid donation: Garden & House £13.40 (ch £6.70). Family ticket £31.90, groups £11.50. Garden or House £8.10 (ch £4.40). Family ticket £19.20, groups £7. King Alfred's Tower £3.20 (ch £1.70). Family ticket £7.20, groups £2.70 **Facilities** licensed (outdoor) (partly accessible) (garden - wheelchair accessible in parts, house - access via 13 steps but stairclimber available) toilets for disabled (wheelchairs, electric buggy, Braille, sensory trail) shop

STOURTON Map 3 ST73

Stourton House Flower Garden

Stourton House BA12 6QF
☎ 01747 840417
dir: 3m NW of Mere, on A303

Set in the attractive village of Stourton, the house has more than four acres of beautifully maintained flower gardens. Many grass paths lead through varied and colourful shrubs and trees. Stourton House also specialises in unusual plants and dried flowers, many of which are for sale. It also has collections of daffodils, delphiniums and hydrangeas, along with a nature garden where visitors can sit and watch the birds, butterflies and other wildlife.

Times Open last 2 Sun Feb & Apr-end Nov, Wed, Thu, Sun & BH Mon 11-6 or dusk if earlier. Also open Dec-Mar, wkdays for plant/dried flower sales* **Facilities** (partly accessible) toilets for disabled (wheelchairs available) shop

SWINDON Map 4 SU18

STEAM - Museum of the Great Western Railway

Kemble Dr SN2 2TA
☎ 01793 466646 📠 01793 466615
e-mail: steampostbox@swindon.gov.uk
web: www.swindon.gov.uk/steam
dir: from M4 junct 16 & A420 follow brown signs to 'Outlet Centre' & Museum

This fascinating day out tells the story of the men and women who built, operated and travelled on the Great Western Railway. Hands-on displays, world-famous locomotives, archive film footage and the testimonies of ex-railway workers bring the story to life. A reconstructed station platform, posters and holiday memorabilia recreate the glamour and excitement of the golden age of steam. Good value group packages, special events, exhibitions and shop.

Times Open daily 10-5. Closed 25-26 Dec & 1 Jan **Fees** £6.40 (ch 3-16 yrs & pen £4.25). Family ticket (2ad+2ch) £17 (2ad+3ch) £20.20* **Facilities** (fully accessible) toilets for disabled (wheelchair/scooter can be pre-booked, induction loop) shop

ENGLAND

Swindon & Cricklade Railway

Blunsdon Station, Tadpole Ln, Blunsdon SN25 2DA
☎ 01793 771615
e-mail: randallchri@yahoo.co.uk
web: www.swindon-cricklade-railway.org
dir: M4 junct 15, take A419, follow signs to Blunsdon Stadium, pass stadium & continue for 2.5m, follow brown signs

Heritage railway in the process of being restored. Steam and diesel locomotives, historic carriages, wagons and a large variety of railway structures from a past era. Last extension to the line opened in June 2010. 2011 marks the 50th Anniversary of the closure of the Midland & South Western Junction Railway.

Times Open 6 Feb-20 Dec, Sat-Sun. Also open BHs (often special events) & Wed in local school hols **Fees** £6 (ch £4). Family £18. Different prices apply for some special events **Facilities** Ⓟ ☕ (outdoor) ♿ (fully accessible) toilets for disabled shop

TEFFONT MAGNA Map 3 ST93

Farmer Giles Farmstead

2 FOR 1

SP3 5QY
☎ 01722 716338
e-mail: farmergiles@farmergiles.co.uk
web: www.farmergiles.co.uk
dir: 11m W of Stonehenge, off A303 to Teffont. Follow brown signs

Forty acres of Wiltshire downland with farm animals to feed, ponds, inside and outside play areas, exhibitions, tractor rides, restaurant and gift shop. Working farm with hands-on rare breed animal feeding, cuddling and grooming. Pony rides, tractor rides, vast indoor and outdoor play areas and exhibitions.

Times Open mid Mar-mid Nov, daily 10-6 (last entry 4), wknds in winters & school hols, 10-dusk. Party bookings all year. Closed 25 & 26 Dec **Fees** £5.95 (ch £4.95, under 2's free & pen £5.50) Family ticket £20 **Facilities** Ⓟ Ⓟ 🍽 licensed (indoor & outdoor) ♿ (fully accessible) toilets for disabled (wheelchairs available) shop

TISBURY Map 3 ST92

Old Wardour Castle

SP3 6RR
☎ 01747 870487
web: www.english-heritage.org.uk
dir: 2m SW

This 14th-century castle stands in a romantic lakeside setting. Landscaped grounds and elaborate rockwork grotto surround the unusual hexagonal ruins. Scenes from *Robin Hood, Price of Thieves*, starring Kevin Costner were filmed here.

Times Open all year, Apr-Jun & Sep, daily 10-5; Jul-Aug, daily 10-6; Oct, daily 10-4; Nov-Mar, Sat-Sun 10-4. Closed 24-26 Dec & 1 Jan **Fees** £3.80 (ch £1.90, concessions £3.20). Prices and opening times are subject to change in March 2011. Please check web site or call 0870 333 1181 for the most up to date prices and opening times when planning your visit **Facilities** Ⓟ ♿ (partly accessible) (some steps, beware of covered well in centre of castle) toilets for disabled #

TOLLARD ROYAL Map 3 ST91

Larmer Tree Gardens

SP5 5PT
☎ 01725 516228 📠 01725 516321
e-mail: larmertree@rushmoreuk.com
web: www.larmertreegardens.co.uk
dir: off A354 Blandford to Salisbury road, follow brown signs with flower

Created by General Pitt Rivers in 1880 as a pleasure ground for 'public enlightenment and entertainment' the gardens are an extraordinary example of Victorian extravagance and vision. The garden contains a wonderful collection of ornate buildings, majestic trees and intimate arbours, retained in an enchanted and tranquil atmosphere. Contact or see website for details of special events.

Times Open Etr-Jun, Sun-Thu 11-4.30* **Fees** £3.75 (ch over 5's £2.50, concessions/groups 15+ £3). Family £12.50* **Facilities** Ⓟ ☕ ♿ (partly accessible) (hard standing path) toilets for disabled shop 🚫

ENGLAND

WESTBURY Map 3 ST85

Brokerswood Country Park **2 FOR 1**

Brokerswood BA13 4EH
☎ 01373 822238 01373 858474
e-mail: info@brokerswood.co.uk
web: www.brokerswoodcountrypark.co.uk
dir: off A36 at Bell Inn, Standerwick. Follow brown signs from A350

Brokerswood Country Park's nature walk leads through 80 acres of woodlands, with a lake and wildfowl. There are two adventure playgrounds, an undercover play area for younger children and the woodland railway; over a third of a mile long operating Easter to October. See website for programme of special events.

Times Open all year; park open daily 10-5. Closed 24-26 Dec & 1 Jan* **Fees** £3.50 (ch 3-16 & concessions £2.50)* **Facilities** (outdoor) (partly accessible) (ramp access to cafe) toilets for disabled shop

WESTWOOD Map 3 ST85

Westwood Manor **2 FOR 1**

BA15 2AF
☎ 01225 863374 01225 867316
e-mail: westwoodmanor@nationaltrust.org.uk
web: www.nationaltrust.org.uk
dir: 1.5m SW of Bradford on Avon, off B3109

This late 15th-century stone manor house was altered in the early 17th century and has late Gothic and Jacobean windows and fine plasterwork. There is a modern topiary garden.

Times Open 4 Apr-29 Sep, Tue, Wed & Sun, 2-5* **Fees** £5.80 (ch £2.90). Family ticket (2ad+3ch) £14.80* **Facilities** (partly accessible) (stairs & steps) (drop off point, Braille & large print guide)

WILTON (NEAR SALISBURY) Map 4 SU03

Wilton House

SP2 0BJ
☎ 01722 746720 & 746729 01722 744447
e-mail: tourism@wiltonhouse.com
web: www.wiltonhouse.com
dir: 3m W of Salisbury, on A30, 10m from Stonehenge & A303

This fabulous Palladian mansion amazes visitors with its treasures, including magnificent art, fine furniture and interiors by Inigo Jones. The traditional and modern gardens, some designed by the 17th Earl, are fabulous throughout the season and continue to delight visitors, whilst the adventure playground is a firm favourite with children.

Times Open House: 10-13 Apr, 2 May-Aug generally closed each Fri & Sat, open BHs Sat 2 May-23 May. The House will not be open on Sat 29 Aug, noon-5 (last admission 4.15). Grounds: 4-19 Apr, 2 May-Aug, daily & wknds in Sep, 11-5.30 (last admission 4.30). For further details see website* **Fees** House and Grounds: £12 (ch 5-15 £6.50, concessions £9.75) Family ticket (2ad+2ch 5-15) £29.50. Grounds, including Adventure Playground £5 (ch 5-15 £3.50, concessions £4.50). Family ticket (2ad+2ch 5-15) £15. For further details see website* **Facilities** licensed (outdoor) (fully accessible) toilets for disabled (induction loop) shop

WOODHENGE Map 4 SU14

Woodhenge **FREE**

web: www.english-heritage.org.uk
dir: 1.5m N of Amesbury, off A345 just S of Durrington

A Neolithic ceremonial monument dating from about 2300 BC, consisting of six concentric rings of timber posts, now marked by concrete piles. The long axis of the rings, which are oval, points to the rising sun on Midsummer Day.

Times Open any reasonable time. Usual facilities may not apply around Summer Solstice 20-22 Jun, please check before visit **Facilities**

WORCESTERSHIRE

Path to North Hill in the Malvern Hills

ENGLAND

BEWDLEY — Map 7 SO77

West Midland Safari & Leisure Park

Spring Grove DY12 1LF
☎ 01299 402114 📠 01299 404519
e-mail: info@wmsp.co.uk
web: www.wmsp.co.uk
dir: on A456 between Kidderminster & Bewdley

Located in the heart of rural Worcestershire, this 200-acre site is the home to a drive-through safari and an amazing range of exotic animals. Animal attractions include Leopard Valley, Twilight Cave, Creepy Crawlies, the Reptile House, Sealion Theatre, and Seaquarium exhibit. There are also a variety of rides, amusements and live shows suitable for all members of the family.

Times Open daily mid Feb-early Nov. Times may change. Seasonal wknd opening early Nov-mid Feb. Check website for up to date opening times and information **Fees** £12.95 (ch 3-15yrs £11.50, ch under 3 free, concessions £11.50). Amusement rides extra* **Facilities** Ⓟ ☕ 🍽 licensed ⛩ (outdoor) ♿ (fully accessible) shop 🚫

See advert on opposite page

BROADWAY — Map 4 SP03

Broadway Tower

WR12 7LB
☎ 01386 852390 📠 01386 858038
e-mail: info@broadwaytower.co.uk
web: www.broadwaytower.co.uk
dir: off A44, 1m SE of village

The 65ft tower was designed by James Wyatt for the 6th Earl of Coventry, and built in 1799. The unique building now houses exhibitions depicting its colourful past and various uses such as holiday retreat to artist and designer William Morris. The viewing platform is equipped with a telescope, giving wonderful views over 13 counties.

Times Open Apr-Oct, daily 10.30-5; Nov-Mar (tower only) wknds weather permitting 11-3 or by prior booking.* **Facilities** Ⓟ ☕ 🍽 licensed ⛩ toilets for disabled shop

BROMSGROVE — Map 7 SO97

Avoncroft Museum of Historic Buildings

Stoke Heath B60 4JR
☎ 01527 831886 & 831363 📠 01527 876934
e-mail: admin@avoncroft.org.uk
web: www.avoncroft.org.uk
dir: 2m S, off A38

A visit to Avoncroft takes you through nearly 700 years of history. Here you can see 25 buildings rescued from destruction and authentically restored on a 15 acre rural site. There are 15th and 16th-century timber framed buildings, 18th-century agricultural buildings and a cockpit. There are industrial buildings and a working windmill from the 19th century, and from the 20th a fully furnished pre-fab.

Times Open all year, Apr-Oct, Tue-Sun 10.30-5, daily Jul-Aug; Nov-Dec & Mar, Fri-Sun 10.30-4.30; open BH Mon, 24-26 Dec* **Facilities** Ⓟ ☕ ⛩ (outdoor) ♿ (partly accessible) (some building interiors may not be fully accessible) toilets for disabled (ramps, wheelchairs available) shop

EVESHAM — Map 4 SP04

The Almonry Heritage Centre

Abbey Gate WR11 4BG
☎ 01386 446944 📠 01386 442348
e-mail: tic@almonry.ndo.co.uk
web: www.almonryevesham.org
dir: on A4184, opposite Merstow Green, main N/S route through Evesham

The 14th-century stone and timber building was the home of the Almoner of the Benedictine Abbey in Evesham. It now houses exhibitions relating to the history of Evesham Abbey, the Battle of Evesham, and the culture and trade of Evesham. Evesham Tourist Information Centre is also located here.

Times Open all year, Mon-Sat & BHs, 10-5, Sun 2-5. Closed Xmas & Sun in Nov-Feb **Fees** £3 (ch under 11 free, concessions £2). Group rates on application **Facilities** Ⓟ ♿ (partly accessible) (only garden accessible) (large print room guide) shop 🚫

GREAT WITLEY — Map 3 SO76

Witley Court

WR6 6JT
☎ 01299 896636
web: www.english-heritage.org.uk
dir: on A433

Discover the spectacular ruins of this once-great house destroyed by fire in 1937. Explore the magnificent landscaped gardens which feature the stunning Perseus and Andromeda fountains and contemporary sculpture, and step back in time with the audio tour.

Times Open all year, Apr-Jun & Sep-Oct, daily 10-5; Jul-Aug, daily 10-6; Nov-Feb, Wed-Sun 10-4; Mar, Wed-Sun 10-5. Closed 24-26 Dec & 1 Jan **Fees** £6 (ch £3, concessions £5.10). Family ticket £15. Prices and opening times are subject to change in March 2011. Please check web site or call 0870 333 1181 for the most up to date prices and opening times when planning your visit **Facilities** Ⓟ ☕ ♿ (partly accessible) (some steps) toilets for disabled (audio tour, hearing loop) shop ⊗ #

HANBURY Map 3 SO96

Hanbury Hall

School Rd WR9 7EA
☎ 01527 821214 📠 01527 821251
e-mail: hanburyhall@nationaltrust.org.uk
web: www.nationaltrust.org.uk/main/w-hanburyhall
dir: 4.5m E of Droitwich, 1m N of B4090 and 1.5m W of B4091

This William and Mary style red-brick house, completed in 1701, was built by a prosperous local family. The house contains outstanding painted ceilings and staircase by Thornhill, and the Watney collection of porcelain. The 18th-century garden has recently been restored with many features including parterre, bowling green and working orangery. 395 acres of beautiful park allow you to enjoy lovely views across the Worcestershire countryside. 2011 sees the centenary celebration of Sir Harry and Lady Georgina's Golden Wedding Anniversary on 17th October 1911. There will be a garden party recreating the one held 100 years ago.

Times House & gardens open 6-21 Feb, Sat-Sun 11.30-3.30 (downstairs only tours); 27 Feb-Oct, Sat-Wed 11-5; 26 Jun-26 Aug, Sat-Thu 11-5; 6 Nov-19 Dec, Sat-Sun 11.30-3.30 (downstairs only tours). Garden & Grounds, open 2 Jan-21 Feb, Sat-Sun 11-4; 27 Feb-Oct, daily 11-5; 6 Nov-26 Dec, Sat-Sun 11-4; 26-31 Dec open daily 11-4* **Fees** House & Garden £8 (ch £4). Family ticket £20. Garden & grounds £5.40 (ch £2.70). Family ticket £13.50* **Facilities** Ⓟ ☕ 𝌆 (outdoor) ♿ (partly accessible) (gardens and ground floor of house are accessible) toilets for disabled (Braille guide, 2 wheelchairs, shuttle from car park) shop ⊗ ✿

KIDDERMINSTER Map 7 SO87

Bodenham Arboretum

Wolverley DY11 5SY
☎ 01562 852444 & 850456 📠 01562 852777
web: www.bodenham-arboretum.co.uk
dir: follow brown signs from Wolverley Church island along the B4189

An award-winning arboretum, with over 3000 species of trees and shrubs, attractively landscaped in 156 acres. The arboretum is incorporated into a working farm. Five miles of paths lead through dells, glades around lakes and pools.

Times Open 23 Feb-23 Dec, Wed-Sun, 11-5. Oct & Dec daily. Also open Jan-Feb half-term, wknds only* **Fees** £5.50 (ch £2.50)* **Facilities** Ⓟ ☕ 🍴 licensed 𝌆 (outdoor) ♿ (partly accessible) toilets for disabled shop

ENGLAND

KIDDERMINSTER *continued*

Severn Valley Railway

Comberton Hill DY10 1QN
☎ 01299 403816 🖹 01299 400839
web: www.svr.co.uk
dir: on A448, clearly signed

The leading standard gauge steam railway, with one of the largest collections of locomotives and rolling stock in the country. Services operate from Kidderminster and Bewdley to Bridgnorth through 16 miles of picturesque scenery along the River Severn. Special steam galas take place during the year along with Santa Specials and many other events.

Times Trains operate wknds throughout the year, daily early May-end of Sep, school hols & half terms, Santa Specials phone for details **Fees** Subject to review. Train fares vary according to journey. Main through ticket £15.50 return. Family ticket £42. Prices include entrance to Engine House at Highley **Facilities** licensed (outdoor) (partly accessible) toilets for disabled (some specially adapted trains, call for details) shop

See advert on opposite page

Worcestershire County Museum 2 FOR 1

Hartlebury Castle, Hartlebury DY11 7XZ
☎ 01299 250416 🖹 01299 251890
e-mail: museum@worcestershire.gov.uk
web: www.worcestershire.gov.uk/museum
dir: 4m S of Kidderminster clearly signed from A449

Housed in the north wing of Hartlebury Castle, the County Museum explores the wonders of Worcestershire and life through the ages. There are unique collections of toys and costume, displays on domestic life, period room settings and horse-drawn vehicles. Visitors can also see a reconstructed forge, a schoolroom, scullery and nursery. Family events at least one weekend each month. Children's craft activities Tue-Fri in school holidays. Phone for details of special events.

Worcestershire County Museum

Times Open 4 Jan-23 Dec, Tue-Fri 10-5; Sat, Sun & BHs 11-5. Closed Good Fri **Fees** £4.50 (ch & concessions £2.25). Family ticket (2ad+2ch) £12 **Facilities** (outdoor) (fully accessible) toilets for disabled (car parking spaces, close to building, lift, hearing loops) shop

REDDITCH Map 4 SP06

Forge Mill Needle Museum & Bordesley Abbey Visitor Centre 2 FOR 1

Forge Mill, Needle Mill Ln, Riverside B98 8HY
☎ 01527 62509
e-mail: museum@redditchbc.gov.uk
web: www.forgemill.org.uk
dir: N side of Redditch, off A441

The Needle Museum tells the fascinating and sometimes gruesome story of how needles are made. Working, water-powered machinery can be seen in an original needle-scouring mill. The Visitor Centre is an archaeological museum showing finds from excavations at the nearby Bordesley Abbey. Children can become an archaeologist for the day and explore the ruins of this fascinating ancient monument. Regularly changing temporary exhibits.

Times Open all year, Etr-Sep, Mon-Fri 11-4.30, Sat-Sun 11-4; Oct-Nov, Tue-Fri 11-4 & Sat-Sun 1-4* **Fees** £4.15 (ch £1.10, pen £3, Reddicard concessions). Family ticket £8.50. Free admission Wed for Redditch residents* **Facilities** (outdoor) (partly accessible) toilets for disabled (wheelchair, museum audio tour, Braille guide, hearing loop) shop

SEVERN STOKE Map 3 SO84

Croome Park **2 FOR 1**

Near High Green WR8 9DW
☎ 01905 371006 📠 01905 371090
e-mail: croomepark@nationaltrust.org.uk
web: www.nationaltrust.org.uk/main/w-croomepark
dir: 8m S of Worcester signed off A38 and B4084

Discover the beauty and space of Croome. Enjoy 18th-century pleasure gardens, 'Capability' Brown's first complete landscape design and see what life was like for the families living at Croome. There is a full programme of special events to enjoy throughout the year. Contact the Park for details.

Times Open all year, Mar-Apr & 3 Sep-26 Oct, Wed-Sun 10-5.30; 31 Mar-Aug, daily 10-5.30 Wed-Sun 10-5.30; Nov-21 Dec & 3 Jan, Sat & Sun 10-4; 26 Dec-1 Jan, daily 10-4* **Fees** £5 (ch £2.50). Family ticket £12.60. Please refer to website for current prices* **Facilities** licensed (outdoor) (partly accessible) (Croome Court only accessible to wheelchair users via stairclimber) toilets for disabled (w/chair, Braille & large print guides, induction loops) shop

SPETCHLEY Map 3 SO85

Spetchley Park Gardens

Spetchley Park WR5 1RS
☎ 01453 810303 📠 01453 511915
e-mail: hb@spetchleygardens.co.uk
web: www.spetchleygardens.co.uk
dir: 2m E of Worcester on A44

The 110-acre deer park and the 30-acre gardens surround an early 19th-century mansion (not open), with sweeping lawns and herbaceous borders, a rose lawn and enclosed gardens with low box and yew hedges. There is a large collection of trees (including 17th-century Cedars of Lebanon), shrubs and plants, many of which are rare or unusual. Various events through the year, check website for details.

Times Open 21 Mar-Sep, Wed-Sun 11-6. BH Mon, 11-6. Oct, Sat & Sun only 11-4 **Fees** £6 (ch free, concessions £5.50). Party 25+ £5* **Facilities** (partly accessible) (Gravel paths and grass are prevalent throughout the gardens. Wet weather would make the grass difficult for disabled access) toilets for disabled shop

STONE Map 7 SO87

Stone House Cottage Gardens

DY10 4BG
☎ 01562 69902
e-mail: louisa@shcn.co.uk
web: www.shcn.co.uk
dir: 2m SE of Kidderminster, on A448

A beautiful walled garden with towers provides a sheltered area of about one acre for rare shrubs, climbers and interesting herbaceous plants. Adjacent to the garden is a nursery with a large selection of unusual plants.

Times Open mid Mar-mid Sep, Wed-Sat, 10-5.* **Facilities** (partly accessible)

WICHENFORD Map 3 SO76

Wichenford Dovecote

☎ 01527 821214
web: www.nationaltrust.org.uk/main/w-wichenforddovecote
dir: N of B4204

17th-century half-timbered black-and-white dovecote, in a picturesque riverside location.

Times Open 26 Feb-Oct, 9-6 or sunset **Fees** £1 **Facilities** (fully accessible)

WORCESTER Map 3 SO85

City Museum & Art Gallery **FREE**

Foregate St WR1 1DT
☎ 01905 25371 📠 01905 616979
e-mail: gallerymuseum@worcestershire.gov.uk
web: www.worcestercitymuseums.org.uk
dir: in city centre, 150mtrs from Foregate St Train Station

The gallery has temporary art exhibitions from both local and national sources. Museum exhibits cover geology, local and natural history. There are collections relating to the Worcestershire Regiment and the Worcestershire Yeomanry Cavalry.

Times Open all year, Tue-Sat 10.30-4.30, Sat 9.30-5. Closed Sun, 25-26 Dec, 1 Jan & Good Fri, Easter Mon and Whitsun BH Mon* **Facilities** (fully accessible) toilets for disabled (lift, induction loop) shop

ENGLAND

WORCESTER *continued*

The Elgar Birthplace Museum **2 FOR 1**

Crown East Ln, Lower Broadheath WR2 6RH
☎ 01905 333224 📠 01905 333426
e-mail: birthplace@elgarmuseum.org
web: www.elgarmuseum.org
dir: 3m W of Worcester, signed off A44 to Leominster

In 2000, the Elgar Centre was opened, to complement the historic Birthplace Cottage and to provide additional exhibition space for more treasures from this unique collection, telling the story of Elgar's musical development and inspirations. Listen to his music as the audio tour guides you round the easily accessible displays.

Times Open Feb-23 Dec, daily 11-5 (last admission 4.15). Closed Xmas-end Jan* **Fees** £7 (ch £3, pen £6, concessions £4)* **Facilities** (outdoor) (partly accessible) (Elgar centre fully accessible, Birthplace Cottage has steps & narrow stairs/doorways) toilets for disabled (large print guides, audio facilities, wheelchair) shop

The Greyfriars

Friar St WR1 2LZ
☎ 01905 23571 📠 01905 739049
e-mail: greyfriars@nationaltrust.org.uk
web: www.nationaltrust.org.uk
dir: in city centre, use public car park on Friar St

Built in 1480, this is a beautiful timber framed merchant's house in the city centre, rescued from demolition and carefully restored. The panelled interior contains interesting textiles and furnishings. An archway leads through to a pleasant walled garden.

Times Open 4 Mar-12 Jun, Wed-Sat; Jul-Aug, Wed-Sun 1-5 **Fees** £4.40 (ch £2.20). Family £11.* **Facilities** (partly accessible) (ground floor is accessible)

Hawford Dovecote

WR3 7SG
☎ 01527 821214 📠 01527 821251
e-mail: hanburyhall@nationaltrust.org
web: www.nationaltrust.org.uk/main/w-hawforddovecote
dir: 3m N of Worcester, 0.5m E of A449

An unusual square, half-timbered 16th-century dovecote. Access on foot only via the entrance drive to the adjoining house.

Times Open 26 Feb-Oct, daily 9-6 or sunset **Fees** £1 **Facilities** (fully accessible)

Worcester Cathedral

WR1 2LH
☎ 01905 28854 & 21004 📠 01905 611139
e-mail: info@worcestercathedral.org.uk
web: www.worcestercathedral.co.uk
dir: city centre, signed from M5 junct 7

Worcester Cathedral is one of England's loveliest cathedrals, with Royal Tombs, medieval cloisters, an ancient crypt and Chapter House and magnificent Victorian stained glass. The tower is open in the summer. There are a number of different celebrations each year, including the Heart of England Food Fair and many concerts.

Times Open all year, daily 7.30-6.* **Facilities** (partly accessible) toilets for disabled (access from College Green) shop

Worcester Porcelain Museum **2 FOR 1**

Severn St WR1 2ND
☎ 01905 21247 📠 01905 617807
e-mail: info.admin@worcesterporcelainmuseum.org
web: www.worcesterporcelainmuseum.org
dir: M5 junct 7, follow signs to city centre, at 7th set of lights take 1st left into Edger St & bear left with road into Severn St. At T-junct bear right & after 700yds take 1st left. Museum on left

Worcester Porcelain Museum is situated amidst the city's Historic Quarter within two minutes walk, the Cathedral, Commandery, Birmingham Canal and River Severn. An informative and entertaining audio tour featuring Henry Sandon and skilled craftsmen is free with entry and tells the story of the factory's history, its famous customers, the talented workforce and everyday life. Gallery displays from 1751 to the 20th century include Oriental simplicity and Victorian extravaganza and offer a glimpse of times past, taking the visitor on a memorable journey from 1751 to the present day.

Times Open all year, Etr-Oct, Mon-Sat 10-5; Nov-Etr, Tue-Sat, 10-4. Closed Sun & BHs **Fees** Museum £6 (concessions £5) **Facilities** (fully accessible) toilets for disabled shop

EAST RIDING OF YORKSHIRE

The lighthouse, Flamborough Head

BEMPTON Map 8 TA17

RSPB Nature Reserve

YO15 1JD
☎ 01262 851179 Fax 01262 851533
e-mail: bempton.cliffs@rspb.org.uk
web: www.rspb.org.uk
dir: take cliff road from B1229, Bempton Village and follow brown tourist signs

Part of the spectacular chalk cliffs that stretch from Flamborough Head to Speeton. This is one of the best sites in England to see thousands of nesting seabirds including gannets and puffins at close quarters. Viewpoints overlook the cliffs, which are best visited from March to September. Over 2 miles of chalk cliffs rising to 400ft with numerous cracks and ledges. Enormous numbers of seabirds nest on these cliffs including guillemots, razorbills, kittiwakes, fulmars and herring gulls. This is the only gannetry in England and is growing annually. Many migrants pass off-shore including terns, skuas and shearwaters. Wheatears, ring ouzels and a wide variety of warblers frequent the cliff top on migration. Grey seal and porpoise are sometimes seen offshore.

Times Visitor centre open all year, Mar-Oct, daily 10-5. Nov-Feb 10-4 **Fees** £3.50 per car for non RSPB **Facilities** Ⓟ ☕ ⛩ (outdoor) ♿ (partly accessible) (some paths not easily accessible for people with limited mobility or wheelchairs) toilets for disabled shop

BEVERLEY Map 8 TA03

The Guildhall

Register Sq HU17 9AU
☎ 01482 392783 Fax 01482 392779
e-mail: fiona.jenkinson@eastriding.gov.uk
web: www.eastriding.gov.uk/museums
dir: in Register Sq, next to post office

A Guildhall has been on this site since 1500, although parts of the building date back to a private dwelling of 1320. The Guildhall has been the home of civic governance in Beverley for over 500 years. The building was re-modelled in the 18th and 19th centuries and features a stunning courtroom with ornate plasterwork by Giuseppe Cortese, a Magistrates Room with original 17th-century furniture and an elegant parlour with a silver collection dating back over several centuries.

Times Open every Fri, 10-4. Please phone for guided tours at other times **Fees** Free on Fri. Charge for guided tours at other times **Facilities** ♿ (partly accessible) (ground floor only accessible) (disabled parking 100yds) ⊗

BURTON AGNES Map 8 TA16

Burton Agnes Hall

Estate Office YO25 0ND
☎ 01262 490324 Fax 01262 490513
e-mail: office@burtonagnes.com
web: www.burtonagnes.com
dir: on A614 between Driffield & Bridlington

Built in 1598, this exquisite Elizabethan house is filled with furniture, pictures and china amassed by one family over four centuries. Lawns with topiary bushes surround the Hall and an award-winning walled garden contains a maze, potager, giant games, jungle garden and more than 4,000 plant species, including campanula and geranium collections. There is a woodland walk, children's playground and picnic area. The Red Bus Gallery presents works by local artists in a London RouteMaster bus.

Times Open Hall & Gardens Apr-Oct, daily 11-5. Xmas opening 14 Nov-22 Dec **Fees** Hall & gardens: £7 (ch 5-15 £3.50, pen £6.50). Gardens only: £4 (ch 5-15 £2.50, pen £3.50)* **Facilities** Ⓟ ☕ ⛩ (outdoor) ♿ (partly accessible) (ground floor of hall, garden, woodland areas, courtyard cafe & shop all accessible) toilets for disabled (scented garden for the blind, wheelchair available) shop

Burton Agnes Manor House FREE

web: www.english-heritage.org.uk
dir: in Burton Agnes, 5m SW of Bridlington on A166

A rare and well-preserved example of a Norman house. Some interesting Norman architectural features can still be seen, but the building was encased in brick during the 17th and 18th centuries. The house is near Burton Agnes Hall and the gardens are privately owned and not managed by English Heritage.

Times Open Apr-Oct, daily 11-5 **Facilities** ⌗

GOOLE Map 8 SE72

The Yorkshire Waterways Museum

Dutch River Side DN14 5TB
☎ 01405 768730 01405 769868
e-mail: info@waterwaysmuseum.org.uk
web: www.waterwaysmuseum.org.uk
dir: M62 junct 36, enter Goole, turn right at next 3 sets of lights onto Dutch River Side. 0.75m and follow brown signs

Discover the story of the Aire & Calder Navigation and the growth of the 'company town' of Goole and its busy port. Find out how to sail and, in the interactive gallery, see how wooden boats were built. Enjoy the unique 'Tom Pudding' story, brought to life through the vessels on the canal and the boat hoist in South Dock. Rediscover the Humber keels and sloops, and Goole's shipbuilding history through the objects, photos and memories of Goole people.

Times Open all year Mon-Fri 9-4, Sat-Sun 10-4. Closed Xmas & New Year **Fees** Free entry to museum. Boat trip £4 (ch under 12 £3) **Facilities** (outdoor) (fully accessible) toilets for disabled (disabled access on boats, nature trail, wheelchair) shop

HORNSEA Map 8 TA14

Hornsea Museum

11 Newbegin HU18 1AB
☎ 01964 533443
web: www.hornseamuseum.com
dir: turn off A165 onto B1244

A former farmhouse whose outbuildings now illustrate local life and history. There are 19th-century period rooms and a dairy, plus craft tools and farming implements. Photographs, local personalities and industries are also featured along with a large display of Hornsea pottery.

Times Open Etr-Sep & Oct half-term hols, Tue-Sat 11-5, Sun 2-5 (last admission 4). Also open BH Mon.* **Facilities** (outdoor) (partly accessible) (two thirds of museum accessible) toilets for disabled (audio interpretation for blind/partially sighted) shop

KINGSTON UPON HULL Map 8 TA02

'Streetlife' - Hull Museum of Transport FREE

High St HU1 1PS
☎ 01482 613902 01482 613710
e-mail: museums@hullcc.gov.uk
web: www.hullcc.gov.uk
dir: A63 from M62, follow signs for Old Town

This purpose built museum uses a 'hands-on' approach to trace 200 years of transport history. With a vehicle collection of national importance, state-of-the-art animatronic displays and authentic scenarios, you can see Hull's Old Town brought vividly to life. The mail coach ride uses the very latest in computer technology to recreate a Victorian journey by four-in-hand.

Times Open all year, Mon-Sat 10-5, Sun 1.30-4.30. Closed 24-25 Dec & Good Fri* **Facilities** (fully accessible) toilets for disabled shop

The Deep

Tower St HU1 4DP
☎ 01482 381000 01482 381018
e-mail: info@thedeep.co.uk
web: www.thedeep.co.uk
dir: follow signs from city centre

The Deep is a conservation and educational charity which runs one of the deepest and most spectacular aquariums in the world. It is a unique blend of stunning marine life, and the latest interactive and audio-visual presentations, which together tell the dramatic story of the world's oceans. Highlights include over 3,500 fish with spectacular sharks and rays, Europe's deepest viewing tunnel and a glass lift ride through a 10m deep tank. Includes 3D movie. The Deep has an annual programme of events all available online.

Times Open all year, daily 10-6. Closed 24-25 Dec (last entry 5) **Fees** £9.50 (ch under 16 £7.50). Family ticket (2ad+2ch) £30, (2ad+3ch) £36. Please check website for up to date admission prices* **Facilities** licensed (indoor & outdoor) (fully accessible) toilets for disabled (signing for the deaf if booked in advance) shop

Maister House FREE

160 High St HU1 1NL
☎ 01482 324114 01482 227003
web: www.nationaltrust.org.uk
dir: Hull city centre

The house is a mid-18th-century rebuilding, notable for its splendid stone and wrought-iron staircase, ornate stucco work and finely carved doors. Only the staircase and entrance hall are open as the house is now let as offices.

Times Open all year, Mon-Fri 10-4. Closed BH* **Facilities** (partly accessible)

KINGSTON UPON HULL *continued*

Maritime Museum FREE

Queen Victoria Square HU1 3DX
☎ 01482 613902 📠 01482 613710
e-mail: museums@hullcc.gov.uk
web: www.hullcc.gov.uk
dir: A63 to town centre, museum is within pedestrian area

Hull's maritime history is illustrated here, with displays on whales and whaling, ships and shipping, and other aspects of this Humber port. This collection has been designated as being of national significance.

Times Open all year, Mon-Sat 10-5 & Sun 1.30-4.30. Closed 25 Dec-2 Jan & Good Fri **Facilities** Ⓟ ♿ (partly accessible) (main entrance is stepped, level access is through side door) (lift to both floors) shop ⊗

Wilberforce House FREE

23-25 High St HU1 1NE
☎ 01482 613902 📠 01482 613710
e-mail: museums@hullcc.gov.uk
web: www.hullcc.gov.uk
dir: A63 from M62 or A1079 from York, follow signs for Old Town

The early 17th-century Merchant's house was the birthplace of William Wilberforce, who became a leading campaigner against slavery. Re-opened in 2007 after full refurbishment the House tells the story of slavery, abolition, the triangular trade and explores modern issues surrounding slavery.

Times Open all year, Mon-Sat 10-5 & Sun 1.30-4.30. Closed 25-26 Dec, 1 Jan & Good Fri.* **Facilities** Ⓟ 卄 (outdoor) ♿ (fully accessible) (large print, video area & audio guides) shop ⊗

POCKLINGTON Map 8 SE84

Burnby Hall Garden & Stewart Museum 2 FOR 1

33 The Balk YO42 2QF
☎ 01759 307125 & 307541 📠 01377 288359
e-mail: brian@brianpetrie.plus.com
web: www.burnbyhallgardens.com
dir: off A1079 at turning for Pocklington off B1247, follow brown tourist signs

The two lakes in this garden have an outstanding collection of 80 varieties of hardy water lilies, designated a National Collection. The lakes stand within nine acres of beautiful gardens including heather beds, a rock garden, a spring and summer bedding area, woodland walk and Victorian garden. The museum contains sporting trophies and ethnic material gathered on Major Stewart's world-wide travels. The Stewart Museum has been completely refurbished. There are band concerts every other Sunday and various events through the season.

Times Open end Mar-mid Oct, daily 10-6 (last admission 5) **Fees** £4.30 (ch 5-15 £2.30, pen £3.60). Party 20+ £3.35 each* **Facilities** 🅟 Ⓟ ☕ 卄 (outdoor) ♿ (fully accessible) toilets for disabled (free wheelchair hire, viewing platform for wheelchairs) shop ⊗

SEWERBY Map 8 TA16

Sewerby Hall & Gardens

Church Ln YO15 1EA
☎ 01262 673769 📠 01262 673090
e-mail: sewerby.hall@eastriding.gov.uk
web: www.sewerby-hall.co.uk
dir: 2m NE of Bridlington on B1255 towards Flamborough

Sewerby Hall and Gardens, set in 50 acres of parkland overlooking Bridlington Bay, dates back to 1715. The Georgian house, with its 19th-century Orangery, contains art galleries, archaeological displays and an Amy Johnson Room with a collection of her trophies and mementoes. The grounds include magnificent walled Old English and Rose gardens and host many events throughout the year. Activities for all the family include a Children's Zoo and play areas, golf, putting, bowls, plus woodland and clifftop walks. Phone for details of special events.

Times Estate open all year, dawn-dusk. Hall open Etr-end Oct. Please contact for further details* **Fees** £4.30 (ch £2.30, pen £3.50) Family ticket (2ad & 3ch) £13* **Facilities** 🅟 Ⓟ ☕ 卄 (outdoor) ♿ (fully accessible) toilets for disabled (ramp, lift to 1st floor) shop

SPROATLEY Map 8 TA13

Burton Constable Hall 2 FOR 1

HU11 4LN
☎ 01964 562400 📠 01964 563229
e-mail: helendewson@btconnect.com
web: www.burtonconstable.com
dir: Follow signs for A165 Bridlington Road towards Sirlaugh, then right towards Hornsea and follow brown historic house signs to Burton Constable

This superb Elizabethan house was built in 1570, but much of the interior was remodelled in the 18th century. There are magnificent reception rooms and a Tudor long gallery with a pendant roof: the contents range from pictures and furniture to a unique collection of 18th-century scientific instruments. Outside are 200 acres of parkland landscaped by 'Capability' Brown, with oaks and chestnuts, and a lake with an island. Various events through the season include a classic car rally in June and a country fair in July.

Times Open, Hall & Grounds Etr Sat-end Oct. Grounds 12.30-5, Hall 1-5 (last admission 4). Closed Fri* **Fees** House £6 (ch £3, pen £5.50). Family ticket £14.50. Grounds only £2.50 (ch £1.25). Family ticket £6.25* **Facilities** 🅟 ☕ 卄 (indoor & outdoor) ♿ (partly accessible) (3 bedrooms not accessible) toilets for disabled (stair lift to first foor, wheelchairs) shop ⊗

NORTH YORKSHIRE

Steam train leaving Goathland, North Yorkshire Moors Railway

ALDBOROUGH Map 8 SE46

Aldborough Roman Site

YO5 9ES

☎ 01423 322768

web: www.english-heritage.org.uk

dir: 0.75m SE of Boroughbridge, on minor road off B6265 within 1m of junct of A1 & A6055

View two spectacular mosaic pavements and discover the remains of the Roman town, the 'capital' of the Romanized Brigantes, the largest tribe in Britain.

Times Open Apr-Sep, Sat-Sun & BH 11-5 **Fees** £3.20 (ch £1.60, concessions £2.70). Prices and opening times are subject to change in March 2011. Please check web site or call 0870 333 1181 for the most up to date prices and opening times when planning your visit **Facilities** picnic shop #

AYSGARTH Map 7 SE08

National Park Centre

DL8 3TH

☎ 01969 662910 fax 01969 662919

e-mail: aysgarth@ytbtic.co.uk

web: www.yorkshiredales.org.uk

dir: off A684, Leyburn to Hawes road at Falls junct, Palmer Flatt Hotel & continue down hill over river, centre 500yds on left

A visitor centre for the Yorkshire Dales National Park, with maps, guides, walks and local information. Interactive displays explain the history and natural history of the area. Plan the day ahead with a light lunch in the coffee shop. Various guided walks begin here throughout the year.

Times Open Apr-Oct, daily 10-5; Winter open Fri-Sun, 10-4* **Fees** Parking: £2.20 2hrs, £3.20 all day* **Facilities** P Ⓟ café picnic (outdoor) ♿ (fully accessible) toilets for disabled (viewing platform at Falls) shop no dogs

BEDALE Map 8 SE28

Bedale Museum

DL8 1AA

☎ 01677 423797

dir: on A684, 1.5m W of A1 at Leeming Bar. Opposite church, at N end of town

Situated in a building dating back to the 17th century, the Bedale is a fascinating museum. The central attraction is the Bedale fire engine, which dates back to 1742. Other artefacts include documents, toys, craft tools and household utensils, which all help to give an absorbing picture of the lifestyle of the times. There is also a large local genealogy archive.

Times Open Apr-Sep, Mon 2-4, Tue 10-12.30 & 2-4, Wed & Fri 2-4.30* **Facilities** P Ⓟ ♿ (partly accessible) (not suitable for blind or partially sighted without an attendant) toilets for disabled shop no dogs

BENINGBROUGH Map 8 SE55

Beningbrough Hall & Gardens

YO30 1DD

☎ 01904 472027

e-mail: beningbrough@nationaltrust.org.uk

web: www.nationaltrust.org.uk/beningbrough

dir: off A19, 8m NW of York

Beningbrough Hall is a Georgian mansion built in 1716 housing over a hundred 18th-century portraits on loan from the National Portrait Gallery in London, including seven interpretation galleries 'Making Faces: Eighteenth Century Style'. A working walled garden supplies the Walled Garden Restaurant. There is a wilderness play area and equipped Victorian laundry and giftshop.

Times Open Sun-Thu & Good Fri, 12-5. Grounds 11-5.30 (3.30 in winter). Galleries winter wknds Nov-Feb, 11-3.30, Feb half term also open Mon-Wed* **Fees** Summer £8.40 (ch £4.20) Winter £5.50 (ch £2.60)* **Facilities** P restaurant licensed picnic (outdoor) ♿ (partly accessible) (all floors of Georgian mansion & 7 interpretation galleries accessible) toilets for disabled (lift) shop no dogs National Trust

BRIMHAM Map 8 SE26

Brimham Rocks

Summerbridge HG3 4DW

☎ 01423 780688

e-mail: brimhamrocks@nationaltrust.org.uk

web: www.nationaltrust.org.uk

dir: 10m NW of Harrogate, off B6265

The rocks stand on National Trust open moorland at a height of 987ft, enjoying spectacular views over the surrounding countryside. The area is filled with strange and fascinating rock formations and is rich in wildlife. Brimham House is now a visitor centre.

Times Open daily until dusk.* **Facilities** P café picnic (outdoor) ♿ (partly accessible) toilets for disabled (adapted path steep in places, Braille/large print guide) shop National Trust

CASTLE BOLTON Map 7 SE09

Bolton Castle **2 FOR 1**

DL8 4ET

☎ 01969 623981 fax 01969 623332

e-mail: harry@boltoncastle.co.uk

web: www.boltoncastle.co.uk

dir: off A684, 6m W of Leyburn

Medieval castle completed in 1399, located in the heart of Wensleydale with stunning views over the Yorkshire Dales. Stronghold of the Scrope family. Mary, Queen of Scots was imprisoned here for six months during 1568 and 1569. The castle was besieged and taken by Parliamentary forces in 1645. Tapestries, tableaux, arms and armour can be seen. Children can dress in period costume before exploring the castle, visit the nursery where they can play with toys and games, enjoy exciting family trails or visit the medieval gardens and maze. There is a full programme of special events. The 2 for 1 voucher admits one child free with each full paying adult.

Times Open end Mar-Oct, Tue-Sun 10-5; BH & school hols (ex 2 Aug). Castle will close at 1.30 on specific dates in Jun-Oct, see website* **Fees** £6.50 (ch 5-18 & concessions £5). Family ticket (2ad+3ch) £20. Groups 15+ £5.50 (concessions £4). Garden only £1* **Facilities** (outdoor) (partly accessible) (stairs in castle) shop

CASTLE HOWARD

See Malton

COXWOLD — Map 8 SE57

Byland Abbey

YO6 4BD

☎ 01347 868614 01347 868204

web: www.english-heritage.org.uk

dir: 2m S of A170 between Thirsk & Helmsley, near Coxwold village

A hauntingly beautiful monastic ruin set in peaceful meadows in the shadow of the Hambleton Hills. Marvel at the collection of medieval floor tiles still in their original setting.

Times Open Apr-Jun, Wed-Mon, 11-6; Jul-Aug, daily 11-6; Sep, Wed-Mon 11-5 **Fees** £4.20 (ch £2.10, concessions £3.60). Prices and opening times are subject to change in March 2011. Please check web site or call 0870 333 1181 for the most up to date prices and opening times when planning your visit **Facilities** (partly accessible) (grass areas may be marshy in wet weather, museum one step) toilets for disabled (ramp, carved stonework to touch in museum)

DANBY — Map 8 NZ70

The Moors National Park Centre

Lodge Ln YO21 2NB

☎ 01439 772737 01287 660308

e-mail: moorscentre@ytbtic.co.uk

web: www.northyorkmoors.org.uk

dir: turn S off A171, follow Moors Centre Danby signs . Left at crossroads in Danby and then 2m, Centre at bend on right

The ideal place to start exploring the North York Moors National Park. There is an exhibition about the area as well continuous exhibition of arts. Also events, video and local walks. The Moorsbus service also operates from this site - phone for details.

Times Open all year, Apr-Oct, daily 10-5; Nov, Dec & Mar daily & Jan-Feb wknds only, 11-4. Closed 24-26 Dec. Please phone to confirm before visit* **Fees** Free admission £2.20 car parking fee (parking charge under review) **Facilities** (outdoor) (fully accessible) toilets for disabled (garden trails, wheelchairs, Braille maps, hearing loops) shop

EASBY — Map 8 NZ10

Easby Abbey — FREE

web: www.english-heritage.org.uk

dir: 1m SE of Richmond off B6271

Set beside the River Swale, this Premonstratensian Abbey was founded in 1155 and dedicated to St Agatha. Extensive remains of the monks' domestic buildings can be seen.

Times Open all year, Apr-Sep, daily 10-6; Oct, daily 10-5; Nov-Mar, daily 10-4. Closed 24-26 Dec & 1 Jan **Facilities**

ELVINGTON — Map 8 SE74

Yorkshire Air Museum & Allied Air Forces Memorial

Halifax Way YO41 4AU

☎ 01904 608595 01904 608246

e-mail: museum@yorkshireairmuseum.co.uk

web: www.yorkshireairmuseum.co.uk

dir: from York take A1079 then immediate right onto B1228, museum is signed on right

This award-winning museum and memorial is based around the largest authentic former WWII Bomber Command Station open to the public. There is a restored tower, an Air Gunners museum, Archives, an Airborne Forces display, Squadron Memorial Rooms, and much more. Among the exhibits are replicas of the pioneering Cayley Glider and Wright Flyer, along with the Halifax

continued

ELVINGTON *continued*

Bomber and modern jets like the Harrier GR3, Tornado GR1 and GR4. An exhibition 'Against The Odds' tells the story of the R.A.F Bomber Command; whilst the history of aviation and its pioneering Yorkshire connections can be explored in the Pioneers Of Aviation display. Please check website for special events.

Yorkshire Air Museum & Allied Forces Memorial

Times Open all year, daily 10-5 (summer); 10-3.30 (winter). Closed 25-26 Dec **Fees** £7 (ch £4 & pen £5). Family (2ad+3ch) £18 **Facilities** Ⓟ ☕ 🍽 licensed ⛩ (outdoor) ♿ (fully accessible) toilets for disabled shop

See advert on page 339

FAIRBURN Map 8 SE42

RSPB Nature Reserve Fairburn Ings

The Visitor Centre, Newton Ln WF10 2BH
☎ 01977 628191
e-mail: fairburn.ings@rspb.org.uk
web: www.rspb.org.uk/fairburnings
dir: W of A1, N of Ferrybridge. Signed from Allerton Bywater off A656. Signed Fairburn Village off A1

One-third of the 700-acre RSPB reserve is open water, and over 270 species of birds have been recorded. A visitor centre provides information, and there is an elevated boardwalk, suitable for disabled visitors.

Times Access to the reserve via car park, open 9-dusk. Centre & car park open daily 9-5. Closed 25-26 Dec* **Facilities** Ⓟ ⛩ (outdoor) ♿ (partly accessible) (immediate boardwalk & visitor centre accessible, trails not accessible to wheelchairs) toilets for disabled shop

GRASSINGTON Map 7 SE06

National Park Centre — FREE

Hebden Rd BD23 5LB
☎ 01756 751690 📠 01756 751699
e-mail: grassington@yorkshiredales.org.uk
web: www.yorkshiredales.org.uk
dir: situated on B6265 in the main Grassington car park

The centre is a useful introduction to the Yorkshire Dales National Park. Maps, guides and local information are available. There is also a 24-hr public access information service and a full tourist information service. The centre has recently been refurbished with the emphasis on agriculture and climate change. A video display explains this.

Times Open all year, Apr-Oct daily 10-5; Nov-Mar Fri & Sat-Sun 10-4 (also daily in school hols). Closed Jan 2011 **Facilities** Ⓟ ⛩ ♿ (fully accessible) toilets for disabled shop

GUISBOROUGH Map 8 NZ61

Gisborough Priory — 2 FOR 1

TS14 6HG
☎ 01287 633801 📠 01287 633801
web: www.english-heritage.org.uk
dir: next to parish church

The Priory was founded in 1119 by Robert the Bruce for the Augustianian order. The gatehouse is the only part of the original building left standing, thanks partly to a fire in 1289 and the destruction wrought during the Dissolution in 1540. The Chaloner family bought the site in 1550, and still own it today. In the early 18th century, formal gardens were established and although some changes have been made since, the garden remains largely the same.

Times Open Jun-Sep, Tue-Sun 9-5; Oct-May, Wed-Sun 9-5 **Fees** £1.80 (ch & concessions 90p) **Facilities** Ⓟ ⛩ (outdoor) ♿ (fully accessible) #

HARROGATE Map 8 SE35

RHS Garden Harlow Carr

Crag Ln, Otley Rd HG3 1QB
☎ 01423 565418 📠 01423 530663
e-mail: harlowcarr@rhs.org.uk
web: www.rhs.org.uk/harlowcarr
dir: off B6162 Otley Rd, 1.5m from Harrogate centre

One of Yorkshire's most relaxing and surprising gardens at the gateway to the Yorkshire Dales. Wander through tranquil surroundings and find inspiration in the innovative and dramatic Rose Revolution and Main Borders. Stroll along the Streamside Garden and explore 'Gardens through Time'; savour the Scented Garden, and take practical ideas from the extensive Kitchen Garden. Year round events for all the family - sculpture, outdoor theatre, guided walks, quiz trails, workshops and free demonstrations.

Times Open all year, daily 9.30-6, Nov-Mar 9.30-4 (last admission 1hr before closing). Closed 25 Dec.* **Fees** £7 (ch under 6 free, ch 6-16 £2.50).* **Facilities** licensed (outdoor) (partly accessible) (some paths with steep gradients - unsuitable for wheelchair users) toilets for disabled (electric and push wheelchairs available, scented garden) shop

The Royal Pump Room Museum

Crown Place HG1 2RY

☎ 01423 556188 01423 556130

e-mail: museums@harrogate.gov.uk

web: www.harrogate.gov.uk/museums

dir: A61 into town centre and follow brown heritage signs

Housed in the pump room, the museum tells the glory of Harrogate's Spa heyday. Also see our stunning Egyptian collection and temporary exhibitions of social history.

Times Open all year, Mon-Sat 10-5, Sun 2-5, Aug open 12-5; 4pm Nov-Mar. Closed 24-27 Dec, 1 Jan, 4-6 Jan* **Facilities** (fully accessible) toilets for disabled shop

HAWES — Map 7 SD88

Dales Countryside Museum & National Park Centre — 2 FOR 1

Station Yard DL8 3NT

☎ 01969 666210

e-mail: hawes@yorkshiredales.org.uk

web: www.yorkshiredales.org.uk

dir: off A684 in Old Station Yard at the east end of Hawes, look for brown signs

Fascinating museum telling the story of the people and landscape of the Yorkshire Dales. Static steam loco and carriages with displays. Added features include hands-on interactive displays for children, Research Room, temporary exhibitions and special events. Free family exhibition every summer with activities for visitors of all ages.

Times Open all year daily 10-5. Closed 24-26 Dec & 1 Jan. Please phone for winter opening hours* **Fees** Museum: £3 (ch free, concessions £2.50). National park centre, temporary exhibitions free* **Facilities** (outdoor) (fully accessible) toilets for disabled (lifts, ramps and parking) shop

HELMSLEY — Map 8 SE68

Duncombe Park

YO62 5EB

☎ 01439 778625 01439 771114

e-mail: liz@duncombepark.com

web: www.duncombepark.com

dir: located within North York Moors National Park, off A170 Thirsk-Scarborough road, 1m from Helmsley market place

Duncombe Park stands at the heart of a spectacular 30-acre early 18th-century landscape garden which is set in 300 acres of dramatic parkland around the River Rye. The house, originally built in 1713, was gutted by fire in 1879 and rebuilt in 1895. Its principal rooms are a fine example of the type of grand interior popular at the turn of the century. Home of the Duncombes for 300 years, for much of this century the house was a girls' school. In 1985 the present Lord and Lady Feversham decided to make it a family home again and after major restoration, opened the house to the public in 1990. Part of the garden and parkland were designated a 250-acre National Nature Reserve in 1994. Special events include a Country Fair (May), an Antiques Fair (June), Steam Fair (July), Antiques Fair (November). Please telephone for details.

Times Open 12 Apr-25 Oct, Sun-Thu; Gardens, Parkland Centre tea room & shop & Parkland walks 11-5.30. House by guided tour only every hour from 12.30-3.30. Closed 10, 11 & 15 Jun* **Facilities** licensed (outdoor) (partly accessible) (garden limited due to steps) toilets for disabled (portable ramp, lift, wheelchair for loan) shop

Helmsley Castle

Castlegate YO6 5AB

☎ 01439 770442 01439 771814

web: www.english-heritage.org.uk

An atmospheric ruin with formidable double earthworks. Also, an exhibition of the history of the castle.

Times Open all year, Mar, Thu-Mon 10-5; Apr-Sep, daily 10-6; Oct, daily 10-5; Nov-Feb, Thu-Mon 10-4. Closed 24-26 Dec & 1 Jan **Fees** £4.70 (ch £2.40, concessions £4). Family ticket £11.80. Prices and opening times are subject to change in March 2011. Please check web site or call 0870 333 1181 for the most up to date prices and opening times when planning your visit **Facilities** (partly accessible) (virtual tour, ramp) shop #

KIRBY MISPERTON — Map 8 SE77

Flamingo Land Theme Park & Zoo

The Rectory YO17 6UX

☎ 01653 668287 01653 668280

e-mail: info@flamingoland.co.uk

web: www.flamingoland.co.uk

dir: turn off A64 onto A169, Pickering to Whitby road

Set in 375 acres of North Yorkshire countryside with over 100 rides and attractions there's something for everyone at Flamingo Land. Enjoy the thrills and spills of 12 white knuckle rides or enjoy a stroll through the extensive zoo where you'll find tigers, giraffes, hippos and rhinos. The theme park also boasts 6 great family shows.

Times Open daily, 30 Mar-28 Oct.* **Facilities** licensed (outdoor) (partly accessible) (some rides by their nature may be inapproriate for use by persons with certain disabilities) toilets for disabled (parking, wheelchair hire) shop

KIRKHAM Map 8 SE76

Kirkham Priory

Whitwell-on-the-Hill YO6 7JS
☎ 01653 618768
web: www.english-heritage.org.uk
dir: 5m SW of Malton on minor road off A64

Discover the ruins of this Augustinian priory, which includes a magnificent carved gatehouse, set in a peaceful and secluded valley by the River Derwent.

Times Open Apr-Jul & Sep, Thu-Mon 10-5; Aug, daily 10-5 **Fees** £3.20 (ch £1.60, concessions £2.70). Prices and opening times are subject to change in March 2011. Please check web site or call 0870 333 1181 for the most up to date prices and opening times when planning your visit **Facilities** Ⓟ ♿ (partly accessible) (steep steps cloister to refectory) #

KNARESBOROUGH Map 8 SE35

Knaresborough Castle & Museum

Castle Yard HG5 8AS
☎ 01423 556188 📠 01423 556130
e-mail: museums@harrogate.gov.uk
web: www.harrogate.gov.uk/museums
dir: off High St towards Market Square, right at police station into Castle Yard

Towering high above the town of Knaresborough, the remains of this 14th-century castle look down over the gorge of the River Nidd. This imposing fortress was once the hiding place of Thomas Becket's murderers and a summer home for the Black Princes. Visit the King's Tower, the secret underground tunnel and the dungeon. Discover Knaresborough's history in the museum and find out about 'Life in a Castle' in our hands-on gallery. Play our computer game "Time Gate: The Prisoner of Knaresborough Castle". Special events include a Medieval Day annually on the third Sunday in June.

Times Open Good Fri-4 Oct, daily 10.30-5. Guided tours regularly available* **Facilities** Ⓟ Ⓟ ♿ (partly accessible) (ground floor of King's Tower accessible) toilets for disabled shop ⊗

MALHAM Map 7 SD96

Malham National Park Centre FREE

BD23 4DA
☎ 01729 833200 📠 01729 833209
e-mail: malham@yorkshiredales.org.uk
web: www.yorkshiredales.org.uk
dir: off A65 at Gargrave opposite petrol station. Malham 7m

The Yorkshire Dales National Park centre has maps, guides and local information together with displays on the remarkable natural history of the area and work of conservation bodies.

Times Open, Apr-Oct, daily 10-5; Winter, Sat-Sun, 10-4. Daily in school hols. Closed Jan **Facilities** Ⓟ ⛩ (outdoor) ♿ (fully accessible) toilets for disabled (radar key scheme for toilet) shop

MALTON Map 8 SE77

Castle Howard

YO60 7DA
☎ 01653 648333 📠 01653 648529
e-mail: house@castlehoward.co.uk
web: www.castlehoward.co.uk
dir: off A64, follow brown heritage signs

A magnificent 18th-century house situated in breathtaking parkland. House guides share the history of the house, family and collections, while outdoor guided tours reveal the secrets of the gardens and architecture. Visitors can also enjoy a changing programme of exhibitions and events; boat trips, adventure playground and various cafes and shops including a farm shop and a chocolate shop. New exhibition "Brideshead Restored" - telling the story of restoration of Castle Howard and the filming of *Brideshead Revisited*.

Times House: 12 Mar-30 Oct, 26 Nov-18 Dec from 11. Gardens, Shops & Cafés open all year from 10 **Fees** £10.50 (ch £6.50, concessions £9.50). Grounds only £8 (ch £5.50, concessions £7.50). Please check updated admission prices on website* **Facilities** Ⓟ ☕ 🍽 licensed ♿ (partly accessible) toilets for disabled (wheelchair lift, free adapted transport to house) shop ⊗

Eden Camp Modern History Theme Museum 2 FOR 1

Eden Camp YO17 6RT
☎ 01653 697777 📠 01653 698243
e-mail: admin@edencamp.co.uk
web: www.edencamp.co.uk
dir: junct of A64 & A169, between York & Scarborough

Housed within the unique setting of an original prisoner of war camp built in 1942 to house Italian and German POW's, this regional and national award-winning museum presents the most comprehensive display of British civilian life during WWII. The period is brought to life through life size tableau and diorama which incorporate sound, light and even smell effects to create the atmosphere of the 1940s. Other sections of the museum cover military and political events of WWII and British military history of the 20th century from WWI to the war in Iraq and

Afghanistan. The museum also houses an extensive collection of military vehicles, artillery and associated equipment. Special Events: WWII re-enactment weekend; Reunion of Escapers and Evaders (April); All Services Commemorative Day and Parade (September); Palestine Veterans Reunion Day (October).

Times Open 2nd Mon in Jan-23 Dec, daily 10-5 (last admission 4) **Fees** £5.50 (ch & concessions £4.50). Party 10+, £1 discount on individual admission prices **Facilities** (indoor & outdoor) (fully accessible) toilets for disabled (taped tours, Braille guides, free loan w/chairs) shop

Malton Museum

Old Town Hall, Market Place YO17 7LP
☎ 01653 695136
web: www.maltonmuseum.co.uk
dir: leave A64, follow signs for Malton town centre

The extensive Roman settlements in the area are represented and illustrated in this museum, including collections from the Roman fort of Derventio. There are also displays of local prehistoric and medieval finds plus changing exhibitions of local interest.

Times Open all year, Mon-Sat 9.30-4* **Facilities** (fully accessible) (stair lift) shop

MASHAM Map 8 SE28

Theakston Brewery & Visitor Centre

The Brewery HG4 4YD
☎ 01765 680000 01765 684330
e-mail: bookings@theakstons.co.uk
web: www.theakstons.co.uk
dir: On A6108, in town centre. Parking for Brewery visitors is in market place. Follow pedestrian signs. Approx 2 min walk

First established in 1827, T&R Theakston Ltd is home of the legendary Old Peculier Ale. Experience the wonderful aromas of hops and malt, used every day to brew their famous beers, as has been done for generations, and sample their legendary ales in the Brewery Tap - The Black Bull in Paradise. There is plenty to do and see including the Cooper's shop where the cooper crafts the wooden barrels - one of the last remaining working cooperages in the country.

Times Open all year from 10.30, closing times vary according to time of year. Closed 24-26 Dec & 1-2 Jan* **Fees** £4.75 (ch £2.50, students £4.50 & concessions £4). Family £12.50 (2ad+2ch). Please check for current prices* **Facilities** (partly accessible) (access to gift shop and brewery tap) toilets for disabled shop

MIDDLEHAM Map 7 SE18

Middleham Castle

Castle Hill DL8 4RJ
☎ 01969 623899
web: www.english-heritage.org.uk
dir: 2m S of Leyburn on A6108

Explore the maze of rooms and passageways at this impressive castle, once the boyhood home of the ill-fated Richard III. Oak viewing gallery of the magnificent views of the 12th-century keep and exhibition.

Times Open all year, Apr-Sep, daily 10-6; Oct-Mar, Sat-Wed 10-4. Closed 24-26 Dec & 1 Jan. **Fees** £4.20 (ch £2.10, concessions £3.60). Prices and opening times are subject to change in March 2011. Please check web site or call 0870 333 1181 for the most up to date prices and opening times when planning your visit **Facilities** (partly accessible) (steep spiral staircase to top of keep) shop

MIDDLESBROUGH Map 8 NZ42

Captain Cook Birthplace Museum FREE

Stewart Park, Marton TS7 8AT
☎ 01642 311211 01642 515659
e-mail: captcookmuseum@middlesbrough.gov.uk
web: www.captcook-ne.co.uk
dir: 3m S on A172

Opened to mark the 250th anniversary of the birth of the voyager in 1728, this museum illustrates the early life of James Cook and his discoveries with permanent and temporary exhibitions. Located in spacious and rolling parkland, the site also offers outside attractions for the visitor. The museum has a special resource centre which has fresh approaches to presentation with computers, films, special effects, interactives and educational aids.

Times Open all year: Mar-Oct, Tue-Sun 10-5.30; Nov-Feb 9-4 (last entry 45 mins before closing). Closed Mon & some BH, 24-26 Dec, 1 Jan & 1st full wk Jan* **Facilities** licensed (outdoor) (fully accessible) toilets for disabled (lift to all floors, car parking, wheelchair) shop

ENGLAND

NEWBY HALL & GARDENS Map 8 SE36

Newby Hall & Gardens

HG4 5AE
☎ 01423 322583 01423 324452
e-mail: info@newbyhall.com
web: www.newbyhall.com
dir: 4m SE of Ripon & 2m W of A1M, off B6265, between Boroughbridge and Ripon

One of Britain's finest Adam houses with Chippendale furniture, Gobelins tapestries and classical statuary, Newby Hall boasts 25 acres of award winning gardens including one of Europe's largest double herbaceous borders. With an enchanting woodland walk and a delightful contemporary sculpture park, younger visitors will also enjoy the miniature railway and exciting adventure gardens.

Times Open Apr-25 Sep, Tue-Sun & BHs, also Mon in Jul & Aug; Gardens 11-5.30; House 12-5 (last admission 5 gardens, 4.30 house) **Fees** House & gardens £12 (ch/disabled £9.50, pen £11). Family (2ad+2ch) £40. Gardens only £8.50 (ch/disabled £7, pen £7.50). Family (2ad+2ch) £30. Please check website for updates* **Facilities** licensed (outdoor) (fully accessible) toilets for disabled (wheelchairs & batricars available) shop

NORTH STAINLEY Map 8 SE27

Lightwater Valley Theme Park

HG4 3HT
☎ 0871 720 0011 0871 721 0011
e-mail: leisure@lightwatervalley.co.uk
web: www.lightwatervalley.co.uk
dir: 3m N of Ripon on A6108

Set in 175 acres of North Yorkshire parkland, Lightwater Valley Theme park, and its Birds of Prey Centre, is renowned for its friendly and welcoming atmosphere. In the Birds of Prey Centre, visitors have the opportunity to see how these amazing birds are trained and handled; as well as being treated to dramatic flying shows at 2pm and 4pm every day. The theme park line-up includes Europe's longest rollercoaster - The Ultimate, as well as the stomach-churning mighty Eagle's Claw and the "splashtastic" Wild River rapids. Step aboard the new terrifying Whirlwind or risk a one-on-one encounter in Raptor Attack's abandoned mineshaft.

Times Selected dates from Apr-Oct. Please check the website for current opening times* **Fees** £19.45 over 1.3mtrs, £16.95 under 1.3mtrs, free under 1m (concessions £10.95). Family (2ad+2ch or 1ad+3ch under 16) £66. Please check website for current prices* **Facilities** licensed (outdoor) (partly accessible) (some rides may be unsuitable, even pathways) toilets for disabled shop

NUNNINGTON Map 8 SE67

Nunnington Hall

YO62 5UY
☎ 01439 748283 01439 748284
e-mail: nunningtonhall@nationaltrust.org.uk
web: www.nationaltrust.org.uk
dir: 4.5m SE of Helmsley

This large 16th to 17th-century house has panelled rooms and a magnificent staircase. The Carlisle collection of miniature rooms is on display. Changing programme of temporary exhibitions.

Times Open 15 Mar-2 Nov, Tue-Sun 12-5; Jun-Aug, Tue-Sun 12-5.30* **Facilities** (outdoor) (partly accessible) toilets for disabled (wheelchairs, Braille guide, scented garden) shop

ORMESBY Map 8 NZ51

Ormesby Hall

2 FOR 1

TS7 9AS
☎ 01642 324188 01642 300937
e-mail: ormesbyhall@nationaltrust.org.uk
web: www.nationaltrust.org.uk
dir: 3m SE of Middlesborough, W of A19 take the A174 to the A172 . Follow signs for Ormesby Hall. Car entrance on Ladgate Lane B1380

An 18th-century mansion, Ormesby Hall has stables attributed to John Carr of York. Plasterwork, furniture and 18th-century pictures are on view. Exhibiting a large model railway.

Times Open 12 Mar-30 Oct Sat, Sun & BHs 1.30-5 **Fees** £5.50 (ch £3.50 under 5's free) Family (2ad+3ch) £14.50 **Facilities** (outdoor) (partly accessible) (wheelchair access ground floor & gardens only) toilets for disabled (parking, Braille guide, special tours, sensory list)

OSMOTHERLEY Map 8 SE49

Mount Grace Priory

DL6 3JG
☎ 01609 883494 01609 883361
web: www.english-heritage.org.uk
dir: 1m NW

The best preserved Carthusian monastery in the country, set in breathtakingly beautiful woodland surroundings and gardens, including fully reconstructed monks cells and herb garden, illustrating the solitary life of the monk.

Times Open all year, Apr-Sep, Thu-Mon, 10-6; Oct-Mar, Thu-Sun, 10-4. Closed 24-26 Dec & 1 Jan. Site opens at noon on days there are summer evening theatre events **Fees** £4.70 (ch £2.40, concessions £4). Family ticket £11.80. NT members free on non-event days. Prices and opening times are subject to change in March 2011. Please check web site or call 0870 333 1181 for the most up to date prices and opening times when planning your visit **Facilities** (partly accessible) (some steps, slight slope, narrow doors, exhibition via stairs) shop

PARCEVALL HALL GARDENS Map 7 SE06

Parcevall Hall Gardens 2 FOR 1

BD23 6DE
☎ 01756 720311 📠 01756 720311
e-mail: parcevallhall@btconnect.com
web: www.parcevallhallgardens.co.uk
dir: Off B6265 between Grassington and Pateley Bridge

Enjoying a hillside setting east of the main Wharfedale Valley, these beautiful gardens surround a Grade II listed house which is used as the Bradford Diocesan Retreat House (not open to the public).

Times Open Apr-Oct, 10-6 (last entry 5) **Fees** £5.75 (ch free, concessions £4.75)* **Facilities** Ⓟ ☕ ⛩ (outdoor)

PATELEY BRIDGE Map 7 SE16

Stump Cross Caverns

Greenhow HG3 5JL
☎ 01756 752780 📠 01756 752780
web: www.stumpcrosscaverns.co.uk
dir: on B6265 between Pateley Bridge & Grassington

Discovered by the brothers Mark and William Newbould in 1860, Stump Cross Caverns have been an attraction for visitors since 1863 when one shilling was charged for entrance. Among the few limestone show caves in Britain, these require no special clothing, experience or equipment, as walkways are gravel and concrete and floodlighting is provided. Stalagmites, stalagtites and calcite precipitation make this an eerie day out.

Times Open all year, daily, Mar-end of Nov, then wknds and school hols Dec, Jan, Feb 10-5.* **Facilities** Ⓟ ⓟ ☕ 🍽 licensed ♿ (partly accessible) (ground floor accessible and gardens) shop ⊗

PICKERING Map 8 SE78

North Yorkshire Moors Railway

Pickering Station YO18 7AJ
☎ 01751 472508 📠 01751 476970
e-mail: admin@nymr.pickering.fsnet.co.uk
web: www.northyorkshiremoorsrailway.com
dir: from A169 take road towards Kirkbymoorside, right at traffic lights, station 400yds on left

Operating through the heart of the North York Moors National Park between Pickering and Grosmont, steam trains cover a distance of 18 miles. The locomotive sheds at Grosmont are open to the public. Events throughout the year include Day Out with Thomas, Steam Gala, Santa Specials.

Times Open 29 Mar-Oct, daily; Dec, Santa specials and Xmas to New Year running. Further information available from Pickering Station.* **Facilities** Ⓟ ⓟ ☕ 🍽 licensed ⛩ (outdoor) toilets for disabled (ramp for trains) shop

Pickering Castle

Castlegate YO6 5AB
☎ 01751 474989
web: www.english-heritage.org.uk

Splendid 12th-century castle, on the edge of the Yorkshire Moors, originally built by William the Conqueror. Visit the exhibition on the castle's history and take in the views from the keep.

Times Open Apr-Jun & Sep, Thu-Mon 10-5; Jul-Aug, daily 10-5 **Fees** £3.70 (ch £1.90, concessions £3.10). Family ticket £9.30. Prices and opening times are subject to change in March 2011. Please check web site or call 0870 333 1181 for the most up to date prices and opening times when planning your visit **Facilities** Ⓟ ⛩ ♿ (partly accessible) (no w/chair access to motte) toilets for disabled (parking) shop ♯

REDCAR Map 8 NZ62

RNLI Zetland Museum FREE

5 King St TS10 3DT
☎ 01642 494311
e-mail: zetland.museum@yahoo.co.uk
dir: on corner of King St and The Promenade

The museum portrays the lifeboat, maritime, fishing and local history of the area, including its main exhibit *The Zetland* - the oldest lifeboat in the world, dating from 1802. There is also a replica of a fisherman's cottage c1900 and almost 2000 other exhibits. The museum is housed in an early lifeboat station, now a listed building.

Times Open May, Wed 11-4, Sat-Sun 12-4; Jun-Sep, Tue-Fri 11-4, Sat-Sun 12-4 **Facilities** ⓟ ♿ (partly accessible) (ground floor only accessible) shop

RICHMOND Map 7 NZ10

Green Howards Museum 2 FOR 1

Trinity Church Square, Market Place DL10 4QN
☎ 01748 826561 📠 01748 821924
e-mail: greenhowardsmus@aol.com
web: www.greenhowards.org.uk
dir: take any turning on A1, between Catterick & South Corner, signed to Richmond. Located in centre cobbled market square, in Holy Trinity Church

This award-winning museum traces the military history of the Green Howards from the late 17th century onwards. The exhibits include uniforms, weapons, medals and a special Victoria Cross exhibition. There is a children's interactive area, family history research centre, interactive computers and a temporary exhibition area.

Times Open Mon-Sat 10-4.30. Closed Sun & Dec-30 Jan **Fees** £3.50 (accompanied ch free, concessions £3)* **Facilities** ⓟ ♿ (partly accessible) (stairlift, lightweight wheelchair) shop ⊗

RICHMOND *continued*

Richmond Castle

Tower Castle DL10 4QW
☎ 01748 822493
web: www.english-heritage.org.uk

Overlooking the River Swale and market town of Richmond, the views from the keep are stunning. Built by William the Conqueror to subdue the rebellious North, the castle now houses an exciting interactive exhibition.

Times Open all year, Apr-Sep, daily 10-6; Oct-Mar, Thu-Mon 10-4. Closed 24-26 Dec & 1 Jan **Fees** £4.50 (ch £2.30, concessions £3.80). Prices and opening times are subject to change in March 2011. Please check web site or call 0870 333 1181 for the most up to date prices and opening times when planning your visit **Facilities** Ⓟ ⛩ ♿ (partly accessible) toilets for disabled shop ⌗

RIEVAULX Map 8 SE58

Rievaulx Abbey

☎ 01439 798228
web: www.english-heritage.org.uk
dir: 2.25m W of Helmsley on minor road off B1257

Explore the magnificent romantic ruin set in a tranquil wooded valley of the River Rye. Find out about monastic life with the help of the audio tour and exhibition.

Times Open all year, Apr-Sep, daily, 10-6; Oct, Thu-Mon, 10-5; Nov-Mar, Thu-Mon, 10-4. Closed 24-26 Dec & 1 Jan **Fees** £5.30 (ch £2.70, concessions £4.50). Prices and opening times are subject to change in March 2011. Please check web site or call 0870 333 1181 for the most up to date prices and opening times when planning your visit **Facilities** 🅟 ⛩ ♿ (partly accessible) (some steps, site on slight slope) (wheelchair hire, hearing loop, audio tour, lift) shop ⌗

Rievaulx Terrace & Temples

YO62 5LJ
☎ 01439 798340 📠 01439 748284
web: www.nationaltrust.org.uk
dir: 2m NW of Helmsley on B1257

This curved terrace, half a mile long, overlooks the abbey, with views of Ryedale and the Hambleton Hills. It has two mock-Greek temples, one built for hunting parties, the other for quiet contemplation. There are also remarkable frescoes by Borgnis, and an exhibition on English landscape design.

Times Open daily 17 Mar-Sep 11-6, Oct 11-5 (last admission 1hr before close)* **Facilities** 🅟 Ⓟ ⛩ (outdoor) ♿ (partly accessible) (w/chair/runaround vehicle/Braille guide/ramp) shop

RIPLEY Map 8 SE26

Ripley Castle

2 FOR 1

HG3 3AY
☎ 01423 770152 📠 01423 771745
e-mail: enquiries@ripleycastle.co.uk
web: www.ripleycastle.co.uk
dir: off A61, Harrogate to Ripon road

Ripley Castle has been home to the Ingilby family for 26 generations and stands at the heart of an estate with deer park, lakes and Victorian walled gardens. The Castle has a rich history and a fine collection of Royalist armour housed in the 1555 tower. There are also tropical hot houses, a children's play trail, tearooms, woodland walks, pleasure grounds and the National Hyacinth collection in spring.

Times Open Oct-Mar, Tue, Thu, Sat & Sun 10.30-3; Apr-Sep, daily 10.30-3; Dec-Feb wknds only, also BH and school hols. Groups all year by prior arrangement. Gardens open daily 9-5 **Fees** Castle & Gardens £8 (ch £5, pen £7). Gardens only £5.50 (ch £3.50, concessions £5). Party £5* **Facilities** 🅟 ☕ 🍽 licensed ♿ (partly accessible) (two of the rooms in the castle on view are upstairs) toilets for disabled (mobility buggy for hire, audio loop) shop

RIPON Map 8 SE37

Fountains Abbey & Studley Royal

HG4 3DY
☎ 01765 608888 📠 01765 601002
e-mail: fountainsenquiries@nationaltrust.org.uk
web: www.fountainsabbey.org.uk
dir: 4m W of Ripon off B6265

A World Heritage Site comprising of the ruin of a 12th-century Cistercian abbey and monastic watermill, an Elizabethan mansion and one of the best surviving examples of a Georgian water garden. Elegant ornamental lakes, canals, temples and cascades provide eye-catching vistas. The site also contains the Victorian St. Mary's Church and medieval deer park.

Times Open all year, daily, Nov-Feb 10-4, Mar-Oct 10-5. Closed Fri Nov-Jan & 24-25 Dec.* **Facilities** 🅟 ☕ 🍽 licensed ⛩ (outdoor) ♿ (partly accessible) toilets for disabled (pre-bk wheelchairs & batricars. Braille/large print guides) shop

Norton Conyers

Wath HG4 5EQ
☎ 01765 640333 📠 01765 640333
e-mail: norton.conyers@bronco.co.uk
dir: from Ripon take A61 to Thirsk. At top of hill just outside Ripon, turn sharp left onto Wath Road

Norton Conyers, the home of Sir James and Lady Graham, has belonged to the Grahams since 1624, but goes back to much older times. It is best known from Charlotte Brontë's visit in 1839; she is said to have been inspired by a family legend to create the mad Mrs Rochester in *Jane Eyre*. The mid 18th-century walled garden stands near the house, and retains the essentials of its original design. Two paths meet at the central pleasure pavilion (open to visitors), with a little pond and a fountain before it. Wide herbaceous borders are flanked by high yew hedges. Other borders hold gold and silver plants, peonies and irises.

Times House closed due to major repairs. Garden open: 5 Jun-8 Aug, Sun-Mon & 6-9 Jul, 2-5; BHs, ex Etr Sun & Mon (last admission 4.40) **Fees** Admission free but donations welcome, except when garden is open for a charity event and an entrance fee is made for the benefit of the charity **Facilities** Ⓟ ♿ (partly accessible) (most of garden accessible except for main path which is gravelled & has a slight uphill slope)

SCARBOROUGH — Map 8 TA08

Scarborough Castle

Castle Rd YO11 1HY
☎ 01723 372451 📠 01723 372451
web: www.english-heritage.org.uk
dir: E of town centre

This 12th-century fortress housed many important figures in history. Enjoy the spectacular coastal view and see the remains of the great keep still standing over three storeys high. Discover the castle's exciting history through the free audio tour.

Times Open all year, Apr-Sep, daily 10-6; Oct-Mar, Thu-Mon 10-4. Closed 24-26 Dec & 1 Jan **Fees** £4.70 (ch £2.40, concessions £4). Family ticket £11.80. Prices and opening times are subject to change in March 2011. Please check web site or call 0870 333 1181 for the most up to date prices and opening times when planning your visit **Facilities** Ⓟ 🛒 ⌗

Sea Life & Marine Sanctuary

Scalby Mills Rd, North Bay YO12 6RP
☎ 01723 376125 📠 01723 376285
web: www.sealife.co.uk
dir: follow brown tourist signs after entering Scarborough. Centre in North Bay Leisure Parks area of town

Made up of three large white pyramids, this impressive marine sanctuary overlooks the white sandy beaches of the North Bay, Scarborough's Castle, and Peasholm Park. The sanctuary features Jurassic seas, jellyfish, Otter River, penguins, and sea turtles.

Times Open all year daily. Closed 25 Dec.* **Facilities** Ⓟ Ⓟ ☕ 🛒 ♿ (partly accessible) toilets for disabled (lift to cafe) shop ⊗

SETTLE — Map 7 SD86

Yorkshire Dales Falconry & Wildlife Conservation Centre

Crows Nest LA2 8AS
☎ 01729 822832 📠 01729 825160
e-mail: mail@falconryandwildlife.com
web: www.falconryandwildlife.com
dir: on A65 follow brown signs

The first privately owned falconry centre in the north of England. The main aim of the centre is to educate and promote awareness that many of the world's birds of prey are threatened with extinction. Successful captive breeding and educational programmes will help to safeguard these creatures. Regular free flying demonstrations throughout the day and falconry courses throughout the week.

Times Open all year summer 10-6; winter 10-4. Closed 25-26 Dec & 1 Jan **Fees** £6.50 (ch £4.50, pen £5.50). Family ticket (2ad+2ch) £19. Group 20+ £5 (ch £4). 1 ad free with 10 ch **Facilities** Ⓟ ☕ 🛒 (indoor & outdoor) ♿ (fully accessible) toilets for disabled (ramp for w/chair into tea room, and giftshop access) shop ⊗

SKINNINGROVE — Map 8 NZ71

Cleveland Ironstone Mining Museum

2 FOR 1

Deepdale TS13 4AP
☎ 01287 642877 📠 01287 642970
e-mail: visits@ironstonemuseum.co.uk
web: www.ironstonemuseum.co.uk
dir: in Skinningrove Valley, just off A174 near coast between Saltburn and Whitby

On the site of the old Loftus Mine, this museum offers visitors a glimpse into the underground world of Cleveland's ironstone mining past. Discover the special skills and customs of the miners who helped make Cleveland the most important ironstone mining district in Victorian and Edwardian England. The museum is not a glass case museum but an experience.

Times Open Apr-Oct, Mon-Fri 10.30-3.30, Sat 1-3.30. Group visits all year by prior arrangement (please phone) **Fees** £5 (ch 5-16 £2.50, concessions £4.50). Family ticket (2ad+2ch) £12.50 **Facilities** Ⓟ Ⓟ 🛒 (outdoor) ♿ (partly accessible) (electric wheelchairs unable to navigate the tour through a narrow doorway) toilets for disabled (2 wheelchairs on site, induction loop) shop ⊗

ENGLAND

SKIPTON Map 7 SD95

Skipton Castle

BD23 1AW
☎ 01756 792442 01756 796100
e-mail: info@skiptoncastle.co.uk
web: www.skiptoncastle.co.uk
dir: in town centre at head of High Street

Skipton Castle is one of the most complete and well-preserved medieval castles in England. Some of the castle dates from the 1650s when it was rebuilt after being partially damaged following the Civil War. However, the original castle was erected in Norman times and became the home of the Clifford family in 1310 and remained so until 1676. Illustrated tour sheets are available in a number of languages. Please see website for special events.

Times Open all year, daily from 10, Sun from noon (last admission 6, 4pm Oct-Feb). Closed 25 Dec **Fees** £6.20 (incl illustrated tour sheet) (ch under 18 £3.70, under 5 free, concessions £5.60). Family ticket £19.50. Party 15+* **Facilities** Ⓟ ☕ 🛋 (indoor & outdoor) ♿ (partly accessible) (access to grounds, shops, tea room) shop

SUTTON-ON-THE-FOREST Map 8 SE56

Sutton Park

2 FOR 1

YO61 1DP
☎ 01347 810249 & 811239 01347 811251
e-mail: suttonpark@statelyhome.co.uk
web: www.statelyhome.co.uk
dir: off A1237 onto B1363 York to Helmsley road. 8m N of York city centre

The early Georgian house contains fine furniture, paintings and porcelain. The grounds have superb, award-winning terraced gardens, a lily pond and a Georgian ice house. There are also delightful woodland walks as well as spaces for caravans.

Times Open Gardens Apr-end Sep, daily 11-5. House open Apr-end Sep, Wed, Sun & BH 1.30-5 (last tour 4) **Fees** Gardens only £3.50 (ch £1.50, concessions £3). House & Gardens £6.50 (ch £4, concessions £5.50)* **Facilities** Ⓟ ☕ 🛋 (outdoor) ♿ (partly accessible) (4 steps up to front of House, 3 steps down in House) toilets for disabled (wheelchair & lift in house, ramps in garden) shop ⊛

THIRSK Map 8 SE48

Falconry UK - Birds of Prey Centre

2 FOR 1

Sion Hill Hall, Kirby Wiske YO7 4EU
☎ 01845 587522
e-mail: mail@falconrycentre.co.uk
web: www.falconrycentre.co.uk
dir: follow brown tourist signs, situated on A167 between Northallerton and Topcliffe

Set up to ensure that birds of prey would survive to provide the public with a rare opportunity to see and enjoy these beautiful birds. Enjoy the excitement of falconry with over 70 birds and 30 species. Three different flying displays with public participation where possible. After each display, handling birds brought out for public to hold.

Times Open Mar-Oct daily 10.30-5. 3 daily flying displays (different birds in each display) at 11.30, 1.30, 3.30 **Fees** £6.50 (ch £4.50, under 3 free, pen £5.50). Family ticket (2ad+2ch) £19 **Facilities** Ⓟ Ⓟ ☕ 🛋 (outdoor) ♿ (fully accessible) toilets for disabled shop ⊛

Monk Park Farm Visitor Centre

Bagby YO7 2AG
☎ 01845 597730 & 07776 195688 01845 597730
web: www.monkparkfarm.co.uk
dir: just off A170 Scarborough road or A19 from York

Monk Park, once a haven for monks who made their living from the land, is now a favourite for children. There is something for all ages to see and do, with indoor and outdoor viewing and feeding areas. The park has been featured in *Blue Peter* and *Vets in Practice.*

Times Open Feb half term-Oct, daily, 10.30-5.30* **Fees** £5 (ch £4 under 2 free, pen £4) **Facilities** Ⓟ ☕ 🛋 (indoor & outdoor) ♿ (partly accessible) (woodland walk might be slightly difficult with wheelchair) toilets for disabled (ramps) shop ⊛

WHITBY Map 8 NZ81

Whitby Abbey

YO22 4JT
☎ 01947 603568 01947 825561
web: www.english-heritage.org.uk
dir: on clifftop E of Whitby town centre

Uncover the full story of these atmospheric ruins in their impressive clifftop location above the picturesque fishing town with associations ranging from Victorian jewellery and whaling, to Count Dracula.

Times Open all year, Apr-Sep, daily 10-6; Oct-Mar, Thu-Mon 10-4. Closed 24-26 Dec & 1 Jan.* **Facilities** Ⓟ ☕ 🛋 shop #

WINTRINGHAM **Map 8 SE87**

Wolds Way Lavender **2 FOR 1**

Deer Farm Park, Sandy Ln, Wintringham YO17 8HW
☎ 01944 758641
e-mail: admin@woldswaylavender.co.uk
web: www.woldswaylavender.co.uk
dir: off A64 between Malton & Scarborough, follow brown signs

The medicinal and therapeutic benefits of lavender are extolled at this 12-acre site close to the Yorkshire Wolds. Six acres are currently planted with lavender, and a wood-burning still for the extraction of lavender oil. Visitors can be calmed by the Sensory Areas, enjoy a cuppa in the tearoom, and purchase all manner of lavender items at the farm shop.

Times Open Apr-Oct, Sun-Thu; Jun-Aug daily 10-5 **Fees** £3.50 (ch & concessions £2.50)* **Facilities** (outdoor) (fully accessible) toilets for disabled (sensory garden, raised flower beds, giant games maze) shop

YORK **Map 8 SE65**

Clifford's Tower

Tower St YO1 1SA
☎ 01904 646940
web: www.english-heritage.org.uk

Visit this proud symbol of the might of England's medieval kings - and enjoy magnificent views over York. The original wooden tower was built to help William the Conqueror subdue the North. It was burned down during the persecution of the Jewish community in 1190 and rebuilt in a rare design of interlocking circles by Henry III in the 13th-century.

Times Open all year, Apr-Sep, daily 10-6; Oct, daily 10-5; Nov-Mar, daily 10-4. Closed 24-26 Dec & 1 Jan **Fees** £3.50 (ch £1.80, concessions £3). Family £8.80. Prices and opening times are subject to change in March 2011. Please check web site or call 0870 333 1181 for the most up to date prices and opening times when planning your visit **Facilities** shop

DIG **2 FOR 1**

St Saviourgate YO1 8NN
☎ 01904 615505 📠 01904 627097
e-mail: jorvik@yorkat.co.uk
web: www.digyork.co.uk
dir: follow A19 or A64 to city centre then pedestrian signs for attraction

Grab a trowel and dig to see what you can find in DIG's specially designed excavation pits. Rediscover some of the amazing finds that the archaeologists have uncovered under the streets of York. Understand how these finds explain how people lived in Roman, Viking, Medieval and Victorian times. Touch real artefacts and work out what they would be used for. Special events scheduled throughout the year.

Times Open all year, daily 10-5. Closed 24-26 Dec* **Fees** £5.50. (ch, concessions £5). Family of 4 £18.50 of 5 £19.60. Group rates available on request* **Facilities** (indoor & outdoor) (fully accessible) toilets for disabled (induction loop, sensory garden, hearing posts) shop

Fairfax House

Castlegate YO1 9RN
☎ 01904 655543
e-mail: info@fairfaxhouse.co.uk
web: www.fairfaxhouse.co.uk
dir: city centre, close to Jorvik Centre and Cliffords Tower

Fairfax House, one of the finest mid-18th-century townhouses in England and a classical architectural masterpiece of its age, is home to the Noel Terry collection of Georgian furniture, clocks and decorative arts. This outstanding collection perfectly complements the house, bringing it to life and creating a special lived-in feeling. The result is a triumphant blend of connoisseurship and conservation. A series of three special exhibitions are scheduled for 2011.

Times Open mid Feb-Dec, Mon-Thu & Sat 11-5, Sun 1.30-5, Fri guided tours only 11 & 2 (last admission 4.30). Closed 24-26 Dec* **Fees** With voluntary gift aid donation: £6 (ch under 16 free when accompanied by an adult, concessions £5)* **Facilities** (partly accessible) (access restricted to ground floor & only possible with assistance. Phone in advance) shop

Guildhall **FREE**

Coney St YO1 9QN
☎ 01904 613161 📠 01904 551052
web: www.york.gov.uk
dir: 5-10mins walk from rail station

The present Hall dates from 1446 but in 1942 an air raid virtually destroyed the building. The present Guildhall was carefully restored as an exact replica and was re-opened in 1960. There is an interesting arch-braced roof decorated with colourful bosses and supported by 12 solid oak pillars. There are also some beautiful stained-glass windows.

Times Open all year, May-Oct, Mon-Fri 9-5, Sat 10-5, Sun 2-5; Nov-Apr, Mon-Fri 9-5.* **Facilities** (fully accessible) toilets for disabled (electric chair lift & ramps)

Jorvik Viking Centre **2 FOR 1**

Coppergate YO1 9WT
☎ 01904 615505 📠 01904 627097
e-mail: jorvik@yorkat.co.uk
web: www.jorvik-viking-centre.com
dir: follow A19 or A64 to York. Jorvik in Coppergate shopping area (city centre) signed

Explore York's Viking history on the very site where archaeologists discovered remains of the city of Jorvik. See over 800 of the items discovered on site and meet the famous Jorvik Vikings in our three exciting exhibitions, learn what life was like here more than 1000 years ago, and journey through a reconstruction of actual Viking streets. A new feature is 'Are You A Viking?', which uses scientific evidence to discover if you have Viking ancestors. 'Unearthed' tells how the people of ancient York lived and died, as revealed by real bone material. Special events throughout the year.

Times Open all year daily, summer10-5; winter 10-4. Closed 24-26 Dec. Opening times subject to change* **Fees** £8.95 (ch 5-15 £6, under 5 free, concessions £7) Family of 4 £26

continued

ENGLAND

YORK *continued*

of 5 £29. Telephone bookings on 01904 615505 (£1 booking fee per transaction at peak times) **Facilities** Ⓟ ☕ ♿ (partly accessible) (wheelchair users are advised to pre-book) toilets for disabled (lift & time car designed to take wheelchair, hearing loop) shop 🚫

Merchant Adventurers' Hall

Fossgate YO1 9XD
☎ 01904 654818 📠 01904 616150
e-mail: enquiries@theyorkcompany.co.uk
web: www.theyorkcompany.co.uk
dir: located in town centre, between Piccadilly and Fossgate

Construction of the Merchant Adventurers' Hall began in 1357 and it is one of the best preserved medieval guild halls in the world. Explore the Great Hall, Undercroft, and Chapel, along with unique collections of art, silver and furniture. Fully accessible to all from Fossgate. 2011 is the 650th anniversary of the completion of the hall.

Times Open all year, Etr-Sep, Mon-Thu, 9-5, Fri & Sat, 9-3.30. Sun 12-4. Oct-Etr, Mon-Sat, 9-3.30, Closed Sun & Xmas period. **Fees** £5 (ch free 16 or under, concessions £4). Family (2ad+2 or more ch) £7 **Facilities** Ⓟ (picnic) (outdoor) ♿ (fully accessible) toilets for disabled (access from Fossgate, lift) 🚫

Micklegate Bar Museum

Micklegate YO1 6JX
☎ 01904 615505 📠 01904 627097
e-mail: micklegate@yorkat.co.uk
web: www.micklegatebar.com
dir: A1036 on SW inner ring road

Situated on the route of York's famous walls walk, Micklegate Bar has stood sentinel to the city for over 800 years. Originally the main entrance into the City of York, visit this ancient gateway and explore the pageantry and barbaric history that has unfolded between these walls. Delve into York's past from Viking invasion to English civil war in this newly refurbished museum.

Times Open daily 10-3 (last admission), Feb-1 Nov (museum will remain closed if city walls are not open) **Fees** £3.50 (ch £2, concessions £2.50). Family ticket (4) £9 & (5) £10* **Facilities** Ⓟ shop 🚫

National Railway Museum

Leeman Rd YO26 4XJ
☎ 01904 621261 📠 01904 611112
e-mail: nrm@nrm.org.uk
web: www.nrm.org.uk
dir: behind rail station. Signed from all major roads and city centre

The National Railway Museum is the world's largest railway museum. From record breakers to history makers the museum is home to a vast collection of locomotives, carriages and wagons, including The Royal Trains, a replica of Stephenson's *Rocket*, the Japanese Bullet Train and the elegant *Duchess*. With three enormous galleries, interactive exhibits and daily events, the National Railway Museum mixes education with fun. A new art gallery opens during 2011.

Times Open all year 10-6. Closed 24-26 Dec **Fees** Free admission but charges may apply for special events & activities **Facilities** 🅟 Ⓟ ☕ 🍴 licensed (picnic) (outdoor) ♿ (fully accessible) toilets for disabled ("Please Touch" evenings usually in June) shop 🚫

See advert on opposite page

Treasurer's House

Minster Yard YO1 7JL
☎ 01904 624247 📠 01904 647372
e-mail: treasurershouse@nationaltrust.org.uk
web: www.nationaltrust.org.uk
dir: in Minster Yard, on N side of Minster, in the centre of York

Named after the Treasurer of York Minster and built over a Roman Road, the house is not all it seems. Nestled behind the Minster, the size, splendour and contents of the house are a constant surprise to visitors - as are the famous ghost stories. Children's trails and access to the tea room free.

Times Open Apr-Oct, daily (ex Fri) 11-5.* **Facilities** Ⓟ ☕ 🍴 licensed ♿ (partly accessible) (Braille guide/tactile pictures/ induction loop/scented path) 🚫 ✱

York Art Gallery

FREE

Exhibition Square YO1 7EW

☎ 01904 687687 📠 01904 697966

web: www.york.trust.museum

dir: 3 min walk from The Minster in city centre

The gallery is remarkable for the range and quality of its collections that provide a survey of most developments in Western European painting over the past six centuries. Works by Parmigianino, Bellotto, Lely, Reynolds, Frith, Boudin, Lowry and Nash are on display. There are also fine collections of watercolours, pottery and changing exhibitions. From late January 2011 the upper Burton gallery will be closed for refurbishment.

Times Open all year, daily 10-5, ex 24 & 31 Dec close at 2. Closed 25-26 Dec & 1 Jan **Facilities** Ⓟ ☕ ♿ (fully accessible) toilets for disabled (disabled access platform lift) shop ⊗

The York Brewery Co Ltd

12 Toft Green YO1 6JT

☎ 01904 621162 📠 01904 621216

e-mail: tony@yorkbrew.co.uk

web: www.yorkbrew.co.uk

dir: 5 min walk from York train station. Turn right out of station, right at lights. Walk under Mickelgate Bar, then left into Toft Green. Brewery 300yds on right

One of the North's finest independent breweries now offers a tour of its premises inside the city walls. Visitors can observe all the processes that go into producing beers like Centurion's Ghost, Yorkshire Terrier, Guzzler, and Stonewall. Those made intolerably thirsty by the sight of all this brewing expertise will be glad to know that the adult ticket price includes one pint of beer.

Times Open all year, daily, tours at 12.30, 2, 3.30 & 5 Mon-Sat (Sun, May-Sep)* **Facilities** Ⓟ ♿ (partly accessible) (12 steps) shop ⊗

York Castle Museum

The Eye of York YO1 1RY

☎ 01904 687687

e-mail: castle.museum@ymt.org.uk

web: www.yorkcastlemuseum.org.uk

dir: city centre, next to Clifford's Tower

Fascinating exhibits that bring memories to life, imaginatively displayed through reconstructions of period rooms and Victorian indoor streets, complete with cobbles and a Hansom cab. The museum is housed in the city's former prison and is based on an extensive collection of 'bygones' acquired at the beginning of the 20th century. It was one of the first folk museums to display a huge range of everyday objects in an authentic scene. The Victorian street includes a pawnbroker, a tallow candle factory and a haberdasher's. There is even a reconstruction of the original sweet shop of the York chocolate manufacturer, Joseph Terry. An extensive collection of many other items ranging from musical instruments to costumes. The museum also has one of Britain's finest collections of Militaria. A special exhibition called 'Seeing it Through' explores the life of York citizens during WWII. The museum includes the cell where highwayman Dick Turpin was held. Please contact the museum for details of exhibitions and events.

Times Open all year, daily 9.30-5* **Facilities** Ⓟ ☕ ♿ (partly accessible) (main galleries accessible, no access up stairs) toilets for disabled shop ⊗

The York Dungeon

2 FOR 1

12 Clifford St YO1 9RD

☎ 01904 632599 📠 01904 612602

e-mail: yorkdungeons@merlinentertainments.biz

web: www.thedungeons.com

dir: A64/A19/A59 to city centre

The York Dungeon invites you to delve into the city's most blood curdling parts of history including the horrible bits. Live actors, shows and special effects transport visitors back to those black and bleak times. Travel to the dark depths of the dungeons of York Prison, where murderer, thief and torturer Dick Turpin, the infamous highwayman, waits for his death at the gallows. Hear the screams and feel the heat of those accused of witchcraft being burnt at the stake. In the most haunted city in England, come and experience the presence of ghosts which will chill the very bones while standing in the silent yet chilling air. Warning - Not recommended for those of a nervous disposition or young children (under 16 must be accompanied by an adult). The York Dungeon will celebrate its 25th Anniversary in 2011.

Times Open all year, Apr-Sep 10.30-5 (last admission); Nov-Jan 11-4; Oct, Feb & Mar 10.30-4.30; Etr & summer hols 10-5.30. Closed 25 Dec. Please check for further details **Fees** £14.50 (ch £10.50, concessions £13.50). Family ticket (2ad+2ch) £48* **Facilities** Ⓟ ♿ (partly accessible) (accessible for w/chairs, no access for motorised w/chairs, York Dungeon limited access to w/chairs) toilets for disabled (w/chair ramps, stairlifts) shop ⊗

YORK *continued*

York Minster

Deangate YO1 7HH
☎ 0844 9390016 📠 01904 557218
e-mail: visitors@yorkminster.org
web: www.yorkminster.org
dir: easy access via A19, A1 or A64

Enjoy the peaceful atmosphere of the largest Gothic cathedral in Northern Europe, a place of worship for over 1,000 years, and a treasure house of stained glass. Take an audio tour of the Undercroft to find out more about the Minster's fascinating history and climb the Tower for amazing views.

Times Open all year, from 7am for services. Visitors Mon-Sat 9-5.30 (9.30 in winter), Sun noon-3.45. Phone for details* **Fees** Minster undercroft, Treasury & Crypt: £8 (ch 16 & under with family group free, concessions £7); Tower: £5 (ch 8-16 £3, under 8 not allowed, concessions £4)* **Facilities** Ⓟ ♿ (partly accessible) (no disabled access to Undercroft or Central Tower) toilets for disabled (tactile model, Braille & large print guide) shop ⊗

Yorkshire Museum

Museum Gardens YO1 7FR
☎ 01904 551800 📠 01904 551802
e-mail: yorkshire.museum@york.gov.uk
web: http://www.york.gov.uk
dir: park & ride service from 4 sites near A64/A19/A1079 & A166, also 3 car parks within short walk

The Yorkshire Museum is set in 10 acres of botanical gardens in the heart of the historic City of York, and displays some of the finest Roman, Anglo-Saxon, Viking and Medieval treasures ever discovered in Britain. The Middleham jewel, a fine example of English Gothic jewellery, is on display, and in the Roman Gallery, visitors can see a marble head of Constantine the Great. The Anglo-Saxon Gallery houses the delicate silver-gilt Ormside bowl and the Gilling sword.

Times Open all year, daily 10-5.* **Facilities** Ⓟ ⛩ toilets for disabled ♿ (ramps & lift) shop ⊗

SOUTH YORKSHIRE

Stanage Edge, Hathersage, Peak District National Park

BARNSLEY Map 8 SE30

Monk Bretton Priory

S71 5QD
web: www.english-heritage.org.uk
dir: 1m E of town centre, off A633

The priory was an important Cluniac house, founded in 1153. The considerable remains of the gatehouse, church and other buildings can be seen.

Times Open all year, daily 10-3; managed by a keykeeper. Closed 24-26 Dec & 1 Jan **Fees** Charge may apply on event days **Facilities** Ⓟ ⌗

CONISBROUGH Map 8 SK59

Conisbrough Castle

DN12 3HH
☎ 01709 863329
web: www.english-heritage.org.uk
dir: NE of town centre off A630

The white, circular keep of this 12th-century castle is a spectacular structure. Made of magnesian limestone, it is the oldest of its kind in England. Recently restored, with two new floors and a roof, it is a fine example of medieval architecture and was the inspiration for Sir Walter Scott's classic novel *Ivanhoe*.

Times Open all year, Apr-Jun & Sep, Sat-Wed 10-5; Jul-Aug, daily 10-5; Oct-Mar, Sat-Wed 10-4. Closed 24-26 Dec & 1 Jan **Fees** £4.20 (ch £2.10, concessions £3.60). Family ticket £10.50. Prices and opening times are subject to change in March 2011. Please check web site or call 0870 333 1181 for the most up to date prices and opening times when planning your visit **Facilities** Ⓟ ☕ ♿ (wheelchair access limited) shop ⊗ ⌗

CUSWORTH Map 8 SE50

Cusworth Hall, Museum and Park Hall — 2 FOR 1

Cusworth Ln DN5 7TU
☎ 01302 782342 📠 01302 800040
e-mail: museum@doncaster.gov.uk
web: www.doncaster.gov.uk
dir: 3m NW of Doncaster off A638. Signed

Cusworth Hall is an 18th-century country house set in a landscaped park. It has displays which illustrate the way local people here lived, worked and entertained themselves over the last 200 years. The Hall and Park have recently reopened following extensive refurbishment, giving visitors access to the magnificent chapel and great kitchen. The Park features a pleasure grounds, 18th-century lake system, lawns and woodland. The Tea Room is noted for its homemade food.

Times Open all year, Mon-Fri 10.30-5, Sat-Sun 1-5. Park open 24hrs* **Fees** £2 (ch 5-16 & concessions £1)* **Facilities** Ⓟ ☕ ♿ (fully accessible) toilets for disabled (wheelchair available) shop ⊗

DONCASTER Map 8 SE50

Brodsworth Hall & Gardens

Brodsworth DN5 7XJ
☎ 01302 722598 📠 01302 337165
web: www.english-heritage.org.uk
dir: between A635 & A638

This Victorian country house has survived largely intact. Imagine how the serving classes fared below stairs, then experience, in contrast, the opulent 'upstairs' apartments. Outside, visitors can enjoy a leisurely stroll around the extensive newly restored gardens.

Times House: open Apr-Sep, Tue-Sun & BHs, 1-5; Oct, Sat-Sun 12-4. Gardens: open Apr-Oct, Tue-Sun & BHs 10-5.30; Nov-Mar, Sat-Sun 10-4. (including Servant's Wing) (last admission half an hour before closing). Closed 24-26 Dec & 1 Jan **Fees** House & Gardens £8.70 (ch £4.40, concessions £7.40). Gardens only £5.30 (ch £2.70, concessions £4.50). Prices and opening times are subject to change in March 2011. Please check web site or call 0870 333 1181 for the most up to date prices and opening times when planning your visit **Facilities** Ⓟ ☕ ♿ (partly accessible) (limited access, some steps, steep slopes) toilets for disabled (ramps, lifts, shuttle service from car parks) shop ⊗ ⌗

Doncaster Museum & Art Gallery — FREE

Chequer Rd DN1 2AE
☎ 01302 734293 📠 01302 735409
e-mail: museum@doncaster.gov.uk
web: www.doncaster.gov.uk/museums
dir: off inner ring road

The wide-ranging collections include fine and decorative art and sculpture. Also ceramics, glass, silver, and displays on history, archaeology and natural history. The historical collection of the Kings Own Yorkshire Light Infantry is housed here. A recent addition is the 'By River and Road' gallery, which details the history of the Doncaster area. Temporary exhibitions are held.

Times Open all year, Mon-Sat 10-5, Sun 2-5. Closed Good Fri, 25-26 Dec & 1 Jan* **Facilities** Ⓟ ℗ ♿ (fully accessible) toilets for disabled (lift, hearing loop in lecture room) shop ⊗

MALTBY Map 8 SK59

Roche Abbey

S66 8NW
☎ 01709 812739
web: www.english-heritage.org.uk
dir: 1.5m S off A634

Visit the enchanting valley designed by 'Capability' Brown and discover the fascinating ruins of Roche Abbey, founded in 1147 by the Cistercians.

Times Open Apr-Sep, Thu-Sun & BHs 11-4 **Fees** £3.20 (ch £1.60, concessions £2.70). Prices and opening times are subject to change in March 2011. Please check web site or call 0870 333 1181 for the most up to date prices and opening times when planning your visit **Facilities** Ⓟ ♿ (partly accessible) (glass slope) toilets for disabled shop ⌗

ROTHERHAM Map 8 SK49

Magna Science Adventure Centre 2 FOR 1

Sheffield Rd, Templeborough S60 1DX
☎ 01709 720002 Fax 01709 820092
e-mail: aholdsworth@magnatrust.co.uk
web: www.visitmagna.co.uk
dir: M1 junct 33/34, follow Templeborough sign off rdbt, then brown heritage signs

Magna is the UK's first Science Adventure Centre, an exciting exploration of Earth, Air, Fire and Water. A chance for visitors to create their own adventure through hands-on interactive challenges. Visit the four Adventure Pavilions, live show and outdoor playgrounds Sci-Tek and Aqua-Tek. In 2011 Magna celebrate their 10th anniversary.

Times Open all year, daily 10-5. Closed 24 Dec-2 Jan. Check website for details seasonal closures & Mon opening **Fees** £9.95 (under 4's free, ch & concessions £8.95). Family ticket (2ad+1ch) £25 **Facilities** P (P) cafe restaurant licensed picnic (indoor & outdoor) disabled access (fully accessible) toilets for disabled (lifts, portable seating, wheelchair hire) shop no dogs

SHEFFIELD Map 8 SK38

Abbeydale Industrial Hamlet FREE

Abbeydale Industrial Hamlet, Abbeydale Road South S7 2QW
☎ 0114 236 7731
e-mail: ask@simt.co.uk
web: www.simt.co.uk
dir: A621 Abbeydale Road, S towards Bakewell

Catch a unique glimpse of life at home and at work in a rural scythe and steelworks dating back to the 18th century at Abbeydale Industrial Hamlet. Worker's houses, water wheels, crucible steel, furnaces, tilt hammers and workshops make up one of the largest water powered industrial complexes on Sheffield's River Sheaf. The site is a Grade I Listed building and a Scheduled Ancient Monument. Watch out for the popular Abbeydale Family Sunday Events Programme, including Traditional Crafts and Skills, Steam Gathering and Lammas Festival, where living history characters bring the Hamlet to life with family activities and Hamlet tours.

Times Open Apr-Oct, Mon-Thu 10-4, Sun 11-4.45. Closed Fri & Sat. Check current opening days and times at Xmas & New Year before travelling* **Facilities** P cafe disabled access (partly accessible) (upper areas - indoor) shop no dogs

Kelham Island Museum 2 FOR 1

Alma St S3 8RY
☎ 0114 272 2106 Fax 0114 275 7847
e-mail: ask@simt.co.uk
web: www.simt.co.uk
dir: 0.5m NW of city centre, from Sheffield Parkway (A57), take A6 North ringroad and follow signs

Set on a man-made island that is over 900 years old, Kelham Island Museum is the showcase of Sheffield's industrial history from early industrialisation to modern times. With the most powerful working steam engine in Europe, reconstructed workshops, and craftspeople demonstrating traditional 'made in Sheffield' skills - this is a 'living' museum. Learn what it was like to live and work in Sheffield's past, and see how steelmaking forged both the city of today and the world. Kelham Island is now the new home of the world renowned Hawley Tool Collection. The 2-for-1 voucher is not valid during Sheffield school holidays as entrance to the museum is free.

Times Open Mon-Thu 10-4, Sun 11-4.45. Closed Fri & Sat. Check opening days & times at Xmas & New Year before travelling* **Fees** £4 (accompanied ch under 16 free, concessions £3). Sheffield's school hols admission free for all* **Facilities** P (P) cafe disabled access (partly accessible) (all main areas fully accessible) toilets for disabled (wheelchair on request, lifts) shop no dogs

Millennium Gallery

Arundel Gate S1 2PP
☎ 0114 278 2600 Fax 0114 278 2604
e-mail: info@museums-sheffield.org.uk
web: www.museums-sheffield.org.uk
dir: Follow signs to city centre, then follow the brown signs marked M

With four different galleries under one roof, the Millennium Gallery has something for everyone. Enjoy new blockbuster exhibitions drawn from the collections of Britain's national galleries and museums, including the Victoria & Albert Museum and Tate Gallery. See the best of contemporary craft and design in a range of exhibitions by established and up-and-coming makers. Be dazzled by Sheffield's magnificent and internationally important collection of decorative and domestic metalwork and silverware. Discover the Ruskin Gallery with its wonderful array of treasures by Victorian artist and writer John Ruskin.

Times Open all year, daily Mon-Sat 10-5, Sun 11-5* **Fees** Admission Free, charge for some special exhibitions (concessions available) **Facilities** (P) cafe restaurant licensed disabled access (fully accessible) toilets for disabled (hearing loop) shop no dogs

WEST YORKSHIRE

Ilkley Moor

BRADFORD Map 7 SE13

Bolling Hall

FREE

Bowling Hall Rd BD4 7LP

☎ 01274 431826 Fax 01274 726220

web: www.bradfordmuseums.org

dir: 1m from city centre off A650

A classic West Yorkshire manor house, complete with galleried 'housebody' (hall), Bolling Hall dates mainly from the 17th century but has medieval and 18th-century sections. It has panelled rooms, plasterwork in original colours, heraldic glass and a rare Chippendale bed.

Times Open all year, Wed-Fri 11-4, Sat 10-5, Sun 12-5. Closed Mon ex BH, Good Fri, 25-26 Dec.* **Facilities** P (P) shop (no dogs)

Bradford Industrial Museum and Horses at Work

FREE

Moorside Mills, Moorside Rd, Eccleshill BD2 3HP

☎ 01274 435900 Fax 01274 636362

web: www.bradfordmuseums.org

dir: off A658

Moorside Mills is an original spinning mill, now part of a museum that brings vividly to life the story of Bradford's woollen industry. There is the machinery that once converted raw wool into cloth, and the mill yard rings with the sound of iron on stone as shire horses pull trams, haul buses and give rides. Daily demonstrations and changing exhibitions.

Times Open all year, Tue-Sat 10-5, Sun 12-5. Closed Mon ex BH, Good Fri, 25-26 Dec & 1 Jan* **Facilities** P (café) (disabled access) (fully accessible) toilets for disabled (induction loop in lecture theatre, lift, ramp) shop (no dogs)

Cartwright Hall Art Gallery

FREE

Lister Park BD9 4NS

☎ 01274 431212 Fax 01274 481045

e-mail: cartwright.hall@bradford.gov.uk

web: www.bradfordmuseums.org

dir: 1m from city centre on A650

Built in dramatic Baroque style in 1904, the gallery has permanent collections of 19th and 20th-century British art, contemporary prints, and older works by British and European masters.

Times Open all year, Tue-Sat 10-5, Sun 1-5. Closed Mon ex BH, Good Fri & 25-26 Dec.* **Facilities** P (P) (disabled access) (partly accessible) toilets for disabled (wheelchair available, lift) shop (no dogs)

National Media Museum

Pictureville BD1 1NQ

☎ 01274 202030 Fax 01274 723155

e-mail: talk@nationalmediamuseum.org.uk

web: www.nationalmediamuseum.org.uk

dir: 2m from end of M606, follow signs for city centre

Journey through popular photography and visit IMAX - the world's powerful giant screen experience, discover the past, present and future of television in Experience TV, watch your favourite TV moments in TV Heaven, play with light, lenses and colour in the Magic Factory and explore the world of animation. There are also temporary exhibitions and various special events are planned, please see the website for details.

Times Open all year, Tue-Sun 10-6, BH Mon & school hols. Closed 24-26 Dec **Fees** Admission to permanent galleries free, IMAX Cinema £7.75 (concessions £5.75). DMR (Feature length films) £9 (£7 concessions). Groups 20% discount. Family tickets available* **Facilities** P (P) (café) (restaurant) licensed (picnic area) (indoor) (disabled access) (fully accessible) toilets for disabled (tailored tours, induction loop, cinema seating) shop (no dogs)

BRAMHAM Map 8 SE44

Bramham Park

LS23 6ND

☎ 01937 846000 Fax 01937 846007

e-mail: enquiries@bramhampark.co.uk

web: www.bramhampark.co.uk

dir: on A1(M), junct 44/45, 4m S of Wetherby, to Bramham/Thorner slip road and follow brown signs

This fine Queen Anne house was built by Robert Benson and is the home of his descendants. The garden has ornamental ponds, cascades, temples and avenues. The landscape is a unique example of early 18th-century design, remaining virtually unchanged. The Bramham International Horse Trials take place here on the first weekend in June, and the Leeds Rock Festival on August bank holiday weekend.

Times Open wkdays by appointment, 31 May-7 Jun 11.30-4.30. Closed 30 May-6 Jun & 8 Aug-26 Sep **Fees** House £10, Gardens £4 (concessions £2)* **Facilities** P (disabled access) (partly accessible) (some steep slopes in garden) toilets for disabled (ramps & lift in house)

ENGLAND

CASTLEFORD Map 8 SE42

Diggerland 2 FOR 1

Willowbridge Ln, Whitwood WF10 5NW

☎ 0871 227 7007 📠 09012 01300

e-mail: mail@diggerland.com

web: www.diggerland.com

dir: M62 junct 31 then north on A655 towards Castleford. Diggerland 0.5m on left immediately before petrol station

An adventure park with a difference. Experience the thrills of driving real earth moving equipment. Choose from various types of diggers and dumpers ranging from 1 ton to 8.5 tons. Complete the Dumper Truck Challenge or dig for buried treasure supervised by an instructor. New rides include JCB Robots, Diggerland Dodgems, Go-karts, Landrover Safari, Spin Dizzy and the Diggerland Tractors.

Times Open 12 Feb-end Oct, 10-5, wknds, BH & school hols only including half terms* **Fees** £15 - all rides & drives included in price.* **Facilities** (outdoor) (fully accessible) toilets for disabled shop

GOMERSAL Map 8 SE22

Red House FREE

Oxford Rd BD19 4JP

☎ 01274 335100 📠 01274 335105

web: www.kirkleesmc.gov.uk/community/museums.museum.shtml

dir: M62 junct 26, take A58 towards Leeds then right onto A651 towards Gomersal. Red House on right

Delightful redbrick house displayed as the 1830s home of a Yorkshire wool clothier and merchant. The house and family was frequently visited by Charlotte Brontë in the 1830s and featured in her novel *Shirley*. The gardens have been reconstructed in the style of the period and there are exhibitions on the Brontë connection and local history in restored barn and cartsheds.

Times Open all year, Mon-Fri 11-5, Sat-Sun 12-5. Telephone for Xmas opening. Closed Good Fri & 1 Jan.* **Facilities** (partly accessible) (ground floor of Red House accessible) toilets for disabled (Braille & T-setting hearing aid available) shop

HALIFAX Map 7 SE02

Bankfield Museum FREE

Boothtown Rd, Akroyd Park HX3 6HG

☎ 01422 354823 & 352334 📠 01422 349020

e-mail: bankfield-museum@calderdale.gov.uk

web: www.calderdale.gov.uk

dir: on A647 Bradford via Queensbury road, 0.5m from Halifax town centre

Built by Edward Akroyd in the 1860s, this Renaissance-style building is set in parkland on a hill overlooking the town. It has an outstanding collection of costumes and textiles from many periods and parts of the world, including a new gallery featuring East European textiles. There is also a section on toys, and the museum of the Duke of Wellington's Regiment is housed here. Temporary exhibitions are held and there is a lively programme of events, workshops and activities. Please ring for details.

Times Open all year, Tue-Sat 10-5, Sun 1-4, BH Mon 10-5. Closed 25-26 Dec & 1 Jan **Facilities** (partly accessible) (2 ramps giving access to ground floor) toilets for disabled (audio guide & tactile objects) shop

Eureka! The National Children's Museum

Discovery Rd HX1 2NE

☎ 01422 330069 📠 01422 330275

e-mail: info@eureka.org.uk

web: www.eureka.org.uk

dir: M62 junct 24 follow brown heritage signs to Halifax centre - A629

With over 400 'must touch' exhibits, interactive activities and challenges, visitors are invited to embark upon a journey of discovery through six main gallery spaces. They can find out how their bodies and senses work, discover the realities of daily life, travel from the familiar 'backyard' to amazing and faraway places and experiment with creating their own sounds and music. A magical place where children play to learn and grown-ups learn to play. It is one of the leading children's museums in the UK and gives children a fun packed day out. The museum has been designed to inspire children to find out about themselves and the world around them.

Times Open all year, wknds, BHs & school hols 10-5; Term time wkdays 10-4. Closed Mon during term time & 24-26 Dec **Fees** £8.95 (ch 1-2 £2.95, ch under 1 free) Family Saver ticket (admits 5) £38.50. Special group rates available. One payment allows unlimited return for one year* **Facilities** (indoor & outdoor) (fully accessible) toilets for disabled (lift, basic sign language, large print, hearing loop) shop

Halifax Visitor Centre and Art Gallery

FREE

HX1 1RE

☎ 01422 368725 & 352334 📠 01422 349020

e-mail: halifax@ytbtic.co.uk

web: www.calderdale.gov.uk

dir: follow brown tourist signs, close to railway station

The merchants of Halifax built the elegant and unique hall in 1770, and it has over 300 merchant's rooms around a courtyard, now housing an art gallery and visitor centre. There are around eight temporary exhibitions each year.

Times Open all year, daily 10-5. Closed 1 Jan & 25-26 Dec **Facilities** Ⓟ (outdoor) ♿ (fully accessible) toilets for disabled (lifts, audio guide available) shop

Shibden Hall

Lister's Rd HX3 6XG

☎ 01422 352246 & 321455 📠 01422 348440

e-mail: shibden.hall@calderdale.gov.uk

web: www.calderdale.gov.uk

dir: 2km E of Halifax on A58

The house dates back to the early 15th century, and its rooms have been laid out to illustrate life in different periods of its history. Craft weekends, featuring over 30 craftworkers demonstrating historic skills, are held, and there's a lively programme of craft events, workshops and family activities. Please apply for details.

Times Open Mar-Nov, Mon-Sat 10-5, Sun 12-5. Dec-Feb, Mon-Sat 10-4, Sun 12-4. Closed 25-26 Dec & 1 Jan **Fees** £3.50 (ch & concessions £2.50). Family ticket £10* **Facilities** Ⓟ (outdoor) ♿ (partly accessible) (grounds and Mereside Visitor Centre accessible) toilets for disabled shop

HAREWOOD — Map 8 SE34

Harewood House & Bird Garden

2 FOR 1

LS17 9LG

☎ 0113 218 1010 📠 0113 218 1002

e-mail: info@harewood.org

web: www.harewood.org

dir: junct A61/A659 Leeds to Harrogate road

Designed in 1759 by John Carr, Harewood House is home to the Queen's cousin, the Earl of Harewood. His mother, HRH Princess Mary, Princess Royal lived at Harewood for 35 years and much of her memorabilia is still displayed. The House, renowned for its stunning architecture and exquisite Adam interiors, contains a rich collection of Chippendale furniture, fine porcelain and outstanding art collections from Italian Renaissance masterpieces and Turner watercolours to contemporary works. The old kitchen contains the best collection of noble household copperware in the country giving visitors a glimpse into below stairs life. The grounds include a restored parterre terrace, oriental rock garden, Himalayan Garden with Buddist Stupa, walled garden, lakeside and woodland walks, a bird garden and for youngsters, an adventure playground.

Times Open 18-27 Feb daily. Below Stairs & Grounds open Apr-30 Oct, State Rooms open 22 Apr-30 Oct **Fees** With Gift Aid donation: 28 Jun-7 Sep plus all BH wknds, £13.50 (ch/student £8.50, pen £12.20) Family (2ad+3ch) £46.50. Without Gift Aid donation: £12 (ch/student £7.70, pen £11) Family (2ad+3ch) £42. Prices will change in the lower season. Grounds & Below Stairs £7.50-£10, Freedom ticket £11-£14.30. **Facilities** Ⓟ (outdoor) ♿ (partly accessible) (the house is fully accessible. The grounds are on a natural slope with some gravel paths) toilets for disabled (electric ramp, wheelchair lift) shop

HAWORTH — Map 7 SE03

Brontë Parsonage Museum

2 FOR 1

Church St BD22 8DR

☎ 01535 642323 📠 01535 647131

e-mail: bronte@bronte.org.uk

web: www.bronte.info

dir: A629 & A6033 follow signs for Haworth, take Rawdon Rd, pass 2 car parks, next left, then right

Haworth Parsonage was the lifelong family home of the Brontës. An intensely close-knit family, the Brontës saw the parsonage as the heart of their world, and the moorland setting provided them with inspiration for their writing. The house contains much personal memorabilia, including the furniture Charlotte bought with the proceeds of her literary success, Branwell's portraits of local worthies, Emily's writing desk and Anne's books and drawings. The museum is currently holding a two year exhibition focusing on Branwell Brontë, who as a child was considered the greatest genius of the family. Branwell declined into alcoholism while his sisters went on to write great novels.

Times Open all year daily, Apr-Sep 10-5.30; Oct-Mar 11-5 (last admission 30 mins before closing). Closed 24-27 Dec & 2-31 Jan **Fees** £6.50 (ch 5-16 £3.50, concessions £5). Family ticket £15* **Facilities** Ⓟ Ⓟ ♿ (partly accessible) (please contact the museum) (info in large type & Braille, loop induction system) shop

Keighley & Worth Valley Railway & Museum

Keighley BD22 8NJ

☎ 01535 645214 & 677777 📠 01535 647317

e-mail: admin@kwvr.co.uk

web: www.kwvr.co.uk

dir: 1m from Keighley on A629 Halifax road, follow brown signs

The line was built mainly to serve the valley's mills, and passes through the heart of Brontë country. Beginning at Keighley (shared with Network Rail), it climbs up to Haworth, and terminates at Oxenhope, which has a storage and restoration building. At Haworth there are locomotive workshops and at Ingrow West, an award-winning museum. Events take place throughout the year, please telephone for details.

Times Open every wknd, please phone for other times.* **Facilities** Ⓟ Ⓟ (outdoor) ♿ (partly accessible) toilets for disabled (level access to all sites, ramps on trains and stations) shop

HUDDERSFIELD Map 7 SE11

Tolson Memorial Museum

Ravensknowle Park, Wakefield Rd HD5 8DJ
☎ 01484 223830 01484 223843
e-mail: tolson.museum@kirkdees.gov.uk
web: www.kirklees.gov.uk/museums
dir: on A629, 1m from town centre

Displays on the development of the cloth industry and a collection of horse-drawn vehicles, together with natural history, archaeology, toys and folk exhibits. There is a full programme of events and temporary exhibitions.

Times Open all year. Mon-Fri 11-5, Sat & Sun noon-5. Please contact for Xmas closures **Fees** Admission free. There may be a small charge for certain activities/events **Facilities** (partly accessible) (ground floor fully accessible, upstairs only accessible by stairs) toilets for disabled (mini-com, induction loop, parking) shop

ILKLEY Map 7 SE14

Manor House Gallery & Museum FREE

Castle Yard, Church St LS29 9DT
☎ 01943 600066 01943 817079
web: www.bradfordmuseums.org
dir: behind Ilkley Parish Church, on A65

This Elizabethan manor house, one of Ilkley's few buildings to pre-date the 19th century, was built on the site of a Roman fort. Part of the Roman wall can be seen, together with Roman objects and displays on archaeology. There is a collection of 17th and 18th-century farmhouse parlour and kitchen furniture, and the art gallery exhibits works by contemporary artists and craftspeople.

Times Open all year, Tue-Sat 1-5, Sun 1-4. Open BH Mon. Closed Good Fri, 25-28 Dec* **Facilities** shop

KEIGHLEY Map 7 SE04

Cliffe Castle Museum & Gallery FREE

Spring Gardens Ln BD20 6LH
☎ 01535 618230 01535 610536
web: www.bradfordmuseums.org
dir: NW of town off A629

Built as a millionaire's mansion, the house displays Victorian interiors, together with collections of local and natural history, ceramics, dolls, geological items and minerals. There is a play area and aviary in the grounds. Temporary exhibitions throughout the year.

Times Open all year, Tue-Sat 10-5, Sun 12-5. Open BH Mon. Closed Good Fri & 25-28 Dec* **Facilities** (partly accessible) (upstairs galleries hard to access by disabled users) toilets for disabled (access trail, bringing the exhibition to life downstairs) shop

East Riddlesden Hall

Bradford Rd BD20 5EL
☎ 01535 607075 01535 691462
e-mail: eastriddlesden@nationaltrust.org.uk
web: www.nationaltrust.org.uk
dir: 1m NE of Keighley on S side of Bradford Rd

The interior of this 17th-century manor house is furnished with textiles, Yorkshire oak and pewter, together with fine examples of 17th-century embroidery. The honeysuckle and rose covered façade ruin of the Starke Wing, provides the backdrop to the garden. Wild flowers, perennials, and a fragrant herb border provide a transition of colour throughout the year.

Times Open 27 Feb-Oct daily (ex Thu & Fri) 12-5. Open Good Fri.* **Facilities** (outdoor) (partly accessible) (Braille and large print guides, sensory photo album) shop

LEEDS Map 8 SE33

Abbey House Museum 2 FOR 1

Abbey Walk, Abbey Rd, Kirkstall LS5 3EH
☎ 0113 230 5492 0113 230 5499
e-mail: abbey.house@leeds.gov.uk
web: www.leeds.gov.uk
dir: 3m W of city centre on A65

Displays at this museum include an interactive childhood gallery and an exploration of life in Victorian Leeds. Three reconstructed streets allow the visitor to immerse themselves in the sights and sounds of the late 19th century, from the glamourous art furnishers shop to the impoverished widow washerwoman.

Times Open all year Tue-Fri 10-5, Sat noon-5, Sun 10-5. Open BH Mon open 10-5 **Fees** £3.60 (ch £1.60, under 5 free, concessions £2.60). Family ticket (2ad+3ch) £6* **Facilities** licensed (outdoor) (fully accessible) toilets for disabled (Braille plaques on wall, tactile tours by request) shop

Kirkstall Abbey 2 FOR 1 FREE

Abbey Rd, Kirkstall LS5 3EH
☎ 0113 230 5492 0113 230 5499
e-mail: kirkstall.abbey@leeds.gov.uk
web: www.leeds.gov.uk
dir: off A65, W of city centre

The most complete 12th-century Cistercian Abbey in the country stands on the banks of the River Aire. Many of the original buildings can still be seen, including the cloister, church and refectory. Regular tours take visitors to areas not normally accessible to the public. During the summer the Abbey hosts plays, fairs and musical events. A visitor centre gives an insight into the history of the Abbey and a true sense of how the monks lived in the 15th century.

Times Open all year, abbey site open dawn to dusk. Visitor centre open: Tue-Thu 10-4, Sat-Sun 10-4. Open BHs **Facilities** (outdoor) (fully accessible) toilets for disabled shop

Leeds Art Gallery FREE

The Headrow LS1 3AA
☎ 0113 247 8256 📠 0113 244 9689
e-mail: city.art.gallery@leeds.gov.uk
web: www.leeds.gov.uk/artgallery
dir: in city centre, next to town hall and library

Leeds Art Gallery has something to offer everyone. Home to one of the best collections of 20th-century British art outside London, as well as Victorian and late 19th-century pictures, an outstanding collection of English watercolours, a display of modern sculpture and temporary exhibitions focusing on contemporary art. The gallery holds an active events programme with talks, demonstrations and workshops regularly planned. Wander through the Tiled Hall to access Leeds Central Library.

Times Open all year, Mon-Tue 10-5, Wed 12-5, Thu-Sat 10-5, Sun 1-5. Closed BHs **Facilities** Ⓟ ☕ 🍽 licensed ♿ (partly accessible) (restricted access to upper floor) toilets for disabled (access ramp) shop ⊗

Leeds Industrial Museum at Armley Mills 2 FOR 1

Canal Rd, Armley LS12 2QF
☎ 0113 263 7861 📠 0113 224 4365
web: www.leeds.gov.uk/armleymills
dir: 2m W of city centre, off A65

Once the world's largest woollen mill, Armley Mills evokes memories of the 18th-century woollen industry, showing the progress of wool from the sheep to knitted clothing. The museum has its own 1930s cinema illustrating the history of cinema projection, including the first moving pictures taken in Leeds. The Museum is set in some lovely scenery, between the Leeds & Liverpool Canal and the River Aire. There are demonstrations of static engines and steam locomotives, a printing gallery and a journey through the working world of textiles and fashion.

Times Open all year, Tue-Sat 10-5, Sun 1-5 (last entry 4). Closed Mon ex BHs **Fees** £3.10 (ch £1.10, concessions £1.60). Family ticket (2ad+2ch) £6* **Facilities** Ⓟ ⛩ (indoor & outdoor) ♿ (partly accessible) (conference room on first floor not accessible) toilets for disabled (chair-lifts between floors) shop ⊗

Middleton Railway

Moor Rd, Hunslet LS10 2JQ
☎ 0113 271 0320 (ansaphone) & 01904 633906 (home)
e-mail: info@middletonrailway.org.uk
web: www.middletonrailway.org.uk
dir: M621 junct 5 or follow signs from A61

This was the first railway authorised by an Act of Parliament (in 1758) and the first to succeed with steam locomotives (in 1812). Steam trains run each weekend in season from Tunstall Road roundabout to Middleton Park. There is a programme of special events.

Times Open Etr-end Nov, Diesel Sat 1-4.20. Heritage & Steam Sun & BH Mon 11-4.20. Both at 40min intervals. Santa specials Sat & Sun in Dec* **Fees** £ 4.50 (ch £2.50). Family £12. Special rates & restrictions may apply for special events* **Facilities** Ⓟ Ⓟ ☕ ♿ (fully accessible) toilets for disabled (ramped access to all areas, disabled parking) shop

Royal Armouries Museum

Armouries Dr LS10 1LT
☎ 0113 220 1866 & 08700 344 344 📠 0113 220 1955
e-mail: enquiries@armouries.org.uk
web: www.royalarmouries.org
dir: off A61 close to Leeds centre, follow brown heritage signs.

The museum is an impressive contemporary home for the renowned national collection of arms and armour. The collection is divided between five galleries: War, Tournament, Self-Defence, Hunting and Oriental. The Hall of Steel features a 100ft-high mass of 3000 pieces of arms and armour. Try the hands-on interactive displays and handling collection or be part of the action at medieval jousting tournaments, falconry displays and live combat demonstrations.

Times Open all year, daily, 10-5. Closed 24-26 Dec **Fees** Free entry. Charges may apply for some activites **Facilities** Ⓟ ☕ 🍽 licensed ⛩ (indoor) ♿ (fully accessible) toilets for disabled (induction loops, wheelchairs, signers, low level counter) shop ⊗

Temple Newsam Estate 2 FOR 1

Temple Newsam Rd, Off Selby Rd, Halton LS15 0AE
☎ 0113 264 7321 (House) & 264 5535 (Estate)
📠 0113 232 6485
e-mail: temple.newsam.house@leeds.gov.uk
web: www.leeds.gov.uk/templenewsam
dir: 4m from city centre on A63 or 2m from M1 junct

Temple Newsam is celebrated as one of the country's great historic houses and estates. Set in 1500 acres of stunning parkland, Temple Newsam House is home to outstanding collections of fine and decorative art, many designated as being of national importance. The Estate includes a working Rare Breeds farm and national plant collections.

Times Open all year. House: Tue-Sun 10.30-5, Nov-28 Dec & Mar, Tue-Sat 10.30-4. Open BHs. Home Farm: Tue-Sun, 10-5 (4 in winter), also open Mon in school hols; Gardens: 10-dusk. Estate: daily, dawn-dusk* **Fees** House: £3.50 (ch £2.50). Family ticket £9. Farm: £3.25 (ch £2). Family ticket £8.50. Joint ticket: £5.75 (ch £3.50). Family ticket £14.50* **Facilities** Ⓟ ☕ ⛩ (outdoor) ♿ (fully accessible) toilets for disabled (ramps for full access to parkland, electric wheelchairs) shop ⊗

LEEDS *continued*

Thackray Museum **2 FOR 1**

Beckett St LS9 7LN
☎ 0113 244 4343 🖷 0113 247 0219
e-mail: info@thackraymuseum.org
web: www.thackraymuseum.org
dir: M1 junct 43, onto M621 junct 4. Follow signs for York & St James Hospital, then brown tourist signs

Your visit transports you into the world of health and medicine - past, present and future. Experience life in the Victorian slums of 1840 and be flabbergasted at the incredible lotions and potions once offered as cures for your ills. See how surgery was performed without the aid of anaesthetics, experience pregnancy by trying on an empathy belly, and step inside the human body in the interactive Life Zone.

Times Open all year, daily 10-5. Closed 24-26 & 31 Dec & 1 Jan **Fees** £6.50 (ch 4-16 £4, concessions £5.50). Family ticket (2ad+3ch) £19. Group rates available 12+* **Facilities** Ⓟ Ⓟ ☕ 🛒 (indoor) ♿ (fully accessible) toilets for disabled (wheelchairs, induction loop, large texts) shop 🚫

Tropical World

Roundhay Park LS8 2ER
☎ 0113 214 5715
e-mail: parks@leeds.gov.uk
web: www.leeds.gov.uk
dir: 3m N of city centre off A58 at Oakwood, also accessible from A610

The atmosphere of the tropics is recreated here as visitors arrive on the beach and walk through the depths of the swamp into the rainforest. A waterfall cascades into a rock-pool and other pools contain terrapins and carp. There are reptiles, insects, meerkats and more than 30 species of butterfly. Feel the dry heat of the desert and look out for fruit bats, monkeys and bush babies in the nocturnal zone. See piranhas and other exotic fish in the depths of the aquarium.

Times Open all year daily, winter 10-4; summer 10-6 (last admission 30mins before close). Closed 25-26 Dec **Fees** £3.25 (ch 5-15 £2, under 5 & Leeds card/Breezecard holders free)* **Facilities** Ⓟ Ⓟ ☕ ♿ (fully accessible) toilets for disabled shop 🚫

LOTHERTON HALL Map 8 SE43

Lotherton Hall **2 FOR 1**

Aberford LS25 3EB
☎ 0113 281 3259 (house) & 264 5535 (estate)
🖷 0113 281 2100
e-mail: lotherton@leeds.gov.uk
web: www.leeds.gov.uk/lothertonhall
dir: off the A1, 0.75m E of junct with B1217

Lotherton Hall is a beautiful, Edwardian country house. It is home to a treasure trove of arts and crafts, housing collections of painting, silver, ceramics and costume. The hall is set within an estate with formal gardens, a red deer park and includes an adventure playground and large bird garden. Please see website for details.

Times Open Hall: Mar-Dec, summer Tue-Sat 10-5, Sun 1-5; winter Tue-Sat 10-4, Sun 12-4 (last admission 45 mins before closing). Estate: 8-8. Bird garden: 10-5, (winter 10-4) open BH's* **Fees** £3 (ch £1, concessions 1.50). Family ticket £6. Discounts for Leeds Card holders* **Facilities** Ⓟ ☕ 🍽 licensed 🛒 (outdoor) ♿ (partly accessible) (access limited to ground floor of hall only) toilets for disabled (scooters available) shop 🚫

MIDDLESTOWN Map 8 SE21

National Coal Mining Museum for England **FREE**

Caphouse Colliery, New Rd WF4 4RH
☎ 01924 848806 🖷 01924 844567
e-mail: info@ncm.org.uk
web: www.ncm.org.uk
dir: on A642 between Huddersfield & Wakefield

A unique opportunity to go 140 metres underground down one of Britain's oldest working mines. Take a step back in time with one of the museum's experienced local miners who will guide parties around the underground workings, where models and machinery depict methods and conditions of mining from the early 1800s to present day. Other attractions include the Hope Pit, pithead baths, Victorian steam winder, nature trail, adventure playground and ponies. Visitors are strongly advised to wear sensible footwear and warm clothing.

Times Open all year, daily 10-5. Closed 24-26 Dec & 1 Jan **Facilities** Ⓟ ☕ 🍽 licensed 🛒 (outdoor) ♿ (fully accessible) toilets for disabled (induction loop, audio tours, 2 w'chairs for underground) shop 🚫

NOSTELL PRIORY Map 8 SE41

Nostell Priory & Parkland

Doncaster Rd WF4 1QE
☎ 01924 863892 📠 01924 866846
e-mail: nostellpriory@nationaltrust.org.uk
web: www.nationaltrust.org.uk/nostellpriory
dir: 5m SE of Wakefield towards Doncaster, on A638

Built by James Paine in the middle of the 18th century, the priory has an additional wing built by Robert Adam in 1766. It contains a notable saloon and tapestry room, and displays pictures and Chippendale furniture. There are lakeside walks within the grounds with rhododendrons and azaleas in bloom in late spring.

Times Open 15 Mar-2 Nov, Wed-Sun 1-5, 6-14 Dec daily 12-4. Grounds: 15 Mar-2 Nov, Wed-Sun 11-5.30, 6-14 Dec daily 11-4.30. Parkland, daily 9-5* **Facilities** (outdoor) (partly accessible) toilets for disabled (Braille guide/tactile books, wheelchair) shop

OAKWELL HALL Map 8 SE22

Oakwell Hall

Nutter Ln, Birstall WF17 9LG
☎ 01924 326240 📠 01924 326249
e-mail: oakwell.hall@kirklees.gov.uk
web: www.kirklees.gov.uk/museums
dir: 6m SE of Bradford, off M62 junct 26/27, follow brown heritage signs, turn off A652 onto Nutter Lane

A moated Elizabethan manor house, furnished as it might have looked in the 1690s. Extensive 110-acre country park with visitor information centre, period gardens, nature trails, arboretum and children's playground.

Times Open all year, Mon-Fri 11-5; Sat & Sun 12-5. Closed 24-26 Dec & 1 Jan **Fees** Hall: £2 (ch £1). Family ticket £5.50* **Facilities** (outdoor) (partly accessible) (gardens, ground floor of hall, visitor centre) toilets for disabled (large print & Braille guide, induction loops) shop

WEST BRETTON Map 8 SE21

Yorkshire Sculpture Park

WF4 4LG
☎ 01924 832631 📠 01924 832600
e-mail: info@ysp.co.uk
web: www.ysp.co.uk
dir: M1 junct 38, follow brown heritage signs to A637. After 1m, left at rdbt, attraction signed

Set in the beautiful grounds and gardens of a 500 acre, 18th-century country estate, Yorkshire Sculpture Park is one of the world's leading open-air galleries and presents a changing programme of international sculpture exhibitions. The landscape provides a variety of magnificent scenic vistas of the valley, lakes, estate buildings and bridges. By organising a number of temporary exhibitions each year in four magnificent galleries, the park ensures that there is always something new to see. The Visitor Centre provides all-weather facilities including a large restaurant, shop, coffee bar, audio-visual auditorium and meeting rooms.

Times Open all year, daily summer 10-6; winter 10-5. Closed 23-25 Dec* **Fees** Free. (Donations welcome). Car parking £4, coaches £10 by prior arrangement* **Facilities** licensed (outdoor) (partly accessible) (some paths difficult for wheelchair users, trail accessible for wheelchairs, all galleries accessible) toilets for disabled (free scooters, parking) shop

GUERNSEY

Plemont Bay, Guernsey

ENGLAND

FOREST — Map 16

German Occupation Museum

GY8 0BG
☎ 01481 238205
dir: Behind Forest Church near the airport

The museum has the Channel Islands' largest collection of Occupation items, with tableaux of a kitchen, bunker rooms and a street during the Occupation. A large selection of displays, dioramas and audio-visual technology illustrates the experiences and stories of islanders during the five years.

Times Open all year, Apr-Oct, daily 10-4.30; Nov-Mar, Tue-Sun 10-12.30 **Fees** £5 (ch £2.50). Free admission for disabled **Facilities** (outdoor) (partly accessible) (steps to street level alternative route available) (ramps & handrails)

ROCQUAINE BAY — Map 16

Fort Grey Shipwreck Museum

GY7 9BY
☎ 01481 265036 01481 263279
e-mail: admin@museums.gov.gg
web: www.museum.gov.gg
dir: on coast road at Rocquaine Bay

The fort is a Martello tower, built in 1804, as part of the Channel Islands' extensive defences. It is nicknamed the 'cup and saucer' because of its appearance, and houses a museum devoted to ships wrecked on the treacherous Hanois reefs nearby.

Times Open 26 Mar-Oct, daily 10-5 **Fees** £3.50 (ch over 7 & students £1, concessions £2.75). Season ticket available **Facilities** (outdoor) shop

ST MARTIN — Map 16

Sausmarez Manor — 2 FOR 1

Sausmarez Rd GY4 6SG
☎ 01481 235571 01481 235572
e-mail: sausmarezmanor@cwgsy.net
web: www.sausmarezmanor.co.uk
dir: halfway between airport & St Peter Port

The Manor has been owned and lived in by the same family for centuries. The style of each room is different, with collections of Oriental, French and English furniture and paintings. Outside take a train ride, enjoy a game of pitch and putt or visit the Formal Garden with its herbaceous borders. The subtropical Woodland Garden, set around two small lakes and a stream, is planted with colourful shrubs, bulbs and wild flowers. Also on view, a sculpture park which is now the most comprehensive in Britain.

Times Open Etr-Oct 10-5 **Fees** House £6.90 (ch £5.50, concessions £6.50). Sculpture Park/Woodland Garden £5.50 (accompanied ch & concessions £5, disabled free) **Facilities** (partly accessible) (partial access to garden, 8 shallow steps to the house) (free disabled admission for gardens) shop

ST PETER PORT — Map 16

Castle Cornet

GY1 1AU
☎ 01481 721657 01481 715177
e-mail: admin@museums.gov.gg
web: www.museums.gov.gg
dir: 5 mins walk from St Peter Port bus terminus

The history of this magnificent castle spans eight centuries and its buildings now house several museums, the Refectory Cafe and a shop. Soldiers fire the noonday gun in a daily ceremony. Look for the Maritime Museum that charts Guernsey's nautical history, the 'Story of Castle Cornet' with its mystery skeleton and the 201 squadron RAF Museum. A refurbished Regimental Museum of the Royal Guernsey Militia and Royal Guernsey Light Infantry is now open. A programme of living history, theatre, music and family events take place throughout the year.

Times Open 26 Mar-Oct, daily 10-5 **Fees** £8 (ch over 7, students & adults after 4 pm £1.50, pen £6). Season ticket available **Facilities** shop

Guernsey Museum & Art Gallery

Candie Gardens GY1 1UG
☎ 01481 726518 01481 715177
e-mail: admin@museums.gov.gg
web: www.museums.gov.gg
dir: On the outskirts of St Peter Port set in the Victorian 'Candie gardens'

The museum, designed around a Victorian bandstand, tells the story of Guernsey and its people. There is an audio-visual theatre and an art gallery, and special exhibitions are arranged throughout the year. It is surrounded by beautiful gardens with superb views over St Peter Port harbour. In 2011 the summer exhibition will be the Works of Mervyn Peake.

Times Open Feb-Dec, daily 10-5 (winter 10-4) **Fees** £5 (ch over 7 & students £1.50, pen £4). Season ticket available **Facilities** (fully accessible) toilets for disabled (audio guides) shop

VALE — Map 16

Rousse Tower — FREE

Rousse Tower Headland
☎ 01489 726518 & 726965 01481 715177
e-mail: admin@museums.gov.gg
web: www.museums.gov.gg
dir: on Island's W coast, signed

One of the original fifteen towers built in 1778-9 in prime defensive positions around the coast of Guernsey. Recently re-furbished, they were designed primarily to prevent the landing of troops on nearby beaches. Musket fire could be directed on invading forces through the loopholes. An interpretation centre displays replica guns.

Times Open Apr-Oct 9-dusk, Nov-Mar, Wed, Sat & Sun 9-4 **Facilities** (partly accessible) (tower can only be viewed from the outside)

JERSEY

St Ouens Bay, Jersey

GOREY — Map 16

Mont Orgueil Castle — 2 FOR 1

JE3 6ET
☎ 01534 853292 📠 01534 854303
e-mail: info@jerseyheritage.org
web: www.jerseyheritage.org
dir: A3 or coast road to Gorey

Standing on a rocky headland, on a site which has been fortified since the Iron Age, this is one of the best-preserved examples in Europe of a medieval concentric castle, and dates from the 12th and 13th centuries.

Times Open daily, Mar-Nov 10-6; winter open Fri-Mon 10-4 (last admission 1hr before close)* **Fees** £10 (ch £6, pen £9, student £6). Family ticket £29* **Facilities** Ⓟ ☕ (outdoor) ♿ (partly accessible) (castle keep accessible) toilets for disabled shop

GROUVILLE — Map 16

La Hougue Bie — 2 FOR 1

JE2 7UA
☎ 01534 853823 📠 01534 856472
e-mail: info@jerseyheritage.org
web: www.jerseyheritage.org
dir: A6 or A7 to Five Oaks, at mini-rdbt take B28 to site

This Neolithic burial mound stands 40ft high, and covers a stone-built passage grave that is still intact and may be entered. The passage is 50ft long, and built of huge stones, the mound is made from earth, rubble and limpet shells. On top of the mound are two medieval chapels, one of which has a replica of the Holy Sepulchre in Jerusalem below. Also on the site is an underground bunker built by the Germans as a communications centre, now a memorial to the slave workers of the Occupation.

Times Open Apr-Oct, daily 10-5* **Fees** £6.70 (ch £4.20, pen £5.70, student £4.20). Family ticket £19.50* **Facilities** Ⓟ (outdoor) shop

LA GREVE DE LECQ — Map 16

Greve de Lecq Barracks — FREE

☎ 01534 483193 & 482238 📠 01534 485434
e-mail: enquiries@nationaltrustjersey.org.je
web: www.nationaltrustjersey.org.je
dir: on side of valley, overlooking beach

Originally serving as an outpost of the British Empire, these barracks, built in 1810, were used for civilian housing from the end of WWI to 1972, when they were bought by the National Trust and made into a museum that depicts the life of soldiers who were stationed here in the 19th century. Also includes a collection of old horse-drawn carriages.

Times Open May-Sep, Wed-Sat, 10-4, Sun 1-4 **Facilities** Ⓟ Ⓟ ♿ (fully accessible) toilets for disabled (wheelchair ramps) shop

ST BRELADE — Map 16

Jersey Lavender Farm

Rue du Pont Marquet JE3 8DS
☎ 01534 742933 📠 01534 745613
e-mail: admin@jerseylavender.co.uk
web: www.jerseylavender.co.uk
dir: on B25 from St Aubin's Bay to Redhouses

Jersey Lavender grows nine acres of lavender, distils out the essential oil and creates a range of fine toiletry products. Visitors are able to see the whole process from cultivating, through to harvesting, distillation and the production of the final product. There is a national collection of lavenders, extensive gardens, herb beds and walks among the lavender fields. There are also other herbs that are grown and distilled, namely eucalyptus, rosemary and tea tree. The harvest season between early June and mid-August and during this time talks are given in the distillery.

Times Open 29 Mar-3 Oct, Tue-Sun 10-5 **Fees** £4.80 (ch under 14 free, pen £4.30)* **Facilities** Ⓟ ☕ ♿ (partly accessible) (main garden & distillery accessible, further afield around farm/ fields not accessible) toilets for disabled (free wheelchair loan) shop

ST CLEMENT — Map 16

Samarès Manor

JE2 6QW
☎ 01534 870551 📠 01534 768949
e-mail: enquiries@samaresmanor.com
web: www.samaresmanor.com
dir: 2m E of St Helier on St Clements Inner Rd

Samarès Manor is a beautiful house, surrounded by exceptional gardens. These include the internationally renowned herb garden, Japanese garden, water gardens and exotic borders. There are tours of the manor house and of the Rural Life and Carriage Museum. Talks on herbs and their uses take place each week day and there is a plant trail and activities for children.

Times Open 3 Apr-16 Oct **Fees** £6.75 (ch under 5 free, 5-16 & students £2.35, concessions £6.20) **Facilities** Ⓟ ☕ licensed ♿ (partly accessible) (ground floor only of the house and part of the water garden as small paths) toilets for disabled shop

ENGLAND

ST HELIER Map 16

Elizabeth Castle 2 FOR 1

JE2 3WU
☎ 01534 723971 01534 610338
e-mail: info@jerseyheritage.org
web: www.jerseyheritage.org
dir: access by causeway or amphibious vehicle

The original Elizabethan fortress was extended in the 17th and 18th centuries, and then refortified by the Germans during the Occupation. Please telephone for details of events, including 'Living History' militia re-enactments.

Times Open Apr-Oct, daily 10-6 (last admission 5)* **Fees** £8.50 (ch £6, pen £7.50, student £6). Family ticket £26* **Facilities** Ⓟ (outdoor) (partly accessible) (castle keep & parade ground accessible) toilets for disabled shop

Jersey Museum and Art Gallery 2 FOR 1

The Weighbridge JE2 3NF
☎ 01534 633300 01534 633301
e-mail: info@jerseyheritage.org
web: www.jerseyheritage.org
dir: near bus station on weighbridge

Home to 'The Story of Jersey', Jersey's art gallery, an exhibition gallery which features a changing programme, a lecture theatre, and an audio-visual theatre. Special exhibitions take place throughout the year.

Times Open all year, daily summer 9.30-5; winter 10-4
Fees £8 (ch & students £4.50, pen £7. Family ticket £22.50*
Facilities Ⓟ licensed (fully accessible) toilets for disabled (audio loop, magnilink viewer, lift, car park) shop

Maritime Museum & Occupation Tapestry Gallery 2 FOR 1

New North Quay JE2 3ND
☎ 01534 811043 01534 874099
e-mail: info@jerseyheritage.org
web: www.jerseyheritage.org
dir: alongside Marina, opposite Liberation Square

This converted 19th-century warehouse houses the tapestry consisting of 12 two-metre panels that tells the story of the occupation of Jersey during World War II. Each of the 12 parishes took responsibility for stitching a panel, making it the largest community arts project ever undertaken on the island. The Maritime Museum celebrates the relationship of islanders and the sea, including an award winning hands-on experience, especially enjoyed by children.

Times Open all year, daily summer 9.30-5; winter 10-4
Fees £7.50 (ch & students £4.50, pen £6.50). Family ticket £22.50* **Facilities** Ⓟ (fully accessible) toilets for disabled (Braille books) shop

ST LAWRENCE Map 16

Hamptonne Country Life Museum

La Rue de la Patente JE3 1HS
☎ 01534 863955 01534 863935
e-mail: info@jerseyheritage.org
web: www.jerseyheritage.org
dir: 5m from St Helier on A1, A10 & follow signs

Here visitors will find a medieval 17th-century home, furnished in authentic style and surrounded by 19th-century farm buildings.

Times Open for special events only, incl 7 Aug, 11 Sep & 16-17 Oct* **Fees** £6.70 (ch & students £4.20, pen £5.70). Family ticket £19.50* **Facilities** (outdoor) (partly accessible) (courtyard & garden accessible) toilets for disabled (sensory garden, designated parking) shop

Jersey War Tunnels

Les Charrieres Malorey JE3 1FU
☎ 01534 860808 01534 860886
e-mail: info@jerseywartunnels.com
web: www.jerseywartunnels.com
dir: bus route 8A from St Helier

On 1 July 1940 the Channel Islands were occupied by German forces, and this vast complex dug deep into a hillside is the most evocative reminder of that Occupation. A video presentation, along with a large collection of memorabilia, illustrates the lives of the islanders at war and a further exhibition records their impressions during 1945, the year of liberation.

Times Open 14 Feb-19 Dec, daily 9.30-5.30 (last admission 4).* **Facilities** Ⓟ licensed toilets for disabled (ramp to restaurant & lift in Visitor Centre to restaurant) shop

ST OUEN Map 16

The Channel Islands Military Museum

Five Mile Rd
☎ 07797 732072
e-mail: damienhorn@jerseymail.co.uk
dir: N end of Five Mile Rd, across road from Jersey Pearl

The museum is housed in a German coastal defence bunker, which formed part of Hitler's Atlantic Wall. It has been restored, as far as possible, to give the visitor an idea of how it looked. The visitor can also see German uniforms, weapons, documents, photographs, other items from the 1940-45 occupation as well as a large collection of civilian items from the time, many of which have not been on display before. The 40th anniversary of the collection is celebrated in 2011.

Times Open Mon before Good Fri-Oct **Fees** £4 (ch £2) Groups by arrangement* **Facilities** Ⓟ (outdoor) (fully accessible) shop

Kempt Tower Visitor Centre

Five Mile Rd

☎ 01534 483651 & 483140 📠 01534 441600

web: www.eco-active.je

Kempt Tower is buzzing with hands on activities for all ages. The centre has displays on history and the wildlife of St Ouen's Bay, including Les Mielles, which is Jersey's miniature national park. There are breath-taking views from the roof of a genuine Martello Tower.

Times Open May-Sep, daily 2-5* **Facilities** Ⓟ (P) (outdoor) shop ®

ST PETER — Map 16

The Living Legend

Rue de Petit Aleval JE3 7ET

☎ 01534 485496 📠 01534 485855

e-mail: info@jerseyslivinglegend.co.je

web: www.jerseyslivinglegend.co.je

dir: from St Helier, along main esplanade & right to Bel Royal. Left and follow road to attraction, signed from German Underground Hospital

Pass through the granite archways into the landscaped gardens and the world of the Jersey Experience where Jersey's exciting past is recreated in a three dimensional spectacle featuring Stephen Tompkinson, Tony Robinson and other well-known names. Learn of the heroes and villains, the folklore and the story of the island's links with the UK and its struggles with Europe. Other attractions include an adventure playground, street entertainment, the Jersey Craft and Shopping Village, a range of shops and the Jersey Kitchen Restaurant. Two 18-hole adventure golf courses are suitable for all ages. Jersey Karting is a formula one style experience. A unique track featuring adult and cadet karts.

Times Open daily Apr-Oct. Mar & Nov, Sat-Wed 9-5 **Fees** The Jersey Story £7.50 (ch £5), Jersey Adventure Golf £6.25 (ch £5.25). Jersey Karting £8.95 **Facilities** Ⓟ licensed ♿ (partly accessible) (Adventure Golf has lots of steps and uneven surfaces) toilets for disabled (wheelchair available) shop ®

Le Moulin de Quetivel

St Peters Valley, Le Mont Fallu

☎ 01534 483193 & 745408 📠 01534 485434

e-mail: enquiries@nationaltrustjersey.org.je

web: www.nationaltrustjersey.org.je

dir: A11 through St Peter's Valley. Attraction located on left, with junct of Le Mont Fallu B58

There has been a water mill on this site since 1309. The present granite-built mill was worked until the end of the 19th century, when it fell into disrepair; during the German Occupation it was reactivated for grinding locally grown corn, but after 1945 a fire destroyed the remaining machinery, roof and internal woodwork. In 1971 the National Trust for Jersey began restoration, and the mill is now producing stoneground flour again.

Times Open May-Sep, Sat only* **Fees** £2 (ch under 16 free, concessions £1.50). Free entry UK National Trust card* **Facilities** Ⓟ (P) shop ®

TRINITY — Map 16

Durrell Wildlife Conservation Trust

Les Augres Manor, La Profunde Rue JE3 5BP

☎ 01534 860000 📠 01534 860001

e-mail: info@durrell.org

web: www.durrell.org

dir: From St Hellier follow A8 to Trinity until B31. Turn right & follow B31, signed

Gerald Durrell's unique sanctuary and breeding centre for many of the world's rarest animals. Visitors can see these remarkable creatures, some so rare that they can only be found here, in modern, spacious enclosures in the gardens of the 16th-century manor house. Major attractions are the magical Aye-Ayes from Madagascar and the world-famous family of Lowland gorillas. There is a comprehensive programme of keeper talks, animal displays and activities.

Times Open all year, daily 9.30-6 (summer); 9.30-5 (winter). Closed 25 Dec **Fees** £12.90 (ch £9.40, pen £10.50). Family ticket £39.95* **Facilities** Ⓟ licensed (outdoor) ♿ (partly accessible) (some indoor areas cannot accommodate wheelchairs/scooters) toilets for disabled (scooters, wheelchairs, quad walker for hire) shop ®

ISLE OF MAN

Cashtal-Yn-Ard standing stones

BALLASALLA Map 6 SC27

Rushen Abbey and The Abbey Restaurant

IM9 3DB
☎ 01624 648000 📠 01624 648001
e-mail: enquiries@mnh.gov.im
web: www.storyofmann.com
dir: right at Whitestone Inn, left at next rdbt, then 1st right over bridge, car park on left

The most substantial and important medieval religious site in the Isle of Man. Remains of medieval buildings, exhibitions and displays, set in beautifully landscaped gardens.

Times Open Etr-Oct, daily 10-5 **Fees** £4 (ch £2) **Facilities** Ⓟ Ⓟ ☕ 🍽 licensed ⛩ (outdoor) ♿ (fully accessible) toilets for disabled shop ⊗

BALLAUGH Map 6 SC39

Curraghs Wild Life Park 2 FOR 1

IM7 5EA
☎ 01624 897323 📠 01624 897327
e-mail: curraghswlp@gov.im
web: www.gov.im/wildlife
dir: on main road halfway between Kirk Michael & Ramsey

This park has been developed adjacent to the reserve area of the Ballaugh Curraghs and a large variety of animals and birds can be seen. Walk-through enclosures let visitors explore the world of wildlife, including local habitats along the Curraghs Nature Trail. The miniature railway runs on Sundays.

Times Open all year Etr-Oct, daily 10-6 (last admission 5); Oct-Etr, Sat-Sun 10-4 **Fees** £8 (ch £4, under 3's free, pen £5.50) Family ticket £18.50* **Facilities** Ⓟ ☕ ⛩ (outdoor) ♿ (partly accessible) (some paths in winter not accessible to wheelchairs) toilets for disabled (loan of wheelchair & electric wheelchair) shop ⊗

CASTLETOWN Map 6 SC26

Castle Rushen

The Quay IM9 1LD
☎ 01624 648000 📠 01624 648001
e-mail: enquiries@mnh.gov.im
web: www.storyofmann.com
dir: centre of Castletown

One of the world's best preserved medieval castles, Castle Rushen is a limestone fortress rising out of the heart of the old capital of the Island, Castletown. Once the fortress of the Kings and Lords of Mann, Castle Rushen is brought alive with rich decorations, and the sounds and smells of a bygone era.

Times Open daily, Etr-Oct, 10-5 **Fees** £5.50 (ch £3). Family ticket £14.50 **Facilities** Ⓟ shop ⊗

Nautical Museum

☎ 01624 648000 📠 01624 648001
e-mail: enquiries@mnh.gov.im
web: www.storyofmann.com
dir: From Castletown centre, cross footbridge over harbour. Museum on right

Set at the mouth of Castletown harbour, The Nautical Museum is home to an 18th-century armed yacht, *The Peggy*, built by a Manxman in 1791. A replica sailmaker's loft, ship model and photographs bring Manx maritime life and trade in the days of sail alive.

Times Open daily, Etr-Oct, 10-5 **Fees** £4 (ch £2). Family ticket £9.50 **Facilities** Ⓟ ♿ (partly accessible) (access to ground floor for w/chair users with assistance) (guided tour) shop ⊗

Old Grammar School FREE

IM9 1LE
☎ 01624 648000 📠 01624 648001
e-mail: enquiries@mnh.gov.im
web: www.storyofmann.com
dir: centre of Castletown, opposite the castle

Built around 1200AD, the former capital's first church, St Mary's, has had a significant role in Manx education. It was a school from 1570 to 1930 and evokes memories of Victorian school life.

Times Open daily, Etr-late Oct, 10-5 **Facilities** Ⓟ Ⓟ ⛩ (outdoor) ♿ (partly accessible) (restricted access narrow door, 3 steps) shop ⊗

The Old House of Keys

IM9 1LA
☎ 01624 648000 📠 01624 648001
e-mail: enquiries@mnh.gov.im
web: www.storyofmann.com
dir: opposite Castletown Rushen in centre of Castletown

The Old House of Keys is a portrayal of the long and often turbulent history of Manx politics. It has been restored to its appearance in 1866 and visitors are invited to participate in a lively debate with interactive Members of Tynwald, the Manx parliament.

Times Open Apr-late Oct, daily 10-5* **Facilities** Ⓟ ⊗

ENGLAND

CREGNEASH — Map 6 SC16

The National Folk Museum at Cregneash

☎ 01624 648000 📠 01624 648001
e-mail: enquiries@mnh.gov.im
web: www.storyofmann.com
dir: 2m from Port Erin/Port St Mary, signed

The Cregneash story begins in Cummal Beg - the village information centre which shows what life was really like in a Manx crofting village during the early 19th century. As you stroll around this attractive village, set in beautiful countryside, call into Harry Kelly's cottage, a Turner's shed, a Weaver's house, and the Smithy. The Manx Four-horned Loghtan Sheep can be seen grazing along with other animals from the village farm.

Times Open Etr-Oct, daily 10-5 **Fees** £4 (ch £2). Family ticket £9.50 **Facilities** (outdoor) shop

DOUGLAS — Map 6 SC37

Manx Museum — FREE

IM1 3LY
☎ 01624 648000 📠 01624 648001
e-mail: enquiries@mnh.gov.im
web: www.storyofmann.com
dir: signed in Douglas

The Island's treasure house provides an exciting introduction to the "Story of Mann" where a specially produced film portrayal of Manx history complements the award-winning displays. Galleries depict natural history, archaeology and the social development of the Island. There are also examples of famous Manx artists in the National Art Gallery, together with the Island's National archive and reference library. Events and exhibitions throughout the year, please visit website for details.

Times Open all year, Mon-Sat, 10-5. Closed 25-26 Dec & 1 Jan **Facilities** licensed (outdoor) (fully accessible) toilets for disabled (lift) shop

Snaefell Mountain Railway

Banks Circus IM1 5PT
☎ 01624 663366 📠 01624 663637
e-mail: info@busandrail.dtl.gov.im
web: www.iombusandrail.info
dir: Manx Electric Railway from Douglas and change at Laxey

Snaefell is the Isle of Man's highest mountain. Running up it is Britain's oldest working mountain railway, which was laid in 1895. From the top of Snaefell, on a clear day, England, Ireland, Scotland and Wales are all visible.

Times Open Apr-Oct. (Regular departures from Laxey station between 10.15-15.45) **Fees** Prices determined by route & type of ticket, single/return. Explorer tickets also available. Contact for current prices* **Facilities** (partly accessible) (limited access, steps) shop

LAXEY — Map 6 SC48

Great Laxey Wheel & Mines Trail

☎ 01624 648000 📠 01624 648001
e-mail: enquiries@mnh.gov.im
web: www.storyofmann.com
dir: signed in Laxey village

Built in 1854, the Great Laxey Wheel, 22 metres in diameter, is the largest working water wheel in the world. It was designed to pump water from the lead and zinc mines, and is an acknowledged masterpiece of Victorian engineering. The wheel is also known as 'Lady Isabella', after the wife of the then Lieutenant Governor of the Isle of Man.

Times Open Etr-Oct 10-5 **Fees** £4 (ch £2). Family ticket £9.50 **Facilities** (outdoor) shop

PEEL — Map 6 SC28

House of Manannan

Mill Rd IM5 1TA
☎ 01624 648000 📠 01624 648001
e-mail: enquiries@mnh.gov.im
web: www.storyofmann.com
dir: signed in Peel

The mythological sea-god Manannan guides visitors through the Island's rich Celtic, Viking and maritime past. Step inside reconstructions of a Manx Celtic roundhouse and a Viking longhouse, discover the stories on magnificent Manx stone crosses, and see *Odin's Raven*, a splendid Viking longship. Displays and exhibitions throughout the year please see website.

Times Open all year, daily 10-5. Closed 25-26 Dec & 1 Jan **Fees** £6 (ch £3). Family ticket £14.50 **Facilities** (fully accessible) toilets for disabled shop

Peel Castle

IM5 1TB
☎ 01624 648000 📠 01624 648001
e-mail: enquiries@mnh.gov.im
web: www.storyofmann.com
dir: on St Patrick's Isle, facing Peel Bay, signed

One of the Island's principle historic centres, this great natural fortress with its imposing curtain wall set majestically at the mouth of Peel Harbour is part of Man's Viking heritage. The sandstone walls of Peel Castle enclose an 11th-century church and Round Tower, the 13th-century St German's Cathedral and the later apartments of the Lords of Mann.

Times Open Etr-Oct, daily 10-5 **Fees** £4 (ch £2). Family ticket £9.50 **Facilities**

PORT ST MARY Map 6 SC26

Sound Visitor Centre

FREE

The Sound IM1 3LY
☎ 01624 648000 & 838123 🖷 01624 648001
e-mail: enquiries@mnh.gov.im
web: www.storyofmann.com
dir: follow coastal road towards Port Erin/Port St Mary. Past Cregneash village towards most S point of Island

The Sound Visitor Centre is set in one of the Island's most scenic areas overlooking the natural wonders of the Sound and the Calf of Man. Along with information and audio presentations about the area, other facilities add to the enjoyment and convenience of visitors.

Times Open Etr-Oct daily 10-5. For winter opening times telephone 01624 838123 **Facilities** licensed (outdoor) (fully accessible) toilets for disabled

RAMSEY Map 6 SC49

The Grove

IM8 3UA
☎ 01624 648000 🖷 01624 648001
e-mail: enquiries@mnh.gov.im
web: www.storyofmann.com
dir: on W side of Andreas Rd. Signed in Ramsey

This Victorian time capsule was a country house built as a summer retreat for a Liverpool shipping merchant. Rooms are filled with period furnishings together with a costume exhibition. In the adjacent farmyard are buildings containing displays on farming and 19th-century vehicles. Around the grounds you may see Loghtan sheep, ducks and perhaps a Manx cat.

Times Open Etr-Oct, daily 10-5 **Fees** £4 (ch £2). Family ticket £9.50 **Facilities** licensed (partly accessible) (ground floor fully accessible, 3 steps to gardens) shop

Milntown

Estate & Gardens, Glen Auldyn IM7 2AB
☎ 01624 812321 & 818091
e-mail: milntown@manx.net
web: www.milntown.org
dir: A3 from Ramsey towards Sulby, located on left side

A wide variety of landscapes await, in this spectacular 15 acre garden, including formal gardens, woodland, water features and open spaces. Part of the Milntown estate, the gardens are planted to provide colour and variety all year. Vegetables grown in the kitchen garden are often used in the restaurant. Nearby the mill and its wheel can be still be found in working order and in May see the Island's biggest rhododendron.

Times Garden open Mar-Oct daily (ex Tue) 10-5 (last admission 4.30). See website for current opening times* **Fees** £2.50 (ch £1, pen £2). 10% discount groups 10+* **Facilities** licensed (partly accessible) (restricted access to some woodland areas, garden fully accessible) toilets for disabled

SCOTLAND

The Rest and Be Thankful, Argyll & Bute

CITY OF ABERDEEN

ABERDEEN Map 15 NJ90

Aberdeen Art Gallery FREE

Schoolhill AB10 1FQ
☎ 01224 523700 📠 01224 632133
e-mail: info@aagm.co.uk
web: www.aberdeencity.gov.uk
dir: located in city centre

Aberdeen's splendid art gallery houses an important fine art collection, a rich and diverse applied art collection and an exciting programme of special exhibitions.

Times Open all year Tue-Sat 10-5, Sun 2-5. Closed Xmas & New Year* **Facilities** Ⓟ ☕ toilets for disabled (ramp, lift) shop ⊗

Aberdeen Maritime Museum FREE

Shiprow AB11 5BY
☎ 01224 337700 📠 01224 213066
e-mail: info@aagm.co.uk
web: www.aberdeencity.gov.uk
dir: located in city centre

The award-winning Maritime Museum brings the history of the North Sea to life. Featuring displays and exhibitions on the offshore oil industry, shipbuilding, fishing and clipper ships.

Times Open all year, Tue-Sat, 10-5, Sun 2-5* **Facilities** Ⓟ ☕ 🍽 licensed ♿ (partly accessible) (2 rooms in Provost Ross's house not accessible due to stairs) toilets for disabled (ramps, lifts, induction loop) shop ⊗

Cruickshank Botanic Garden FREE

The Chanonry AB24 3UU
☎ 01224 272704 📠 01224 272703
web: http://www.abdn.ac.uk/pss/cruickshank
dir: enter by gate in Chanonry, in Old Aberdeen

Developed at the end of the 19th century, the 11 acres include rock and water gardens, a rose garden, a fine herbaceous border, an arboretum and a patio garden. There are collections of spring bulbs, gentians and alpine plants, and a fine array of trees and shrubs.

Times Open all year, Mon-Fri 9-4.30; also Sat & Sun, May-Sep 2-5* **Facilities** Ⓟ ♿ (partly accessible) (some steep, narrow paths) ⊗

The Gordon Highlanders Museum

St Luke's, Viewfield Rd AB15 7XH
☎ 01224 311200 📠 01224 319323
e-mail: museum@gordonhighlanders.com
web: www.gordonhighlanders.com

Presenting a large collection of artefacts, paintings, films and reconstructions, the Gordon Highlanders Museum is the perfect day out for anyone interested in Scottish military history, and is also the former home of 19th-century artist, Sir George Reid. The exhibition includes interactive maps, original film footage, scaled reproductions, life-size models, touch screens, uniforms, medals and an armoury. The grounds also contain a tea-room, shop and gardens. See the website for details of changing exhibitions and events.

Times Open Apr-Oct, Tue-Sat 10-4.30, Sun 12.30-4.30; Nov, Feb & Mar Thu-Sat 10-4. Open by appointment only at other times* **Facilities** 🅟 Ⓟ ☕ ♿ (fully accessible) toilets for disabled (low level cases, hearing loop, lift) shop ⊗

Provost Skene's House

FREE

Guestrow, off Broad St AB10 1AS
☎ 01224 641086
e-mail: info@aagm.co.uk
web: www.aberdeencity.gov.uk
dir: located in town centre

16th century town house with a stunning series of period room settings. Painted Gallery and changing displays of local history.

Times Open all year Mon-Sat 10-5* **Facilities** Ⓟ ☕ ⊗

Satrosphere Science Centre

179 Constitution St AB24 5TU
☎ 01224 640340 📠 01224 622211
e-mail: info@satrosphere.net
web: www.satrosphere.net
dir: located very close to Beach Esplanade. Follow signs to fun beach, then attraction

Satrosphere is Scotland's first science and discovery centre and with over 50 hands-on exhibits and live science shows, a visit to Satrosphere will not only inspire the scientist within but will entertain the whole family. Satrosphere's exhibits offer interactive ways for visitors to discover more about the world around them and the science of how things work.

Times Open all year, Mar-Oct, daily 10-5; Nov-Feb, Tue-Sun 10-5. Closed 25-26 Dec & 1 Jan **Fees** £5.75 (ch 3+ £4.50, concessions £4.50). Please visit website for up to date prices* **Facilities** 🅟 Ⓟ ☕ ♿ (fully accessible) toilets for disabled (lift) shop ⊗

PETERCULTER — Map 15 NJ80

Drum Castle

AB31 5EY
☎ 0844 493 2161 📠 0844 493 2162
e-mail: information@nts.org.uk
web: www.nts.org.uk
dir: Off A93, 3m W of Peterculter

The great 13th-century Square Tower is one of the three oldest tower houses in Scotland and has associations with Robert the Bruce. The handsome mansion, added in 1619, houses a collection of family memorabilia. The grounds contain the 100-acre Old Wood of Drum, a natural oak wood and an old rose garden.

Times Castle: May-Jun & Sep, daily (ex Tue & Fri) 11.30-5; Jul-Aug, daily 11.30-5. Garden of Historic Roses: Apr-Oct, daily 10-6. Grounds: all year, daily; Jul-Aug daily 11.30-5 (last admission 45 mins before closing). Property open BH wknds from Fri-Mon inclusive* **Facilities** 🅟 ☕ ⛩ ♿ (partly accessible) (access to ground floor, but limited access to main floor) (wheelchair available, Braille, touch tours, scented garden) shop ⊗ 🏰

ABERDEENSHIRE

ALFORD — Map 15 NJ51

Alford Valley Railway

AB33 8AD
☎ 019755 64236 & 07879 293934
e-mail: info@alfordvalleyrailway.org.uk
web: www.alfordvalleyrailway.org.uk
dir: A944 Alford Village

Alford Valley Railway is a narrow-gauge passenger railway between Alford and Haughton Park, about one mile long. Santa specials at Christmas during the first two week-ends in December. The line travels through a golf course - spectacular views.

Times Open last wknd of Mar, all wknds in Apr; May-4 Oct 11.30-4* **Fees** £2.50 (ch £1.50) return fare. Family weekly pass £15 (2ad+2ch). Season ticket May-Sep £30* **Facilities** 🅟 Ⓟ ⛩ (outdoor) ♿ (fully accessible) (ramps at station platforms) shop

Craigievar Castle

AB33 8JF
☎ 0844 493 2174 📠 0844 493 2163
e-mail: information@nts.org.uk
web: www.nts.org.uk
dir: on A980, 6m S of Alford

A fairytale like castle, the Great Tower completed in 1626. The collection includes family portraits and 17th and 18th century furniture. There are extensive wooded grounds with a waymarked trail.

Times Castle: Mar-Jun, Fri-Tue 12-5.30; Jul-Aug, daily 12-5.30* **Facilities** 🅟 ⛩ ♿ (partly accessible) (access to castle difficult, many steps & spiral stairs to all rooms) (touch tours, radio microphone) shop ⊗ 🏰

SCOTLAND

SCOTLAND

BALMORAL Map 15 NO29

Balmoral Castle Grounds & Exhibition

AB35 5TB
☎ 013397 42534 📠 013397 42034
e-mail: info@balmoralcastle.com
web: www.balmoralcastle.com
dir: on A93 between Ballater & Braemar

Queen Victoria and Prince Albert first rented Balmoral Castle in 1848, and Prince Albert bought the property four years later. He commissioned William Smith to build a new castle, which was completed by 1856 and is still the Royal Family's Highland residence. Explore the exhibitions, grounds, gardens and trails as well as the magnificent Castle Ballroom.

Times Open Apr-Jul, daily 10-5 (last admission 4.30)* **Facilities** Ⓟ ☕ ⛩ (outdoor) ♿ (fully accessible) toilets for disabled (wheelchairs & battricars available, reserved parking) shop

BANCHORY Map 15 NO69

Banchory Museum FREE

Bridge St AB31 5SX
☎ 01771 622807 📠 01771 623558
e-mail: heritage@aberdeenshire.gov.uk
web: www.aberdeenshire.gov.uk/museums
dir: in Bridge St beside tourist information centre

The museum has displays on Scott Skinner (The 'Strathspey King'), natural history, royal commemorative china, local silver artefacts and a variety of local history displays.

Times Open Jan-Jun & Sep-Dec, Mon, Fri-Sat 11-1 & 2-4; Jul-Aug also open Tue & Wed **Facilities** Ⓟ ♿ (fully accessible) toilets for disabled 🚭

BANFF Map 15 NJ66

Banff Museum FREE

High St AB45 1AE
☎ 01771 622807 📠 01771 623558
e-mail: museums@aberdeenshire.gov.uk
web: www.aberdeenshire.gov.uk/museums

Displays of geology, natural history, local history, Banff silver, arms and armour, and displays relating to James Ferguson (18th-century astronomer) and Thomas Edward (19th-century Banff naturalist).

Times Open Jun-Sep, Mon-Sat 10-12.30 **Facilities** Ⓟ ♿ (partly accessible) (ground floor only accessible) 🚭

Duff House

AB45 3SX
☎ 01261 818181
web: www.historic-scotland.gov.uk
dir: 0.5m S, access S of town

The house was designed by William Adam for William Duff, later Earl of Fife. The main block was roofed in 1739, but the planned wings were never built. Although it is incomplete, the house is still considered one of Britain's finest Georgian baroque buildings. Duff House is a Country House Gallery of the National Galleries of Scotland.

Times Telephone for details of opening dates and times **Fees** Telephone for details of admission charges **Facilities** Ⓟ 🍽 licensed ⛩ toilets for disabled shop 🚭 🏛

CORGARFF Map 15 NJ20

Corgarff Castle

AB36 8YP
☎ 01975 651460
web: www.historic-scotland.gov.uk
dir: 8m W of Strathdon village

The 16th-century tower was besieged in 1571 and is associated with the Jacobite risings of 1715 and 1745. It later became a military barracks. Its last military use was to control the smuggling of whisky between 1827 and 1831.

Times Open all year, Apr-Sep, daily 9.30-5.30; Oct-Mar, wknds only 9.30-4.30. Closed 25-26 Dec & 1-2 Jan **Fees** £4.70 (ch £2.80, concessions £3.80). Please phone or check website for further details* **Facilities** Ⓟ shop 🏛

CRATHES Map 15 NO79

Crathes Castle Garden & Estate

AB31 5QJ
☎ 0844 4932166 📠 0844 4932169
e-mail: information@nts.org.uk
web: www.nts.org.uk
dir: On A93, 3m E of Banchory, 15m W of Aberdeen

This impressive 16th-century castle with magnificent interiors has royal associations dating from 1323. There is a large walled garden and a notable collection of unusual plants, including yew hedges dating from 1702. The grounds contain six nature trails, one suitable for disabled visitors, and an adventure playground.

Times Open daily 1-19 Apr & then wknds until 4 May, 10.30-4.30; 4 May-Jun & Sep-Oct, Sat-Thu 10.30-4.30; Jul-Aug, daily 10.30-5.30 (last entry 45mins before close). Gardens & Estate open all year, daily 9-sunset* **Facilities** Ⓟ 🍽 licensed ⛩ ♿ (partly accessible) (only lower garden accessible for wheelchairs) toilets for disabled (tape for visually impaired) shop 🚭 ♞

HUNTLY Map 15 NJ53

Brander Museum FREE

The Square AB54 8AE
☎ 01771 622807 📠 01771 623558
e-mail: heritage@aberdeenshire.gov.uk
web: www.aberdeenshire.gov.uk/museums
dir: in centre of Huntly, sharing building with library, museum on ground floor

The museum has displays of local and church history, plus the 19th-century Anderson Bey and the Sudanese campaigns.

Exhibits connected with George MacDonald, author and playwright, can also be seen.

Times Open all year, Tue-Sat 2-4.30 **Facilities** Ⓟ ♿ (fully accessible) (ramped access to front door of museum ground floor)

Huntly Castle

AB54 4SH

☎ 01466 793191

web: www.historic-scotland.gov.uk

The original medieval castle was rebuilt a number of times and destroyed, once by Mary, Queen of Scots. It was rebuilt for the last time in 1602, in palatial style, and is now an impressive ruin, noted for its ornate heraldic decorations. It stands in wooded parkland.

Times Open all year, Apr-Sep, daily 9.30-5.30; Oct, 9.30-4.30; Nov-Mar, Mon-Wed & Sat-Sun 9.30-4.30. Closed 25-26 Dec & 1-2 Jan **Fees** £4.70 (ch £2.80, concessions £3.80). Please phone or check website for further details* **Facilities** P toilets for disabled shop

INVERURIE — Map 15 NJ72

Carnegie Museum FREE

Town House, The Square AB51 3SN

☎ 01771 622807 01771 623558

e-mail: museums@aberdeenshire.gov.uk

web: www.aberdeenshire.gov.uk/museums

dir: in centre of Inverurie, on left side of townhouse building, above library

This fine museum contains displays on local history and archaeology, including Pictish stones, Bronze Age material and the Great North of Scotland Railway.

Times Open all year, Mon & Wed-Fri 12.30-3, Sat 10-1 & 2-4. Closed Tue & PH **Facilities** Ⓟ ♿ (partly accessible) (access to museum 1st floor via chairlift, ramped access to library)

KEMNAY — Map 15 NJ71

Castle Fraser

AB51 7LD

☎ 0844 493 2164 0844 493 2165

e-mail: information@nts.org.uk

web: www.nts.org.uk

dir: off A944, 4m N of Dunecht

The massive Z-plan castle was built between 1575 and 1636 and is one of the grandest of the Castles of Mar. The interior was remodelled in 1838 and decoration and furnishings of that period survive in some of the rooms. A formal garden inside the old walled garden, estate trails, a children's play area and a programme of concerts are among the attractions.

Times Castle open Apr-Jun, Thu-Sun 12-5; Jul-Aug, daily 11-5; Sep-Oct, Thu-Sun 12-5 & BH Mons* **Facilities** P ♿ (partly accessible) (access restricted to ground floor of Castle & walled garden) toilets for disabled (printed room guides, photos, scented garden) shop

KILDRUMMY — Map 15 NJ41

Kildrummy Castle

AB33 8RA

☎ 01975 571331

web: www.historic-scotland.gov.uk

dir: 10m SW of Alford

An important part of Scottish history, at least until it was dismantled in 1717, this fortress was the seat of the Earls of Mar. Now it is a ruined, but splendid, example of a 13th-century castle, with four round towers, hall and chapel all discernible. Some parts of the building, including the Great Gatehouse, are from the 15th and 16th centuries.

Times Open Apr-Sep, daily 9.30-5.30 **Fees** £3.70 (ch £2.20, concessions £3). Please phone or check website for further details* **Facilities** P toilets for disabled shop

Kildrummy Castle Gardens

AB33 8RA

☎ 019755 71277 & 71203 019755 71277

e-mail: information@kildrummy-castle-gardens.co.uk

web: www.kildrummy-castle-gardens.co.uk

dir: on A97 off A944. 10m W of Alford

With the picturesque ruin as a backdrop, these beautiful gardens include an alpine garden in an ancient quarry and a water garden. There's a small museum and a children's play area.

Times Open Apr-Oct, daily 10-5* **Facilities** P Ⓟ ♿ (partly accessible) toilets for disabled shop

MACDUFF — Map 15 NJ76

Macduff Marine Aquarium

11 High Shore AB44 1SL

☎ 01261 833369 01261 831052

e-mail: macduff.aquarium@aberdeenshire.gov.uk

web: www.macduff-aquarium.org.uk

dir: off A947 and A98 to Macduff, aquarium signed

Exciting displays feature local sealife. The central exhibit, unique in Britain, holds a living kelp reef. Divers feed the fish in this tank. Other displays include an estuary exhibit, splash tank, rock pools, deep reef tank and ray pool. Young visitors especially enjoy the touch pools. There are talks, video presentations and feeding shows throughout the week.

Times Open all year, daily 10-5 (last admission 4.15). Closed 25-27 & 31 Dec, 1-3 Jan **Fees** £5.65 (ch £2.80, pen £3.50). Family ticket £15.60* **Facilities** P Ⓟ (outdoor) ♿ (fully accessible) toilets for disabled (audio tour for visually impaired) shop

SCOTLAND

SCOTLAND

MARYCULTER Map 15 NO89

Storybook Glen

AB12 5FT
☎ 01224 732941 01224 732941
web: www.storybookglenaberdeen.co.uk
dir: 5m W of Aberdeen on B9077

This is a child's fantasy land, where favourite nursery rhyme and fairytale characters are brought to life. Grown-ups can enjoy the nostalgia and also the 20 acres of Deeside country, full of flowers, plants, trees and waterfalls.

Times Open all year, Mar-Oct, daily 10-6; Nov-Feb 10-4 **Fees** £5.40 (ch £3.85, concessions £4.05)* **Facilities** licensed (outdoor) (fully accessible) toilets for disabled shop

METHLICK Map 15 NJ83

Haddo House

AB41 7EQ
☎ 0844 493 2179 0844 493 2180
e-mail: information@nts.org.uk
web: www.nts.org.uk
dir: off B999, 4m N of Pitmedden

It is a splendid Palladian-style mansion built in the 1730s to designs by William Adam. Home to the Earls of Aberdeen, the house was refurbished in the 1880s in the 'Adam Revival' style. The adjoining country park offers beautiful woodland walks.

Times House: (Pre-booked guided tours only) 10 Apr-Jun & Sep-25 Oct, Fri-Mon 11.30, 1.30 & 3.30; Jul-Aug daily 11.30, 1.30 & 3.30. (Pre-booked group tours any time). Garden & grounds open daily.* **Facilities** licensed (partly accessible) (wheelchair access restricted in garden) toilets for disabled (lift, wheelchair, large print & hearing impaired guides) shop

MINTLAW Map 15 NJ94

Aberdeenshire Farming Museum FREE

Aden Country Park AB42 5FQ
☎ 01771 624590 & 622807 01771 623558
e-mail: museums@aberdeenshire.gov.uk
web: www.aberdeenshire.gov.uk/museums
dir: 1m W of Mintlaw on A950

Housed in 19th-century farm buildings, once part of the estate which now makes up the Aden Country Park. Two centuries of farming history and innovation are illustrated, and the story of the estate is also told. The reconstructed farm of Hareshowe shows how a family in the north-east farmed during the 1950s - access by guided tour only.

Times Open Apr-Sep, daily 11-4.30 (last admission 30 mins before closing). Park open all year, Apr-Sep 7-10; winter 7-7 **Facilities** (outdoor) (partly accessible) (1st floor not accessible) toilets for disabled (sensory garden) shop

OLD DEER Map 15 NJ94

Deer Abbey FREE

☎ 01667 460232
web: www.historic-scotland.gov.uk
dir: 2m W of Mintlaw on A950

The remains of the Cistercian Abbey, founded in 1218, include the infirmary, Abbot's House and the southern claustral range. The University Library at Cambridge now houses the famous Book of Deer.

Times Open at all reasonable times **Facilities**

OYNE Map 15 NJ62

Archaeolink Prehistory Park

Berryhill AB52 6QP
☎ 01464 851500 01464 851544
e-mail: info@archaeolink.co.uk
web: www.archaeolink.co.uk
dir: 1m off A96 on B9002

A stunning audio-visual show, a Myths and Legends Gallery and a whole range of interpretation techniques help visitors to explore what it was like to live 6000 years ago. In addition there are landscaped walkways, and outdoor activity areas including an Iron Age farm, Roman marching camp and Stone Age settlement in the 40-acre park. Enjoy daily hands-on activities for all ages, guided tours with costumed guides or relax in the coffee shop. Special weekend events held regularly.

Times Open Apr-Oct, daily 10-5* **Facilities** licensed (outdoor) (partly accessible) toilets for disabled (induction loop in theatre, wheelchair) shop

PETERHEAD — Map 15 NK14

Arbuthnot Museum — FREE

St Peter St AB42 1QD
☎ 01771 622807 Fax 01771 623558
e-mail: museums@aberdeenshire.gov.uk
web: www.aberdeenshire.gov.uk/museums
dir: at St.Peter St & Queen St x-roads, above library

Specialising in local exhibits, particularly those relating to the fishing industry, this museum also displays Arctic and whaling specimens and a British coin collection. The regular programme of exhibitions changes approximately every six weeks.

Times Open all year, Mon-Tue & Thu-Sat 11-1 & 2-4.30, Wed 11-1. Closed Sun and BHs **Facilities** Ⓟ ⊗

PITMEDDEN — Map 15 NJ82

Pitmedden Garden

AB41 7PD
☎ 0844 493 2177 Fax 0844 493 2178
e-mail: information@nts.org.uk
web: www.nts.org.uk
dir: 1m W of Pitmedden on A920

The fine 17th-century walled garden, with sundials, pavilions and fountains dotted among the parterres, has been authentically restored, and there is a Museum of Farming Life and a woodland walk.

Times Garden, Museum: May-Oct, daily 10-5.30 (last admission 5); grounds: all year, daily* **Facilities** Ⓟ ☕ ⛩ ♿ (partly accessible) toilets for disabled (2 wheelchairs available, scented plants) shop ♉

Tolquhon Castle

AB41 7LP
☎ 01651 851286
web: www.historic-scotland.gov.uk
dir: 2m NE off B999

Now roofless, this late 16th-century quadrangular mansion encloses an early 15th-century tower. There is a fine gatehouse and a splendid courtyard.

Times Open all year, Apr-Sep, daily, 9.30-5.30; Oct-Mar, wknds only 9.30-4.30. Closed 25-26 Dec & 1-2 Jan **Fees** £3.70 (ch £2.20, concessions £3). Please phone or check website for further details* **Facilities** Ⓟ ⛩ toilets for disabled shop ⊗ ▮

RHYNIE — Map 15 NJ42

Leith Hall, Garden & Estate

Kennethmont AB54 4NQ
☎ 0844 493 2175 Fax 0844 493 2176
e-mail: information@nts.org.uk
web: www.nts.org.uk
dir: on B9002, 1m W of Kennethmont

Home of the Leith family for over 300 years, the house, which is no longer open to the public, dates back to 1650. It is surrounded by charming gardens and extensive grounds, with marked trails.

Times Garden: all year, daily 9-sunset. Grounds: all year, daily* **Facilities** Ⓟ ☕ ⛩ ♿ (partly accessible) (sloping walled garden, path to viewpoint & pond walk accessible with assistance) toilets for disabled (wheelchair, parking next to hall, scented garden) ⊗ ♉

STONEHAVEN — Map 15 NO88

Dunnottar Castle

AB39 2TL
☎ 01569 762173
e-mail: info@dunechtestates.co.uk
web: www.dunnottarcastle.co.uk
dir: 2m S of Stonehaven on A92

This once-impregnable fortress, now a spectacular ruin, was the site of the successful protection of the Scottish Crown Jewels from the might of Cromwell. A must for anyone who takes Scottish history seriously.

Times Open all year, Spring & Autumn, Mon-Sat 9-6 Sun 2-5; Summer, daily 9-6; Winter, Fri-Mon (last entry 30mins before closing)* **Facilities** Ⓟ ⛩ (indoor & outdoor) ♿ (partly accessible) (many steps)

Tolbooth Museum — FREE

Old Pier AB39 2JU
☎ 01771 622807 Fax 01771 623558
e-mail: museums@aberdeenshire.gov.uk
web: www.aberdeenshire.gov.uk/museums
dir: on harbour front

Built in the late 16th century as a storehouse for the Earls Marischal at Dunnottar Castle, the building was the Kincardineshire County Tollbooth from 1600-1767. Displays feature local history and fishing.

Times Open 3 Apr-Sep, Wed-Mon 1.30-4.30 **Facilities** Ⓟ ♿ (partly accessible) (lower ground floor not accessible) ⊗

SCOTLAND

SCOTLAND

TURRIFF Map 15 NJ75

Fyvie Castle

Fyvie AB53 8JS
☎ 0844 493 2182 📠 0844 493 2181
e-mail: information@nts.org.uk
web: www.nts.org.uk
dir: 8m SE of Turriff off A947

This superb castle, founded in the 13th century, has five towers, each built in a different century, and is one of the grandest examples of Scottish Baronial. It contains the finest wheel stair in Scotland, and a 17th-century morning room, lavishly furnished in Edwardian style. The collection of portraits is exceptional, and there are also displays of arms and armour and tapestries.

Times Castle: Apr-Jun & Sep-Oct, Sat-Tue 12-5; Jul-Aug daily 11-5 (last admission 4.15). Garden: all year, daily 9-sunset. Open BH wknds from Fri-Mon incl. Grounds: open all year, daily* **Facilities** (partly accessible) (steps to various rooms) toilets for disabled (small lift, Braille sheets, scented gardens) shop

ANGUS

ARBROATH Map 12 NO64

Arbroath Abbey

DD11 1EG
☎ 01241 878756
web: www.historic-scotland.gov.uk

The 'Declaration of Arbroath' - declaring Robert the Bruce as king - was signed at the 12th-century abbey on 6 April 1320. The abbot's house is well preserved, and the church remains are also interesting.

Times Open all year daily, Apr-Sep 9.30-5.30; Oct-Mar 9.30-4.30. Closed 25-26 Dec & 1-2 Jan **Fees** £4.70 (ch £2.80, concessions £3.80). Please phone or check website for further details* **Facilities**

Arbroath Signal Tower Museum FREE

Signal Tower, Ladyloan DD11 1PU
☎ 01241 875598
e-mail: signal.tower@angus.gov.uk
web: www.angus.gov.uk/history/museums
dir: on A92 adjacent to harbour. 16m NE of Dundee

Located by Arbroath's historic harbour, the Signal Tower tells the stories of Arbroath's maritime history including that of the Bell Rock Lighthouse. The lighthouse was constructed in 1811, on a rock eleven miles offshore from Arbroath, and "Signal Tower" was the original shore station, housing keepers' families. The museum will be the focus of "The Year of the Light", a programme of events celebrating the bicentenary of the Bell Rock Lighthouse in 2011. See museum website for details.

Times Re-opening in Feb 2011 after complete re-display of museum collections. Please call to confirm opening hours **Facilities** (outdoor) (partly accessible) (access restricted to ground floor, no lift) (induction loop) shop

BRECHIN Map 15 NO66

Brechin Town House Museum FREE

28 High St DD9 7AA
☎ 01356 625536
e-mail: brechin.museum@angus.gov.uk
web: www.angus.gov.uk/history/museum
dir: off A90 at sign for Brechin, 2m into town centre

Within a former courtroom, debtor's prison and seat of local government, this museum covers the history of the little City of Brechin from the earliest settlement, through the market town to industrialisation in the form of flax, jute mills, distilling, weaving and engineering. Brechin's fascinating history of development is portrayed in vivid displays. The Museum also houses the Tourist Information Office.

Times Open Mon-Tue & Thu-Sat 10-5, Wed 10-1. Closed 25-26 Dec, 1-2 Jan **Facilities** (fully accessible) toilets for disabled (induction loop) shop

Pictavia Visitor Centre

Brechin Castle Centre, Haughmuir DD9 6RL
☎ 01356 626241 📠 01307 467357
e-mail: ecdev@angus.gov.uk
web: www.pictavia.org.uk
dir: off A90 at Brechin

Find about more about the ancient pagan nation of the Picts, who lived in Scotland nearly 2000 years ago. Visitors can learn about Pictish culture, art and religion through film, interactive displays and music. Special events and exhibitions take place throughout the year, for full details please refer to website.

Times Open all year, Mar-Oct, Mon-Sat 9-5, Sun 10-5; Nov-Feb, Sat 9-5, Sun 10-5 **Fees** £3.25 (under 5 free, ch & concessions £2.25). Family ticket £10. Group rates available for large parties & educational groups **Facilities** licensed (outdoor) (fully accessible) toilets for disabled shop

CARNOUSTIE Map 12 NO53

Barry Mill

Barry DD7 7RJ
☎ 0844 493 2140 📠 0844 493 2140
e-mail: information@nts.org.uk
web: www.nts.org.uk
dir: N of Barry village between A92 & A930, 2m W of Carnoustie

This restored 18th-century mill works on a demonstration basis. Records show that the site has been used for milling since the 16th century. Displays highlight the important place the mill held in the community. There is a waymarked walk and picnic area.

Times Open 2 Apr-Oct, Thu-Mon 12-5, Sun 1-5* **Facilities** (partly accessible) (ground floor & lower ground floor accessible only, stairs to first floor) toilets for disabled (ramp from car park to mill)

EDZELL Map 15 NO56

Edzell Castle and Garden

DD9 7UE
☎ 01356 648631
web: www.historic-scotland.gov.uk
dir: on B966

The 16th-century castle has a remarkable walled garden built in 1604 by Sir David Lindsay. Flower-filled recesses in the walls are alternated with heraldic and symbolic sculptures of a sort not seen elsewhere in Scotland. There are ornamental and border gardens and a garden house.

Times Open all year, Apr-Sep, daily 9.30-5.30; Oct, 9.30-4.30; Nov-Mar, Mon-Wed & Sat-Sun 9.30-4.30. Closed 25-26 Dec & 1-2 Jan **Fees** £4.70 (ch £2.80, concessions £3.80). Please phone or check website for further details* **Facilities** shop

FORFAR Map 15 NO45

The Meffan Museum & Art Gallery FREE

20 West High St DD8 1BB
☎ 01307 464123
e-mail: the.meffan@angus.gov.uk
web: www.angus.gov.uk/museums
dir: off A90. Attraction in town centre

This lively, ever-changing contemporary art gallery and museum is full of surprises. Walk down a cobbled street full of shops, ending up at a witch-burning scene. Carved Pictish stones and a diorama of an archaeological dig complete the vibrant displays.

Times Open all year Mon-Sat. Closed 25-26 Dec & 1-2 Jan* **Facilities** (fully accessible) toilets for disabled shop

GLAMIS Map 15 NO34

Angus Folk Museum

Kirkwynd Cottages DD8 1RT
☎ 0844 493 2141 📠 0844 493 2141
e-mail: information@nts.org.uk
web: www.nts.org.uk
dir: off A94, in Glamis, 5m SW of Forfar

A row of stone-roofed, late 18th-century cottages now houses the splendid Angus Folk Collection of domestic equipment and cottage furniture. Across the wynd, an Angus stone steading houses 'The Life on the Land' exhibition.

Times Open 4 Apr-28 Jun, wknds only 12-5, 29 Jun-Aug daily 12-5, 5 Sep-1 Nov wknds only 12-5, BH Mon's* **Facilities** (fully accessible) toilets for disabled

Glamis Castle 2 FOR 1

DD8 1RJ
☎ 01307 840393 📠 01307 840733
e-mail: enquiries@glamis-castle.co.uk
web: www.glamis-castle.co.uk
dir: 5m W of Forfar on A94, turn off after Coupar Angus, direction Forfar

Glamis Castle is the family home of the Earls of Strathmore and Kinghorne and has been a royal residence since 1372. It is the childhood home of the late Queen Mother, the birthplace of her daughter the late Princess Margaret, and the setting for Shakespeare's play *Macbeth*. Guided Tours, Garden walks, Nature Trail, Shopping, children's activities and exhibitions.

Times Open all year, Mar-Oct, 10-6 (last admission 4.30); Nov-Dec 10.30-4.30 (last admission 3.30)* **Fees** Castle & grounds £8.50 (ch £5.30, pen £7.50). Family ticket £23.50* **Facilities** licensed (outdoor) (partly accessible) toilets for disabled (castle tour not suitable, audio visual film of tour) shop

KIRRIEMUIR Map 15 NO35

J M Barrie's Birthplace

9 Brechin Rd DD8 4BX
☎ 0844 493 2142 📠 0844 493 2142
e-mail: information@nts.org.uk
web: www.nts.org.uk
dir: on A90/A926 in Kirriemuir, 6m NW of Forfar

The creator of Peter Pan, Sir James Barrie, was born in Kirriemuir in 1860. The upper floors of No 9 Brechin Road are furnished as they may have been when Barrie lived there, and the adjacent house, No 11, houses an exhibition about him. The wash-house outside was his first 'theatre' and gave him the idea for Wendy's house in *Peter Pan*.

Times Open 4 Apr-28 Jun & 31 Aug-1 Nov, Sat-Wed 12-5; 29 Jun-30 Aug, daily 11-5* **Facilities** (partly accessible) (steps to reception room, wheelchair access restricted to museum & wash house) (stairlift, induction loop, Braille info sheets) shop

SCOTLAND

SCOTLAND

KIRRIEMUIR *continued*

Kirriemuir Gateway to the Glens Museum FREE

The Town House, 32 High St DD8 4BB
☎ 01575 575479
e-mail: kirrie.gateway@angus.gov.uk
web: www.angus.gov.uk/history/museum
dir: in town centre, 30mins N of Dundee, on A90

Housed in the town house dating from 1604, this museum covers the history of Kirriemuir and the Angus Glens from prehistoric times. A realistic model of Kirriemuir on market day in 1604 can be seen and local voices can be heard telling their part in the area's history from sweet making to linen weaving. Animals and birds can be seen at close range in the Wildlife diorama. The museum also houses Kirriemuir tourist information centre.

Times Open all year, Jan-Mar & Oct-Dec, Mon-Wed, Fri-Sat 10-5, Thu 2-5; Apr-Sep, Mon-Sat 10-5. Closed 25-26 Dec & 1-2 Jan **Facilities** Ⓟ ♿ (partly accessible) (ground floor accessible, steps to first floor) toilets for disabled (induction loop, multi media displays) shop

MONTROSE Map 15 NO75

House of Dun

DD10 9LQ
☎ 0844 493 2144 📠 0844 493 2145
e-mail: information@nts.org.uk
web: www.nts.org.uk
dir: on A935, 3m W of Montrose

This Georgian house, overlooking the Montrose Basin, was built for Lord Dun in 1730 and is noted for the exuberant plasterwork of the interior. Family portraits, fine furniture and porcelain are on display, and royal mementos connected with a daughter of King William IV and the actress Mrs Jordan, who lived here in the 19th century. There is a walled garden and woodland walks.

Times Open House: Apr-28 Jun & 2 Sep-Oct, Wed-Sun 12-5; 29 Jun-Aug, daily 11-5 (last admission 45 mins before closing). Garden: All year, daily 9-sunset. Grounds: All year daily. Open BH wknds from Fri-Mon incl. (Occasional closures for weddings)* **Facilities** Ⓟ licensed ♿ (partly accessible) (access to first floor & basement via a stair lift) toilets for disabled (Braille sheets, wheelchair & stair lift, subtitled video) shop

Montrose Museum & Art Gallery FREE

Panmure Place DD10 8HE
☎ 01674 673232
e-mail: montrose.museum@angus.gov.uk
web: www.angus.gov.uk/history/museum
dir: opposite Montrose Academy in town centre, approach via A92 from Aberdeen or Dundee

Montrose Museum opened in 1842, one of the earliest purpose built museums. This neo-classical building with its iconic columns holds extensive local collections covering prehistoric times, the maritime history of the port, the natural history of Angus and local art. The museum has regular changing exhibitions. It also houses Montrose Tourist Information.

Times Open all year, Mon-Sat 10-5. Closed 25-26 Dec & 1-2 Jan* **Facilities** Ⓟ ♿ (fully accessible) toilets for disabled (induction loop) shop

ARGYLL & BUTE

ARDUAINE Map 10 NM71

Arduaine Garden

PA34 4XQ
☎ 0844 493 2216 📠 0844 493 2216
e-mail: information@nts.org.uk
web: www.nts.org.uk
dir: 20m S of Oban, on A816, 19m N of Lochgilphead

An outstanding 18-acre garden on a promontory bounded by Loch Melfort and the Sound of Jura, climatically favoured by the North Atlantic Drift. It is famous for its rhododendrons and azalea species and other rare trees and shrubs.

Times Garden open all year, daily 9.30-sunset, Reception centre Apr-Sep daily, 9.30-4.30* **Facilities** Ⓟ ♿ (partly accessible) (a large part of the garden is accessible to the less mobile) toilets for disabled (scented flowers for the blind)

ARROCHAR Map 10 NN20

Argyll Forest Park FREE

Forestry Commission, Ardgartan Visitor Centre G83 7AR
☎ 01301 702432 📠 01301 702597
web: www.forestry.gov.uk/argyllforest
dir: on A83 at foot of "The Rest and Be Thankful"

This park extends over a large area of hill ground and forest, noted for its rugged beauty. Numerous forest walks and picnic sites allow exploration; the Arboretum walks and the route between Younger Botanic Gardens and Puck's Glen are particularly lovely. Wildlife viewing facilities include live footage of nesting birds in season. Bird and red squirrel hides at Glenbranter, Ardentinny and Puck's Glenn.

Times Open Etr-Oct, daily 10-5 **Facilities** Ⓟ (outdoor) ♿ (fully accessible) shop

AUCHINDRAIN Map 10 NN00

Auchindrain Museum

PA32 8XN
☎ 01499 500235 📠 01499 500235
e-mail: manager@auchindrain-museum.org.uk
web: www.auchindrain-museum.org.uk
dir: 6m SW of Inveraray on A83

Auchindrain is an extraordinary attraction that brings an original Township or farming village back to life. On entering the Museum visitors step back in time to witness how the local community lived, worked and played. The original Township buildings are furnished and give a fascinating glimpse into the lives of the people who once lived and worked at Auchindrain. See the website for special events.

Times Open Apr-Oct, daily 10-5 (last admission 4)* **Facilities** (indoor & outdoor) (partly accessible) (some areas are accessible but steep paths) shop

BARCALDINE — Map 10 NM94

Scottish Sea Life Sanctuary

PA37 1SE
01631 720386 01631 720529
e-mail: obansealife@merlinentertainments.biz
web: www.sealsanctuary.co.uk
dir: 10m N of Oban on A828 towards Fort William

Set in one of Scotland's most picturesque locations, the Scottish Sea Life Sanctuary provides dramatic views of native undersea life including stingrays, seals, octopus and catfish. There are daily talks and feeding demonstrations and during the summer young seals can be viewed prior to their release back into the wild. Recent additions include Otter Creek - a large naturally landscaped enclosure with deep diving pool with underwater viewing and cascading streams through other pools, and 'Into the Deep', a themed interactive area displaying living creatures from the deep. There is a restaurant, gift shop, children's play park and a nature trail.

Times Open daily at 10. Please call for last admissions* **Facilities** (outdoor) (fully accessible) toilets for disabled (assistance available for wheelchairs) shop

BENMORE — Map 10 NS18

Benmore Botanic Garden — 2 FOR 1

PA23 8QU
01369 706261 01369 706369
e-mail: benmore@rbge.org.uk
web: www.rbge.org.uk
dir: 7m N of Dunoon on A815

From the formal gardens, through the hillside woodlands, follow the paths to a stunning viewpoint with a spectacular outlook across the garden and the Holy Loch to the Firth of Clyde and beyond. Amongst many highlights are the stately conifers, the magnificent avenue of giant redwoods, and an extensive magnolia and rhododendron collection. Visit the restored Victorian Fernery.

Times Open Mar & Oct, daily 10-5; Apr-Sep, daily 10-6 **Fees** £5 (ch 5-16yrs £1, concessions £4). Family £10* **Facilities** licensed (partly accessible) toilets for disabled shop

CARNASSARIE CASTLE — Map 10 NM80

Carnassarie Castle — FREE

PA31 8RQ
web: www.historic-scotland.gov.uk
dir: 2m N of Kilmartin off A816

A handsome combined tower house and hall, home of John Carswell, first Protestant Bishop of the Isles and translator of the first book printed in Gaelic. Very fine architectural details of the late 16th century.

Times Open at all reasonable times **Facilities**

HELENSBURGH — Map 10 NS28

Hill House

Upper Colquhoun St G84 9AJ
0844 493 2208 0844 493 2209
e-mail: information@nts.org.uk
web: www.nts.org.uk
dir: off B832, between A82 & A814 23m NW of Glasgow

The Hill House is a handsome example of Charles Rennie Mackintosh's work, modern but part-inspired by Scottish tower houses. It was commissioned by the publisher Walter Blackie. The gardens are being restored to Blackie's design, with features reflecting the suggestions of Mackintosh. There is also a special display about Mackintosh.

Times Open Apr-Oct, daily 1.30-5.30* **Facilities** (partly accessible) (no wheelchair access to upper floors) (Braille guidebook) shop

INVERARAY — Map 10 NN00

Bell Tower of All Saints' Church

The Avenue PA32 8YX
01838 200293
dir: through the arches on Front St, into Avenue car park

The tower stands next to All-Saints Church but is separate from it. Built by the 10th Duke of Argyll as a war memorial to the dead of Clan Campbell, it was completed in 1931. It has the second heaviest peal of bells in the world, and these are rung once a month. The tower is 126 feet high and has a narrow circular staircase of 176 steps, which are not suitable for the infirm. From the top is a spectacular view of Inverary, Loch Fyne and the surrounding hills.

Times Tower open May-Sep, daily, 10-1 & 2-5. Church open Mar-Oct* **Facilities** (outdoor)

Inveraray Castle & Garden

PA32 8XE
01499 302203 01499 302421
e-mail: enquiries@inveraray-castle.com
web: www.inveraray-castle.com
dir: on A83 Glasgow to Campbeltown road

The Castle is currently home to the Duke of Argyll, Head of the Clan Campbell, whose family have lived in Inveraray since the 15th century. Designed by Roger Morris and decorated by Robert Mylne, the fairytale exterior belies the grandeur of the gracious interior. The Armoury Hall contains some 1300 pieces including Brown Bess muskets, Lochaber axes, 18th-century Scottish broadswords, and swords from the Battle of Culloden. Other rooms contain fine French tapestries, Scottish, English and French furniture, and a wealth of other works of art. There is also a unique collection of china, silver and family artefacts.

Times Open Apr-Oct, daily 10-5.45 (last admission 5) **Fees** Castle & Gardens £9 (concessions £7.50) Family ticket £25. Groups 20+ 20% discount **Facilities** (outdoor) (partly accessible) toilets for disabled shop

INVERARAY *continued*

Inveraray Jail

Church Square PA32 8TX
☎ 01499 302381 🖷 01499 302195
e-mail: info@inverarayjail.co.uk
web: www.inverarayjail.co.uk
dir: on A82/A83 Campbeltown road

Enter Inveraray Jail and step back in time. See furnished cells and experience prison sounds and smells. Ask the 'prisoner' how to pick oakum. Turn the heavy handle of an original crank machine, take 40 winks in a hammock or listen to Matron's tales of day-to-day prison life. Visit the magnificent 1820 courtroom and hear trials in progress. Imaginative exhibitions including 'Torture, Death and Damnation' and 'In Prison Today'. Also a fully preserved "Black Maria", built in 1891.

Times Open all year, Nov-Mar, daily 10-5; Apr-Oct, daily 9.30-6 (last admission 1hr before close). Closed 25-26 Dec **Fees** £8.25 (ch £4.95, concessions £6.95) **Facilities** Ⓟ ♿ (partly accessible) (lots of old steep staircases) toilets for disabled (wheelchair ramp at rear, induction loop in courtroom) shop

SCOTLAND

KILMARTIN — Map 10 NR89

Dunadd Fort — FREE

web: www.historic-scotland.gov.uk
dir: 2m S of Kilmartin on A816

Dunadd was one of the ancient capitals of Dalriada from which the Celtic kingdom of Scotland was formed. Near to this prehistoric hill fort (now little more than an isolated hillock) are carvings of a boar and a footprint; these probably marked the spot where early kings were invested with their royal power.

Times Open at all reasonable times **Facilities**

Kilmartin House Museum

PA31 8RQ
☎ 01546 510278 🖷 01546 510330
e-mail: museum@kilmartin.org
web: www.kilmartin.org
dir: in centre of village, adjacent to church

People have lived in the Kilmartin area for thousands of years, gradually shaping the extraordinary landscape you see today. More than 350 prehistoric and historic sites lie within six miles of this quiet village; burial cairns, rock-carvings, standing stones, stone circles and the fortress of the earliest Scottish Kings, medieval castles, ancient gravestones depicting warriors, early Christian crosses and deserted croft houses. This remarkable concentration and diversity of ancient sites is celebrated at Kilmartin House Museum. Explore enigmatic monuments, see ancient objects and learn more about the people who made them.

Times Open Mar-Oct, daily, 10-5.30. Nov-Xmas 11-4* **Facilities** 🅟 Ⓟ licensed (outdoor) ♿ (partly accessible) (stairs to audio visual theatre) toilets for disabled shop

LOCHAWE — Map 10 NN12

Cruachan Power Station

Visitor Centre, Dalmally PA33 1AN
☎ 01866 822618 🖷 01866 822509
e-mail: visit.cruachan@scottishpower.com
web: www.visitcruachan.co.uk
dir: A85 18m E of Oban

A vast cavern hidden deep inside Ben Cruachan, which contains a 440,000-kilowatt hydro-electric power station, driven by water drawn from a high-level reservoir up the mountain. A guided tour takes you inside the mountain and reveals the generators in their underground cavern.

Times Open Apr-Oct, daily 9.30-4.45; Feb-Mar & Nov-Dec, Mon-Fri 10-3.45. Closed 20 Dec-1 Feb **Fees** £6 (ch 6-16 £2.50, concessions £5) **Facilities** 🅟 ♿ (partly accessible) (visitor centre fully accessible, guided tours not accessible) toilets for disabled shop

MINARD — Map 10 NR99

Crarae Garden

PA32 8YA
☎ 0844 493 2210 🖷 0844 493 2210
e-mail: information@nts.org.uk
web: www.nts.org.uk
dir: 10m S of Inveraray on A83

Set beside Loch Fyne, these gardens are among Scotland's loveliest, noted for their rhododendrons, azaleas, conifers and ornamental shrubs, which include a number of rare species.

Times Visitor centre Apr-Oct, daily 10-5; Garden all year, daily 9.30-sunset* **Facilities** 🅟 ♿ (partly accessible) (only lower garden accessible for wheelchairs & terrain on some routes steep with steps) toilets for disabled shop

OBAN — Map 10 NM83

Dunstaffnage Castle and Chapel

PA37 1PZ
☎ 01631 562465
web: www.historic-scotland.gov.uk
dir: 3m N on peninsula

Now ruined, this four-sided stronghold has a gatehouse, two round towers and walls 10 feet thick. It was once the prison of Flora MacDonald.

Times Open all year, Apr-Sep, daily, 9.30-5.30; Oct, 9.30-4.30; Nov-Mar, Mon-Wed & Sat-Sun, 9.30-4.30. Closed 25-26 Dec & 1-2 Jan **Fees** £3.70 (ch £2.20, concessions £3). Please phone or check website for further details* **Facilities** 🅟 shop

TAYNUILT Map 10 NN03

Bonawe Historic Iron Furnace

PA35 1JQ
☎ 01866 822432
web: www.historic-scotland.gov.uk
dir: 0.75m NE off B845

The furnace is a restored charcoal blast-furnace for iron-smelting and making cast-iron. It was established in 1753 and worked until 1876. The works exploited the Forest of Lorne to provide charcoal for fuel.

Times Open Apr-Sep, daily 9.30-5.30 **Fees** £4.20 (ch £2.50, concessions £3.40). Please phone or check website for further details* **Facilities** Ⓟ toilets for disabled shop

CLACKMANNANSHIRE

ALLOA Map 11 NS89

Alloa Tower

Alloa Park FK10 1PP
☎ 0844 493 2129 Fax 0844 493 2129
e-mail: information@nts.org.uk
web: www.nts.org.uk
dir: Off A907, close to town centre

Beautifully restored, the tower, completed in 1467, is the only remaining part of the ancestral home of the Earls of Mar. The structure retains rare medieval features, notably the complete timber roof structure and groin vaulting. A superb loan collection of portraits and chattels of the Erskine family includes paintings by Raeburn.

Times Open Apr-Oct, daily 1-5 (last entry 4.15). Morning visits available for pre-booked groups. Costumed guided tours by arrangement* **Facilities** Ⓟ ♿ (partly accessible) (ground floor accessible for wheelchair users, slides of portraits & film about property available) toilets for disabled (large print interpretation, induction loop)

DOLLAR Map 11 NS99

Castle Campbell and Gardens

FK14 7PP
☎ 01259 742408
web: www.historic-scotland.gov.uk
dir: 10m E of Stirling on A91

Traditionally known as the 'Castle of Gloom', the 15th to 17th-century tower stands in the picturesque Ochil Hills, gives wonderful views, and can be reached by a walk through the magnificent Dollar Glen. Care must be taken in or after rain when the path may be dangerous.

Times Open all year, Apr-Sep, daily, 9.30-5.30; Oct-Mar, 9.30-4.30. Closed Thu & Fri in winter, 25-26 Dec & 1-2 Jan **Fees** £4.70 (ch £2.80, concessions £3.80). Please phone or check website for further details* **Facilities** Ⓟ licensed shop

DUMFRIES & GALLOWAY

ARDWELL Map 10 NX14

Ardwell House Gardens

DG9 9LY
☎ 01776 860227 Fax 01776 860288
dir: 10m S of Stranraer, on A716

Country house gardens and grounds with flowering shrubs and woodland walks. Plants for sale. House not open to the public.

Times Open Apr-Oct, 10-5. Walled garden & greenhouses close at 5 **Fees** £3 (ch & concessions £2)* **Facilities** Ⓟ (outdoor) toilets for disabled

CAERLAVEROCK Map 11 NY06

Caerlaverock Castle

Glencaple DG1 4RU
☎ 01387 770244
web: www.historic-scotland.gov.uk
dir: 8m SE of Dumfries, on B725

This ancient seat of the Maxwell family is a splendid medieval stronghold dating back to the 13th century. It has high walls and round towers, with machicolations added in the 15th century.

Times Open all year daily, Apr-Sep 9.30-5.30; Oct-Mar 9.30-4.30. Closed 25-26 Dec & 1-2 Jan **Fees** £5.20 (ch £3.10, concessions £4.20). Please phone or check website for further details* **Facilities** Ⓟ Ⓟ licensed toilets for disabled shop

SCOTLAND

CAERLAVEROCK *continued*

WWT Caerlaverock

Eastpark Farm DG1 4RS
☎ 01387 770200 📠 01387 770539
e-mail: info@caerlaverock@wwt.org.uk
web: www.wwt.org.uk
dir: 9m SE of Dumfries, signed from A75

This internationally important wetland is the winter home of the Barnacle goose, whose entire Svalbard population spend the winter on the Solway Firth. Observation facilities include 20 hides, 3 towers and a heated observatory. A wide variety of other wildlife can be seen, notably the rare Natterjack Toad and a family of Barn Owls and ospreys which can be observed via a CCTV system. Swan feeds daily at 11-2. For a wide range of special events please see website for details.

Times Open daily 10-5. Closed 25 Dec **Fees** £6.70 (ch £3.30, concessions £5.05). Family ticket £18* **Facilities** Ⓟ ☕ ⛩ (outdoor) ♿ (partly accessible) (all hides and observatories accessible except farmhouse tower and small avenue hides) toilets for disabled shop ㊗

CARDONESS CASTLE — Map 11 NX55

Cardoness Castle

DG7 2EH
☎ 01557 814427
web: www.historic-scotland.gov.uk
dir: 1m SW of Gatehouse of Fleet, off A75

A 15th-century stronghold overlooking the Water of Fleet. It was once the home of the McCullochs of Galloway. The architectural details inside the tower are of very high quality.

Times Open all year, Apr-Sep, daily 9.30-5.30; Oct-Mar open wknds only 9.30-4.30. Closed 25-26 Dec & 1-2 Jan **Fees** £3.70 (ch £2.20, concessions £3). Please phone or check website for further details* **Facilities** Ⓟ shop

CASTLE DOUGLAS — Map 11 NX76

Threave Castle

DG7 1TJ
☎ 07711 223101
web: www.historic-scotland.gov.uk
dir: 3m W on A75

Archibald the Grim built this lonely castle in the late 14th century. It stands on an islet in the River Dee, and is four storeys high with round towers guarding the outer wall. The island is reached by boat.

Times Open Apr-Sep, daily 9.30-5 **Fees** £4.20 (ch £2.50, concessions £3.40). Charge includes ferry trip. Please phone or check website for further details* **Facilities** Ⓟ ⛩ toilets for disabled ㊗

Threave Garden & Estate

DG7 1RX
☎ 08449 4932245 📠 0844 4932243
e-mail: information@nts.org.uk
web: www.nts.org.uk
dir: 1m W of Castle Douglas, off A75

The best time to visit is in spring when there is a dazzling display of daffodils. The garden is a delight in all seasons, however, and is home to the National Trust for Scotland's School of Practical Gardening.

Times Garden, visitor & countryside centre: Apr-Oct daily 10-5; Nov-20 Dec & Feb-Mar, Fri-Sun 10-5. House: Apr-Oct, Wed-Fri & Sun 11-3.30 (visit by guided tour only). Estate: all year daily* **Facilities** Ⓟ 🍽 licensed ⛩ ♿ (fully accessible) toilets for disabled (manual & electric wheelchairs available) shop ㊗

CREETOWN — Map 11 NX45

Creetown Gem Rock Museum — 2 FOR 1

Chain Rd DG8 7HJ
☎ 01671 820357 & 820554 📠 01671 820554
e-mail: enquiries@gemrock.net
web: www.gemrock.net
dir: follow signs from A75 at Creetown bypass

The Gem Rock is the leading independent museum of its kind in the UK, and is renowned worldwide. Crystals, gemstones, minerals, jewellery and fossils, the Gem Rock displays some of the most breathtaking examples of nature's wonders. See the audio-visual 'Fire in the Stones', the latest attraction 'Olga', a 50,000 year old cave bear skeleton, explore the Crystal Cave, relax in the Prospector's Study, and sample the home-baked Scottish cakes in the café. 2011 celebrates the museum's 30th year.

Times Open daily, Feb-Mar 10-4; Apr-Sep 9.30-5.30, Oct-22 Dec 10-4. Closed 23 Dec-Jan **Fees** £3.75 (ch £2.25, under 5 free, concessions £3.25). Family ticket (2ad+3ch) £9.75 **Facilities** Ⓟ Ⓟ ☕ ⛩ (outdoor) ♿ (fully accessible) toilets for disabled (ideal attraction for wheelchair users) shop ㊗

DRUMCOLTRAN TOWER — Map 11 NX86

Drumcoltran Tower — FREE

web: www.historic-scotland.gov.uk
dir: 7m NE of Dalbeattie, in farm buildings off A711

A well-preserved tower from the mid-16th century, simply planned and built, set in a busy modern farmyard.

Times Open at any reasonable time **Facilities** Ⓟ ㊗

DUMFRIES Map 11 NX97

Burns Mausoleum

FREE

St Michael's Churchyard
☎ 01387 255297 Fax 01387 265081
e-mail: dumfriesmuseum@dumgal.gov.uk
web: www.dumgal.gov.uk/museums
dir: at junct of Brooms Rd (ATS) and St Michael's St (B725)

The mausoleum is in the form of a Greek temple, and contains the tombs of Robert Burns, his wife Jean Armour, and their five sons. A sculptured group shows the Muse of Poetry flinging her cloak over Burns at the plough.

Times House: Phone for details. Grounds: Unrestricted access **Facilities** Ⓟ ♿ (partly accessible) (visitors with mobility difficulties tel 01387 255297)

Dumfries Museum & Camera Obscura

2 FOR 1

The Observatory, Rotchell Rd DG2 7SW
☎ 01387 253374 Fax 01387 265081
e-mail: dumfriesmuseum@dumgal.gov.uk
web: www.dumgal.gov.uk/museums
dir: A75 from S Carlisle or SW from Castle Douglas, museum in Maxwellton area of Dumfries

Situated in and around the 18th-century windmill tower, the museum's collections were started over 150 years ago and exhibitions trace the history of the people and landscape of Dumfries & Galloway. The Camera Obscura, open on dry days between April and September, is on the top floor of the windmill tower. 2 for 1 voucher valid at Camera Obscura.

Times Open all year, Apr-Sep, Mon-Sat 10-5, Sun 2-5; Oct-Mar, Tue-Sat 10-1 & 2-5. Camera Obscura open daily Apr-Sep, Mon-Sat 10-5, Sun 2-5 **Fees** Free except Camera Obscura £2.30 (concessions £1.15)* **Facilities** 🅟 Ⓟ (outdoor) ♿ (partly accessible) (spiral staircase) toilets for disabled (parking available) shop

Old Bridge House Museum

Mill Rd DG2 7BE
☎ 01387 256904 Fax 01387 265081
e-mail: dumfriesmuseum@dumgal.gov.uk
web: www.dumgal.gov.uk/museums
dir: at W end of Devorgilla's Bridge

The Old Bridge House was built in 1660, and is the oldest house in Dumfries. A museum of everyday life in the town, it has an early 20th-century dentist's surgery, a Victorian nursery and kitchens of the 1850s and 1900s.

Times Open Apr-Sep, Mon-Sat 10-5 & Sun 2-5 **Fees** Free addmission. Donations welcome **Facilities** 🅟 Ⓟ ♿ (partly accessible) (step to front door please phone for details) shop

Robert Burns Centre

Mill Rd DG2 7BE
☎ 01387 264808 Fax 01387 265081
e-mail: dumfriesmuseum@dumgal.gov.uk
web: www.dumgal.gov.uk/museums
dir: on Westbank of River Nith

This award-winning centre explores the connections between Robert Burns and the town of Dumfries. Situated in the town's 18th-century watermill, the centre tells the story of Burns' last years spent in the busy streets and lively atmosphere of Dumfries in the 1790s. In the evening the centre shows feature films in the Film Theatre.

Times Open all year, Apr-Sep, Mon-Sat 10-8, Sun 2-5; Oct-Mar, Tue-Sat 10-1 & 2-5* **Facilities** 🅟 Ⓟ licensed (outdoor) ♿ (fully accessible) toilets for disabled (induction loop hearing system in auditorium, chairlift) shop

Robert Burns House

Burns St DG1 2PS
☎ 01387 255297 Fax 01387 265081
e-mail: dumfriesmuseum@dumgal.gov.uk
web: www.dumgal.gov.uk/museums
dir: signed from Brooms Rd [ATS] car park

It was in this house that Robert Burns spent the last three years of his short life; he died here in 1796. It retains much of its 18th-century character and contains many fascinating items connected with the poet. There is the chair in which he wrote his last poems, many original letters and manuscripts, and the famous Kilmarnock and Edinburgh editions of his work.

Times Open all year, Apr-Sep, Mon-Sat 10-5, Sun 2-5; Oct-Mar, Tue-Sat 10-1 & 2-5 **Fees** Free admission but donations welcome **Facilities** Ⓟ ♿ (partly accessible) (steps to front door, please phone for details) shop

DUNDRENNAN Map 11 NX74

Dundrennan Abbey

DG6 4QH
☎ 01557 500262
web: www.historic-scotland.gov.uk
dir: 6.5m SE of Kirkcudbright, on A711

The now ruined abbey was founded for the Cistercians. The east end of the church and the chapter house are of exceptional architectural quality. Mary, Queen of Scots is thought to have spent her last night in Scotland here on 15 May 1568, before seeking shelter in England, where she was imprisoned and eventually executed.

Times Open all year, Apr-Sep, daily 9.30-5.30; Oct-Mar wknds only 9.30-4.30. Closed 25-26 Dec & 1-2 Jan **Fees** £3.20 (ch £1.90, concessions £2). Please phone or check website for further details* **Facilities** 🅟

SCOTLAND

SCOTLAND

GLENLUCE Map 10 NX15

Glenluce Abbey

DG8 0AF
☎ 01581 300541
web: www.historic-scotland.gov.uk
dir: 2m NW, off A75

The abbey was founded for the Cistercians in 1192 by Roland, Earl of Galloway. The ruins include a vaulted chapter house, and stand in a beautiful setting.

Times Open Apr-Sep daily 9.30-5.30 **Fees** £3.20 (ch £1.90, concessions £2.70). Please phone or check website for further details* **Facilities** Ⓟ ☕ ⊗ ▮

KIRKCUDBRIGHT Map 11 NX65

Broughton House & Garden

12 High St DG6 4JX
☎ 0844 493 2246 📠 0844 493 2246
e-mail: information@nts.org.uk
web: www.nts.org.uk
dir: off A711/A755

An 18th-century house where Edward A Hornel, one of the 'Glasgow Boys' group of artists, lived and worked from 1901-1933. It features a collection of his work, an extensive library of local history, including rare editions of Burns' works, and a Japanese-style garden that he created.

Times Garden only : Feb-Mar, Mon-Fri 11-4. House & garden: Apr-Oct, daily 12-5* **Facilities** Ⓟ ♿ (partly accessible) (steps to front door - alternative disabled access via side lane. Wheelchair access to lower and upper ground floors only, narrow paths in garden) (large print info, garden viewing area) ⊗

Galloway Wildlife Conservation Park

2 FOR 1

Lochfergus Plantation DG6 4XX
☎ 01557 331645 📠 01557 331645
e-mail: info@gallowaywildlife.co.uk
web: www.gallowaywildlife.co.uk
dir: follow brown signs from A75, 1m from Kirkcudbright on B727

Galloway is the wild animal conservation centre for southern Scotland, set in 27 acres of mixed woodland. A varied zoological collection of over 150 animals from all over the world. Close animal encounters and nature trails are some of the features giving an insight into wildlife conservation. Picnic area: Café and Gift Shop, baby facilities and play area.

Times Open Feb-Nov, daily 10-5, summer 10-6 **Fees** £7 (ch 4-15 £5, under 4 free, concessions £6) **Facilities** Ⓟ ☕ ⛩ (outdoor) ♿ (partly accessible) (due to the rising terrain, the nature trail is not accessible) toilets for disabled (British sign language) shop ⊗

MacLellan's Castle

DG6 4JD
☎ 01557 331856
web: www.historic-scotland.gov.uk
dir: in Kirkcudbright on A711

This handsome structure has been a ruin since the mid 18th-century. It was once an imposing castellated mansion, elaborately planned with fine architectural detail. Something of its 16th-century grandeur still remains.

Times Open Apr-Sep, daily 9.30-5.30 **Fees** £3.70 (ch £2.20, concessions £3). Please phone or check website for further details* **Facilities** Ⓟ shop ⊗ ▮

Stewartry Museum

FREE

St Mary St DG6 4AQ
☎ 01557 331643 📠 01557 331643
e-mail: david.devereux@dumgal.gov.uk
web: www.dumgal.gov.uk/museums
dir: from A711 through town, pass parish church, museum approx 200mtrs on right

A large and varied collection of archaeological, social history and natural history exhibits relating to the Stewartry district.

Times Open all year, May, Jun & Sep, Mon-Sat 11-5, Sun 2-5; Jul-Aug, Mon-Sat 10-5, Sun 2-5; Oct, Mon-Sat 11-4, Sun 2-5; Nov-Apr, Mon-Sat 11-4 **Facilities** Ⓟ (outdoor) ♿ (partly accessible) (access to ground floor only) shop

Tolbooth Art Centre

FREE

High St DG6 4JL
☎ 01557 331556 📠 01557 331643
e-mail: david.devereux@dumgal.gov.uk
web: www.dumgal.gov.uk/museums
dir: from A711, through town pass parish church & Stewartry Museum, 1st right into High St

Dating from 1629, the Tolbooth was converted into an art centre and provides an interpretive introduction to the Kirkcudbright artists's colony, which flourished in the town from the 1880s. It also provides studio and exhibition space for contemporary local and visiting artists. There is a programme of exhibitions from March to October.

Times Open all year, May, Jun & Sep, Mon-Sat 11-5, Sun 2-5; Jul & Aug, Mon-Sat 10-5, Sun 2-5; Oct, Mon-Sat 11-4, Sun 2-5; Nov-Apr, Mon-Sat 11-4 **Facilities** Ⓟ ♿ (partly accessible) (step to small studio) toilets for disabled (lift for access to upper floors) shop

NEW ABBEY — Map 11 NX96

National Museum of Costume Scotland

Shambellie House DG2 8HQ
☎ 0131 247 4030
e-mail: info@nms.ac.uk
web: www.nms.ac.uk/costume
dir: 7m S of Dumfries, on A710

Become a dedicated follower of fashion. Shambellie House, a 19th-century country home in wooded grounds, is the perfect setting for discovering 100 years of costume, from the 1850s through to the 1950s. Put yourself in the shoes of those who wore the trends of the time. The museum holds special events and activities throughout the year.

Times Open Apr-Oct, daily, 10-5 **Fees** £4 (ch under 12 & members free, concessions £3) **Facilities** Ⓟ (outdoor) ♿ (partly accessible) (ramp & wheelchair lift provide access to ground floor of museum, tearoom & toilets) (ramp and w/chair lift at main entrance) shop

New Abbey Corn Mill

DG2 8BX
☎ 01387 850260
web: www.historic-scotland.gov.uk
dir: 7m S of Dumfries on A710

Built in the late 18th century, this water-driven corn mill is still in working order, and regular demonstrations are held.

Times Open all year, Apr-Sep, daily, 9.30-5.30; Oct, 9.30-4.30; Nov-Mar, Mon-Wed & Sat-Sun, 9.30-4.30. Closed 25-26 Dec & 1-2 Jan **Fees** £4.20 (ch £2.50, concessions £3.40). Please phone or check website for further details* **Facilities** Ⓟ shop

Sweetheart Abbey

DG2 8BU
☎ 01387 850397
web: www.historic-scotland.gov.uk
dir: on A710

Lady Devorgilla of Galloway founded Balliol College, Oxford in memory of her husband John Balliol; she also founded this abbey in his memory in 1273. When she died in 1289 she was buried in front of the high altar with the heart of her husband resting on her bosom; hence the name 'Sweetheart Abbey'. The abbey features an unusual precinct wall of enormous boulders.

Times Open all year, Apr-Sep, daily, 9.30-5.30; Oct, 9.30-4.30; Nov-Mar, Mon-Wed & Sat-Sun, 9.30-4.30. Closed 25-26 Dec & 1-2 Jan **Fees** £3 (ch £1.80, concessions £3). Please phone or check website for further details* **Facilities** Ⓟ

PALNACKIE — Map 11 NX85

Orchardton Tower

FREE

web: www.historic-scotland.gov.uk
dir: 6m SE of Castle Douglas on A711

A charming little tower house from the mid-15th-century. It is, uniquely, circular in plan.

Times Open all reasonable times. Closed 25-26 Dec **Facilities** Ⓟ

PORT LOGAN — Map 10 NX04

Logan Botanic Garden

DG9 9ND
☎ 01776 860231 📠 01776 860333
e-mail: logan@rbge.org.uk
web: www.rbge.org.uk
dir: on B7065, 14m S of Stranraer

Logan's exceptionally mild climate allows a colourful array of tender plants to thrive out-of-doors. Amongst the many highlights are tree ferns, cabbage palms, unusual shrubs, climbers and tender perennials found within the setting of the walled, water, terrace and woodland gardens.

Times Open Mar & Oct daily 10-5. Apr-Sep 10-6* **Facilities** Ⓟ licensed ♿ (partly accessible) toilets for disabled (wheelchairs available for loan) shop

SCOTLAND

SCOTLAND

RUTHWELL Map 11 NY16

Ruthwell Cross FREE

☎ 131 550 7612
web: www.historic-scotland.gov.uk
dir: sited within the parish church on B724

Now in a specially built apse in the parish church, the carved cross dates from the 7th or 8th centuries. Two faces show scenes from the Life of Christ; the others show scroll work, and parts of an ancient poem in Runic characters. It was broken up in the 18th century, but pieced together by a 19th-century minister.

Times Open all reasonable times. Key available locally
Facilities

Savings Banks Museum FREE

DG1 4NN
☎ 01387 870640
e-mail: savingsbanksmuseum@tiscali.co.uk
web: www.lloydstsb.com/savingsbankmuseum
dir: off B724, 10m E of Dumfries & 7m W of Annan

Housed in the building where Savings Banks first began, the museum traces their growth and development from 1810 up to the present day. The museum also traces the life of Dr Henry Duncan, father of savings banks, and restorer of the Ruthwell Cross. Multi-lingual leaflets available.

Times Open all year, Apr-Sep, Tue-Sat; Oct-Mar, Thu-Sat 10-4. Open on BHs except Xmas Day & New Year **Facilities** (fully accessible) (touch facilities for blind, guide available)

SANQUHAR Map 11 NS70

Sanquhar Tolbooth Museum FREE

High St DG4 6BN
☎ 01659 250186 01387 265081
e-mail: dumfriesmuseum@dumgal.gov.uk
web: www.dumgal.gov.uk/museums
dir: on A76 Dumfries-Kilmarnock road

Housed in the town's fine 18th-century tolbooth, the museum tells the story of the mines and miners of the area, its earliest inhabitants, native and Roman, the history and customs of the Royal Burgh of Sanquhar and local traditions.

Times Open Apr-Sep, Tue-Sat 10-1 & 2-5 & Sun 2-5
Facilities (partly accessible) (museum up steps, phone for info) shop

STRANRAER Map 10 NX06

Castle Kennedy & Gardens 2 FOR 1

Stair Estates, Rephad DG9 8BX
☎ 01776 702024 & 01581 400225 01776 706248
e-mail: info@castlekennedygardens.co.uk
web: www.castlekennedygardens.co.uk
dir: 3m E of Stranraer on A75, signed at Castle Kennedy Village

Perfect for exploring, these stunning 18th-century gardens are uniquely situated between two lochs. As well as rhododendrons, rare plants, a walled garden, Lochinch Castle and the romantic ruined Castle Kennedy, there is a charming tearoom, gift shop, plant centre and seasonal children's activities. New for visitors is the Snowdrop Trail, open at weekends in February and March.

Times Gardens open all year & tea room: Apr-Sep, daily 10-5; Feb-Mar & Oct, wknds only 10-5 **Fees** £4 (ch £1, concessions £3). Family £10. Party 20+ 10% discount **Facilities** (outdoor) (partly accessible) (undulating walks, all grass paths, wet ground conditions) toilets for disabled (free wheelchair) shop

See advert on opposite page

Glenwhan Gardens

Dunragit DG9 8PH
☎ 01581 400222 🖷 01581 400222
e-mail: tess@glenwhan.freeserve.co.uk
web: www.glenwhangardens.co.uk
dir: 7m E of Stranraer, signed

Enjoying spectacular views over the Mull of Galloway and Luce Bay, Glenwhan is a beautiful 12-acre garden set on a hillside. There are two lakes filled with rare species, alpines, scree plants, heathers, conifers, roses, woodland walks and fascinating garden sculpture. A 17 acre moorland walk with wild flowers is open to the public.

Times Open Apr-Sep, daily 10-5 **Fees** £4.50 (ch £2, concessions £3.50). Family ticket up to 3 ch £10. Season ticket £10 **Facilities** licensed (partly accessible) (some hilly areas) toilets for disabled (wheelchair provided) shop

THORNHILL Map 11 NX89

Drumlanrig Castle, Gardens & Country Park

DG3 4AQ
☎ 01848 331555 🖷 01848 331682
e-mail: enquiries@drumlanrig.com
web: www.drumlanrig.com
dir: 4m N of Thornhill off A7

This unusual pink sandstone castle was built in the late 17th century in Renaissance style. It contains a outstanding collection of fine art. There is also French furniture, as well as silver and relics of Bonnie Prince Charlie. The old stable block has a craft centre with resident craft workers, and the grounds offer an extensive garden plant centre, mountain bike hire and woodland walks. The Scottish cycle museum and shop have been recently renovated. Contact for details of special events.

Times Castle open 2 Apr-Aug, daily 11-4 (last tour)* **Facilities** licensed (outdoor) (partly accessible) (some areas of garden not easily accessible to wheelchair users) toilets for disabled (lift) shop

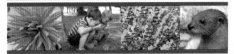

WANLOCKHEAD Map 11 NS81

Hidden Treasures Museum of Lead Mining

2 FOR 1

ML12 6UT
☎ 01659 74387 🖷 01659 74481
e-mail: miningmuseum@hotmail.com
web: www.leadminingmuseum.co.uk
dir: signed from M74 and A76

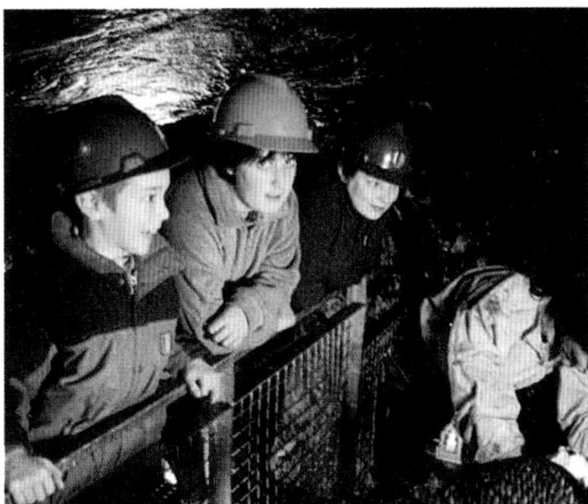

Wanlockhead is Scotland's highest village, set in the beautiful Lowther Hills. Visitors can see miners' cottages, and the miners' library as well as the 18th-century lead mine. Visitors can also pan for gold.

continued

SCOTLAND

SCOTLAND

WANLOCKHEAD *continued*

Times Open Apr-Nov, daily 11-4.30; Jul-Aug & BHs 10-5 **Fees** £7.25 (ch & concessions £5.25). Family tickets available **Facilities** Ⓟ Ⓟ licensed (outdoor) (fully accessible) toilets for disabled shop

WHITHORN Map 10 NX44

Whithorn Priory and Museum

DG8 8PY

☎ 01988 500700

web: www.historic-scotland.gov.uk

dir: on A746

The first Christian church in Scotland was founded here by St Ninian in 397AD, but the present ruins date from the 12th century. These ruins are sparse but there is a notable Norman door, the Latinus stone of the 5th century and other early Christian monuments.

Times Open Apr-Oct, daily 10.30-5 **Fees** £4.50 (ch £2.25, concessions £3). Please phone or check website for further details* **Facilities** Ⓟ

The Whithorn Story

45-47 George St DG8 8NS

☎ 01988 500508

e-mail: enquiries@whithorn.com

web: www.whithorn.com

dir: follow directions S from junct at Newton Stewart & Glenluce A75. Centre on main street in centre of Whithorn

The Whithorn Story tells the story of the first Christian settlement in Scotland - the Candida Casa (or White House) built by St Ninian circa 397AD. There is an audio-visual element, an exhibition, Priory ruins and a Historic Scotland Museum. The Festival of St Ninian takes place from the end of July to mid-September.

Times Open daily, Apr or Etr-Oct 10.30-5* **Facilities** Ⓟ (outdoor) (fully accessible) toilets for disabled (one short staircase with 'stairmatic') shop

CITY OF DUNDEE

DUNDEE Map 11 NO43

Broughty Castle Museum FREE

Castle Approach, Broughty Ferry DD5 2TF

☎ 01382 436916 01382 436951

e-mail: broughty@dundeecity.gov.uk

web: www.dundeecity.gov.uk/broughtycastle

dir: turn S off A930 at traffic lights by Eastern Primary School in Broughty Ferry

This 15th-century coastal fort has faced many battles and sieges, and was rebuilt in the 19th century as part of the River Tay's coastal defence system. It now houses a fascinating museum featuring displays on the life and times of Broughty Ferry, its people, the environment and the wildlife that lives close by. Don't miss the Orchar Gallery which features a selection of paintings from the Orchar Collection - one of the most important collections of Scottish Victorian art in the country. Enjoy the spectacular views over the River Tay.

Times Open all year, Tue-Sat 10-4, Sun 12.30-4; also open Mon, Apr-Sep. Closed 25-26 Dec & 1-3 Jan **Facilities** Ⓟ (unsuitable for wheelchairs) shop

Camperdown Country Park

Coupar Angus Rd DD2 4TF

☎ 01382 431818 01382 431810

e-mail: leisure.communities@dundeecity.gov.uk

web: www.camperdownpark.com

dir: A90 to Dundee then onto A923 (Coupar-Angus road), left at 1st rdbt to attraction

Camperdown is Dundee's largest park, covers an area of over 400 acres and is home to some 190 species of tree. Facilities include an 18-hole golf course, a putting green, boating pond, children's play area, footpaths, woodland trails, and Camperdown Wildlife Centre. There is also a year-round calendar of special events, contact for details.

Times Open Park: all year. Wildlife Centre: daily, Mar-Sep 10-4.30; Oct-Feb 10-3.30 (last admission 45mins before close) **Fees** Park - free admission. Wildlife Centre charged, £3.50 (ch 3-17 & concessions £2.80, under 3 £1). Family (2ad+3ch) £10. Group rate available for 12 people or more* **Facilities** Ⓟ (outdoor) (fully accessible) toilets for disabled (ramps) shop

Discovery Point & RRS Discovery

Discovery Quay DD1 4XA

☎ 01382 309060 01382 225891

e-mail: info@dundeeheritage.co.uk

web: www.rrsdiscovery.com

dir: follow brown heritage signs for Historic Ships

Discovery Point is the home of *RRS Discovery*, Captain Scott's famous Antarctic ship. Spectacular lighting, graphics and special effects re-create key moments in the *Discovery* story. The restored bridge gives a captain's view over the ship and the River Tay. Learn what happened to the ship after the expedition, during the First World War and the Russian Revolution, and find out about her involvement in the first survey of whales' migratory patterns.

Times Open all year, Apr-Oct, Mon-Sat 10-6. Sun 11-6; Nov-Mar, Mon-Sat 10-5, Sun 11-5 **Fees** £7.75 (ch £4.75, concessions £5). Family ticket £22* **Facilities** licensed (outdoor) (partly accessible) (access to exhibition on top deck, no access to lower deck, but virtual tour available) toilets for disabled (in-house wheelchairs & lifts, parking, ramps onto ship) shop

HM Frigate Unicorn — 2 FOR 1

Victory Dock DD1 3BP
01382 200900 & 200893
e-mail: mail@frigateunicorn.org
web: www.frigateunicorn.org
dir: from W follow A85 from A90 at Invergowrie. From E follow A92. Near N end of Tay Road Bridge. Follow signs for City Quay

The *Unicorn* is the oldest British-built warship afloat, and Scotland's only example of a wooden warship. Today she houses a museum of life in the Royal Navy during the days of sail, with guns, models and displays.

Times Open all year, Apr-Oct, daily 10-5; Nov-Mar, Wed-Fri 12-4, Sat-Sun 10-4. Closed Mon-Tue & 2 weeks at Xmas & New Year **Fees** £5 (ch £3, concessions £4). Family ticket (1ad+2ch) £10 or (2ad+2ch) £13. Groups 10+ £3 each **Facilities** (partly accessible) (wheelchair access to main gun deck only) (AV presentations, introductory video, virtual tour) shop

The McManus: Dundee's Art Gallery & Museum — FREE

Albert Square DD1 1DA
01382 307200 01382 307207
e-mail: mcmanus.galleries@dundeecity.gov.uk
web: www.themcmanus-dundee.gov.uk
dir: off A90, attraction in city centre

Recently re-opened to the public following an extensive refurbishment programme. Beautiful open gallery spaces have been created; where displays of art, history and the environment combine to offer a fascinating insight into Dundee. Activities and workshops take place regularly in the new creative learning suite. A new retail area and café with an outdoor terrace are just some of the other highlights, this Victorian, gothic building has to offer.

Times Open all year. Mon-Sat 10-5, Sun 12.30-4.30 (last admission 4.15) **Facilities** licensed (fully accessible) toilets for disabled (w/chairs, lift, larger text sizes, induction loops) shop

Mills Observatory

Balgay Park, Glamis Rd DD2 2UB
01382 435967 01382 435962
e-mail: mills.observatory@dundeecity.gov.uk
web: www.dundeecity.gov.uk/mills
dir: 1m W of city centre, in Balgay Park, on Balgay Hill. Vehicle entrance at Glamis Rd gate to Balgay Park

Mills Observatory is Britain's only full-time public observatory. See breathtaking views of the stars and planets through the impressive Victorian refracting telescope. The telescope with state-of-the-art technology, allows you to move from one object to another more quickly than ever before. During October to March, the Planetarium Shows provide the chance to learn about constellations, planets and other jewels of the night sky. There are also displays on the solar system and space exploration.

Times Open all year, Apr-Sep, Tue-Fri 11-5, Sat & Sun 12.30-4; Oct-Mar, Mon-Fri 4pm-10pm, Sat & Sun 12.30-4. Closed 25-26 Dec & 1-3 Jan **Fees** Free entry, small charge for public Planetarium shows and groups* **Facilities** (outdoor) (partly accessible) (ground floor accessible) toilets for disabled (portable telescopes available, images on screen) shop

SCOTLAND

Verdant Works

West Henderson's Wynd DD2 5BT
01382 309060 01382 225891
e-mail: info@dundeeheritage.co.uk
web: www.verdantworks.com
dir: follow brown tourist signs

Dating from 1830, this old Jute Mill covers 50,000 square feet and has been restored as a living museum of Dundee and Tayside's textile history and award-winning European Industrial Museum. Phase I explains what jute is, where it comes from and why Dundee became the centre of its production. Working machinery illustrates the production process from raw jute to woven cloth. Phase II deals with the uses of jute and its effects on Dundee's social history.

Times Open all year, Apr-Oct, Mon-Sat 10-6, Sun 11-6; Nov-Mar, Mon-Sat 10-4.30, Sun 11-4.30 (Venue closes 1hr after last entry). Please check for winter opening times. Closed 25-26 Dec & 1-2 Jan* **Fees** £7 (ch £4, concessions £5.25). Family ticket (2ad+2ch) £19* **Facilities** licensed (fully accessible) toilets for disabled (wheelchairs, induction loops) shop

EAST AYRSHIRE

GALSTON — Map 11 NS53

Loudoun Castle Theme Park

KA4 8PE
01563 822296 01563 822408
e-mail: loudouncastle@btinternet.com
web: www.loudouncastle.co.uk
dir: signed from A74(M), from A77 and from A71

Loudoun Castle Theme Park is a great day out for the whole family. Theme park rides, live entertainment and McDougals Farm are just a taster of what's on offer.

Times Open Etr-end of Sep. Please phone for further details* **Facilities** licensed (indoor & outdoor) toilets for disabled shop

KILMARNOCK Map 10 NS43

Dick Institute Museum & Art Galleries FREE

Elmbank Ave KA1 3BU
☎ 01563 554902 📠 01563 554344
web: www.east-ayrshire.gov.uk
dir: follow brown tourist signs from A77 S of Glasgow, into town centre

Temporary and permanent exhibitions spread over two floors of this grand Victorian building. Fine art, social and natural history feature upstairs, whilst the downstairs galleries house temporary exhibitions of art and craft.

Times Open all year, Tue-Sat 11-5. Closed PH **Facilities** Ⓟ Ⓟ ♿ (fully accessible) toilets for disabled (wheelchair available) shop

EAST DUNBARTONSHIRE

BEARSDEN Map 11 NS57

Antonine Wall: Bearsden Bath-house FREE

Roman Rd G61 2SG
web: www.historic-scotland.gov.uk
dir: signed from Bearsden Cross on A810

Considered to be the best surviving visible Roman building in Scotland, the bath-house was discovered in 1973 during excavations for a construction site. It was originally built for use by the Roman garrison at Bearsden Fort, which is part of the Antonine Wall defences. This building dates from the 2nd century AD. Visitors should wear sensible footwear.

Times Open all reasonable times **Facilities**

MILNGAVIE Map 11 NS57

Mugdock Country Park FREE

Craigallian Rd G62 8EL
☎ 0141 956 6100 & 6586
web: www.mugdock-country-park.org.uk
dir: N of Glasgow on A81, signed

This country park incorporates the remains of Mugdock and Craigend castles, set in beautiful landscapes as well as an exhibition centre, craft shops, orienteering course and many walks.

Times Open all year, daily summer 9-9, winter 9-6 **Facilities** Ⓟ Ⓟ licensed (outdoor) ♿ (partly accessible) (full access to cafe, theatre, restaurant, gift shop, arts & crafts gallery) toilets for disabled (mobility equipment, audio leaflet, large print media) shop

EAST LOTHIAN

ABERLADY Map 12 NT47

Myreton Motor Museum 2 FOR 1

EH32 0PZ
☎ 01875 870288 & 07947 066666 📠 01368 860199
e-mail: myreton.motor.museum@aberlady.org
dir: 1.5m from A198, 2m from A1

The museum has on show a large collection, from 1899, of cars, bicycles, motor cycles and commercials. There is also a large collection of period advertising, posters and enamel signs.

Times Open all year, Mar-Oct daily 10.30-4.30, Nov-Feb, wknds only 11-3 **Fees** £7 (ch £3, concessions £6) **Facilities** Ⓟ (outdoor) ♿ (fully accessible)

DIRLETON Map 12 NT58

Dirleton Castle and Gardens

EH39 5ER
☎ 01620 850330
web: www.historic-scotland.gov.uk
dir: on A198

The oldest part of this romantic castle dates from the 13th century. It was besieged by Edward I in 1298, rebuilt and expanded, and then destroyed in 1650. Now the sandstone ruins have a beautiful mellow quality. Within the castle grounds is a garden established in the 16th century, with ancient yews and hedges around a bowling green.

Times Open all year daily, Apr-Sep 9.30-5.30; Oct-Mar 9.30-4.30. Closed 25-26 Dec & 1-2 Jan **Fees** £4.70 (ch £2.80, concessions £3.80). Please phone or check website for further details* **Facilities** Ⓟ shop

EAST FORTUNE Map 12 NT57

National Museum of Flight Scotland 2 FOR 1

East Fortune Airfield EH39 5LF
☎ 0131 225 7534
e-mail: info@nms.ac.uk
web: www.nms.ac.uk/flight
dir: signed from A1 near Haddington. Onto B1347, past Athelstaneford, 20m E of Edinburgh

The National Museum of Flight is situated on 63 acres of one of Britain's best preserved wartime airfields. The museum has four hangars, with more than 50 aeroplanes, plus engines, rockets and memorabilia. Items on display include two Spitfires, a Vulcan bomber and Britain's oldest surviving aeroplane, built in 1896; recent exhibits also include a Phantom jet fighter, and a Harrier jump-jet. The Concorde Experience is free with admission to the Museum, but boarding passes are limited. The Concorde Experience explores the story of this historic plane through the lives of those who worked or travelled on it.

Times Open all year, Apr-Oct, daily, 10-5; Nov-Mar, wknds only, 10-4. (Contact for details of seasonal variations in opening times) **Fees** £9 (ch under 12 & NMS members free, concessions £7)* **Facilities** (outdoor) (partly accessible) (no wheelchair access to Concorde's passenger cabin, most display areas are on ground floor) toilets for disabled (wheelchair loan) shop

EAST LINTON Map 12 NT57

Hailes Castle

FREE

web: www.historic-scotland.gov.uk
dir: 1.5m SW of East Linton on A1

A beautiful sited ruin incorporating a fortified manor of 13th-century date, extended in the 14th and 15th centuries. There are two vaulted pit-prisons.

Times Open at all reasonable times **Facilities**

Preston Mill & Phantassie Doocot

EH40 3DS
0844 493 2128
e-mail: information@nts.org.uk
web: www.nts.org.uk
dir: Off A1, in East Linton, 23m east of Edinburgh

This attractive mill, with conical, pantiled roof, is the oldest working water-driven meal mill to survive in Scotland, and was last used commercially in 1957. Nearby is the charming Phantassie Doocot (dovecote), built for 500 birds.

Times Open Jun-Sep, Thu-Mon 1-5.* **Facilities** (partly accessible) toilets for disabled shop

INVERESK Map 11 NT37

Inveresk Lodge Garden

24 Inveresk Village EH21 7TE
0844 493 2126 0844 493 2126
e-mail: information@nts.org.uk
web: www.nts.org.uk
dir: A6124, S of Musselburgh, 6m E of Edinburgh

This charming terraced garden, set in the historic village of Inveresk, specialises in plants, shrubs and roses suitable for growing on small plots. The 17th-century house makes an elegant backdrop.

Times Open all year, daily 10-6 or dusk if earlier* **Facilities** (outdoor) (partly accessible) (steps to entrance, access to top terrace & upper reaches of the garden not accessible to all) (Scented plants, interpretation guides)

NORTH BERWICK Map 12 NT58

Scottish Seabird Centre

The Harbour EH39 4SS
01620 890202 01620 890222
e-mail: info@seabird.org
web: www.seabird.org
dir: A1 from Edinburgh, then A198 to North Berwick. Brown heritage signs clearly marked from A1

Escape to another world at this award-winning wildlife visitor attraction. Breathtaking panoramic views over the sea and sandy beaches. See wildlife close up with amazing live cameras - puffins spring-cleaning their burrows, gannets with fluffy white chicks, seals sunning themselves and occasional sightings of dolphins and whales. The Discovery Centre has a Wildlife cinema, Environment Zone, Kids' Play Zone and Migration Flyway. Boat trips around the islands from April to October. There is a packed programme of festivals and events, see the website for details.

Times Open all year, Feb, Mar & Oct Mon-Fri 10-5, Sat-Sun 10-5.30; Apr-Sep daily 10-6. Nov-Jan Mon-Fri 10-4, Sat-Sun 10-5 **Fees** £7.95 (ch £4.50, concessions £5.95)* **Facilities** licensed (outdoor) (fully accessible) toilets for disabled (1 w/chair, parking on site, walking frame, lift) shop

Tantallon Castle

EH39 5PN
01620 892727
web: www.historic-scotland.gov.uk
dir: 3m E, off A198

A famous 14th-century stronghold of the Douglases facing towards the lonely Bass Rock from the rocky Firth of Forth shore. Nearby 16th and 17th-century earthworks.

Times Open all year, Apr-Sep, daily, 9.30-5.30; Oct, 9.30-4.30; Nov-Mar, Mon-Wed & Sat-Sun, 9.30-4.30. Closed 25-26 Dec & 1-2 Jan **Fees** £4.70 (ch £2.80, concessions £3.80). Please phone or check website for further details* **Facilities** shop

PRESTONPANS Map 11 NT37

Prestongrange Museum

FREE

Prestongrange
0131 653 2904 01620 828201
e-mail: elms@eastlothian.gov.uk
web: www.prestongrange.org
dir: on B1348 coast road between Prestonpans & Musselburgh

The oldest documented coal mining site in Scotland, with 800 years of history, this museum shows a Cornish Beam Engine and on-site evidence of associated industries such as brickmaking and pottery. It is located next to a 16th-century customs port. Contact for details of special events or see website.

Times Open Apr-Oct, daily, 11.30-4.30 **Facilities** (outdoor) (partly accessible) (grounds partly accessible) toilets for disabled shop

SCOTLAND

SCOTLAND

CITY OF EDINBURGH

BALERNO Map 11 NT16

Malleny Garden

EH14 7AF
☎ 0844 493 2123
e-mail: information@nts.org.uk
web: www.nts.org.uk
dir: off A70 Lanark road

The delightful gardens are set round a 17th-century house (not open to the public). Shrub roses, a woodland garden, and a group of four clipped yews, survivors of a group planted in 1603, are among its notable features. The National Bonsai Collection for Scotland is also at Malleny.

Times Open all year, daily 10-6 or dusk if earlier* **Facilities** (fully accessible)

EDINBURGH Map 11 NT27

Brass Rubbing Centre

Trinity Apse, Chalmers Close, High St EH1 1SS
☎ 0131 556 4364 0131 557 3346
e-mail: moc@edinburgh.gov.uk
web: www.cac.org.uk
dir: located on the Royal Mile

Housed in the 15th-century remnant of Trinity Apse, the Centre offers the chance to make your own rubbing from a wide range of replica monumental brasses and Pictish stones. Tuition is available.

Times Open Apr-Sep, Mon-Sat 10-5, Sun during Aug 12-5* **Facilities** (partly accessible) toilets for disabled shop

Camera Obscura and World of Illusions

Castlehill, Royal Mile EH1 2ND
☎ 0131 226 3709 0131 225 4239
e-mail: info@camera-obscura.co.uk
web: www.camera-obscura.co.uk
dir: next to Edinburgh Castle

A unique view of Edinburgh - as the lights go down, a brilliant moving image of the surrounding city appears. See three other floors of optical illusions and hands on inter-active fun. An expanded exhibition space includes more hands-on exhibits. Walk on water, shake hands with your ghost, hear cats sing or spy on people from inside a giant camera. At Camera Obscura, anything is possible.

Times Open all year, daily, Apr-Oct 9.30-6; Jul-Aug open until 7.30; Nov-Mar 10-5. Closed 25 Dec **Fees** £9.25 (ch £6.25)* **Facilities** (partly accessible) (access restricted to ground floor, 15 steps to view camera, not wheelchair accessible) toilets for disabled shop

City Art Centre

2 Market St EH1 1DE
☎ 0131 529 3993 0131 529 3977
e-mail: cityartcentre@edinburgh.gov.uk
web: www.cac.org.uk
dir: opposite rear of Waverley Stn

The City Art Centre houses the city's permanent fine art collection and stages a constantly changing programme of temporary exhibitions from all parts of the world. It has six floors of display galleries (linked by an escalator).

Times Open all year, Mon-Sat 10-5 & Sun 12-5* **Facilities** licensed (fully accessible) toilets for disabled (induction loop, lifts, Braille signage, escalator) shop

Craigmillar Castle

EH16 4SY
☎ 0131 661 4445
web: www.historic-scotland.gov.uk
dir: 2.5m SE, off A68

Mary, Queen of Scots retreated to this 14th-century stronghold after the murder of Rizzio. The plot to murder Darnley, her second husband, was also hatched here. There are 16th and 17th-century apartments.

Times Open all year, Apr-Sep, daily, 9.30-5.30; Oct, 9.30-4.30; Nov-Mar, Mon-Wed & Sat-Sun, 9.30-4.30. Closed 25-26 Dec & 1-2 Jan **Fees** £4.20 (ch £2.50, concessions £3.40). Please phone or check website for further details* **Facilities** toilets for disabled shop

Dean Gallery

75 Belford Rd EH4 3DS
☎ 0131 624 6200 0131 343 3250
e-mail: enquiries@nationalgalleries.org
web: www.nationalgalleries.org
dir: 20 min walk from Edinburgh Haymarket stn & Princes St

Opened in March 1999, the Dean Gallery provides a home for the Eduardo Paolozzi gift of sculpture and graphic art, the Gallery of Modern Art's renowned Dada and Surrealist collections, a major library and archive centre, and temporary exhibition space for modern and contemporary art.

Times Open all year, daily 10-5 (6 in Aug). Closed 25-26 Dec* **Fees** Admission to permanent collections free, charge may be made for special exhibitions **Facilities** (outdoor) (fully accessible) toilets for disabled (ramps & lift) shop

Dynamic Earth

Holyrood Rd EH8 8AS
☎ 0131 550 7800 0131 550 7801
e-mail: enquiries@dynamicearth.co.uk
web: www.dynamicearth.co.uk
dir: on edge of Holyrood Park, opposite Palace of Holyrood House

Explore our planet's past, present and future. Featuring Scotland's only 4D experience, this is the Mother Earth of all adventures.

Times Open all year Apr-Oct, daily 10-5.30; Nov-Mar, Wed-Sun 10-5.30; Jul-Aug, daily 10-6* **Fees** £10.50 (ch £7, concessions

£9)* **Facilities** Ⓟ (indoor & outdoor) (fully accessible) toilets for disabled (audio guides, large print gallery guides) shop

Edinburgh Castle

EH1 2NG

0131 225 9846

web: www.edinburghcastle.gov.uk

This historic stronghold stands on the precipitous crag of Castle Rock. One of the oldest parts is the 11th-century chapel of the saintly Queen Margaret, but most of the present castle evolved later, during its stormy history of sieges and wars, and was altered again in Victorian times. The Scottish crown and other royal regalia are displayed in the Crown Room. Also notable is the Scottish National War Memorial.

Times Open all year, Apr-Sep, daily, 9.30-6; Oct-Mar 9.30-5; 1 Jan, 11-4.30. Closed 25-26 Dec **Fees** £14 (ch from 5yrs £7.50, concessions £11.20). Please phone or check website for further details* **Facilities** licensed (partly accessible) toilets for disabled (free transport to top of Castle Hill lift) shop

The Edinburgh Dungeon

31 Market St EH1 1QB

0131 240 1000 & 240 1002 0131 240 1002

e-mail: edinburghdungeon@merlinentertainments.biz

web: www.thedungeons.com

dir: close to Waverley Train Station

From the same team at The London Dungeon, there comes a Scottish "feast of fun with history's horrible bits". A mixture of live actors, rides, shows and special effects take the brave visitor back into a dark past that includes such delights as the Judgement of Sinners, the Plague, Burke & Hare: Bodysnatchers, and Clan Wars, which attempts to recreate the horror of the Glencoe Massacre of 1692. Visit the Inferno, and explore the Great Fire of Edinburgh in 1828.

Times Open all year ex Xmas. Please telephone for times* **Facilities** Ⓟ toilets for disabled shop

Edinburgh Zoo

134 Corstorphine Rd, Murrayfield EH12 6TS

0131 334 9171 0131 314 0382

e-mail: info@rzss.org.uk

web: www.edinburghzoo.org.uk

dir: 3m W of city centre on A8 towards Glasgow

Scotland's largest wildlife attraction set in 82 acres of leafy hillside parkland, just ten minutes from the city centre. With over 1,000 animals ranging from the UK's only koalas to massive Indian rhinos, including many other threatened species. See the world's largest penguin pool or visit the chimpanzees in the world-class Budongo Trail.

Times Open all year, daily Apr-Sep, 9-6; Oct & Mar, 9-5; Nov-Feb, 9-4.30 **Fees** £15.50 (ch £11, concessions £13). Family ticket (2ad+2ch) £47.70. Carers for disabled visitors are free when displaying relevant documentation **Facilities** Ⓟ licensed (indoor & outdoor) (partly accessible) (Zoo is on a hillside, but there is a free hilltop safari to the top of the hill) toilets for disabled (wheelchair loan free, 1 helper free - phone in advance) shop

The Georgian House

7 Charlotte Square EH2 4DR

0844 493 2118 0844 493 2118

e-mail: information@nts.org.uk

web: www.nts.org.uk

dir: 2 mins walk W end of Princes St

The house is part of Robert Adam's splendid north side of Charlotte Square, the epitome of Edinburgh New Town architecture. The lower floors of No 7 have been restored in the style of the early 1800s, when the house was new. There also videos of life in the New Town, and this house in particular.

Times Open 2-29 Mar, daily 11-4; 30 Mar-Jun & 31 Aug-Oct, daily 10-5; Jul-30 Aug, daily 10-6; Nov, daily 11-3 (last admission 30 mins before closing)* **Facilities** Ⓟ (partly accessible) (stairs into building, first floor & basement) (induction loop, Braille guide, subtitled video) shop

Gladstone's Land

477b Lawnmarket EH1 2NT

0844 493 2120 0844 493 2119

e-mail: information@nts.org.uk

web: www.nts.org.uk

dir: 5 mins walk from Princes St via Mound

Built in 1620, this six-storey tenement, once a merchant's house, still has its arcaded front - a rare feature now. Visitors can also see unusual tempera paintings on the walls and ceilings. It is furnished as a typical 17th-century merchant's home, complete with ground-floor shop front and goods of the period.

Times Open Apr-Jun & 31 Aug-Oct, daily 10-5; Jul-Aug, daily 10-7 (last admission 30 mins before closing)* **Facilities** Ⓟ (partly accessible) (steep steps from road, pavement ramp 100 metres, turnpike stairs in building) (large print, Braille guidebook) shop

John Knox House

Scottish Story Telling Centre, 43-45 High St EH1 1SR

0131 556 9579 0131 557 5224

e-mail: reception@scottishstorytellingcentre.com

web: www.scottishstorytellingcentre.co.uk

dir: Between The Castle and Holyrood House, halfway along Edinburgh's Royal Mile

John Knox the Reformer is said to have died in the house, which was built by the goldsmith to Mary, Queen of Scots. Renovation work has revealed the original floor in the Oak Room, and a magnificent painted ceiling. Audio tour available.

Times Open all year, Mon-Sat 10-6. Jul-Aug, Sun 12-6. Closed 25-26 Dec & 1-2 Jan **Fees** £4 (ch £1, under 7's free, concessions £3.50) **Facilities** Ⓟ (partly accessible) (access to ground floor only, virtual computer tour for rest of house) toilets for disabled (Braille, hearing loops, tours for blind) shop

SCOTLAND

EDINBURGH *continued*

Lauriston Castle

Cramond Rd South, Davidson's Mains EH4 5QD
☎ 0131 336 2060 0131 312 7165
e-mail: lauriston.castle@tiscali.co.uk
web: www.cac.org.uk
dir: NW outskirts of Edinburgh, 1m E of Cramond overlooking the Forth at Silverknowles

The castle is a late 16th-century tower house with 19th-century additions but is most notable as a classic example of the Edwardian age. It has a beautifully preserved Edwardian interior and the feel of a country house, and the spacious grounds are very pleasant.

Times Guided tours: Apr-Oct, daily (ex Fri), 11, 12, 2, 3 & 4; Nov-Mar 12, 2 & 3* **Facilities** Ⓟ Ⓟ (outdoor) ♿ (partly accessible) (chair lift to upper floor) toilets for disabled shop

SCOTLAND

Museum of Childhood FREE

42 High St, Royal Mile EH1 1TG
☎ 0131 529 4142 0131 558 3103
e-mail: moc@edinburgh.gov.uk
web: www.edinburghmuseums.org.uk
dir: On the Royal Mile

The whole family will enjoy seeing toys and games from the past, and finding out about childhood through the years, from school days and baby care to clubs and hobbies. Visit the website for details of events and exhibitions.

Times Open all year, Mon-Sat 10-5, Sun 12-5. Closed 25-26 Dec & 1-2 Jan **Facilities** Ⓟ ♿ (partly accessible) (3 floors only) toilets for disabled shop

Museum of Edinburgh FREE

142 Canongate, Royal Mile EH8 8DD
☎ 0131 529 4143 0131 557 3346
e-mail: moe@edinburgh.gov.uk
web: www.cac.org.uk
dir: on the Royal Mile

Housed in one of the best-preserved 16th-century buildings in the Old Town. It was built in 1570 and later became the headquarters of the Incorporation of Hammermen. Now a museum of local history, it has collections of silver, glassware, pottery, and other items such as street signs.

Times Open all year, Mon-Sat 10-5. Sun in Aug noon-5 **Facilities** Ⓟ toilets for disabled shop

National Gallery Complex

The Mound, Princess St EH2 2EL
☎ 0131 624 6200 0131 343 3250
e-mail: enquiries@nationalgalleries.org
web: www.nationalgalleries.org
dir: off Princes St

The National Gallery complex consists of three magnificent buildings, right in the heart of Edinburgh: The National Gallery of Scotland, home to Scotland's prestigious national collection; The Royal Scottish Academy, one of Europe's premier exhibition centres; and The Weston Link which houses the café, restaurant and lecture rooms.

Times Open all year, daily 10-5; Thu until 7; 1 Jan noon-5. Closed 25-26 Dec **Fees** Free. Admission charged to some major exhibitions.* **Facilities** Ⓟ licensed ♿ (fully accessible) toilets for disabled (ramps, lift) shop

National Museum of Scotland FREE

Chambers St EH1 1JF
☎ 0131 225 7534
e-mail: info@nms.ac.uk
web: www.nms.ac.uk
dir: situated in Chambers St in Old Town. A few mins walk from Princes St and The Royal Mile

Scotland - past, present and future. The Museum's collections tell you the story of Scotland - land, people and culture. What influence has the world had on Scotland, and Scotland on the world? For generations the museum has collected key exhibits from all over Scotland and beyond. Viking brooches, Pictish stones, ancient chessmen and Queen Mary's clarsach. Connect with Dolly the sheep, design a robot, test drive a Formula One car or blast off into outer space. See website for special exhibitions and events. Re-opening after refurbishment of part of the Victorian Royal Museum in summer 2011.

Times Open all year, daily 10-5 **Facilities** Ⓟ licensed ♿ (fully accessible) toilets for disabled (lifts, wheelchair loan, audio guides, induction loops) shop

National War Museum Scotland

Edinburgh Castle EH1 2NG
☎ 0131 225 7534 0131 225 3848
e-mail: info@nms.ac.uk
web: www.nms.ac.uk
dir: at Edinburgh Castle, a few minutes walk up the Royal Mile to Castlehill

Explore the Scottish experience of war and military service over the last 400 years. A chance to experience the poignant stories of the Scots who went to war, through their letters and personal treasures. See website for special exhibitions and events.

Times Open all year, daily, Apr-Sep 9.45-5.45; Oct-Mar 9.45-4.45. Closed 25-26 Dec. **Fees** Standard Fares £13 (ch £7, ch under 5 free, concessions £10.40). NMS members £11.70. Free entry to museum with admission to Edinburgh Castle. Peak Fares £14 (ch £7.50, concessions £11.20). NMS Members £12.60* **Facilities** Ⓟ ♿ (fully accessible) toilets for disabled (courtesy vehicle runs from Castle ticket kiosk) shop

Nelson Monument

Calton Hill EH7 5AA
☎ 0131 556 2716 0131 557 3346
e-mail: museums&galleries@edinburgh.gov.uk
web: www.cac.org.uk
dir: Calton Hill (Overlooking east end of city)

Designed in 1807 the monument dominates the east end of Princes Street. The views are superb, and every day except Sunday the time ball drops at 1pm as the gun at the castle goes off.

Times Open all year, Apr-Sep, Mon 1-6 & Tue-Sat 10-6; Oct-Mar, Mon-Sat 10-3* **Facilities** Ⓟ Ⓟ ㊗

Palace of Holyroodhouse

EH8 8DX
☎ 0131 556 5100 📠 020 7930 9625
e-mail: bookinginfo@royalcollection.org.uk
web: www.royalcollection.org.uk
dir: at east end of Royal Mile

The Palace grew from the guest house of the Abbey of Holyrood, said to have been founded by David I after a miraculous apparition. Mary, Queen of Scots had her court here from 1561 to 1567, and 'Bonnie' Prince Charlie held levees at the Palace during his occupation of Edinburgh. Today the Royal Apartments are used by HM The Queen for state ceremonies and official entertaining, and are finely decorated with works of art from the Royal Collection.

Times Open all year, daily, Apr-Oct 9.30-6; Nov-Mar 9.30-4.30 (last admission 1hr before close). Closed Good Fri, 25-26 Dec and during Royal visits* **Fees** £10.50 (ch £6.50, concessions £9.50). Family ticket (2ad+3ch) £28. Provides unlimited admission for 12 months. See website for current prices* **Facilities** Ⓟ ☕ ♿ (partly accessible) (historic apartments accessible by spiral staircase) toilets for disabled (first floor by lift, wheelchair available, virtual tour) shop ㊗

Parliament House FREE

Supreme Courts, 2-11 Parliament Square EH1 1RQ
☎ 0131 225 2595 📠 0131 225 9485
e-mail: dlundie@scotcourts.gov.uk
web: www.scotcourts.gov.uk
dir: behind St Giles Cathedral on the high street

Scotland's independent parliament last sat in 1707, in this 17th-century building hidden behind an 1829 façade, now the seat of the Supreme Law Courts of Scotland. A large stained glass window depicts the inauguration of the Court of Session in 1540.

Times Open all year, Mon-Fri 10-4 **Facilities** Ⓟ ☕ 🍴 licensed ♿ (partly accessible) (cannot access restaurant if unable to use stairlift) toilets for disabled ㊗

The People's Story Museum FREE

Canongate Tolbooth, 163 Canongate, Royal Mile EH8 8BN
☎ 0131 529 4057 📠 0131 556 3439
e-mail: socialhistory@edinburgh.gov.uk
web: www.edinburghmuseums.org.uk
dir: on the Royal Mile

The museum, housed in the 16th-century tolbooth, tells the story of the ordinary people of Edinburgh from the late 18th century to the present day. Reconstructions include a prison cell, 1930s pub and 1940s kitchen supported by photographs, displays, sounds and smells.

Times Open all year, Mon-Sat 10-5. Also open Sun in Aug 12-5 **Facilities** Ⓟ ♿ (partly accessible) (first floor wheelchair accessible) toilets for disabled (lift, induction loop in video room) ㊗

The Real Mary King's Close

2 Warriston's Close, High St EH1 1PG
☎ 08702 430160 📠 0131 225 0671
e-mail: info@realmarykingsclose.com
web: www.realmarykingsclose.com
dir: off High St, opposite St. Giles Cathedral

Hidden deep beneath the Royal Mile lies Edinburgh's deepest secret; a warren of hidden 'closes' or streets where people lived, worked and died. For centuries they have lain forgotten and abandoned... until now. This award-winning underground attraction is a curious network of streets, town houses and rooms. Step back in time as you meet the characters from days gone by and enjoy stories of life on the Close from the perspective of a one-time resident.

Times Open all year, daily Apr-Oct 10-9 (last tour), Aug 9-9 (last tour); Nov-Mar Fri-Sun 10-4 (last tour), Sat 10-9 (last tour). Closed 25 Dec **Fees** £11 (ch £6, concessions £10)* **Facilities** Ⓟ ♿ (partly accessible) (ramped access provided to information and retail outlet) toilets for disabled (hearing loop) shop ㊗

Royal Botanic Garden Edinburgh

Inverleith Row EH3 5LR
☎ 0131 552 7171 📠 0131 248 2901
e-mail: info@rbge.org.uk
web: www.rbge.org.uk
dir: 1m N of city centre, off A902

Established in 1670, on an area the size of a tennis court, the Garden is now over 70 acres of beautifully landscaped grounds. Spectacular features include the Rock Garden and the Chinese Hillside. The amazing glasshouses feature Britain's tallest palm house and the magnificent woodland gardens and arboretum.

Times Open all year, daily; Apr-Sep, 10-7; Mar & Oct, 10-6; Nov-Feb, 10-4. Closed 25 Dec & 1 Jan. (Facilities close 30 mins before Garden)* **Facilities** Ⓟ ☕ 🍴 licensed ♿ (partly accessible) toilets for disabled (wheelchairs available at east/ west gates) shop ㊗

SCOTLAND

EDINBURGH *continued*

The Royal Yacht Britannia

Ocean Terminal, Leith EH6 6JJ
☎ 0131 555 5566 📠 0131 555 8835
e-mail: enquiries@tryb.co.uk
web: www.royalyachtbritannia.co.uk
dir: follow signs to North Edinburgh & Leith. Situated within Ocean Terminal

Visit the *Royal Yacht Britannia*, now in Edinburgh's historic port of Leith. The experience starts in the Visitor Centre where you can discover *Britannia*'s fascinating story. Then step aboard for a self-led audio tour which takes you around five decks giving you a unique insight into what life was like for the Royal Family, officers and yachtsmen. Highlights include the State Apartments, Admiral's Cabin, Engine Room, Laundry and Sick Bay. Visit the new Royal Deck tea room.

Times Open all year daily from 10; Jul & Aug from 9.30; (last admission 4 Apr-Jul & Sep-Oct;, 4.30 Aug; 3.30 Nov-Mar). Closed 25 Dec & 1 Jan **Fees** £10.50 (ch 5-17 £6.75, concessions £9) Family ticket (2ad+3ch) £31* **Facilities** (fully accessible) toilets for disabled (lift to ship, areas ramped, written scripts, audio tour) shop

Scotch Whisky Experience

354 Castlehill, The Royal Mile EH1 2NE
☎ 0131 220 0441 📠 0131 220 6288
e-mail: info@scotchwhiskyexperience.co.uk
web: www.scotchwhiskyexperience.co.uk
dir: next to Edinburgh Castle

Take a barrel ride and become part of the Whisky making process. Experience the varying aromas of our regional whiskies of fruity, sweet or smoky flavours. The experts will help with selecting the prefect dram. Enter the World's largest collection of Scotch Whiskies and enjoy a special tutored nosing and tasting of a dram. Whisky bar with over 300 single malts, blends, Scotch whisky, liqueurs and cocktails.

Times Open all year, daily, 10-5 (extended in summer). Closed 25 Dec **Fees** £11.50 (ch 5-17 £5.95, concessions £9). Family £27* **Facilities** licensed (fully accessible) toilets for disabled (Braille script, tour script, lift) shop

Scottish National Gallery of Modern Art

75 Belford Rd EH4 3DR
☎ 0131 624 6200 📠 0131 343 3250
e-mail: enquiries@nationalgalleries.org
web: www.nationalgalleries.org
dir: in West End, 20 min walk from Haymarket station

An outstanding collection of 20th-century painting, sculpture and graphic art. Includes major works by Matisse, Picasso, Bacon, Moore and Lichtenstein and an exceptional group of Scottish paintings. Set in leafy grounds with a sculpture garden.

Times Open all year, daily 10-5, 1 Jan noon-5. Closed 25-26 Dec **Fees** Free. Admission charged to some major exhibitions **Facilities** (fully accessible) toilets for disabled (ramps & lift) shop

Scott Monument

East Princes Street Gardens, Princes St EH2 2EJ
☎ 0131 529 4068
dir: Overlooking city centre

Since the Scott Monument opened in 1846, millions of people have climbed the 200 foot structure to admire its commanding views of the city, the exhibition on Scott's life and the statuettes of characters from his novels.

Times Open all year Apr-Sep, daily 10-7, Oct-Mar, Mon-Sat 9-3, Sun 10-3.* **Fees** £3* **Facilities**

The Writers' Museum FREE

Lady Stair's House, Lady Stair's Close, Lawnmarket EH1 2PA
☎ 0131 529 4901 📠 0131 220 5057
e-mail: museumsandgalleries@edinburgh.gov.uk
web: www.edinburghmuseums.org.uk
dir: off the Royal Mile

Situated in the historic Lady Stair's House which dates from 1622, the museum houses various objects associated with Robert Burns, Sir Walter Scott and Robert Louis Stevenson. Temporary exhibitions are planned throughout the year.

Times Open all year, Mon-Sat 10-5. (Aug only, Sun 12-5) **Facilities** shop

GOGAR **Map 11 NT17**

Suntrap Garden

43 Gogarbank EH12 9BY
☎ 0131 339 7283 📠 0131 339 2891
e-mail: suntrap@btopenworld.com
web: www.suntrap-garden.org.uk
dir: between A8 & A71 W of city bypass

The three-acre garden consists of many gardens within a single garden, including Italian, Rock, Peat and Woodland.

Times Open all year 10-5.* **Facilities** (outdoor) (partly accessible) toilets for disabled (limited access to toilet facilities at wknds)

SOUTH QUEENSFERRY Map 11 NT17

Dalmeny House

EH30 9TQ
☎ 0131 331 1888 0131 331 1788
e-mail: events@dalmeny.co.uk
web: www.dalmeny.co.uk

This is the home of the Earl and the Countess of Rosebery, whose family have lived here for over 300 years. The house, however, dates from 1815 when it was built in Tudor Gothic style. There is fine French furniture, tapestries and porcelain from the Rothschild Mentmore collection. Early Scottish furniture is also shown, with 18th-century portraits, Rosebery racing mementoes, a display of pictures and one of the world's most important Napoleonic collections.

Times Open Jun-Jul, guided tours only 2.15 & 3.30 **Fees** £6 (ch 10-16 £4, concessions £5)* **Facilities** (partly accessible) (rough surface to car park, access restricted to main collection ground floor and tearoom) toilets for disabled (designated car parking and access)

Hopetoun House

EH30 9SL
☎ 0131 331 2451 0131 319 1885
e-mail: marketing@hopetoun.co.uk
web: www.hopetoun.co.uk
dir: 2m W of Forth Road Bridge, off A904

Hopetoun House at South Queensferry is just a short drive from Edinburgh and has all the ingredients for a great family day out. Whether it is a leisurely stroll, afternoon tea or a touch of nostalgia, Hopetoun fits the bill. Built around 300 years ago, it is a delight to wander the corridors and historical rooms of one of the most splendid examples of the work of Scottish architects, Sir William Bruce and William Adam. It shows some of the finest examples in Scotland of carving, wainscoting and ceiling painting. With 100 acres of parkland including a deer park, the gardens are a colourful carpet of seasonal flowers. Summer fair in July, Christmas shopping fair in November.

Times Open daily Etr-25 Sep* **Fees** £8 (ch £4.25). Grounds £3.70 (ch £2.20)* **Facilities** (outdoor) (partly accessible) (ramps to tearoom, lift to first floor of house) toilets for disabled (touch screens showing photos of upstairs room) shop

Inchcolm Abbey and Island

Inchcolm Island KY3 0SL
☎ 01383 823332
web: www.historic-scotland.gov.uk
dir: 1.5m S of Aberdour. Access by ferry Apr-Sep

Situated on a green island on the Firth of Forth, the Augustinian abbey was founded in about 1192 by Alexander I. The well-preserved remains include a fine 13th-century octagonal chapter house and a 13th-century wall painting.

Times Open Apr-Sep, daily 9.30-5.30; Oct 9.30-4.30 **Fees** £4.70 (ch £2.80, concessions £3.80). Additional charge for ferry trip. Please phone or check website for further details* **Facilities** toilets for disabled shop

Queensferry Museum FREE

53 High St EH30 9HP
☎ 0131 331 5545 0131 557 3346
web: www.cac.org.uk
dir: A90 from Edinburgh

The museum commands magnificent views of the two great bridges spanning the Forth and traces the history of the people of Queensferry and Dalmeny, the historic ferry passage to Fife, the construction of the rail and road bridges and the wildlife of the Forth estuary. An ancient annual custom, in August, is the Burry Man, who is clad from head to toe in burrs, and parades through the town. See the full size model of the Burry Man in the museum.

Times Open all year, Mon & Thu-Sat 10-1, 2.15-5, Sun noon-5 (last admission 30 mins before closing). Closed 25-26 Dec & 1-2 Jan **Facilities** (partly accessible) (induction loop at reception) shop

FALKIRK

BIRKHILL Map 11 NS97

Birkhill Fireclay Mine

EH51 9AQ
☎ 01506 825855 & 822298 01506 828766
e-mail: mine@srps.org.uk
web: www.srps.org.uk
dir: A706 from Linlithgow, A904 from Grangemouth, follow brown signs to Steam Railway & Fireclay Mine. Main access is by train from Bo'ness

Tour guides will meet you at Birkhill station and lead you down into the Fireclay Mine. Once inside and wearing a protective hard hat, the mysteries of the caves and tunnels start to unfold. 300-million-year-old fossils and mysterious water filled caverns will excite and enthral visitors. Although the 100 plus steps from the station may restrict those with mobility difficulties, it is possible to enjoy the meadowland and ancient woodland of the Avon Gorge.

Times Open wknds Apr-Oct, daily in Jul-Aug **Fees** Mine & Train £9 (ch £5, concessions £7.50). Family ticket (2ad+2ch) £23. Mine only £3.10 (ch £2.10, concessions £2.60). Family ticket £8.25* **Facilities** (outdoor) toilets for disabled (not suitable for wheelchair users due to steps)

SCOTLAND

BO'NESS Map 11 NT08

Bo'ness & Kinneil Railway 2 FOR 1

Bo'ness Station, Union St EH51 9AQ
☎ 01506 825855 & 822298 📠 01506 828766
e-mail: enquiries.railway@srps.org.uk
web: www.srps.org.uk
dir: A904 from all directions, signed

Historic railway buildings, including the station and train shed, have been relocated from sites all over Scotland. The Scottish Railway Exhibition tells the story of the development of railways and their impact on the people of Scotland. A return trip by steam train to the tranquil country station at Birkhill now includes crossing the River Avon Viaduct on to Manuel. Thomas the Tank Engine weekends in May, August and September, and Santa Specials in December. Booking is essential for these special events and 2-for-1 Voucher cannot be used. 2011 is the 50th anniversary of The Scottish Railway Preservation Society.

Times Open wknds Apr-Oct, daily Jul-Aug, ex 1, 2, 5, 12 Jul & 30-31 Aug* **Fees** Return fare £9 (ch 5-15 £5, concessions £7.50). Family ticket £23. (Ticket for return train fare & tour of Birkhill Fireclay Mine)* **Facilities** (outdoor) (fully accessible) toilets for disabled (ramps to station & adapted carriage) shop

Kinneil Museum & Roman Fortlet FREE

Duchess Anne Cottages, Kinneil Estate EH51 0PR
☎ 01506 778530
web: www.falkirk.gov.uk/cultural
dir: follow tourist signs from Heritage Railway, off M9. Establishment at E end of town accessed via Dean Rd

The museum is in a converted stable block of Kinneil House. The ground floor has displays on the industrial history of Bo'ness, while the upper floor looks at the history and environment of the Kinneil Estate. The remains of the Roman fortlet can be seen nearby. An audio-visual presentation shows 2000 years of history.

Times Open all year, Mon-Sat 12.30-4 **Facilities** shop

FALKIRK Map 11 NS88

Callendar House FREE

Callendar Park FK1 1YR
☎ 01324 503770 📠 01324 503771
e-mail: callendar.house@falkirk.gov.uk
web: www.falkirk.gov.uk/cultural
dir: On southside of town centre, Callendar House is signed. Easily accessible from M9

Mary, Queen of Scots, Oliver Cromwell, Bonnie Prince Charlie, noble earls and wealthy merchants all feature in the history of Callendar House. Costumed interpreters describe early 19th-century life in the kitchens and the 900-year history of the house is illustrated in the 'Story of Callendar House' exhibition. The house is set in parkland, offering boating and woodland walks. Regular temporary heritage, natural history and visual arts exhibitions in Callendar House's Large Gallery.

Times Open all year, Mon-Sat, 10-5 (Sun Apr-Sep only 2-5) **Facilities** (outdoor) (partly accessible) (ramped access, lift to all floors, no wheelchair access to shop/reception) toilets for disabled (induction loop) shop

Rough Castle FREE

web: www.historic-scotland.gov.uk
dir: 1m E of Bonnybridge, signed from B816

The impressive earthworks of a large Roman fort on the Antonine Wall can be seen here. The buildings have disappeared, but the mounds and terraces are the sites of barracks, and granary and bath buildings. Running between them is the military road, which once linked all the forts on the wall and is still well defined.

Times Open any reasonable time **Facilities**

FIFE

ABERDOUR Map 11 NT18

Aberdour Castle and Gardens

KY3 0SL
☎ 01383 860519
web: www.historic-scotland.gov.uk
dir: in Aberdour, 5m E of Forth Bridge on A921

The earliest surviving part of the castle is the 14th-century keep. There are also later buildings, and the remains of a terraced garden, a bowling green and a fine 16th-century doocot (dovecote).

Times Open all year, Apr-Sep, daily 9.30-5.30; Oct, 9.30-4.30; Nov-Mar, 9.30-4.30; closed Thu-Fri & 25-26 Dec & 1-2 Jan **Fees** £4.20 (ch £2.50, concessions £3.40). Please phone or check website for further details* **Facilities** licensed (partly accessible) toilets for disabled (wheelchairs) shop

ANSTRUTHER Map 12 NO50

Scottish Fisheries Museum

St Ayles, Harbour Head KY10 3AB
☎ 01333 310628 📠 01333 310628
e-mail: info@scotfishmuseum.org
web: www.scotfishmuseum.org
dir: A917 through St Monans & Pittenweem to Anstruther

This award-winning national museum tells the story of Scottish fishing and its people from the earliest times to the present. With 10 galleries, 2 large boatyards, and a restored fisherman's cottage, which contain many fine paintings and photographs, boat models and 17 actual boats, clothing and items of daily life to see, a visit to the museum makes for an exceptional day out. Contact the museum for details of events.

Times Open all year, Apr-Sep, Mon-Sat 10-5.30, Sun 11-5; Oct-Mar, Mon-Sat 10-4.30, Sun 12-4.30. Closed 25-26 Dec & 1-2 Jan (last admission 1 hr before closing)* **Facilities** Ⓟ ☕ ♿ (fully accessible) toilets for disabled (ramps throughout to provide full access) shop ⊗

BURNTISLAND Map 11 NT28

Burntisland Edwardian Fair Museum

FREE

102 High St KY3 9AS
☎ 01592 583213
e-mail: kirkcaldy.museum@fife.gov.uk
dir: in the centre of Burntisland

Burntisland Museum has recreated a walk through the sights and sounds of the town's fair in 1910, based on a painting of the scene by local artist Andrew Young. See reconstructed rides, stalls and side shows of the time.

Times Open all year, Mon, Wed, Fri & Sat 10-1 & 2-5; Tue & Thu 10-1 & 2-7. Closed PH **Facilities** Ⓟ ⊗

CULROSS Map 11 NS98

Culross Palace, Town House & The Study

West Green House KY12 8JH
☎ 0844 4932189 📠 0844 493 2190
e-mail: information@nts.org.uk
web: www.nts.org.uk
dir: off A985, 4m E of Kincardine Bridge

A Royal Burgh, Culross dates from the 16th and 17th centuries and has remained virtually unchanged since. It prospered from the coal and salt trades, and when these declined in the 1700s, Culross stayed as it was. It owes its present appearance to the National Trust for Scotland, which has been gradually restoring it. In the Town House is a visitor centre and exhibition; in the building called The Study can be seen a drawing room with a Norwegian painted ceiling, and The Palace has painted rooms and terraced gardens.

Times Palace, Study, Town House 2 Apr-May, Thu-Mon 12-5; Jun-Aug, daily 12-5; 3-29 Sep, Thu-Mon 12-5; Oct, Thu-Mon 12-4. Access to Study & Town House is by guided tour only, Tours depart every hour from Palace reception (starting at 1, last tour departs 4, in Oct last tour departs at 3). Garden all year, daily 10-6 or sunset if earlier* **Facilities** 🅟 Ⓟ ☕ ⛩ ♿ (partly accessible) (Palace, study & town house unsuitable for visitors with limited mobility due to uneven surfaces and spiral staircases) toilets for disabled (Braille guide, large print) shop ⊗ 🏰

CUPAR Map 11 NO31

Hill of Tarvit Mansionhouse & Garden

KY15 5PB
☎ 0844 493 2185 📠 01334 653127
e-mail: information@nts.org.uk
web: www.nts.org.uk
dir: 2.5m S of Cupar, off A916

Built in the first decade of the 20th century, the Mansionhouse is home to a notable collection of paintings, tapestries, furniture and Chinese porcelain. The grounds include formal gardens, and there is a regular programme of concerts and art exhibitions.

Times Open all year, 2 Apr-May, Thu-Mon 1-5; Jun-Aug, daily 1-5; Sep-Oct, Thu-Mon 1-5. Garden & grounds open all year, daily (closes at dusk).* **Facilities** 🅟 ☕ ⛩ ♿ (partly accessible) toilets for disabled (ramps, visual information, room sheets) shop ⊗ 🏰

The Scottish Deer Centre

2 FOR 1

Bow-of-Fife KY15 4NQ
☎ 01337 810391 📠 01337 810477
e-mail: info@tsdc.co.uk
web: www.tsdc.co.uk
dir: From S M90 junct 8 to A91 Cupar, from N M90 junct 9 to A912, join A91. Follow brown tourist sign

Guided tours take about 30 minutes and allow you to meet and feed deer. There are indoor and outdoor adventure play areas. Other features include daily falconry displays and a tree top walkway. European wolves are fed every-day (except Friday) at 3pm. Trailer rides through fields and paddocks available. A photography workshop is held the last weekend of each month and there are various events from May to October.

Times Open all year, daily, Winter 10-4, Summer 10-5, 5.30 Jul-Aug **Fees** £6.95 (ch 3-15 £4.95)* **Facilities** 🅟 ☕ ⛩ (indoor & outdoor) ♿ (fully accessible) toilets for disabled (special parking bay, loan of wheelchairs) shop ⊗

SCOTLAND

DUNFERMLINE Map 11 NT08

Abbot House Heritage Centre

Abbot House, Maygate KY12 7NE
☎ 01383 733266 📠 01383 624908
e-mail: dht@abbothouse.co.uk
web: www.abbothouse.co.uk
dir: in city centre

SCOTLAND

For the better part of a millennium, pilgrims have beaten a path to Dunfermline's door. Today visitors can still share the rich royal heritage of the capital of Fife's Magic Kingdom. The volunteer-run Abbot House Heritage Centre - dubbed 'The People's Tardis' - propels the traveller through time from the days of the Picts - a time warp peopled by a veritable Who's Who of characters from Dunfermline's past: Scotland's royal saint, Braveheart's Wallace and Bruce, Scotland's Chaucer, steel magnate Andrew Carnegie and a whole panoply of kings, ending with the birth of ill-starred Charles I.

Times Open Mar-Oct daily, 10-5; Nov-Feb, Sun-Fri 10-4, Sat 10-5. Closed 25-26 Dec & 1 Jan **Fees** £4 (accompanied ch under 16 free, concessions £3). Party 20+* **Facilities** Ⓟ ☕ ♿ (partly accessible) (ground floor fully accessible) toilets for disabled (parking on site, virtual tour of inaccessible areas) shop 🚫

Andrew Carnegie Birthplace Museum — FREE

Moodie St KY12 7PL
☎ 01383 724302 📠 01383 749799
e-mail: info@carnegiebirthplace.com
web: www.carnegiebirthplace.com
dir: 400yds S from Abbey

The museum tells the story of the handloom weaver's son, born here in 1835, who created the biggest steel works in the USA and then became a philanthropist on a huge scale. The present-day work of the philanthropic Carnegie Trust is also explained. A series of temporary exhibitions will take place in the main hall throughout the year.

Times Open Mar-Dec, Mon-Sat 10-5, Sun 2-5 **Facilities** 🅟 Ⓟ ☕ ♿ (partly accessible) (cottage inaccessible, main hall and shop accessible) toilets for disabled (photo album, cd audio tape in cottage) shop 🚫

Dunfermline Abbey and Palace

Pittencrieff Park KY12 7PE
☎ 01383 739026
web: www.historic-scotland.gov.uk

The monastery was a powerful Benedictine house, founded by Queen Margaret in the 11th century. A modern brass in the choir marks the grave of King Robert the Bruce. The monastery guest house became a royal palace, and was the birthplace of Charles I.

Times Open all year, Apr-Sep, daily 9.30-5.30; Oct, 9.30-4.30; Nov-Mar, daily, 9.30-4.30, closed Thu (pm), Fri & Sun (am). Closed 25-26 Dec & 1-2 Jan **Fees** £3.70 (ch £2.20, concessions £3). Please phone or check website for further details* **Facilities** Ⓟ shop 🚫

Pittencrieff House Museum — FREE

Pittencrieff Park KY12 8QH
☎ 01383 722935 & 723042
e-mail: dunfermline.museum@fife.gov.uk
dir: off A994 into Pittencriefff Park Car Park. Attraction on W edge of town

A fine 17th-century house standing in the beautiful park gifted to the town by Andrew Carnegie. Accessible displays tell the story of the park's animals and plants, with plenty of photographs of people enjoying the park over the last 100 years.

Times Open all year, daily Jan-Mar & Oct-Dec 11-4; Apr-Sep 11-5 **Facilities** Ⓟ ♿ (fully accessible) toilets for disabled (ramp) shop 🚫

FALKLAND Map 11 NO20

Falkland Palace & Garden

KY15 7BU
☎ 0844 493 2186 📠 0844 493 2188
e-mail: information@nts.org.uk
web: www.nts.org.uk
dir: off A912, 10m from M90, junct 8

The hunting palace of the Stuart monarchs, this fine building, with a French-Renaissance style south wing, stands in the shelter of the Lomond Hills. The beautiful Chapel Royal and King's Bedchamber are its most notable features, and it is also home to the oldest royal tennis court in Britain (1539). The garden has a spectacular delphinium border. Recorded sacred music is played hourly in the Chapel. Please telephone for details of concerts, recitals etc.

Times Palace & Garden: 2 Mar-Oct, Mon-Sat 10-5, Sun 1-5* **Facilities** 🅟 Ⓟ ♿ (partly accessible) (building not suitable for wheelchairs, some gravel paths in garden) (audio wand, scented garden, wheelchair available) shop 🚫

KELLIE CASTLE & GARDENS Map 12 NO50

Kellie Castle & Gardens

KY10 2RF
☎ 0844 493 2184 📠 0844 493 2183
e-mail: information@nts.org.uk
web: www.nts.org.uk
dir: On B9171, 3m NNW of Pittenweem

The oldest part dates from about 1360, but it is for its 16th and 17th-century domestic architecture (designed by Sir Robert Lorimer) that Kellie is renowned. It has notable plasterwork and painted panelling, and there are also interesting Victorian gardens.

Times Castle: 3 Apr-May & Sep-Oct, Fri-Tue 1-5; Jun-Aug, daily 1-5. Garden: same dates as Castle, 10-5.* **Facilities** (outdoor) (partly accessible) toilets for disabled (induction loop, video, tour facility, photo albums) shop

KIRKCALDY Map 11 NT29

Kirkcaldy Museum & Art Gallery FREE

War Memorial Gardens KY1 1YG
☎ 01592 583213
e-mail: kirkcaldy.museum@fife.gov.uk
web: www.fifedirect.org.uk/museums
dir: next to train station

Set in the town's lovely memorial gardens, the museum houses a collection of fine and decorative art, including 18th to 21st-century Scottish paintings, among them the works of William McTaggart and S J Peploe. An award-winning display 'Changing Places' tells the story of the social, industrial and natural heritage of the area.

Times Open all year, Mon-Sat 10.30-5, Sun 2-5. Closed local hols **Facilities** (fully accessible) toilets for disabled (ramp to main entrance & lift to 1st floor galleries) shop

NORTH QUEENSFERRY Map 11 NT17

Deep Sea World

Forthside Ter KY11 1JR
☎ 01383 411880 📠 01383 410514
e-mail: info@deepseaworld.co.uk
web: www.deepseaworld.com/
dir: from N, M90 take exit for Inverkeithing. From S follow signs to Forth Rd Bridge, 1st exit left

The UK's longest underwater tunnel gives you a diver's eye view of an underwater world. Come face to face with Sand Tiger sharks, and watch divers hand-feed a wide array of sea life. Visit the Amazon Experience with ferocious piranhas and the amazing amphibian display featuring the world's most poisonous frog. Also featuring the Seal Sanctuary, dedicated to the rehabilitation and release of injured and orphaned seal pups. Please telephone or visit website for details of events running throughout the year.

Times Open all year, daily from 10. See website for seasonal closing times.* **Facilities** (outdoor) (fully accessible) toilets for disabled (ramps & disabled parking, hearing loop) shop

ST ANDREWS Map 12 NO51

British Golf Museum 2 FOR 1

Bruce Embankment KY16 9AB
☎ 01334 460046 & 460051 📠 01334 460064
e-mail: judychance@randa.org
web: www.britishgolfmuseum.co.uk
dir: opposite Royal & Ancient Golf Club

Where better to find out about golf than in St Andrews, the home of golf. Using diverse and exciting interactive displays, this museum explores the history of golf from its origins to the personalities of today. For a chance to play with replica clubs and balls visit the Royal and Ancient gallery.

Times Open all year, Apr-Oct, Mon-Sat 9.30-5, Sun 10-5; Nov-Mar, Mon-Sun 10-4 **Fees** £6 (ch £3, concessions £5). Family ticket £15.50* **Facilities** (fully accessible) toilets for disabled shop

Castle & Visitor Centre

KY16 9AR
☎ 01334 477196

This 13th-century stronghold castle was the scene of the murder of Cardinal Beaton in 1546. The new visitor centre incorporates an exciting multi-media exhibition describing the history of the castle and nearby cathedral.

Times Open all year daily, Apr-Sep 9.30-6.30; Oct-Mar 9.30-4.30. Closed 25-26 Dec & 1-2 Jan* **Facilities** toilets for disabled shop

Cathedral (& Museum)

KY16 9QU
☎ 01334 472563

The cathedral was the largest in Scotland, and is now an extensive ruin. The remains date mainly from the 12th and 13th centuries, and large parts of the precinct walls have survived intact. Close by is St Rule's church, which the cathedral was built to replace. St Rule's probably dates from before the Norman Conquest, and is considered the most interesting Romanesque church in Scotland.

Times Open all year daily, Apr-Sep 9.30-6.30; Oct-Mar 9.30-4.30. Closed 25-26 Dec & 1-2 Jan* **Facilities** shop

St Andrews Aquarium

The Scores KY16 9AS
☎ 01334 474786 📠 01334 475985
web: www.standrewsaquarium.co.uk
dir: signed in town centre

This continually expanding aquarium is home to shrimps, sharks, eels, octopi, seals and much much more. Special features include the Seahorse Parade, and the Sea Mammal Research Unit, which is committed to the care of sea mammals and their environment.

Times Open all year, daily from 10. Please phone for winter opening* **Facilities** licensed toilets for disabled shop

SCOTLAND

SCOTLAND

CITY OF GLASGOW

GLASGOW Map 11 NS56

Burrell Collection FREE

Pollok Country Park, 2060 Pollokshaws Rd G43 1AT
☎ 0141 287 2550 🖷 0141 287 2597
e-mail: museums@csglasgow.org
web: www.glasgowmuseums.com
dir: 3.5m S of city centre, signed from M77 junct 2

Set in Pollok Country Park, this award-winning building makes the priceless works of art on display seem almost part of the woodland setting. Shipping magnate Sir William Burrell's main interests were medieval Europe, Oriental art and European paintings. Colourful paintings and stained glass show the details of medieval life. Furniture, paintings, sculpture, armour and weapons help to complete the picture. Rugs, ceramics and metalwork represent the art of Islam. There is also a strong collection of Chinese and other Oriental ceramics. Paintings on display include works by Bellini, Rembrandt and the French Impressionists.

Times Open all year, Mon-Thu & Sat 10-5, Fri & Sun 11-5. Closed 25-26 & 31 (pm) Dec & 1-2 Jan* **Facilities** licensed (fully accessible) toilets for disabled (wheelchairs available, tape guides, lifts) shop

Clydebuilt - Scottish Maritime Museum at Braehead 2 FOR 1

Braehead Shopping Centre, King Inch Rd G51 4BN
☎ 0141 886 1013 🖷 0141 886 1015
e-mail: clydebuilt@scotmaritime.org.uk
web: www.scottishmaritimemuseum.org
dir: M8 junct 25A, 26, follow signs for Braehead Shopping Centre, then Green car park

On the banks of the River Clyde, home of the Scottish shipbuilding industry, visitors can discover how Glasgow's famous ships were built, from the design stages through to the launch. There are also displays on the textile and cotton industries, iron and steel, and tobacco. Hands-on activities allow you to operate a real ship's engine, become a ship's riveter, and steer a virtual ship up the Clyde. See the QE2 exhibition celebrating her last visit to the place of her birth. A new exhibition about the 'Blockade Runners' opened autumn 2010.

Times Open all year, Mon-Sat 10-5.30, Sun 11-5.30 **Fees** £4.25 (ch £2.50, concessions £3). Family ticket £10 **Facilities** (outdoor) (fully accessible) toilets for disabled (lift, ramps, wheelchairs from shopping centre) shop

Gallery of Modern Art

Royal Exchange Square G1 3AH
☎ 0141 287 3050 🖷 0141 287 3062
e-mail: museums@csglasgow.org
web: www.glasgowmuseums.com
dir: just off Buchanan St & close to Central Station & Queen St Stn

GoMA offers a thought-provoking programme of temporary exhibitions and workshops. It displays work by local and international artists, as well as addressing contemporary social issues through its major biennial projects.

Times Open all year, Mon-Tue & Sat 10-5, Thu 10-8, Fri & Sun 11-5. Closed 25-26 & 31 Dec (pm), 1-2 Jan* **Facilities** (fully accessible) toilets for disabled shop

Glasgow Botanic Gardens FREE

730 Great Western Rd G12 0UE
☎ 0141 276 1614 🖷 0141 276 1615
e-mail: gbg@land.glasgow.gov.uk
dir: From M8 junct 17 onto A82 Dumbarton. Approx 2-3m the Botanic Gardens are on the right

Home of the national collections of Dendrobium Orchids, Begonias and tree ferns, the Gardens consist of an arboretum, herbaceous borders, a herb garden, rose garden, and unusual vegetables. The Kibble Palace contains carnivorous plants, island flora and temperate plant collections.

Times Open all year. Gardens open daily 7-dusk. Glasshouses 10-6 (4.15 in winter) **Facilities** (partly accessible) (all areas accessible except small section on river Kelvin Walway) toilets for disabled

Glasgow Cathedral FREE

Castle St G4 0QZ
☎ 0141 552 6891
web: www.historic-scotland.gov.uk
dir: M8 junct 15, in centre of Glasgow

The only Scottish mainland medieval cathedral to have survived the Reformation complete (apart from its western towers). Built during the 13th to 15th centuries over the supposed site of the tomb of St Kentigern. Notable features in this splendid building are the elaborately vaulted crypt, which includes an introductory display and collection of carved stones, the stone screen of the early 15th century and the unfinished Blackadder Aisle.

Times Open all year, Apr-Sep, daily, 9.30-5.30, Sun, 1-5; Oct-Mar, daily, 9.30-4.30, Sun 1-4.30. Closed 25-26 Dec & 1-2 Jan **Facilities** (partly accessible) (telephone for disabled access details) shop

Glasgow Museums Resource Centre FREE

200 Woodhead Rd, South Nitshill Ind Estate G53 7NN
☎ 0141 276 9300 📠 0141 276 9305
web: www.glasgowmuseums.com
dir: on S side, close to Rail Stn

GMRC is the first publicly-accessible store for the city's museum service, offering a behind-the-scenes look at 200,000 treasures held in storage. Please note that access to the stores is by guided tour only. Viewings of a specific object can be arranged, with two weeks prior notice. Activities, tours and talks are held throughout the year - see website or phone for details.

Times Open all year Mon-Thu & Sat 10-5, Fri-Sun 11-5. Guided tours for public at 2.30 Access is only by guided tours. **Facilities** 🅟 toilets for disabled ㊗

Glasgow Science Centre

50 Pacific Quay G51 1EA
☎ 0141 420 5000 📠 0141 420 5011
e-mail: admin@glasgowsciencecentre.org
web: www.glasgowsciencecentre.org
dir: M8 junct 24 or M77 junct 21, follow brown signs, across Clyde from SECC

The centre is home to many entertaining and exciting attractions and contains hundreds of interactive exhibits over 2 acres of science floors. Highlights include the Planetarium, Scotland's only IMAX cinema and the 127 metre Glasgow Tower, a remarkable free-standing structure that gives breathtaking views of the city (check availability before visiting). GSC presents the world of science and technology in new and exciting ways.

Times Open all year, 29 Oct-30 Mar, 10-5 Tue-Sun; 30 Mar-29 Oct daily 10-5 **Fees** £9.95 (ch & concessions £7.95). Tower, Planetarium, & Imax Science Film £2.50 each* **Facilities** 🅟 Ⓟ ☕ 🛋 (indoor & outdoor) ♿ (fully accessible) toilets for disabled (induction loops) shop ㊗

Greenbank Garden

Flenders Rd, Clarkston G76 8RB
☎ 0844 493 2201 📠 0844 493 2200
e-mail: information@nts.org.uk
web: www.nts.org.uk
dir: off A726 on southern outskirts of city, 6m S of Glasgow

The spacious, walled woodland gardens are attractively laid out in the grounds of an elegant Georgian house, and best seen between April and October. A wide range of flowers and shrubs are grown, with the idea of helping private gardeners to look at possibilities for their own gardens. A greenhouse and garden designed for the disabled gardener also displays specialised tools.

Times Garden open daily all year, 9.30-sunset. House Apr-Oct, Sun 2-4* **Facilities** 🅟 ☕ ♿ (partly accessible) (8 steps to front door of house, gentle slopes in garden) toilets for disabled (wheelchairs available, scented/textured plants) shop ㊗ 🐕

Holmwood House

61-63 Netherlee House, Cathcart G44 3YG
☎ 0844 493 2204 📠 0844 493 2204
e-mail: information@nts.org.uk
web: www.nts.org.uk
dir: off Clarkston Rd

Completed in 1858, Holmwood is considered to be the finest domestic design by the architect Alexander 'Greek' Thomson. Many rooms are richly ornamented in wood, plaster and marble.

Times Open Apr-Oct, Thu-Mon 12-5* **Facilities** 🅟 ☕ 🛋 ♿ (partly accessible) (access to first floor via lift) (audio tour, room guides) shop ㊗ 🐕

House for an Art Lover

10 Dumbreck Rd, Bellahouston Park G41 5BW
☎ 0141 353 4770 📠 0141 353 4771
e-mail: info@houseforanartlover.co.uk
web: www.houseforanartlover.co.uk
dir: M8 W junct 23 signed B768, left at top of slip road onto Dumbreck Rd. Bellahouston Park on right

Inspired by a portfolio of drawings by Charles Rennie Mackintosh in 1901, this fascinating artistic attraction and private dining venue opened in 1996. Visitors can view the Mackintosh suite of rooms and learn from a DVD presentation about the development of the building and its contents. There is a full programme of changing art exhibitions, dinner concerts and afternoon musical recitals. Contact for more details.

Times Open all year, Apr-Sep, Mon-Wed 10-4 & Thu-Sun 10-1; Oct-Mar, Sat-Sun 10-1, telephone for wkday opening times* **Facilities** 🅟 🍽 licensed ♿ (fully accessible) toilets for disabled (lift to 1st floor) shop ㊗

Hunterian Art Gallery

82 Hillhead St, The University of Glasgow G12 8QQ
☎ 0141 330 5431 📠 0141 330 3618
e-mail: hunter@museum.gla.ac.uk
web: www.hunterian.gla.ac.uk
dir: on University of Glasgow Campus in Hillhead District, 2m W of city centre

The founding collection is made up of paintings bequeathed in the 18th century by Dr William Hunter, including works by Rembrandt and Stubbs. The Gallery now has works by James McNeill Whistler, major displays of paintings by the Scottish Colourists, and a graphics collection holding some 300,000 prints. A popular feature of the Charles Rennie Mackintosh collection is the re-construction of the interiors of The Mackintosh House.

Times Open all year, Mon-Sat 9.30-5. Telephone for BH closures **Fees** Free admission for the Art Gallery. Admission charged for the Mackintosh House £3 (concessions £2) **Facilities** Ⓟ ♿ (partly accessible) (Art Gallery full access, in the Mackintosh House ground floor orientation room, hall & dining-room only accessible) toilets for disabled (lift, wheelchair available) shop ㊗

SCOTLAND

GLASGOW *continued*

Hunterian Museum FREE

Gilbert Scott Building, The University of Glasgow G12 8QQ
☎ 0141 330 4221 0141 330 3617
e-mail: hunter@museum.gla.ac.uk
web: www.hunterian.gla.ac.uk
dir: on University of Glasgow campus in Hillhead District, 2m W of city centre

The museum tells the story of the handloom weaver's son, born here in 1835, who created the biggest steel works in the USA and then became a philanthropist on a huge scale. The present-day work of the philanthropic Carnegie Trust is also explained.

Times Open all year, Mon-Fri 9.30-5. Closed certain BHs phone for details. The main hall is closed to the public until spring 2011 to allow for the installation of a new roof but other areas of the Museum are open. For an update on what is currently on display please call 0141 330 4221* **Facilities** (partly accessible) toilets for disabled (lift) shop

Hutchesons' Hall FREE

158 Ingram St G1 1EJ
☎ 0844 493 2199 0844 493 2198
e-mail: information@nts.org.uk
web: www.nts.org.uk
dir: near SE corner of George Square

This handsome early 19th-century building was designed by David Hamilton and houses a visitor centre and shop. There is a video about Glasgow's merchant city, and the Hall can be booked for functions. Telephone for details of concerts, recitals, etc. The Trust is considering some new initiatives at Hutchesons' Hall and as a result opening times may change. Please call in advance before making a visit.

Times Please call in advance to check opening times.* **Facilities** (partly accessible) toilets for disabled shop

Kelvingrove Art Gallery & Museum

Argyle St G3 8AG
☎ 0141 276 9599 0141 276 9540
e-mail: museums@csglasgow.org
web: www.glasgowmuseums.com
dir: 1m W of city centre

Glasgow's favourite building re-opened in July 2006 after a three-year, £35 million restoration project. On display are 8000 objects, including a Spitfire, a 4-metre ceratosaur and Salvador Dali's *Christ of St John of the Cross*. A new 'Mackintosh and the Glasgow Style Gallery' explores the genius of Charles Rennie Mackintosh. Exciting temporary exhibitions take place throughout the year. Organ recitals take place each day and there are a range of tours and activities available for all ages.

Times Open all year, Mon-Thu & Sat 10-5; Fri & Sun 11-5. Closed 25-26 & 31 Dec (pm) & 1-2 Jan* **Facilities** licensed (outdoor) (fully accessible) toilets for disabled shop

The Lighthouse

11 Mitchell Ln G1 3NU
☎ 0141 221 6362 0141 221 6395
e-mail: enquiries@thelighthouse.co.uk
web: www.thelighthouse.co.uk
dir: in city centre

Scotland's National Centre for Architecture, Design and the City. Extending over six floors and one of the biggest centres of its kind in Europe. Home to the award-winning Mackintosh Centre, devoted to the art, architecture and design of Charles Rennie Mackintosh (1868-1928). There are also temporary exhibition spaces with a thought provoking programme. A place of discovery and learning, another feature of The Lighthouse is the uninterrupted view over Glasgow's cityscape. Climb the helical staircase in the Mackintosh Tower or use the lift to the Level 6 Viewing Platform and spot some significant buildings that make up Glasgow's architectural tapestry.

Times Open all year, Mon & Wed-Sat, 10.30-5, Tue 11-5, Sun noon-5* **Facilities** licensed (partly accessible) (Mackintosh tower inaccessible) toilets for disabled (induction loop, large print brochures) shop

Museum of Transport FREE

1 Bunhouse Rd G3 8DP
☎ 0141 287 2720 0141 287 2692
e-mail: museums@csglasgow.org
web: www.glasgowmuseums.com
dir: 1.5m W of city centre

Visit the Museum of Transport and the first impression is of gleaming metalwork and bright paint. All around you there are cars, caravans, carriages and carts, fire engines, buses, steam locomotives, prams and trams. The museum uses its collections of vehicles and models to tell the story of transport by land and sea, with a unique Glasgow flavour. Visitors can even go window shopping along the recreated Kelvin Street of 1938. Upstairs 250 ship models tell the story of the great days of Clyde shipbuilding. The Museum of Transport has something for everyone.

Times Glasgow's Museum of Transport is now closed. The new Riverside Museum: Scotland's Museum of Transport and Technology will open in Spring 2011. For more information on this innovative new attraction, visit website* **Facilities** (fully accessible) toilets for disabled (assistance available) shop

People's Palace FREE

Glasgow Green G40 1AT
☎ 0141 276 0788 📠 0141 276 0787
e-mail: museums@csglasgow.org
web: www.glasgowmuseums.com
dir: 1m SE of city centre

Glasgow grew from a medieval town located by the Cathedral to the Second City of the British Empire. Trade with the Americas, and later industry, made the city rich. But not everyone shared in Glasgow's wealth. The People's Palace on historic Glasgow Green shows how ordinary Glaswegians worked, lived and played. Visitors can discover how a family lived in a typical one-room Glasgow 'single end' tenement flat, see Billy Connolly's amazing banana boots, learn to speak Glesga, take a trip 'doon the watter' and visit the Winter Gardens.

Times Open all year, Mon-Thu & Sat 10-5, Fri & Sun 11-5. Closed 25-26 & 31 Dec (pm) & 1-2 Jan* **Facilities** Ⓟ ♿ (fully accessible) toilets for disabled (lifts) shop ㊅

Pollok House

Pollok Country Park, 2060 Pollokshaws Rd G43 1AT
☎ 0141 616 6410 📠 0141 616 6521
e-mail: pollokhouse@nts.org.uk
web: www.nts.org.uk
dir: 3.5m S of city centre, off M77 junct 2, follow signs for Burrell Collection

The house is one of Glasgow's most elegant, and was built by the Maxwell family in the 18th century and expanded between 1890 and 1901, including extensive servants' quarters. The rooms are decorated with 18th-century plasterwork, fine furniture and the Stirling Maxwell art collection, including works by El Greco, Goya and William Blake.

Times Open all year, house: daily 10-5. Closed 25-26 Dec & 1-2 Jan. Park: open all year, daily* **Facilities** Ⓟ Ⓟ 🍽 licensed ♿ (partly accessible) (no access to first floor) toilets for disabled (large print guide, visual record book) shop ㊅

Provand's Lordship

3 Castle St G4 0RB
☎ 0141 552 8819 📠 0141 552 4744
e-mail: museums@csglasgow.org
web: www.glasgowmuseums.com
dir: 1m E of city centre, adjacent to St Mungo Museum of religious life & Art, Glasgow Cathedral & the Necropolis

Provand's Lordship is the only house to survive from Medieval Glasgow. For over 500 years it has watched the changing fortunes of the city and the nearby Cathedral. Bishop Andrew Muirhead built the house as part of St Nicholas' Hospital in 1571. The prebendary of Barlanark later bought it for use as a manse. Inside, the displays recreate home life in the middle ages. Behind the house is the St Nicholas Garden, built in 1997. It is a medical herb garden, in keeping with the original purpose of the house.

Times Open all year, Tue-Thu & Sat 10-5, Fri & Sun 11-5. Closed 25-26 & 31 Dec (pm), 1-2 Jan **Fees** Free admission. Donations welcome **Facilities** Ⓟ ♿ (partly accessible) (ground floor only accessible) ㊅

St Mungo Museum of Religious Life & Art

2 Castle St G4 0RH
☎ 0141 276 1625 📠 0141 276 1626
e-mail: museums@csglasgow.org
web: www.glasgowmuseums.com
dir: 1m NE of city centre, adjacent to Glasgow Cathedral & Necropolis

The award-winning St Mungo Museum explores the importance of religion in peoples' everyday lives and art. It aims to promote understanding and respect between people of different faiths and of none. The museum features stained glass, objects, statues and video footage. In the grounds is Britain's first Japanese Zen garden.

Times Open all year, Tue-Thu & Sat 10-5, Fri & Sun 11-5. Closed 25-26 & 31 Dec (pm) & 1-2 Jan **Fees** Free admission. Donations welcome **Facilities** Ⓟ ☕ ♿ (fully accessible) toilets for disabled (taped information, large print & Braille & lift) shop ㊅

SCOTLAND

Scotland Street School Museum FREE

225 Scotland St G5 8QB
☎ 0141 287 0500 📠 0141 287 0515
e-mail: museums@csglasgow.org
web: www.glasgowmuseums.com

Designed by Charles Rennie Mackintosh between 1903 and 1906 for the School Board of Glasgow, and now a museum telling the story of education in Scotland from 1872 to the late 20th century. Also hosts temporary exhibitions.

Times Open all year daily 10-5, Fri & Sun 11-5. Closed 25-26 & 31 Dec & pm 1 & 2 Jan **Facilities** Ⓟ ☕ ♿ (fully accessible) toilets for disabled shop ㊅

The Scottish Football Museum 2 FOR 1

Hampden Park G42 9BA
☎ 0141 616 6139 📠 0141 616 6101
e-mail: info@scottishfootballmuseum.org.uk
web: www.scottishfootballmuseum.org.uk
dir: 3m S of city centre, follow brown tourist signs

Using 2500 pieces of footballing memorabilia, the Scottish Football Museum covers such themes as football's origins, women's football, fan culture, other games influenced by football, and even some social history. The exhibits include the World's oldest football trophy, a ticket and cap from the first International Match in 1872, a reconstructed 1903 changing room and press box, and items of specific import, such as Kenny Dalglish's silver cap, Jimmy McGrory's boots, and the ball from Scotland's 5-1 win over England in 1928. Visit the Scottish Football Hall of Fame, and take the guided Hampden Stadium tour.

Times Open all year, Mon-Sat 10-5, Sun 11-5. Closed match days, special events and Xmas/New Year. Please telephone in advance for confirmation **Fees** Museum £6 (ch 16 & concessions £3) Stadium £6 (ch 16 & concessions £3). Combined Ticket £9 (ch 16 & concessions £4.50) under 5's free* **Facilities** Ⓟ Ⓟ ☕ ♿ (fully accessible) toilets for disabled (ramps throughout, lifts) shop ㊅

SCOTLAND

GLASGOW *continued*

The Tall Ship at Glasgow Harbour

100 Stobcross Rd G3 8QQ
☎ 0141 222 2513 ▤ 0141 222 2536
e-mail: info@thetallship.com
web: www.thetallship.com
dir: from M8 junct 19 onto A814 follow signs for attraction

Visit The Tall Ship at Glasgow Harbour and step back in time to the days of sail. Experience Glasgow's maritime history at first hand and explore the UK's only remaining Clydebuilt sailing ship, the Glenlee. Exhibitions on board and in the visitor centre on the quayside tell the story of the ship and the Glasgow Harbour area. If you have ever wondered what it would have been like to be a sailor on a tall ship, this is your chance to find out. Children can have fun by joining in the hunt for Jock, the ship's cat. An unmissable experience, The Tall Ship offers guided tours, changing exhibitions, children's activities, a nautical gift shop and café.

Times Open all year, daily Mar-Oct 10-5; Nov-Feb 10-4* **Facilities** Ⓟ Ⓟ ☕ ⛩ (indoor & outdoor) toilets for disabled shop

The Tenement House

145 Buccleuch St, Garnethill G3 6QN
☎ 0844 493 2197 ▤ 0844 493 2197
e-mail: information@nts.org.uk
web: www.nts.org.uk
dir: N of Charing Cross

This shows an unsung but once-typical side of Glasgow life: it is a first-floor flat, built in 1892, with a parlour, bedroom, kitchen and bathroom, furnished with the original recess beds, kitchen range, sink, and coal bunker, among other articles. The home of Agnes Toward from 1911 to 1965, the flat was bought by an actress who preserved it as a 'time capsule'. The contents vividly portray the life of one section of Glasgow society.

Times Open Mar-Oct, daily 1-5* **Facilities** Ⓟ ♿ (partly accessible) (steps to first floor) (Braille guide, object handling collection) shop

Trades Hall of Glasgow — FREE

85 Glassford St G1 1UH
☎ 0141 552 2418 ▤ 0141 552 5053
e-mail: info@tradeshallglasgow.co.uk
web: www.tradeshallglasgow.co.uk
dir: in city centre in Merchant City. Accessible from George Square & Argyle St

The Trades Hall is one of Glasgow's most historic buildings and was home to the 14 incorporated crafts who regulated trade and played a vital role in shaping and making Glasgow the city it is today. Visitors can explore the impressive rooms of the building taking in the Grand Hall with its spectacular soaring windows, baroque chandeliers and striking dome, and the Saloon which features an original Adam fireplace and beautiful stained glass windows.

Times Open all year, Mon-Fri 10-4, Sat 9.30-12.30 subject to availability **Facilities** Ⓟ ♿ (fully accessible) toilets for disabled (electronic ramps for rise in levels of 3 & 4 stairs)

HIGHLAND

AVIEMORE — Map 14 NH81

Strathspey Steam Railway

Aviemore Station, Dalfaber Rd PH22 1PY
☎ 01479 810725
e-mail: strathtrains@strathspeyrailway.co.uk
web: www.strathspeyrailway.co.uk
dir: from A9 take B970 for Coylumbridge, on B9152, left after railway bridge, car park 0.25m on left. Other stations: Boat of Garten in village; Broomhill, off A95, 3.5m S of Grantown-on-Spey

This steam railway covers the ten miles from Aviemore via Boat of Garten to Broomhill. The journey takes about 40 minutes, but allow around two hours for the round trip. Shorter trips are possible and timetables are available from the station and the tourist information centre. Telephone, visit website or see local press for details of events running throughout the year.

Times Please telephone for details **Fees** Basic roundtrip £11 (ch £5.50) Family £27. Day Rover £18 (ch £8) **Facilities** Ⓟ Ⓟ ☕ 🍽 licensed ⛩ (outdoor) ♿ (partly accessible) (ramps) toilets for disabled shop

BALMACARA — Map 14 NG82

Balmacara Estate & Lochalsh Woodland Garden

Lochalsh House IV40 8DN
☎ 0844 493 2233 ▤ 0844 493 2235
e-mail: information@nts.org.uk
web: www.nts.org.uk
dir: 3m E of Kyle of Lochalsh, off A87

The Balmacara Estate comprises some 5,600 acres and seven crofting villages, including Plockton, a conservation area. There are excellent views of Skye, Kintail and Applecross. The main attraction is the Lochalsh Woodland Garden, but the whole area is excellent for walking.

Times Estate open all year daily, Woodland Garden all year daily 9-sunset, Reception Kiosk Apr-Sep daily 9-5, Balmacara Square Visitor Centre Apr-Sep daily 9-5 (Fri 9-4)* **Facilities** Ⓟ ♿ (partly accessible) (visual & audio information)

BETTYHILL — Map 14 NC76

Strathnaver Museum

KW14 7SS
☎ 01641 521418
e-mail: strathnavermus@ukonline.co.uk
dir: By the A836 on outskirts of Bettyhill on the E of the village

The museum has displays on the Clearances, with a fine collection of Strathnaver Clearances furnishings, domestic and farm implements, and local books. There is also a Clan Mackay room. The museum's setting is a former church, a handsome stone building with a magnificent canopied pulpit dated 1774. The churchyard contains a carved stone known as the Farr

Stone, which dates back to the 9th century and is a fine example of Pictish art.

Times Open Apr-Oct, Mon-Sat 10-5 **Fees** £2 (ch 50p, under 5's free, concessions £1.50, student/groups £1)* **Facilities** Ⓟ (P) ♿ (partly accessible) (ground floor only accessible) (DVD tour, portable player, small wheelchair) shop ⊗

BOAT OF GARTEN **Map 14 NH91**

RSPB Loch Garten Osprey Centre

RSPB Reserve Abernethy Forest, Forest Lodge, Nethybridge PH25 3EF
☎ 01479 821894 📠 01479 821069
dir: signed from B970 & A9 at Aviemore, follow 'RSPB Ospreys' signs

Home of the Loch Garten Osprey site, this reserve holds one of the most important remnants of Scots Pine forest in the Highlands. Within its 30,760 acres are forest bogs, moorland, mountain top, lochs and crofting land. In addition to the regular pair of nesting ospreys, there are breeding Scottish crossbills, capercaillies, black grouse and many others. The ospreys can be viewed through telescopes and there is a live TV link to the nest. Please telephone for details of special events running throughout the year.

Times Osprey Centre open daily, Apr-Aug 10-6* **Facilities** Ⓟ ♿ (partly accessible) toilets for disabled (low level viewing slots & optics) shop ⊗

CARRBRIDGE **Map 14 NH92**

Landmark Forest Adventure Park

PH23 3AJ
☎ 01479 841613 & 0800 731 3446 📠 01479 841384
e-mail: landmarkcentre@btconnect.com
web: www.landmark-centre.co.uk
dir: off A9 between Aviemore & Inverness

This amazing Adventure Park is designed to provide a fun and educational visit for all ages. There is also a 70ft forest viewing tower and a treetop trail. Demonstrations of timber sawing, on a steam-powered sawmill and log hauling by a Clydesdale horse throughout the day. Attractions include a 3-track Watercoaster, a maze and a large covered adventure play area, mini electric cars and remote-controlled truck arena. New features include; 'RopeworX', the Tarzan Trail aerial highwire obstacle courses, and 'Skydive', a parachute jump simulator; Bamboozeleum, an exhibition of illusions, puzzle sand, special effects and a rollercoaster "Runaway Timber Train".

Times Open all year, daily, Apr-mid Jul 10-6; mid Jul-mid Aug 10-7; Sep-Oct 10-5.30; Nov-Mar 10-5. Closed 25 Dec, 1 Jan **Fees** Apr-Oct £11.50 (ch & pen £9.50), Nov-Mar £3.50 (ch & pen £2.65) **Facilities** Ⓟ (P) ☕ 🍴 licensed ♿ (partly accessible) (all areas accessible, some attractions not suitable) toilets for disabled shop

CAWDOR **Map 14 NH85**

Cawdor Castle

IV12 5RD
☎ 01667 404401 📠 01667 404674
e-mail: info@cawdorcastle.com
web: www.cawdorcastle.com
dir: on B9090, off A96

Home of the Thanes of Cawdor since the 14th century, this lovely castle has a drawbridge, an ancient tower built round a tree, and a freshwater well inside the house. Gardens Weekend takes place from May to September in 2010 - guided tours of gardens with the head gardener. In 1510, Muriel Calder married Sir John Campbell and thus the Calders became the Campbells of Cawdor.

Times Open May-10 Oct, daily 10-5.30 (last admission 5)* **Facilities** Ⓟ ☕ 🍴 licensed ⛩ (outdoor) ♿ (partly accessible) (ramps to restaurant, shops and garden, ground floor only of castle accessible) toilets for disabled shop ⊗

CLAVA CAIRNS **Map 14 NH74**

Clava Cairns

FREE

☎ 01667 460232
web: www.historic-scotland.gov.uk
dir: 6m E of Inverness, signed from B9091

A well-preserved Bronze Age cemetery complex of passage graves, ring cairns, kerb cairn and standing stones in a beautiful setting. In addition, the remains of a chapel of unknown date can be seen at this site.

Times Open at all reasonable times **Facilities** Ⓟ ⊗ 🏰

CROMARTY **Map 14 NH76**

Hugh Miller Museum & Birth Place Cottage

Church St IV11 8XA
☎ 0844 493 2158
e-mail: information@nts.org.uk
web: www.nts.org.uk
dir: Via Kessock Bridge and A832 in Cromarty, 22m NE of Inverness.

The cottage houses an exhibition on the life and work of Hugh Miller, a stonemason born here in 1802 who became an eminent geologist and writer. It was built by his great-grandfather around 1698, and now has a charming cottage garden.

Times Open Apr-Oct, Sun-Wed 1-5* **Facilities** (P) ♿ (partly accessible) (limited access, not suitable for wheelchair users) (touch screens) ⊗ 🏵

SCOTLAND

SCOTLAND

CULLODEN MOOR Map 14 NH74

Culloden Battlefield

IV2 5EU
☎ 0844 493 2159 Fax 0844 493 2160
e-mail: information@nts.org.uk
web: www.nts.org.uk
dir: B9006, 5m E of Inverness

A cairn recalls this last battle fought on mainland Britain, on 16 April 1746, when the Duke of Cumberland's forces routed 'Bonnie' Prince Charles Edward Stuart's army. The battlefield has been restored to its state on the day of the battle, and in summer there are 'living history' enactments. This is a most atmospheric evocation of tragic events. Telephone for details of guided tours. A Visitors' Centre exploring the impact of the battle opened in 2007.

Times Open all year: Visitor Centre, Restaurant & Shop: 4 Feb-Mar & Nov-Dec, daily 10-4; Apr-Oct, daily 9-6. Closed 24-26 Dec. Site: all year, daily* **Facilities** licensed (fully accessible) toilets for disabled (wheelchair, induction loop, raised map, Braille guidebook) shop

DRUMNADROCHIT Map 14 NH52

Loch Ness Centre & Exhibition **2 FOR 1**

IV3 6TU
☎ 01456 450573 & 450218 Fax 01456 450770
web: www.lochness.com
dir: on A82, 12m S Inverness

This award-winning centre has a fascinating and popular multi-media presentation lasting 30 minutes. Seven themed areas cover the story of the Loch Ness Monster, from the pre-history of Scotland, through the cultural roots of the legend in Highland folklore, and into the 50-year controversy which surrounds it. The centre uses the latest technology in computer animation, lasers and multi-media projection systems.

Times Open all year; Nov-end Jan, 10-3.30, Xmas hols 10-5, Feb-end May & Oct 9.30-5, Jun & Sep, 9-6, Jul & Aug 9-6.30 **Fees** £6.50 (ch 6-16 £4.50, students £5.50, pen £5). Family ticket (2ad+2 or 3 ch) £18* **Facilities** licensed (outdoor) (fully accessible) toilets for disabled (parking) shop

Urquhart Castle

IV63 6XJ
☎ 01456 450551
web: www.historic-scotland.gov.uk
dir: on A82

The castle was once Scotland's biggest and overlooks Loch Ness. It dates mainly from the 14th century, when it was built on the site of an earlier fort, and was destroyed before the 1715 Jacobite rebellion.

Times Open all year, Apr-Sep, daily, 9.30-6.30; Oct, 9.30-5; Nov-Mar, daily 9.30-4.30. Closed 25-26 Dec **Fees** £7 (ch £4.20, concessions £5.60). Please phone or check website for further details* **Facilities** shop

DUNBEATH Map 15 ND12

Laidhay Croft Museum

KW6 6EH
☎ 01593 731244
dir: 1m N of Dunbeath on A9

The museum gives visitors a glimpse of a long-vanished way of life. The main building is a thatched Caithness longhouse, with the dwelling quarters, byre and stable all under one roof. It dates back some 200 years, and is furnished as it might have been 100 years ago. A collection of early farm tools and machinery is also shown. Near the house is a thatched winnowing barn with its roof supported on three 'Highland couples', or crucks.

Times Open Jun-Sep, Mon-Sat 9.30-4.30 **Fees** £2 (ch 50p). Please check for current prices* **Facilities** (fully accessible) toilets for disabled

FORT GEORGE Map 14 NH75

Fort George

IV2 7TD
☎ 01667 460232
web: www.historic-scotland.gov.uk
dir: 11m NE of Inverness

Built following the Battle of Culloden as a Highland fortress for the army of George II, this is one of the outstanding artillery fortifications in Europe and still an active army barracks.

Times Open all year, Apr-Sep, daily, 9.30-5.30; Oct-Mar 9.30-4.30. Closed 25-26 Dec **Fees** £6.70 (ch £4, concessions £5.40). Please phone or check website for further details* **Facilities** licensed toilets for disabled shop

The Highlanders Regimental Museum

IV2 7TD
☎ 0131 310 8701 Fax 0131 310 8701
e-mail: info@thehighlandersmuseum.com
web: www.thehighlandersmuseum.com
dir: off A96 5m from Inverness

Fort George has been a military barracks since it was built in 1748-69, and was the Depot of the Seaforth Highlanders until 1961. The museum of the Queen's Own Highlanders (Seaforth and Camerons) is sited in the former Lieutenant Governor's house, where uniforms, medals and pictures are displayed.

Times Open all year, Apr-Sep, daily 9.30-5.15; Oct-Mar, Mon-Fri 10-4. Closed 24-25 Dec & BHs **Fees** Free admission but admission charged by Historic Scotland for entry to Fort George **Facilities** (partly accessible) (2nd floor accessible via stairs) toilets for disabled (stair lift to 1st floor, wheelchair on 1st floor) shop

FORT WILLIAM Map 14 NN17

Inverlochy Castle FREE

PH33 6SN
web: www.historic-scotland.gov.uk
dir: 2m NE of Fort William, off A82

A fine well-preserved 13th-century castle of the Comyn family; in the form of a square, with round towers at the corners. The largest tower was the donjon or keep. This is one of Scotland's earliest castles.

Times Open at all reasonable times **Facilities**

West Highland Museum

Cameron Square PH33 6AJ
☎ 01397 702169 01397 701927
e-mail: info@westhighlandmuseum.org.uk
web: www.westhighlandmuseum.org.uk
dir: Cameron Square, centre of High Street

The displays illustrate traditional Highland life and history, with numerous Jacobite relics. One of them is the 'secret portrait' of Bonnie Prince Charlie, which looks like meaningless daubs of paint but reveals a portrait when reflected in a metal cylinder.

Times Open all year, with seasonal variations. Please contact or see website for further information **Fees** £4 (ch 12-18 yrs £1, under 12 free, concessions £3)* **Facilities** (partly accessible) (access restricted to ground floor, no lift, access to 4 out of 7 rooms) toilets for disabled shop

GAIRLOCH Map 14 NG87

Gairloch Heritage Museum

Achtercairn IV21 2BP
☎ 01445 712287 & 08458 648001
e-mail: info@gairlochheritagemuseum.org
web: www.gairlochheritagemuseum.org
dir: on junct of A382 & B8021 near police station & public car park

A converted farmstead now houses the award-winning museum, which shows the way of life in this West Highland parish from early times to the 20th century. There are hands-on activities for children and reconstructions of a croft house room, a school room, a shop, and a smugglers' cave. You can also view Gairloch through one of the largest lenses assembled by the Northern Lighthouse Board. Please visit website for details of regular events, such as craft demonstrations, free open evenings and special exhibitions.

Times Open Etr-Oct, Mon-Sat 10-5. Winter months by arrangement. **Fees** £4 (ch 5-16 £1, under 5 free, concessions £3). Group rates available* **Facilities** (partly accessible) (Computer access to archive photographs) shop

GLENCOE Map 14 NN15

Glencoe & Dalness

NTS Visitor Centre PH49 4LA
☎ 0844 493 2222 0844 493 2223
e-mail: information@nts.org.uk
web: www.nts.org.uk
dir: on A82, 17m S of Fort William

Glencoe has stunning scenery and some of the most challenging climbs and walks in the Highlands. Red deer, wildcats, eagles and ptarmigan are among the wildlife. It is also known as a place of treachery and infamy. The Macdonalds of Glencoe were hosts to a party of troops who, under government orders, fell upon the men, women and children, in a bloody massacre in 1692. The Visitor Centre tells the story.

Times Open all year: Visitor centre, shop, exhibition & cafe: 3 Jan-28 Feb, Thu-Sun 10-4; Mar-Oct, daily 9-6; Nov-13 Dec, Thu-Sun 10-4, 27-31 Dec, 10-4 (last entry to exhibition 45 mins before centre closes). Site: all year daily* **Facilities** (partly accessible) (visitors centre, café, shop suitable for wheelchairs) toilets for disabled (induction loop in video programme room, objects to handle) shop

Glencoe & North Lorn Folk Museum 2 FOR 1

PH49 4HS
☎ 01855 811664
e-mail: info@glencoemuseum.com
web: www.glencoefolkmuseum.com
dir: turn off A82 at Glencoe x-roads then immediately right into Glencoe village

Two heather-thatched cottages in the main street of Glencoe now house items connected with the Macdonalds and the Jacobite risings. A variety of local domestic and farming exhibits, dairying and slate-working equipment, costumes and embroidery are also shown. Activities for all ages inside the museum, plus special events, please see the website for details.

Times Open Apr-Oct, Mon-Sat 10-5.30 **Fees** £3 (ch free, concessions £2) **Facilities** (fully accessible) (disabled parking outside) shop

GLENFINNAN Map 14 NM98

Glenfinnan Monument

NTS Visitor Centre PH37 4LT
☎ 0844 493 2221 0844 493 2221
e-mail: information@nts.org.uk
web: www.nts.org.uk
dir: on A830, 18.5m W of Fort William

The monument commemorates the Highlanders who fought for Bonnie Prince Charlie in 1745. It stands in an awe-inspiring setting at the head of Loch Shiel. There is a visitor centre with information (commentary in four languages) on the Prince's campaign.

Times Visitor Centre open daily, Apr-Jun & Sep-Oct 10-5; Jul-Aug 9.30-5.30* **Facilities** (partly accessible) (wheelchair available, audio commentary) shop

SCOTLAND

SCOTLAND

GOLSPIE Map 14 NH89

Dunrobin Castle

KW10 6SF
☎ 01408 633177 & 633268 01408 634081
e-mail: info@dunrobincastle.net
web: www.dunrobincastle.co.uk
dir: 1m NE on A9, from Golspie

The ancient seat of the Earls and Dukes of Sutherland is a splendid, gleaming, turreted structure, thanks largely to 19th-century rebuilding, and has a beautiful setting overlooking the sea. Paintings, furniture and family heirlooms are on display, and the gardens are on a grand scale to match the house. There are also falconry displays in the gardens.

Times Open Apr-15 Oct, Mon-Sat 10.30-4.30, Sun 12-4.30; Jun, Jul & Aug 10.30-5.30 (last admission half hour before closing) **Fees** £8.50 (ch £5, concessions £7). Family ticket (2ad+2ch) £22. Group rates for 10+ £6.50 (ch £4.70, pen £6)* **Facilities** (outdoor) (partly accessible) (garden access by prior arrangement) toilets for disabled shop

HELMSDALE Map 14 ND01

Timespan

Dunrobin St KW8 6JX
☎ 01431 821327
e-mail: enquiries@timespan.org.uk
web: www.timespan.org.uk
dir: off A9 in centre of village, by Telford Bridge

Located in a historic fishing village, this museum relates to the social and natural history of the area, and the art gallery has changing exhibitions of contemporary art and works by local artists. The garden has over 100 varieties of herbs and plants. There is a gift shop, and a café with beautiful views of the Telford Bridge.

Times Open Etr-end Oct, Mon-Sat 10-5, Sun 12-5. Reduced hrs Nov-Mar, Tue 2-5, Sat-Sun 12-5 (winter hours) **Fees** £4 (ch £2, concessions £3). Family ticket £10 **Facilities** (outdoor) (fully accessible) toilets for disabled (lift) shop

KINCRAIG Map 14 NH80

Highland Wildlife Park

PH21 1NL
☎ 01540 651270 01540 651236
e-mail: info@highlandwildlifepark.org
web: www.highlandwildlifepark.org
dir: on B9152, 7m S of Aviemore

As you drive through the main reserve, you can see awe-inspiring European bison grazing alongside wild horses, red deer and highland cattle plus a wide variety of other species. Then in the walk-round forest, woodland and moorland habitats prepare for close encounters with animals such as wolves, capercaillies, arctic foxes, wildcats, pine martens, otters and owls. Visit the snow monkeys in their beautiful loch side enclosure and the red pandas usually found climbing high up the trees. Meet Mercedes, the UK's only polar bear and Amur tigers endangered in the wild.

Times Open all year, Jul-Aug 10-6; Apr-Oct 10-5; Nov-Mar 10-4 (last entry 1 hr before close) **Fees** £13.50 (ch £10, concessions £11.50). Family ticket (2ad+2ch) £43.50 **Facilities** (outdoor) (partly accessible) (some steep inclines & rocky roads can restrict wheelchair access) toilets for disabled (wheelchair) shop

KINGUSSIE Map 14 NH70

Ruthven Barracks

FREE

☎ 01667 460232
web: www.historic-scotland.gov.uk
dir: 1m SE from Kingussie, signed from A9 and A86

An infantry barracks erected in 1719 following the Jacobite rising of 1715, with two ranges of quarters and a stable block. Captured and burnt by Prince Charles Edward Stuart's army in 1746.

Times Open at any reasonable time **Facilities**

KIRKHILL Map 14 NH54

Moniack Castle (Highland Winery)

IV5 7PQ
☎ 01463 831283 01463 831419
e-mail: jg@moniackcastle.co.uk
web: www.moniackcastle.co.uk
dir: 7m from Inverness on A862, near Beauly, on S side of Beauly Firth

This unique attraction, situated in a 16th-century castle, offers a warm welcome and the opportunity to taste 20 liqueurs, country wines and preserves, including whisky and ginger liqueur; mead and sloe gin.

Times Open all year, Apr-Oct, Mon-Sat 10-5; Nov-Mar, Mon-Fri 11-4 **Fees** Admission free, but £1 made for coach parties which includes a video presentation and wine tasting **Facilities** (outdoor) (partly accessible) shop

NEWTONMORE — Map 14 NN79

Clan Macpherson House & Museum

Main St PH20 1DE
☎ 01540 673332 📠 01540 673332
e-mail: museum@clan-macpherson.org
web: www.clan-macpherson.org
dir: off A9 at junct of Newtonmore and Kingussie, museum on left after entering village

Containing relics and memorials of the clan chiefs and other Macpherson families as well as those of Prince Charles Edward Stuart, this museum also displays the Prince's letters to the Clan Chief of 1745 and one to the Prince from his father, the Old Pretender, along with royal warrants and the green banner of the clan. Other interesting historic exhibits include James Macpherson's fiddle, swords, pictures, decorations and medals.

Times Open Apr-Oct, Mon-Sat 10-5, Sun 12-5. Other times by appointment **Fees** Free admission. Donations welcome **Facilities** (fully accessible) toilets for disabled (ramp entrance from car park, subtitles on DVD) shop

Highland Folk Museum — FREE

Aultlarie Croft PH20 1AY
☎ 01540 673551 📠 01540 673693
e-mail: highland.folk@highland.gov.uk
web: www.highlandfolk.com
dir: on A86, follow signs off A9

An early 18th-century farming township with turf houses has been reconstructed at this award-winning museum. A 1930s school houses old world maps and little wooden desks. Other attractions include a working croft and tailor's workshop. Squirrels thrive in the pinewoods and there is an extensive play area at reception. A vintage bus runs throughout the site.

Times Open daily Etr-Aug, 10.30-5.30; Sep-Oct, 11-4.30 **Facilities** (outdoor) (partly accessible) toilets for disabled (vintage bus with full disabled access) shop

POOLEWE — Map 14 NG88

Inverewe Garden

IV22 2LG
☎ 0844 493 2225 📠 0844 493 2227
e-mail: information@nts.org.uk
web: www.nts.org.uk
dir: 6m NE of Gairloch, on A832 by Poolewe

The influence of the North Atlantic Drift enables this remarkable garden to grow rare and sub-tropical plants. At its best in early June, but full of beauty from March to October, Inverewe has a backdrop of magnificent mountains and stands to the north of Loch Maree.

Times Open all year daily: Garden: Jan-Mar 10-3; Apr-3 May 10-9 or sunset if earlier; 4 May-Aug 9.30-9 or sunset if earlier; Sep-Oct 10-sunset; Nov-Dec 10-3. Visitor Centre & Shop: 8 Apr-3 May 10-5; 4-31 May 9.30-5.30; Jun-Aug 9.30-6; Sep 10-5; Oct 10-4* **Facilities** licensed (partly accessible) (some areas not accessible for wheelchair users due to gradients & tree roots) toilets for disabled (audio tour, mobility scooter) shop

ROSEMARKIE — Map 14 NH75

Groam House Museum — FREE

High St IV10 8UF
☎ 01381 620961 & 01463 811883 📠 01463 811883
e-mail: curator@groamhouse.org.uk
web: www.groamhouse.org.uk
dir: off A9 at Tore onto A832

Opened in 1980, this community-based museum explores the history, culture and crafts of the mysterious Picts, who faded from history over a thousand years ago. Visitors can see the Rosemarkie symbol-bearing cross-slab and other Pictish sculptured stones; a replica Pictish harp, and a collection of photographs of Pictish stones all over the country. Thanks to a generous donation, the museum now holds the George Bain Collection of Celtic art for the Scottish Nation. Annual exhibitions take place, often with loans from other major museums.

Times Open Etr week, daily 2-4.30; May-Oct, Mon-Sat, 10-5, Sun 2-4.30; Apr, Sat-Sun 2-4.30. Nov-mid Dec, Sat-Sun 2-4 **Facilities** (partly accessible) (wheelchair access to ground floor only) (Key held for disabled public toilets) shop

STRATHPEFFER — Map 14 NH45

Highland Museum of Childhood — 2 FOR 1

The Old Station IV14 9DH
☎ 01997 421031
e-mail: info@highlandmuseumofchildhood.org.uk
web: www.highlandmuseumofchildhood.org.uk
dir: 5m W of Dingwall on A834

Located in a renovated Victorian railway station of 1885, the museum tells the story of childhood in the Highlands amongst the crofters and townsfolk; a way of life recorded in oral testimony, displays and evocative photographs. An award-winning video, A Century of Highland Childhood is shown. There are also doll and toy collections.

Times Open Apr-Oct, daily 10-5, Sun 2-5. Other times by arrangement **Fees** £2.50 (ch £1.50, concessions £2). Family ticket (2ad+4ch) £6 **Facilities** (outdoor) (fully accessible) (tape tour with induction loop, large print guide) shop

SCOTLAND

SCOTLAND

THURSO Map 15 ND17

The Castle & Gardens of Mey

KW14 8XH
☎ 01847 851473 & 851227 📠 01847 851475
e-mail: enquiries@castleofmey.org.uk
web: www.castleofmey.org.uk
dir: 5m W of John O'Groats on A836

Built in the 1560s, The Castle of Mey was bought by The Queen Mother in 1952. She restored the castle and created the beautiful gardens that can be seen today. For almost half a century The Queen Mother spent many happy summers at Mey. Children will enjoy the animal centre.

Times Open May-Sep, 10.20 (last entry 4). Closed 10 days late Jul-early Aug **Fees** £10 (ch 5-16 £4.50, under 5 free, concessions & groups £9). Family ticket £24 **Facilities** Ⓟ ☕ (outdoor) ♿ (partly accessible) (visitors' centre, garden & grounds fully accessible, 1st floor of castle possible, but not 2nd) toilets for disabled shop

TORRIDON Map 14 NG85

Torridon Countryside Centre

The Mains IV22 2EZ
☎ 0844 493 2229 📠 0844 493 2229
e-mail: information@nts.org.uk
web: www.nts.org.uk
dir: N of A896, 9m SW of Kinlochewe

Set amid some of Scotland's finest mountain scenery, the centre offers audio-visual presentations on the local wildlife. At the Mains nearby visitors may see deer.

Times Countryside Centre: Apr-Sep, Mon-Fri & Sun 10-5. Estate, Deer Enclosure & Deer Museum (unstaffed): all year daily* **Facilities** Ⓟ ♿ (partly accessible) (2 steps into deer museum) toilets for disabled (ramp into centre, parking at centre)

WICK Map 15 ND35

Castle of Old Wick FREE

☎ 01667 460232
web: www.historic-scotland.gov.uk
dir: 1m S on Shore Rd

The ruin of the best-preserved Norse castle in Scotland. Dating from the 12th-century this spectacular site is on a spine of rock projecting into the sea, between two deep, narrow gullies. Visitors must take great care and wear sensible shoes.

Times Open at all reasonable times **Facilities**

Wick Heritage Museum

18-27 Bank Row KW1 5EY
☎ 01955 605393 📠 01955 605393
e-mail: museum@wickheritage.org
web: www.wickheritage.org
dir: close to the harbour

The heritage centre is near the harbour in a complex of eight houses, yards and outbuildings. The centre illustrates local history from Neolithic times to the herring fishing industry. In addition, there is a complete working 19th-century lighthouse, and the famous Johnston collection of photographs.

Times Open Apr-Oct, Mon-Sat 10-5 (last admission 3.45)* **Facilities** Ⓟ (outdoor) ♿ (partly accessible) toilets for disabled

INVERCLYDE

GREENOCK Map 10 NS27

McLean Museum & Art Gallery FREE

15 Kelly St PA16 8JX
☎ 01475 715624
e-mail: museum@inverclyde.gov.uk
web: www.inverclyde.gov.uk/
dir: close to Greenock West Railway Station and Greenock Bus Station

James Watt was born in Greenock, and various exhibits connected with him are shown. The museum also has an art collection, and displays on shipping, local and natural history, Egyptology and ethnography. In summer 2011, exhibition to mark the 300th anniversary of the Foundation of Scott's the Shipbuilders and celebration of the 150th anniversary of the Greenock Philosophical Society season (2011-2012).

Times Open all year, Mon-Sat 10-5. Closed some local & national PHs **Facilities** Ⓟ ♿ (partly accessible) (only ground floor accessible, ramped entrance with automatic doors) toilets for disabled (induction loop) shop

PORT GLASGOW Map 10 NS37

Newark Castle

PA14 5NH
☎ 01475 741858
web: www.historic-scotland.gov.uk
dir: on A8

The one-time house of the Maxwells, dating from the 15th and 17th centuries. The courtyard and hall are preserved. Fine turrets and the remains of painted ceilings can be seen, and the hall carries an inscription of 1597.

Times Open Apr-Sep, daily 9.30-5.30 **Fees** £3.70 (ch £2.20, concessions £3). Please phone or check website for further details* **Facilities** Ⓟ shop

MIDLOTHIAN

CRICHTON Map 11 NT36

Crichton Castle

EH37 5XA
☎ 01875 320017
web: www.historic-scotland.gov.uk
dir: 2.5m SW of Pathhead, off A68

The castle dates back to the 14th century, but most of what remains today was built over the following 300 years. A notable feature is the 16th-century wing built by the Earl of Bothwell in Italian style, with an arcade below.

Times Open Apr-Sep, daily 9.30-5.30 **Fees** £3.70 (ch £2.20, concessions £3). Please phone or check website for further details* **Facilities** Ⓟ

DALKEITH Map 11 NT36

Edinburgh Butterfly & Insect World

Dobbies Garden World, Mellville Nursery, Lasswade EH18 1AZ
☎ 0131 663 4932 0131 654 2774
e-mail: info@edinburgh-butterfly-world.co.uk
web: www.edinburgh-butterfly-world.co.uk
dir: 0.5m S of Edinburgh city bypass at Gilmerton exit or at Sherrifhall rdbt

Rich coloured butterflies from all over the world can be seen flying among exotic rainforest plants, trees and flowers. The tropical pools are filled with giant waterlilies, colourful fish and are surrounded by lush vegetation. There are daily animal handling sessions and opportunities to see the leaf-cutting ants, scorpions, poison frogs, snakes, tarantulas and other remarkable creatures. There is also a unique honeybee hive that can be visited in season.

Times Open all year daily, summer 9.30-5.30; winter 10-5. Closed 25-26 Dec & 1 Jan* **Facilities** Ⓟ licensed (outdoor) ♿ (fully accessible) toilets for disabled shop

NEWTONGRANGE Map 11 NT36

Scottish Mining Museum

Lady Victoria Colliery EH22 4QN
☎ 0131 663 7519 0131 654 0952
e-mail: visitorservices@scottishminingmuseum.com
web: www.scottishminingmuseum.com
dir: 10m S of Edinburgh on A7, signed from bypass

Based at Scotland's National Coalmining Museum offering an outstanding visit to Britains' finest Victorian colliery. Guided tours with miners, magic helmets, exhibitions, theatres, interactive displays and a visit to the coal face. Home to Scotland's largest steam engine.

Times Open all year, daily Mar-Oct 10-5, Nov-Feb 10-4
Fees £6.50 (ch free, concessions £4.50). Party 12+ £5.50
Facilities Ⓟ Ⓟ licensed (outdoor) ♿ (fully accessible) toilets for disabled (tactile opportunities, audio tours, induction loop) shop

MORAY

BALLINDALLOCH Map 15 NJ13

The Glenlivet Distillery

Glenlivet AB37 9DB
☎ 01340 821720 & 821738 01340 821718
e-mail: betty.munro@chivas.com
web: www.theglenlivet.com
dir: 10m N of Tomintoul, off B9008

The visitor centre includes a guided tour of the whisky production facilities and a chance to see inside the vast bonded warehouses where the spirit matures. The multimedia exhibition and interactive presentations communicate the unique history, and traditions of the Glenlivet Scotch Whisky. A complimentary dram is offered on return from the tour. New extension fully accessible to all visitors with disabilities.

Times Open 4 Apr-28 Oct, Mon-Sat 9.30-4, Sun 12-4 **Fees** Free admission (ch under 8 not permitted into production area) **Facilities** Ⓟ ♿ (fully accessible) toilets for disabled (cafeteria, lift to exhibition) shop

SCOTLAND

BRODIE CASTLE Map 14 NH95

Brodie Castle

IV36 2TE
☎ 0844 493 2156 ⎙ 0844 493 2157
e-mail: information@nts.org.uk
web: www.nts.org.uk
dir: 4.5m W of Forres, off A96 24m E of Inverness

The Brodie family lived here for hundreds of years before passing the castle to the NTS in 1980. It contains many treasures, including furniture, porcelain and paintings. The extensive grounds include a woodland walk and an adventure playground. Wheelchairs for disabled visitors are available. Please telephone for details of recitals, concerts, open-air theatre etc.

Times Castle open Apr daily 10.30-4.30; May-Jun & Sep-Oct, Sun-Wed 10.30-5; Jul-Aug, daily 10.30-5 (last tour starts at 3.30); Grounds open all year daily* **Facilities** (partly accessible) (4 steps to ground floor, accessible with assistance) toilets for disabled (audio tape, large print guide, wheel chair & stairclimber) shop

CRAIGELLACHIE Map 15 NJ24

Speyside Cooperage Visitor Centre

Dufftown Rd AB38 9RS
☎ 01340 871108 ⎙ 01340 881437
e-mail: enquiries@speysidecooperage.co.uk
web: www.speysidecooperage.co.uk
dir: 1m S of Craigellachie, on A941

A working cooperage with unique visitor centre, where skilled coopers and their apprentices practise this ancient craft. Each year they repair around 100,000 oak casks - barrels, hogsheads, butts and puncheons; which will be used to mature many different whiskies. Savour the sights, sounds and smells of our bustling workshops and why not have a go at building a demonstration cask? There is also a spacious gift shop which specialises in quality goods crafted from wood.

Times Open all year, Mon-Fri 9.30-4. Closed 25 Dec & 1 Jan **Fees** £3.30 (ch £2, concesssions £2.70). Family ticket £8.50. Party 15+* **Facilities** (outdoor) (fully accessible) toilets for disabled (picnic table, disabled viewing point) shop

DUFFTOWN Map 15 NJ34

Balvenie Castle

AB55 4DH
☎ 01340 820121
web: www.historic-scotland.gov.uk
dir: on A941

The ruined castle was the ancient stronghold of the Comyns, and became a stylish house in the 16th century.

Times Open Apr-Sep, daily 9.30-5.30 **Fees** £3.70 (ch £2.20, concessions £3). Please phone or check website for further details* **Facilities** toilets for disabled

Glenfiddich Distillery

AB55 4DH
☎ 01340 820373 ⎙ 01340 822083
web: www.glenfiddich.com
dir: N of town, off A941

Set close to Balvenie Castle, the distillery was founded in 1887 by William Grant and has stayed in the hands of the family ever since. Visitors can see the whisky-making process in its various stages and then sample the finished product.

Times Open all year, Mon-Sat 9.30-4.30, Sun 12-4.30. Closed 25 Dec & 1 Jan **Fees** Standard tours free. Charge for special tours **Facilities** licensed (outdoor) (partly accessible) (all areas accessible except fermentation ie. most of tour, coffee shop & gift shop) toilets for disabled (ramp access to production area & warehouse gallery) shop

DUFFUS Map 15 NJ16

Duffus Castle FREE

☎ 01667 460232
web: www.historic-scotland.gov.uk
dir: 5m NW of Elgin on B9012 to Burghead

One of the finest examples of a motte and bailey castle in Scotland with a later, very fine, stone hall house and curtain wall. The original seat of the Moray family.

Times Open at all reasonable times **Facilities**

ELGIN Map 15 NJ26

Elgin Cathedral

North College St IV30 1HU
☎ 01343 547171
web: www.historic-scotland.gov.uk

Founded in 1224, the cathedral was known as the Lantern of the North and the Glory of the Kingdom because of its beauty. In 1390 it was burnt, along with most of the town. Although it was rebuilt, it fell into ruin after the Reformation. The ruins are quite substantial, however, and there is still a good deal to admire, including the fine west towers and the octagonal chapter house.

Times Open all year, Apr-Sep, daily, 9.30-5.30; Oct, 9.30-4.30; Nov-Mar, Mon-Wed & Sat-Sun, 9.30-4.30. Closed 25-26 Dec & 1-2 Jan **Fees** £4.70 (ch £2.80, concessions £3.80). Please phone or check website for further details* **Facilities** shop

Elgin Museum 2 FOR 1

1 High St IV30 1EQ
☎ 01343 543675 ⎙ 01343 543675
e-mail: curator@elginmuseum.org.uk
web: www.elginmuseum.org.uk
dir: E end of High St, follow brown heritage signs

This award-winning museum is internationally famous for its fossil fish and fossil reptiles, and for its Pictish stones. The displays relate to the natural and human history of Moray.

Times Open Apr-Oct, Mon-Fri 10-5, Sat 11-4 **Fees** £4 (ch £1.50, concessions £2). Family ticket £8* **Facilities** (partly accessible) toilets for disabled (handrails, case displays at sitting level with large fonts) shop

Pluscarden Abbey

FREE

IV30 8UA

☎ 01343 890257 📠 01343 890258

web: www.pluscardenabbey.org

dir: 6m SW of Elgin on unclass road

The original monastery was founded in 1230 by King Alexander II for monks of the Valliscaulian order from Burgundy, but it later became a Benedictine house. Monastic life was abandoned after the Reformation and the house passed through a succession of lay owners until it was bought by the third Marquess of Bute in 1898. His third son, Lord Colum Crichton Stuart gave the monastery to the Benedictines of Prinknash Abbey near Gloucester, and monastic life was recommenced in 1948. Today there are about twenty monks who lead a life of prayer, study and manual work. The services in the Abbey church are sung in Latin with Gregorian chant and are all open to the public.

Times Open all year, daily 4.45am-8.30pm. See website for special occasions **Facilities** (fully accessible) toilets for disabled (induction loop, ramp, main entrance assistance required) shop

FORRES — Map 14 NJ05

Dallas Dhu Distillery

IV36 2RR

☎ 01309 676548

web: www.historic-scotland.gov.uk

dir: 1m S of Forres, off A940

A perfectly preserved time capsule of the distiller's art. It was built in 1898 to supply malt whisky for Wright and Greig's 'Roderick Dhu' blend. Visitors are welcome to wander at will through this fine old Victorian distillery, or to take a guided tour, dram included.

Times Open all year, Apr-Sep, daily, 9.30-5.30; Oct, 9.30-4.30; Nov-Mar, Mon-Wed & Sat-Sun, 9.30-4.30. Closed 25-26 Dec & 1-2 Jan **Fees** £5.20 (ch £3.10, concessions £4.20). Please phone or check website for further details* **Facilities** toilets for disabled shop

Falconer Museum

Tolbooth St IV36 1PH

☎ 01309 673701

e-mail: museums@moray.gov.uk

web: www.moray.gov.uk/museums

dir: 11m W of Elgin, 25m E of Inverness on A96

Founded in 1871, the Falconer Museum contains a wealth of Moray's heritage. From social history and archaeology to natural history and crime, the family friendly Falconer Museum is an essential stop for locals and visitors alike. This Victorian gem was built to house Hugh Falconer's eclectic collection of fossils and souvenirs from his stay in India.

Times Open all year Apr-Oct, Mon-Sat 10-5, Jul-Aug daily, Sun 1-4; Nov-Mar, Mon-Fri 10-5 **Fees** Donations welcome **Facilities** (fully accessible) toilets for disabled (induction loop system, lift) shop

Sueno's Stone

FREE

☎ 01667 460232

web: www.historic-scotland.gov.uk

dir: E end of Forres, off A96

The most remarkable sculptured monument in Britain, probably a cenotaph, standing over 20 feet high and dating back to the end of the first millennium AD. Covered by a protective glass enclosure.

Times Open at all reasonable times **Facilities**

KEITH — Map 15 NJ45

Strathisla Distillery

Seafield Av AB55 5BS

☎ 01542 783044 & 783000 📠 01542 783056

e-mail: jeanett.grant@chivas.com

web: www.chivas.com

dir: A96 Aberdeen to Inverness road, attraction signed midway through town

Tour the oldest distillery in the highlands, founded in 1786. A welcome dram of Chivas Regal 12-year-old is offered whilst guests view a DVD. A further dram of Chivas Regal 18 year old or Strathisla 12-year-old single malt is offered on return from the distillery tour.

Times Open 4 Apr-28 Oct, daily 9.30-4, Sun 12-4 **Fees** £6 (ch under 18 free, ch under 8 not admitted to production area, but welcome in visitor centre) **Facilities** (partly accessible) (partial accessibility to Still House, Dram Room & gift shop) toilets for disabled shop

MARYPARK — Map 15 NJ13

Glenfarclas Distillery

2 FOR 1

AB37 9BD

☎ 01807 500345 & 500257 📠 01807 500234

e-mail: info@glenfarclas.co.uk

web: www.glenfarclas.co.uk

dir: 4m S of Aberlour on A95 to Grantown-on-Spey

Established in 1836, Glenfarclas Distillery is proud of its independence. There is a guided tour illustrating their whisky's history and production, followed by a dram in the splendour of the Ships Room or a chance to browse in the gift shop. Glenfarclas celebrates its 175th anniversary of licensed distilling in 2011.

Times Open all year, Jan-Mar, Mon-Fri 10-4; Apr-Sep, Mon-Fri 10-5 (Jul-Sep also open Sat 10-4) Oct-Dec, Mon-Fri 10-4 (last tour 1.5hr before closing)* **Fees** £3.50 (free admission under 18)* **Facilities** (partly accessible) (only visitor centre is accessible) toilets for disabled shop

SCOTLAND

SCOTLAND

ROTHES Map 15 NJ24

Glen Grant Distillery

Elgin Rd AB38 7BS
☎ 01340 832118 📠 01340 832104
e-mail: visitorcentre@glengrant.com
web: www.glengrant.com
dir: on A941 Elgin-Rothes road

Founded in 1840 in a sheltered glen by the two Grant brothers. Discover the secrets of the distillery, including the delightful Victorian garden originally created by Major Grant, and now restored to its former glory.

Times Open mid Jan-Apr & Nov-mid Dec, Mon-Sat 9.30-5, Sun 12-5; May-Oct, daily 9.30-5 **Fees** £3.50 (under 18 free)* **Facilities** (outdoor) (partly accessible) (access to ground floor only) toilets for disabled (reception centre & still house, video) shop

SPEY BAY Map 15 NJ36

The WDCS Wildlife Centre FREE

IV32 7PJ
☎ 01343 820339 📠 01343 829065
e-mail: wildlifecentre@wdcs.org
web: www.wdcs.org/wildlifecentre
dir: off A96 onto B9014 at Fochabers, follow road approx 5m to village of Spey Bay. Turn left at Spey Bay Hotel and follow road for 500mtrs

The centre, owned and operated by the Whale and Dolphin Conservation Society, lies at the mouth of the River Spey and is housed in a former salmon fishing station, built in 1768. There is a free exhibition about the Moray Firth dolphins and the wildlife of Spey Bay. Visitors can browse through a well-stocked gift shop and enjoy refreshments in the cosy tea room.

Times Open daily 27 Mar-Oct 10.30-5 **Facilities** (outdoor) (partly accessible) (some rough paths) toilets for disabled shop

TOMINTOUL Map 15 NJ11

Tomintoul Museum

The Square AB37 9ET
☎ 01807 580285
e-mail: museums@moray.gov.uk/museums
web: www.moray.gov.uk
dir: on A939, 13m E of Grantown

Discover the heritage of the 'highest village in the Highlands'. The old village smithy and a traditional farmhouse kitchen are recreated here, along with displays on peat cutting and local wildlife. Marvel at the early skiing equipment in this staging post for the ski slopes.

Times Open Apr-Oct, Mon-Sat 10-5, Jul-Aug daily 10-5, Sun 1-5 **Fees** Free admission. Donations welcome **Facilities** (outdoor) (fully accessible) (induction loop, sound commentaries) shop

NORTH AYRSHIRE

IRVINE Map 10 NS34

Scottish Maritime Museum 2 FOR 1

Harbourside KA12 8QE
☎ 01294 278283 📠 01294 313211
e-mail. dam@scotmaritime.org.uk
web: www.scottishmaritimemuseum.org
dir: Follow signs for Irvine & the Harbourside & signs for Maritime Museum

The museum has displays that reflect all aspects of Scottish maritime history. Vessels can be seen afloat in the harbour and undercover. Experience life in a 1910 shipyard worker's tenement flat. Visit the Linthouse Engine Shop originally built in 1872, which is being developed and holds a substantial part of the museum's collection. Displays include PS Lochlomond Gallery, machine pits, puffer exhibition and three new interactive ones.

Times Open daily Apr-Oct, 10-5 **Fees** £3.50 (ch & concessions £2.50). Family ticket £9.50 **Facilities** licensed (outdoor) (fully accessible) toilets for disabled shop

LARGS Map 10 NS25

Kelburn Castle and Country Centre

Fairlie KA29 0BE
☎ 01475 568685 📠 01475 568121
e-mail: admin@kelburncountrycentre.com
web: www.kelburnstate.com
dir: 2m S of Largs, on A78

Historic home of the Earls of Glasgow, Kelburn is famous for its romantic Glen, family gardens, unique trees and spectacular views over the Firth of Clyde. Glen walks, riding and trekking centre, adventure course, Kelburn Story Cartoon Exhibition and a family museum. The "Secret Forest" at the centre, Scotland's most unusual attraction, is a chance to explore the Giant's Castle, maze of the Green Man and secret grotto. Also included is an indoor Sawmill Adventure Playground.

Times Open all year, Etr-end Oct, daily 10-6; Nov-Mar, 11-dusk. Grounds & Adventure Playbarn, wknds only* **Fees** £7.50 (ch & concessions £5). Family ticket £25* **Facilities** licensed (outdoor) (partly accessible) (wheelchair access limited to main square area) toilets for disabled (Ranger service to assist disabled) shop

Vikingar!

Greenock Rd KA30 8QL
☎ 01475 689777 📠 01475 689444
e-mail: cmcnaught@kaleisure.com
web: www.kaleisure.com
dir: on A78, 0.5m into Largs, opposite RNLI lifeboat station

A multi-media experience that takes you from the first Viking raids in Scotland to their defeat at the Battle of Largs.

Times Open daily Apr-Sep, 10.30-4.30; Oct & Mar, 10.30-3.30; Nov & Feb, wknds only 10.30-3.30. Closed Dec & Jan **Fees** £4.50 (ch 4-15 £3.50, concessions £3.50). Family £14* **Facilities** Ⓟ ☕ ♿ (fully accessible) toilets for disabled (ramp to main door, automatic doors) shop ⊛

SALTCOATS **Map 10 NS24**

North Ayrshire Museum FREE

Manse St, Kirkgate KA21 5AA
☎ 01294 464174 📠 01294 464174
e-mail: namuseum@north-ayrshire.gov.uk
web: www.north-ayrshire.gov.uk/museums

This museum is housed in an 18th-century church, and features a rich variety of artefacts from the North Ayrshire area, including archaeological and social history material. There is a continuing programme of temporary exhibitions.

Times Open all year Tue-Sat, 10-1 & 2-5.* **Facilities** Ⓟ ♿ (fully accessible) toilets for disabled shop ⊛

NORTH LANARKSHIRE

COATBRIDGE **Map 11 NS76**

Summerlee Industrial Museum FREE

Heritage Way, West Canal St ML5 1QD
☎ 01236 638460 📠 01236 638454
e-mail: museums@northlan.gov.uk
web: www.visitlanarkshire.com/summerlee
dir: follow main routes towards town centre, adjacent to Coatbridge central station

A 20-acre museum of social and industrial history centering on the remains of the Summerlee Ironworks which were put into blast in the 1830s. The exhibition hall features displays of social and industrial history including working machinery, hands-on activities and recreated workshop interiors. Outside, Summerlee operates the only working tram in Scotland, a coal mine and reconstructed miners' rows with interiors dating from 1840.

Times Open summer 10-5, winter 10-4* **Facilities** Ⓟ Ⓟ ☕ ⛩ (outdoor) ♿ (partly accessible) (coal mine tour not accessible, miner's cottages narrow doors and single step) toilets for disabled (wheelchair available & staff assistance) shop ⊛

MOTHERWELL **Map 11 NS75**

Motherwell Heritage Centre FREE

High Rd ML1 3HU
☎ 01698 251000 📠 01698 268867
e-mail: museums@northlan.gov.uk
web: www.northlan.gov.uk
dir: A723 for town centre. Left at top of hill, after pedestrian crossing and just before railway bridge

The award-winning audio-visual experience, 'Technopolis', traces the history of the area from Roman times to the rise of 19th-century industry and the post-industrial era. There is also a fine viewing tower, an exhibition gallery and family history research facilities. A mixed programme of community events and touring exhibitions occur throughout the year.

Times Open all year Wed-Sat 10-5 (Thu 10-7), Sun 12-5. Closed Mon-Tue (ex local PH). Local studies library closed Sun **Facilities** Ⓟ Ⓟ ♿ (fully accessible) toilets for disabled (lifts, audio info & Braille buttons) shop ⊛

PERTH & KINROSS

ABERFELDY **Map 14 NN84**

Dewar's World of Whisky

Aberfeldy Distillery PH15 2EB
☎ 01887 822010 📠 01887 822012
e-mail: worldofwhisky@dewars.com
web: www.dewars.com
dir: from A9 take A827 for Aberfeldy at Ballinluig

This is an all-round whisky experience which challenges the skills and senses, and will educate you about the people and innovations of Dewar's. Try a dram of Aberfeldy single malt or Dewar's 12 before heading off for a guided tour of the working distillery.

Times Open all year, Apr-Oct, Mon-Sat 10-6, Sun noon-4; Nov-Mar, Mon-Sat 10-4. Closed Xmas & New Year* **Fees** £6.50 (ch £4, concessions £5)* **Facilities** Ⓟ ☕ ⛩ (outdoor) ♿ (partly accessible) (some parts of tour are inaccessible to wheelchair users) toilets for disabled (lift) shop ⊛

BLAIR ATHOLL Map 14 NN86

Blair Castle

2 FOR 1

PH18 5TL
☎ 01796 481207 01796 481487
e-mail: office@blair-castle.co.uk
web: www.blair-castle.co.uk
dir: 7m NW of Pitlochry, off A9 at Blair Atholl & follow signs to attraction

Blair Castle is at the heart of the Atholl Estates set among glorious Highland scenery. The castle has been the ancient seat of the Dukes and Earls of Atholl for almost 740 years and is home to the Atholl Highlanders, Europe's only remaining private army. There are 30 rooms open to visitors, as well as historic gardens and grounds which include a magnificent walled garden, a peaceful wooded grove, a ruined Celtic Kirk, a red deer park and a whimsical gothic folly. Children will also enjoy the castle's woodland adventure playground. Highland Games in May, Horse Trials and Country Fair in August.

Times Open daily Apr-28 Oct, 9.30-5.30 (last admission 4.30) **Fees** £8.95 (ch £5.50, pen & students £7.75). Family ticket £24.75 **Facilities** Ⓟ licensed (outdoor) ♿ (partly accessible) (access to ground floor only) toilets for disabled (scooter, parking) shop

CRIEFF Map 11 NN82

The Famous Grouse Experience

The Hosh PH7 4HA
☎ 01764 656565 01764 654366
e-mail: enquiries@thefamousgrouse.com
web: www.thefamousgrouse.com
dir: 1.5m NW off A85

A trip to Crieff is incomplete without a visit to The Famous Grouse Experience, set in Scotland's oldest, most visited and award-winning distillery. Opened in July 2002, this attraction is a fun and interesting day out which combines the traditional distillery visit with a unique exciting sensory experience. Spend a relaxing few hours absorbing the history of the brand. Test your senses and see if you have what it takes to become a 'Whisky Nose'. Have lunch, a snack or even a barbecue at the family restaurant. Visit the well-stocked shop or enjoy a peaceful woodland walk over The Brig O' Dram.

Times Open all year, daily 9-6 (last tour 4.30). Closed 25-26 Dec & 1 Jan* **Facilities** Ⓟ licensed (outdoor) ♿ (partly accessible) toilets for disabled (lifts in all areas) shop

Innerpeffray Library

PH7 3RF
☎ 01764 652819
e-mail: info@innerpeffraylibrary.co.uk
web: www.innerpeffraylibrary.co.uk
dir: 4.5m SE on B8062

This is Scotland's oldest free lending public library, founded in 1680. This Georgian Library (1762) with its associated school (1847), chapel (1508) and castle form an early complete group of educational and religious buildings. It houses the original 400 books in English, French, German, Latin and Italian presented by David Drummond, Lord Madertie, the Library's founder. It also has the books on law, history, geography, maths and works by most of the Enlightenment authors. There are research facilities available, special events are planned.

Times Open Wed-Sat 10-12.45 & 2-4.45, Sun 2-4. Nov-Feb by arrangement* **Facilities** Ⓟ (outdoor) ♿ (partly accessible)

DUNKELD Map 11 NO04

The Ell Shop & Little Houses

FREE

The Cross PH8 0AN
☎ 0844 4932192
e-mail: information@nts.org.uk
web: www.nts.org.uk
dir: off A9, 15m N of Perth

The National Trust owns two rows of 20 houses in Dunkeld, and has preserved their 17th/18th-century character. They are not open to the public, but there is a display and audio-visual show in the Information Centre.

Times Open all year: Ell Shop: Apr-Oct, Mon-Sat 10-5.30, Sun 12.30-5.30, Nov-23 Dec, Mon-Sat 10-4.30, Sun 12.30-4.30. Closed for 30mins lunch. Riverbanks & Stanley Hill: all year, daily.* **Facilities** Ⓟ ♿ (partly accessible) (small step into shop) toilets for disabled shop

KILLIECRANKIE Map 14 NN96

Killiecrankie Visitor Centre FREE

NTS Visitor Centre PH16 5LG
☎ 0844 493 2194
e-mail: information@nts.org.uk
web: www.nts.org.uk
dir: 3m N of Pitlochry on B8079

The visitor centre features an exhibition on the battle of 1689, when the Jacobite army routed the English, although the Jacobite leader, 'Bonnie Dundee', was mortally wounded in the attack. The wooded gorge is a notable beauty spot, admired by Queen Victoria, and there are some splendid walks.

Times Visitor Centre: Open Apr-1 Nov, daily 10-5.30. Site: open all year daily.* **Facilities** (outdoors) (partly accessible) (footpath down into the pass is steep with uneven path and steps) toilets for disabled (large print exhibition text) shop

KINROSS Map 11 NO10

Kinross House Gardens

KY13 8ET
☎ 01577 862900 01577 863372
e-mail: jm@kinrosshouse.com
web: www.kinrosshouse.com
dir: M90 [Edinburgh to Perth] junct 6 to Kinross, signed in village

Yew hedges, roses and herbaceous borders are the elegant attractions of these formal gardens. The 17th-century house was built by Sir William Bruce, but is not generally open to the public.

Times Gardens only open Apr-Sep, daily 10-7* **Facilities** (fully accessible)

Lochleven Castle

Castle Island KY13 8UF
☎ 01577 862670
web: www.historic-scotland.gov.uk
dir: on an island in Loch Leven accessible by boat from Kinross

Mary, Queen of Scots was imprisoned here in this five-storey castle in 1567 - she escaped 11 months later and so gave the 14th-century castle its special place in history.

Times Open Apr-Sep, daily 9.30-5.30; Oct, 9.30-4.30 **Fees** £4.70 (ch £2.80, concessions £3.80). Charge includes ferry trip. Please phone or check website for further details* **Facilities** shop

RSPB at Loch Leven, Vane Farm Nature Reserve

By Loch Leven KY13 9LX
☎ 01577 862355 01577 862013
e-mail: vane.farm@rspb.org.uk
web: www.rspb.org.uk
dir: 2m E of M90 junct 5, on S shore of Loch Leven, entered off B9097 to Glenrothes, 5 mins from junct 5

Well placed beside Loch Leven, with a heritage trail to Kinross, hides overlooking the Loch and a woodland trail with stunning panoramic views. Noted for its pink-footed geese, the area also attracts whooper swans, greylag geese and great spotted woodpeckers, among others. Details of special events are available from the Visitors' Centre and the RSPB website.

Times Open all year daily, 10-5. Closed 25-26 Dec & 1-2 Jan. Trails, hides & car park always open **Fees** £3 (ch 5-18 50p, concessions £2). Family ticket £6. RSPB members & Wildlife Explorer free* **Facilities** (outdoor) (partly accessible) (Visitor Centre accessible but not reserve without assistance, new w/chair & pushchair accessible path) toilets for disabled (wheelchair extensions, ramps, telescopes) shop

MILNATHORT Map 11 NO10

Burleigh Castle FREE

KY13 7XZ
web: www.historic-scotland.gov.uk
dir: 0.5m E of Milnathort on A911

The roofless but otherwise complete ruin of a tower house of about 1500, with a section of defensive barmkin wall and a remarkable corner tower with a square cap-house corbelled out. This castle was often visited by James IV.

Times Open summer only. Keys available locally, telephone 01786 45000 **Facilities**

MUTHILL Map 11 NN81

Drummond Gardens

PH7 4HZ
☎ 01764 681433 01764 681642
e-mail: thegardens@drummondcastle.sol.co.uk
web: www.drummondcastlegardens.co.uk
dir: 2m S of Crieff on A822

The gardens of Drummond Castle were originally laid out in 1630 by John Drummond, 2nd Earl of Perth. In 1830, the parterre was changed to an Italian style. The multi-faceted sundial was designed by John Mylne, Master Mason to Charles I. These are Scotland's largest formal gardens and amongst the finest in Europe.

Times Open Gardens May-Oct, daily 1-6 (last admission 5). Also Etr for 4 days* **Facilities** (outdoor) (partly accessible) (viewing platform, wheelchair friendly route) toilets for disabled shop

SCOTLAND

PERTH — Map 11 NO12

The Black Watch Castle & Museum

2 FOR 1

Balhousie Castle, Hay St PH1 5HR
☎ 01738 638 152 📠 01738 643245
e-mail: museum@theblackwatch.co.uk
web: www.thoblackwatch.co.uk
dir: follow signs to Perth & attraction, approach via Dunkeld Rd

The Black Watch Regimental Museum is housed in the dramatic and historic Balhousie Castle. The Castle is set in its own beautiful gardens and grounds, and is ideally situated close to the centre of Perth, beside the pleasant parkland walks of the North Inch on the banks of the River Tay. This unique and special collection consists of two and a half centuries of treasures of Scotland's oldest Highland Regiment. Uniforms, fine paintings, medals, photographs, weapons and military equipment linked to film, reminiscences and dioramas, bring to life the proud military heritage of this family Regiment.

Times Open all year. Apr-Oct, Mon-Sat 9.30-5, Sun 10-3.30 (ex Etr Sun). Closed last Sat in Jun; Nov-Mar, Mon-Fri 9.30-5. Closed during festive period (please contact for details). Other times & parties 16+ by appointment **Fees** £4 (ch 5-16 £2, under 5 free, concessions £2). Family ticket (2ad max) £10. Serving with Armed Forces £3. Black Watch Association members & serving with the Royal Regiment of Scotland free **Facilities** (partly accessible) (ground floor access only) toilets for disabled (1 bay parking for disabled) shop

Branklyn Garden

116 Dundee Rd PH2 7BB
☎ 0844 493 2193
e-mail: information@nts.org.uk
web: www.nts.org.uk
dir: on A85, Dundee Road, N of Perth

The gardens cover two acres and are noted for their collections of rhododendrons, shrubs and alpines. Garden tours and botanical painting courses are held.

Times Open Apr-Oct, daily 10-5. (Shop times may vary)* **Facilities** (partly accessible) (entrance is set on a hillside, but some paths are accessible by wheelchair)

Caithness Glass Factory & Visitor Centre

FREE

Inveralmond PH1 3TZ
☎ 01738 492320 📠 01738 492300
e-mail: visitorcentre@caithnessglass.co.uk
web: www.caithnessglass.co.uk
dir: on Perth Western Bypass, A9, at Inveralmond Roundabout

All aspects of paperweight-making can be seen from the purpose-built viewing galleries. Visitors can now enter the glasshouse on a route which enables them to watch the glassmakers closely. There are talks in the glasshouse regularly throughout the day from Monday to Friday. There is also a factory shop, a best shop, children's play area and tourist information centre with internet access.

Times Open all year, Factory shop & restaurant Mon-Sat 9-5, Sun 10-5 (Jan-Feb 12-5). Glassmaking daily 9-4.30.* **Facilities** licensed (outdoor) (fully accessible) toilets for disabled (wheelchair available) shop

Huntingtower Castle

PH1 3JL
☎ 01738 627231
web: www.historic-scotland.gov.uk
dir: 2m W

Formerly known as Ruthven Castle and famous as the scene of the so-called 'Raid of Ruthven' in 1582, this structure was built in the 15th and 16th centuries and features a painted ceiling.

Times Open all year, Apr-Sep, daily 9.30-5.30; Oct, 9.30-4.30; Nov-Mar, Mon-Wed & Sat-Sun 9.30-4.30. Closed 25-26 Dec & 1-2 Jan **Fees** £4.20 (ch £2.50, concessions £3.40). Please phone or check website for further details* **Facilities** shop

Perth Museum & Art Gallery

FREE

78 George St PH1 5LB
☎ 01738 632488 📠 01738 443505
e-mail: museum@pkc.gov.uk
web: www.pkc.gov.uk
dir: in town centre, adjacent to Perth Concert Hall

Visit Perth Museum and Art Gallery for a fascinating look into Perthshire throughout the ages. Collections cover silver, glass, art, natural history, archaeology and human history.

Times Open all year, Mon-Sat 10-5, Sun 1-4.30, May-Sep. Closed Xmas-New Year.* **Facilities** (partly accessible) toilets for disabled (ramp, lifts, induction loops) shop

PITLOCHRY — Map 14 NN95

Edradour Distillery

PH16 5JP
☎ 01796 472095 📠 01796 472002
e-mail: info@signatoryvintage.com
web: www.edradour.co.uk
dir: 2.5m E of Pitlochry on A924

It was in 1825 that a group of local farmers founded Edradour, naming it after the bubbling burn that runs through it. It is Scotland's smallest distillery and is virtually unchanged since Victorian times. Have a dram of whisky while watching an audio-visual in the malt barn and then take a guided tour through the distillery itself. Well stocked tasting bar and shop.

Times Open Jan-Feb, Mon-Sat 10-4, Sun closed; Mar-Apr, Mon-Sat 10-4, Sun 12-4; May & Oct, Mon-Sat 10-5, Sun 12-5; Jun-Sep, Mon-Sat 9.30-5, Sun 12-5; Nov-Dec, Mon-Sat 10-4, Sun 12-4 (last tour 1hr before closing time). Private tours arranged for an additional fee. Closed 25-26 Dec, 1-2 Jan **Fees** £5 (ch 5-16 £2.50) **Facilities** (partly accessible) toilets for disabled shop

Scottish Hydro Electric Visitor Centre, Dam & Fish Pass — FREE

PH16 5ND

☎ 01796 473152 🖷 01796 473152

dir: off A9, 24m N of Perth

The visitor centre features an exhibition showing how electricity is brought from the power station to the customer, and there is access to the turbine viewing gallery. The salmon ladder viewing chamber allows you to see the fish as they travel upstream to their spawning ground.

Times Open Apr-Oct, Mon-Fri 10-5. Wknd opening Jul, Aug & BHs **Facilities** Ⓟ Ⓟ ♿ (partly accessible) (access to shop only) toilets for disabled (monitor viewing of salmon fish pass) shop

QUEEN'S VIEW — Map 14 NN85

Queen's View Visitor Centre — FREE

PH16 5NR

☎ 01350 727284 🖷 01350 728635

e-mail: peter.fullarton@forestry.gsi.gov.uk

web: www.forestry.gov.uk

dir: 7m W of Pitlochry on B8019

Queen Victoria admired the view on a visit here in 1866; it is possibly one of the most famous views in Scotland. The area, in the heart of the Tay Forest Park, has a variety of woodlands that visitors can walk or cycle in.

Times Open Apr-Nov, daily 10-6.* **Facilities** Ⓟ Ⓟ (outdoor) toilets for disabled shop

SCONE — Map 11 NO12

Scone Palace — 2 FOR 1

PH2 6BD

☎ 01738 552300 🖷 01738 552588

e-mail: visits@scone-palace.co.uk

web: www.scone-palace.co.uk

dir: 2m NE of Perth on A93

Visit Scone Palace, the crowning place of Scottish Kings and the home of the Earls of Mansfield. The Palace dates from 1803 but incorporates 16th century and earlier buildings, and is a unique treasury of furniture, fine art and other objets d'art. As well as beautiful gardens the grounds are home to the Murray Star Maze, the Pinetum, Plant Hunters Pavilion, Cyril the Squirrel's Wildlife Trail and an adventure playground, livestock, Highland cattle and champion trees.

Times Open Apr-Oct, daily 9.30-5.30 (Sat last admission 4) **Fees** Palace & grounds £9 (ch £6, concessions £7.90). Family ticket £26. Grounds only £5.10 (ch £3.50, concessions £4.50). Group £7.90 (ch £5.50 concessions £6.75). Please contact for current details* **Facilities** Ⓟ licensed (outdoor) ♿ (fully accessible) toilets for disabled (stairlift which gives access to all state rooms) shop

See advert on this page

WEEM — Map 14 NN84

Castle Menzies

PH15 2JD

☎ 01887 820982 🖷 01887 820982

e-mail: castlem@tiscali.co.uk

web: www.menzies.org

dir: Follow signs from main roads

Restored seat of the Chiefs of Clan Menzies, and a fine example of a 16th-century Z-plan fortified tower house. Prince Charles Edward Stuart stayed here briefly on his way to Culloden in 1746. The whole of the 16th-century building can be explored, and there's a small clan museum.

Times Open Apr-mid Oct, Mon-Sat 10.30-5, Sun 2-5* **Facilities** Ⓟ Ⓟ (outdoor) toilets for disabled shop

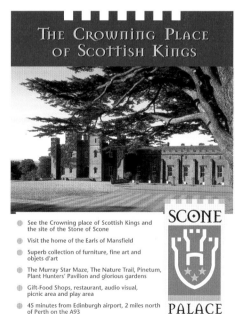

SCOTLAND

RENFREWSHIRE

KILBARCHAN — Map 10 NS46

Weaver's Cottage

The Cross PA10 2JG
☎ 0844 493 2205
e-mail: information@nts.org.uk
web: www.nts.org.uk
dir: off A737, 12m SW of Glasgow

The weaving craft is regularly demonstrated at this delightful 18th-century cottage museum, and there is a collection of weaving equipment and other domestic utensils.

Times Open Apr-Sep, Fri-Tue 1-5* **Facilities** Ⓟ ♿ (partly accessible) (steps into cottage, uneven sloping garden) (scented plants, subtitled audio visual programme).

SCOTLAND

LANGBANK — Map 10 NS37

Finlaystone Country Estate — 2 FOR 1

PA14 6TJ
☎ 01475 540505 📠 01475 540505
e-mail: info@finlaystone.co.uk
web: www.finlaystone.co.uk
dir: off A8 W of Langbank, 10m W of Glasgow Airport, follow Thistle signs

A beautiful country estate with historic formal gardens which are renowned for their natural beauty, with extensive woodland walks, picnic, BBQ and play areas. A tea room in the old walled garden, a gift shop and The 'Dolly Mixture', an international collection of dolls, can be seen in the Visitor Centre.

Times Open all year. Woodland & Gardens daily, 10-5 (winter 12-4) **Fees** Garden & Woods £4 (ch & pen £2.50). 'The Dolly Mixture' Doll Museum free* **Facilities** Ⓟ (outdoor) ♿ (partly accessible) (gardens and most walks accessible for wheelchairs incl tea room & visitor centre) toilets for disabled shop

LOCHWINNOCH — Map 10 NS35

RSPB Lochwinnoch Nature Reserve — 2 FOR 1

Largs Rd PA12 4JF
☎ 01505 842663 📠 01505 843026
e-mail: lochwinnoch@rspb.org.uk
web: www.rspb.org.uk/reserves/lochwinnoch
dir: on A760, Largs road, opposite Lochwinnoch station, 16m SW of Glasgow

The reserve, part of Clyde Muirshiel Regional Park and a Site of Special Scientific Interest, comprises two shallow lochs fringed by marsh which in turn is fringed by scrub and woodland. There are two trails with hides and a visitor centre with a viewing area. Please visit website for details of events running throughout the year.

Times Open all year, daily 10-5. Closed 1-2 Jan & 25-26 Dec **Fees** Trails £2 (ch 50p, concessions £1). Family ticket £4 **Facilities** Ⓟ Ⓟ (outdoor) ♿ (partly accessible) (visitor centre, trails and hides all accessible, tower inaccessible) toilets for disabled (wheelchair hire, ramps, disabled parking bays) shop

PAISLEY — Map 11 NS46

Coats Observatory — FREE

High St PA1 2BA
☎ 0141 889 2013 📠 0141 889 9240
e-mail: ram.els@renfrewshire.gov.uk
web: www.renfrewshire.gov.uk
dir: M8 junct 27, follow signs to town centre until Gordon St (A761). Left onto Causeyside St, left onto Stone St then left onto High St

The Observatory, funded by Thomas Coats and designed by John Honeyman, was opened in 1883. It houses a 5 inch telescope under the dome at the top. Weather recording activities have been carried out here continuously since 1884. There is also earthquake-measuring equipment and the Renfrewshire Astronomical Society holds regular meetings here. There are displays on the solar system, earthquakes and the telescope.

Times Open all year, Tue-Sat 10-5, Sun 2-5 (last entry 15 mins before closing)* **Facilities** Ⓟ shop

Paisley Museum — FREE

High St PA1 2BA
☎ 0141 889 3151 📠 0141 889 9240
e-mail: ram.els@renfrewshire.gov.uk
web: www.renfrewshire.gov.uk
dir: M8 junct 27 (A741), rdbt 2nd exit (A761-town centre). At traffic lights take left lane towards Kilbride. Onto Gordon St, right onto Causeyside St, left onto New St, left onto High St

Pride of place here is given to a world-famous collection of Paisley shawls. Other collections illustrate local industrial and natural history, while the emphasis of the art gallery is on 19th-century Scottish artists and an important studio ceramics collection.

Times Open all year, Tue-Sat 10-5, Sun 2-5. BH 10-5* **Facilities** Ⓟ ♿ (partly accessible) (level access available through side entrance, lift gives access to main gallery, Shawl gallery only available via rear entrance) toilets for disabled shop

SCOTTISH BORDERS

COLDSTREAM Map 12 NT84

The Hirsel

Douglas & Angus Estates, Estate Office, The Hirsel TD12 4LP
☎ 01890 830279 & 830293 📠 01890 830279
e-mail: john.letham2@btinternet.com
web: www.hirselcountrypark.co.uk
dir: 0.5m W on A697, on N outskirts of Coldstream

The seat of the Home family, the grounds of which are open all year. The focal point is the Homestead Museum, craft centre and workshops. From there, nature trails lead around the lake, along the Leet Valley and into woodland noted for its rhododendrons and azaleas.

Times Garden & Grounds open all year, daylight hours. Museum 10-5. Craft Centre Mon-Fri, 10-5, wknds noon-5 **Fees** £2.50 per car **Facilities** licensed (outdoor) (fully accessible) toilets for disabled shop

DRYBURGH Map 12 NT53

Dryburgh Abbey

TD6 0RQ
☎ 01835 822381
web: www.historic-scotland.gov.uk
dir: 5m SE of Melrose on B6404

The abbey was one of the Border monasteries founded by David I, and stands in a lovely setting on the River Tweed. The ruins are equally beautiful, and the church has the graves of Sir Walter Scott and Earl Haig.

Times Open all year daily, Apr-Sep, 9.30-5.30; Oct-Mar, 9.30-4.30. Closed 25-26 Dec & 1-2 Jan **Fees** £4.70 (ch £2.80, concessions £3.80). Please phone or check website for further details* **Facilities** shop

DUNS Map 12 NT75

Manderston

TD11 3PP
☎ 01361 883450 & 882636 📠 01361 882010
e-mail: palmer@manderston.co.uk
web: www.manderston.co.uk
dir: 2m E of Duns on A6105

This grandest of grand houses gives a fascinating picture of Edwardian life above and below stairs. Completely remodelled for the millionaire racehorse owner Sir James Miller, the architect was told to spare no expense, and so the house boasts the world's only silver staircase. The staterooms are magnificent, and there are fine formal gardens, with a woodland garden and lakeside walks. Manderston has been the setting for a number of films.

Times Open 6 May-26 Sep, Thu & Sun (also late May & Aug English BH Mons). Gardens open, 11.30-dusk. House open, 1.30-4.15* **Fees** House & Gardens £8.50 (ch £4.50); Gardens only £4.50* **Facilities** (partly accessible) shop

EYEMOUTH Map 12 NT96

Eyemouth Museum

Auld Kirk, Manse Rd TD14 5JE
☎ 018907 50678
dir: off A1 onto A1107, follow signs to town centre

The museum was opened in 1981 as a memorial to the 129 local fishermen lost in the Great Fishing Disaster of 1881. Its main feature is the 15ft Eyemouth tapestry, which was made for the centenary. There are also displays on local history.

Times Open Apr-Jun & Sep, Mon-Sat 10-5, Sun 10-1; Jul-Aug, Mon-Sat 10-5; Sun 10-2; Oct, Mon-Sat 10-4 (closed Sun)* **Facilities** Ⓟ shop

GORDON Map 12 NT64

Mellerstain House

TD3 6LG
☎ 01573 410225 📠 01573 410636
e-mail: enquiries@mellerstain.com
web: www.mellerstain.com
dir: signed on A6089 Kelso-Gordon road, 1m W. From A68 Jedburgh to Edinburgh road through Earlston, then follow minor road for Smailholm

One of Scotland's finest Georgian houses, begun by William Adam and completed by his son Robert in the 1770s. It has beautiful plasterwork, period furniture and pictures, terraced gardens and a lake.

Times Open Etr, May-Jun & Sep, Sun, Wed, & BH; Jul-Aug Sun-Mon & Wed-Thu; Oct, Sun 12.30-5 (last admission 4.15)* **Fees** House & Gardens £7 (ch £3.50, under 5's free); Garden only £4 (ch £2, under 5's free)* **Facilities** (partly accessible) (main floor only accessible) toilets for disabled

HERMITAGE Map 12 NY59

Hermitage Castle

TD9 0LU
☎ 01387 376222
web: www.historic-scotland.gov.uk
dir: 5.5m NE of Newcastleton, on B6399

A vast, eerie ruin of the 14th and 15th centuries, associated with the de Soulis, the Douglases and Mary, Queen of Scots. Much restored in the 19th century.

Times Open Apr-Sep, daily 9.30-5.30 **Fees** £3.70 (ch £2.20, concessions £3). Please phone or check website for further details* **Facilities**

SCOTLAND

SCOTLAND

INNERLEITHEN Map 11 NT33

Robert Smail's Printing Works

7/9 High St EH44 6HA
☎ 0844 493 2259
e-mail: information@nts.org.uk
web: www.nts.org.uk
dir: 30m S of Edinburgh, A272, 6m from Peebles. (Innerleithen Road)

These buildings contain a Victorian office, a paper store with reconstructed waterwheel, a composing room and a press room. The machinery is in full working order and visitors may view the printer at work and experience typesetting in the composing room.

Times Open 2 Apr-Oct, Thu-Mon 12-5, (Sun 1-5)* **Facilities** Ⓟ ♿ (partly accessible) (stairs to caseroom) (guidebook) shop

JEDBURGH Map 12 NT62

Jedburgh Abbey

TD8 6JQ
☎ 01835 863925
web: www.historic-scotland.gov.uk

Standing as the most complete of the Border monasteries (although it has been sacked and rebuilt many times) Jedburgh Abbey has been described as 'the most perfect and beautiful example of the Saxon and early Gothic in Scotland'. David I founded it as a priory in the 12th century and remains of some of the domestic buildings have been uncovered during excavations.

Times Open all year daily, Apr-Sep 9.30-5.30; Oct-Mar 9.30-4.30. Closed 25-26 Dec & 1-2 Jan **Fees** £5.20 (ch £3.10, concessions £4.20). Please phone or check website for details* **Facilities** Ⓟ toilets for disabled shop

Jedburgh Castle Jail & Museum FREE

Castlegate TD8 6QD
☎ 01835 864750 01835 864750
web: www.scotborders.gov.uk/museums
dir: off A68 towards town centre, follow signs to top of Castlegate

Relive the harsh realities of prison life in the 19th century with a visit to Jedburgh Castle Jail, built in the 1820s on the site of the Royal Burgh's medieval castle. Displays in the cell blocks recreate the lives of prisoners and staff, while the Jailer's House explores the history of the town. A children's activity guide is available, and there are plenty of hands-on activities for all the family.

Times Open late Mar-end Oct, Mon-Sat, 10-4.30, Sun 1-4 **Facilities** Ⓟ Ⓟ (outdoor) ♿ (partly accessible) (assisted wheelchair access to ground floor displays, half of displays on 1st floor) toilets for disabled (audio guide, touch screen, hearing loop, new guide book) shop

KELSO Map 12 NT73

Floors Castle

Roxburghe Estates Office TD5 7SF
☎ 01573 223333 01573 226056
e-mail: cnewton@floorscastle.com
web: www.floorscastle.com
dir: from town centre follow Roxburghe St to main gates

The home of the 10th Duke of Roxburghe, the Castle's lived-in atmosphere enhances the superb collection of French furniture, tapestries and paintings. The house was designed by William Adam in 1721 and enjoys a magnificent setting overlooking the River Tweed and the Cheviot Hills beyond. Regular events include massed pipe bands, open-air theatre, and garden festivals.

Times Open Etr-Oct, daily 11-5 (last admission 4.30) **Fees** £7.50 (ch £3.50, concessions £6.50). Family ticket £19* **Facilities** Ⓟ licensed (outdoor) ♿ (fully accessible) toilets for disabled (lift) shop

Kelso Abbey FREE

☎ 0131 668 8800
web: www.historic-scotland.gov.uk

Founded by David I in 1128 and probably the greatest of the four famous Border abbeys, Kelso became extremely wealthy and acquired extensive lands. In 1545 it served as a fortress when the town was attacked by the Earl of Hertford, but now only fragments of the once-imposing abbey church give any clue to its long history.

Times Open at any reasonable time **Facilities**

LAUDER Map 12 NT54

Thirlestane Castle

TD2 6RU
☎ 01578 722430 01578 722761
e-mail: admin@thirlestanecastle.co.uk
web: www.thirlestanecastle.co.uk
dir: off A68, S of Lauder

This fairy-tale castle has been the home of the Maitland family, the Earls of Lauderdale, since the 12th century. Some of the most splendid plasterwork ceilings in Britain may be seen in the 17th-century state rooms. The family nurseries house a sizeable collection of antique toys and dolls. The informal riverside grounds, with their views of the grouse moors, include a woodland walk, picnic tables and adventure playground. Please visit website for details of events running throughout the year.

Times Open Etr, May-Jun & Sep; Sun, Wed-Thu & BHs; Jul-Aug; Sun-Thu. All days 10-3 for castle, 10-5 for grounds* **Fees** Castle & grounds: £10 (ch £6, pen £7). Family (2ad&3ch) £25. Grounds only £3 (ch £1.50). Group castle & grounds £8* **Facilities** (outdoor) toilets for disabled shop

MELROSE Map 12 NT53

Abbotsford

TD6 9BQ
☎ 01896 752043 01896 752916
e-mail: enquiries@scottsabbotsford.co.uk
web: www.scottsabbotsford.co.uk
dir: 2m W off A6091, on B6360

Set on the River Tweed, Sir Walter Scott's romantic mansion remains much the same as it was in his day. Inside there are many mementoes and relics of his remarkable life and also his historical collections, armouries and library, with some 9,000 volumes. Scott built the mansion between 1811 and 1822, and lived here until his death ten years after its completion.

Times Open daily from 3rd Mon in Mar-Oct, Mon-Sat 9.30-5. Mar-May & Oct, Sun 2-5. Jun-Sep, Sun 9.30-5* **Facilities** (outdoor) (partly accessible) (ramps at entrance, show rooms, gift shop and tea rooms accessible) toilets for disabled shop

Harmony Garden

St Mary's Rd TD6 9LJ
☎ 0844 493 2251
e-mail: information@nts.org.uk
web: www.nts.org.uk
dir: opposite Melrose Abbey, off A6091 in Melrose

Set around the early 19th-century Harmony Hall (not open to visitors), this attractive walled garden has magnificent views of Melrose Abbey and the Eildon Hills. The garden comprises lawns, herbaceous and mixed borders, vegetable and fruit areas, and a rich display of spring bulbs.

Times Open Apr-Oct, Mon-Sat 10-5, Sun 1-5* **Facilities** (fully accessible)

Melrose Abbey & Abbey Museum

TD6 9LG
☎ 01896 822562
web: www.historic-scotland.gov.uk

The ruin of this Cistercian abbey is probably one of Scotland's finest, and has been given added glamour by its connection with Sir Walter Scott. The abbey was repeatedly wrecked during the Scottish wars of independence, but parts survive from the 14th century. The heart of Robert the Bruce is buried somewhere within the church.

Times Open all year daily, Apr-Sep 9.30-5.30; Oct-Mar 9.30-4.30. Closed 25-26 Dec & 1-2 Jan **Fees** £5.20 (ch £3.10, concessions £4.20). Please phone or check website for further details* **Facilities** shop

Priorwood Garden & Dried Flower Shop

TD6 9PX
☎ 0844 493 2257 01896 822965
e-mail: information@nts.org.uk
web: www.nts.org.uk
dir: off A6091, in Melrose, adjacent to Abbey. On National Cycle Route 1

This small garden specialises in flowers suitable for drying. It is formally designed with herbaceous and everlasting annual borders, and the attractive orchard has a display of 'apples through the ages'.

Times Garden Apr-24 Dec (same opening times as shop). Shop open 5 Jan-Mar, Mon-Sat 12-4; Apr-24 Dec, Mon-Sat 10-5, Sun 1-5* **Facilities** (partly accessible) (ramps, paths) shop

PEEBLES Map 11 NT24

Kailzie Gardens

EH45 9HT
☎ 01721 720007 01721 720007
e-mail: info@kailziegardens.com
web: www.kailziegardens.com
dir: 2.5m SE on B7062

These extensive grounds, with their fine old trees, provide a burnside walk flanked by bulbs, rhododendrons and azaleas. A walled garden contains herbaceous, shrub rose borders, greenhouses and a formal rose garden. A garden for all seasons - don't miss the snowdrops. A large stocked trout pond and rod hire available, and an 18-hole putting green, plus an open bait pond, ornamental duck pond and osprey viewing centre.

Times Open daily 25 Mar-Oct, 11-5.30 (Grounds close 5.30). Garden open all year* **Facilities** licensed (outdoor) (partly accessible) (most paths accessible) toilets for disabled (ramps in garden) shop

SCOTLAND

SCOTLAND

SELKIRK Map 12 NT42

Bowhill House and Country Estate

TD7 5ET
☎ 01750 22204 01750 23893
e-mail: bht@buccleuch.com
web: www.bowhill.org
dir: 3m W of Selkirk off A708

An outstanding collection of pictures, including works by Van Dyck, Canaletto, Reynolds, Gainsborough and Claude Lorraine are displayed here. Memorabilia and relics of people such as Queen Victoria and Sir Walter Scott, and a restored Victorian kitchen add further interest inside the house. Outside, the wooded grounds are perfect for walking. A small theatre provides a full programme of music and drama.

Times House open: May BH wknds, Jul-Aug daily. Estate open: Etr fortnight then wknds & BHs Apr-Jun (call for times) **Fees** House & estate £8 (ch £3.50, concessions £7). Estate only £3.50 (ch £2.50) **Facilities** (outdoor) (fully accessible) toilets for disabled (guided tours for the blind by appointment) shop

Halliwells House Museum FREE

Halliwells Close, Market Place TD7 4BC
☎ 01750 20096 01750 23282
e-mail: museums@scotborders.gov.uk
dir: off A7 in town centre

A row of late 18th-century town cottages converted into a museum. Displays recreate the building's former use as an ironmonger's shop and home, and tell the story of the Royal Burgh of Selkirk. The Robson Gallery hosts a programme of contemporary art and craft exhibitions.

Times Open Apr-Sep, Mon-Sat 10-5, Sun 10-12; Jul-Aug, Mon-Sat 10-5.30, Sun 10-12; Oct, Mon-Sat 10-4 **Facilities** (fully accessible) toilets for disabled (lift to first floor, ramp, large print, interpretation) shop

Lochcarron of Scotland Visitor Centre

Waverley Mill, Rodgers Rd TD7 5DX
☎ 01750 726000 01750 724100
e-mail: quality@lochcarron.com
web: www.quality@lochcarron.com
dir: On A7, follow signs to mill

The museum brings the town's past to life and the focal point is a display on the woollen industry. Guided tours of the mill take about 40 minutes. Please note that disabled toilets are built for members of staff who are disabled but are not in wheelchairs.

Times Open all year, Mon-Sat 9-5, Sun (Jun-Sep) 12-5. Mill tours Mon-Thu at 10.30, 11.30, 1.30 & 2.30, Fri am only* **Facilities** (fully accessible) toilets for disabled shop

Sir Walter Scott's Courtroom FREE

Market Place TD7 4BT
☎ 01750 20096 01750 23282
e-mail: museums@scotborders.gov.uk
dir: on A7 in town centre

Built in 1803-4 as a sheriff court and town hall this is where the famous novelist, Sir Walter Scott dispensed justice when he was Sheriff of Selkirkshire from 1804-1832. Displays tell of Scott's time as Sheriff, and of his place as a novelist as well as those of his contemporaries, writer, James Hogg and the explorer, Mungo Park.

Times Open Apr-Sep, Mon-Fri 10-4, Sat 10-2; May-Aug also Sun 10-2; Oct, Mon-Sat 1-4 **Facilities** (partly accessible) (ramp at rear of building) toilets for disabled shop

SMAILHOLM Map 12 NT63

Smailholm Tower

TD5 7PG
☎ 01573 460365
web: www.historic-scotland.gov.uk
dir: 6m W of Kelso on B6937

An outstanding example of a classic Border tower-house, probably erected in the 15th century. It is 57 feet high and well preserved. The tower houses an exhibition of dolls and a display based on Sir Walter Scott's book *Minstrels of the Border.*

Times Open Apr-Sep, daily 9.30-5.30; Oct-Mar, wknds only 9.30-4.30. Closed 25-26 Dec & 1-2 Jan **Fees** £3.70 (ch £2.20, concessions £3). Please phone or check website for further details* **Facilities** shop

STOBO Map 11 NT13

Dawyck Botanic Garden

EH45 9JU
☎ 01721 760254 01721 760214
e-mail: dawyck@rbge.org.uk
web: www.rbge.org.uk
dir: 8m SW of Peebles on B712

From the landscaped walks of this historic arboretum an impressive collection of mature specimen trees can be seen - some over 40 metres tall and including the unique Dawyck beech-stand. Notable features include the Swiss Bridge, a fine estate chapel and stonework/terracing produced by Italian craftsmen in the 1820s.

Times Open daily, Feb & Nov 10-4. Mar & Oct 10-5. Apr-Sep 10-6* **Facilities** (outdoor) toilets for disabled shop

TRAQUAIR Map 11 NT33

Traquair House

2 FOR 1

EH44 6PW

☎ 01896 830323 📠 01896 830639
e-mail: enquiries@traquair.co.uk
web: www.traquair.co.uk
dir: at Innerleithen take B709, house in 1m

Said to be Scotland's oldest inhabited house, dating back to the 12th century, 27 Scottish monarchs have stayed at Traquair House. William the Lion Heart held court here, and the house has associations with Mary, Queen of Scots and the Jacobite risings. The Bear Gates were closed in 1745, not to be reopened until the Stuarts should once again ascend the throne. There is a maze and woodland walks by the River Tweed, craft workshops and a children's adventure playground. Also an 18th-century working brewery with museum shop and tastings. Award-winning 1745 Cottage Restaurant open for lunches and teas.

Times Open daily Apr-May & Sep 12-5; Jun-Aug 10.30-5; Oct 11-4; Nov 11-3 (wknds only) **Fees** House & Grounds £7.60 (ch £4.10, pen £6.90). Family ticket £21.20. Grounds only £4 (concessions £2.50) **Facilities** Ⓟ ☕ 🍽 licensed ⛩ (outdoor) ♿ (partly accessible) (ground floor of house only accessible) toilets for disabled shop

SOUTH AYRSHIRE

ALLOWAY Map 10 NS31

Burns National Heritage Park

Murdoch's Lone KA7 4PQ

☎ 01292 443700 📠 01292 441750
e-mail: info@burnsheritagepark.com
web: www.burnsheritagepark.com
dir: 2m S of Ayr

The birthplace of Robert Burns, Scotland's National Poet set in the gardens and countryside of Alloway. An introduction to the life of Robert Burns, with an audio-visual presentation - a multi-screen 3D experience describing the Tale of Tam O'Shanter. This attraction consists of the museum, Burn's Cottage, visitor centre, tranquil landscaped gardens and historical monuments. Please telephone for further details.

Times Open all year, Apr-Sep 10-5.30, Oct-Mar 10-5. Closed 25-26 Dec & 1-2 Jan* **Facilities** Ⓟ Ⓟ ☕ 🍽 licensed ♿ (partly accessible) (access limited in some parts of property) toilets for disabled (wheelchair available) shop 🚫

CULZEAN CASTLE Map 10 NS21

Culzean Castle & Country Park

KA19 8LE

☎ 0844 493 2149 📠 0844 493 2150
e-mail: information@nts.org.uk
web: www.nts.org.uk
dir: 4m W of Maybole, off A77, 12m S of Ayr

This 18th-century castle stands on a cliff in spacious grounds and was designed by Robert Adam for the Earl of Cassillis. It is noted for its oval staircase, circular drawing room and plasterwork. The Eisenhower Room explores the American General's links with Culzean. The 563-acre country park has a wide range of attractions - shoreline, woodland walks, parkland, an adventure playground and gardens.

Times Castle, Visitor centre & other facilities: Apr-1 Nov, daily 10.30-5 (last entry 4). (Visitor centre off season: 2 Nov-29 Mar, Sat-Sun 11-4). Walled garden: all year, daily 9.30-5 (sunset if earlier). Country Park: open all year 9.30-sunset* **Facilities** Ⓟ ☕ 🍽 licensed ⛩ (outdoor) ♿ (partly accessible) toilets for disabled (wheelchairs, lift in castle, Braille guides, induction loop) shop 🚫 🐾

SCOTLAND

KIRKOSWALD Map 10 NS20

Souter Johnnie's Cottage

Main Rd KA19 8HY

☎ 0844 493 2147 Fax 0844 493 2147

e-mail: information@nts.org.uk

web: www.nts.org.uk

dir: on A77, 4m SW of Maybole

'Souter' means cobbler and the village cobbler who lived in this 18th-century cottage was the inspiration for Burns' character Souter Johnnie, in his ballad *Tam O'Shanter*. The cottage is now a Burns museum and life-size stone figures of the poet's characters can be seen in the restored ale-house in the cottage garden.

Times Open: Burns Night, 25 Jan 11.30-5, 30 Apr-Sep, Fri-Tue 11.30-5* **Facilities** Ⓟ ♿ (partly accessible) (cobblestones front property, gentle slope to garden)

MAYBOLE Map 10 NS20

Crossraguel Abbey

KA19 5HQ

☎ 01655 883113

web: www.historic-scotland.gov.uk

dir: 2m S

The extensive remains of this 13th-century Cluniac monastery are impressive and architecturally important. The monastery was founded by Duncan, Earl of Carrick and the church, claustral buildings, abbot's house and an imposing castellated gatehouse can be seen.

Times Open Apr-Sep, daily 9.30-5.30 **Fees** £3.70 (ch £2.20, concessions £3). Please phone or check website for further details* **Facilities** 🅟

OLD DAILLY Map 10 NX29

Bargany Gardens

KA26 9PH

☎ 01465 871249 Fax 01465 871282

e-mail: bargany@btinternet.com

dir: 4m NE on B734 from Girvan

Woodland walks with a fine show of azaleas and rhododendrons. Plants on sale from the gardens.

Times Open May 10-5 **Fees** £2 (ch under 12 free)* **Facilities** 🅟 (outdoor) ♿ (partly accessible) (rock garden not accessible)

TARBOLTON Map 10 NS42

Bachelors' Club

Sandgate St KA5 5RB

☎ 0844 493 2146 Fax 0844 493 2146

e-mail: information@nts.org.uk

web: www.nts.org.uk

dir: In Tarbolton, off A77 S of Kilmarnock & off A76 at Mauchline, 7.5m NE of Ayr

In this 17th-century thatched house, Robert Burns and his friends formed a debating club in 1780. Burns attended dancing lessons and was initiated into freemasonry here in 1781. The house is furnished in the style of the period.

Times Open Burns Night, 25 Jan 1-5, Apr-Sep, Fri-Tue 1-5* **Facilities** Ⓟ ♿ (partly accessible) (limited access 12 steps to upper room)

SOUTH LANARKSHIRE

BIGGAR Map 11 NT03

Gladstone Court Museum

ML12 6DT

☎ 01899 221050 Fax 01899 221050

e-mail: suzanne.bmt@googlemail.com

web: www.biggarmuseumtrust.co.uk

dir: On A702 entrance by 113 High St

An old-fashioned village street is portrayed in this museum, which is set out in a century-old coach-house. On display are reconstructed shops, complete with old signs and advertisements - a bank, telephone exchange, photographer's booth and other interesting glimpses into the recent past.

Times Open May-Sep, Mon-Sat 11-4.30, Sun 2-4.30* **Facilities** 🅟 Ⓟ shop

Greenhill Covenanters House

Burn Braes ML12 6DT

☎ 01899 221050 Fax 01899 221050

e-mail: suzanne.bmt@googlemail.com

web: www.biggarmuseum.co.uk

dir: On A702, 30m from Edinburgh, 40m from Glasgow

This 17th-century farmhouse was brought, stone by stone, ten miles from Wiston and reconstructed at Biggar. It has relics of the turbulent 'Covenanting' period, when men and women defended the right to worship in Presbyterian style. Audio presentations.

Times Open mid May-Sep, wknds only 2-4.30* **Facilities** 🅟 Ⓟ (outdoor)

Moat Park Heritage Centre

Kirkstyle ML12 6DT
☎ 01899 221050
e-mail: suzanne.bmt@googlemail.com
web: www.biggarmuseumtrust.co.uk
dir: On A702

The centre illustrates the history, archaeology and geology of the Upper Clyde and Tweed valleys with interesting displays.

Times Open all year, May-Sep, Mon-Sat 11.30-4.30, Sun 2-4.30; Oct-Apr, open by appointment only* **Facilities** (outdoor) (partly accessible) (upper floor with assistance on request) toilets for disabled shop

BLANTYRE — Map 11 NS65

David Livingstone Centre

165 Station Rd G72 9BT
☎ 0844 493 2207 📠 0844 493 2206
e-mail: information@nts.org.uk
web: www.nts.org.uk
dir: M74 junct 5 onto A725, then A724, follow signs for Blantyre, right at lights. Centre is at foot of hill

Share the adventurous life of Scotland's greatest explorer, from his childhood in the Blantyre Mills to his explorations in the heart of Africa, dramatically illustrated in the historic tenement where he was born. Various events are planned throughout the season.

Times Open Apr-24 Dec, Mon-Sat 10-5, Sun 12.30-5*
Facilities (fully accessible) toilets for disabled (audio transcripts) shop

BOTHWELL — Map 11 NS75

Bothwell Castle

G71 8BL
☎ 01698 816894
web: www.historic-scotland.gov.uk
dir: approach from Uddingston off B7071

Besieged, captured and 'knocked about' several times in the Scottish-English wars, the castle is a splendid ruin. Archibald the Grim built the curtain wall; later, in 1786, the Duke of Buccleuch carved graffiti - a coronet and initials - beside a basement well.

Times Open all year, Apr-Sep, daily 9.30-5.30; Oct-Mar, 9.30-4.30, closed Thu & Fri in winter, 25-26 Dec & 1-2 Jan. **Fees** £3.70 (ch £2.20, concessions £3). Please phone or check website for further details.* **Facilities** shop

EAST KILBRIDE — Map 11 NS65

National Museum of Rural Life Scotland

Wester Kittochside, Philipshill Rd, (off Stewartfield Way) G76 9HR
☎ 0131 225 7534
e-mail: info@nms.ac.uk
web: www.nms.ac.uk/rural
dir: From Glasgow take A749 to East Kilbride. From Edinburgh follow M8 to Glasgow, turn off junct 6 onto A725 to East Kilbride. Museum clearly signed before East Kilbride

Get a healthy dose of fresh air. Take in the sights, sounds and smells as you explore this 1950s working farm. Discover what life was like for country people in the past and how this has shaped Scotland's countryside today. Explore the museum and farmhouse, hitch a ride on our farm explorer, meet Mairi the horse and the sheep, cows and hens. See the website for details of a wide range of special events and exhibitions.

Times Open daily 10-5. Closed 25-26 Dec & 1 Jan* **Fees** £6 (ch 12 & under free, concessions £5) NMS and NTS members free. Charge for some special events* **Facilities** (outdoor) (fully accessible) toilets for disabled (disabled parking, induction loop, site transport, ramps) shop

HAMILTON — Map 11 NS75

Chatelherault Country Park — FREE

Ferniegair ML3 7UE
☎ 01698 426213 📠 01698 427741
e-mail: phyllis.crosbie@southlanarkshire.gov.uk
web: www.southlanarkshire.gov.uk
dir: 2.5km SE of Hamilton on A72 Hamilton-Larkhall/Lanark Clyde Valley tourist route

Designed as a hunting lodge by William Adam in 1732, Chatelherault, built of unusual pink sandstone, has been described as a gem of Scottish architecture. Situated close to the motorway, there is a visitor's centre, shop and adventure playground. Also a herd of white Cadzow cattle.

Times Visitor Centre, open all year, Mon-Sat 10-5, Sun 12-5. House closed Fri & Sat* **Facilities** (outdoor) (partly accessible) toilets for disabled (ramps, parking, large print guide) shop

SCOTLAND

HAMILTON *continued*

Low Parks Museum

FREE

129 Muir St ML3 6BJ
☎ 01698 328232 📠 01698 328412
e-mail: lowparksmuseum@southlanarkshire.gov.uk
web: www.southlanarkshire.gov.uk
dir: off M74 junct 6, by Asda Superstore

The museum tells the story of both South Lanarkshire and The Cameronians (Scottish Rifles). The Cameronians were unique as they were the only Scottish rifle regiment, and the museum details their fascinating history from 1689 to 1968. Housed in the town's oldest building, dating from 1696, the museum also features a restored 18th-century assembly room and exhibitions on Hamilton Palace and The Covenanters.

Times Open all year, daily, Mon-Sat 10-5, Sun 12-5* **Facilities** Ⓟ Ⓟ ☕ toilets for disabled shop ⊗

SCOTLAND

NEW LANARK — Map 11 NS84

New Lanark Visitor Centre

2 FOR 1

Mill 3, New Lanark Mills ML11 9DB
☎ 01555 661345 📠 01555 665738
e-mail: trust@newlanark.org
web: www.newlanark.org
dir: 1m S of Lanark. Signed from all major routes. Around 1hr from Glasgow (M74/A72) and Edinburgh (A70)

Founded in 1785, New Lanark became well known in the early 19th century as a model community managed by enlightened industrialist and educational reformer Robert Owen. Close to the Falls of Clyde, this unique world heritage site explores the philosophies of Robert Owen, using theatre, interactive displays, and the 'Annie McLeod Experience', a magical ride through history. The village is also home to the Scottish Wildlife Trust's Falls of Clyde Reserve. There is a wide variety of exciting, fun and educational events every year. A roof garden and viewing platform provide a bird's eye view of this historic village and the surrounding woodland.

Times Open all year daily, Jun-Aug 10.30-5; Sep-May 11-5. Closed 25 Dec & 1 Jan **Fees** £6.95 (ch, concessions £5.95). Family ticket (2ad+2ch) £21.95 or (2ad+4ch) £27.95* **Facilities** Ⓟ ☕ 🍴 licensed ⛩ (outdoor) ♿ (fully accessible) toilets for disabled (ramps, disabled parking, wheelchairs) shop ⊗

STIRLING

BANNOCKBURN — Map 11 NS89

Bannockburn

Glasgow Rd FK7 0LJ
☎ 0844 493 2139 📠 0844 493 2138
e-mail: information@nts.org.uk
web: www.nts.org.uk
dir: 2m S of Stirling off M80/M9 junct 9, on A872

The Heritage Centre stands close to what is traditionally believed to have been Robert the Bruce's command post before the 1314 Battle of Bannockburn, a famous victory for the Scots and a turning point in Scottish history.

Times Heritage Centre 2 Mar-Oct daily, 10-5. Grounds all year daily, until dusk* **Facilities** Ⓟ ☕ ♿ (partly accessible) toilets for disabled (induction loop, visual info, w/chair) shop ⊗

BLAIR DRUMMOND — Map 11 NS79

Blair Drummond Safari & Leisure Park

FK9 4UR
☎ 01786 841456 & 841396 📠 01786 841491
e-mail: enquiries@blairdrummond.com
web: www.blairdrummond.com
dir: M9 junct 10, 4m on A84 towards Callander

Drive through the wild animal reserves where North American bison, antelopes, lions, tigers, white rhino and camels can be seen at close range. Other attractions include the sea lion show, a ride on the boat safari around Chimp Island, an adventure playground, giant astraglide, and pedal boats. There are also African elephants, giraffes, zebras, a bear and ostriches. Bird of Prey Centre and daily displays. Lemur Land and Pets' Farm.

Times Open 19 Mar-3 Oct, daily 10-5.30 (last admission 4.30)* **Fees** £11.50 (under 3 free, ch 3-14, concessions, special needs & carers with ID £8)* **Facilities** Ⓟ ☕ 🍴 licensed ⛩ (outdoor) ♿ (fully accessible) toilets for disabled shop ⊗

DOUNE — Map 11 NN70

Doune Castle

FK16 6EA
☎ 01786 841742
web: www.historic-scotland.gov.uk
dir: 8m S of Callander on A84

The 14th-century stronghold with its two fine towers has been restored. It stands on the banks of the River Teith, and is associated with 'Bonnie Prince Charlie' and Sir Walter Scott.

Times Open all year, Apr-Sep, daily, 9.30-5.30; Oct, 9.30-4.30; Nov-Mar, Mon-Wed & Sat-Sun, 9.30-4.30. Closed 25-26 Dec & 1-2 Jan **Fees** £4.20 (ch £2.50, concessions £3.40). Please phone or check website for further details* **Facilities** Ⓟ ⛩ shop

KILLIN — Map 11 NN53

Breadalbane Folklore Centre

Falls of Dochart FK21 8XE
☎ 01567 820254 01567 820764
e-mail: info@breadalbanefolklorecentre.com
web: www.breadalbanefolklorecentre.com
dir: A827 from Aberfeldy & Kenmore or A85 from Cairnlarich

Overlooking the beautiful Falls of Dochart, the centre gives a fascinating insight into the legends of Breadalbane - Scotland's 'high country'. Learn of the magical deeds of St Fillan and hear tales of mystical giants, ancient prophesies, traditional folklore and clan history. Housed in historic St Fillans Mill which features a restored waterwheel. Tourist Information and gift shop.

Times Open Apr-Oct, daily (ex Tue) 10-4 **Fees** £2.95 (ch £1.95 concessions £2.50). Family ticket £7.85 **Facilities** Ⓟ shop

PORT OF MENTEITH — Map 11 NN50

Inchmahome Priory

FK8 3RA
☎ 01877 385294
web: www.historic-scotland.gov.uk
dir: 4m E of Aberfoyle, off A81

Walter Comyn founded this Augustinian house in 1238, and it became famous as the retreat of the infant Mary, Queen of Scots in 1547. The ruins of the church and cloisters are situated on an island in the Lake of Monteith.

Times Open Apr-Sep, daily 9.30-4.30; Oct 9.30-3.30 **Fees** £4.70 (ch £2.80, concessions £3.80). Charge includes ferry trip. Please phone or check website for further details* **Facilities** Ⓟ shop

STIRLING — Map 11 NS79

Mar's Wark — FREE

Broad St FK8 1EE
web: www.historic-scotland.gov.uk

A remarkable Renaissance mansion built by the Earl of Mar, Regent for James VI in 1570 and later used as the town workhouse. It was never completed and now the facade can be seen.

Times Open all reasonable times **Facilities**

The National Wallace Monument

Hillfoots Rd, Causewayhead FK9 5LF
☎ 01786 472140 01786 461322
e-mail: info@nationalwallacemonument.com
web: www.nationalwallacemonument.com
dir: Monument is signed from city centre & A91

Meet Scotland's national hero, Sir William Wallace, and join his epic struggle for a free Scotland. Step into Westminster Hall and witness his trial. Climb the 220 foot tower and experience one of the finest views in Scotland. Each August there is an 'Encounter with Wallace', a programme of dramatic performances including traditional Scottish music.

Times Open all year, daily Apr-Jun & Sep-Oct 10-5; Jul-Aug 10-6; Nov-Mar 10.30-4 **Fees** £7.50 (ch £4.50, concessions £6). Family ticket £19.50 **Facilities** Ⓟ (outdoor) ♿ (partly accessible) (visitor reception centre & legends coffee house fully accessible) shop

The Regimental Museum of the Argyll & Sutherland Highlanders

The Castle FK8 3PA
☎ 01786 475165 01786 446038
e-mail: museum@argylls.co.uk
web: www.argylls.co.uk
dir: museum in Stirling Castle

Situated in the King's Old Building in Stirling Castle, the museum tells the history of the Regiment from 1794 to the present day. Displays include uniforms, medals, silver, paintings, colours, pipe banners, and commentaries.

Times Open daily Etr-Sep, 9.30-5; Sep-Etr, 10-4.15 **Fees** Free admission to Museum. Entry fee to Castle (see website) **Facilities** Ⓟ ♿ (partly accessible) (restricted access, turret & stone steps) shop

SCOTLAND

STIRLING *continued*

Stirling Castle

Upper Castle Hill FK8 1EJ
☎ 01786 450000
web: www.stirlingcastle.gov.uk

Sitting on top of a 250ft rock, Stirling Castle has a strategic position on the Firth of Forth. As a result it has been the scene of many events in Scotland's history. James II was born at the castle in 1430. Mary, Queen of Scots spent some years there, and it was James IV's childhood home. Among its finest features are the splendid Renaissance palace built by James V, and the Chapel Royal, rebuilt by James VI.

Times Open all year daily, Apr-Sep 9.30-6; Oct-Mar 9.30-5. Closed 25-26 **Fees** £9 (ch £5.40, concessions £7.20). Please phone or check website for further details* **Facilities** licensed toilets for disabled shop

Stirling Old Town Jail

Saint John St FK8 1EA
☎ 01786 450050 01786 471301
e-mail: info@oldtownjail.com
web: www.oldtownjail.com
dir: Located on St John's St (main route to Stirling Castle)

Step inside an authentic Victorian jail at the heart of historic Stirling for a fascinating live prison tour. You'll meet the warden, the convict desperate to escape, and even the hangman. Look out from the rooftop viewpoint for a wonderful view, visit the exhibition area, and just for children, join the Beastie Hunt.

Times Open 27 May-Oct, daily 10-5 **Fees** £6.50 (ch £4, concessions £5). Family ticket £14.50-£17 **Facilities** toilets for disabled shop

Stirling Smith Art Gallery & Museum

Dumbarton Rd FK8 2RQ
☎ 01786 471917 01786 449523
e-mail: museum@smithartgallery.demon.co.uk
web: www.smithartgallery.demon.co.uk
dir: M9 junct 10, follow Stirling Castle signs

This award-winning museum and gallery presents a variety of exhibitions drawing on its own rich collections and works from elsewhere. Please telephone for details of events running throughout the year. 2011 will be the centenary of the Barnwell Brothers air flight in Stirling.

Times Open all year, Tue-Sat 10.30-5, Sun 2-5. Closed 25-26 Dec & 1-2 Jan **Fees** Small charge for special events* **Facilities** (indoor & outdoor) (partly accessible) (wheelchair ramp available) toilets for disabled (wheelchair lift, induction loop in theatre) shop

WEST DUNBARTONSHIRE

DUMBARTON Map 10 NS37

Dumbarton Castle

G82 1JJ
☎ 01389 732167
web: www.historic-scotland.gov.uk

The castle, set on the 240ft Dumbarton Rock above the River Clyde, dominates the town (the capital of the Celtic kingdom of Strathclyde) and commands spectacular views. Most of what can be seen today dates from the 18th and 19th centuries, but there are a few earlier remains.

Times Open all year, Apr-Sep, daily, 9.30-5.30; Oct, 9.30-4.30; Nov-Mar, Mon-Wed & Sat-Sun, 9.30-4.30. Closed 25-26 Dec & 1-2 Jan **Fees** £4.20 (ch £2.50, concessions £3.40). Please phone or check website for further details* **Facilities** shop

WEST LOTHIAN

LINLITHGOW Map 11 NS97

Blackness Castle

EH49 7NH
☎ 01506 834807
web: www.historic-scotland.gov.uk
dir: 4m NE

This was once one of the most important fortresses in Scotland. Used as a state prison during covenanting time and in the late 19th-century as a powder magazine, it was one of four castles left fortified by the Articles of Union. Most impressive are the massive 17th-century artillery emplacements.

Times Open all year, Apr-Sep, daily 9.30-5.30; Oct, 9.30-4.30; Nov-Mar, 9.30-4.30, closed Thu & Fri in winter, 25-26 Dec & 1-2 Jan **Fees** £4.20 (ch £2.50, concessions £3.40). Please phone or check website for further details* **Facilities** shop

House of The Binns

EH49 7NA
☎ 0844 493 2127
e-mail: information@nts.org.uk
web: www.nts.org.uk
dir: 4m E of Linlithgow, off A904

An example of changing architectural tastes from 1612 onwards, this house reflects the transition from fortified stronghold to spacious mansion. The original three-storey building, with small windows and twin turrets, evolved into a fine crenellated house with beautiful moulded plaster ceilings - the ancestral home of the Dalyell family. There is a magnificent display of snowdrops and daffodils in spring.

Times Open House: Jun-Sep, Sat-Wed 2-5. Estate all year daily* **Facilities** (partly accessible) (access restricted to ground floor) (Braille sheets, photo album, audio info)

Linlithgow Palace

EH49 7AL
☎ 01506 842896
web: www.historic-scotland.gov.uk
dir: off M9

The magnificent ruin of a great Royal Palace, set in its own park or 'peel'. All the Stuart kings lived here, and work commissioned by James I, III, IV, and VI can be seen. The great hall and the chapel are particularly fine. James V was born here in 1512 and Mary, Queen of Scots in 1542.

Times Open all year daily, Apr-Sep 9.30-5.30; Oct-Mar 9.30-4.30. Closed 25-26 Dec & 1-2 Jan **Fees** £5.20 (ch £3.10, concessions £4.20). Please phone or check website for details* **Facilities** P shop

LIVINGSTON **Map 11 NT06**

Almond Valley Heritage Trust

Millfield EH54 7AR
☎ 01506 414957 01506 497771
e-mail: info@almondvalley.co.uk
web: www.almondvalley.co.uk
dir: 2m from M8 junct 3

A combination of fun and educational potential ideal for children, Almond Valley has a petting zoo of farm animals, an interactive museum on the shale oil industry, a narrow gauge railway, and tractor rides. Please telephone for details of events running throughout the year.

Times Open all year, daily 10-5. Closed Dec 25-26, Jan 1-2* **Facilities** P (indoor & outdoor) (fully accessible) toilets for disabled shop

SCOTTISH ISLANDS

ARRAN, ISLE OF

BRODICK **Map 10 NS03**

Brodick Castle, Garden & Country Park

KA27 8HY
☎ 0844 493 2152 0844 493 2153
e-mail: information@nts.org.uk
web: www.nts.org.uk
dir: Ferry from Ardrossan-Brodick or Lochranza-Kintyre - frequent in summer, limited in winter

The site has been fortified since Viking times, but the present castle dating from the 13th century was a stronghold of the Dukes of Hamilton. Splendid silver, fine porcelain and paintings acquired by generations of owners can be seen, including many sporting pictures and trophies. There is a magnificent woodland garden, started by the Duchess of Montrose in 1923, world famous for its rhododendrons and azaleas.

Times Castle Apr-Oct, Sun-Thu 11-4, (closes at 3 in Oct). Country Park all year, daily 9.30-sunset. Reception Centre, Walled Garden & shop Apr-Oct, daily 10-4.30, Nov-21 Dec, Fri-Sun 10-3.30. Goatfell all year, daily* **Facilities** P licensed (partly accessible) (access limited to ground floor castle & some areas of the garden unsuitable for wheelchairs) toilets for disabled (Braille, wheelchairs, motorised buggy & stairlift) shop

Isle of Arran Heritage Museum

Rosaburn KA27 8DP
☎ 01770 302636
e-mail: tom.macleod@arranmuseum.co.uk
web: www.arranmuseum.co.uk
dir: right at Brodick Pier, approx 1m

The setting is an 18th-century croft farm, including a cottage restored to its pre-1920 state and a 'smiddy' where a blacksmith worked until the late 1960s. There are also several demonstrations of horse-shoeing, sheep-shearing and weaving and spinning throughout the season - please ring for details. There is a large archaeology and geology section with archive, where help with research is available. Also, a school room set in the 1940's and a new geology display which reflects the importance of Arran in geological terms.

Times Open Apr-Oct, daily 10.30-4.30 **Fees** £3 (ch £1.50, pen £2). Family £7 **Facilities** P (outdoor) (fully accessible) toilets for disabled shop

LOCHRANZA **Map 10 NR95**

Isle of Arran Distillery Visitor Centre

KA27 8HJ
☎ 01770 830264 01770 830364
e-mail: visitorcentre@arranwhisky.com
web: www.arranwhisky.com
dir: from Brodick Ferry Terminal take coast road N for 14m. Distillery on left upon entering village

Located amidst beautiful surroundings, the distillery was built to revive the dormant traditions of Arran single malt whisky production. After a guided tour of the distillery, visitors can now taste the highly-acclaimed 10 year old single malt and cask-matured whisky. 12 year old whisky awarded 'Best Island non-Islay single malt whisky 12 years and under' in the World Whisky Awards 2009.

Times Open all year, Jan-Feb & Nov-Dec, Mon, Wed, Fri-Sat 10-4; Mar-Oct, Mon-Sat 10-6, Sun 11-6* **Facilities** P (outdoor) (partly accessible) (ground floor, shop, eating area, display area and toilets are accessible) toilets for disabled shop

SCOTLAND

BUTE, ISLE OF

ROTHESAY Map 10 NS06

Ardencraig FREE

9 Ardencraig Ln, High Craigmore PA20 9EZ
☎ 01700 504644
e-mail: enquiries@argyll-bute.gov.uk
web: www.argyll-bute.gov.uk
dir: 1m off A844, S of Rothesay

Particular attention has been paid to improving the layout of the garden and introducing rare plants. The greenhouse and walled garden produce plants for floral displays throughout the district. A variety of fish is kept in the ornamental ponds and the aviaries have some interesting birds.

Times Open May-Sep, Mon-Thu 9-4, Fri 9-3.30, Sat-Sun 1-4.30 **Facilities** (outdoor) (partly accessible) (75% nursery wheelchair accessible using ramps) toilets for disabled

Bute Museum

7 Stuart St PA20 0EP
☎ 01700 505067
e-mail: info@butemuseum.org
dir: on road behind castle

Local and natural history displays, including birds, mammals and seashore items; varied collections of recent bygones, information on WWII (especially midget submarines), a collection of early Christian crosses, and flints and pots from various Mesolithic and Neolithic burial cairns.

Times Open all year, Apr-Sep, Mon-Sat 10.30-4.30, Sun 2.30-4.30; Oct-Mar, Tue-Sat 2.30-4.30 **Fees** £2 (ch £1, pen £1.50). Please check for current admission prices* **Facilities** (partly accessible) (touch table for blind, ramps) shop

Rothesay Castle

PA20 0DA
☎ 01700 502691
web: www.historic-scotland.gov.uk

The focal point of Rothesay is this 13th-century castle. It has lofty curtain walls defended by drum towers that enclose a circular courtyard.

Times Open all year, Apr-Sep, daily, 9.30-5.30; Oct, 9.30-4.30; Nov-Mar, Mon-Wed & Sat-Sun, 9.30-4.30. Closed 25-26 Dec & 1-2 Jan **Fees** £4.20 (ch £2.50, concessions £3.40). Please phone or check website for further details* **Facilities** shop

GREAT CUMBRAE ISLAND

MILLPORT Map 10 NS15

Museum of the Cumbraes FREE

Garrison Grounds KA28 0DG
☎ 01475 531191
e-mail: namuseum@north-ayrshire.gov.uk
web: www.north-ayrshire.gov.uk/museums
dir: Ferry to Millport, from Largs Cal-Mac Terminal. Bus meets each ferry

A small museum which displays the history and life of the Cumbraes. There is also a fine collection of local photographs.

Times Open Etr-Sep, daily from 9 (Sat & Sun from 12).* **Facilities** (fully accessible) shop

HARRIS, ISLE OF

DRINISHADER Map 13 NG29

Ardbuidhe Cottage Gallery FREE

3 Drinishader HS3 3DX
☎ 01859 511218 & 511140
e-mail: williefulton@hebrides.net
web: www.williefulton.com
dir: turn off Golden Road at Drinishader

A small art gallery run by owner-artist Willie Fulton can be found in a beautiful setting in the corner of the bay in Drinishader. The gallery in a traditional Hebridean dwelling, has been converted to provide ground floor exhibition space for the artist work. Inspired by his surroundings, Willie's art is influenced by what lies outside his own studio door and the unique Harris landscape.

Times Open Apr-Oct 10-5 (at all other times by appt only) **Facilities** (outdoor) (fully accessible)

LEWIS, ISLE OF

ARNOL Map 13 NB34

The Blackhouse, Arnol

HS2 9DB
☎ 01851 710395
web: www.historic-scotland.gov.uk
dir: 11m NW of Stornoway on A858

A traditional Hebridean dwelling, built without mortar and roofed with thatch on a timber framework. It has a central peat fire in the kitchen, no chimney and a byre under the same roof.

Times Open all year, Apr-Sep, Mon-Sat 9.30-5.30; Oct-Mar, Mon-Sat 9.30-4.30. Closed 25-26 Dec & 1-2 Jan **Fees** £2.50 (ch £1.50, concessions £2). Please phone or check website for further details* **Facilities** toilets for disabled shop

CALLANISH Map 13 NB23

Calanais Visitor Centre

2 FOR 1

HS2 9DY
☎ 01851 621422 📠 01851 621446
e-mail: info@callanishvisitorcentre.co.uk
web: www.callanishvisitorcentre.co.uk
dir: 12m W of Stornoway off A859

An avenue of 19 monoliths leads north from a circle of 13 stones with rows of more stones fanning out to south, east and west. Probably constructed between 3000 and 1500BC, this is a unique cruciform of megaliths.

Times Site accessible at all times. Visitor Centre open Apr-May & Sep, Mon-Sat 10-6; Jun-Aug, Mon-Sat 10-8; Oct-Mar, Tue-Sat 10-4 **Fees** £2.50 (ch £1.20, concessions £1.90)* **Facilities** licensed (fully accessible) toilets for disabled shop

CARLOWAY Map 13 NB24

Dun Carloway Broch

FREE

☎ 1851 710395
web: www.historic-scotland.gov.uk
dir: 1.5m S of Carloway on A858

Brochs are late-prehistoric circular stone towers, and their origins are mysterious. One of the best examples can be seen at Dun Carloway, where the tower still stands about 30ft high.

Times Open at all reasonable times **Facilities**

MULL, ISLE OF

CRAIGNURE Map 10 NM73

Mull & West Highland Narrow Gauge Railway

Craignure (old pier) Station PA65 6AY
☎ 01680 812494 (in season) & 812567 📠 01680 300595
e-mail: mullrail@dee-emm.co.uk
web: www.mullrail.co.uk
dir: 0.25m from Craignure Ferry Terminal, just off road to Iona, by police station

The first passenger railway on a Scottish island, opened in 1983. Both steam and diesel trains operate on the ten-and-a-quarter inch gauge line, which runs from Craignure to Torosay Castle. The 1.25 mile line offers dramatic woodland and mountain views taking in Ben Nevis, Glencoe and the Isle of Lismore.

Times Open Etr-end Oct, 11-5* **Facilities** (outdoor) (partly accessible) (provision to carry person seated in wheelchair on trains) shop

Torosay Castle & Gardens

PA65 6AY
☎ 01680 812421 📠 01680 812470
e-mail: info@torosay.com
web: www.torosay.com
dir: 1.5m S of Ferry Terminal at Craignure

The Scottish baronial architecture of this Victorian castle is complemented by the magnificent setting, and inside the house there are displays of portraits and wildlife pictures, family scrapbooks and a study of the Antarctic. The gardens include a statue walk and water garden, an avenue of Australian gum trees, and an Oriental garden. Within the grounds there is a narrow gauge steam and diesel railway.

Times Open end Apr-Oct, daily 10.30-5. Gardens all year* **Facilities** (outdoor) shop

ORKNEY

BIRSAY Map 16 HY22

Earl's Palace

FREE

KW15 1PD
☎ 01856 721205 & 841815
web: www.historic-scotland.gov.uk
dir: on A966

The gaunt remains of the residence of the 16th-century Earl of Orkney, constructed round a courtyard.

Times Open at all reasonable times **Facilities**

DOUNBY Map 16 HY22

Brough of Birsay

KW17 2LX
☎ 01856 841815
web: www.historic-scotland.gov.uk
dir: off A966

This ruined Romanesque church stands next to the remains of a Norse village. The nave, chancel and semicircular apse can be seen, along with claustral buildings. Crossings must be made on foot at low-water - there is no boat.

Times Open mid Jun-Sep (tides permitting), daily 9.30-5.30 **Fees** £3.20 (ch £1.90, concessions £2.70)* **Facilities**

Click Mill

FREE

☎ 01856 841815
web: www.historic-scotland.gov.uk
dir: 2.5m from Dounby on B905

The last surviving horizontal water mill in Orkney, of a type well represented in Shetland and Lewis. The mill is in working condition and visitors should wear sensible footwear.

Times Open at all reasonable times **Facilities**

SCOTLAND

DOUNBY *continued*

Skara Brae Prehistoric Village

KW16 3LR
☎ 01856 841815
web: www.historic-scotland.gov.uk
dir: 19m W of Kirkwall on B9056

Engulfed in drift sand, this remarkable group of well-preserved Stone Age dwellings is the most outstanding survivor of its kind in Britain. Stone furniture and a fireplace can be seen.

Times Open all year daily, Apr-Sep 9.30-5.30; Oct-Mar 9.30-4.30. Closed 25-26 Dec & 1-2 Jan **Fees** £6.70 (ch £4, concessions £5.40). Winter: Skara Brae only £5.70 (ch £3.40, concessions £4.70) Please phone or check website for details* **Facilities** licensed toilets for disabled shop

FINSTOWN — Map 16 HY31

Maeshowe Chambered Cairn

KW16 3HA
☎ 01856 761606
web: www.historic-scotland.gov.uk
dir: 9m W of Kirkwall, on A965

The masonry of Britain's finest megalithic tomb is in a remarkably good state of preservation. Dating from neolithic times, it contains Viking carvings and runes.

Times Open all year, Apr-Sep, daily 9.30-5; Oct-Mar, daily 9.30-4.30. Closed 25-26 Dec & 1-2 Jan. (Visits must be pre-booked) **Fees** £5.20 (ch £3.10, concessions £4.20). Please phone or check website for further details* **Facilities** licensed shop

Stones of Stenness Circle and Henge — FREE

☎ 01856 841815
web: www.historic-scotland.gov.uk
dir: 5m NE of Stromness on B9055

Dating back to the second millennium BC, the remains of this stone circle are near the Ring of Brogar - a splendid circle of upright stones surrounded by a ditch.

Times Open at any reasonable time* **Facilities**

HARRAY — Map 16 HY31

Corrigall Farm & Kirbuster Museum — FREE

KW17 2JR
☎ 01856 771411 & 771268
e-mail: museum@orkney.gov.uk
web: www.orkneyheritage.com
dir: Off A986, main road through parish of Harray to parish of Birsay

The museum consists of two Orkney farmhouses with outbuildings. Kirbuster (Birsay) has the last surviving example of a 'Firehoose' with its central hearth; Corrigall (Harray) represents an improved farmhouse and steading of the late 1800s.

Times Open Mar-Oct, Mon-Sat 10.30-1 & 2-5, Sun 12-5 **Facilities** (outdoor) (fully accessible) toilets for disabled shop

KIRKWALL — Map 16 HY41

Bishop's & Earl's Palaces

KW15 1PD
☎ 01856 871918
web: www.historic-scotland.gov.uk
dir: In Kirkwall on A960

The Bishop's Palace is a hall-house of the 12th century, later much altered, with a round tower built by Bishop Reid in 1541-48. A later addition was made by the notorious Patrick Stewart, Earl of Orkney, who built the adjacent Earl's Palace between 1600 and 1607 in a splendid Renaissance style.

Times Open Apr-Sep, daily 9.30-5.30 **Fees** £3.70 (ch £2.20, concessions £3). Please phone or check website for further details* **Facilities** shop

The Orkney Museum — FREE

Broad St KW15 1DH
☎ 01856 87355 ext 2523 📠 01856 871560
e-mail: museum@orkney.gov.uk
web: www.orkney.gov.uk
dir: town centre

One of the finest vernacular town houses in Scotland, this 16th-century building now contains a museum of Orkney history, including the islands' fascinating archaeology and social history.

Times Open all year, Oct-Apr, Mon-Sat 10.30-12.30 & 1.30-5; May-Sep, Mon-Sat 10.30-5 **Facilities** (partly accessible) (5 galleries at ground level, 8 galleries require use of stair lift) toilets for disabled shop

Scapa Flow Visitor Centre & Museum — FREE

Lyness, Hoy KW16 3NU
☎ 01856 791300 📠 01856 871560
e-mail: museum@orkney.gov.uk
web: www.orkney.gov.uk
dir: on A964 to Houton, ferry crossing takes 30 mins, visitors centre 2 mins walk from ferry terminal

Also known as the Lyness Interpretation Centre, this fascinating museum is home to a large collection of military equipment used in the defence of the Orkneys during the First and Second World Wars. There are also guns salvaged from the German ships scuppered in WWII. Visitors arrive at the island after a short boat trip from the Orkney mainland.

Times Open Mar-Oct, Mon-Fri 9-4.30 (mid May-Sep also Sat-Sun 10.30-3.30) **Facilities** (fully accessible) toilets for disabled shop

STROMNESS Map 16 HY20

Orkney Maritime & Natural History Museum 2 FOR 1

52 Alfred St KW16 3DF
☎ 01856 850025
e-mail: curator@stromnessmuseum.co.uk
web: www.orkneycommunities/stromnessmuseum
dir: 0.5m from Stromess pier head

The museum focuses on Orkney's broad maritime connections, including fishing, whaling, the Hudson's Bay Company, the German Fleet in Scapa Flow, and the award-winning Pilot's House extension. The Natural History Gallery is fully restored, displaying a fine collection of curios and rare and interesting exhibits.

Times Open all year, Apr-Sep, Mon-Sun 10-5; Oct-Mar, Mon-Sat 11-3.30. Closed Xmas, New Year & 3 wks Feb-Mar **Fees** £3.50 (ch £1, concessions £2.50). Family ticket £7. All tickets are valid for 1 week* **Facilities** Ⓟ ♿ (partly accessible) (chair lift to natural history gallery) toilets for disabled (stair lift and ramps) shop

Pier Arts Centre FREE

KW16 3AA
☎ 01856 850209 📠 01856 851462
e-mail: info@pierartscentre.com
web: www.pierartscentre.com

A permanent collection of modern art and sculpture including works by Barbara Hepworth and Ben Nicholson, given to Orkney by the late Margaret Gardiner. These works are housed in a landmark 18th-century building that has served as merchant's offices, a cooperage, stores and private lodgings.

Times Open all year, Mon-Sat 10.30-5, Jul-Aug open Sun 12-4 **Facilities** Ⓟ ♿ (fully accessible) toilets for disabled shop

WESTRAY Map 16 HY44

Noltland Castle FREE

☎ 01856 841815
web: www.historic-scotland.gov.uk
dir: 1m W of Pierowall village

A fine, ruined Z-plan tower, built between 1560 and 1573 but never completed. The tower is remarkable for its large number of gun loops and impressive staircase.

Times Open mid Jun-Sep, daily 9.30-5.30 **Facilities**

SHETLAND

LERWICK Map 16 HU44

Clickimin Broch FREE

ZE1 0QX
☎ 01667 460232
web: www.historic-scotland.gov.uk
dir: 1m SW of Lerwick on A970

The remains of a prehistoric settlement that was fortified at the beginning of the Iron Age with a stone-built fort. The site was occupied for over 1000 years. The remains include a partially demolished broch (round tower) which still stands to a height of 17ft.

Times Open at all reasonable times. Key available locally
Facilities

Fort Charlotte FREE

ZE1 0JN
☎ 01667 460232
web: www.historic-scotland.gov.uk
dir: in centre of Lerwick

A five-sided artillery fort with bastions projecting from each corner. The walls are high and massive. It was built in 1665 to protect the Sound of Bressay from the Dutch, but taken by them and burned in 1673. It was rebuilt in 1781.

Times Open at all reasonable times. Key available locally
Facilities

Shetland Museum and Archives FREE

Hay's Dock ZE1 0WP
☎ 01595 695057 📠 01595 696729
e-mail: info@shetlandmuseumandarchives.org.uk
web: www.shetlandmuseumandarchives.org.uk

The Shetland Museum and Archives occupies a restored 19th century unique dockside setting and is home to 3000 artefacts telling the story of Shetland from its geological beginnings to the present day.

Times Open all year, Jan-mid May & mid Sep-Dec, Mon-Sat 10-4, Sun 12-4, mid May-mid Sep, Mon-Sat 10-5, Sun 12-5. Closed 25-26 Dec & 1-2 Jan **Facilities** Ⓟ Ⓟ licensed ♿ (fully accessible) toilets for disabled (lift, wheelchair available) shop

SCOTLAND

MOUSA ISLAND **Map 16 HU42**

Mousa Broch

FREE

☎ 01667 460232
web: www.historic-scotland.gov.uk
dir: accessible by boat from Sandwick

This broch is the best-preserved example of an Iron Age drystone tower in Scotland. The tower is nearly complete and rises to a height of 40ft. The outer and inner walls both contain staircases that may be climbed to the parapet. Boat not available all year. Contact 01950 431367 for more information.

Times Open at all reasonable times **Facilities**

SCALLOWAY **Map 16 HU33**

Scalloway Castle

FREE

ZE1 0TP
☎ 01667 460232
web: www.historic-scotland.gov.uk
dir: 6m from Lerwick on A970

The ruins of a castle designed on the medieval two-step plan. The castle was actually built in 1600 by Patrick Stewart, Earl of Orkney. When the Earl, who was renowned for his cruelty, was executed in 1615, the castle fell into disuse.

Times Telephone for details of opening times **Facilities** Ⓟ

SUMBURGH **Map 16 HU30**

Jarlshof Prehistoric & Norse Settlement

ZE3 9JN
☎ 01950 460112
web: www.historic-scotland.gov.uk
dir: at Sumburgh Head, approx 22m S of Lerwick

One of the most remarkable archaeological sites in Europe. There are remains of Bronze Age, Iron Age and Viking settlements as well as a medieval farm. There is also a 16th-century Laird's House, once the home of the Earls Robert and Patrick Stewart, and the basis of 'Jarlshof' in Sir Walter Scott's novel *The Pirate*.

Times Open Apr-Sep, daily 9.30-5.30 **Fees** £4.70 (ch £2.80, concessions £3.80). Please phone or check website for further details* **Facilities** Ⓟ shop

SKYE, ISLE OF

ARMADALE **Map 13 NG60**

Armadale Castle Gardens & Museum of the Isles

IV45 8RS
☎ 01471 844305 & 844227 01471 844275
e-mail: office@clandonald.com
web: www.clandonald.com
dir: 16m S of Broadford on A851. Follow Clan Donald Centre or Armadale Castle Gardens & Museum of the Isles signs. Easily reached by Skye Bridge or the Mallaig A830 to Armdale Ferry

Armadale Castle and Gardens were built in 1815 as the home of Lord Macdonald. The warming effect of the Gulf Stream allows exotic trees and plants to flourish. Within the 40 acres of gardens is the Museum of the Isles, where visitors can discover the history of the Highlands.

Times Open daily 9.30-5.30. Garden & Museum open Apr-Oct* **Facilities** Ⓟ licensed (outdoor) (fully accessible) toilets for disabled (wheelchairs available) shop

DUNVEGAN **Map 13 NG24**

Dunvegan Castle and Gardens

IV55 8WF
☎ 01470 521206 01470 521205
e-mail: info@dunvegancastle.com
web: www.dunvegancastle.com
dir: follow A87 over Skye Bridge. Turn onto A863 at Sligachan and continue to castle

Dunvegan Castle is the oldest continuously inhabited castle in Scotland and has been the stronghold of the chiefs of MacLeod for nearly 800 years. Originally designed to keep people out, it was first opened to visitors in 1933. Romantic and historic, the castle is set amid stunning scenery and beautiful formal gardens. The castle and estate are steeped in history and clan legend, and you can take a boat trip onto Loch Dunvegan to see the seal colony, or stay in one of the charming estate cottages. Previous visitors to the castle have included Sir Walter Scott, Dr Johnson, Queen Elizabeth II and the Japanese Emperor Akihito.

Times Open Apr-15 Oct, daily 10-5.30 (last entry 5), 16 Oct-Mar open by appointment **Fees** Castle & Gardens: £8 (ch 5-15 yrs £4, pen, students & groups £6.50)* **Facilities** Ⓟ Ⓟ licensed (outdoor) (partly accessible) (gardens, restaurant and shop fully accessible, parts of the castle are not accessible) toilets for disabled (restaurant has ramps for wheelchair access) shop

WALES

Conwy Castle at dusk

ANGLESEY, ISLE OF

BEAUMARIS Map 6 SH67

Beaumaris Castle

LL58 8AP
☎ 01248 810361
web: www.cadw.wales.gov.uk

Beaumaris was built by Edward I and took from 1295 to 1312 to complete. In later centuries it was plundered for its lead, timber and stone. Despite this it remains one of the most impressive and complete castles built by Edward I. It has a perfectly symmetrical, concentric plan, with a square inner bailey and curtain walls, round corner towers and D-shaped towers in between. There are also two great gatehouses, but these were never finished.

Times Open all year, daily, Mar-Jun & Sep-Oct 9.30-5, Jul-Aug 9.30-6; Nov-Feb, Mon-Sat 10-4, Sun 11-4 **Fees** £3.60 (ch 5-15, concessions £3.20, disabled visitors and assisting companion free). Family ticket (2ad+all ch/grandch under 16) £10.40. Group rates available. Prices quoted apply until 31 Mar 2011* **Facilities** shop

BRYNCELLI DDU Map 6 SH57

Bryn Celli Ddu Burial Chamber FREE

☎ 01443 336000
web: www.cadw.wales.gov.uk
dir: 3m W of Menai Bridge off A4080

Excavated in 1865, and then again in 1925-9, this is a prehistoric circular cairn covering a passage grave with a polygonal chamber.

Times Open all year, access available at all reasonable times, which will normally be 10-4 daily **Facilities**

BRYNSIENCYN Map 6 SH46

Anglesey Sea Zoo

LL61 6TQ
☎ 01248 430411 📠 01248 430213
e-mail: info@angleseyseazoo.co.uk
web: www.angleseyseazoo.co.uk
dir: 1st turning off Britannia Bridge onto Anglesey then follow Lobster signs along A4080 to zoo

Nestling by the Menai Straits, this all-weather undercover attraction contains a shipwreck bristling with conger eels, a lobster hatchery, a seahorse nursery, crashing waves and the enchanting fish forest.

Times Open Feb half term-late Oct half term. Telephone for times* **Facilities** licensed (outdoor) (partly accessible) toilets for disabled (2 wheelchairs available, Braille tour notes) shop

HOLYHEAD Map 6 SH28

RSPB Nature Reserve South Stack Cliffs

Plas Nico, South Stack LL65 1YH
☎ 01407 764973
e-mail: south.stack@rspb.org.uk
web: www.rspb.org.uk/reserves/southstack
dir: A5 or A55 to Holyhead follow town centre then follow brown heritage signs

South Stack Cliffs is an expanse of heathland with dramatic sea cliffs and tremendous views. In summer breeding seabirds, including puffins, can be seen from the Information Centre at Ellins Tower where telescopes are provided and staff are on hand to help. There are also large screen televisions displaying live images of the seabirds which staff can control from the information centre to give visitors an amazing 'Big Brother' type view of the breeding seabirds.

Times Open: Information Centre Etr-Sep, daily 10-5.30. Reserve open daily at all times **Fees** Free but donations to continue work are welcome **Facilities** (outdoor) (partly accessible) (natural surface paths and tracks) toilets for disabled (path RSPB car park to Ellins Tower, interactive display)

LLANALLGO Map 6 SH58

Din Llugwy Ancient Village FREE

☎ 01443 336000
web: www.cadw.wales.gov.uk
dir: 0.75m NW off A5025

The remains of a 4th-century village can be seen here. There are two circular and seven rectangular buildings, still standing up to head height and encircled by a pentagonal stone wall some 4 to 5ft thick.

Times Open all year, access available at all reasonable times, which will normally be 10-4 daily **Facilities**

PLAS NEWYDD Map 6 SH56

Plas Newydd 2 FOR 1

LL61 6DQ
☎ 01248 714795 📠 01248 713673
e-mail: plasnewydd@nationaltrust.org.uk
web: www.nationaltrust.org.uk/main/plasnewydd
dir: 2m S of Llanfairpwll, on A4080

Set amidst breathtakingly beautiful scenery and with spectacular views of Snowdonia, this elegant 18th-century house was built by James Wyatt and is an interesting mixture of Classical and Gothic. The comfortable interior, restyled in the 1930s, is famous for its association with Rex Whistler, whose largest painting is here. There is also an exhibition about his work. A military museum contains campaign relics of the 1st Marquess of Anglesey, who commanded the cavalry at the Battle of Waterloo. There is a fine spring garden and Australasian arboretum with an understorey of shrubs and wild flowers, as well as a summer terrace and, later, massed hydrangeas and autumn colour. A woodland walk gives access to a marine walk on the Menai Strait.

Times Open Apr-Oct, Sat-Wed. House 12-5, Garden 11-5.30 (last admission 4.30) **Fees** With voluntary Gift Aid donation: Home & Garden: £9 (ch £4.50). Family ticket £22.50. Garden only: £7 (ch £3.50). Visitors can choose to pay standard admission prices displayed. Check website for current prices **Facilities** (outdoor) (partly accessible) (ground floor accessible for manual wheelchairs) toilets for disabled (close parking, wheelchairs, garden shuttle, Braille guide) shop

BRIDGEND

BRIDGEND — Map 3 SS97

Newcastle — FREE

01443 336000
web: www.cadw.wales.gov.uk

The small castle dates back to the 12th century. It is ruined, but a rectangular tower, a richly carved Norman gateway and massive curtain walls enclosing a polygonal courtyard can still be seen.

Times Open all year, access available at all reasonable times, which will normally be 10-4 daily. Key keeper arrangement **Facilities**

COITY — Map 3 SS98

Coity Castle — FREE

CF35 6BG
01443 336000
web: www.cadw.wales.gov.uk
dir: 2m NE of Bridgend, off A4061

A 12th to 16th-century stronghold, with a hall, chapel and the remains of a square keep.

Times Open all year, access available at all reasonable times, which will normally be 10-4 daily. Key keeper arrangement **Facilities**

CAERPHILLY

CAERPHILLY — Map 3 ST18

Caerphilly Castle

CF8 1JL
029 2088 3143
web: www.cadw.wales.gov.uk
dir: on A469

The concentrically planned castle was begun in 1268 by Gilbert de Clare and completed in 1326. It is the largest in Wales, and has extensive land and water defences. A unique feature is the ruined tower - the victim of subsidence - which manages to out-lean even Pisa! The south dam platform, once a tournament-field, now displays replica medieval siege-engines.

Times Open all year, daily Mar-Jun & Sep-Oct 9.30-5, Jul-Aug 9.30-6: Nov-Feb, Mon-Sat 10-4, Sun 11-4 **Fees** £3.60 (ch 5-15, concessions £3.20, disabled visitors and assisting companion free). Family ticket (2ad+all ch/grandch under 16) £10.40. Group rates available. Prices quoted apply until 31 Mar 2011* **Facilities** shop

Llancaiach Fawr Manor — 2 FOR 1

Gelligaer Rd, Nelson CF46 6ER
01443 412248 01443 412688
e-mail: llancaiachfawr@caerphilly.gov.uk
web: www.llancaiachfawr.co.uk
dir: M4 junct 32, A470 to Merthyr Tydfil. Towards Ystrad Mynach A472, follow brown heritage signs

Step back in time to the Civil War period at this fascinating living history museum. The year is 1645 and visitors are invited into the Manor to meet the servants of 'Colonel' Edward Prichard - from the puritanical to the gossipy. Please telephone for details of events running throughout the year or see website.

Times Open daily 10-5 (last admission 1hr before closing). Closed Mon, Nov-Feb & 24 Dec-1 Jan **Fees** £6.50 (ch £5, concessions £5.50). Family ticket (2ad+2ch) £19* **Facilities** licensed (outdoor) (partly accessible) (2nd & 3rd floors not accessible as no lift, visitor centre & education block fully accessible) toilets for disabled (DVD players) shop

CWMCARN — Map 3 ST29

Cwmcarn Forest & Campsite

Nantcarn Rd NP11 7FA
01495 272001 01495 279306
e-mail: cwmcarn-vc@caerphilly.gov.uk
web: www.cwmcarnforest.co.uk
dir: 8m N of Newport on A467, follow brown tourist signs

A seven-mile scenic drive with spectacular views over the Bristol Channel and surrounding countryside. Facilities include barbecues, picnic and play areas, and forest and mountain walks. There is also a mountain bike trail and downhill trail on site. Special events are held throughout the year, please ring for details or visit the website.

Times Open Forest Drive: Mar & Oct 11-5; Apr-Aug 11-7; Sep, 11-6; Nov-Feb 11-4 (wknds only). Visitor Centre open daily; Etr-Sep Mon-Thu 9-5, Fri-Sun 9-5; Oct-Etr, Mon-Thu & Sat-Sun 9-5, Fri 9-4.30 (last entry 1 hr before closing). Please phone for Xmas & New Year opening times **Fees** Cars & Motorcycles £5, Minibus £10, Coaches £20. Car season ticket £20* **Facilities** (outdoor) (fully accessible) toilets for disabled shop

WALES

CARDIFF

CARDIFF Map 3 ST17

Cardiff Castle

Castle St CF10 3RB
☎ 029 2087 8100 🖷 029 2023 1417
e-mail: cardiffcastle@cardiff.gov.uk
web: www.cardiffcastle.com
dir: from M4, A48 & A470 follow signs to city centre

Cardiff Castle is situated in the heart of the city. Contained within its mighty walls is a history spanning nearly 2000 years, dating from the coming of the Romans to the Norman Conquest and beyond. Discover spectacular interiors and enjoy magnificent views of the city from the top of the 12th-century Norman keep. The new Interpretation Centre includes a film presentation and a audio guide around the Castle grounds. Regular events throughout the year include an open air theatre, medieval and Roman re-enactments and much more.

Times Open all year daily, Mar-Oct 9-6; Nov-Feb 9-5 (last entry 1 hr before close). Closed 25-26 Dec & 1 Jan **Fees** Essential ticket: £10.50 (ch £7.95, pen £9). Premium Tour Ticket £13.50 (ch £10, pen £11.50)* **Facilities** Ⓟ ☕ ♿ (partly accessible) (Castle apartments and Norman Keep not accessible to wheelchair users, cobblestone path at entrance, castle grounds accessible) toilets for disabled (ramp & lift within Interpretation Centre, audio guide) shop 🚫

Dyffryn Gardens

St Nicholas CF5 6SU
☎ 029 2059 3328 🖷 029 2059 1966
e-mail: dyffryn@valeofglamorgan.gov.uk
web: www.dyffryngardens.org.uk
dir: A4232 towards Barry, rdbt take 1st exit, exit at junct with A48/A4050. At Culverhouse Cross rdbt take 4th exit A48 signed Cowbridge. Left at lights in St Nicholas village, Dyffryn on right after 1.5m

Set in the heart of the Vale of Glamorgan, this exceptional example of Edwardian garden design is the result of a unique collaboration between landscape architect Thomas Mawson and plant collector Reginald Cory. The 55 acres of garden boast splendid lawns, an arboretum of rare and unusual trees, and a beautiful selection of intimate outdoor garden rooms.

Times Open all year, Apr-Oct 10-6; Nov-Feb 10-4 **Fees** £6.50 (ch £2.50, concessions £4.50, disabled £2.50) Family (2ad&4ch) £17* **Facilities** Ⓟ ☕ 🧺 (outdoor) ♿ (partly accessible) (arboretum not suitable for wheelchairs) toilets for disabled (wheelchairs for hire, parking) shop

Llandaff Cathedral

Llandaff CF5 2LA
☎ 029 2056 4554 🖷 029 2056 3897
e-mail: office@llandaffcathedral.org.uk
web: www.llandaffcathedral.org.uk
dir: W on M4 junct 29 to A48(M), then onto A48 and follow brown signs. E on M4 junct 32 onto A470 towards Cardiff, leave A48 and follow brown signs

A medieval cathedral begun in the 12th century on the site of an early Christian place of worship. The cathedral was severely damaged during the bombing raids on Cardiff during World War II. The interior is dominated by a modernistic post-war 'Christ in Majesty' sculpture by Epstein. Please visit website for details of events running throughout the year.

Times Open all year, daily 8-7; Sun 7-7 & Mon 8.30-7* **Facilities** Ⓟ ♿ (partly accessible) (wheelchair access is provided at the East and West ends of the Cathedral) (wheelchair available) shop 🚫

Millennium Stadium Tours

Millennium Stadium, Westgate St, Gate 3 CF10 1JA
☎ 029 2082 2228 🖷 029 2082 2151
e-mail: mgibbons@wru.co.uk
web: www.millenniumstadium.com/tours
dir: A470 to city centre. Westgate St opposite Castle far end. Turn by Angel Hotel on corner of Westgate Street.

In the late 1990s this massive stadium was completed as part of an effort to revitalise Welsh fortunes. It replaced Cardiff Arms Park, and now hosts major music events, exhibitions, and international rugby and soccer matches. Its capacity of around 75,000 and its retractable roof make it unique in Europe. The home of Welsh Rugby and Welsh Football.

Times Open all year, Mon-Sat 10-5; Sun 10-4 **Fees** £6.50 (ch up to 16 £4, ch under 5 free, concessions £4.50). Family (2ad+3ch) £18* **Facilities** Ⓟ ♿ (fully accessible) toilets for disabled (lifts, escalators, disabled parking) shop 🚫

National Museum Cardiff

Cathays Park CF10 3NP
☎ 029 2039 7951 🖷 029 2057 3321
e-mail: post@museumwales.ac.uk
web: www.museumwales.ac.uk
dir: in Civic Centre. M4 junct 32, A470, 5 mins walk from city centre & 20 mins walk from bus & train station

National Museum Cardiff is home to spectacular collections from Wales and all over the world. The Museum showcases displays of art, archaeology, geology and natural history all under one roof. The new archaeology gallery, 'Origins in search of early Wales', traces life in Wales from the earliest humans 230,000 years ago. Explore the past through themes such as conflict, power, wealth, family and the future - are we really so different today? Discover stories behind some of Wales' most famous works of art in the new art galleries, which now include activity stations and touch screens to help bring the paintings to life. You can also enjoy changing displays drawn from the collection of Impressionist and Post-Impressionist paintings, including work by Monet, Renoir and Cézanne. Or how about a close encounter with The

Big Bang, erupting volcanoes, dinosaurs and woolly mammoths on the journey through time and space?

Times Open all year, Tue-Sun 10-5, open most BHs. Telephone for Xmas opening times **Fees** Free admission but charge may be made for some events **Facilities** licensed (fully accessible) toilets for disabled (wheelchair available, Tel 029 2057 3509 for access guide) shop

Techniquest

Stuart St CF10 5BW

029 2047 5475 029 2048 2517

e-mail: info@techniquest.org

web: www.techniquest.org

dir: A4232 to Cardiff Bay

Located in the heart of the Cardiff Bay, there's always something new to explore at this exciting science discovery centre. Journey into space in the planetarium, enjoy an interactive Science Theatre Show or experience one of the 120 hands-on exhibits. Please visit website for details of events running throughout the year.

Times Open all year, school days 9.30-4.30; all other times 10-5. Closed Xmas* **Facilities** (fully accessible) toilets for disabled (lift, hearing loop) shop

ST FAGANS — Map 3 ST17

St Fagans: National History Museum

CF5 6XB

029 2057 3500 029 2057 3490

web: www.museumwales.ac.uk

dir: 4m W of Cardiff on A4232. From M4 exit at junct 33 and follow brown signs

A stroll around the indoor galleries and 100 acres of beautiful grounds will give you a fascinating insight into how people in Wales have lived, worked and spent their leisure hours since Celtic times. You can see people practising the traditional means of earning a living, the animals they kept and at certain times of year, the ways in which they celebrated the seasons.

Times Open all year daily, 10-5. Closed 24-26 Dec **Fees** Free admission. Charge may apply to some events **Facilities** licensed (outdoor) (partly accessible) (wheelchair access possible to most parts) toilets for disabled (wheelchairs, motorised buggy-must pre-book) shop

TONGWYNLAIS — Map 3 ST18

Castell Coch

CF15 7JS

029 2081 0101

web: www.cadw.wales.gov.uk

dir: A470 to Tongwynlais junct, then B4262 to castle on top of hill

Castell Coch is Welsh for 'red castle', an appropriate name for this fairy-tale building with its red sandstone walls and conical towers. The castle was originally built in the 13th century but fell into ruins, and the present castle is a late-19th-century creation. Inside, the castle is decorated in fantasy style.

Times Open all year, daily Mar-Jun & Sep-Oct 9.30-5, Jul-Aug 9.30-6: Nov-Feb, Mon-Sat 10-4, Sun 11-4. Closed for conservation 1-28 Jan **Fees** £3.60 (ch 5-15, concessions £3.20, disabled visitors and assisting companion free). Family ticket (2ad+all ch/grandch under 16) £10.40. Group rates available. Prices quoted apply until 31 Mar 2011* **Facilities** shop

CARMARTHENSHIRE

ABERGWILI — Map 2 SN42

Carmarthenshire County Museum — FREE

SA31 2JG

01267 228696 01267 223830

e-mail: museums@carmarthenshire.gov.uk

web: www.carmarthenshire.gov.uk/

dir: 2m E of Carmarthen, just off A40, at Abergwili rdbt

Housed in the old palace of the Bishop of St David's and set in seven acres of grounds, the museum offers a wide range of local subjects to explore, from geology and prehistory to butter making, Welsh furniture and folk art. Temporary exhibitions are held.

Times Open all year, Mon-Sat 10-4.30. Closed Xmas-New Year **Facilities** (outdoor) (fully accessible) toilets for disabled (lift) shop

CARREG CENNEN CASTLE — Map 3 SN61

Carreg Cennen Castle

SA19 6UA

01558 822291

web: www.cadw.wales.gov.uk

dir: unclass road from A483 to Trapp village

A steep path leads up to the castle, which is spectacularly sited on a limestone crag. It was first built as a stronghold of the native Welsh and then rebuilt in the late 13th century. Most remarkable among the impressive remains is a mysterious passage, cut into the side of the cliff and lit by loopholes. The farm at the site has a rare breeds centre.

Times Open all year daily, Apr-Oct 9.30-6.30; Nov-Mar 9.30-4 **Fees** £3.60 (ch 5-15, concessions £3.20, disabled visitors & assisting companion free). Family ticket (2ad+all ch/grandch under 16) £10.40. Group rates available. Prices quoted apply until 31 Mar 2011* **Facilities** shop

WALES

DRE-FACH FELINDRE Map 2 SN33

National Woollen Museum

SA44 5UP
☎ 01559 370929 📠 01559 371592
e-mail: post@museumwales.ac.uk
web: www.museumwales.ac.uk
dir: 16m W of Carmarthen off A484, 4m E of Newcastle Emlyn

The museum is housed in the former Cambrian Mills and has a comprehensive display tracing the evolution of the industry from its beginnings to the present day. Demonstrations of the fleece to fabric process are given on 19th-century textile machinery.

Times Open all year, Apr-Sep, daily 10-5; Oct-Mar, Tue-Sat 10-5. Phone for details of Christmas opening times **Fees** Free admission but charge may be made for some events **Facilities** (outdoor) (fully accessible) toilets for disabled (wheelchair access to ground floor & ample seating) shop

DRYSLWYN Map 2 SN52

Dryslwyn Castle

FREE

☎ 01443 336000
web: www.cadw.wales.gov.uk
dir: on B4279

The ruined 13th-century castle was a stronghold of the native Welsh. It stands on a lofty mound, and was important in the struggles between English and Welsh. It is gradually being uncovered by excavation.

Times Open-entrance by arrangement with Dryslwyn Farm **Facilities**

KIDWELLY Map 2 SN40

Kidwelly Castle

SA17 5BQ
☎ 01554 890104
web: www.cadw.wales.gov.uk
dir: via A484

This is an outstanding example of late 13th-century castle design, with its 'walls within walls' defensive system. There were later additions made to the building, the chapel dating from about 1400. Of particular interest are two vast circular ovens.

Times Open all year, daily Mar-Jun & Sep-Oct 9.30-5, Jul-Aug 9.30-6: Nov-Feb, Mon-Sat 10-4, Sun 11-4 **Fees** £3 (ch 5-15, concessions £2.60, disabled visitors & assisting companion free). Family ticket (2ad+all ch/grandch under 16) £8.60. Group rates available. Prices quoted apply until 31 Mar 2011* **Facilities** toilets for disabled shop

Kidwelly Industrial Museum

Broadford SA17 4LW
☎ 01554 891078
dir: signed from Kidwelly bypass & town, stack visible from bypass

Two of the great industries of Wales are represented in this museum: tinplate and coal mining. The original buildings and machinery of the Kidwelly tinplate works, where tinplate was hand made, are now on display to the public. There is also an exhibition of coal mining with pit-head gear and a winding engine, while the more general history of the area is shown in a separate exhibition.

Times Open Etr, Jun-Sep, BH wknds, Mon-Fri 10-5, Sat-Sun 12-5 (last admission 4). Other times by arrangement for parties only* **Facilities** (outdoor) (fully accessible) toilets for disabled (ramps on entrances) shop

LAUGHARNE Map 2 SN31

Dylan Thomas' Boat House

Dylans Walk SA33 4SD
☎ 01994 427420 📠 01994 427420
e-mail: dylanthomas@carmarthenshire.gov.uk
web: www.dylanthomasboathouse.com
dir: 14m SW of Carmarthen

The home of Dylan Thomas and his family during the last four turbulent and creative years of his life. The house and its surrounding estuary, town and countryside feature considerably in the poet's work, including his famous *Under Milk Wood*. The house contains interpretive display, original furniture, bookshop and tearoom. Please telephone for details of events running throughout the year.

Times Open all year daily, May-Oct & Etr wknd 10-5.30; Nov-Apr 10.30-3.30 (last admission 30 mins before close)* **Facilities** (not accessible for wheelchairs) shop

Laugharne Castle

King St SA33 4SA
☎ 01994 427906
web: www.cadw.wales.gov.uk
dir: on A4066

Newly opened to the public, picturesque Laugharne Castle stands on a low ridge overlooking the wide Taff Estuary. A medieval fortress converted into an Elizabethan mansion, it suffered a civil war siege and later became the backdrop for elaborate Victorian gardens, now recreated. Laugharne Castle has also inspired two modern writers - Richard Hughes and Dylan Thomas.

Times Open Apr-Oct, daily 10-5 **Fees** £3 (ch 5-15, concessions £2.60, disabled visitors & assisting companion free). Family ticket (2ad+all ch/grandch under 16) £8.60. Group rates available. Prices quoted apply until 31 Mar 2011* **Facilities** toilets for disabled shop

WALES

LLANARTHNE Map 2 SN52

The National Botanic Garden of Wales

SA32 8HG
☎ 01558 668768 01558 668933
e-mail: info@gardenofwales.org.uk
web: www.gardenofwales.org.uk
dir: 8m E of Carmarthen on A48, dedicated intersection - signed

Set amongst 568 acres of Parkland in the beautiful Towy Valley in West Wales, just 7 miles from Carmarthen. The Gardens centrepiece is the Great Glasshouse, an amazing tilted glass dome with a six-metre ravine. The Mediterranean landscape enables the visitor to experience the aftermath of an Australian bush fire, pause in an olive grove or wander through Fuchsia collections from Chile. The Tropical House features orchids, palms and other tropical plants. A 220 metre herbaceous board walk forms the spine of the garden and leads to the children's play area and our 360°-surround screen cinema to the Old Stables Courtyard. Here the visitor can view art exhibitions, wander in the gift shop or enjoy a meal in the restaurant. Land train tours will take the visitor around the necklace of lakes, which surround the central garden.

Times Open all year, 24 Mar-26 Oct 10-6; 27 Oct-22 Mar 10-4.30* **Facilities** licensed (outdoor) (partly accessible) toilets for disabled (Braille interpretation, wheelchairs/scooters shuttle service) shop

LLANDEILO Map 3 SN62

Dinefwr Park and Castle 2 FOR 1

SA19 6RT
☎ 01558 823902 & 825912 01558 822036
e-mail: dinefwr@nationaltrust.org.uk
web: www.nationaltrust.org.uk/main/w-dinefwrpark
dir: off A40 Carmarthenshire, on W outskirts of Llandeilo

At the heart of Welsh history for a thousand years, the Park as we know it today took shape in the years after 1775 when the medieval castle, house, gardens, woods and deer park were integrated into one vast and breathtaking landscape. The 'hands-on' Newton House gives visitors an atmospheric experience set in 1912.

Times Open daily 14 Feb-Jun & Sep-Oct, 11-5; Jul-Aug 11-6; 5 Nov-19 Dec 11-4 (last admission 30 mins before close) **Fees** With Gift Aid donation £6.70 (ch £3.35). Family ticket £16.75. Party 15+ £5.70. Without Gift Aid donation £6.09 (ch £3.04). Family ticket £15.22* **Facilities** (outdoor) (partly accessible) (some walks around property are not suitable for wheelchairs) toilets for disabled shop

LLANELLI Map 2 SN50

WWT National Wetland Centre Wales

Llwynhendy SA14 9SH
☎ 01554 741087 01554 744101
e-mail: info.llanelli@wwt.org.uk
web: www.wwt.org.uk
dir: 3m E of Llanelli, off A484

Stretching over 97 hectares on the Burry Inlet, the centre is Wales' premier site for water birds and waders and is home to countless wild species as diverse as dragonflies and Little Egrets. The beautifully landscaped grounds are home to over 650 of some of the world's most spectacular ducks, swans, geese and flamingos - many so tame they feed from the hand. There is also a discovery centre and outdoor activities for visitors including a Canoe Safari, Water Vole City, Pond Dipping Zone and Bike Trail.

Times Open all year, daily 9.30-5 (ex 24-25 Dec). Grounds open until 6 in the summer* **Facilities** licensed (indoor & outdoor) (partly accessible) (tower inaccessible) toilets for disabled (wheelchair/mobility scooter, special viewing areas) shop

LLANGATHEN Map 2 SN52

Aberglasney Gardens

SA32 8QH
☎ 01558 668998 01558 668998
e-mail: info@aberglasney.org
web: www.aberglasney.org
dir: 4m W of Llandeilo, follow signs from A40

Aberglasney is a 10-acre garden, containing a variety of rare and unusual plants, providing interest throughout the seasons. At its heart is a unique and fully restored Elizabethan/Jacobean cloister and parapet walk, plus the award-winning garden created within the ruinous courtyard of the mansion. Please telephone for details of events running throughout the year.

Times Open all year daily, Apr-Oct 10-6 (last entry 5); Nov-Mar 10.30-4. Closed 25 Dec **Facilities** licensed (outdoor) (partly accessible) (access to garden restricted in some areas, steps, uneven ground & slopes) toilets for disabled (garden route map, wheelchairs available, parking) shop

WALES

LLANSTEFFAN Map 2 SN31

Llansteffan Castle FREE

☎ 01443 336000
web: www.cadw.wales.gov.uk
dir: off B4312

The ruins of this 11th to 13th century stronghold stand majestically on the west side of the Towy estuary.

Times Open all year, access available at all reasonable times, which will normally be 10-4 daily. Key keeper arrangement **Facilities**

PUMSAINT Map 3 SN64

Dolaucothi Gold Mines 2 FOR 1

SA19 8US
☎ 01558 650177 & 825912 01588 651919
e-mail: dolaucothi@nationaltrust.org.uk
web: www.nationaltrust.org.uk/main/w-dolaucothigoldmines
dir: on A482, signed both directions

Turn prospector in the only known Roman goldmine in Britain. Explore the underground working, wearing a miner's lamp and helmet on a guided tour. Have a go at gold panning and take the opportunity to experience the frustrations of searching for specks of gold.

Times Open mid Mar-Jun & Sep-Oct, daily 11-5; Jul-Aug 10-6 **Fees** With Gift Aid donation: £3.60 (ch £1.80). Family ticket £9. Without Gift aid donation: £3.27 (ch £1.63) Family ticket £8.18. Guided underground tours £3.80 (ch £1.90). Family ticket £9.50* **Facilities** (outdoor) (partly accessible) (only one underground tour accessible, most other areas accessible, walks vary in accessibility) toilets for disabled shop

WALES

CEREDIGION

ABERAERON Map 2 SN46

Llanerchaeron

Llanerchaeron, Ciliau Aeron SA48 8DG
☎ 01545 570200 01545 571759
e-mail: llanerchaeron@nationaltrust.org.uk
web: www.nationaltrust.org.uk
dir: 2.5m E of Aberaeron off A482

Llanerchaeron, a few miles inland from Aberaeron on the Cardigan Bay coast, is centred round a Regency Villa designed by John Nash. The self sufficient country estate, villa, service courtyard, grounds, working organic farm and outbuildings remain virtually unaltered. The 18th-century estate features; the Walled Garden and farm complex, mature woodland and ornamental lake, vast parkland and farmland containing Llanwennog sheep and Welsh Black Cattle. Produce and plants from the walled gardens are sold in the visitor building. Please telephone for details of events running throughout the year.

Times Open Feb-Dec, 11-5 (last admission 1hr before closing). Also open some evenings. Please check website for updates **Fees** £7.10 (ch £3.60). Family ticket (2ad+2ch) £17.80. Special group rates available **Facilities** (outdoor) (partly accessible) (upstairs of villa not accessible) toilets for disabled (ramp access to villa, wheelchair, Braille guide) shop

ABERYSTWYTH Map 6 SN58

The National Library of Wales

Penglais SY23 3BU
☎ 01970 632800 01970 615709
e-mail: holi@llgc.org.uk
web: www.llgc.org.uk
dir: Off Penglais Hill, A487 in N area of Aberystwyth

The largest library in Wales celebrated its hundred birthday in 2007. Its collections include books, manuscripts, archival documents, maps and photographs as well as paintings, film, video and sound recordings. The library is recognised as the leading research centre for Welsh and Celtic studies, and is popular with those studying family history. Lectures, screenings and conferences throughout the year. There are constantly changing exhibitions in the galleries and exhibition halls. Free guided tour every Monday morning at 11am. Group guided tours available by prior arrangement.

Times Open Mon-Fri 9.30-6, Sat 9.30-5.30 (Gallery closes at 4.30) **Fees** Free. Admission to reading rooms available by readers ticket, two proofs of identity required, one including address. Free admission to all exhibitions* **Facilities** licensed (outdoor) (fully accessible) toilets for disabled (lift) shop

CENARTH Map 2 SN24

The National Coracle Centre

Cenarth Falls SA38 9JL
☎ 01239 710980
e-mail: martinfowler7@aol.com
web: www.coracle-centre.co.uk
dir: on A484 between Carmarthen and Cardigan, centre of Cenarth village, beside bridge and river

Situated by the beautiful Cenarth Falls, this fascinating museum has a unique collection from all over the world, including Tibet, India, Iraq, Vietnam, and North America. Cenarth has long been a centre for coracle fishing, and coracle rides are often available in the village during the summer holiday. Look out for the salmon leap by the flour mill.

Times Open Etr-Oct, daily 10.30-5.30. All other times by appointment* **Facilities** (partly accessible) (top floor of mill inaccessible for disabled) shop

EGLWYS FACH **Map 6 SN69**

RSPB Nature Reserve Ynys-hir

Visitor Centre, Cae'r Berllan SY20 8TA
☎ 01654 700222 01654 700333
e-mail: ynyshir@rspb.org.uk
web: www.rspb.org.uk
dir: 6m S of Machynlleth on A487 in Eglwysfach. Signed from main road

The mixture of different habitats is home to an abundance of birds and wildlife. The saltmarshes in winter support the only regular wintering flock of Greenland white-fronted geese in England and Wales, in addition to peregrines, hen harriers and merlins. The sessile oak woodland is home to pied flycatchers, wood warblers, and redstarts in the summer, but woodpeckers, nuthatches, red kites, sparrowhawks and buzzards are here all year round. Otters, polecats, 30 butterfly and 15 dragonfly species are also present. Guided walks and children's activities. Please telephone for details of events running throughout the year.

Times Open all year, daily 9am-9pm (or sunset if earlier). Visitor Centre: Apr-Oct daily 9-5; Nov-Mar Wed-Sun 10-4* **Facilities** (outdoor) (partly accessible) (can take car to viewpoint) shop

FELINWYNT **Map 2 SN25**

Felinwynt Rainforest Centre

SA43 1RT
☎ 01239 810882 & 810250 01239 810465
e-mail: dandjdevereux@btinternet.com
web: www.butterflycentre.co.uk
dir: from A487 Blaenannerch Airfield turning, onto B4333. Signed 6m N of Cardigan

A chance to wander amongst free-flying exotic butterflies accompanied by the recorded wildlife sounds of the Peruvian Amazon. A waterfall, ponds and streams contribute to a humid tropical atmosphere and provide a habitat for fish and native amphibians. See the exhibition of rainforests of Peru and around the world. Free paper and crayons to borrow for children.

Times Open daily, Apr-Oct, 10-5; Oct 11-4 **Fees** £4.50 (ch 3-14 £2.50, concessions £4.25)* **Facilities** (outdoor) (fully accessible) toilets for disabled shop

STRATA FLORIDA **Map 3 SN76**

Strata Florida Abbey

SY25 6ES
☎ 01974 831261
web: www.cadw.wales.gov.uk
dir: unclassified road from Pontrhydfendigaid, accessed from B4340

Little remains of the Cistercian abbey founded in 1164, except the ruined church and cloister. Strata Florida was an important centre of learning in the Middle Ages, and it is believed that the 14th-century poet Dafyd ap Gwilym was buried here.

Times Open Apr-Sep, 10-5. Open 10-4 daily and unstaffed with no admission charge at all other times **Fees** £3 (ch 5-15, concessions £2.60, disabled visitors & assisting companion free). Family ticket (2ad+all ch/grandch under 16) £8.60. Group discounts available. Prices quoted apply until 31 Mar 2011* **Facilities** shop

CONWY

BETWS-Y-COED **Map 6 SH75**

Conwy Valley Railway Museum

Old Goods Yard LL24 0AL
☎ 01690 710568 01690 710132
e-mail: info@conwyrailwaymuseum.co.uk
web: www.conwyrailwaymuseum.co.uk
dir: signed from A5 into Old Church Rd, adjacent to train station

The two large museum buildings have displays on both the narrow and standard-gauge railways of North Wales, including railway stock and other memorabilia. There are working model railway layouts, a steam-hauled miniature railway in the grounds, which cover over four acres, and a 15inch-gauge tramway to the woods. The latest addition is the quarter-size steam 'Britannia' loco that is now on display. For children there are mini-dodgems, Postman Pat, a school bus and Toby Tram. There is a large model railway in the B R Coach.

Times Open all year daily, 10-5.30. Closed 25-26 Dec
Fees £1.50 (ch & concessions 80p). Family ticket £4. Steam train ride £1.50. Tram ride £1 **Facilities** licensed (outdoor) (fully accessible) toilets for disabled (ramps & clearances for wheelchairs) shop

CERRIGYDRUDION **Map 6 SH94**

Llyn Brenig Visitor Centre

LL21 9TT
☎ 01490 420463 01490 420694
e-mail: llyn.brenig@dwrcymru.com
web: www.dwrcymru.com
dir: on B4501 between Denbigh & Cerrigydrudion

The 1800-acre estate has a unique archaeological trail and round-the-lake walk of 10 miles. A hide is available and disabled anglers are catered for with a specially adapted fishing boat and an annual open day. The centre has an exhibition on archaeology, history and conservation, and an audio-visual programme.

Times Open mid Mar-Oct, daily 9-5* **Facilities** (outdoor) (fully accessible) toilets for disabled (boats for disabled & fishing open days) shop

WALES

COLWYN BAY — Map 6 SH87

Welsh Mountain Zoo

Old Highway LL28 5UY
☎ 01492 532938 🖷 01492 530498
e-mail: info@welshmountainzoo.org
web: www.welshmountainzoo.org
dir: A55 junct 20 signed Rhos-on-Sea. Zoo signed

Set high above Colwyn Bay with panoramic views and breath-taking scenery, this caring conservation zoo is set among beautiful gardens. Among the animals are many rare and endangered species, and there are daily shows which include Penguins Playtime, Chimp Encounter, Sealion Feeding and Birds of Prey.

Times Open all year daily, Apr-Oct 9.30-6; Nov-Mar 9.30-5. Closed 25 Dec **Fees** £9.85 (ch 3-15 & students £7.25, pen £8.60). Family ticket (2ad+3ch) £31.10. Admission is free for visitors confined to a wheelchair* **Facilities** licensed (outdoor) (partly accessible) (approx 70% of exhibits are viewable by wheelchair) toilets for disabled (wheelchairs for hire) shop

CONWY — Map 6 SH77

Aberconwy House

LL32 8AY
☎ 01492 592246 🖷 01492 564818
e-mail: aberconwyhouse@nationaltrust.org.uk
web: www.nationaltrust.org.uk
dir: Llanerchaeron is situated 2.5m E of Aberdeen off the A482 & signed off the A55 expressway

This house dates from the 14th century; it is the only medieval merchant's house in Conwy to have survived the centuries of turbulence, fire and pillage in this frontier town. Furnished rooms and an audio-visual presentation show daily life in the house at different periods in its history.

Times Open 31 Mar-4 Nov, Wed-Mon 11-5 (last admission 30 mins before closing)* **Facilities** Ⓟ shop

Conwy Castle

LL32 8AY
☎ 01492 592358
web: www.cadw.wales.gov.uk
dir: via A55 or B5106

The castle is a magnificent fortress, built 1283-7 by Edward I. There is an exhibition on castle chapels on the ground floor of the Chapel Tower. The castle forms part of the same defensive system as the extensive town walls, which are among the most complete in Europe.

Times Open all year, daily Mar-Jun & Sep-Oct 9.30-5, Jul-Aug 9.30-6: Nov-Feb, Mon-Sat 10-4, Sun 11-4 **Fees** £4.60 (ch 5-15, concessions £4.10, disabled visitors & assisting companion free). Family ticket £13.30. Joint ticket for both monuments £6.85 (ch 5-15 & concessions £5.85, disabled visitors & assisting companion free). Family £19.55. Group rates available. Prices quoted apply until 31 Mar 2011* **Facilities** toilets for disabled shop

Conwy Suspension Bridge

LL32 8LD
☎ 01492 573282 🖷 01492 564818
e-mail: david.jennings@nationaltrust.org.uk
web: www.nationaltrust.org.uk
dir: adjacent to Conwy Castle

Designed by Thomas Telford, one of the greatest engineers of the late 18th and early 19th century, this was the first bridge to span the river at Conwy. The bridge has been restored and the toll house furnished as it would have been a century ago.

Times Open daily 27 Mar-1 Nov, 10-5* **Facilities** Ⓟ (partly accessible)

Plas Mawr

High St LL32 8DE
☎ 01492 580167
web: www.cadw.wales.gov.uk

Plas Mawr is an excellent example of an Elizabethan townhouse. Built by Robert Wynn between 1576 and 1585, the interior remains almost unaltered and displays decorated plaster ceilings and wooden screens.

Times Open Apr-Sep, Tue-Sun 9-5, open BH Mon; Oct, Tue-Sun 9.30-4 **Fees** £4.95 (ch 5-15, concessions £4.60, disabled visitors & assisting companion free). Family ticket £14.50. Joint ticket for both monuments £6.85 (ch 5-15 & concessions £5.85, disabled visitors & assisting companion free). Family £19.55. Group rates available. Prices quoted apply until 31 Mar 2011* **Facilities** shop

Smallest House — 2 FOR 1

The Quay LL32 8BB
☎ 01492 593484
dir: leave A55 at Conwy sign, through town, at bottom of High St for the quay, turn left

The 'Guinness Book of Records' lists this as the smallest house in Britain. Just 6ft wide by 10ft high, it is furnished in the style of a mid-Victorian Welsh cottage.

Times Open Apr-May & Oct 10-5; Jul-Sep 10-6 **Fees** £1 (ch 5-16 50p, under 5 free) **Facilities** Ⓟ (partly accessible) (access to ground floor only) shop

DOLWYDDELAN — Map 6 SH75

Dolwyddelan Castle

LL25 0JD
☎ 01690 750366
web: www.cadw.wales.gov.uk
dir: on A470 Blaenau Ffestiniog to Betws-y-Coed

The castle is reputed to be the birthplace of Llywelyn the Great. It was captured in 1283 by Edward I, who immediately began strengthening it for his own purposes. A restored keep of around 1200, and a 13th-century curtain wall can be seen. An exhibition on the castles of the Welsh Princes is located in the keep.

Times Open Apr-Sep, Mon-Sat 10-5 & Sun 11.30-4; Oct-Mar, Mon-Sat 10-4, Sun 11.30-4 **Fees** £2.60 (ch 5-15, concessions

£2.25, disabled visitors & assisting companion free). Family ticket (2ad+all ch/grandch under 16) £7.50. Group rates available. Prices quoted apply until 31 Mar 2011* **Facilities**

LLANDUDNO Map 6 SH78

Great Orme Bronze Age Copper Mines

Pyliau Rd, Great Orme LL30 2XG
☎ 01492 870447
e-mail: gomines@greatorme.freeserve.co.uk
web: www.greatormemines.info
dir: Follow 'ancient mine' signs from Llandudno

Browse in the visitor centre with a model of a Bronze Age village. Take a look at some original 4,000 year old artefacts and a selection of mining tools. After watching two short films take a helmet and make your way down to the mines. Walking through tunnels mined nearly 4,000 years ago look into some of the smaller tunnels and get a feel for the conditions our prehistoric ancestors faced in their search for valuable copper ores. Excavation on the surface will continue for decades and one of the team is usually available to answer visitor's questions as they walk around the site and view the prehistoric landscape being uncovered.

Times Open mid Mar-end Oct, daily 10-5 **Fees** £6 (ch £4, under 5's free). Family ticket (2ad+2ch) £16, extra child £3* **Facilities** (outdoor) (partly accessible) (no wheelchair access to underground mine) toilets for disabled (paved walkways and ramps) shop

LLANDUDNO JUNCTION Map 6 SH77

RSPB Nature Reserve Conwy 2 FOR 1

LL31 9XZ
☎ 01492 584091
e-mail: conwy@rspb.org.uk
web: www.rspb.org.uk/conwy
dir: signed from junct 18 of A55

Explore the quiet nature trails, get close up experience with birds and other wildlife, or enjoy a leisurely cup of coffee or lunch while drinking in the magnificent views of Conwy Castle and Snowdonia. Lots of activities to keep small people happy and lots to interest big kids too. 2011 is RSPB Cymru's centenary year so check website for details of special events taking place to mark the event.

Times Open all year, daily 9.30-5. Closed 25 Dec **Fees** £2.50 (ch £1, concessions £1.50). Family £5 **Facilities** (outdoor) (fully accessible) toilets for disabled (free use of wheelchair) shop

LLANRWST Map 6 SH86

Gwydyr Uchaf Chapel FREE

☎ 01492 640578
web: www.cadw.wales.gov.uk
dir: 0.5m SW off B5106

Built in the 17th century by Sir John Wynn of Gwydir Castle, the chapel is noted for its painted ceiling and wonderfully varied woodwork.

Times Open all year, access available at all reasonable times, which will normally be 10-4 daily. Key keeper arrangement **Facilities**

PENMACHNO Map 6 SH75

Ty Mawr Wybrnant

LL25 0HJ
☎ 01690 760213
e-mail: tymawrwybrnant@nationaltrust.org.uk
web: www.nationaltrust.org.uk
dir: From A5 3m S of Betws-y-Coed take B4406 to Penmachno. House is 2.5m NW of Penmachno by forest road

Situated in the beautiful, secluded Wybrnant Valley, Ty Mawr was the birthplace of Bishop William Morgan (1545-1604), the first translator of the Bible into Welsh. The house has been restored to give an idea of its 16th-17th century appearance. The Wybrnant Nature Trail, a short walk, covers approximately one mile.

Times Open 5 Apr-28 Oct, Thu-Sun & BH Mon 12-5; Oct, Thu, Fri & Sun 12-4 (last admission 30 mins before closing)* **Fees** £3 (ch £1.50). Family ticket £7.50. Party 15+(£2.50 each)* **Facilities** (outdoor)

TAL-Y-CAFN Map 6 SH77

Bodnant Garden

LL28 5RE
☎ 01492 650460 01492 650448
e-mail: ann.smith@nationaltrust.org.uk
web: www.bodnant-garden.co.uk
dir: 8m S of Llandudno & Colwyn Bay off A470. Signed from the A55 exit at junct 19

Set above the River Conwy with beautiful views over Snowdonia, this garden is a delight. Five Italian style terraces were constructed below the house - on the lowest terrace is a canal pool with an open-air yew hedge stage and a reconstructed Pin Mill. The garden is renowned for its collections of magnolias, camellias, rhododendrons and azaleas and the famous Laburnum Arch. The colourful displays in summer and autumn are a spectacular sight. Contact for details of events programme.

Times Open daily 28 Feb-1 Nov, 10-5; 2-15 Nov, 10-4 (last admission 30 mins before close)* **Facilities** (partly accessible) (Garden is steep in places with many steps and is not easily accessible for wheelchairs) toilets for disabled (ramps to gardens, wheelchairs & Braille guides) shop

WALES

TREFRIW Map 6 SH76

Trefriw Woollen Mills

Main Rd LL27 0NQ
☎ 01492 640462
e-mail: info@t-w-m.co.uk
web: www.t-w-m.co.uk
dir: on B5106 in centre of Trefriw, 5m N of Betws-y-Coed

Established in 1859, the mill is situated beside the fast-flowing Afon Crafnant, which drives two hydro-electric turbine to power the looms. All the machinery of woollen manufacture can be seen here: blending, carding, spinning, dyeing, warping and weaving. In the Weaver's Garden, there are plants traditionally used in the textile industry, mainly for dyeing. Hand-spinning demonstrations. Traditional Welsh bedspreads, 'tapestries' and tweeds woven on site are available to purchase.

Times Mill Museum open Etr-Oct, Mon-Fri 10-1 & 2-5 (ex BH's). Weaving & turbine house: open all year (ex festive season), Mon-Fri 10-1 & 2-5. Handspinning & weaver's garden open Jun-Sep, Tue-Thu. Shop open all year, daily **Fees** Free admission but no school parties.* **Facilities** Ⓟ ☕ ♿ (partly accessible) (access limited to ground floor of Mill, stairs to top 2 floors) (ramp access to shop, cafe, weaving & turbine house) shop ⊗

WALES

DENBIGHSHIRE

BODELWYDDAN Map 6 SJ07

Bodelwyddan Castle **2 FOR 1**

LL18 5YA
☎ 01745 584060 📠 01745 584563
e-mail: enquiries@bodelwyddan-castle.co.uk
web: www.bodelwyddan-castle.co.uk
dir: just off junct 25 of A55, between St Asaph & Abergele, follow brown signs

Bodelwyddan Castle houses over 100 portraits from the National Portrait Gallery's 19th-century collection. The portraits hang in beautifully refurbished rooms and are complemented by sculpture and period furnishings. Interactive displays show how portraits were produced and used in the Victorian era. The Castle Gallery hosts a programme of temporary exhibitions and events. The castle is set within 200 acres of parkland, including formal gardens, an aviary, woodlands, a butterfly glade and an adventure playground. Regularly changing gallery exhibitions and outdoor events throughout the year. Please refer to website for details.

Times Open Oct-Mar wknds & half terms 10.30-4; Apr wknds 10.30-5; May-Sep daily 10.30-5, closed some Fri **Fees** £6 (ch 5-16 £2.50, ch under 5 free, disabled adult £3.50 (carers special rates) concessions £5). Family ticket (2ad+2ch) £15 (1ad+3ch) £12* **Facilities** Ⓟ Ⓟ ☕ 🍽 licensed ⛩ (outdoor) ♿ (partly accessible) (some rooms not accessible by wheelchair, some gravel paths & steps in garden, but alternative paved routes available) toilets for disabled (lift to first floor, Braille & audio guides) shop ⊗

CORWEN Map 6 SJ04

Ewe-Phoria Sheepdog Centre

Glanrafon, Llangwm LL21 0PE
☎ 01490 460369
e-mail: info@adventure-mountain.co.uk
web: www.ewe-phoria.co.uk
dir: off A5 to Llangwm, follow signs

Ewe-Phoria is an Agri-Theatre and Sheepdog Centre that details the life and work of the shepherd on a traditional Welsh farm. The Agri-Theatre has unusual living displays of sheep with accompanying lectures on their history and breed, while outside sheepdog handlers put their dogs through their paces. Try your hand at quad biking and off-road rally karting on Adventure Mountain.

Times Open Etr-end Oct, Wed-Fri & Sun. Closed Sat & Mon ex BHs* **Facilities** Ⓟ ☕ 🍽 licensed ⛩ ♿ (fully accessible) toilets for disabled shop ⊗

Rug Chapel

Rug LL21 9BT
☎ 01490 412025
web: www.cadw.wales.gov.uk

Rug Chapel was built in 1637 for Colonel William Salusbury, famous Civil War defender of Denbigh Castle. A rare, little altered example of a 17th-century private chapel, it reflects the Colonel's High Church religious views. Prettily set in a wooded landscape, the chapel's modest exterior gives little hint of the interior where local artists and carvers were given a free reign, with some spectacular results.

Times Open Apr-Oct, Wed-Sun, 10-5. Access to Llangar is arranged Wed-Sun, 1-2.30 through Custodian at Rug Chapel, telephone 01490 412025 for details. Both monuments closed Mon & Tue (ex BH wknds) between Apr-Oct & are closed at all other times **Fees** £3.60 (ch 5-15, concessions £3.20, disabled visitors & assisting companion free). Family ticket (2ad+all ch/grandch under 16) £10.40. Group rates available. Prices quoted apply until 31 Mar 2011* **Facilities** Ⓟ toilets for disabled shop ⊗

DENBIGH Map 6 SJ06

Denbigh Castle

LL16 3NB
☎ 01745 813385
web: www.cadw.wales.gov.uk
dir: via A525, A543 & B5382

The castle was begun by Henry de Lacy in 1282 and has an inspiring and impressive gatehouse, with a trio of towers and a superb archway, which is surmounted by a figure believed to be that of Edward I.

Times Open Apr-Oct, 10-5. Open 10-4 daily, unstaffed with no admission charge at all other times **Fees** £3 (ch 5-15, concessions £2.60, disabled visitors & assisting companion free). Family ticket (2ad+all ch/grandch under 16) £8.60. Group rates available. Prices quoted apply until 31 Mar 2011* **Facilities** Ⓟ shop ⊗

LLANGOLLEN Map 7 SJ24

Horse Drawn Boats Centre

The Wharf, Wharf Hill LL20 8TA
☎ 01978 860702 🖷 01978 860702
e-mail: bill@horsedrawnboats.co.uk
web: www.horsedrawnboats.co.uk
dir: A5 onto Llangollen High St, across river bridge to T-junct. Wharf opposite, up the hill

Take a horse drawn boat trip along the beautiful Vale of Llangollen. There is also a narrow boat trip that crosses Pontcysyllte Aqueduct, the largest navigable aqueduct in the world. Full bar on board, commentary throughout. Tea room serving light meals and breakfast.

Times Open Etr-end Oct, daily, 9.30-5; Tea room Nov-Mar, wknds 10-4.30 **Fees** Horse Drawn Boat Trip from £6 (ch £3). Family £15. Aquaduct Trip £11 (ch £9)* **Facilities** Ⓟ ☕ ♿ (partly accessible) (no access to motor boat, access to tea room & Horse Drawn Boats) toilets for disabled (alighting/pick-up point available) shop ㉿

Llangollen Railway

Abbey Rd LL20 8SN
☎ 01978 860979 & 860951 (timetable) 🖷 01978 869247
e-mail: llangollen.railway@btinternet.com
web: www.llangollen-railway.co.uk
dir: Llangollen Station - off A5 at Llangollen lights onto A539, cross river bridge. Station on left at T-junct. Carrog Station - from A5 at Llidiart-y-Parc take B5437, station on right downhill after crossing railway bridge

Heritage Railway featuring steam and classic diesel services along the picturesque Dee Valley. The journey consists of a 15-mile roundtrip between Llangollen and Carrog. A special coach for the disabled is available on all services. Please contact for more information.

Times Open: Services most wknds, daily services Apr-Oct, principally steam hauled. (Refer to timetable for diesel hauled services and off peak) **Fees** £11 (ch 5.50, pen £9) Family ticket (2ad+2ch) £27.50. Dogs/cycles £1* **Facilities** Ⓟ ☕ ⛩ (outdoor) ♿ (fully accessible) toilets for disabled (special coach for disabled on all trains) shop

Plas Newydd **2 FOR 1**

Hill St LL20 8AW
☎ 01978 861314 & 862834 🖷 01824 708258
e-mail: heritage@denbighshire.gov.uk
web: www.denbighshire.gov.uk
dir: follow brown heritage signs from A5

The 'Ladies of Llangollen', Lady Eleanor Butler and Sarah Ponsonby, lived here from 1780 to 1831. The original stained-glass windows, carved panels, and domestic miscellany of two lives are exhibited along with prints, pictures and letters.

Times Open Apr-Oct, daily, 10-5 **Fees** £5.50 (ch & pen £4.50). Family £16* **Facilities** 🅟 Ⓟ ☕ ⛩ (outdoor) ♿ (partly accessible) (no physical access upstairs) toilets for disabled (virtual, signed & touch tours) shop ㉿

Valle Crucis Abbey

LL20 8DD
☎ 01978 860326
web: www.cadw.wales.gov.uk
dir: on B5103, off A5 W of Llangollen

Set in a deep, narrow valley, the abbey was founded for the Cistercians in 1201 by Madog ap Gruffydd. Substantial remains of the church can be seen, and some beautifully carved grave slabs have been found. There is a small exhibition on the Cistercian monks and the abbey.

Times Open Apr-Oct, 10-5. Open 10-4 daily and unstaffed with no admission charge at all other times **Fees** £2.60 (ch 5-15, concessions £2.25, disabled visitors & assisting companion free). Family ticket (2ad and all ch/grandch under 16) £7.45. Group rates available. Prices quoted apply until 31 Mar 2011* **Facilities** 🅟 shop ㉿ ✣

RHUDDLAN Map 6 SJ07

Rhuddlan Castle

LL18 5AD
☎ 01745 590777
web: www.cadw.wales.gov.uk

The castle was begun by Edward I in 1277, on a simple 'diamond' plan with round towers linked by sections of 9 foot thick curtain wall. The moat was linked to a deep-water canal, allowing Edward's ships to sail from the sea right up to the castle.

Times Open Apr-Oct, daily 10-5 **Fees** £3 (ch 5-15, concessions £2.60, disabled visitors & assisting companion free). Family ticket (2ad+all ch/grandch under 16) £8.60. Group discounts available. Prices quoted apply until 31 Mar 2011* **Facilities** 🅟 shop ㉿ ✣

FLINTSHIRE

EWLOE Map 7 SJ36

Ewloe Castle **FREE**

☎ 01443 336000
web: www.cadw.wales.gov.uk
dir: 1m NW of village on B5125

Standing in Ewloe Wood are the remains of Ewloe Castle. It was a native Welsh castle, and Henry II was defeated nearby in 1157. Part of the Welsh Tower in the upper ward still stands to its original height, and there is a well in the lower ward. Remnants of walls and another tower can also be seen.

Times Open all year, access available at all reasonable times, which will normally be 10-4 daily **Facilities** ㉿ ✣

FLINT Map 7 SJ27

Flint Castle FREE

CH6 5PH
☎ 01443 336000
web: www.cadw.wales.gov.uk
dir: NE side of Flint

The castle was started by Edward I in 1277 and overlooks the River Dee. It is exceptional for its great tower, or Donjon, which is separated by a moat. Other buildings would have stood in the inner bailey, of which parts of the walls and corner towers remain.

Times Open all year, access available at all reasonable times, which will normally be 10-4 daily. Key keeper arrangement **Facilities**

HOLYWELL Map 7 SJ17

Basingwerk Abbey FREE

Greenfield Valley Heritage Pk, Greenfield CH8 7GH
☎ 01443 336000
web: www.cadw.wales.gov.uk
dir: just S of A458

The abbey was founded around 1131 by Ranulf de Gernon, Earl of Chester. The first stone church dates from the beginning of the 13th century. The last abbot surrendered the house to the crown in 1536. The Abbey is close to the Heritage Park Visitor Centre and access to the Museum and Farm Complex at Greenfield Valley.

Times Open all year, access available at all reasonable times, which will normally be 10-4 daily **Facilities** licensed (partly accessible) toilets for disabled (disabled facilities in Heritage Park) shop

WALES

GWYNEDD

BANGOR Map 6 SH57

Penrhyn Castle

LL57 4HN
☎ 01248 353084 01248 371281
e-mail: penrhyncastle@nationaltrust.org.uk
web: www.nationaltrust.org.uk
dir: 1m E of Bangor, off A5122 at Llandegai

A massive 19th-century castle built on the profits of Jamaican sugar and Welsh slate, crammed with fascinating artefacts such as a one-ton slate bed made for Queen Victoria and a grand staircase that took ten years to build. Also houses a doll museum, two railway museums and one of the finest collections of Old Master paintings in Wales. Regular programme of events throughout the season.

Times Open 19 Mar-2 Nov, daily (ex Tue) Castle 12-5. Grounds and stableblock exhibitions 11-5; Jul & Aug 10-5 (last admission 4.30, last audio tour 4)* **Facilities** licensed (outdoor) (partly accessible) toilets for disabled (wheelchairs & golf buggies pre bookable) shop

BEDDGELERT Map 6 SH54

Sygun Copper Mine 2 FOR 1

LL55 4NE
☎ 01766 890595 01766 890595
e-mail: sygunmine@hotmail.com
web: www.syguncoppermine.co.uk
dir: 1m E of Beddgelert on A498

Spectacular audio-visual underground experience where visitors can explore the workings of this 19th-century coppermine and see the magnificent stalactite and stalagmite formations. Other activities include archery, panning for gold, metal detecting and coin making. Marvel at the fantastic coin collection from Julius Caesar to Queen Elizabeth II, and visit the Time-Line Museum with Bronze Age and Roman artefacts.

Times Open Mar-end Oct 9.30-5. Feb half term, 10-4 **Fees** £8.75 (ch £6.75, pen £7.75). Family Ticket £28. Please check website for current prices* **Facilities** (outdoor) (partly accessible) (gift shop, cafe & museum accessible for wheelchairs) shop

BLAENAU FFESTINIOG Map 6 SH74

Llechwedd Slate Caverns

LL41 3NB
☎ 01766 830306 01766 831260
e-mail: quarrytours@aol.com
web: www.llechwedd-slate-caverns.co.uk
dir: beside A470, 1m from Blaenau Ffestiniog

The Miners' Tramway travels deep into the mountainside with tour guides who introduce you to the tools of the trade and working conditions underground. There is also an audio-visual tour through ten spectacular caverns. Free surface attractions include various exhibitions, museums, and the Victorian village with shops, bank, Miners Arms pub, chemist and viewpoint.

Times Open all year, daily from 10 (last tour Etr-Sep, 5.15, Sep-Etr, 4.15). Closed 25-26 Dec & 1 Jan* **Facilities** licensed (outdoor) (partly accessible) (access to underground mine tours via steps, some areas of loose slate chipping) toilets for disabled shop

CAERNARFON Map 6 SH46

Caernarfon Castle

LL55 2AY
☎ 01286 677617
web: www.cadw.wales.gov.uk

Edward I began building the castle and extensive town walls in 1283 after defeating the last independent ruler of Wales. Completed in 1328, it has unusual polygonal towers, notably the 10-sided Eagle Tower. There is a theory that these features were copied from the walls of Constantinople, to reflect a tradition that Constantine was born nearby. Edward I's son and heir was born and presented to the Welsh people here, setting a precedent that was followed in 1969, when Prince Charles was invested as Prince of Wales.

Times Open all year, daily Mar-Jun & Sep-Oct 9.30-5, Jul-Aug 9.30-6: Nov-Feb, Mon-Sat 10-4, Sun 11-4 **Fees** £4.95 (ch 5-15, pen & students £4.60, disabled visitors & assisting companion free). Family ticket (2 ad & all ch/grandch under 16) £14.50. Group rates available. Prices quoted apply until 31 Mar 2011*
Facilities P shop

Segontium Roman Museum

FREE

Beddgelert Rd LL55 2LN
☎ 01286 675625 📠 01286 678416
e-mail: info@segontium.org.uk
web: www.segontium.org.uk
dir: on A4085 to Beddgelert approx 1m from Caernarfon

Segontium Roman Museum tells the story of the conquest and occupation of Wales by the Romans and displays the finds from the auxiliary fort of Segontium, one of the most famous in Britain. You can combine a visit to the museum with exploration of the site of the Roman Fort, which is in the care of Cadw: Welsh Historic Monuments. The exciting discoveries displayed at the museum vividly portray the daily life of the soldiers stationed in this most westerly outpost of the Roman Empire.

Times Open all year, Tue-Sun 12.30-4. Closed Mon except BH*
Facilities Ⓟ shop

Welsh Highland Railway

St. Helen's Rd LL55 2YD
☎ 01286 677018 & 01766 516000 📠 01286 677018
e-mail: enquiries@festrail.co.uk
web: www.festrail.co.uk
dlr: SW of Caernarfon Castle beside harbour. Follow brown signs

The Welsh Highland Railway is one of the Great Little Trains of Wales and was voted Heritage Railway of the Year in 2009. A recently opened piece of track now takes the line from Caernarfon to Pont Croesor, just 2.5 miles from Porthmadog. Passengers can enjoy the wonderful scenery of Snowdonia whilst travelling in modern comfortable carriages. There is a refreshment service on all trains. A first class panorama vehicle, recently named by Her Majesty The Queen is at the rear of some trains.

Times Open Apr-Oct. Santa trains in Dec. Open between Xmas & New Year **Fees** Caernarfon-Rhyd Ddu £18.50, Beddgelert £22.80 (1 ch free for each ad, concessions 10% discount). Pont Croesor, new terminus £28* **Facilities** P Ⓟ ♿ (partly accessible) (most main service trains, main stations & buildings accessible) toilets for disabled (ramps, Braille & large print guides) shop

CRICCIETH Map 6 SH43

Criccieth Castle

LL52 0DP
☎ 01766 522227
web: www.cadw.wales.gov.uk
dir: off A497

The castle dates from the 13th century and was taken and destroyed by Owain Glyndwr in 1404. Evidence of a fierce fire can still be seen. The gatehouse leading to the inner ward remains impressive, and parts of the walls are well preserved.

Times Open all year, Apr-Oct, daily 10-5; Nov-Mar, Fri & Sat 9.30-4, Sun 11-4. Monument open and unstaffed with no admission charge 10-4 at all other times **Fees** £3 (ch 5-15, concessions £2.60, disabled visitors & assisting companion free). Family ticket (2ad+all ch/grandch under 16) £8.60. Group rates available. Prices quoted apply until 31 Mar 2011*
Facilities P Ⓟ toilets for disabled shop

WALES

CYMER ABBEY Map 6 SH71

Cymer Abbey FREE

☎ 01443 336000
web: www.cadw.wales.gov.uk
dir: 2m NW of Dolgellau on A494

The abbey was built for the Cistercians in the 13th century. It was never very large, and does not seem to have been finished. The church is the best-preserved building, with ranges of windows and arcades still to be seen. The other buildings have been plundered for stone, but low outlines remain.

Times Open all year, access available at all reasonable times, which will normally be 10-4 daily. Key keeper arrangement **Facilities** Ⓟ

FAIRBOURNE Map 6 SH61

Fairbourne Railway

Beach Rd LL38 2EX
☎ 01341 250362 01341 250240
web: www.fairbournerailway.com
dir: on A493 follow signs for Fairbourne, main terminus is just past level crossing on left

One of the most unusual of Wales's 'little trains'; built in 1890 as a horse-drawn railway to carry building materials it was later converted to steam, and now covers two-and-a-half miles. Its route passes one of the loveliest beaches in Wales, with views of the beautiful Mawddach Estuary.

Times Open half term hols 13-21 Feb, 23-31 Oct. Open Tue-Thu & wknds off peak. Open daily 10 Jul-Aug. Refer to webiste for further details **Fees** Return £7.80 (ch £4.20, pen £6.50). Family (2ad&3ch) £18.95 **Facilities** Ⓟ ♿ (partly accessible) toilets for disabled (wheelchair carriage available upon request) shop

GROESLON Map 6 SH45

Inigo Jones Slateworks 2 FOR 1

LL54 7UE
☎ 01286 830242 01286 831247
e-mail: slate@inigojones.co.uk
web: www.inigojones.co.uk
dir: on A487, 6m S of Caernarfon towards Porthmadog

Inigo Jones was established in 1861 primarily to make school writing slates. Today the company uses the same material to make architectural, monumental and craft products. A self-guided audio/video tour takes visitors round the slate workshops, and displays the various processes used in the extraction and working of Welsh slate. In 2011 the company established in 1861, will celebrate its 150th Anniversary.

Times Open all year, daily 9-5. Closed 25-26 Dec & 1 Jan **Fees** £5 (ch & concessions £4.50) **Facilities** Ⓟ toilets for disabled shop

HARLECH Map 6 SH53

Harlech Castle

LL46 2YH
☎ 01766 780552
web: www.cadw.wales.gov.uk
dir: from A496

Harlech Castle was built in 1283-89 by Edward I, with a sheer drop to the sea on one side. Owain Glyndwr starved the castle into submission in 1404 and made it his court and campaigning base. Later, the defence of the castle in the Wars of the Roses inspired the song *Men of Harlech*. Today the sea has slipped away, and the castle's great walls and round towers stand above the dunes.

Times Open all year, daily Mar-Jun & Sep-Oct 9.30-5, Jul-Aug 9.30-6: Nov-Feb, Mon-Sat 10-4, Sun 11-4 **Fees** £3.60 (ch 5-15, concessions £3.20, disabled visitors & assisting companion free). Family ticket (2ad+all ch/grandch under 16) £10.40. Group rates available. Prices quoted apply until 31 Mar 2011* **Facilities** Ⓟ shop

LLANBERIS Map 6 SH56

Dolbadarn Castle FREE

LL55 4UD
☎ 01443 336000
web: www.cadw.wales.gov.uk
dir: A4086

Built by Llywelyn the Great in the early 13th century, this Welsh castle overlooks Llyn Padarn in the Llanberis Pass.

Times Open all year, access available at all reasonable times, which will normally be 10-4 daily **Facilities** Ⓟ

Llanberis Lake Railway

Padarn Country Park LL55 4TY
☎ 01286 870549 01286 870549
e-mail: info@lake-railway.co.uk
web: www.lake-railway.co.uk
dir: off A4086 at Llanberis

Starting near the foot of Snowdon, these vintage narrow-gauge steam trains, dating from 1889 to 1922, take you on a five mile return journey along the shore of Lake Padarn, following the route of the old slate railway. Passengers are treated to spectacular views of Snowdon and nearby mountains. The main station is adjacent to the Welsh Slate Museum in Padarn Country Park. There are Santa Train weekends in December, and an Easter Egg Hunt on Easter weekend, please telephone for details of these and other events. During 2011 the railway will be celebrating 40 years since it first re-opened in 1971 as a tourist railway.

Times Open mid Mar-end Oct, Sun-Fri, 11-4; also Sat Jun-Aug; Nov-mid Mar limited dates, send for free timetable or check the website **Fees** £7.40 (ch £4.50). Family ticket (2ad+2ch) £19.80. Reduced rates for groups **Facilities** Ⓟ Ⓟ (outdoor) ♿ (fully accessible) toilets for disabled (disabled carriage available) shop

National Slate Museum

Gilfach Ddu, Padarn Country Park LL55 4TY
☎ 01286 870630 📠 01286 871906
e-mail: slate@museumwales.ac.uk
web: www.museumwales.ac.uk
dir: 0.25m off A4086. Museum within Padarn Country Park

Set among the towering quarries at Llanberis, the Welsh Slate Museum is a living, working site located in the original workshops of Dinorwig Quarry, which once employed 15,000 men and boys. You can see the foundry, smithy, workshops and mess room which make up the old quarry, and view original machinery, much of which is still in working order.

Times Open all year, Etr-Oct, daily 10-5; Nov-Etr, Sun-Fri 10-4 **Fees** Some events may incur a charge. **Facilities** (partly accessible) toilets for disabled (all parts accessible except patten loft) shop

Snowdon Mountain Railway

LL55 4TY
☎ 01286 870223 📠 01286 872518
e-mail: info@snowdonrailway.co.uk
web: www.snowdonrailway.co.uk
dir: on A4086, Caernarfon to Capel Curig road. 7.5m from Caernarfon

The journey of just over four-and-a-half miles takes passengers more than 3,000ft up to the summit of Snowdon; breathtaking views include, on a clear day, the Isle of Man and the Wicklow Mountains in Ireland. The round trip to the summit and back takes two and a half hours including a half hour at the summit.

Times Open daily mid Mar-Oct, (weather permitting) **Fees** Return £23 (ch £16). Early bird discount on 9am train, pre-booking only. 3/4 distance return £16 (ch £12)* **Facilities** (outdoor) (partly accessible) (some carriages suitable for wheelchairs - must notify) toilets for disabled shop

LLANFIHANGEL-Y-PENNANT Map 6 SH60

Castell-y-Bere FREE

☎ 01443 336000
web: www.cadw.wales.gov.uk
dir: off B4405

The castle was begun around 1221 by Prince Llewelyn ap Iorwerth of Gwynedd to guard the southern flank of his principality. It is typically Welsh in design with its D-shaped towers. Although a little off the beaten track, the castle lies in a spectacular setting, overshadowed by the Cader Idris range.

Times Open all year, access available at all reasonable times, which will normally be 10-4 daily **Facilities**

LLANGYBI Map 6 SH44

St Cybi's Well FREE

☎ 01443 336000
web: www.cadw.wales.gov.uk
dir: off B4354

Cybi was a sixth-century Cornish saint, known as a healer of the sick, and St Cybi's Well (or Ffynnon Gybi) has been famous for its curative properties through the centuries. The corbelled beehive vaulting inside the roofless stone structure is Irish in style and unique in Wales.

Times Open all year, access available at all reasonable times, which will normally be 10-4 daily. **Facilities**

LLANUWCHLLYN Map 6 SH83

Bala Lake Railway

The Station LL23 7DD
☎ 01678 540666
web: www.bala-lake-railway.co.uk
dir: off A494 Bala to Dolgellau road

Steam locomotives which once worked in the slate quarries of North Wales now haul passenger coaches for four-and-a-half miles from Llanuwchllyn Station along the lake to Bala. The railway has one of the few remaining double-twist lever-locking framed GWR signal boxes, installed in 1896. Some of the coaches are open and some closed, so passengers can enjoy the beautiful views of the lake and mountains in all weathers.

Times Open Etr-last wknd in Sep, daily. Closed certain Mon & Fri, telephone for details **Fees** £8.50 (pen £8). Family ticket (2ad+2ch) £18* **Facilities** (outdoor) (partly accessible) (wheelchairs can be taken on train) shop

LLANYSTUMDWY Map 6 SH43

Lloyd George Museum

LL52 0SH
☎ 01766 522071 📠 01766 522071
e-mail: amgueddfeydd-museums@gwynedd.gov.uk
web: www.gwynedd.gov.uk/museums
dir: on A497 between Pwllheli & Criccieth

Explore the life and times of David Lloyd George in this museum and Highgate. His boyhood home is recreated as it would have been when he lived there between 1864 and 1880, along with his Uncle Lloyd's shoemaking workshop. 2011 is the centenary of the introduction of the National Insurance Act 1911 by Lloyd George.

Times Open Etr, daily 10.30-5; Apr-May, Mon-Fri 10.30-5 (open Sat in Jun); Jul-Sep daily 10.30-5; Oct, Mon-Fri, 11-4. Open BHs; Other times by appointment, telephone 01286 679098 for details **Fees** £4 (ch, concessions & pen £3). Family ticket £10* **Facilities** (outdoor) (partly accessible) (museum fully accessible, Highgate cottage & garden partly accessible as no w/chair to 1st floor of cottage) toilets for disabled (induction loop in audio visual theatre, shop & cottage) shop

WALES

PENARTH FAWR Map 6 SH43

Penarth Fawr

FREE

☎ 01443 336000
web: www.cadw.wales.gov.uk
dir: 3.5m NE of Pwllheli off A497

The hall, buttery and screen are preserved in this house which was probably built in the 15th century.

Times Open all year, access available at all reasonable times, which will normally be 10-4 daily **Facilities**

PLAS-YN-RHIW Map 6 SH22

Plas-yn-Rhiw

LL53 8AB
☎ 01758 780219 01758 780219
e-mail: plasynrhiw@nationaltrust.org.uk
web: www.nationaltrust.org.uk
dir: 12m from Pwllheli signed from B4413 to Aberdaron

This is a small manor house, part medieval, with Tudor and Georgian additions. The ornamental gardens have flowering trees and shrubs including sub-tropical specimens, divided by box hedges and grass paths. There is a stream and waterfall, which descends from the snowdrop wood behind.

Times Open Apr-29 May, Thu-Mon, 12-5; 31 May-Sep, Wed-Mon, 12-5; 1-22 Oct, Sat-Sun, 12-4. 23-29 Oct, daily, 12-4* **Facilities** (partly accessible) toilets for disabled (Braille guides/scented plants) shop

PORTHMADOG Map 6 SH53

Ffestiniog Railway

Harbour Station LL49 9NF
☎ 01766 516000 01766 516006
e-mail: enquiries@festrail.co.uk
web: www.festrail.co.uk
dir: SE end of town beside the harbour, on A487

One of the Great Little Train of Wales, this railway runs for 13.5 through Snowdonia. Originally built to carry slate from the quarries at Blaenau Ffestiniog to the harbour at Porthmadog, the little trains now carry passengers through the beautiful scenery of the national park. A licensed at-your-seat refreshment service is available on all main trains. Day rover tickets allow you to break your journey to make the most of your day. First class observation carriage on all trains. 2011 marks the 200th anniversary of the building of the mile long embankment across the estuary, carrying both railway and road into Porthmadog.

Times Open late Mar-late Oct daily. Limited Winter service mid wk trains Nov & early Dec. Santa specials in Dec. Open Xmas wk & Feb half term **Fees** Full distance return £18.50 (1 ch under 16 free, concessions £16.65). Other fares available* **Facilities** licensed (outdoor) (partly accessible) (most train services accessible, phone in advance, main station/platforms & restaurant accessible, Tan y Bwlch station & cafe accessible) toilets for disabled (wheelchair ramps, Braille and large print guides) shop

PORTMEIRION Map 6 SH53

Portmeirion

LL48 6ER
☎ 01766 770000 01766 771331
e-mail: info@portmeirion-village.com
web: www.portmeirion-village.com
dir: off A487 at Minffordd

Welsh architect Sir Clough Williams Ellis built his fairy-tale, Italianate village on a rocky, tree-clad peninsula on the shores of Cardigan Bay. A bell-tower, castle and lighthouse mingle with a watch-tower, grottoes and cobbled squares among pastel-shaded picturesque cottages let as holiday accommodation. The 60-acre Gwyllt Gardens include miles of dense woodland paths and are famous for their fine displays of rhododendrons, azaleas, hydrangeas and sub-tropical flora. There is a mile of sandy beach and a playground for children. The village is probably best known as the major location for 1960s cult TV show, *The Prisoner*.

Times Open daily Oct-Mar, 9.30-5.30; Apr-Sep, 9.30-7.30* **Facilities** licensed (outdoor) (partly accessible) (steep slopes and many steps make access difficult to some areas) toilets for disabled (w/chair available, disabled parking) shop

WALES

TYWYN Map 6 SH50

Talyllyn Railway

Wharf Station LL36 9EY
☎ 01654 710472 📠 01654 711755
e-mail: enquiries@talyllyn.co.uk
web: www.talyllyn.co.uk
dir: A493 Machynlleth to Dolgellau for Tywyn station, B4405 for Abergynolwyn

The oldest 27in-gauge railway in the world, built in 1865 to run from Tywyn on Cardigan Bay to Abergynolwyn slate mine some seven miles inland. The railway climbs the steep sides of the Fathew Valley and with stops on the way at Dolgoch Falls and the Nant Gwernol forest. The return trip takes 2.5 hours. All scheduled passenger trains are steam hauled. There is a children's play area at Abergynolwyn. 2011 is the 60th anniversary of the first train in the world operated by a volunteer preservation society. To mark this anniversary there will be celebrations throughout the year.

Times Open Feb half term, Sun in Mar, Etr-Oct daily & Xmas **Fees** £12.50 Day Rover (ch accompanied £3, under 5 free). Other fares available (prices subject to change)* **Facilities** Ⓟ Ⓟ ☕ 🍽 licensed ⛩ (outdoor) ♿ (fully accessible) toilets for disabled (prior notice useful, wheelchair ramps into carriages) shop

Y FELINHELI Map 6 SH56

Greenwood Forest Park

LL56 4QN
☎ 01248 670076 & 671493 📠 01248 670069
e-mail: info@greenwoodforestpark.co.uk
web: www.greenwoodforestpark.co.uk
dir: A55 junct 11, follow Llanberis signs onto A4244, signed from next rdbt. Located between Bangor and Caernarfon, follow brown tourist signs

For family adventure, visit Greenwood Forest Park, North Wales' premier eco attraction. Ride the World's first eco-friendly rollercoaster, zoom down Wales' longest sledge run, and take a stroll on the invigorating Barefoot Trail. Scramble up Tree Top Towers, reach for the sky on the super bouncy Giant Jumper and enjoy a Jungle Boat Adventure. Aim for gold at Archery, stagger on stilts, and new for the under 3s is Little Forest Play Barn. With fabulous Forest Theatre entertainment and cool crafts (main season only), no two visits are the same.

Times Open mid Mar-late Oct, daily 10-5.30; Feb half-term & Sep-Oct 11-5 **Fees** Seasonal from £7.60 (ch from £6.35, disabled & carers 50% discount). Family ticket from £25* **Facilities** Ⓟ ☕ 🍽 licensed ⛩ (indoor & outdoor) ♿ (partly accessible) (grounds mostly accessible, some activities may not be accessible for visitors with disabilities) toilets for disabled (parking) shop

MERTHYR TYDFIL

MERTHYR TYDFIL Map 3 SO00

Brecon Mountain Railway

Pant Station Dowlais CF48 2UP
☎ 01685 722988 📠 01685 384854
web: www.breconmountainrailway.co.uk
dir: follow Mountain Railway signs from A470 or A465 N of Merthyr Tydfil

Opened in 1980, this narrow-gauge railway follows part of an old British Rail route which closed in 1964 when the iron industry in South Wales fell into decline. The present route starts at Pant Station and continues for 3.5 miles through the beautiful scenery of the Brecon Beacons National Park, as far as Taf Fechan reservoir. The train is pulled by a vintage steam locomotive and is one of the most popular railways in Wales.

Times Opening times on application to The Brecon Mountain Railway, Pant Station, Merthyr Tydfil **Fees** £10 (ch free, seniors £9.25)* **Facilities** Ⓟ ☕ 🍽 licensed ⛩ (indoor & outdoor) ♿ (partly accessible) (no disabled access to toilets at Pontsticill Station) toilets for disabled (adapted carriage) shop

Cyfarthfa Castle Museum & Art Gallery FREE

Cyfarthfa Park CF47 8RE
☎ 01685 723112 📠 01685 723112
e-mail: museum@merthyr.gov.uk
web: www.museums.merthyr.gov.uk
dir: off A470, N towards Brecon, follow brown heritage signs

Set in wooded parkland beside a beautiful lake, this imposing Gothic mansion now houses a superb museum and art gallery. Providing a fascinating glimpse into 3,000 years of history, the museum displays wonderful collections of fine art, social history and objects from around the world in a Regency setting.

Times Open Apr-Sep, daily, 10-5.30 (last admission 5); Oct-Mar, Tue-Fri 10-4, Sat-Sun 12-4. Closed between Xmas & New Year **Facilities** Ⓟ Ⓟ ☕ ⛩ (outdoor) ♿ (fully accessible) toilets for disabled (stair lift & wheelchair available) shop ⊗

WALES

MONMOUTHSHIRE

CAERWENT — Map 3 ST49

Caerwent Roman Town — FREE

☎ 01443 336000
web: www.cadw.wales.gov.uk
dir: just off A48

A complete circuit of the town wall of 'Venta Silurum', together with excavated areas of houses, shops and a temple.

Times Open - access throughout the year. There is a facilitator on site each Tue. For group bookings Tel: (01633) 430576
Facilities

CALDICOT — Map 3 ST48

Caldicot Castle & Country Park — 2 FOR 1

Church Rd NP26 4HU
☎ 01291 420241 📠 01291 435094
e-mail: caldicotcastle@monmouthshire.gov.uk
web: www.caldicotcastle.co.uk
dir: M4 junct 23A onto B4245. From M48 junct 2 follow A48 & B4245. Signed from B4245

Caldicot Castle's well-preserved fortifications were founded by the Normans and fully developed by the late 14th century. Restored as a family home by a wealthy Victorian, the castle offers the chance to explore medieval walls and towers in a setting of tranquil gardens and wooded country parkland, plus the opportunity to play giant chess or draughts. The 2 for 1 voucher is not valid for special events.

Times Open Apr-Oct, daily 11-5 **Fees** £3.75 (ch, pen, student & disabled £2.50). Family (2ad+3ch) £12. Party 10+*
Facilities (outdoor) (partly accessible) (access to courtyard) toilets for disabled (taped tour, level trails, induction loop, access guide) shop

CHEPSTOW — Map 3 ST59

Chepstow Castle

NP16 5EY
☎ 01291 624065
web: www.cadw.wales.gov.uk

Built by William FitzOsbern, Chepstow is the first recorded Norman stone castle. It stands in a strategic spot above the Wye. The castle was strengthened in the following centuries, but was not besieged (as far as is known) until the Civil War, when it was twice lost to the Parliamentarians. The remains of the domestic rooms and the massive gatehouse with its portcullis grooves and ancient gates are still impressive, as are the walls and towers.

Times Open all year, daily Mar-Jun & Sep-Oct 9.30-5, Jul-Aug 9.30-6: Nov-Feb, Mon-Sat 10-4, Sun 11-4 **Fees** £3.60 (ch 5-15, concessions £3.20, disabled visitors and assisting companion free). Family ticket (2ad+all ch/grandch under 16) £10.40. Group rates available. Prices quoted apply until 31 Mar 2011*
Facilities shop

GROSMONT — Map 3 SO42

Grosmont Castle — FREE

☎ 01981 240301
web: www.cadw.wales.gov.uk
dir: on B4347

Grosmont is one of the 'trilateral' castles of Hubert de Burgh (see also Skenfrith and White Castle). It stands on a mound with a dry moat, and the considerable remains of its 13th-century great hall can be seen. Three towers once guarded the curtain wall, and the western one is well preserved.

Times Open all year, access available at all reasonable times, which will normally be 10-4 daily **Facilities**

LLANTHONY — Map 3 SO22

Llanthony Priory — FREE

☎ 01443 336000
web: www.cadw.wales.gov.uk

William de Lacey discovered the remains of a hermitage dedicated to St David. By 1108 a church had been consecrated on the site and just over a decade later the priory was complete. After the priory was brought to a state of siege in an uprising, Hugh de Lacey provided the funds for a new church, and it is this that makes the picturesque ruin seen today. Visitors can still make out the west towers, north nave arcade and south transept.

Times Open all year, access available at all reasonable times, which will normally be 10-4 daily **Facilities** toilets for disabled

LLANTILIO CROSSENNY — Map 3 SO31

Hen Gwrt — FREE

☎ 01443 336000
web: www.cadw.wales.gov.uk
dir: off B4233

The rectangular enclosure of the former medieval house, still surrounded by a moat.

Times Open all year, access available at all reasonable times, which will normally be 10-4 daily **Facilities**

MONMOUTH Map 3 SO51

The Nelson Museum & Local History Centre

FREE

New Market Hall, Priory St NP25 3XA
☎ 01600 710630
e-mail: nelsonmuseum@monmouthshire.gov.uk
dir: in town centre

One of the world's major collections of Admiral Nelson-related items, including original letters, glass, china, silver, medals, books, models, prints and Nelson's fighting sword feature here. The local history displays deal with Monmouth's past as a fortress market town, and include a section on the co-founder of the Rolls Royce company, Charles Stewart Rolls, who was also a pioneer balloonist, aviator and, of course, motorist.

Times Open all year, Mar-Oct, Mon-Sat & BH 11-1 & 2-5, Sun 2-5; Nov-Feb, Mon-Sat 11-1 & 2-4, Sun 2-4 **Facilities** Ⓟ ♿ (partly accessible) (mezzanine display area accessible only by stairs - 25% of whole museum display area) toilets for disabled shop

RAGLAN Map 3 SO40

Raglan Castle

NP15 2BT
☎ 01291 690228
web: www.cadw.wales.gov.uk
dir: signed off A40

This magnificent 15th-century castle is noted for its 'Yellow Tower of Gwent'. It was built by Sir William ap Thomas and destroyed during the Civil War, after a long siege. The ruins are still impressive however, and the castle's history is illustrated in an exhibition situated in the closet tower and two rooms of the gate passage.

Times Open all year, daily Mar-Jun & Sep-Oct 9.30-5, Jul-Aug 9.30-6: Nov-Feb, Mon-Sat 10-4, Sun 11-4 **Fees** £3 (ch 5-15, concessions £2.60, disabled visitors & assisting companion free). Family ticket (2ad+all ch/grandch under 16) £8.60. Group rates available. Prices quoted apply until 31 Mar 2011* **Facilities** Ⓟ shop

SKENFRITH Map 3 SO42

Skenfrith Castle

FREE

☎ 01443 336000
web. www.cadw.wales.gov.uk
dir: on B4521

This 13th-century castle has a round keep set inside an imposing towered curtain wall. Hubert de Burgh built it as one of three 'trilateral' castles to defend the Welsh Marches.

Times Open all year, access available at all reasonable times, which will normally be 10-4 daily. Key keeper arrangement **Facilities** Ⓟ

TINTERN PARVA Map 3 SO50

Tintern Abbey

NP16 6SE
☎ 01291 689251
web: www.cadw.wales.gov.uk
dir: via A466

The ruins of this Cistercian monastery church are still surprisingly intact. The monastery was established in 1131 and became increasingly wealthy well into the 15th century. During the Dissolution, the monastery was closed and most of the buildings were completely destroyed. During the 18th century many poets and artists came to see the ruins and recorded their impressions.

Times Open all year, daily Mar-Jun & Sep-Oct 9.30-5, Jul-Aug 9.30-6: Nov-Feb, Mon-Sat 10-4, Sun 11-4 **Fees** £3.60 (ch 5-15, concessions £3.20, disabled visitors & assisting companion free). Family ticket (2ad+all ch/grandch under 16) £10.40. Group rates available. Prices quoted apply until 31 Mar 2011* **Facilities** Ⓟ toilets for disabled shop

WHITE CASTLE Map 3 SO31

White Castle

NP7 8UD
☎ 01600 780380
web: www.cadw.wales.gov.uk
dir: 7m NE of Abergavenny, unclass road N of B4233

The impressive 12th to 13th-century moated stronghold was built by Hubert de Burgh to defend the Welsh Marches. Substantial remains of walls, towers and a gatehouse can be seen. This is the finest of a trio of castles, the others being at Skenfrith and Grosmont.

Times Open Apr-Oct, 10-5 daily. Open 10-4 daily and unstaffed with no admission charge at all other times **Fees** £2.60 (ch 5-15, concessions £2.25, disabled visitors & assisting companion free). Family ticket (2ad+all ch/grandch under 16) £7.45. Group rates available. Prices quoted apply until 31 Mar 2011* **Facilities** Ⓟ

WALES

NEATH PORT TALBOT

ABERDULAIS Map 3 SS79

Aberdulais Falls 2 FOR 1

SA10 8EU
☎ 01639 636674 📠 01639 645069
e-mail: aberdulais@nationaltrust.org.uk/main
web: www.nationaltrust.org.uk
dir: M4 junct 43, take A465 signed Vale of Neath. Onto A4109 signed Seven Sisters & follow brown tourist signs

The industrial heritage of this area goes back to 1584, when copper was first manufactured. Iron smelting and corn milling followed, with a tin plate works being built around 1830. As well as powering industries for over 400 years, this magnificent waterfall inspired artist J. M. W. Turner in 1795. Today, the site houses Europe's largest electricity-generating water wheel. An exciting exhibition and film show how Aberdulais Falls played an important role in the industrialisation of South Wales.

Times Open Jan-Mar, Mon-Fri 11-4; Apr-Oct, daily 10-5; Nov-Dec Fri-Sun 11-4 **Fees** £4.40 (ch 5-18 £2.20) Family ticket (2ad+2ch) £11 **Facilities** Ⓟ ☕ ⛩ (outdoor) ♿ (fully accessible) toilets for disabled (lifts for disabled to view falls, ramp into tearoom) shop

CRYNANT Map 3 SN70

Cefn Coed Colliery Museum FREE

SA10 8SN
☎ 01639 750556 📠 01639 750556
e-mail: colliery@btconnect.com
web: www.neath-porttalbot.gov.uk
dir: 1m S of Crynant, on A4109

The museum is on the site of a former working colliery, and tells the story of mining in the Dulais Valley. A steam-winding engine has been kept and is now operated by electricity, and there is also a simulated underground mining gallery, boilerhouse, compressor house, and exhibition area. Outdoor exhibits include a stationary colliery locomotive. Exhibitions relating to the coal mining industry are held on a regular basis. The museum is now home to the Dulais Valley Historical Model Railway Society who, with the help from the Heritage Lottery Fund have created an ever increasing layout depicting the Neath-Brecon railway through the valley.

Times Open Apr-Oct, daily 10.30-5; Nov-Mar, groups welcome by prior arrangement.* **Facilities** Ⓟ ⛩ (outdoor) ♿ (partly accessible) (access to exhibition areas, but not to underground gallery) toilets for disabled shop

NEATH Map 3 SS79

Gnoll Estate Country Park

SA11 3BS
☎ 01639 635808 📠 01639 635694
e-mail: e.ford@npt.gov.uk
web: www.neath-porttalbot.gov.uk
dir: follow brown heritage signs from town centre

The extensively landscaped Gnoll Estate offers tranquil woodland walks, picnic areas, stunning views, children's play areas, adventure playground, 9-hole golf course, and coarse fishing. Varied programme of events and school holiday activities.

Times Open all year. Vistor centre: daily from 10. Closed 24 Dec-2 Jan* **Facilities** Ⓟ ☕ ⛩ (outdoor) ♿ (partly accessible) toilets for disabled (wheelchair & scooter for hire, designated parking) shop

Neath Abbey FREE

SA10 7DW
☎ 01443 336000
web: www.cadw.wales.gov.uk
dir: 1m W off A465

These ruins were originally a Cistercian abbey founded in 1130 by Richard de Grainville.

Times Open all year, access available at all reasonable times, which will normally be 10-4 daily. Key keeper arrangement. **Facilities** Ⓟ

NEWPORT

CAERLEON Map 3 ST39

Caerleon Roman Baths FREE

NP18 1AE
☎ 01663 422518
web: www.cadw.wales.gov.uk
dir: on B4236

Caerleon was an important Roman military base, with accommodation for thousands of men. The foundations of barrack lines and parts of the ramparts can be seen, with remains of the cookhouse, latrines and baths. The amphitheatre nearby is one of the best examples in Britain.

Times Open all year, Apr-Oct, daily 9.30-5; Nov-Mar, Mon-Sat, 9.30-5, Sun 11-4 **Facilities** Ⓟ shop

WALES

National Roman Legion Museum

High St NP18 1AE
☎ 01633 423134 01633 422869
e-mail: roman@museumwales.ac.uk
web: www.museumwales.ac.uk
dir: close to Newport, 20 min from M4, follow signs from Cardiff & Bristol

The museum illustrates the history of Roman Caerleon and the daily life of its garrison. On display are arms, armour and equipment, with a collection of engraved gemstones, a labyrinth mosaic and finds from the legionary base at Usk. Please telephone for details of children's holiday activities.

Times Open all year: Mon-Sat 10-5, Sun 2-5 **Fees** Free - there may be a charge for some events **Facilities** Ⓟ ♿ (fully accessible) toilets for disabled shop

NEWPORT Map 3 ST38

Tredegar House & Park

NP10 8YW
☎ 01633 815880 01633 815895
e-mail: tredegar.house@newport.gov.uk
web: www.newport.gov.uk
dir: 2m W of Newport, signed from A48 & M4 junct 28

Tredegar House is a magnificent 17th-century country house, which was the ancestral home of the Morgan family for 500 years. Parts of the house date back to medieval times, but most of it was built between 1664 and 1672. The house is set in 90 acres of landscaped park, and feature formal gardens, self-guided trails and craft workshops.

Times Open Etr-late Sep, Wed-Sun 11-4* **Facilities** Ⓟ licensed (outdoor) ♿ (partly accessible) (1st floor not accessible) toilets for disabled (wheelchairs for loan) shop

PEMBROKESHIRE

AMROTH Map 2 SN10

Colby Woodland Garden

SA67 8PP
☎ 01834 811885
e-mail: colby@nationaltrust.org.uk
web: www.nationaltrust.org.uk/main
dir: 1.5m inland from Amroth beside Carmarthen Bay, follow brown signs from A477 Tenby-Carmarthen road, or off coast road at Amroth Castle Caravan Park

From early spring to the end of June the garden is a blaze of colour, from the masses of daffodils to the rich hues of rhododendrons, azaleas and bluebells. Followed by hydrangeas in shaded walks through summer to glorious shades of autumn.

Times Open 19 Feb-30 Oct, daily 10-5 **Fees** £4.60 (ch £2.30). Family ticket £11.50. Group £4 (ch £2) NT members free **Facilities** Ⓟ (outdoor) ♿ (partly accessible) (grounds partly accessible -map of accessible route available) toilets for disabled shop

CAREW Map 2 SN00

Carew Castle & Tidal Mill

SA70 8SL
☎ 01646 651782 01646 651782
e-mail: enquiries@carewcastle.com
web: www.carewcastle.com
dir: on A4075, just off A477 Pembroke to Kilgetty road

This magnificent Norman castle has royal links with Henry Tudor and was the setting for the Great Tournament of 1507. Nearby is the Carew Cross (Cadw), an impressive 13ft Celtic cross dating from the 11th century. Carew Mill is one of only four restored tidal mills in Britain, with records dating back to 1558.

Times Open Castle Jan-Etr, Nov-Dec, daily 11-3 (closed Xmas). Castle & Mill Etr-Oct, daily 10-5* **Facilities** Ⓟ Ⓟ (outdoor) ♿ (partly accessible) (ground floors, toilets and shop are acccessible) toilets for disabled (audio tours, sign language, tours by arrangement) shop

CILGERRAN Map 2 SN14

Cilgerran Castle

SA43 2SF
☎ 01239 621339
web: www.cadw.wales.gov.uk
dir: off A484 & A478

Set above a gorge of the River Teifi - famed for its coracle fishermen - Cilgerran Castle dates from the 11th to 13th centuries. It decayed gradually after the Civil War, but its great round towers and high walls give a vivid impression of its former strength.

Times Open all year, Apr-Oct, daily 10-5; open and unstaffed with no admission charge at all other times daily 10-4 **Fees** £3 (ch 5-15, concessions £2.60, disabled visitors & assisting companion free). Family ticket (2ad+all ch/grandch under 16) £8.60 Group rates available. Prices quoted apply until 31 Mar 2011* **Facilities** shop

CRYMYCH Map 2 SN13

Castell Henllys Iron Age Fort 2 FOR 1

Pant-Glas, Meline SA41 3UT
☎ 01239 891319 📠 01239 891319
e-mail: celts@castellhenllys.com
web: www.castellhenllys.com
dir: off A487 between Cardigan and Newport

This Iron Age hill fort is set in the beautiful Pembrokeshire Coast National Park. Excavations began in 1981 and three roundhouses have been reconstructed, another roundhouse has been completed and is the largest on the site. The roundhouses have been constructed in the original way using hazel wattle walls, oak rafters and thatched conical roofs. A forge, smithy and looms can be seen, with other attractions such as trails and a herb garden. Please telephone for details of special events.

Times Open all year, Etr-Oct daily 10-5; Nov-Mar 11-3 (last entry 30 mins before close). Closed 24-31 Dec **Fees** £4.50 (concessions £3). Family ticket £12* **Facilities** Ⓟ ⛩ (indoor & outdoor) ♿ (fully accessible) toilets for disabled (ramp to shop, hearing loop, lift, buggy, tramper bike) shop

WALES

FISHGUARD Map 2 SM93

OceanLab

The Parrog, Goodwick SA64 0DE
☎ 01348 874737 📠 01348 872528
e-mail: fishguardharbour.tic@pembrokeshire.gov.uk
web: www.ocean-lab.co.uk
dir: A40 to Fishguard, turn at by-pass, follow signs for Stenaline ferry terminal, pass 2 garages, turn right at rdbt & follow signs to attraction

Overlooking the Pembrokeshire coastline, OceanLab is a multifunctional centre, which aims to provide a fun-filled experience for the family. There is also a hands-on ocean quest exhibition, a soft play area and a cybercafé. An exhibition is centred around 'Ollie the Octopus's Garden', with hands-on displays and activities.

Times Open Apr-Oct, 9.30-5 (6 wk summer hols 9.30-6); Nov-Mar 10-4* **Facilities** Ⓟ ⓟ ☕ ⛩ (outdoor) ♿ (fully accessible) toilets for disabled (lift, flat even ground, low counter) shop

LAMPHEY Map 2 SN00

Lamphey Bishop's Palace

SA71 5NT
☎ 01646 672224
web: www.cadw.wales.gov.uk
dir: off A4139

This ruined 13th-century palace once belonged to the Bishops of St David's.

Times Open Apr-Mar, daily 10-5. The Visitor Centre will be closed at times during the winter, but the side gate will be left open for access to the site between 10-4 **Fees** £3 (ch 5-15, concessions £2.60, disabled visitors & assisting companion free). Family ticket (2ad+all ch/grandch under 16) £8.60. Group rates available. Price quoted apply until 31 Mar 2011* **Facilities** Ⓟ toilets for disabled shop

LLAWHADEN Map 2 SN01

Llawhaden Castle FREE

☎ 01443 336000
web: www.cadw.wales.gov.uk
dir: off A40, 3m NW of Narberth

The castle was first built in the 12th century to protect the possessions of the Bishops of St David's. The 13th and 14th-century remains of the bishops' hall, kitchen, bakehouse and other buildings can be seen, all surrounded by a deep moat.

Times Open all year, access available at all reasonable times, which will normally be 10-4 daily. Key keeper arrangement **Facilities**

NARBERTH Map 2 SN11

Oakwood Theme Park

Canaston Bridge SA67 8DE
☎ 01834 861889 📠 01834 891380
e-mail: info@oakwoodthemepark.co.uk
web: www.oakwoodthemepark.co.uk
dir: M4 W junct 49, take A48 to Carmarthen, signed

Oakwood Theme Park is a top ten UK theme park with over 30 rides and attractions. Thrill seekers can brave Speed, the UK's first roller-coaster with a beyond vertical drop, the award-winning wooden roller coaster Megafobia celebrating its 15th anniversary, the 50 metre high sky coaster Vertigo, and shot n' drop tower coaster The Bounce. Cool off on Hydro, the steepest and wettest ride in Europe. There are also plenty of family rides and lots of fun to be had for smaller kids, with a designated children's area available with smaller rides.

Times Open Etr-Oct, days & times vary, call for details **Fees** £19.95 (under 2's free, ch 3-12 £14.25, pen & disabled £12.25). Please call or see website for up to date prices* **Facilities** Ⓟ ☕ 🍴 licensed ⛩ (indoor & outdoor) ♿ (partly accessible) (most areas of park are accessible apart from a few rides) toilets for disabled (wheelchair hire, special access to some rides) shop

NEWPORT Map 2 SN03

Pentre Ifan Burial Chamber FREE

☎ 01443 336000
web: www.cadw.wales.gov.uk
dir: 3m SE from B4329 or A487

Found to be part of a vanished long barrow when excavated in 1936-37, the remains of this chamber include the capstone, three uprights and a circular forecourt.

Times Open all year, access available at all reasonable times, which will normally be 10-4 daily **Facilities**

PEMBROKE Map 2 SM90

Pembroke Castle

SA71 4LA
☎ 01646 681510 & 684585 📠 01646 622260
e-mail: info@pembrokecastle.co.uk
web: www.pembrokecastle.co.uk
dir: W end of main street

This magnificent castle commands stunning views over the Milford estuary. Discover its rich medieval history, and that of Henry VII, the first Tudor king, through a variety of exhibitions. There are lively guided tours and events each Sunday in July and August. Before leaving, pop into the Brass Rubbing Centre and make your own special souvenir. To complete the day, wander round the tranquil millpond and medieval town walls, which surround other architectural gems from Tudor and Georgian times. Special Events: 1st week in Sep 'Pembroke Festival'. Please telephone for details.

Times Open all year, daily, Apr-Sep 9.30-6; Mar & Oct 10-5; Nov-Feb, 10-4. Closed 24-26 Dec & 1 Jan* **Facilities** Ⓟ ☕ ⛩ (outdoor) ♿ (partly accessible) toilets for disabled (induction loop, handrails, portable ramp) shop

ST DAVID'S Map 2 SM72

St David's Bishop's Palace

SA62 6PE
☎ 01437 720517
web: www.cadw.wales.gov.uk
dir: on A487

These extensive and impressive ruins are all that remain of the principal residence of the Bishops of St David's. The palace shares a quiet valley with the cathedral, which was almost certainly built on the site of a monastery founded in the 6th century by St David. The Bishop's Palace houses an exhibition: 'Lords of the Palace'.

Times Open all year, Apr-Oct, daily 9-5; Nov-Mar, Mon-Sat 9.30-4, Sun 11-4 **Fees** £3 (ch 5-15, concessions £2.60, disabled visitors & assisting companion free). Family ticket (2ad+all ch/grandch under 16) £8.90. Group rates available. Prices quoted apply until 31 Mar 2011* **Facilities** 🅟 toilets for disabled shop ⊗ ✣

St David's Cathedral

The Close SA62 6PE
☎ 01437 720202 📠 01437 721885
e-mail: info@stdavidscathedral.org.uk
web: www.stdavidscathedral.org.uk
dir: from Haverfordwest A487 into St Davids, pass Cross Sq, left into car park

Begun 1181 on the reputed site of St David's 6th-century monastic settlement, the present building was altered during the 12th to the 14th centuries and again in the 16th. The ceilings of oak, painted wood and stone vaulting are of considerable interest.

Times Open all year 8.30-5 **Fees** Free - Suggested donation of £3 **Facilities** Ⓟ ☕ ♿ (fully accessible) toilets for disabled (hearing loop) shop ⊗

SCOLTON Map 2 SM92

Scolton Manor Museum & Country Park

Scolton Manor SA62 5QL
☎ 01437 731328 (Museum) & 731457 (Park)
📠 01437 731743
dir: 5m N of Haverfordwest, on B4329

Scolton Manor Museum is situated in Scolton Country Park. The early Victorian mansion, refurbished stables and the exhibition hall illustrate the history and natural history of Pembrokeshire. There are new displays in the house and stables, plus a 'Pembrokeshire Railways' exhibition. The 60-acre grounds, partly a nature reserve, have fine specimen trees and shrubs. Environmentally friendly Visitor Centre, alternative energy and woodland displays, guided walks and children's play areas. Classic Car show in June and Model Air show in July.

Times Open Museum Etr-Oct, daily & BHs 10.30-5.30 (last entry 4.30); Country Park Apr-Oct 9.30-5.30, Nov-Mar 9.30-4.30. Closed 25-26 Dec **Fees** Museum: £2 (ch £1, concessions £1.50). Country Park car park £1 all day* **Facilities** 🅟 Ⓟ ☕ ⛩ (outdoor) ♿ (partly accessible) (ground floor only accessible for wheelchairs) toilets for disabled shop ⊗

WALES

TENBY Map 2 SN10

Tenby Museum & Art Gallery **2 FOR 1**

Castle Hill SA70 7BP
☎ 01834 842809 📠 01834 842809
e-mail: info@tenbymuseum.org.uk
web: www.tenbymuseum.org.uk
dir: near town centre above Harbour

The museum is situated on Castle Hill. It covers the local heritage from prehistory to the present in galleries devoted to archaeology, geology, maritime history, natural history, militaria and bygones. The art galleries concentrate on local associations with an important collection of works by Augustus John, Gwen John and others. There are child-friendly trails and art exhibitions that change monthly, as well as a bilingual audio tour.

Times Open all year, 10-5; winter Mon-Fri only (last admission 4.30) **Fees** £4 (ch £2, concessions £3). Family ticket £9 **Facilities** Ⓟ ☕ ♿ (fully accessible) toilets for disabled (lifts, levelled floors, ramps, stair lift) shop ⊛

Tudor Merchant's House

Quay Hill SA70 7BX
☎ 01834 842279 📠 01834 842279
e-mail: alyson.bush@nationaltrust.org.uk
web: www.nationaltrust.org.ukmain-w-tudormerchantshouse
dir: turn left off lower end of High St, past Lifeboat PH and Caldey Shop

Recalling Tenby's history as a thriving and prosperous port, the Tudor Merchant's house is a fine example of gabled 15th-century architecture. There is a good Flemish chimney and on three walls the remains of seccos can be seen. A small herb garden has been created which is open, weather permitting. Children can try on Tudor costume and play with replica toys.

Times Open 30 Mar-1 Nov, Sun-Fri 11-5 (last admission 4.30), open Sat BH wknds **Fees** £3 (ch £1.50). Family ticket £7.50. Group 15+ £2.55 (ch £1.30). NT members & under 5's free **Facilities** Ⓟ ♿ (partly accessible) (3 steps to entrance, ground floor has steps, uneven floors, stairs to other floors) (Braille guide, photo album, induction loop) shop ⊛

POWYS

ABERCRAF Map 3 SN81

Dan-Yr-Ogof The National Showcaves Centre for Wales

SA9 1GJ
☎ 01639 730284 📠 01639 730293
e-mail: info@showcaves.co.uk
web: www.showcaves.co.uk
dir: M4 junct 45, midway between Swansea & Brecon on A4067, follow brown tourist signs for Dan-Yr-Ogof

This award-winning attraction includes three separate caves, dinosaur park, Iron Age Farm, museum, shire horse centre and covered children's play area.

Times Open Apr-Oct, daily from 10.30 (last admission 3) **Fees** £13 (ch 3-16 £7)* **Facilities** 🅟 ☕ ⛩ (outdoor) toilets for disabled shop ⊛

BERRIEW Map 7 SJ10

Glansevern Hall Gardens

Glansevern SY21 8AH
☎ 01686 640644 📠 01686 640829
e-mail: glansevern@yahoo.co.uk
web: www.glansevern.co.uk
dir: signed on A483 between Welshpool and Newtown

Built in the Greek Revival style for Arthur Davies Owen, who chose a romantically positioned site on the banks of the River Severn. The current owners have developed the gardens, respecting the plantings and features of the past, and added a vast collection of new and interesting species. There are many fine and unusual trees, a lakeside walk, walled garden, water gardens and a rock garden with grotto.

Times Open May-Sep, BH Mon & Thu-Sat 12-5. Parties other dates by arrangement **Fees** £5 (pen £4.50)* **Facilities** 🅟 ☕ 🍽 licensed ⛩ (outdoor) ♿ (partly accessible) (most areas accessible) toilets for disabled shop

BRECON Map 3 SO02

Brecknock Museum & Art Gallery **2 FOR 1**

Captain's Walk LD3 7DS
☎ 01874 624121 📠 01874 614046
e-mail: brecknock.museum@powys.gov.uk
web: www.powys.gov.uk/breconmuseum
dir: near town centre at junct of The Watton & Glamorgan St

A wealth of local history is explored at the museum, which has archaeological and historical exhibits, with sections on folk life, decorative arts and natural history. Victorian Assize Court is interpreted with life-size figures, sound and light and there is one of the finest collections of Welsh Lovespoons. The museum also runs a lively programme of Welsh contemporary art exhibitions.

Times Open all year, Mon-Fri 10-5, Sat 10-1 & 2-5. Closed Good Fri, 25-26 Dec & 1 Jan **Fees** £1 (ch & residents free, concessions 50p)* **Facilities** 🅟 Ⓟ ♿ (fully accessible) toilets for disabled (limited parking, must be accompanied by able-bodied) shop ⊛

Regimental Museum of The Royal Welsh

The Barracks, The Watton LD3 7EB
☎ 01874 613310 📠 01874 613275
e-mail: swb@rrw.org.uk
web: www.rrw.org.uk
dir: close to town centre, well signed

The museum of the South Wales Borderers and Monmouthshire Regiment (now the Royal Welsh), which was raised in 1689 and has been awarded 23 Victoria Crosses. Amongst the collections is the Zulu War Room, devoted to the war and in particular to the events at Rorke's Drift, 1879, when 121 men fought 4,500 Zulus.

Times Open all year wkdys 10-5, Apr-Sep Sat & BHs 10-4. Call for special Sun opening times* **Facilities** Ⓟ ♿ (fully accessible) toilets for disabled shop

LLANFAIR CAEREINION Map 6 SJ10

Welshpool & Llanfair Light Railway 2 FOR 1

SY21 0SF
☎ 01938 810441 📠 01938 810861
e-mail: info@wllr.org.uk
web: www.wllr.org.uk
dir: beside A458, Shrewsbury-Dolgellau road

The Llanfair Railway is one of the Great Little Trains of Wales. It offers a 16-mile round trip through glorious scenery by narrow-gauge steam train. The line is home to a collection of engines and coaches from all round the world. Please ring for details for special events.

Times Open Etr-late Oct wknds, (some extra days during Jun, Jul & Sep) daily during holiday periods, phone for timetable enquiries **Fees** £11.80 return (one ch £1 per adult, extra ch £5.90, concessions £10.80)* **Facilities** Ⓟ Ⓟ ☕ (outdoor) ♿ (partly accessible) (both termini have ramped access, no access from intermediate stations) toilets for disabled (three coaches adapted for wheelchairs) shop

MACHYNLLETH Map 6 SH70

Bards' Quest

Corris Craft Centre, Corris SY20 9RF
☎ 01654 761584 📠 01654 761575
e-mail: info@kingarthurslabyrinth.co.uk
web: www.kingarthurslabyrinth.com
dir: Situated at Corris Craft Centre on main A487 rd between Machynlleth & Dolgellau

Take on the challenge of the Bard's Quest and search for legends and stories lost along the paths of time. Once found sit, enjoy and be enthralled by some great Welsh stories, and like the Bard, pass them on for others to enjoy. Bards Quest is self-guided and easy to get around, with level paths and seating.

Times Open Mar-Oct, daily 10-5 **Fees** £4.10 (ch £2.35, concessions £3.60)* **Facilities** Ⓟ ☕ (outdoor) ♿ (fully accessible) toilets for disabled (designated parking nr entrance) shop

Centre for Alternative Technology 2 FOR 1

SY20 9AZ
☎ 01654 705950
e-mail: visit@cat.org.uk
web: www.cat.org.uk
dir: 3m N of Machynlleth, on A487

The Centre for Alternative Technology promotes practical ideas and information on sustainable technologies. The exhibition includes displays of wind, water and solar power, organic gardens, low-energy buildings, and a unique water-powered railway which ascends a 200ft cliff from the car park. Free children's activities and guided tours during the summer holidays.

Times Open all year 10-5.30 or dusk in winter. Closed Dec 23-27 & 3-14 Jan **Fees** Summer £8.50 (ch over 5 £4, concessions £7.50); Winter, £6.50 (ch over 5 £4, concessions £5.50). Discounts available for cyclists, walkers and users of public transport* **Facilities** Ⓟ 🍽 licensed (indoor & outdoor) ♿ (fully accessible) toilets for disabled (assisted wheelchair access, mobility scooter available) shop

Corris Craft Centre FREE

Corris SY20 9RF
☎ 01654 761584 📠 01654 761575
e-mail: info@corriscraftcentre.co.uk
web: www.corriscraftcentre.co.uk
dir: on main A487 rd between Machynlleth & Dolgellau

A large collection of workshops where visitors can meet the craftspeople and see them at work every day. The range of crafts include glassware, leatherwork, pottery, jewellery, traditional wooden toys, candles, rustic furniture, designer cards and herbal lotions and remedies. A perfect place to find unusual items for the home and garden. Drop in for pottery painting, candle-dipping and a chance to make herbals.

Times Open daily Mar-Nov. From Nov-Mar many workshops open please call to check dates and times **Facilities** Ⓟ ☕ (outdoor) ♿ (fully accessible) toilets for disabled (disabled parking spaces near entrance) shop

King Arthur's Labyrinth

Corris SY20 9RF
☎ 01654 761584 📠 01654 761575
e-mail: info@kingarthurslabyrinth.co.uk
web: www.kingarthurslabyrinth.com
dir: on A487 between Machynlleth and Dolgellau

An underground storytelling adventure where visitors travel by boat deep inside the vast caverns of the labyrinth, and far back into the past. Tales of King Arthur and other legends are re-told as you explore the spectacular underground setting. Complete with dramatic scenes, light shows and sound effects, this is a fascinating attraction for all ages.

Times Open Mar-Oct, daily 10-5 **Fees** £7.50 (ch £5, pen £6.75)* **Facilities** Ⓟ ☕ (outdoor) ♿ (partly accessible) (full access to reception, shop & units of craft centre. Labyrinth tour includes 0.5m walk through caverns) toilets for disabled shop

MONTGOMERY Map 7 SO29

Montgomery Castle

FREE

☎ 01443 336000
web: www.cadw.wales.gov.uk

Initially an earth and timber structure guarding an important ford in the River Severn, Montgomery was considered a 'suitable spot for the erection of an impregnable castle' in the 1220s. Building and modifications continued until 1251-53, but the final conquest of Wales by Edward I meant the castle lost much of its role.

Times Open all year, access available at all reasonable times, which will normally be 10-4 daily **Facilities**

PRESTEIGNE Map 3 SO36

The Judge's Lodging

2 FOR 1

Broad St LD8 2AD
☎ 01544 260650
e-mail: info@judgeslodging.org.uk
web: www.judgeslodging.org.uk
dir: in town centre, off B4362, signed from A44 & A49

A restored Victorian town house with integral courtroom, cells and service areas - step back into the 1860s, accompanied by an 'eavesdropping' audio tour of voices from the past. Explore the fascinating world of the Victorian judges, their servants and felonious guests at this award-winning, historic house. Various special events take place throughout the year, please telephone for details.

Times Open Mar-Oct, Tue-Sun 10-5; Nov, Wed-Sun & Dec, Sat-Sun 10-4. Closed Mon ex BH **Fees** £5.95 (ch £3.95, concessions £4.95). Family ticket £16. Party rates available **Facilities** Ⓟ ♿ (partly accessible) (access to ground floor only) (lift, inaccessible items pack, audio/large print guides) shop

RHAYADER Map 6 SN96

Gilfach Nature Discovery Centre and Reserve

St Harmon LD6 5LF
☎ 01597 823298
e-mail: info@rwtwales.org
web: www.rwtwales.org
dir: From A470 turn right into reserve, before cattle grid turn right and follow road

Situated in the Cambrian Mountains, Gilfach is locally unique due to its wide variety of habitats; high moorland to enclosed meadow, oak woodland to rocky upland river. The reserve therefore supports a tremendous abundance of plants and animals within a relatively small area. This richness of wildlife has adapted to living in the various habitats created over the centuries through the practice of traditional farming. Visitors can take a number of planned walks including the Nature Trail, the Monks Trod Trail, and the Oakwood Path. The Nature Discovery Centre offers the opportunity to learn about the various habitats and wildlife featuring footage from cameras in nestboxes, games and quizzes.

Times Open Reserve all year. Visitor Centre & Nature Discovery Centre open Etr-Sep during wknds, BHs & school hols* **Facilities** Ⓟ Ⓟ ☕ (outdoor) ♿ (partly accessible) (the centre & otter hide is accessible) toilets for disabled (wheelchair access path to viewpoint) shop

TRETOWER Map 3 SO12

Tretower Court & Castle

NP8 1RD
☎ 01874 730279
web: www.cadw.wales.gov.uk
dir: 3m NW of Crickhowell, off A479

The castle is a substantial ruin of an 11th-century motte and bailey, with a three-storey tower and 9ft-thick walls. Nearby is the Court, a 14th-century fortified manor house which has been altered and extended over the years. The two buildings show the shift from medieval castle to more domestic accommodation over the centuries.

Times Open end May-Oct daily 10-5; Nov-Mar, Fri & Sat 10-4, Sun 11-4 **Fees** £3 (ch 5-15, concessions £2.60, disabled visitors & assisting companion free). Family ticket (2ad+all ch/grandch under 16) £8.60. Group rates available. Prices quoted apply until 31 Mar 2011* **Facilities** Ⓟ toilets for disabled shop

WELSHPOOL Map 7 SJ20

Powis Castle & Garden

SY21 8RF
☎ 01938 551920 & 551929 Fax 01938 554336
e-mail: powis.castle@nationaltrust.org.uk
web: www.nationaltrust.org.uk
dir: 1m S of Welshpool, signed off A483

Laid out in the Italian and French styles, the Garden retains its original lead statues, an Orangery and an aviary on the terraces. The medieval castle contains one of the finest collections of paintings and furniture in Wales and a beautiful collection of treasures from India. Please visit website for details of events running throughout the year.

Times Open 6 Apr-29 Oct, Thu-Mon; Wed-Mon Jul-Aug, castle & museum 1-5, gardens 11-6* **Facilities** Ⓟ licensed (outdoor) ♿ (partly accessible) (please phone for details) toilets for disabled (photos of interior, braille guides, virtual tour) shop

RHONDDA CYNON TAFF

TREHAFOD — Map 3 ST09

Rhondda Heritage Park

Lewis Merthyr Colliery, Coed Cae Rd CF37 2NP
☎ 01443 682036 & 680932 Fax 01443 687420
e-mail: info@rhonddaheritagepark.com
web: www.rhonddaheritagepark.com
dir: between Pontypridd & Porth, off A470, follow brown heritage signs from M4 junct 32

Based at the Lewis Merthyr Colliery, the Heritage Park is a fascinating 'living history' attraction. You can take the Cage Ride to 'Pit Bottom' and explore the underground workings of a 1950s pit, guided by men who were miners themselves. There are children's activities, an art gallery and a museum illustrating living conditions in the Rhondda Valley. Special events throughout the year, phone for details.

Times Open all year daily 9-4.30 (last admission 4); Oct-Etr, daily (ex Mon). Closed 25 Dec-early Jan **Fees** £5.60 (ch £4.30, pen £4.95). Family ticket (4) from £16.50, (6) £21 **Facilities** licensed (indoor & outdoor) (partly accessible) (assistance required underground) toilets for disabled (wheelchair available, accessible parking, lifts) shop

SWANSEA

LLANRHIDIAN — Map 2 SS49

Weobley Castle

SA3 1HB
☎ 01792 390012
web: www.cadw.wales.gov.uk
dir: from B4271 or B4295

A 12th-to 14th-century fortified manor house with an exhibition on the history of Weobley and other historic sites on the Gower peninsula.

Times Open all year, Apr-Oct, daily 9.30-6; Nov-Mar, daily 9.30-5 **Fees** £2.60 (ch 5-15, concessions £2.25, disabled visitors & assisting companion free). Family ticket (2ad+all ch/grandch under 16) £7.50. Group rates available. Prices quoted apply until 31 Mar 2011* **Facilities** shop

OXWICH — Map 2 SS48

Oxwich Castle

SA3 1NG
☎ 01792 390359
web: www.cadw.wales.gov.uk
dir: A4118 from Swansea

Situated on the Gower peninsula, this Tudor mansion is a striking testament in stone to the pride and ambitions of the Mansel dynasty of Welsh gentry. The E-shaped wing houses an exhibition on historical Gower and 'Chieftains and Princes of Wales'.

Times Open Apr-Sep, daily 10-5 **Fees** £2.60 (ch 5-15, concessions £2.25, disabled visitors & assisting companion free). Family ticket (2ad+all ch/grandch under 16) £7.45. Group rates available. Prices quoted apply until 31 Mar 2011* **Facilities** toilets for disabled (Radar key toilet)

PARKMILL — Map 2 SS58

Gower Heritage Centre — 2 FOR 1

Y Felin Ddwr SA3 2EH
☎ 01792 371206 Fax 01792 371471
e-mail: info@gowerheritagecentre.co.uk
web: www.gowerheritagecentre.co.uk
dir: follow signs for South Gower on A4118 W from Swansea. W side of Parkmill village

Based around a 12th-century water-powered cornmill, the site also contains a number of craft workshops, two play areas, animals, a museum and a miller's cottage, all set in attractive countryside in an Area of Outstanding Natural Beauty.

Times Open all year, daily, Mar-Oct 10-5.30; Nov-Feb 10-4.30. Closed 25 Dec **Fees** £5.50 (ch & pen £4.50). Family ticket (2ad+4ch) £18* **Facilities** licensed (partly accessible) (95% of site accessible, some steps & uneven floors) toilets for disabled (ramp entrance access, amplification system guided tours) shop

SWANSEA — Map 3 SS69

Glynn Vivain Art Gallery

Alexandra Rd SA1 5DZ
☎ 01792 516900 Fax 01792 516903
e-mail: glynn.vivian.gallery@swansea.gov.uk
web: www.glynnviviangallery.org
dir: M4 junct 42 along Fabian Way A483 up Wind St. Left at train station opposite Swansea Metropolitan University Art College

A broad spectrum of visual arts form the original bequest of Richard Glynn Vivian, including old masters and an international collection of porcelain and Swansea china. The 20th century is also well represented with modern painting and sculpture by British and foreign artists, with the emphasis on Welsh artists. On-going temporary exhibitions showcase the work of contemporary artists.

Times Open all year, Tue-Sun & BH Mon 10-5. Closed 25-26 Dec & 1 Jan* **Facilities** (partly accessible) toilets for disabled (hearing loop, audio guides) shop

WALES

SWANSEA *continued*

Plantasia **2 FOR 1**

Parc Tawe SA1 2AL

☎ 01792 474555 📠 01792 464743

e-mail: swansea.plantasia@swansea.gov.uk

web: www.plantasia.org

dir: M4 Junct 42, follow A483 into Swansea, follow car park signs for attraction

Plantasia is a unique tropical haven of exotic plants and animals. Within the impressive glass pyramid is a luscious rainforest filled with over 500 tropical plants and a terraced waterfall flowing into a fish-filled lagoon. There is also a mini-zoo where monkeys, reptiles, birds and insects can be seen

Times Open daily 10-5, including BHs. Closed Mon in Dec, Xmas & first two weeks of Jan* **Fees** £3.90 (ch & concessions £2.95). Family ticket £13* **Facilities** Ⓟ Ⓟ ☕ ♿ (fully accessible) toilets for disabled shop ⊗

Swansea Museum **FREE**

Victoria Rd, Maritime Quarter SA1 1SN

☎ 01792 653763 📠 01792 652585

e-mail: swansea.museum@swansea.gov.uk

web: www.swanseaheritage.net

dir: M4 junct 42, on main road into city centre, just past Sainsurys on left

This is the oldest museum in Wales, showing the history of Swansea from the earliest times until today. The museum has a Tramshed and floating boats to explore (summer only). There is a continuous programme of temporary exhibitions and events all year around. The collections centre is nearby which is open to the public every Wednesday.

Times Open all year, Tue-Sun 10-5 (last admission 4.45). Closed Mon except BH Mon, 25-26 Dec & 1 Jan **Facilities** Ⓟ Ⓟ ⛩ (outdoor) ♿ (fully accessible) toilets for disabled shop ⊗

TORFAEN

BLAENAVON — Map 3 SO20

Big Pit National Coal Museum **FREE**

NP4 9XP

☎ 01495 790311 📠 01495 792618

e-mail: post@museumwales.ac.uk

web: www.museumwales.ac.uk

dir: M4 junct 25/26, follow signs on A4042 & A4043 to Pontypool & Blaenavon. Signed off A465

The Real Underground Experience, Big Pit is the UK's leading mining museum. It is a real colliery and was the place of work for hundreds of men, woman and children for over 200 years. A daily struggle to extract the precious mineral that stoked furnaces and lit household fires across the world.

Times Open all year 9.30-5. Please call for underground guided tour availability* **Facilities** Ⓟ ☕ ♿ (partly accessible) toilets for disabled (underground tours by prior arrangement) shop ⊗

Blaenavon Ironworks **FREE**

North St NP4 9RN

☎ 01495 792615

web: www.cadw.wales.gov.uk

The Blaenavon Ironworks were a milestone in the history of the Industrial Revolution. Constructed in 1788-99, they were the first purpose-built, multi-furnace ironworks in Wales. By 1796, Blaenavon was the second largest ironworks in Wales, eventually closing down in 1904.

Times Open all year, Apr-Oct, daily 10-5; Nov-Mar, Fri-Sat 9.30-4, Sun 11-4 **Facilities** Ⓟ ⊗ ✣

CWMBRAN — Map 3 ST29

Greenmeadow Community Farm **2 FOR 1**

Greenforge Way NP44 5AJ

☎ 01633 647662 📠 01633 647671

e-mail: greenmeadowcommunityfarm@torfaen.gov.uk

web: www.greenmeadowcommunityfarm.org.uk

dir: M4 junct 26. Follow signs for Cwmbran then brown signs with white sheep

Greenmeadow Community Farm has been a working farm for over 250 years. Set in over 150 acres, it has a wide range of pedigree and rare animals which you can meet up close. Nestled in the heart of Cwmbran, this is a community farm in every sense of the word, working closely with and serving the local community and welcoming visitors from far and wide. The cosy farmhouse café offers a selection of homemade specials. Milking demonstrations held daily, tractor and trailer rides, a farm trail and lots more.

Times Open all year, daily, Apr-Oct 10-6; Nov-Mar 10-4.30 (last admission 1 hr before close) **Fees** £4.50 (ch £3.50). Family ticket (2ad+3ch) £16, Nov-Mar; £5 (ch £4). Family ticket (2 ad+2ch) £18 Apr-Oct. Season tickets available **Facilities** Ⓟ Ⓟ ☕ ⛩ (outdoor) ♿ (partly accessible) (some slopes and uneven paths, some rooms accessible by stairs only) toilets for disabled (tractor & trailer rides for wheelchair users) shop

VALE OF GLAMORGAN

BARRY — Map 3 ST16

Welsh Hawking Centre **2 FOR 1**

Weycock Rd CF62 3AA

☎ 01446 734687 📠 01446 739620

e-mail: norma@welsh-hawking.co.uk

dir: on A4226

There are over 200 birds of prey here, including eagles, hawks, owls, buzzards and falcons. They can be seen and photographed in the mews and some of the breeding aviaries. There are flying demonstrations at regular intervals during the day. A variety of tame, friendly animals, such as guinea pigs, horses and rabbits will delight younger visitors.

Times Open late Mar-late Sep, daily 10.30-5 (1hr before dusk in winter) **Fees** £5 (ch £3)* **Facilities** (outdoor) (fully accessible) toilets for disabled shop

OGMORE Map 3 SS87

Ogmore Castle FREE

01443 336000
web: www.cadw.wales.gov.uk
dir: 2.5m SW of Bridgend, on B4524

Standing on the River Ogmore, the west wall of this castle is 40ft high. A hooded fireplace is preserved in the 12th-century, three-storey keep and a dry moat surrounds the inner ward.

Times Open all year, access available at all reasonable times, which will normally be 10-4 daily. Key keeper arrangement. **Facilities**

PENARTH Map 3 ST17

Cosmeston Lakes Country Park & Medieval Village

Lavernock Rd CF64 5UY
029 2070 1678 029 2070 8686
e-mail: NColes@valeofglamorgan.gov.uk
web: www.valeofglamorgan.gov.uk
dir: on B4267 between Barry and Penarth

Deserted during the plagues and famines of the 14th century, the original village was rediscovered through archaeological excavations. The buildings have been faithfully reconstructed on the excavated remains, creating a living museum of medieval village life. Special events throughout the year include re-enactments and Living History.

Times Open all year, daily 11-5 summer, 11-4 winter. Closed 25 Dec. Country park open at all times **Facilities** licensed (partly accessible) toilets for disabled (access ramps & wheelchair hire) shop

ST HILARY Map 3 ST07

Old Beaupre Castle FREE

01443 336000
web: www.cadw.wales.gov.uk
dir: 1m SW, off A48

This ruined manor house was rebuilt during the 16th century. Its most notable features are an Italianate gatehouse and porch. The porch is an unusual three-storeyed structure.

Times Open all year, access available at all reasonable times, which will normally be 10-4 daily. Key keeper arrangement **Facilities**

WREXHAM

CHIRK Map 7 SJ23

Chirk Castle

LL14 5AF
01691 777701 01691 774706
e-mail: chirkcastle@nationaltrust.org.uk
web: www.nationaltrust.org.uk/main/w-chirkcastle
dir: 8m S of Wrexham, signed off A483, 5m from Llangollen signed off A5

Chirk Castle is one of a chain of late 13th-century Marcher castles. Its high walls and drum towers have hardly changed, but the inside shows the varied tastes of 700 years of occupation. One of the least altered parts is The Adam Tower. Many of the medieval-looking decorations were created by Pugin in the 19th century. Varied furnishings include fine tapestries. In the garden there are beautiful views that take in seven counties.

Times Open 9 Mar-Jun, Wed-Sun 11-5; Jul-Oct, daily 11-5; Garden 2 Feb-1 Mar, Sat-Sun 10-4; 2 Mar-Jun, Wed-Sun 10-6; Jul-Oct, daily 10-6. Open BH Mon **Fees** Full Castle £10 (ch £5). Family ticket £25. Garden & Tower £7.20 (ch £3.60). Family ticket £18 **Facilities** (outdoor) (partly accessible) (access to east wing, garden, laundries, servants hall) toilets for disabled (stairclimber, hearing loop, coach from car park) shop

WREXHAM Map 7 SJ35

Erddig

LL13 0YT
01978 355314 01978 313333
e-mail: erddig@nationaltrust.org.uk
web: www.nationaltrust.org.uk
dir: off A525, 2m S of Wrexham & A483/A5152

Built in 1680, the house was enlarged and improved by a wealthy London lawyer with a passion for gilt and silver furniture. Original furnishings remain, including a magnificent state bed in Chinese silk. The house is notable for the view it gives of both 'upstairs' and 'downstairs' life. The gardens, unusually, have been changed very little since the 18th century. The country park includes part of Wat's Dyke, a cup and saucer waterfall, examples of ridge and furrow field systems and a motte and bailey castle. Woodland walks and carriage rides available. Special events take place in spring, summer and autumn, please contact for details.

Times Open 13 Mar-Oct, Sat-Wed (open Good Fri & Thu in Jul-Aug), house 12-5, garden 11-6* **Facilities** licensed (outdoor) (partly accessible) (no access to first floor of house) toilets for disabled (4 wheelchairs available) shop

WALES

NORTHERN IRELAND

Giants Causeway, Co Antrim

CO ANTRIM

ANTRIM Map 1 D5

Antrim Round Tower FREE

BT41 1BJ
☎ 028 9023 5000 028 9031 0288
web: www.ehsni.gov.uk
dir: N of town

Antrim round tower stands among lawns and trees but it was once surrounded by monastic buildings. Antrim was an important early monastery, probably a 6th-century foundation, closely linked with Bangor.

Times Open all year. **Facilities** Ⓟ

BALLYCASTLE Map 1 D6

Bonamargy Friary FREE

☎ 028 9023 5000 028 9031 0288
web: www.ehsni.gov.uk
dir: E of town, at golf course

Founded by Rory MacQuillan around 1500 and later passed on to the MacDonnells, Earls of Antrim, there are still remains of the friary gatehouse, church and cloister for visitors to see.

Times Open all year. **Facilities** Ⓟ

BALLYLUMFORD Map 1 D5

Ballylumford Dolmen FREE

☎ 028 9023 5000 028 9031 0288
web: www.ehsni.gov.uk
dir: on B90 on NW tip of Island Magee

Incorporated in the front garden of a house in Ballylumford Road are the remains of this huge 4-5,000-year-old single-chamber Neolithic tomb, also known as the Druid's Altar.

Times Open all year.

BALLYMENA Map 1 D5

Ecos Visitor & Conference Centre FREE

Ecos Centre, Kernohams Ln, Broughshane Rd BT43 7QA
☎ 028 2566 4400 028 2563 8984
web: www.ballymena.gov.uk/ecos
dir: follow signs from M2 bypass at Ballymena

Plenty of fun and adventure for all the family with duck feeding, toy tractors and sand pit. The centre hosts two interactive galleries, one on sustainability and one on biodiversity, and you can stroll through the willow tunnel and enjoy the play park.

Times Open Etr-Oct, Mon-Fri 9-5; Jun-Aug, Sat-Sun 12-5 (last admission 4)* **Facilities** Ⓟ (outdoor) (fully accessible) toilets for disabled shop

Harryville Motte FREE

☎ 028 9023 5000 028 9031 0288
web: www.ehsni.gov.uk
dir: N bank of River Braid

On a ridge to the south of the town, this Norman fort, with its 40ft-high motte and rectangular bailey, is one of the finest examples of Norman earthworks left in Northern Ireland.

Times Open all year. **Facilities** Ⓟ

BALLYMONEY Map 1 C6

Leslie Hill Open Farm 2 FOR 1

Leslie Hill BT53 6QL
☎ 028 2766 6803 028 2766 6803
web: www.lesliehillopenfarm.co.uk
dir: 1m NW of Ballymoney on MacFin Rd

An 18th-century estate with a Georgian house, magnificent period farm buildings, and fine grounds with paths, lakes and trees. Attractions include an extensive collection of rare breeds, poultry, horsedrawn machinery and carriages, exhibition rooms, a museum, working forge, deer park, walled garden and an adventure playground.

Times Open Jul-Aug, Mon-Sat 11-6, Sun 2-6; Jun, Sat-Sun & BHs 2-6; Etr-May, Sun & BHs 2-6, open all Etr wk 11-6 **Fees** £4 (ch £3). Family ticket £12* **Facilities** Ⓟ (indoor & outdoor) (fully accessible) toilets for disabled (ramps) shop

BUSHMILLS Map 1 C6

Old Bushmills Distillery

BT57 8XH
☎ 028 2073 1521 028 2073 1339
e-mail: sheelagh.croskery@diageo.com
web: www.bushmills.com
dir: on Castlecatt Rd, in Bushmills Village

Old Bushmills was granted its licence in 1608 and is the oldest licenced whiskey distillery in the world. There's a guided tour, and afterwards you can take part in a comparative tasting session and become a whiskey expert.

Times Open all year, Apr-Oct, Mon-Sat 9.30-5.30, Sun 12-5.30 (last tour 4); Nov-Mar, Mon-Fri 5 tours daily, 10.30, 11.30, 1.30, 2.30 & 3.30. Sat & Sun 3 tours, 1.30, 2.30, 3.30. Closed 12 Jul, Good Fri pm, Xmas & New Year* **Facilities** Ⓟ licensed (partly accessible) toilets for disabled (audio visual theatre, shops & restaurant) shop

IRELAND

CARRICK-A-REDE — Map 1 D6

Carrick-a-rede Rope Bridge and Larrybane Visitor Centre

BT54 6LS
☎ 028 2076 9839 & 2073 1582 (office) 028 2073 2963
e-mail: carrickarede@nationaltrust.org.uk
web: www.nationaltrust.org.uk
dir: E of Ballintoy on B15

On the North Antrim Coastal Path is one of Northern Ireland's best-loved attractions: Carrick-a-Rede Rope Bridge and the disused limestone quarry of Larrybane. The island of Carrick is known as 'the rock in the road', as it is an obstacle on the path of migrating salmon, and fishermen have taken advantage of this to net the fish here for over 300 years.

Times Open Bridge daily (weather permitting), 28 Feb-24 May & Sep-1 Nov 10-6, 25 May-Aug 10-7. (last admission 45 mins before closing). Coastal path open all year* **Facilities** (outdoor) (partly accessible) toilets for disabled (information centre, telescope at wheelchair height)

CARRICKFERGUS — Map 1 D5

Carrickfergus Castle

Marine Highway BT38 7BG
☎ 028 9335 1273
web: www.ehsni.gov.uk
dir: on N shore of Belfast Lough

Imposingly placed on a rocky headland overlooking Belfast Lough, this is the best preserved and probably the most fought-over Norman castle in Ireland. Built by John de Courcy, Earl of Ulster, after 1180, it served a military purpose for more than eight centuries. Exhibits include a giant model of the castle, a short film, and a banqueting suite. The castle is often used as a venue for medieval banquets and fairs. There is a visitors' centre, shop and refreshment point.

Times Open all year, daily, Etr-end Sep, 10-6; Oct-Etr 10-4 (last admission 30mins before closing)* **Facilities** toilets for disabled shop

Town Walls — FREE

☎ 028 9023 5000 028 9031 0288
web: www.ehsni.gov.uk

Lord Deputy Sir Arthur Chichester enclosed Carrickfergus with stone walls from 1611 onwards and more than half the circuit is still visible, often to its full height of 4 metres to the wall walk.

Times Visible at all times. **Facilities**

CHURCHTOWN — Map 1 D5

Cranfield Church — FREE

☎ 028 9023 5000 028 9031 0288
web: www.ehsni.gov.uk
dir: 3.75m SW of Randalstown

This small medieval church is situated on the shores of Lough Neagh. Beside it is a famous holy well.

Times Open all year. **Facilities**

GIANT'S CAUSEWAY — Map 1 C6

Giant's Causeway Centre

44 Causeway Rd BT57 8SU
☎ 028 2073 1855 028 2073 2537
e-mail: causewaytic@hotmail.com
web: www.northantrim.com
dir: 2m N of Bushmills on B146

This dramatic rock formation is undoubtedly one of the wonders of the natural world. The Centre provides an exhibition and audio-visual show, and Ulsterbus provides a minibus service to the stones and there are guided walks, and special facilities for the disabled.

Times Open all year, daily from 10 (closes 7 Jul & Aug). Closed 1 wk Xmas* **Facilities** licensed (partly accessible) toilets for disabled (mini bus transport with wheelchair hoist, reserved parking) shop

LARNE — Map 1 D5

Olderfleet Castle — FREE

☎ 028 9023 5000 028 9031 0288
web: www.ehsni.gov.uk

A 16th-century tower house, the last surviving of three which defended Larne.

Times Open at all times.

LISBURN — Map 1 D5

Duneight Motte and Bailey — FREE

☎ 028 9023 5000 028 9031 0288
web: www.ehsni.gov.uk
dir: 2.3m S beside Ravernet River

Impressive Anglo-Norman earthwork castle with high mound-embanked enclosure, making use of the defences of an earlier pre-Norman fort.

Times Open all year.

Irish Linen Centre & Lisburn Museum

FREE

Market Square BT28 1AG
☎ 028 9266 3377 📠 028 9267 2624
e-mail: irishlinencentre@lisburn.gov.uk
web: www.lisburncity.gov.uk
dir: Signed both in and outside town centre. Follow tourist signs from M1

The centre tells the story of the Irish linen industry past and present. The recreation of individual factory scenes brings the past to life and a series of imaginative hands-on activities describe the linen manufacturing processes. The Museum has a range of temporary exhibitions of local interest.

Times Open all year, Mon-Sat, 9.30-5.* **Facilities** Ⓟ ☕ ♿ (fully accessible) toilets for disabled (lift, induction loop, staff trained in sign language) shop ⊗

PORTBALLINTRAE — Map 1 C6

Dunluce Castle

87 Dunluce Rd BT57 8UY
☎ 028 2073 1938 📠 028 2073 2850
web: www.ehsni.gov.uk
dir: off A2

Extensive and picturesque ruins of a 16th-century castle perched on a rocky crag high above the sea. Stronghold of the MacQuillans and MacDonnells, who significantly altered the original stonebuilt fortress. Randal MacDonnell built a house in the centre of the castle, of which parts of the Great Hall remain, as do the towers and early 17th-century gatehouse. The castle has new displays and there is an audio-visual show. The cave below the ruins provided a secret way into and out of the castle from the sea.

Times Open all year, daily, Etr-end Sep, 10-6; Oct-Etr, 10-4 (last admission 30 mins before closing)* **Facilities** 🅟 ⛩ ♿ (partly accessible) (areas of original paving & cobbles make wheelchair access difficult) toilets for disabled shop

TEMPLEPATRICK — Map 1 D5

Pattersons Spade Mill

2 FOR 1

751 Antrim Rd BT39 0AP
☎ 028 9443 9713 📠 028 9443 9713
e-mail: pattersons@nationaltrust.org.uk
web: www.nationaltrust.org.uk/main/w-pattersonsspademill
dir: 2m SE of Templepatrick on A6

See history literally forged in steel at the last working water-driven spade mill in daily use in the British Isles. Hear the hammers, smell the grit, feel the heat and witness the thrills of traditional spade making. Guided tours virtually capture life during the Industrial Revolution and dig up the history and culture of the humble spade.

Times Open 14 Mar-May & 5-27 Sep, wknds & BHs; 10-19 Apr, daily; Jun-Aug Wed-Mon 2-6 **Fees** £5 (ch £2.80). Family Ticket £12.80* **Facilities** 🅟 ⛩ (outdoor) ♿ (fully accessible) toilets for disabled (ramps, wheelchair available) 🌿

Templetown Mausoleum

FREE

BT39
web: www.ntni.org.uk
dir: in Castle Upton graveyard on A6, Belfast-Antrim road

Situated in the graveyard of Castle Upton, this family mausoleum is in the shape of a triumphal arch and was designed by Robert Adam.

Times Open daily during daylight hours. **Facilities** 🅟 Ⓟ 🌿

CO ARMAGH

ARMAGH — Map 1 C5

Armagh County Museum

FREE

The Mall East BT61 9BE
☎ 028 3752 3070 📠 028 3752 2631
e-mail: acm.info@nmni.com
web: www.nmni.com/acm
dir: in city centre

Housed in a 19th-century schoolhouse, this museum contains an art gallery and library, as well as a collection of local folkcrafts, natural history, costume and railway material. Special events are planned throughout the year.

Times Open all year, Mon-Fri 10-5, Sat 10-1 & 2-5 **Facilities** Ⓟ ♿ (fully accessible) toilets for disabled shop ⊗

Armagh Friary

FREE

☎ 028 9023 5000 📠 028 9031 0288
web: www.ehsni.gov.uk
dir: SE edge of town

Situated just inside the gates of the former Archbishop's Palace are the remains of the longest friary church in Ireland (163ft). The friary was established in 1263 by Archbishop O'Scanail and destroyed by Shane O'Neill in the middle of the 16th century to prevent it being garrisoned by Elizabethan soldiers.

Times Open all year. **Facilities** 🅟

Armagh Planetarium

College Hill BT61 9DB
☎ 028 3752 3689 & 4725 📠 028 3752 6187
e-mail: info@armaghplanet.com
web: www.armaghplanet.com
dir: on Armagh-Belfast road close to mall, city centre

The Planetarium is home to The Digital Theatre, a multi-media environment equipped with the latest Planetarium projector technology and state-of-the-art sound system. Also featured are the space displays in the Galileo Hall, Copernicus Hall, Tycho, Cassini and Kepler rooms and surrounding the Planetarium is the Astropark, a 25-acre area where you can walk through the Solar System and the Universe.

Times Open all year, Sat-Sun 11.30-5. Mon during term time; May-Jun & Sep-Dec wkdys 1-5, Jul-Aug daily 11.30-5* **Fees** £6 (ch & concessions £5). Family ticket (2ad&3ch) £20. Exhibition area only £2* **Facilities** 🅟 Ⓟ ☕ ⛩ (outdoor) ♿ (fully accessible) toilets for disabled (loop system in theatre, lifts/ramps) shop ⊗

IRELAND

ARMAGH *continued*

Navan Centre & Fort 2 FOR 1

81 Killylea Rd BT60 4LD
☎ 028 3752 9655 🖷 028 3752 6431
e-mail: navan@armagh.gov.uk
web: www.navan.com
dir: 2.5m W on A28

Navan was once known as Emain Macha, the ancient seat of kings and earliest capital of Ulster. Today it is an impressive archaeological site with its own museum and visitor centre located in a building that blends into the landscape. The Navan Centre uses audio-visuals and interactive devices to unravel history from myth. Travel into the 'Real World' of archaeology and the 'Other World' to hear the legends of the Ulster Cycle.

Times Open daily, Oct-Mar 10-4 (last admission 3); Apr-Sep 10-7 (last admission 5.30) **Fees** £5.50 (ch £3.75, pens £4.50). Family ticket £15.75* **Facilities** (outdoor) (fully accessible) toilets for disabled (loop for hearing aids, parking, full disabled facilities) shop

Saint Patrick's Trian Visitor Complex 2 FOR 1

40 English St BT61 7BA
☎ 028 3752 1801 🖷 028 3751 0180
e-mail: info@saintpatrickstrian.com
web: www.visitarmagh.com
dir: in city centre

An exciting visitor complex in the heart of the city. Incorporating three major exhibitions - The Armagh story: traces Armagh's historic Pagan monuments through to the coming of St Patrick and Celtic Christianity to the modern day city. Patrick's Testament: takes a closer look at Ireland's patron saint through the writings found in ancient manuscript the Book of Armagh. The Land of Lilliput: Jonathan Swift's most famous book, *Gulliver's Travels* is narrated by a 20-foot giant.

Times Open all year, Mon-Sat 10-5, Sun 2-5. Closed 12 Jul **Fees** £5.50 (ch £3.75, pen £4.50). Family ticket £15.75* **Facilities** licensed (fully accessible) toilets for disabled (specially designed for disabled) shop

IRELAND

CAMLOUGH Map 1 D5

Killevy Churches FREE

☎ 028 9023 5000 🖷 028 9031 0288
web: www.ehsni.gov.uk
dir: 3m S lower eastern slopes of Slieve Gullion

The ruins of the two churches (10th and 13th-century) stand back to back, at the foot of Slieve Gullion sharing a common wall, but with no way through from one to the other. The churches stand on the site of an important nunnery founded by St Monenna in the 5th century. A huge granite slab in the graveyard supposedly marks the founder's grave. A holy well can be reached by climbing the path north of the graveyard. The nunnery was in use until the Dissolution in 1542.

Times Open all year.

JONESBOROUGH Map 1 D5

Kilnasaggart Inscribed Stone FREE

☎ 028 9023 5000 🖷 028 9031 0288
web: www.ehsni.gov.uk
dir: 1.25m S

A granite pillar stone dating back to the 8th century, with numerous crosses and a long Irish inscription carved on it.

Times Open all year.

MOY Map 1 C5

The Argory

Derrycaw Rd BT71 6NA
☎ 028 8778 4753 🖷 028 8778 9598
e-mail: argory@nationaltrust.org.uk
web: www.nationaltrust.org.uk
dir: 3m NE

Built in the 1820s, this handsome Irish gentry house sits surveying the surrounding 320 acre wooded riverside estate. The former home of the McGeough family, a tour of this neo-classical masterpiece reveals it is unchanged since 1900 - the eclectic interior still evoking the family's Edwardian tastes and interests.

Times Grounds: Open daily Feb-Apr & Oct-Jan; May-Sep, 10-6. House: Open 14 Mar-Jun & 5-27 Sep, wknds & BH; Good Fri-19 Apr, Jul & Aug daily 1-5.30. (last admission 1hr before closing)* **Facilities** (outdoor) (partly accessible) toilets for disabled (parking facilities, wheelchair available, Braille) shop

NEWRY Map 1 D5

Moyry Castle FREE

☎ 028 9023 5000 🖷 028 9031 0288
web: www.ehsni.gov.uk
dir: 7.5m S

This tall, three-storey keep was built by Lord Mountjoy, Queen Elizabeth's deputy, in 1601, its purpose to secure the Gap of the North which was the main route into Ulster.

Times Open all year

OXFORD ISLAND Map 1 D5

Lough Neagh Discovery Centre

Oxford Island National Nature, Reserve BT66 6NJ
☎ 028 3832 2205 🖷 028 3831 1699
e-mail: oxford.island@craigavon.gov.uk
web: www.oxfordisland.com
dir: signed from M1 junct 10

In a spectacular setting on the water's edge, discover natural history, wildlife, family walks and much more.

Times Open all year, Apr-Sep, Mon-Fri 9-5, Sat 10-5, Sun 10-6; Oct-Mar, Mon-Fri 9-5, Sat-Sun 10-5 **Fees** Free except for events **Facilities** (outdoor) (fully accessible) toilets for disabled (bird watching hides) shop

PORTADOWN Map 1 D5

Ardress House

64 Ardress Rd, Annaghmore BT62 1SQ
☎ 028 3885 1236 & 8778 4753 📠 028 3885 1236
e-mail: ardress@nationaltrust.org.uk
web: www.nationaltrust.org.uk
dir: on B28, 5m from Moy, 5m from Portadown, 3m from M1 junct 13

A charming 17th-century farmhouse, elegantly remodelled in Georgian times by its visionary architect-owner George Ensor. The grounds are beautifully unspoilt and there is a traditional farmyard with livestock (popular with children) and a display of farm implements. Explore the apple orchards and scenic walks, and see the table where George V signed the Constitution of Northern Ireland in 1921.

Times Open 14 Mar-27 Sep, wknds, BH/PHs 2-6; 21-22 Feb 12-4; Jul & Aug also open Thu; Etr, daily 2-6 (last admission 1hr before closing)* **Facilities** Ⓟ (outdoor) (partly accessible) toilets for disabled shop

TYNAN Map 1 C5

Village Cross FREE

☎ 028 9023 5000 📠 028 9031 0288
web: www.ehsni.gov.uk

A carved High Cross, 11ft tall, which lay broken in two pieces for many years, but was skilfully mended in 1844.

Times Open all year **Facilities** Ⓟ

BELFAST

BELFAST Map 1 D5

Belfast Zoological Gardens

Antrim Rd BT36 7PN
☎ 028 9077 6277 📠 028 9037 0578
e-mail: info@belfastzoo.co.uk
web: www.belfastzoo.co.uk
dir: M2 junct 4 signed to Glengormley. Follow signs off rdbt to Zoo

The 50-acre zoo has a dramatic setting on the face of Cave Hill, enjoying spectacular views. Attractions include the primate house (gorillas and chimpanzees), penguin enclosure, free-flight aviary, African enclosure, and underwater viewing of sealions and penguins. There are also red pandas, lemurs and a group of very rare spectacled bears. Recent additions to the collection include capybara, crowned lemurs, tawny frogmouth and laughing kookaburra, tree kangaroo and giant anteater.

Times Open all year, Apr-Sep, daily 10-7 (last admission 5); Oct-Mar 10-4 (last admission 2.30). Closed 25-26 Dec* **Facilities** Ⓟ Ⓟ licensed (outdoor) (fully accessible) toilets for disabled (free admission, reserved parking, scooters available) shop

Botanic Gardens FREE

3 College Park, Off Botanic Ave. BT7 1LP
☎ 028 9032 4902 📠 028 9032 4902
e-mail: maxwellr@belfastcity.gov.uk
web: www.belfastcity.gov.uk
dir: from City Hall, Bedford St then Dublin road for Botanic Avenue

One highlight of the park is the beautiful glass-domed Victorian Palm House, built between 1839-52. This palm house pre-dates the one in Kew Gardens and is one of the earliest curved glass and iron structures in the world. Another feature is the Tropical Ravine - stand on a balcony to get a wonderful view through a steamy ravine full of exotic plants.

Times Open Palm House Tropical Ravine: Open all year, Apr-Sep 10-12, 1-5; Oct-Mar 10-12, 1-4. Sat, Sun & BHs 1-5 summer, 1-4 winter **Facilities** Ⓟ toilets for disabled

Giant's Ring FREE

☎ 028 9023 5000 📠 028 9031 0288
web: www.ehsni.gov.uk
dir: 0.75m S of Shaws Bridge

Circular, Bronze-age enclosure nearly 200 feet in diameter similar in style to Stonehenge, with a stone chambered grave in the centre and bordered by banks 20 feet wide and 12 feet high. Very little is known for certain about this site, except that it was used for ritual burial.

Times Open all times. **Facilities** Ⓟ

Ulster Museum FREE

Botanic Gardens BT9 5AB
☎ 028 9044 0000 📠 028 9038 3003
e-mail: info@nmni.com
web: www.nmni.com
dir: 1m S of city centre on Stranmillis road

The Ulster Museum, winner of the 2010 Art Fund prize, is the perfect place to explore the arts, ancient and modern history, and the nature of Ireland. Come face to face with dinosaurs, meet an Ancient Egyptian mummy and see modern masterpieces. Art displays change regularly but always include a rich variety of Irish and international paintings, drawings and sculpture, along with ceramics, glass and costume. The history galleries tell the story of the north of Ireland from the Ice Age to the present day. The natural environment is explored in the Habitas galleries. There is a programme of special events throughout the year.

Times Open all year daily, Tue-Sun 10-5; open NI BHs **Facilities** Ⓟ (fully accessible) toilets for disabled (lifts, ramps, hand rails) shop

BELFAST *continued*

W5 at Odyssey

2 Queens Quay BT3 9QQ
☎ 028 9046 7700 028 9046 7707
web: www.w5online.co.uk

W5 investigates Who? What? Where? When? Why?... and that pretty much sums up the intent behind Ireland's first purpose built discovery centre. Visitors of any age will want to get their hands on interactive science and technology displays that include the laser harp, the fog knife, microscopes, robots and computers. W5 is part of a massive Millennium Landmark Project in the heart of Belfast.

Times Open all year Mon-Sat 10-6, Sun 12-6. Closed 25-26 Dec & 12 Jul* **Facilities** licensed (partly accessible) toilets for disabled (hearing loop) shop

CO DOWN

BALLYWALTER — Map 1 D5

Grey Abbey — FREE

☎ 028 9054 6552
web: www.ehsni.gov.uk
dir: on E edge of village

Founded in 1193 by Affreca, daughter of the King of the Isle of Man, these extensive ruins of a Cistercian abbey, sitting in lovely sheltered parkland, are among the best preserved in Northern Ireland. The chancel, with its tall lancet windows, magnificent west doorway and an effigy tomb - believed to be Affreca's - in the north wall, are particularly interesting. The abbey was burned down in 1572, and then re-used as a parish church. There are many 17th and 18th-century memorials to be seen in the church ruins, which occupy a pleasant garden setting. The abbey now has a beautiful medieval herb garden, with over 50 varieties of plants, and a visitors' centre.

Times Open Apr-Sep; Tue-Sat 9-6, Sun 2-6; Oct-Mar, wknds 10-4.* **Facilities** toilets for disabled

CASTLEWELLAN — Map 1 D5

Drumena Cashel — FREE

☎ 028 9023 5000 028 9031 0288
web: www.ehsni.gov.uk
dir: 2.25m SW

There are many stone ring forts in Northern Ireland, but few so well preserved as Drumena. Dating back to early Christian times, the fort is 30 metre in diameter and has an 11 metre accessible underground stone-built passage, probably used as a refuge and for storage.

Times Open all times

COMBER — Map 1 D5

WWT Castle Espie — 2 FOR 1

Ballydrain Rd BT23 6EA
☎ 028 9187 4146 028 9187 3857
e-mail: info.castleespie@wwt.org.uk
web: www.wwt.org.uk
dir: 12m SE of Belfast. A22 from Comber towards Killyleagh, 1st left into Ballydrain Rd

Home to the largest collection of wildfowl in Ireland. Comfortable hides enable you to watch the splendour of migratory waders and wildfowl. Beautiful landscaped gardens, a taxidermy collection and fine paintings by wildlife artists can also be seen. Thousands of birds migrate to the reserve in winter and birdwatch mornings are held on the last Thursday of every month. The Centre's effluent is treated in a reed bed filtration system which can be seen on one walk.

Times Open daily Nov-Jan, 10.30-4.30; Feb-Jun & Sep-Oct, daily 10.30-5; Jul-Aug daily 10.30-5.30. Closed 24-25 Dec **Fees** £6.10 (ch £3.05, under 4's free, concessions £4.65) Family (2ad&2ch) £16.50. Carers assisting disabled visitors free* **Facilities** (outdoor) (fully accessible) toilets for disabled (hides have wheelchair platforms, wheelchairs) shop

DOWNPATRICK — Map 1 D5

Down County Museum — FREE

The Mall BT30 6AH
☎ 028 4461 5218 028 4461 5590
e-mail: museum@downdc.gov.uk
web: www.downcountymuseum.com
dir: on entry to town follow brown signs to museum

The museum is located in the restored buildings of the 18th-century county gaol. In addition to restored cells that tell the stories of some of the prisoners, there are exhibitions on the history of County Down. Plus temporary exhibits, events, tea-room and shop.

Times Open all year, Mon-Fri 10-5, wknds 1-5* **Facilities** (outdoor) (partly accessible) toilets for disabled (wheelchair available, handling boxes on application) shop

Inch Abbey

☎ 028 9023 5000 028 9031 0288
web: www.ehsni.gov.uk
dir: 0.75m NW off A7

Beautiful riverside ruins of a Cistercian abbey founded by John de Courcy around 1180. Of particular note is the tall, pointed, triple east window.

Times Open all year Apr-Sep 10-7, Sun 2-7. Oct-Mar free access* **Facilities**

IRELAND

Loughinisland Churches FREE

☎ 028 9023 5000 📠 028 9031 0288
web: www.ehsni.gov.uk
dir: 4m W

This remarkable group of three ancient churches stands on an island in the lough, accessible by a causeway. The middle church is the oldest, probably dating back to the 13th century, with a draw-bar hole to secure the door. The large North church was built in the 15th century, possibly to replace the middle church and continued in use until 1720. The smallest and most recent church is the South (MacCartan's) church.

Times Open all times **Facilities** Ⓟ

Mound of Down FREE

☎ 028 9023 5000 📠 028 9031 0288
web: www.ehsni.gov.uk
dir: on Quoile Marshes, from Mount Crescent

A hill fort from the Early Christian period, conquered by Anglo-Norman troops in 1177, who then built an earthwork castle on top. This mound in the marshes, beside the River Quoile, was the first town before the present Downpatrick.

Times Open all times **Facilities** Ⓟ

The St Patrick Centre 2 FOR 1

St Patrick Visitor Centre, Market St BT30 6LZ
☎ 028 4461 9000 📠 028 4461 9111
e-mail: director@saintpatrickcentre.com
web: www.saintpatrickcentre.com
dir: A7 from Belfast, follow brown heritage signs

This 21st-century multimedia, interactive, audio-visual feast is dedicated to the fascinating story of Ireland's Patron Saint Patrick, who brought Christianity to Ireland in the 5th century. The Centre is located beside the saint's grave, in the heart of St. Patrick's country, forty minutes from Belfast and two hours from Dublin. Major events usually take place around the 17th of March, St Patrick's Day.

Times Open all year Oct-Mar, Mon-Sat 10-5 & St Patricks Day 9.30-7; Apr-May & Sep, Mon-Sat 9.30-5.30, Sun 1-5.30 (morning opening on request), Jun-Aug Mon-Sat 9.30-6, Sun 10-6. (last admission 1.5 hrs before closing) **Fees** £4.95 (ch £2.55, concessions £3.35). Family ticket (2ad+2ch) £11.75. Groups (25+) £3.30. Children's groups (25+) £2.25. Senior Citizen Groups (25+) £2.70* **Facilities** Ⓟ Ⓟ ♿ (fully accessible) toilets for disabled (lifts, wheelchairs, sensory garden) shop

Struell Wells FREE

☎ 028 9023 5000 📠 028 9031 0288
web: www.ehsni.gov.uk
dir: 1.5m E

Pilgrims come to collect the healing waters from these holy drinking and eye wells which are fed by a swift underground stream. Nearby are the ruins of an 18th-century church, and, even more interesting, single-sex bath-houses. The men's bath-house is roofed, has an anteroom and a sunken bath, while the ladies' is smaller and roofless.

Times Open all times **Facilities** Ⓟ

DROMARA Map 1 D5

Legananny Dolmen FREE

☎ 028 9023 5000 📠 028 9031 0288
web: www.ehsni.gov.uk
dir: 4m S

Theatrically situated on the slopes of Slieve Croob, this tripod dolmen with its three tall uprights and huge capstone is the most graceful of Northern Ireland's Stone Age monuments. There are views to the Mourne Mountains.

Times Open at all times **Facilities**

HILLSBOROUGH Map 1 D5

Hillsborough Fort FREE

☎ 028 9268 3285 📠 028 9031 0288
web: www.ehsni.gov.uk

On a site that dates back to early Christian times, the existing fort was built in 1650 by Colonel Arthur Hill to command a view of the road from Dublin to Carrickfergus. The building was ornamented in the 18th century. It is set in a forest park with a lake and pleasant walks.

Times Open all year; summer, Mon-Sat 10-7, Sun 2-7; winter, Mon-Sat 10-4, Sun 2-4 **Facilities** Ⓟ

HOLYWOOD

Ulster Folk and Transport Museum

Cultra BT18 0EU
☎ 028 9042 8428
e-mail: info@nmni.com
web: www.nmni.com
dir: 7m E of Belfast on A2 Banger Rd

Step back in time and uncover a way of life from 100 years ago. Discover town and countryside with cottages, farms, schools and shops to explore as you wander through the beautiful parkland of the Folk Museum. Chat to costumed visitor guides as they demonstrate traditional crafts. Climb on and off majestic steam locomotives or experience the sensation of flight in the transport museum bursting with horse drawn carriages, electric trams, boats, motorbikes, fire engines and vintage cars. In May 2011, a new Titanic Exhibition will open and mark the 100th Anniversary of the ship leaving Belfast.

Times Open all year Mar-Sep, Tue-Sun 10-5; Oct-Feb, Tue-Fri 10-4, Sat & Sun 11-4. Closed Mon ex BHs & 24-26 Dec **Fees** Price for one site £6.50 (ch 5-18 under 4 free & concessions £4). Family (2 ad+up to 3ch) £18.50, (1ad+up to 3ch) £16.50. Dual £8 (ch 5-18 under 4 free & concessions £4.50). Family (2 ad+up to 3ch) £21.50 (1ad+up to 3ch) £16.50. Prices valid until Apr 2011* **Facilities** Ⓟ (outdoor) ♿ (partly accessible) (transport museum full access, folk park upstairs in small number of exhibit buildings not accessible to w/chairs) toilets for disabled (free disabled admission) shop

IRELAND

KILKEEL Map 1 D4

Greencastle

☎ 028 9181 1491
web: www.ehsni.gov.uk
dir: 4m SW

Looking very much like an English Norman castle with its massive keep, gatehouse and curtain wall, this 13th-century royal fortress stands on the shores of Carlingford Lough, with fine views of the Mourne Mountains. Greencastle has an eventful military history, it was beseiged and taken by Edward Bruce in 1316, attacked and spoiled by the Irish at least twice later in the 14th century, and maintained as a garrison for Elizabeth in the 1590s.

Times Open Jul-Aug, daily 10-6* **Facilities** (partly accessible) (limited access for wheelchair users & those with walking difficulties)

KILLINCHY Map 1 D5

Sketrick Castle FREE

☎ 028 9023 5000 028 9031 0288
web: www.ehsni.gov.uk
dir: 3m E on W tip of Sketrick Islands

A badly ruined tall tower house, probably 15th century. The ground floor rooms include a boat bay and prison. An underground passage leads from the north-east of the bawn to a freshwater spring.

Times Open at all times. **Facilities**

NEWCASTLE Map 1 D5

Dundrum Castle FREE

☎ 028 9054 6518
web: www.ehsni.gov.uk
dir: 4m N

This medieval castle, one of the finest in Ireland, was built in 1777 by John De Courcy in a strategic position overlooking Dundrum Bay, a position which offers visitors fine views over the sea and to the Mourne Mountains. The castle was captured by King John in 1210 and was badly damaged by Cromwellian troops in 1652. Still an impressive ruin, it shows a massive round keep with walls 16 miles high and 2 miles thick, surrounded by a curtain wall, and a gatehouse which dates from the 13th century.

Times Open Apr-Sep, Tue-Sat 10-7, Sun 2-7; Oct-Mar, wknds, Sat 10-4, Sun 2-4. **Facilities** toilets for disabled

Maghera Church FREE

☎ 028 9023 5000 028 9031 0288
web: www.ehsni.gov.uk
dir: 2m NNW

The stump of a round tower, blown down in a storm in the early 18th century, survives from the early monastery, with a ruined 13th-century church nearby.

Times Open all year. **Facilities**

NEWTOWNARDS Map 1 D5

Mount Stewart House & Gardens 2 FOR 1

Greyabbey BT22 2AD
☎ 028 4278 8387 028 4278 8569
e-mail: mountstewart@nationaltrust.org.uk
web: www.nationaltrust.org.uk
dir: 5m SE off A20

On the east shore of Strangford Lough, is this fascinating house which has survived for three centuries, famous for its many illustrious owners and guests and well renowned for its magnificent gardens created by Edith Lady Londonderry, wife of the 7th Marquess. In the inspired gardens, which are now a nominated world heritage site, many rare and subtropical trees thrive. Located by the shore is the Temple of the Winds, built by James 'Athenian' Stuart in 1782 for the first Marquess.

Times Lakeside Gardens & Walks: Open all year daily, 10-6. Closed 25 Dec. Formal Gardens: daily, 12 Mar-Oct 10-6. House: daily 12 Mar-Oct 12-6. Temple of the Winds, Sun only, 13 Mar-30 Oct 2-5. Open all BH Mons & PH in NI incl. 17 Mar (last admission 1hr before closing) **Fees** Gift Aid prices. £7 (ch £3.50). Family £17.50. Std Admission £6.36 (ch £3.18). Family £15.90. Groups £6 (out of hours group visits call property to arrange) **Facilities** licensed (outdoor) (partly accessible) toilets for disabled (4 wheelchairs (2 electric) available) shop

Scrabo Tower FREE

Scrabo Country Park, 203A Scrabo Rd BT23 4SJ
☎ 028 9181 1491 028 9182 0695
web: www.ehsni.gov.uk
dir: 1m W

The 135 foot high Scrabo Tower, one of Northern Ireland's best-known landmarks, dominates the landscape of North Down and is also the centre of a country park around the slopes of Scrabo Hill. The Tower provides a fascinating series of interpretative displays about the surrounding countryside and the viewing platform boasts spectacular views over Strangford Lough and County Down. The park provides walks through fine beech and hazel woodlands and the unique sandstone quarries display evidence of volcanic activity as well as being breeding sites for peregrine falcons.

Times Open late Mar-mid Sep, Sat-Thu 10.30-6. **Facilities** toilets for disabled shop

PORTAFERRY Map 1 D5

Exploris Aquarium

The Rope Walk, Castle St BT22 1NZ
☎ 028 4272 8062 028 4272 8396
e-mail: info@exploris.org.uk
web: www.exploris.org.uk
dir: A20 or A2 or A25 to Strangford Ferry Service

Exploris Aquarium is Northern Ireland's only public aquarium and now includes a seal sanctuary. Situated in Portaferry on the shores of Strangford Lough it houses some of Europe's finest displays. The Open Sea Tank holds 250 tonnes of sea water. The complex includes a park with duck pond, picnic area, children's playground, caravan site, woodland and bowling green.

Times Open all year, Mon-Fri 10-6, Sat 11-6, Sun 1-6. (Sep-Mar closing 1 hr earlier)* **Facilities** (outdoor) (fully accessible) toilets for disabled (2 lifts within complex) shop

SAINTFIELD Map 1 D5

Rowallane Garden

BT24 7LH
028 9751 0131 028 9751 1242
e-mail: rowallane@nationaltrust.org.uk
web: www.nationaltrust.org.uk
dir: 1m S of Saintfield on A7

Beautiful and exotic 52-acre gardens, started by the Rev John Moore in 1860, containing exquisite plants from all over the world. They are particularly noted for their rhododendrons and azaleas and for the wonderful floral displays in spring and summer.

Times Open all year daily, Jan-Feb & Nov-Dec 10-4; Mar-Apr & Sep-Oct 10-6; May-Aug 10-8. Closed 24-25 Dec & 1 Jan **Fees** £4.54 (ch £2.27) Family £11.36. Groups £3.70 each.* **Facilities** (partly accessible) (grass steep paths) toilets for disabled (parking facilities, manual wheelchairs, scented plants) shop

STRANGFORD Map 1 D5

Castle Ward

BT30 7LS
028 4488 1204 028 4488 1729
e-mail: castleward@nationaltrust.org.uk
web: www.nationaltrust.org.uk
dir: 0.5m W of Strangford on A25

Explore this exceptional 820-acre walled demesne dramatically set overlooking Strangford Lough and marvel at the quirky mid-Georgian mansion. An architectural curiosity, it is built inside and out in distinctly different styles of classical and gothic. Winding woodland, lakeside and parkland walks afford amazing unexpected vistas.

Times Open Ground Oct-Mar, daily 10-4; Apr-Sep, daily 10-8. House; 21 Feb-29 Jun, wknds, BH/PH 1-5; 10-19 Apr & 4 Jul-Aug, daily 1-5; 5 Sep-1 Nov, wknds 1-5. Wildlife Centre 21-22 Feb, noon-5 & 28 Feb-May, noon-5 wknds & BH/PH* **Facilities** (outdoor) (partly accessible) (no access to upper floor of house) toilets for disabled (wheelchair available, may be driven to house, Braille) shop

CO FERMANAGH

BELLEEK Map 1 B5

Belleek Pottery **2 FOR 1**

3 Main St BT93 3FY
028 6865 9300 & 6865 8501 028 6865 8625
e-mail: visitorcentre@belleek.ie
web: www.belleek.ie
dir: A46 from Enniskillen to Belleek. Pottery at entrance to village

Discover the secrets that make Belleek Pottery one of the most enduring success stories in Irish Craftsmanship. The award winning visitor centre offers guided tours along with a restaurant, audiovisual centre, showroom and museum. Belleek Pottery enters its 3rd decade at the top of Irish Tourism. Visitors have the opportunity to truly immerse themselves in the Belleek experience when they visit Ireland's oldest working pottery.

Times Open all year, Jan-Jun, Mon-Fri 9-5.30, Mar-Jun also Sat 10-5.30, Sun 2-5.30; Jul-Oct, Mon-Fri 9-6, Sat 10-6, Sun 12-5.30; Nov-Dec, Mon-Fri 9-5.30, Sat 10-5. Closed Xmas, New Year & 17 Mar **Fees** Guided tours £4 (ch under 12 free, concessions £2) **Facilities** licensed (outdoor) (fully accessible) toilets for disabled (2 wheelchairs available) shop

IRELAND

CASTLE ARCHDALE BAY Map 1 C5

White Island Church

☎ 028 6862 1156
dir: in Castle Archdale Bay; ferry from marina

Lined up on the far wall of a small, roofless 12th-century church are eight uncanny carved-stone figures. Part Christian and part pagan in appearance, their significance has been the subject of great debate. The church ruins sit on an early monastic site.

Times Open Etr-Jun wknds 10-6, Jul-Aug daily 10-6, Oct-Mar wknds 2-6* **Facilities**

DERRYGONNELLY Map 1 C5

Tully Castle FREE

☎ 028 9054 6552
web: www.ehsni.gov.uk
dir: 3m N, on W shore of Lower Lough Erne

Extensive ruins of a Scottish-style stronghouse with enclosing bawn overlooking Lough Erne. Built by Sir John Hume in the early 1600s, the castle was destroyed, and most of the occupants slaughtered, by the Maguires in the 1641 Rising. There is a replica of a 17th-century garden in the bawn.

Times Open Etr-Sep, 10-6. **Facilities**

ENNISKILLEN Map 1 C5

Castle Coole

BT74 6JY
☎ 028 6632 2690 028 6632 5665
e-mail: castlecoole@nationaltrust.org.uk
web: www.nationaltrust.org.uk
dir: on A4, 1.5m from Enniskillen towards Belfast

Savour the exquisite stately grandeur of this stunning 18th-century mansion, set in a historic wooded landscape park - ideal for family walks. As one of Ireland's finest neo-classical houses, the sumptuous Regency interior, boasting an especially fine state bedroom prepared for George IV, provides a rare treat for visitors to glimpse what life was like in the home of the Earls of Belmore.

Times Open Grounds, 14 Mar-Sep, daily 10-8. House: 14 Mar-May wknds & BH/PH 1-6; 10-19 Apr daily 1-6; Jun daily (ex Thu) 1-6, Jul-Aug daily 12-6; 5-27 Sep wknds 1-6 (last tour 1hr before closing)* **Facilities** (partly accessible) toilets for disabled (may be driven to house, large print guide) shop

Enniskillen Castle 2 FOR 1

Castle Barracks BT74 7HL
☎ 028 6632 5000
e-mail: castle@fermanagh.gov.uk
web: www.enniskillencastle.co.uk
dir: The Castle is located on the Wellington Rd within walking distance of the town centre

Overlooking Lough Erne, this castle, a three-storey keep surrounded by massive stone-built barracks and with a turreted fairytale 17th-century water gate, now houses two museums and a heritage centre. In the castle keep is a small museum displaying Royal Enniskillen Fusiliers regimental exhibits, while the other rooms contain the Fermanagh County Museum's collection of local antiquities.

Times Open all year, Mon 2-5, Tue-Fri 10-5, May-Sep, Sat 2-5; Jul-Aug, Sun 2-5 **Fees** £3.50 (ch & concessions £2.50p). Family (2ad+3ch under 16yrs) £9.50* **Facilities** (partly accessible) (no lift in the Castle Keep, virtual tour on the ground floor) shop

Florence Court

BT92 1DB
☎ 028 6634 8249 028 6634 8873
e-mail: florencecourt@nationaltrust.org.uk
web: www.nationaltrust.org.uk
dir: 8m SW of Enniskillen via A4, then A32 to Swanlibar, well signed

An 18th-century mansion overlooking wild and beautiful scenery towards the Mountains of Cuilcagh. The interior of the house, particularly noted for its flamboyant rococo plasterwork, was gutted by fire in 1955, but has been restored. There are pleasure grounds with an ice house, summer house, water powered sawmill and also a walled garden.

Times Open Grounds, 21 Feb-9 Apr daily 10-6; 10 Apr-1 Nov daily 10-8; 2 Nov-20 Feb daily 10-4. House: 21 Feb-10 May wknds & BH/PH, 10-19 Apr & 1-13 Sep daily 1-6; 16 May-Jun daily (ex Tue) 1-6; Jul-Aug daily noon-6; 19 Sep-1 Nov wknds 1-5 (last tour 1hr before closing)* **Facilities** licensed (outdoor) (fully accessible) toilets for disabled (electric wheelchair available, Braille) shop

Marble Arch Caves Global Geopark

Marlbank Scenic Loop BT92 1EW
☎ 028 6634 8855 028 6634 8928
e-mail: mac@fermanagh.gov.uk
web: www.marblearchcaves.net
dir: off A4 Enniskillen to Sligo road. Left onto A32 and follow signs

One of Europe's finest cave systems, under Cuilcagh Mountain. Visitors are given a tour of a wonderland of stalagmites, stalactites and underground rivers and lakes, starting with a boat trip on the lower lake. The streams, which feed the caves, flow down into the mountain then emerge at Marble Arch, a 30ft detached limestone bridge. The geological, historical and economic benefits of Marble Arch Caves and Cuilcagh Mountain Park were recognised on an international scale when they were jointly awarded the title of European Geopark by UNESCO in 2001.

Times Open late Mar-Sep daily 10-4.30, Jul & Aug 10-5* **Facilities** (outdoor) (partly accessible) (cave not accessible) toilets for disabled (induction loop in AV theatre) shop

Monea Castle

FREE

☎ 028 9023 5000 📠 028 9031 0288
web: www.ehsni.gov.uk
dir: 6m NW

A fine example of a plantation castle still with much of its enclosing bawn wall intact, built around 1618. Of particular interest is the castle's stone corbelling - the Scottish method of giving additional support to turrets.

Times Open at any reasonable time. **Facilities** P

The Sheelin Irish Lace Shop & Museum

Ballanaleck BT92 2BA
☎ 028 6634 8052 📠 028 6634 8041
e-mail: rosemary.cathcart@virgin.net
web: www.antiqueirishlace.co.uk
dir: from Enniskillen take A4 onto A509. Thatched Sheelin Museum on left after 3m

The Irish Lace Museum has the largest and most comprehensive display of antique lace anywhere in Ireland. There are around 700 exhibits, representing the five main types of Irish lace: Inishmacsaint Needlelace, Crochet, Limerick, Carrickmacross, and Youghal Needlelace. The history of the Irish lace-making industry is described, and antique items can be bought in the museum shop.

Times Museum open Apr-Oct, lace shop all year **Fees** £4 (ch free). Party 15+ £2 each* **Facilities** P Ⓟ ♿ (fully accessible) toilets for disabled shop ⊗

LISNASKEA Map 1 C5

Castle Balfour

FREE

☎ 028 9023 5000 📠 028 9031 0288
web: www.ehsni.gov.uk

Dating from 1618 and refortified in 1652, this is a T-plan house with vaulted rooms. Badly burnt in the early 1800s, this house has remained in ruins.

Times Open at all times.

NEWTOWNBUTLER Map 1 C5

Crom

BT92 8AP
☎ 028 6773 8118 & 8174 📠 028 6773 8118
e-mail: crom@nationaltrust.org.uk
web: www.nationaltrust.org.uk
dir: 3m from A34, well signed from Newtownbutler

Featuring 2,000 acres of woodland, parkland and wetland, the Crom Estate is one of Northern Ireland's most important conservation areas. Nature trails are signposted through woodlands to the ruins of the old castle, and past the old boat house and picturesque summer house. Day tickets for pike fishing and boat hire are available from the Visitor Centre.

Times Open Grounds: 14 Mar-May & Sep-1 Nov, daily 10-6; Jun-Aug, daily 10-7. Visitor centre: 14-29 Mar, wknds & BH/PH 10-6; 4 Apr-13 Sep daily & BH/PH 10-6; 14 Sep-11 Oct wknds 10-5; 12 Oct-1 Nov Sun 10-5 (last admission 1hr before closing)* **Facilities** P Ⓟ ☕ ⛩ toilets for disabled shop ✿

CO LONDONDERRY

COLERAINE Map 1 C6

Hezlett House

107 Sea Rd, Castlerock BT51 4TW
☎ 028 7084 8728 📠 028 7084 8728
e-mail: hezletthouse@nationaltrust.org.uk
web: www.nationaltrust.org.uk
dir: 5m W on Coleraine/Downhill coast road 1m from Castlerock

A low, thatched cottage built around 1690 with an interesting cruck truss roof, constructed by using pairs of curved timbers to form arches and infilling around this frame with clay, rubble and other locally available materials.

Times Open 4-19 Apr, Fri-Tue 11-5; 25 Apr-28 Jun, wknds & BH/PH 11-5; Jul-Aug, Thu-Mon 11-5; 5-27 Sep, wknds 11-5* **Facilities** P ⛩ (outdoor) toilets for disabled ⊗ ✿

Mount Sandel

FREE

☎ 028 9023 0560 📠 028 9031 0288
web: www.ehsni.gov.uk
dir: 1.25m SSE

This 200ft oval mound overlooking the River Bann is believed to have been fortified in the Iron Age. Nearby is the earliest known inhabited place in Ireland, where post holes and hearths of wooden dwellings, and flint implements dating back to 6650BC have been found. The fort was a stronghold of de Courcy in the late 12th century and was refortified for artillery in the 17th century.

Times Open at all times. **Facilities** P

DOWNHILL Map 1 C6

Mussenden Temple and Downhill Demesne

Mussenden Rd BT51 4RP
☎ 028 7084 8728 📠 028 7084 8728
e-mail: downhillcastle@nationaltrust.org.uk
web: www.nationaltrust.org.uk
dir: 1m W of Castlerock off A2, 6m from Coleraine

Spectacularly placed on a cliff edge overlooking the Atlantic, this perfect 18th-century rotunda was modelled on the Temple of Vesta at Tivoli. Visitors entering by the Bishop's Gate can enjoy a beautiful glen walk up to the headland where the temple stands. If you enjoy open windswept walks with views that stretch over the whole of the north coast of Ireland, then you must visit Downhill.

Times Open Grounds: all year, dawn-dusk. Temple: 28 Mar-4 Oct daily & BH/PH 10-5* **Facilities** P Ⓟ ⛩ toilets for disabled ✿

DUNGIVEN Map 1 C5

Banagher Church FREE

☎ 028 9023 5000 📠 028 9031 0288
web: www.ehsni.gov.uk
dir: 2m SW

This church was founded by St Muiredach O'Heney in 1100 and altered in later centuries. Today impressive ruins remain. The nave is the oldest part and the square-headed lintelled west door is particularly impressive. Just outside, the perfect miniature stone house, complete with pitched roof and the sculpted figures of a saint at the doorway, is believed to be the tomb of St Muiredach. The saint was said to have endowed his large family with the power of bringing good luck. All they had to do was to sprinkle whoever or whatever needed luck with sand taken from the base of the saint's tomb.

Times Open at all times. **Facilities** Ⓟ

Dungiven Priory FREE

☎ 028 9023 5000 📠 028 9031 0288
web: www.ehsni.gov.uk
dir: SE of town overlooking River Roe

Up until the 17th century Dungiven was the stronghold of the O'Cahan chiefs, and the Augustinian priory, of which extensive ruins remain, was founded by the O'Cahans around 1150. The church, which was altered many times in later centuries, contains one of Northern Ireland's finest medieval tombs. It is the tomb of Cooey na Gall O'Cahan who died in 1385. His sculpted effigy, dressed in Irish armour, lies under a stonework canopy. Below are six kilted warriors.

Times Open Church at all times, chancel only when caretaker available. Check with house at end of lane. **Facilities** Ⓟ

LIMAVADY Map 1 C6

Rough Fort FREE

☎ 028 7084 8728 📠 028 7084 8728
e-mail: downhillcastle@nationaltrust.org.uk
web: www.ntni.org.uk
dir: 1m W off A2

Early Christian rath picturesquely surrounded by pine and beech trees, making it a significant landscape feature. The Rough Fort is one of the best examples of an earthwork ring fort in Ireland.

Times Open at all times. **Facilities**

LONDONDERRY Map 1 C5

City Walls

☎ 028 7126 7284 📠 028 7137 7992
e-mail: info@derryvisitor.com
web: www.ehsni.gov.uk

The finest and most complete city walls to be found in Ireland. The walls, 20-25ft high, are mounted with ancient cannon, and date back to the 17th century. The walled city is a conservation area with many fine buildings. Visitors can walk round the city ramparts - a circuit of one mile.

Times Open all times* **Facilities** Ⓟ ♿ (partly accessible) (limited wheelchair access to Walls)

Tower Museum 2 FOR 1

Union Hall Place BT48 6LU
☎ 028 7137 2411 📠 028 7137 7633
e-mail: museums@derrycity.gov.uk
web: www.derrycity.gov.uk/museums
dir: behind city wall, facing Guildhall

Opened in 1992, the museum has won the Irish and British Museum of the Year Awards. It has two permanent exhibitions as well as hosting temporary and travelling exhibitions throughout the year. The multimedia 'Story of Derry' exhibition has reopened following extensive refurbishment. There is also an exhibition about the Spanish Armada which includes artefacts from a galleon shipwrecked in Kinnagoe Bay in 1588.

Times Open all year, Sep-Jun, Tue-Sat 10-5. Jul-Aug, Mon-Sat 10-5, Sun 12-4. Please check local press for opening details on BH.* **Fees** £4 (concessions £2.50). Families £9 **Facilities** Ⓟ ♿ (fully accessible) toilets for disabled

MAGHERA Map 1 C5

Maghera Church FREE

☎ 028 9023 5000 📠 028 9031 0288
web: www.ehsni.gov.uk
dir: E approach to the town

Important 6th-century monastery founded by St Lurach, later a bishop's see and finally a parish church. This much-altered church has a magnificently decorated 12th-century west door. A cross-carved stone to the west of the church is supposed to be the grave of the founder.

Times Key from Leisure Centre. **Facilities** Ⓟ

MONEYMORE Map 1 C5

Springhill House 2 FOR 1

BT45 7NQ
☎ 028 8674 8210 & 8674 7880 📠 028 8674 8210
e-mail: springhill@nationaltrust.org.uk
web: www.nationaltrust.org.uk
dir: 1m from Moneymore on B18 to Coagh

Pretty 17th-century 'plantation' home with a significant costume collection. Today much of the family furniture, books and bric-a-brac have been retained. Outside, the laundry, stables,

IRELAND

brewhouse, and old dovecote make interesting viewing. Inside is a family home with portraits, furniture and decorative arts that bring to life the many generations of the Lenox-Conynghams who lived here from 1680. Living history days through the year, historical re-enactments of life in the house through various periods

Times Open House: 14 Mar-28 Jun wknds & BH/PH 1-6; 10-14 Apr & Jul-Aug daily 1-6; 18-19 Apr & 5-27 Sep wknds 1-6. Grounds & Costume Collection: Feb-Apr & Oct-Jan daily 10-4; May-Sep daily 10-6* **Fees** £6.60 (ch £3.40). Family ticket £16.60. Group rate £5.25 each **Facilities** (outdoor) (partly accessible) (2 rooms upstairs not accessible) toilets for disabled (lift, photograph album, wheelchair, scented plants) shop

CO TYRONE

ARDBOE — Map 1 C5

Ardboe Cross — FREE

☎ 028 9023 5000 Fax 028 9031 0288
web: www.ehsni.gov.uk
dir: off B73

Situated at Ardboe Point, on the western shore of Lough Neagh, is the best example of a high cross to be found in Northern Ireland. Marking the site of an ancient monastery, the cross has 22 sculpted panels, many recognisably biblical, including Adam and Eve and the Last Judgment. It stands over 18ft high and dates back to the 10th century. It is still the rallying place of the annual Lammas, but praying at the cross and washing in the lake has been replaced by traditional music-making, singing and selling of local produce. The tradition of 'cross reading' or interpreting the pictures on the cross, is an honour passed from generation to generation among the men of the village.

Times Open at all times. **Facilities**

BALLYGAWLEY — Map 1 C5

U S Grant Ancestral Homestead

Dergenagh Rd BT70 1TW
☎ 028 8555 7133 Fax 028 8555 7133
e-mail: killymaddy.reception@dungannon.gov.uk
web: www.dungannon.gov.uk
dir: off A4, 2m on Dergenagh road, signed

Ancestral homestead of Ulysses S Grant, 18th President of the United States of America. The homestead and farmyard have been restored to the style and appearance of a mid-19th-century Irish smallholding. There are many amenities including a children's play area, purpose built barbecue and picnic tables and butterfly garden.

Times Open all year daily 9-5* **Facilities** (outdoor) (fully accessible) (wide doorway to audio-visual area/entrances/exits)

BEAGHMORE — Map 1 C5

Beaghmore Stone Circles and Alignments — FREE

☎ 028 9023 5000 Fax 028 9031 0288
web: www.ehsni.gov.uk

Discovered in the 1930s, these impressive, ritualistic stones have been dated back to the early Bronze, and maybe even Neolithic Ages. There are three pairs of stone circles, one single circle, stone rows or alignments and cairns, which range in height from one to four feet. This is an area littered with historic monuments, many discovered by people cutting turf.

Times Open at all times. **Facilities**

BENBURB — Map 1 C5

Benburb Castle — FREE

☎ 028 9023 5000 Fax 028 9031 0288
web: www.ehsni.gov.uk

The castle ruins - three towers and massive walls - are dramatically placed on a cliff-edge 120ft above the River Blackwater. The northwest tower is now restored and has dizzy cliff-edge views. The castle, built by Sir Richard Wingfield around 1615, is actually situated in the grounds of the Servite Priory. There are attractive walks down to the river.

Times Castle grounds open at all times. Special arrangements, made in advance, necessary for access to flanker tower. **Facilities**

CASTLECAULFIELD — Map 1 C5

Castle Caulfield — FREE

☎ 028 9023 5000 Fax 028 9031 0288
web: www.ehsni.gov.uk

Sir Toby Caulfield, an Oxfordshire knight and ancestor of the Earls of Charlemont, built this manor house in 1619 on the site of an ancient fort. It was badly burnt in 1641, repaired and lived in by the Caulfield/Charlemont family until 1670. It boasts the rare distinction of having had Saint Oliver Plunkett and John Wesley preach in its grounds. Some fragments of the castle are re-used in the fine, large 17th-century parish church.

Times Open at all times.

COOKSTOWN Map 1 C5

Tullaghoge Fort

FREE

☎ 028 9023 5000 Fax 028 9031 0288
web: www.ehsni.gov.uk
dir: 2m S

This large hilltop earthwork, planted with trees, was once the headquarters of the O'Hagans, Chief Justices of the old kingdom of Tyrone. Between the 12th and 16th centuries the O'Neill Chiefs of Ulster were also crowned here - the King Elect was seated on a stone inauguration chair, new sandals were placed on his feet and he was then anointed and crowned. The last such ceremony was held here in the 1590s; in 1600 the stone throne was destroyed by order of Lord Mountjoy.

Times Open at all times. **Facilities** P

Wellbrook Beetling Mill

20 Wellbrook Rd, Corkhill BT80 9RY
☎ 028 8675 1735 & 8675 1715
e-mail: wellbrook@nationaltrust.org.uk
web: www.nationaltrust.org.uk
dir: 4m W, 0.5m off A505

This 18th-century water-powered beetling mill was used for beetling and, until 1961, for finishing Irish linen. Beetling was the name given to the final process in linen making, when the material was beaten by 30 or so hammers (beetles) to achieve a smooth and slightly shiny finish. The only mill left as a remainder of the linen industry in Ireland that beetles linen.

Times Open 14 Mar-28 Jun wknds & BH/PH 2-6; 10-14 Apr daily 12-6; 18-19 Apr wknd 12-6; Jul-Aug daily (ex Fri) 2-6; Sep wknds only 2-6* **Fees** £4 (ch £2.30). Family ticket £10.30. Group rate £3.20 each* **Facilities** P (outdoor) (partly accessible) toilets for disabled shop

NEWTOWNSTEWART Map 1 C5

Harry Avery's Castle

FREE

☎ 028 9023 5000 Fax 028 9031 0288
web: www.ehsni.gov.uk
dir: 0.75m SW

The hilltop ruins of a Gaelic stone castle, built around the 14th century by one of the O'Neill chiefs, are the remains of the oldest surviving Irish-built castle in the north. Only the great twin towers of the gatehouse are left. A stairway enables the public to gain access to one of these.

Times Open at all times. **Facilities**

OMAGH Map 1 C5

Ulster American Folk Park

2 Mellon Rd, Castletown BT78 5QY
☎ 028 8224 3292
e-mail: info@nmni.com
web: www.nmni.com
dir: 4m NW Omagh on A5 to Strabane

Immerse yourself in the story of Irish Emigration at the museum that brings it to life. Experience the adventure that takes you from the thatched cottages of Ulster, on board a full scale emigrant sailing ship, to the log cabins of the American Frontier. Meet an array of costumed characters on your way demonstrating traditional crafts, with tales to tell and food to share.

Times Open all year Apr-Oct, daily 10.30-6, Sun & BH 11-6.30; Nov-Mar, Mon-Fri 10.30-5 (last admission 1hr 30mins before closing) **Fees** £6.50 (under 5 free, ch 5-18 & concessions £4). Family (2ad+up to 3ch) £18.50. Family (1ad+up to 3ch) £13* **Facilities** P (outdoor) (partly accessible) (galleries fully accessible, some exhibit buildings not accessible to wheelchair users) toilets for disabled (free admission for people with access needs) shop

STEWARTSTOWN Map 1 C5

Mountjoy Castle

FREE

Magheralamfield
☎ 028 9023 5000 Fax 028 9031 0288
web: www.ehsni.gov.uk
dir: 3m SE, off B161

Ruins of an early 17th-century brick and stone fort, with four rectangular towers, overlooking Lough Neagh. The fort was built for Lord Deputy Mountjoy during his campaign against Hugh O'Neill, Earl of Tyrone. It was captured and re-captured by the Irish and English during the 17th century and was also used by the armies of James II and William III.

Times Open at all times. **Facilities** P

STRABANE Map 1 C5

Gray's Printing Press

49 Main St BT82 8AU
☎ 028 7188 0055 & 867 48210 Fax 028 7188 0055
e-mail: grays@nationalturst.org.uk
web: www.nationaltrust.org.uk
dir: in centre of Strabane

Behind this 18th-century shopfront in the heart of Strabane, visitors can step back in time and hear the story of printing in what was once the leading printing town in Ulster. A treasure trove of history that tells the indelible story of ink, presses and emigration in the 18th-century printing house where John Dunlap, printer of the American Declaration of Independence, and James Wilson, grandfather of US President Woodrow Wilson, learnt their trade.

Times Please contact Property Manager 028 8674 8210* **Facilities** P (partly accessible) toilets for disabled

IRELAND

REPUBLIC OF IRELAND

Ha'penny Bridge over the River Liffey, Dublin

CO CLARE

BALLYVAUGHAN — Map 1 B3

Aillwee Cave & the Burren Birds of Prey Centre — 2 FOR 1

065 7077036 065 7077107
e-mail: barbara@aillweecave.ie
web: www.aillweecave.ie
dir: 3m S of Ballyvaughan. Signed from Galway and Ennis

An underground network of caves beneath the world famous Burren. Guided tours take you through large caverns, over bridged chasms and alongside thunderous waterfalls. There is a craftshop, a dairy where cheese is made, a speciality food shop and a tearoom. Santa uses the cave as a workshop around Christmas time, while Easter sees a massive egg hunt in the woods. The Burren Birds of Prey Centre, home to the largest display of birds of prey in Ireland. Visitors have the opportunity to view the magnificent birds in open fronted aviaries. Special Events: Santa's Workshop, appointments necessary.

Times Open all year, daily 10-5.30; mid Nov & all Dec by appointment only **Fees** €17 (ch €10, pen €15). Family ticket €39-€49 (all prices are joint tickets) **Facilities** licensed (outdoor) (partly accessible) (cave not accessible, but main cave building and birds of prey centre fully accessible) toilets for disabled shop

BUNRATTY — Map 1 B3

Bunratty Castle & Folk Park

061 360788 061 361020
e-mail: reservations@shannonheritage.com
web: www.shannonheritage.com
dir: approx 11km from Shannon Airport just off the main dual carriageway (N18) between Limerick and Ennis. Follow the tourist sign from the N18

Magnificent Bunratty Castle was built around 1425. The restored castle contains mainly 15th and 16th century furnishings and tapestries. Within its grounds is Bunratty Folk Park where 19th-century Irish life is tellingly recreated. Rural farmhouses, a village street and Bunratty House with its formal Regency gardens are recreated and furnished, as they would have appeared at the time. Medieval Banquets in the castle throughout the year (5.30pm & 8.45pm sitting, booking necessary) and an Irish Night operates in the Folk Park from April to October (reservations necessary).

Times Open all year, Jan-May & Sep-Dec 9-5.30; Jun-Aug, Mon-Fri 9-5.30 (last admission 4.15), Sat-Sun 9-6 (last admission 5.15). (Last admission to the castle is 4pm year round). Closed 24-26 Dec. Opening times may be subject to change* **Facilities** licensed (outdoor) (partly accessible) (castle is not accessible to wheelchair users) toilets for disabled shop

KILLALOE — Map 1 B3

Brian Boru Heritage Centre

061 360788 061 361020
e-mail: reservations@shannonheritage.com
web: www.shannonheritage.com
dir: off the N7 between Limerick & Nenagh, take the R494 to Killaloe & Ballina

The 11th-century High King of Ireland, Brian Boru one of the most influential and colourful figures in Irish history. The heritage centre reveals the story of Brian Boru through a series of colourful exhibits, graphic illustrations and inter-active audio-visual presentation.

Times Open May-Sep, daily 10-5 (last admission 4.30) Opening times may be subject to change* **Facilities** shop

LISCANNOR — Map 1 B3

Cliffs of Moher Visitors Experience

065 7086141 065 7086142
e-mail: info@cliffsofmoher.ie
web: www.cliffsofmoher.ie
dir: 6m NW of Lahinch

The Cliffs of Moher stand as a giant natural rampart against the aggressive might of the Atlantic Ocean. They rise in places to 700ft, and stretch for almost 5 miles. O'Brien's Tower was built in the early 19th century as a viewing point for tourists on the highest point. The famous site is the location for a Visitor Experience, including a state-of-the-art interpretation element, Atlantic Edge, as well as extensive visitor facilities.

Times Open all year, Jan-Feb, 9-5.30; Mar-Apr & Oct, 9-6.30; May, 9-7; Jun-Aug, 9-9; Sep, 9-7.30; Nov-Dec, 9-5* **Fees** €6 (ch under 16 free, concessions €4) **Facilities** licensed (outdoor) (fully accessible) toilets for disabled (induction loops, AV theatre, large print leaflet, w/chairs) shop

QUIN — Map 1 B3

Craggaunowen The Living Past Experience

061 360788 061 361020
e-mail: reservations@shannonheritage.com
web: www.shannonheritage.com
dir: off the R469 near Quin

Craggaunowen is situated on 50 acres of wooded grounds and the park interprets Ireland's pre-historic and early Christian eras. It features a stunning recreation of some of the homesteads, animals and artefacts which existed in Ireland during those time periods. Visitors can for example see a replica of a Crannog (Lake dwelling), Ring Fort, an Iron Age roadway and an outdoor cooking site. Other features include the 'Brendan Boat' and 16th-century Craggaunowen Castle. See rare animal breeds such as Soay sheep and wid boar - specimens of the pre-historic era.

Times Open mid Apr-Sep, daily 10-5 (last admission 4). Opening times may be subject to change* **Facilities** (outdoor) (partly accessible) (castle not accessible) toilets for disabled shop

Knappogue Castle & Walled Garden

061 360788 061 361020
e-mail: reservations@shannonheritage.com
web: www.shannonheritage.com
dir: on R469 near Quin

Built in 1467, Knappogue has a long and varied history. Occupied by Cromwell's troops in 1641 and completely restored in the mid-19th century, the castle fell into disrepair in the 1900s. In 1966 the careful restoration was completed and today the castle is famous for its medieval events. The attractive restored Victorian walled garden includes among many of its features a collection of plants from the Victorian era. Medieval banquets operate in the castle on evenings from April to October (reservations necessary)'

Times Open May-mid Sep daily 10-4.30 (last admission 4). Opening times may be subject to change* **Facilities** (partly accessible) (ground floor & garden) toilets for disabled shop

CO CORK

BLARNEY — Map 1 B2

Blarney Castle & Rock Close

021 4385252 021 4381518
e-mail: info@blarneycastle.ie
web: www.blarneycastle.ie
dir: 5m from Cork on main road towards Limerick

The site of the famous Blarney Stone, known the world over for the eloquence it is said to impart to those who kiss it. The stone is in the upper tower of the castle, and, held by your feet, you must lean backwards down the inside of the battlements in order to receive the 'gift of the gab'. There is also a large area of garden open to the public all year round, woodland walks, lake, fern garden, rock close (laid out in the 18th century) and stable yard.

Times Open Blarney Castle & Rock Close. Mon-Fri, May & Sep 10-4, Jun-Aug 9-7. Oct-Apr 9-sundown or 6. Sun, Summer 9.30-5.30, Winter 9.30-sundown. Closed 24-25 Dec **Fees** Blarney Castle & Rock Close €10 (ch 8-14 €3.50, concessions €8). Family ticket (2ad+2ch) €23.50* **Facilities** (partly accessible) shop

CARRIGTWOHILL (CARRIGTOHILL) — Map 1 B2

Fota Arboretum & Gardens

Fota Estate
021 4812728 021 4812728
e-mail: info@heritageireland.ie
web: www.heritageireland.ie
dir: 14km from Cork on Cobh road

Fota Arboretum contains an extensive collection of trees and shrubs extending over an area of approx 27 acres and includes features such as an ornamental pond and Italian walled gardens. The collection includes many tender plants that could not be grown at inland locations, with many examples of exotic plants from the Southern Hemisphere.

Times Arboretum: Open all year, Apr-Oct, daily 9-6; Nov-Mar, daily 9-5. Walled Gardens: Apr-Oct, Mon-Thu 9-4.30, Fri 9-3.30, Apr-Sep, Sat & BH 11-5, Sun 2-5 **Fees** Free admission. Parking fee €3 **Facilities** toilets for disabled

Fota Wildlife Park

Fota Estate
021 4812678 021 4812744
e-mail: info@fotawildlife.ie
web: www.fotawildlife.ie
dir: 16km E of Cork. From N25 (Cork to Waterford road) take Cobh road

Established with the primary aim of conservation, Fota has more than 90 species of exotic wildlife in open, natural surroundings. Many of the animals wander freely around the park. Giraffes, zebras, ostriches, antelope, cheetahs and a wide array of waterfowl are among the species here.

Times Open all year, 17 Mar-Oct, daily, 10-6; Sun 11-6; Nov-17 Mar 10-4.30; Sun 11-4.30 (last admission 1 hr before closing)* **Facilities** (outdoor) (fully accessible) toilets for disabled shop

CLONAKILTY — Map 1 B2

West Cork Model Village Railway

Inchydoney Rd
023 8833224
e-mail: modelvillage@eircom.net
web: www.modelvillage.ie
dir: From Cork N71 West Cork left at junct for Inchydoney Island, signed at road junct. Village on bay side of Clonakilty

This miniature world depicts Irish towns as they were in the 1940s, with models of the West Cork Railway and various animated scenes. The tea room is set in authentic railway carriages that overlook picturesque Clonakilty Bay. Also take a guided tour of Clonakilty and the surrounding area on the road train. Kids will enjoy the indoor and outdoor play areas.

Times Open all year daily 11-5 (Jul-Aug 10-6)* **Facilities** (outdoor) (fully accessible) toilets for disabled shop

COBH Map 1 B2

The Queentown Story 2 FOR 1

Cobh Railway Station
☎ 021 4813591 🖹 021 4813595
e-mail: info@cobhheritage.com
web: www.cobhheritage.com
dir: off N25, follow signs for Cobh. Attraction at Deepwater Quay, adjacent to train station

A dramatic exhibition of the origins, history and legends of Cobh. Between 1848 and 1950 over 3 million Irish people were deported from Cobh on convict ships. Visitors can explore the conditions onboard these vessels and learn about the harbour's connections with the *Lusitania* and the *Titanic*.

Times Open daily, 5 Jan-22 Dec 9.30-5; Jun-1 Sep, 9.30-6 (last admission 1hr before closing) **Fees** €7.10 (ch €4, concessions €6). Family ticket €20* **Facilities** licensed (fully accessible) toilets for disabled (wide access) shop

CORK Map 1 B2

Cork City Gaol 2 FOR 1

Convent Av, Sundays Well
☎ 021 4305022 🖹 021 4307230
e-mail: corkgaol@indigo.ie
web: www.corkcitygaol.com
dir: 2km NW from Patrick St off Sundays Well Rd

A restored 19th-century prison building. Furnished cells, lifelike characters and sound effects combine to allow visitors to experience day-to-day life for prisoners and gaoler. There is an audio-visual presentation of the social history of Cork City. Individual sound tours are available in a number of languages. A permanent exhibition, the Radio Museum Experience, is located in the restored 1920s broadcasting studio, home to Cork's first radio station, 6CK.

Times Open all year, daily Mar-Oct 9.30-5; Nov-Feb 10-4. Closed 23-28 Dec **Fees** £7.50 (ch £4.50, pen £6.50) **Facilities** (outdoor) (partly accessible) (3 cells on the first/second floor inaccessible to w/chair users) toilets for disabled shop

Cork Public Museum FREE

Fitzgerald Park, Mardyke
☎ 021 4270679 🖹 021 4270931
e-mail: museum@corkcity.ie
dir: N of University College

Displays illustrating the history of the city are housed in this museum. The collections cover the economic, social and municipal history from the Mesolithic period onwards. There are fine collections of Cork Silver and Glass.

Times Open all year, Mon-Fri, 11-1 & 2.15-5; Sat 11-1 & 2.15-4; Sun (Apr-Oct only) 3-5.* **Facilities** (fully accessible) toilets for disabled

GLENGARRIFF Map 1 B2

Garinish Island

☎ 027 63040 🖹 027 63149
dir: 1.5km boat trip from Glengarriff

Ilnacullin is a small island of 37 acres known to horticulturists and lovers of trees and shrubs all around the world as an island garden of rare beauty. The gardens of Ilnacullin owe their existence to the creative partnership, some 80 years ago, of Annan Bryce, then owner of the island and Harold Peto, architect and garden designer.

Times Open Mar & Oct, Mon-Sat 10-4, Sun 1-5; Apr, Mon-Sat 10-6.30, Sun 1-6.30; May & Sep, Mon-Sat 10-6.30, Sun 12-6.30; Jun, Mon-Sat 10-6.30, Sun 11-6.30, Jul & Aug, Mon-Sat 9.30-6.30, Sun 11- 6.30 (last landing 1hr before closing) **Fees** €4 (ch & students €2, pen €3) Family ticket €10. Group rate €3 each **Facilities** toilets for disabled

KINSALE Map 1 B2

Charles Fort

Summer Cove
☎ 021 4772263 🖹 021 4774347
e-mail: charlesfort@opw.ie
web: www.heritageireland.ie
dir: 3km from Kinsale

Built as part of the fortifications of the Irish coast in the late 17th century, Charles Fort was named after King Charles II. After the Battle of the Boyne in 1690, Williamite forces attacked and successfully besieged Charles Fort and the nearby James Fort, both of which held out for King James. The Fort also played a role in the Napoleonic Wars and was made a National Monument in 1973.

Times Open all year, mid Mar-Oct, daily 10-6; Nov-mid Mar, daily 10-5. (last admission 1hr before closing) **Fees** €4 (ch & students €2, pen €3). Family ticket €10. Group rate €3 each **Facilities** toilets for disabled (lift)

Desmond Castle

Cork St
☎ 021 4774855
e-mail: desmondcastle@opw.ie
web: www.desmondcastle.ie
dir: R600 from Cork city to Kinsdale. From post office, 1st left then right, opposite Regional Museum then left and right again, castle on left

Built by the Earl of Desmond around the beginning of the 16th century, this tower was originally a custom house, but has also served as an ordnance office, prison, workhouse, stable and meeting place for the Local Defence Force during World War II. In 1938 it was declared a National Monument and restored. The Castle now houses the International Museum of Wine.

Times Open early Apr-late Sep, daily 10-6. (last admission 1 hr before closing) **Fees** €3, (ch & students €1, pen €2). Family €8 **Facilities**

IRELAND

MIDLETON Map 1 C2

Jameson Experience 2 FOR 1

The Old Distillery
☎ 021 4613594 🖷 021 4613642
e-mail: bookings@omd.ie
web: www.jamesonwhiskey.com
dir: E end of main street on left. Well signed

A tour of the Old Midleton Distillery commences with a 15-minute audio/visual presentation, followed by a 35-minute guided tour of the Old Distillery and then back to the Jameson Bar for a whiskey tasting - mineral water is available for children. The guided tour and audio-visual are available in seven languages.

Times Open all year daily, Nov-Feb tours 11.30, 1, 2.30 & 4; Mar-Oct 10-6 (last tour 5). Closed Good Fri, 24-26 & 31 Dec & 1 Jan **Fees** €13.50 Family ticket €30 **Facilities** licensed (fully accessible) toilets for disabled shop

CO DONEGAL

BALLYSHANNON Map 1 B5

The Water Wheels FREE

Abbey Assaroe
☎ 071 9851580
dir: cross Abbey River on Rossnowlagh Rd, next turning left & follow signs

Abbey Assaroe was founded by Cistercian Monks from Boyle Abbey in the late 12th century, who excelled in water engineering and canalised the river to turn water wheels for mechanical power. Two restored 12th-century mills, one is used as coffee shop and restaurant; the other houses a small museum related to the history of the Cistercians. Interesting walks in the vicinity with views of the Erne Estuary and Atlantic Ocean.

Times Open May-Oct, daily 10.30-6.30 **Facilities** licensed (outdoor) (fully accessible) toilets for disabled shop

DONEGAL Map 1 B5

Donegal Castle

☎ 074 9722405 🖷 074 9722436
e-mail: donegalcastle@opw.ie
dir: in town centre

This restored 15th-century castle and adjoining 17th-century ruined English manor house contain exhibitions of Irish historical events. Guided tours are available.

Times Open all year, Etr-mid Sep, daily 10-6; mid Sep-early Apr, Thu-Mon 9.30-4.30. (last admission 45mins before closing) **Fees** €4 (ch & students €2, pen €3). Family ticket (2ad+3ch) €10 **Facilities**

LETTERKENNY Map 1 C5

Glebe House & Gallery

Churchill
☎ 074 9137071 🖷 074 9137521
web: www.glebegallery@opw.ie
dir: signed from Letterkenny on R251

This Regency house, set in beautiful woodland gardens along the shore of Lough Gartan, was given to the nation along with his art collection by artist Derek Hill. The interior of the house is decorated with original wallpapers and textiles by William Morris.

Times Open Etr, daily 10-6.30; May-Jun & Sep, Sat-Thu 11-6.30; Jul-Aug, daily 11-6.30. (last admission 1hr before closing) **Fees** €3 (ch & student €1, pen €2). Family ticket €8. Group rate €2 each **Facilities**

Glenveagh National Park & Castle 2 FOR 1

Churchill
☎ 074 9137090 (ext 3609) & 9137262 🖷 074 9137072
e-mail: tres.connaghan@environ.ie
web: www.glenreaghnationalpark.ie
dir: left off N56 from Letterkenny

Over 40,000 acres of mountains, glens, lakes and woods. A Scottish-style castle is surrounded by one of the finest gardens in Ireland, contrasting with the rugged surroundings.

Times Open all year, daily 9.30-6 (winter times may change) **Fees** Castle tour: €5 (concessions €3, student €2) Family €10. Buses €3 (concessions €2) **Facilities** licensed (outdoor) (partly accessible) (no lift access to first floor) toilets for disabled (buses equipped to take wheelchair users) shop

IRELAND

LIFFORD Map 1 C5

Cavanacor Historic House & Art Gallery

Ballindrait
☎ 074 9141143 📠 074 9141143
e-mail: art@cavanacorgallery.ie
web: www.cavanacorgallery.ie
dir: 1.5m from town off N14 Strabane/Letterkenny road

Built in the early 1600s and commanding a view of the Clonleigh Valley and the River Deele, Cavanacor House is the ancestral home of James Knox Polk, 11th President of the USA (1845-1849). King James II dined under the sycamore tree in front of the house in 1689. There are over 10 acres of landscaped gardens and an old-fashioned walled garden. The Art Gallery will feature exhibitions of new work by national and international artists.

Times House open 1-24 Feb; May-14 Jun. Art gallery open all year **Fees** €7 (ch & concessions €5)* **Facilities** Ⓟ Ⓟ ♿ (partly accessible) (ground floor & gallery accessible)

The Old Courthouse

Visitor Centre, The Diamond
☎ 091 41733 📠 091 41228
e-mail: info@liffordoldcourthouse.com
web: www.liffordoldcourthouse.com

This old courthouse and jail provides an insight into legal history and some of the terrible conditions endured by prisoners in the 18th century. Witness re-enactments of famous trials held in this historic building.

Times Open all year, Mon-Fri, 10-5 & Sun 12.30-5 (last tour 4). Closed Sat & BHs.* **Facilities** Ⓟ licensed (outdoor) toilets for disabled shop

IRELAND

CO DUBLIN

BALBRIGGAN Map 1 D4

Ardgillan Castle

☎ 01 8492212 📠 01 8492786
dir: R127 or M1 past Dublin Airport then follow signs

A large and elegant country manor house built in 1738, set in 194 acres of parkland, overlooking the sea and coast as far as the Mourne Mountains. There is a permanent exhibition of the 17th-century 'Down Survey' maps and various temporary exhibitions. Tours of the Gardens (June, July and August) begin at 3.30pm every Thursday. Guided tours of the house are conducted daily.

Times Open all year, Apr-Sep, Tue-Sun & BHs 11-6 (daily Jul-Aug); Oct-Mar, Wed-Sun & BHs 11-4.30. Closed 23 Dec-1 Jan* **Facilities** Ⓟ (outdoor) ♿ (partly accessible) (ground floor, toilet & tearooms accessible) toilets for disabled shop

DONABATE Map 1 D4

Newbridge House and Traditional Farm

Newbridge Demesne
☎ 01 8436534 & 8462184 📠 01 8436535
e-mail: newbridgehouse@fingalcoco.ie
web: www.newbridgehouseandfarm.com
dir: Take N1 and follow signs for Donabate.

Newbridge House was designed by James Gibbs and built in 1737 for Charles Cobbe, Archbishop of Dublin. Set in 350 acres of parkland, the house contains many splendidly refurbished rooms featuring plasterwork, furniture and paintings. The house also features a fully restored courtyard surrounded by; a dairy, estate workers house, carpenters shop and blacksmiths forge. The grounds contain a 29 acre traditional farm with many rare breeds and children's playground.

Times Open all year, Apr-Sep, Mon-Sat 10-5, Sun & BH 12-6; Oct-Mar, Sat-Sun & PH 2-5. Parties at other times by arrangement* **Facilities** Ⓟ (outdoor) shop

DUN LAOGHAIRE Map 1 D4

The James Joyce Museum **2 FOR 1**

Joyce Tower, Sandycove
☎ 01 2809265 & 8722077 📠 01 2809265
e-mail: joycetower@dublintourism.ie
web: www.visitdublin.com/museums
dir: 1m SE Dun Laoghaire by coast road to Sandycove Point or turn off main Dun Laoghaire-Dalkey road

Built by the British as a defence against a possible invasion by Napoleon, the tower has walls approximately 8ft thick and an original entrance door 13ft above the ground. The tower was once the temporary home of James Joyce, who depicted this setting in the opening scene of *Ulysses*. The structure is now a museum devoted to the author. Bloomsday, the day in 1904 on which all the action of *Ulysses* is set, is celebrated annually on 16th June. On this day, the museum is open from 8-6 for visits, readings from *Ulysses* and performances of various kinds, Edwardian costume is encouraged.

Times Open Apr-Aug, Tue-Sat 10-1 & 2-5, Sun 2-6; Closed Mon & BHs. Oct-Mar by arrangement* **Fees** €6 (ch €4, concessions €5) Family €15* **Facilities** Ⓟ ♿ (partly accessible) (access to ground floor only) shop

MALAHIDE Map 1 D4

Malahide Castle

☎ 01 8462184 📠 01 8462537
e-mail: malahidecastle@dublintourism.ie
web: www.malahidecastle.com
dir: from Dublin city centre follow signs for Malahide, then approaching village, main entrance to castle is signed to right off main road

One of Ireland's oldest castles, this romantic and beautiful structure, set in 250 acres of grounds, has changed very little in 800 years. Tours offer views of Irish period furniture and historical portrait collections. Additional paintings from the

National Gallery depict figures from Irish life over the last few centuries.

Times Open Jan-Dec, Mon-Sat 10-5; Apr-Sep, Sun & PHs, 10-6; Oct-Mar, Sun & PHs 11-5* **Facilities** licensed (outdoor) shop

Talbot Botanic Gardens

Malahide Castle
01 8462456 01 8463620
e-mail: gemma.ecarr@finga/coco.ie
web: www.finga/coco.ie
dir: signed off M1/N1 Dublin-Belfast & Dublin-Malahide Rd

Malahide Castle has long been associated with ornamental gardening. Over seven hectares of shrubbery, and a Walled Garden of nearly two hectares are mainly the creation of Lord Milo Talbot de Malahide, whose family had lived at the estate for 800 years until his death in 1973. Lord Milo Talbot had travelled the world and brought home many exotic plants from Australia and Chile, among others. Visitors follow a path through the gardens, which gives them the best view of this impressive botanic garden.

Times Open May-Sep, daily 2-5. Groups by appointment only. Guided tour of Walled Garden on Wed at 2 **Fees** €4.50 (ch under 12 & pen free). Guided tour €4.50. Groups €4 each* **Facilities** licensed (outdoor) (fully accessible) shop

SKERRIES Map 1 D4

Skerries Mills 2 FOR 1

01 8495208 01 8495213
e-mail: skerriesmills@indigo.ie
web: www.skerriesmills.org
dir: signed off M1 via Lusk or Balbriggan

A collection of restored mills, including a watermill, a five-sail, and a four-sail windmill, all in working order. The site dates from the 16th century and was originally part of a monastic establishment. It came into private ownership in 1538, and a bakery has been there since 1840. Nature lovers will enjoy the millpond, nearby wetlands and town park, of which the mills are the focal landmark.

Times Open all year, daily Apr-Sep 10-5.30; Oct-Mar 10-4.30. Closed 24-27 Dec & 31 Dec-2 Jan **Fees** Guided tours €6.50 (ch €3.50, pen & students €5). Family ticket €13. Groups on request* **Facilities** licensed (partly accessible) toilets for disabled (stair lift, interactive tour) shop

DUBLIN

DUBLIN Map 1 D4

The Casino

off Malahide Rd, Marino
01 8331618 01 8332636
e-mail: casinomarino@opw.ie
web: www.heritageireland.ie
dir: Turn left at pedestrian lights after Dublin Five Brigade Training HQ

Designed in 1757 by Sir William Chambers as a pleasure house for James Caulfield, 1st Earl of Charlemont, the Casino is possibly one of the finest 18th-century neo-Classical buildings in Europe. Its name means "small house", but the Casino surprisingly contains 16 finely-decorated rooms.

Times Open end Apr-Oct, daily 10-5 (last admission 45mins before closing) **Fees** €3 (ch & students €1, pen €2). Family ticket €8 **Facilities**

Chester Beatty Library FREE

Dublin Castle
01 4070750 01 4070760
e-mail: info@cbl.ie
web: www.cbl.ie
dir: 2 min walk from Dame St via the Palace St gate of Dublin Castle, 5 mins from Trinity College

Situated in the heart of the city centre, the Chester Beatty Library is an art museum and library which houses the great collection of manuscripts, miniature paintings, prints, drawings, rare books and decorative arts assembled by Sir Alfred Chester Beatty (1875-1968). The exhibitions open a window on the artistic treasures of the great cultures and religions of the world. Egyptian papyrus texts, beautifully illustrated copies of the Qur'an and the Bible, and European medieval and renaissance manuscripts are among the highlights of the collection. Turkish and Persian miniatures and striking Buddhist paintings are also on display, as are Chinese dragon robes and Japanese woodblock prints.

Times Open all year, May-Sep, Mon-Fri 10-5; Oct-Apr, Tue-Fri 10-5, Sat 11-5, Sun 1-5. Closed 24-26 Dec, 1 Jan, Good Fri & BH Mons **Facilities** licensed (fully accessible) toilets for disabled (Braille leaflet, wheelchairs) shop

DUBLIN *continued*

Christ Church Cathedral

Christchurch Place
☎ 01 6778099 📠 01 6798991
e-mail: welcome@cccdub.ie
web: www.cccdub.ie
dir: at top end of Dame St

Founded in 1030, the present building dates from 1180 with a major restoration in the 1870s. The crypt is the second largest medieval crypt in Britain or Ireland. There are daily services and choral services on Sundays and during the week.

Times Open all year, daily Sep-May 9.45-5; Jun-Aug 9.45-7 (last entry 45 mins before close). Please check website for details of services. Closed St Stephens Day & 27 Dec **Fees** €6 (pen €4, student €3) **Facilities** Ⓟ (outdoor) ♿ (partly accessible) (main cathedral accessible except area behind high altar) shop

Drimnagh Castle

Long Mile Rd, Drimnagh D12
☎ 01 4502530 & 4508927 📠 01 4508927
e-mail: drimnaghcastle@eircom.net
dir: Dame St, left at Christchurch Cathedral into Patrick St, right into Cork St, through Dolphins Barn up to Crumlin Rd, past Halfway House. 500yds on right

The last surviving medieval castle in Ireland with a flooded moat, Drimnagh dates back to the 13th century and was inhabited until 1954. The Castle consists of a restored Great Hall and medieval undercroft, a tall battlement tower and lookout posts, and other separate buildings including stables, an old coach house and a folly. One of the most attractive features of Drimnagh is the garden, a formal 17th-century layout with box hedges, yews and mop heads.

Times Open all year, Apr-Oct Wed & Sun 12-5, Nov-Mar Sun 2-5 (last tour 4). Other times by appointment. Large groups advisable to book **Fees** €4 (ch €2, concessions & students €3.50). Groups 20+ €3 each* **Facilities** Ⓟ Ⓟ ♿ (partly accessible) (limited access gravel courtyard and gardens)

Dublin Castle

Dame St
☎ 01 6458813 📠 01 6797831
dir: City centre off Dame St, behind City Hall

With two towers and a partial wall, this is the city's most outstanding legacy of the Middle Ages. Of interest are the Record Tower, state apartments, Church of the Most Holy Trinity and Heraldic Museum. The inauguration of the President of Ireland and related ceremonies are held in St. Patrick's Hall, an elegant state apartment.

Times Open all year, daily 10-4.45; Sun & BHs 2-4.45 Advance booking for groups required. Dublin Castle can be closed at short notice for Government Business. State Apts may be close occasionally for State Functions. Closed 24-28 Dec, 1 Jan & Good Fri **Fees** €4.50 (ch & concessions €3.50, ch under 12 €2) **Facilities** Ⓟ licensed ♿ (partly accessible) toilets for disabled shop

Dublin City Gallery The Hugh Lane FREE

Charlemont House, Parnell Square
☎ 01 2222550 📠 01 8741132
e-mail: info.hughlane@dublincity.ie
web: www.hughlane.ie
dir: Off O'Connell St Parnell Monument. At the top of Parnell Square

Situated in Charlemont House, a fine Georgian building, the gallery's collection includes one of the most extensive collections of 20th-century Irish art. A superb range of international and Irish paintings, sculpture, works on paper and stained glass is also on show. Possibly the most fascinating aspect of the gallery is Francis Bacon's Studio, a complete reconstruction of the painter's studio, and a complete database of all the items in it. There are public lectures every Sunday and regular concerts (at noon on Sundays) throughout the year.

Times Open all year, Tue-Thu 10-6, Fri-Sat 10-5, Sun 11-5. Closed Mon, Good Fri & 24-25 Dec **Facilities** Ⓟ ♿ (fully accessible) toilets for disabled (ramp & reserved parking) shop

Dublinia & The Viking World

St Michael's Hill, Christ Church
☎ 01 6794611 📠 01 6797116
e-mail: info@dublinia.ie
web: www.dublinia.ie
dir: in city centre

The story of medieval Dublin. Housed in the former Synod Hall beside Christ Church Cathedral and developed by the Medieval Trust, Dublinia recreates the period from the arrival of Strongbow and the Anglo-Normans in 1170 to the closure of the monasteries by Henry VIII in 1540. Also included is the exhibition on the Viking World which tells the story of their way of life and turbulent voyages. New history hunters' exhibition unearths the world of archaeology.

Times Open all year daily 10-5 **Fees** €6.95 (ch €3.95, concessions €5.95). Family ticket (2ad+3ch) €20. Please check website for current details* **Facilities** Ⓟ ♿ (partly accessible) (3 floors accessible, but bridge and tower are not) toilets for disabled shop

Dublin Writers Museum

18 Parnell Square
☎ 01 8722077 📠 01 8722231
e-mail: writers@dublintourism.ie
web: www.writersmuseum.com
dir: on Parnell Sq, at North end of O'Connell St

The Dublin Writers Museum is housed in a restored 18th-century mansion and is a collection featuring personal items, portraits, books and letters relating to Dublin's most important literary figures, including Swift, Sheridan, Shaw, Wilde, Yeats, Joyce and Beckett. The mansion is a pleasure in itself, with sumptuous plasterwork and decorative stained windows. There is a special room dedicated to children's literature and a full programme of workshops, lectures and receptions.

Times Open all year, Mon-Sat 10-5, Sun & BH 11-5 **Fees** €7.50 (ch under 12 €4.70, concessions €6.30)* **Facilities** Ⓟ licensed shop

Dublin Zoo

Phoenix Park
☎ 01 4748900 📠 01 6771660
e-mail: info@dublinzoo.ie
web: www.dublinzoo.ie
dir: 10mins bus ride from city centre

Dublin Zoo first opened to the public in 1830, making it one of the oldest zoos in the world and has consistently been Ireland's favourite attraction. The Kaziranga Forest Trail is the latest development within Dublin Zoo. Visitors wander along winding paths to glimpse a breeding herd of Asian elephants. Dublin Zoo is a modern zoo with conservation, education and study as its mission. The majority of the animals here have been born and bred in zoos and are part of global breeding programmes to ensure their continued survival.

Times Open all year, Mar-Oct, Mon-Sat 9.30-6, Sun 10.30-6; Nov-Feb, daily 10.30-dusk* **Facilities** licensed (outdoor) (partly accessible) toilets for disabled (wheelchairs available) shop

Guinness Storehouse

St James's Gate Brewery
☎ 01 4084800 & 4714634 📠 01 4084965
e-mail: guinness-storehouse@guinness.com
web: www.guinness-storehouse.com
dir: from Dame St near Trinity College keep straight, follow road around passing Christchurch on right into Thomas St. Pass main brewery gates on left. At junct of James's St & Echlin St take left turn. At top of road turn left then 1st left on to Market St - pedestrian entrance on left

The Guinness Storehouse is located in the heart of the Guinness brewery at St James's Gate. Housed in an old fermentation plant, this seven storey visitor experience tells the history of the making of this world famous beer. It is a dramatic story that begins 250 years ago and ends in Gravity Bar where visitors receive a complimentary pint of Guinness while relaxing and enjoying spectacular views over Dublin. The adventure begins the moment you walk through the door into the building's giant, pint-shaped heart of glass. You will discover what goes into making the "Black Stuff", the ingredients, the process, the passion. You'll learn about Arthur Guinness and find out how the drink that carries his name has been transported around the world.

Times Open daily 9.30-5 (last admission 5). Late summer opening Jul & Aug until 7. Closed Good Fri & 25-26 Dec
Fees €15 (ch 6-12 €5, pen & students over 18 €11, students under 18 €9). Family (2ad+2ch) €34 **Facilities** licensed (fully accessible) toilets for disabled shop

Howth Castle Rhododendron Gardens

FREE

Howth
☎ 01 8322624 & 8322256 📠 01 8392405
e-mail: sales@deerpark.iol.ie
dir: 9m NE of city centre, by coast road to Howth. Before Howth follow signs for Deer Park Hotel

Overlooking the sea on the north side of Dublin Bay, the rhododendron walks command spectacular views of the Castle and Ireland's Eye. The flowers are at their best in May and June. Visitors should be aware that the gardens are in some disrepair and the paths somewhat rough and overgrown in parts.

Times Open all year, daily 8am-dusk. Closed 25 Dec.
Facilities licensed (partly accessible) (garden unsuitable) toilets for disabled (ramped entrance)

Irish Museum of Modern Art

FREE

Royal Hospital, Military Rd, Kilmainham
☎ 01 6129900 📠 01 6129999
e-mail: info@imma.ie
web: www.imma.ie
dir: 3.5km from city centre, just off N7 opposite Heuston Station

Housed in the Royal Hospital Kilmainham, an impressive 17th-century building, the Irish Museum of Modern Art is Ireland's leading national institution for the collection and presentation of modern and contemporary art. It presents a wide variety of art and artists' ideas in a dynamic programme of exhibitions, which regularly includes bodies of work from the museum's own collection, its award-winning Education and Community Department and the Studio and National Programmes.

Times Please contact Kilmainham Gaol to arrange tours: May-Sep. (Tel: 01 4535984) **Facilities** toilets for disabled shop

James Joyce Centre

35 North Great George's St
☎ 01 8788547 📠 01 8788488
e-mail: info@jamesjoyce.ie
web: www.jamesjoyce.ie
dir: signed from N end of O'Connell Street and Parnell Square

Situated in a beautifully restored 18th-century Georgian town house, the Centre is dedicated to the promotion of a greater interest in, and understanding of, the life and works of James Joyce. Visitors follow a self-guided tour through the house, that includes the door to No.7 Eccles Street, home of Leopold Bloom, the hero of *Ulysses*; furniture from Joyce's Paris flat, computer installations, video documentaries and a reconstruction of period rooms. Events are centred every year around 'Bloomsday', the 16th of June, which is when the events of *Ulysses* take place.

Times Open all year, Tue-Sat 10-5, Sun 12-5. Closed Xmas to New Year **Fees** Exhibition €5 (concessions €4). Walking Tour €10 (concessions €8). Group 10+ €4.50 (concessions €3.50)
Facilities toilets for disabled shop

IRELAND

DUBLIN *continued*

Kilmainham Gaol

Inchicore Rd
☎ 01 4535984 📠 01 4532037
web: www.kilmainhamgaol.opw.ie
dir: 3.5km from city centre

One of the largest unoccupied gaols in Europe, covering some of the most heroic and tragic events in Ireland's emergence as a modern nation from the 1720s. Attractions include a major exhibition detailing the political and penal history of the prison and its restoration.

Times Open all year, Apr-Sep, daily 9.30-6 (last admission 5); Oct-Mar, Mon-Sat 9.30-5.30 (last admission 4), Sun 10-6 (last admission 5). Access by guided tour only **Fees** €6 (ch & students €2, pen €4). Family ticket €14 **Facilities** Ⓟ ☕ ♿ (partly accessible) toilets for disabled (tours available by prior appointment) 🚭

Marsh's Library

St Patrick's Close
☎ 01 4543511 📠 01 4543511
e-mail: keeper@marshlibrary.ie
web: www.marshlibrary.ie
dir: beside St Patrick Cathedral

The first public library in Ireland, dating from 1701. Designed by William Robinson, the interior has been unchanged for 300 years. The collection is of approximately 25,000 volumes of 16th, 17th and early 18th-century books.

Times Open all year, Mon & Wed-Fri, 9.30-1 & 2-5, Sat 10-1* **Facilities** Ⓟ 🚭

National Botanic Gardens

Glasnevin
☎ 01 8040300 📠 01 8360080
e-mail: botanicgardens@opw.ie
web: www.botanicgardens.ie
dir: on Botanic Road, between N1 and N2

Ireland's premier Botanic Gardens, covers a total area of 19.5 hectares (48 acres), part of which is the natural flood plain of the River Tolka. The Gardens contain a large plant collection, which includes approximately 20,000 species and cultivated varieties. There are four ranges of glasshouses including the restored Curvilinear Range and the Great Palm House. Notable features include herbaceous borders, rose garden, rockery, alpine yard, arboretum, extensive shrub collections, wall plants and vegetable garden.

Times Open all year daily, mid Feb-mid Nov 9-6; mid Nov-mid Feb 9-4.30 **Fees** Free admission. Parking €2 **Facilities** 🅟 Ⓟ ☕ 🍽 licensed toilets for disabled 🚭

National Gallery of Ireland

Merrion Square
☎ 01 6615133 📠 01 6615372
e-mail: info@ngi.ie
web: www.nationalgallery.ie
dir: N11, M50, follow signs to City Centre

The gallery, founded in 1854 by an Act of Parliament, houses the national collections of Irish art and European Old Masters including Rembrandt, Caravaggio, Poussin, and El Greco. There is also a special room dedicated to Jack B Yeats, and a National Portrait Collection.

Times Open all year, Mon-Sat 9.30-5.30, Thu 9.30-8.30, Sun 12-5. Closed 24-26 Dec & Good Fri* **Facilities** Ⓟ ☕ 🍽 licensed ♿ (fully accessible) toilets for disabled (Braille/audio tours, lifts, ramps, disabled parking) shop 🚭

National Library of Ireland FREE

Kildare St
☎ 01 6030200 📠 01 6766690
e-mail: info@nli.ie
web: www.nli.ie

Founded in 1877 the National Library holds an estimated 8 million items including collections of printed books, manuscripts, prints and drawings, photographs, maps, newspapers and magazines. Explore the poetry of Ireland's greatest poet in the award-winning exhibition of WB Yeats. The library's new exhibition 'Discover Your National Library: Explore Reflect, Connect' showcases some of the fine items from the collection. In addition the library provides a free Genealogy Advisory Service for family history research.

Times Open all year, Mon-Wed 9.30-9 (Kildare Street); Thu-Fri 9.30-5, Sat 9.30-1 (reading rooms); 9.30-4.30 (Yeats exhibitions & Discover). Opening times may vary during PH **Facilities** Ⓟ 🍽 licensed ♿ (fully accessible) toilets for disabled shop 🚭

National Museum of Ireland - Natural History FREE

Merrion St
☎ 01 6777444 📠 01 6777828
e-mail: marketing@museum.ie
web: www.museum.ie
dir: in city centre, SW corner of Merrion Square

The Natural History Museum, which is part of The National Museum of Ireland, is a zoological museum containing diverse collections of world wildlife. The Irish Room, on the ground floor, is devoted largely to Irish mammals, sea creatures and insects. It includes the extinct giant Irish deer and the skeleton of a basking shark. The World Collection, has as its centre piece, the skeleton of a 60ft whale suspended from the roof. Other displays include the Giant Panda and a Pygmy Hippopotamus.

Times Open all year, Tue-Sat 10-5, Sun 2-5. Closed Mon, 25 Dec & Good Fri **Facilities** Ⓟ ♿ (partly accessible) (ground floor only accessible) toilets for disabled shop 🚭

National Photographic Archive FREE

Meeting House Square, Temple Bar
☎ 01 6030200 & 6030374 📠 01 6777451
e-mail: photoarchive@nli.ie
web: www.nli.ie
dir: opposite The Gallery of Photography

The National Photographic Archive, which is part of the National Library of Ireland, was opened in 1998 in an award-winning building in the Temple Bar area of Dublin. The archive holds an unrivalled collection of photographic images relating to Irish history, topography and cultural and social life. The collection is especially rich in late 19th and early 20th-century topographical views and studio portraits, but also includes photographs taken during the Rebellion of 1916 and the subsequent War of Independence and Civil War, as well as other historic events.

Times Open all year, Mon-Sat 10-5, Sun & BHs 12-5* **Facilities** ♿ (fully accessible) toilets for disabled shop ⊗

Number Twenty Nine 2 FOR 1

29 Lower Fitzwilliam St Dublin 2
☎ 01 7026165 📠 01 7027796
e-mail: numbertwentynine@esb.ie
web: www.esb.ie/no29
dir: on corner of Lower Fitzwilliam St & Mount Street Upper; adjacent to Merrion Square

Number Twenty-Nine is a lovingly restored middle class Dublin home from the late 18th and early 19th century, filled with a unique collection of original pieces, with excellent examples of Irish and international craftsmanship. Visitors are guided through the house from the basement kitchen to the attic nursery. 2011 is the 20th anniversary of the opening of the museum.

Times Open all year, Tue-Sat 10-5, Sun 12-5. Closed 2 wks Xmas **Fees** €6 (ch under 16 free, concessions €3)* **Facilities** Ⓟ ☕ ♿ (partly accessible) (basement & ground floor accessible) toilets for disabled shop ⊗

Old Jameson Distillery

Bow St, Smithfield
☎ 01 8072355 & 8072348
e-mail: bookings@ojd.ie
web: www.jamesonwhiskey.com
dir: M25 to Midleton, 15min from Cork.

Set in the heart of Ireland's capital city, The Old Jameson Distillery captures the spirit and imagination of Ireland. Take a guided tour and discover the smooth taste of Jameson Irish Whiskey.

Times Open all year, daily, 9-6 (last tour 5.30). Closed 22 Apr, Good Fri, 24-26 Dec **Fees** €13.50 (ch under 18 €8, concessions €10) Group rate €10 **Facilities** 🅟 Ⓟ 🍽 licensed ⛩ (outdoor) ♿ (fully accessible) toilets for disabled shop ⊗

Phoenix Park Visitor Centre FREE

Phoenix Park
☎ 01 6770095 📠 01 6726454
e-mail: phoenixparkvisitorcentre@opw.ie
dir: 4km from Dublin

Situated in Phoenix Park, the Visitor Centre provides an historical interpretation of the park from 3500BC, through a series of attractive displays. Part of the building is devoted to nature and there is a colourful film of Phoenix Park. The castle, probably dating from the early 17th century, has been restored to its former glory.

Times Open all year, Nov-mid Mar, Wed-Sun 9.30-5.30; mid Mar-Oct, daily 10-5.45 **Facilities** 🅟 ☕ ⛩ toilets for disabled ⊗

CO GALWAY

GALWAY Map 1 B3

Galway Atlantaquaria

Salthill
☎ 091 585100 📠 091 584360
e-mail: atlantaquaria@eircom.net
web: www.nationalaquarium.ie
dir: follow signs for Salthill. Next to Tourist Office at seafront rdbt

Concentrating on the native Irish marine ecosystem, the Galway Atlantiquaria contains some 170 species of fish and sealife, and features both fresh and saltwater exhibits.

Times Open all year, Apr-Jun & Sep, daily 10-5; Jul & Aug, daily, 10-6; Oct-Mar, Wed-Sun, 10-5* **Facilities** 🅟 Ⓟ ☕ 🍽 licensed toilets for disabled shop ⊗

Nora Barnacle House Museum

Bowling Green
☎ 091 564743
e-mail: norabarnaclehouse@eircom.net
web: www.norabarnacle.com
dir: close to St Nicholas Collegiate Church, in city centre

The smallest museum in Ireland, this tiny turn-of-century house was the home of Nora Barnacle, companion, wife and lifelong inspiration of James Joyce. It was here in 1909, sitting at the kitchen table that Joyce first met his darling's mother. Letters, photographs and other exhibits of the lives of James Joyce and Nora Barnacle make a visit here a unique experience.

Times Open Jun-Aug, days may change during the week, opening times posted on window*

GALWAY *continued*

Royal Tara China Gift Centre

FREE

Tara Hall, Mervue
☎ 091 705602 📠 091 757574
e-mail: mkilroy@royal-tara.com
web: www.royal-tara.com
dir: N6 from Tourist Office. At rdbt take 2nd left & at lights turn right

Royal Tara China visitor centre, located minutes from Galway City Centre, operates from a 17th-century house situated on five acres.

Times Open all year, Mon-Sat 9-5, Sun 10-5* **Facilities** P ♿ (fully accessible) toilets for disabled (all facilities accessible for disabled) shop

GORT — Map 1 B3

Coole Park & Gardens

FREE

Coole Nature Reserve
☎ 091 631804 📠 091 631653
e-mail: info@coolepark.ie
web: www.coolepark.ie
dir: 3km N of Gort on N18 Limerick-Galway road, left turn signed

Once the home of Lady Gregory, dramatist and co-founder of the Abbey Theatre with W.B. Yeats and Edward Martyn, now a nature reserve, the Seven Woods celebrated by Yeats is part of a nature trail taking in woods and river to Coole lake. The restored courtyard has a visitor centre with exhibits and displays of Coole Park's history. Events around Biodiversity Day in May, and Heritage week at the end of August.

Times Park open all year. Visitor Centre open Apr-Aug, daily 10-5 **Facilities** P licensed (outdoor) ♿ (partly accessible) (visitor centre is fully accessible. Nature trails are partly accessible. All main features are accessible) toilets for disabled

Thoor Ballylee

☎ 091 631436 & 537700 📠 091 631436
dir: 1km off N18 & N66

This tower house is the former home of the poet William Butler Yeats and is where he completed most of his literary works. The tower, restored to appear exactly as it was when he lived there, houses an Interpretative Centre with audio-visual presentations and displays of his work.

Times Open end May-Sep, Mon-Sat 9.30-5. Opening details under review please phone for further information* **Fees** €6 (ch €1.50-£2.50). Family ticket €12. Tour (ad & concessions) €5.50* **Facilities** P ♿ (partly accessible) (ground floor area only accessible) toilets for disabled (multilingual audio-visual presentation) shop

KINVARA — Map 1 B3

Dunguaire Castle

☎ 061 360768 📠 061 361020
e-mail: reservations@shannonheritage.com
web: www.shannonheritage.com
dir: near Kinvara off N18 Limerick/Galway road

Picturesque Dunguaire Castle, situated on the shores of Galway Bay, was built in 1520. Explore the castle and learn about the people who have lived there since the 16th century. Banquets are also held in the castle on evenings from April to October. (reservations necessary)

Times Open mid Apr-Sep, daily 10-5 (last admission 4.30). Opening times may be subject to change* **Facilities** Ⓟ shop

PORTUMNA — Map 1 B3

Portumna Castle & Gardens

☎ 090 9741658 📠 090 9741889
e-mail: portumnacastle@opw.ie

The great semi-fortified house at Portumna was built before 1618 by Richard Burke or de Burgo, 4th Earl of Clanricarde. This important Jacobean house, while influenced by Renaissance and English houses, remains distinctively Irish. It was the main seat of the de Burgo family for over 200 years, until it was gutted by fire in 1826. The ground floor of the house is now open to the public. To the north of the house is a formal, geometrically laid out garden, a feature often associated with large Jacobean mansions.

Times Open early Apr-Sep, daily 9.30-6 (last admission 45mins before closing) **Fees** €3 (ch & concessions €1). Family ticket €8. Group rate €2 each **Facilities** Ⓟ

ROSSCAHILL — Map 1 B4

Brigit's Garden

2 FOR 1

Pollagh
☎ 091 550905 📠 091 550491
e-mail: info@brigitsgarden.ie
web: www.brigitsgarden.ie
dir: signed from N59 between Moycullen & Oughterard

At the heart of Brigit's Garden are four unique gardens based on the old Celtic festivals and representing the cycle of life. Features include Irish sculpture and crafts designed to reflect the West of Ireland landscape. There are 11 acres of woodland and wildflower meadows to explore with a nature trail, a wind chamber, an original ring fort and the impressively large Brigit's Sundial. Special events all year round, including on Bealtaine (May Day) and the Summer Solstice.

Times Open Feb-Oct, daily, 10-5.30 **Fees** €7.50 (ch €5, under 5 free, concessions €6). Family (2ad+3ch) €22* **Facilities** P (outdoor) ♿ (partly accessible) (buildings and gardens fully accessible, only section of nature trail not accessible) toilets for disabled shop

IRELAND

ROUNDSTONE Map 1 A4

Roundstone Music, Crafts & Fashion

FREE

Craft Centre
☎ 095 35875 📠 095 35980
e-mail: bodhran@iol.ie
web: www.bodhran.com
dir: N59 from Galway to Clifden. After approx 50m turn left at Roundstone sign, 7m to village. Attraction at top of village

The Roundstone Music Craft and Fashion shop is located within the walls of an old Franciscan Monastery. Here you can see Ireland's oldest craft: the Bodhran being made, and regular talks and demonstrations are given. The 1st RiverDance stage drums were made here and are still on display in the Craftsman's Craftshop. There is an outdoor picnic area in a beautiful location alongside the bell tower by the water where the dolphins swim up to the wall in summer.

Times Open Apr-Oct 9.30-6, Jul-Sep 9-7, Winter 6 days 11-6 **Facilities** (indoor & outdoor) (fully accessible) toilets for disabled shop

CO KERRY

CASTLEISLAND Map 1 B2

Crag Cave

2 FOR 1

☎ 066 7141244 📠 066 7142352
e-mail: info@cragcave.com
web: www.cragcave.com
dir: 1m N, signed off N21

Crag Cave is one of the longest surveyed cave systems in Ireland, with a total length of 3.81km. It is a spectacular world, where pale forests of stalagmites and stalactites, thousands of years old, throw eerie shadows around vast echoing caverns complemented by dramatic sound and lighting effects. Now features new indoor and outdoor soft play areas, which are priced seperately. Tours of the caves last about 30 minutes.

Times Open all year, daily 10-6. Jan-Feb closed Mon & Tue (last tour 5.30) **Fees** €12 (ch €5, concessions €9)* **Facilities** licensed (outdoor) (partly accessible) toilets for disabled (ramp to visitor centre) shop

KILLARNEY Map 1 B2

Muckross House, Gardens & Traditional Farms

Muckross
☎ 064 6670144 📠 066 33926
e-mail: mucros@iol.ie
web: www.muckross-house.ie
dir: 4m on Kenmare road

The 19th-century mansion house of the formerly private Muckross Estate. It now houses a museum of Kerry folklife. In the basement craft centre, a weaver, blacksmith and potter demonstrate their trades. The grounds include Alpine and bog gardens, rhododendrons, azaleas and a rock garden.

Times Open all year, daily Nov-mid Mar 9.30-5; mid Mar-Jun & Sep-Oct 9-6; Jul-Aug 9-7 **Fees** €7 (ch & students €3, pen €5.50) Family ticket €17.50. Group ticket €5.50 **Facilities** licensed toilets for disabled shop

Museum of Irish Transport

Scotts Hotel Gardens
☎ 064 34677 📠 064 36656
dir: town centre, opposite railway station

A unique collection of Irish veteran, vintage and classic cars, motorcycles, bicycles, carriages and fire engines. Exhibits include the 1907 Silver Stream, reputed to be the rarest car in the world, it was designed and built by an Irishman and he only made one!

Times Open Apr & Oct 11-4; May & Sep 11-5; Jun, Jul & Aug 10-6* **Facilities**

TRALEE Map 1 A2

Kerry County Museum

Ashe Memorial Hall, Denny St
☎ 066 7127777 📠 066 7127444
e-mail: info@kerrymuseum.com
web: www.kerrymuseum.com
dir: in town centre, follow signs for museum & tourist information office

The museum tells the story of Kerry (and Ireland) from the Stone Age to the present day. Archaeological treasures are displayed in the Museum Gallery, while a stroll through the Medieval Experience reveals the streets of Tralee as they were in 1450, with all the sights, sounds and smells of a bustling community. Discover what people wore, what they ate and where they lived, and find out why the Earls of Desmond, who founded the town, also destroyed it.

Times Open all year, Jan-Mar, Tue-Fri 10-4.30; Apr-May, Tue-Sat 9.30-5.30; Jun-Aug, daily 9.30-5.30; Sep-Dec, Tue-Sat 9.30-5; BH wknds Sun & Mon 10-5* **Facilities** (partly accessible) toilets for disabled (special time car through Medieval Experience) shop

IRELAND

VALENCIA ISLAND Map 1 A2

The Skellig Experience

☎ 066 9476306 📠 066 9476351
e-mail: info@skelligexperience.com
web: www.skelligexperience.com
dir: Ring of Kerry road, signed after Cahersiveen then Valentia bridge, or ferry from Rena Rd Point

The Skellig Rocks are renowned for their scenery, sea bird colonies, lighthouses, Early Christian monastic architecture and rich underwater life. The two islands - Skellig Michael and Small Skellig - stand like fairytale castles in the Atlantic Ocean, rising to 218 metres and their steep cliffs plunging 50 metres below the sea. The Heritage Centre, (on Valentia Island, reached from the mainland via a bridge), tells the story of the Skellig Islands in an exciting multimedia exhibition. Cruises around Valentia Harbour are also available.

Times Open May-Jun 10-6; Jul-Aug 10-7; Sep 10-6. Mar, Apr & Oct-Nov 10-5* **Facilities** Ⓟ ☕ toilets for disabled shop ⊗

CO KILDARE

CELBRIDGE Map 1 D4

Castletown

☎ 01 6288252 📠 01 6271811
e-mail: castletown@opw.ie
web: www.heritageireland.ie
dir: 13m from Dublin, follow signs to Celbridge from N4

Ireland's largest and finest Palladian country house, begun c1722 for William Conolly, Speaker of the Irish House of Commons. The state rooms include the 'Pompeian' Long Gallery with its Venetian chandeliers, green silk drawing room and magnificent staircase hall with Lafranchini plasterwork. There is a fine collection of 18th-century Irish furniture and paintings.

Times Open mid Mar-Oct, Tue-Sun & BHs 10-6; Open Xmas season **Fees** €4.50 (ch & concessions €3.50). Family ticket €12.50. Pre-booked groups 20+ €3.50 **Facilities** Ⓟ Ⓟ ☕ toilets for disabled ⊗

KILDARE Map 1 C3

Irish National Stud, Gardens & Horse Museum — 2 FOR 1

Irish National Stud, Tully
☎ 045 521617 📠 045 522964
e-mail: reservations@instourism.net
web: www.irish-national-stud.ie
dir: off M7, exit 13 then R415 towards Nurney & Kildare. Attraction well signed from rdbt

Situated in the grounds of the Irish National Stud, the gardens were established by Lord Wavertree between 1906 and 1910, and symbolise 'The Life of Man' in a Japanese-style landscape. You can also visit the Horse Museum which includes the skeleton of Arkle, an Irish racehorse that won a number of major races in the 1960s. The Commemorative Millennium Garden of St Fiachra has 4 acres of woodland and lakeside walks and features a Waterford Crystal garden and monastic cells of limestone.

Times Open 12 Feb-23 Dec, daily 9.30-5 **Fees** €11. Concessions for seniors & students **Facilities** Ⓟ ☕ 🍽 licensed ⛩ (outdoor) ♿ (partly accessible) (all parts of stud, garden & house accessible. Japanese gardens partly accessible) toilets for disabled shop

CO KILKENNY

KILKENNY Map 1 C3

Kilkenny Castle

☎ 056 7704100 📠 056 776 3488

Situated in a beautiful 50-acre park, the castle dates from 1172. The first stone castle was built 20 years later by William Marshall, Earl of Pembroke. It was the home of the very powerful Butler family, Earls and Dukes of Ormonde from 1391 to 1935. Due to major restoration works, the central block now includes a library, drawing room, and bedrooms decorated in 1830s splendour, as well as the beautiful Long Gallery.

Times Open all year, Apr-Sep, daily 9.30-5.30; Oct-Feb, daily 9.30-4.30; Mar 9.30-5. Check with site for opening arrangements over Xmas & New Year **Fees** €6 (ch & students €2.50). Family ticket €14. Group rate €4 each **Facilities** Ⓟ ☕ shop ⊗

CO LIMERICK

BRUFF Map 1 C3

Lough Gur Stone Age Centre

Bruff Rd
☎ 061 360788 📠 061 361020
e-mail: reservations@shannonheritage.com
web: www.shannonheritage.com
dir: 17km S of Limerick, off R512 towards Kilmallock

Lough Gur introduces visitors to the habitat of Neolithic Man on one of Ireland's most important archaeological sites. The visitor centre interprets the history of the area which dates back to 3000BC.

Times Open May-mid Sep, daily 10.30-5 (last admission 4.30). Opening times may be subject to change* **Facilities** ⛩ (outdoor) ♿ (fully accessible) toilets for disabled shop ⊗

IRELAND

FOYNES Map 1 B3

Foynes Flying Boat Museum

☎ 069 65416 📠 069 65416
e-mail: info@flyingboatmuseum.com
web: www.flyingboatmuseum.com
dir: on N69 in Foynes

The museum recalls the era of the flying boats during the 1930s and early 1940s when Foynes was an important airport for air traffic between the United States and Europe. There is a comprehensive range of exhibits, graphic illustrations and a 1940s style cinema featuring a 17-minute film - all original footage from the 30s and 40s. This is where Irish coffee was first invented by chef, Joe Sheridan, in 1942. Fly our B314 flight simulators and go on board the world's only full scale B314 flying boat model.

Times Open daily Mar-Oct 10-6, Nov 10-4 (last admission 1hr before closing)* **Facilities** Ⓟ Ⓟ ☕ ♿ (fully accessible) toilets for disabled shop ⊗

LIMERICK Map 1 B3

The Hunt Museum 2 FOR 1

The Custom House, Rutland St
☎ 061 312833 & 490083 📠 061 312834
e-mail: info@huntmuseum.com
web: www.huntmuseum.com
dir: a short walk from Arthur's Quay

On show at the Hunt Museum is one of Ireland's finest private collections of art and antiquities. Reflecting Ireland's Celtic past as well as displaying artefacts from the ancient civilisations of Egypt, Greece and Rome. Set in an 18th-century Custom House beside the River Shannon.

Times Open all year Mon-Sat 10-5, Sun 2-5, ex Good Fri, 25 Dec & 1 Jan **Fees** €8 (ch €4.25, concessions €6.25). Family ticket €18. Free admission Sun **Facilities** Ⓟ ☕ 🍽 licensed ♿ (fully accessible) toilets for disabled (wheelchair on request) shop ⊗

King John's Castle

Nicholas St
☎ 061 360788 📠 061 361020
e-mail: reservations@shannonheritage.com
web: www.shannonheritage.com
dir: on Kings Island in city

King John's Castle was built between 1200 and 1210 and was repaired and extended many times in the following centuries. The Castle overlooks the broad majestic River Shannon. Explore 800 years of history brought to life in the imaginative historical exhibition, excavated pre-Norman houses, fortifications, siege mines, and the battlement walks.

Times Open all year, Jan-Feb & Nov-Dec 10-4.30; Mar-Apr & Sep-Oct: 9.30-5.30; May-Aug, Mon-Fri 10-5, Sat & Sun-10-5.30 (last admission 1 hr before closing). Closed 24-26 Dec. Opening times may be subject to change* **Facilities** Ⓟ Ⓟ 🪑 (outdoor) ♿ (partly accessible) toilets for disabled (lifts and ramps) shop ⊗

CO LONGFORD

KEENAGH Map 1 C4

Corlea Trackway Visitor Centre FREE

☎ 043 3322386 📠 043 22442
e-mail: ctrackwayvisitorcentre@opw.ie
dir: off R397, 3km from village, 15km from Longford

The centre interprets an Iron Age bog road which was built in the year 148BC across the boglands close to the River Shannon. The oak road is the largest of its kind to have been uncovered in Europe and was excavated over the years by Professor Barry Raferty of University College Dublin. Inside the building, an 18-metre stretch of preserved road is on permanent display in a specially designed hall with humidifiers to prevent the ancient wood from cracking in the heat.

Times Open early Apr-Sep, daily 10-6 **Facilities** Ⓟ ☕ 🪑 toilets for disabled ⊗

CO MAYO

BALLYCASTLE Map 1 B5

Céide Fields

☎ 096 43325 📠 096 43261
e-mail: ceidefields@opw.ie
web: www.heritageireland.ie
dir: 5m W of Ballycastle on R314

Beneath the wild boglands of North Mayo lies Céide Fields, the most extensive Stone-age monument in the world; field systems, dwelling areas and megalithic tombs of 5,000 years ago. In addition, the wild flora of the bog is of international importance and is bounded by some of the most spectacular rock formations and cliffs in Ireland.

Times Open early Apr-May & 1-27 Oct, 10-5; Jun-Sep, daily 10-6. Available for group bookings in winter months (last tour 1hr before closing) **Fees** €4 (ch & students €2, pen €3). Family ticket €10. Group rate €3 each **Facilities** Ⓟ ☕ toilets for disabled ⊗

WESTPORT

Westport House & Pirate Adventure Park

☎ 098 27766 & 098 25430 📠 098 25206
e-mail: info@westporthouse.ie
web: www.westporthouse.ie
dir: On R335, 3.2km from Westport towards Louisburgh, right at Westport Quay.

Privately owned by the Browne family, who are direct descendants of the 16th-century Pirate Queen, Grace O'Malley, this Georgian mansion has over 30 rooms on display as well as magnificent grounds and an enviable art collection. In addition to culture and heritage, a whole range of family fun awaits at the Pirate Adventure Park which includes a log flume, pirate ship ride, miniature railway, a climbing wall, soft play area, playground, pitch and putt, caravan and camping park and lots more.

Times Open: House Mar-Oct daily 10-4, Dec wknds, 8, 23 & 24 noon-6; Adventure Park 18 Apr-2 May & Sun in May noon-6, Jun-1 Sep daily 10-7, Oct mid-term wk 10-4. **Fees** House €12 (ch €6.50) Park €22 (ch €18.50) 1 day family pass for House & Park €75 (€99 for two days). More pricing options available on website **Facilities** licensed (outdoor) (partially accessible - house not accessible) toilets for disabled shop

CO MONAGHAN

INNISKEEN Map 1 C4

Patrick Kavanagh Rural & Literary Resource Centre

Candlefort
☎ 042 9378560 📠 042 9378560
e-mail: infoatpkc@eircom.net
web: www.patrickkavanaghcountry.com
dir: from Dublin take N2, exit at Carrickmacross, left along R178 to Essexford. Left at Kelly's pub for Inniskeen

Birthplace of Patrick Kavanagh, one of Ireland's foremost 20th-century poets. The village grew around the ancient monastery of St Daig MacCairill, founded in 562, and its strong, 10th-century round tower still stands. The centre, housed in the former parish church, chronicles the ancient history of the region and its role in developing Kavanagh's work.

Times Open all year Tue-Fri 11-4.30; Jun-Sep also open Sun 2-5* **Facilities** (fully accessible) toilets for disabled shop

MONAGHAN Map 1 C5

Monaghan County Museum FREE

1-2 Hill St
☎ 047 82928 📠 047 71189
e-mail: comuseum@monghancoco.ie
web: www.monaghan.ie
dir: near town centre, opposite market house exhibition galleries

This is an award-winning museum of local archaeology, history, arts and crafts. Throughout the year various special exhibitions take place.

Times Open all year, Mon-Fri 11-5, Sat 12-5. Closed Sun & BHs **Facilities** (partly accessible)

CO OFFALY

BIRR Map 1 C3

Birr Castle Demesne

☎ 05791 20336 📠 05791 21583
e-mail: mail@birrcastle.com
web: www.birrcastle.com
dir: N52 to Birr, turn right into Town Sq. At castle wall turn left, entrance is on right

These award-winning gardens are the largest in the country, spanning over 120 acres of natural landscapes, with five miles of paths. The impressive plant collection boasts rare species from around the world, including over 40 champion trees of the British Isles. The Formal Gardens include the world's tallest box hedges and beautiful pathways of hornbeam arches. The Demesne is also home to Ireland's Historic Science Centre which allows visitors to travel back to the time of the earlier Earls and Countesses of Rosse, when the Castle was a hub of scientific discovery and innovation. Many special events take place throughout the year. Please see the website for details.

Times Open all year, Mar-Oct 9-6; Nov-Mar 10-4 **Fees** €9 (ch €5 under 5 free, concessions €7.50). Family (2ad+2ch) €25 **Facilities** (indoor & outdoor) (fully accessible) toilets for disabled shop

CO ROSCOMMON

BOYLE Map 1 B4

King House - Georgian Mansion & Military Barracks 2 FOR 1

☎ 071 9663242 📠 071 9663243
e-mail: kinghouse@roscommoncoco.ie
web: www.kinghouse.ie
dir: in Boyle town centre, 1km from N4 Dublin to Sligo rd

King House is a magnificently restored Georgian mansion built around 1730 by Sir Henry King, whose family were one of the most powerful and wealthy in Ireland. After its first life as a home, King House became a military barracks to the famous Connaught Rangers from 1788-1922. In more recent years it has also been a barracks for the National Irish Army. Today visitors can explore and delve into its history with interactive presentations on: Gaelic Ireland, the lives of the King family, the architecture and restoration of the building and its military history. Visitors can also discover the connection between the famous Hollywood actress Maureen O'Sullivan and King House. The Boyle Arts Festival takes place in the last week of July

Times Open Apr-Sep, Tue-Sat 11 (last admission 4). Also open BH Sun & Mon during season. Pre-booked groups welcome all year round* **Fees** €7 (ch €4, concessions €5). Family ticket €18. Group rates available* **Facilities** licensed (outdoor) (fully accessible) toilets for disabled (lift to all areas, ramps, wide doors, parking) shop

STROKESTOWN — Map 1 C4

Strokestown Park House Garden & Famine Museum

Strokestown Park
☎ 071 9633013 071 9633712
e-mail: info@strokestownpark.ie
web: www.strokestownpark.ie
dir: 23km from Longford on N5

A fine example of an early 18th-century gentleman farmer's country estate. Built in Palladian style the house reflects perfectly the confidence of the newly emergent ruling class. The pleasure garden has also been restored, and the Famine Museum, located in the stable yard, commemorates the Great Irish Famine of the 1840s.

Times Open 17 Mar-Oct, daily 11-5* **Facilities** licensed (outdoor) (partly accessible) (House - ground floor accessible, Famine Museum & Gardens - accessible) toilets for disabled shop

CO TIPPERARY

CASHEL — Map 1 C3

Brú Ború Heritage Centre

☎ 062 61122 062 62700
e-mail: bruboru@comhaltas.com
web: www.comhaltas.com
dir: below Rock of Cashel in town

At the foot of the Rock of Cashel, a 4th-century stone fort, this Heritage Centre is dedicated to the study and celebration of native Irish music, song, dance, story telling, theatre and Celtic studies. There's a Folk Theatre where performances are held daily in the summer, and in the evening, banquets evoke the Court of Brian Ború, 11th-century High King of Ireland with music, song and dance. Promoted by Comhaltas Ceoltóiri Éireann. There is also a Subterranean, "Sounds of History", experience.

Times Open all year, Jan-May & Oct-Dec, Mon-Fri 9-5; Jun-Sep, Mon-Sat 9-11.30* **Facilities** licensed (fully accessible) toilets for disabled (wheelchair bay in theatre) shop

CO WATERFORD

LISMORE — Map 1 C2

Lismore Castle Gardens & Art Gallery

☎ 058 54424 058 54896
e-mail: lismoreestates@eircom.net
web: www.lismorecastle.com
dir: on N72 near town centre

Lismore Castle is the Irish home of the Duke of Devonshire. The beautifully situated walled and woodland gardens contain a fine collection of camellias, magnolias and other shrubs and a remarkable Yew Walk. Several pieces of contemporary sculpture have been installed in the garden. The West Wing has been converted into a contemporary art space and is planning to host art exhibitions from around the world.

Times Open 17 Mar-Sep, daily 11-4.45* **Facilities** (partly accessible) (some of the grounds are accessible, stairs to upper gardens)

WATERFORD — Map 1 C2

Waterford Crystal Visitor Centre

Kilbarry
☎ 051 332500 051 332716
e-mail: visitorreception@waterford.ie
web: www.waterfordvisitorcentre.com
dir: on N25, 1m from city centre

There are factory tours to see mastercraftsmen mouth-blow and hand-cut this famous crystal. You can talk to the master engravers and see the crystal being sculpted. In the gallery there is the finest display of Waterford Crystal in the world.

Times Factory tours: open all year, Mar-Oct daily 8.30-4.15; Nov-Feb closed Sat & Sun* **Facilities** licensed (fully accessible) toilets for disabled (special tours on request) shop

IRELAND

CO WEXFORD

FERRYCARRIG Map 1 D3

The Irish National Heritage Park 2 FOR 1

☎ 053 9120733 Fax 053 9120911
e-mail: info@inhp.com
web: www.inhp.com
dir: 3m from Wexford, on N11

Sixteen historical sites set in a magnificent 35-acre mature forest explaining Ireland's history from the Stone and Bronze Ages, through the Celtic period and concluding with the Vikings and Normans. Among the exhibits are a reconstructed Mesolithic camp, a Viking boatyard with two full-size ships and a Norman motte and bailey. Please visit website for details of events running throughout the year.

Times Open all year daily, May-Aug 9.30-6.30; Sep-Apr 9.30-5.30* **Fees** €8 (concessions €6.50). Family (2ad&upto3 ch) €20. Group rates available on request* **Facilities** P licensed (outdoor) (fully accessible) toilets for disabled shop

NEW ROSS Map 1 C3

Dunbrody Abbey Visitors Centre

Dunbrody Abbey, Campile
☎ 051 88603
e-mail: patrickbelfast@aol.com
web: www.dunbrodyabbey.com
dir: 10m from New Ross at base of Hook Peninsular

The visitor centre is based around the Abbey itself and Dunbrody Castle. There is an intriguing yew hedge maze with 1,550 yew trees and a museum. In addition there is a golf pitch-and-putt course, a local craft centre and Dunbrody Abbey Cookery School.

Times Open May-Sep 11-5.30 **Fees** Abbey €2 (ch €1). Family ticket €5. Maze/Golf €5 (ch €2). Family ticket €12* **Facilities** P licensed (outdoor) (fully accessible) shop

John F Kennedy Arboretum

☎ 051 388171 Fax 051 388172
e-mail: jfkarboretum@opn.ie
dir: 12km S of New Ross, off R733

The Arboretum covers 623 acres across the hill of Slievecoiltia which overlooks the Kennedy ancestral home at Dunganstown. There are 4,500 types of trees and shrubs representing the temperate regions of the world, and laid out in botanical sequence. There's a lake and a visitor centre.

Times Open all year daily, Oct-Mar 10-5; Apr & Sep 10-6.30; May-Aug 10-8 (last admission 45 mins before closing) **Fees** €3 (ch & student €1, pen €2). Family ticket €8 **Facilities** P toilets for disabled shop

WEXFORD Map 1 D3

The Irish Agricultural Museum

Johnstown Castle Estate
☎ 053 9184671 & 9171247
e-mail: info@irishagrimuseum.ie
web: www.irishagrimuseum.ie
dir: 4m SW of town, signed off N25

This museum is located in the old farm and stable buildings of the Johnstown castle Estate. There are a vast range of artefacts relating to a bygone era. Farming and rural life are the main themes explored, with exhibits covering rural transport, farming and the activities of the farmyard and farmhouse; and includes a large exhibition on the history of the potato and the Great Famine (1845-49). Large scale replicas of different workshops, including a blacksmith, cooper and basket worker, and include displays on the Ferguson tractor system and the history of the estate. Johnstown Castle Garden is a delightful 50 acres of ornamental grounds surrounding a Victorian castle. Famous architect Daniel Robertson designed both Johnstown Castle Gardens and Powerscourt Gardens. The grounds contain a wide variety of trees and shrubs, as well as two lakes and various follies.

Times Open all year: Museum Apr-Oct, Mon-Fri 9-5, Sat-Sun & BHs 11-5; Nov-Mar, Mon-Fri 9-5. Closed for lunch 12.30-1.30, wknds & BHs. Grounds open daily 9-5 **Fees** Museum €6 (ch & students €4, concessions & group €5)* **Facilities** P (outdoor) (partly accessible) (ground floor accessible) toilets for disabled shop

Johnstown Castle Gardens

Johnstown Castle Estate
☎ 053 9184671 & 9171247
e-mail: info@irishagrimuseum.ie
web: www.irishagrimuseum.ie
dir: 4m SW of town, signed off N25

Johnstown Castle Garden is a fairy setting consisting of an exquisite Victorian castle set within 50 acres of onarmental grounds. The famous architect Daniel Robertson designed both Johnstown castle grounds and Powerscourt gardens. The grounds contain a wide variety of trees and shrubs representing the best aspects of a formal and wild garden. The grounds are greatly enhanced by two lakes with folly towers and are populated with a wide range of waterfowl. The Irish Agricultural Museum is located in the old farm and stable buildings of Johnstown Castle estate. Please note that Johnstown Castle itself is not open to the public.

Times Open all year, daily 9-5. Closed 25 Dec **Fees** Car (inc passengers) €6. Pedestrians €2 (ch & students €0.50). Small coach €20, large coach €30. Charges apply May-Sep, Oct-Apr free.* **Facilities** P (outdoor) (fully accessible) toilets for disabled shop

IRELAND

Wexford Wildfowl Reserve FREE

North Slob
☎ 053 9123129 📠 053 24785
e-mail: info@heritageireland.ie
dir: 8km NE from Wexford

The reserve is of international importance for Greenland white-fronted geese, Brent geese, Bewick's swans and wigeon. The reserve is a superb place for birdwatching and there are hides and a tower hide available as well as a visitor centre.

Times Open all year, daily 9-5. Other hours by arrangement with the warden. Closed 25 Dec. Notice on gate if reserve closed **Facilities** Ⓟ ⛩ toilets for disabled ⊗

CO WICKLOW

ENNISKERRY Map 1 D4

Powerscourt House & Gardens

Powerscourt Estate
☎ 01 2046000 📠 01 2046900
web: www.powerscourt.ie
dir: From Dublin city centre take N11 S, after 12m take exit left to Bray S, Enniskerry. Left at rdbt, over flyover, rejoin N11 N. Take 1st left for Enniskerry Village, entrance 600mtrs out of village

In the foothills of the Wicklow Mountains, these gardens were begun by Richard Wingfield in the 1740s, and are a blend of formal plantings, sweeping terraces, statuary and ornamental lakes together with secret hollows, rambling walks and walled gardens. The gardens cover 19 hectares and contain more than two hundred varieties of trees and shrubs. The house itself incorporates an audio visual exhibition which traces the history of the estate, and tells the story of the disastrous fire of 1974 which gutted the house. The grounds also contain Powerscourt Waterfall, Ireland's highest at 398ft, 6km from the main estate.

Times Open all year: Gardens & House daily 9.30-5.30 (Gardens close at dusk in winter), closed 25-26 Dec. Waterfall open daily, Mar-Apr & Sep-Oct 9.30-5.30; May-Aug 9.30-7; Nov-Feb 10.30-4 (closed 2 wks before Xmas). Ballroom & Garden rooms open every Sun & Mon 9.30-1.30 (May-Sep)* **Fees** House & Gardens €8 (ch under 13 €5 ch under 5 free, concessions €7). Waterfall €5 (ch under 13 €3.50 ch under 2 free, concessions €4.50)* **Facilities** Ⓟ ⓟ ☕ 🍴 licensed ♿ (partly accessible) (some areas in gardens are flat and suitable for wheelchair users) toilets for disabled (lift to first floor, 2 wheelchairs available) shop ⊗

KILQUADE Map 1 D3

National Garden Exhibition Centre

☎ 01 2819890 📠 01 2810359
e-mail: ngec@eircom.net
web: www.gardenexhibition.ie
dir: 7m S of Bray - turn off N11 for Kilquade

This Exhibition Centre has over 20 different gardens designed by some of Ireland's leading landscapers and designers. Ring for details and a calendar of events. The exhibitions are constantly changing and enjoy a high standard of maintenance. All plants are clearly labelled.

Times Open all year, Mon-Sat 9-5.30; Sun 1-5.30 **Fees** €5 (ch under 16 free, concessions €3.50) **Facilities** Ⓟ ⓟ ☕ 🍴 licensed ♿ (partly accessible) shop ⊗

RATHDRUM Map 1 D3

Avondale House & Forest Park 2 FOR 1

☎ 0404 46111 📠 0404 46333
e-mail: costelloe_j@coillte.ie
web: www.coillteoutdoors.ie
dir: S of Dublin on N11. At Rathnew on R752 to Glenealy and Rathdrum, L2149 to Avondale

It was here in 1846 that one of the greatest political leaders of modern Irish history, Charles Stewart Parnell, was born. Parnell spent much of his time at Avondale until his death in October 1891. The house is set in a magnificent forest park with miles of forest trails, plus a children's play area, deer pen, orienteering courses and picnic areas. House open to visit with many original features, audio visual presentation.

Times Open: Etr-Oct. Please see website for dates & times **Fees** €7 (concessions €6.50). Family ticket (2ad+2ch) €19.50 **Facilities** Ⓟ ☕ 🍴 licensed ⛩ (outdoor) ♿ (partly accessible) (ground floor in house & one forest trail accessible) (special car park, ramp to cafe) ⊗

IRELAND

County Maps

The county map shown here will help you identify the counties within each country. You can look up each county in the guide using the county names at the top of each page. To find towns featured in the guide use the atlas and the index.

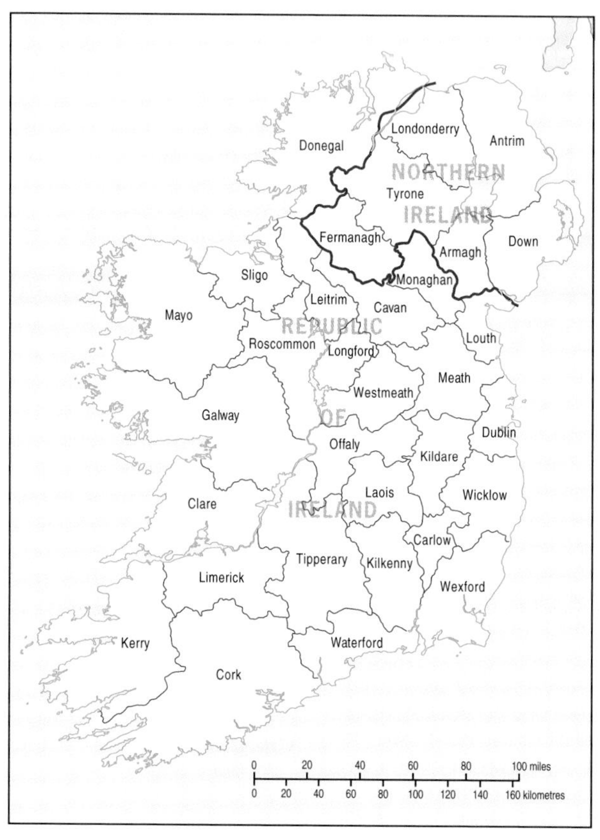

England

1 Bedfordshire
2 Berkshire
3 Bristol
4 Buckinghamshire
5 Cambridgeshire
6 Greater Manchester
7 Herefordshire
8 Hertfordshire
9 Leicestershire
10 Northamptonshire
11 Nottinghamshire
12 Rutland
13 Staffordshire
14 Warwickshire
15 West Midlands
16 Worcestershire

Scotland

17 City of Glasgow
18 Clackmannanshire
19 East Ayrshire
20 East Dunbartonshire
21 East Renfrewshire
22 Perth & Kinross
23 Renfrewshire
24 South Lanarkshire
25 West Dunbartonshire

Wales

26 Blaenau Gwent
27 Bridgend
28 Caerphilly
29 Denbighshire
30 Flintshire
31 Merthyr Tydfil
32 Monmouthshire
33 Neath Port Talbot
34 Newport
35 Rhondda Cynon Taff
36 Torfaen
37 Vale of Glamorgan
38 Wrexham

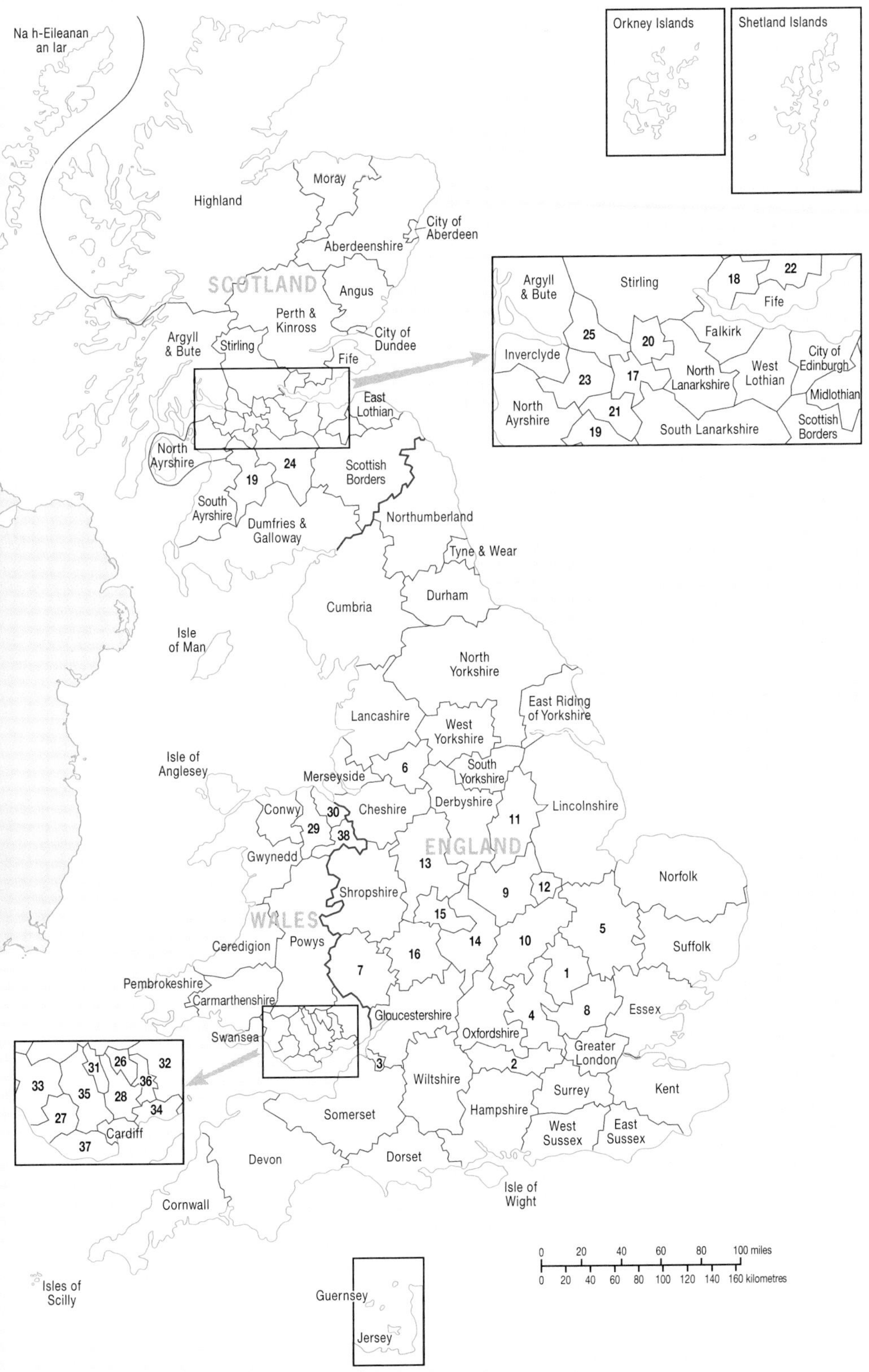

Na h-Eileanan an Iar
Orkney Islands
Shetland Islands
Highland
Moray
City of Aberdeen
Aberdeenshire
SCOTLAND
Angus
Perth & Kinross
City of Dundee
Argyll & Bute
Stirling
Fife
East Lothian
North Ayrshire
19
24
Scottish Borders
South Ayrshire
Dumfries & Galloway
Northumberland
Tyne & Wear
Durham
Cumbria
Isle of Man
North Yorkshire
East Riding of Yorkshire
Lancashire
West Yorkshire
Isle of Anglesey
Merseyside
6
South Yorkshire
Conwy
30
Cheshire
Derbyshire
Lincolnshire
29
38
11
Gwynedd
ENGLAND
13
Norfolk
12
Shropshire
9
15
5
WALES
Ceredigion
Powys
14
10
Suffolk
16
7
1
Pembrokeshire
Carmarthenshire
8
Essex
4
Gloucestershire
Swansea
Oxfordshire
Greater London
3
2
Wiltshire
Surrey
Kent
Hampshire
Somerset
West Sussex
East Sussex
Devon
Dorset
Isle of Wight
Cornwall
Isles of Scilly
Guernsey
Jersey
Argyll & Bute
Stirling
18
22
Fife
Falkirk
25
20
Inverclyde
City of Edinburgh
North Lanarkshire
West Lothian
23
17
Midlothian
North Ayrshire
21
Scottish Borders
19
South Lanarkshire
33
31
26
32
36
35
28
34
27
Cardiff
37
0 20 40 60 80 100 miles
0 20 40 60 80 100 120 140 160 kilometres

KEY TO ATLAS

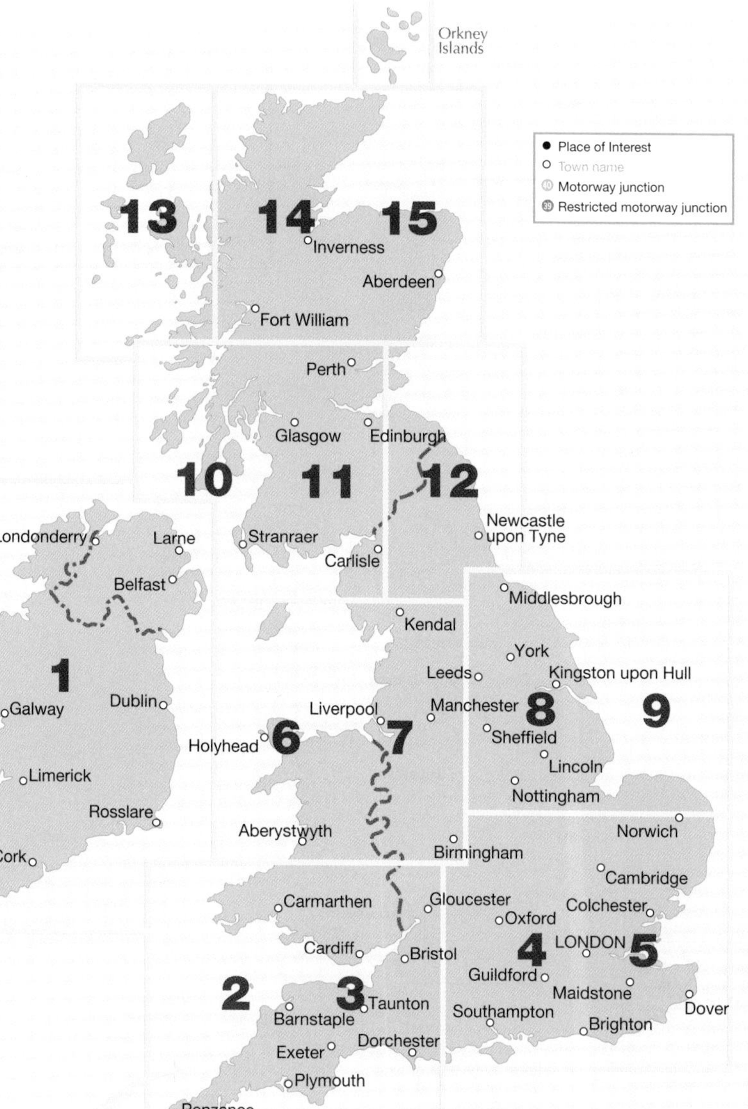

Shetland Islands
Orkney Islands
16
Place of Interest
Town name
Motorway junction
Restricted motorway junction
13
14
15
Inverness
Aberdeen
Fort William
Perth
Glasgow
Edinburgh
10
11
12
Newcastle upon Tyne
Londonderry
Larne
Stranraer
Carlisle
Belfast
Middlesbrough
Kendal
1
York
Leeds
Kingston upon Hull
Galway
Dublin
Liverpool
Manchester
8
9
Holyhead
6
7
Sheffield
Lincoln
Limerick
Nottingham
Rosslare
Norwich
Aberystwyth
Cork
Birmingham
Cambridge
Carmarthen
Gloucester
Colchester
Oxford
Cardiff
Bristol
4
LONDON
5
Guildford
2
3
Taunton
Maidstone
Dover
Barnstaple
Southampton
Brighton
Exeter
Dorchester
Plymouth
Penzance
Isles of Scilly
Channel Islands
16

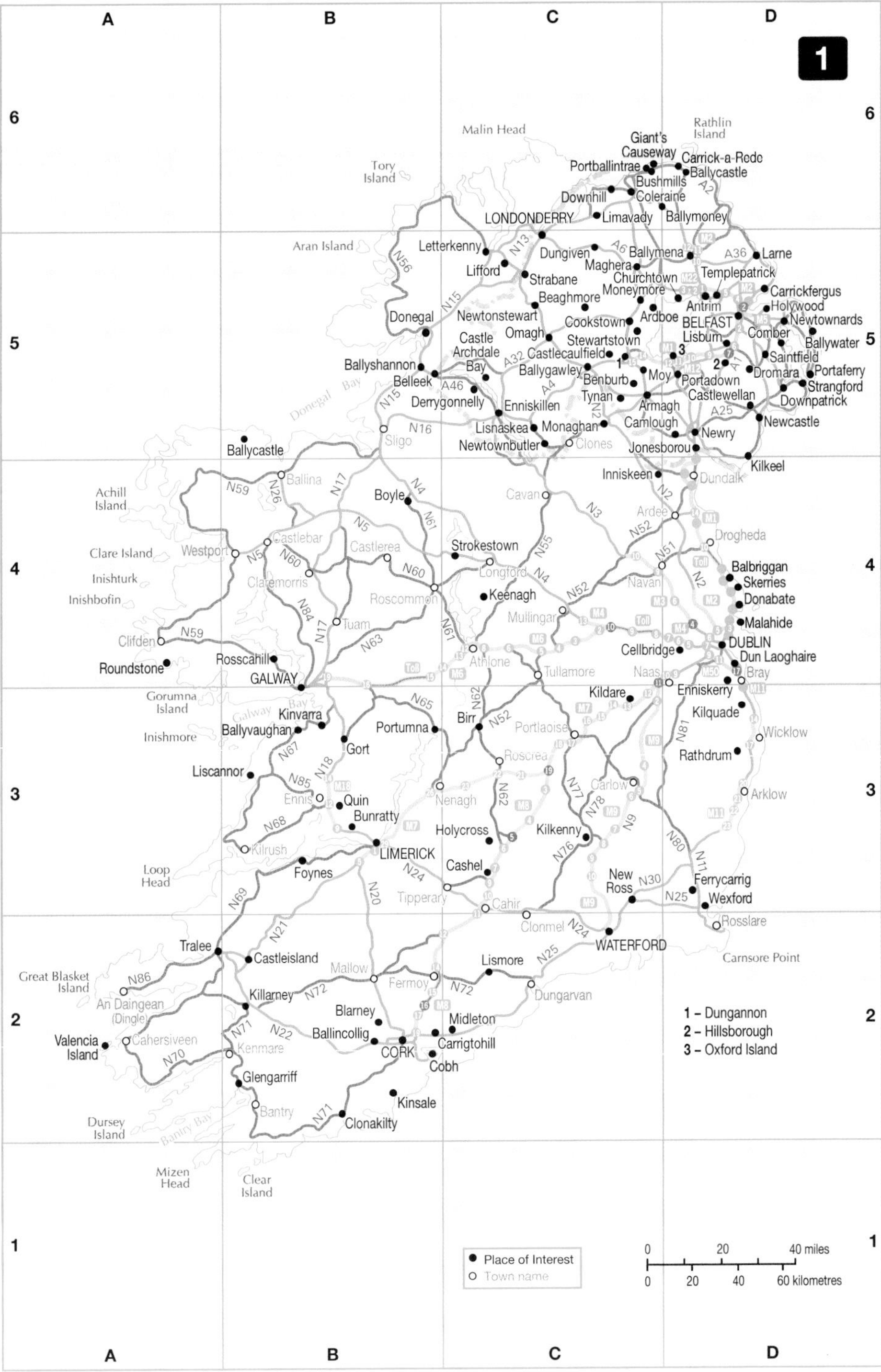
1
A
B
C
D
6
5
4
3
2
1
Malin Head
Rathlin Island
Tory Island
Giant's Causeway
Portballintrae
Carrick-a-Rede
Ballycastle
Bushmills
Downhill
Coleraine
LONDONDERRY
Limavady
Ballymoney
Aran Island
Letterkenny
Lifford
Dungiven
Ballymena
Larne
Maghera
Templepatrick
Strabane
Churchtown
Moneymore
Carrickfergus
Beaghmore
Antrim
Holywood
Donegal
Newtonstewart
Ardboe
Cookstown
BELFAST
Newtownards
Omagh
Lisburn
Comber
Castle Archdale Bay
Stewartstown
Ballywater
Ballyshannon
Castlecaulfield
Saintfield
Belleek
Ballygawley
Benburb
Moy
Dromara
Portaferry
Portadown
Strangford
Derrygonnelly
Tynan
Castlewellan
Downpatrick
Donegal Bay
Enniskillen
Armagh
Camlough
Newcastle
Lisnaskea
Monaghan
Newry
Sligo
Newtownbutler
Clones
Jonesborou
Ballycastle
Kilkeel
Inniskeen
Dundalk
Achill Island
Ballina
Boyle
Cavan
Ardee
Drogheda
Castlebar
Clare Island
Westport
Castlerea
Strokestown
Inishturk
Claremorris
Longford
Balbriggan
Skerries
Navan
Inishbofin
Roscommon
Keenagh
Donabate
Mullingar
Malahide
Tuam
Clifden
Cellbridge
DUBLIN
Dun Laoghaire
Rosscahill
Roundstone
Athlone
Tullamore
Naas
Bray
GALWAY
Enniskerry
Gorumna Island
Kildare
Galway Bay
Kinvarra
Kilquade
Ballyvaughan
Portumna
Birr
Inishmore
Portlaoise
Wicklow
Gort
Roscrea
Rathdrum
Liscannor
Carlow
Ennis
Quin
Nenagh
Arklow
Bunratty
Holycross
Kilkenny
Kilrush
LIMERICK
Loop Head
Foynes
Cashel
New Ross
Ferrycarrig
Tipperary
Cahir
Wexford
Clonmel
Rosslare
Tralee
WATERFORD
Castleisland
Lismore
Carnsore Point
Great Blasket Island
Mallow
Fermoy
An Daingean (Dingle)
Killarney
Dungarvan
Blarney
Midleton
Valencia Island
Cahersiveen
Ballincollig
Carrigtohill
Kenmare
CORK
Cobh
Glengarriff
Kinsale
Bantry
Dursey Island
Bantry Bay
Clonakilty
Mizen Head
Clear Island
1 – Dungannon
2 – Hillsborough
3 – Oxford Island
Place of Interest
Town name
0 20 40 miles
0 20 40 60 kilometres

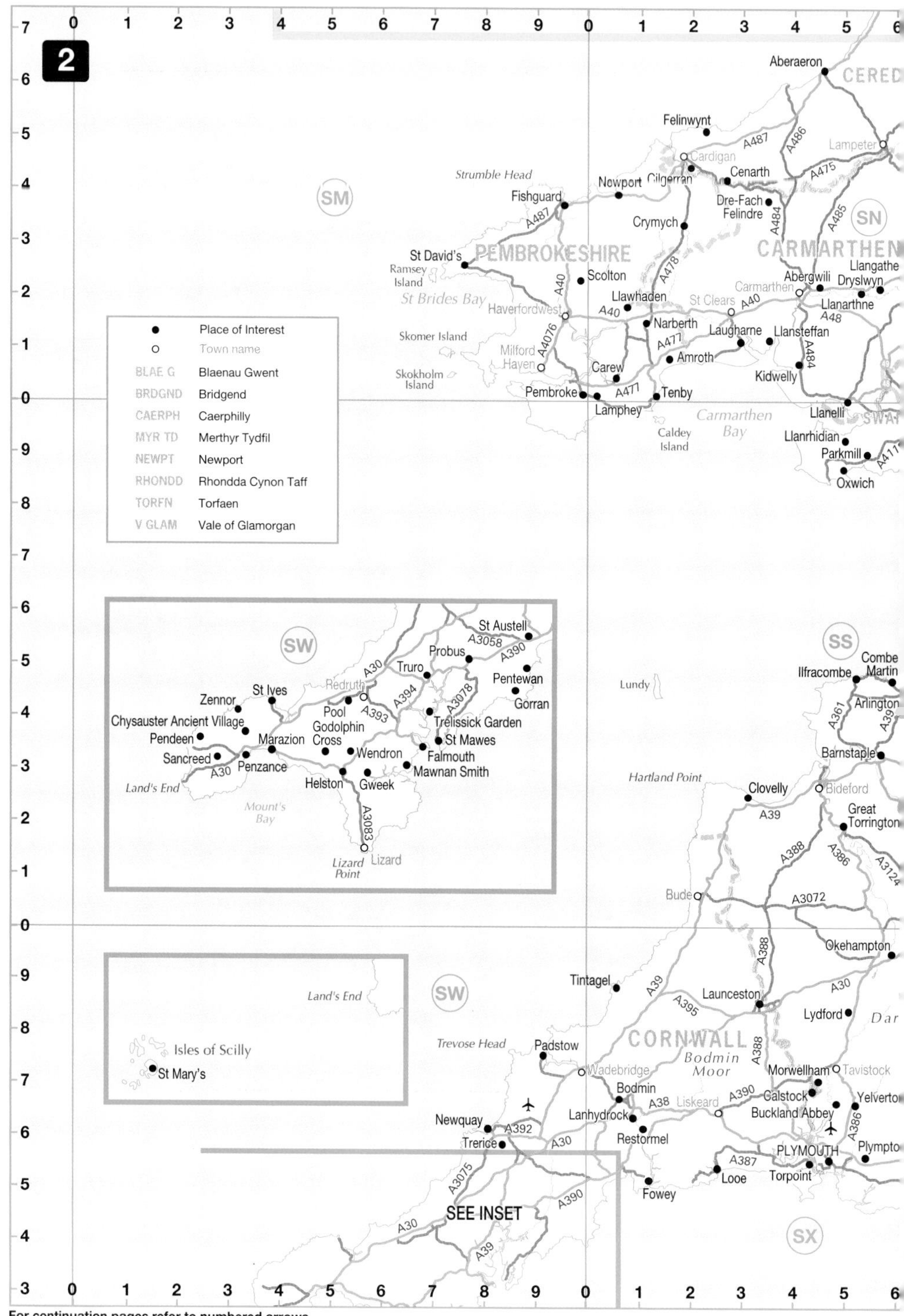
2
Place of Interest
Town name
BLAE G Blaenau Gwent
BRDGND Bridgend
CAERPH Caerphilly
MYR TD Merthyr Tydfil
NEWPT Newport
RHONDD Rhondda Cynon Taff
TORFN Torfaen
V GLAM Vale of Glamorgan
Aberaeron
Felinwynt
Cardigan
Cilgerran
Cenarth
Newport
Fishguard
Strumble Head
Dre-Fach Felindre
Lampeter
Crymych
PEMBROKESHIRE
CARMARTHEN
St David's
Ramsey Island
St Brides Bay
Scolton
Llawhaden
Haverfordwest
Carmarthen
Abergwili
Dryslwyn
Llangathe
Llanarthne
St Clears
Narberth
Laugharne
Llansteffan
Skomer Island
Milford Haven
Skokholm Island
Carew
Amroth
Kidwelly
Pembroke
Lamphey
Tenby
Caldey Island
Carmarthen Bay
Llanelli
Llanrhidian
Parkmill
Oxwich
St Austell
Probus
Truro
Pentewan
Gorran
Redruth
St Ives
Zennor
Chysauster Ancient Village
Pendeen
Sancreed
Pool
Godolphin Cross
Trelissick Garden
St Mawes
Marazion
Wendron
Falmouth
Penzance
Helston
Gweek
Mawnan Smith
Land's End
Mount's Bay
Lizard Point
Lizard
Lundy
Ilfracombe
Combe Martin
Arlington
Barnstaple
Hartland Point
Clovelly
Bideford
Great Torrington
Bude
Okehampton
Tintagel
Launceston
Lydford
Isles of Scilly
St Mary's
Trevose Head
Padstow
CORNWALL
Bodmin Moor
Wadebridge
Morwellham
Tavistock
Bodmin
Liskeard
Calstock
Buckland Abbey
Yelverton
Newquay
Lanhydrock
Restormel
Trerice
PLYMOUTH
Plympton
Looe
Torpoint
Fowey
SEE INSET
For continuation pages refer to numbered arrows

3
6
7
4
Strata Florida
Presteigne
Croft
Burford
Great Witley
Hanbury
Redditch
Llandrindod Wells
Kington
Leominster
Ashton
Wichenford
WORCESTERSHIRE
WARWICKSHIRE
Builth Wells
Brockhampton
WORCESTER
Spetchley
Stratford-upon-Avon
HEREFORDSHIRE
Great Malvern
Pumsaint
Hay-on-Wye
Swainshill
Severn Stoke
Evesham
Llandovery
POWYS
SO
HEREFORD
Ledbury
SHIRE
Brecon
Llanthony
Ross-on-Wye
Deerhurst
SP
Llandeilo
Brecon Beacons
Grosmont
Newent
CHELTENHAM
Carreg Cennen Castle
Tretower
Skenfrith
Goodrich
GLOUCESTER
RHONDD
White Castle
Abergavenny
Llantilio Crossenny
Monmouth
GLOUCESTERSHIRE
Abercraf
Merthyr Tydfil
Westbury on Severn
Cranham
Soudley
Painswick
Clearwell
Slimbridge
NEATH PORT TALBOT
Crynant
Blaenavon
Raglan
Tintern Parva
Stroud
Cirencester
Lydney
Berkeley
Owlpen
Neath
Aberdulais
Cwmbran
Cwmcarn
Chepstow
Uley
SWANSEA
Trehafod
Caerleon
Tetbury
Port Talbot
BRDGND
CAERPH
Caerphilly
Caerwent
Caldicot
Westonbirt
NEWPORT
Swansea Bay
Coity
Tongwyniais
SWINDON
Bridgend
CARDIFF
Ogmore
St Fagans
St Hilary
Dyrham
Chippenham
BRISTOL
Calne
Clevedon
V GLAM
Penarth
Corsham
Barry
BATH
Lacock
Bristol Channel
Weston-super-Mare
Bradford-on-Avon
Holt
Farleigh Hungerford
Westwood
WILTSHIRE
Axbridge
Wookey Hole
Midsomer Norton
Salisbury Plain
Lynton
Minehead
Burnham-on-Sea
ST
Frome
Westbury
SU
East Huntspill
Wells
Nunney
Warminster
Blackmoor Gate
Dunster
Washford
Nether Stowey
Shepton Mallet
Cranmore
Longleat
Exmoor
Glastonbury
Bridgwater
Stourhead
Teffont Magna
Street
Stoke St Gregory
Stourton
South Molton
SOMERSET
Kingsdon
Sparkford
Wincanton
Tisbury
SALISBURY
Chittlehampton
Taunton
Muchelney
Yeovilton
Knightshayes Court
East Lambrook
Tintinhull
Shaftesbury
Tollard Royal
Barrington
Stoke-Sub-Hamdon
Yeovil
Sherborne
Tiverton
Montacute
Uffculme
Chard
Cullompton
Cricket St Thomas
Minterne Magna
Blandford Forum
New Forest
Killerton House & Garden
Honiton
Beaminster
Wimborne
Crediton
Athelhampton
Tolpuddle
Sticklepath
EXETER
Clyst St Mary
Bridport
DORSET
Bovington Camp
Organford
Poole
Drewsteignton
Beer
Dorchester
BOURNEMOUTH
DEVON
Powderham
Otterton
Branscombe
Abbotsbury
Brownsea Island
Dartmoor
Bicton
Wool
Corfe Castle
Exmouth
Chesil Beach
West Lulworth
SZ
Chudleigh
Dawlish
Lyme Bay
Weymouth
Swanage
Newton Abbot
Portland
Buckfastleigh
Compton
TORQUAY
Portland Bill
SY
Totnes
Paignton
Churston Ferrers
Dartmouth
Kingswear
Kingsbridge
Salcombe
Prawle Point
0 10 20 miles
0 10 20 30 kilometres

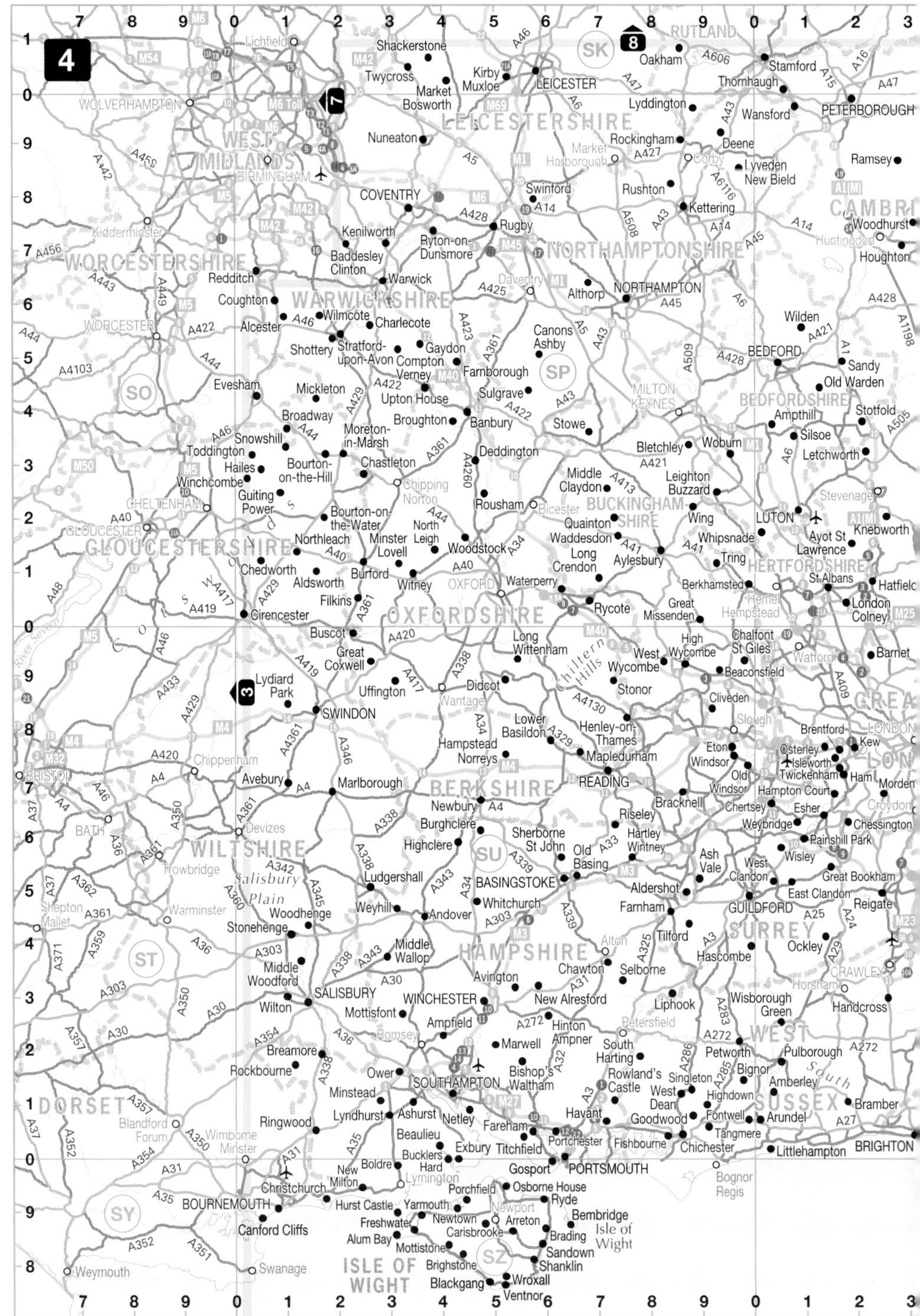

For continuation pages refer to numbered arrows

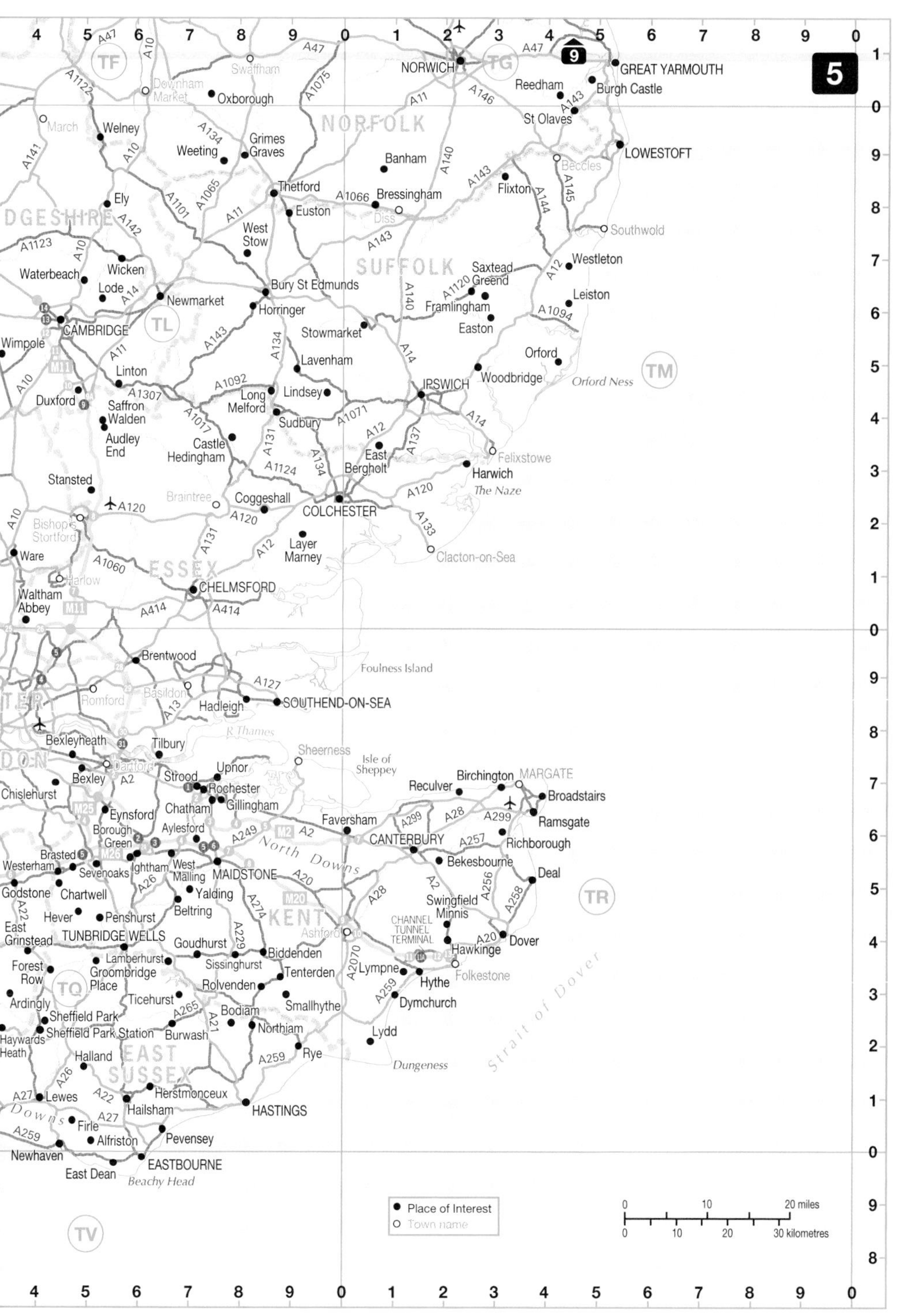
5
NORFOLK
SUFFOLK
ESSEX
KENT
EAST SUSSEX
NORWICH
GREAT YARMOUTH
Burgh Castle
Reedham
St Olaves
LOWESTOFT
Beccles
Southwold
Oxborough
Swaffham
Downham Market
March
Welney
Weeting
Grimes Graves
Banham
Thetford
Bressingham
Diss
Flixton
Euston
Ely
West Stow
Wicken
Waterbeach
Lode
Newmarket
Bury St Edmunds
Horringer
Saxtead Greend
Framlingham
Easton
Westleton
Leiston
Wimpole
CAMBRIDGE
Stowmarket
Orford
Orford Ness
Lavenham
Woodbridge
Linton
IPSWICH
Lindsey
Duxford
Saffron Walden
Long Melford
Sudbury
Audley End
Castle Hedingham
East Bergholt
Felixstowe
Harwich
The Naze
Stansted
Braintree
Coggeshall
COLCHESTER
Bishop's Stortford
Layer Marney
Clacton-on-Sea
Ware
Harlow
CHELMSFORD
Waltham Abbey
Brentwood
Foulness Island
Romford
Basildon
Hadleigh
SOUTHEND-ON-SEA
R Thames
Bexleyheath
Tilbury
Sheerness
Isle of Sheppey
Dartford
Bexley
Upnor
Strood
Rochester
Chislehurst
Chatham
Gillingham
Reculver
Birchington
MARGATE
Broadstairs
Ramsgate
Eynsford
Faversham
Borough Green
Aylesford
CANTERBURY
Richborough
Brasted
North Downs
Bekesbourne
Westerham
Sevenoaks
Ightham
West Malling
MAIDSTONE
Deal
Godstone
Chartwell
Yalding
Beltring
Swingfield Minnis
Hever
Penshurst
East Grinstead
TUNBRIDGE WELLS
Goudhurst
Ashford
CHANNEL TUNNEL TERMINAL
Dover
Hawkinge
Biddenden
Forest Row
Lamberhurst
Groombridge Place
Sissinghurst
Tenterden
Lympne
Folkestone
Hythe
Rolvenden
Ardingly
Ticehurst
Smallhythe
Dymchurch
Strait of Dover
Sheffield Park
Bodiam
Sheffield Park Station
Burwash
Northiam
Lydd
Haywards Heath
Halland
Rye
Dungeness
Herstmonceux
Lewes
Hailsham
HASTINGS
Downs
Firle
Alfriston
Pevensey
Newhaven
EASTBOURNE
East Dean
Beachy Head
TF
TG
TL
TM
TQ
TR
TV
Place of Interest
Town name
0 10 20 miles
0 10 20 30 kilometres

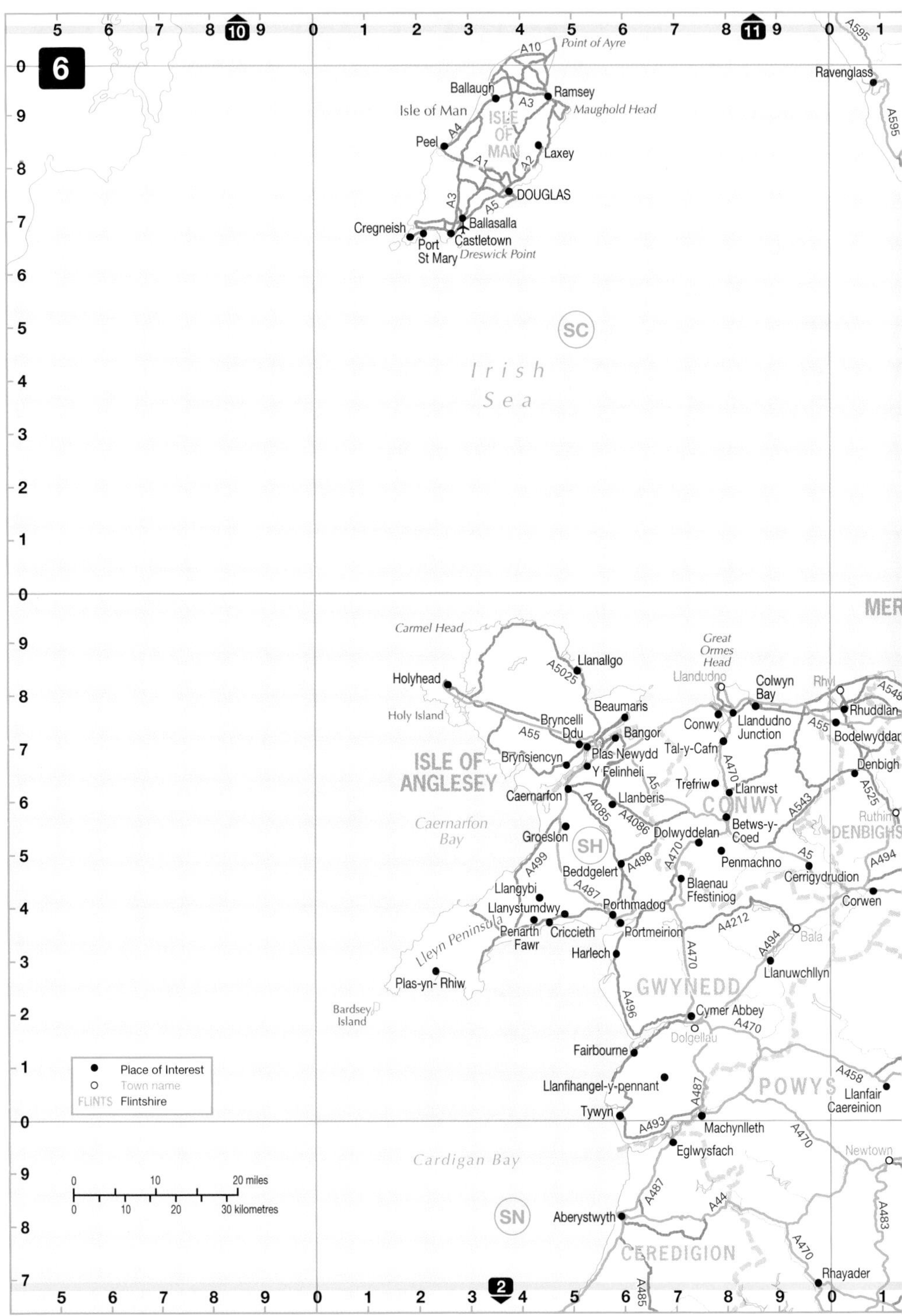

For continuation pages refer to numbered arrows

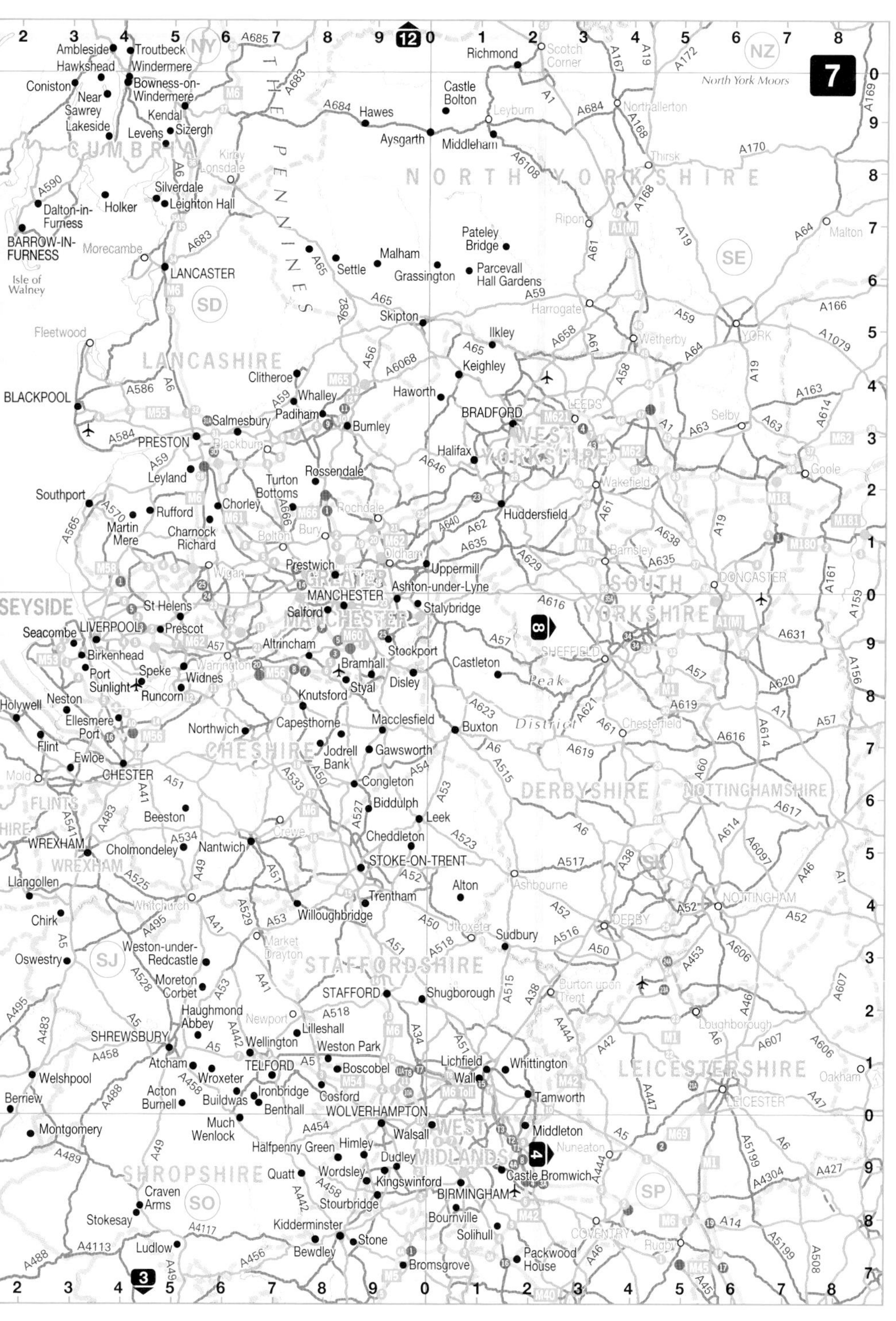
7
12
8
4
3
NY
NZ
SD
SE
SJ
SK
SO
SP
North York Moors
CUMBRIA
THE PENNINES
NORTH YORKSHIRE
LANCASHIRE
WEST YORKSHIRE
GREATER MANCHESTER
SEYSIDE
SOUTH YORKSHIRE
CHESHIRE
FLINTS
WREXHAM
DERBYSHIRE
NOTTINGHAMSHIRE
STAFFORDSHIRE
LEICESTERSHIRE
WEST MIDLANDS
SHROPSHIRE
Peak District
Ambleside
Troutbeck
Hawkshead
Windermere
Coniston
Bowness-on-Windermere
Near Sawrey
Lakeside
Kendal
Levens
Sizergh
Kirby Lonsdale
Silverdale
Leighton Hall
Dalton-in-Furness
Holker
BARROW-IN-FURNESS
Isle of Walney
Morecambe
LANCASTER
Fleetwood
BLACKPOOL
Richmond
Scotch Corner
Castle Bolton
Hawes
Aysgarth
Leyburn
Middleham
Northallerton
Thirsk
Ripon
Malton
Pateley Bridge
Malham
Settle
Grassington
Parcevall Hall Gardens
Skipton
Harrogate
Ilkley
Wetherby
YORK
Keighley
Haworth
Clitheroe
Whalley
Padiham
Burnley
Salmesbury
PRESTON
Blackburn
BRADFORD
LEEDS
Selby
Halifax
Goole
Leyland
Rossendale
Turton Bottoms
Southport
Rufford
Chorley
Martin Mere
Charnock Richard
Rochdale
Bury
Bolton
Wakefield
Huddersfield
Barnsley
DONCASTER
Oldham
Wigan
Prestwich
Uppermill
MANCHESTER
Ashton-under-Lyne
Salford
Stalybridge
St Helens
Prescot
LIVERPOOL
Seacombe
Birkenhead
Altrincham
Stockport
Castleton
SHEFFIELD
Warrington
Bramhall
Port Sunlight
Speke
Widnes
Runcorn
Styal
Disley
Holywell
Neston
Knutsford
Ellesmere Port
Northwich
Capesthorne
Macclesfield
Buxton
Chesterfield
Flint
Jodrell Bank
Gawsworth
Ewloe
Mold
CHESTER
Congleton
Biddulph
Leek
Beeston
Crewe
Cheddleton
WREXHAM
Cholmondeley
Nantwich
STOKE-ON-TRENT
Llangollen
Alton
Ashbourne
Trentham
NOTTINGHAM
Whitchurch
Willoughbridge
Chirk
DERBY
Uttoxeter
Sudbury
Market Drayton
Weston-under-Redcastle
Oswestry
Moreton Corbet
STAFFORD
Shugborough
Burton upon Trent
Loughborough
Haughmond Abbey
Newport
Lilleshall
SHREWSBURY
Wellington
Weston Park
Lichfield
Whittington
Atcham
TELFORD
Boscobel
Wall
Oakham
Welshpool
Wroxeter
Acton Burnell
Buildwas
Ironbridge
Cosford
Tamworth
LEICESTER
Berriew
Benthall
WOLVERHAMPTON
Much Wenlock
Walsall
Middleton
Montgomery
Halfpenny Green
Himley
Dudley
Nuneaton
Quatt
Wordsley
Kingswinford
Castle Bromwich
Craven Arms
BIRMINGHAM
Stourbridge
Stokesay
Bournville
COVENTRY
Kidderminster
Solihull
Rugby
Stone
Ludlow
Bewdley
Packwood House
Bromsgrove

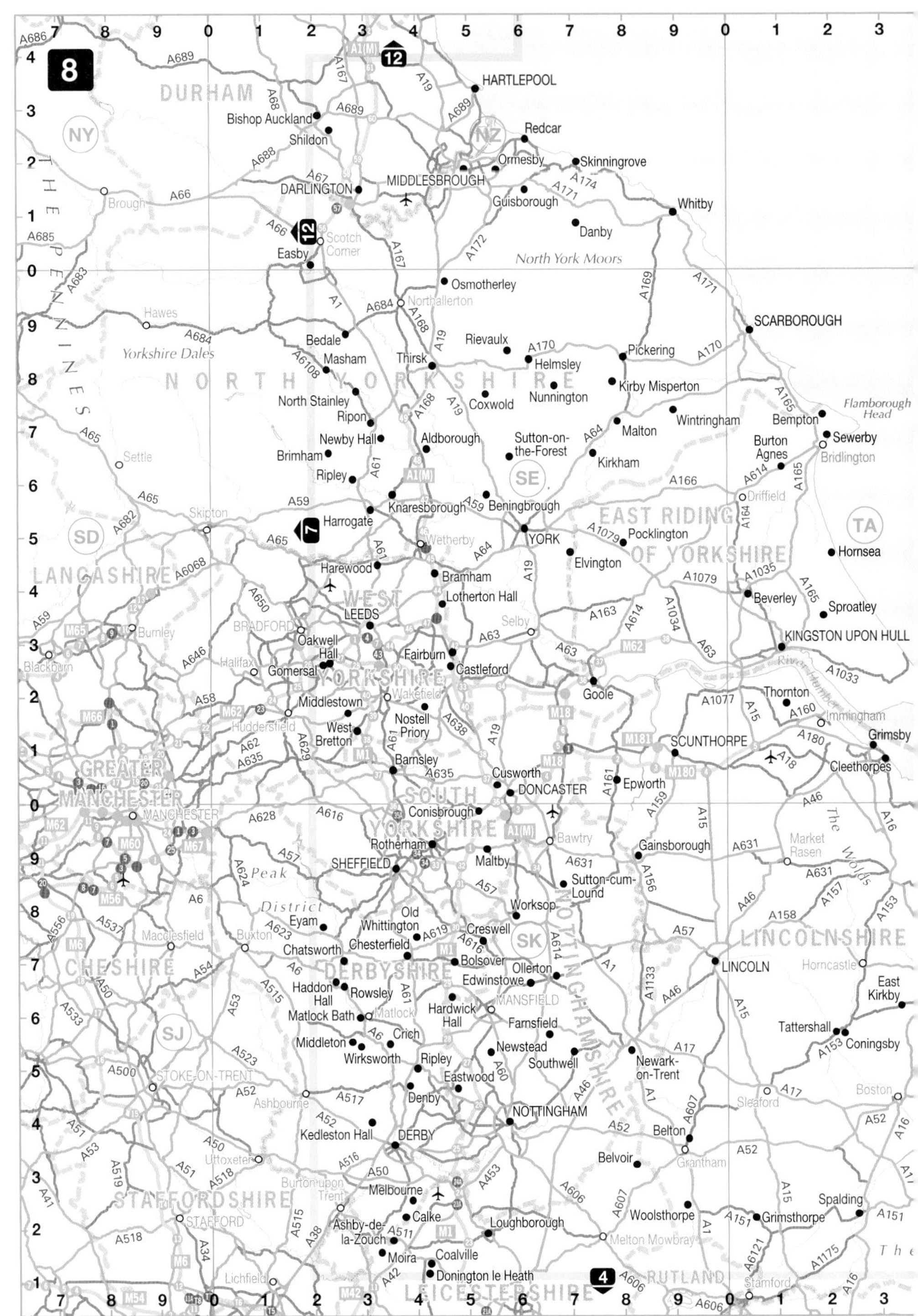

For continuation pages refer to numbered arrows

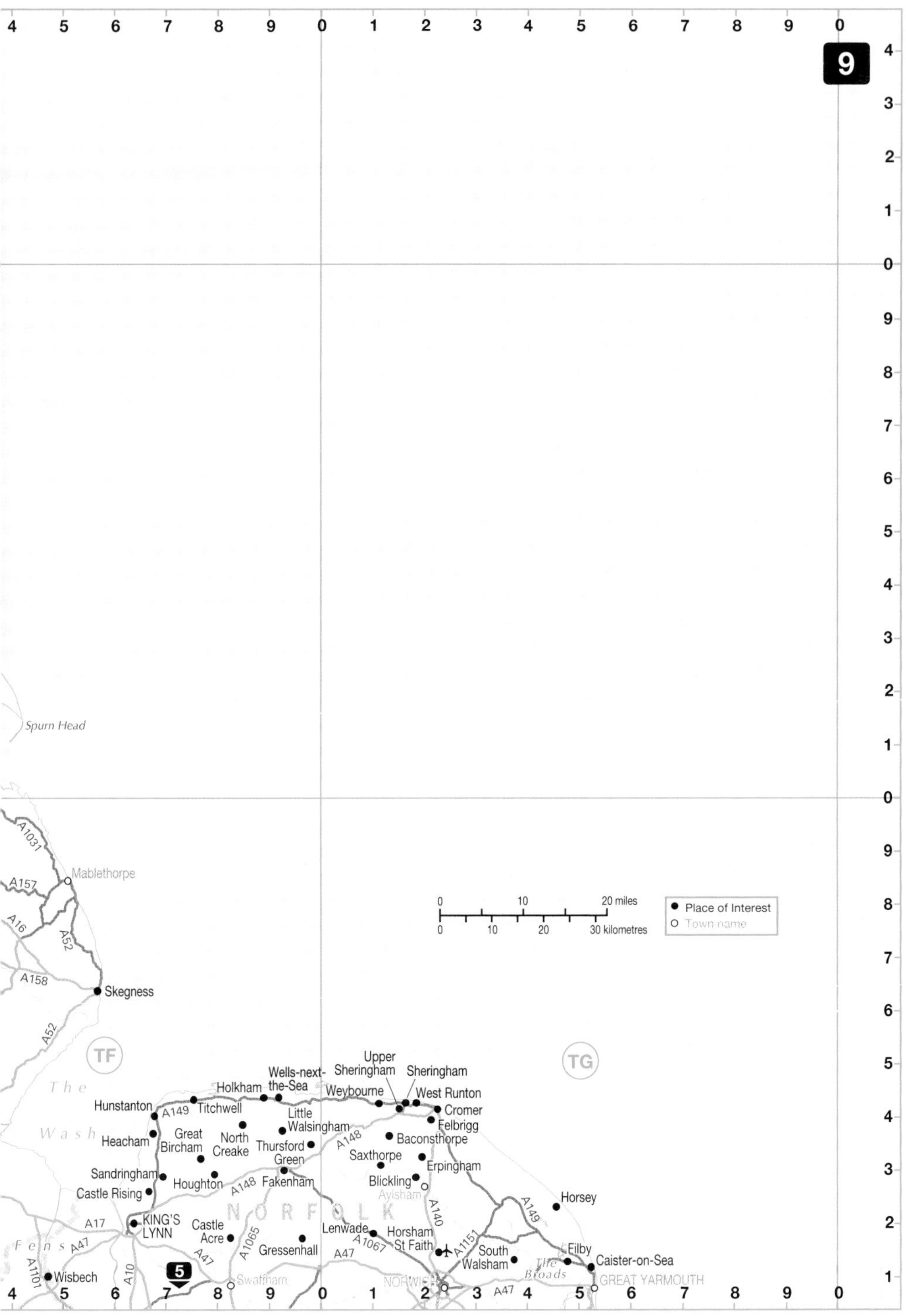
9
Spurn Head
Mablethorpe
Skegness
TF
TG
The Wash
Fens
Hunstanton
Holkham
Wells-next-the-Sea
Titchwell
Heacham
Great Bircham
North Creake
Little Walsingham
Thursford Green
Sandringham
Houghton
Fakenham
Castle Rising
KING'S LYNN
Castle Acre
Gressenhall
Swaffham
Wisbech
NORFOLK
Upper Sheringham
Sheringham
Weybourne
West Runton
Cromer
Felbrigg
Baconsthorpe
Saxthorpe
Erpingham
Blickling
Aylsham
Lenwade
Horsham St Faith
NORWICH
South Walsham
Horsey
Filby
The Broads
Caister-on-Sea
GREAT YARMOUTH
A1031
A157
A16
A52
A158
A149
A148
A17
A47
A1101
A10
A1065
A1067
A140
A1151
0 10 20 miles
0 10 20 30 kilometres
Place of Interest
Town name
5

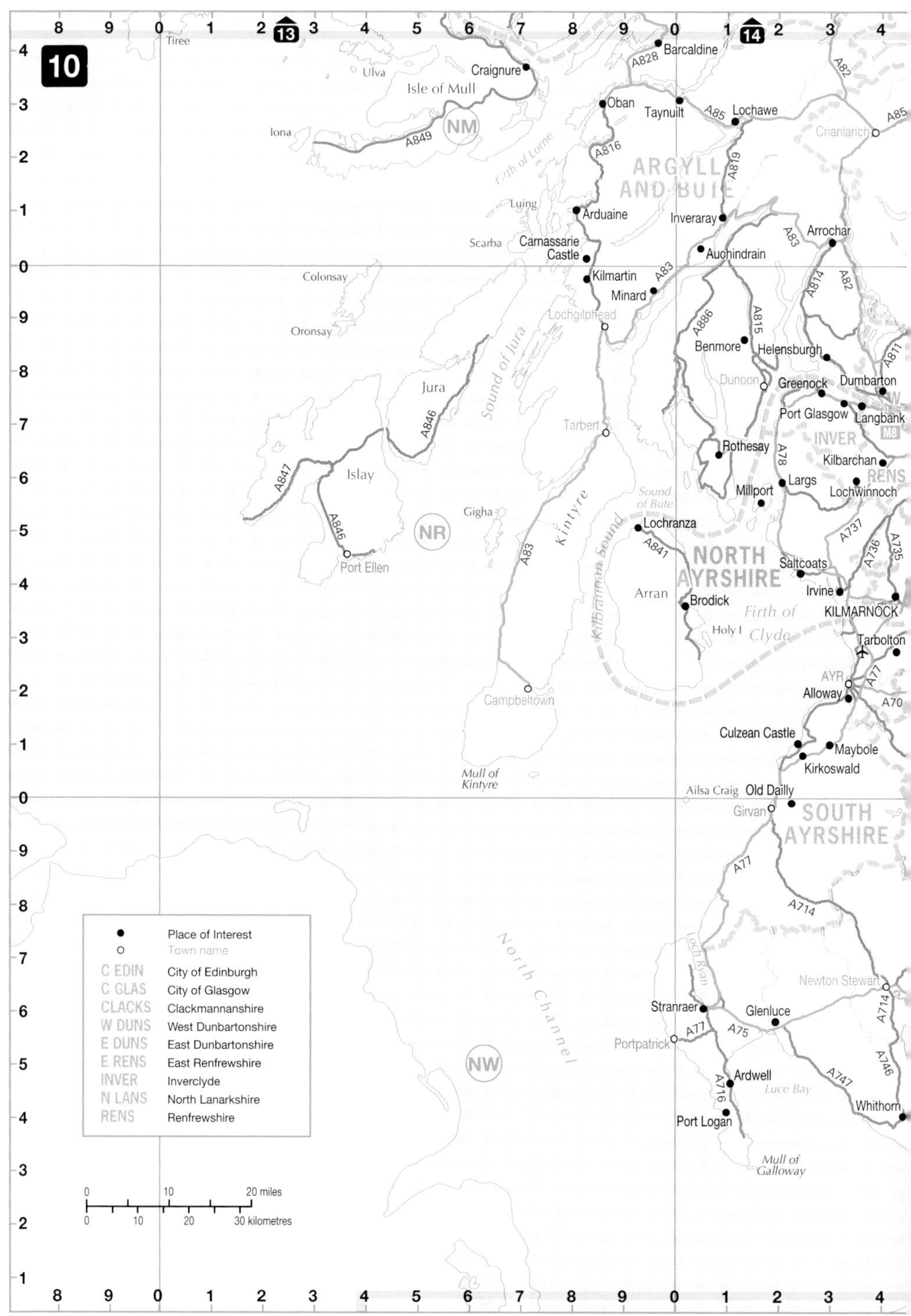

For continuation pages refer to numbered arrows

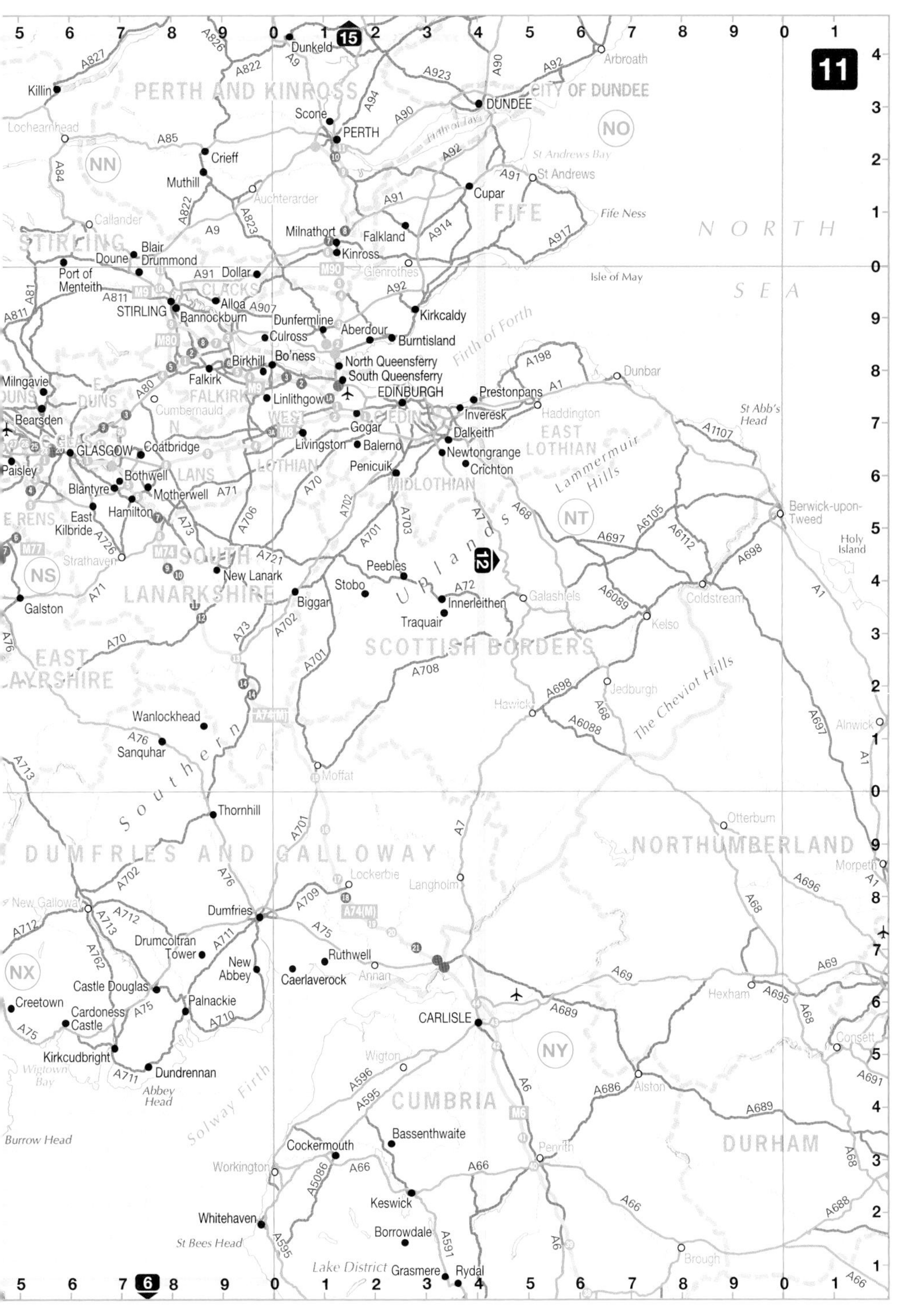
11
15
12
6
PERTH AND KINROSS
CITY OF DUNDEE
STIRLING
CLACKS
FIFE
FALKIRK
WEST LOTHIAN
EDINBURGH
MIDLOTHIAN
EAST LOTHIAN
S LANS
SOUTH LANARKSHIRE
EAST AYRSHIRE
E RENS
SCOTTISH BORDERS
DUMFRIES AND GALLOWAY
NORTHUMBERLAND
CUMBRIA
DURHAM
NORTH SEA
NN
NO
NS
NT
NX
NY
Killin
Lochearnhead
Crieff
Muthill
Auchterarder
Callander
Doune
Blair Drummond
Port of Menteith
Dollar
Dunkeld
Scone
PERTH
DUNDEE
Arbroath
Firth of Tay
St Andrews Bay
St Andrews
Cupar
Fife Ness
Falkland
Milnathort
Kinross
Glenrothes
Isle of May
STIRLING
Bannockburn
Alloa
Dunfermline
Culross
Aberdour
Burntisland
Kirkcaldy
Firth of Forth
Bo'ness
Birkhill
Falkirk
North Queensferry
South Queensferry
Linlithgow
Milngavie
Bearsden
Cumbernauld
GLASGOW
Coatbridge
Paisley
Livingston
Gogar
Balerno
Prestonpans
Inveresk
Dalkeith
Newtongrange
Crichton
Penicuik
Haddington
Dunbar
St Abb's Head
Lammermuir Hills
Bothwell
Blantyre
Motherwell
Hamilton
East Kilbride
Strathaven
New Lanark
Biggar
Peebles
Stobo
Innerleithen
Traquair
Galashiels
Southern Uplands
Berwick-upon-Tweed
Holy Island
Coldstream
Kelso
Galston
Jedburgh
Hawick
The Cheviot Hills
Alnwick
Wanlockhead
Sanquhar
Moffat
Thornhill
Otterburn
Morpeth
Lockerbie
Langholm
New Galloway
Dumfries
Drumcoltran Tower
New Abbey
Caerlaverock
Ruthwell
Annan
Castle Douglas
Creetown
Cardoness Castle
Palnackie
Kirkcudbright
Dundrennan
Wigtown Bay
Abbey Head
Burrow Head
Solway Firth
CARLISLE
Hexham
Consett
Wigton
Alston
Cockermouth
Bassenthwaite
Workington
Penrith
Keswick
Whitehaven
Borrowdale
St Bees Head
Lake District
Grasmere
Rydal
Brough
A827
A826
A822
A9
A923
A90
A92
A94
A85
A84
A822
A823
A91
A914
A917
A81
A811
A907
M90
M9
M80
A80
M8
M77
M74
A726
A71
A70
A706
A702
A703
A701
A7
A721
A72
A68
A198
A1
A1107
A6105
A6112
A697
A698
A6089
A708
A73
A74(M)
A76
A713
A702
A712
A762
A711
A75
A710
A709
A6088
A696
A69
A695
A689
A6
M6
A596
A595
A5086
A66
A591
A686
A691
A688

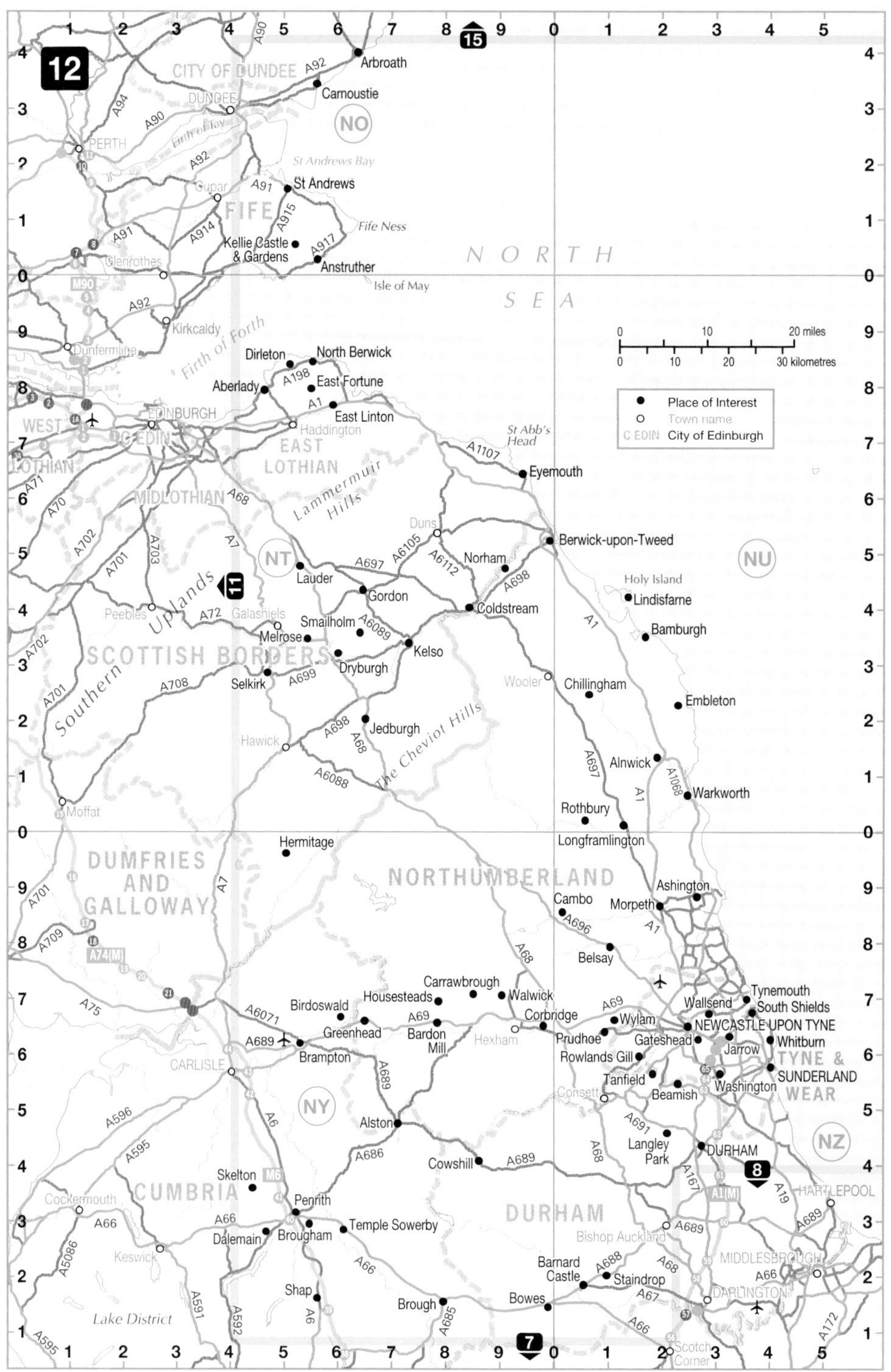

For continuation pages refer to numbered arrows

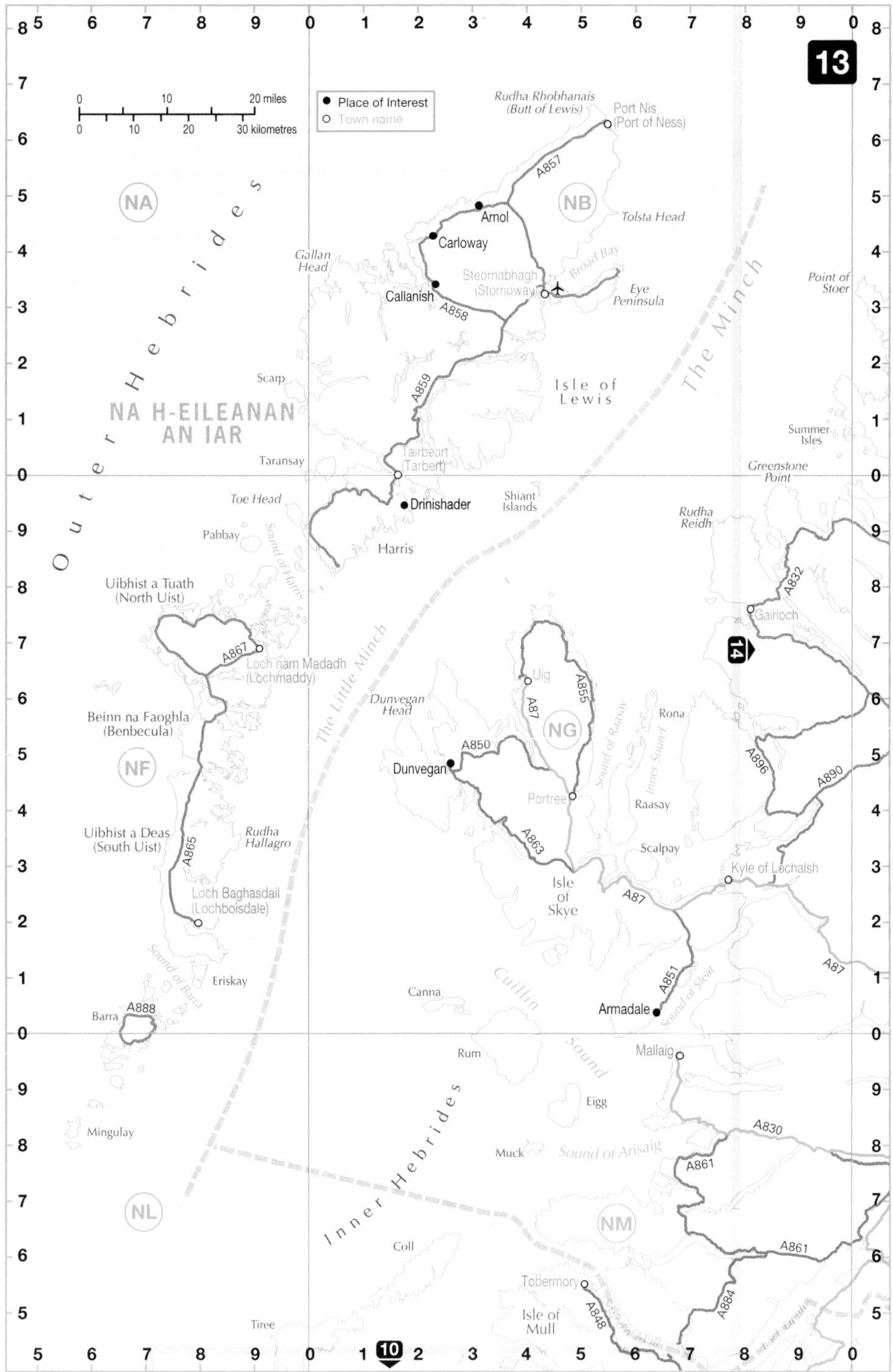
13
0 10 20 miles
0 10 20 30 kilometres
Place of Interest
Town name
Rudha Rhobhanais (Butt of Lewis)
Port Nis (Port of Ness)
A857
NA
NB
Arnol
Tolsta Head
Carloway
Gallan Head
Broad Bay
Steornabhagh (Stornoway)
Eye Peninsula
Callanish
A858
Point of Stoer
The Minch
Outer Hebrides
Scarp
A859
Isle of Lewis
NA H-EILEANAN AN IAR
Summer Isles
Taransay
Tairbeart (Tarbert)
Greenstone Point
Toe Head
Drinishader
Shiant Islands
Rudha Reidh
Pabbay
Sound of Harris
Harris
Uibhist a Tuath (North Uist)
A832
Gairloch
A867
Loch nam Madadh (Lochmaddy)
The Little Minch
Uig
A855
14
Dunvegan Head
A87
Beinn na Faoghla (Benbecula)
NG
Rona
Sound of Raasay
Inner Sound
A850
NF
Dunvegan
A896
A890
Portree
Raasay
Uibhist a Deas (South Uist)
Rudha Hallagro
A865
A863
Scalpay
Kyle of Lochalsh
Isle of Skye
Loch Baghasdail (Lochboisdale)
A87
Sound of Barra
Cuillin Sound
A851
Eriskay
Canna
A87
Barra
A888
Armadale
Sound of Sleat
Rum
Mallaig
Inner Hebrides
Eigg
Mingulay
A830
Muck
Sound of Arisaig
A861
NL
NM
Coll
A861
Tobermory
A884
A848
Isle of Mull
Tiree
Sound of Mull
Loch Linnhe
10

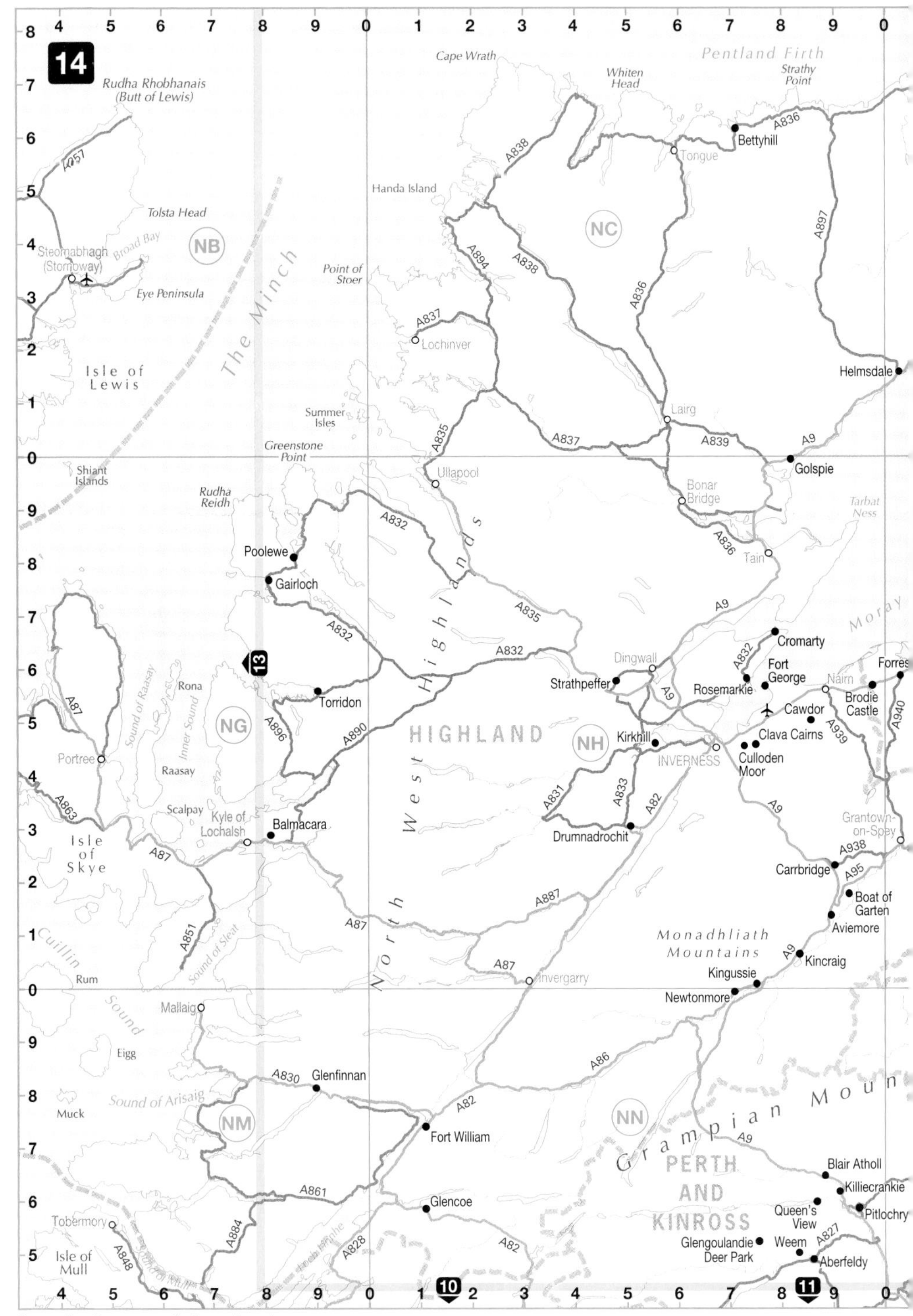

For continuation pages refer to numbered arrows

15
Dunnet Head
Island of Stroma
Duncansby Head
John o' Groats
Thurso
Noss Head
Wick
Dunbeath
ND
NK
NJ
NO
Duffus
Lossiemouth
Spey Bay
Banff
Macduff
Fraserburgh
Elgin
MORAY
Rothes
Keith
Turriff
Mintlaw
Peterhead
Old Deer
Craigellachie
Marypark
Dufftown
Huntly
Methlick
Ballindalloch
Ellon
Rhynie
Oyne
Pitmedden
Tomintoul
Inverurie
Kildrummy
Alford
Kemnay
CITY OF ABERDEEN
ABERDEENSHIRE
ABERDEEN
Corgarff
Peterculter
Maryculter
Ballater
Banchory
Crathes
Balmoral
Braemar
Stonehaven
Edzell
ANGUS
Brechin
Montrose
Kirriemuir
Lunan Bay
Forfar
Glamis
Blairgowrie
12
Place of Interest
Town name
20 miles
30 kilometres

16
Place of Interest
Town name
0 10 20 miles
0 10 20 30 kilometres
HY
ND
Westray
Westray
Rousay
Sanday
Birsay
Mainland
Eday
Stronsay
Dounby
Harray
Shapinsay
Finstown
Kirkwall
Stromness
Hoy
South Ronaldsay
Orkney Islands

0 10 20 miles
0 10 20 30 kilometres
HP
Unst
Yell
Fetlar
Whalsay
Mainland
Lerwick
Scalloway
Bressay
HU
Mousa Island
Sumburgh
Shetland Islands

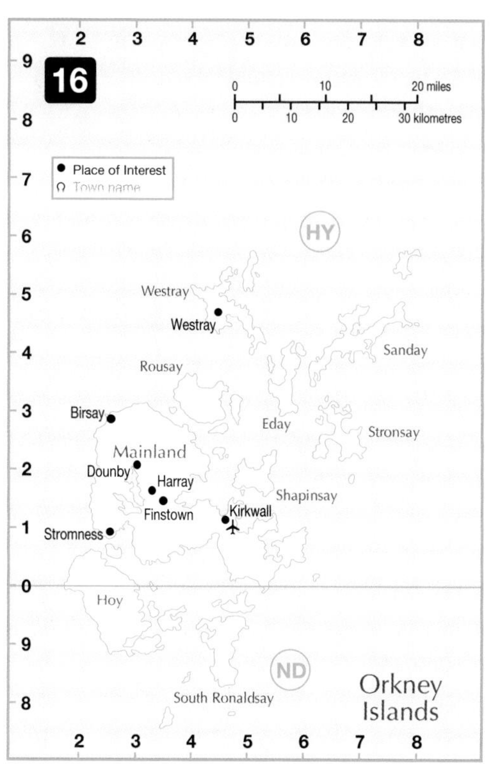

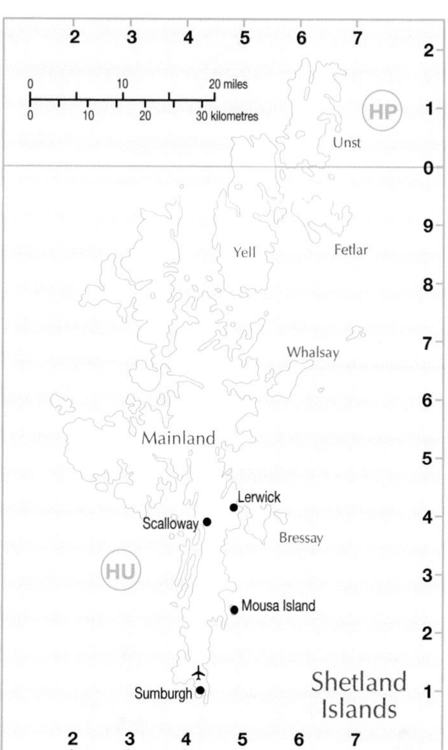

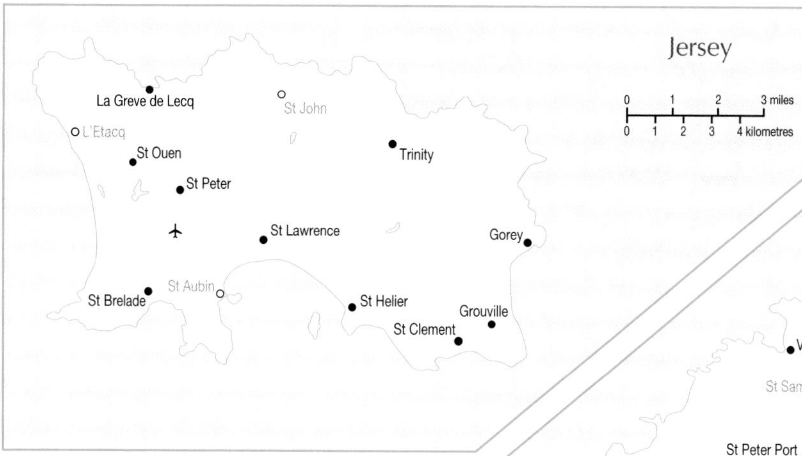

Jersey
0 1 2 3 miles
0 1 2 3 4 kilometres
La Greve de Lecq
St John
L'Etacq
St Ouen
Trinity
St Peter
St Lawrence
Gorey
St Aubin
St Brelade
St Helier
Grouville
St Clement

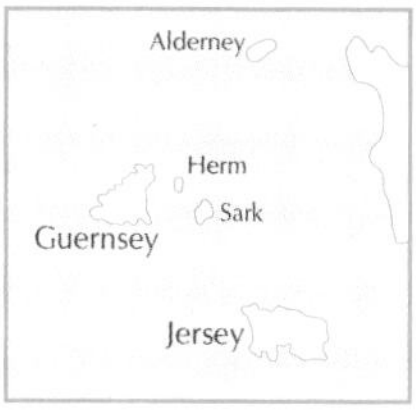

Alderney
Herm
Sark
Guernsey
Jersey

Guernsey
0 1 2 3 miles
0 1 2 3 4 kilometres
Vale
St Sampson
St Peter Port
St Andrew
Rocquaine Bay
St Martin
Forest

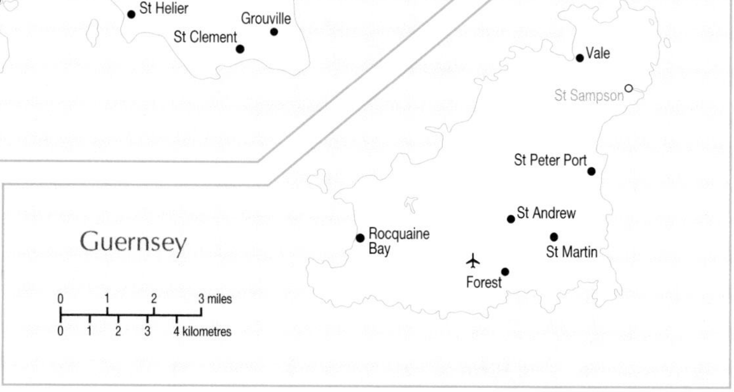

Index to Days Out

C

D

E

H

I

J

K

L

M

N

O

P

T

U

V

The Automobile Association would like to thank the following photographers, companies and picture libraries for their assistance in the preparation of this book.

Abbreviations for the picture credits are as follows: (t) top; (b) bottom; (l) left; (r) right; (c) centre; (AA) AA World Travel Library.

1 AA/J Miller; 2 AA/S Day; 3t AA/R Coulam; 3bl AA/J Tims; 3br AA/L Whitwam; 4 AA/P Baker; 5t AA/R Coulam; 5c AA; 7 AA/T Mackie; Bedfordshire AA/M Birkitt; Berkshire AA/J Miller; Bristol AA/S Day; Buckinghamshire AA/C Jones; Cambridgeshire AA/T Mackie; Cheshire AA/V Bates; Cornwall & Isles of Scilly AA/J Wood; Cumbria AA/T Mackie; Derbyshire AA/T Mackie; Devon AA/N Hicks; Dorset AA/A Burton; Durham AA/R Coulam; Essex AA/N Setchfield; Gloucestershire AA/F Stephenson; Greater Manchester AA/S Day; Hampshire AA/W Voysey; Hereford AA/H Palmer; Hertfordshire AA/M Moody; Kent AA/M Busselle; Lancashire AA/D Clapp; Leicestershire AA/M Birkitt; Lincolnshire AA/M Birkitt; London AA/J Tims; Merseyside AA/D Clapp; Norfolk AA/T Mackie; Northamptonshire AA/M Birkitt; Northumberland, AA/R Coulam; Nottinghamshire, AA/J Tims; Oxfordshire AA/J Tims; Rutland Colin Underhill/Alamy; Shropshire AA/C Jones; Somerset AA/J Tims; Staffordshire AA/T Mackie; Suffolk AA/T Mackie; Surrey AA/J Tims; East Sussex AA/D Forss; West Sussex AA/J Miller; Tyne & Wear AA/R Coulam; Warwickshire AA/H Palmer; West Midlands AA/C Jones; Isle of Wight AA/A Burton; Wiltshire AA/W Voysey; Worcestershire AA/C Jones; East Riding of Yorkshire AA/D Clapp; North Yorkshire AA/M Kipling; South Yorkshire AA/N Coates; West Yorkshire AA/T Mackie; Guernsey Jon Arnold Images Ltd/Alamy; Jersey Jon Arnold Images Ltd/Alamy; Isle of Man AA/V Bates; Scotland AA/D W Robertson; Wales AA/M Bauer; Northern Ireland AA/C Coe; Republic of Ireland AA/K Blackwell

Readers' Report Form

Please send this form to:
Editor, The Days Out Guide,
Lifestyle Guides,
The Automobile Association,
Fanum House,
Basingstoke RG21 4EA

e-mail: lifestyleguides@theAA.com

Please use this form to recommend any visitor attraction you have been to, whether it is in the guide or not currently listed. Feedback from readers helps us to keep our guide accurate and up to date. Please note, however, that if you have a complaint to make during a visit, we strongly recommend that you discuss the matter with the establishment management there and then so that they have a chance to put things right before your visit is spoilt. The AA does not undertake to arbitrate between you and the attraction's management, or to obtain compensation or engage in correspondence.

Date:

Your name (block capitals)

Your address (block capitals)

....

....

....

....

....

e-mail address:

Comments (Please include the name & address of the establishment) ....

....

....

....

....

....

....

....

....

....

(please attach a separate sheet if necessary)

Please tick here if you DO NOT wish to receive details of AA offers or products ☐

PTO

Have you bought this Guide before? Yes No

What other Days Out guides have you bought recently?

....

....

....

Why did you buy this Guide? (circle all that apply)

family holiday short break school holidays special occasion

other ....

How often do you have a Day Out? (circle one choice)

more than once a month once a month once in 2-3 months

once in six months once a year less than once a year

Please answer these questions to help us make improvements to the guide:

Which of these factors are most important when choosing a Day Out?

price location previous experience

recommendation type of attraction

other (please state) ....

Do you use the location atlas? Yes No

What elements of the guide do you find the most useful when choosing somewhere to visit?

description photo advertisement

Can you suggest any improvements to the guide?

....

....

....

....

Thank you for returning this form

Readers' Report Form

Please send this form to:
Editor, The Days Out Guide,
Lifestyle Guides,
The Automobile Association,
Fanum House,
Basingstoke RG21 4EA

e-mail: lifestyleguides@theAA.com

Please use this form to recommend any visitor attraction you have been to, whether it is in the guide or not currently listed. Feedback from readers helps us to keep our guide accurate and up to date. Please note, however, that if you have a complaint to make during a visit, we strongly recommend that you discuss the matter with the establishment management there and then so that they have a chance to put things right before your visit is spoilt. The AA does not undertake to arbitrate between you and the attraction's management, or to obtain compensation or engage in correspondence.

Date:

Your name (block capitals)

Your address (block capitals)

....

....

....

....

....

e-mail address:

Comments (Please include the name & address of the establishment) ....

....

....

....

....

....

....

....

....

....

(please attach a separate sheet if necessary)

Please tick here if you DO NOT wish to receive details of AA offers or products ☐

PTO

The Days Out Guide 2011

Have you bought this Guide before? Yes No

What other Days Out guides have you bought recently?

....

....

....

Why did you buy this Guide? (circle all that apply)

family holiday short break school holidays special occasion

other ....

How often do you have a Day Out? (circle one choice)

more than once a month once a month once in 2-3 months

once in six months once a year less than once a year

Please answer these questions to help us make improvements to the guide:

Which of these factors are most important when choosing a Day Out?

price location previous experience

recommendation type of attraction

other (please state) ....

Do you use the location atlas? Yes No

What elements of the guide do you find the most useful when choosing somewhere to visit?

description photo advertisement

Can you suggest any improvements to the guide?

....

....

....

....

Thank you for returning this form

Readers' Report Form

Please send this form to:
Editor, The Days Out Guide,
Lifestyle Guides,
The Automobile Association,
Fanum House,
Basingstoke RG21 4EA

e-mail: lifestyleguides@theAA.com

Please use this form to recommend any visitor attraction you have been to, whether it is in the guide or not currently listed. Feedback from readers helps us to keep our guide accurate and up to date. Please note, however, that if you have a complaint to make during a visit, we strongly recommend that you discuss the matter with the establishment management there and then so that they have a chance to put things right before your visit is spoilt. The AA does not undertake to arbitrate between you and the attraction's management, or to obtain compensation or engage in correspondence.

Date:

Your name (block capitals)

Your address (block capitals)

....

....

....

....

....

e-mail address:

Comments (Please include the name & address of the establishment) ....

....

....

....

....

....

....

....

....

....

(please attach a separate sheet if necessary)

Please tick here if you DO NOT wish to receive details of AA offers or products ☐

PTO

The Days Out Guide 2011

Have you bought this Guide before? Yes No

What other Days Out guides have you bought recently?

....

....

....

Why did you buy this Guide? (circle all that apply)

family holiday short break school holidays special occasion

other ....

How often do you have a Day Out? (circle one choice)

more than once a month once a month once in 2-3 months

once in six months once a year less than once a year

Please answer these questions to help us make improvements to the guide:

Which of these factors are most important when choosing a Day Out?

price location previous experience

recommendation type of attraction

other (please state) ....

Do you use the location atlas? Yes No

What elements of the guide do you find the most useful when choosing somewhere to visit?

description photo advertisement

Can you suggest any improvements to the guide?

....

....

....

....

Thank you for returning this form

Please send this form to:
Editor, The Days Out Guide,
Lifestyle Guides,
The Automobile Association,
Fanum House,
Basingstoke RG21 4EA

e-mail: lifestyleguides@theAA.com

Readers' Report Form

Please use this form to recommend any visitor attraction you have been to, whether it is in the guide or not currently listed. Feedback from readers helps us to keep our guide accurate and up to date. Please note, however, that if you have a complaint to make during a visit, we strongly recommend that you discuss the matter with the establishment management there and then so that they have a chance to put things right before your visit is spoilt. The AA does not undertake to arbitrate between you and the attraction's management, or to obtain compensation or engage in correspondence.

Date:

Your name (block capitals)

Your address (block capitals)

....

....

....

....

....

e-mail address:

Comments (Please include the name & address of the establishment) ....

....

....

....

....

....

....

....

....

....

(please attach a separate sheet if necessary)

Please tick here if you DO NOT wish to receive details of AA offers or products ☐

PTO

The Days Out Guide 2011

Have you bought this Guide before? Yes No

What other Days Out guides have you bought recently?

....

....

....

Why did you buy this Guide? (circle all that apply)

family holiday short break school holidays special occasion

other ....

How often do you have a Day Out? (circle one choice)

more than once a month once a month once in 2-3 months

once in six months once a year less than once a year

Please answer these questions to help us make improvements to the guide:

Which of these factors are most important when choosing a Day Out?

price location previous experience

recommendation type of attraction

other (please state) ....

Do you use the location atlas? Yes No

What elements of the guide do you find the most useful when choosing somewhere to visit?

description photo advertisement

Can you suggest any improvements to the guide?

....

....

....

....

Thank you for returning this form

2 FOR 1

Terms: This voucher is valid at any venue specified as accepting vouchers within the AA 'The Days Out Guide 2011'. This voucher admits one adult or child free when presented at the time of purchase of one fully priced adult ticket. Valid until 31 Oct 2011. Subject to availability at the venue when presented. Photocopies will not be accepted.

AA Lifestyle Guides

2 FOR 1

Terms: This voucher is valid at any venue specified as accepting vouchers within the AA 'The Days Out Guide 2011'. This voucher admits one adult or child free when presented at the time of purchase of one fully priced adult ticket. Valid until 31 Oct 2011. Subject to availability at the venue when presented. Photocopies will not be accepted.

AA Lifestyle Guides

2 FOR 1

Terms: This voucher is valid at any venue specified as accepting vouchers within the AA 'The Days Out Guide 2011'. This voucher admits one adult or child free when presented at the time of purchase of one fully priced adult ticket. Valid until 31 Oct 2011. Subject to availability at the venue when presented. Photocopies will not be accepted.

AA Lifestyle Guides

2 FOR 1

Terms: This voucher is valid at any venue specified as accepting vouchers within the AA 'The Days Out Guide 2011'. This voucher admits one adult or child free when presented at the time of purchase of one fully priced adult ticket. Valid until 31 Oct 2011. Subject to availability at the venue when presented. Photocopies will not be accepted.

AA Lifestyle Guides

2 FOR 1

Terms: This voucher is valid at any venue specified as accepting vouchers within the AA 'The Days Out Guide 2011'. This voucher admits one adult or child free when presented at the time of purchase of one fully priced adult ticket. Valid until 31 Oct 2011. Subject to availability at the venue when presented. Photocopies will not be accepted.

AA Lifestyle Guides

2 FOR 1

Terms: This voucher is valid at any venue specified as accepting vouchers within the AA 'The Days Out Guide 2011'. This voucher admits one adult or child free when presented at the time of purchase of one fully priced adult ticket. Valid until 31 Oct 2011. Subject to availability at the venue when presented. Photocopies will not be accepted.

AA Lifestyle Guides

2 FOR 1

Terms: This voucher is valid at any venue specified as accepting vouchers within the AA 'The Days Out Guide 2011'. This voucher admits one adult or child free when presented at the time of purchase of one fully priced adult ticket. Valid until 31 Oct 2011. Subject to availability at the venue when presented. Photocopies will not be accepted.

AA Lifestyle Guides

2 FOR 1

Terms: This voucher is valid at any venue specified as accepting vouchers within the AA 'The Days Out Guide 2011'. This voucher admits one adult or child free when presented at the time of purchase of one fully priced adult ticket. Valid until 31 Oct 2011. Subject to availability at the venue when presented. Photocopies will not be accepted.

AA Lifestyle Guides

2 FOR 1

Terms: This voucher is valid at any venue specified as accepting vouchers within the AA 'The Days Out Guide 2011'. This voucher admits one adult or child free when presented at the time of purchase of one fully priced adult ticket. Valid until 31 Oct 2011. Subject to availability at the venue when presented. Photocopies will not be accepted.

AA Lifestyle Guides

2 FOR 1

Terms: This voucher is valid at any venue specified as accepting vouchers within the AA 'The Days Out Guide 2011'. This voucher admits one adult or child free when presented at the time of purchase of one fully priced adult ticket. Valid until 31 Oct 2011. Subject to availability at the venue when presented. Photocopies will not be accepted.

AA Lifestyle Guides

AA Lifestyle Guides

Conditions: Only one voucher per person or party accepted.
No change given. This voucher is valid during the published opening times for the establishments concerned, and will not be valid after 31 Oct 2011.
This voucher cannot be used in conjunction with any other discount voucher or special offer.
Redeemable cash value .01p.
No cash alternative available.

AA Lifestyle Guides

Conditions: Only one voucher per person or party accepted.
No change given. This voucher is valid during the published opening times for the establishments concerned, and will not be valid after 31 Oct 2011.
This voucher cannot be used in conjunction with any other discount voucher or special offer.
Redeemable cash value .01p.
No cash alternative available.

AA Lifestyle Guides

Conditions: Only one voucher per person or party accepted.
No change given. This voucher is valid during the published opening times for the establishments concerned, and will not be valid after 31 Oct 2011.
This voucher cannot be used in conjunction with any other discount voucher or special offer.
Redeemable cash value .01p.
No cash alternative available.

AA Lifestyle Guides

Conditions: Only one voucher per person or party accepted.
No change given. This voucher is valid during the published opening times for the establishments concerned, and will not be valid after 31 Oct 2011.
This voucher cannot be used in conjunction with any other discount voucher or special offer.
Redeemable cash value .01p.
No cash alternative available.

AA Lifestyle Guides

Conditions: Only one voucher per person or party accepted.
No change given. This voucher is valid during the published opening times for the establishments concerned, and will not be valid after 31 Oct 2011.
This voucher cannot be used in conjunction with any other discount voucher or special offer.
Redeemable cash value .01p.
No cash alternative available.

AA Lifestyle Guides

Conditions: Only one voucher per person or party accepted.
No change given. This voucher is valid during the published opening times for the establishments concerned, and will not be valid after 31 Oct 2011.
This voucher cannot be used in conjunction with any other discount voucher or special offer.
Redeemable cash value .01p.
No cash alternative available.

AA Lifestyle Guides

Conditions: Only one voucher per person or party accepted.
No change given. This voucher is valid during the published opening times for the establishments concerned, and will not be valid after 31 Oct 2011.
This voucher cannot be used in conjunction with any other discount voucher or special offer.
Redeemable cash value .01p.
No cash alternative available.

AA Lifestyle Guides

Conditions: Only one voucher per person or party accepted.
No change given. This voucher is valid during the published opening times for the establishments concerned, and will not be valid after 31 Oct 2011.
This voucher cannot be used in conjunction with any other discount voucher or special offer.
Redeemable cash value .01p.
No cash alternative available.

AA Lifestyle Guides

Conditions: Only one voucher per person or party accepted.
No change given. This voucher is valid during the published opening times for the establishments concerned, and will not be valid after 31 Oct 2011.
This voucher cannot be used in conjunction with any other discount voucher or special offer.
Redeemable cash value .01p.
No cash alternative available.

AA Lifestyle Guides

Conditions: Only one voucher per person or party accepted.
No change given. This voucher is valid during the published opening times for the establishments concerned, and will not be valid after 31 Oct 2011.
This voucher cannot be used in conjunction with any other discount voucher or special offer.
Redeemable cash value .01p.
No cash alternative available.